SECOND

PDR®

Drug Guide for Mental Health Professionals

THOMSON

PDR

Contents

PDR® Drug Guide
for Mental Health Professionals

SECOND EDITION

Foreword by Harris B. Stratyner, PhD, CASAC
Director, Addiction Recovery Services
New York Presbyterian Hospital, Payne Whitney Westchester
Asst. Professor, Weill Cornell Medical College

Manager, Editorial Services: Bette LaGow
Senior Pharmacy Manager: Tammy Chernin, RPh
Senior Editor: Lori Murray
Production Editor: Gwynned Kelly
Drug Information Specialists: Min Ko, PharmD; Sheila Talatala, PharmD
Project Manager: Lynn S. Wilhelm
Production Specialist: Christina Klinger
Production Design Manager: Adeline Rich
Senior Electronic Publishing Designer: Livio Udina
Electronic Publishing Designers: Bryan Dix, Rosalia Sberna

PHYSICIANS' DESK REFERENCE

Executive Vice President, PDR: David Duplay
Vice President, Sales and Marketing: Dikran N. Barsamian
Vice President, PDR Services: Brian Holland
Senior Director, Brand and Product Management: Valerie Berger
Director, Brand and Product Management: Carmen Mazzatta
Associate Product Managers: Michael Casale, Andrea Colavecchio
Senior Director, Publishing Sales and Marketing: Michael Bennett
Director of Trade Sales: Bill Gaffney
Associate Director of Marketing: Jennifer Fronzaglia
Director of Operations: Robert Klein
Director of PDR Content: Jeffrey D. Schaefer
Clinical Content Operations Manager: Thomas Fleming, PharmD
Manager, Production Purchasing: Thomas Westburgh

ISBN: 1-56363-511-9

Foreword

The mental health profession is one that clearly must keep abreast of the constantly evolving biopsychosocial developments and societal changes. For instance, scientific breakthroughs have resulted in human beings living longer, but this comes at a great cost. Physical ailments, the accompanying aches and pains, possible decline in mental faculties, and depression and anxiety due to the loss of loved ones or difficulty coping with an ever-changing world have resulted in the consumption of more over-the-counter drugs and prescription medications (including psychotropic prescriptions). With increased consumption comes increased risk for misuse and abuse.

Another example involves the development of a group of drugs known as selective serotonin reuptake inhibitors (SSRIs), which have proved to be quite effective for the treatment of depression. These drugs have been embroiled in controversy, however, when prescribed for children and adolescents under the age of 18 for fear that some may increase the risk of suicidal ideation. This is particularly important because some studies have indicated that depression may affect as many as 2.5% of children and 8.3% of adolescents—this translates into *millions* of young lives.

The advent of "club drugs" such as GHB, Rohypnol, and MDMA have resulted in increased visits to emergency rooms and hospital admissions related to rape, heat exhaustion, and cardiovascular collapse. Ingestion of these chemicals in combination with other drugs and alcohol has resulted in death in some cases.

When one ponders these examples, it is clear that today's clinician must have a working knowledge of the myriad medications and substances that their patients may be prescribed or abusing.

Unquestionably, today's mental health professional works at a time when research studies are being conducted with greater proficiency and abundance, due in large measure to advances in computer science and technology. As a result, the field is exploding with information. Combine this with shorter lengths of stay in inpatient units, abridged outpatient programs, consumers being treated in both mental health and substance abuse settings, and you have the necessity for mental health professionals to know more than the breadth and scope of their own discipline. The nonphysician clinician working in the mental health field can no longer afford to simply say to his or her patient, "Speak to your psychiatrist about that."

Mental health practitioners today must be as knowledgeable as possible about psychotropics, herbal and psychotropic supplements, street drugs, and any medications that may be causing interaction effects or clinical symptoms so they can monitor their patients and effectively communicate with psychiatrists and psychopharmacologists (as well as the many general practitioners that have been known to prescribe these agents). That is why I am so pleased with this second edition of the *PDR® Drug Guide for Mental Health Professionals*. Not only does this volume provide all of the sections and indices included in the first edition (i.e., clearly written detailed descriptions of the most commonly prescribed psychotropic medications; drugs that interact with these medications; commonly prescribed Rx drugs; medications that can cause psychological side effects; psychotropic herbs and supplements; and drugs that have great potential for abuse), but what makes it particularly invaluable is the inclusion of a new section on street drugs.

In my 25 years working in the mental health profession, my primary focus has been in the area of treating individuals with co-occurring disorders. Conservative estimates state that as many as 30% to 50% of mental health consumers may have a co-occurring substance abuse/addiction disorder—and this takes into consideration only AXIS I psychopathology. Stemming from my research, I have developed an approach to treat these individuals that I have termed "carefrontation." This approach stresses that an individual with a psychiatric and substance abuse diagnosis must be treated with respect and dignity, without being shamed or blamed for his or her disorder, but instead *held responsible* for dealing with it. This includes taking psychotropic medication if necessary, and not using illicit substances or abusing prescribed substances.

If the patient is held responsible, the clinician must also be held responsible—responsible for knowing all he or she can about "what is out there." Since the helping profession is comprised of many practitioners with various credentials and orientations, the nonphysician clinician may approach the area of co-occurring disorders from a very different place than a colleague. For example, in the substance abuse field, many nonphysician clinicians lack a full understanding of psychotropic medications. *PDR Drug Guide for Mental Health Professionals*, written in a clear, easy-to-comprehend manner, will provide the necessary information they need about psychotropic drugs, as well as serving as an excellent reference guide on all aspects of street drugs. On the other hand, for the nonphysician clinician working in the mental health field who does not have a strong background in the area of substance abuse, this book will provide definitive information on street drugs, as well as offer complete information on psychotropic medications. For this reason alone, I view this drug guide as mandatory reading and a reference source for every mental health professional. Indeed, *PDR Drug Guide for Mental Health Professionals* may just be the bridge between disciplines that finally leads to better communication and longer-lasting, integrated clinical out-comes.

Harris Stratyner, PhD, CASAC
Director of Addiction Recovery Services
New York Presbyterian Hospital, Payne Whitney Westchester
Assistant Professor, Weill Cornell Medical College

Psychotropic Drug Profiles

In this section you'll find detailed overviews of 80 medications commonly used in the treatment of mental and emotional disorders. The drugs are organized alphabetically by brand name and cross-referenced by generic name. The information is drawn from the drug's government-approved product labeling as submitted for publication in *Physicians' Desk Reference*®. Included are the drug's potential side effects and interactions, reasons the drug should *not* be prescribed, necessary precautions, typical dosage regimens, and signs of overdose. A more detailed review of each drug's possible interactions with other medications can be found in Section 2.

ABILIFY
Aripiprazole

Why is this drug prescribed?

Abilify is used in the treatment of schizophrenia. The drug is thought to work by modifying sensitivity to two of the brain's chief chemical messengers, serotonin and dopamine.

Most important fact about this drug

Abilify can cause tardive dyskinesia, a condition marked by involuntary movements in the face and body, including chewing movements, puckering, puffing the cheeks, and sticking out the tongue. This condition may be permanent and appears to be most common among older adults, especially women.

How should this medication be taken?

Abilify should be taken once a day. It may be taken with or without food.

● *Missed dose...*
  Generally, forgotten doses should be taken as soon remembered. However, if it is almost time for the next dose, patients should skip the one they missed and return to their regular schedule. Doses should never be doubled.

● *Storage instructions...*
  Store at room temperature.

What side effects may occur?

Side effects cannot be anticipated. If any develop or change in intensity, patients should inform their doctor as soon as possible.

● *Side effects may include:*
  Anxiety, blurred vision, constipation, cough, headache, insomnia, light-headedness, nausea, rash, restlessness, runny nose, sleepiness, tremors, vomiting, weakness

A variety of other reactions have been reported on extremely rare occasions. Any new or unusual symptom should be checked with the doctor.

Why should this drug not be prescribed?

If Abilify causes an allergic reaction, the patient will be unable to use it.

Special warnings about this medication

The risk of tardive dyskinesia (see "Most important fact about this drug") increases with the total amount of Abilify that a patient has taken. To reduce the risk, the doctor will prescribe the lowest effective dose and resort to long-term therapy only if necessary. Patients who develop symptoms of tardive dyskinesia should see their doctor immediately. Therapy with Abilify may have to be discontinued.

In rare cases, Abilify has been known to cause a potentially fatal condition called neuroleptic malignant syndrome (NMS). Symptoms include high fever, rigid muscles, irregular pulse or blood pressure, rapid heartbeat, excessive perspiration, altered mental status, and changes in heart rhythm. Patients who develop these symptoms need to alert their doctor immediately. Abilify should be discontinued.

Certain antipsychotic drugs are associated with an increased risk of developing high blood sugar, which on rare occasions has led to coma or death. To date, there have been only a few reports of blood sugar problems during treatment with Abilify. Even so, all patients taking this drug should be monitored closely by their doctor for signs of high blood sugar, especially those with risk factors for diabetes.

Because Abilify tends to make some people sleepy, patients should be cautious about operating hazardous machinery such as cars until they are certain the drug will not impair their ability.

In a few people, Abilify can cause an abrupt drop in blood pressure when they stand up, leading to light-headedness or even fainting. Abilify should be used with caution by anyone with a heart or circulatory problem, people who take blood pressure medication, and those who tend to become dehydrated.

Abilify has triggered seizures in a very small number of patients, and can also interfere with the swallowing mechanism. The risk of either problem is greater among older adults. If a patient has ever had a seizure, the doctor should be made aware of it. Abilify should be used with caution.

Drugs such as Abilify can cause the body to overheat. Patients should be cautious in hot weather and when exercising strenuously, and should be sure to get plenty of liquids.

Abilify has not been tested in children or teenagers. Older adults should use the drug with caution.

Possible food and drug interactions when taking this medication

The doctor will need to reduce the dosage of Abilify when patients take the following additional drugs:

Fluoxetine (Prozac)
Ketoconazole (Nizoral)
Paroxetine (Paxil)
Quinidine (Quinidex)

On the other hand, the dosage of Abilify should be increased for patients taking carbamazepine (Tegretol).

Caution is in order when taking Abilify with blood pressure medications classified as alpha-adrenergic blockers, including Hytrin and Cardura. Caution is also advised when combining Abilify with drugs that act on the brain, including tranquilizers, antidepressants, sleeping pills, narcotic painkillers, and other schizophrenia medications.

Although Abilify does not interact with alcohol, the manufacturer recommends avoiding the combination.

Special information about pregnancy and breastfeeding

The effects of Abilify during pregnancy have not been adequately studied. The drug is recommended only if its benefits are thought to outweigh the potential risk to the baby. If a patient is pregnant or planning to become pregnant, she should inform her doctor immediately.

Breastfeeding is not recommended during Abilify therapy.

Recommended dosage

ADULTS

The usual dose is 10 or 15 milligrams taken once a day. The doctor will wait at least 2 weeks before prescribing an increased dosage.

Overdosage

Any medication taken in excess can have serious consequences. If an overdose is suspected, seek medical attention immediately.

- *Symptoms of Abilify overdose may include:*
  Sleepiness, vomiting

ADDERALL

Amphetamines
Other brand name: Adderall XR

Why is this drug prescribed?

Adderall is prescribed in the treatment of attention deficit hyperactivity disorder (ADHD). It is used as part of a broader treatment plan that includes psychological, educational, and social measures. An extended-release form of the drug, called Adderall XR, is available for once-daily treatment of ADHD.

The regular form of Adderall is also prescribed for narcolepsy.

Most important fact about this drug

Adderall, like all amphetamines, has a high potential for abuse. If used in large doses over long periods of time, it can cause dependence and addiction. It's important for patients to use Adderall only as prescribed.

How should this medication be taken?

Patients should use no more than the prescribed amount of Adderall. It should not be taken for a longer time or for any other purpose than prescribed.

The first dose should be taken upon awakening. If additional doses are prescribed, they should be taken at intervals of 4 to 6 hours. Patients should avoid late evening doses, which can interfere with sleep.

Adderall XR capsules can be taken whole, or the contents can be sprinkled on applesauce. The applesauce should be eaten immediately, without chewing. Patients should be sure to use the entire contents of the capsule.

● *Missed dose...*
If the patient is taking 1 dose a day, and at least 6 hours remain before bedtime, the dose should be taken as soon as remembered. If it's not remembered until the next day, the patient should skip the dose and go back to the regular schedule.

If the patient is taking more than 1 dose a day, and remembers within an hour or so of the scheduled time, the missed dose should be taken immediately. Otherwise, the patient should skip the dose and go back to the regular schedule.

Patients should never take 2 doses at once.

● *Storage instructions...*
Adderall should be stored at room temperature in a tight, light-resistant container.

What side effects may occur?
Side effects cannot be predicted. If any develop or change in intensity, patients should inform their doctor as soon as possible.

● *Side effects of Adderall may include:*
Dry mouth, high blood pressure, hives, impotence, overstimulation, rapid or pounding heartbeat, stomach and intestinal disturbances, weight loss

● *Side effects of Adderall XR may include:*
Abdominal pain, diarrhea, dizziness, fever, infection (including viral), insomnia, loss of appetite, mood swings, nausea, nervousness, vomiting, weakness, weight loss

Why should this drug not be prescribed?
Adderall should never be prescribed for patients with any of the following conditions:

Heart disease
Hardening of the arteries
High blood pressure
High pressure in the eye (glaucoma)
Overactive thyroid gland

Patients should avoid using Adderall within 14 days of taking a drug classified as an MAO inhibitor, such as the antidepressants Nardil and Parnate. A potentially life-threatening spike in blood pressure could result.

Adderall should not be prescribed for patients who have ever had a reaction to similar stimulant drugs. Adderall is also contraindicated for patients who appear agitated or are prone to substance abuse.

Special warnings about this medication

Adderall should be used with caution if the patient has even a mild case of high blood pressure. Patients should be careful, too, about driving or operating machinery until they know how this drug affects them. It may impair judgment and coordination.

Adderall can make tics and twitches worse. If the patient or a family member has this problem (or the condition called Tourette's syndrome), the doctor should be made aware of it. Amphetamines such as Adderall have also been known to aggravate symptoms in patients with psychosis.

If the problem is attention-deficit disorder, the doctor should do a complete history and evaluation before prescribing Adderall, taking particular account of the severity of the symptoms and the age of the child. If the problem is a temporary reaction to a stressful situation, Adderall is probably not called for.

There are no data on long-term Adderall therapy in children. However, other amphetamine-based medications have been known to stunt growth, so the child should be watched carefully.

Possible food and drug interactions when taking this medication

If Adderall is taken with certain other drugs, the effects of either could be increased, decreased, or altered. Here is an overview of the drugs that may cause a problem:

Acetazolamide (Diamox)
Antihistamines such as Benadryl and Chlor-Trimeton
Antipsychotic drugs such as Haldol and chlorpromazine
Drugs classified as MAO inhibitors, including the antidepressants
  Nardil and Parnate
Drugs that make the urine more acid, such as Uroquid-Acid No. 2
Glutamic acid (an amino acid related to MSG)
High blood pressure medications such as Calan, guanethidine,
  HydroDIURIL, Hytrin, Procardia, and reserpine
Lithium (Eskalith, Lithobid)
Meperidine (Demerol)
Methenamine (Urised)
Norepinephrine (Levophed)
Propoxyphene (Darvon)
Seizure medications such as Dilantin, phenobarbital, and Zarontin
Tricyclic antidepressants such as Norpramin, Tofranil, and Vivactil
Vitamin C

Special information about pregnancy and breastfeeding

Heavy use of amphetamines during pregnancy can lead to premature birth or low birth weight. Pregnant women should avoid taking Adderall unless absolutely necessary.

Amphetamines do find their way into breast milk, so patients should not take Adderall while breastfeeding.

Recommended dosage

Whether the problem is attention-deficit disorder or narcolepsy, the dosage should be kept as low as possible.

ATTENTION DEFICIT HYPERACTIVITY DISORDER

Adderall

Children 3 to 5 Years of Age: The usual starting dose is 2.5 milligrams daily. Each week, the daily dosage may be increased by 2.5 milligrams until the condition is under control.

Children 6 Years of Age and Older: The usual starting dose is 5 milligrams once or twice a day. Each week, the daily dosage may be increased by 5 milligrams. Only in rare cases will a child need more than 40 milligrams per day.

Therapy may be interrupted occasionally to see if the drug is still needed.

Adderall XR

Children 6 Years of Age and Older: The usual starting dose for children taking Adderall for the first time is 10 milligrams once daily in the morning. At weekly intervals, the doctor may increase the daily dosage by 5 or 10 milligrams, up to a maximum of 30 milligrams a day.

Children already taking regular Adderall are prescribed a single dose of Adderall XR equal to their previous daily total.

Adderall XR has not been tested on children under 6 years old.

NARCOLEPSY

Adderall

Adults: The usual total daily dose ranges from 5 to 60 milligrams, taken as 2 or more smaller doses.

Children under 12 Years of Age: The usual starting dose is 5 milligrams daily. Each week, the daily dose may be raised by 5 milligrams until the condition is under control.

Children 12 Years of Age and Older: The usual starting dose is 10 milligrams daily, with weekly increases of 10 milligrams daily until the drug takes effect.

Overdosage

A large overdose of Adderall can be fatal. Warning signs of a massive overdose include convulsions and coma.

- *Symptoms of Adderall overdose may include:*
  Abdominal cramps, changes in blood pressure, combative behavior, confusion, diarrhea, hallucinations, heightened reflexes, high fever, irregular heartbeat, nausea, panic, rapid breathing, restlessness, tremor, vomiting

If an overdose is suspected, seek emergency treatment immediately.

Alprazolam *See Xanax, page 234*

AMBIEN

Zolpidem tartrate

Why is this drug prescribed?

Ambien is used for short-term treatment of insomnia. A relatively new drug, it is chemically different from other common sleep medications such as Halcion and Dalmane.

Most important fact about this drug

Sleep problems are usually temporary and require medication for a week or two at most. Insomnia that lasts longer could be a sign of another medical problem. Patients should check with their doctor if they find that they need this medicine for more than 7 to 10 days.

How should this medication be taken?

Ambien works very quickly. Patients should take it just before going to bed, and should take no more than the prescribed dose.

- *Missed dose...*
  Ambien should be taken only as needed. Patients should never double the dose.

- *Storage instructions...*
  May be stored at room temperature. Protect from extreme heat.

What side effects may occur?

Side effects cannot be predicted. If any develop or change in intensity, patients should inform their doctor as soon as possible.

- *Side effects may include:*
  Confusion, dependence on Ambien, dizziness, drowsiness, drugged feeling, headache, indigestion, muscle aches, nausea

Why should this drug not be prescribed?

There are no known situations in which Ambien cannot be used.

Special warnings about this medication

When sleep medications are used every night for more than a few weeks, some may lose their effectiveness. People can also become dependent on sleep medications if they are used for a long time or at high doses. Anyone who has had previous problems with addiction to alcohol or drugs should make sure the doctor knows about it.

Some people using Ambien—especially those taking serotonin-boosting antidepressants—have experienced unusual changes in their thinking and/or behavior. Patients should alert the doctor if they notice a change.

Ambien and other sleep medicines can cause a special type of memory loss. It should not be taken on an overnight airplane flight of less than 7 to 8 hours, since "traveler's amnesia" may occur.

Until patients know whether the medication will have any "carry over" effect the next day, they should use extreme care while doing anything that requires complete alertness, such as driving a car or operating machinery. Older adults, in particular, should be aware that they may be more apt to fall.

Patients with liver problems should use Ambien with caution. It will take longer for its effects to wear off.

Patients should consult with their doctor before stopping Ambien if they've taken it for more than 1 or 2 weeks. Sudden discontinuation of a sleep medicine can bring on withdrawal symptoms ranging from unpleasant feelings to vomiting and cramps.

When taking Ambien, patients should not drink alcohol. It can increase the drug's side effects.

Patients with breathing problems may find that the condition worsens while they use Ambien.

Possible food and drug interactions when taking this medication

If Ambien is used with certain other drugs, the effects of either drug could be increased, decreased, or altered. Here is an overview of drugs that can cause a problem:

The antipsychotic agent chlorpromazine
The antidepressant drug imipramine (Tofranil)
Serotonin-boosting antidepressants such as Paxil, Prozac, and Zoloft
Drugs that depress the central nervous system, including Valium,
 Percocet, and Benadryl

Special information about pregnancy and breastfeeding

Patients should inform their doctor immediately if they are pregnant or plan to become pregnant. Babies whose mothers take some sedative/

hypnotic drugs may have withdrawal symptoms after birth and may seem limp and flaccid. Ambien is not recommended for use by nursing mothers.

Recommended dosage

ADULTS

The recommended dosage for adults is 10 milligrams right before bedtime. The doctor will prescribe a smaller dose if the patient is likely to be sensitive to the drug or has a liver problem. No one should ever take more than 10 milligrams of Ambien per day.

CHILDREN

Safety and effectiveness have not been established in children below the age of 18.

OLDER ADULTS

Because older people and those in a weakened condition may be more sensitive to Ambien's effects, the recommended starting dosage is 5 milligrams just before bedtime.

Overdosage

People who take too much Ambien may become excessively sleepy or even go into a light coma. The symptoms of overdose are more severe if the person is also taking other drugs that depress the central nervous system. Some cases of multiple overdose have been fatal. If an overdose is suspected, seek medical attention immediately.

Amitriptyline *See Elavil, page 61*

Amitriptyline with Chlordiazepoxide *See Limbitrol, page 98*

Amitriptyline with Perphenazine *See Triavil, page 213*

AMOXAPINE

Why is this drug prescribed?

Amoxapine relieves the symptoms of depression. It belongs to the class of antidepressants known as tricyclics and is believed to work by balancing certain natural chemicals in the brain.

Most important fact about this drug

Serious, sometimes fatal, reactions can occur when drugs such as amoxapine are taken with the type of antidepressant classified as an MAO inhibitor. Drugs in this category include Nardil and Parnate. Amoxapine should be avoided within two weeks of taking one of these drugs.

How should this medication be taken?

It's not unusual to feel no immediate effect from this medication. However, relief of symptoms usually begins within 2 weeks, and sometimes in as few as 4 to 7 days.

Amoxapine can cause dry mouth. Sucking hard candy or chewing gum can help this problem.

* *Missed dose...*
  Patients who take amoxapine once a day at bedtime and don't remember until morning should skip the missed dose. If they take several doses per day, the forgotten dose should be taken as soon as it's remembered. If it is almost time for the next dose, they should skip the one they missed and return to their regular schedule. Doses should never be doubled.

* *Storage instructions...*
  Amoxapine can be stored at room temperature. It should be protected from excessive heat.

What side effects may occur?

Side effects cannot be predicted. If any develop or change in intensity, patients should inform their doctor as soon as possible.

* *Side effects may include:*
  Blurred vision, constipation, drowsiness, dry mouth

Why should this drug not be prescribed?

Amoxapine must be avoided by anyone taking an MAO inhibitor. (See "Most important fact about this drug.") Patients should also avoid this medication if recovering from a heart attack, or if they have ever had an allergic reaction to amoxapine or dibenzoxazepine medications.

Special warnings about this medication

Amoxapine may cause the facial and body twitching known as tardive dyskinesia. This happens more often in older adults, especially older women. Patients who develop involuntary facial or body movements should see their doctor immediately.

Neuroleptic malignant syndrome (NMS) has also occurred in people using amoxapine. NMS is characterized by extremely high body temperature, rigid muscles, excessive perspiration, altered mental state, and irregular pulse, blood pressure, and heartbeat. If any of these symptoms develop, they should be reported to the doctor immediately.

Amoxapine should be used with care in patients who have difficulty urinating, and in those who suffer from increased pressure within the eye (glaucoma). It should also be used cautiously by anyone who has a seizure disorder or has had one in the past.

The antidepressant drug Prozac can increase the effects of amoxapine. If the patient is switching from Prozac to amoxapine, the doctor may wait 5 weeks or more before starting the new drug.

Patients with a heart condition should use amoxapine with caution. There have been reports of heart attack and stroke in patients taking this type of antidepressant.

Antidepressants can cause allergic reactions such as skin rashes or fever in some people. This usually occurs during the first few days of treatment. Patients should stop taking the medication and consult their doctor if these symptoms develop.

Amoxapine may cause drowsiness. Caution is warranted when driving, operating machinery or appliances, or doing any activity that requires full mental alertness until it's known how the patient reacts on amoxapine.

Possible food and drug interactions when taking this medication

Amoxapine may increase the effects of alcohol. Patients should not drink alcohol while taking this medication.

If amoxapine is taken with certain other drugs, the effects of either could be increased, decreased, or altered. Here is an overview of drugs that can cause a problem:

Antipsychotic drugs such as Mellaril and chlorpromazine
Barbiturates/sedatives such as phenobarbital and Seconal
Cimetidine (Tagamet)
Flecainide (Tambocor)
Fluoxetine (Prozac)
MAO inhibitors such as the antidepressant drugs Nardil and Parnate
Other central nervous system depressants such as Percocet and Halcion
Paroxetine (Paxil)
Propafenone (Rythmol)
Quinidine (Quinaglute)
Sertraline (Zoloft)

Special information about pregnancy and breastfeeding

Although the effects of amoxapine during pregnancy have not been adequately studied, stillbirths and decreased birth weight have appeared in animal studies. Amoxapine should be used only if the potential benefits outweigh the potential risks. Patients should inform their doctors immediately if they are pregnant or plan to become pregnant.

Amoxapine appears in breast milk and could affect a nursing infant. If this medication is essential to the patient's health, her doctor may advise her to stop breastfeeding until her treatment is finished.

Recommended dosage

Effective dosages of amoxapine may vary from one person to another.

ADULTS

The usual starting dosage is 50 milligrams 2 or 3 times daily. If the patient tolerates the drug well, the doctor may increase the dosage to 100 milligrams 2 or 3 times daily by the end of the first week. If that dose is not effective after 2 weeks, the doctor may increase the dose even further.

When the effective dosage has been established, the doctor may prescribe a single dose (not to exceed 300 milligrams) at bedtime.

CHILDREN

Safety and effectiveness have not been established in children under the age of 16.

OLDER ADULTS

In general, lower dosages are recommended for older people. The recommended starting dosage of amoxapine is 25 milligrams 2 or 3 times daily. If this is well tolerated, the doctor may increase the dosage by the end of the first week to 50 milligrams 2 or 3 times daily. A daily dosage of 100 to 150 milligrams may be enough for many older people, but some may need up to 300 milligrams.

Overdosage

Any medication taken in excess can have serious consequences. If an overdose is suspected, seek medical treatment immediately.

- *Symptoms of amoxapine overdose may include:*
  Coma, convulsions, kidney failure, severe, protracted epileptic seizures

Amphetamines *See Adderall, page 3*

ANAFRANIL

Clomipramine hydrochloride

Why is this drug prescribed?

Anafranil, a chemical cousin of tricyclic antidepressant medications such as Tofranil and Elavil, is used in the treatment of obsessive-compulsive disorder.

Most important fact about this drug

Serious, even fatal, reactions have been known to occur when drugs such as Anafranil are taken along with drugs classified as MAO inhibitors. Drugs in this category include the antidepressants Nardil and Parnate. Anafranil must never be combined with one of these drugs.

How should this medication be taken?

Anafranil should be taken with meals at first, to avoid stomach upset. After a regular dosage has been established, patients can take 1 dose at bedtime to avoid sleepiness during the day.

This medicine may cause dry mouth. Hard candy, chewing gum, or bits of ice may relieve this problem.

- *Missed dose...*
  Patients who take 1 dose at bedtime should consult their doctor if they miss a dose. The missed dose should not be taken in the morning. Patients who take 2 or more doses a day can take the missed dose as soon as they remember. If it is almost time for their next dose, they should skip the one they missed and go back to their regular schedule. Doses should never be doubled.

- *Storage instructions...*
  Anafranil should be stored at room temperature in a tightly closed container, away from moisture.

What side effects may occur?

Side effects cannot be predicted. If any develop or change in intensity, patients should inform their doctor as soon as possible.

The most significant risk is that of seizures. Headache, fatigue, and nausea can be problems. Men are likely to experience problems with sexual function. Unwanted weight gain is a potential problem for many people who take Anafranil, although a small number actually lose weight.

- *Side effects may include:*
  Constipation, dizziness, dry mouth, impotence, increased appetite, increased sweating, indigestion, libido change, nausea, nervousness, sleepiness, tremor, twitching, visual changes, weight gain, weight loss

Why should this drug not be prescribed?

This medication cannot be used by patients who are sensitive to or have ever had an allergic reaction to a tricyclic antidepressant such as Tofranil, Elavil, or Tegretol.

Anafranil must be avoided if the patient is taking, or has taken within the past 14 days, an MAO inhibitor such as the antidepressants Parnate or Nardil. Combining Anafranil with one of these medications could lead to fever, seizures, coma, and even death.

Patients who have recently had a heart attack should not take Anafranil.

Special warnings about this medication

If the patient has narrow-angle glaucoma (increased pressure in the eye) or is having difficulty urinating, Anafranil could make these conditions worse. Anafranil should also be used with caution in patients with limited kidney function.

If the patient has a tumor of the adrenal gland, this medication could cause blood pressure to rise suddenly and dangerously.

Because Anafranil poses a possible risk of seizures, and because it may impair mental or physical ability to perform complicated tasks, patients should take special precautions if they need to drive a car, operate complicated machinery, or take part in activities such as swimming or climbing in which suddenly losing consciousness could be dangerous. Note that the risk of seizures is increased if the patient:

Has ever had a seizure
Has a history of brain damage or alcoholism
Is taking another medication that increases the risk of seizures

As with Tofranil, Elavil, and other tricyclic antidepressants, an overdose of Anafranil can be fatal. To minimize the risk of overdose, the doctor may prescribe only a small quantity of Anafranil at a time.

Anafranil may cause the skin to become more sensitive to sunlight. Prolonged exposure to sunlight should be avoided.

Before any kind of surgery involving the use of general anesthesia, the doctor or dentist should be informed that the patient is taking Anafranil. The drug may have to be temporarily discontinued.

When it is time to stop taking Anafranil, patients should not quit abruptly. Their doctor will have them taper off gradually to avoid withdrawal symptoms such as dizziness, fever, general feeling of illness, headache, high fever, irritability or worsening of emotional or mental problems, nausea, sleep problems, and vomiting.

Possible food and drug interactions when taking this medication

Patients should avoid alcoholic beverages while taking Anafranil.

If Anafranil is taken with certain other drugs, the effects of either could be increased, decreased, or altered. Here is an overview of the drugs that may cause a problem.

Antipsychotic drugs such as Haldol and chlorpromazine
Barbiturates such as phenobarbital
Certain blood pressure drugs such as Ismelin and Catapres-TTS
Cimetidine (Tagamet)
Digoxin (Lanoxin)
Drugs that ease spasms, such as Donnatal, Cogentin, and Bentyl
Flecainide (Tambocor)
Methylphenidate (Ritalin)
MAO inhibitors such as Nardil and Parnate
Phenytoin (Dilantin)
Propafenone (Rythmol)
Quinidine (Quinidex)
Serotonin-boosting drugs such as the antidepressants fluvoxamine,

Paxil, Prozac, and Zoloft
Thyroid medications such as Synthroid
Tranquilizers such as Xanax and Valium
Warfarin (Coumadin)

Special information about pregnancy and breastfeeding

The doctor should be informed immediately if the patient is pregnant or plans to become pregnant. Some babies born to women who took Anafranil have had withdrawal symptoms such as jitteriness, tremors, and seizures. Anafranil should be used during pregnancy only if absolutely necessary.

Anafranil appears in breast milk. Patients should not breastfeed while taking this medication.

Recommended dosage

ADULTS

The usual recommended initial dose is 25 milligrams daily. The doctor may gradually increase this dosage to 100 milligrams during the first 2 weeks. During this period the patient should take this drug, divided into smaller doses, with meals. The maximum daily dosage is 250 milligrams. After the ideal dose has been determined, the doctor may switch the patient to a single dose at bedtime, to avoid sleepiness during the day.

CHILDREN

The usual recommended initial dose is 25 milligrams daily, divided into smaller doses and taken with meals. Within 2 weeks, the doctor may gradually increase the dose to 100 milligrams or 3 milligrams per 2.2 pounds of body weight per day, whichever is smaller. The maximum dose is 200 milligrams or 3 milligrams per 2.2 pounds of body weight, whichever is smaller. Once the dose has been determined, the child can take it in a single dose at bedtime.

Overdosage

An overdose of Anafranil can be fatal. If an overdose is suspected, seek medical attention immediately.

- *Critical signs and symptoms of Anafranil overdose may include:*
  Impaired brain activity (including coma), irregular heartbeat, seizures, severely low blood pressure

- *Other signs and symptoms of overdosage may include:*
  Agitation, bluish skin color, breathing difficulty, delirium, dilated pupils, high fever, incoordination, little or no urine output, muscle rigidity, overactive reflexes, rapid heartbeat, restlessness, severe perspiration, shock, stupor, twitching or twisting movements, vomiting

There is a danger of heart malfunction and, in rare cases, heart attack.

ARICEPT
Donepezil hydrochloride

Why is this drug prescribed?
Aricept is used to treat mild to moderate Alzheimer's disease. This progressive, degenerative disorder causes physical changes in the brain that disrupt the flow of information and interfere with memory, thinking, and behavior. Aricept can temporarily improve brain function in some Alzheimer's sufferers, although it does not halt the progress of the underlying disease.

Most important fact about this drug
To maintain any improvement, Aricept must be taken regularly. If the drug is stopped, its benefits will soon be lost. Patience is in order when starting the drug. It can take up to 3 weeks for any positive effects to appear.

How should this medication be taken?
Aricept should be taken once a day just before bedtime. Caregivers should make sure it's taken every day. If Aricept is not taken regularly, it won't work. It can be taken with or without food.

● *Missed dose...*
  It should be made up as soon as it's remembered. If it is almost time for the next dose, caregivers should skip the one that was missed and go back to the regular schedule. Doses should never be doubled.

● *Storage instructions...*
  Aricept may be stored at room temperature.

What side effects may occur?
Side effects cannot be predicted. If any develop or change in intensity, the doctor should be informed as soon as possible.

   Side effects are more likely with higher doses. The most common are diarrhea, fatigue, insomnia, loss of appetite, muscle cramps, nausea, and vomiting. When one of these effects occurs, it is usually mild and gets better as treatment continues.

● *Other side effects may include:*
  Abnormal dreams, arthritis, bruising, depression, dizziness, fainting, frequent urination, headache, pain, sleepiness, weight loss

Why should this drug not be prescribed?
There are two reasons to avoid Aricept: an allergic reaction to the drug itself, or an allergy to the group of antihistamines that includes Claritin, Allegra, Atarax, Periactin, and Optimine.

Special warnings about this medication

Aricept can aggravate asthma and other breathing problems, and can increase the risk of seizures. It can also slow the heartbeat, cause heartbeat irregularities, and lead to fainting episodes. The doctor should be contacted if any of these problems occur.

In patients who have had stomach ulcers, and those who take a nonsteroidal anti-inflammatory drug such as Advil, Nuprin, or Aleve, Aricept can make stomach side effects worse. Aricept should be used with caution in such patients, and all side effects should be reported to the doctor.

Possible food and drug interactions when taking this medication

Aricept will increase the effects of certain anesthetics. The doctor should be made aware of Aricept therapy prior to any surgery.

If Aricept is taken with certain other drugs, the effects of either could be increased, decreased, or altered. Here is an overview of the drugs that may cause a problem:

Drugs that quell spasms, including Bentyl, Cogentin, and Donnatal
Bethanechol chloride (Urecholine)
Carbamazepine (Tegretol)
Dexamethasone (Decadron)
Ketoconazole (Nizoral)
Phenobarbital
Phenytoin (Dilantin)
Quinidine (Quinidex)
Rifampin (Rifadin, Rifamate)

Special information about pregnancy and breastfeeding

Since it is not intended for women of child-bearing age, Aricept's effects during pregnancy have not been studied, and it is not known whether it appears in breast milk.

Recommended dosage

ADULTS

The usual starting dose is 5 milligrams once a day at bedtime for at least 4 to 6 weeks. The dose should not be increased during this period unless directed. The doctor may then change the dosage to 10 milligrams once a day if response to the drug warrants it.

CHILDREN

The safety and effectiveness of Aricept have not been established in children.

Overdosage

Any medication taken in excess can have serious consequences. If an overdose is suspected, seek medical attention immediately.

- *Symptoms of Aricept overdose may include:*
  Collapse, convulsions, extreme muscle weakness (possibly ending in death if breathing muscles are affected), low blood pressure, nausea, salivation, slowed heart rate, sweating, vomiting

Aripiprazole *See Abilify, page 1*

ATARAX

Hydroxyzine hydrochloride
Other brand name: Vistaril

Why is this drug prescribed?

Atarax is an antihistamine used to relieve the symptoms of common anxiety and tension and, in combination with other medications, to treat anxiety that results from physical illness. It also relieves itching from allergic reactions and can be used as a sedative before and after general anesthesia. Antihistamines work by decreasing the effects of histamine, a chemical the body releases that narrows air passages in the lungs and contributes to inflammation. Antihistamines reduce itching and swelling and dry up secretions from the nose, eyes, and throat.

Most important fact about this drug

Atarax is not intended for long-term use (more than 4 months). The doctor should reevaluate the prescription periodically.

How should this medication be taken?

This medication should be taken exactly as prescribed.

- *Missed dose...*
  Generally, the dose should be taken as soon as remembered. However, if it is almost time for the next dose, the patient should skip the missed dose and go back to the regular schedule. Doses should never be doubled.

- *Storage instructions...*
  Tablets and syrup should be stored away from heat, light, and moisture. Syrup should be kept from freezing.

What side effects may occur?

Side effects cannot be predicted. If any develop or change in intensity, patients should inform their doctor as soon as possible.

Drowsiness, the most common side effect of Atarax, is usually temporary and may disappear in a few days or when dosage is reduced. Other side effects include dry mouth, twitches, tremors, and convulsions. The last two usually occur with higher-than-recommended doses of Atarax.

Why should this drug not be prescribed?

Atarax should not be taken in early pregnancy. It should be avoided by anyone who is sensitive to or has ever had an allergic reaction to it.

Special warnings about this medication

Atarax increases the effects of drugs that depress the activity of the central nervous system. If the patient is taking narcotics, non-narcotic analgesics, or barbiturates in combination with Atarax, the dosage should be reduced.

This medication can cause drowsiness. Driving or operating dangerous machinery or participating in any hazardous activity that requires full mental alertness is not recommended until patients know how they react to Atarax.

Possible food and drug interactions when taking this medication

Atarax may increase the effects of alcohol. Patients should avoid alcohol while taking this medication.

If Atarax is taken with certain other drugs, the effects of either could be increased, decreased, or altered. Here is an overview of the drugs that may cause a problem:

Barbiturates such as Seconal and phenobarbital
Narcotics such as Demerol and Percocet
Non-narcotic analgesics such as Motrin and Tylenol

Special information about pregnancy and breastfeeding

Although the effects of Atarax during pregnancy have not been adequately studied in humans, birth defects have appeared in animal studies with this medication. Patients should avoid Atarax in early pregnancy, and inform their doctor immediately if they are pregnant or plan to become pregnant.

Atarax may appear in breast milk and could affect a nursing infant. If this medication is essential to the patient's health, the doctor may advise her to discontinue breastfeeding until her treatment is finished.

Recommended dosage

When treatment begins with injections, it can be continued in tablet form. The doctor will adjust dosage based on the patient's response to the drug.

FOR ANXIETY AND TENSION

Adults: The usual dose is 50 to 100 milligrams 4 times per day.

Children under Age 6: The total dose is 50 milligrams daily, divided into several smaller doses.

Children over Age 6: The total dose is 50 to 100 milligrams daily, divided into several smaller doses.

FOR ITCHING DUE TO ALLERGIC CONDITIONS

Adults: The usual dose is 25 milligrams 3 or 4 times a day.

Children under Age 6: The total dose is 50 milligrams daily, divided into several smaller doses.

Children over Age 6: The total dose is 50 to 100 milligrams daily, divided into several smaller doses.

BEFORE AND AFTER GENERAL ANESTHESIA

Adults: The usual dose is 50 to 100 milligrams.

Children: The usual dose is 0.6 milligram per 2.2 pounds of body weight.

Overdosage

Any medication taken in excess can have serious consequences. If an overdose of Atarax is suspected, seek medical attention immediately.

The most common symptom of Atarax overdose is excessive calm; blood pressure may drop, although it is not likely.

ATIVAN

Lorazepam

Why is this drug prescribed?

Ativan is used in the treatment of anxiety disorders, and for short-term (up to 4 months) relief of the symptoms of anxiety. It belongs to a class of drugs known as benzodiazepines.

Most important fact about this drug

Tolerance and dependence can develop with the use of Ativan. Patients may experience withdrawal symptoms if they stop using it abruptly. A change in dose or discontinuation of the drug should be done only under the supervision of a doctor.

How should this medication be taken?

This medication should be taken exactly as prescribed.

- *Missed dose...*
  If it is within an hour or so of the scheduled time, the forgotten dose should be taken as soon as remembered. Otherwise, it should be skipped and the patient should go back to the regular schedule. Doses should never be doubled.

- *Storage instructions...*
  Ativan should be stored at room temperature in a tightly closed container, away from light.

What side effects may occur?
Side effects cannot be predicted. If any develop or change in intensity, patients should inform their doctor as soon as possible.

If any side effects develop, they will usually surface at the beginning of treatment. They will probably disappear as the patient continues to take the drug, or if the dosage is reduced.

● *Side effects may include:*
Dizziness, memory problems, sedation, transient amnesia, unsteadiness, weakness

● *Side effects due to rapid decrease in dose or abrupt withdrawal from Ativan:*
Abdominal and muscle cramps, convulsions, depressed mood, inability to fall or stay asleep, sweating, tremors, vomiting

Why should this drug not be prescribed?
Patients who are sensitive to or have ever had an allergic reaction to Ativan or similar drugs such as Valium should not take this medication.

Ativan should also be avoided if the patient has acute narrow-angle glaucoma (a type of high pressure in the eyes).

Anxiety or tension related to everyday stress usually does not require treatment with Ativan. Symptoms should be thoroughly evaluated prior to treatment.

Special warnings about this medication
Ativan may cause patients to become drowsy or less alert. Therefore, driving or operating dangerous machinery or participating in any hazardous activity that requires full mental alertness is not recommended.

This drug should be used with caution in patients who are severely depressed or have suffered from severe depression. A risk of suicide exists.

Ativan should also be used cautiously in patients with decreased kidney or liver function.

Older patients and those who have been using Ativan for a prolonged period of time should be closely watched for stomach and upper intestinal problems.

Possible food and drug interactions when taking this medication
Ativan may intensify the effects of alcohol. Patients should avoid alcohol while taking this medication.

If Ativan is taken with certain other drugs, the effects of either could be increased, decreased, or altered. It is especially important for patients to check with their doctor before combining Ativan with barbiturates (phenobarbital, Seconal, Amytal) or sedative-type medications such as Valium and Halcion.

Special information about pregnancy and breastfeeding

The patient should avoid Ativan if she is pregnant or planning to become pregnant. There is an increased risk of birth defects.

It is not known whether Ativan appears in breast milk like other drugs in this class. However, breastfeeding is not recommended.

Recommended dosage

ADULTS

The recommended starting dose is 2 to 3 milligrams per day taken in 2 or 3 smaller doses. The usual dosage range is a total of 2 to 6 milligrams per day divided into smaller doses. The largest dose should be taken at bedtime. The daily dose may vary from 1 to 10 milligrams.

For insomnia due to anxiety, a single daily dose of 2 to 4 milligrams may be taken, usually at bedtime.

CHILDREN

The safety and effectiveness of Ativan have not been established in children under 12 years of age.

OLDER ADULTS

To avoid oversedation, the usual starting dosage for older adults and those in a weakened condition should not exceed a total of 1 to 2 milligrams per day, divided into smaller doses. This dose can be adjusted by the doctor as needed.

Overdosage

Any medication taken in excess can have serious consequences. An overdose of Ativan can be fatal, though this is rare. If an overdose is suspected, seek medical attention immediately.

- *Symptoms of Ativan overdose may include:*
  Coma, confusion, drowsiness, hypnotic state, lack of coordination, low blood pressure, sluggishness

Atomoxetine *See Strattera, page 197*

Aventyl *See Pamelor, page 131*

Bupropion *See Wellbutrin, page 229*

BUSPAR
Buspirone hydrochloride

Why is this drug prescribed?
BuSpar is used in the treatment of anxiety disorders and for short-term relief of the symptoms of anxiety.

Most important fact about this drug
BuSpar should not be used with drugs classified as monoamine oxidase (MAO) inhibitors, such as the antidepressants Nardil and Parnate.

How should this medication be taken?
Patients should not be discouraged if they feel no immediate effect. The full benefit of this drug may not be seen for 1 to 2 weeks.

- *Missed dose...*
  Patients should take a forgotten dose as soon as they remember, unless it is almost time for the next dose. If that's the case, they should skip the one they missed and go back to their regular schedule. Doses should never be doubled.

- *Storage instructions...*
  BuSpar should be stored at room temperature in a tightly closed container, away from light.

What side effects may occur?
Side effects cannot be predicted. If any develop or change in intensity, patients should inform their doctor as soon as possible.

- *Side effects may include:*
  Dizziness, dry mouth, fatigue, headache, light-headedness, nausea, nervousness, unusual excitement

Why should this drug not be prescribed?
This drug should be avoided by patients who are sensitive to or have ever had an allergic reaction to BuSpar or similar mood-altering drugs. BuSpar is also inappropriate for people with severe kidney or liver damage.

Anxiety or tension related to everyday stress usually does not require treatment with BuSpar. Symptoms should be thoroughly assessed prior to treatment.

Special warnings about this medication
The effects of BuSpar on the central nervous system are unpredictable. Patients should avoid driving, operating dangerous machinery, or participating in any hazardous activity while they are taking BuSpar.

Possible food and drug interactions when taking this medication

Although BuSpar does not intensify the effects of alcohol, it is best to avoid alcohol while taking this medication.

If BuSpar is taken with certain other drugs, the effects of either can be increased, decreased, or altered. Here is an overview of the drugs that may cause a problem:

The blood-thinning drug Coumadin
Haloperidol (Haldol)
MAO inhibitors such as the antidepressants Nardil and Parnate
Trazodone (Desyrel)

Special information about pregnancy and breastfeeding

The effects of BuSpar during pregnancy have not been adequately studied. Patients should inform their doctor immediately if they are pregnant or plan to become pregnant.

It is not known whether BuSpar appears in breast milk. If this medication is essential to the patient's health, the doctor may advise her to discontinue breastfeeding until her treatment is finished.

Recommended dosage

ADULTS

The recommended starting dose is a total of 15 milligrams per day divided into smaller doses, usually 5 milligrams 3 times a day. Every 2 to 3 days, the doctor may increase the dosage 5 milligrams per day as needed. The daily dose should not exceed 60 milligrams.

CHILDREN

The safety and effectiveness of BuSpar have not been established in children under 18 years of age.

Overdosage

Any medication taken in excess can have serious consequences. If an overdose of BuSpar is suspected, seek medical attention immediately.

- *Symptoms of BuSpar overdose may include:*
  Dizziness, drowsiness, nausea or vomiting, severe stomach upset, unusually small pupils

Buspirone *See BuSpar, page 23*

CELEXA

Citalopram hydrobromide

Why is this drug prescribed?

Celexa is used to treat major depression. Like the antidepressant medications Paxil, Prozac, and Zoloft, Celexa is thought to work by boosting serotonin levels in the brain. Serotonin, one of the nervous system's primary chemical messengers, is known to elevate mood.

Most important fact about this drug

Celexa must not be taken for 2 weeks before or after using an antidepressant known as an MAO inhibitor. Drugs in this category include Nardil and Parnate. Combining Celexa with one of these medications could lead to a serious—even fatal—reaction.

How should this medication be taken?

Celexa is available in tablet and liquid forms. The drug is taken once a day, in the morning or evening, with or without food. It's important to take Celexa regularly, even when feeling better. Depression typically begins to lift in 1 to 4 weeks, but it takes several months for the medication to yield its full benefits.

- *Missed dose...*
  Generally, the forgotten dose should be taken as soon as remembered. However, if it is almost time for the next dose, patients should skip the one they missed and go back to their regular schedule. Doses should never be doubled.

- *Storage instructions...*
  Celexa may be stored at room temperature.

What side effects may occur?

Side effects cannot be predicted. If any develop or change in intensity, patients should inform their doctor as soon as possible.

- *Side effects may include:*
  Agitation, anxiety, diarrhea, dry mouth, ejaculation disorder, increased sweating, indigestion, insomnia, nausea, runny nose, skeletal pain, sleepiness, vomiting, weight loss

Why should this drug not be prescribed?

If Celexa gives the patient an allergic reaction, it cannot be used. Also remember that Celexa must never be combined with an MAO inhibitor (see "Most important fact about this drug," above).

Special warnings about this medication

The FDA has issued a public health advisory to alert healthcare professionals about reports of worsening depression and suicidality (both suicidal thoughts and suicide attempts) during antidepressant drug therapy in adult and pediatric patients with major depressive disorder. Healthcare professionals and family members are advised to watch for signs of worsening depression and to be aware of the suicide statement present in all antidepressant labeling. Celexa is currently not approved for treating major depression in pediatric patients.

Serotonin-boosting antidepressants could potentially cause stomach bleeding, especially in older patients or those taking nonsteroidal anti-inflammatory drugs (NSAIDs) such as aspirin, ibuprofen (Advil, Motrin), naproxen (Aleve), and ketoprofen (Orudis KT). Advise patients to consult their doctor before combining Celexa with NSAIDs or blood-thinning medications.

In recommended doses, Celexa does not seem to impair judgment or motor skills. However, a theoretical possibility of such problems remains, so caution is advisable when driving or operating dangerous equipment until Celexa's effect is known.

There is a slight chance that Celexa will trigger a manic episode. Celexa should be used with caution in patients who suffer from bipolar disorder. Caution is also warranted in patients who are over 60 years old, have liver or kidney problems, suffer from heart disease or high blood pressure, or have ever had seizures.

Possible food and drug interactions when taking this medication

Celexa does not increase the effects of alcohol. Nevertheless, it's considered unwise to combine Celexa with alcohol or any other drug that affects the brain.

Remember that Celexa must never be combined with an MAO inhibitor (see "Most important fact about this drug").

If Celexa is taken with certain other drugs, the effects of either could be increased, decreased, or altered. It's best to check with the doctor before combining any new prescription or over-the-counter drugs with Celexa. Here's an overview of the drugs most likely to cause a problem:

Carbamazepine (Tegretol)
Cimetidine (Tagamet)
Erythromycin (Eryc, Ery-Tab)
Fluconazole (Diflucan)
Itraconazole (Sporanox)
Ketoconazole (Nizoral)
Lithium (Eskalith, Lithobid)
Metoprolol (Lopressor)
Omeprazole (Prilosec)
Other antidepressants such as Elavil, Norpramin, Pamelor, and Tofranil
Sumatriptan (Imitrex)
Warfarin (Coumadin)

Special information about pregnancy and breastfeeding

The effects of Celexa during pregnancy have not been adequately studied, and the potential for harm has not been ruled out. There have been reports of serious complications in newborns who were exposed to Celexa late in the third trimester. Any patient who becomes pregnant or plans to become pregnant while on Celexa therapy should contact her doctor immediately.

Celexa may appear in breast milk and could affect a nursing infant. If this medication is essential to the patient's health, the doctor may advise her to discontinue breastfeeding until her treatment with Celexa is finished.

Recommended dosage

ADULTS

The recommended starting dose of Celexa tablets or oral solution is 20 milligrams once a day. Dosage is usually increased to 40 milligrams once daily after at least a week has passed. Doses above 40 milligrams a day are generally not recommended.

For older adults and those who have liver problems, the recommended dose is 20 milligrams once a day.

Overdosage

Any medication taken in excess can have serious consequences. If an overdose is suspected, seek medical attention immediately.

- *Symptoms of Celexa overdose may include:*
  Amnesia, bluish or purplish discoloration of the skin, coma, confusion, convulsions, dizziness, drowsiness, hyperventilation, nausea, rapid heartbeat, sweating, tremor, vomiting

Chlordiazepoxide *See Librium, page 95*

CHLORPROMAZINE

Why is this drug prescribed?

Chlorpromazine is used to treat schizophrenia. It is also prescribed for the short-term treatment of severe behavioral disorders in children, including explosive hyperactivity and combativeness; and for the manic phase of bipolar disorder.

Chlorpromazine is also used to control nausea and vomiting, and to relieve restlessness and apprehension before surgery. It is used as an aid in the treatment of tetanus, and is prescribed for uncontrollable hiccups and acute intermittent porphyria (attacks of severe abdominal pain sometimes accompanied by psychiatric disturbances, cramps in the arms and legs, and muscle weakness).

Most important fact about this drug

Chlorpromazine may cause tardive dyskinesia—a condition marked by involuntary muscle spasms and twitches in the face and body. This condition may be permanent, and appears to be most common among the elderly, especially women.

How should this medication be taken?

Patients taking chlorpromazine in a liquid concentrate form will need to dilute it with a liquid such as a carbonated beverage, coffee, fruit juice, milk, tea, tomato juice, or water. Puddings, soups, and other semisolid foods may also be used. Chlorpromazine should not be mixed with alcoholic beverages. It will taste best if it is diluted immediately prior to use.

Antacids such as Gelusil should not be taken at the same time as chlorpromazine. At least 1 to 2 hours should be allowed between doses of the two drugs.

- *Missed dose...*
  Patients taking 1 dose a day should take the missed dose as soon as they remember. If they do not remember until the next day, they should skip the missed dose and go back to their regular schedule.

  Patient who take more than 1 dose a day should take the missed dose if it is within an hour or so of the scheduled time. If they do not remember until later, they should skip the missed dose and go back to their regular schedule. Doses should never be doubled.

- *Storage instructions...*
  Chlorpromazine should be stored away from heat, light, and moisture. The liquid should be protected from freezing. Since the liquid concentrate form of chlorpromazine is light-sensitive, it should be stored in a dark place, but it does not need to be refrigerated.

What side effects may occur?

Side effects cannot be predicted. If any develop or change in intensity, patients should inform their doctor as soon as possible.

- *Side effects may include:*
  Anticholinergic effects (such as constipation, dry mouth, rapid heartbeat), drowsiness, involuntary muscle spasms and twitches (tardive dyskinesia), jaundice, low blood pressure, low white blood-cell count (agranulocytosis), movements similar to Parkinson's disease, physical restlessness, neuroleptic malignant syndrome (see "Special warnings about this medication"), vision changes

Why should this drug not be prescribed?

Chlorpromazine should not be combined with large amounts of any substance that slows down mental function, such as alcohol, barbiturates, or narcotics. It should be avoided by anyone who has ever had an allergic reaction to a member of the phenothiazine family of antipsychotic medications.

Special warnings about this medication

Chlorpromazine should be used with caution if the patient has asthma, a brain tumor, breast cancer, intestinal blockage, emphysema, glaucoma, heart problems, kidney or liver disease, a severe respiratory infection, seizures, or an abnormal bone marrow or blood condition. Caution is also advisable if the patient is exposed to pesticides or extreme heat.

Due to its ability to prevent vomiting, chlorpromazine can mask symptoms of an overdose of other drugs. It could also mask symptoms of brain tumor, intestinal blockage, and the neurological condition known as Reye's syndrome. The drug should be avoided in children and adolescents who have symptoms that could indicate Reye's syndrome, including persistent or recurrent vomiting, listlessness, irritability, combativeness, and disorientation.

Patients should be aware that chlorpromazine contains sulfites and could cause an allergic reaction.

Stomach inflammation, dizziness, nausea, vomiting, and tremors may result if chlorpromazine is stopped suddenly. Therapy should be discontinued only under a doctor's supervision.

This drug may impair the ability to drive a car or operate potentially dangerous machinery. Patients should not participate in any activities that require full alertness if they are unsure about their ability.

This drug can increase sensitivity to light. Patients should avoid being out in the sun too long.

Chlorpromazine can cause a potentially fatal group of symptoms called neuroleptic malignant syndrome. Symptoms include extremely high body temperature, rigid muscles, mental changes, irregular pulse or blood pressure, rapid heartbeat, sweating, and changes in heart rhythm. The doctor should be alerted immediately if these symptoms develop. Chlorpromazine therapy will need to be discontinued.

Patients on chlorpromazine for a prolonged period should see their doctor for regular evaluations, since side effects can get worse over time.

Chlorpromazine may cause false-positive phenylketonuria (PKU) tests.

Possible food and drug interactions when taking this medication

If chlorpromazine is taken with certain other drugs, the effects of either could be increased, decreased, or altered. Here is an overview of drugs that may cause a problem:

Anesthetics
Antacids such as Gelusil
Antiseizure drugs such as Dilantin
Antispasmodic drugs such as Cogentin
Atropine (Donnatal)
Barbiturates such as phenobarbital

Blood-thinning drugs such as Coumadin
Captopril (Capoten)
Cimetidine (Tagamet)
Diuretics such as Dyazide
Drugs classified as MAO inhibitors, such as the antidepressants Nardil
    and Parnate
Epinephrine (EpiPen)
Guanethidine
Lithium (Lithobid, Eskalith)
Narcotics such as Percocet
Propranolol (Inderal)

Extreme drowsiness and other potentially serious effects can result if
chlorpromazine is combined with alcohol and other mental depressants
such as narcotic painkillers like Demerol.

Because chlorpromazine prevents vomiting, it can hide the signs and
symptoms of overdose of other drugs.

Special information about pregnancy and breastfeeding

The effects of chlorpromazine during pregnancy have not been adequately studied. Patients who are pregnant or plan to become pregnant should
notify their doctor. Pregnant women should use chlorpromazine only if
clearly needed.

Chlorpromazine appears in breast milk and may affect a nursing
infant. If this medication is essential to the mother's health, the doctor
may advise her not to breastfeed until treatment is finished.

Recommended dosage

Dosage recommendations shown here are for the oral and rectal forms of
the drug. In some cases, chlorpromazine is also given by injection. The
following indications and dosages are for adults unless otherwise noted.

SCHIZOPHRENIA AND MANIA

The doctor will gradually increase the dosage until symptoms are controlled. Full improvement may not be seen for weeks or even months.

Initial dosages may range from 30 to 75 milligrams daily. The amount
is divided into equal doses and taken 3 or 4 times a day. If needed, the
doctor may increase the dosage by 20 to 50 milligrams at semiweekly
intervals.

NAUSEA AND VOMITING

The usual tablet dosage is 10 to 25 milligrams, taken every 4 or 6 hours,
as needed.

One 100-milligram suppository can be used every 6 to 8 hours.

UNCONTROLLABLE HICCUPS

Dosages may range from 75 to 200 milligrams daily, divided into 3 or 4 equal doses.

ACUTE INTERMITTENT PORPHYRIA

Dosages may range from 75 to 200 milligrams daily, divided into 3 or 4 equal doses.

SEVERE BEHAVIOR PROBLEMS OR NAUSEA AND VOMITING IN CHILDREN

Dosages are based on the child's weight. Chlorpromazine is generally not prescribed for children younger than 6 months.

Oral: The daily dose is one-quarter milligram for each pound of the child's weight, taken every 4 to 6 hours, as needed.

Rectal: The usual dose is one-half milligram per pound of body weight, taken every 6 to 8 hours, as necessary.

OLDER ADULTS

In general, older people take lower dosages of chlorpromazine, and any increase in dosage will be gradual. Because of a greater risk of low blood pressure, the doctor will watch the patient closely. Remember that older people (especially older women) may be more susceptible to tardive dyskinesia.

Overdosage

An overdose of chlorpromazine can be fatal. If an overdose is suspected, seek medical help immediately.

- *Symptoms of chlorpromazine overdose may include:*
  Agitation, coma, convulsions, difficulty breathing, difficulty swallowing, dry mouth, extreme sleepiness, fever, intestinal blockage, irregular heart rate, low blood pressure, restlessness

Citalopram *See Celexa, page 25*

Clomipramine *See Anafranil, page 12*

Clonazepam *See Klonopin, page 86*

Clorazepate *See Tranxene, page 210*

Clozapine *See Clozaril, page 32*

CLOZARIL

Clozapine

Why is this drug prescribed?

Clozaril is prescribed for people with severe schizophrenia who have failed to respond to standard treatments. It is also used to help reduce the risk of suicidal behavior in people with schizophrenia. Like all antipsychotic agents, Clozaril is not a cure, but it can help some people return to more normal lives.

Most important fact about this drug

Even though it does not produce some of the disturbing side effects of other antipsychotic medications, Clozaril may cause agranulocytosis, a potentially lethal disorder of the white blood cells. Because of the risk of agranulocytosis, anyone who takes Clozaril is required to have a blood test once a week for the first 6 months. The drug is carefully controlled so that those taking it must get their weekly blood test before receiving the following week's supply of medication. After 6 months of acceptable blood counts, patients are allowed to switch to an every-other-week testing schedule. Anyone whose blood test results are abnormal will be taken off Clozaril either temporarily or permanently, depending on the results of an additional 4 weeks of testing.

How should this medication be taken?

It is important to take Clozaril exactly as directed. Because of the significant risk of serious side effects associated with this drug, patients should be periodically reassessed for continuation of Clozaril therapy. Clozaril is distributed only through the Clozaril Patient Management System, which ensures regular white blood cell testing, monitoring, and pharmacy services prior to delivery of the next supply.

Clozaril may be taken with or without food.

* *Missed dose...*
  Generally, the forgotten dose should be taken as soon as remembered. However, if it is almost time for the next dose, patients should skip the one they missed and go back to their regular schedule. Doses should never be doubled.

  If the patient stops taking Clozaril for more than 2 days, it should not be started again without first consulting the physician.

* *Storage instructions...*
  Clozaril may be stored at room temperature.

What side effects may occur?

Side effects cannot be predicted. If any develop or change in intensity, patients should inform their doctor as soon as possible.

The most feared side effect is agranulocytosis, a dangerous drop in the number of a certain kind of white blood cells. Symptoms include fever, lethargy, sore throat, and weakness. If not caught in time, agranulocytosis can be fatal. That is why all people who take Clozaril must have a blood test every week. About 1 percent develop agranulocytosis and must stop taking the drug.

Seizures are another potential side effect, occurring in some 5 percent of people who take Clozaril. The higher the dosage, the greater the risk of seizures.

- *Other side effects may include:*
  Blood disorders, constipation, drowsiness, dry mouth, fainting, fever, headache, low blood pressure, nausea, rapid heartbeat, salivation, sweating, tremor, vertigo, visual disturbances

Why should this drug not be prescribed?

Clozaril is considered a somewhat risky medication because of its potential to cause agranulocytosis and seizures. It should be taken only by people whose condition is serious, and who have not been helped by more traditional antipsychotic medications such as Haldol or Mellaril. Clozaril should not be used if the patient:

Has a bone marrow disease or disorder
Has epilepsy that is not controlled
Has ever developed an abnormal white blood cell count while taking Clozaril
Is currently taking some other drug, such as Tegretol, that could cause a decrease in white blood cell count or a drug that could affect the bone marrow
Has ever had an allergic reaction to any of Clozaril's ingredients

Special warnings about this medication

Clozaril can cause drowsiness, especially at the start of treatment. For this reason, and also because of the potential for seizures, patients should not drive, swim, climb, or operate dangerous machinery while taking this medication, at least in the early stages of treatment.

Even though blood tests are done weekly for the first 6 months of treatment and every other week after that, patients need to stay alert for early symptoms of agranulocytosis: weakness, lethargy, fever, sore throat, a general feeling of illness, a flu-like feeling, or ulcers of the lips, mouth, or other mucous membranes. If any such symptoms develop, they should contact their doctor immediately.

Especially during the first 3 weeks of treatment, a fever may develop. If this happens, the patient should notify the doctor.

Instruct patients to check with their doctor before drinking alcohol or using drugs of any kind, including over-the-counter medicines.

Patients with an enlarged prostate or the eye condition called narrow-angle glaucoma must be closely monitored by the doctor. Clozaril could make these conditions worse.

Certain antipsychotic drugs, including Clozaril, are associated with an increased risk of developing high blood sugar, which on rare occasions has led to coma or death. Patients should see their doctor right away if they develop signs of high blood sugar, including dry mouth, thirst, increased urination, and tiredness. Patients who have diabetes or have a high risk of developing it should see their doctor regularly for blood sugar testing.

On rare occasions, Clozaril can cause intestinal problems—constipation, impaction, or blockage—that can, in extreme cases, be fatal.

In very rare cases, Clozaril has been known to cause a potentially fatal inflammation of the heart. This problem is most likely to surface during the first month of treatment, but has also occurred later. Warning signs include unexplained fatigue, shortness of breath, fever, chest pain, and a rapid or pounding heartbeat. Patients should see their doctor immediately if they develop these symptoms. Even a suspicion of heart inflammation warrants discontinuation of Clozaril.

Especially when starting Clozaril therapy, patients may be troubled by a dramatic drop in blood pressure whenever they first stand up. This can lead to light-headedness, fainting, or even total collapse and cardiac arrest. Clozaril also tends to increase the heart rate. Both problems are more dangerous for someone with a heart problem. If a patient suffers from heart disease, make sure the doctor knows about it.

Patients with kidney, liver, or lung disease, or a history of seizures or prostate problems, should discuss the problem with their doctor before taking Clozaril. Nausea, vomiting, loss of appetite, and a yellow tinge to the skin and eyes are signs of liver trouble. The doctor should be contacted immediately if a patient develops these symptoms.

Drugs such as Clozaril can sometimes cause a set of symptoms called neuroleptic malignant syndrome. Symptoms include high fever, muscle rigidity, irregular pulse or blood pressure, rapid heartbeat, excessive perspiration, and changes in heart rhythm. The patient will be taken off Clozaril while this condition is being treated.

There is also a risk of developing tardive dyskinesia, a condition of involuntary, slow, rhythmical movements. This happens more often in older adults, especially older women.

In very rare instances, Clozaril may also cause a blood clot in the lungs. Patients should call their doctor immediately if they develop severe breathing problems or chest pain.

Possible food and drug interactions when taking this medication

If Clozaril is taken with certain other drugs, the effects of either could be increased, decreased, or altered. Here's an overview of the drugs that can cause a problem:

Alcohol
Antidepressants such as Paxil, Prozac, and Zoloft
Antipsychotic drugs such as chlorpromazine and Mellaril
Blood pressure medications such as Aldomet and Hytrin
Caffeine
Chemotherapy drugs
Cimetidine (Tagamet)
Digitoxin (Crystodigin)
Digoxin (Lanoxin)
Drugs that depress the central nervous system such as phenobarbital
  and Seconal
Drugs that contain atropine such as Donnatal and Levsin
Epilepsy drugs such as Tegretol and Dilantin
Epinephrine (EpiPen)
Erythromycin (E-Mycin, Eryc, others)
Fluvoxamine
Heart rhythm stabilizers such as Rythmol, Quinidex, and Tambocor
Nicotine
Rifampin (Rifadin)
Tranquilizers such as Valium and Xanax
Warfarin (Coumadin)

Special information about pregnancy and breastfeeding

The effects of Clozaril during pregnancy have not been adequately studied. Patients who are pregnant or plan to become pregnant should inform their doctor immediately. Clozaril treatment should be continued during pregnancy only if absolutely necessary.

Breastfeeding is not recommended during Clozaril therapy, since the drug may appear in breast milk.

Recommended dosage

ADULTS

Dosage should be carefully individualized and monitored. The usual recommended initial dose is half of a 25-milligram tablet (12.5 milligrams) 1 or 2 times daily. The doctor may increase the dosage in increments of 25 to 50 milligrams a day to achieve a daily dose of 300 to 450 milligrams by the end of 2 weeks. Dosage increases after that will be made only once or twice a week and will be no more than 100 milligrams each time. Dosage is increased gradually because rapid increases and higher doses are more likely to cause seizures and changes in heart rhythm. The highest recommended dosage is 900 milligrams a day divided into 2 or 3 doses.

CHILDREN

Safety and efficacy have not been established for children up to 16 years of age.

Overdosage

Any medication taken in excess can have serious consequences. If an overdose is suspected, seek emergency medical attention immediately.

- *Symptoms of overdose with Clozaril may include:*
  Coma, delirium, drowsiness, excess salivation, low blood/pressure, faintness, pneumonia, rapid heartbeat, seizures, shallow breathing or absence of breathing

COGNEX
Tacrine hydrochloride

Why is this drug prescribed?
Cognex is used for the treatment of mild to moderate Alzheimer's disease. This progressive, degenerative disorder causes physical changes in the brain that disrupt the flow of information and affect memory, thinking, and behavior. Like other Alzheimer's drugs, Cognex can temporarily improve brain function in some Alzheimer's sufferers, although it does not halt the progress of the underlying disease.

Most important fact about this drug
Cognex treatment should not be stopped, or the dosage reduced, without consulting the doctor. A sudden reduction can cause the patient to become more disturbed and forgetful. Giving more Cognex than the doctor advises can also cause serious problems. Dosage should not be changed without instructions from the doctor.

How should this medication be taken?
This medication will work better if taken at regular intervals, usually 4 times a day. Cognex is best taken between meals. However, if it is irritating to the stomach, the doctor may advise taking it with meals. If Cognex is not taken regularly, as the doctor directs, the condition may get worse.

- *Missed dose...*
  Generally, the forgotten dose should be given as soon as possible. If it is within 2 hours of the next dose, caregivers should skip the missed dose and go back to the regular schedule. Doses should never be doubled.

- *Storage instructions...*
  Cognex should be stored at room temperature away from moisture.

What side effects may occur?

Side effects cannot be predicted. If any develop or change in intensity, caregivers should tell the doctor as soon as possible.

- *Side effects may include:*
  Diarrhea, indigestion, liver problems, loss of muscle coordination, muscle aches, nausea, vomiting, weight loss

Caregivers should report any symptoms that develop while on Cognex therapy. They should alert the doctor if the patient develops nausea, vomiting, loose stools, or diarrhea at the start of therapy or when the dosage is increased. Later in therapy, they should be on the lookout for rash or fever, yellowing of the eyes and skin, or changes in the color of the stool.

Why should this drug not be prescribed?

People who are sensitive to or have ever had an allergic reaction to Cognex (including symptoms such as rash or fever) should not take this medication. If during previous Cognex therapy the patient developed jaundice (yellow skin and eyes), which signals that something is wrong with the liver, Cognex should not be used again.

Special warnings about this medication

Cognex should be used with caution if the patient has a history of liver disease, certain heart disorders, stomach ulcers, or asthma.

Because of the risk of liver problems when taking Cognex, the doctor will schedule blood tests to monitor liver function every other week from at least the fourth week to the sixteenth week of treatment. After 16 weeks, blood tests will be given monthly for 2 months and every 3 months after that. If the patient develops any liver problems, the doctor may temporarily discontinue Cognex treatment until further testing shows that the liver has returned to normal. If the doctor resumes Cognex treatment, regular blood tests will be conducted again.

Before having any surgery, including dental surgery, caregivers should tell the doctor that the patient is being treated with Cognex.

Cognex can cause seizures, and may cause problems with urination.

Possible food and drug interactions when taking this medication

If Cognex is taken with certain other drugs, the effects of either could be increased, decreased, or altered. Here is an overview of drugs that can cause a problem:

Drugs that quell spasms, including Bentyl and Levsin
Bethanechol chloride (Urecholine)
Cimetidine (Tagamet)
Fluvoxamine
Muscle stimulants such as Mestinon, Mytelase, and Prostigmin
Nonsteroidal anti-inflammatory drugs such as Aleve, Motrin, and Naprosyn

The Parkinson's medications Artane and Cogentin
Theophylline (Theo-Dur)

Special information about pregnancy and breastfeeding
The effects of Cognex during pregnancy have not been studied; and it is
not known whether Cognex appears in breast milk.

Recommended dosage
ADULTS

The usual starting dose is 10 milligrams 4 times a day, for at least 4
weeks. The dose should not be increased during this 4-week period unless
the doctor directs.

Depending on the patient's tolerance of the drug, dosage may then be
increased at 4-week intervals, first to 20 milligrams, then to 30, and finally to 40, always taken 4 times a day.

CHILDREN

The safety and effectiveness of Cognex have not been established in
children.

Overdosage
Any medication taken in excess can have serious consequences. If an
overdose is suspected, seek medical attention immediately.

- *Symptoms of Cognex overdose may include:*
  Collapse, convulsions, extreme muscle weakness, possibly ending in
  death (if breathing muscles are affected), low blood pressure, nausea,
  salivation, slowed heart rate, sweating, vomiting

Compazine *See Prochlorperazine, page 149*

Concerta *See Ritalin, page 176*

CYLERT
Pemoline

Why is this drug prescribed?
Cylert is used to help treat children who have attention deficit hyperactivity disorder (ADHD). Because it has been known to cause liver damage, it is usually prescribed only when other drugs have failed. Drugs
such as Cylert should be used as part of a comprehensive treatment plan
offering psychological and educational support to help the child become
more stable.

Most important fact about this drug
Although cases of liver damage are rare, some have been serious enough
to be fatal. Children taking Cylert should have their liver function tested

every 2 weeks. If the child develops any signs of liver damage, the doctor should be called immediately. Warning signs include fatigue, loss of appetite, digestive problems, yellow skin or eyes, and pain in the upper right section of the abdomen.

How should this medication be taken?

Cylert should be taken once a day, in the morning.

● *Missed dose...*
The child should take it as soon as remembered, then go back to the regular schedule. If it's not remembered until the next day, it should be skipped and the child should go back to the regular schedule. Doses should never be doubled.

● *Storage instructions...*
Cylert may be stored at room temperature.

What side effects may occur?

Side effects cannot be predicted. If any develop or change in intensity, caregivers should inform the child's doctor as soon as possible.

● *Side effects may include:*
Aplastic anemia (rare), dizziness, drowsiness, growth suppression, insomnia, liver problems, mental depression, nausea, rash, seizures, stomach pain, weight loss

Why should this drug not be prescribed?

Cylert cannot be used if the child is allergic to it or has liver problems.

Special warnings about this medication

Cylert may cause dizziness. Patients should be careful climbing stairs or participating in activities that require mental alertness.

Although there have been no reports that Cylert is physically addictive, it is chemically similar to a class of drugs that are potentially addictive. It is important that the child be given no more than the prescribed dosage.

Children who take this drug on a long-term basis should be carefully monitored for signs of stunted growth.

The doctor will be extra cautious if the child has kidney problems.

Children who have a psychiatric illness and take Cylert may experience increasingly disordered thoughts and behavioral disturbances.

Possible food and drug interactions when taking this medication

If Cylert is taken with certain other drugs, the effects of either could be increased, decreased, or altered. Here is an overview of drugs that may cause a problem:

Seizure medications such as Tegretol
Other drugs that affect the central nervous system, such as Ritalin

Special information about pregnancy and breastfeeding

This drug is for use only in children, and its effects in pregnancy have not been adequately studied. Cylert should be used during pregnancy only if it is clearly necessary. It is not known whether the drug appears in breast milk, but caution is advised.

Recommended dosage

The recommended beginning dose is 37.5 milligrams daily. Dosages may be gradually increased if needed. Most children take doses ranging from 56.25 to 75 milligrams a day. The maximum recommended daily dose of Cylert is 112.5 milligrams. Significant improvement is gradual and may not be apparent until the third or fourth week of treatment with Cylert.

The doctor may occasionally stop treatment with Cylert to see whether behavioral problems return and whether further treatment with Cylert is necessary.

Overdosage

Any medication taken in excess can have serious consequences. If an overdose is suspected, seek medical help immediately.

- *Symptoms of Cylert overdose may include:*
  Agitation, coma, confusion, convulsions, delirium, dilated pupils, exaggerated feeling of well-being, extremely high temperature, flushing, hallucinations, headache, high blood pressure, increased heart rate, increased reflex reactions, muscle twitches, sweating, tremors, vomiting

DALMANE

Flurazepam hydrochloride

Why is this drug prescribed?

Dalmane is used for the relief of insomnia—difficulty falling asleep, waking up frequently at night, or waking up early in the morning. It can be used by people whose insomnia keeps coming back and in those who have poor sleeping habits. It belongs to a class of drugs known as benzodiazepines.

Most important fact about this drug

Tolerance and dependence can occur with the use of Dalmane. Patients may experience withdrawal symptoms if they stop using this drug abruptly. They should discontinue or change their dose only in consultation with their doctor.

How should this medication be taken?

Dalmane is taken in a single dose at bedtime. It is important to take this medication exactly as prescribed.

- *Missed dose...*
  Dalmane should be taken only as needed. Doses should never be doubled.

- *Storage instructions...*
  Dalmane should be stored away from heat, light, and moisture.

What side effects may occur?

Side effects cannot be predicted. If any develop or change in intensity, patients should inform their doctor as soon as possible.

- *Side effects may include:*
  Confusion, dizziness, drowsiness, impaired muscle coordination, light-headedness

- *Side effects due to rapid decrease in dose or abrupt withdrawal from Dalmane:*
  Abdominal and muscle cramps, convulsions, depressed mood, inability to fall asleep or stay asleep, sweating, tremors, vomiting

Why should this drug not be prescribed?

Dalmane cannot be used by anyone who is sensitive to or has had an allergic reaction to it or similar drugs such as Valium.

Special warnings about this medication

Patients should avoid driving, operating dangerous machinery, or participating in any hazardous activity that requires full mental alertness after taking Dalmane.

This drug should be used with caution in patients who are severely depressed, or have suffered from severe depression.

Caution is also warranted in patients who have decreased kidney or liver function or chronic respiratory or lung disease.

Possible food and drug interactions when taking this medication

Alcohol intensifies the effects of Dalmane. Patients should avoid drinking alcohol while taking this medication.

If Dalmane is taken with certain other drugs, the effects of either could be increased, decreased, or altered. Here is an overview of drugs that may cause a problem:

Antidepressants such as Elavil and Tofranil
Antihistamines such as Benadryl and Tavist
Antipsychotic drugs such as Mellaril and chlorpromazine
Barbiturates such as Seconal and phenobarbital
Narcotic painkillers such as Demerol and Tylenol with Codeine
Sedatives such as Xanax and Halcion
Tranquilizers such as Librium and Valium

Special information about pregnancy and breastfeeding

Dalmane should not be used during pregnancy. There is an increased risk of birth defects. This drug may appear in breast milk and could affect a nursing infant. It may be advisable to discontinue breastfeeding until treatment with Dalmane is finished.

Recommended dosage

ADULTS

The usual recommended dose is 30 milligrams at bedtime; however 15 milligrams may be all that is necessary. The doctor should adjust the dose to the patient's needs.

CHILDREN

Safety and effectiveness of Dalmane have not been established in children under 15 years of age.

OLDER ADULTS

The doctor will limit the dosage to the smallest effective amount to avoid oversedation, dizziness, confusion, or lack of muscle coordination. The usual starting dose is 15 milligrams.

Overdosage

Any medication taken in excess can have serious consequences. If an overdose is suspected, seek medical attention immediately.

- *The symptoms of Dalmane overdose may include:*
  Coma, confusion, low blood pressure, sleepiness

DEPAKOTE

Divalproex sodium (Valproic acid)

Why is this drug prescribed?

Depakote, in both delayed-release tablet and capsule form, is used to treat certain types of seizures and convulsions. It may be prescribed alone or with other epilepsy medications.

The delayed-release tablets are also used to control the manic episodes that occur in bipolar disorder.

An extended-release form of this drug, Depakote ER, is prescribed to prevent migraine headaches. The delayed-release tablets are also used for this purpose.

Most important fact about this drug

Depakote can cause serious or even fatal liver damage, especially during the first 6 months of treatment. Children under 2 years of age are the most vulnerable, especially if they are also taking other anticonvulsant medicines and have certain other disorders such as mental retardation. The risk of liver damage decreases with age; but patients should always be alert for the following symptoms: loss of seizure control, weakness, dizziness, drowsiness, a general feeling of ill health, facial swelling, loss of appetite, vomiting, and yellowing of the skin and eyes. The doctor should be alerted immediately if a liver problem is suspected.

Depakote has also been known to cause life-threatening damage to the pancreas. This problem can surface at any time, even after years of treatment. Patients should call the doctor immediately if they develop any of the following warning signs: abdominal pain, loss of appetite, nausea, or vomiting.

How should this medication be taken?

Patients should take the Depakote tablet with water and swallow it whole (don't chew it or crush it). It has a special coating to avoid upsetting the stomach.

The sprinkle capsule can be swallowed whole or opened and sprinkled on a teaspoon of soft food such as applesauce or pudding. The food should be swallowed immediately, without chewing. The sprinkle capsules are large enough to be opened easily.

Depakote can be taken with meals or snacks to avoid stomach upset.

- *Missed dose...*
  If a patient takes Depakote once a day, the missed dose should be taken as soon as remembered. If it isn't remembered until the next day, the patient should skip the missed dose and return to the regular schedule.

  If a patient takes more than one dose a day, the missed dose should be taken right away if it's within 6 hours of the scheduled time, and the rest of the day's doses should be taken at equal intervals during the remainder of the day. Doses should never be doubled.

- *Storage instructions...*
  Depakote may be stored at room temperature.

What side effects may occur?

Side effects cannot be predicted. If any develop or change in intensity, patients should inform their doctor as soon as possible. Because Depakote is often used with other antiseizure drugs, it may not be possible to determine whether a side effect is due to Depakote alone. Only the doctor can determine if it is safe to continue taking Depakote.

- *Side effects may include:*
  Abdominal pain, blurred vision, diarrhea, double vision, headache, impaired muscle coordination, indigestion, nausea, rapid eye movement, sleepiness, tremor, vomiting, weakness, weight loss or gain

Why should this drug not be prescribed?

This medication must be avoided by anyone with liver disease, poor liver function, or the genetic abnormality known as urea cycle disorder (UCD).

It is also contraindicated for those who are sensitive to or have ever had an allergic reaction to Depakote.

Special warnings about this medication

This medication can severely damage the liver (see "Most important fact about this drug"). The doctor should test the patient's liver function before starting therapy with this medication and at regular intervals thereafter.

Also remember that the drug can damage the pancreas (see "Most important fact about this drug"). This problem can worsen very rapidly. Patients should contact their doctor without delay if they develop any symptoms.

In people with a rare set of genetic abnormalities called urea cycle disorder, Depakote may adversely affect the brain. Signs of a developing problem include lack of energy, repeated attacks of vomiting, and mental changes. Patients who suspect a problem should see their doctor immediately. Depakote may have to be discontinued.

Depakote causes some people to become drowsy or less alert. Patients should not drive, operate dangerous machinery, or participate in any hazardous activity that requires full mental alertness until they are certain the drug does not effect them this way.

This medication should not be stopped abruptly. A gradual reduction in dosage is usually required under a physician's supervision.

Depakote prolongs the time it takes blood to clot, which increases the chances of serious bleeding.

This drug can also increase the effect of painkillers and anesthetics. Before any surgery or dental procedure, the doctor should be informed that the patient is taking Depakote.

Patients taking Depakote to prevent migraine should remember that it will not cure a headache once it has started.

Some coated particles from the capsules may appear in the stool. This is to be expected, and is not a cause for worry.

Possible food and drug interactions when taking this medication

Depakote depresses activity of the central nervous system, and may increase the effects of alcohol. Patient's should not drink alcohol while taking this medication.

If Depakote is taken with certain other drugs, the effects of either could be increased, decreased, or altered. Here is an overview of drugs that can cause a problem:

Amitriptyline (Elavil)
Aspirin
Barbiturates such as phenobarbital and Seconal
Blood thinners such as Coumadin

Cyclosporine (Sandimmune, Neoral)
Nortriptyline (Pamelor)
Other seizure medications, including carbamazepine (Tegretol), clo-
  nazepam (Klonopin), ethosuximide (Zarontin), felbamate (Felbatol),
  lamotrigine (Lamictal), phenytoin (Dilantin), and primidone
  (Mysoline)
Rifampin (Rifater)
Sleep aids such as Halcion
Tolbutamide (Orinase)
Tranquilizers such as Valium and Xanax
Zidovudine (Retrovir)

Special information about pregnancy and breastfeeding

Depakote may produce birth defects when taken during pregnancy.
Patients who are pregnant or plan to become pregnant should inform their
doctor immediately. Depakote should be used during pregnancy only if it
is essential for seizure control.

Depakote appears in breast milk and could affect a nursing infant. If
Depakote is essential to the patient's health, the doctor may advise her to discontinue breastfeeding until her treatment with this medication is finished.

Recommended dosage

EPILEPSY

Dosage for adults and children 10 years of age or older is determined
by body weight. The usual recommended starting dose is 10 to 15 milligrams per 2.2 pounds per day, depending on the type of seizure. The
doctor may increase the dose at 1-week intervals by 5 to 10 milligrams
per 2.2 pounds per day until the seizures are controlled or the side effects
become too severe. The maximum dose is 60 milligrams per 2.2 pounds
per day. If the total dosage is more than 250 milligrams a day, the doctor
will divide it into smaller individual doses.

Older adults usually begin taking this medication at lower dosages,
and the dosage is increased more slowly.

MANIC EPISODES

The usual starting dose for those aged 18 and over is 750 milligrams a
day, divided into smaller doses. The doctor will adjust the dose for best
results.

MIGRAINE PREVENTION

Delayed-Release Tablets
The usual starting dose for those aged 16 and over is 250 milligrams
twice a day. The doctor will adjust the dose, up to a maximum of 1,000
milligrams a day.

Extended-Release Tablets
The usual starting dose is 500 milligrams once a day for 1 week. The dose may then be increased to 1,000 milligrams once a day.

Depakote delayed-release and extended-release tablets work differently and cannot be substituted for each other.

Researchers have not established the safety and effectiveness of Depakote for prevention of migraines in children or in adults over 65.

Overdosage
An overdose of Depakote can be fatal. If an overdose is suspected, seek medical attention immediately.

* *Symptoms of Depakote overdose may include:*
  Coma, extreme sleepiness, heart problems

Desipramine *See Norpramin, page 129*

DESOXYN
Methamphetamine hydrochloride

Why is this drug prescribed?
Desoxyn is used to treat attention deficit hyperactivity disorder (ADHD). This drug is given as part of a total treatment program that includes psychological, educational, and social measures.

Desoxyn also may be used for a short time as part of an overall diet plan for weight reduction. Desoxyn is given only when other weight loss drugs and weight loss programs have been unsuccessful.

Most important fact about this drug?
Excessive doses of this medication can produce addiction. Individuals who stop taking this medication after taking high doses for a long time may suffer withdrawal symptoms, including extreme tiredness, depression, and sleep disorders. Signs of excessive use of Desoxyn include severe skin inflammation, difficulty sleeping, irritability, hyperactivity, personality changes, and psychiatric problems.

Desoxyn can lose its effectiveness in decreasing the appetite after a few weeks. If this happens, the medication should be stopped. Patients should never take more than the recommended dose in an attempt to increase the drug's effect.

How should this medication be taken?
It is important to follow the doctor's directions carefully. The doctor will prescribe the lowest effective dose of Desoxyn; it should never be increased without approval.

Patients should avoid taking this medication late in the evening; it can cause difficulty sleeping.

- *Missed dose . . .*
  Generally, the forgotten dose should be taken as soon as remembered. However, if it is almost time for the next dose, the patient should skip the missed dose and return to the regular schedule. Doses should never be doubled.

- *Storage instructions . . .*
  Desoxyn may be stored at room temperature.

What side effects may occur?

Side effects cannot be predicted. If any develop or change in intensity, patients should inform their doctor as soon as possible.

- *Side effects may include:*
  Changes in sex drive, constipation, diarrhea, dizziness, dry mouth, hives, impotence, increased blood pressure, rapid or irregular heartbeat, sleeplessness, tremor

Why should this drug not be prescribed?

Desoxyn must never be combined with a monoamine oxidase (MAO) inhibitor drug such as Nardil or Parnate. Patients should allow 14 days between stopping an MAO inhibitor and beginning therapy with Desoxyn.

Desoxyn should not be taken by anyone who has high pressure in the eyes (glaucoma), advanced hardening of the arteries, heart disease, moderate to severe high blood pressure, thyroid problems, or sensitivity to this type of drug. This medication should also be avoided by anyone who suffers from tics (repeated, involuntary twitches) or Tourette's syndrome or who has a family history of these conditions.

People who are in an agitated state or who have a history of drug abuse should not take this medication.

Desoxyn should not be used to treat children whose symptoms may be caused by stress or a psychiatric disorder.

Special warnings about this medication

Desoxyn is not appropriate for all children with symptoms of ADHD. The doctor will do a complete history and evaluation before prescribing this medication. The doctor will take into account the duration and severity of the symptoms as well as the child's age.

This type of medication can affect the growth of children, so the doctor will monitor them carefully while they are taking this drug. The long-term effects of this type of medication in children have not been established.

Desoxyn should be used with caution by people with mild high blood pressure.

Desoxyn may affect the patient's ability to perform potentially hazardous activities, such as operating machinery or driving a car.

Desoxyn should not be used to combat fatigue or to replace rest.

Possible food and drug interactions when taking this medication

If Desoxyn is taken with certain other drugs, the effects of either could be increased, decreased, or altered. Here is an overview of drugs that may cause a problem:

Antidepressants classified as tricyclics, such as Elavil, Pamelor, and Tofranil

Drugs classified as monoamine oxidase (MAO) inhibitors, such as the antidepressants Nardil and Parnate

Drugs classified as phenothiazines, such as the antipsychotic medications prochlorperazine and chlorpromazine

Guanethidine

Insulin

Special information about pregnancy and breastfeeding

Infants born to women taking this type of drug have a risk of prematurity and low birth weight. Drug dependence may occur in newborns when the mother has taken this drug prior to delivery. Patients who are pregnant or plan to become pregnant should tell their doctor immediately.

Desoxyn makes its way into breast milk. Women should not breastfeed while taking this medication.

Recommended dosage

ATTENTION DEFICIT HYPERACTIVITY DISORDER

For children 6 years and older, the usual starting dose is 5 milligrams of Desoxyn taken once or twice a day. The doctor may increase the dose by 5 milligrams a week until the child responds to the medication. The typical effective dose is 20 to 25 milligrams a day, usually divided into two doses.

The doctor may periodically discontinue this drug in order to reassess the child's condition and see whether therapy is still needed.

Desoxyn should not be given to children under 6 years of age to treat attention deficit disorder; the safety and effectiveness in this age group have not been established.

WEIGHT LOSS

For adults and children 12 years and older, the usual starting dose is 5 milligrams taken one-half hour before each meal. Treatment should not continue for longer than a few weeks. The safety and effectiveness of Desoxyn for weight loss have not been established in children under age 12.

Overdosage

Any drug taken in excess can have dangerous consequences. If an overdose is suspected, seek medical attention immediately.

- *Symptoms of Desoxyn overdose may include:*
  Abdominal cramps, agitation, blood pressure changes, confusion, convulsions (may be followed by coma), depression, diarrhea, exaggerated reflexes, fatigue, hallucinations, high fever, irregular heartbeat, kidney failure, muscle aches and weakness, nausea, panic attacks, rapid breathing, restlessness, shock, tremor, vomiting

---

DESYREL

Trazodone hydrochloride

Why is this drug prescribed?

Desyrel is prescribed for the treatment of depression. The drug is thought to work by altering levels of serotonin in the brain; however, it's not chemically related to other serotonin-boosting antidepressants such as Paxil and Prozac.

Most important fact about this drug

Desyrel does not provide immediate relief. It may take up to 4 weeks before its benefits are felt, although most patients notice improvement within 2 weeks.

How should this medication be taken?

Desyrel should be taken shortly after a meal or light snack. Patients are more apt to feel dizzy or light-headed if they take the drug before eating.

Desyrel may cause dry mouth. Sucking on a hard candy, chewing gum, or melting bits of ice in the mouth can relieve the problem.

- *Missed dose...*
  Generally, patients should take a forgotten dose as soon as they remember. However, if it is within 4 hours of their next dose, they should skip the one they missed and go back to their regular schedule. Doses should never be doubled.

- *Storage instructions...*
  Desyrel should be stored at room temperature in a tightly closed container away from light and excessive heat.

What side effects may occur?

Side effects cannot be predicted. If any develop or change in intensity, patients should inform their doctor as soon as possible.

● *Side effects may include:*
Blurred vision, confusion, dizziness, drowsiness, dry mouth, fatigue,headache, insomnia, low blood pressure, muscle and/or bone pain, nausea, nervousness, swelling, vomiting

Why should this drug not be prescribed?
Anyone who is sensitive to or has ever had an allergic reaction to Desyrel or similar drugs cannot take this medication.

Special warnings about this medication
Desyrel may cause patients to become drowsy or less alert and may affect judgment. They should avoid driving, operating dangerous machinery, or participating in any hazardous activity that requires full mental alertness until they know how this drug affects them.

Desyrel has been associated with priapism, a persistent, painful erection of the penis. Men who experience prolonged or inappropriate erections should stop taking this drug and consult their doctor.

In a medical emergency, and before surgery or dental treatment, patients should notify the doctor or dentist that they are taking this drug. The doctor will ask them to stop using the drug if they are going to have elective surgery.

Caution is warranted in patients with heart disease. Desyrel can cause irregular heartbeats.

Possible food and drug interactions when taking this medication
Desyrel may intensify the effects of alcohol. Patient should avoid drinking alcohol while taking this medication.

If Desyrel is taken with certain other drugs, the effects of either could be increased, decreased, or altered. Here is an overview of drugs that may cause a problem:

Antidepressants such as Prozac and Norpramin
Carbamazepine (Tegretol)
Drugs classified as MAO inhibitors, including the antidepressants
  Nardil and Parnate
Barbiturates such as Seconal
Central nervous system depressants such as Demerol and Halcion
Chlorpromazine
Digoxin (Lanoxin)
Drugs for high blood pressure such as Aldomet and Catapres
Indinavir (Crixivan)
Ketoconazole (Nizoral)
Phenytoin (Dilantin)
Ritonavir (Norvir)
Warfarin (Coumadin)

Special information about pregnancy and breastfeeding

The effects of Desyrel during pregnancy have not been adequately studied. Patients should inform their doctor immediately if they are pregnant or planning to become pregnant. This medication may appear in breast milk. If treatment with this drug is essential to the patient's health, the doctor may advise her to discontinue breastfeeding until her treatment is finished.

Recommended dosage

ADULTS

The usual starting dosage is a total of 150 milligrams per day, divided into 2 or more smaller doses. The doctor may increase the dose by 50 milligrams per day every 3 or 4 days. Total dosage should not exceed 400 milligrams per day, divided into smaller doses. Once a patient has responded well to the drug, the doctor may gradually reduce the dose. Because this medication causes drowsiness, the doctor may schedule the largest dose at bedtime.

CHILDREN

The safety and effectiveness of Desyrel have not been established in children below 18 years of age.

Overdosage

Any medication taken in excess can have serious consequences. An overdose of Desyrel in combination with other drugs can be fatal. If an overdose is suspected, seek medical attention immediately.

- *Symptoms of a Desyrel overdose may include:*
  Breathing failure, drowsiness, irregular heartbeat, prolonged, painful erection, seizures, vomiting

---

DEXEDRINE

Dextroamphetamine sulfate

Why is this drug prescribed?

Dexedrine, a stimulant drug available in tablet or sustained-release capsule form, is prescribed to help treat the following conditions:

1. Narcolepsy (recurrent "sleep attacks")
2. Attention deficit hyperactivity disorder (The total treatment program should include social, psychological, and educational guidance along with Dexedrine.)

Most important fact about this drug

Because it is a stimulant, this drug has high abuse potential. The stimulant effect may give way to a letdown period of depression and fatigue.

Although the letdown can be relieved by taking another dose, this soon becomes a vicious circle.

Patients should be aware that if they habitually take Dexedrine in doses higher than recommended, or if they take it over a long period of time, they may eventually become dependent on the drug and suffer withdrawal symptoms when it is unavailable.

How should this medication be taken?

It is important to take Dexedrine exactly as prescribed. If it is prescribed in tablet form, patients may need up to 3 doses a day. The first dose should be taken upon awakening; the next 1 or 2 doses should be taken at intervals of 4 to 6 hours. The sustained-release capsules are taken only once a day.

It is best to avoid taking Dexedrine late in the day, since this could cause insomnia. If patients experience insomnia or loss of appetite while taking this drug, they should notify their doctor; they may need a lower dosage.

The doctor is likely to periodically take the patient off Dexedrine to determine whether the drug is still needed.

Patients should avoid chewing or crushing the sustained-release form, Dexedrine Spansules. They should never increase the dosage, except on their doctor's advice. Dexedrine should not be used to improve mental alertness or to stay awake. It should not be shared with others.

● *Missed dose...*
Patients who take 1 dose a day should take it as soon as they remember, but not within 6 hours of going to bed. If they do not remember until the next day, they should skip the missed dose and go back to their regular schedule.

Patients who take 2 or 3 doses a day should take the missed dose immediately if it is within an hour or so of the scheduled time. Otherwise, they should skip the dose and go back to their regular schedule. Warn against taking 2 doses at once.

● *Storage instructions...*
Dexedrine should be stored at room temperature in a tightly closed container, away from light.

What side effects may occur?

Side effects cannot be predicted. If any develop or change in intensity, patients should inform their doctor as soon as possible.

● *Side effects may include:*
Dry mouth, gastrointestinal problems, high blood pressure, hives, impotence, insomnia, overstimulation, rapid or pounding heartbeat, restlessness, weight loss

- *Effects of chronic heavy abuse of Dexedrine may include:*
Hyperactivity, irritability, personality changes, schizophrenia-like thoughts and behavior, severe insomnia, severe skin disease

Why should this drug not be prescribed?
Dexedrine must not be taken by anyone who is sensitive to or has ever had an allergic reaction to it. It should be avoided for at least 14 days after taking a monoamine oxidase inhibitor (MAO inhibitor) such as the antidepressants Nardil and Parnate. Dexedrine and MAO inhibitors may interact to cause a sharp, potentially life-threatening rise in blood pressure.

Dexedrine must also be avoided by anyone suffering from one of the following conditions:
Agitation
Cardiovascular disease
Glaucoma
Hardening of the arteries
High blood pressure
Overactive thyroid gland
Substance abuse

Special warnings about this medication
Patients should be aware that one of the inactive ingredients in Dexedrine is a yellow food coloring called tartrazine (Yellow No. 5). In a few people, particularly those who are allergic to aspirin, tartrazine can cause a severe allergic reaction.

Dexedrine may impair judgment or coordination. Patients should avoid driving or operating dangerous machinery until they know how they react to the medication.

There is some concern that Dexedrine may stunt a child's growth. For the sake of safety, any child who takes Dexedrine should have his or her growth monitored.

Possible food and drug interactions when taking this medication
If Dexedrine is taken with certain foods or drugs, the effects of either could be increased, decreased, or altered. Here is an overview of drugs that may cause a problem:

- *Substances that dampen the effects of Dexedrine:*
Ammonium chloride
Chlorpromazine
Fruit juices
Glutamic acid hydrochloride
Guanethidine
Haloperidol (Haldol)

Lithium (Eskalith, Lithobid)
Methenamine (Urised)
Reserpine
Sodium acid phosphate
Vitamin C (as ascorbic acid)

- *Substances that boost the effects of Dexedrine:*
Acetazolamide (Diamox)
MAO inhibitors such as Nardil and Parnate
Propoxyphene (Darvon)
Sodium bicarbonate (baking soda)
Thiazide diuretics such as Diuril

- *Substances that have decreased effect when taken with Dexedrine:*
Antihistamines such as Benadryl
Blood pressure medications such as Catapres, Hytrin, and Minipress
Ethosuximide (Zarontin)
Veratrum alkaloids (found in certain blood pressure drugs)

- *Substances that have increased effect when taken with Dexedrine:*
Antidepressants such as Norpramin
Meperidine (Demerol)
Norepinephrine (Levophed)
Phenobarbital
Phenytoin (Dilantin)

Special information about pregnancy and breastfeeding

If a patient is pregnant or plans to become pregnant, she should inform her doctor immediately. Babies born to women taking Dexedrine may be premature or have low birth weight. They may also be depressed, agitated, or apathetic due to withdrawal symptoms.

Since Dexedrine appears in breast milk, it should not be taken by a nursing mother.

Recommended dosage

Patients should take no more Dexedrine than prescribed. Intake should be kept to the lowest level that proves effective.

NARCOLEPSY

Adults: The usual dose is 5 to 60 milligrams per day, divided into smaller, equal doses.

Children: Narcolepsy seldom occurs in children under 12 years of age; however, when it does, Dexedrine may be used.

The suggested initial dose for children between 6 and 12 years of age is 5 milligrams per day. The doctor may increase the daily dose in increments of 5 milligrams at weekly intervals until it becomes effective.

Children 12 years of age and older will be started with 10 milligrams daily. The daily dosage may be raised in increments of 10 milligrams at weekly intervals until effective. If side effects such as insomnia or loss of appetite appear, the dosage will probably be reduced.

ATTENTION DEFICIT HYPERACTIVITY DISORDER

This drug is not recommended for children under 3 years of age.

Children from 3 to 5 Years of Age: The usual starting dose is 2.5 milligrams daily, in tablet form. The doctor may raise the daily dosage by 2.5 milligrams at weekly intervals until the drug becomes effective.

Children 6 Years of Age and Older: The usual starting dose is 5 milligrams once or twice a day. The doctor may raise the dose by 5 milligrams at weekly intervals until he or she is satisfied with the response. Only in rare cases will the child take more than 40 milligrams per day.

The child should take the first dose upon awakening; the remaining 1 or 2 doses are taken at intervals of 4 to 6 hours. Alternatively, the doctor may prescribe "Spansule" capsules that are taken once a day. The doctor may interrupt the schedule occasionally to see if behavioral symptoms come back enough to require continued therapy.

Overdosage

An overdose of Dexedrine can be fatal. If an overdose is suspected, seek medical attention immediately.

- *Symptoms of an acute Dexedrine overdose may include:*
  Abdominal cramps, assaultiveness, coma, confusion, convulsions, depression, diarrhea, fatigue, hallucinations, high fever, heightened reflexes, high or low blood pressure, irregular heartbeat, nausea, panic, rapid breathing, restlessness, tremor, vomiting

Dexmethylphenidate *See Focalin, page 74*

Dextroamphetamine *See Dexedrine, page 51*

Diazepam *See Valium, page 223*

Divalproex *See Depakote, page 42*

Donepezil *See Aricept, page 16*

DORAL

Quazepam

Why is this drug prescribed?

Doral, a sleeping medication available in tablet form, is taken as short-term treatment for insomnia. Symptoms of insomnia may include difficulty falling asleep, frequent awakenings throughout the night, or very early morning awakening.

Most important fact about this drug

Doral is a chemical cousin of Valium and is potentially addictive. Over time, the body will get used to the prescribed dosage of Doral, and a patient will no longer derive any benefit from it. If the patient were to increase the dosage against medical advice, the drug would again work as a sleeping pill–but only until the body adjusted to the higher dosage. This is a vicious circle that can lead to addiction. To avoid this danger, Doral must be used only as prescribed.

How should this medication be taken?

Doral must be used exactly as prescribed, one dose per day, at bedtime. Patients should keep in touch with their doctor. If they respond very well, it may be possible to cut their dosage in half after the first few nights. The older or more run-down the patient is, the more desirable it is to try for this early dosage reduction.

After taking Doral regularly for 6 weeks or so, patients may experience withdrawal symptoms if they stop suddenly, or even if they reduce the dosage without specific instructions on how to do it. They should see their doctor for instructions on how to taper off gradually from Doral.

- *Missed dose...*
  This medication should be taken only if needed.

- *Storage instructions...*
  Doral should be stored at room temperature, away from moisture.

What side effects may occur?

Side effects cannot be predicted. If any develop or change in intensity, patients should inform their doctor as soon as possible.

- *More common side effects may include:*
  Drowsiness during the day, headache

- *Less common side effects may include:*
  Changes in sex drive, dizziness, dry mouth, fatigue, inability to urinate, incontinence, indigestion, irregular menstrual periods, irritability, muscle spasms, slurred or otherwise abnormal speech, yellowed eyes and skin

In rare instances, Doral produces agitation, sleep disturbances, hallucinations, or stimulation—exactly the opposite of the desired effect. If this should happen, the patient should see the doctor, who will stop the medication.

Why should this drug not be prescribed?

Doral cannot be used by anyone who is sensitive to it or has ever had an allergic reaction to it or to another Valium-type medication.

Doral should not be used by patients with known or suspected sleep apnea (short periods of interrupted breathing that occur during sleep).

Doral must not be taken during pregnancy.

Special warnings about this medication

Because Doral may decrease daytime alertness, patients should not drive, climb, or operate dangerous machinery until they find out how the drug affects them. In some cases, Doral's sedative effect may last for several days after the last dose.

Doral may aggravate depression in patients with depressive disorders.

Patients with a history of alcohol or drug abuse are at special risk for addiction to Doral. It is important for patients to avoid increasing the dosage of Doral on their own. They should tell the doctor right away if the medication no longer seems to be working.

Possible food and drug interactions when taking this medication

If Doral is taken with certain other drugs, the effects of either could be increased, decreased, or altered. Here is an overview of drugs that may cause a problem:

Antihistamines such as Benadryl
Antipsychotic drugs such as chlorpromazine and Clozaril
Antiseizure medications such as Dilantin and Tegretol
Tranquilizers such as Xanax and Valium

Patients should avoid drinking alcohol while taking Doral; it can increase the drug's effects.

Special information about pregnancy and breastfeeding

Because Doral may cause harm to the unborn child, it should not be taken during pregnancy. Patients should discontinue Doral before getting pregnant.

Babies whose mothers are taking Doral at the time of birth may experience withdrawal symptoms from the drug. Such babies may be "floppy" (flaccid) instead of having normal muscle tone.

Since Doral finds its way into breast milk, patients should not take this medication while nursing a baby.

Recommended dosage

ADULTS

The recommended initial dose is 15 milligrams daily. The doctor may later reduce this dosage to 7.5 milligrams.

CHILDREN

Safety and efficacy of Doral in children under 18 years old have not been established.

OLDER ADULTS

Older patients may be more sensitive to this drug, and the doctor may reduce the dosage after only 1 or 2 nights.

Overdosage

Any medication taken in excess can have serious consequences. If an overdose of Doral is suspected, seek medical attention immediately.

- *Symptoms of an overdose of Doral may include:*
  Coma, confusion, extreme sleepiness

Doxepin *See Sinequan, page 192*

EFFEXOR

Venlafaxine hydrochloride
Other brand name: Effexor XR

Why is this drug prescribed?

Effexor is prescribed for the treatment of depression. Effexor XR is also prescribed to relieve generalized anxiety disorder and social anxiety disorder. The drug is thought to work by boosting levels of serotonin and norepinephrine, two important chemical messengers in the brain.

Most important fact about this drug

Serious, sometimes fatal reactions have occurred when Effexor is used in combination with drugs classified as MAO inhibitors, including the anti-depressants Nardil and Parnate. Effexor must never be taken with one of these drugs; or within 14 days of discontinuing treatment with one of them. It is also important to allow at least 7 days between the last dose of Effexor and the first dose of an MAO inhibitor.

How should this medication be taken?

Effexor should be taken with food, exactly as prescribed. It may take several weeks before an effect is seen.

Effexor must be taken 2 or 3 times daily. The extended-release form, Effexor XR, permits once-a-day dosing. (It should be taken at the same time each day.) The capsule should be swallowed whole with water. It must not be divided, crushed, or chewed. However, if the patient has trouble swallowing pills, he or she may take Effexor XR by carefully opening the capsule and sprinkling the entire contents on a spoonful of applesauce, followed by a glass of water.

- *Missed dose...*
  It is not necessary to make up a forgotten dose. Patients should skip the missed dose and continue with the next scheduled dose. They should never take 2 doses at once.

- *Storage instructions...*
  Effexor should be stored in a tightly closed container at room temperature and protected from excessive heat and moisture.

What side effects may occur?

Side effects cannot be predicted. If any develop or change in intensity, patients should inform their doctor as soon as possible.

- *Side effects of Effexor may include:*
  Abnormal ejaculation/orgasm, anxiety, blurred vision, constipation, dizziness, dry mouth, impotence, insomnia, nausea, nervousness, sleepiness, sweating, tremor, vomiting, weakness, weight loss

- *Side effects of Effexor XR may include:*
  Abnormal dreams, abnormal ejaculation, constipation, dizziness, dry mouth, headache, insomnia, nausea, nervousness, sleepiness, sweating, weakness, weight loss

Why should this drug not be prescribed?

Remember that Effexor must never be combined with an MAO inhibitor. (See "Most important fact about this drug.") This drug should also be avoided by anyone who has had an allergic reaction to it.

Special warnings about this medication

The FDA has issued a public health advisory to alert healthcare professionals about reports of worsening depression and suicidality (both suicidal thoughts and suicide attempts) during antidepressant drug therapy in adult and pediatric patients with major depression. In pediatric clinical trials of Effexor, hostility and suicide-related adverse events such as suicidal thoughts and self-harm have been reported, especially in children with major depression. Healthcare professionals and family members are advised to watch for signs of worsening depression and to be aware of the suicide statement present in all antidepressant labeling. Effexor is currently not approved for treating pediatric patients.

Serotonin-boosting antidepressants such as Paxil and Prozac have been linked to stomach bleeding, especially in older patients or those taking nonsteroidal anti-inflammatory drugs (NSAIDs) such as aspirin, Advil, or Aleve. Because Effexor also affects serotonin, patients should consult their doctor before combining it with NSAIDs or blood-thinning medications.

Effexor should be used with caution in patients with high blood pressure; heart, liver, or kidney disease; or a history of seizures or mania. It's important for patients to discuss all of their medical problems with their doctor before taking Effexor.

Effexor sometimes causes an increase in blood pressure. If this happens, the doctor may need to reduce the dose or discontinue the drug.

Effexor also tends to increase the heart rate, especially at higher doses. Effexor must be used cautiously in patients who have recently had a heart attack, suffer from heart failure, or have an overactive thyroid gland.

Effexor may increase cholesterol levels if it's taken for 3 months or longer. This effect is more common among patients taking higher doses.

Antidepressants such as Effexor may cause fluid retention, especially in older adults.

Effexor may cause patients to feel drowsy or less alert and may affect their judgment. They should avoid driving or operating dangerous machinery, or participating in any hazardous activity that requires full mental alertness, until they know how this drug affects them.

The doctor should regularly check any patient who has glaucoma (high pressure in the eye), or is at risk of developing it.

This drug should be discontinued only under supervision of a doctor. If it is stopped suddenly, patients may have withdrawal symptoms, even though Effexor does not seem to be habit-forming. The doctor will have them taper off gradually. If they have ever been addicted to drugs, they should tell the doctor before starting Effexor.

Patients who develop a skin rash or hives while taking Effexor should notify their doctor immediately. Effexor may also cause bleeding or bruising of the skin.

Possible food and drug interactions when taking this medication

Combining Effexor with MAO inhibitors could cause a fatal reaction. (See "Most important fact about this drug.")

Although Effexor does not interact with alcohol, the manufacturer recommends avoiding alcohol while taking this medication.

Patients who have high blood pressure or liver disease, or are elderly, should check with their doctor before combining Effexor with cimetidine (Tagamet).

Patients should consult their doctor before combining Effexor with other drugs that affect the central nervous system, including lithium, migraine medications such as Imitrex, weight-loss products such as phentermine, narcotic painkillers, sleep aids, tranquilizers, antipsychotic medicines such as Haldol, and other antidepressants such as Celexa, Prozac, Tofranil, and Zoloft.

Effexor has been found to reduce blood levels of the HIV drug Crixivan. It's best for patients to check with their doctor before combining Effexor with any other drug or herbal product.

Special information about pregnancy and breastfeeding

The effects of Effexor during pregnancy have not been adequately studied. There have been reports of serious complications in newborns who were exposed to Effexor late in the third trimester. Patients should consult their doctor immediately if they are pregnant or are planning to become pregnant. Effexor should be used during pregnancy only if clearly needed.

Effexor appears in breast milk and could cause serious side effects in a nursing infant. Patients will need to choose between nursing their baby or continuing their treatment with Effexor.

Recommended dosage

EFFEXOR

The usual starting dose is 75 milligrams a day, divided into 2 or 3 smaller doses, and taken with food. If needed, the doctor may gradually increase the daily dose in steps of no more than 75 milligrams at a time up to a maximum of 375 milligrams per day.

If the patient has kidney or liver disease or is taking other medications, the doctor will adjust the dosage accordingly.

EFFEXOR XR

For both depression and anxiety the usual starting dose is 75 milligrams once daily taken with food, although some people begin with a dose of 37.5 milligrams for the first 4 to 7 days. The doctor may gradually increase the dose, in steps of no more than 75 milligrams, up to a maximum of 225 milligrams daily. As with regular Effexor, the doctor will make adjustments in the dosage for patients with kidney or liver disease.

Overdosage

An overdose of Effexor, combined with other drugs or alcohol, can be fatal. If an overdose is suspected, seek medical attention immediately.

- *Symptoms of Effexor overdose may include:*
  Sleepiness, vertigo, rapid or slow heartbeat, low blood pressure, seizures, coma

---

ELAVIL
Amitriptyline hydrochloride

Why is this drug prescribed?

Elavil is prescribed for the relief of major depression. It is a member of the group of drugs called tricyclic antidepressants. Some doctors also prescribe Elavil to treat bulimia (an eating disorder), to control chronic pain, to prevent migraine headaches, and to treat a pathological weeping and laughing syndrome associated with multiple sclerosis.

Most important fact about this drug

Elavil must be taken regularly for several weeks before it becomes fully effective. It's important that patients not skip any doses, even if they seem to make no difference or don't seem necessary.

How should this medication be taken?

Elavil must be taken exactly as prescribed. Patients may experience side effects, such as mild drowsiness, early in therapy. However, these problems usually disappear after a few days.

Elavil may cause dry mouth. Sucking a hard candy, chewing gum, or melting bits of ice in the mouth can provide relief.

● *Missed dose...*
Generally, the forgotten dose should be taken as soon as remembered. However, if it is almost time for their next dose, patients should skip the one they missed and go back to their regular schedule. Doses should never be doubled.

Patients who take a single daily dose at bedtime should not make up for it in the morning. It may cause side effects during the day.

● *Storage instructions...*
Elavil should be stored at room temperature in a tightly closed container, and protected from light and excessive heat.

What side effects may occur?

Side effects cannot be predicted. If any develop or change in intensity, patients should inform their doctor as soon as possible.

Older adults are especially liable to certain side effects of Elavil, including rapid heartbeat, constipation, dry mouth, blurred vision, sedation, and confusion, and are in greater danger of sustaining a fall.

● *Side effects may include:*
Blurred vision, bone marrow depression, bowel problems, breast enlargement (in males and females), constipation, dry mouth, hair loss, heart attack, high body temperature, problems urinating, rash, seizure, stroke, swelling of the testicles, water retention

● *Side effects due to rapid decrease in dose or abrupt withdrawal from Elavil may include:*
Headache, nausea, vague feeling of bodily discomfort

● *Side effects due to gradual dosage reduction may include:*
Dream and sleep disturbances, irritability, restlessness

These side effects do not signify an addiction to the drug.

Why should this drug not be prescribed?

Anyone who is sensitive to or has ever had an allergic reaction to Elavil or similar drugs such as Norpramin and Tofranil should not take this medication. Patients should be careful to make the doctor aware of any drug reactions they have experienced.

Elavil cannot be used by anyone taking an MAO inhibitor such as the antidepressants Nardil and Parnate. Unless the doctor says otherwise, it should also be avoided by patients recovering from a heart attack.

Special warnings about this medication

Elavil should not be stopped abruptly, especially if the patient has been taking large doses for a long time. The doctor will schedule a gradual reduction in dosage that will help prevent a possible relapse and will reduce the possibility of withdrawal symptoms.

Elavil may make the skin more sensitive to sunlight. Patients should stay out of the sun, wear protective clothing, and apply a sunblock.

Elavil can make patients drowsy or less alert. They should avoid driving, operating dangerous machinery, or participating in any hazardous activity that requires full mental alertness until they know how this drug affects them.

While taking this medication, patients may feel dizzy or light-headed or actually faint when getting up from a lying or sitting position. If getting up slowly doesn't help or if this problem continues, the doctor should be notified.

Elavil should be used with caution in patients with a history of seizures, urinary retention, glaucoma or other chronic eye conditions, a heart or circulatory system disorder, or liver problems. Caution is also warranted in patients who are receiving thyroid medication. The doctor should be apprised of all the patient's medical problems before the start of Elavil therapy.

Patients should tell doctors they are taking Elavil before having surgery, dental treatment, or any diagnostic procedure. Certain drugs used during surgery, such as anesthetics and muscle relaxants, and drugs used in certain diagnostic procedures may react badly with Elavil.

Possible food and drug interactions when taking this medication

Elavil may intensify the effects of alcohol. Patients should avoid drinking alcohol while taking this medication.

If Elavil is taken with certain other drugs, the effects of either could be increased, decreased, or altered. Here is an overview of drugs that may cause a problem:

Airway-opening drugs such as Sudafed and Proventil
Antidepressants known as MAO inhibitors, such as Nardil and Parnate
Antidepressants that raise serotonin levels, such as Paxil, Prozac, and Zoloft

Other antidepressants, such as amoxapine
Antihistamines such as Benadryl and Tavist
Antipsychotic medications such as Mellaril and chlorpromazine
Barbiturates such as phenobarbital
Certain blood pressure medicines such as Catapres
Cimetidine (Tagamet)
Disulfiram (Antabuse)
Drugs that control spasms, such as Bentyl and Donnatal
Estrogen drugs such as Premarin and oral contraceptives
Ethchlorvynol (Placidyl)
Medications for irregular heartbeat, such as Tambocor and Rythmol
Painkillers such as Demerol and Percocet
Parkinson's drugs such as Cogentin and Larodopa
Quinidine (Quinidex)
Seizure medications such as Tegretol and Dilantin
Sleep medicines such as Halcion and Dalmane
Thyroid hormones (Synthroid)
Tranquilizers such as Librium and Xanax
Warfarin (Coumadin)

Special information about pregnancy and breastfeeding

The effects of Elavil during pregnancy have not been adequately studied. Patients should inform their doctor immediately if they are pregnant or are planning to become pregnant.

This medication appears in breast milk. If Elavil is essential to a patient's health, the doctor may advise her to discontinue breastfeeding until treatment is finished.

Recommended dosage

ADULTS

The usual starting dosage is 75 milligrams per day divided into 2 or more smaller doses. The doctor may gradually increase this dose to 150 milligrams per day. The total daily dose is generally never higher than 200 milligrams.

Alternatively, the doctor may start patients with 50 milligrams to 100 milligrams at bedtime. This bedtime dose may be gradually increased by 25 or 50 milligrams up to a total of 150 milligrams a day.

For long-term use, the usual dose ranges from 40 to 100 milligrams taken once daily, usually at bedtime.

CHILDREN

Use of Elavil is not recommended for children under 12 years of age.

The usual dose for adolescents 12 years of age and over is 10 milligrams, 3 times a day, with 20 milligrams taken at bedtime.

OLDER ADULTS

The usual dose is 10 milligrams taken 3 times a day, with 20 milligrams taken at bedtime.

Overdosage

An overdose of Elavil can prove fatal.

- *Symptoms of Elavil overdose may include:*
  Abnormally low blood pressure, confusion, convulsions, dilated pupils and other eye problems, disturbed concentration, drowsiness, hallucinations, impaired heart function, rapid or irregular heartbeat, reduced body temperature, stupor, unresponsiveness or coma

- *Symptoms contrary to the usual effect of this medication are:*
  Agitation, extremely high body temperature, overactive reflexes, rigid muscles, vomiting

If an overdose is suspected, seek medical attention immediately.

Escitalopram *See Lexapro, page 92*

ESKALITH
Lithium carbonate
Other brand names: Eskalith CR, Lithobid

Why is this drug prescribed?

Eskalith is used to treat the manic episodes of bipolar disorder. Once the mania subsides, Eskalith treatment may be continued over the long term, at a somewhat lower dosage, to prevent or reduce the intensity of future manic episodes.

Some doctors also prescribe lithium for premenstrual tension, eating disorders such as bulimia, certain movement disorders, and sexual addictions.

Most important fact about this drug

If the Eskalith dosage is too low, patients derive no benefit; if it is too high, they could suffer lithium poisoning. Patient and doctor must work together to find the correct dosage. Initially, this means frequent blood tests to find out how much of the drug is actually circulating in the patient's bloodstream. Later, the patient must stay alert for side effects. Signs of lithium poisoning include vomiting, unsteady walking, diarrhea, drowsiness, tremor, and weakness. If any of these symptoms develop, the patient should stop taking the drug and call the doctor.

How should this medication be taken?

To avoid stomach upset, Eskalith should be taken immediately after meals or with food or milk.

It is unwise to change from one brand of lithium to another without consulting a doctor or pharmacist. The drug should be taken exactly as prescribed.

While taking Eskalith, patients should drink 10 to 12 glasses of water or fluid a day. To minimize the risk of harmful side effects, they should eat a balanced diet that includes some salt and lots of liquids. Patients who have been sweating a great deal or have had diarrhea should be sure to get extra liquids and salt.

Patients should keep in close touch with their doctor if they develop an infection with a fever. They may need to cut back on their Eskalith dosage or even quit taking it temporarily.

Long-acting forms of lithium, such as Eskalith CR or Lithobid, should be swallowed whole. They should not be chewed, crushed, or broken.

- *Missed dose...*
  Patients need to check with the doctor; requirements vary for each individual. Doses should never be doubled.

- *Storage instructions...*
  Eskalith may be stored at room temperature.

What side effects may occur?

The possibility of side effects varies with the level of lithium in the bloodstream. Patients should inform their doctor as soon as possible if they experience unfamiliar symptoms of any kind.

- *Side effects may include:*
  Diarrhea, discomfort, drowsiness, frequent urination, hand tremor, lack of coordination, mild thirst, muscle weakness, nausea, vomiting

Why should this drug not be prescribed?

Although doctors are cautious under certain conditions, lithium may be prescribed for anyone.

Special warnings about this medication

Eskalith may affect judgment or coordination. Patients should avoid driving, climbing, or performing hazardous tasks until they find out how this drug affects them.

Eskalith should be used with extra caution in patients who have a heart or kidney problem, brain or spinal cord disease, or a weak, run-down, or dehydrated condition. It's important for patients to make sure the doctor is aware of any medical problems they may have, including diabetes, epilepsy, thyroid problems, Parkinson's disease, and difficulty urinating.

Patients should avoid activities that cause heavy sweating. They should also avoid drinking large amounts of coffee, tea, or cola, which can cause dehydration through increased urination. It is unwise for patients to make a major change in eating habits or to go on a weight loss diet without consulting the doctor. The loss of water and salt from the body could lead to lithium poisoning.

Possible food and drug interactions when taking this medication

If Eskalith is taken with certain other drugs, the effects of either could be increased, decreased, or altered. Here is an overview of drugs that may cause a problem:

ACE-inhibitor blood pressure drugs such as Capoten or Vasotec
Acetazolamide (Diamox)
Amphetamines such as Dexedrine
Antidepressant drugs that boost serotonin levels, including Paxil, Prozac, and Zoloft
Antipsychotic medications such as Haldol and chlorpromazine
Bicarbonate of soda
Caffeine (No-Doz)
Calcium-blocking blood pressure drugs such as Calan and Cardizem
Carbamazepine (Tegretol)
Diuretics such as Lasix or HydroDIURIL
Iodine-containing preparations such as potassium iodide (Quadrinal)
Methyldopa (Aldomet)
Metronidazole (Flagyl)
Nonsteroidal anti-inflammatory drugs such as Advil, Celebrex, Feldene, Indocin, and Vioxx
Phenytoin (Dilantin)
Sodium bicarbonate
Tetracyclines such as Achromycin V and Sumycin
Theophylline (Theo-Dur, Quibron, others)

Special information about pregnancy and breastfeeding

The use of Eskalith during pregnancy can harm the developing baby. Patients should inform the doctor immediately if they are pregnant or plan to become pregnant.

Eskalith appears in breast milk and is considered potentially harmful to a nursing infant. If this medication is essential to the patient's health, the doctor may advise her to discontinue breastfeeding while she is taking it.

Recommended dosage

ADULTS

Acute Episodes

The usual dosage is a total of 1,800 milligrams per day. Immediate-release forms are taken in 3 or 4 doses per day; long-acting forms are taken twice a day.

Dosage is individualized according to the levels of the drug in the patient's blood. Blood levels will be checked at least twice a week when the drug is first prescribed and on a regular basis thereafter.

Long-term Control

Dosage will vary from one individual to another, but a total of 900 milligrams to 1,200 milligrams per day is typical. Immediate-release forms are taken in 3 or 4 doses per day; long-acting forms are taken twice a day. Blood levels in most cases should be checked every 2 months.

CHILDREN

Safety and effectiveness of Eskalith in children under 12 years of age have not been established.

OLDER ADULTS

Older people often need less Eskalith and may show signs of overdose at a dosage that younger people can handle well.

Overdosage

Any medication taken in excess can have serious consequences. If an overdose of Eskalith is suspected, seek medical attention immediately.

The harmful levels are close to those needed for treatment. Patients need to watch for early signs of overdose, such as diarrhea, drowsiness, lack of coordination, vomiting, and weakness. If they develop any of these signs, they should stop taking the drug and call the doctor.

Estazolam *See ProSom, page 156*

Etrafon *See Triavil, page 213*

EXELON

Rivastigmine tartrate

Why is this drug prescribed?

Exelon is used in the treatment of mild to moderate Alzheimer's disease. This progressive, degenerative disorder causes physical changes in the brain that disrupt the flow of information and interfere with memory, thinking, and behavior. By boosting levels of the chemical messenger acetylcholine, Exelon can temporarily improve brain function in some Alzheimer's sufferers, though it does not halt the progress of the underlying disease. Like other drugs for Alzheimer's, Exelon may become less effective as the disease progresses.

Most important fact about this drug

Patience is in order when starting this drug. It can take up to 12 weeks before Exelon's full benefits appear.

How should this medication be taken?

Exelon should be taken with food in the morning and in the evening.

- *Missed dose...*

  Generally, the forgotten dose should be given as soon as remembered. However, if it is almost time for the next dose, caregivers should skip the one they missed and go back to the regular schedule. Doses should never be doubled.

- *Storage instructions...*

  Exelon should be stored at room temperature in a tightly closed container.

What side effects may occur?

Side effects cannot be predicted. If any develop or change in intensity, caregivers should inform the doctor as soon as possible.

- *Side effects may include:*

  Abdominal pain, constipation, diarrhea, dizziness, fatigue, headache, indigestion, nausea, sleepiness, vomiting, weakness, weight loss

Why should this drug not be prescribed?

Exelon cannot be used if it causes an allergic reaction.

Special warnings about this medication

Exelon often causes nausea and vomiting, especially at the beginning of treatment. The problem is more likely in women, but it can lead to significant weight loss in both women and men. The doctor should be informed immediately if these side effects occur.

The chance of severe vomiting increases when Exelon is given after an interruption of several days. Caregivers should check with the doctor before starting to give the drug again. Dosage may need to be reduced to the lowest starting level.

Exelon may aggravate asthma and other breathing problems and can increase the risk of seizures. Other drugs of its type are also known to increase the chance of ulcers, stomach bleeding, and urinary obstruction, although these problems have not been noted with Exelon. Drugs in this category can also slow the heartbeat, possibly causing fainting in people who have a heart condition. The doctor should be alerted if any of these problems occur.

Exelon has not been tested in children.

Possible food and drug interactions when taking this medication

If Exelon is taken with certain other drugs, the effects of either could be increased, decreased, or altered. Here is an overview of drugs that may cause a problem:

Bethanechol (Urecholine)

Drugs that control spasms, such as Bentyl, Donnatal, and Levsin

Special information about pregnancy and breastfeeding
Exelon is not intended for women of child-bearing age, and its effects during pregnancy and breastfeeding have not been studied.

Recommended dosage
ADULTS

The usual starting dose is 1.5 milligrams 2 times a day for at least 2 weeks. At 2-week intervals, the doctor may then increase the dose to 3 milligrams, 4.5 milligrams, and finally 6.0 milligrams 2 times a day. Higher doses tend to be more effective. The maximum dosage is 12 milligrams daily.

If side effects such as nausea and vomiting begin to develop, the doctor may recommend skipping a few doses, then starting again at the same or the next lowest dosage.

Overdosage
Any medication taken in excess can have serious consequences. If an overdose is suspected, seek emergency medical attention immediately.

- *Symptoms of Exelon overdose may include:*
  Collapse, convulsions, breathing difficulty, extreme muscle weakness (possibly ending in death if breathing muscles are affected), low blood pressure, salivation, severe nausea, slow heartbeat, sweating, vomiting

Fluoxetine *See Prozac, page 161*

Fluphenazine *See Prolixin, page 153*

Flurazepam *See Dalmane, page 40*

FLUVOXAMINE MALEATE

Why is this drug prescribed?
Fluvoxamine is prescribed for obsessive-compulsive disorder. It belongs to the class of drugs known as selective serotonin reuptake inhibitors (SSRIs), although it is chemically unrelated to other SSRIs such as Prozac and Zoloft.

Most important fact about this drug
Before starting therapy with fluvoxamine, patients should tell the doctor what medications they are taking—both prescription and over-the-counter—since combining fluvoxamine with certain drugs may cause serious or even life-threatening effects. Fluvoxamine should never be combined with thioridazine (Mellaril) or pimozide (Orap). In addition, it

should not be used within 14 days of taking any antidepressant drug classified as an MAO inhibitor, including Nardil and Parnate.

How should this medication be taken?
This medication should be taken only as directed by the doctor. It may be taken with or without food.

* *Missed dose...*
  Patients who are taking 1 dose a day should skip the missed dose and go back to their regular schedule. Patients who are taking 2 doses a day should take the missed dose as soon as possible, then go back to their regular schedule. They should never take 2 doses at the same time.

* *Storage instructions...*
  Fluvoxamine should be stored at room temperature and protected from humidity.

What side effects may occur?
Side effects cannot be predicted. If any develop or change in intensity, patients should tell the doctor immediately.

* *Side effects may include:*
  Abnormal ejaculation, agitation, anxiety, diarrhea, dizziness, dry mouth, headache, indigestion, insomnia, nausea, nervousness, sleepiness, sweating, tremor, vomiting, weakness, weight loss

Why should this drug not be prescribed?
Patients who are sensitive to or have ever had an allergic reaction to fluvoxamine or similar drugs, such as Prozac and Zoloft, should not take this medication.

Fluvoxamine should never be combined with Mellaril or Orap, or taken within 14 days of taking an MAO inhibitor such as Nardil or Parnate. (See "Most important fact about this drug.")

Special warnings about this medication
The FDA has issued a public health advisory to alert healthcare professionals about reports of worsening depression and suicidality (both suicidal thoughts and suicide attempts) during therapy with various antidepressants (including SSRIs) in adult and pediatric patients with major depressive disorder. Healthcare professionals are advised that these drugs must be used with caution and to be aware of the suicide statement present in all SSRI labeling. Fluvoxamine is currently not approved for treating major depression.

Patients should discuss all medical problems with their doctor before starting therapy with fluvoxamine, as certain physical conditions or diseases may affect their reaction to the drug.

This medication should be used cautiously by anyone with a history of seizures. Patients who experience a seizure while taking fluvoxamine should stop taking the drug and call the doctor immediately.

The dosage of fluvoxamine may need adjustment if the patient has ever had suicidal thoughts. The drug should be used with caution by patients who have a history of mania.

The doctor will need to adjust the dosage if the patient has liver disease.

Fluvoxamine may cause patients to become drowsy or less alert and may affect their judgment. They should avoid driving, operating dangerous machinery, or participating in any hazardous activity that requires full mental alertness until they know how this medication affects them.

Fluvoxamine can also deplete the body's supply of salt, especially in older adults and people who take diuretics or suffer from dehydration. Under these conditions, the doctor will check salt levels regularly.

Serotonin-boosting drugs could potentially cause stomach bleeding, especially in older patients or those taking nonsteroidal anti-inflammatory drugs (NSAIDs) such as aspirin, ibuprofen (Advil, Motrin), naproxen (Aleve), and ketoprofen (Orudis KT). Advise patients to consult their doctor before combining fluvoxamine with NSAIDs or blood-thinning medications.

If the patient develops a rash or hives, or any other allergic-type reaction, the physician should be notified immediately.

Possible food and drug interactions when taking this medication

Patients should not drink alcohol while taking this medication. If they smoke, they should tell the doctor before starting fluvoxamine therapy, as their dosage may need adjustment.

If fluvoxamine is taken with certain other drugs, the effects of either could be increased, decreased, or altered. Here is an overview of drugs that may cause a problem:

Anticoagulant drugs such as Coumadin
Antidepressant medications such as Anafranil, Elavil, and Tofranil, as well as the MAO inhibitors Nardil and Parnate
Blood pressure medications known as beta blockers, including Inderal and Lopressor
Carbamazepine (Tegretol)
Clozapine (Clozaril)
Diltiazem (Cardizem)
Lithium (Eskalith, Lithobid)
Methadone (Dolophine)
Mexiletine (Mexitil)
Phenytoin (Dilantin)
Pimozide (Orap)

Quinidine (Quinidex)
Sumatriptan (Imitrex)
Tacrine (Cognex)
Theophylline (Theo-Dur)
Thioridazine (Mellaril)
Tranquilizers and sedatives such as Halcion, Valium, Versed, and Xanax
Tryptophan

Special information about pregnancy and breastfeeding

The effects of fluvoxamine in pregnancy have not been adequately studied. Patients who are pregnant or plan to become pregnant should consult their doctor immediately.

Fluvoxamine passes into breast milk and may cause serious reactions in a nursing baby. If this medication is essential to the mother's health, her doctor may advise her to discontinue breastfeeding until her treatment with fluvoxamine is finished.

Recommended dosage

ADULTS

The usual starting dose is one 50-milligram tablet taken at bedtime. The doctor may increase the dose, depending on response. The maximum daily dose is 300 milligrams. If the patient takes more than 100 milligrams a day, the doctor will divide the total amount into 2 doses; if the doses are not equal, the larger dose is taken at bedtime.

CHILDREN

For children aged 8 to 17, the recommended starting dose is 25 milligrams taken at bedtime. The dose may be increased to a maximum of 200 milligrams daily. Larger daily dosages are divided in two, as for adults.

OLDER ADULTS

Older adults and people with liver problems may need a reduced dosage.

Overdosage

An overdose of fluvoxamine can be fatal. If an overdose is suspected, seek medical help immediately.

- *Symptoms of fluvoxamine overdose may include:*
  Coma, breathing difficulties, sleepiness, rapid heartbeat, nausea, vomiting
  Other possible symptoms include convulsions, tremor, diarrhea, exaggerated reflexes, and slow or irregular heartbeat. After recovery, some overdose victims have been left with kidney complications, bowel damage, an unsteady gait, or dilated pupils.

FOCALIN

Dexmethylphenidate hydrochloride

Why is this drug prescribed?

Focalin is a mild central nervous system stimulant used to treat attention deficit hyperactivity disorder (ADHD) in children. The drug is a modified version of Ritalin (a common medication for attention disorders) and contains only the most active component of Ritalin. Because of this special formulation, the usual dose of Focalin is half the amount of the Ritalin dose. Focalin should be given as part of a total treatment program that includes psychological, educational, and social measures.

Most important fact about this drug

Excessive doses of Focalin over a long period of time can produce addiction. It is also possible to develop tolerance to the drug, so that larger doses are needed to produce the original effect. Because of these dangers, the doctor should be consulted before making any change in dosage; and the drug should be withdrawn only under a doctor's supervision.

How should this medication be taken?

Focalin can be taken with or without food. The drug is usually taken twice a day, at least 4 hours apart, but the doctor may adjust the schedule depending on the child's response.

- *Missed dose...*
  The dose should be given to the child as soon as it's remembered. If it is almost time for the next dose, the missed dose should be skipped and the child should return to the regular schedule. Doses should never be doubled.

- *Storage instructions...*
  Like all drugs, this one should be kept out of reach of children. It should be stored below 86 degrees Fahrenheit in a tightly closed, light-resistant container. It should not be stored in hot, damp, or humid places.

What side effects may occur?

Side effects cannot be predicted. If any develop or change in intensity, the caregiver should inform the child's doctor as soon as possible.

- *Side effects may include:*
  Fever, insomnia, loss of appetite, nausea, nervousness, and stomach pain

The most common side effects reported for drugs that are similar to Focalin (including Ritalin) are nervousness and the inability to fall asleep or stay asleep. In children, loss of appetite, stomach pain, weight loss during long-term treatment, inability to fall asleep or stay asleep, and abnormally fast heartbeat are the more common side effects.

Why should this drug not be prescribed?

Focalin should not be used by people who suffer from anxiety, tension, and agitation, since the drug may aggravate these symptoms.

If Focalin, or similar drugs such as Ritalin, cause an allergic reaction, the drug should be avoided. It should not be taken by anyone with the eye condition known as glaucoma. It should also be avoided by anyone who suffers from motion tics (repeated, uncontrollable twitches) or verbal tics (uncontrollable repetition of words or sounds), or someone who suffers from, or has a family history of, Tourette's syndrome (severe and multiple tics).

Focalin should not be taken with drugs classified as monoamine oxidase (MAO) inhibitors, such as the antidepressants Nardil and Parnate, or within 14 days of stopping this type of medication.

Special warnings about this medication

The doctor will do a complete history and evaluation before prescribing Focalin. It is important to remember that the drug is only part of the overall management of ADHD, and that the doctor should also recommend counseling or other therapy.

There is no information about the safety and effectiveness of long-term Focalin treatment in children. However, suppression of growth has been seen with the long-term use of stimulants, so it's important to watch the child carefully while he or she is taking this drug. If the child is not growing or gaining weight as expected, the doctor may have to stop Focalin treatment. This drug should not be given to children under 6 years of age; safety and effectiveness in this age group have not been established.

Blood pressure should be monitored in anyone taking Focalin, especially those with high blood pressure or abnormal heart rate or rhythm. Caution is also advised in those with heart or thyroid problems.

The doctor should be alerted if the child develops blurred vision while taking Focalin; some people have reported visual disturbances while taking stimulants similar to this drug.

The use of Focalin by anyone with a seizure disorder or psychosis is not recommended. Caution is also advisable for anyone with a history of emotional instability or substance abuse, due to the danger of addiction. Focalin should not be used for the prevention or treatment of normal fatigue, nor should it be used for the treatment of severe depression.

Focalin should not be shared with anyone else, and the child should be given only the number of tablets prescribed by the doctor. Caregivers should keep track of the number of tablets in a bottle so they can tell if any are missing. Incorrect use of Focalin can lead to dependence. The doctor should be consulted *immediately* if the drug is being used in more than the prescribed amount.

Possible food and drug interactions when taking this medication

If Focalin is taken with certain other drugs, the effects of either can be increased, decreased, or altered. Here is an overview of drugs that may cause a problem:

Antidepressant drugs, including MAO inhibitors (Nardil, Parnate), tricyclics (Elavil, Tofranil), and serotonin reuptake inhibitors (Prozac, Paxil)
Antiseizure drugs such as phenobarbital, Dilantin, and Mysoline
Blood pressure drugs such as Catapres
Blood thinners such as Coumadin
Herbal remedies such as ephedra and St. John's wort

Special information about pregnancy and breastfeeding

The effects of Focalin during pregnancy have not been adequately studied. Caregivers should tell the doctor immediately if the patient becomes pregnant. Focalin should be used during pregnancy only if clearly needed.

It is not known whether Focalin appears in breast milk. Caution is advised if the patient is nursing a baby.

Recommended dosage

For patients who are not currently taking Ritalin, the usual starting dose is 5 milligrams a day. For those who are switching from Ritalin, the starting Focalin dose is half the amount of the Ritalin dose. In either case, the total daily dose of Focalin should be divided into 2 doses taken at least 4 hours apart.

Depending on the response, the doctor may increase the dose by 2.5 to 5 milligrams a day, up to a maximum daily dose of 20 milligrams (10 milligrams twice a day). Increases are usually made at weekly intervals.

Overdosage

If an overdose is suspected, seek medical attention immediately.

- *Symptoms of Focalin overdose may include:*
  Abnormal reflexes, agitation, confusion, convulsions (may be followed by coma), delirium, dryness of mucous membranes, enlarged pupils in the eyes, exaggerated feeling of elation, extremely elevated body temperature, flushing, hallucinations, headache, high blood pressure, irregular or rapid heartbeat, muscle twitching, palpitations, sweating, tremors, vomiting

Galantamine *See Reminyl, page 168*

GEODON
Ziprasidone hydrochloride

Why is this drug prescribed?
Geodon is used in the treatment of schizophrenia. Researchers believe that it works by opposing the action of serotonin and dopamine, two of the brain's major chemical messengers. Because of its potentially serious side effects, Geodon is typically prescribed only after other medications have proved inadequate. An intramuscular injection is available for use in agitated patients.

Most important fact about this drug
In some people with heart problems or a slow heartbeat, Geodon can cause serious and potentially fatal heartbeat irregularities. The chance of a problem is greater if the patient is taking a water pill (diuretic) or a medication that prolongs a part of the heartbeat known as the QT interval. Many of the drugs prescribed for heartbeat irregularities prolong the QT interval and should never be combined with Geodon. Other drugs to avoid when taking Geodon include Anzemet, Avelox, chlorpromazine, Halfan, Inapsine, Lariam, Mellaril, Nebupent, Orap, Orlaam, Pentam, Probucol, Prograf, Serentil, Tequin, Trisenox, and Zagam. Patients should check with their doctor before combining Geodon with any drug they're unsure of.

How should this medication be taken?
Geodon capsules should be taken twice a day with food.

- *Missed dose...*
  Generally, the forgotten dose should be taken as soon as remembered. However, if it is almost time for the next dose, patients should skip the one they missed and go back to their regular schedule. Doses should never be doubled.

- *Storage instructions...*
  Geodon may be stored at room temperature.

What side effects may occur?
Side effects cannot be predicted. If any develop or change in intensity, patients should inform their doctor as soon as possible.

- *Side effects may include:*
  Accidental injury, cold symptoms, constipation, cough, diarrhea, dizziness, drowsiness, dry mouth, headache, indigestion, involuntary muscle contractions, muscle tightness, nausea, rash, stuffy and runny nose, upper respiratory infection, vision problems, vomiting, weakness

Why should this drug not be prescribed?
Geodon cannot be taken by anyone who has the heartbeat irregularity known as QT prolongation, has had a recent heart attack, or suffers from

heart failure. This drug should also be avoided if it causes an allergic reaction.

Special warnings about this medication

Remember that Geodon can cause dangerous—even fatal—heartbeat irregularities. Warning signs include dizziness, palpitations, and fainting. The doctor should be consulted immediately if any of these symptoms develop.

Particularly during the first few days of therapy, Geodon can cause low blood pressure, with accompanying dizziness, fainting, and rapid heartbeat. The doctor should be notified of any of these side effects. To minimize such problems, the doctor will increase the dose gradually. If a patient is prone to low blood pressure, takes blood pressure medicine, becomes dehydrated, or has heart disease or poor circulation in the brain, Geodon should be used with caution.

Geodon may cause drowsiness and can impair judgment, thinking, and motor skills. Patients should use caution while driving and should avoid operating potentially dangerous machinery until they know how this drug affects them.

Antipsychotic drugs such as Geodon are associated with an increased risk of developing high blood sugar, which on rare occasions has led to coma or death. Patients should see their doctor right away if they develop signs of high blood sugar, including dry mouth, thirst, increased urination, and tiredness. Patients who have diabetes or have a high risk of developing it should see their doctor regularly for blood sugar testing.

Animal studies suggest that Geodon may increase the risk of breast cancer, although human studies have not confirmed such a risk. Advise patients with a history of breast cancer to see their doctor regularly for checkups.

Geodon poses a very slight risk of seizures, especially if a patient is over age 65, has a history of seizures, or has Alzheimer's disease.

Drugs such as Geodon sometimes cause a condition called neuroleptic malignant syndrome. Symptoms include high fever, muscle rigidity, irregular pulse or blood pressure, rapid heartbeat, excessive perspiration, and changes in heart rhythm. If these symptoms appear, the doctor should be informed immediately. The patient will need to stop taking Geodon while the condition is under treatment.

There also is the risk of developing tardive dyskinesia, a condition marked by slow, rhythmical, involuntary movements. This problem is more likely to occur in mature adults, especially older women. When it does, use of Geodon is usually stopped.

Geodon can suppress the cough reflex, making it difficult to clear the airway. Some people taking Geodon also develop a rash. If this happens, the doctor should be informed. If the rash doesn't clear up with treatment, the drug may have to be discontinued.

Other antipsychotic medications have been known to interfere with the body's temperature-regulating mechanism, causing the body to overheat. Although this problem has not occurred with Geodon, caution is still advisable. Patients should avoid exposure to extreme heat, strenuous exercise, and dehydration. There also is a remote chance that this medication may cause abnormal, prolonged and painful erections.

Possible food and drug interactions when taking this medication

Patients should be careful to avoid drugs that prolong the QT interval of the heartbeat. They should check with their doctor before combining any other medication with Geodon.

If Geodon is taken with certain other drugs, the effects of either could be increased, decreased, or altered. Here is an overview of drugs that may cause a problem:

Carbamazepine (Tegretol)
Certain blood pressure medications
Drugs that boost the effects of dopamine such as Mirapex, Parlodel, Permax, and Requip
Drugs that affect the brain and nervous system, such as sedatives, tranquilizers, and antidepressants
Ketoconazole (Nizoral)
Levodopa (Larodopa, Sinemet)

Special information about pregnancy and breastfeeding

Geodon has caused fetal harm when tested in animals. It should be taken during pregnancy only if the benefits outweigh the potential risk. Patients should notify their doctor as soon as they become pregnant or plan to become pregnant.

It is not known whether Geodon appears in breast milk, and breastfeeding is not recommended.

Recommended dosage

The usual starting dose is 20 milligrams twice a day. If needed, the dosage may be increased at several-week intervals up to a maximum of 80 milligrams twice a day.

Intramuscular injections of 10 milligrams may be given every 2 hours. Injections of 20 milligrams may be given every 4 hours. The maximum daily dose by injection is 40 milligrams. Patients who are elderly or have kidney or liver problems may need to have their injection dosage adjusted.

Overdosage

Any medication taken in excess can have serious consequences. If an overdose is suspected, seek medical help immediately.

- *Symptoms of Geodon overdose may include:*
  Drowsiness, slurred speech, high blood pressure

HALCION
Triazolam

Why is this drug prescribed?
Halcion is used for short-term treatment of insomnia. It is a member of the benzodiazepine class of drugs, many of which are used as tranquilizers.

Most important fact about this drug
Sleep problems are usually temporary, requiring treatment for only a short time, usually 1 or 2 days and no more than 1 to 2 weeks. Insomnia that lasts longer than this may be a sign of another medical problem. If patients find they need this medicine for more than 7 to 10 days, they should check with their doctor.

How should this medication be taken?
This medication must be taken exactly as directed. It is important to never take more than the doctor has prescribed.

- *Missed dose...*
  Halcion should be taken only as needed.

- *Storage instructions...*
  This medication should be kept in the container it came in, tightly closed, and out of reach of children. It may be stored at room temperature.

What side effects may occur?
Side effects cannot be predicted. If any develop or change in intensity, patients should inform their doctor as soon as possible.

- *Side effects may include:*
  Coordination problems, dizziness, drowsiness, headache, light-headedness, nausea/vomiting, nervousness

Why should this drug not be prescribed?
Halcion should not be taken during pregnancy. Patients should also avoid it if they have had an allergic reaction to it or to other benzodiazepine drugs such as Valium. It should never be combined with the antifungal medications Nizoral or Sporanox, or the antidepressant Serzone.

Special warnings about this medication
When Halcion is used every night for more than a few weeks, it loses its effectiveness. This is known as tolerance. Also, it can cause dependence, especially when it is used regularly for longer than a few weeks or at high doses.

Abrupt discontinuation of Halcion should be avoided, since it has been associated with withdrawal symptoms (convulsions, cramps, tremor, vomiting, sweating, feeling ill, perceptual problems, and insomnia). A gradual dosage tapering schedule is usually recommended for patients taking more than the lowest dose of Halcion for longer than a few weeks. The usual treatment period is 7 to 10 days.

If patients develop unusual and disturbing thoughts or behavior—including increased anxiety or depression—during treatment with Halcion, they should discuss them with their doctor immediately.

Traveler's amnesia has been reported by patients who took Halcion to induce sleep while traveling. To avoid this condition, patients should not take Halcion on an overnight airplane flight of less than 7 to 8 hours.

Some people suffer increased anxiety during the daytime while taking Halcion.

Because Halcion could have a carryover effect the next day, patients first starting therapy should use extreme care while doing anything that requires complete alertness, such as driving a car or operating machinery.

After discontinuing the drug, patients may experience rebound insomnia for the first 2 nights.

They should be aware that anterograde amnesia (forgetting events after an injury) has been associated with benzodiazepine drugs such as Halcion.

Halcion should be used with caution by anyone who has liver or kidney problems, lung problems, or a tendency to temporarily stop breathing while asleep.

Possible food and drug interactions when taking this medication

Patients should avoid alcoholic beverages and grapefruit juice while taking Halcion.

If Halcion is taken with certain other drugs, the effects of either could be increased, decreased, or altered. Here is an overview of drugs that may cause a problem:

Amiodarone (Cordarone)
Antidepressant medications, including tricyclic drugs such as Elavil and
  MAO inhibitors such as Nardil and Parnate
Antihistamines such as Benadryl and Tavist
Antipsychotic medications such as Mellaril and chlorpromazine
Barbiturates such as phenobarbital and Seconal
Cimetidine (Tagamet)
Clarithromycin (Biaxin)
Cyclosporine (Sandimmune, Neoral)
Diltiazem (Cardizem)
Ergotamine (Cafergot)
Erythromycin (E.E.S., PCE, E-Mycin, others)
Fluvoxamine
Isoniazid (Nydrazid)
Itraconazole (Nizoral)
Ketoconazole (Sporanox)

Narcotic painkillers such as Demerol
Nefazodone
Nicardipine (Cardene)
Nifedipine (Adalat)
Oral contraceptives
Other tranquilizers such as BuSpar, Valium, and Xanax
Paroxetine (Paxil)
Ranitidine (Zantac)
Seizure medications such as Dilantin and Tegretol
Sertraline (Zoloft)
Verapamil (Calan)

Special information about pregnancy and breastfeeding

Since benzodiazepines have been associated with damage to the developing baby, women should not take Halcion if they are pregnant, think they may be pregnant, or are planning to become pregnant. Halcion must also be avoided while breastfeeding.

Recommended dosage

ADULTS

The usual dose is 0.25 milligram before bedtime. The dose should never be more than 0.5 milligram.

CHILDREN

Safety and effectiveness for children under the age of 18 have not been established.

OLDER ADULTS

To decrease the possibility of oversedation, dizziness, or impaired coordination, the usual starting dose is 0.125 milligram. This may be increased to 0.25 milligram if necessary.

Overdosage

Any medication taken in excess can have serious consequences. Severe overdosage of Halcion can be fatal. If an overdose is suspected, seek medical help immediately.

- *Symptoms of Halcion overdose may include:*
  Apnea (temporary cessation of breathing), coma, confusion, excessive sleepiness, problems in coordination, seizures, shallow or difficult breathing, slurred speech

HALDOL
Haloperidol

Why is this drug prescribed?
Haldol is used to reduce the symptoms of mental disorders such as schizophrenia. It is also prescribed to control tics (uncontrolled muscle contractions of face, arms, or shoulders) and the unintended utterances that mark Tourette's syndrome. It is used in the short-term treatment of children with severe behavior problems such as combative hyperexcitability. It is also prescribed for the short-term treatment of hyperactive children with conduct disorders marked by some or all of the following symptoms: impulsivity, difficulty sustaining attention, aggressivity, mood lability, and poor frustration tolerance.

Some doctors also prescribe Haldol to relieve severe nausea and vomiting caused by cancer drugs, to treat drug problems such as LSD flashback and PCP intoxication, and to control symptoms of hemiballismus, a condition that causes involuntary writhing of one side of the body.

Most important fact about this drug
Haldol may cause tardive dyskinesia—a condition characterized by involuntary muscle spasms and twitches in the face and body. This condition can be permanent, and appears to be most common among the elderly, especially women.

How should this medication be taken?
Haldol may be taken with food or after eating. If taking Haldol in a liquid concentrate form, patients will need to dilute it with milk or water.

Haldol should not be taken with coffee, tea, or other caffeinated beverages, or with alcohol.

Haldol causes dry mouth. Sucking on a hard candy or ice chips may help alleviate the problem.

- *Missed dose...*
  The forgotten dose should be taken as soon as remembered. The rest of the doses for that day should follow at equally spaced intervals. Doses should never be doubled.

- *Storage instructions...*
  Haldol should be stored away from heat, light, and moisture in a tightly closed container. The liquid should be protected from freezing.

What side effects may occur?
Side effects cannot be predicted. If any develop or change in intensity, patients should inform their doctor as soon as possible.

- *Side effects may include:*
  Anticholinergic effects (such as constipation, dry mouth, rapid heartbeat), breast development in men, breathing problems, cataracts,

drowsiness, insomnia, involuntary muscle contractions, skin reactions, tardive dyskinesia (see "Most important fact about this drug"), tightness of the throat muscles, weight loss

Why should this drug not be prescribed?

Haldol should be avoided by anyone who has Parkinson's disease or is sensitive to or allergic to the drug.

Special warnings about this medication

Haldol should be used with caution by patients who have had or currently have breast cancer, a severe heart or circulatory disorder, chest pain, the eye condition known as glaucoma, seizures, or any drug allergies.

Temporary muscle spasms and twitches may occur if Haldol is stopped abruptly. Patients need to follow the doctor's instructions closely when discontinuing the drug.

This drug may impair the ability to drive a car or operate potentially dangerous machinery. Patients should avoid any activities that require full alertness if they are unsure of their reaction to Haldol.

Haldol may make the skin more sensitive to sunlight. Patients should use a sunscreen or wear protective clothing when spending time in the sun.

Patients should avoid exposure to extreme heat or cold. Haldol interferes with the body's temperature-regulating mechanism, so they could become overheated or suffer severe chills.

Possible food and drug interactions when taking this medication

Extreme drowsiness and other potentially serious effects can result if Haldol is combined with alcohol, narcotics, painkillers, sleeping medications, or other drugs that slow down the central nervous system.

If Haldol is taken with certain other drugs, the effects of either could be increased, decreased, or altered. Here is an overview of drugs that may cause a problem:

Antiseizure drugs such as Dilantin or Tegretol
Blood-thinning medications such as Coumadin
Certain antidepressants, including Elavil, Tofranil, and Prozac
Drugs that quell spasms, such as Bentyl and Cogentin
Epinephrine (EpiPen)
Lithium (Eskalith, Lithobid)
Methyldopa (Aldomet)
Propranolol (Inderal)
Rifampin (Rifadin)

Special information about pregnancy and breastfeeding

The effects of Haldol during pregnancy have not been adequately studied. Pregnant women should use Haldol only if clearly needed. Patients should inform their doctor immediately if they are pregnant or plan to become pregnant. Haldol should not be used by women who are breast-feeding an infant.

Recommended dosage

ADULTS

Moderate Symptoms
The usual dosage is 1 to 6 milligrams daily. This amount should be divided into 2 or 3 smaller doses.

Severe Symptoms
The usual dosage is 6 to 15 milligrams daily, divided into 2 or 3 smaller doses.

CHILDREN

Children younger than 3 years old should not take Haldol. For children between the ages of 3 and 12, weighing approximately 33 to 88 pounds, doses should start at 0.5 milligram per day. The doctor will increase the dose if needed.

For Psychotic Disorders
The daily dose may range from 0.05 milligram to 0.15 milligram for every 2.2 pounds of body weight.

For Non-Psychotic Behavior Disorders and Tourette's Syndrome
The daily dose may range from 0.05 milligram to 0.075 milligram for every 2.2 pounds of body weight.

OLDER ADULTS

In general, older people take dosages of Haldol in the lower ranges. Older adults (especially older women) may be more susceptible to tardive dyskinesia. Doses may range from 1 to 6 milligrams daily.

Overdosage

Any medication taken in excess can have serious consequences. If an overdose is suspected, seek medical help immediately.

- *Symptoms of Haldol overdose may include:*
  Catatonic (unresponsive) state, coma, decreased breathing, low blood pressure, rigid muscles, sedation, tremor, weakness

Haloperidol *See Haldol, page 83*

Hydroxyzine *See Atarax, page 18*

Imipramine *See Tofranil, page 207*

KLONOPIN

Clonazepam

Why is this drug prescribed?

Klonopin has two major uses. In the mental health field it is prescribed for panic disorder. In neurology it is used, alone or along with other medications, to treat convulsive disorders such as epilepsy. Klonopin belongs to the class of drugs known as benzodiazepines.

Most important fact about this drug

Klonopin works best when there is a constant amount in the bloodstream. It is important for patients to take their doses at regularly spaced intervals and to avoid missing any if possible.

How should this medication be taken?

Klonopin should be taken exactly as prescribed. If patients are taking it for panic disorder and find it makes them sleepy, the doctor may recommend a single dose at bedtime.

- *Missed dose...*
  If it is within an hour after the scheduled time, the dose should be taken as soon as remembered. If it's not remembered until later, the patient should skip it and go back to the regular schedule. Doses should never be doubled.

- *Storage instructions...*
  Klonopin should be stored at room temperature away from heat, light, and moisture.

What side effects may occur?

Side effects cannot be predicted. If any develop or change in intensity, patients should inform their doctor as soon as possible.

- *Side effects in panic disorder may include:*
  Allergic reaction, constipation, coordination problems, depression, dizziness, fatigue, inflamed sinuses or nasal passages, flu, memory problems, menstrual problems, nervousness, reduced thinking ability, respiratory infection, sleepiness, speech problems, vaginal inflammation

- *Side effects in seizure disorders may include:*
  Behavior problems, drowsiness, lack of muscular coordination

  Klonopin can also cause aggressive behavior, agitation, anxiety, excitability, hostility, irritability, nervousness, nightmares, sleep disturbances, and vivid dreams.

- *Side effects due to rapid decrease in dose or abrupt withdrawal from Klonopin may include:*
  Abdominal and muscle cramps, behavior disorders, convulsions,

depressed feeling, hallucinations, restlessness, sleeping difficulties, tremors

Why should this drug not be prescribed?

This medication should be avoided by anyone who is sensitive to or has ever had an allergic reaction to it or to similar drugs, such as Librium and Valium. Klonopin also cannot be used in patients with severe liver disease or the eye condition known as acute narrow-angle glaucoma.

Special warnings about this medication

Klonopin makes some people drowsy or less alert. Patients should avoid driving, operating dangerous machinery, or participating in any hazardous activity that requires full mental alertness until they know how this drug affects them.

If a patient suffers from several types of seizures, this drug may increase the possibility of grand mal seizures (epilepsy). Patients should inform their doctor immediately if this occurs. The doctor may wish to prescribe an additional anticonvulsant drug or increase the dose of Klonopin.

Klonopin can be habit-forming and can lose its effectiveness as patients build up a tolerance to it. They may experience withdrawal symptoms—such as convulsions, hallucinations, tremor, and abdominal and muscle cramps—if they stop using this drug abruptly. Patients should discontinue or change their dose only in consultation with their doctor.

Possible food and drug interactions when taking this medication

Klonopin slows the nervous system, and its effects may be intensified by alcohol. Patients should avoid alcohol while taking this medication.

If Klonopin is taken with certain other drugs, the effects of either could be increased, decreased, or altered. Here is an overview of drugs that may cause a problem:

Antianxiety drugs such as Valium
Antidepressant drugs such as Elavil, Nardil, Parnate, and Tofranil
Antipsychotic medications such as Haldol, Navane, and chlorpromazine
Barbiturates such as phenobarbital
Carbamazepine (Tegretol)
Narcotic pain relievers such as Demerol and Percocet
Oral antifungal drugs such as Fungizone, Mycelex, and Mycostatin
Other anticonvulsants such as Dilantin, Depakene, and Depakote
Sedatives such as Halcion

Special information about pregnancy and breastfeeding

Klonopin should be avoided if at all possible during the first 3 months of pregnancy; there is a risk of birth defects. When taken later in pregnancy, the drug can cause other problems, such as withdrawal symptoms in the newborn. Patients who are pregnant or plan to become pregnant should inform their doctor immediately.

Klonopin appears in breast milk and could affect a nursing infant. Mothers taking this drug should not breastfeed.

Recommended dosage

PANIC DISORDER

Adults: The starting dose is 0.25 milligram twice a day. After 3 days, the doctor may increase the dose to 1 milligram daily. Some people need as much as 4 milligrams a day.

Children: For panic disorder, safety and effectiveness have not been established in children under age 18.

SEIZURE DISORDERS

Adults: The starting dose should be no more than 1.5 milligrams per day, divided into 3 doses. The doctor may increase the daily dosage by 0.5 to 1 milligram every 3 days until the patient's seizures are controlled or the side effects become too bothersome. The maximum daily dosage is 20 milligrams.

Children: The starting dose for infants and children up to 10 years old or up to 66 pounds should be 0.01 to 0.03 milligram—no more than 0.05 milligram—per 2.2 pounds of body weight daily. The daily dosage should be given in 2 or 3 smaller doses. The doctor may increase the dose by 0.25 to 0.5 milligram every 3 days until seizures are controlled or side effects become too bad. If the dose cannot be divided into 3 equal doses, the largest dose should be given at bedtime. The maximum maintenance dose is 0.1 to 0.2 milligram per 2.2 pounds daily.

DOSAGE ADJUSTMENT

Klonopin tends to build up in the body if the kidneys are weak—a common problem among older adults. Higher doses of the drug also tend to cause more drowsiness and confusion in older patients. People over age 65 are therefore started on low doses of Klonopin and watched with extra care.

Overdosage

Any medication taken in excess can have serious consequences. If an overdose is suspected, seek medical attention immediately.

- *Symptoms of Klonopin overdose may include:*
  Coma, confusion, sleepiness, slowed reaction time

LAMICTAL

Lamotrigine
Other brand name: Lamictal CD

Why is this drug prescribed?

Lamictal is used to help prevent the manic and/or depressive phases of bipolar disorder.

This drug is also prescribed to control partial seizures in people with epilepsy and the epileptic condition known as Lennox-Gastaut syndrome. Lamictal is used in combination with other antiepileptic drugs or as a replacement for another medication such as Tegretol, Dilantin, phenobarbital, or Mysoline.

Most important fact about this drug

Lamictal may cause a rash during the first 2 to 8 weeks of therapy, particularly if the patient is also taking Depakene or Depakote. If this happens, the doctor should be notified immediately. The rash could become severe and even dangerous, particularly in children. A slight possibility of this problem remains for up to 6 months.

How should this medication be taken?

Instruct patients to take Lamictal exactly as instructed by their doctor. Taking more than the prescribed amount can increase the risk of developing a serious rash. Patients should not stop taking this medication without first discussing it with their doctor. An abrupt halt could increase the risk of seizures and other adverse effects.

Lamictal Chewable Dispersible (CD) tablets may be swallowed whole, chewed, or dissolved in liquid. When chewing the tablets, patients should drink a small amount of water or diluted fruit juice to aid in swallowing. When dissolving the tablets, patients should add them to a small amount of water or diluted fruit juice (about 1 teaspoonful), and wait 1 minute until the tablets are completely dissolved. They should swirl and drink the solution immediately. Patients should not try to cut the dose by drinking only part of the solution.

- *Missed dose...*
  Patients should take the forgotten dose as soon as they remember. If it is almost time for their next dose, patients should skip the one they missed and go back to their regular schedule. Patients should never try to "catch up" by doubling the dose.

- *Storage instructions...*
  Lamictal should be stored in a tightly closed container at room temperature. It should be kept dry and protected from light.

What side effects may occur?

Side effects cannot be predicted. If any develop or change in intensity, patients should inform their doctor as soon as possible.

- *Side effects may include:*
  Abdominal pain, back pain, blurred vision, constipation, coordination problems, dizziness, double vision, dry mouth, fatigue, headache, increased cough, insomnia, nausea, rash (sometimes serious), runny nose, sleepiness, sore throat, vomiting

- *Additional side effects in children may include:*
  Bronchitis, convulsions, ear problems, eczema, facial swelling, hemorrhage, infection, indigestion, light sensitivity, lymph node problems, nervousness, penis disorder, sinus infection, swelling, tooth problems, urinary tract infection, vertigo, vision problems

Why should this drug not be prescribed?

This medication should be avoided by anyone who is sensitive to or has ever had an allergic reaction to Lamictal.

Special warnings about this medication

Remind patients to be alert for the development of any type of rash, especially during the first 2 to 8 weeks of treatment. They should contact their doctor immediately at the first sign of an allergic reaction, including fever, swollen lymph nodes, or rash.

Lamictal may cause some people to become drowsy, dizzy, or less alert. Patients should not drive or operate dangerous machinery or participate in any hazardous activity until they know how the drug affects them.

Before starting Lamictal therapy, patients should tell their doctor about any history of medical problems. Patients with heart problems or kidney or liver disease should use this drug with caution.

Lamictal may cause vision problems. If any develop, patients should notify their doctor immediately.

Patients with bipolar disorder should be aware that Lamictal should not be used to stop an episode of mania or depression once it has started. Patients who are taking Lamictal for seizure control should tell their doctor right away if their seizures get worse.

There are no clinical studies to prove the safety and effectiveness of Lamictal for treating bipolar disorder in children less than 18 years old.

Possible food and drug interactions when taking this medication

If Lamictal is taken with certain other drugs, the effects of either could be increased, decreased, or altered. Here is an overview of drugs that may cause a problem:

Carbamazepine (Tegretol)
Drugs that inhibit folate metabolism, such as methotrexate and Septra
Oral contraceptives
Phenobarbital
Phenytoin (Dilantin)
Primidone (Mysoline)
Valproic acid (Depakene, Depakote)

Special information about pregnancy and breastfeeding

The effects of Lamictal during pregnancy have not been adequately studied. Patients who are pregnant or plan to become pregnant should tell their doctor immediately.

This medication appears in breast milk, and breastfeeding is not recommended during Lamictal therapy.

Recommended dosage

The following indications and dosages are for adults unless otherwise noted.

BIPOLAR DISORDER

Lamictal NOT combined with Depakene, Depakote, Tegretol, Dilantin, Phenobarbital, or Mysoline

One 25-milligram dose of Lamictal per day for weeks 1 and 2, then 50 milligrams per day for weeks 3 and 4, then 100 milligrams a day for week 5. After that, the doctor will have the patient take a total of 200 milligrams a day.

Lamictal combined with Depakene or Depakote

One 25-milligram dose of Lamictal every other day for weeks 1 and 2, then 25 milligrams once a day for weeks 3 and 4, then 50 milligrams a day for week 5. After that, the doctor will have the patient take a total of 100 milligrams a day.

Lamictal combined with Tegretol, Dilantin, Phenobarbital, or Mysoline

One 50-milligram dose of Lamictal per day for weeks 1 and 2, then 50 milligrams twice a day for weeks 3 and 4, then 100 milligrams twice a day for week 5. After that, the doctor will have the patient take a total of 300 to 400 milligrams a day, divided into 2 doses.

SEIZURES

Lamictal combined with Tegretol, Dilantin, Phenobarbital, and Mysoline

One 50-milligram dose per day for 2 weeks, then two 50-milligram doses per day for 2 weeks. After that, the doctor may have the patient take a total of 300 milligrams to 500 milligrams a day, divided into 2 doses.

Lamictal combined with Depakene or Depakote, whether taken alone or with any of the above medications

One 25-milligram dose every other day for 2 weeks, then 25 milligrams once a day for 2 weeks. After that, the doctor will prescribe a total of 100 milligrams to 400 milligrams a day, taken in 1 or 2 doses.

Lamictal as a replacement for Tegretol, Dilantin, Phenobarbital, or Mysoline

While patients continue to take the other drug, the doctor will add Lamictal, starting at a dose of 50 milligrams per day, then gradually increase the daily dose. Once the patient has reached a dosage of 500 milligrams per day divided into 2 doses, the doctor will then begin to gradually reduce the dosage of the other drug until, after 4 weeks, it has been completely eliminated.

The doctor will adjust the patient's dose accordingly when treatment with any of the above medications is stopped, or when patients start or stop taking oral contraceptives or psychiatric drugs.

Due to the lack of clinical studies, Lamictal should be used cautiously in people with liver or kidney problems. The doctor may have these patients take less than the usual dose and raise it based on their body's response.

SEIZURES IN CHILDREN 2 YEARS OF AGE AND OLDER

Lamictal can be added to other epilepsy drugs prescribed for children under 16 who have partial seizures or a serious form of epilepsy known as Lennox-Gastaut syndrome. Doses for children under 12 are based on the child's weight. Children 12 and older receive the adult dose. Doses are increased gradually from a low starting level to limit the risk of severe rash. Lamictal is not used as a replacement drug for children under 16.

Overdosage

A massive overdose of Lamictal can be fatal. If an overdose is suspected, seek medical treatment immediately.

• *Symptoms of Lamictal overdose may include:*
Decreased level of consciousness, delayed heartbeat, coma, increased seizures, lack of coordination, rolling eyeballs

Lamotrigine *See Lamictal, page 89*

LEXAPRO
Escitalopram oxalate

Why is this drug prescribed?

Lexapro is prescribed for major depression and generalized anxiety disorder. The drug is a close chemical cousin of the antidepressant medication Celexa.

Lexapro belongs to the class of drugs known as selective serotonin reuptake inhibitors (SSRIs). Serotonin is one of the chemical messengers believed to govern moods. Ordinarily, it is quickly reabsorbed after its release at the junctures between nerves. Reuptake inhibitors such as Lexapro slow this process, thereby boosting the levels of serotonin available in the brain.

Most important fact about this drug

Patients should be careful to avoid taking Lexapro for 2 weeks before or after taking any drug classified as an MAO inhibitor. Drugs in this category include the antidepressants Marplan, Nardil, and Parnate. Combining these drugs with Lexapro can cause serious and even fatal reactions marked by such symptoms as fever, rigidity, twitching, and agitation leading to delirium and coma.

How should this medication be taken?

Patients need to take Lexapro exactly as prescribed, even after they begin to feel better. Although improvement usually begins within 1 to 4 weeks, treatment typically continues for several months. Lexapro can be taken with or without food.

- *Missed dose...*
  The forgotten dose should be taken as soon as it's remembered. However, if it is almost time for the next dose, patients should skip the one they missed and return to their regular schedule. Doses should never be doubled.

- *Storage instructions...*
  Lexapro should be stored at room temperature.

What side effects may occur?

Side effects cannot be anticipated. If any develop or change in intensity, patients should inform their doctor as soon as possible.

- *Side effects may include:*
  Diarrhea, ejaculation disorder, fatigue, insomnia, nausea, sleepiness, sweating

A variety of very rare side effects have also been reported. Patients should check with their doctor if they develop any new or unusual symptoms.

Why should this drug not be prescribed?

Patients should not use Lexapro if it causes an allergic reaction, or if they've ever had an allergic reaction to the related drug Celexa. Also remember that Lexapro, like all serotonin-boosting drugs, must never be combined with an MAO inhibitor such as Marplan, Nardil, or Parnate.

Special warnings about this medication

The FDA has issued a public health advisory to alert healthcare professionals about reports of worsening depression and suicidality (both suicidal thoughts and suicide attempts) during antidepressant drug therapy in adults and pediatric patients with major depression. Healthcare professionals and family members are advised to watch for signs of worsening depression and to be aware of the suicide statement present in all antidepressant labeling. Lexapro is currently not approved for treating major depression or anxiety disorders in pediatric patients.

Lexapro may cause patients to become drowsy or less alert. Until they know how the drug affects them, patients should use caution when driving a car or operating other hazardous machinery.

In rare cases, Lexapro can trigger mania (unreasonably high spirits and excess energy). If a patient has ever had this problem, it's important to make sure the doctor is aware of it.

It's also important to alert the doctor if a patient has liver problems or severe kidney disease. The dosage of Lexapro may need adjustment.

Convulsions have been reported during Lexapro treatment. Patients with a history of seizures should use this drug with caution.

Serotonin-boosting antidepressants could potentially cause stomach bleeding, especially in older patients or those taking nonsteroidal anti-inflammatory drugs (NSAIDs) such as aspirin, ibuprofen (Advil, Motrin), naproxen (Aleve), and ketoprofen (Orudis KT). Advise patients to consult their doctor before combining Lexapro with NSAIDs or blood-thinning medications.

Patients should never stop taking Lexapro without consulting the doctor. An abrupt decrease in dose could cause withdrawal symptoms such as mood problems, lethargy, insomnia, and tingling sensations.

Possible food and drug interactions when taking this medication

Patients should not use Lexapro if they are taking the related drug Celexa. In addition, Lexapro must never be combined with MAO inhibitors such as Marplan, Nardil, and Parnate.

Although Lexapro does not interact with alcohol, the manufacturer recommends avoiding alcoholic beverages.

If Lexapro is taken with certain other drugs, the effects of either could be increased, decreased, or altered. Here is an overview of the drugs that may cause a problem:

Aspirin
Carbamazepine (Tegretol)
Cimetidine (Tagamet)
Desipramine (Norpramin)
Drugs that act on the brain, including antidepressants, painkillers,
  sedatives, and tranquilizers

Ketoconazole (Nizoral)
Linezolid (Zyvox)
Lithium (Eskalith, Lithobid)
Metoprolol (Lopressor)
Narcotic pain killers
Nonsteroidal anti-inflammatory drugs such as Advil and Motrin
Sumatriptan (Imitrex)
Warfarin (Coumadin)

Special information about pregnancy and breastfeeding

The effects of Lexapro during pregnancy have not been adequately studied, and the potential for harm has not been ruled out. There have been reports of newborns developing serious complications after exposure to Lexapro late in the third trimester. Patients who are pregnant or plan to become pregnant should inform their doctor immediately.

Lexapro appears in breast milk and can affect a nursing infant. If a patient decides to breastfeed, Lexapro is not recommended.

Recommended dosage

ADULTS

The recommended dose of Lexapro is 10 milligrams once a day. If necessary, the doctor may increase the dose to 20 milligrams after a minimum of 1 week. For most older adults or patients with severe kidney disease or liver problems, the recommended dose is 10 milligrams once a day.

Overdosage

In rare cases, a massive overdose of Lexapro—especially when combined with alcohol or other drugs—can be fatal. If an overdose is suspected, seek emergency treatment immediately.

- *Symptoms of Lexapro overdose may include:*
  Dizziness, drowsiness, nausea, rapid heartbeat, seizures, sweating, tremors, vomiting

  Rarely, an overdose may also cause memory loss, confusion, coma, breathing problems, muscle wasting, irregular heartbeat, and a bluish tinge to the skin.

LIBRIUM
Chlordiazepoxide

Why is this drug prescribed?

Librium is used in the treatment of anxiety disorders. It is also prescribed for short-term relief of the symptoms of anxiety, symptoms of withdrawal in acute alcoholism, and anxiety and apprehension before surgery. It belongs to a class of drugs known as benzodiazepines.

Most important fact about this drug

Librium is habit-forming and can lead to dependency. Warn patients that they could experience withdrawal symptoms if they stop taking the drug abruptly (see "What side effects may occur?"). They should discontinue or change their dose only on the advice of their doctor.

How should this medication be taken?

Instruct patients to take this medication exactly as prescribed.

- *Missed dose...*
  Patients should take the forgotten dose as soon as they remember if it is within an hour or so of the scheduled time. If they do not remember until later, they should skip the missed dose and go back to their regular schedule. Warn against taking 2 doses at once.

- *Storage instructions...*
  Librium should be stored away from heat, light, and moisture.

What side effects may occur?

Side effects cannot be predicted. If any develop or change in intensity, patients should inform their doctor as soon as possible.

- *Side effects may include:*
  Confusion, constipation, drowsiness, fainting, increased or decreased sex drive, liver problems, lack of muscle coordination, minor menstrual irregularities, nausea, skin rash or eruptions, swelling due to fluid retention, yellow eyes and skin

- *Side effects due to rapid decrease in dose or abrupt withdrawal from Librium may include:*
  Abdominal and muscle cramps, convulsions, exaggerated feeling of depression, sleeplessness, sweating, tremors, vomiting

Why should this drug not be prescribed?

This medication should be avoided by anyone who is sensitive to or has ever had an allergic reaction to Librium or similar tranquilizers.

Anxiety or tension related to everyday stress usually does not require treatment with Librium. Patients should discuss their symptoms thoroughly with the doctor.

Special warnings about this medication

Librium may cause patients to become drowsy or less alert. They should not drive or operate dangerous machinery or participate in any hazardous activity that requires full mental alertness until they know how they react to this drug.

Patients who are severely depressed or have suffered from severe depression should consult with their doctor before taking this medication.

If Librium has been prescribed for a hyperactive, aggressive child, the doctor should be informed of contrary reactions such as excitement, stimulation, or acute rage.

Patients should check with their doctor before taking Librium if they are being treated for porphyria (a rare metabolic disorder) or kidney or liver disease.

Possible food and drug interactions when taking this medication

Librium is a central nervous system depressant and may intensify the effects of alcohol or have an additive effect. Warn patients against drinking alcohol while taking this medication.

If Librium is taken with certain other drugs, the effects of either can be increased, decreased, or altered. Here is an overview of drugs that may cause a problem:

Antacids such as Maalox and Mylanta
Antipsychotic medications such as chlorpromazine and trifluoperazine
Drugs classified as MAO inhibitors, including the antidepressants
  Nardil and Parnate
Barbiturates such as phenobarbital
Blood-thinning drugs such as Coumadin
Cimetidine (Tagamet)
Disulfiram (Antabuse)
Levodopa (Larodopa)
Narcotic pain relievers such as Demerol and Percocet
Oral contraceptives

Special information about pregnancy and breastfeeding

Women should not take Librium if they are pregnant or planning to become pregnant. There may be an increased risk of birth defects.

This drug may appear in breast milk and could affect a nursing infant. If Librium is essential to the patient's health, her doctor may advise her to discontinue breastfeeding until her treatment with the drug is finished.

Recommended dosage

ANXIETY IN ADULTS

Mild or Moderate Symptoms: The usual dose is 5 or 10 milligrams, 3 or 4 times a day.

Severe Symptoms: The usual dose is 20 to 25 milligrams, 3 or 4 times a day.

Apprehension and Anxiety Before Surgery: On days preceding surgery, the usual dose is 5 to 10 milligrams, 3 or 4 times a day.

ANXIETY IN CHILDREN

The usual dose for children 6 years of age and older is 5 milligrams, 2 to 4 times per day. Some children may need to take 10 milligrams 2 or 3 times per day. The drug is not recommended for children under 6.

WITHDRAWAL SYMPTOMS OF ACUTE ALCOHOLISM

The usual starting oral dose is 50 to 100 milligrams; the doctor will repeat this dose, up to a maximum of 300 milligrams per day, until agitation is controlled. The dose will then be reduced as much as possible.

OLDER ADULTS

The doctor will limit the dose to the smallest effective amount in order to avoid oversedation or lack of coordination. The usual dose is 5 milligrams, 2 to 4 times per day.

Overdosage

Any medication taken in excess can cause symptoms of overdose. If an overdose is suspected, seek medical attention immediately.

- *Symptoms of Librium overdose may include:*
  Coma, confusion, sleepiness, slow reflexes

LIMBITROL

Amitriptyline hydrochloride with Chlordiazepoxide
Other brand name: Limbitrol DS

Why is this drug prescribed?

Limbitrol is a combination of an antidepressant and an antianxiety drug. It is used in the treatment of moderate to severe depression associated with moderate to severe anxiety.

Most important fact about this drug

Limbitrol is habit-forming and can lead to dependency. Patients could experience withdrawal symptoms if they stop taking it abruptly (see "What side effects may occur?"). They should discontinue or change their dose only on the advice of their doctor.

How should this medication be taken?

It is important that this medication be taken exactly as prescribed.

- *Missed dose...*
  Patients should skip the missed dose and go back to their regular schedule. They should never take 2 doses at once.

● *Storage instructions...*
Limbitrol should be stored away from heat, light, and moisture.

What side effects may occur?

Side effects cannot be predicted. If any develop or change in intensity, patients should inform their doctor as soon as possible.

● *Side effects may include:*
Bloating, blurred vision, constipation, dizziness, drowsiness, dry mouth, fatigue, restlessness, weakness, weight loss

● *Side effects due to rapid decrease in dose or abrupt withdrawal from Limbitrol may include:*
Abdominal and muscle cramps, convulsions, exaggerated feeling of depression, headache, inability to fall asleep or stay asleep, nausea, restlessness, sweating, tremors, vague bodily discomfort, vomiting

Why should this drug not be prescribed?

Limbitrol should be avoided by anyone who is sensitive to or has ever had an allergic reaction to related drugs—benzodiazepine tranquilizers and tricyclic antidepressants.

Limbitrol should not be used by patients who have just had a heart attack.

Patients who are taking an antidepressant drug classified as an MAO inhibitor (Nardil, Parnate) should not take Limbitrol. Convulsions and death have occurred when the drugs were combined. (MAO inhibitors are long-lasting. A minimum of 14 days should be allowed between stopping an MAO inhibitor and starting Limbitrol.)

Special warnings about this medication

Limbitrol may cause patients to become drowsy or less alert. They should not drive or participate in any hazardous activity that requires full mental alertness until they know how this drug affects them.

This drug, especially when given in high doses, can cause irregular heartbeat, an increase in heart rate, heart attack, or stroke. Patients who are being treated for a heart or circulatory disorder should consult their doctor before taking Limbitrol.

Patients who are severely depressed or have been treated for severe depression should check with their doctor before taking this medication.

They should also double check with the doctor before taking this medication if they are being treated for the eye condition known as angle-closure glaucoma or for inability to pass urine. The doctor should also be alerted if they have a thyroid condition or liver or kidney problems, or if they have ever had seizures.

Before elective surgery, the doctor will discontinue Limbitrol several days prior to the operation. Limbitrol should be used with caution in patients who are getting electroconvulsive therapy.

Possible food and drug interactions when taking this medication

Limbitrol is a central nervous system depressant and may intensify the effects of alcohol. Patients should not drink alcohol while taking this medication.

If Limbitrol is taken with certain other drugs, the effects of either could be increased, decreased, or altered. Here is an overview of drugs that may cause a problem:

Antipsychotic medications such as chlorpromazine and Mellaril
Any type of antidepressant drug
Barbiturates such as phenobarbital
Cimetidine (Tagamet)
Disulfiram (Antabuse)
Flecainide (Tambocor)
Guanethidine
Levodopa (Larodopa)
Oral contraceptives
Other mood-altering drugs
Propafenone (Rythmol)
Quinidine (Quinidex)
Thyroid medication such as Synthroid

Severe constipation may occur if Limbitrol is combined with spasm-quelling drugs such as Donnatal or Bentyl.

Special information about pregnancy and breastfeeding

Women who are pregnant or plan to become pregnant should avoid Limbitrol. There is an increased risk of birth defects.

This drug may appear in breast milk and could affect a nursing infant. If this medication is essential to the patient's health, the doctor may advise her to discontinue breastfeeding until her treatment is finished.

Recommended dosage

ADULTS

Limbitrol Tablets

The usual starting dosage is a total of 3 or 4 tablets per day in several small doses. The larger portion of the daily dose may be taken at bedtime. A single bedtime dose may be sufficient.

Limbitrol DS (Double-strength)

The usual starting dosage is a total of 3 or 4 tablets per day divided into smaller doses. The doctor may increase the dose to 6 tablets per day or decrease it to 2 tablets per day, depending on response.

CHILDREN

Safety and effectiveness have not been established in children under 12 years old.

OLDER ADULTS

The doctor will prescribe the smallest amount possible in order to avoid side effects such as oversedation, confusion, and loss of muscle control.

Overdosage

Any medication taken in excess can have serious conseqences. If an over-dose is suspected, seek medical attention immediately.

- *Symptoms of Limbitrol overdose may include:*
  Abnormally fast heart rate, agitation, coma, confusion, congestive heart failure, convulsions, dilated pupils, disturbed concentration, drowsiness, exaggerated reflexes, hallucinations, high fever, irregular heartbeat, muscle rigidity, reduction of body temperature, severe low blood pressure, stupor, vomiting

Lithium *See Eskalith, page 65*

Lithobid *See Eskalith, page 65*

Lorazepam *See Ativan, page 20*

LUDIOMIL
Maprotiline hydrochloride

Why is this drug prescribed?

Ludiomil is used to treat depression and anxiety associated with depression. It is also used for depression in people with manic-depressive illness.

Ludiomil is classified as a tetracyclic antidepressant. It is thought to work by boosting sensitivity at nerve junctions in the brain.

Most important fact about this drug

Seizures have been associated with Ludiomil, particularly when the drug was taken in amounts larger than prescribed, the dosage was increased too fast, or it was taken with certain other drugs such as Stelazine and Thorazine. To reduce the risk of seizures, patients should be sure to follow the doctor's instructions for taking this medication.

How should this medication be taken?

The doctor may prescribe a single daily dose or several smaller doses.

Improvement may not be evident for 2 to 3 weeks. Patients should not let this discourage them. They should continue Ludiomil therapy until instructed otherwise by the doctor.

- *Missed dose...*

  Patients who take 1 dose at bedtime should check with their doctor. Taking it in the morning may cause side effects during the day.

  Patients who take more than 1 dose a day should take the forgotten dose as soon as they remember. If it is almost time for the next dose, they should skip the one they missed and go back to their regular schedule. They should never try to "catch up" by doubling the dose.

- *Storage instructions...*

  Ludiomil should be stored at room temperature in a tightly closed container.

What side effects may occur?

Side effects cannot be predicted. If any develop or change in intensity, patients should inform the doctor as soon as possible.

- *Side effects may include:*

  Anxiety, blurred vision, constipation, dizziness, drowsiness, dry mouth, fatigue, headache, nervousness, tremors, weakness

Why should this drug not be prescribed?

Ludiomil should not be used by anyone who has had a recent heart attack. It should be avoided by patients who have taken one of the antidepressant drugs known as MAO inhibitors, including Parnate and Nardil, within the preceding 14 days. It should not be used by people who have had seizures. It should not be taken by individuals known to be hypersensitive to it.

Special warnings about this medication

Ludiomil should be used cautiously if the patient has ever had glaucoma (excessive pressure in the eyes), heart disease, heart attacks, irregular heartbeats, strokes, thyroid disease, or difficulty urinating.

This drug may impair patients' ability to drive a car or operate potentially dangerous machinery. They should not participate in any activities that require full alertness if they are unsure of their response to the drug.

Ludiomil may cause sensitivity to light. Patients should avoid prolonged exposure to the sun; they should use sunscreens and wear protective clothing until they learn their tolerance.

Possible food and drug interactions when taking this medication

Ludiomil should not be combined with MAO inhibitors such as Nardil.

If Ludiomil is taken with certain other drugs, the effects of either could be increased, decreased, or altered. Here is an overview of drugs that may cause a problem:

Airway-opening drugs such as Ventolin
Antipsychotic medications such as chlorpromazine and trifluperazine
Choline
Cimetidine (Tagamet)
Drugs that control spasms, such as Bentyl
Fluoxetine (Prozac)
Guanethidine
Phenytoin (Dilantin)
Thyroid medications such as Synthroid
Tranquilizers such as Valium and Xanax

Extreme drowsiness and other potentially serious effects can result if Ludiomil is combined with alcohol, sleeping medications such as Seconal, and other drugs that depress the central nervous system.

Special information about pregnancy or breastfeeding

The effects of Ludiomil during pregnancy have not been adequately studied. Pregnant women should use Ludiomil only if clearly needed.

Ludiomil appears in breast milk and could affect a nursing infant. Women who nurse infants should use the drug cautiously and only when the potential benefits clearly outweigh the potential risks.

Recommended dosage

ADULTS

For Mild to Moderate Depression

Dosages usually start at 75 milligrams a day, taken as a single daily dose or divided into smaller doses. The doctor may increase the dose gradually to a maximum of 150 milligrams daily.

For Moderate to Severe Depression

For those who are hospitalized, dosages as high as 225 milligrams daily may be prescribed.

CHILDREN

Safety and effectiveness for children under 18 years old have not been established.

OLDER ADULTS

For Mild to Moderate Depression

Dosages usually start at 25 milligrams a day and may range up to 50 to 75 milligrams daily.

Overdosage

An overdose of Ludiomil can be fatal. If an overdose is suspected, seek medical help immediately.

- *Symptoms of Ludiomil overdose may include:*
  Agitation, bluish skin, coma, convulsions, dilated pupils, drowsiness, heart failure, high fever, irregular heart rate, lack of coordination, loss of consciousness, muscle rigidity, rapid heartbeat, restlessness, severely low blood pressure, shock, vomiting, writhing movement of the hands

Luvox *See Fluvoxamine maleate, page 70*

Maprotiline *See Ludiomil, page 101*

MEBARAL
Mephobarbital sodium

Why is this drug prescribed?

Mebaral is a barbiturate used as a sedative for the relief of anxiety, tension, and apprehension. It also works as an anticonvulsant and is prescribed to treat certain types of epilepsy, including grand mal and petit mal seizures.

Most important fact about this drug

If taken for a long enough time, Mebaral can cause physical and psychological addiction. An overdose can be fatal. Mebaral should be used in the smallest possible amount, and it should always be stored in child-resistant containers.

How should this medication be taken?

Mebaral should be taken exactly as prescribed. Patients should never increase the dose or use the drug more often than the doctor has instructed.

Patients who are using Mebaral to control seizures should take it at bedtime if the attacks generally occur at night, and during the day if the attacks happen in the daytime.

- *Missed dose...*
  Patients should take the forgotten dose as soon as they remember. If it is almost time for their next dose, they should skip the one they missed and go back to their regular schedule. Patients should never take two doses at once.

- *Storage instructions...*
  Mebaral should be stored at room temperature.

What side effects may occur?

Side effects cannot be predicted. If any develop or change in intensity, patients should inform their doctor as soon as possible.

- *Side effects may include:*
  Abnormal or increased muscle movement, agitation, confusion, fainting, headache, impaired coordination, low blood pressure, nausea, shallow or slowed breathing, slowed heartbeat, stoppage of breathing (apnea), sleepiness, vomiting

Why should this drug not be prescribed?

People with the rare blood disorder porphyria and those who are allergic or sensitive to barbiturates must avoid Mebaral.

Special warnings about this medication

Mebaral must not be stopped abruptly. Doing so can result in severe withdrawal symptoms and even death. To reduce any possible withdrawal symptoms, patients should follow their doctor's instructions closely when stopping this drug. Minor withdrawal symptoms may appear 8 to 12 hours after the last dose, and usually occur in the following order: anxiety, muscle twitching, tremors of hands and fingers, progressive weakness, dizziness, visual problems, nausea, vomiting, insomnia, and light-headedness on standing up. Major withdrawal symptoms include convulsions and delirium, which may occur within 16 hours of abruptly stopping Mebaral and can last up to 5 days.

Barbiturates such as Mebaral should be used cautiously, if at all, in patients who have a history of depression, suicidal tendencies, or drug abuse.

In some people, Mebaral may cause excitement rather than sedation. Others experience depression and confusion. Such reactions are more likely in elderly or debilitated patients.

The doctor will prescribe this drug cautiously in patients with any of the following: liver damage, kidney impairment, heart problems, breathing difficulties, the muscle disorder myasthenia gravis, or myxedema (a type of skin swelling associated with poor thyroid function). Caution is also advised in patients with acute or chronic pain, since Mebaral treatment could induce paradoxical excitement or mask important pain symptoms.

Mebaral may impair the ability to drive a car or operate potentially dangerous machinery. Patients should not participate in any activities that require full alertness if they are unsure of the drug's effects.

Mebaral may cause vitamin D deficiency. Patients should ask their doctor about increasing their vitamin D intake.

Mebaral could lessen the effectiveness of oral contraceptives. Women who take this drug may need to consider another type of birth control.

Barbiturates such as Mebaral may lose their effect when taken regularly. If this happens, patients should contact the doctor. They should never increase the dose in an effort to get the drug to work again.

Possible food and drug interactions when taking this medication

If Mebaral is taken with certain other drugs, the effects of either could be increased, decreased, or altered. Here is an overview of drugs that may cause a problem:

Antidepressant drugs classified as MAO inhibitors, such as Nardil and Parnate
Antihistamines such as Benadryl
Blood-thinning medications such as Coumadin
Doxycycline (Vibramycin)
Griseofulvin (Gris-PEG)
Hormonal medications such as Premarin
Oral contraceptives
Phenytoin (Dilantin)
Sedatives such as Halcion and Dalmane
Steroids such as prednisone
Tranquilizers such as Xanax and Valium
Valproate (Depakene, Depakote)

Warn patients not to drink alcohol while using Mebaral. Combining the two could cause serious effects due to central nervous system depression.

Special information about pregnancy and breastfeeding

Mebaral can cause damage to developing babies and withdrawal symptoms in newborns. Patients who are pregnant or plan to become pregnant should inform their doctor immediately.

This drug appears in breast milk and should be used with caution by nursing mothers.

Recommended dosage

SEDATION

Adults: The recommended optimum dose is 50 milligrams 3 to 4 times a day. The effective dosage can range from 32 to 100 milligrams 3 to 4 times a day.

Children: Dosages for children range from 16 to 32 milligrams 3 to 4 times a day

EPILEPSY

Adults: The average dose is 400 to 600 milligrams a day.

Children 5 years of age and older: 32 to 64 milligrams 3 to 4 times a day.

Children under 5 years of age: 16 to 32 milligrams 3 to 4 times a day.

Patients who are taking Mebaral with other anticonvulsants, particularly phenobarbital, may be prescribed a reduced dosage. The doctor will also prescribe lower dosages for patients who are elderly, debilitated, or suffering from liver or kidney problems.

Overdosage

An overdose of Mebaral can be fatal. If an overdose is suspected, seek medical help immediately.

* *Symptoms or complications of Mebaral overdose may include:*
  Coma, constriction (or sometimes dilation) of pupils, difficulty breathing, fluid in the lungs, heart failure, kidney failure, lack of reflexes, low blood pressure, low body temperature, pneumonia, rapid or irregular heartbeat, reduced flow of urine

---

MELLARIL

Thioridazine hydrochloride

Why is this drug prescribed?

Mellaril is used to treat schizophrenia. Because Mellaril has been known to cause dangerous heartbeat irregularities, it is usually prescribed only when at least two other medications have failed. Patients should receive an electrocardiogram before the drug is prescribed and periodically during Mellaril therapy.

Most important fact about this drug

The danger of potentially fatal cardiac irregularities increases when Mellaril is combined with any medication that prolongs a part of the heartbeat known as the QT interval. Many of the drugs prescribed for heartbeat irregularities (including Cordarone, Inderal, Quinaglute, Quinidex, and Rythmol) prolong the QT interval and should never be combined with Mellaril. Other drugs to be avoided during Mellaril therapy include fluvoxamine, Norvir, Paxil, pindolol, Prozac, Rescriptor, and Tagamet. Patients should make sure the doctor knows they are taking Mellaril whenever a new drug is prescribed.

How should this medication be taken?

Patients taking Mellaril in a liquid concentrate form can dilute it with a liquid such as distilled water, soft tap water, or juice just before taking it.

Patients should not change from one brand of thioridazine to another without consulting their doctor.

* *Missed dose...*
  Patients who take 1 dose a day and remember later in the day should take the dose immediately. If they don't remember until the next day,

they should skip the dose and go back to their regular schedule.

Patients who take more than 1 dose a day and remember the forgotten dose within an hour or so after its scheduled time should take it immediately. If they don't remember until later, they should skip the dose and go back to their regular schedule.

Patients should never try to "catch up" by doubling a dose.

- *Storage instructions...*
  Mellaril should be stored at room temperature, tightly closed, in the container the medication came in.

What side effects may occur?

Side effects cannot be predicted. If any develop or change in intensity, patients should inform the doctor as soon as possible.

- *Side effects may include:*
  Blurred vision, breast development in men, breast milk secretion, constipation, diarrhea, drowsiness, dry mouth, impotence, nausea, swelling in the arms and legs (edema), tardive dyskinesia (see "Special warnings about this medication"), vomiting

Why should this drug not be prescribed?

Due to the danger of cardiac irregularities, Mellaril must never be combined with drugs that increase its effects or prolong the part of the heartbeat known as the QT interval. (See "Most important fact about this drug.") It is also important to avoid combining Mellaril with excessive amounts of central nervous system depressants such as alcohol, barbiturates, or narcotics. It should not be used by anyone who has heart disease accompanied by severe high or low blood pressure.

Special warnings about this medication

Warning signs of the heartbeat irregularities that may be triggered by Mellaril include dizziness, palpitations, and fainting. Any patient who develops these symptoms should check with the doctor immediately.

Mellaril may cause tardive dyskinesia—a condition marked by involuntary muscle spasms and twitches in the face and body. This condition may be permanent, and appears to be most common among the elderly, especially women.

Drugs such as Mellaril are also known to cause a potentially fatal condition known as neuroleptic malignant syndrome. Symptoms of this problem include high fever, rigid muscles, altered mental status, sweating, fast or irregular heartbeat, and changes in blood pressure. Patients who develop these symptoms should see their doctor immediately. Mellaril therapy may have to be permanently discontinued.

Animal studies suggest that antipsychotics such as Mellaril may increase the risk of breast cancer, although human studies have not confirmed such a risk. Advise patients with a history of breast cancer to see their doctor regularly for checkups.

In rare cases, Mellaril has been known to trigger blood disorders and seizures. It can cause dizziness or faintness upon first standing up. High doses can also cause vision problems, including blurring, brownish coloring of vision, and poor night vision.

This drug may impair the ability to drive a car or operate potentially dangerous machinery. Patients should not participate in any activities that require full alertness until they are certain the drug will not interfere.

Possible food and drug interactions when taking this medication

Remember that combining Mellaril with certain drugs can increase the danger of potentially fatal heartbeat irregularities. Among the drugs to avoid are the following:

Amiodarone (Cordarone)
Cimetidine (Tagamet)
Delavirdine (Rescriptor)
Fluoxetine (Prozac)
Fluvoxamine
Paroxetine (Paxil)
Pindolol
Propafenone (Rythmol)
Propranolol (Inderal)
Quinidine (Quinaglute, Quinidex)
Ritonavir (Norvir)

Extreme drowsiness and other potentially serious effects can result if Mellaril is combined with alcohol or other central nervous system depressants such as narcotics, painkillers, and sleeping medications. Patients should check with their doctor before adding any new drug to their regimen.

Special information about pregnancy and breastfeeding

Pregnant women should use Mellaril only if clearly needed. Patients who are pregnant or plan to become pregnant should inform their doctor immediately.

There is no information on the effects of Mellaril during breastfeeding. The doctor may advise the patient to stop nursing until her treatment with this medication is finished.

Recommended dosage

The doctor will tailor the dose to the patient's needs, using the smallest effective amount.

ADULTS

The starting dose ranges from 50 to 100 milligrams 3 times a day. The doctor may gradually increase the dosage to as much as 800 milligrams a day, taken in 2 to 4 small doses. Once the symptoms improve, the doctor will decrease the dosage to the lowest effective amount.

CHILDREN

The usual starting dose for schizophrenic children is 0.5 milligrams per 2.2 pounds of body weight per day, divided into smaller doses. The dose may be gradually increased to a maximum of 3 milligrams per 2.2 pounds per day.

Overdosage

An overdose of Mellaril can be fatal. If an overdose is suspected, seek medical help immediately.

● *Symptoms of Mellaril overdose may include:*
Agitation, blurred vision, coma, confusion, constipation, difficulty breathing, dilated or constricted pupils, diminished flow of urine, dry mouth, dry skin, excessively high or low body temperature, extremely low blood pressure, fluid in the lungs, heart abnormalities, inability to urinate, intestinal blockage, nasal congestion, restlessness, sedation, seizures, shock

Memantine *See Namenda, page 115*

Mephobarbital *See Mebaral, page 104*

Meprobamate *See Miltown, page 110*

Mesoridazine *See Serentil, page 185*

Metadate *See Ritalin, page 176*

Methamphetamine *See Desoxyn, page 46*

Methylin *See Ritalin, page 176*

Methylphenidate *See Ritalin, page 176*

MILTOWN
Meprobamate

Why is this drug prescribed?

Miltown is a tranquilizer used in the treatment of anxiety disorders and for short-term relief of the symptoms of anxiety.

Most important fact about this drug

Miltown can be habit-forming. Patients can develop tolerance and dependence, and may experience withdrawal symptoms if they stop using this drug abruptly. They should discontinue this drug or change the dose only on their doctor's advice.

How should this medication be taken?

Miltown should be taken exactly as prescribed.

● *Missed dose...*
   The dose should be taken as soon as remembered if it is within an hour of the scheduled time. If it's not remembered until later, the patient should skip it and go back to the regular schedule. Doses should never be doubled.

● *Storage instructions...*
   Miltown should be stored at room temperature in a tightly closed container.

What side effects may occur?

Side effects cannot be predicted. If any develop or change in intensity, patients should inform their doctor as soon as possible.

● *Side effects may include:*
   Broken blood vessels, diarrhea, drowsiness, impaired coordination, irregular or rapid heartbeat, low red blood-cell count, nausea, rash, slurred speech, vertigo, vomiting, weakness

● *Side effects due to rapid decrease in dose or abrupt withdrawal from Miltown:*
   Anxiety, confusion, convulsions, hallucinations, inability to fall or stay asleep, loss of appetite, loss of coordination, muscle twitching, tremors, vomiting

Withdrawal symptoms usually become apparent within 12 to 48 hours after discontinuation of this medication and should disappear in another 12 to 48 hours.

Why should this drug not be prescribed?

Miltown should be avoided by anyone who is sensitive to or has ever had an allergic reaction to it or related drugs such as carisoprodol (Soma).

Miltown should not be taken by individuals with acute intermittent porphyria, an inherited disease of the body's metabolism. It can make the symptoms worse.

Anxiety or tension related to everyday stress usually does not require treatment with Miltown.

Special warnings about this medication

Patients who develop a skin rash, sore throat, fever, or shortness of breath should contact their doctor immediately. They may be having an allergic reaction to the drug.

Miltown may cause patients to become drowsy or less alert. They should not drive, operate dangerous machinery, or participate in any hazardous activity that requires full mental alertness until they know how this drug affects them.

Long-term use of this drug should be evaluated by the doctor periodically for its usefulness.

If the patient has liver or kidney disorders, the doctor should be made aware of these conditions before therapy begins.

Use of this drug may bring on seizures in people with epilepsy. They need to consult with their doctor before taking this medication.

Possible food and drug interactions when taking this medication

Miltown may intensify the effects of alcohol. Patients should not drink alcohol while taking this medication.

If Miltown is taken with certain other drugs, the effects of either could be increased, decreased, or altered. Interactions are particularly likely with mood-altering drugs and central nervous system depressants such as the following:

Antidepressant drugs such as Elavil, Nardil, and Tofranil
Antipsychotics such as chlorpromazine and Mellaril
Barbiturates such as Seconal and phenobarbital
Narcotics such as Percocet or Demerol
Tranquilizers such as Halcion, Restoril, and Valium

Special information about pregnancy and breastfeeding

Miltown should not be taken by patients who are pregnant or are planning to become pregnant. There is an increased risk of birth defects.

Miltown appears in breast milk and could affect a nursing infant. If this medication is essential to the mother's health, the doctor may advise her to discontinue breastfeeding until her treatment is finished.

Recommended dosage

ADULTS

The usual dosage is 1,200 milligrams to 1,600 milligrams per day divided into 3 or 4 doses. The maximum dosage is 2,400 milligrams a day.

CHILDREN

The usual dose for children 6 to 12 years of age is 200 to 600 milligrams per day divided into 2 or 3 doses.

Miltown is not recommended for children under age 6.

OLDER ADULTS

The doctor will limit the dose to the smallest effective amount to avoid oversedation.

Overdosage

Any medication taken in excess can have serious consequences. If an overdose is suspected, seek emergency medical attention immediately.

- *Symptoms of Miltown overdose may include:*
  Coma, drowsiness, loss of muscle control, severely impaired breathing, shock, sluggishness, and unresponsiveness

Mirtazapine *See Remeron, page 166*

MOBAN

Molindone hydrochloride

Why is this drug prescribed?

Moban is used in the treatment of schizophrenia.

Most important fact about this drug?

Moban can cause tardive dyskinesia, a condition marked by involuntary movements in the face and body, including chewing movements, puckering, puffing the cheeks, and sticking out the tongue. This condition may be permanent and appears to be most common among the elderly, especially elderly women.

How should this medication be taken?

Moban should be taken exactly as prescribed. It should not be taken with alcohol.

- *Missed dose...*
  Generally, the forgotten dose should be taken as soon as remembered. However, if it is almost time for the next dose, the missed dose should be skipped and the patient should return to the regular schedule. Doses should never be doubled.

- *Storage instructions...*
  Moban should be stored at room temperature and protected from light.

What side effects may occur?

Side effects cannot be predicted. If any develop or change in intensity, patients should inform their doctor as soon as possible.

- *The most common side effect is:*
  Drowsiness (especially at the start of therapy)

• *Other side effects may include:*
Blurred vision, depression, dry mouth, euphoria, hyperactivity, nausea, Parkinson's–like movements, restlessness

Why should this drug not be prescribed?
Moban should not be combined with alcohol, barbiturates (sleep aids), narcotics (painkillers), or other substances that slow down the nervous system, nor should it be given to anyone in a comatose state. Moban cannot be used by anyone who is hypersensitive to the drug. The concentrate form of Moban contains a sulfite that may cause life-threatening allergic reactions in some people, especially in those with asthma.

Special warnings about this medication
Drugs such as Moban can cause a potentially fatal condition called neuroleptic malignant syndrome. Symptoms include high fever, rigid muscles, irregular pulse or blood pressure, rapid heartbeat, excessive perspiration, and changes in heart rhythm. If patients develop these symptoms, they need to contact their doctor immediately. Moban should be discontinued.

Moban should be used with caution by anyone who has ever had breast cancer. The drug stimulates production of a hormone that promotes the growth of certain types of tumors.

Because this drug may cause drowsiness, patients should not participate in activities that require full alertness, such as driving or operating machinery, until they are sure how this medicine affects them.

Moban may mask signs of a brain tumor or intestinal blockage. It causes increased activity in some people. On rare occasions, it causes seizures.

Possible food and drug interactions when taking this medication
Remember that Moban must never be combined with alcohol, barbiturates, or narcotics. In addition, Moban tablets contain calcium, which may interfere with the absorption of tetracycline antibiotics (Achromycin V, Sumycin) and phenytoin (Dilantin).

Special information about pregnancy and breastfeeding
The safety and effectiveness of Moban during pregnancy have not been adequately studied. Patients who are pregnant or planning to become pregnant should tell their doctor immediately. Moban should be used during pregnancy only if the benefits outweigh the potential risks.

It is not known whether Moban appears in breast milk. Patients should check with their doctor before deciding to breastfeed.

Recommended dosage

ADULTS

The usual starting dose is 50 to 75 milligrams a day. The doctor may increase the dose to 100 milligrams a day after 3 or 4 days of treatment.

The long-term maintenance dose depends on the patient's response to the medication. The usual maintenance dose for treatment of mild symptoms is 5 milligrams to 15 milligrams taken 3 or 4 times a day. For moderate symptoms it is 10 milligrams to 25 milligrams taken 3 or 4 times a day. For severe symptoms, up to 225 milligrams a day may be prescribed. Older adults generally take lower dosages of Moban.

CHILDREN

The safety and effectiveness of Moban in children under age 12 have not been established.

Overdosage

Any medication taken in excess can have serious consequences. If an overdose of Moban is suspected, seek medical help immediately.

Modafinil *See Provigil, page 158*

Molindone *See Moban, page 113*

NAMENDA

Memantine

Why is this drug prescribed?

Namenda is used to treat moderate to severe Alzheimer's disease. While other Alzheimer's drugs work to prevent the breakdown of the brain chemical acetylcholine, Namenda works by targeting glutamate. Both chemicals are associated with memory and learning.

Studies show that Namenda can help improve the mental state and daily functioning of some—but not all—people with Alzheimer's disease. As with other Alzheimer's drugs, Namenda does not cure or slow the progression of the disease; it merely treats the symptoms.

Most important fact about this drug

Namenda treatment should not be stopped, or the dose changed, without consulting a doctor. Caregivers need to pay particular attention to the doctor's instructions on dose increases. Giving doses that are higher than recommended provides no additional benefit. It can take up to 4 weeks for any positive effects to appear.

How should this medication be taken?

Caregivers should give Namenda exactly as prescribed. The dose of Namenda is increased gradually at 1-week intervals. Using doses that are higher than recommended provides no additional benefit and could increase the risk of side effects.

Namenda can be given with or without food.

- *Missed dose...*
  It should be given as soon as it's remembered. However, if it is almost time for the next dose, caregivers should skip the one they missed and return to the regular schedule. Doses should never be doubled.

- *Storage instructions...*
  Store at room temperature.

What side effects may occur?

Side effects cannot be predicted. If any develop or change in intensity, the doctor should be informed as soon as possible.

- *Side effects may include:*
  Confusion, constipation, coughing, dizziness, hallucinations, headache, high blood pressure, pain, sleepiness, vomiting

Why should this drug not be prescribed?

People who have ever had an allergic reaction to Namenda should not take this medication.

Special warnings about this medication

Namenda is not recommended for patients with severe kidney impairment.

Certain conditions can alter the alkaline balance of the urine, which may cause a buildup of Namenda in the body. Caregivers should alert the doctor about any major dietary changes, kidney problems such as renal acidosis, or urinary tract infections.

The doctor should be told about any history of seizures. Namenda has not been formally studied in people with seizure disorders.

Possible food and drug interactions when taking this medication

If Namenda is taken with certain other drugs, the effects of either could be increased, decreased, or altered. Here is an overview of drugs that can cause a problem:

Amantadine (Symmetrel)
Cimetidine (Tagamet, Tagamet HB)
Cough suppressants that contain dextromethorphan (usually denoted as "DM")
Glaucoma drugs such as Diamox and Neptazane
Hydrochlorothiazide (HydroDIURIL)
Ketamine (Ketalar)
Nicotine (Nicoderm patch, Nicorette gum)
Quinidine (Quinidex)

Ranitidine (Zantac)
Sodium bicarbonate (baking soda, Alka-Seltzer)
Triamterine (Dyrenium)

Special information about pregnancy and breastfeeding

Namenda is not usually prescribed for women of childbearing age. The effects of Namenda during pregnancy have not been studied; and it is not known whether Namenda appears in breast milk.

Recommended dosage

ADULTS

The recommended dosage is 10 milligrams twice a day. The doctor will start treatment at 5 milligrams once a day for at least 7 days, and gradually increase the dose by 5 milligrams every 7 days, up to a maximum total daily dose of 20 milligrams.

If Namenda causes side effects, the doctor may wait more than 1 week to increase the dose. People who have impaired kidney function may require lower doses.

Overdosage

Any medication taken in excess can have serious consequences. If an overdose is suspected, seek emergency treatment immediately.

- *Symptoms of Namenda overdose may include:*
  Loss of consciousness, hallucinations, psychosis, restlessness, sleepiness, stupor

---

NARDIL
Phenelzine sulfate

Why is this drug prescribed?

Nardil is a monoamine oxidase (MAO) inhibitor used to treat depression as well as anxiety or phobias mixed with depression. MAO is an enzyme responsible for breaking down certain neurotransmitters in the brain. By inhibiting MAO, Nardil boosts the levels of these neurotransmitters and helps restore more normal mood states. Unfortunately, MAO inhibitors such as Nardil also block MAO activity throughout the body, an action that can have serious, even fatal, side effects—especially if MAO inhibitors are combined with certain foods or drugs.

Most important fact about this drug

It is essential that patients avoid the following foods, beverages, and medications while taking Nardil and for 2 weeks thereafter:

Beer (including alcohol-free or reduced-alcohol beer)
Caffeine (in excessive amounts)
Cheese (except for cottage cheese and cream cheese)

Chocolate (in excessive amounts)

Dry sausage (including Genoa salami, hard salami, pepperoni, and
  Lebanon bologna)

Fava bean pods

Liver

Meat extract

Pickled herring

Pickled, fermented, aged, or smoked meat, fish, or dairy products

Sauerkraut

Spoiled or improperly stored meat, fish, or dairy products

Wine (including alcohol-free or reduced-alcohol wine)

Yeast extract (including large amounts of brewer's yeast)

Yogurt

Medications to avoid:

Amphetamines

Appetite suppressants such as Redux and Tenuate

Antidepressants and related medications such as fluvoxamine,
  nefazodone, Prozac, Effexor, Paxil, Remeron, Celexa, Wellbutrin,
  Zoloft, Elavil, Triavil, Tegretol, and Flexeril

Asthma inhalants such as Proventil and Ventolin

Cold and cough preparations including those with dextromethorphan,
  such as Robitussin DM

Hay fever medications such as Contac and Dristan

L-tryptophan-containing products

Nasal decongestants in tablet, drop, or spray form such as Sudafed

Sinus medications such as Sinutab

Stimulants such as Ritalin and epinephrine (EpiPen)

Taking Nardil with any of the above foods, beverages, or medications can
cause serious, potentially fatal, high blood pressure. When taking Nardil
patients should immediately report the occurrence of a headache, heart
palpitations, or any other unusual symptom. In addition, patients should
be sure to inform any physician or dentist they see that they are currently taking Nardil or have taken Nardil within the last 2 weeks.

How should this medication be taken?

Nardil may be taken with or without food. It can take up to 4 weeks for
the drug to begin working.

Use of Nardil may complicate other medical treatment. Patients should
carry a card that says they are taking Nardil, or wear a Medic Alert bracelet.

- *Missed dose...*
  Generally, the dose should be taken as soon as remembered. However,
  if it is within 2 hours of the next dose, the patient should skip the
  missed dose and go back to the regular schedule. Doses should never
  be doubled.

- *Storage instructions...*
  Nardil may be stored at room temperature.

What side effects may occur?

Side effects cannot be predicted. If any develop or change in intensity, patients should inform their doctor as soon as possible.

- *Side effects may include:*
  Constipation, dizziness, drowsiness, dry mouth, headache, liver problems, low blood pressure upon standing, sexual problems, sleep disturbances, stomach and intestinal problems, water retention, weight gain

Why should this drug not be prescribed?

This drug cannot be taken by anyone with pheochromocytoma (a tumor of the adrenal gland), congestive heart failure, a history of liver disease, or an allergy to the drug's ingredients.

Nardil should not be combined with medications that may increase blood pressure (such as amphetamines, cocaine, allergy and cold medications, or Ritalin), other MAO inhibitors, L-dopa, methyldopa (Aldomet), phenylalanine, L-tryptophan, L-tyrosine, fluoxetine (Prozac), buspirone (BuSpar), bupropion (Wellbutrin), guanethidine (Ismelin), meperidine (Demerol), dextromethorphan, or substances that slow the central nervous system such as alcohol and narcotics. It is also important to avoid foods, beverages, or medications listed in the "Most important fact about this drug" section.

Special warnings about this medication

Patients *must* follow the food and drug limitations established by the physician; failure to do so may lead to potentially fatal side effects. While taking Nardil, they should promptly report the occurrence of a headache or any other unusual symptoms.

The doctor should prescribe Nardil with caution if the patient has diabetes, since it is not clear how MAO inhibitors affect blood sugar levels.

Patients need to tell the doctor that they are taking Nardil before deciding to have elective surgery.

Abrupt discontinuation of Nardil may trigger withdrawal symptoms. They may include nightmares, agitation, strange behavior, and convulsions.

Possible food and drug interactions when taking this medication

If Nardil is taken with certain other drugs, the effects of either could be increased, decreased, or altered. It is important for patients to closely follow the doctor's dietary and medication limitations when taking Nardil. Consult the "Most important fact about this drug" and "Why should this drug not be prescribed?" sections for lists of the foods, beverages, and medications that should be avoided while taking Nardil.

In addition, blood pressure medications (including water pills and beta blockers) should be used with caution by anyone taking Nardil, since excessively low blood pressure may result. Symptoms of low blood pressure include dizziness when rising from a lying or sitting position, fainting, and tingling in the hands or feet.

Special information about pregnancy and breastfeeding

The effects of Nardil during pregnancy have not been adequately studied. Nardil should be used during pregnancy only if the benefits of therapy clearly outweigh the potential risks to the fetus. If a patient is pregnant or plans to become pregnant, she should inform her doctor immediately.

Nursing mothers should use Nardil only after consulting their physician, since it is not known whether Nardil appears in breast milk.

Recommended dosage

ADULTS

The usual starting dose is 15 milligrams (1 tablet) 3 times a day. The doctor may increase the dosage to 90 milligrams per day.

It may be 4 weeks before the drug starts to work. Once the patient responds, the doctor may gradually reduce the dose, possibly to as low as 15 milligrams daily or every 2 days.

OLDER ADULTS

Because older people are more likely to have poor liver, kidney, or heart function, or other diseases that could increase the likelihood of side effects, a relatively low dose of Nardil is usually recommended at the start.

CHILDREN

Nardil is not recommended, since safety and efficacy for children under the age of 16 have not been determined.

Overdosage

An overdose of Nardil can be fatal. If an overdose is suspected, seek medical help immediately.

- *Symptoms of Nardil overdose may include:*
  Agitation, backward arching of the head, neck, and back, cool, clammy skin, coma, convulsions, difficult breathing, dizziness, drowsiness, faintness, hallucinations, high blood pressure, high fever, hyperactivity, irritability, jaw muscle spasms, low blood pressure, pain in the heart area, rapid and irregular pulse, rigidity, severe headache, sweating

NAVANE
Thiothixene

Why is this drug prescribed?
Navane is used to treat schizophrenia. Researchers theorize that this type of antipsychotic medication works by lowering levels of dopamine, a neurotransmitter in the brain.

Most important fact about this drug
Navane may cause tardive dyskinesia—a condition marked by involuntary muscle spasms and twitches in the face and body. This condition can be permanent and appears to be most common among the elderly, especially women.

How should this medication be taken?
Navane may be taken in liquid or capsule form. For the liquid form, a dropper is supplied.

- *Missed dose...*
  Generally, it should be taken as soon as remembered. However, if it is within 2 hours of the next dose, patients can skip the missed dose and go back to their regular schedule. Doses should never be doubled.

- *Storage instructions...*
  Navane should be stored at room temperature away from heat, light, and moisture. The liquid form should not be allowed to freeze.

What side effects may occur?
Side effects cannot be predicted. If any develop or change in intensity, patients should inform their doctor as soon as possible.

- *Side effects may include:*
  Agitation, blood disorders, blurred vision, drowsiness, dry mouth, exaggerated reflexes, fainting, high blood pressure, insomnia, lightheadedness, low blood pressure, Parkinson's–like movements, profuse sweating, rapid or irregular heartbeat, rash, sensitivity to sunlight, skin color changes

Why should this drug not be prescribed?
Navane should not be given to comatose individuals. It should be avoided by anyone known to be hypersensitive to it. Also, it should not be used when the activity of the central nervous system is slowed down for any—example, by a sleeping medication, circulatory system collapse, or an abnormal bone marrow or blood condition.

Special warnings about this medication
Navane may hide symptoms of brain tumor and intestinal obstruction. The doctor will prescribe Navane cautiously if the patient has or has ever had a brain tumor, breast cancer, a convulsive disorder, the eye condition

called glaucoma, intestinal blockage, or heart disease. It should also be avoided by patients exposed to extreme heat and those recovering from alcohol addiction.

This drug may impair the ability to drive a car or operate potentially dangerous machinery. Patients should not participate in any activities that require full alertness if they are unsure of their ability.

Possible food and drug interactions when taking this medication

If Navane is taken with certain other drugs, the effects of either could be increased, decreased, or altered. Here is an overview of drugs that may cause a problem:

Antihistamines such as Benadryl
Barbiturates such as phenobarbital
Drugs that contain atropine, such as Donnatal

Extreme drowsiness and other potentially serious effects can result if Navane is combined with alcohol or other central nervous system depressants such as painkillers, narcotics, or sleeping medications.

Special information about pregnancy and breastfeeding

If a patient is pregnant or plans to become pregnant, she should inform her doctor immediately; pregnant women should use Navane only if clearly needed. The doctor may also advise her to avoid breastfeeding while she is taking Navane.

Recommended dosage

Dosages of Navane are tailored to the individual. Usually treatment begins with a small dose, which is increased if needed.

ADULTS

For Milder Conditions

The usual starting dosage is a daily total of 6 milligrams, divided into doses of 2 milligrams and taken 3 times a day. The doctor may increase the dose to a total of 15 milligrams a day.

For More Severe Conditions

The usual starting dosage is a daily total of 10 milligrams, taken in 2 doses of 5 milligrams each. The doctor may increase this dose to a total of 60 milligrams a day.

Taking more than 60 milligrams a day rarely increases the benefits of Navane.

Some people are able to take Navane once a day. Patients should check with their doctor to see whether they can follow this schedule.

CHILDREN

Navane is not recommended for children younger than 12 years old.

OLDER ADULTS

In general, older adults are prescribed dosages of Navane in the lower ranges. Because older adults may develop low blood pressure while taking Navane, their doctors will monitor them closely. Older adults (especially women) may be more susceptible to such side effects as involuntary muscle spasms and twitches in the face and body.

Overdosage

Any medication taken in excess can have serious consequences. If an overdose is suspected, seek medical help immediately.

- *Symptoms of Navane overdose may include:*
  Central nervous system depression, coma, difficulty swallowing, dizziness, drowsiness, head tilted to the side, low blood pressure, muscle twitching, rigid muscles, salivation, tremors, walking disturbances, weakness

---

NEFAZODONE HYDROCHLORIDE

Why is this drug prescribed?

Nefazodone is prescribed for the treatment of major depression. Researchers believe it works by boosting levels of two of the brain's key chemical messengers, serotonin and norepinephrine. However, the drug is chemically unrelated to the family of serotonin-boosters that includes Prozac and Paxil.

Most important fact about this drug

Nefazodone has been known to produce very rare cases of potentially fatal liver failure. Ordinarily, the drug is not prescribed for people with liver disease, and the doctor may periodically test the patient's liver function. If a patient develops warning signs of liver problems—such as nausea, abdominal pain, loss of appetite, unusually dark urine, or yellowing of the skin or eyes—the doctor should be alerted immediately. Treatment with nefazodone will probably have to be stopped.

How should this medication be taken?

Patients must take nefazodone exactly as prescribed, even if they no longer feel depressed.

- *Missed dose...*
  Generally, a missed dose should be taken as soon as remembered. However, if it is within 4 hours of the next dose, patients should skip the one they missed and go back to their regular schedule. Doses should never be doubled.

• *Storage instructions...*
Nefazodone should be stored at room temperature in a tightly closed container.

What side effects may occur?

Side effects cannot be predicted. If any develop or change in intensity, patients should tell their doctor as soon as possible.

• *Side effects may include:*
Agitation, blurred or abnormal vision, confusion, constipation, dizziness, dry mouth, insomnia, lack of coordination, light-headedness, liver problems (sometimes severe), nausea, sleepiness, weakness

Why should this drug not be prescribed?

This medication should be avoided by anyone who is sensitive to or has ever had an allergic reaction to it or to similar drugs, such as Desyrel. Likewise, patients should not take nefazodone if previous treatment had to be stopped due to signs of liver injury.

Serious, sometimes fatal reactions have occurred when nefazodone is used in combination with drugs known as MAO inhibitors, including the antidepressants Nardil and Parnate. Nefazodone must never be taken with one of these drugs or within 14 days of discontinuing treatment with one of them. Also, patients should allow at least 7 days between the last dose of nefazodone and the first dose of an MAO inhibitor.

Nefazodone should also be avoided by people taking terfenadine, astemizole, cisapride, Halcion, or Tegretol, and should never be combined with Orap, as heart problems could result.

Special warnings about this medication

The doctor will prescribe nefazodone with caution if the patient has a history of suicide attempts, seizures, mania, or heart or liver disease. Nefazodone should also be used with caution in patients who have had a heart attack, stroke, or angina; take drugs for high blood pressure; or suffer from dehydration. Under these circumstances, nefazodone could cause an unwanted drop in blood pressure. Patients should discuss all of their medical problems with the doctor before taking this drug.

The FDA has issued a public health advisory to alert healthcare professionals about reports of worsening depression and suicidality (both suicidal thoughts and suicide attempts) during antidepressant drug therapy in adult and pediatric patients with major depressive disorder. Healthcare professionals and family members are advised to watch for signs of worsening depression and to be aware of the suicide statement present in all antidepressant labeling. Nefazodone is not approved to treat pediatric patients less than 18 years old.

Nefazodone may cause patients to become drowsy or less alert and may affect their judgment. They should not drive, operate dangerous machinery, or participate in any hazardous activity that requires full mental alertness until they know how the drug affects them.

Before having surgery, dental treatment, or any diagnostic procedure requiring anesthesia, patients should tell the doctor or dentist they are taking nefazodone. If they develop an allergic reaction such as a skin rash or hives while taking nefazodone, they should notify the doctor. Men who experience a prolonged or inappropriate erection while taking nefazodone should discontinue the drug and call their doctor.

Nefazodone should be used with caution in people who have been addicted to drugs.

Serotonin-boosting antidepressants such as Paxil and Prozac have been linked to stomach bleeding, especially in older patients or those taking nonsteroidal anti-inflammatory drugs (NSAIDs) such as aspirin, Advil, or Aleve. Because nefazodone also affects serotonin, patients should consult their doctor before combining it with NSAIDs or blood-thinning medications.

Possible food and drug interactions when taking this medication

If nefazodone is taken with certain other drugs, the effects of either could be increased, decreased, or altered. Here is an overview of drugs that may cause a problem:

Alcohol
Alprazolam (Xanax)
Antidepressants that boost serotonin levels, including Celexa,
  fluvoxamine Paxil, Prozac, and Zoloft
Buspirone (BuSpar)
Carbamazepine (Tegretol)
Cholesterol-lowering drugs that could affect liver function, including
  Lipitor, Mevacor, and Zocor
Cyclosporine (Neoral and Sandimmune)
Digoxin (Lanoxin)
Haloperidol (Haldol)
MAO inhibitors, including Nardil and Parnate
Pimozide (Orap)
Triazolam (Halcion)

Special information about pregnancy and breastfeeding

The effects of nefazodone during pregnancy have not been adequately studied. Women who are pregnant or are planning to become pregnant should tell their doctor immediately. Nefazodone should be used during pregnancy only if clearly needed.

Nefazodone may appear in breast milk. If this medication is essential to the patient's health, the doctor may tell her to discontinue breastfeeding until treatment with nefazodone is finished.

Recommended dosage

ADULTS

The usual starting dose is 200 milligrams a day, divided into 2 doses. If needed, the doctor may increase the dose gradually to 300 to 600 milligrams a day. Remind patients that it may take several weeks before they feel the full antidepressant effects.

CHILDREN

The safety and effectiveness of nefazodone have not been established in children under 18 years of age.

OLDER ADULTS

The usual starting dose for older people and those in a weakened condition is 100 milligrams a day, taken in 2 doses. The doctor will adjust the dose according to the patient's response.

Overdosage

Any medication taken in excess can have serious consequences. If an overdose is suspected, seek medical attention immediately.

- *Symptoms of nefazodone overdose may include:*
  Nausea, sleepiness, vomiting

NEMBUTAL
Pentobarbital sodium

Why is this drug prescribed?

Nembutal is used as a sedative. It is prescribed on a short-term basis to help people fall asleep. After 2 weeks, it appears to lose its effectiveness as a sleep aid.

Most important fact about this drug

If taken for a long enough time, Nembutal can cause physical and psychological addiction. An overdose can be fatal. Nembutal should be used in the smallest possible amount, and it should always be stored in child-resistant containers.

How should this medication be taken?

Nembutal should be taken at bedtime, only as prescribed.

- *Missed dose...*
  This drug is for use only at bedtime. The dose should never be doubled.

- *Storage instructions...*
  Nembutal may be stored at room temperature.

What side effects may occur?

Side effects cannot be predicted. If any develop or change in intensity, patients should inform their doctor as soon as possible.

- *More common side effects may include:*
  Extreme sleepiness

- *Less common or rare side effects may include:*
  Agitation, anemia, anxiety, central nervous system depression, confusion, constipation, difficulty breathing, disturbed thinking, dizziness, fainting, fever, hallucinations, headache, insomnia, lack of coordination, low blood pressure, nausea, nervousness, nightmares, overactivity, skin inflammation and flaking, skin rash, slow heartbeat, temporary failure to breathe, vomiting

Why should this drug not be prescribed?

People with the rare blood disorder porphyria and those who are allergic or sensitive to barbiturates must avoid Nembutal.

Special warnings about this medication

Nembutal must not be stopped abruptly. Doing so can result in withdrawal symptoms and even death. To reduce any possible withdrawal symptoms, patients should follow the doctor's instructions closely when stopping Nembutal.

Minor withdrawal symptoms may include increased dreams or nightmares. Other minor withdrawal symptoms usually occur in the following order: anxiety, muscle twitching, tremors of hands and fingers, progressive weakness, dizziness, visual problems, nausea, vomiting, insomnia, and light-headedness on standing up. Major withdrawal symptoms may include convulsions and delirium.

The doctor will prescribe Nembutal cautiously if the patient has had liver disease or has a history of depression or substance abuse.

Patients should tell the doctor if they suffer from pain. Nembutal may hide pain-causing symptoms that require treatment.

Older adults may become confused, depressed, or excited while taking Nembutal, and should be prescribed lower doses. People with kidney or liver problems should also use lower doses.

Nembutal may lessen the effectiveness of oral contraceptives. Women who take Nembutal may need to consider another type of birth control.

This drug may impair the ability to drive a car or operate potentially dangerous machinery. Patients should not participate in any activities that require full alertness if they are unsure of their ability.

Nembutal may lose its effect when taken regularly. Patients should not increase the dose in an effort to get the drug to work again. Instead, they should contact the doctor.

Possible food and drug interactions when taking this medication

If Nembutal is taken with certain other drugs, the effects of either could be increased, decreased, or altered. Here is an overview of drugs that may cause a problem:

Antidepressant drugs classified as MAO inhibitors, including Nardil and Parnate
Antihistamines such as Benadryl
Blood-thinning medications such as Coumadin
Doxycycline (Vibramycin)
Epilepsy drugs such as Dilantin and Depakene
Griseofulvin (Gris-PEG)
Hormonal medications such as Premarin
Oral contraceptives
Sedatives such as Halcion and Dalmane
Steroids such as prednisone
Tranquilizers such as Xanax and Valium

Extreme drowsiness and other potentially serious effects can result if Nembutal is combined with alcohol or drugs that slow down the central nervous system such as Percocet and Demerol.

Special information about pregnancy and breastfeeding

Nembutal causes damage to developing babies and withdrawal symptoms in newborns. Patients who are pregnant or plan to become pregnant should inform their doctor immediately.

This drug appears in breast milk and should be used with caution by nursing mothers.

Recommended dosage

ADULTS

The usual dose is 100 milligrams at bedtime.

CHILDREN

Dosages for children should be based on the child's age and weight.

OLDER ADULTS

Because older adults may be more sensitive to Nembutal, it will be prescribed at lower dosages.

Overdosage

An overdose of Nembutal can be fatal. If an overdose is suspected, seek medical help immediately.

● *Symptoms of Nembutal overdose may include:*
Coma, constriction (or sometimes dilation) of pupils, difficulty breathing, fluid in the lungs, heart failure, kidney failure, lack of reflexes, low

blood pressure, low body temperature, pneumonia, rapid or irregular heartbeat, reduced flow of urine

NORPRAMIN

Desipramine hydrochloride

Why is this drug prescribed?

Norpramin is used in the treatment of depression. It is one of a family of drugs called tricyclic antidepressants. Drugs in this class are thought to work by affecting the levels of neurotransmitters in the brain, and adjusting the brain's response to them.

Norpramin has also been used to treat bulimia and attention deficit disorders, and to help with cocaine withdrawal.

Most important fact about this drug

Serious, sometimes fatal, reactions have been known to occur when drugs such as Norpramin are taken with another type of antidepressant called an MAO inhibitor. Drugs in this category include Nardil and Parnate. Norpramin cannot be taken within two weeks of taking one of these drugs.

How should this medication be taken?

Patients should continue taking Norpramin even if they feel no immediate effect. It can take up to 2 or 3 weeks for improvement to begin.

Norpramin can cause dry mouth. Sucking hard candy or chewing gum can help this problem.

● *Missed dose...*
Patients who take several doses per day should take the forgotten dose as soon as they remember, then take any remaining doses for the day at evenly spaced intervals. If the patient takes Norpramin once a day at bedtime and doesn't remember until morning, the missed dose should be skipped. Doses should never be doubled in an effort to "catch up."

● *Storage instructions...*
Norpramin can be stored at room temperature. It should be protected from excessive heat.

What side effects may occur?

Side effects cannot be predicted. If any develop or change in intensity, patients should inform their doctor as soon as possible.

● *Side effects may include:*
Anxiety, confusion, dizziness, dry mouth, frequent urination or problems urinating, high blood pressure, hallucinations, hives, impaired coordination, irregular heartbeat, low blood pressure, numbness, rapid heartbeat, sensitivity to sunlight, sex drive changes, tingling, tremors

Why should this drug not be prescribed?

Norpramin should not be used by anyone known to be hypersensitive to it, or by someone who has had a recent heart attack.

People who take antidepressant drugs known as MAO inhibitors (including Nardil and Parnate) should not take Norpramin.

Special warnings about this medication

Norpramin should be used with caution in patients who have heart or thyroid disease, a seizure disorder, a history of being unable to urinate, or high pressure in the eyes (glaucoma).

Nausea, headache, and uneasiness can result if Norpramin is discontinued abruptly. Patients should consult their doctor and follow instructions closely when discontinuing Norpramin.

This drug may impair the ability to drive a car or operate potentially dangerous machinery. Patients should not participate in any activities that require full alertness if they are unsure about their ability.

Norpramin may increase the skin's sensitivity to sunlight. Overexposure could cause rash, itching, redness, or sunburn. Patients should avoid direct sunlight or wear protective clothing.

Patients planning to have elective surgery should make sure that the doctor is aware that they are taking Norpramin. It should be discontinued as soon as possible prior to surgery.

The doctor should be alerted if a fever and sore throat develop during Norpramin therapy. He may want to do some blood tests.

Possible food and drug interactions when taking this medication

People who take antidepressant drugs known as MAO inhibitors (including Nardil and Parnate) should not take Norpramin.

If Norpramin is taken with certain other drugs, the effects of either could be increased, decreased, or altered. Here is an overview of drugs that may cause a problem:

Cimetidine (Tagamet)
Drugs that improve breathing, such as Proventil
Drugs that quell spasms, such as Bentyl
Fluoxetine (Prozac)
Guanethidine
Paroxetine (Paxil)
Sedatives/hypnotics (Halcion, Valium)
Sertraline (Zoloft)
Thyroid medications (Synthroid)

Extreme drowsiness and other potentially serious effects can result if Norpramin is combined with alcohol or other depressants, including narcotic painkillers such as Percocet and Demerol, sleeping medications such as Halcion and Nembutal, and tranquilizers such as Valium and Xanax.

Special information about pregnancy and breastfeeding
Pregnant women or mothers who are nursing an infant should use Norpramin only when the potential benefits clearly outweigh the potential risks. If a patient is pregnant or planning to become pregnant, she should inform her doctor immediately.

Recommended dosage
Doses are tailored to individual needs.

ADULTS

The usual dosage ranges from 100 to 200 milligrams per day, taken in 1 dose or divided into smaller doses. If needed, dosage may gradually be increased to 300 milligrams a day. Dosages above 300 milligrams per day are not recommended.

CHILDREN

Norpramin is not recommended for children.

OLDER ADULTS AND ADOLESCENTS

The usual dose ranges from 25 to 100 milligrams per day. If needed, dosage may gradually be increased to 150 milligrams a day. Dosages above 150 milligrams per day are not recommended.

Overdosage
An overdose of Norpramin can be fatal. If an overdose is suspected, seek medical help immediately.

- *Symptoms of Norpramin overdose may include:*
  Agitation, coma, confusion, convulsions, dilated pupils, disturbed concentration, drowsiness, extremely low blood pressure, hallucinations, high fever, irregular heart rate, low body temperature, overactive reflexes, rigid muscles, stupor, vomiting

Nortriptyline *See Pamelor, page 131*

Olanzapine *See Zyprexa, page 241*

Olanzapine and fluoxetine *See Symbyax, page 202*

Oxazepam *See Serax, page 183*

PAMELOR
Nortriptyline hydrochloride
Other brand name: Aventyl

Why is this drug prescribed?
Pamelor is prescribed to relieve the symptoms of depression. It is one of the drugs known as tricyclic antidepressants.

Most important fact about this drug

Pamelor must be taken regularly to be effective, and it may be several weeks before the patient begins to feel better. It's important to keep taking regular doses, even if they seem to make no difference.

How should this medication be taken?

Pamelor should be taken exactly as prescribed. This drug can make the mouth dry. Sucking on hard candy, chewing gum, or melting ice chips in the mouth can provide relief.

- *Missed dose...*
  A forgotten dose should be taken as soon as remembered, unless it is almost time for the next dose. If that's the case, the missed dose should be skipped and the patient should return to the regular schedule. Patients who take Pamelor once a day at bedtime and miss a dose should not take it in the morning, since disturbing side effects could occur. Doses should never be doubled.

- *Storage instructions...*
  Pamelor should be kept in the container it came in, tightly closed and away from light. It is especially important to keep this drug out of reach of children; an overdose is particularly dangerous in the young. Pamelor may be stored at room temperature.

What side effects may occur?

Side effects cannot be predicted. If any develop or change in intensity, patients should inform their doctor as soon as possible.

- *Side effects may include:*
  Anxiety, blurred vision, confusion, dry mouth, hallucinations, heart attack or vascular heart blockage, heartbeat irregularities, high blood pressure, insomnia, loss of muscle coordination, low blood pressure, rapid heartbeat, sensitivity to sunlight, skin rash, stroke, tremors, weight loss

- *Side effects due to rapid decrease in dose or abrupt withdrawal from Pamelor after prolonged treatment include:*
  Headache, nausea, vague feeling of bodily discomfort

These side effects do not indicate addiction to this drug.

Why should this drug not be prescribed?

Anyone who is sensitive to or has ever had an allergic reaction to Pamelor or similar drugs should not take this medication.

Pamelor must be avoided by people who are taking—or have taken within the past 14 days—a drug classified as an MAO inhibitor. Drugs in this category include the antidepressants Nardil and Parnate. Combining these drugs with Pamelor can cause fever and convulsions, and could even be fatal.

Unless directed to do so by a doctor, patients should not take this medication while recovering from a heart attack or taking any other antidepressant drugs.

Patients who have been taking Prozac typically have to wait at least 5 weeks before beginning therapy with Pamelor. Otherwise, a drug interaction could result.

Special warnings about this medication

Pamelor may cause patients to become drowsy or less alert. They should not drive, operate dangerous machinery, or participate in any hazardous activity that requires full mental alertness until they know how this drug affects them.

Pamelor should be used with caution in people who have a history of seizures, difficulty urinating, diabetes, or chronic eye conditions such as glaucoma. Caution is also warranted with patients who have heart disease, high blood pressure, or an overactive thyroid, and with those who are receiving thyroid medication.

If a patient is being treated for a severe mental disorder (schizophrenia or manic depression), the doctor should be made aware of this before Pamelor therapy begins.

Pamelor may make the skin more sensitive to sunlight. Patients should stay out of the sun, wear protective clothing, and apply a sunblock.

Before any surgery, dental treatment, or diagnostic procedure is undertaken, the doctor should be informed that the patient is taking Pamelor. Certain drugs used during these procedures, such as anesthetics and muscle relaxants, may interact with Pamelor.

Possible food and drug interactions when taking this medication

Combining Pamelor and MAO inhibitors can be fatal.

Pamelor may intensify the effects of alcohol. Patients should avoid alcohol while taking this medication.

If Pamelor is taken with certain other drugs, the effects of either can be increased, decreased, or altered. Here is an overview of drugs that may cause a problem:

Airway-opening drugs such as Ventolin and Proventil
Antidepressants such as Wellbutrin and Desyrel
Antidepressants that act on serotonin, such as Prozac, Paxil, and Zoloft
Antipsychotic medications such as chlorpromazine and Mellaril
Blood pressure medications such as Catapres
Cimetidine (Tagamet)
Chlorpropamide (Diabinese)
Drugs for heart irregularities, such as Tambocor and Rythmol
Drugs that control spasms, such as Donnatal and Bentyl
Levodopa (Larodopa)

Quinidine (Quinidex)
Reserpine (Diupres)
Stimulants such as Dexedrine
Thyroid medications such as Synthroid
Warfarin (Coumadin)

Special information about pregnancy and breastfeeding

The effects of Pamelor during pregnancy have not been adequately studied. Patients who are pregnant or planning to become pregnant should inform their doctor immediately. The doctor should also be consulted about breastfeeding.

Recommended dosage

This medication is available in tablet and liquid form. Only tablet dosages are listed. For liquid dosages, check with the doctor.

ADULTS

Doctors monitor response to this medication carefully, and gradually increase or decrease the dose to suit the patient's needs. Some doctors use blood tests to help determine the ideal dose.

The usual starting dosage is 25 milligrams, 3 or 4 times per day. Alternatively, the doctor may instruct that the total daily dose be taken once a day. Doses above 150 milligrams per day are not recommended.

CHILDREN

The safety and effectiveness of Pamelor have not been established for children and its use is not recommended. However, adolescents may be given 30 to 50 milligrams per day, either in a single dose or divided into smaller doses, as determined by the doctor.

OLDER ADULTS

The usual dose is 30 to 50 milligrams taken in a single dose or divided into smaller doses, as determined by the doctor.

Overdosage

An overdose of this type of antidepressant can be fatal. If an overdose is suspected, seek medical help immediately.

* *Symptoms of Pamelor overdose may include:*
  Agitation, coma, confusion, congestive heart failure, convulsions, dilated pupils, disturbed concentration, drowsiness, excessive reflexes, extremely high fever, fluid in the lungs, hallucinations, irregular heartbeat, low body temperature, restlessness, rigid muscles, severely low blood pressure, shock, stupor, vomiting.

PARNATE

Tranylcypromine sulfate

Why is this drug prescribed?

Parnate is prescribed for the treatment of major depression. A member of the class of drugs known as monoamine oxidase (MAO) inhibitors, it works by increasing concentrations of the brain chemicals epinephrine, norepinephrine, and serotonin.

Most important fact about this drug

Parnate is a potent drug with the capability of producing serious side effects. It is typically prescribed only if other antidepressants fail, and then only for adults who are under close medical supervision. It is considered especially risky because it can interact with a long list of drugs and foods to produce life-threatening side effects (see "Possible food and drug interactions when taking this medication").

How should this medication be taken?

Dosage is adjusted according to the patient's individual needs and response. The drug usually produces improvement within 48 hours to 3 weeks after starting therapy.

- *Missed dose...*
  Generally, the forgotten dose should be taken as soon as remembered. However, if it is within 2 hours of the next dose, the missed dose should be skipped and the patient should return to the regular schedule. Doses should never be doubled.

- *Storage instructions...*
  Parnate should be stored at room temperature.

What side effects may occur?

Side effects cannot be predicted. If any develop or change in intensity, patients should inform their doctor as soon as possible.

- *Side effects may include:*
  Blood disorders, diarrhea, dizziness, drowsiness, dry mouth, insomnia, muscle spasm, nausea, overstimulation, rapid or irregular heartbeat, restlessness, ringing in the ears, water retention, weakness, weight loss

Why should this drug not be prescribed?

Parnate should be avoided by anyone in danger of a stroke, by those who have heart or liver disease, high blood pressure, or a history of headaches, by individuals who have a type of tumor known as pheochromocytoma, and by anyone who will be undergoing elective surgery requiring general anesthesia.

Special warnings about this medication

The most dangerous reaction to Parnate is a surge in blood pressure, which has sometimes been fatal. For this reason, patients should report promptly to their doctor any of the following symptoms: constriction or pain in the throat or chest, dizziness, fever, headache, irregular heartbeat, light sensitivity, nausea, neck stiffness or soreness, palpitations, pupil dilation, sweating, or vomiting.

A number of people who take Parnate experience low blood pressure, faintness, or drowsiness. Great care should be exercised when performing potentially hazardous tasks, such as driving a car or operating machinery.

Some people become physically dependent on Parnate and experience withdrawal symptoms when the drug is stopped, including restlessness, anxiety, depression, confusion, hallucinations, headache, weakness, and diarrhea.

If the patient has kidney problems, the doctor should be made aware of it. The doctor may need to reduce the dosage of Parnate to avoid a buildup of the drug. Parnate should also be used with caution by people who have an overactive thyroid gland.

MAO inhibitors can suppress heart pain that would otherwise serve as a warning sign of a heart attack. For this reason and others, it should be used with caution by older adults. Also, it should be used with caution by diabetics and people with epilepsy or other convulsive disorders because it can alter the level of drugs used to treat these conditions.

Possible food and drug interactions when taking this medication

Parnate should never be combined with the following drugs; the combination can trigger seizures or a dangerous spike in blood pressure:

Other MAO inhibitors such as Nardil
Antidepressant drugs classified as tricyclics, such as Anafranil, Elavil, and Tofranil
Carbamazepine (Tegretol)
Cyclobenzaprine (Flexeril)

When switching from one of these drugs to Parnate, or vice versa, patients must allow an interval of at least 1 week between medications.

Parnate should also be avoided by people taking any of the following:

Antidepressant drugs classified as selective serotonin reuptake inhibitors, such as Paxil, Prozac, and Zoloft
Amphetamines such as Adderall and Dexedrine
Anesthetics
Antihistamines such as Allegra, Benadryl, and Clarinex
Blood pressure medications such as Accupril, Lotensin, and Prinivil
Bupropion (Wellbutrin)

Buspirone (BuSpar)
Cold and hay fever remedies that constrict blood vessels
Cough remedies containing dextromethorphan
Demerol and other narcotic painkillers such as Percodan, OxyContin, and Vicodin
Disulfiram (Antabuse)
Guanethidine
Methyldopa
Over-the-counter weight reduction aids
Parkinson's disease medications such as Parlodel, Requip, and Sinemet
Reserpine
Sedatives such as Halcion, Nembutal, and Seconal
Tryptophan
Water pills such as HydroDIURIL

While taking Parnate, patients should also avoid foods that contain a high amount of a substance called tyramine, including:

Anchovies
Avocados
Bananas
Beer (including nonalcoholic beer)
Caviar
Cheese (especially strong and aged varieties)
Chianti wine
Chocolate
Dried fruits (including raisins, prunes, and figs)
Liqueurs
Liver
Meat extracts or meat prepared with tenderizers
Overripe fruit
Pickled herring
Pods of broad beans like fava beans
Raspberries
Sauerkraut
Sherry
Sour cream
Soy sauce
Yeast extracts
Yogurt

Likewise, patients taking Parnate should avoid alcohol and large amounts of caffeine.

Special information about pregnancy and breastfeeding

Patients who are pregnant or plan to become pregnant should inform their doctor immediately. Parnate should be used during pregnancy only if its benefits outweigh potential risks.

Parnate makes its way into breast milk. If the drug is essential to the patient's health, the doctor may advise her to stop nursing until her treatment is finished.

Recommended dosage

ADULTS

The usual dosage is 30 milligrams per day, divided into smaller doses. If ineffective, the dosage may be slowly increased under the doctor's supervision to a maximum of 60 milligrams per day.

Overdosage

Any medication taken in excess can have serious consequences. If an overdose of Parnate is suspected, seek medical help immediately.

* *Symptoms of Parnate overdose may include:*
  Agitation, confusion, coma, dizziness, drowsiness, high fever, incoherence, rigid muscles, severe headache, twitching, weakness

Paroxetine *See Paxil, page 138*

PAXIL

Paroxetine hydrochloride
Other brand name: Paxil CR

Why is this drug prescribed?

Paxil relieves a variety of emotional problems. It can be prescribed for major depressive disorder, obsessive-compulsive disorder (OCD), panic disorder, generalized anxiety disorder, social anxiety disorder (also known as social phobia), and post-traumatic stress disorder.

Paxil CR, the controlled-release version, is indicated for major depressive disorder, panic disorder, social anxiety disorder, and severe premenstrual symptoms classified as premenstrual dysphoric disorder.

Paxil belongs to the class of drugs known as selective serotonin reuptake inhibitors (SSRIs). Serotonin is one of the chemical messengers believed to govern moods. Ordinarily, it is quickly reabsorbed after its release at the junctures between nerves. Reuptake inhibitors such as Paxil slow this process, thereby boosting the levels of serotonin available in the brain.

Most important fact about this drug

Improvement may be noted within 1 to 4 weeks after treatment begins. Patients should continue taking the medication even if they begin to feel better.

How should this medication be taken?

Paxil is taken once a day, with or without food, usually in the morning. The oral suspension must be thoroughly shaken before each use. Paxil CR should be swallowed whole; it should not be chewed or crushed.

- *Missed dose...*
  Patients should skip the forgotten dose and go back to their regular schedule with the next dose. They should not take a double dose to make up for the one they missed.

- *Storage instructions...*
  Paxil tablets and suspension can be stored at room temperature.

What side effects may occur?

Side effects cannot be predicted. If any develop or change in intensity, patients should inform their doctor as soon as possible.

During the first 4 to 6 weeks, patients may find some side effects less troublesome (nausea and dizziness, for example) than others (dry mouth, drowsiness, and weakness).

- *Side effects of Paxil may include:*
  Constipation, decreased appetite, decreased libido, diarrhea, dizziness, dry mouth, ejaculation problems, impotence, insomnia, nausea, sleepiness, sweating, tremors, vomiting, weakness, yawning

- *Side effects of Paxil CR may include:*
  Dry mouth, impaired concentration, nausea, sleepiness, weakness

Why should this drug not be prescribed?

Dangerous and even fatal reactions are possible when Paxil is combined with thioridazine (Mellaril) or drugs classified as monoamine oxidase (MAO) inhibitors, such as the antidepressants Nardil and Parnate. Paxil must not be taken with any of these medications, or within 2 weeks of starting or stopping use of an MAO inhibitor. Paxil must also be avoided if it causes an allergic reaction.

Special warnings about this medication

The FDA has issued a public health advisory to alert healthcare professionals about reports of worsening depression and suicidality (both suicidal thoughts and suicide attempts) during antidepressant drug therapy in adult and pediatric patients with major depressive disorder. Healthcare professionals and family members are advised to watch for signs of worsening depression and to be aware of the suicide statement present in all antidepressant labeling. Paxil is currently not approved for use in pediatric patients.

SSRI antidepressants could potentially cause stomach bleeding, especially in older patients or those taking nonsteroidal anti-inflammatory drugs (NSAIDs) such as aspirin, ibuprofen (Advil, Motrin), naproxen (Aleve), and ketoprofen (Orudis KT). Advise patients to consult their doctor before combining Paxil with NSAIDs or blood-thinning drugs.

Paxil should be used cautiously by people with a history of manic disorders and those with high pressure in the eyes (glaucoma). Caution is also warranted if the patient has a disease or condition that affects the metabolism or blood circulation.

If the patient has a history of seizures, the doctor should be informed about it. Paxil must be used with caution in this situation. If the patient develops seizures once therapy has begun, the drug should be discontinued.

Paxil may impair judgment, thinking, or motor skills. Patients should not drive, operate dangerous machinery, or participate in any hazardous activity that requires full mental alertness until they are sure the medication is not affecting them in this way.

It's best to avoid an abrupt discontinuation of Paxil therapy. It can lead to symptoms such as dizziness, abnormal dreams, and tingling sensations. To prevent such problems, the dosage is reduced gradually.

Possible food and drug interactions when taking this medication

Remember that Paxil must never be combined with Mellaril or MAO inhibitors such as Nardil and Parnate, or taken within 2 weeks of starting or stopping an MAO inhibitor.

If Paxil is taken with certain other drugs, the effects of either could be increased, decreased, or altered. Here is an overview of drugs that may cause a problem:

Alcohol
Antidepressants such as Elavil, Tofranil, Norpramin, Pamelor, Prozac
Cimetidine (Tagamet)
Diazepam (Valium)
Digoxin (Lanoxin)
Flecainide (Tambocor)
Lithium (Eskalith, Lithobid)
Nonsteroidal anti-inflammatory drugs (NSAIDs) such as aspirin, ibuprofen (Advil, Motrin), naproxen (Aleve), and ketoprofen (Orudis KT)
Phenobarbital
Phenytoin (Dilantin)
Procyclidine (Kemadrin)
Propafenone (Rythmol)

Propranolol (Inderal, Inderide)
Quinidine (Quinidex)
Sumatriptan (Imitrex)
Theophylline
Tryptophan
Warfarin (Coumadin)

Special information about pregnancy and breastfeeding

The effects of Paxil during pregnancy have not been adequately studied. There have been reports of serious complications in newborns who were exposed to Paxil late in the third trimester. Patients who are pregnant or plan to become pregnant should inform their doctor immediately.

Paxil appears in breast milk and could affect a nursing infant. If this medication is essential to the patient's health, the doctor may advise her to discontinue breastfeeding until her treatment with Paxil is finished.

Recommended dosage

The following indications and dosages are for adults. The safety and effectiveness of Paxil have not been established in children.

DEPRESSION

Paxil: The usual starting dose is 20 milligrams a day, taken as a single dose, usually in the morning. At intervals of at least 1 week, the dosage may be increased by 10 milligrams a day, up to a maximum of 50 milligrams a day.

Paxil CR: The recommended starting dose is 25 milligrams a day, usually taken in the morning. At intervals of at least 1 week, the dosage may be increased by 12.5 milligrams a day, up to a maximum of 62.5 milligrams a day.

OBSESSIVE-COMPULSIVE DISORDER

Paxil: The usual starting dose is 20 milligrams a day, typically taken in the morning. At intervals of at least 1 week, the dosage may be increased by 10 milligrams a day. The recommended long-term dosage is 40 milligrams daily. The maximum is 60 milligrams a day.

PANIC DISORDER

Paxil: The usual starting dose is 10 milligrams a day, taken in the morning. At intervals of 1 week or more, the dosage may be increased by 10 milligrams a day. The target dose is 40 milligrams daily; dosage should never exceed 60 milligrams.

Paxil CR: The recommended starting dose is 12.5 milligrams a day, usually taken in the morning. At intervals of at least 1 week, the dosage may be increased by 12.5 milligrams a day, up to a maximum of 75 milligrams a day.

GENERALIZED ANXIETY DISORDER

Paxil: The recommended dose is 20 milligrams taken once a day, usually in the morning.

SOCIAL ANXIETY DISORDER

Paxil: The recommended dose is 20 milligrams taken once a day, usually in the morning.

Paxil CR: The recommended starting dose is 12.5 milligrams a day, usually taken in the morning. At intervals of at least 1 week, the dosage may be increased by 12.5 milligrams a day, up to a maximum of 37.5 milligrams a day.

POST-TRAUMATIC STRESS DISORDER

Paxil: The recommended dose is 20 milligrams taken once a day, usually in the morning.

PREMENSTRUAL DYSPHORIC DISORDER

Paxil CR: The recommended starting dose is 12.5 milligrams a day, usually taken in the morning. The doctor will instruct the patient to take the dose either every day of the month or only during the 2 weeks before menstruation begins (the luteal phase of their cycle). If needed, the dose can be increased to 25 milligrams a day.

DOSAGE ADJUSTMENT

For older adults, the weak, and those with severe kidney or liver disease: Starting doses of Paxil are reduced to 10 milligrams daily, and later doses are limited to no more than 40 milligrams a day. Starting doses of Paxil CR are limited to 12.5 milligrams daily, and later doses are limited to no more than 50 milligrams a day.

Overdosage

Any medication taken in excess can have serious consequences. If an overdose is suspected, seek medical attention immediately.

* *Symptoms of Paxil overdose may include:*
  Coma, dizziness, drowsiness, facial flushing, nausea, sweating, tremor, vomiting

Pemoline *See Cylert, page 38*

Pentobarbital *See Nembutal, page 126*

Perphenazine *See Trilafon, page 220*

Phenelzine *See Nardil, page 117*

PHENERGAN
Promethazine hydrochloride

Why is this drug prescribed?

Phenergan is an antihistamine. Because antihistamines of this type cause drowsiness, the drug is used as a sedative and sleep aid for both children and adults.

Like other antihistamines, Phenergan is also prescribed to relieve the nasal stuffiness and inflammation and red, inflamed eyes caused by hay fever and other allergies. It is used to treat itching, swelling, and redness from hives and other rashes; allergic reactions to blood transfusions; and, with other medications, anaphylactic shock (severe allergic reaction). It is prescribed to prevent and control nausea and vomiting before and after surgery and to prevent and treat motion sickness. It is also used, with other medications, for pain after surgery.

Antihistamines work by decreasing the effects of histamine, a chemical the body releases in response to certain irritants. Histamine narrows air passages in the lungs and contributes to inflammation. Antihistamines reduce itching and swelling and dry up secretions from the nose, eyes, and throat.

Most important fact about this drug

Because Phenergan may cause considerable drowsiness, patients should not drive, operate dangerous machinery, or participate in any hazardous activity that requires full mental alertness until they know how they react to Phenergan. Children should be carefully supervised while they are bike-riding, roller-skating, or playing until the drug's effect on them is established.

How should this medication be taken?

Phenergan should be taken exactly as prescribed.

* *Missed dose...*
  If Phenergan is being taken on a regular schedule, the forgotten dose should be taken as soon as remembered. If it is almost time for the next dose, patients should skip the one they missed and go back to their regular schedule. Doses should never be doubled.

* *Storage instructions...*
  Tablets should be stored at room temperature, away from light. Suppositories should be stored in the refrigerator, in a tightly closed container.

What side effects may occur?

Side effects cannot be predicted. If any develop or change in intensity, patients should inform their doctor as soon as possible.

* *Side effects may include:*
  Blurred vision, dizziness, drowsiness, dry mouth, increased or decreased blood pressure, nausea, rash, sedation, vomiting

Why should this drug not be prescribed?

Phenergan should be avoided by anyone who has ever had an allergic reaction to it or to related medications, such as Thorazine, Mellaril, Stelazine, or Prolixin. Phenergan is not for use in comatose patients, and should not be used to treat asthma or other breathing problems.

Special warnings about this medication

If the patient is taking other medications that cause sedation, the doctor may reduce the dosage of these medications or eliminate them during Phenergan therapy.

In people who have a seizure disorder, Phenergan may cause seizures to occur more often.

Phenergan can cause a serious—even fatal—decline in the breathing function. This medication should be avoided by people with chronic breathing problems such as emphysema, and those who suffer from sleep apnea (periods during sleep when breathing stops).

Phenergan can also cause a potentially fatal condition called neuroleptic malignant syndrome. Symptoms include high fever, rigid muscles, sweating, and a rapid or irregular heartbeat. Patients who develop these symptoms should stop taking Phenergan and see their doctor immediately.

Phenergan should be used with caution by anyone who has heart disease, high blood pressure or circulatory problems, liver problems, the eye condition called narrow-angle glaucoma, peptic ulcer or other abdominal obstructions, or urinary bladder obstruction due to an enlarged prostate.

Phenergan may affect the results of pregnancy tests and can raise blood sugar.

Some people have developed jaundice (yellow eyes and skin) while on this medication.

The doctor should be notified if the patient develops any uncontrolled movements or seems to be unusually sensitive to sunlight.

Remember that Phenergan can cause drowsiness.

Phenergan should not be given to children under 2 years of age, and should be used with caution in older children, due to the danger of impaired breathing. Large doses have been known to cause hallucinations, seizures, and sudden death, especially in children who are dehydrated. Drugs such as Phenergan are not recommended for the treatment of vomiting in children unless the problem is severe. Phenergan should also be avoided if the child has the serious neurological disease known as Reye's syndrome or any disease of the liver.

Possible food and drug interactions when taking this medication

Phenergan may increase the effects of alcohol. Patients should avoid alcohol, or at least substantially reduce the amount they drink, while taking this medication.

If Phenergan is taken with certain other drugs, the effects of either could be increased, decreased, or altered. Here is an overview of drugs that may cause a problem:

Certain antidepressant drugs, including Elavil and Tofranil
Drugs that control spasms, such as Cogentin
Drugs that reduce bone-marrow function (certain cancer drugs)
MAO inhibitors such as the antidepressants Nardil and Parnate
Narcotic pain relievers such as Demerol and Dilaudid
Sedatives such as Halcion, Dalmane, and Seconal
Tranquilizers such as Xanax and Valium

Special information about pregnancy and breastfeeding
The effects of Phenergan during pregnancy have not been adequately studied. If the patient is pregnant or plans to become pregnant, she should inform her doctor immediately.

Although it is not known whether Phenergan appears in breast milk, there is a chance that it could cause a nursing infant serious harm. The use of Phenergan is not recommended during breastfeeding.

Recommended dosage
Phenergan is available in tablet, syrup, and suppository form. The suppositories are for rectal use only. Phenergan tablets and suppositories are not recommended for children under 2 years of age.

INSOMNIA

Adults: The usual dose is 25 to 50 milligrams for nighttime sedation.

Children: The usual dose is 12.5 to 25 milligrams by tablets or rectal suppository at bedtime.

Older Adults: The dosage is usually reduced for people over 60.

ALLERGY

Adults: The average oral dose is 25 milligrams taken before bed. However, the doctor may prescribe 12.5 milligrams before meals and before bed.

Children: The usual dose is a single 25-milligram dose at bedtime, or 6.25 to 12.5 milligrams 3 times daily.

MOTION SICKNESS

Adults: The average adult dose is 25 milligrams taken twice daily. The first dose should be taken one-half to 1 hour before the patient plans to travel, and the second dose 8 to 12 hours later, if necessary. On travel days after that, the recommended dose is 25 milligrams upon arising and again before the evening meal.

Children: The usual dose of Phenergan tablets, syrup, or rectal suppositories is 12.5 to 25 milligrams taken twice a day.

NAUSEA AND VOMITING

The average dose of Phenergan for nausea and vomiting in children or
adults is 25 milligrams. When oral medication cannot be tolerated, use
the rectal suppository. The doctor may prescribe 12.5 to 25 milligrams
every 4 to 6 hours, if necessary.

For nausea and vomiting in children, the dose is usually calculated at
0.5 milligram per pound of body weight and will also be based on the age
of the child and the severity of the condition being treated. Phenergan and
other anti-vomiting drugs should not be given to children if the cause of
the problem is unknown.

Overdosage

An overdose of Phenergan can be fatal. If an overdose is suspected, seek
medical treatment immediately.

● *Symptoms of Phenergan overdose may include:*
Difficulty breathing, dry mouth, fixed and dilated pupils, flushing,
heightened reflexes, loss of consciousness, muscle tension, poor coordination, seizures, slowdown in brain activity, slowed heartbeat, stomach and intestinal problems, very low blood pressure, writhing
movements

Children may become overstimulated and have nightmares. Older adults
may also become overstimulated.

PHENOBARBITAL

Why is this drug prescribed?

Phenobarbital, a barbiturate, is used as a sleep aid and in the treatment of
certain types of epilepsy, including generalized or grand mal seizures and
partial seizures.

Most important fact about this drug

Phenobarbital can be habit-forming. One can become tolerant (needing
more and more of the drug to achieve the same effect) and physically and
psychologically dependent with continued use. Patients should never
increase the amount of phenobarbital they take without first checking
with their doctor.

How should this medication be taken?

It is important to take this medication exactly as prescribed.

Patients taking phenobarbital for seizures should not discontinue it
abruptly.

- *Missed dose...*

  Generally, a forgotten dose should be taken as soon as remembered. However, if it is almost time for the next dose, patients should skip the one they missed and go back to their regular schedule. Doses should never be doubled.

- *Storage instructions...*

  Phenobarbital may be stored at room temperature in a tightly closed container.

What side effects may occur?

Side effects cannot be predicted. If any develop or change in intensity, patients should notify their doctor as soon as possible.

- *Side effects may include:*

  Allergic reaction, drowsiness, headache, lethargy, nausea, oversedation, sleepiness, slowed or delayed breathing, vertigo, vomiting

Why should this drug not be prescribed?

Phenobarbital should not be used by anyone suffering from porphyria (an inherited metabolic disorder), liver disease, or a lung disease that causes blockages or breathing difficulties, or by anyone who has ever had an allergic reaction to or is sensitive to phenobarbital or other barbiturates.

Special warnings about this medication

Remember that phenobarbital may be habit-forming. It must be taken exactly as prescribed.

Phenobarbital should be used with extreme caution, or not at all, by people who are depressed, or have a history of drug abuse.

Patients should tell the doctor if they are in pain, or if they have constant pain, before they take phenobarbital.

Phenobarbital may cause excitement, depression, or confusion in elderly or weakened individuals, and excitement in children.

People with liver disease or poorly functioning adrenal glands should use phenobarbital with extra caution.

Barbiturates such as phenobarbital can cause people to become tired or less alert. Patients should be careful driving, operating machinery, or doing any activity that requires full mental alertness until they know how they react to this medication.

Possible food and drug interactions when taking this medication

Phenobarbital may increase the effects of alcohol. Patients should avoid alcoholic beverages while taking phenobarbital.

If phenobarbital is taken with certain other drugs, the effects of either could be increased, decreased, or altered. Here is an overview of drugs that may cause a problem:

Antihistamines such as Benadryl
Blood-thinning medications such as Coumadin
Doxycycline (Doryx, Vibramycin)
Griseofulvin (Fulvicin-P/G, Grifulvin V)
MAO inhibitors, including the antidepressants Nardil and Parnate
Narcotic pain relievers such as Percocet
Oral contraceptives
Other epilepsy drugs such as Dilantin, Depakene, and Depakote
Other sedatives such as Nembutal and Seconal
Steroids such as Medrol and Deltasone
Tranquilizers such as Xanax and Valium

Special information about pregnancy and breastfeeding

Barbiturates such as phenobarbital may cause damage to the developing baby during pregnancy. Withdrawal symptoms may occur in an infant whose mother took barbiturates during the last 3 months of pregnancy. Patients who are pregnant or plan to become pregnant should inform their doctor immediately.

Phenobarbital appears in breast milk and could affect a nursing infant. If phenobarbital is essential to the patient's health, the doctor may advise her to stop breastfeeding until her treatment is finished.

Recommended dosage

The following indications and dosages are for adults unless otherwise noted.

SEDATION

The usual initial dose of phenobarbital is a single dose of 30 to 120 milligrams. The doctor may repeat this dose at intervals, depending on the patient's response to this medication. The maximum amount allowable during a 24-hour period is 400 milligrams.

DAYTIME SEDATION

The usual dose is 30 to 120 milligrams a day, divided into 2 to 3 doses.

TO INDUCE SLEEP

The usual dose is 100 to 200 milligrams.

ANTICONVULSANT USE

Adults: Phenobarbital dosage must be individualized on the basis of specific laboratory tests. The usual dose is 60 to 200 milligrams daily.

Children: The phenobarbital dosage must be individualized on the basis of specific laboratory tests. The usual dose is 3 to 6 milligrams per 2.2 pounds of body weight per day.

DOSAGE ADJUSTMENT

For all indications, the doctor will need to prescribe a lower dosage for older adults, the weak, and those with liver or kidney disease.

Overdosage

Barbiturate overdose can be fatal. If an overdose is suspected, seek medical treatment immediately.

- *Symptoms of phenobarbital overdose may include:*
  Congestive heart failure, diminished breathing, extremely low body temperature, fluid in lungs, involuntary eyeball movements, irregular heartbeat, kidney failure, lack of muscle coordination, low blood pressure, poor reflexes, skin reddening or bloody blisters, slowdown of the central nervous system

PROCHLORPERAZINE

Why is this drug prescribed?

Prochlorperazine is used to treat symptoms of mental disorders such as schizophrenia, and is occasionally prescribed for anxiety. It is also used to control severe nausea and vomiting.

Most important fact about this drug

Prochlorperazine may cause tardive dyskinesia—involuntary muscle spasms and twitches in the face and body. This condition may be permanent. It appears to be most common among the elderly, especially women. Patients should see their doctor immediately at the first sign of this problem (spasms in the tongue may be an early warning). Antipsychotic medications usually must be discontinued if these symptoms appear.

How should this medication be taken?

Patients should never take more prochlorperazine than prescribed. Doing so can increase the risk of serious side effects.

If patients are using the suppository form of prochlorperazine and find it is too soft to insert, they can chill it in the refrigerator for about 30 minutes or run cold water over it before removing the wrapper.

To insert a suppository, patients should first remove the wrapper and moisten the suppository with cold water. They should then lie down on their side and use a finger to push the suppository well up into the rectum.

- *Missed dose...*
  Generally, the forgotten dose should be taken as soon as remembered. However, if it is almost time for the next dose, patients should skip the one they missed and go back to their regular schedule. Doses should never be doubled.

● *Storage instructions...*
Prochlorperazine may be stored at room temperature. Protect from heat and light.

What side effects may occur?

Side effects cannot be predicted. If any develop or change in intensity, patients should inform their doctor as soon as possible.

● *Side effects may include:*
Blurred vision, dizziness, drowsiness, jaundice, low blood pressure, menstrual irregularities, neuroleptic malignant syndrome (see "Special warnings about this medication"), skin reactions

Why should this drug not be prescribed?

Prochlorperazine must be avoided by anyone who is sensitive to or has ever had an allergic reaction to prochlorperazine or other phenothiazine drugs such as chlorpromazine, Prolixin, Triavil, Mellaril, or trifluoperazine.

Prochlorperazine should not be given to children who are undergoing surgery.

Special warnings about this medication

Patients should never take large amounts of alcohol, barbiturates, or narcotics when taking prochlorperazine. Serious problems can result.

If prochlorperazine is stopped suddenly, patients may experience a change in appetite, dizziness, nausea, vomiting, and tremors. Therapy should be discontinued only under a doctor's supervision.

Prochlorperazine should be used with caution if the patient is being treated for a brain tumor, intestinal blockage, heart disease, breast cancer, seizures, glaucoma, or an abnormal bone marrow or blood condition such as leukemia. Caution is also advised if the patient is exposed to pesticides or extreme heat.

Due to its ability to prevent vomiting, prochlorperazine can mask symptoms of an overdose of other drugs. It could also mask symptoms of brain tumor, intestinal blockage, and the neurological condition known as Reye's syndrome.

Prochlorperazine should be used cautiously in children suffering from dehydration or an acute illness such as chickenpox, measles, or other infection. The drug should be avoided altogether in children and adolescents who have symptoms that could indicate Reye's syndrome, including persistent or recurrent vomiting, listlessness, irritability, combativeness, and disorientation.

Prochlorperazine can cause a potentially fatal group of symptoms called neuroleptic malignant syndrome. Symptoms include extremely high body temperature, rigid muscles, mental changes, irregular pulse or blood pressure, rapid heartbeat, sweating, and changes in heart rhythm.

The doctor should be alerted immediately if these symptoms develop. Prochlorperazine therapy will need to be discontinued.

This drug may impair the ability to drive a car or operate potentially dangerous machinery. Patients should avoid any activities that require full alertness if they are unsure about their ability.

Patients should try to stay out of the sun while taking prochlorperazine. They should use sunblock and wear protective clothing. Their eyes may become more sensitive to sunlight, too, so they should keep sunglasses handy.

Prochlorperazine interferes with the body's ability to shed extra heat. Caution is warranted in hot weather.

Patients taking prochlorperazine for a prolonged period should see their doctor for regular evaluations, since side effects can get worse over time.

Prochlorperazine may cause false-positive phenylketonuria (PKU) tests.

Possible food and drug interactions when taking this medication

If prochlorperazine is taken with certain other drugs, the effects of either could be increased, decreased, or altered. Here is an overview of drugs that may cause a problem:

Antiseizure drugs such as Dilantin and Tegretol
Anticoagulants such as Coumadin
Guanethidine
Lithium (Lithobid, Eskalith)
Narcotic painkillers such as Demerol and Tylenol with Codeine
Other central nervous system depressants such as Xanax, Valium,
  Seconal, and Halcion
Propranolol (Inderal)
Thiazide diuretics such as Dyazide

Special information about pregnancy and breastfeeding

Prochlorperazine is not usually recommended for pregnant women, although it is sometimes prescribed for severe nausea and vomiting if the potential benefits of the drug outweigh the potential risks.

Prochlorperazine appears in breast milk and may affect a nursing infant. Patients are typically instructed to stop breastfeeding until their treatment is finished.

Recommended dosage

The following dosages are for adults unless otherwise noted.

NONPSYCHOTIC ANXIETY

Tablets: The usual dose is 5 milligrams, taken 3 or 4 times a day.

"Spansule" Capsules: The usual starting dose is one 15-milligram capsule on getting up or one 10-milligram capsule every 12 hours.

Treatment should not continue for longer than 12 weeks, and daily doses should not exceed 20 milligrams.

SCHIZOPHRENIA

Relatively Mild Symptoms: The usual dose is 5 or 10 milligrams, taken 3 or 4 times daily.

Moderate to Severe Symptoms: Dosages usually start at 10 milligrams, taken 3 or 4 times a day. If needed, dosage may be gradually increased; 50 to 75 milligrams daily has been helpful for some people.

Very Severe Symptoms: Dosages may range from 100 to 150 milligrams per day.

SEVERE NAUSEA AND VOMITING

Tablets: The usual dosage is one 5-milligram or 10-milligram tablet 3 or 4 times a day.
"Spansule" Capsules: The usual starting dose is one 15-milligram capsule on getting out of bed or one 10-milligram capsule every 12 hours.

The usual rectal dosage (suppository) is 25 milligrams, taken 2 times a day.

SCHIZOPHRENIA IN CHILDREN

Children 2 to 5 Years Old: The starting oral or rectal dose is 2-1/2 milligrams 2 or 3 times daily. Do not exceed 10 milligrams the first day and 20 milligrams thereafter.

Children 6 to 12 Years Old: The starting oral or rectal dose is 2-1/2 milligrams 2 or 3 times daily. Do not exceed 10 milligrams the first day and 25 milligrams thereafter.

SEVERE NAUSEA AND VOMITING IN CHILDREN

An oral or rectal dose of prochlorperazine is usually not needed for more than 1 day.

Children 20 to 29 Pounds: The usual dose is 2-1/2 milligrams 1 or 2 times daily. Total daily amount should not exceed 7.5 milligrams.

Children 30 to 39 Pounds: The usual dose is 2-1/2 milligrams 2 or 3 times daily. Total daily amount should not exceed 10 milligrams.

Children 40 to 85 Pounds: The usual dose is 2-1/2 milligrams 3 times daily, or 5 milligrams 2 times daily. Total daily amount should not exceed 15 milligrams.

NOTE: Children under 2 years of age or weighing less than 20 pounds should not be given prochlorperazine. If a child becomes restless or excited after taking prochlorperazine, the child should not get another dose.

DOSAGE ADJUSTMENT

In general, weak or older patients take lower dosages of prochlorperazine. Because they may develop low blood pressure while taking the drug, the doctor should monitor them closely. Older people (especially women) may be more susceptible to tardive dyskinesia.

Overdosage

An overdose of prochlorperazine can be fatal. If an overdose is suspected, seek medical help immediately.

- *Symptoms of prochlorperazine overdose may include:*
  Agitation, coma, convulsions, dry mouth, extreme sleepiness, fever, intestinal blockage, irregular heart rate, restlessness

---

PROLIXIN

Fluphenazine hydrochloride

Why is this drug prescribed?

Prolixin is used to reduce the symptoms of severe mental disturbances such as schizophrenia.

Most important fact about this drug

Prolixin may cause tardive dyskinesia—a condition marked by involuntary muscle spasms and twitches in the face and body. This condition may be permanent and appears to be most common among the elderly, especially women.

How should this medication be taken?

The elixir form of Prolixin should be examined before it's taken. The flavoring oils may have separated from the solution, causing globs or a wispy appearance. If this happens, the bottle should be gently shaken. The oil should blend in, and the solution should look clear. If the solution is not clear, it should not be used.

Prolixin Concentrate can be mixed with homogenized milk, noncaffeinated soft drinks, or fruit juice. It should not be mixed with caffeine-containing beverages, tea, or apple juice.

- *Missed dose...*
  Patients who take 1 dose a day should take the forgotten dose as soon as they remember, then go back to their regular schedule. If they do not remember until the next day, they should skip the dose they missed and go back to their regular schedule.

  If they take more than 1 dose a day, they should take the forgotten dose as soon as they remember if it is within an hour or so of their scheduled time. If they do not remember until later, they should skip the dose they missed and go back to their regular schedule. Doses should never be doubled.

- *Storage instructions...*
  Prolixin should be stored at room temperature in a tightly closed container, away from light. The liquid forms should not be frozen. The tablets should be protected from excessive heat.

What side effects may occur?

Side effects cannot be predicted. If any develop or change in intensity, patients should inform their doctor as soon as possible.

- *Side effects may include:*
  Allergic reactions, constipation, dry mouth, headache, high blood pressure, increased urination, liver problems, loss of appetite, low blood pressure, nausea, salivation, sweating, tardive dyskinesia (see "Most important fact about this drug")

Why should this drug not be prescribed?

Do not give Prolixin to someone in a comatose state. This drug should not be taken by anyone who is also taking large doses of hypnotic drugs such as Seconal, Halcion, and phenobarbital, who is very depressed, who has had brain or liver damage, or who has an abnormal bone marrow or blood condition. It should also be avoided by anyone who has ever had an allergic reaction to it or similar major tranquilizers.

Special warnings about this medication

Prolixin should be used with caution by anyone who has ever had breast cancer; convulsive disorders; heart or kidney disease; or certain tumors. Caution is warranted, too, if the patient is exposed to extreme heat or certain pesticides.

Stomach inflammation, dizziness, nausea, vomiting, and tremors can result if Prolixin is suddenly stopped. Patients must follow their doctor's instructions closely when discontinuing Prolixin.

Prolixin can cause a collection of symptoms called neuroleptic malignant syndrome. If the patient develops high fever, rigid muscles, changed mental state, irregular pulse or blood pressure, rapid or abnormal heartbeat, or excessive perspiration, the doctor should be notified immediately.

The doctor will periodically check your liver, kidneys, and blood during Prolixin therapy.

This drug may impair the ability to drive a car or operate potentially dangerous machinery. Patients should not participate in any activities that require full alertness if they are unsure of their ability.

Prolixin 2.5-, 5-, and 10-milligram tablets contain a coloring agent that can cause an allergic reaction in some people, especially those who are also allergic to aspirin.

Possible food and drug interactions when taking this medication

Prolixin should not be used with epinephrine (EpiPen). Extreme drowsiness and other potentially serious effects can result if Prolixin is combined with alcohol, narcotic pain relievers such as Percocet, sleeping medications such as Seconal, antihistamines such as Benadryl, or tranquilizers such as Valium. Prolixin may also interact with Atropine.

Special information about pregnancy and breastfeeding

Pregnant women should use Prolixin only if clearly needed. Patients who are pregnant or plan to become pregnant should inform their doctor immediately.

Prolixin may appear in breast milk and could affect a nursing infant. If this medication is essential to the patient's health, the doctor may advise her not to breastfeed while taking it.

Recommended dosage

ADULTS

The usual beginning total daily dose is 2.5 to 10 milligrams. This amount is divided into 3 or 4 equal doses and taken 6 or 8 hours apart.

If necessary, the doctor may increase the total dosage to 40 milligrams daily. When symptoms are under control, the doctor may decrease the dose. A daily maintenance dose may range from 1 to 5 milligrams, usually taken once daily.

CHILDREN

Safety and efficacy of Prolixin in children have not been established.

OLDER ADULTS

Older people may start with a daily dose of 1 to 2.5 milligrams. In general, they will take dosages of Prolixin in the lower ranges. Older people (especially older women) may be more susceptible to tardive dyskinesia—a possibly permanent condition characterized by involuntary muscle spasms and twitches in the face and body.

Overdosage

Any medication taken in excess can have serious consequences. If an overdose of Prolixin is suspected, seek medical help immediately.

Promethazine *See Phenergan, page 143*

PROSOM
Estazolam

Why is this drug prescribed?

ProSom, a sleeping pill, is given for the short-term treatment of insomnia. Insomnia may involve difficulty falling asleep, frequent awakenings during the night, or too-early awakening in the morning.

Most important fact about this drug

As a chemical cousin of Valium and similar tranquilizers, ProSom is potentially addictive. It should be used only as a temporary sleeping aid. Even after relatively short-term use of ProSom, withdrawal symptoms may occur when the medication is stopped.

How should this medication be taken?

ProSom must be taken exactly as prescribed. A typical schedule is 1 tablet at bedtime. For small, physically run-down, or older people, one-half a tablet may be a safer starting dose.

- *Missed dose...*
  ProSom should be taken at bedtime only as needed. It is not necessary to make up a missed dose.

- *Storage instructions...*
  ProSom may be stored at room temperature.

What side effects may occur?

Side effects cannot be predicted. If any develop or change in intensity, patients should inform their doctor as soon as possible.

- *Side effects may include:*
  Abnormal coordination, constipation, decreased movement or activity, dizziness, dry mouth, general feeling of illness, hangover, headache, leg and foot pain, memory problems, nausea, nervousness, sleepiness, weakness

Why should this drug not be prescribed?

ProSom should not be taken by anyone who is sensitive or allergic to it, or by anyone who has ever had an adverse reaction to another Valium-type medication.

ProSom should be avoided during pregnancy. Drugs in this class may cause damage to the unborn child.

Special warnings about this medication

Since ProSom may cloud thinking, impair judgment, or interfere with normal physical coordination, patients should not drive, climb, or perform hazardous tasks until they know their reaction to this medication. It is important to remember that a tablet taken in the evening may continue to have effects well into the following day.

People who are older or physically run-down and those who have liver or kidney damage or breathing problems are particularly vulnerable to side effects from ProSom. They should use this medication with special caution.

Patients who have ever had seizures should not abruptly stop taking ProSom, even if they are taking antiseizure medication. Instead, they should taper off from ProSom under their doctor's supervision.

Even if a patient has never had a seizure, it is better to taper off from ProSom than to stop taking the medication abruptly. Experience suggests that tapering off can help prevent drug withdrawal symptoms.

Typically, the only withdrawal symptoms caused by ProSom are mild and temporary insomnia or irritability. Occasionally, however, withdrawal can involve considerable discomfort or even danger, with symptoms such as abdominal and muscle cramps, convulsions, sweating, tremors, and vomiting.

Possible food and drug interactions when taking this medication

Patients should not drink alcohol while taking ProSom; this combination could make them comatose or dangerously slow their breathing.

For the same reason, it is unwise to combine ProSom with any other medication that might calm or slow the functioning of the central nervous system. Among such drugs are:

Antipsychotic medications such as Haldol and Mellaril
Antiseizure drugs such as Dilantin, Tegretol, and Depakene
Antihistamines such as Benadryl and Chlor-Trimeton
Barbiturates such as phenobarbital
MAO inhibitors such as the antidepressants Nardil and Parnate
Narcotics such as Percodan and Tylox
Tranquilizers such as Valium and Xanax

Smokers tend to process and eliminate ProSom fairly quickly compared with nonsmokers.

Special information about pregnancy and breastfeeding

ProSom should not be used during pregnancy; it could cause birth defects in the developing baby.

When a pregnant woman takes ProSom or a similar medication shortly before giving birth, her baby is likely to have poor muscle tone (flaccidity) and/or experience drug withdrawal symptoms.

Because ProSom is thought to pass into breast milk, this medication should not be used while breastfeeding.

Recommended dosage

ADULTS

The recommended initial dose is 1 milligram at bedtime. Some people may need a 2-milligram dose.

CHILDREN

There is no information on the safety and effectiveness of ProSom in people under age 18.

OLDER ADULTS

The recommended usual dosage for older adults is 1 milligram. Some may require only 0.5 milligram.

Overdosage

Any medication taken in excess can have serious consequences. If an overdose is suspected, seek medical attention immediately.

- *Symptoms of a ProSom overdose may include:*
  Confusion, depressed breathing, drowsiness and eventually coma, lack of coordination, slurred speech

Protriptyline *See Vivactil, page 226*

PROVIGIL
Modafinil

Why is this drug prescribed?

Provigil is a stimulant drug used to treat unusually sleepy people who have been diagnosed with narcolepsy, obstructive sleep apnea/hypopnea syndrome, or shift work sleep disorder. The patient should be medically diagnosed with one of these sleep disorders before taking Provigil, since sleepiness can be a symptom of other medical conditions.

Most important fact about this drug

Provigil will not cure any sleep disorder; it merely treats the symptom of sleepiness. This medication should not be used in place of getting enough sleep. The patient should follow the doctor's advice about maintaining good sleep habits.

Provigil, like other stimulants, has the potential for abuse. It can alter mood, perception, thinking, and feelings, providing an artificial "lift" and potentially leading to a certain degree of dependence (although discontinuation of the drug does not produce physical withdrawal symptoms). Patients should take only the prescribed dose; they should never increase the dose or take additional doses.

How should this medication be taken?

Food does not reduce the effectiveness of this medication. However, it will delay the onset of action by approximately 1 hour.

● *Missed dose...*
  The forgotten dose should be taken as soon as possible. If it's not remembered until the next day, patients should skip the forgotten dose and go back to their regular schedule. Doses should never be doubled.

● *Storage instructions...*
  Store at room temperature.

What side effects may occur?

Side effects cannot be predicted. If any develop or change in intensity, patients should inform their doctor as soon as possible.

● *Side effects may include:*
  Anxiety, headache, infection, insomnia, nausea, nervousness

Why should this drug not be prescribed?

Provigil should be avoided by anyone who has ever had an allergic reaction to it.

Special warnings about this medication

Provigil should be used with caution by patients with high blood pressure, liver or kidney problems, or a history of psychosis or drug abuse. The doctor should know the patient's complete medical history before prescribing this drug.

Provigil should be avoided by people with certain types of heart problems such as mitral valve prolapse. Patients should tell the doctor about any heart problems they have before taking this drug.

Leukopenia (low white blood-cell count) has been reported in pediatric patients taking Provigil.

Provigil may impair judgment, thinking, or motor skills. Patients should not drive a car or operate hazardous machinery until they know how this drug affects them. Likewise, patients should be aware that Provigil may not restore complete wakefulness in certain people.

Provigil may interfere with the effectiveness of oral and implantable contraceptives. Patients should use an additional method of contraception while taking Provigil and for 1 month after discontinuing it.

Possible food and drug interactions when taking this medication

The effect of combining Provigil with alcohol has not been studied. It's best to avoid alcohol while taking this drug.

If Provigil is taken with certain other drugs, the effects of either could be increased, decreased, or altered. Here is an overview of drugs that may cause a problem:

Antidepressants such as Effexor, Elavil, Pamelor, Paxil, Prozac, and
  Tofranil
Carbamazepine (Tegretol)
Clomipramine (Anafranil)
Cyclosporine (Sandimmune)
Dextroamphetamine (Dexedrine)
Diazepam (Valium)
Itraconazole (Sporanox)
Ketoconazole (Nizoral)
MAO inhibitors such as the antidepressants Nardil and Parnate
Methylphenidate (Ritalin)
Oral contraceptives and hormonal implants
Phenobarbital
Phenytoin (Dilantin)
Propranolol (Inderal)
Rifampin (Rifater)
Theophylline (Theo-Dur)
Triazolam (Halcion)
Warfarin (Coumadin)

Special information about pregnancy and breastfeeding

The possibility of harmful effects during pregnancy has not been ruled
out. Patients who are pregnant or plan to become pregnant should inform
their doctor immediately.

It is not known whether Provigil appears in breast milk. Nursing mothers should use Provigil with caution and only when clearly needed.

Recommended dosage

ADULTS

The usual dose of Provigil is 200 milligrams taken as a single dose in the
morning. Patients with shift work sleep disorder should take Provigil
about 1 hour before their shift starts.

CHILDREN

Children younger than 16 years old should not use Provigil.

OLDER ADULTS

People over 65 may need a lower dose if they have liver or kidney disease,
which reduces the body's ability to metabolize this medication.

Overdosage

Any medication taken in excess can have serious consequences. If an
overdose is suspected, seek medical treatment immediately.

- *Symptoms of Provigil overdose may include:*
Aggressiveness, agitation, anxiety, confusion, diarrhea, fluttering heartbeat, insomnia, irritability, nausea, nervousness, sleep disturbances, slow blood clotting, tremor

PROZAC

Fluoxetine hydrochloride
Other brand names: Prozac Weekly, Sarafem

Why is this drug prescribed?

Prozac is prescribed for the treatment of major depression, panic disorder, and obsessive-compulsive disorder. The drug is also used in the treatment of bulimia and has been used to treat other eating disorders and obesity. Prozac Weekly is approved for treating major depression.

In children and adolescents, Prozac is approved to treat major depression and obsessive-compulsive disorder.

Under the brand name Sarafem, the active ingredient in Prozac is also prescribed for the treatment of premenstrual dysphoric disorder (PMDD). Symptoms of PMDD include mood problems such as anxiety, depression, irritability or persistent anger, mood swings, and tension. Physical problems that accompany PMDD include bloating, breast tenderness, headache, and joint and muscle pain. Symptoms typically begin 1 to 2 weeks before a woman's menstrual period and are severe enough to interfere with day-to-day activities and relationships.

Prozac belongs to the class of drugs called selective serotonin reuptake inhibitors (SSRIs). Serotonin is one of the chemical messengers believed to govern moods. Ordinarily, it is quickly reabsorbed after its release at the junctures between nerves. Reuptake inhibitors such as Prozac slow this process, thereby boosting the levels of serotonin available in the brain.

Most important fact about this drug

Serious, sometimes fatal, reactions have been known to occur when Prozac is used in combination with drugs known as MAO inhibitors, including the antidepressants Nardil and Parnate; and when Prozac is discontinued and an MAO inhibitor is started. Prozac should never be taken with one of these drugs or within at least 14 days of discontinuing therapy with one of them; and 5 weeks or more should be allowed between stopping Prozac and starting an MAO inhibitor. Caution is especially warranted if the patient has been taking Prozac in high doses or for a long time.

In addition, Prozac should never be combined with thioridazine (Mellaril) due to the risk of life-threatening drug interactions; and a minimum of 5 weeks should be allowed between stopping Prozac and starting Mellaril.

Patients who are taking any prescription or nonprescription drugs should notify their doctor before taking Prozac.

How should this medication be taken?

Prozac should be taken exactly as prescribed. It usually is taken once or twice a day. To be effective, it should be taken regularly. Patients should make a habit of taking it at the same time they do some other daily activity.

It may be 4 weeks before a patient feels any relief from depression, but the drug's effects should last about 9 months after a 3-month treatment regimen. For obsessive-compulsive disorder, the full effect may take 5 weeks to appear.

* *Missed dose...*
  The forgotten dose should be taken as soon as the patient remembers. If several hours have passed, the dose should be skipped. Patients should never try to "catch up" by doubling the dose.

* *Storage instructions...*
  Store at room temperature.

What side effects may occur?

Side effects cannot be predicted. If any develop or change in intensity, patients should inform their doctor as soon as possible.

* *Side effects may include:*
  Anxiety, decreased libido, diarrhea, dizziness, dry mouth, headache, impaired coordination, indigestion, insomnia, nausea, nervousness, sleepiness, sweating, tremor, weight loss

A wide variety of other very rare reactions have been reported during Prozac therapy. Patients who develop any new or unexplained symptoms should tell their doctor without delay.

Why should this drug not be prescribed?

This drug should be avoided by anyone who is sensitive to or has ever had an allergic reaction to it or to similar drugs such as Paxil and Zoloft. Remember, too, that Prozac should never be combined with thioridazine or an MAO inhibitor (see "Most important fact about this drug").

Special warnings about this medication

The FDA has issued a public health advisory to alert healthcare professionals about reports of worsening depression and suicidality (both suicidal thoughts and suicide attempts) during antidepressant drug therapy in adult and pediatric patients with major depression. Healthcare professionals and family members are advised to watch for signs of worsening depression and to be aware of the suicide statement present in all antidepressant labeling. Prozac is approved for treating major depression in children 8 years and older and for obsessive-compulsive disorder in children 7 years and older.

SSRI antidepressants could potentially cause stomach bleeding, especially in older patients or those taking nonsteroidal anti-inflammatory drugs (NSAIDs) such as aspirin, ibuprofen (Advil, Motrin), naproxen (Aleve), and ketoprofen (Orudis KT). Advise patients to consult their doctor before combining Prozac with NSAIDs or blood-thinning medications.

Unless the doctor directs, this medication should not be taken by anyone who is recovering from a heart attack or has liver disease or diabetes.

Prozac may cause patients to become drowsy or less alert and may affect their judgment. Therefore, driving, operating dangerous machinery, or participating in any hazardous activity that requires full mental alertness is not recommended.

While taking this medication, some people may feel dizzy or lightheaded or actually faint when getting up from a lying or sitting position. If getting up slowly doesn't help, or if this problem continues, the doctor should be notified.

Patients who develop a skin rash or hives while taking Prozac should discontinue use of the medication and notify the doctor immediately.

Prozac should be used with caution if the patient has a history of mania or seizures. All the patient's medical conditions should be discussed with the doctor before this medication is taken.

Prozac can occasionally cause decreased appetite and weight loss, especially in depressed people who are already underweight and in those with bulimia. The doctor should be alerted if the patient has a significant change in weight or appetite.

There have been rare reports of prolonged seizures in patients who received electroconvulsive therapy (ECT) while taking Prozac. To date, there are no clinical studies establishing the benefit of combined treatment with Prozac and ECT.

Possible food and drug interactions when taking this medication

Remember that combining Prozac with thioridazine (Mellaril) or MAO inhibitors is dangerous. Alcohol should also be avoided by people on Prozac.

If Prozac is taken with certain other drugs, the effects of either could be increased, decreased, or altered. Here is an overview of drugs that may cause a problem:

Alprazolam (Xanax)
Any other antidepressants
Carbamazepine (Tegretol)
Clozapine (Clozaril)

Diazepam (Valium)
Digitoxin (Crystodigin)
Drugs that impair brain function, such as Xanax
Flecainide (Tambocor)
Haloperidol (Haldol)
Lithium (Eskalith)
Nonsteroidal anti-inflammatory drugs (NSAIDs) such as aspirin,
  ibuprofen (Advil, Motrin), naproxen (Aleve), and ketoprofen
  (Orudis KT)
Phenytoin (Dilantin)
Pimozide (Orap)
Sumatriptan (Imitrex)
Tryptophan
Vinblastine (Velban)
Warfarin (Coumadin)

Special information about pregnancy and breastfeeding

The effects of Prozac during pregnancy have not been adequately studied. Patients who are pregnant or plan to become pregnant should inform their doctor immediately. This medication appears in breast milk, and breast-feeding is not recommended during Prozac therapy.

Recommended dosage

DEPRESSION

It may take 4 weeks before the full antidepressant effect of Prozac is seen.

Adults: The recommended starting dose is 20 milligrams a day, usually taken in the morning. If needed, the doctor may gradually increase the dose up to a maximum of 80 milligrams a day. The usual daily dose ranges from 20 to 60 milligrams. Daily doses above 20 milligrams should be taken in the morning or in two smaller doses taken in the morning and at noon.

Children 8 years and older: The usual starting dose is 10 or 20 milligrams a day. Children starting at 10 milligrams will have their dose increased to 20 milligrams a day after 1 week. Underweight children may need to remain at the 10-milligram dose.

Prozac Weekly: Patients need to wait at least 7 days after stopping their daily dose of Prozac before switching to the once-weekly formulation. One Prozac Weekly capsule contains 90 milligrams of medication.

OBSESSIVE-COMPULSIVE DISORDER

It may take 5 weeks before the full effects of Prozac are seen.

Adults: The recommended starting dose is 20 milligrams a day, usually taken in the morning. If needed, the doctor may gradually increase the dose up to a maximum of 80 milligrams a day. The usual daily dose ranges from 20 to 60 milligrams. Daily doses above 20 milligrams should be taken in the morning or in two smaller doses taken in the morning and at noon.

Children 7 years and older: The recommended starting dose is 10 milligrams a day. After 2 weeks, the doctor will increase the dose to 20 milligrams. If needed, the doctor may further increase the dose up to a maximum of 60 milligrams a day. The recommended dosage range for underweight children is 10 to 30 milligrams a day.

BULIMIA

Adults: The recommended dose is 60 milligrams a day taken in the morning. The doctor may start the patient at a lower dose and gradually increase it over a period of several days.

PANIC DISORDER

Adults: The recommended starting dose is 10 milligrams a day. After 1 week, the doctor will increase the dose to 20 milligrams. If no improvement is seen after several weeks, the doctor may increase the dose to a maximum of 60 milligrams a day.

PREMENSTRUAL DYSPHORIC DISORDER

Adults: The usual dose of Sarafem is 20 milligrams a day. The doctor will instruct the patient to take the dose either every day of the month or only during the 2 weeks before menstruation begins (the luteal phase of her cycle). If there's no improvement after several weeks, the dose can be increased, usually to 60 milligrams a day. The maximum dose is 80 milligrams daily.

DOSAGE ADJUSTMENT

For all indications, the doctor may need to prescribe a lower dose for patients who are elderly, have liver disease, or are taking other medications.

Overdosage

An overdose of Prozac can be fatal. In addition, combining Prozac with certain other drugs can cause symptoms of overdose. If an overdose is suspected, seek medical attention immediately.

- *Common symptoms of Prozac overdose include:*
  Nausea, rapid heartbeat, seizures, sleepiness, vomiting

- *Other symptoms of Prozac overdose include:*
  Coma, delirium, fainting, high fever, irregular heartbeat, low blood pressure, mania, rigid muscles, sweating, stupor

Quazepam *See Doral, page 56*

Quetiapine *See Seroquel, page 188*

REMERON
Mirtazapine
Other brand name: Remeron SolTab

Why is this drug prescribed?
Remeron is prescribed for the treatment of major depression. It belongs to the class of drugs known as tetracyclics and is chemically unrelated to other antidepressants such as serotonin reuptake inhibitors and MAO inhibitors. Remeron is thought to work by adjusting the balance of the brain's natural chemical messengers, especially norepinephrine and serotonin.

Most important fact about this drug
Remeron makes some people drowsy or less alert, and may affect judgment and thinking. Patients should avoid driving or participating in any hazardous activity that requires full mental alertness until they know whether Remeron has this effect on them.

How should this medication be taken?
Remeron may be taken with or without food. It is preferable to take it in the evening before going to bed. Even though improvement may begin in 1 to 4 weeks, it is important for the patient to continue taking this medication exactly as prescribed. Regular daily doses are needed for the drug to work properly.

Patients using Remeron SolTabs, an orally disintegrating form of the drug, should make sure their hands are dry before removing the tablet from the blister pack and should immediately place the tablet on their tongue. They should not attempt to split the tablet; it will fall apart rapidly and can be swallowed with saliva.

- *Missed dose...*
  If the forgotten dose is remembered within a few hours, it should be taken immediately. Otherwise, it should be skipped. Doses should never be doubled.

- *Storage instructions...*
  Remeron should be stored at room temperature in a tight, light-resistant container.

What side effects may occur?
Side effects cannot be predicted. If any develop or change in intensity, patients should tell their doctor as soon as possible.

- *Side effects may include:*
  Abnormal dreams and thinking, constipation, dizziness, dry mouth, flu-like symptoms, increased appetite, sleepiness, weakness, weight gain

Why should this drug not be prescribed?

Anyone who has ever had an allergic reaction to Remeron or similar drugs such as Ludiomil and Desyrel should not take this medication. It is important for patients to tell the doctor about any drug reactions they have experienced.

Remeron must also be avoided by anyone taking the antidepressants Nardil or Parnate (see "Special warnings about this medication").

Special warnings about this medication

The FDA has issued a public health advisory to alert healthcare professionals about reports of worsening depression and suicidality (both suicidal thoughts and suicide attempts) during antidepressant drug therapy in adult and pediatric patients with major depressive disorder. Healthcare professionals and family members are advised to watch for signs of worsening depression and to be aware of the suicide statement present in all antidepressant labeling. Remeron is currently not approved for use in pediatric patients.

Serious, sometimes fatal, reactions have been known to occur when drugs such as Remeron are taken in combination with other drugs known as MAO inhibitors, including the antidepressants Nardil and Parnate. Remeron should never be taken with one of these drugs or within 14 days of discontinuing therapy with one of them. Patients should also allow at least 14 days between stopping Remeron and starting an MAO inhibitor.

Patients who develop flu-like symptoms, a sore throat, chills or fever, mouth sores, or any other signs of infection should call their doctor; these symptoms may signal a serious underlying condition.

Remeron tends to raise cholesterol levels in some people. If the patient has a cholesterol problem, it should be mentioned to the doctor before Remeron therapy begins.

Remeron should be used with caution by people with active liver or kidney disease, or heart or blood pressure problems. The doctor should also be alerted if the patient has a history of seizures, mania, hypomania (mild excitability), drug use, or any other physical or emotional problems.

While first taking this medication, some people feel dizzy or lightheaded, especially when getting up from a lying or sitting position. If getting up slowly doesn't help, or if this problem continues, the doctor should be notified.

People who must avoid phenylalanine should not use the SolTab form of Remeron, which contains this substance.

Possible food and drug interactions when taking this medication

Remeron should never be combined with an MAO inhibitor; and patients should not drink alcohol while taking this medication. If Remeron is taken with certain other drugs, the effects of either could be increased, decreased, or altered. It is especially important for patients to check with the doctor before combining Remeron with tranquilizers such as Valium, Xanax, and Ativan.

Special information about pregnancy and breastfeeding

The effects of Remeron during pregnancy have not been adequately studied. If the patient is pregnant or plans to become pregnant, she should tell her doctor immediately. It is not known whether Remeron appears in breast milk. However, because many drugs do make their way into breast milk, caution is advised.

Recommended dosage

ADULTS

The usual starting dose is 15 milligrams taken daily before going to sleep. Depending upon the patient's response, the dosage may be increased to as much as 45 milligrams a day.

CHILDREN

The safety and effectiveness of Remeron have not been established in children.

Overdosage

Any medication taken in excess can have serious consequences. If you suspect an overdose, seek medical attention immediately.

- *Symptoms of Remeron overdose may include:*
  Drowsiness, impaired memory, mental confusion, rapid heartbeat

---

REMINYL

Galantamine

Why is this drug prescribed?

Reminyl can delay mental decline in some patients with mild to moderate Alzheimer's disease. It is thought to work by boosting levels of the chemical messenger acetylcholine in the brain. (In Alzheimer's disease, the cells that produce acetylcholine slowly deteriorate.)

Like other Alzheimer's drugs, Reminyl is a temporary remedy. It doesn't work for everyone, and it doesn't halt the underlying disease.

Most important fact about this drug

Reminyl therapy starts at a low dose and increases over several months. It is important to wait 4 weeks between dosage adjustments. If treatment with Reminyl is interrupted for several days or longer, the patient will need to start over again at the lowest dose, increasing the dose at 4-week intervals until the former dose is achieved.

How should this medication be taken?

Reminyl should be taken twice a day, preferably with the morning and evening meals. The drug is available in tablet form and as an oral solution. If the solution is used, the required amount should be drawn into the measuring pipette that comes with the bottle and emptied into 3 to 4 ounces of a non-alcoholic beverage. The mixture should be stirred well and administered immediately.

● *Missed dose...*
 Generally, it should be given as soon as remembered. However, if it is almost time for the next dose, the missed dose should be skipped and the next dose given on schedule. Doses should never be doubled.

● *Storage instructions...*
 Both the tablets and the oral solution may be stored at room temperature. The solution should be protected from freezing.

What side effects may occur?

Side effects cannot be predicted. If any develop or change in intensity, caregivers should inform the doctor as soon as possible.

● *Side effects may include:*
 Abdominal pain, anemia, blood in urine, depression, diarrhea, dizziness, fatigue, headache, inability to sleep, indigestion, loss of appetite, nausea, runny nose, sleepiness, tremor, urinary tract infection, vomiting, weight loss

Why should this drug not be prescribed?

Reminyl cannot be used if it gives the patient an allergic reaction. This drug is not recommended for patients with severe liver disease or kidney disease.

Special warnings about this medication

Reminyl should be used with caution if the patient has severe asthma, obstructive lung disease, or a history of stomach ulcers.

Reminyl can slow the heart rate and cause fainting episodes. Caution is especially important if the patient has a heart irregularity.

Before surgery, the doctor should be made aware of the use of Reminyl.

Possible food and drug interactions when taking this medication

If Reminyl is taken with certain other drugs, the effect of either may be increased, decreased, or altered. Here is an overview of drugs that may cause a problem:

Certain Parkinson's drugs such as Artane and Cogentin
Cimetidine (Tagamet)
Erythromycin (E.E.S., Eryc, PCE)
Ketoconazole (Nizoral)
Meclizine (Antivert)
Nonsteroidal anti-inflammatory drugs such as Motrin and Voltaren
Paroxetine (Paxil)
Urinary tract medications such as Urispas and Urecholine

Special information about pregnancy and breastfeeding

Reminyl is not usually prescribed for women of childbearing age. It should be used during pregnancy only if the potential benefit justifies the risk to the developing baby. Reminyl should not be used by nursing mothers.

Recommended dosage

ADULTS

The recommended starting dose of Reminyl is 4 milligrams twice a day. Four weeks later, the dose should be increased to 8 milligrams twice a day. After waiting an additional four weeks, the doctor may increase the dose to 12 milligrams twice a day if necessary.

For patients with mild to moderate liver problems and kidney problems, dosage should not exceed 16 milligrams per day.

Overdosage

Any medication taken in excess can have serious consequences. A massive overdose of Reminyl could prove fatal. If you suspect an overdose, seek medical attention immediately.

- *Symptoms of Reminyl overdose may include:*
  Convulsions, drooling, fainting, incontinence, low blood pressure, muscle weakness, severe nausea, slow or irregular heartbeat, stomach cramps, sweating, teary eyes, twitching, weak breathing, vomiting

---

RESTORIL

Temazepam

Why is this drug prescribed?

Restoril is used for the relief of insomnia (difficulty in falling asleep, waking up frequently at night, or waking up early in the morning). It belongs to a class of drugs known as benzodiazepines.

Most important fact about this drug

Sleep problems are usually temporary, requiring treatment for only a short time, usually 1 or 2 days and no more than 2 to 3 weeks. Insomnia that lasts longer than this may be a sign of another medical problem.

Needing this medicine for more than 7 to 10 days is a signal to check with the doctor.

How should this medication be taken?

It is important to take this medication exactly as directed, and in no more than the prescribed amount.

- *Missed dose...*
  Restoril should be taken only as needed.

- *Storage instructions...*
  This medication should be kept in the container it came in, tightly closed, and out of the reach of children. It may be stored at room temperature.

What side effects may occur?

Side effects cannot be predicted. If any develop or change in intensity, patients should inform their doctor as soon as possible.

- *Side effects may include:*
  Dizziness, drowsiness, fatigue, headache, nausea, nervousness, sluggishness

- *Side effects due to rapid decrease in dose or abrupt withdrawal from Restoril:*
  Abdominal and muscle cramps, convulsions, feeling of discomfort, inability to fall asleep or stay asleep, sweating, tremors, vomiting

Why should this drug not be prescribed?

Women who are pregnant or plan to become pregnant should not take this medication. It poses a potential risk to the developing baby.

Special warnings about this medication

When Restoril is used every night for more than a few weeks, it loses its effectiveness to promote sleep. This is known as tolerance. Patients can also develop physical dependence on this drug, especially if they take it regularly for more than a few weeks, or take high doses.

When patients first start taking Restoril, until they know whether the medication will have any carryover effect the next day, they should use extreme care while doing anything that requires complete alertness such as driving a car or operating machinery.

Patients who are severely depressed, or have suffered from severe depression in the past, should double-check with their doctor before taking this medication. They should also make sure the doctor is aware of any kidney ailments, liver problems, or chronic lung disease they may have.

After stopping Restoril, patients may have more trouble sleeping than they had before they started taking it. This is called rebound insomnia and should clear up after 1 or 2 nights.

Possible food and drug interactions when taking this medication

Restoril may intensify the effects of alcohol. Patients should avoid alcohol while taking this medication.

If Restoril is taken with certain other drugs, the effects of either could be increased, decreased, or altered. Here is an overview of drugs that may cause a problem:

Antidepressant drugs such as Elavil, Nardil, Parnate, and Tofranil
Antihistamines such as Benadryl
Antipsychotic medications such as Mellaril and chlorpromazine
Barbiturates such as phenobarbital and Seconal
Narcotic pain relievers such as Percocet and Demerol
Tranquilizers such as Valium and Xanax

Special information about pregnancy and breastfeeding

Women who are pregnant or planning to become pregnant should avoid Restoril. There is an increased risk of birth defects.

This drug may appear in breast milk and could affect a nursing infant. If this medication is considered essential to a woman's health, her doctor may advise her to discontinue breastfeeding until her treatment with this medication is finished.

Recommended dosage

ADULTS

The usual recommended dose is 15 milligrams at bedtime. However, 7.5 milligrams may be all that is necessary, while some people may need 30 milligrams. Your doctor will tailor your dose to your needs.

CHILDREN

The safety and effectiveness of Restoril have not been established in children under 18 years of age.

OLDER ADULTS

The doctor will prescribe the smallest effective amount in order to avoid side effects such as oversedation, dizziness, confusion, and lack of muscle coordination. The usual starting dose is 7.5 milligrams.

Overdosage

Any medication taken in excess can have serious consequences. If an overdose is suspected, seek medical attention immediately.

- *Symptoms of Restoril overdose may include:*
  Coma, confusion, diminished reflexes, loss of coordination, low blood pressure, labored or difficult breathing, seizures, sleepiness, slurred speech

RISPERDAL

Risperidone
Other brand name: Risperdal M-Tab

Why is this drug prescribed?

Risperdal is prescribed for the treatment of schizophrenia and for the short-term treatment of mania associated with bipolar disorder. It is thought to work by muting the impact of dopamine and serotonin, two of the brain's key chemical messengers.

Most important fact about this drug

Risperdal may cause tardive dyskinesia, a condition that causes involuntary muscle spasms and twitches in the face and body. This condition can become permanent and is most common among older people, especially women. Patients should see their doctor immediately if they begin to have any involuntary movements. They may need to discontinue Risperdal therapy.

How should this medication be taken?

It is important for patients to take exactly the amount of Risperdal prescribed. Higher doses are more likely to cause unwanted side effects.

Risperdal may be taken with or without food.

Risperdal oral solution comes with a calibrated pipette to use for measuring. The oral solution can be taken with water, coffee, orange juice, and low-fat milk, but not with cola drinks or tea.

Risperdal M-Tabs are orally disintegrating tablets that come in blister packs. The tablets should not be removed from the package until patients are ready to take them. When it's time for their dose, patients should use dry fingers to peel back the foil of the blister pack to remove the tablet; they should *not* push the tablet through the foil because this could damage the tablet. Once removed, the tablet should be placed immediately on the tongue. The medication dissolves in the mouth quickly and can be swallowed with or without liquid. Risperdal M-Tabs should not be split or chewed.

- *Missed dose...*
  Generally, the dose should be taken as soon as remembered. However, if it is almost time for the next dose, patients should skip the one they missed and go back to their regular schedule. Doses should never be doubled.

- *Storage instructions...*
  Risperdal may be stored at room temperature. The tablets should be protected from light and moisture; the oral solution should be protected from light and freezing.

What side effects may occur?

Side effects cannot be predicted. If any develop or change in intensity, patients should inform their doctor as soon as possible.

* *Side effects may include:*
  Agitation, anxiety, constipation, dizziness, hallucination, headache, indigestion, insomnia, rapid or irregular heartbeat, restlessness, runny nose, sleepiness, vomiting, weight change

Why should this drug not be prescribed?

Risperdal cannot be taken by anyone who is sensitive to or has ever had an allergic reaction to it or to other antipsychotic medications.

Risperdal should not be used to treat elderly patients who have dementia because the drug could increase the risk of stroke.

Special warnings about this medication

Risperdal should be used with caution in patients who have kidney, liver, or heart disease, seizures, breast cancer, thyroid disorders, or any other diseases that affect the metabolism. Caution is also warranted in patients exposed to extremes of temperature.

Be aware that Risperdal may mask signs and symptoms of drug overdose and of conditions such as intestinal obstruction, brain tumor, and Reye's syndrome (a dangerous neurological condition that may follow viral infections, usually occurring in children).

Risperdal may cause neuroleptic malignant syndrome, a condition marked by muscle stiffness or rigidity, fast heartbeat or irregular pulse, increased sweating, high fever, and high or low blood pressure. Unchecked, this condition can prove fatal. Patients should call their doctor immediately if they notice any of these symptoms. Risperdal therapy should be discontinued.

Certain antipsychotic drugs, including Risperdal, are associated with an increased risk of developing high blood sugar, which on rare occasions has led to coma or death. Patients should see their doctor right away if they develop signs of high blood sugar, including dry mouth, thirst, increased urination, and tiredness. Patients who have diabetes or have a high risk of developing it should see their doctor regularly for blood sugar testing.

Patients at high risk of suicide attempts should be prescribed the lowest dose possible to reduce the risk of intentional overdose.

This drug may impair the ability to drive a car or operate potentially dangerous machinery. Patients should avoid participating in any activities that require full alertness if they are unsure of their ability.

Risperdal can cause orthostatic hypotension (low blood pressure when rising to a standing position), with dizziness, rapid heartbeat, and fainting, especially at the start of therapy. This problem should be reported to the doctor if it develops. The dosage can be adjusted to reduce the symptoms.

Risperdal is prescribed for the short-term treatment of rapid-onset bipolar mania; it is not approved for preventing future episodes. The effectiveness of the drug for treating mania for more than 3 weeks has not been studied.

People who have phenylketonuria and must avoid the amino acid phenylalanine should not use Risperdal M-Tabs, which contain this substance.

The safety and effectiveness of Risperdal have not been studied in children.

Possible food and drug interactions when taking this medication

If Risperdal is taken with certain other drugs, the effects of either can be increased, decreased, or altered. Here is an overview of drugs that may cause a problem:

Blood pressure medicines such as Aldomet, Procardia, and Vasotec
Bromocriptine mesylate (Parlodel)
Carbamazepine (Tegretol)
Clozapine (Clozaril)
Fluoxetine (Prozac)
Levodopa (Sinemet, Larodopa)
Paroxetine (Paxil)
Phenobarbital
Phenytoin (Dilantin)
Quinidine (Quinidex)
Rifampin (Rifadin)
Valproic acid (Depakene, Depakote)

Risperdal tends to increase the effect of blood pressure medicines.

Patients may experience drowsiness and other potentially serious effects if Risperdal is combined with alcohol and other drugs that slow the central nervous system such as Valium, Percocet, Demerol, or Haldol.

Patients should check with their doctor before taking any new medications.

Special information about pregnancy and breastfeeding

The safety and effectiveness of Risperdal during pregnancy have not been adequately studied. Patients who are pregnant or plan to become pregnant should tell their doctor immediately.

Risperdal makes its way into breast milk, so women taking Risperdal must avoid breastfeeding.

Recommended dosage

SCHIZOPHRENIA

Adults: Doses of Risperdal can be taken once a day, or divided in half and taken twice daily. The usual dose on the first day is 2 milligrams or 2 milliliters of oral solution. On the second day, the dose increases to 4 milligrams or milliliters, and on the third day rises to 6 milligrams or milliliters. Further dosage adjustments can be made at intervals of 1 week. Over the long term, typical daily doses range from 2 to 8 milligrams or milliliters.

BIPOLAR MANIA (SHORT-TERM TREATMENT OF ACUTE EPISODES)

Adults: The recommended starting dose is 2 to 3 milligrams (or milliliters of oral solution) per day, given as a single dose. If needed, the doctor will adjust the dose by 1 milligram at intervals of at least 24 hours. The effective dosage range is 1 to 6 milligrams a day.

DOSAGE ADJUSTMENT

The doctor will prescribe lower doses for patients who are weak, elderly, have liver or kidney disease, or have a high risk for low blood pressure. The usual starting dose is 0.5 milligram (or 0.5 milliliter of oral solution) twice a day. The doctor may switch the patient to a once-a-day dosing schedule after the first 2 to 3 days of treatment.

If needed, each dose may be increased by increments of no more than 0.5 milligram. Increases to dosages above 1.5 milligrams twice a day should generally me made at intervals of at least 1 week.

Patients taking certain medications may also need their Risperdal dose adjusted. The list includes Dilantin, Paxil, phenobarbital, Prozac, Rifadin, and Tegretol.

Overdosage

Any medication taken in excess can have serious consequences. If an overdose of Risperdal is suspected, seek medical attention immediately.

- *Symptoms of Risperdal overdose may include:*
  Drowsiness, low blood pressure, rapid heartbeat, sedation

Risperidone *See Risperdal, page 173*

RITALIN

Methylphenidate hydrochloride
Other brand names: Concerta, Metadate, Methylin

Why is this drug prescribed?

Ritalin and other brands of methylphenidate are mild central nervous system stimulants used in the treatment of attention deficit hyperactivity disorder (ADHD) in children. With the exception of Ritalin LA, Concerta, and Metadate CD, these products are also used in adults to treat narcolepsy.

When given for ADHD, this drug should be an integral part of a total treatment program that includes psychological, educational, and social measures.

Most important fact about this drug

Excessive doses of this drug over a long period of time can produce addiction. It is also possible to develop tolerance to the drug, so that larger doses are needed to produce the original effect. Because of these dangers, dosage should be changed only as directed, and the drug should be withdrawn only under a doctor's supervision.

How should this medication be taken?

The doctor's directions should be followed carefully. It is recommended that methylphenidate be taken 30 to 45 minutes before meals. If the drug interferes with sleep, the child should receive the last dose before 6 p.m. Ritalin-SR, Ritalin LA, Metadate CD, Methylin ER, and Concerta are long-acting forms of the drug, taken less frequently. They should be swallowed whole, never crushed or chewed. (Ritalin LA and Metadate CD may also be given by sprinkling the contents of the capsule on a tablespoon of cool applesauce and administering immediately, followed by a drink of water.)

- *Missed dose...*
  It should be given as soon as remembered. The remaining doses for the day should then be administered at regularly spaced intervals. Doses should never be doubled.

- *Storage instructions...*
  This drug should be kept out of reach of children and stored below 86 degrees Fahrenheit in a tightly closed, light-resistant container. Ritalin-SR should be protected from moisture.

What side effects may occur?

Side effects cannot be predicted. If any develop or change in intensity, patients should inform their doctor as soon as possible.

- *Side effects may include:*
  Dizziness, headache, heart problems, inability to fall or stay asleep, nausea, nervousness

These side effects can usually be controlled by reducing the dosage and omitting the drug in the afternoon or evening.

In children, loss of appetite, abdominal pain, weight loss during long-term therapy, inability to fall or stay asleep, and abnormally fast heartbeat are more common side effects.

Why should this drug not be prescribed?

This drug should not be prescribed for anyone experiencing anxiety, tension, and agitation, since the drug may aggravate these symptoms.

Anyone sensitive or allergic to this drug should not take it.

This medication should not be taken by anyone with the eye condition known as glaucoma, anyone who suffers from tics (repeated, involuntary twitches), or someone with a family history of Tourette's syndrome (severe and multiple tics).

This drug is not intended for use in children whose symptoms may be caused by stress or a psychiatric disorder.

This medication should not be used for the prevention or treatment of normal fatigue, nor should it be used for the treatment of severe depression.

This drug should not be taken during treatment with drugs classified as monoamine oxidase inhibitors, such as the antidepressants Nardil and Parnate, nor for the 2 weeks following discontinuation of these drugs.

Special warnings about this medication

The doctor should do a complete history and evaluation before prescribing this drug. He or she will take into account the severity of the symptoms, as well as the child's age.

This drug should not be given to children under 6 years of age; safety and effectiveness in this age group have not been established.

There is no information regarding the safety and effectiveness of long-term treatment in children. However, suppression of growth has been seen with the long-term use of stimulants, so the child should be monitored carefully while taking this drug.

Blood pressure should be monitored in anyone taking this drug, especially those with high blood pressure.

Some people have had visual disturbances such as blurred vision while being treated with this drug.

The use of this drug by anyone with a seizure disorder is not recommended. Make sure the doctor is aware of any problem in this area. Caution is also advisable for anyone with a history of emotional instability or substance abuse, due to the danger of addiction.

Possible food and drug interactions when taking this medication

If this medication is taken with certain other drugs, the effects of either can be increased, decreased, or altered. Here is an overview of drugs that may cause a problem:

Antiseizure drugs such as phenobarbital, Dilantin, and Mysoline
Antidepressant drugs such as Tofranil, Anafranil, Norpramin, and
 Effexor
Blood thinners such as Coumadin

Clonidine (Catapres-TTS)
Drugs that restore blood pressure, such as EpiPen
Guanethidine
MAO inhibitors (drugs such as the antidepressants Nardil and Parnate)
Phenylbutazone

Special information about pregnancy and breastfeeding

The effects of this drug during pregnancy have not been adequately studied. Patients who are pregnant or plan to become pregnant should inform their doctor immediately.

It is not known if this drug appears in breast milk. If this medication is essential to a patient's health, the doctor may advise her to discontinue nursing until her treatment with this medication is finished.

Recommended dosage

ADULTS

Ritalin and Methylin Tablets
The average dosage is 20 to 30 milligrams a day, divided into 2 or 3 doses, preferably taken 30 to 45 minutes before meals. Some people may need 40 to 60 milligrams daily, others only 10 to 15 milligrams. The doctor will determine the best dose.

Ritalin-SR, Methylin ER, and Metadate ER Tablets
These tablets keep working for 8 hours. They may be used in place of Ritalin tablets if they deliver a comparable dose over an 8-hour period.

CHILDREN

This drug should not be given to children under 6 years of age.

Ritalin and Methylin Tablets
The usual starting dose is 5 milligrams taken twice a day, before breakfast and lunch. The doctor will increase the dose by 5 to 10 milligrams a week, up to a maximum of 60 milligrams a day. If improvement fails to appear after 1 month, the doctor may decide to discontinue the drug.

Ritalin-SR, Methylin ER, and Metadate ER Tablets
These tablets continue working for 8 hours. The doctor will decide if they should be used in place of the regular tablets.

Ritalin LA Capsules
The recommended starting dose is 20 milligrams once daily in the morning. At weekly intervals, the doctor may increase the dose by 10 milligrams, up to a maximum of 60 milligrams once a day.

Concerta Tablets
The recommended starting dose is 18 milligrams once daily in the morning. At weekly intervals, the doctor may increase the dose in 18-milligram steps, up to a maximum of 54 milligrams each morning.

Metadate CD Capsules

The recommended starting dose is 20 milligrams once daily before breakfast. If necessary, the doctor may increase the dose in 20-milligram steps to a maximum of 60 milligrams once a day.

The doctor will periodically discontinue the drug in order to reassess the child's condition. Drug treatment should not, and need not, be indefinite, and usually can be discontinued after puberty.

Overdosage

If an overdose is suspected, seek medical attention immediately.

- *Symptoms of Ritalin overdose may include:*
  Agitation, confusion, convulsions (may be followed by coma), delirium, dryness of mucous membranes, enlarging of the pupil of the eye, exaggerated feeling of elation, extremely elevated body temperature, flushing, hallucinations, headache, high blood pressure, irregular or rapid heartbeat, muscle twitching, sweating, tremors, vomiting

Rivastigmine *See Exelon, page 68*

Sarafem *See Prozac, page 161*

Secobarbital *See Seconal, page 180*

SECONAL

Secobarbital sodium

Why is this drug prescribed?

Seconal is a barbiturate used to treat insomnia on a short-term basis. After 2 weeks, Seconal appears to lose its effectiveness as a sleep aid.

Seconal is also used as a sedative to relieve anxiety before surgery.

Most important fact about this drug

If taken for a long enough time, Seconal can cause physical addiction. Taken in a large enough amount, it can cause death.

How should this medication be taken?

Seconal should be taken only at bedtime, and only in the prescribed amount. It should not be taken with alcohol.

- *Missed dose...*
  Seconal is taken only as needed. It is not necessary to make up for a missed dose. Doses should never be doubled.

- *Storage instructions...*
  Seconal should be stored at room temperature in a tightly closed container.

What side effects may occur?

Side effects cannot be predicted. If any develop or change in intensity, patients should inform their doctor as soon as possible.

- *Side effects may include:*
  Agitation, anemia, anxiety, confusion, constipation, difficulty breathing, disturbed thinking, dizziness, fainting, fever, fluid retention, hallucinations, headache, insomnia, lack of coordination, low blood pressure, nausea, nervousness, nightmares, overactivity, slow heartbeat, skin rash, inflammation and/or peeling, temporary interruptions of breathing, vomiting

Why should this drug not be prescribed?

Seconal should be avoided by anyone who has the rare blood disorder porphyria, liver damage, or a lung disease that makes breathing difficult. The drug cannot be used by people who have ever had an allergic reaction to barbiturates.

Special warnings about this medication

Seconal should not be stopped suddenly, since this may result in severe withdrawal symptoms and even death. To reduce the possibility of withdrawal symptoms, patients should follow the doctor's instructions closely when discontinuing Seconal.

Minor withdrawal symptoms include (in order of occurrence): anxiety, muscle twitching, tremors of hands and fingers, progressive weakness, dizziness, visual problems, nausea, vomiting, insomnia, and light-headedness upon first standing up. Major withdrawal symptoms include convulsions and delirium.

Seconal should be used with caution by people who have had liver disease or have a history of depression or substance abuse.

Patients should inform the doctor if they have any pain. Seconal may hide pain-causing disorders that require treatment.

Children may become excited while taking Seconal. Elderly people may become confused, depressed, or excited.

Seconal may lessen the effectiveness of oral contraceptives. Women who take Seconal may need to consider another type of birth control.

This drug may impair the ability to drive a car or operate potentially dangerous machinery. Patients should not participate in any activities that require full alertness if they are unsure about their ability.

Possible food and drug interactions when taking this medication

If Seconal is taken with certain other drugs, the effects of either could be increased, decreased, or altered. Here is an overview of drugs that may cause a problem:

Antihistamines such as Benadryl

Blood thinners such as Coumadin
Doxycycline (Vibramycin)
Griseofulvin (Gris-PEG)
Drugs classified as MAO inhibitors, such as the antidepressant drugs
  Nardil and Parnate
Oral contraceptives
Phenytoin (Dilantin)
Sedatives such as Halcion
Sodium valproate (Depakote)
Steroids such as prednisone
Tranquilizers such as Xanax and Valium
Valproic acid (Depakene, Depakote)

Extreme drowsiness and other potentially serious effects can result if
Seconal is combined with alcohol and other drugs that slow the activity
of the brain.

Special information about pregnancy and breastfeeding

Studies have shown Seconal to have a potentially harmful effect on the
unborn child. Patients who are pregnant or plan to become pregnant
should inform their doctor immediately. This drug should be used during
pregnancy only if clearly needed and only if potential benefits outweigh
possible risks.

Small amounts of Seconal appear in breast milk. The doctor should be
consulted before breastfeeding is undertaken.

Recommended dosage

ADULTS

For insomnia, the usual dose is 100 milligrams, taken at bedtime. To
relieve anxiety before surgery, the usual dose is 200 to 300 milligrams,
given 1 to 2 hours before the operation.

CHILDREN

Dosages for children, generally given to reduce anxiety before an
operation, are based on the child's weight. The usual dose is 2 to 6 milligrams per 2.2 pounds of body weight, up to a maximum of 100
milligrams.

DOSAGE ADJUSTMENT

Because older people may be more sensitive to Seconal, they should take
lower dosages; this is also true for people whose kidneys are not functioning properly and those who have liver disease.

Overdosage

An overdose of Seconal can be fatal. If an overdose is suspected, seek
medical help immediately.

- *Symptoms of Seconal overdose may be seen within 15 minutes and may include:*
  Blood blisters, difficulty breathing, extreme drowsiness, extreme low body temperature, fluid in the lungs, irregular heartbeat, low blood pressure

---

SERAX
Oxazepam

Why is this drug prescribed?
Serax is used in the treatment of anxiety disorders, including anxiety associated with depression.

This drug seems to be particularly effective for anxiety, tension, agitation, and irritability in older people. It is also prescribed to relieve symptoms of acute alcohol withdrawal.

Serax belongs to a class of drugs known as benzodiazepines.

Most important fact about this drug
Serax can be habit-forming or addicting and can lose its effectiveness over time as patients develop a tolerance for it. They may experience withdrawal symptoms if they stop using the drug abruptly. When discontinuing the drug, the doctor will reduce the dose gradually.

How should this medication be taken?
Serax should be taken exactly as prescribed.

- *Missed dose...*
  If remembered within an hour or so, the dose should be taken immediately. If not remembered until later, the dose should be skipped and the patient should return to the regular schedule. Doses should never be doubled.

- *Storage instructions...*
  Serax should be stored at room temperature in a tightly closed container.

What side effects may occur?
Side effects cannot be predicted. If any develop or change in intensity, patients should inform their doctor as soon as possible. The doctor should periodically reassess the need for this drug.

- *Side effects may include:*
  Dizziness, drowsiness, headache, memory impairment, paradoxical excitement, transient amnesia, vertigo

- *Side effects due to rapid decrease in dose or abrupt withdrawal from Serax:*
  Abdominal and muscle cramps, convulsions, depressed mood, inability to fall or stay asleep, sweating, tremors, vomiting

Why should this drug not be prescribed?

Anyone who is sensitive to or has ever had an allergic reaction to Serax or other tranquilizers such as Valium should not take this medication. Patients should make sure the doctor is aware of any drug reactions they have experienced.

Anxiety or tension related to everyday stress usually does not require treatment with Serax. Patients should discuss their symptoms thoroughly with their doctor.

Serax should not be prescribed for people who are being treated for mental disorders more serious than anxiety.

Special warnings about this medication

Serax may cause patients to become drowsy or less alert. They should not drive, operate dangerous machinery, or participate in any hazardous activity that requires full mental alertness until they know how this drug affects them.

Serax may cause a drop in blood pressure. People with heart problems should check with their doctor before taking this medication.

Possible food and drug interactions when taking this medication

Serax may intensify the effects of alcohol. It may be best to avoid alcohol while taking this medication.

If Serax is taken with certain other drugs, the effects of either could be increased, decreased, or altered. Here is an overview of drugs that may cause a problem:

Antihistamines such as Benadryl
Narcotic painkillers such as Percocet and Demerol
Sedatives such as Seconal and Halcion
Tranquilizers such as Valium and Xanax

Special information about pregnancy and breastfeeding

Patients should not take Serax if they are pregnant or planning to become pregnant. There is an increased risk of birth defects.

Serax may appear in breast milk and could affect a nursing infant. If this drug is essential to the patient's health, the doctor may advise her to stop breastfeeding until her treatment with this medication is finished.

Recommended dosage

ADULTS

Mild to Moderate Anxiety with Tension, Irritability, or Agitation
The usual dose is 10 to 15 milligrams 3 or 4 times per day.

Severe Anxiety, Depression with Anxiety, or Alcohol Withdrawal
The usual dose is 15 to 30 milligrams 3 or 4 times per day.

CHILDREN

Safety and effectiveness have not been established for children under 6 years of age, nor have dosage guidelines been established for children 6 to 12 years old. The doctor will adjust the dosage to fit the child's needs.

OLDER ADULTS

The usual starting dose is 10 milligrams 3 times a day. The doctor may increase the dose to 15 milligrams 3 or 4 times a day, if needed.

Overdosage

An overdose of Serax can be fatal. If an overdose is suspected, seek medical attention immediately.

- *Symptoms of mild Serax overdose may include:*
  Confusion, drowsiness, lethargy

- *Symptoms of more serious overdose may include:*
  Coma, hypnotic state, lack of coordination, limp muscles, low blood pressure

---

SERENTIL
Mesoridazine besylate

Why is this drug prescribed?

Serentil is prescribed to treat schizophrenia. Because of its dangerous side effects, this medication is recommended only after at least two other drugs have failed to provide relief.

Most important fact about this drug?

Serentil may cause dangerous and even fatal cardiac irregularities by prolonging a part of the heartbeat known as the QT interval. The likelihood of such irregularities increases when Serentil is combined with other medications known to prolong the QT interval, such as the heart medications Cordarone, Inderal, Quinaglute, Quinidex, and Rythmol. These drugs must never be taken with Serentil, and it's advisable for patients to check with their doctor before taking any new medications.

Symptoms of a possible heart irregularity include palpitations, dizziness, and fainting. Patients should call the doctor immediately if they experience any of these symptoms.

How should this medication be taken?

It is important to take Serentil exactly as prescribed. Patients taking Serentil in a liquid concentrate form can dilute it with distilled water, orange juice, or grape juice just before swallowing it.

If Serentil is given by injection, the patient should remain lying down for at least one-half hour after the injection.

- *Missed dose . . .*
  Generally, the forgotten dose should be taken as soon as remembered. However, if it is almost time for the next dose, the patient should skip the missed dose and return to the regular schedule. Doses should never be doubled.

- *Storage instructions . . .*
  Serentil should be stored at room temperature in a tightly closed container and protected from light.

What side effects may occur?

Side effects cannot be predicted. If any develop or change in intensity, patients should inform their doctor as soon as possible. Side effects generally occur when high doses are given early in treatment.

- *Side effects may include:*
  Blurred vision, drowsiness, dry mouth, impotence, incontinence, low blood pressure, nausea, rash, rigidity, slowed heartbeat, tremor, vomiting

Why should this drug not be prescribed?

Serentil must be avoided by anyone who has a history of heartbeat irregularities, and all those who are taking other medications that may cause an irregular heartbeat (see "Most important fact about this drug"). Serentil should not be combined with other substances that slow the nervous system, such as alcohol, barbiturates (sleep aids), and narcotics (painkillers), nor should it be given to anyone in a comatose state. People who have shown a hypersensitivity to Serentil cannot take this drug.

Special warnings about this medication

Before using Serentil, patients should tell the doctor if they have a history of heart problems. The doctor will perform tests to check the health of their heart before prescribing this medication.

Serentil can cause tardive dyskinesia, a condition marked by involuntary muscle spasms and twitches in the face and body, including chewing movements, puckering, puffing the cheeks, and sticking out the tongue. This condition may be permanent and appears to be most common among older adults, especially older women.

Drugs such as Serentil can also cause a potentially fatal condition called neuroleptic malignant syndrome. Symptoms include high fever, rigid muscles, irregular pulse or blood pressure, rapid heartbeat, excessive perspiration, and changes in heart rhythm. If a patient develops these symptoms, the doctor should be alerted immediately. Serentil therapy should be discontinued.

This type of drug can cause vision problems. If patients suffer a change in vision while taking this medication, they should inform the doctor.

Serentil may impair the ability to drive a car or operate machinery. Patients should not participate in any activities that require full alertness until they are sure of their reaction to this drug.

Serentil should be used with caution by anyone who has ever had breast cancer. The drug stimulates production of a hormone that promotes the growth of certain types of tumors.

Serentil may cause a condition called agranulocytosis, a dangerous drop in the number of certain kinds of white blood cells. Symptoms include fever, lethargy, sore throat, and weakness.

Possible food and drug interactions when taking this medication

Remember that Serentil must never be combined with alcohol, barbiturates, or narcotics. It's also best to avoid combining it with other drugs prescribed for schizophrenia, depression, or anxiety, or with the spasm-quelling drug atropine (Donnatal). Be careful, too, to avoid exposure to phosphorus insecticides.

Special information about pregnancy and breastfeeding

The effects of Serentil during pregnancy have not been adequately studied. Patients who are pregnant or plan to become pregnant should tell the doctor immediately. Pregnant women should use Serentil only if clearly needed.

It is not known whether Serentil appears in breast milk. Patients should talk with their doctor before deciding to breastfeed.

Recommended dosage

The doctor will tailor the dose of Serentil to the patient's needs. Once symptoms improve, the doctor will gradually reduce the dosage to the lowest effective dose.

ADULTS

Tablets and Oral Soulution

The usual starting dose of Serentil tablets or oral solution is 50 milligrams taken 3 times daily. Over the long term, the usual daily dose ranges from 100 to 400 milligrams per day.

CHILDREN

The safety and effectiveness of Serentil in children have not been established.

Overdosage

An overdose of Serentil can be fatal. If an overdose is suspected, seek medical attention immediately.

- *Symptoms of Serentil overdose may include:*
  Absence of reflexes, agitation, blurred vision, coma, confusion, convulsions, difficulty breathing, disorientation, drowsiness, dry mouth,

enlarged pupils, heartbeat irregularities, heart failure or arrest, high temperature, nasal congestion, overactive reflexes, rigid muscles, stupor, swollen throat, throat spasms, vomiting

SEROQUEL
Quetiapine fumarate

Why is this drug prescribed?
Seroquel is prescribed for the treatment of schizophrenia and for the short-term treatment of mania associated with bipolar disorder. It is the first in a new class of antipsychotic medications. Researchers believe that it works by diminishing the action of dopamine and serotonin, two of the brain's chief chemical messengers.

Most important fact about this drug
Seroquel may cause tardive dyskinesia, a condition characterized by uncontrollable muscle spasms and twitches in the face and body. This problem can be permanent, and appears to be most common among older adults, especially women.

How should this medication be taken?
Dosage is increased gradually until the drug takes effect. Patients who stop taking Seroquel for more than 1 week will need to build up to their ideal dosage once again.

● *Missed dose...*
Generally, a missed dose should be taken as soon as remembered. However, if it is almost time for the next dose, patients should skip the one they missed and go back to their regular schedule. Doses should never be doubled.

● *Storage instructions...*
Seroquel should be stored at room temperature.

What side effects may occur?
Side effects cannot be predicted. If any develop or change in intensity, patients should inform their doctor as soon as possible.

● *Side effects may include:*
Constipation, dizziness, dry mouth, headache, indigestion, low blood pressure upon standing, rapid or irregular heartbeat, sleepiness

Why should this drug not be prescribed?
If Seroquel causes an allergic reaction, the patient will not be able to use this drug.

Special warnings about this medication

Patients who develop muscle stiffness, confusion, irregular or rapid heartbeat, excessive sweating, and high fever should call their doctor immediately. These are signs of neuroleptic malignant syndrome, a serious—and potentially fatal—reaction to the drug. Patients should be especially wary if they have a history of heart attack, heart disease, heart failure, circulation problems, or irregular heartbeat.

Particularly during the first few days of therapy, Seroquel can cause low blood pressure, with accompanying dizziness, fainting, and rapid heartbeat. To minimize these effects, the doctor will increase the dose gradually. People who are prone to low blood pressure, take blood pressure medication, or become dehydrated should use Seroquel with caution.

Seroquel also tends to cause drowsiness, especially at the start of therapy, and can impair judgment, thinking, and motor skills. Until patients are certain of the drug's effect, they need to use caution when operating machinery or driving a car.

Certain antipsychotic drugs, including Seroquel, are associated with an increased risk of developing high blood sugar, which on rare occasions has led to coma or death. Patients should see their doctor right away if they develop signs of high blood sugar, including dry mouth, thirst, increased urination, and tiredness. Patients who have diabetes or have a high risk of developing it should see their doctor regularly for blood sugar testing.

Patients at high risk of suicide attempts should be prescribed the lowest dose possible to reduce the risk of intentional overdose.

Seroquel should be used cautiously in older patients and those with Alzheimer's disease. Antipsychotic drug treatment has been associated with swallowing and breathing problems (aspiration).

Animal studies suggest that Seroquel may increase the risk of breast cancer, although human studies have not confirmed such a risk. Advise patients with a history of breast cancer to see their doctor regularly for checkups.

Patients should report any vision problems to the doctor. There is a chance that Seroquel may cause cataracts, and some people may be asked to see an eye doctor when they start Seroquel therapy, and every 6 months thereafter.

Seroquel poses a very slight risk of seizures, especially in people who are over 65 or have epilepsy or Alzheimer's disease. The drug can also suppress an underactive thyroid, and generally causes a minor increase in cholesterol levels. There is also a remote chance that it will trigger a prolonged and painful erection.

Other antipsychotic medications have been known to interfere with the body's temperature-regulating mechanism, causing patients to overheat. Although this problem has not occurred with Seroquel, caution is still advisable. Patients should avoid exposure to extreme heat, strenuous exercise, and dehydration.

Seroquel is prescribed for the short-term treatment of rapid-onset bipolar mania; it is not approved for preventing future episodes. The effectiveness of the drug for treating mania for more than 3 weeks has not been studied.

The safety and effectiveness of Seroquel have not been studied in children.

Possible food and drug interactions when taking this medication

Seroquel increases the effects of alcohol. Patients should avoid alcoholic beverages while on Seroquel therapy.

If Seroquel is taken with certain other drugs, the effects of either could be increased, decreased, or altered. Here is an overview of drugs that may cause a problem:

Barbiturates such as phenobarbital
Carbamazepine (Tegretol)
Cimetidine (Tagamet)
Erythromycin (Eryc, Ery-Tab)
Fluconazole (Diflucan)
Itraconazole (Sporanox)
Ketoconazole (Nizoral)
Levodopa (Sinemet)
Lorazepam (Ativan)
Phenytoin (Dilantin)
Rifampin (Rifadin, Rifamate, Rimactane)
Steroid medications such as hydrocortisone and prednisone
Thioridazine (Mellaril)

Special information about pregnancy and breastfeeding

The possibility of harm to a developing baby has not been ruled out. Women should take Seroquel during pregnancy only if the benefits outweigh this potential risk. They should notify their doctor as soon as they become pregnant or decide to become pregnant.

It is not known whether Seroquel appears in breast milk, and breastfeeding is not recommended.

Recommended dosage

SCHIZOPHRENIA

Adults: The usual dosage range is 300 to 400 milligrams a day, divided into two or three smaller doses. Doses as low as 150 milligrams a day sometimes prove effective, and the dose rarely exceeds 750 milligrams per day. Doses above 800 milligrams per day have not been tested for safety.

The dose is gradually increased over 4 days until the most effective dose is reached.

Day 1: Patients take 25 milligrams twice a day.
Days 2, 3, and 4: Each daily dose is increased by 25 to 50 milligrams, taken either two or three times a day.
Day 5 and up: If needed, the doctor may increase each dose by 25 to 50 milligrams every 2 or more days.

BIPOLAR MANIA (SHORT-TERM TREATMENT OF ACUTE EPISODES)

Adults: The usual dosage range is 400 to 800 milligrams a day. Doses above 800 milligrams a day have not been tested for safety. The dosage will be gradually increased over 4 to 6 days until the most effective dose is reached.

Day 1: Patients take 50 milligrams twice a day.
Day 2: The dose is increased to 100 milligrams twice a day.
Day 3: The dose is increased to 150 milligrams twice a day.
Day 4: The dose is increased to 200 milligrams twice a day.
Days 5 and 6: If needed, the doctor may increase each dose by no more than 200-milligram increments to a total daily dose of 800 milligrams.

DOSAGE ADJUSTMENT

Patients with liver problems will be started at 25 milligrams a day. The doctor will increase the dose as needed in increments of 25 to 50 milligrams a day based on the patient's tolerability.

The dosage may also need to be lowered for older adults, those prone to low blood pressure reactions, and the debilitated. Patients taking certain drugs—including Dilantin, Tegretol, and phenobarbital—may also need their dose adjusted.

Overdosage

Any medication taken in excess can have serious consequences. If an overdose is suspected, seek medical help immediately.

* *Symptoms of Seroquel overdose may include:*
 Dizziness, drowsiness, fainting, rapid heartbeat

Sertraline *See Zoloft, page 237*

Serzone *See Nefazodone, page 123*

SINEQUAN

Doxepin hydrochloride

Why is this drug prescribed?

Sinequan is used in the treatment of depression and anxiety. It helps relieve tension, improve sleep, elevate mood, increase energy, and generally ease feelings of fear, guilt, apprehension, and worry. It is effective in treating people whose depression and/or anxiety is psychological, associated with alcoholism, or a result of another disease (cancer, for example). It is also prescribed for major depression and bipolar disorder. It is in the family of drugs called tricyclic antidepressants.

Most important fact about this drug

Serious, sometimes fatal, reactions have occurred when Sinequan is used in combination with drugs known as MAO inhibitors, including the antidepressants Nardil and Parnate. Any drug of this type should be discontinued at least 2 weeks prior to starting treatment with Sinequan, and the patient should be carefully monitored by the doctor.

Patients should consult their doctor before combining Sinequan with any other prescription or nonprescription drugs.

How should this medication be taken?

This medication must be taken exactly as prescribed. It may take several weeks for its beneficial effects to appear.

- *Missed dose...*
  Patients taking several doses a day should take the missed dose as soon as they remember, then take any remaining doses for that day at evenly spaced intervals. If it is almost time for the next dose, they should skip the one they missed and go back to their regular schedule.

  Patients who take a single dose at bedtime and do not remember until the next morning should skip the dose. Doses should never be doubled.

- *Storage instructions...*
  Sinequan may be stored at room temperature.

What side effects may occur?

Side effects cannot be predicted. If any develop or change in intensity, patients should inform their doctor as soon as possible.

- *Side effects may include:*
  Blurred vision, constipation, dizziness, drowsiness, dry mouth, itchy or scaly skin (pruritus), light sensitivity, low blood pressure, nausea, rapid or irregular heartbeat, rash, trouble urinating, water retention

Why should this drug not be prescribed?

Anyone who is sensitive to or has ever had an allergic reaction to Sinequan or similar antidepressants should not take this medication. Sinequan should also be avoided by patients with the eye condition known as glaucoma and by those who have difficulty urinating.

Special warnings about this medication

Sinequan may cause the patient to become drowsy or less alert. Driving, operating dangerous machinery, or participating in any hazardous activity that requires full mental alertness is not recommended.

In a medical emergency, and before surgery or dental treatment, the doctor or dentist should be made aware that the patient is taking Sinequan.

Possible food and drug interactions when taking this medication

Alcohol increases the danger in a Sinequan overdose. Patients should not drink alcohol while taking this medication.

Sinequan should never be combined with drugs known as MAO inhibitors. Medications in this category include the antidepressants Nardil and Parnate.

Patients switching from Prozac should wait at least 5 weeks after their last dose of Prozac before starting Sinequan.

If Sinequan is taken with certain other drugs, the effects of either could be increased, decreased, or altered. Here is an overview of drugs that may cause a problem:

Antidepressants that boost serotonin, such as Celexa, Lexapro, Prozac, Zoloft, and Paxil
Other antidepressants such as Elavil and nefazodone
Antipsychotic medications such as chlorpromazine, Mellaril, and prochlorperazine
Carbamazepine (Tegretol)
Cimetidine (Tagamet)
Clonidine (Catapres)
Flecainide (Tambocor)
Guanethidine
Propafenone (Rythmol)
Quinidine (Quinidex)
Tolazamide (Tolinase)

Special information about pregnancy and breastfeeding

The effects of Sinequan during pregnancy have not been adequately studied. Women who are pregnant or are planning to become pregnant should inform their doctor immediately.

Sinequan may appear in breast milk and could affect a nursing infant. If this medication is essential to the patient's health, the doctor may advise her to discontinue breastfeeding until treatment is finished.

Recommended dosage

ADULTS

The starting dose for mild to moderate illness is usually 75 milligrams per day. This dose can be increased or decreased by the doctor according to individual need. The usual ideal dose ranges from 75 milligrams per day to 150 milligrams per day, although it can be as low as 25 to 50 milligrams per day. The total daily dose can be given once a day or divided into smaller doses. For people taking this drug once a day, the recommended dose is 150 milligrams at bedtime.

The 150-milligram capsule strength is intended for long-term therapy only and is not recommended as a starting dose.

For more severe illness, gradually increased doses of up to 300 milligrams may be required as determined by the doctor.

CHILDREN

Safety and effectiveness have not been established for use in children under 12 years of age.

OLDER ADULTS

Due to a greater risk of drowsiness and confusion, older people are usually started on a low dose.

Overdosage

An overdose of Sinequan can be fatal. The following symptoms signal the need for immediate medical attention.

- *Symptoms of Sinequan overdose may include:*
  Agitation, coma, confusion, convulsions, dilated pupils, disturbed concentration, drowsiness, hallucinations, high or low body temperature, irregular heartbeat, overactive reflexes, rigid muscles, severely low blood pressure, stupor, vomiting

---

SONATA

Zaleplon

Why is this drug prescribed?

Sonata is prescribed for people who have trouble falling asleep at bedtime. Because it has a short duration of action, it doesn't help those who suffer from frequent awakenings during the night or those who wake too early in the morning. It is intended only for short-term use (7 to 10 days).

Most important fact about this drug

Problems with sleep are usually temporary and require only short-term treatment with medication. Patients should call their doctor immediately if it seems the medication is making the problem worse, or if they notice any unusual changes in their thinking or behavior, such as hallucinations, amnesia, agitation, or a lack of inhibition. The emergence of new symptoms could be a sign of an undiagnosed medical or psychiatric condition.

How should this medication be taken?

Sonata is very fast-acting and should be taken only at bedtime.

- *Missed dose...*
  Sonata should be taken only when the patient is ready to sleep. The dose should never be doubled.

- *Storage instructions...*
  Sonata should be stored at room temperature in a light-resistant container.

What side effects may occur?

Side effects cannot be predicted. If any develop or change in intensity, patients should inform their doctor as soon as possible.

- *Side effects may include:*
  Abdominal pain, amnesia, dizziness, eye pain, headache, menstrual problems, nausea, sleepiness, weakness

A variety of other symptoms have been reported on very rare occasions. If Sonata is suspected of causing any sort of problem, it would be wise to check with the doctor.

Why should this drug not be prescribed?

Sonata is not recommended for people with severe liver disease and is best avoided during pregnancy.

Sonata contains FD&C Yellow No. 5 (tartrazine). Patients who are allergic to this dye, or any other ingredient in Sonata, should not take this drug. Tartrazine allergy may be more likely in people with aspirin sensitivity.

Special warnings about this medication

Sonata should not be used unless the patient plans to be in bed for at least four hours after taking it. Those who need to be alert and active in less than four hours may find that their performance is impaired. No one should attempt to drive a car or operate other dangerous machinery right after taking Sonata.

Sonata should be used only for temporary relief of insomnia; sleep medicines tend to lose their effect when taken for more than a few weeks. Remember, too, that taking sleeping pills for extended periods or in high doses can lead to physical dependence and the danger of a withdrawal reaction when the drug is abruptly stopped. Special caution is warranted for patients who have had addiction problems with alcohol or other drugs.

Severe allergic reactions—sometimes life-threatening—have been reported. Patients who develop any of the following symptoms should seek medical attention immediately: agitation, difficulty breathing, sudden drop in blood pressure, fainting, tingling sensations, itchy and flushed skin, hives, or swelling.

The safety and effectiveness of Sonata have not been established in children.

Possible food and drug interactions when taking this medication

Patients should avoid alcoholic beverages when taking Sonata; the drug increases alcohol's effect. They should also forgo high-fat meals immediately before taking Sonata; they tend to slow or reduce the drug's effect.

If Sonata is used with certain other drugs, the effects of either could be increased, decreased, or altered. Here is an overview of drugs that may cause a problem:

Carbamazepine (Tegretol)
Cimetidine (Tagamet)
Diphenhydramine (Benadryl)
Imipramine (Tofranil)
Phenobarbital
Rifampin (Rifadin)
Thioridazine (Mellaril)

Special information about pregnancy and breastfeeding

Sonata can affect a developing baby, especially during the last weeks before delivery, and is therefore not recommended for use during pregnancy. This drug also appears in breast milk and should not be used by nursing mothers.

Recommended dosage

ADULTS

The usual dose is 10 milligrams taken once daily at bedtime. The doctor may adjust the dose according to individual need, especially for those who are in a weakened condition or have a low body weight. A dose of 5 milligrams is recommended if the patient has liver disease or uses the drug cimetidine.

OLDER ADULTS

The usual dose for older adults is 5 milligrams, as they may be more sensitive to the effects of Sonata.

Overdosage

An overdose of drugs such as Sonata can be fatal. If an overdose is suspected, seek medical attention immediately.

• *Symptoms of Sonata overdose may include:*
Drowsiness, mental confusion, grogginess, lack of coordination, flaccid muscles, labored breathing, coma

Stelazine *See Trifluoperazine hydrochloride, page 217*

STRATTERA
Atomoxetine hydrochloride

Why is this drug prescribed?

Strattera is used in the treatment of attention deficit hyperactivity disorder (ADHD). Medications such as Strattera should always be part of a comprehensive treatment program that includes psychological, educational, and social measures designed to remedy the problem.

Strattera is the first ADHD medication to avoid classification as a controlled substance (a drug with potential for abuse). It is thought to work by boosting levels of norepinephrine, one of the brain chemicals responsible for regulating activity. It is prescribed for children and adults.

Most important fact about this drug

During clinical trials, researchers found that Strattera slowed children's average rate of growth. It's not known whether final adult height and weight are affected, but the manufacturer recommends interrupting use of the drug if a child is not growing or gaining weight at the expected rate.

How should this medication be taken?

Strattera should be taken exactly as prescribed; higher-than-recommended doses provide no additional benefit. Strattera may be taken with or without food.

• *Missed dose...*
The forgotten dose should be taken as soon as remembered. However, patients should take no more than the prescribed daily total during any 24-hour period.

• *Storage instructions...*
Store at room temperature.

What side effects may occur?

Side effects cannot be anticipated. If any develop or change in intensity, patients should inform their doctor as soon as possible.

- *Side effects in children may include:*
  Cough, decreased appetite, dizziness, headache, irritability, sleepiness, stomach pain, vomiting

- *Side effects in adults may include:*
  Constipation, decreased appetite, dry mouth, ejaculation problems, headache, insomnia, menstrual problems, nausea

Why should this drug not be prescribed?

Strattera must not be taken within 2 weeks of taking any drug classified as an MAO inhibitor, such as the antidepressants Nardil and Parnate. The combination can cause severe—even fatal—reactions, including symptoms such as high fever, rigid muscles, rapid changes in heart rate, delirium, and coma.

Patients should also avoid Strattera if they have narrow angle glaucoma (high pressure in the eye), or if the drug causes an allergic reaction.

Special warnings about this medication

Strattera can speed up the heart and boost blood pressure. It should be used with caution if the patient has high blood pressure, a rapid heart rate, heart disease, or any other circulation problem.

On the other hand, Strattera can also cause an attack of low blood pressure when the patient first stands up. Caution is warranted when the patient has a condition, such as severe dehydration, that can cause low blood pressure.

Because Strattera sometimes causes sluggishness, patients should be careful when operating machinery or driving until they know how the drug affects them.

Possible food and drug interactions when taking this medication

Remember that Strattera must never be combined with MAO inhibitors (see "Why should this drug not be prescribed?"). Also, the doctor will probably prescribe a lower dose of Strattera if the patient is taking one of the following:

Fluoxetine (Prozac)
Paroxetine (Paxil)
Quinidine (Quinidex)

Due to the possibility of boosted effects, patients should check with the doctor before combining Strattera with the following:

Proventil and similar asthma medications
Drugs that raise blood pressure, such as the phenylephrine in some
  over-the-counter cold medications

If patients are unsure about a particular medication—whether prescription or over-the-counter—they should make a point of asking their doctor.

Special information about pregnancy and breastfeeding

Strattera has not been studied in pregnant women. If a woman is pregnant or plans to become pregnant, she should notify her doctor immediately. Strattera should not be taken during pregnancy unless its benefits justify the potential risk to the baby.

It is not known whether Strattera makes its way into breast milk. Caution is warranted if the patient plans to nurse.

Recommended dosage

The daily dose of Strattera can be taken as a single dose in the morning, or divided into two equal doses taken in the morning and late afternoon or early evening.

CHILDREN

For children and teenagers weighing up to 154 pounds, the usual starting dosage is 0.5 milligram per 2.2 pounds of body weight per day. After at least 3 days, the doctor may increase the daily total to a recommended level of 1.2 milligrams per 2.2 pounds. Daily doses should never exceed 1.4 milligrams per 2.2 pounds or a total of 100 milligrams, whichever is less.

Strattera has not been tested in children under 6 years of age.

ADULTS

For adults and teenagers weighing over 154 pounds, the usual starting dosage is 40 milligrams per day. After at least 3 days, the doctor may increase the daily total to a recommended level of 80 milligrams. After another 2 to 4 weeks, dosage may be increased to a maximum of 100 milligrams daily.

DOSAGE ADJUSTMENT

If the patient has liver problems, the dosage will be reduced.

Overdosage

There is limited information on Strattera overdose. However, any medication taken in excess can have serious consequences. If an overdose is suspected, seek emergency treatment immediately.

- *Symptoms of a Strattera overdose may include:*
  Abnormal behavior, agitation, dilated pupils, dry mouth, hyperactivity, rapid or irregular heartbeat, sleepiness, stomach and intestinal problems

SURMONTIL
Trimipramine maleate

Why is this drug prescribed?

Surmontil is used to treat depression. It is a member of the family of drugs known as tricyclic antidepressants.

Most important fact about this drug

Serious, sometimes fatal, reactions have been known to occur when drugs such as Surmontil are taken with drugs classified as MAO inhibitors. Drugs in this category include the antidepressants Nardil and Parnate. Surmontil must not be used within 2 weeks of taking one of these drugs.

How should this medication be taken?

Surmontil may be taken in 1 dose at bedtime. Alternatively, the total daily dosage may be divided into smaller amounts taken during the day. The single bedtime dose is preferred for people on long-term therapy with Surmontil.

It is important to take Surmontil exactly as prescribed, even if the drug seems to have no effect. It may take up to 4 weeks for its benefits to appear.

Surmontil can make the mouth dry. Sucking hard candy or chewing gum can help this problem.

• *Missed dose...*
Generally, a missed dose should be taken as soon as remembered. However, if it is almost time for the next dose, patients should skip the one they missed and go back to their regular schedule. Doses should never be doubled.

Patients who take Surmontil once a day at bedtime and miss a dose should not take it in the morning. It could cause disturbing side effects during the day.

• *Storage instructions...*
Surmontil should be stored at room temperature in a tightly closed container. Capsules in blister strips should be protected from moisture.

What side effects may occur?

Side effects cannot be predicted. If any develop or change in intensity, patients should inform their doctor as soon as possible.

• *Side effects may include:*
Allergic reactions, blood disorders, blurred vision, breast development in men, confusion, dry mouth, heartbeat irregularities, high blood pressure, insomnia, lack of coordination, low blood pressure, stomach and intestinal problems, urination problems

Why should this drug not be prescribed?

Surmontil should not be used by anyone recovering from a recent heart attack. It should not be taken by people who are sensitive to it or have ever had an allergic reaction to it or to similar drugs such as Tofranil.

Special warnings about this medication

Surmontil should be used with caution by patients who have a seizure disorder, the eye condition known as glaucoma, heart disease, or a liver disorder. Caution is also warranted if they have thyroid disease or are taking thyroid medication. People who have had problems urinating should also be careful about taking Surmontil.

Nausea, headache, and a general feeling of illness may result if Surmontil is stopped suddenly. This does not signify addiction, but the doctor's instructions should be followed closely when discontinuing the drug.

This drug may impair the ability to drive a car or operate potentially dangerous machinery. Patients should not participate in any activities that require full alertness if they are unsure of the drug's effect.

Possible food and drug interactions when taking this medication

People who are taking antidepressants known as MAO inhibitors (Parnate and Nardil) should not take Surmontil. They need to wait 2 weeks after stopping an MAO inhibitor before starting Surmontil.

If Surmontil is taken with certain other drugs, the effects of either could be increased, decreased, or altered. Here is an overview of drugs that may cause a problem:

Antidepressants such as Desyrel and Wellbutrin
Antidepressants that act on serotonin, such as Prozac, Paxil, and Zoloft
Antipsychotic medications such as chlorpromazine and Mellaril
Cimetidine (Tagamet)
Drugs for heartbeat irregularities, such as Rythmol and Tambocor
Drugs that quell spasms, such as Donnatal and Cogentin
Guanethidine
Local anesthetics containing epinephrine
Local decongestants such as Dristan Nasal Spray
Quinidine (Quinidex)
Stimulants such as Proventil, Sudafed, and EpiPen
Thyroid medications such as Synthroid

Extreme drowsiness and other potentially serious effects may result if the patient drinks alcoholic beverages while taking Surmontil.

Special information about pregnancy and breastfeeding

The effects of Surmontil in pregnancy have not been adequately studied. Pregnant women should use Surmontil only when the potential benefits clearly outweigh the potential risks.

There is no information on whether Surmontil appears in breast milk. The doctor may tell the patient to stop nursing until her treatment is finished.

Recommended dosage

ADULTS

The usual starting dose is 75 milligrams per day, divided into equal smaller doses. The doctor may gradually increase the dose to 150 milligrams per day, divided into smaller doses. Doses over 200 milligrams a day are not recommended. Doses in long-term therapy may range from 50 to 150 milligrams daily. This total daily dosage at bedtime can be taken at bedtime or spread out through the day.

CHILDREN

Safety and effectiveness of Surmontil in children have not been established.

OLDER ADULTS AND ADOLESCENTS

Dosages usually start at 50 milligrams per day. The doctor may increase the dose to 100 milligrams a day, if needed.

Overdosage

An overdose of Surmontil can be fatal. If an overdose is suspected, seek medical help immediately.

* *Symptoms of Surmontil overdose may include:*
  Agitation, coma, confusion, convulsions, dilated pupils, disturbed concentration, drowsiness, hallucinations, high fever, irregular heart rate, low body temperature, muscle rigidity, overactive reflexes, severely low blood pressure, stupor, vomiting

Also possible are any of the symptoms listed under "What side effects may occur?"

SYMBYAX
Olanzapine and Fluoxetine hydrochloride

Why is this drug prescribed?

Symbyax is used to treat depressive episodes associated with bipolar disorder. The drug is a combination of the active ingredients in Prozac (fluoxetine), used to treat depression and other conditions; and Zyprexa (olanzapine), used to treat the manic phase of bipolar disorder as well as other conditions.

Most important fact about this drug

Serious, sometimes fatal, reactions have been known to occur when fluoxetine, one of the ingredients in Symbyax, is taken with other antidepressant drugs called MAO inhibitors, including Nardil and Parnate. Such reactions have also occurred when fluoxetine is discontinued and an MAO inhibitor is started. Patients should never take Symbyax with an MAO inhibitor, or within 14 days of discontinuing therapy with an MAO inhibitor. A minimum of 5 weeks should be allowed between stopping Symbyax and starting an MAO inhibitor. Caution is especially warranted if patients have been taking Symbyax in high doses or for a long time.

In addition, Symbyax should never be combined with thioridazine (Mellaril) due to the risk of life-threatening drug interactions; and a minimum of 5 weeks should be allowed between stopping Symbyax and starting Mellaril.

How should this medication be taken?

Symbyax should be taken exactly as prescribed. It is usually taken once a day in the evening. To be effective, Symbyax must be taken every day, even if the patient starts to feel better. Patients should never change the dosage or stop taking the drug without consulting their doctor.

- *Missed dose...*
  Patients should take the forgotten dose as soon as they remember. However, if it is almost time for their next dose, patients should skip the one they missed and return to their regular schedule. They should never take two doses at once.

- *Storage instructions...*
  Symbyax should be stored at room temperature in a tightly closed container. The drug should also be protected from moisture.

What side effects may occur?

Side effects cannot be predicted. If any develop or change in intensity, patients should inform their doctor as soon as possible.

- *Side effects may include:*
  Abnormal thinking, increased appetite, lack of coordination, sleepiness, sore throat, swelling (especially in the arms and legs), tremor, weight gain

Why should this drug not be prescribed?

Symbyax should be avoided by anyone who has ever had an allergic reaction to it or to the drugs Prozac or Zyprexa. Patients need to alert their doctor about any drug reaction they have experienced.

Remember, too, that Symbyax should never be combined with an MAO inhibitor or Mellaril (see "Most important fact about this drug").

Special warnings about this medication

Certain antipsychotic drugs—including olanzapine, one of the ingredients in Symbyax—are associated with an increased risk of developing high blood sugar, which on rare occasions has led to coma or death. Patients should see their doctor right away if they develop signs of high blood sugar, including dry mouth, thirst, increased urination, and tiredness. Patients who have diabetes or have a high risk of developing it should see their doctor regularly for blood sugar testing.

Symbyax should be used with caution in patients who have a history of heart disease, heart rhythm problems, stroke, seizures, or liver problems. Caution is also advised in patients who are at risk of developing low blood pressure or dehydration, and in those taking drugs to lower their blood pressure.

Patients with bipolar disorder are at a high risk of suicide. The FDA has issued a public health advisory to alert healthcare professionals about reports of worsening depression and suicidality (both suicidal thoughts and suicide attempts) during antidepressant drug therapy in adults and pediatric patients with major depressive disorder. Healthcare professionals and family members are advised to watch for signs of worsening depression and to be aware of the suicide statement present in all antidepressant labeling. The safety and effectiveness of Symbyax have not been studied in children.

Serotonin-boosting antidepressants such as fluoxetine, one of the ingredients in Symbyax, could potentially cause stomach bleeding. This is especially likely in older adults or those taking nonsteroidal anti-inflammatory drugs (NSAIDs) such as aspirin, ibuprofen (Advil, Motrin), naproxen (Aleve), and ketoprofen (Orudis KT). Advise patients to consult their doctor before combining Symbyax with NSAIDs or blood-thinning medications.

Symbyax has not been studied in people with certain diseases. However, the individual ingredients in this drug have been known to cause problems in people with specific illnesses. Patients should tell the doctor if they have a history of the following: heart attack, heart disease, an enlarged prostate, high or low blood pressure, abnormal bleeding, narrow-angle glaucoma, paralysis of the intestines, trouble swallowing, Alzheimer's disease, or dementia (in patients older than 65).

Animal studies suggest that olanzapine, one of the ingredients in Symbyax, may increase the risk of breast cancer, although human studies have not confirmed such a risk. Advise patients with a history of breast cancer to see their doctor regularly for checkups.

Symbyax can cause dizziness and even fainting when getting up from sitting or lying down (orthostatic hypotension). Patients who experience this should notify the doctor.

The ingredients in this drug could cause an allergic reaction. Patients should alert the doctor immediately if they develop a skin rash or hives.

Olanzapine and other antipsychotic drugs sometimes cause a condition called neuroleptic malignant syndrome. Symptoms include high fever, muscle rigidity, irregular pulse or blood pressure, rapid heartbeat, excessive perspiration, and changes in heart rhythm. If these symptoms appear, patients should alert the doctor immediately. The doctor will need to stop therapy with Symbyax while the condition is being treated.

Symbyax could increase the risk of developing tardive dyskinesia, a condition marked by slow, rhythmic, involuntary movements. This problem is more likely to surface in older adults, especially women. If it does, treatment with Symbyax will usually be stopped.

Symbyax could trigger a manic episode. The patient should be watched closely for symptoms of mania.

Medications such as Symbyax can interfere with regulation of body temperature. Patients should avoid getting overheated or becoming dehydrated while taking Symbyax. They should avoid extreme heat and drink plenty of fluids.

Symbyax sometimes causes drowsiness and can impair judgment, thinking, and motor skills. Patients should use caution while driving and shouldn't operate dangerous machinery until they know how the drug affects them.

Prolonged seizures have occurred in people receiving electroconvulsive therapy (ECT) while taking fluoxetine, one of the ingredients in Symbyax. To date, there are no clinical studies establishing the benefit of combined treatment with fluoxetine and ECT.

Possible food and drug interactions when taking this medication

Patients should avoid alcohol while taking Symbyax. The combination can cause a sudden drop in blood pressure.

Remember that Symbyax should never be combined with MAO inhibitors or Mellaril (see "Most important fact about this drug").

Symbyax should be used cautiously, if at all, with Zyprexa, Zyprexa Zydis, Prozac, Prozac Weekly, or Sarafem. Symbyax contains the same active ingredients as these medications.

If Symbyax is taken with certain other drugs, the effects of either can be increased, decreased, or altered. Here is an overview of drugs that may cause a problem:

Antidepressants known as tricyclics, such as Elavil
Blood pressure medications
Carbamazepine (Tegretol)
Clozapine (Clozaril)
Diazepam (Valium)
Dopamine-boosting drugs, such as the Parkinson's medications
  Mirapex, Parlodel, Permax, and Requip
Fluvoxamine
Haloperidol (Haldol)
Levodopa (Larodopa)
Lithium (Eskalith, Lithobid)

Nonsteroidal anti-inflammatory drugs (NSAIDs) such as aspirin, ibupro-
fen (Advil, Motrin), naproxen (Aleve), and ketoprofen (Orudis KT)
Phenytoin (Dilantin)
Pimozide (Orap)
Sumatriptan (Imitrex)
Tryptophan
Warfarin (Coumadin)

Patients should let the doctor know if they smoke cigarettes, since this
could affect how the body processes Symbyax.

Special information about pregnancy and breastfeeding
Patients who are pregnant or planning to become pregnant should notify
their doctor immediately. Symbyax should be used during pregnancy only
if absolutely necessary.

Symbyax appears in breast milk and is considered potentially harmful
to a nursing infant. The patient will need to discuss with her doctor whether
she should avoid breastfeeding or discontinue therapy with Symbyax.

Recommended dosage

ADULTS

The usual starting dose is one capsule containing 6 milligrams of olanzapine and 25 milligrams of fluoxetine, taken once a day in the evening. If
needed, the doctor may gradually increase the dose. The usual dosage
range is 6 to 12 milligrams of olanzapine and 25 to 50 milligrams of
fluoxetine.

CHILDREN

The safety and effectiveness of Symbyax have not been studied in children.

DOSAGE ADJUSTMENT

The doctor may adjust the dosage if patients have liver problems, a high
risk of low blood pressure, or a combination of factors that may slow the
body's processing of Symbyax (female, older age, nonsmoker).

Overdosage
Overdose with fluoxetine, one of the ingredients in Symbyax, can be
fatal. There have been reports of patients dying after overdosing on fluoxetine and olanzapine taken as separate drugs at the same time. If an
overdose is suspected, seek emergency treatment immediately.

- *Symptoms of Symbyax overdose may include:*
  Aggressive behavior, agitation, coma, confusion, convulsions, heart problems, irregular or fast heartbeat, loss of consciousness, problems with
  muscle coordination, problems with speech, sleepiness, sluggishness

Tacrine *See Cognex, page 36*

Temazepam *See Restoril, page 170*

Thioridazine *See Mellaril, page 107*

Thiothixene *See Navane, page 121*

Thorazine *See Chlorpromazine, page 27*

TOFRANIL
Imipramine hydrochloride
Other brand name: Tofranil-PM

Why is this drug prescribed?
Tofranil is used to treat major depression. It is a member of the family of drugs called tricyclic antidepressants.

Tofranil is also used on a short term basis, along with behavioral therapies, to treat bed-wetting in children aged 6 and older. Its effectiveness may decrease with longer use.

Off-label uses of Tofranil include bulimia, attention deficit disorder in children, obsessive-compulsive disorder, and panic disorder.

Tofranil-PM, which is usually taken once daily at bedtime, is approved to treat major depression.

Most important fact about this drug
Serious, sometimes fatal, reactions have been known to occur when drugs such as Tofranil are taken with another type of antidepressant called an MAO inhibitor. Drugs in this category include Nardil and Parnate. Tofranil must not be taken within 2 weeks of taking one of these drugs.

How should this medication be taken?
Tofranil may be taken with or without food. It should not be combined with alcohol.

Patients should keep taking Tofranil even if they feel no immediate effect. It can take from 1 to 3 weeks for improvement to begin.

Tofranil can cause dry mouth. Sucking hard candy or chewing gum can help this problem.

- *Missed dose...*
  Patients who take 1 dose a day at bedtime should contact their doctor. They should not take the dose in the morning because of possible side effects.

  If they take 2 or more doses a day, they should take the forgotten dose as soon as they remember. However, if it is almost time for the next dose, they should skip the one they missed and go back to their regular schedule. Doses should never be doubled.

- *Storage instructions...*
Tofranil should be stored at room temperature in a tightly closed container.

What side effects may occur?
Side effects cannot be predicted. If any develop or change in intensity, patients should inform their doctor as soon as possible.

- *Side effects may include:*
Breast development in males, breast enlargement in females, breast milk production, confusion, diarrhea, dry mouth, hallucinations, hives, high blood pressure, low blood pressure upon standing, nausea, numbness, tremors, vomiting

- *The most common side effects in children being treated for bed-wetting are:*
Nervousness, sleep disorders, stomach and intestinal problems, tiredness

- *Other side effects in children are:*
Anxiety, collapse, constipation, convulsions, emotional instability, fainting

Why should this drug not be prescribed?
Tofranil should not be used by anyone recovering from a recent heart attack.

People who take drugs known as MAO inhibitors, such as the antidepressants Nardil and Parnate, should not take Tofranil. The drug should also be avoided by those who are sensitive or allergic to it.

Special warnings about this medication
Tofranil should be used with caution by people who have or have ever had narrow-angle glaucoma (increased pressure in the eye); difficulty urinating; heart, liver, kidney, or thyroid disease; or seizures. Caution is also warranted for those taking thyroid medication.

General feelings of illness, headache, and nausea can result if Tofranil is stopped abruptly. Patients need to follow the doctor's instructions closely when discontinuing Tofranil.

The doctor should be alerted if a sore throat or fever develops during Tofranil therapy.

This drug may impair the ability to drive a car or operate potentially dangerous machinery. Patients should avoid any activities that require full alertness if they are unsure about their ability.

Both increased and decreased blood sugar levels have been reported during Tofranil therapy. Patients with diabetes or low blood sugar (hypoglycemia) should be closely monitored by their doctors.

Tofranil could cause a manic episode in patients with bipolar disorder or a psychotic episode in those with schizophrenia. Such patients should be watched closely for signs of any problems during Tofranil therapy.

Unless it's absolutely essential, Tofranil is not recommended for patients undergoing electroconvulsive therapy (ECT).

This drug can make people sensitive to light. Patients should stay out of the sun as much as possible.

Tofranil should be discontinued before elective surgery.

Possible food and drug interactions when taking this medication

Tofranil must never be combined with an MAO inhibitor (see "Most important fact about this drug"). If Tofranil is taken with certain other drugs, the effects of either could be increased, decreased, or altered. Here is an overview of drugs that may cause a problem:

Albuterol (Proventil, Ventolin)
Antidepressants that act on serotonin, including Prozac, Paxil, and
  Zoloft
Other antidepressants such as Elavil and Pamelor
Antipsychotic medications such as Mellaril and chlorpromazine
Barbiturates such as Nembutal and Seconal
Blood pressure medications such as Catapres
Carbamazepine (Tegretol)
Cimetidine (Tagamet)
Decongestants such as Sudafed
Drugs that control spasms, such as Cogentin
Epinephrine (EpiPen)
Flecainide (Tambocor)
Guanethidine
Methylphenidate (Ritalin)
Norepinephrine
Phenytoin (Dilantin)
Propafenone (Rythmol)
Quinidine (Quinidex)
Thyroid medications such as Synthroid
Tranquilizers and sleep aids such as Halcion, Xanax, and Valium

Extreme drowsiness and other potentially serious effects can result if Tofranil is combined with alcohol or other mental depressants, such as narcotic painkillers (Percocet), sleeping medications (Halcion), or tranquilizers (Valium).

Patients switching from Prozac should wait at least 5 weeks after the last dose of Prozac before starting Tofranil.

Special information about pregnancy and breastfeeding

The effects of Tofranil during pregnancy have not been adequately studied. Pregnant women should use Tofranil only when the potential benefits clearly outweigh the potential risks. If a patient is pregnant or plans to become pregnant, she should inform her doctor immediately.

Tofranil may appear in breast milk and could affect a nursing infant. If this medication is essential to the patient's health, the doctor may advise her to stop breastfeeding until treatment is finished.

Recommended dosage

ADULTS

The usual starting dose is 75 milligrams a day. The doctor may increase this to 150 milligrams a day. The maximum daily dose is 200 milligrams.

CHILDREN

Tofranil should be used in children only for the short-term treatment of bed-wetting. Safety and effectiveness in children under 6 years old have not been established. Tofranil-PM should not be used in children for any reason.

Total daily dosages for children should not exceed 2.5 milligrams for each 2.2 pounds of the child's weight. Doses usually begin at 25 milligrams per day, taken an hour before bedtime. If needed, this dose may be increased after 1 week to 50 milligrams (ages 6 through 11) or 75 milligrams (ages 12 and up), taken in one dose at bedtime or divided into 2 doses, 1 taken at mid-afternoon and 1 at bedtime.

OLDER ADULTS AND ADOLESCENTS

People in these two age groups should start with 25 to 50 milligrams per day of Tofranil tablets, since Tofranil-PM capsules are not available in these dosage strengths. The dose may be increased as necessary, but effective dosages usually do not exceed 100 milligrams a day. Patients who need to take 75 milligrams or more a day may use Tofranil-PM capsules instead of the regular tablets.

Overdosage

An overdose of Tofranil can be fatal. It has been reported that children are more sensitive than adults to overdoses of Tofranil. If an overdose is suspected, seek medical help immediately.

- *Symptoms of Tofranil overdose may include:*
  Coma, convulsions, difficulty breathing, heart failure, high fever, involuntary movements, irregular or rapid heartbeat, lack of coordination, low blood pressure, shock, stupor, sweating, vomiting

---

TRANXENE
Clorazepate dipotassium
Other brand names: Tranxene-SD, Tranxene-SD Half Strength

Why is this drug prescribed?
Tranxene belongs to a class of drugs known as benzodiazepines. It is used to treat anxiety disorders and for short-term relief of anxiety symptoms.

It is also used to relieve the symptoms of acute alcohol withdrawal and to help in treating certain convulsive disorders such as epilepsy.

Most important fact about this drug

Tranxene can be habit-forming if taken regularly over a long period. Withdrawal symptoms may occur if this drug is stopped abruptly. Patients should consult the doctor before discontinuing Tranxene or making any change in their dose.

How should this medication be taken?

Tranxene should be taken exactly as prescribed.

* *Missed dose...*
  If it is within an hour or so of the scheduled time, the forgotten dose should be taken immediately. If it's not remembered until later, the patient should skip the dose and go back to the regular schedule. Doses should never be doubled.

* *Storage instructions...*
  Tranxene should be stored at room temperature and protected from excessive heat.

What side effects may occur?

Side effects cannot be predicted. If any develop or change in intensity, patients should inform their doctor as soon as possible.

* *Side effects may include:*
  Blurred vision, dizziness, drowsiness, dry mouth, headache, mental confusion, nervousness, stomach and intestinal problems

* *Side effects due to rapid decrease in dose or abrupt withdrawal from Tranxene may include:*
  Abdominal cramps, convulsions, diarrhea, difficulty in sleeping or falling asleep, hallucinations, impaired memory, irritability, muscle aches, nervousness, tremors, vomiting

Why should this drug not be prescribed?

Anyone who is sensitive to or has ever had an allergic reaction to Tranxene should not take this medication. It should also be avoided by people with the eye condition known as acute narrow-angle glaucoma.

Anxiety or tension related to everyday stress usually does not require treatment with such a strong drug. Patients should discuss their symptoms thoroughly with the doctor.

Tranxene is not recommended for use in more serious conditions such as depression or severe psychological disorders.

Special warnings about this medication

Tranxene may cause patients to become drowsy or less alert. They should not drive, operate dangerous machinery, or participate in any hazardous activity that requires full mental alertness until they know how this drug affects them.

Patients who have anxiety along with depression may be at an increased risk of suicide. In these patients, the doctor will prescribe the lowest amount possible to avoid the risk of overdose.

Patients taking Tranxene for prolonged periods will need to have their blood counts and liver function checked periodically.

The elderly and people in a weakened condition are more apt to become unsteady or oversedated when taking Tranxene.

Possible food and drug interactions when taking this medication

Tranxene slows down the central nervous system and may intensify the effects of alcohol. Patients should avoid alcohol while taking this medication.

If Tranxene is taken with certain other drugs, the effects of either could be increased, decreased, or altered. Here is an overview of drugs that may cause a problem:

Antidepressant drugs known as MAO inhibitors (Nardil, Parnate) and
  other antidepressants such as Elavil and Prozac
Antipsychotic medications such as Mellaril and chlorpromazine
Barbiturates such as Nembutal and Seconal
Narcotic pain relievers such as Demerol and Percodan
Other drugs that slow down the central nervous system

Special information about pregnancy and breastfeeding

The effects of Tranxene during pregnancy have not been adequately studied. However, because there is an increased risk of birth defects associated with this class of drug, its use during pregnancy should be avoided.

Tranxene may appear in breast milk and could affect a nursing infant. If this medication is essential to the patient's health, the doctor may advise her to discontinue breastfeeding until treatment with this medication is finished.

Recommended dosage

ANXIETY

Adults: The usual daily dosage is 30 milligrams divided into several smaller doses. A normal daily dose can be as little as 15 milligrams. The doctor may increase the dosage gradually to as much as 60 milligrams, according to the patient's individual needs. For older adults, the usual starting dose is 7.5 to 15 milligrams a day.

Tranxene can also be taken in a single bedtime dose. The initial dose is 15 milligrams. The doctor may increase it if necessary.

Tranxene-SD, a 22.5-milligram tablet, and Tranxene-SD Half Strength, an 11.25-milligram tablet, can be taken once every 24 hours. The doctor may switch patients to this form of the drug after they have been taking Tranxene for several weeks.

ACUTE ALCOHOL WITHDRAWAL

Tranxene can be used in a multi-day program for relief of the symptoms of acute alcohol withdrawal. Dosages are usually increased in the first 2 days from 30 to 90 milligrams and then reduced over the next 2 days to lower levels. The doctor will continue to lower the dose until the drug is no longer necessary.

WHEN USED WITH ANTIEPILEPTIC DRUGS

Tranxene can be used in conjunction with antiepileptic drugs. Recommended dosages must be followed carefully to avoid drowsiness.

Adults and Children over 12 Years Old: The starting dose is 7.5 milligrams 3 times a day. The doctor may increase the dosage by 7.5 milligrams per week to a maximum of 90 milligrams a day.

Children 9 to 12 Years Old: The starting dose is 7.5 milligrams twice a day. The doctor may increase the dosage by 7.5 milligrams a week to a maximum of 60 milligrams a day. Safety and effectiveness in children under 9 years of age have not been established.

Overdosage

Any medication taken in excess can have serious consequences. If an overdose is suspected, seek medical treatment immediately.

* *Symptoms of Tranxene overdose may include:*
  Coma, low blood pressure, sedation

Tranylcypromine *See Parnate, page 135*

Trazodone *See Desyrel, page 49*

TRIAVIL
Amitriptyline hydrochloride with Perphenazine
Other brand name: Etrafon

Why is this drug prescribed?

Triavil is used to treat anxiety, agitation, and depression. It is a combination of a tricyclic antidepressant (amitriptyline) and a tranquilizer (perphenazine).

Triavil can also help people with schizophrenia who are depressed and people with insomnia, fatigue, loss of interest, loss of appetite, or a slowing of physical and mental reactions.

Most important fact about this drug

Triavil may cause tardive dyskinesia—a condition marked by involuntary muscle spasms and twitches in the face and body. This condition may be permanent and appears to be most common among the elderly, especially women.

How should this medication be taken?

Triavil may be taken with or without food. It should not be taken with alcohol. Triavil should not be taken within 2 hours of antacids or diarrhea medication.

- *Missed dose...*
  Generally, a forgotten dose should be taken as soon as remembered. However, if it is within 2 hours of the next dose, patients should skip the one they missed and go back to their regular schedule. Doses should never be doubled.

- *Storage instructions...*
  Triavil should be stored at room temperature in a tightly closed container. Triavil 2-10 tablets should be protected from light.

What side effects may occur?

Side effects cannot be predicted. If any develop or change in intensity, patients should inform their doctor as soon as possible.

- *Side effects may include:*
  Disorientation, dry mouth, high or low blood pressure, nervous system disorders, sedation

Why should this drug not be prescribed?

Triavil must never be combined with drugs that slow down the central nervous system, including alcohol, barbiturates, analgesics, antihistamines, or narcotics.

It should not be used by anyone who is recovering from a recent heart attack or has an abnormal bone marrow condition. It should be avoided by patients who have had an allergic reaction to phenothiazines or amitriptyline.

People who are taking antidepressant drugs known as MAO inhibitors (including Nardil and Parnate) should not take Triavil.

Special warnings about this medication

Triavil should be used with caution by anyone who has ever had glaucoma; difficulty urinating; breast cancer; breathing problems, seizures; or heart, liver, kidney, or thyroid disease. Caution is also in order if the patient is exposed to extreme heat or pesticides. Be aware that Triavil may mask signs of brain tumor, intestinal blockage, and overdose of other drugs.

Drugs such as Triavil are known to trigger a potentially fatal condition known as neuroleptic malignant syndrome. Symptoms include high fever, muscle rigidity, altered mental status, unstable blood pressure, rapid or irregular heartbeat, and excessive sweating. If any of these symptoms develop, patients should see their doctor immediately. Triavil therapy will need to be discontinued.

People who are severely depressed are at an increased risk of suicide. Patients should be watched closely for signs of suicidal thoughts and behavior. The doctor will prescribe the lowest amount of drug possible to avoid the risk of overdose.

Any significant increase in body temperature should be reported to the doctor immediately. This could be an early warning sign that the patient cannot tolerate Triavil.

Triavil could make patients more sensitive to sunlight. Encourage them to stay out of the sun, wear protective clothing, and use sunblock.

Triavil could also trigger a manic episode in bipolar patients, although the drug's tranquilizing effects seem to reduce this risk.

While taking this medication, patients may feel dizzy or light-headed or actually faint when getting up from a lying or sitting position. If getting up more slowly doesn't help or if the problem continues, patients should alert the doctor.

Patients should tell the doctor or dentist they're taking Triavil before having any surgery, dental work, or diagnostic procedure. Triavil could interact with anesthetics, muscle relaxants, and other drugs used during surgical procedures.

Nausea, headache, and a general ill feeling can result if Triavil is stopped abruptly. Patients need to follow the doctor's instructions closely when discontinuing Triavil. If the dose is gradually reduced, they may still experience irritability, restlessness, and dream and sleep disturbances, but these effects will not last.

This drug may impair the ability to drive a car or operate potentially dangerous machinery. Patients should not participate in any activities that require full alertness if they are unsure about their ability.

Possible food and drug interactions when taking this medication

Triavil contains the same active ingredients as Elavil and Trilafon and should not be used with these drugs.

If Triavil is taken with certain other drugs, the effects of either could be increased, decreased, or altered. Here is an overview of drugs that may cause a problem:

Airway-opening drugs such as Proventil

Antidepressants classified as MAO inhibitors, including Nardil and Parnate

Antidepressants that boost serotonin, including fluvoxamine, Paxil,

Prozac, and Zoloft
Antiseizure drugs such as Dilantin
Antihistamines such as Benadryl
Atropine (Donnatal)
Barbiturates such as phenobarbital
Blood pressure medications
Blood-thinning drugs such as Coumadin
Cimetidine (Tagamet)
Disulfiram (Antabuse)
Drugs that quell spasms, such as Bentyl
Epinephrine (EpiPen)
Ethchlorvynol (Placidyl)
Flecainide (Tambocor)
Fluphenazine (Prolixin)
Furazolidone (Furoxone)
Guanethidine
Major tranquilizers such as Haldol
Narcotic analgesics such as Percocet
Quinidine (Quinidex)
Phosphorus insecticides
Propafenone (Rythmol)
Thioridazine (Mellaril)
Thyroid medications such as Synthroid

Extreme drowsiness and other potentially serious effects can result if Triavil is combined with alcohol or other central nervous system depressants such as narcotics, painkillers, and sleep medications.

Special information about pregnancy and breastfeeding

Triavil may cause false-positive results on pregnancy tests. Triavil should not be used by pregnant women or mothers who are breastfeeding.

Recommended dosage

Each patient's dose must be individualized. The maximum dose is 8 tablets a day. It may be a few days to a few weeks before the patient notices any improvement.

The following dosages are for adults; older patients and adolescents usually take lower doses. Triavil is not recommended for use in children since the proper dosage has not been established.

NONPSYCHOTIC ANXIETY AND DEPRESSION

The usual dose is 1 tablet of Triavil 2-25 or 4-25 taken 3 or 4 times a day.

ANXIETY IN PEOPLE WITH SCHIZOPHRENIA

The usual dose is 2 tablets of Triavil 4-25 taken 3 times a day. The doctor may prescribe another tablet of Triavil 4-25 at bedtime, if needed. For patients who continue taking Triavil, the doctor will probably reduce the dosage to 1 tablet of Triavil 2-25 or 4-25 from 2 to 4 times a day.

Overdosage

Any medication taken in excess can have serious consequences. An overdose of Triavil can be fatal. If you suspect an overdose, seek medical help immediately.

* *Symptoms of Triavil overdose may include:*
  Abnormalities of posture and movements, agitation, coma, convulsions, dilated pupils, drowsiness, extreme low body temperature, eye movement problems, high fever, heart failure, overactive reflexes, rapid or irregular heartbeat, rigid muscles, stupor, very low blood pressure, vomiting

Triazolam *See Halcion, page 80*

TRIFLUOPERAZINE HYDROCHLORIDE

Why is this drug prescribed?

Trifluoperazine is used to treat schizophrenia. It is also prescribed for anxiety that does not respond to ordinary tranquilizers.

Most important fact about this drug

Trifluoperazine may cause tardive dyskinesia—a condition marked by involuntary muscle spasms and twitches in the face and body. This condition may be permanent and appears to be most common among the elderly, especially women.

How should this medication be taken?

Patients taking trifluoperazine in a liquid concentrate form will need to dilute it with a liquid such as a carbonated beverage, coffee, fruit juice, milk, tea, tomato juice, or water. It can also be mixed with puddings, soups, and other semisolid foods. It should not be mixed with alcohol.

Trifluoperazine should be diluted just before it's taken.

* *Missed dose...*
  Patients taking 1 dose a day should take the missed dose as soon as they remember. If they do not remember until the next day, they should skip the missed dose and go back to their regular schedule.

  Patients who take more than 1 dose a day should take the missed dose if it is within an hour or so of the scheduled time. If they do not remember until later, they should skip the missed dose and go back to their regular schedule. Doses should never be doubled.

* *Storage instructions...*
  Trifluoperazine may be stored at room temperature. The concentrate

should be protected from light.

What side effects may occur?

Side effects cannot be predicted. If any develop or change in intensity, patients should inform their doctor as soon as possible.

- *Side effects may include:*
  Blood disorders, convulsions, dry mouth, headache, muscle stiffness or rigidity, nausea, restlessness, Parkinson's–like movements, tardive dyskinesia (see "Most important fact about this drug")

Why should this drug not be prescribed?

Trifluoperazine should be avoided by people with liver damage and those who are taking central nervous system depressants such as alcohol, barbiturates, or narcotic pain relievers. It is also contraindicated for people who have an abnormal bone marrow or blood condition.

Special warnings about this medication

Trifluoperazine should be used with caution by anyone who has ever had a brain tumor, breast cancer, intestinal blockage, the eye condition called glaucoma, heart or liver disease, or seizures. Caution is warranted, too, if the patient is exposed to certain pesticides or extreme heat.

Trifluoperazine may hide the signs of overdose of other drugs and may make it more difficult for the doctor to diagnose intestinal obstruction, brain tumor, and the dangerous neurological condition called Reye's syndrome.

Patients should inform the doctor if they have ever had an allergic reaction to any antipsychotic medication similar to trifluoperazine.

Dizziness, nausea, vomiting, and tremors can result if a patient suddenly stops taking trifluoperazine. The drug should be discontinued under a doctor's supervision.

The doctor should be alerted immediately if a patient experiences symptoms such as a fever or sore throat, mouth, or gums. These signs of infection may signal the need to stop trifluoperazine treatment. The doctor should be notified, too, of flu-like symptoms with fever.

This drug may impair the ability to drive a car or operate potentially dangerous machinery, especially during the first few days of treatment. Patients should not participate in any activities that require full mental alertness if they are unsure about their ability.

Any vision problems that develop should be reported to the doctor.

Trifluoperazine concentrate contains a sulfite that may cause allergic reactions in some people, especially in those with asthma.

Trifluoperazine can cause a potentially fatal condition called neuroleptic malignant syndrome. Signs are high body temperature, rigid muscles, irregular pulse or blood pressure, rapid or abnormal heartbeat, and excessive perspiration. These symptoms should be reported to the doctor immediately. Antipsychotic therapy will have to be discontinued.

Possible food and drug interactions when taking this medication

Extreme drowsiness and other potentially serious effects can result if trifluoperazine is combined with alcohol, tranquilizers such as Valium, narcotic painkillers such as Percocet, antihistamines such as Benadryl, and barbiturates such as phenobarbital.

If trifluoperazine is taken with certain other drugs, the effects of either could be increased, decreased, or altered. Here is an overview of drugs that may cause a problem:

Antiseizure drugs such as Dilantin
Atropine (Donnatal)
Blood thinners such as Coumadin
Guanethidine
Lithium (Eskalith, Lithobid)
Propranolol (Inderal)
Thiazide diuretics such as Dyazide

Special information about pregnancy and breastfeeding

Pregnant women should use trifluoperazine only if clearly needed. The effects of trifluoperazine during pregnancy have not been adequately studied.

Trifluoperazine appears in breast milk and may affect a nursing infant. If this medication is essential to the patient's health, the doctor may have her discontinue breastfeeding while she is taking it.

Recommended dosage

NONPSYCHOTIC ANXIETY

Adults: Doses usually range from 2 to 4 milligrams daily. This amount should be divided into 2 equal doses and taken twice a day. The maximum dose is 6 milligrams a day. Treatment should continue for no more than 12 weeks.

SCHIZOPHRENIA

Adults: The usual starting dose is 4 to 10 milligrams a day, divided into 2 equal doses; doses range from 15 to 40 milligrams daily.

Children 6 to 12 Years Old Who Are Closely Monitored or Hospitalized: Doses are based on the child's weight and the severity of his or her symptoms. The starting dose is 1 milligram a day, taken all at once or divided into 2 doses. The doctor will increase the dosage gradually, up to 15 milligrams a day.

DOSAGE ADJUSTMENT

Older people usually take trifluoperazine at lower doses. Because they may develop low blood pressure while taking this drug, the doctor will watch them closely.

Overdosage

Any medication taken in excess can have serious consequences. If you suspect an overdose of trifluoperazine, seek medical help immediately.

- *Symptoms of trifluoperazine overdose may include:*
  Agitation, coma, convulsions, difficulty breathing, difficulty swallowing, dry mouth, extreme sleepiness, fever, intestinal blockage, irregular heart rate, low blood pressure, restlessness

TRILAFON

Perphenazine

Why is this drug prescribed?

Trilafon is used to treat schizophrenia and to control severe nausea and vomiting in adults. It is a member of the phenothiazine family of antipsychotic medications, which includes such drugs as Mellaril, chlorpromazine, and trifluoperazine.

Most important fact about this drug

Trilafon can cause tardive dyskinesia, a condition marked by involuntary muscle spasms and twitches in the face and body, including chewing movements, puckering, puffing the cheeks, and sticking out the tongue. This condition may be permanent and appears to be most common among older adults, especially older women.

How should this medication be taken?

Trilafon should be taken exactly according to physician instructions and for no longer than necessary.

- *Missed dose...*
  If it is within an hour or so after the scheduled time, the forgotten dose should be taken as soon as remembered. If they do not remember until later, patients should skip the dose and go back to their regular schedule. They should never double the dose.

- *Storage instructions...*
  Trilafon should be stored at room temperature.

What side effects may occur?

Side effects cannot be predicted. If any develop or change in intensity, patients should inform their doctor as soon as possible.

- *Side effects may include:*

Aching or numbness of the limbs, brain swelling, breast milk production, diarrhea, drowsiness, dry mouth, low blood pressure upon standing, nausea, rapid or irregular heartbeat, restlessness, salivation, seizures, vomiting

Why should this drug not be prescribed?

People who are comatose or who are at reduced levels of consciousness or alertness should not take Trilafon. Nor should those who are taking large amounts of any substance that slows brain function, including barbiturates, alcohol, narcotics, pain killers, and antihistamines.

Trilafon should also be avoided by people who have blood disorders, liver problems, or brain damage It cannot be taken by anyone who is hypersensitive to its ingredients or to related drugs.

Special warnings about this medication

Drugs such as Trilafon are capable of triggering a potentially fatal condition known as neuroleptic malignant syndrome. Symptoms include high fever, muscle rigidity, altered mental status, unstable blood pressure, a rapid or irregular heartbeat, and excessive sweating. If any of these symptoms develop, patients should see their doctor immediately. Trilafon therapy will need to be discontinued.

Any significant increase in body temperature should also be reported to the doctor. It could be an early warning that the drug cannot be tolerated.

Patients should alert their physician before taking Trilafon if they are going through alcohol withdrawal, suffer from convulsions or seizures, or have a depressive disorder. They will have to use the drug with caution.

Trilafon should also be used with caution by anyone who has a history of eye disorders such as glaucoma; difficulty urinating; breast cancer; breathing problems; or heart, liver, kidney, or thyroid disease. Caution is also advised if the patient is exposed to extreme heat or pesticides. Be aware that Trilafon may mask signs of brain tumor, intestinal blockage, and overdose of other drugs.

Trilafon should be used cautiously in people who are severely depressed and may be at risk for suicide. Patients should be watched closely for signs of suicidal thoughts and behavior. The doctor will prescribe the lowest amount of drug possible to avoid the risk of overdose.

While taking this medication, patients may feel dizzy or light-headed or actually faint when getting up from a lying or sitting position. If getting up more slowly doesn't help or if the problem continues, patients should alert the doctor.

Trilafon could make patients more sensitive to sunlight. Encourage them to stay out of the sun, wear protective clothing, and use sunblock.

Patients should tell the doctor or dentist they're taking Trilafon before having any surgery, dental work, or diagnostic procedure. Trilafon could interact with anesthetics, muscle relaxants, and other drugs used during surgical procedures.

Trilafon may impair the mental or physical abilities needed to drive a car or operate heavy machinery. Patients should not participate in any activities that require full alertness until they know how this drug affects them.

Stomach inflammation, dizziness, nausea, vomiting, and tremors may result if Trilafon is stopped suddenly. Therapy should be discontinued only under a doctor's supervision.

Trilafon is not recommended for children under the age of 12 years.

Possible food and drug interactions when taking this medication

If Trilafon is taken with certain other drugs, the effects of either could be increased, decreased, or altered. Here is an overview of drugs that may cause a problem:

Antidepressants such as Elavil, Nardil, Prozac, and Triavil
Antihistamines such as Benadryl and Tavist
Antipsychotic medications such as Mellaril and chlorpromazine
Antiseizure drugs such as Dilantin
Barbiturates such as Nembutal and Seconal
Blood pressure medications
Drugs that quell spasms, such as Donnatal and Levsin
Narcotic painkillers such as Percodan and Vicodin
Phosphorus insecticides
Tranquilizers and sleep aids such as Halcion, Valium, and Xanax

Extreme drowsiness and other potentially serious effects can result if Trilafon is combined with alcohol or other central nervous system depressants such as narcotics, painkillers, and sleep medications.

Special information about pregnancy and breastfeeding

Trilafon may cause false-positive results on pregnancy tests. Patients who are pregnant or planning to become pregnant should tell their doctor immediately. The safe use of Trilafon during pregnancy has not been established. The possible benefits of using this medication must be weighed against the possible hazards to the mother and child.

Drugs similar to Trilafon appear in breast milk. If this medication is essential to the patient's health, the doctor may advise her to avoid breastfeeding until her treatment is finished.

Recommended dosage

The dosage of Trilafon is adjusted according to the severity of the condition and the drug's effect. Doctors aim for the lowest effective dose.

SCHIZOPHRENIA

The usual initial dosage of Trilafon tablets is 4 to 8 milligrams 3 times daily, up to a maximum daily dose of 24 milligrams. Hospitalized patients are usually given 8 to 16 milligrams 2 to 4 times daily, up to a maximum daily dose of 64 milligrams.

SEVERE NAUSEA AND VOMITING IN ADULTS

For this problem, the usual dosage of Trilafon tablets is 8 to 16 milligrams daily divided into smaller doses. Up to 24 milligrams daily is occasionally necessary.

Overdosage

Anyone suspected of having taken on overdose of Trilafon should be hospitalized immediately for emergency treatment.

- *Usual symptoms of Trilafon overdose include:*
  Stupor, coma, convulsions (in children)

Victims may also exhibit symptoms such as rigid muscles, twitches and involuntary movements, hair-trigger reflexes, loss of coordination, rolling eyeballs, and slurred speech.

Trimipramine *See Surmontil, page 200*

VALIUM

Diazepam

Why is this drug prescribed?

Valium is used for treatment of anxiety disorders and for short-term relief of the symptoms of anxiety. It belongs to a class of drugs known as benzodiazepines.

Valium is also used to relieve the symptoms of acute alcohol withdrawal, to relax muscles, to relieve the uncontrolled muscle movements caused by disorders such as cerebral palsy, to control involuntary movement of the hands (athetosis), to relax tight, aching muscles, and, along with other medications, to treat convulsive disorders such as epilepsy.

Most important fact about this drug

Valium can be habit-forming or addictive. Some patients may experience withdrawal symptoms if they stop using this drug abruptly. Patients should consult their doctor before discontinuing the drug or making any change in their dose.

How should this medication be taken?

This medication must be taken exactly as prescribed. People taking the drug for epilepsy should be sure to take it at the same times every day.

- *Missed dose...*
  If it is within an hour or so of the scheduled time, the forgotten dose should be taken as soon as remembered. Otherwise, it should be skipped and the patient should return to the regular schedule. Doses should never be doubled.

- *Storage instructions...*
  Valium should be stored away from heat, light, and moisture.

What side effects may occur?
Side effects cannot be predicted. If any develop or change in intensity, patients should inform their doctor as soon as possible.

- *Side effects may include:*
  Drowsiness, fatigue, lack of coordination, paradoxical reactions such as anxiety

- *Side effects due to rapid decrease in dose or abrupt withdrawal from Valium:*
  Abdominal and muscle cramps, convulsions, sweating, tremors, vomiting

Why should this drug not be prescribed?
Anyone who is sensitive to or has ever had an allergic reaction to Valium should not take this medication. It should also be avoided by those with the eye condition known as acute narrow-angle glaucoma.

Anxiety or tension related to everyday stress usually does not require treatment with such a powerful drug as Valium. Patients should discuss their symptoms thoroughly with the doctor.

Valium should not be prescribed for patients who are being treated for mental disorders more serious than anxiety.

Special warnings about this medication
Valium causes some people to become drowsy or less alert. Patients should not drive, operate dangerous machinery, or participate in any hazardous activity that requires full mental alertness until they know how this drug affects them.

This medication should be used cautiously by people with liver or kidney problems.

Possible food and drug interactions when taking this medication
Valium slows down the central nervous system and may intensify the effects of alcohol. Patients should avoid alcohol while taking this medication.

If Valium is taken with certain other drugs, the effects of either could be increased, decreased, or altered. Here is an overview of drugs that may cause a problem:

Antiseizure drugs such as Dilantin
Antidepressant drugs such as Elavil and Prozac
Antipsychotic medications such as Mellaril and chlorpromazine
Barbiturates such as phenobarbital
Cimetidine (Tagamet)
Digoxin (Lanoxin)
Disulfiram (Antabuse)
Isoniazid (Rifamate)
Levodopa (Larodopa, Sinemet)
MAO inhibitors such as the antidepressant drugs Nardil and Parnate
Narcotics such as Percocet
Omeprazole (Prilosec)
Oral contraceptives
Propoxyphene (Darvon)
Ranitidine (Zantac)
Rifampin (Rifadin)

Special information about pregnancy and breastfeeding

Valium should not be taken during pregnancy. There is an increased risk of birth defects. The doctor may also advise against breastfeeding until treatment with this drug is finished.

Recommended dosage

The following dosages are for adults unless otherwise noted.

ANXIETY DISORDERS AND SHORT-TERM
RELIEF OF ANXIETY SYMPTOMS

The usual dose ranges from 2 milligrams to 10 milligrams 2 to 4 times daily, depending upon severity of symptoms.

ACUTE ALCOHOL WITHDRAWAL

The usual dose is 10 milligrams 3 or 4 times during the first 24 hours, then 5 milligrams 3 or 4 times daily as needed.

RELIEF OF MUSCLE SPASM

The usual dose is 2 milligrams to 10 milligrams 3 or 4 times daily.

CONVULSIVE DISORDERS

The usual dose is 2 milligrams to 10 milligrams 2 to 4 times daily.

DOSAGE ADJUSTMENT IN CHILDREN

Valium should not be given to children under 6 months of age.

The usual starting dose for children over 6 months is 1 to 2.5 milligrams 3 or 4 times a day. The doctor may increase the dosage gradually if needed.

DOSAGE ADJUSTMENT IN OLDER ADULTS

The usual starting dose is 2 milligrams to 2.5 milligrams once or twice a day. The doctor will increase the dose as needed, but will limit it to the smallest effective amount because older people are more apt to become oversedated or uncoordinated.

Overdosage

Any medication taken in excess can have serious consequences. If an overdose is suspected, seek medical attention immediately.

- *Symptoms of Valium overdose may include:*
  Coma, confusion, diminished reflexes, sleepiness

Venlafaxine *See Effexor, page 58*

Vistaril *See Atarax, page 18*

VIVACTIL

Protriptyline hydrochloride

Why is this drug prescribed?

Vivactil is used to treat the symptoms of mental depression in people who are under close medical supervision. It is particularly suitable for those who are inactive and withdrawn.

   Vivactil is a member of the family of drugs called tricyclic antidepressants. Researchers don't know exactly how it works. Unlike the class of antidepressants known as monoamine oxidase inhibitors (MAOIs), it does not act primarily through stimulation of the central nervous system. It tends to work more rapidly than some other tricyclic antidepressants. Improvement sometimes begins within a week.

Most important fact about this drug

For patients prone to anxiety or agitation, Vivactil can make the problem worse. It can also exaggerate the symptoms of manic-depression and schizophrenia. If this seems to be happening, the doctor should be alerted immediately. The dose of Vivactil may need reduction, or addition of another drug may be required.

How should this medication be taken?

Vivactil should be taken exactly as prescribed. It should not be taken with alcohol.

- *Missed dose . . .*
  Generally, the forgotten dose should be taken as soon as remembered. However, if it is almost time for the next dose, the missed dose should be skipped and the patient should return to the regular schedule. Doses should never be doubled.

- *Storage instructions . . .*
  Vivactil should be stored at room temperature in a tightly closed container.

What side effects may occur?

Side effects cannot be predicted. If any develop or change in intensity, patients should inform their doctor as soon as possible.

- *Side effects may include:*
  Anxiety, blood disorders, confusion, decreased libido, dizziness, flushing, headache, impotence, insomnia, low blood pressure, nightmares, rapid or irregular heartbeat, rash, seizures, sensitivity to sunlight, stomach and intestinal problems

Why should this drug not be prescribed?

Due to the possibility of life-threatening side effects, Vivactil must never be taken with drugs classified as MAO inhibitors, such as the antidepressants Nardil and Parnate. At least 14 days should be allowed between the last dose of one of these drugs and the first dose of Vivactil.

Vivactil should not be used during recovery from a heart attack. It also cannot be used by anyone who has had an allergic reaction to it.

Special warnings about this medication

Drugs such as Vivactil sometimes cause heartbeat irregularities. Vivactil should be used with caution by people who have heart problems or a thyroid disorder. Caution is also advisable for those who have a history of seizures, difficulty urinating, glaucoma, or alcohol abuse.

This drug is not recommended during electroconvulsive therapy.

Vivactil should be discontinued several days before any surgery.

Vivactil may impair the physical and/or mental abilities required to drive a car or operate heavy machinery. Patients should not participate in any activities that require full alertness until they know how this drug affects them.

Possible food and drug interactions when taking this medication

Remember that Vivactil must never be combined with MAO inhibitors such as Nardil and Parnate.

If Vivactil is taken with certain other drugs, the effects of either could be increased, decreased, or altered. Here is an overview of drugs that may cause a problem.

Antidepressants that boost serotonin, including Paxil, Prozac, and Zoloft
Antipsychotic medications such as Mellaril and chlorpromazine
Barbiturates such as Nembutal and Seconal
Certain blood pressure medications such as guanethidine

Cimetidine (Tagamet)
Decongestants such as Sudafed
Drugs that quell spasms, such as Donnatal and Levsin
Epinephrine (EpiPen)
Flecainide (Tambocor)
Narcotic painkillers such as Percodan and Vicodin
Norepinephrine
Other antidepressants such as Elavil and Tofranil
Propafenone (Rythmol)
Quinidine (Quinidex)
Tramadol (Ultram)
Tranquilizers and sleep aids such as Halcion, Valium, and Xanax

Special information about pregnancy and breastfeeding

The effects of Vivactil during pregnancy have not been adequately studied. It should be used during pregnancy only if its benefits outweigh the
potential risk. Patients who are pregnant or planning to become pregnant
should inform their doctor immediately.

It is not known whether Vivactil makes its way into breast milk.
Patients should consult with their doctor before deciding to breastfeed.

Recommended dosage

The doctor will start with a low dose and increase it gradually, watching
for side effects and a positive response

ADULTS

The usual adult dosage is 15 to 40 milligrams in 3 or 4 doses per day. The
maximum dosage is 60 milligrams daily. Increases are made in the morning dose.

CHILDREN

The safety and efficacy of Vivactil in children have not been established.

OLDER ADULTS AND ADOLESCENTS

Lower dosages are recommended for adolescents and older adults. Five
milligrams 3 times a day may be given initially, followed by a gradual
increase if necessary. Heart function must be monitored in older adults
who are taking 20 or more milligrams per day.

Overdosage

An overdose of Vivactil can be fatal. If an overdose is suspected, seek
medical help immediately.

- *Critical signs of Vivactil overdose may include:*
  Convulsions, irregular heartbeat, severely low blood pressure, reduced
  level of consciousness or even coma

- *Other signs of Vivactil overdose may include:*
  Agitation, confusion, dilated pupils, disturbed concentration, drowsiness, fever, hyperactive reflexes, low body temperature, muscle rigidity, sporadic hallucinations, stupor, vomiting, or any of the other symptoms listed in the "side effects" section

WELLBUTRIN

Bupropion hydrochloride
Other brand name: Wellbutrin SR, Wellbutrin XL

Why is this drug prescribed?

Wellbutrin is prescribed to treat major depression. It is thought to work by altering levels of the brain chemicals norepinephrine and dopamine. Wellbutrin is not chemically related to other antidepressants such as MAO inhibitors (Nardil, Parnate), tricyclics (Elavil), or serotonin inhibitors (Prozac).

Most important fact about this drug

Wellbutrin is associated with an increased risk of seizures. This risk is greater at higher doses (approximately 4 in 1,000 patients at dosages of 300 to 450 milligrams a day). Certain factors increase the risk of seizure, including:

A history of head trauma or previous seizure
Central nervous system tumor
Severe liver disease such as cirrhosis
A history of eating disorders, including anorexia and bulimia
Excessive use of alcohol, or abrupt withdrawal from alcohol or
  sedatives
Taking medications that lower the seizure threshold (see "Possible food
  and drug interactions when taking this medication")

To minimize the risk of seizures, dose increases should be done gradually, and the total daily dose of Wellbutrin should not exceed 450 milligrams. Additionally, patients need to inform their doctor about all medical conditions and not take any other medications (both prescription and over-the-counter) unless the doctor approves.

How should this medication be taken?

Wellbutrin should be taken exactly as prescribed. The usual dosing regimen is 3 equal doses spaced evenly throughout the day. At least 6 hours should elapse between doses. The doctor will probably start at a low dosage and gradually increase it; this helps minimize side effects.

Wellbutrin SR, the sustained-release form, should be taken in 2 doses at least 8 hours apart. Wellbutrin XL extended-release tablets should be taken once a day in the morning. Wellbutrin SR and Wellbutrin XL tablets must be swallowed whole; not chewed, divided, or crushed.

If Wellbutrin proves effective, the doctor will probably continue therapy for at least several months.

- *Missed dose...*
  Generally, a forgotten dose should be taken as soon as remembered. However, if it is within 4 hours of the next dose, the missed dose should be skipped and the patient should go back to the regular schedule. Doses should never be doubled.

- *Storage instructions...*
  Wellbutrin should be stored at room temperature and should be protected from light and moisture.

What side effects may occur?

Side effects cannot be predicted. If any develop or change in intensity, patients should inform their doctor as soon as possible.

- *Side effects of Wellbutrin may include:*
  Agitation, constipation, dizziness, dry mouth, excessive sweating, headache, nausea, vomiting, skin rash, sleep disturbances, tremor

- *Side effects of Wellbutrin SR may include:*
  Agitation, constipation, dizziness, dry mouth, insomnia, nausea, rash, sweating, weight loss

- *Side effects of Wellbutrin XL may include:*
  Abdominal pain, agitation, anxiety, constipation, diarrhea, dizziness, dry mouth, heart palpitations, increased urination, insomnia, muscle soreness, nausea, rash, ringing in the ears, sore throat, sweating,

Why should this drug not be prescribed?

Anyone who is sensitive to or has ever had an allergic reaction to Wellbutrin should avoid it.

Since Wellbutrin causes seizures in some people, it should not be taken by anyone who has any type of seizure disorder. It should also be avoided by people who are taking another medication containing bupropion, such as Zyban, the quit-smoking aid.

Wellbutrin must be avoided by patients who currently have, or formerly had, an eating disorder. For some reason, people with a history of anorexia nervosa or bulimia seem to be more likely to experience Wellbutrin-related seizures.

Wellbutrin should not be used if, within the past 14 days, the patient has taken a monoamine oxidase inhibitor (MAO inhibitor) drug such as the antidepressants Nardil and Parnate. This particular drug combination could cause a sudden, dangerous rise in blood pressure.

Wellbutrin must also be avoided by patients undergoing abrupt discontinuation of alcohol or sedatives (including benzodiazepines such as Valium and Xanax).

Special warnings about this medication

Patients who have had any kind of heart trouble or liver or kidney disease should be sure to alert the doctor before they start taking this drug. It must be used with extreme caution by people with severe cirrhosis of the liver. A reduced dosage may be needed by those with any sort of liver or kidney problem.

Although Wellbutrin occasionally causes weight gain, a more common effect is weight loss. Some 28 percent of people who take this medication lose 5 pounds or more. If depression has already caused a decline in weight, and if further weight loss would be detrimental to the patient's health, Wellbutrin may not be the best choice.

The FDA has issued a public health advisory to alert healthcare professionals about reports of worsening depression and suicidality (both suicidal thoughts and suicide attempts) during antidepressant drug therapy in adult and pediatric patients with major depressive disorder. Healthcare professionals and family members are advised to watch for signs of worsening depression and to be aware of the suicide statement present in all antidepressant labeling. The safety and effectiveness of Wellbutrin have not been established in pediatric patients less than 18 years old.

Like all antidepressants, Wellbutrin could trigger a manic episode. Patients with bipolar disorder should be watched closely for symptoms of mania.

Healthcare professionals and family members are also advised to alert the doctor immediately at the first sign of serious psychological side effects, including anxiety, agitation, panic attacks, insomnia, irritability, hostility, impulsivity, elation or inappropriate excitement, worsening depression, and suicidal thoughts or behaviors.

Patients should stop taking Wellbutrin and call the doctor immediately if they have difficulty breathing or swallowing; notice swelling in the face, lips, tongue, or throat; develop swollen arms and legs; or break out with itchy eruptions. These are warning signs of a potentially severe allergic reaction.

Wellbutrin may impair coordination or judgment. Patients should not drive or operate dangerous machinery until they know how the medication affects them.

Possible food and drug interactions when taking this medication

Patients should avoid alcohol while taking Wellbutrin; an interaction between alcohol and Wellbutrin could increase the possibility of a seizure.

Wellbutrin should not be combined with drugs that lower the seizure threshold, including:

Antidepressants classified as MAO inhibitors, such as Nardil and Parnate
Other antidepressants such as Elavil, Norpramin, Pamelor, Paxil,
  Prozac, Tofranil, and Zoloft
Antipsychotics such as chlorpromazine, Haldol, Risperdal, and Mellaril
Cocaine
Diabetes medications such as Glucotrol and Prandin
Insulin
Opiates such as heroin and morphine
Sedatives, including benzodiazepines such as Xanax and Valium
Steroid medications such as prednisone
Stimulants, including over-the-counter diet drugs
Theophylline (Theo-Dur)

If Wellbutrin is taken with certain other drugs, the effects of either could be increased, decreased, or altered. Here is an overview of additional drugs that may cause a problem:

Beta blockers (used for high blood pressure and heart conditions) such as
Inderal, Lopressor, and Tenormin
Carbamazepine (Tegretol)
Cimetidine (Tagamet)
Cyclophosphamide (Cytoxan)
Heart-stabilizing drugs such as Rythmol and Tambocor
Levodopa (Larodopa)
Nicotine patches such as Habitrol, NicoDerm CQ, and Nicotrol patch
Orphenadrine (Norgesic)
Phenobarbital
Phenytoin (Dilantin)

Special information about pregnancy and breastfeeding
Patients who are pregnant or plan to become pregnant should notify their doctor immediately. Wellbutrin should be taken during pregnancy only if clearly needed.

Wellbutrin does pass into breast milk and may cause serious reactions in a nursing baby. New mothers will need to choose between breastfeeding or continuing this medication.

Recommended dosage
No single dose of Wellbutrin should exceed 150 milligrams.

ADULTS

Wellbutrin
At the beginning, the dose will probably be 200 milligrams per day, taken as 100 milligrams 2 times a day. After at least 3 days at this dose, the doc-

tor may increase the dosage to 300 milligrams per day, taken as 100 milligrams 3 times a day, with at least 6 hours between doses. This is the usual adult dose. The maximum recommended dosage is 450 milligrams per day taken in doses of no more than 150 milligrams each.

Wellbutrin SR

The usual starting dose is 150 milligrams in the morning. After 3 days, if the patient responds well, the doctor will prescribe another 150 milligrams at least 8 hours after the first dose. It may be 4 weeks before the patient feels the benefit and therapy may continue for several months. The maximum recommended dose is 400 milligrams a day, taken in doses of 200 milligrams each.

For people with severe cirrhosis of the liver, the dosage should be no more than 75 milligrams once a day. With less serious liver and kidney problems, the dosage will be reduced as needed.

Wellbutrin XL

The usual starting dose is 150 milligrams taken once a day in the morning. If this dose is well tolerated after a minimum of 3 days, the doctor may increase the dose to 300 milligrams, also taken once a day in the morning. If no improvement is seen after several weeks of treatment, the doctor may increase the dose to a maximum of 450 milligrams once a day.

Patients with severe liver damage should use this drug with extreme caution. Their dose should not exceed 150 milligrams every *other* day. Patients with mild to moderate liver damage or kidney impairment will be prescribed a lower dose as well.

CHILDREN

The safety and effectiveness in children under 18 years old have not been established.

Overdosage

There have been rare reports of death after an overdose of Wellbutrin. Any medication taken in excess can have serious consequences. If an overdose of Wellbutrin is suspected, seek medical attention immediately.

- *Symptoms of Wellbutrin overdose may include:*
  Hallucinations, heart failure, loss of consciousness, rapid heartbeat, seizures

- *Symptoms of Wellbutrin SR overdose may include:*
  Blurred vision, confusion, jitteriness, lethargy, light-headedness, nausea, seizures, vomiting

- *An overdose that involves other drugs in combination with Wellbutrin may also cause these symptoms:*
  Breathing difficulties, coma, fever, rigid muscles, stupor

XANAX

Alprazolam
Other brand name: Xanax XR

Why is this drug prescribed?

Xanax is a tranquilizer used for the treatment of anxiety disorders and the short-term relief of symptoms of anxiety. Xanax is also used in the treatment of panic disorder and anxiety associated with depression. Some doctors prescribe Xanax to treat alcohol withdrawal, fear of open spaces and strangers, depression, irritable bowel syndrome, and premenstrual syndrome.

Xanax XR is prescribed to treat panic disorder.

Most important fact about this drug

Tolerance and dependence can occur with the use of Xanax. Withdrawal symptoms may occur if the drug is stopped abruptly or the dosage is reduced. Patients should discontinue the drug or change the dose only under a doctor's supervision. Withdrawal symptoms are listed under "What side effects may occur?"

How should this medication be taken?

Xanax must be taken exactly as prescribed. It may be taken with or without food. Xanax XR tablets should be swallowed whole; they should not be broken in half, chewed, or crushed.

* *Missed dose...*
  If it is less than 1 hour late, the dose should be taken as soon as remembered. Otherwise it should be skipped and the patient should go back to the regular schedule. Doses should never be doubled.

* *Storage instructions...*
  Store Xanax at room temperature.

What side effects may occur?

Side effects cannot be predicted. If any develop or change in intensity, patients should inform their doctor as soon as possible.

Side effects of Xanax are usually seen at the beginning of treatment and disappear with continued medication. However, if dosage is increased, side effects will be more likely.

* *Side effects of Xanax may include:*
  Decreased libido, drowsiness, fatigue, impaired coordination, memory impairment, speech difficulties, weight changes

* *Side effects of Xanax XR may include:*
  Constipation, decreased libido, depression, drowsiness, fatigue, impaired coordination, memory problems, mental impairment, nausea, sedation, sleepiness, speech difficulties, weight changes

- *Side effects due to decrease in dose or abrupt withdrawal from Xanax:*
  Blurred vision, decreased concentration, decreased mental clarity, diarrhea, heightened awareness of noise or bright lights, impaired sense of smell, loss of appetite, loss of weight, muscle cramps, seizures, tingling sensation, twitching

Why should this drug not be prescribed?

Anyone who is sensitive to or has ever had an allergic reaction to Xanax or other antianxiety agents should not take this medication. It should be avoided by people who have the eye condition called narrow-angle glaucoma. It must not be combined with the antifungal drugs Sporanox or Nizoral.

Anxiety or tension related to everyday stress usually does not require treatment with Xanax. Patients should discuss their symptoms thoroughly with the doctor. The doctor should periodically reassess the need for this drug.

Special warnings about this medication

Xanax may cause patients to become drowsy or less alert. Driving, operating dangerous machinery, or participating in any hazardous activity that requires full mental alertness is not recommended.

Individuals being treated for panic disorder may need a higher dose of Xanax than those being treated for anxiety alone. High doses—more than 4 milligrams a day—taken for long intervals may cause emotional and physical dependence. The doctor should monitor such patients carefully.

As with all antianxiety medication, there is a slight chance that Xanax could encourage suicidal thoughts or manic episodes. The doctor should be alerted immediately if any new or unusual symptoms appear.

Xanax should be used with caution in older or weak patients, and in those with lung disease, alcoholic liver disease, or any disorder that could hinder the elimination of the drug.

Possible food and drug interactions when taking this medication

Xanax may intensify the effect of alcohol. Patients should avoid alcohol while taking this medication.

Xanax should never be combined with Sporanox or Nizoral. These drugs cause a buildup of Xanax in the body.

If Xanax is taken with certain other drugs, the effects of either could be increased, decreased, or altered. Here is an overview of drugs that may cause a problem:

Amiodarone (Cordarone)
Antihistamines such as Benadryl and Tavist
Antipsychotic medications such as Mellaril and chlorpromazine

Carbamazepine (Tegretol)
Certain antibiotics such as Biaxin and erythromycin
Certain antidepressant drugs, including Elavil, Norpramin, and Tofranil
Cimetidine (Tagamet)
Cyclosporine (Neoral, Sandimmune)
Digoxin (Lanoxin)
Diltiazem (Cardizem)
Disulfiram (Antabuse)
Ergotamine
Fluoxetine (Prozac)
Fluvoxamine
Grapefruit juice
Isoniazid (Rifamate)
Nefazodone
Nicardipine (Cardene)
Nifedipine (Adalat, Procardia)
Oral contraceptives
Other central nervous system depressants such as Valium and Demerol
Paroxetine (Paxil)
Propoxyphene (Darvon)
Sertraline (Zoloft)

Special information about pregnancy and breastfeeding

Xanax should be avoided by patients who are pregnant or plan to become pregnant. There is an increased risk of respiratory problems and muscular weakness in the baby. Infants may also experience withdrawal symptoms.

Xanax may appear in breast milk and could affect a nursing infant. If this medication is essential to the mother's health, the doctor may advise her to stop breastfeeding until treatment is finished.

Recommended dosage

The following dosages are for adults. The safety and effectiveness of Xanax have not been established in children less than 18 years old.

ANXIETY DISORDER

Xanax

The usual starting dose is 0.25 to 0.5 milligram taken three times a day. The dose may be increased every 3 to 4 days to a maximum daily dose of 4 milligrams, divided into smaller doses.

PANIC DISORDER

Xanax

The usual starting dose is 0.5 milligram three times a day. The dose may be increased by 1 milligram a day every 3 or 4 days. The daily dose ranges from 1 milligram up to a total of 10 milligrams, according to the patient's needs. A typical dose is 5 to 6 milligrams a day.

Xanax XR

The usual starting dose is 0.5 to 1 milligram taken once a day, preferably in the morning. If needed, the dose can be increased by no more than 1 milligram a day every 3 or 4 days. The usual effective dose ranges from 3 to 6 milligrams a day, but doses as high as 10 milligrams a day have occasionally been needed.

DOSAGE ADJUSTMENT

In patients who are older, weak, or have advanced liver disease, the usual starting dose of Xanax is 0.25 milligram, 2 or 3 times a day. For Xanax XR, the starting dose is 0.5 milligram taken once a day, preferably in the morning. If needed, the doctor will increase the dose gradually based on the patient's tolerance.

Overdosage

An overdose of Xanax, alone or after combining it with alcohol, can be fatal. If an overdose is suspected, seek medical attention immediately.

* *Symptoms of Xanax overdose may include:*
  Confusion, coma, impaired coordination, sleepiness, slowed reaction time

Zaleplon *See Sonata, page 194*

Ziprasidone *See Geodon, page 77*

ZOLOFT

Sertraline

Why is this drug prescribed?

Zoloft is prescribed for major depressive disorder and obsessive-compulsive disorder. It is also used for the treatment of panic disorder, social anxiety disorder, premenstrual dysphoric disorder (PMDD), and posttraumatic stress disorder.

Zoloft is a member of the family of drugs called selective serotonin reuptake inhibitors (SSRIs). Serotonin is one of the chemical messengers believed to govern moods. Ordinarily, it is quickly reabsorbed after its release at the junctures between nerves. Reuptake inhibitors such as Zoloft slow this process, thereby boosting the levels of serotonin available in the brain.

Most important fact about this drug

Zoloft must not be used within 2 weeks of taking any drug classified as an MAO inhibitor, such as the antidepressants Nardil and Parnate. When serotonin boosters such as Zoloft are combined with MAO inhibitors, serious and sometimes fatal reactions can occur.

How should this medication be taken?

Zoloft should be taken exactly as prescribed, once a day in either the morning or the evening.

Zoloft is available in capsule and oral concentrate forms. Zoloft oral concentrate should be prepared with the dropper provided. The amount of concentrate prescribed by the doctor should be mixed with 4 ounces of water, ginger ale, lemon/lime soda, lemonade, or orange juice. (No other type of beverage should be used.) The mixture must be taken immediately; it should not be prepared in advance for later use. At times, a slight haze may appear after mixing, but this is normal.

Improvement with Zoloft may not be seen for several days to a few weeks. Treatment typically lasts for at least several months.

Zoloft may make the mouth dry. Sucking a hard candy, chewing gum, or melting bits of ice in the mouth can provide temporary relief.

● *Missed dose...*
Generally, the forgotten dose should be taken as soon as remembered. However, if several hours have passed, it should be skipped and the patient should return to the regular schedule. Doses should never be doubled.

● *Storage instructions...*
Zoloft may be stored at room temperature.

What side effects may occur?

Side effects cannot be predicted. If any develop or change in intensity, patients should inform their doctor as soon as possible.

● *Side effects may include:*
Abdominal pain, agitation, anxiety, constipation, decreased sex drive, diarrhea or loose stools, difficulty with ejaculation, dizziness, dry mouth, fatigue, gas, headache, decreased appetite, increased sweating, indigestion, insomnia, nausea, nervousness, rash, sleepiness, tingling or pins and needles, tremor, vision problems, vomiting

● *Zoloft may also cause mental or emotional symptoms such as:*
Abnormal dreams or thoughts, aggressiveness, exaggerated feeling of well-being, depersonalization ("unreal" feeling), hallucinations, impaired concentration, memory loss, paranoia, rapid mood shifts, suicidal thoughts, tooth-grinding, worsened depression

Many people lose a pound or two of body weight while taking Zoloft. This usually poses no problem but may be a concern if depression has already caused a great deal of weight loss.

In a few people, Zoloft may trigger the grandiose, inappropriate, out-of-control behavior called mania or the similar, but less dramatic, "hyper" state called hypomania.

Why should this drug not be prescribed?

Anyone who has ever had an allergic reaction to Zoloft should not take it.

This drug should never be combined with pimozide (Orap) or an MAO inhibitor (see "Most important fact about this drug"). Due to its alcohol content, Zoloft oral concentrate cannot be used with the anti-alcohol medication Antabuse.

Special warnings about this medication

Patients with a kidney or liver disorder, and those with a history of heart disease, seizures, or bleeding problems, need to take Zoloft cautiously and under close medical supervision.

The FDA has issued a public health advisory to alert healthcare professionals about reports of worsening depression and suicidality (both suicidal thoughts and suicide attempts) during antidepressant drug therapy in adults and pediatric patients with major depression. Healthcare professionals and family members are advised to watch for signs of worsening depression and to be aware of the suicide statement present in all antidepressant labeling. Zoloft is only approved for treating obsessive-compulsive disorder in children 6 years and older.

Zoloft could cause weight loss in children. The manufacturer recommends regular monitoring of weight and growth during long-term treatment in pediatric patients.

SSRI antidepressants could potentially cause stomach bleeding, especially in older patients or those taking nonsteroidal anti-inflammatory drugs (NSAIDs) such as aspirin, ibuprofen (Advil, Motrin), naproxen (Aleve), and ketoprofen (Orudis KT). Advise patients to consult their doctor before combining Zoloft with NSAIDs or blood-thinning medications.

Like all antidepressants, Zoloft could trigger a manic episode. Patients with bipolar disorder should be watched closely for symptoms of mania.

Zoloft has not been found to impair the ability to drive or operate machinery. Nevertheless, the manufacturer recommends caution until patients know how the drug affects them.

People who are sensitive to latex should use caution when handling the dropper provided with the oral concentrate.

Possible food and drug interactions when taking this medication

Remember that Zoloft must never be combined with pimozide (Orap) or an MAO inhibitor (see "Most important fact about this drug").

Although alcohol does not appear to interact with Zoloft, the manufacturer recommends avoiding the combination. Likewise, over-the-counter remedies should be used with caution. Although none is known to interact with Zoloft, interactions remain a possibility.

If Zoloft is taken with certain other drugs, the effects of either could be increased, decreased, or altered. Here is an overview of drugs that may cause a problem:

Antidepressants that boost serotonin such as Paxil and Prozac
Other antidepressants, including tricyclics such as Elavil and Pamelor
Cimetidine (Tagamet)
Diazepam (Valium)
Digitoxin (Crystodigin)
Flecainide (Tambocor)
Lithium (Eskalith, Lithobid)
Propafenone (Rythmol)
Sumatriptan (Imitrex)
Tolbutamide (Orinase)
Warfarin (Coumadin)

Special information about pregnancy and breastfeeding

The effects of Zoloft during pregnancy have not been adequately studied. Patients who are pregnant or plan to become pregnant should inform their doctor immediately. Zoloft should be taken during pregnancy only if it is clearly needed.

It is not known whether Zoloft appears in breast milk. Caution is advised when using Zoloft during breastfeeding.

Recommended dosage

The following indications and dosages are for adults only unless otherwise noted

DEPRESSIVE DISORDER, OBSESSIVE-COMPULSIVE DISORDER, OR PMDD

The usual starting dose is 50 milligrams once a day, taken either in the morning or in the evening. The doctor may increase the dose depending upon the patient's response. For patients with PMDD, the doctor will assess whether Zoloft should be taken throughout the menstrual cycle or only during the week or so before menstruation begins (the luteal phase). The maximum dose for PMDD is 150 milligrams daily. For other disorders, the maximum dose is 200 milligrams a day.

PANIC DISORDER, SOCIAL ANXIETY DISORDER,
OR POSTTRAUMATIC STRESS DISORDER

During the first week, the usual dose is 25 milligrams once a day. After that, the dose increases to 50 milligrams once a day. Depending on response, the doctor may continue to increase the dose up to a maximum of 200 milligrams a day.

OBSESSIVE-COMPULSIVE DISORDER IN CHILDREN

The starting dose for children 6 to 12 years old is 25 milligrams, and for adolescents 13 to 17 years old, the initial dose is 50 milligrams. The doctor will adjust the dose as necessary.

Safety and effectiveness have not been established for children under 6 years old.

The doctor will need to reduce the dosage for patients with liver disease.

Overdosage

An overdose of Zoloft can be fatal. If an overdose is suspected, seek medical attention immediately.

- *Common symptoms of Zoloft overdose may include:*
  Agitation, dizziness, nausea, rapid heartbeat, sleepiness, tremor, vomiting

Other possible symptoms include coma, stupor, fainting, convulsions, delirium, hallucinations, mania, high or low blood pressure, and slow, rapid, or irregular heartbeat.

Zolpidem *See Ambien, page 7*

ZYPREXA

Olanzapine

Why is this drug prescribed?

Zyprexa helps manage symptoms of schizophrenia, the manic phase of bipolar disorder, and other psychotic disorders. It is thought to work by opposing the action of serotonin and dopamine, two of the brain's major chemical messengers. The drug is available as Zyprexa tablets and Zyprexa Zydis, which dissolves rapidly with or without liquid.

Most important fact about this drug

At the start of Zyprexa therapy, the drug can cause extreme low blood pressure, increased heart rate, dizziness, and, in rare cases, a tendency to faint when first standing up. These problems are more likely if the patient is dehydrated, has heart disease, or takes blood pressure medicine. To avoid such problems, the doctor may start with a low dose of Zyprexa and increase the dosage gradually.

How should this medication be taken?

Zyprexa should be taken once a day with or without food. To use Zyprexa Zydis, patients should open the sachet, peel back the foil on the blister pack, remove the tablet, and place the entire tablet in their mouth. The tablet should not be pushed through the foil. The medication can be taken with or without water; saliva will cause the tablet to dissolve.

- *Missed dose...*
  Generally, a forgotten dose should be taken as soon as remembered. However, if it is almost time for the next dose, the missed dose should

be skipped and the patient should go back to the regular schedule. Doses should never be doubled.

- *Storage instructions...*
  Zyprexa should be stored at room temperature away from light and moisture.

What side effects may occur?

Side effects cannot be predicted. If any develop or change in intensity, patients should inform their doctor as soon as possible.

- *Side effects may include:*
  Agitation, change in personality, constipation, dizziness, dry mouth, increased appetite, indigestion, low blood pressure upon standing, sleepiness, tremor, weakness, weight gain

Why should this drug not be prescribed?

Anyone who is allergic to Zyprexa cannot use this drug.

Special warnings about this drug

Certain antipsychotic drugs, including Zyprexa, are associated with an increased risk of developing high blood sugar, which on rare occasions has led to coma or death. Patients should see their doctor right away if they develop signs of high blood sugar, including dry mouth, thirst, increased urination, and tiredness. Patients who have diabetes or have a high risk of developing it should see their doctor regularly for blood sugar testing.

Zyprexa should not be used to treat elderly patients who have dementia because the drug could increase the risk of stroke.

Animal studies suggest that Zyprexa may increase the risk of breast cancer, although human studies have not confirmed such a risk. Advise patients with a history of breast cancer to see their doctor regularly for checkups.

Patients at high risk of suicide attempts should be prescribed the lowest dose possible to reduce the risk of intentional overdose.

Zyprexa sometimes causes drowsiness and can impair judgment, thinking, and motor skills. Patients should use caution while driving and shouldn't operate dangerous machinery until they know how the drug affects them.

Medicines such as Zyprexa can interfere with regulation of the body's temperature. Patients should avoid getting overheated or becoming dehydrated while taking Zyprexa. They need to stay away from extreme heat and drink plenty of fluids.

People with the following conditions should use Zyprexa with caution: Alzheimer's disease, trouble swallowing, narrow angle glaucoma (high pressure in the eye), an enlarged prostate, heart irregularities, heart disease, heart failure, liver disease, or a history of heart attack, seizures, or intestinal blockage.

Drugs such as Zyprexa sometimes cause a condition called neuroleptic malignant syndrome. Symptoms include high fever, muscle rigidity, irregular pulse or blood pressure, rapid heartbeat, excessive perspiration, and changes in heart rhythm. If these symptoms appear, the doctor will discontinue Zyprexa while the condition is under treatment.

There is also a risk of developing tardive dyskinesia, a condition marked by slow, rhythmical, involuntary movements. This problem is more likely to surface in older adults, especially elderly women. When it does, use of Zyprexa is usually stopped.

Zyprexa can cause low blood pressure upon standing, resulting in dizziness, rapid heartbeat, and fainting, especially at the start of therapy. Patients who experience this should alert the doctor; the dosage can be adjusted to reduce the symptoms.

Patients who have phenylketonuria and must avoid the amino acid phenylalanine should not take the rapidly disintegrating form of this drug, Zyprexa Zydis, which contains this substance.

The safety and effectiveness of Zyprexa have not been studied in children.

Possible food and drug interactions when taking this medication

Patients should avoid alcohol while taking Zyprexa. The combination can cause a sudden drop in blood pressure.

If Zyprexa is taken with certain other drugs, the effects of either can be increased, decreased, or altered. Patients should check with the doctor before taking any prescription or over-the-counter drugs. Medications of particular concern include the following:

Blood pressure medications
Carbamazepine (Tegretol)
Diazepam (Valium)
Drugs that boost the effect of dopamine, such as the Parkinson's
  medications Mirapex, Parlodel, Permax, and Requip
Fluvoxamine
Levodopa (Larodopa)
Omeprazole (Prilosec)
Rifampin (Rifadin, Rimactane)

Special information about pregnancy and breastfeeding

Patients who are pregnant or plan to become pregnant should inform their doctor immediately. Zyprexa should be used during pregnancy only if absolutely necessary.

This drug may appear in breast milk; women on Zyprexa therapy should not breastfeed.

Recommended dosage

SCHIZOPHRENIA

Adults: The usual starting dose is 5 to 10 milligrams once a day. If the patient starts at the lower dose, after a few days the doctor will increase it to 10. After that, the dosage will be increased no more than once a week, 5 milligrams at a time, up to a maximum of 20 milligrams a day.

MANIC EPISODES IN BIPOLAR DISORDER

Adults: The usual starting dose is 10 to 15 milligrams once a day. If needed, the dose can be increased every 24 hours by 5 milligrams a day, up to a maximum daily dose of 20 milligrams. After the patient is stabilized, the doctor may continue maintenance therapy at a dosage range of 5 to 20 milligrams a day. If Zyprexa is being combined with lithium or valproate (Depakene, Depakote), the usual starting dose is 10 milligrams a day.

DOSAGE ADJUSTMENT

The doctor will need to lower the dosage in debilitated patients, those prone to low blood pressure, and nonsmoking women over 65 (because they tend to have a slower metabolism). The recommended starting dose is 5 milligrams a day. Any dose increases should be done cautiously.

Overdosage

An overdose of Zyprexa is usually not life-threatening, but fatalities have been reported. If an overdose is suspected, seek medical attention immediately.

- *Symptoms of Zyprexa overdose may include:*
  Agitation, drowsiness, rapid or irregular heartbeat, slurred or disrupted speech, stupor

Overdoses of Zyprexa have also led to breathing difficulties, changes in blood pressure, excessive perspiration, fever, muscle rigidity, cardiac arrest, coma, and convulsions.

Section 2

Interactions with Psychotropic Drugs

Listed in this section are over 1,600 possible interactions with the psychotropic medications profiled in Section 1. Entries are organized alphabetically, first by the generic name of the psychotropic drug, then by the generic name of the potentially interactive medication. Each entry includes a brief description of the possible results of concurrent use, plus ratings of the interaction's rapidity of onset, degree of severity, and level of supporting documentation. A key to these ratings follows.

Onset
  0 = Unspecified
  1 = Rapid: Develops within 24 hours
  2 = Delayed: Will not occur during the first 24 hours

Severity
  1 = Contraindicated: The interaction may be life-threatening. Concomitant use of the interacting agents is contraindicated.
  2 = Major: The interaction may be life-threatening and/or require medical intervention to minimize or prevent serious adverse effects.
  3 = Moderate: The interaction may result in an exacerbation of the patient's condition and/or require an alteration in therapy.
  4 = Minor: The interaction would have limited clinical effects. Manifestations may include an increase in the frequency or severity of side effects but generally would not require a major alteration in therapy.

Evidence
  1 = Excellent: Controlled studies have clearly established the existence of the interaction.
  2 = Good: Documentation strongly suggests the interaction exists, but well-controlled studies are lacking.
  3 = Fair: Available documentation is fair, but pharmacologic considerations lead clinicians to suspect the interaction exists; or, documentation is good for a pharmacologically similar drug.
  4 = Poor: Documentation is poor (such as limited case reports), but the interaction is theoretically possible.

The information in this section is extracted from the DRUG-REAX System, a drug therapy screening program produced by *Physicians' Desk Reference*® affiliate Micromedex, Inc., the world leader in specialized information on pharmaceuticals. The entries are based on an independent review of the medical literature by a staff of more than 100 clinicians, and may vary from the summary information presented in Section 1.

Alprazolam

INTERACTION	ONSET	SEVERITY	EVIDENCE
CIMETIDINE Concurrent use may result in an increased risk of alprazolam toxicity (central nervous system depression).	1	3	3
CLARITHROMYCIN Concurrent use may result in increased alprazolam toxicity (central nervous system depression, ataxia, lethargy).	2	3	3
ERYTHROMYCIN Concurrent use may result in increased alprazolam toxicity (central nervous system depression, ataxia, lethargy).	2	3	3
ETHANOL Concurrent use may result in increased sedation.	1	3	2
FLUCONAZOLE Concurrent use may result in increased alprazolam serum concentrations and potential alprazolam toxicity (sedation, slurred speech, central nervous system depression).	2	1	3
FLUOXETINE Concurrent use may result in an increased risk of alprazolam toxicity (somnolence, dizziness, ataxia, slurred speech, hypotension, psychomotor impairment).	1	3	2
FLUVOXAMINE Concurrent use may result in elevated plasma alprazolam levels and an increased risk of side effects (central nervous system depression).	2	3	2
ITRACONAZOLE Concurrent use may result in increased alprazolam serum concentrations and potential alprazolam toxicity (sedation, slurred speech, central nervous system depression).	2	1	3
JOSAMYCIN Concurrent use may result in increased alprazolam toxicity (central nervous system depression, ataxia, lethargy).	2	3	3
KETOCONAZOLE Concurrent use may result in increased alprazolam serum concentrations and potential alprazolam toxicity (sedation, slurred speech, central nervous system depression).	2	1	3
NEFAZODONE Concurrent use may result in psychomotor impairment and sedation.	1	3	2
OMEPRAZOLE Concurrent use may result in alprazolam toxicity (central nervous system depression, ataxia, lethargy).	2	3	3
ORAL CONTRACEPTIVE Concurrent use may result in an increased risk of alprazolam toxicity (central nervous system depression, hypotension).	2	3	3

Onset: 0=Unspecified 1=Rapid 2=Delayed
Severity: 1=Contraindicated 2=Major 3=Moderate 4=Minor
Evidence: 1=Excellent 2=Good 3=Fair 4=Poor

INTERACTION	ONSET	SEVERITY	EVIDENCE
PROPOXYPHENE Concomitant administration may result in additive respiratory depression.	0	2	3
RITONAVIR Concurrent use may result in increased plasma concentrations of alprazolam and enhanced alprazolam effects.	2	3	3
ROXITHROMYCIN Concurrent use may result in increased alprazolam toxicity (central nervous system depression, ataxia, lethargy).	2	3	3
THEOPHYLLINE Concurrent use result in decreased alprazolam effectiveness.	1	3	2
TROLEANDOMYCIN Concurrent use may result in increased alprazolam toxicity (central nervous system depression, ataxia, lethargy).	2	3	3

Amitriptyline

INTERACTION	ONSET	SEVERITY	EVIDENCE
ACENOCOUMAROL Concurrent use may result in an increased risk of bleeding.	2	3	3
AMPRENAVIR Concurrent use may result in increased amitriptyline serum concentrations and potential toxicity (anticholinergic effects, sedation, confusion, cardiac arrhythmias).	2	2	3
ANISINDIONE Concurrent use may result in an increased risk of bleeding.	2	3	3
BEPRIDIL Concurrent use may result in an increased risk of cardiotoxicity (QT prolongation, torsade de pointes, cardiac arrest).	1	1	3
BETHANIDINE Concurrent use may result in decreased antihypertensive effectiveness.	1	3	2
CARBAMAZEPINE Concurrent use may result in decreased amitriptyline effectiveness.	2	3	3
CIMETIDINE Concurrent use may result in amitriptyline toxicity (dry mouth, blurred vision, urinary retention).	2	3	2
CISAPRIDE Concurrent use may result in cardiotoxicity (QT prolongation, torsade de pointes, cardiac arrest).	1	1	3
CLONIDINE Concurrent use may result in decreased antihypertensive effectiveness.	2	2	3

INTERACTION	ONSET	SEVERITY	EVIDENCE
CLORGYLINE Concurrent use may result in neurotoxicity, seizures, or serotonin syndrome (hypertension, hyperthermia, myoclonus, mental status changes).	2	1	3
DICUMAROL Concurrent use may result in an increased risk of bleeding.	2	3	3
DROPERIDOL Concurrent use may result in an increased risk of cardiotoxicity (QT prolongation, torsade de pointes, cardiac arrest).	0	2	3
EPINEPHRINE Concurrent use may result in hypertension, cardiac arrhythmias, and tachycardia.	1	2	2
ETHANOL Concurrent use may result in enhanced central nervous system depression and impairment of motor skills.	1	3	1
ETILEFRINE Concurrent use may result in hypertension, cardiac arrhythmias, and tachycardia.	1	2	2
FLUCONAZOLE Concurrent use result in an increased risk of amitriptyline toxicity and an increased risk of cardiotoxicity (QT prolongation, torsade de pointes, cardiac arrest).	2	2	3
FLUOXETINE Concurrent use may result in amitriptyline toxicity (dry mouth, urinary retention, sedation) and an increased risk of cardiotoxicity (QT prolongation, torsade de pointes, cardiac arrest).	0	2	3
FLUVOXAMINE Concurrent use may result in amitriptyline toxicity (dry mouth, urinary retention, sedation).	2	3	3
FURAZOLIDONE Concurrent use may result in neurotoxicity, seizures, or serotonin syndrome (hypertension, hyperthermia, myoclonus, mental status changes).	2	1	3
GREPAFLOXACIN Concurrent use may result in an increased risk of cardiotoxicity (QT prolongation, torsade de pointes, cardiac arrest).	2	1	3
GUANADREL Concurrent use may result in decreased antihypertensive effectiveness.	2	3	3
GUANETHIDINE Concurrent use may result in decreased antihypertensive effectiveness.	2	3	2

Onset: 0=Unspecified 1=Rapid 2=Delayed
Severity: 1=Contraindicated 2=Major 3=Moderate 4=Minor
Evidence: 1=Excellent 2=Good 3=Fair 4=Poor

INTERACTION	ONSET	SEVERITY	EVIDENCE
GUANFACINE Concurrent use may result in decreased antihypertensive effectiveness.	2	3	3
HALOFANTRINE Concurrent use may result in an increased risk of cardiotoxicity (QT prolongation, torsade de pointes, cardiac arrest).	2	2	3
IPRONIAZID Concurrent use may result in neurotoxicity, seizures, or serotonin syndrome (hypertension, hyperthermia, myoclonus, mental status changes).	2	1	3
ISOCARBOXAZID Concurrent use may result in neurotoxicity, seizures, or serotonin syndrome (hypertension, hyperthermia, myoclonus, mental status changes).	2	1	3
LEVOMETHADYL Concurrent use may result in an increased risk of cardiotoxicity (QT prolongation, torsade de pointes, cardiac arrest).	2	1	3
METHOXAMINE Concurrent use may result in hypertension, cardiac arrhythmias, and tachycardia.	1	2	2
MIDODRINE Concurrent use may result in hypertension, cardiac arrhythmias, and tachycardia.	1	2	2
MOCLOBEMIDE Concurrent use may result in neurotoxicity, seizures, or serotonin syndrome (hypertension, hyperthermia, myoclonus, mental status changes).	2	1	3
NEFAZODONE Concurrent use may result in increased risk of serotonin syndrome (hypertension, hyperthermia, myoclonus, mental status changes).	1	2	3
NIALAMIDE Concurrent use may result in neurotoxicity, seizures, or serotonin syndrome (hypertension, hyperthermia, myoclonus, mental status changes).	2	1	3
NOREPINEPHRINE Concurrent use may result in hypertension, cardiac arrhythmias, and tachycardia.	1	2	2
OXILOFRINE Concurrent use may result in hypertension, cardiac arrhythmias, and tachycardia.	1	2	2
PARGYLINE Concurrent use may result in neurotoxicity, seizures, or serotonin syndrome (hypertension, hyperthermia, myoclonus, mental status changes).	2	1	3

INTERACTION	ONSET	SEVERITY	EVIDENCE
PHENELZINE Concurrent use may result in neurotoxicity, seizures, or serotonin syndrome (hypertension, hyperthermia, myoclonus, mental status changes).	2	1	3
PHENINDIONE Concurrent use may result in an increased risk of bleeding.	2	3	3
PHENPROCOUMON Concurrent use may result in an increased risk of bleeding.	2	3	3
PHENYLEPHRINE Concurrent use may result in hypertension, cardiac arrhythmias, and tachycardia.	1	2	2
PIMOZIDE Concurrent use may result in an increased risk of cardiotoxicity (QT prolongation, torsade de pointes, cardiac arrest).	0	1	3
PROCARBAZINE Concurrent use may result in neurotoxicity, seizures.	2	1	3
SELEGILINE Concurrent use may result in neurotoxicity, seizures, or serotonin syndrome (hypertension, hyperthermia, myoclonus, mental status changes).	2	1	3
SERTRALINE Concurrent use may result in elevated amitriptyline serum levels or possible serotonin syndrome (hypertension, hyperthermia, myoclonus, mental status changes).	2	2	3
SPARFLOXACIN Concurrent use may result in prolongation of the QTc interval and/or torsade de pointes.	2	1	3
TOLOXATONE Concurrent use may result in neurotoxicity, seizures, or serotonin syndrome (hypertension, hyperthermia, myoclonus, mental status changes).	2	1	3
TRAMADOL Concurrent use may result in an increased risk of seizures.	1	2	3
TRANYLCYPROMINE Concurrent use may result in neurotoxicity, seizures, or serotonin syndrome (hypertension, hyperthermia, myoclonus, mental status changes).	2	1	3
WARFARIN Concurrent use may result in an increased risk of bleeding.	2	3	3

Onset: 0=Unspecified 1=Rapid 2=Delayed
Severity: 1=Contraindicated 2=Major 3=Moderate 4=Minor
Evidence: 1=Excellent 2=Good 3=Fair 4=Poor

Amoxapine

INTERACTION	ONSET	SEVERITY	EVIDENCE
ACENOCOUMAROL Concurrent use may result in increased risk of bleeding.	2	3	3
AMPRENAVIR Concurrent use may result in increased amoxapine serum concentrations and potential toxicity (anticholinergic effects, sedation, confusion, cardiac arrhythmias).	2	2	3
ANISINDIONE Concurrent use may result in increased risk of bleeding.	2	3	3
BEPRIDIL Concurrent use may result in an increased risk of cardiotoxicity (QT prolongation, torsade de pointes, cardiac arrest).	1	1	3
CIMETIDINE Concurrent use result in amoxapine toxicity (dry mouth, urinary retention, blurred vision).	2	3	3
CISAPRIDE Concurrent use may result in cardiotoxicity (QT prolongation, torsade de pointes, cardiac arrest).	1	1	3
CLONIDINE Concurrent use may result in decreased antihypertensive effectiveness.	2	2	3
CLORGYLINE Concurrent use may result in neurotoxicity, seizures, or serotonin syndrome (hypertension, hyperthermia, myoclonus, mental status changes).	2	2	3
DICUMAROL Concurrent use may result in increased risk of bleeding.	2	3	3
DROPERIDOL Concurrent use may result in an increased risk of cardiotoxicity (QT prolongation, torsade de pointes, cardiac arrest).	0	2	3
EPINEPHRINE Concurrent use may result in hypertension, cardiac arrhythmias, and tachycardia.	1	2	2
ETILEFRINE Concurrent use may result in hypertension, cardiac arrhythmias, and tachycardia.	1	2	2
FLUOXETINE Concurrent use may result in amoxapine antidepressant toxicity (dry mouth, urinary retention, sedation) and an increased risk of cardiotoxicity (QT prolongation, torsade de pointes, cardiac arrest).	0	2	3

INTERACTION	ONSET	SEVERITY	EVIDENCE
GREPAFLOXACIN Concurrent use may result in an increased risk of cardiotoxicity (QT prolongation, torsade de pointes, cardiac arrest).	2	1	3
GUANADREL Concurrent use may result in decreased antihypertensive effectiveness.	2	3	3
HALOFANTRINE Concurrent use may result in an increased risk of cardiotoxicity (QT prolongation, torsade de pointes, cardiac arrest).	2	2	3
ISOCARBOXAZID Concurrent use may result in neurotoxicity, seizures, or serotonin syndrome (hypertension, hyperthermia, myoclonus, mental status changes).	2	1	3
LEVOMETHADYL Concurrent use may result in an increased risk of cardiotoxicity (QT prolongation, torsade de pointes, cardiac arrest).	2	1	3
METHOXAMINE Concurrent use may result in hypertension, cardiac arrhythmias, and tachycardia.	1	2	2
MIDODRINE Concurrent use may result in hypertension, cardiac arrhythmias, and tachycardia.	1	2	2
MOCLOBEMIDE Concurrent use may result in neurotoxicity, seizures, or serotonin syndrome (hypertension, hyperthermia, myoclonus, mental status changes).	2	2	3
NOREPINEPHRINE Concurrent use may result in hypertension, cardiac arrhythmias, and tachycardia.	1	2	2
OXILOFRINE Concurrent use may result in hypertension, cardiac arrhythmias, and tachycardia.	1	2	2
PHENELZINE Concurrent use may result in neurotoxicity, seizures, or serotonin syndrome (hypertension, hyperthermia, myoclonus, mental status changes).	2	2	3
PHENINDIONE Concurrent use may result in increased risk of bleeding.	2	3	3
PHENPROCOUMON Concurrent use may result in increased risk of bleeding.	2	3	3
PHENYLEPHRINE Concurrent use may result in hypertension, cardiac arrhythmias, and tachycardia.	1	2	2

Onset: 0=Unspecified 1=Rapid 2=Delayed
Severity: 1=Contraindicated 2=Major 3=Moderate 4=Minor
Evidence: 1=Excellent 2=Good 3=Fair 4=Poor

INTERACTION	ONSET	SEVERITY	EVIDENCE
PIMOZIDE			
Concurrent use may result in an increased risk of cardiotoxicity (QT prolongation, torsade de pointes, cardiac arrest).	0	1	3
PROCARBAZINE			
Concurrent use may result in neurotoxicity, seizures.	2	2	3
SELEGILINE			
Concurrent use may result in neurotoxicity, seizures, or serotonin syndrome (hypertension, hyperthermia, myoclonus, mental status changes).	2	2	3
TRAMADOL			
Concurrent use may result in an increased risk of seizures.	1	2	3
TRANYLCYPROMINE			
Concurrent use may result in neurotoxicity, seizures, or serotonin syndrome (hypertension, hyperthermia, myoclonus, mental status changes).	2	2	3
WARFARIN			
Concurrent use may result in an increased risk of bleeding.	2	3	3

Amphetamine

INTERACTION	ONSET	SEVERITY	EVIDENCE
ACETAZOLAMIDE			
Concurrent use may result in amphetamine toxicity (hypertension, hyperpyrexia, seizures).	2	4	3
CLORGYLINE			
Concurrent use may result in hypertensive crisis (headache, hyperpyrexia, hypertension).	1	1	3
GUANETHIDINE			
Concurrent use may result in decreased guanethidine effectiveness.	1	3	2
IPRONIAZID			
Concurrent use may result in hypertensive crisis (headache, hyperpyrexia, hypertension).	1	1	3
ISOCARBOXAZID			
Concurrent use may result in hypertensive crisis (headache, hyperpyrexia, hypertension).	1	1	3
MOCLOBEMIDE			
Concurrent use may result in hypertensive crisis (headache, hyperpyrexia, hypertension).	1	1	3
NIALAMIDE			
Concurrent use may result in hypertensive crisis (headache, hyperpyrexia, hypertension).	1	1	3
PARGYLINE			
Concurrent use may result in hypertensive crisis (headache, hyperpyrexia, hypertension).	1	1	3

INTERACTION	ONSET	SEVERITY	EVIDENCE
PHENELZINE Concurrent use may result in hypertensive crisis (headache, hyperpyrexia, hypertension).	1	1	2
PROCARBAZINE Concurrent use may result in hypertensive crisis (headache, hyperpyrexia, hypertension).	1	1	3
SELEGILINE Concurrent use may result in hypertensive crisis (headache, hyperpyrexia, hypertension).	1	1	2
SIBUTRAMINE Concurrent use may result in an increased risk of hypertension and tachycardia.	1	1	3
SODIUM BICARBONATE Concurrent use may result in amphetamine toxicity (hypertension, hyperpyrexia, seizures).	2	3	3
TOLOXATONE Concurrent use may result in hypertensive crisis (headache, hyperpyrexia, hypertension).	1	1	3
TRANYLCYPROMINE Concurrent use may result in hypertensive crisis (headache, hyperpyrexia, hypertension).	1	1	2

Aripiprazole

INTERACTION	ONSET	SEVERITY	EVIDENCE
CARBAMAZEPINE Concurrent use may result in decreased aripiprazole concentrations.	2	2	3
FLUOXETINE Concurrent use may cause increased aripiprazole plasma levels.	2	2	3
KETOCONAZOLE Concurrent use may result in increased aripiprazole concentrations.	2	2	3
PAROXETINE Concurrent use may cause increased aripiprazole plasma levels.	2	2	3
QUINIDINE Concurrent use may result in increased aripiprazole plasma levels.	2	2	3

Atomoxetine

INTERACTION	ONSET	SEVERITY	EVIDENCE
ALBUTEROL Concurrent use may result in an increase in heart rate and blood pressure.	0	2	3

Onset: 0=Unspecified 1=Rapid 2=Delayed
Severity: 1=Contraindicated 2=Major 3=Moderate 4=Minor
Evidence: 1=Excellent 2=Good 3=Fair 4=Poor

INTERACTION	ONSET	SEVERITY	EVIDENCE
AMITRIPTYLINE Concurrent use may result in an increase in atomoxetine steady-state plasma concentrations.	0	3	3
AMOXAPINE Concurrent use may result in an increase in atomoxetine steady-state plasma concentrations.	0	3	3
CLOMIPRAMINE Concurrent use may result in an increase in atomoxetine steady-state plasma concentrations.	0	3	3
CLORGYLINE Concurrent use may result in an increased risk of serotonin syndrome (hypertension, hyperthermia, myoclonus, mental status changes).	0	1	3
DESIPRAMINE Concurrent use may result in an increase in atomoxetine steady-state plasma concentrations.	0	3	3
DIBENZEPIN Concurrent use may result in an increase in atomoxetine steady-state plasma concentrations.	0	3	3
DOTHIEPIN Concurrent use may result in an increase in atomoxetine steady-state plasma concentrations.	0	3	3
DOXEPIN Concurrent use may result in an increase in atomoxetine steady-state plasma concentrations.	0	3	3
FLUOXETINE Concurrent use may result in an increase in atomoxetine steady-state plasma concentrations.	0	3	3
IMIPRAMINE Concurrent use may result in an increase in atomoxetine steady-state plasma concentrations.	0	3	3
ISOCARBOXAZID Concurrent use may result in an increased risk of serotonin syndrome (hypertension, hyperthermia, myoclonus, mental status changes).	0	1	3
LAZABEMIDE Concurrent use may result in an increased risk of serotonin syndrome (hypertension, hyperthermia, myoclonus, mental status changes).	0	1	3
LOFEPRAMINE Concurrent use may result in an increase in atomoxetine steady-state plasma concentrations.	0	3	3
MOCLOBEMIDE Concurrent use may result in an increased risk of serotonin syndrome (hypertension, hyperthermia, myoclonus, mental status changes).	0	1	3

INTERACTION	ONSET	SEVERITY	EVIDENCE
NORTRIPTYLINE Concurrent use may result in an increase in atomoxetine steady-state plasma concentrations.	0	3	3
OPIPRAMOL Concurrent use may result in an increase in atomoxetine steady-state plasma concentrations.	0	3	3
PAROXETINE Concurrent use may result in an increase in atomoxetine steady-state plasma concentrations.	0	3	3
PHENELZINE Concurrent use may result in an increased risk of serotonin syndrome (hypertension, hyperthermia, myoclonus, mental status changes).	0	1	3
PROTRIPTYLINE Concurrent use may result in an increase in atomoxetine steady-state plasma concentrations.	0	3	3
QUINIDINE Concurrent use may result in an increase in atomoxetine steady-state plasma concentrations.	0	3	3
SELEGILINE Concurrent use may result in an increased risk of serotonin syndrome (hypertension, hyperthermia, myoclonus, mental status changes).	0	1	3
TRANYLCYPROMINE Concurrent use may result in an increased risk of serotonin syndrome (hypertension, hyperthermia, myoclonus, mental status changes).	0	1	3

Bupropion

INTERACTION	ONSET	SEVERITY	EVIDENCE
CLORGYLINE Concurrent use may result in bupropion toxicity.	1	1	3
DROPERIDOL Concurrent use may result in an increased risk of cardiotoxicity (QT prolongation, torsade de pointes, cardiac arrest).	1	2	3
ETHANOL Concurrent use may result in an increased risk of seizures.	2	2	3
IPRONIAZID Concurrent use may result in bupropion toxicity (seizures, agitation, psychotic changes).	1	1	3
ISOCARBOXAZID Concurrent use may result in bupropion toxicity (seizures, agitation, psychotic changes).	1	1	3

Onset: 0=Unspecified 1=Rapid 2=Delayed
Severity: 1=Contraindicated 2=Major 3=Moderate 4=Minor
Evidence: 1=Excellent 2=Good 3=Fair 4=Poor

INTERACTION	ONSET	SEVERITY	EVIDENCE
MOCLOBEMIDE Concurrent use may result in bupropion toxicity (seizures, agitation, psychotic changes).	1	1	3
NIALAMIDE Concurrent use may result in bupropion toxicity (seizures, agitation, psychotic changes).	1	1	3
PARGYLINE Concurrent use may result in bupropion toxicity (seizures, agitation, psychotic changes).	1	1	3
PHENELZINE Concurrent use may result in bupropion toxicity (seizures, agitation, psychotic changes).	1	1	3
PROCARBAZINE Concurrent use may result in bupropion toxicity (seizures, agitation, psychotic changes).	1	1	3
SELEGILINE Concurrent use may result in bupropion toxicity (seizures, agitation, psychotic changes).	1	1	3
TOLOXATONE Concurrent use may result in bupropion toxicity (seizures, agitation, psychotic changes).	1	1	3
TRANYLCYPROMINE Concurrent use may result in bupropion toxicity (seizures, agitation, psychotic changes).	1	1	3

Buspirone

INTERACTION	ONSET	SEVERITY	EVIDENCE
CLORGYLINE Concurrent use may result in hypertensive crisis.	1	2	3
DILTIAZEM Concurrent use may result in an increased risk of enhanced buspirone effects.	1	3	3
ERYTHROMYCIN Concurrent use may result in increased buspirone plasma concentrations; increased buspirone side effects (impaired psychomotor performance, sedation).	1	3	3
GRAPEFRUIT JUICE Concurrent use may result in an increased risk of buspirone toxicity (dizziness, sedation).	1	3	3
IPRONIAZID Concurrent use may result in hypertensive crisis.	1	2	3
ISOCARBOXAZID Concurrent use may result in hypertensive crisis.	1	1	3

INTERACTION	ONSET	SEVERITY	EVIDENCE
ITRACONAZOLE Concurrent use may result in increased buspirone plasma concentrations; increased buspirone side effects (impaired psychomotor performance, sedation).	1	3	3
MOCLOBEMIDE Concurrent use may result in hypertensive crisis.	1	2	3
NIALAMIDE Concurrent use may result in hypertensive crisis.	1	2	3
PARGYLINE Concurrent use may result in hypertensive crisis.	1	2	3
PHENELZINE Concurrent use may result in hypertensive crisis.	1	1	3
PROCARBAZINE Concurrent use may result in hypertensive crisis.	1	2	3
RIFAMPIN Concurrent use may result in reduced anxiolytic effects of buspirone.	1	3	3
SELEGILINE Concurrent use may result in hypertensive crisis.	1	2	3
TOLOXATONE Concurrent use may result in hypertensive crisis.	1	2	3
TRANYLCYPROMINE Concurrent use may result in hypertensive crisis.	1	1	3
VERAPAMIL Concurrent use may result in an increased risk of enhanced buspirone effects.	1	3	3

Chlordiazepoxide

INTERACTION	ONSET	SEVERITY	EVIDENCE
CIMETIDINE Concurrent use may result in chlordiazepoxide toxicity (central nervous system depression).	1	4	3
DISULFIRAM Concurrent use may result in an increased risk of chlordiazepoxide toxicity (central nervous system depression).	2	4	3
ETHANOL Concurrent use may result in increased sedation.	1	3	1
KETOCONAZOLE Concurrent use may result in increased chlordiazepoxide serum concentrations and potential chlordiazepoxide toxicity (sedation, slurred speech, central nervous system depression).	2	1	3

Onset: 0=Unspecified   1=Rapid   2=Delayed
Severity: 1=Contraindicated   2=Major   3=Moderate   4=Minor
Evidence: 1=Excellent   2=Good   3=Fair   4=Poor

INTERACTION	ONSET	SEVERITY	EVIDENCE
THEOPHYLLINE Concurrent use may result in decreased chlordiazepoxide effectiveness.	1	3	2

Chlorpromazine

INTERACTION	ONSET	SEVERITY	EVIDENCE
ANTACIDS Concurrent use may result in decreased chlorpromazine effectiveness.	2	4	3
ATENOLOL Concurrent use may result in hypotension and/or chlorpromazine toxicity.	1	3	2
BELLADONNA Concurrent use may result in increased manic, agitated reactions, or enhanced anticholinergic effects resulting in cardiorespiratory failure, especially in cases of belladonna overdose.	1	3	2
BENZTROPINE Concurrent use may result in decreased chlorpromazine serum concentrations, decreased chlorpromazine effectiveness, enhanced anticholinergic effects (ileus, hyperpyrexia, sedation, dry mouth).	2	3	3
CABERGOLINE Concurrent use may result in the decreased therapeutic effect of both drugs.	1	3	3
CISAPRIDE Concurrent use may result in cardiotoxicity (QT prolongation, torsade de pointes, cardiac arrest).	1	1	3
DROPERIDOL Concurrent use may result in an increased risk of cardiotoxicity (QT prolongation, torsade de pointes, cardiac arrest).	0	2	3
EPINEPHRINE Concurrent use may result in hypotension and tachycardia.	1	3	3
ETHANOL Concurrent use may result in increased sedation.	1	3	2
FOSPHENYTOIN Concurrent use may result in increased or decreased phenytoin levels and possibly reduced chlorpromazine levels.	2	4	3
GREPAFLOXACIN Concurrent use may result in an increased risk of cardiotoxicity (QT prolongation, torsade de pointes, cardiac arrest).	2	1	3
GUANETHIDINE Concurrent use may result in decreased guanethidine effectiveness.	1	3	2

INTERACTION	ONSET	SEVERITY	EVIDENCE
HALOFANTRINE Concurrent use may result in an increased risk of cardiotoxicity (QT prolongation, torsade de pointes, cardiac arrest).	0	2	3
LEVODOPA Concurrent use may result in loss of levodopa efficacy.	1	3	2
LEVOMETHADYL Concurrent use may result in an increased risk of cardiotoxicity (QT prolongation, torsade de pointes, cardiac arrest).	2	1	3
LITHIUM Concurrent use may result in weakness, dyskinesias, increased extrapyramidal symptoms, encephalopathy, and brain damage.	2	2	1
MEPERIDINE Concurrent use result in an increase in central nervous system and respiratory depression.	1	3	2
METOPROLOL Concurrent use may result in hypotension and/or chlorpromazine toxicity.	1	3	2
NOREPINEPHRINE Concurrent use may result in decreased norepinephrine effectiveness.	1	3	3
ORPHENADRINE Concurrent use may result in decreased chlorpromazine serum concentrations, decreased chlorpromazine effectiveness, enhanced anticholinergic effects (ileus, hyperpyrexia, sedation, dry mouth).	2	3	3
PHENMETRAZINE Concurrent use may result in decreased phenmetrazine effectiveness.	1	3	2
PHENOBARBITAL Concurrent use result in decreased chlorpromazine effectiveness.	1	3	3
PHENYTOIN Concurrent use may result in increased or decreased phenytoin levels and possibly reduced chlorpromazine levels.	2	4	3
PORFIMER Concurrent use may result in excessive intracellular damage in photosensitized tissues.	2	3	3
PROCYCLIDINE Concurrent use may result in decreased chlorpromazine serum concentrations, decreased chlorpromazine effectiveness, enhanced anticholinergic effects (ileus, hyperpyrexia, sedation, dry mouth).	2	3	3

Onset: 0=Unspecified 1=Rapid 2=Delayed
Severity: 1=Contraindicated 2=Major 3=Moderate 4=Minor
Evidence: 1=Excellent 2=Good 3=Fair 4=Poor

INTERACTION	ONSET	SEVERITY	EVIDENCE
PROPRANOLOL Concurrent use may result in chlorpromazine toxicity (sedation, extrapyramidal effects, delirium), seizures.	2	3	3
SPARFLOXACIN Concurrent use may result in prolongation of the QTc interval and/or torsade de pointes.	2	1	3
TRAMADOL Concurrent use may result in an increased risk of seizures.	1	2	3
TRIHEXYPHENIDYL Concurrent use may result in decreased chlorpromazine serum concentrations, decreased chlorpromazine effectiveness, enhanced anticholinergic effects (ileus, hyperpyrexia, sedation, dry mouth).	2	3	3
ZIPRASIDONE Concurrent use may result in an increased risk of cardiotoxicity (QT prolongation, torsade de pointes, cardiac arrest).	0	1	3

Citalopram

INTERACTION	ONSET	SEVERITY	EVIDENCE
ALMOTRIPTAN Concurrent use may result in weakness, hyperreflexia, and/or incoordination.	0	3	3
CLORGYLINE Concurrent use may result in central nervous system toxicity or serotonin syndrome (hypertension, hyperthermia, myoclonus, mental status changes).	1	1	3
DEXFENFLURAMINE Concurrent use may result in serotonin syndrome (hypertension, hyperthermia, myoclonus, mental status changes).	1	2	3
DROPERIDOL Concurrent use may result in an increased risk of cardiotoxicity (QT prolongation, torsade de pointes, cardiac arrest).	1	2	3
FENFLURAMINE Concurrent use may result in serotonin syndrome (hypertension, hyperthermia, myoclonus, mental status changes).	1	2	3
FURAZOLIDONE Concurrent use may result in weakness, hyperreflexia, and incoordination.	2	1	3
HYDROXYTRYPTOPHAN Concurrent use may result in an increased risk of serotonin syndrome (hypertension, hyperthermia, myoclonus, mental status changes).	1	3	3

INTERACTION	ONSET	SEVERITY	EVIDENCE
IPRONIAZID Concurrent use may result in central nervous system toxicity or serotonin syndrome (hypertension, hyperthermia, myoclonus, mental status changes).	1	1	3
ISOCARBOXAZID Concurrent use may result in central nervous system toxicity or serotonin syndrome (hypertension, hyperthermia, myoclonus, mental status changes).	1	1	3
LEVOMETHADYL Concurrent use may result in an increased risk of cardiotoxicity (QT prolongation, torsade de pointes, cardiac arrest).	2	1	3
MOCLOBEMIDE Concurrent use may result in serotonin syndrome (hypertension, hyperthermia, myoclonus, mental status changes).	1	1	3
NIALAMIDE Concurrent use may result in central nervous system toxicity or serotonin syndrome (hypertension, hyperthermia, myoclonus, mental status changes).	1	1	3
PARGYLINE Concurrent use may result in central nervous system toxicity or serotonin syndrome (hypertension, hyperthermia, myoclonus, mental status changes).	1	1	3
PHENELZINE Concurrent use may result in central nervous system toxicity or serotonin syndrome (hypertension, hyperthermia, myoclonus, mental status changes).	1	1	3
PROCARBAZINE Concurrent use may result in central nervous system toxicity or serotonin syndrome (hypertension, hyperthermia, myoclonus, mental status changes).	1	1	3
SELEGILINE Concurrent use may result in central nervous system toxicity or serotonin syndrome (hypertension, hyperthermia, myoclonus, mental status changes).	1	1	3
SIBUTRAMINE Concurrent use may result in an increased risk of serotonin syndrome (hypertension, hypothermia, myoclonus, mental status changes).	1	2	3
TOLOXATONE Concurrent use may result in central nervous system toxicity or serotonin syndrome (hypertension, hyperthermia, myoclonus, mental status changes).	1	1	3

Onset: 0=Unspecified 1=Rapid 2=Delayed
Severity: 1=Contraindicated 2=Major 3=Moderate 4=Minor
Evidence: 1=Excellent 2=Good 3=Fair 4=Poor

INTERACTION	ONSET	SEVERITY	EVIDENCE
TRAMADOL Concurrent use may result in an increased risk of seizures and serotonin syndrome (hypertension, hyperthermia, myoclonus, mental status changes).	1	2	2
TRANYLCYPROMINE Concurrent use may result in central nervous system toxicity or serotonin syndrome (hypertension, hyperthermia, myoclonus, mental status changes).	1	1	3

Clomipramine

INTERACTION	ONSET	SEVERITY	EVIDENCE
ACENOCOUMAROL Concurrent use may result in increased risk of bleeding.	2	3	3
AMPRENAVIR Concurrent use may result in increased clomipramine serum concentrations and potential toxicity (anticholinergic effects, sedation, confusion, cardiac arrhythmias).	2	2	3
ANISINDIONE Concurrent use may result in increased risk of bleeding.	2	3	3
BEPRIDIL Concurrent use may result in an increased risk of cardiotoxicity (QT prolongation, torsade de pointes, cardiac arrest).	1	1	3
BETHANIDINE Concurrent use may result in decreased antihypertensive effectiveness.	1	3	3
CIMETIDINE Concurrent use may result in clomipramine toxicity (dry mouth, blurred vision, urinary retention).	2	3	3
CISAPRIDE Concurrent use may result in cardiotoxicity (QT prolongation, torsade de pointes, cardiac arrest).	1	1	3
CLONIDINE Concurrent use may result in decreased antihypertensive effectiveness.	2	2	3
CLORGYLINE Concurrent use may result in neurotoxicity, seizures, or serotonin syndrome (hypertension, hyperthermia, myoclonus, mental status changes).	2	2	3
DICUMAROL Concurrent use may result in increased risk of bleeding.	2	3	3
EPINEPHRINE Concurrent use may result in hypertension, cardiac arrhythmias, and tachycardia.	1	2	2

INTERACTION	ONSET	SEVERITY	EVIDENCE
ETILEFRINE Concurrent use may result in hypertension, cardiac arrhythmias, and tachycardia.	1	2	2
FLUVOXAMINE Concurrent use may result in clomipramine toxicity (dry mouth, urinary retention, sedation).	2	3	3
GREPAFLOXACIN Concurrent use may result in an increased risk of cardiotoxicity (QT prolongation, torsade de pointes, cardiac arrest).	2	1	3
GUANADREL Concurrent use may result in decreased antihypertensive effectiveness.	2	3	3
HALOFANTRINE Concurrent use may result in an increased risk of cardiotoxicity (QT prolongation, torsade de pointes, cardiac arrest).	2	2	3
ISOCARBOXAZID Concurrent use may result in neurotoxicity, seizures, or serotonin syndrome (hypertension, hyperthermia, myoclonus, mental status changes).	2	1	3
METHOXAMINE Concurrent use may result in hypertension, cardiac arrhythmias, and tachycardia.	1	2	2
MIDODRINE Concurrent use may result in hypertension, cardiac arrhythmias, and tachycardia.	1	2	2
MOCLOBEMIDE Concurrent use may result in neurotoxicity, seizures, or serotonin syndrome (hypertension, hyperthermia, myoclonus, mental status changes).	1	2	3
NOREPINEPHRINE Concurrent use may result in hypertension, cardiac arrhythmias, and tachycardia.	1	2	2
OLANZAPINE Concurrent use may result in an increased risk of seizures.	2	2	2
OXILOFRINE Concurrent use may result in hypertension, cardiac arrhythmias, and tachycardia.	1	2	2
PHENELZINE Concurrent use may result in neurotoxicity, seizures, or serotonin syndrome (hypertension, hyperthermia, myoclonus, mental status changes).	2	2	3

Onset: 0=Unspecified **1**=Rapid **2**=Delayed
Severity: **1**=Contraindicated **2**=Major **3**=Moderate **4**=Minor
Evidence: **1**=Excellent **2**=Good **3**=Fair **4**=Poor

INTERACTION	ONSET	SEVERITY	EVIDENCE
PHENINDIONE Concurrent use may result in increased risk of bleeding.	2	3	3
PHENPROCOUMON Concurrent use may result in increased risk of bleeding.	2	3	3
PHENYLEPHRINE Concurrent use may result in hypertension, cardiac arrhythmias, and tachycardia.	1	2	2
PROCARBAZINE Concurrent use may result in neurotoxicity, seizures.	2	2	3
SELEGILINE Concurrent use may result in neurotoxicity, seizures, or serotonin syndrome (hypertension, hyperthermia, myoclonus, mental status changes).	2	2	3
TRAMADOL Concurrent use may result in an increased risk of seizures.	1	2	3
TRANYLCYPROMINE Concurrent use may result in neurotoxicity, seizures, or serotonin syndrome (hypertension, hyperthermia, myoclonus, mental status changes).	2	2	3
WARFARIN Concurrent use may result in an increased risk of bleeding.	2	3	3

Clonazepam

INTERACTION	ONSET	SEVERITY	EVIDENCE
CARBAMAZEPINE Concurrent use may result in reduced plasma levels of clonazepam.	2	3	3
CIMETIDINE Concurrent use may result in clonazepam toxicity (central nervous system depression).	1	4	3
KETOCONAZOLE Concurrent use may result in increased clonazepam serum concentrations and potential clonazepam toxicity (sedation, slurred speech, central nervous system depression).	2	1	3
THEOPHYLLINE Concurrent use may result in decreased clonazepam effectiveness.	1	3	2

Clorazepate

INTERACTION	ONSET	SEVERITY	EVIDENCE
CIMETIDINE Concurrent use may result in clorazepate toxicity (central nervous system depression).	1	4	3
ETHANOL Concurrent use may result in increased sedation.	1	3	2

INTERACTION	ONSET	SEVERITY	EVIDENCE
KETOCONAZOLE Concurrent use may result in increased clorazepate serum concentrations and potential clorazepate toxicity (sedation, slurred speech, central nervous system depression).	2	1	3
THEOPHYLLINE Concurrent use may result in decreased clorazepate effectiveness.	1	3	2

Clozapine

INTERACTION	ONSET	SEVERITY	EVIDENCE
CARBAMAZEPINE Concurrent use may result in an increased risk of bone marrow suppression, asterixis, or decreased serum clozapine levels.	2	2	3
DROPERIDOL Concurrent use may result in an increased risk of cardiotoxicity (QT prolongation, torsade de pointes, cardiac arrest).	1	1	3
ERYTHROMYCIN Concurrent use may result in increased clozapine serum concentrations and risk of side effects (sedation, incoordination, slurred speech, seizures, hematologic abnormalities).	2	3	3
FLUOXETINE Concurrent use may result in an increased risk of clozapine toxicity (sedation, seizures, hypotension).	2	3	3
FOSPHENYTOIN Concurrent use may result in decreased clozapine plasma levels associated with marked worsening of psychosis.	2	3	3
GUARANA Concomitant administration may lead to increased clozapine levels, (leukopenia, agranulocytosis, seizures) or increased guarana levels, (headache, insomnia, restlessness, diuresis, tachycardia).	2	3	3
LITHIUM Concurrent use may result in weakness, dyskinesias, increased extrapyramidal symptoms, encephalopathy, and brain damage.	2	2	1
LORAZEPAM Concurrent use may result in central nervous system depression.	1	4	3
PHENOBARBITAL Concurrent use may result in decreased clozapine plasma levels associated with marked worsening of psychosis.	2	3	3

Onset: 0=Unspecified 1=Rapid 2=Delayed
Severity: 1=Contraindicated 2=Major 3=Moderate 4=Minor
Evidence: 1=Excellent 2=Good 3=Fair 4=Poor

INTERACTION	ONSET	SEVERITY	EVIDENCE
PHENYTOIN Concurrent administration may result in decreased clozapine plasma levels associated with marked worsening of psychosis.	2	3	3
SERTRALINE Concurrent use may result in an increased risk of clozapine toxicity (sedation, seizures, hypotension).	2	3	3
TRAMADOL Concurrent use may result in an increased risk of seizures.	1	2	3

Desipramine

INTERACTION	ONSET	SEVERITY	EVIDENCE
ACENOCOUMAROL Concurrent use may result in increased risk of bleeding.	2	3	3
AMPRENAVIR Concurrent use may result in increased desipramine serum concentrations and potential toxicity (anticholinergic effects, sedation, confusion, cardiac arrhythmias).	2	2	3
ANISINDIONE Concurrent use of may result in increased risk of bleeding.	2	3	3
BEPRIDIL Concurrent use may result in an increased risk of cardiotoxicity (QT prolongation, torsade de pointes, cardiac arrest).	1	1	3
BETHANIDINE Concurrent use may result in decreased antihypertensive effectiveness.	1	3	2
CIMETIDINE Concurrent use may result in desipramine toxicity (dry mouth, blurred vision, urinary retention).	2	3	2
CISAPRIDE Concurrent use may result in cardiotoxicity (QT prolongation, torsade de pointes, cardiac arrest).	1	1	3
CLONIDINE Concurrent use may result in decreased antihypertensive effectiveness.	2	2	2
CLORGYLINE Concurrent use may result in neurotoxicity, seizures, or serotonin syndrome (hypertension, hyperthermia, myoclonus, mental status changes).	2	2	3
DICUMAROL Concurrent use may result in increased risk of bleeding.	2	3	3
DROPERIDOL Concurrent use may result in an increased risk of cardiotoxicity (QT prolongation, torsade de pointes, cardiac arrest).	0	2	3

INTERACTION	ONSET	SEVERITY	EVIDENCE
EPINEPHRINE Concurrent use may result in hypertension, cardiac arrhythmias, and tachycardia.	1	2	2
ETILEFRINE Concurrent use may result in hypertension, cardiac arrhythmias, and tachycardia.	1	2	2
FLUOXETINE Concurrent use may result in desipramine toxicity (dry mouth, urinary retention, sedation) and an increased risk of cardiotoxicity (QT prolongation, torsade de pointes, cardiac arrest).	0	2	3
GREPAFLOXACIN Concurrent use may result in an increased risk of cardiotoxicity (QT prolongation, torsade de pointes, cardiac arrest).	2	1	3
GUANADREL Concurrent use may result in decreased antihypertensive effectiveness.	2	3	3
GUANETHIDINE Concurrent use may result in decreased antihypertensive effectiveness.	2	3	1
HALOFANTRINE Concurrent use may result in an increased risk of cardiotoxicity (QT prolongation, torsade de pointes, cardiac arrest).	2	2	3
ISOCARBOXAZID Concurrent use may result in neurotoxicity, seizures, or serotonin syndrome.	2	1	3
LEVOMETHADYL Concurrent use may result in an increased risk of cardiotoxicity (QT prolongation, torsade de pointes, cardiac arrest).	2	1	3
METHOXAMINE Concurrent use may result in hypertension, cardiac arrhythmias, and tachycardia.	1	2	2
MIDODRINE Concurrent use may result in hypertension, cardiac arrhythmias, and tachycardia.	1	2	2
MOCLOBEMIDE Concurrent use may result in neurotoxicity, seizures, or serotonin syndrome (hypertension, hyperthermia, myoclonus, mental status changes).	2	2	3
NOREPINEPHRINE Concurrent use may result in hypertension, cardiac arrhythmias, and tachycardia.	1	2	2

Onset: 0=Unspecified 1=Rapid 2=Delayed
Severity: 1=Contraindicated 2=Major 3=Moderate 4=Minor
Evidence: 1=Excellent 2=Good 3=Fair 4=Poor

INTERACTION	ONSET	SEVERITY	EVIDENCE
OXILOFRINE Concurrent use may result in hypertension, cardiac arrhythmias, and tachycardia.	1	2	2
PHENELZINE Concurrent use may result in neurotoxicity, seizures, or serotonin syndrome (hypertension, hyperthermia, myoclonus, mental status changes).	2	2	3
PHENINDIONE Concurrent use may result in increased risk of bleeding.	2	3	3
PHENPROCOUMON Concurrent use may result in increased risk of bleeding.	2	3	3
PHENYLEPHRINE Concurrent use may result in hypertension, cardiac arrhythmias, and tachycardia.	1	2	2
PIMOZIDE Concurrent use may result in an increased risk of cardiotoxicity (QT prolongation, torsade de pointes, cardiac arrest).	0	1	3
PROCARBAZINE Concurrent use may result in neurotoxicity, seizures.	2	2	3
QUINIDINE Concurrent use may result in an increased risk of cardiotoxicity (QT prolongation, torsade de pointes, cardiac arrest).	0	2	3
RITONAVIR Concurrent use may result in increased desipramine plasma concentrations and potential desipramine toxicity (dry mouth, urinary retention, sedation, blurred vision).	2	3	3
SELEGILINE Concurrent use may result in neurotoxicity, seizures, or serotonin syndrome (hypertension, hyperthermia, myoclonus, mental status changes).	2	2	3
SPARFLOXACIN Concurrent use may result in prolongation of the QTc interval and/or torsade de pointes.	2	1	3
TRAMADOL Concurrent use may result in an increased risk of seizures.	1	2	3
TRANYLCYPROMINE Concurrent use may result in neurotoxicity, seizures, or serotonin syndrome (hypertension, hyperthermia, myoclonus, mental status changes).	2	2	3
WARFARIN Concurrent use may result in an increased risk of bleeding.	2	3	3

Dexmethylphenidate

INTERACTION	ONSET	SEVERITY	EVIDENCE
CLORGYLINE Concurrent use may result in hypertensive crisis (headache, palpitation, neck stiffness).	1	1	3
COUMARIN Concurrent use may result in an increased risk of bleeding.	1	3	3
IPRONIAZID Concurrent use may result in hypertensive crisis (headache, palpitation, neck stiffness).	1	1	3
ISOCARBOXAZID Concurrent use may result in hypertensive crisis (headache, palpitation, neck stiffness).	1	1	3
LAZABEMIDE Concurrent use may result in hypertensive crisis (headache, palpitation, neck stiffness).	1	1	3
MOCLOBEMIDE Concurrent use may result in hypertensive crisis (headache, palpitation, neck stiffness).	1	1	3
NIALAMIDE Concurrent use may result in hypertensive crisis (headache, palpitation, neck stiffness).	1	1	3
PARGYLINE Concurrent use may result in hypertensive crisis (headache, palpitation, neck stiffness).	1	1	3
PHENELZINE Concurrent use may result in hypertensive crisis (headache, palpitation, neck stiffness).	1	1	3
PHENOBARBITAL Concurrent use may result in an increase in phenobarbital plasma concentrations.	1	3	3
PHENYTOIN Concurrent use may result in an increase in phenytoin plasma concentrations.	1	3	3
PRIMIDONE Concurrent use may result in an increase in primidone plasma concentrations.	1	3	3
PROCARBAZINE Concurrent use may result in hypertensive crisis (headache, palpitation, neck stiffness).	1	1	3
SELEGILINE Concurrent use may result in hypertensive crisis (headache, palpitation, neck stiffness).	1	1	3

Onset: 0=Unspecified 1=Rapid 2=Delayed
Severity: 1=Contraindicated 2=Major 3=Moderate 4=Minor
Evidence: 1=Excellent 2=Good 3=Fair 4=Poor

INTERACTION	ONSET	SEVERITY	EVIDENCE
TOLOXATONE Concurrent use may result in hypertensive crisis (headache, palpitation, neck stiffness).	1	1	3
TRANYLCYPROMINE Concurrent use may result in hypertensive crisis (headache, palpitation, neck stiffness).	1	1	3

Dextroamphetamine

INTERACTION	ONSET	SEVERITY	EVIDENCE
ACETAZOLAMIDE Concurrent use may result in amphetamine toxicity (hypertension, hyperpyrexia, seizures).	1	3	2
ACIDIC FOODS Concurrent use may result in altered serum concentrations.	1	4	2
CLORGYLINE Concurrent use may result in a hypertensive crisis (headache, hyperpyrexia, hypertension).	1	1	3
FURAZOLIDONE Concurrent use may result in a hypertensive crisis (headache, hyperpyrexia, hypertension).	1	1	3
IPRONIAZID Concurrent use may result in a hypertensive crisis (headache, hyperpyrexia, hypertension).	1	1	3
ISOCARBOXAZID Concurrent use may result in a hypertensive crisis (headache, hyperpyrexia, hypertension).	1	1	3
MOCLOBEMIDE Concurrent use may result in a hypertensive crisis (headache, hyperpyrexia, hypertension).	1	1	3
NIALAMIDE Concurrent use may result in a hypertensive crisis (headache, hyperpyrexia, hypertension).	1	1	3
PARGYLINE Concurrent use may result in a hypertensive crisis (headache, hyperpyrexia, hypertension).	1	1	1
PHENELZINE Concurrent use may result in a hypertensive crisis (headache, hyperpyrexia, hypertension).	1	1	3
PROCARBAZINE Concurrent use may result in a hypertensive crisis (headache, hyperpyrexia, hypertension).	1	1	3
SELEGILINE Concurrent use may result in a hypertensive crisis (headache, hyperpyrexia, hypertension).	1	1	3
SIBUTRAMINE Concurrent use may result in an increased risk of hypertension and tachycardia.	1	1	3

INTERACTION	ONSET	SEVERITY	EVIDENCE
SODIUM BICARBONATE Concurrent use may result in amphetamine toxicity (hypertension, hyperpyrexia, seizures).	2	3	3
TOLOXATONE Concurrent use may result in a hypertensive crisis (headache, hyperpyrexia, hypertension).	1	1	3
TRANYLCYPROMINE Concurrent use may result in a hypertensive crisis (headache, hyperpyrexia, hypertension).	1	1	3

Diazepam

INTERACTION	ONSET	SEVERITY	EVIDENCE
CIMETIDINE Concurrent use may result in diazepam toxicity (central nervous system depression).	1	4	2
CLARITHROMYCIN Concurrent use may result in increased diazepam toxicity (central nervous system depression, ataxia, lethargy).	2	3	3
DISULFIRAM Concurrent use may result in an increased risk of central nervous system depression.	2	3	3
ERYTHROMYCIN Concurrent use may result in increased diazepam toxicity (central nervous system depression, ataxia, lethargy).	2	3	3
ETHANOL Concurrent use may result in increased sedation.	1	3	1
FLUOXETINE Concurrent use may result in higher serum concentrations of diazepam.	2	4	3
FLUVOXAMINE Concurrent use may result in diazepam and N-desmethyldiazepam accumulation.	2	3	2
FOOD Concurrent use may result in increased diazepam concentrations.	1	4	3
ITRACONAZOLE Concurrent use may result in increased diazepam serum concentrations and potential diazepam toxicity (sedation, slurred speech, central nervous system depression).	2	1	3
JOSAMYCIN Concurrent use may result in increased diazepam toxicity (central nervous system depression, ataxia, lethargy).	2	3	3

Onset: 0=Unspecified 1=Rapid 2=Delayed
Severity: 1=Contraindicated 2=Major 3=Moderate 4=Minor
Evidence: 1=Excellent 2=Good 3=Fair 4=Poor

INTERACTION	ONSET	SEVERITY	EVIDENCE
KETOCONAZOLE Concurrent use may result in increased diazepam serum concentrations and potential diazepam toxicity (sedation, slurred speech, central nervous system depression).	2	1	3
RIFAMPIN Concurrent use may result in decreased diazepam effectiveness.	2	3	3
ROXITHROMYCIN Concurrent use may result in increased diazepam toxicity (central nervous system depression, ataxia, lethargy).	2	3	3
THEOPHYLLINE Concurrent use may result in decreased diazepam effectiveness.	1	3	2
TROLEANDOMYCIN Concurrent use may result in increased diazepam toxicity (central nervous system depression, ataxia, lethargy).	2	3	3

Donepezil

INTERACTION	ONSET	SEVERITY	EVIDENCE
SUCCINYLCHOLINE Concurrent use may result in prolonged neuromuscular blockade.	1	2	3

Doxepin

INTERACTION	ONSET	SEVERITY	EVIDENCE
ACENOCOUMAROL Concurrent use may result in increased risk of bleeding.	2	3	3
AMPRENAVIR Concurrent use may result in increased doxepin serum concentrations and potential toxicity (anticholinergic effects, sedation, confusion, cardiac arrhythmias).	2	2	3
ANISINDIONE Concurrent use may result in increased risk of bleeding.	2	3	3
BEPRIDIL Concurrent use may result in an increased risk of cardiotoxicity (QT prolongation, torsade de pointes, cardiac arrest).	1	1	3
BETHANIDINE Concurrent use may result in decreased antihypertensive effectiveness.	1	3	2
CIMETIDINE Concurrent use may result in doxepin toxicity (dry mouth, blurred vision, urinary retention).	2	3	2
CISAPRIDE Concurrent use may result in cardiotoxicity (QT prolongation, torsade de pointes, cardiac arrest).	1	1	3

INTERACTION	ONSET	SEVERITY	EVIDENCE
CLONIDINE Concurrent use may result in decreased antihypertensive effectiveness.	2	2	3
CLORGYLINE Concurrent use may result in neurotoxicity, seizures, or serotonin syndrome (hypertension, hyperthermia, myoclonus, mental status changes).	2	2	3
DICUMAROL Concurrent use may result in increased risk of bleeding.	2	3	3
DROPERIDOL Concurrent use may result in an increased risk of cardiotoxicity (QT prolongation, torsade de pointes, cardiac arrest).	0	2	3
EPINEPHRINE Concurrent use may result in hypertension, cardiac arrhythmias, and tachycardia.	1	2	2
ETILEFRINE Concurrent use may result in hypertension, cardiac arrhythmias, and tachycardia.	1	2	2
FLUOXETINE Concurrent use may result in doxepin toxicity (dry mouth, urinary retention, sedation) and an increased risk of cardiotoxicity (QT prolongation, torsade de pointes, cardiac arrest).	0	2	3
GREPAFLOXACIN Concurrent use may result in an increased risk of cardiotoxicity (QT prolongation, torsade de pointes, cardiac arrest).	2	1	3
GUANADREL Concurrent use may result in decreased antihypertensive effectiveness.	2	3	3
GUANETHIDINE Concurrent use may result in decreased antihypertensive effectiveness.	2	3	3
HALOFANTRINE Concurrent use may result in an increased risk of cardiotoxicity (QT prolongation, torsade de pointes, cardiac arrest).	2	2	3
ISOCARBOXAZID Concurrent use may result in neurotoxicity, seizures, or serotonin syndrome (hypertension, hyperthermia, myoclonus, mental status changes).	2	1	3
METHOXAMINE Concurrent use may result in hypertension, cardiac arrhythmias, and tachycardia.	1	2	2

Onset: 0=Unspecified 1=Rapid 2=Delayed
Severity: 1=Contraindicated 2=Major 3=Moderate 4=Minor
Evidence: 1=Excellent 2=Good 3=Fair 4=Poor

INTERACTION	ONSET	SEVERITY	EVIDENCE
MIDODRINE Concurrent use may result in hypertension, cardiac arrhythmias, and tachycardia.	1	2	2
MOCLOBEMIDE Concurrent use may result in neurotoxicity, seizures, or serotonin syndrome (hypertension, hyperthermia, myoclonus, mental status changes).	2	2	3
NOREPINEPHRINE Concurrent use may result in hypertension, cardiac arrhythmias, and tachycardia.	1	2	2
OXILOFRINE Concurrent use may result in hypertension, cardiac arrhythmias, and tachycardia.	1	2	2
PHENELZINE Concurrent use may result in neurotoxicity, seizures, or serotonin syndrome (hypertension, hyperthermia, myoclonus, mental status changes).	2	2	3
PHENINDIONE Concurrent use may result in increased risk of bleeding.	2	3	3
PHENPROCOUMON Concurrent use may result in increased risk of bleeding.	2	3	3
PHENYLEPHRINE Concurrent use may result in hypertension, cardiac arrhythmias, and tachycardia.	1	2	2
PIMOZIDE Concurrent use may result in an increased risk of cardiotoxicity (QT prolongation, torsade de pointes, cardiac arrest).	0	1	3
PROCARBAZINE Concurrent use may result in neurotoxicity, seizures.	2	2	3
SELEGILINE Concurrent use may result in neurotoxicity, seizures, or serotonin syndrome (hypertension, hyperthermia, myoclonus, mental status changes).	2	2	3
TRAMADOL Concurrent use may result in an increased risk of seizures.	1	2	3
TRANYLCYPROMINE Concurrent use may result in neurotoxicity, seizures, or serotonin syndrome (hypertension, hyperthermia, myoclonus, mental status changes).	2	2	3
WARFARIN Concurrent use may result in an increased risk of bleeding.	2	3	3

Escitalopram

INTERACTION	ONSET	SEVERITY	EVIDENCE
ALMOTRIPTAN Concurrent use may result in weakness, hyperreflexia, and/or incoordination.	0	3	3
CLORGYLINE Concurrent use may result in central nervous system toxicity or serotonin syndrome (hypertension, hyperthermia, myoclonus, mental status changes).	1	1	3
ENTACAPONE Concurrent use may result in decreased catecholamine metabolism.	1	2	3
ETHANOL Concurrent use may result in the potentiation of the cognitive and motor effects of alcohol.	0	3	3
FURAZOLIDONE Concurrent use may result in weakness, hyperreflexia, and incoordination.	2	1	3
HYDROXYTRYPTOPHAN Concurrent use may result in an increased risk of serotonin syndrome (hypertension, hyperthermia, myoclonus, mental status changes).	1	3	3
ISOCARBOXAZID Concurrent use may result in central nervous system toxicity or serotonin syndrome (hypertension, hyperthermia, myoclonus, mental status changes).	1	1	3
LAZABEMIDE Concurrent use may result in central nervous system toxicity or serotonin syndrome (hypertension, hyperthermia, myoclonus, mental status changes).	1	1	3
LINEZOLID Concurrent use may result in central nervous system toxicity or serotonin syndrome (hypertension, hyperthermia, myoclonus, mental status changes).	1	2	3
LITHIUM Concurrent use may result in possible lithium toxicity (weakness, tremor, excessive thirst, confusion, dizziness).	2	3	3
MOCLOBEMIDE Concurrent use may result in central nervous system toxicity or serotonin syndrome (hypertension, hyperthermia, myoclonus, mental status changes).	1	1	3
PHENELZINE Concurrent use may result in central nervous system toxicity or serotonin syndrome (hypertension, hyperthermia, myoclonus, mental status changes).	1	1	3

Onset: 0=Unspecified 1=Rapid 2=Delayed
Severity: 1=Contraindicated 2=Major 3=Moderate 4=Minor
Evidence: 1=Excellent 2=Good 3=Fair 4=Poor

INTERACTION	ONSET	SEVERITY	EVIDENCE
SELEGILINE Concurrent use may result in central nervous system toxicity or serotonin syndrome (hypertension, hyperthermia, myoclonus, mental status changes).	1	1	3
SIBUTRAMINE Concurrent use may result in an increased risk of serotonin syndrome (hypertension, hypothermia, myoclonus, mental status changes).	1	2	3
ST. JOHN'S WORT Concurrent use may result in an increased risk of serotonin syndrome (hypertension, hyperthermia, myoclonus, mental status changes).	1	2	3
SUMATRIPTAN Concurrent use may result in an increased risk of weakness, hyperreflexia, incoordination.	0	3	3
TOLCAPONE Concurrent use may result in decreased catecholamine metabolism.	1	2	3
TRAMADOL Concurrent use may result in an increased risk of seizures and serotonin syndrome (hypertension, hyperthermia, myoclonus, mental status changes).	1	2	3
TRANYLCYPROMINE Concurrent use may result in central nervous system toxicity or serotonin syndrome (hypertension, hyperthermia, myoclonus, mental status changes).	1	1	3
ZOLMITRIPTAN Concurrent use may result in weakness, hyperreflexia, and incoordination.	1	3	3

Estazolam

INTERACTION	ONSET	SEVERITY	EVIDENCE
CIMETIDINE Concurrent use may result in estazolam toxicity (central nervous system depression).	1	4	3
KETOCONAZOLE Concurrent use may result in increased estazolam serum concentrations and potential estazolam toxicity (sedation, slurred speech, central nervous system depression).	2	1	3
THEOPHYLLINE Concurrent use may result in decreased estazolam effectiveness.	1	3	2

Fluoxetine

INTERACTION	ONSET	SEVERITY	EVIDENCE
ALMOTRIPTAN Concurrent use may result in weakness, hyperreflexia, and/or incoordination.	0	3	3

INTERACTION	ONSET	SEVERITY	EVIDENCE
ALPRAZOLAM			
Concurrent use may result in an increased risk of alprazolam toxicity (somnolence, dizziness, ataxia, slurred speech, hypotension, psychomotor impairment).	1	3	2
AMITRIPTYLINE			
Concurrent use may result in amitriptyline toxicity (dry mouth, urinary retention, sedation) and an increased risk of cardiotoxicity (QT prolongation, torsade de pointes, cardiac arrest).	0	2	3
AMOXAPINE			
Concurrent use may result in amoxapine toxicity (dry mouth, urinary retention, sedation) and an increased risk of cardiotoxicity (QT prolongation, torsade de pointes, cardiac arrest).	0	2	3
ASTEMIZOLE			
Concurrent use may result in cardiotoxicity (QT interval prolongation, torsade de pointes, cardiac arrest).	1	2	3
CLORGYLINE			
Concurrent use may result in central nervous system toxicity or serotonin syndrome (hypertension, hyperthermia, myoclonus, mental status changes).	1	1	2
CLOZAPINE			
Concurrent use may result in an increased risk of clozapine toxicity (sedation, seizures, hypotension).	2	3	3
DESIPRAMINE			
Concurrent use may result in desipramine toxicity (dry mouth, urinary retention, sedation) and an increased risk of cardiotoxicity (QT prolongation, torsade de pointes, cardiac arrest).	0	2	3
DEXFENFLURAMINE			
Concurrent use may result in serotonin syndrome (hypertension, hyperthermia, myoclonus, mental status changes).	1	2	3
DEXTROMETHORPHAN			
Concurrent use may result in possible dextromethorphan toxicity (nausea, vomiting, blurred vision, hallucinations) or serotonin syndrome (hypertension, hyperthermia, myoclonus, mental status changes).	1	2	3
DIAZEPAM			
Concurrent use may result in higher serum concentrations of diazepam.	2	4	3
DOXEPIN			
Concurrent use may result in doxepin toxicity (dry mouth, urinary retention, sedation) and an increased risk of cardiotoxicity (QT prolongation, torsade de pointes, cardiac arrest).	0	2	3

Onset: 0=Unspecified 1=Rapid 2=Delayed
Severity: 1=Contraindicated 2=Major 3=Moderate 4=Minor
Evidence: 1=Excellent 2=Good 3=Fair 4=Poor

INTERACTION	ONSET	SEVERITY	EVIDENCE
DROPERIDOL Concurrent use may result in an increased risk of cardiotoxicity (QT prolongation, torsade de pointes, cardiac arrest).	0	2	3
FENFLURAMINE Concurrent use may result in serotonin syndrome (hypertension, hyperthermia, myoclonus, mental status changes).	1	2	3
FOSPHENYTOIN Concurrent use of may result in an increased risk of phenytoin toxicity (ataxia, hyperreflexia, nystagmus, tremor).	2	3	3
FURAZOLIDONE Concurrent use may result in weakness, hyperreflexia, and incoordination.	2	1	3
HYDROXYTRYPTOPHAN Concurrent use may result in an increased risk of serotonin syndrome (hypertension, hyperthermia, myoclonus, mental status changes).	1	3	3
IMIPRAMINE Concurrent use may result in imipramine toxicity (dry mouth, urinary retention, sedation) and an increased risk of cardiotoxicity (QT prolongation, torsade de pointes, cardiac arrest).	0	2	3
IPRONIAZID Concurrent use may result in central nervous system toxicity or serotonin syndrome (hypertension, hyperthermia, myoclonus, mental status changes).	1	1	2
ISOCARBOXAZID Concurrent use may result in central nervous system toxicity or serotonin syndrome (hypertension, hyperthermia, myoclonus, mental status changes).	1	1	2
LEVOMETHADYL Concurrent use may result in an increased risk of cardiotoxicity (QT prolongation, torsade de pointes, cardiac arrest).	2	1	3
MOCLOBEMIDE Concurrent use may result in central nervous system toxicity or serotonin syndrome (hypertension, hyperthermia, myoclonus, mental status changes).	1	1	3
NIALAMIDE Concurrent use may result in central nervous system toxicity or serotonin syndrome (hypertension, hyperthermia, myoclonus, mental status changes).	1	1	2
NORTRIPTYLINE Concurrent use may result in nortriptyline toxicity (dry mouth, urinary retention, sedation) and an increased risk of cardiotoxicity (QT prolongation, torsade de pointes, cardiac arrest).	0	2	3

INTERACTION	ONSET	SEVERITY	EVIDENCE
PARGYLINE Concurrent use may result in central nervous system toxicity or serotonin syndrome (hypertension, hyperthermia, myoclonus, mental status changes).	1	1	2
PHENELZINE Concurrent use may result in central nervous system toxicity or serotonin syndrome (hypertension, hyperthermia, myoclonus, mental status changes).	1	1	2
PHENYTOIN Concurrent use may result in an increased risk of phenytoin toxicity (ataxia, hyperreflexia, nystagmus, tremor).	2	3	3
PROCARBAZINE Concurrent use may result in central nervous system toxicity or serotonin syndrome (hypertension, hyperthermia, myoclonus, mental status changes).	1	1	2
SELEGILINE Concurrent use may result in central nervous system toxicity or serotonin syndrome (hypertension, hyperthermia, myoclonus, mental status changes).	1	1	2
SIBUTRAMINE Concurrent use may result in an increased risk of serotonin syndrome (hypertension, hypothermia, myoclonus, mental status changes).	1	2	3
THIORIDAZINE Concurrent use may result in an increased risk of cardiotoxicity (QT prolongation, torsade de pointes, cardiac arrest).	1	1	3
TOLOXATONE Concurrent use may result in central nervous system toxicity or serotonin syndrome (hypertension, hyperthermia, myoclonus, mental status changes).	1	1	2
TRAMADOL Concurrent use may result in an increased risk of seizures and serotonin syndrome (hypertension, hyperthermia, myoclonus, mental status changes).	1	2	2
TRANYLCYPROMINE Concurrent use may result in central nervous system toxicity or serotonin syndrome (hypertension, hyperthermia, myoclonus, mental status changes).	1	1	2
TRAZODONE Concurrent use may result in trazodone toxicity (sedation, dry mouth, urinary retention) or serotonin syndrome (hypertension, hyperthermia, myoclonus, mental status changes).	2	2	3

Onset: 0=Unspecified 1=Rapid 2=Delayed
Severity: 1=Contraindicated 2=Major 3=Moderate 4=Minor
Evidence: 1=Excellent 2=Good 3=Fair 4=Poor

INTERACTION	ONSET	SEVERITY	EVIDENCE
TRIMIPRAMINE Concurrent use may result in trimipramine toxicity (dry mouth, urinary retention, sedation) and an increased risk of cardiotoxicity (QT prolongation, torsade de pointes, cardiac arrest).	0	2	3
TRYPTOPHAN Concurrent use may result in serotonin syndrome (hypertension, hyperthermia, myoclonus, mental status changes).	2	2	3
WARFARIN Concurrent use may result in an increased risk of bleeding.	2	3	3

Fluphenazine

INTERACTION	ONSET	SEVERITY	EVIDENCE
BELLADONNA Concurrent use may result in increased manic, agitated reactions, or enhanced anticholinergic effects resulting in cardiorespiratory failure, especially in cases of belladonna overdose.	1	3	2
BENZTROPINE Concurrent use may result in decreased fluphenazine serum concentrations, decreased fluphenazine effectiveness, enhanced anticholinergic effects (ileus, hyperpyrexia, sedation, dry mouth).	2	3	3
CABERGOLINE Concurrent use may result in the decreased therapeutic effect of both drugs.	1	3	3
CISAPRIDE Concurrent use may result in cardiotoxicity (QT prolongation, torsade de pointes, cardiac arrest).	1	1	3
ETHANOL Concurrent use may result in increased central nervous system depression and an increased risk of extrapyramidal reactions.	1	3	2
FOSPHENYTOIN Concurrent use may result in increased or decreased phenytoin levels and possibly reduced fluphenazine levels.	2	4	3
GREPAFLOXACIN Concurrent use may result in an increased risk of cardiotoxicity (QT prolongation, torsade de pointes, cardiac arrest).	2	1	3
LEVODOPA Concurrent use may result in loss of levodopa efficacy.	1	3	2
LITHIUM Concurrent use may result in weakness, dyskinesias, increased extrapyramidal symptoms, encephalopathy, and brain damage.	2	2	1

INTERACTION	ONSET	SEVERITY	EVIDENCE
MEPERIDINE Concurrent use may result in an increase in central nervous system and respiratory depression.	1	3	2
ORPHENADRINE Concurrent use may result in decreased fluphenazine serum concentrations, decreased fluphenazine effectiveness, enhanced anticholinergic effects (ileus, hyperpyrexia, sedation, dry mouth).	2	3	3
PHENYTOIN Concurrent use may result in increased or decreased phenytoin levels and possibly reduced fluphenazine levels.	2	4	3
PORFIMER Concurrent use may result in excessive intracellular damage in photosensitized tissues.	2	3	3
PROCYCLIDINE Concurrent use may result in decreased fluphenazine serum concentrations, decreased fluphenazine effectiveness, enhanced anticholinergic effects (ileus, hyperpyrexia, sedation, dry mouth).	2	3	3
TRAMADOL Concurrent use may result in an increased risk of seizures.	1	2	3
TRIHEXYPHENIDYL Concurrent use may result in decreased fluphenazine serum concentrations, decreased fluphenazine effectiveness, enhanced anticholinergic effects (ileus, hyperpyrexia, sedation, dry mouth).	2	3	3

Flurazepam

INTERACTION	ONSET	SEVERITY	EVIDENCE
CIMETIDINE Concurrent use may result in flurazepam toxicity (central nervous system depression).	2	4	3
KETOCONAZOLE Concurrent use may result in increased flurazepam serum concentrations and potential flurazepam toxicity (sedation, slurred speech, central nervous system depression).	2	1	3
THEOPHYLLINE Concurrent use may result in decreased flurazepam. effectiveness.	1	3	2

Fluvoxamine

INTERACTION	ONSET	SEVERITY	EVIDENCE
ACECLOFENAC Concurrent use may result in an increased risk of bleeding.	0	3	2
ACEMETACIN Concurrent use may result in an increased risk of bleeding.	0	3	2

Onset: 0=Unspecified 1=Rapid 2=Delayed
Severity: 1=Contraindicated 2=Major 3=Moderate 4=Minor
Evidence: 1=Excellent 2=Good 3=Fair 4=Poor

INTERACTION	ONSET	SEVERITY	EVIDENCE
ALCLOFENAC Concurrent use may result in an increased risk of bleeding.	0	3	2
ALMOTRIPTAN Concurrent use may result in weakness, hyperreflexia, and/or incoordination.	0	3	3
ALPRAZOLAM Concurrent use may result in elevated plasma alprazolam levels and an increased risk of side effects (central nervous system depression).	2	3	2
AMITRIPTYLINE Concurrent use may result in amitriptyline toxicity (dry mouth, urinary retention, sedation).	2	3	3
ASPIRIN Concurrent use may result in an increased risk of bleeding.	0	3	2
ASTEMIZOLE Concurrent use may result in cardiotoxicity (QT prolongation, torsade de pointes, cardiac arrest).	1	1	3
BENOXAPROFEN Concurrent use may result in an increased risk of bleeding.	0	3	2
BROMFENAC Concurrent use may result in an increased risk of bleeding.	0	3	2
BUFEXAMAC Concurrent use may result in an increased risk of bleeding.	0	3	2
CARPROFEN Concurrent use may result in an increased risk of bleeding.	0	3	2
CELECOXIB Concurrent use may result in an increased risk of bleeding.	0	3	2
CISAPRIDE Concurrent use may result in cardiotoxicity (QT prolongation, torsade de pointes, cardiac arrest).	1	1	3
CLOMIPRAMINE Concurrent use may result in clomipramine toxicity (dry mouth, urinary retention, sedation).	2	3	3
CLONIXIN Concurrent use may result in an increased risk of bleeding.	0	3	2
CLORGYLINE Concurrent use may result in central nervous system toxicity or serotonin syndrome (hypertension, hyperthermia, myoclonus, mental status changes).	1	2	2
CLOZAPINE Concurrent use may result in increased serum clozapine concentrations.	2	3	3
DEXFENFLURAMINE Concurrent use may result in serotonin syndrome (hypertension, hyperthermia, myoclonus, mental status changes).	1	2	3

INTERACTION	ONSET	SEVERITY	EVIDENCE
DEXKETOPROFEN Concurrent use may result in an increased risk of bleeding.	0	3	2
DIAZEPAM Concurrent use may result in diazepam and N-desmethyldiazepam accumulation.	2	3	2
DICLOFENAC Concurrent use may result in an increased risk of bleeding.	0	3	2
DIFLUNISAL Concurrent use may result in an increased risk of bleeding.	0	3	2
DIHYDROERGOTAMINE Concurrent use may result in an increased risk of ergotism (nausea, vomiting, vasospastic ischemia).	1	1	3
DIPYRONE Concurrent use may result in an increased risk of bleeding.	0	3	2
DROPERIDOL Concurrent use may result in an increased risk of cardiotoxicity (QT prolongation, torsade de pointes, cardiac arrest).	1	2	3
DROXICAM Concurrent use may result in an increased risk of bleeding.	0	3	2
ERGOLOID MESYLATES Concurrent use may result in an increased risk of ergotism (nausea, vomiting, vasospastic ischemia).	1	1	3
ERGONOVINE Concurrent use may result in an increased risk of ergotism (nausea, vomiting, vasospastic ischemia).	1	1	3
ERGOTAMINE Concurrent use may result in an increased risk of ergotism (nausea, vomiting, vasospastic ischemia).	1	1	3
ETODOLAC Concurrent use may result in an increased risk of bleeding.	0	3	2
ETOFENAMATE Concurrent use may result in an increased risk of bleeding.	0	3	2
ETORICOXIB Concurrent use may result in an increased risk of bleeding.	0	3	2
FELBINAC Concurrent use may result in an increased risk of bleeding.	0	3	2
FENBUFEN Concurrent use may result in an increased risk of bleeding.	0	3	2
FENFLURAMINE Concurrent use may result in serotonin syndrome (hypertension, hyperthermia, myoclonus, mental status changes).	1	2	3

Onset: 0=Unspecified 1=Rapid 2=Delayed
Severity: 1=Contraindicated 2=Major 3=Moderate 4=Minor
Evidence: 1=Excellent 2=Good 3=Fair 4=Poor

INTERACTION	ONSET	SEVERITY	EVIDENCE
FENOPROFEN Concurrent use may result in an increased risk of bleeding.	0	3	2
FENTIAZAC Concurrent use may result in an increased risk of bleeding.	0	3	2
FLOCTAFENINE Concurrent use may result in an increased risk of bleeding.	0	3	2
FLUFENAMIC ACID Concurrent use may result in an increased risk of bleeding.	0	3	2
FLURBIPROFEN Concurrent use may result in an increased risk of bleeding.	0	3	2
FOSPHENYTOIN Concurrent use may result in an increased risk of phenytoin toxicity (ataxia, hyperreflexia, nystagmus, tremors).	2	3	3
FURAZOLIDONE Concurrent use may result in weakness, hyperreflexia, and incoordination.	2	1	3
GRAPEFRUIT JUICE Concurrent use may result in increased fluvoxamine exposure.	1	4	2
GUARANA Concomitant administration may result in symptoms of excessive caffeine (insomnia, headache, restlessness, nervousness, palpitations, and arrhythmias).	1	3	3
HYDROXYTRYPTOPHAN Concurrent use may result in an increased risk of serotonin syndrome (hypertension, hyperthermia, myoclonus, mental status changes).	1	3	3
IBUPROFEN Concurrent use may result in an increased risk of bleeding.	0	3	2
IMIPRAMINE Concurrent use may result in imipramine toxicity (dry mouth, urinary retention, sedation).	2	3	3
INDOMETHACIN Concurrent use may result in an increased risk of bleeding.	0	3	2
INDOPROFEN Concurrent use may result in an increased risk of bleeding.	0	3	2
IPRONIAZID Concurrent use may result in central nervous system toxicity or serotonin syndrome (hypertension, hyperthermia, myoclonus, mental status changes).	1	2	2
ISOCARBOXAZID Concurrent use may result in central nervous system toxicity or serotonin syndrome (hypertension, hyperthermia, myoclonus, mental status changes).	1	1	2
ISOXICAM Concurrent use may result in an increased risk of bleeding.	0	3	2

INTERACTION	ONSET	SEVERITY	EVIDENCE
KETOPROFEN Concurrent use may result in an increased risk of bleeding.	0	3	2
KETOROLAC Concurrent use may result in an increased risk of bleeding.	0	3	2
LEVOMETHADYL Concurrent use may result in an increased risk of cardiotoxicity (QT prolongation, torsade de pointes, cardiac arrest).	2	1	3
LINEZOLID Concurrent use may result in central nervous system toxicity or serotonin syndrome (hypertension, hyperthermia, myoclonus, mental status changes).	1	1	2
LITHIUM Concurrent use may result in possible lithium toxicity (weakness, tremor, excessive thirst, confusion, dizziness).	2	3	3
LORNOXICAM Concurrent use may result in an increased risk of bleeding.	0	3	2
MECLOFENAMATE Concurrent use may result in an increased risk of bleeding.	0	3	2
MEFENAMIC ACID Concurrent use may result in an increased risk of bleeding.	0	3	2
MELATONIN Concurrent use may result in increased central nervous system depression.	1	4	3
MELOXICAM Concurrent use may result in an increased risk of bleeding.	0	3	2
METHADONE Concurrent use may result in increased plasma methadone levels.	2	3	3
METHYLERGONOVINE Concurrent use may result in an increased risk of ergotism (nausea, vomiting, vasospastic ischemia).	1	1	3
MIDAZOLAM Concurrent use may result in elevated serum midazolam concentrations.	2	3	3
MOCLOBEMIDE Concurrent use may result in central nervous system toxicity or serotonin syndrome (hypertension, hyperthermia, myoclonus, mental status changes).	1	2	2

Onset: 0=Unspecified 1=Rapid 2=Delayed
Severity: 1=Contraindicated 2=Major 3=Moderate 4=Minor
Evidence: 1=Excellent 2=Good 3=Fair 4=Poor

INTERACTION	ONSET	SEVERITY	EVIDENCE
MORNIFLUMATE Concurrent use may result in an increased risk of bleeding.	0	3	2
NABUMETONE Concurrent use may result in an increased risk of bleeding.	0	3	2
NAPROXEN Concurrent use may result in an increased risk of bleeding.	0	3	2
NIALAMIDE Concurrent use may result in central nervous system toxicity or serotonin syndrome (hypertension, hyperthermia, myoclonus, mental status changes).	1	2	2
NIFLUMIC ACID Concurrent use may result in an increased risk of bleeding.	0	3	2
NIMESULIDE Concurrent use may result in an increased risk of bleeding.	0	3	2
OLANZAPINE Concurrent use may result in an increased risk of olanzapine adverse effects.	2	3	3
OXAPROZIN Concurrent use may result in an increased risk of bleeding.	0	3	2
PARECOXIB Concurrent use may result in an increased risk of bleeding.	0	3	2
PARGYLINE Concurrent use may result in central nervous system toxicity or serotonin syndrome (hypertension, hyperthermia, myoclonus, mental status changes).	1	2	2
PHENELZINE Concurrent use may result in central nervous system toxicity or serotonin syndrome (hypertension, hyperthermia, myoclonus, mental status changes).	1	1	2
PHENYLBUTAZONE Concurrent use may result in an increased risk of bleeding.	0	3	2
PHENYTOIN Concurrent use may result in an increased risk of phenytoin toxicity (ataxia, hyperreflexia, nystagmus, tremors).	2	3	3
PIRAZOLAC Concurrent use may result in an increased risk of bleeding.	0	3	2
PIROXICAM Concurrent use may result in an increased risk of bleeding.	0	3	2
PIRPROFEN Concurrent use may result in an increased risk of bleeding.	0	3	2
PROCARBAZINE Concurrent use may result in central nervous system toxicity or serotonin syndrome (hypertension, hyperthermia, myoclonus, mental status changes).	1	2	2

INTERACTION	ONSET	SEVERITY	EVIDENCE
PROPRANOLOL Concurrent use may result in bradycardia and hypotension.	2	3	3
PROPYPHENAZONE Concurrent use may result in an increased risk of bleeding.	0	3	2
PROQUAZONE Concurrent use may result in an increased risk of bleeding.	0	3	2
ROFECOXIB Concurrent use may result in an increased risk of bleeding.	0	3	2
ROPIVACAINE Concurrent use may result in increased plasma levels of ropivacaine.	1	3	3
SELEGILINE Concurrent use may result in central nervous system toxicity or serotonin syndrome (hypertension, hyperthermia, myoclonus, mental status changes).	1	2	2
SIBUTRAMINE Concurrent use may result in an increased risk of serotonin syndrome (hypertension, hypothermia, myoclonus, mental status changes).	1	2	3
ST. JOHN'S WORT Concurrent use may result in an increased risk of serotonin syndrome (hypertension, hyperthermia, myoclonus, mental status changes).	1	2	3
SULINDAC Concurrent use may result in an increased risk of bleeding.	0	3	2
SUMATRIPTAN Concurrent use may result in an increased risk of weakness, hyperreflexia, and incoordination.	2	2	3
SUPROFEN Concurrent use may result in an increased risk of bleeding.	0	3	2
TACRINE Concurrent use may result in an increase in the plasma concentration of tacrine.	1	3	3
TENIDAP Concurrent use may result in an increased risk of bleeding.	0	3	2
TENOXICAM Concurrent use may result in an increased risk of bleeding.	0	3	2
TERFENADINE Concurrent use may result in cardiotoxicity (QT prolongation, torsade de pointes, cardiac arrest).	1	1	3
THEOPHYLLINE Concurrent use may result in theophylline toxicity (nausea, vomiting, palpitations, seizures).	2	2	3

Onset: 0=Unspecified 1=Rapid 2=Delayed
Severity: 1=Contraindicated 2=Major 3=Moderate 4=Minor
Evidence: 1=Excellent 2=Good 3=Fair 4=Poor

INTERACTION	ONSET	SEVERITY	EVIDENCE
THIORIDAZINE Concurrent use may result in an increased risk of thioridazine toxicity, cardiotoxicity (QT prolongation, torsade de pointes, cardiac arrest).	1	1	3
TIAPROFENIC ACID Concurrent use may result in an increased risk of bleeding.	0	3	2
TOBACCO Concurrent use may result in increased fluvoxamine metabolism.	2	4	3
TOLMETIN Concurrent use may result in an increased risk of bleeding.	0	3	2
TOLOXATONE Concurrent use may result in central nervous system toxicity or serotonin syndrome (hypertension, hyperthermia, myoclonus, mental status changes).	1	2	2
TRAMADOL Concurrent use may result in an increased risk of seizures and serotonin syndrome (hypertension, hyperthermia, myoclonus, mental status changes).	1	2	2
TRANYLCYPROMINE Concurrent use may result in central nervous system toxicity or serotonin syndrome (hypertension, hyperthermia, myoclonus, mental status changes).	1	2	2
TRIAZOLAM Concurrent use may result in elevated serum triazolam concentrations.	2	3	3
VALDECOXIB Concurrent use may result in an increased risk of bleeding.	0	3	2
WARFARIN Concurrent use may result in an increased risk of bleeding.	2	3	3
ZOLMITRIPTAN Concurrent use may result in weakness, hyperreflexia, and incoordination.	1	3	3
ZOMEPIRAC Concurrent use may result in an increased risk of bleeding.	0	3	2

Haloperidol

INTERACTION	ONSET	SEVERITY	EVIDENCE
BENZTROPINE Concurrent use may result in excessive anticholinergic effects (sedation, constipation, dry mouth).	2	3	2
CABERGOLINE Concurrent use may result in the decreased therapeutic effect of both drugs.	1	3	3
CARBAMAZEPINE Concurrent use may result in decreased haloperidol effectiveness.	2	3	2

INTERACTION	ONSET	SEVERITY	EVIDENCE
DROPERIDOL Concurrent use may result in an increased risk of cardiotoxicity (QT prolongation, torsade de pointes, cardiac arrest).	0	2	3
LITHIUM Concurrent use may result in weakness, dyskinesias, increased extrapyramidal symptoms, encephalopathy, and brain damage.	2	2	1
RIFAMPIN Concurrent use may result in decreased haloperidol effectiveness.	2	3	3
SPARFLOXACIN Concurrent use may result in prolongation of the QTc interval and/or torsade de pointes.	2	1	3
TRAMADOL Concurrent use may result in an increased risk of seizures.	1	2	3

Imipramine

INTERACTION	ONSET	SEVERITY	EVIDENCE
ACENOCOUMAROL Concurrent use may result in increased risk of bleeding.	2	3	3
AMPRENAVIR Concurrent use may result in increased imipramine serum concentrations and potential toxicity (anticholinergic effects, sedation, confusion, cardiac arrhythmias).	2	2	3
ANISINDIONE Concurrent use may result in increased risk of bleeding.	2	3	3
BEPRIDIL Concurrent use may result in an increased risk of cardiotoxicity (QT prolongation, torsade de pointes, cardiac arrest).	1	1	3
BETHANIDINE Concurrent use may result in decreased antihypertensive effectiveness.	1	3	2
CARBAMAZEPINE Concurrent use may result in decreased imipramine effectiveness.	2	3	3
CIMETIDINE Concurrent use may result in imipramine toxicity (dry mouth, urinary retention, blurred vision).	2	3	2
CISAPRIDE Concurrent use may result in cardiotoxicity (QT prolongation, torsade de pointes, cardiac arrest).	1	1	3
CLONIDINE Concurrent use may result in decreased antihypertensive effectiveness.	2	2	3

Onset: 0=Unspecified 1=Rapid 2=Delayed
Severity: 1=Contraindicated 2=Major 3=Moderate 4=Minor
Evidence: 1=Excellent 2=Good 3=Fair 4=Poor

INTERACTION	ONSET	SEVERITY	EVIDENCE
CLORGYLINE Concurrent use may result in neurotoxicity, seizures, or serotonin syndrome (hypertension, hyperthermia, myoclonus, mental status changes).	2	2	3
DICUMAROL Concurrent use may result in increased risk of bleeding.	2	3	3
DILTIAZEM Concurrent use may result in imipramine toxicity (dry mouth, sedation).	2	4	3
DROPERIDOL Concurrent use may result in an increased risk of cardiotoxicity (QT prolongation, torsade de pointes, cardiac arrest).	0	2	3
EPINEPHRINE Concurrent use may result in hypertension, cardiac arrhythmias, and tachycardia.	1	2	2
ETILEFRINE Concurrent use may result in hypertension, cardiac arrhythmias, and tachycardia.	1	2	2
FLUOXETINE Concurrent use of may result in imipramine antidepressant toxicity (dry mouth, urinary retention, sedation) and an increased risk of cardiotoxicity (QT prolongation, torsade de pointes, cardiac arrest).	0	2	3
FLUVOXAMINE Concurrent use may result in imipramine toxicity (dry mouth, urinary retention, sedation).	2	3	3
GREPAFLOXACIN Concurrent use may result in an increased risk of cardiotoxicity (QT prolongation, torsade de pointes, cardiac arrest).	2	1	3
GUANADREL Concurrent use may result in decreased antihypertensive effectiveness.	2	3	3
GUANETHIDINE Concurrent use may result in decreased antihypertensive effectiveness.	2	3	2
GUANFACINE Concurrent use may result in decreased antihypertensive effectiveness.	2	3	3
HALOFANTRINE Concurrent use may result in an increased risk of cardiotoxicity (QT prolongation, torsade de pointes, cardiac arrest).	2	2	3
ISOCARBOXAZID Concurrent use may result in neurotoxicity, seizures, or serotonin syndrome (hypertension, hyperthermia, myoclonus, mental status changes).	2	1	3

INTERACTION	ONSET	SEVERITY	EVIDENCE
LABETALOL Concurrent use may result in imipramine toxicity (dry mouth, urinary retention, sedation).	2	3	3
LEVOMETHADYL Concurrent use may result in an increased risk of cardiotoxicity (QT prolongation, torsade de pointes, cardiac arrest).	2	1	3
METHOXAMINE Concurrent use may result in hypertension, cardiac arrhythmias, and tachycardia.	1	2	2
MIDODRINE Concurrent use may result in hypertension, cardiac arrhythmias, and tachycardia.	1	2	2
MOCLOBEMIDE Concurrent use may result in neurotoxicity, seizures, or serotonin syndrome (hypertension, hyperthermia, myoclonus, mental status changes).	2	2	3
NOREPINEPHRINE Concurrent use may result in hypertension, cardiac arrhythmias, and tachycardia.	1	2	2
OXILOFRINE Concurrent use may result in hypertension, cardiac arrhythmias, and tachycardia.	1	2	2
PHENELZINE Concurrent use may result in neurotoxicity, seizures, or serotonin syndrome (hypertension, hyperthermia, myoclonus, mental status changes).	2	2	3
PHENINDIONE Concurrent use may result in increased risk of bleeding.	2	3	3
PHENPROCOUMON Concurrent use may result in increased risk of bleeding.	2	3	3
PHENYLEPHRINE Concurrent use may result in hypertension, cardiac arrhythmias, and tachycardia.	1	2	2
PHENYTOIN Concurrent use may result in an increased risk of phenytoin toxicity (ataxia, hyperreflexia, nystagmus, tremors).	2	3	3
PIMOZIDE Concurrent use may result in an increased risk of cardiotoxicity (QT prolongation, torsade de pointes, cardiac arrest).	0	1	3
PROCARBAZINE Concurrent use may result in neurotoxicity, seizures.	2	2	3

Onset: 0=Unspecified 1=Rapid 2=Delayed
Severity: 1=Contraindicated 2=Major 3=Moderate 4=Minor
Evidence: 1=Excellent 2=Good 3=Fair 4=Poor

INTERACTION	ONSET	SEVERITY	EVIDENCE
QUINIDINE Concurrent use may result in an increased risk of cardiotoxicity (QT prolongation, torsade de pointes, cardiac arrest).	0	2	3
QUINIDINE Concurrent use may result in imipramine toxicity (dry mouth, sedation) and an increased risk of cardiotoxicity QT prolongation, torsade de pointes, cardiac arrest).	2	3	3
SELEGILINE Concurrent use may result in neurotoxicity, seizures, or serotonin syndrome (hypertension, hyperthermia, myoclonus, mental status changes).	2	2	3
SPARFLOXACIN Concurrent use may result in prolongation of the QTc interval and/or torsade de pointes.	2	1	3
TOBACCO Concurrent use may result in decreased imipramine concentrations.	2	3	3
TRAMADOL Concurrent use may result in an increased risk of seizures.	1	2	3
TRANYLCYPROMINE Concurrent use may result in neurotoxicity, seizures, or serotonin syndrome (hypertension, hyperthermia, myoclonus, mental status changes).	2	2	3
VERAPAMIL Concurrent use may result in imipramine toxicity (dry mouth, sedation, urinary retention).	2	4	2
WARFARIN Concurrent use may result in an increased risk of bleeding.	2	3	3

Lamotrigine

INTERACTION	ONSET	SEVERITY	EVIDENCE
CARBAMAZEPINE Concurrent use may result in reduced lamotrigine efficacy, loss of seizure control, and a potential risk of neurotoxicity (nausea, vertigo, nystagmus, ataxia).	2	3	3
EVENING PRIMROSE Concurrent use may result in reduced lamotrigine effectiveness.	2	3	3
FOSPHENYTOIN Concurrent use may result in reduced lamotrigine efficacy.	2	3	3
GINKGO Concurrent use may result in decreased lamotrigine effectiveness.	2	3	3
METHSUXIMIDE Concurrent use may result in reduced lamotrigine concentrations and possible loss of seizure control.	2	3	3

INTERACTION	ONSET	SEVERITY	EVIDENCE
ORAL CONTRACEPTIVE Concurrent use may result in altered (increased or decreased) plasma lamotrigine concentrations.	2	3	2
OXCARBAZEPINE Concurrent use may result in reduced lamotrigine concentrations and possible loss of seizure control.	2	3	3
PHENOBARBITAL Concurrent use may result in reduced lamotrigine efficacy, loss of seizure control.	2	3	2
PHENYTOIN Concurrent use may result in reduced lamotrigine efficacy.	2	3	3
PRIMIDONE Concurrent use may result in decreased lamotrigine efficacy.	2	3	1
RITONAVIR Concurrent use may result in decreased lamotrigine serum concentrations.	2	3	3
VALPROIC ACID Concurrent use may result in increased elimination half-life of lamotrigine leading to lamotrigine toxicity (fatigue, drowsiness, ataxia) and an increased risk of life-threatening rashes.	2	2	3

Lithium

INTERACTION	ONSET	SEVERITY	EVIDENCE
ACETAZOLAMIDE Concurrent use may result in decreased lithium effectiveness or increased lithium concentrations and lithium toxicity (weakness, tremor, excessive thirst, confusion).	2	3	3
ACETOPHENAZINE Concurrent use may result in weakness, dyskinesias, increased extrapyramidal symptoms, encephalopathy, and brain damage.	2	2	1
AZOSEMIDE Concurrent use may result in increased lithium concentrations and lithium toxicity (weakness, tremor, excessive thirst, confusion).	2	2	3
BEMETIZIDE Concurrent use may result in lithium toxicity (weakness, tremor, excessive thirst, confusion).	2	2	3
BENDROFLUMETHIAZIDE Concurrent use may result in increased lithium concentrations and lithium toxicity (weakness, tremor, excessive thirst, confusion).	2	2	3

Onset: 0=Unspecified 1=Rapid 2=Delayed
Severity: 1=Contraindicated 2=Major 3=Moderate 4=Minor
Evidence: 1=Excellent 2=Good 3=Fair 4=Poor

INTERACTION	ONSET	SEVERITY	EVIDENCE
BENZTHIAZIDE Concurrent use may result in increased lithium concentrations and lithium toxicity (weakness, tremor, excessive thirst, confusion).	2	2	3
BROMPERIDOL Concurrent use may result in weakness, dyskinesias, increased extrapyramidal symptoms, encephalopathy, and brain damage.	2	2	1
BUMETANIDE Concurrent use may result in increased lithium concentrations and lithium toxicity (weakness, tremor, excessive thirst, confusion).	2	2	3
BUTHIAZIDE Concurrent use may result in increased lithium concentrations and lithium toxicity (weakness, tremor, excessive thirst, confusion).	2	2	3
CANRENOATE Concurrent use may result in increased lithium concentrations and an increased risk of lithium toxicity (weakness, tremor, excessive thirst, confusion).	2	2	3
CHLOROTHIAZIDE Concurrent use may result in increased lithium concentrations and lithium toxicity (weakness, tremor, excessive thirst, confusion).	2	2	3
CHLORPROMAZINE Concurrent use may result in weakness, dyskinesias, increased extrapyramidal symptoms, encephalopathy, and brain damage.	2	2	1
CHLORPROTHIXENE Concurrent use may result in weakness, dyskinesias, increased extrapyramidal symptoms, encephalopathy, and brain damage.	2	2	1
CHLORTHALIDONE Concurrent use may result in increased lithium concentrations and lithium toxicity (weakness, tremor, excessive thirst, confusion).	2	2	3
CLOZAPINE Concurrent use may result in weakness, dyskinesias, increased extrapyramidal symptoms, encephalopathy, and brain damage.	2	2	1
CYCLOTHIAZIDE Concurrent use may result in increased lithium concentrations and lithium toxicity (weakness, tremor, excessive thirst, confusion).	2	2	3
DICLOFENAC Concurrent use may result in lithium toxicity (weakness, tremor, excessive thirst, confusion).	2	3	3

INTERACTION	ONSET	SEVERITY	EVIDENCE
DILTIAZEM Concurrent use may result in neurotoxicity, psychosis.	2	3	3
DOMPERIDONE Concurrent use may result in weakness, dyskinesias, increased extrapyramidal symptoms, encephalopathy, and brain damage.	2	2	1
DROPERIDOL Concurrent use may result in weakness, dyskinesias, increased extrapyramidal symptoms, encephalopathy, and brain damage.	2	2	1
ESCITALOPRAM Concurrent use may result in possible lithium toxicity (weakness, tremor, excessive thirst, confusion, dizziness).	2	3	3
ETHACRYNIC ACID Concurrent use may result in increased lithium concentrations and lithium toxicity (weakness, tremor, excessive thirst, confusion).	2	2	3
ETHOPROPAZINE Concurrent use may result in weakness, dyskinesias, increased extrapyramidal symptoms, encephalopathy, and brain damage.	2	2	1
FILGRASTIM Concurrent use may result in a greater than expected increase in white blood cell count.	2	3	3
FLUPENTHIXOL Concurrent use may result in weakness, dyskinesias, increased extrapyramidal symptoms, encephalopathy, and brain damage.	2	2	1
FLUPHENAZINE Concurrent use may result in weakness, dyskinesias, increased extrapyramidal symptoms, encephalopathy, and brain damage.	2	2	1
FLUVOXAMINE Concurrent use may result in possible lithium toxicity (weakness, tremor, excessive thirst, confusion, dizziness).	2	3	3
FOOD Concurrent use may result in increased lithium concentrations.	1	3	3
FOSINOPRIL Concurrent use may result in lithium toxicity (weakness, tremor, excessive thirst, confusion) and/or nephrotoxicity.	2	3	3
FUROSEMIDE Concurrent use may result in increased lithium concentrations and lithium toxicity (weakness, tremor, excessive thirst, confusion).	2	2	3

Onset: 0=Unspecified 1=Rapid 2=Delayed
Severity: 1=Contraindicated 2=Major 3=Moderate 4=Minor
Evidence: 1=Excellent 2=Good 3=Fair 4=Poor

INTERACTION	ONSET	SEVERITY	EVIDENCE
GUARANA Concomitant administration may cause alterations in serum lithium levels.	2	3	3
HALOPERIDOL Concurrent use may result in weakness, dyskinesias, increased extrapyramidal symptoms, encephalopathy, and brain damage.	2	2	1
HYDROCHLOROTHIAZIDE Concurrent use may result in increased lithium concentrations and lithium toxicity (weakness, tremor, excessive thirst, confusion).	2	2	2
HYDROFLUMETHIAZIDE Concurrent use may result in increased lithium concentrations and lithium toxicity (weakness, tremor, excessive thirst, confusion).	2	2	3
IBUPROFEN Concurrent use may result in an increased risk of lithium toxicity (weakness, tremor, excessive thirst, confusion).	2	3	3
INDAPAMIDE Concurrent use may result in increased lithium concentrations and lithium toxicity (weakness, tremor, excessive thirst, confusion).	2	2	3
INDOMETHACIN Concurrent use may result in an increased risk of lithium toxicity (weakness, tremor, excessive thirst, confusion).	2	3	3
KETOROLAC Concurrent use may result in lithium toxicity (weakness, tremor, excessive thirst, confusion).	2	3	2
LISINOPRIL Concurrent use may result in lithium toxicity (weakness, tremor, excessive thirst, confusion) and/or nephrotoxicity.	2	3	3
LOXAPINE Concurrent use may result in weakness, dyskinesias, increased extrapyramidal symptoms, encephalopathy, and brain damage.	2	2	1
MEFENAMIC ACID Concurrent use may result in lithium toxicity (weakness, tremor, excessive thirst, confusion).	2	3	3
MELOXICAM Concurrent use may result in elevation of plasma lithium levels and reduced renal lithium clearance.	1	3	3
MELPERONE Concurrent use may result in weakness, dyskinesias, increased extrapyramidal symptoms, encephalopathy, and brain damage.	2	2	1

INTERACTION	ONSET	SEVERITY	EVIDENCE
MESORIDAZINE Concurrent use may result in weakness, dyskinesias, increased extrapyramidal symptoms, encephalopathy, and brain damage.	2	2	1
METHOTRIMEPRAZINE Concurrent use may result in weakness, dyskinesias, increased extrapyramidal symptoms, encephalopathy, and brain damage.	2	2	1
METHYCLOTHIAZIDE Concurrent use may result in increased lithium concentrations and lithium toxicity (weakness, tremor, excessive thirst, confusion).	2	2	3
METHYLDOPA Concurrent use may result in an increased risk of lithium toxicity (tremor, weakness, excessive thirst, confusion).	2	3	3
METOLAZONE Concurrent use may result in increased lithium concentrations and lithium toxicity (weakness, tremor, excessive thirst, confusion).	2	2	3
METRONIDAZOLE Concurrent use may result in elevated lithium plasma levels and lithium toxicity (weakness, tremor, excessive thirst, confusion).	2	3	3
MOLINDONE Concurrent use may result in weakness, dyskinesias, increased extrapyramidal symptoms, encephalopathy, and brain damage.	2	2	1
NAPROXEN Concurrent use may result in elevated lithium plasma levels and lithium toxicity (weakness, tremor, excessive thirst, confusion).	2	3	3
OLANZAPINE Concurrent use may result in weakness, dyskinesias, increased extrapyramidal symptoms, encephalopathy, and brain damage.	2	2	1
PEGFILGRASTIM Concurrent use may result in a greater than expected increase in white blood cell count.	2	3	3
PENFLURIDOL Concurrent use may result in weakness, dyskinesias, increased extrapyramidal symptoms, encephalopathy, and brain damage.	2	2	1
PERICIAZINE Concurrent use may result in weakness, dyskinesias, increased extrapyramidal symptoms, encephalopathy, and brain damage.	2	2	1

Onset: 0=Unspecified 1=Rapid 2=Delayed
Severity: 1=Contraindicated 2=Major 3=Moderate 4=Minor
Evidence: 1=Excellent 2=Good 3=Fair 4=Poor

INTERACTION	ONSET	SEVERITY	EVIDENCE
PERPHENAZINE Concurrent use may result in weakness, dyskinesias, increased extrapyramidal symptoms, encephalopathy, and brain damage.	2	2	1
PHENYLBUTAZONE Concurrent use may result in lithium toxicity (weakness, tremor, excessive thirst, confusion).	2	3	3
PIMOZIDE Concurrent use may result in weakness, dyskinesias, increased extrapyramidal symptoms, encephalopathy, and brain damage.	2	2	1
PIPAMPERONE Concurrent use may result in weakness, dyskinesias, increased extrapyramidal symptoms, encephalopathy, and brain damage.	2	2	1
PIPOTIAZINE Concurrent use may result in weakness, dyskinesias, increased extrapyramidal symptoms, encephalopathy, and brain damage.	2	2	1
PIRETANIDE Concurrent use may result in increased lithium concentrations and lithium toxicity (weakness, tremor, excessive thirst, confusion).	2	2	3
PIROXICAM Concurrent use may result in lithium toxicity (weakness, tremor, excessive thirst, confusion).	2	3	3
POLYTHIAZIDE Concurrent use may result in increased lithium concentrations and lithium toxicity (weakness, tremor, excessive thirst, confusion).	2	2	3
PROCHLORPERAZINE Concurrent use may result in weakness, dyskinesias, increased extrapyramidal symptoms, encephalopathy, and brain damage.	2	2	1
PROMAZINE Concurrent use may result in weakness, dyskinesias, increased extrapyramidal symptoms, encephalopathy, and brain damage.	2	2	1
PROMETHAZINE Concurrent use may result in weakness, dyskinesias, increased extrapyramidal symptoms, encephalopathy, and brain damage.	2	2	1
QUINETHAZONE Concurrent use may result in increased lithium concentrations and lithium toxicity (weakness, tremor, excessive thirst, confusion).	2	2	3

INTERACTION	ONSET	SEVERITY	EVIDENCE
REMOXIPRIDE Concurrent use may result in weakness, dyskinesias, increased extrapyramidal symptoms, encephalopathy, and brain damage.	2	2	1
RISPERIDONE Concurrent use may result in weakness, dyskinesias, increased extrapyramidal symptoms, encephalopathy, and brain damage.	2	2	1
SERTINDOLE Concurrent use may result in weakness, dyskinesias, increased extrapyramidal symptoms, encephalopathy, and brain damage.	2	2	1
SIBUTRAMINE Concurrent use may result in an increased risk of serotonin syndrome (hypertension, hypothermia, myoclonus, mental status changes).	1	2	3
SODIUM BICARBONATE Concurrent use may result in decreased lithium effectiveness.	2	3	3
SPIRONOLACTONE Concurrent use may result in increased lithium concentrations and lithium toxicity (weakness, tremor, excessive thirst, confusion).	2	2	3
SULPIRIDE Concurrent use may result in weakness, dyskinesias, increased extrapyramidal symptoms, encephalopathy, and brain damage.	2	2	1
TENIDAP Concurrent use may result in increased lithium serum levels and possible lithium toxicity (weakness, tremor, excessive thirst, confusion).	2	3	3
THEOPHYLLINE Concurrent use may result in decreased lithium effectiveness.	2	3	2
THIOPROPAZATE Concurrent use may result in weakness, dyskinesias, increased extrapyramidal symptoms, encephalopathy, and brain damage.	2	2	1
THIOPROPERAZINE Concurrent use may result in weakness, dyskinesias, increased extrapyramidal symptoms, encephalopathy, and brain damage.	2	2	1
THIORIDAZINE Concurrent use may result in weakness, dyskinesias, increased extrapyramidal symptoms, encephalopathy, and brain damage.	2	2	1

Onset: 0=Unspecified 1=Rapid 2=Delayed
Severity: 1=Contraindicated 2=Major 3=Moderate 4=Minor
Evidence: 1=Excellent 2=Good 3=Fair 4=Poor

INTERACTION	ONSET	SEVERITY	EVIDENCE
THIOTHIXENE Concurrent use may result in weakness, dyskinesias, increased extrapyramidal symptoms, encephalopathy, and brain damage.	2	2	1
TIAPRIDE Concurrent use may result in weakness, dyskinesias, increased extrapyramidal symptoms, encephalopathy, and brain damage.	2	2	1
TRICHLORMETHIAZIDE Concurrent use may result in increased lithium concentrations and lithium toxicity (weakness, tremor, excessive thirst, confusion).	2	2	3
TRIFLUOPERAZINE Concurrent use may result in weakness, dyskinesias, increased extrapyramidal symptoms, encephalopathy, and brain damage.	2	2	1
TRIFLUPROMAZINE Concurrent use may result in weakness, dyskinesias, increased extrapyramidal symptoms, encephalopathy, and brain damage.	2	2	1
TRIMEPRAZINE Concurrent use may result in weakness, dyskinesias, increased extrapyramidal symptoms, encephalopathy, and brain damage.	2	2	1
VALDECOXIB Concurrent use may result in increased lithium plasma concentrations and an increased risk of lithium toxicity (weakness, tremor, excessive thirst, confusion).	2	3	3
XIPAMIDE Concurrent use may result in increased lithium concentrations and lithium toxicity (weakness, tremor, excessive thirst, confusion).	2	2	3
ZOTEPINE Concurrent use may result in weakness, dyskinesias, increased extrapyramidal symptoms, encephalopathy, and brain damage.	2	2	1
ZUCLOPENTHIXOL Concurrent use may result in weakness, dyskinesias, increased extrapyramidal symptoms, encephalopathy, and brain damage.	2	2	1

Lorazepam

INTERACTION	ONSET	SEVERITY	EVIDENCE
CLOZAPINE Concurrent use may result in central nervous system depression.	1	4	3
ETHANOL Concurrent use may result in increased sedation.	1	3	1

INTERACTION	ONSET	SEVERITY	EVIDENCE
ORAL CONTRACEPTIVE Concurrent use may result in decreased lorazepam effectiveness.	2	4	3
THEOPHYLLINE Concurrent use may result in decreased lorazepam effectiveness.	1	3	2

Maprotiline

INTERACTION	ONSET	SEVERITY	EVIDENCE
CISAPRIDE Concurrent use may result in cardiotoxicity (QT prolongation, torsade de pointes, cardiac arrest).	1	1	3
CLORGYLINE Concurrent use may result in neurotoxicity, seizures.	2	1	3
IPRONIAZID Concurrent use may result in neurotoxicity, seizures.	2	1	3
ISOCARBOXAZID Concurrent use may result in neurotoxicity, seizures.	2	1	3
MOCLOBEMIDE Concurrent use may result in neurotoxicity, seizures.	2	1	3
NIALAMIDE Concurrent use may result in neurotoxicity, seizures.	2	1	3
PARGYLINE Concurrent use may result in neurotoxicity, seizures.	2	1	3
PHENELZINE Concurrent use may result in neurotoxicity, seizures.	2	1	3
PROCARBAZINE Concurrent use may result in neurotoxicity, seizures.	2	1	3
SELEGILINE Concurrent use may result in neurotoxicity, seizures.	2	1	3
TOLOXATONE Concurrent use may result in neurotoxicity, seizures.	2	1	3
TRANYLCYPROMINE Concurrent use may result in neurotoxicity, seizures.	2	1	3

Memantine

INTERACTION	ONSET	SEVERITY	EVIDENCE
ACETAZOLAMIDE Concurrent use may result in reduced clearance of memantine.	0	3	3
CIMETIDINE Concurrent use may result in altered plasma levels of memantine and cimetidine.	0	3	3

Onset: 0=Unspecified 1=Rapid 2=Delayed
Severity: 1=Contraindicated 2=Major 3=Moderate 4=Minor
Evidence: 1=Excellent 2=Good 3=Fair 4=Poor

INTERACTION	ONSET	SEVERITY	EVIDENCE
DICHLORPHENAMIDE Concurrent use may result in reduced clearance of memantine.	0	3	3
HYDROCHLOROTHIAZIDE Concurrent use may result in altered plasma levels of memantine and hydrochlorothiazide.	0	3	3
METHAZOLAMIDE Concurrent use may result in reduced clearance of memantine.	0	3	3
NICOTINE Concurrent use may result in altered plasma levels of memantine and nicotine.	0	3	3
QUINIDINE Concurrent use may result in altered plasma levels of memantine and quinidine.	0	3	3
RANITIDINE Concurrent use may result in altered plasma levels of memantine and ranitidine.	0	3	3
SODIUM BICARBONATE Concurrent use may result in reduced renal clearance of memantine.	0	3	3
TRIAMTERENE Concurrent use may result in altered plasma levels of memantine and triamterene.	0	3	3

Mephobarbital

INTERACTION	ONSET	SEVERITY	EVIDENCE
ANISINDIONE Concurrent use may result in decreased anticoagulant effectiveness.	2	2	2
DICUMAROL Concurrent use may result in decreased anticoagulant effectiveness.	2	2	2
ETHANOL Concurrent use may result in excessive central nervous system depression.	1	3	1
EVENING PRIMROSE Concurrent use may result in reduced anticonvulsant effectiveness.	2	3	3
GINKGO Concurrent use may result in decreased anticonvulsant effectiveness.	2	3	3
PHENINDIONE Concurrent use may result in decreased anticoagulant effectiveness.	2	2	2

INTERACTION	ONSET	SEVERITY	EVIDENCE
PHENPROCOUMON Concurrent use may result in decreased anticoagulant effectiveness.	2	2	2
PREDNISOLONE Concurrent use may result in decreased therapeutic effect of prednisolone.	2	3	2
PREDNISONE Concurrent use may result in decreased therapeutic effect of prednisone.	2	3	2
PROCARBAZINE Concurrent use may result in central nervous system depression.	0	3	3
QUETIAPINE Concurrent use may result in decreased serum quetiapine concentrations.	0	2	3
VALERIAN Concurrent use may result in increased central nervous system depression.	1	3	3
VORICONAZOLE Concurrent use may result in reduced systemic exposure to voriconazole.	0	1	3
WARFARIN Concurrent use may result in decreased anticoagulant effectiveness.	2	3	2

Meprobamate

INTERACTION	ONSET	SEVERITY	EVIDENCE
ETHANOL Concurrent use may result in increased sedation.	1	3	1

Mesoridazine

INTERACTION	ONSET	SEVERITY	EVIDENCE
BELLADONNA Concurrent use may result in increased manic, agitated reactions, or enhanced anticholinergic effects resulting in cardiorespiratory failure, especially in cases of belladonna overdose.	1	3	2
BENZTROPINE Concurrent use may result in decreased mesoridazine serum concentrations, decreased mesoridazine effectiveness, enhanced anticholinergic effects (ileus, hyperpyrexia, sedation, dry mouth).	2	3	3
CABERGOLINE Concurrent use may result in the decreased therapeutic effect of both drugs.	1	3	3

Onset: 0=Unspecified 1=Rapid 2=Delayed
Severity: 1=Contraindicated 2=Major 3=Moderate 4=Minor
Evidence: 1=Excellent 2=Good 3=Fair 4=Poor

INTERACTION	ONSET	SEVERITY	EVIDENCE
CISAPRIDE Concurrent use may result in cardiotoxicity (QT prolongation, torsade de pointes, cardiac arrest).	1	1	3
DISOPYRAMIDE Concurrent use may result in an increased risk of cardiotoxicity (QT prolongation, torsade de pointes, cardiac arrest).	0	1	3
DROPERIDOL Concurrent use may result in an increased risk of cardiotoxicity (QT prolongation, torsade de pointes, cardiac arrest).	0	1	3
ETHANOL Concurrent use may result in increased central nervous system depression and an increased risk of extrapyramidal reactions.	1	3	2
FOSPHENYTOIN Concurrent use may result in increased or decreased phenytoin levels and possibly reduced mesoridazine levels.	2	4	3
GREPAFLOXACIN Concurrent use may result in an increased risk of cardiotoxicity (QT prolongation, torsade de pointes, cardiac arrest).	2	1	3
HALOFANTRINE Concurrent use may result in an increased risk of cardiotoxicity (QT prolongation, torsade de pointes, cardiac arrest).	0	1	3
IBUTILIDE Concurrent use may result in an increased risk of cardiotoxicity (QT prolongation, torsade de pointes, cardiac arrest).	0	1	3
LEVODOPA Concurrent use may result in loss of levodopa efficacy.	1	3	2
LEVOMETHADYL Concurrent use may result in an increased risk of cardiotoxicity (QT prolongation, torsade de pointes, cardiac arrest).	0	1	3
LITHIUM Concurrent use may result in weakness, dyskinesias, increased extrapyramidal symptoms, encephalopathy, and brain damage.	2	2	1
MEPERIDINE Concurrent use may result in an increase in central nervous system and respiratory depression.	1	3	2
ORPHENADRINE Concurrent use may result in decreased mesoridazine serum concentrations, decreased mesoridazine effectiveness, enhanced anticholinergic effects (ileus, hyperpyrexia, sedation, dry mouth).	2	3	3

INTERACTION	ONSET	SEVERITY	EVIDENCE
PHENYTOIN Concurrent use may result in increased or decreased phenytoin levels and possibly reduced mesoridazine levels.	2	4	3
PORFIMER Concurrent use may result in excessive intracellular damage in photosensitized tissues.	2	3	3
PROCAINAMIDE Concurrent use may result in an increased risk of cardiotoxicity (QT prolongation, torsade de pointes, cardiac arrest).	0	1	3
PROCYCLIDINE Concurrent use may result in decreased mesoridazine serum concentrations, decreased mesoridazine effectiveness, enhanced anticholinergic effects (ileus, hyperpyrexia, sedation, dry mouth).	2	3	3
QUINIDINE Concurrent use may result in an increased risk of cardiotoxicity (QT prolongation, torsade de pointes, cardiac arrest).	0	1	3
SPARFLOXACIN Concurrent use may result in prolongation of the QTc interval and/or torsade de pointes.	2	1	3
TRAMADOL Concurrent use may result in an increased risk of seizures.	1	2	3
TRIHEXYPHENIDYL Concurrent use may result in decreased mesoridazine serum concentrations, decreased mesoridazine effectiveness, enhanced anticholinergic effects (ileus, hyperpyrexia, sedation, dry mouth).	2	3	3
ZIPRASIDONE Concurrent use may result in an increased risk of cardiotoxicity (QT prolongation, torsade de pointes, cardiac arrest).	0	1	3

Methamphetamine

INTERACTION	ONSET	SEVERITY	EVIDENCE
CLORGYLINE Concurrent use may result in hypertensive crisis.	1	1	3
GUANETHIDINE Concurrent use may result in decreased guanethidine effectiveness.	1	3	2
IPRONIAZID Concurrent use may result in hypertensive crisis.	1	1	3
ISOCARBOXAZID Concurrent use may result in hypertensive crisis.	1	1	3

Onset: 0=Unspecified 1=Rapid 2=Delayed
Severity: 1=Contraindicated 2=Major 3=Moderate 4=Minor
Evidence: 1=Excellent 2=Good 3=Fair 4=Poor

INTERACTION	ONSET	SEVERITY	EVIDENCE
MOCLOBEMIDE Concurrent use may result in hypertensive crisis.	1	1	3
NIALAMIDE Concurrent use may result in hypertensive crisis.	1	1	3
PARGYLINE Concurrent use may result in hypertensive crisis.	1	1	3
PHENELZINE Concurrent use may result in hypertensive crisis.	1	1	3
PROCARBAZINE Concurrent use may result in hypertensive crisis.	1	1	3
SELEGILINE Concurrent use may result in hypertensive crisis.	1	1	3
TOLOXATONE Concurrent use may result in hypertensive crisis.	1	1	3
TRANYLCYPROMINE Concurrent use may result in hypertensive crisis.	1	1	3

Methylphenidate

INTERACTION	ONSET	SEVERITY	EVIDENCE
CLORGYLINE Concurrent use may result in hypertensive crisis (headache, palpitation, neck stiffness).	1	1	3
GUANETHIDINE Concurrent use may result in decreased guanethidine effectiveness.	1	3	3
IPRONIAZID Concurrent use may result in hypertensive crisis (headache, palpitation, neck stiffness).	1	1	3
ISOCARBOXAZID Concurrent use may result in hypertensive crisis (headache, palpitation, neck stiffness).	1	1	3
LAZABEMIDE Concurrent use may result in hypertensive crisis (headache, palpitation, neck stiffness).	1	1	3
MOCLOBEMIDE Concurrent use may result in hypertensive crisis (headache, palpitation, neck stiffness).	1	1	3
NIALAMIDE Concurrent use may result in hypertensive crisis (headache, palpitation, neck stiffness).	1	1	3
PARGYLINE Concurrent use may result in hypertensive crisis (headache, palpitation, neck stiffness).	1	1	3
PHENELZINE Concurrent use may result in hypertensive crisis (headache, palpitation, neck stiffness).	1	1	3

INTERACTION	ONSET	SEVERITY	EVIDENCE
PROCARBAZINE Concurrent use may result in hypertensive crisis (headache, palpitation, neck stiffness).	1	1	3
SELEGILINE Concurrent use may result in hypertensive crisis (headache, palpitation, neck stiffness).	1	1	3
TOLOXATONE Concurrent use may result in hypertensive crisis (headache, palpitation, neck stiffness).	1	1	3
TRANYLCYPROMINE Concurrent use may result in hypertensive crisis (headache, palpitation, neck stiffness).	1	1	3

Mirtazapine

INTERACTION	ONSET	SEVERITY	EVIDENCE
CLONIDINE Concurrent use may result in hypertension, decreased antihypertensive effectiveness.	2	2	3
CLORGYLINE Concurrent use may result in neurotoxicity, seizures.	2	1	3
IPRONIAZID Concurrent use may result in neurotoxicity, seizures.	2	1	3
ISOCARBOXAZID Concurrent use may result in neurotoxicity, seizures.	2	1	3
MOCLOBEMIDE Concurrent use may result in neurotoxicity, seizures.	2	1	3
NIALAMIDE Concurrent use may result in neurotoxicity, seizures.	2	1	3
PARGYLINE Concurrent use may result in neurotoxicity, seizures.	2	1	3
PHENELZINE Concurrent use may result in neurotoxicity, seizures.	2	1	3
PROCARBAZINE Concurrent use may result in neurotoxicity, seizures.	2	1	3
SELEGILINE Concurrent use may result in neurotoxicity, seizures.	2	1	3
TOLOXATONE Concurrent use may result in neurotoxicity, seizures.	2	1	3
TRANYLCYPROMINE Concurrent use may result in neurotoxicity, seizures.	2	1	3

Onset: 0=Unspecified 1=Rapid 2=Delayed
Severity: 1=Contraindicated 2=Major 3=Moderate 4=Minor
Evidence: 1=Excellent 2=Good 3=Fair 4=Poor

Molindone

INTERACTION	ONSET	SEVERITY	EVIDENCE
DROPERIDOL Concurrent use may result in an increased risk of cardiotoxicity (QT prolongation, torsade de pointes, cardiac arrest).	1	1	3
LITHIUM Concurrent use may result in weakness, dyskinesias, increased extrapyramidal symptoms, encephalopathy, and brain damage.	2	2	1
TRAMADOL Concurrent use may result in an increased risk of seizures.	1	2	3

Nefazodone

INTERACTION	ONSET	SEVERITY	EVIDENCE
ALMOTRIPTAN Concurrent use may result in weakness, hyperreflexia, and/or incoordination.	0	3	3
ALPRAZOLAM Concurrent use may result in psychomotor impairment and sedation.	1	3	2
AMITRIPTYLINE Concurrent use may result in increased risk of serotonin syndrome (hypertension, hyperthermia, myoclonus, mental status changes).	1	2	3
ASTEMIZOLE Concurrent use may result in cardiotoxicity (QT interval prolongation, torsade de pointes, cardiac arrest).	1	1	3
ATORVASTATIN Concurrent use may result in an increased risk of myopathy or rhabdomyolysis.	2	2	3
CARBAMAZEPINE Concurrent use may result in an increased risk of carbamazepine toxicity (ataxia, nystagmus, diplopia, headache, vomiting, apnea, seizures, coma).	2	3	3
CISAPRIDE Concurrent use may result in an increased risk of cardiotoxicity (QT prolongation, torsade de pointes, cardiac arrest).	1	1	2
CLORGYLINE Concurrent use may result in hyperthermia, rigidity, myoclonus, seizures, fluctuations of vital signs, or mental status changes.	1	2	2
CYCLOSPORINE Concurrent use may result in an increased risk of cyclosporine toxicity (renal dysfunction, cholestasis, paresthesias).	2	3	3

INTERACTION	ONSET	SEVERITY	EVIDENCE
DIGOXIN Concurrent use may result in an increase in digoxin serum concentrations and possibly increase the risk of digoxin toxicity (nausea, vomiting, cardiac arrhythmias).	2	3	3
DROPERIDOL Concurrent use may result in an increased risk of cardiotoxicity (QT prolongation, torsade de pointes, cardiac arrest).	1	2	3
ETHANOL Concurrent use may result in an increased risk of central nervous system side effects.	1	4	3
FURAZOLIDONE Concurrent use may result in weakness, hyperreflexia, and incoordination.	2	1	3
IPRONIAZID Concurrent use may result in central nervous system toxicity or serotonin syndrome (hypertension, hyperthermia, myoclonus, mental status changes).	1	2	2
ISOCARBOXAZID Concurrent use may result in hyperthermia, rigidity, myoclonus, seizures, fluctuations of vital signs, or mental status changes.	1	1	2
LOVASTATIN Concurrent use may result in an increased risk of myopathy or rhabdomyolysis.	2	2	3
MOCLOBEMIDE Concurrent use may result in central nervous system toxicity or serotonin syndrome (hypertension, hyperthermia, myoclonus, mental status changes).	1	2	2
NIALAMIDE Concurrent use may result in central nervous system toxicity or serotonin syndrome (hypertension, hyperthermia, myoclonus, mental status changes).	1	2	2
PARGYLINE Concurrent use may result in central nervous system toxicity or serotonin syndrome (hypertension, hyperthermia, myoclonus, mental status changes).	1	2	2
PHENELZINE Concurrent use may result in hyperthermia, rigidity, myoclonus, seizures, fluctuations of vital signs, or mental status changes.	1	1	2
PIMOZIDE Concurrent use may result in an increased risk of cardiotoxicity (QT prolongation, torsade de pointes, cardiac arrest).	1	1	3

Onset: 0=Unspecified 1=Rapid 2=Delayed
Severity: 1=Contraindicated 2=Major 3=Moderate 4=Minor
Evidence: 1=Excellent 2=Good 3=Fair 4=Poor

INTERACTION	ONSET	SEVERITY	EVIDENCE
PROCARBAZINE Concurrent use may result in central nervous system toxicity or serotonin syndrome (hypertension, hyperthermia, myoclonus, mental status changes).	1	2	2
PROPRANOLOL Concurrent use may result in decreased beta blocker efficacy.	1	4	3
SELEGILINE Concurrent use may result in hyperthermia, rigidity, myoclonus, seizures, fluctuations of vital signs, or mental status changes.	1	2	2
SIBUTRAMINE Concurrent use may result in an increased risk of serotonin syndrome (hypertension, hypothermia, myoclonus, mental status changes).	1	2	3
SIMVASTATIN Concurrent use may result in an increased risk of myopathy or rhabdomyolysis.	2	2	2
TERFENADINE Concurrent use may result in serious, even fatal, cardiovascular events (QT interval prolongation, torsade de pointes, or cardiac arrest).	1	1	2
TOLOXATONE Concurrent use may result in central nervous system toxicity or serotonin syndrome (hypertension, hyperthermia, myoclonus, mental status changes).	1	2	2
TRANYLCYPROMINE Concurrent use may result in hyperthermia, rigidity, myoclonus, seizures, fluctuations of vital signs, or mental status changes.	1	2	2
TRIAZOLAM Concurrent use may result in psychomotor impairment and excessive sedation.	1	3	2

Nortriptyline

INTERACTION	ONSET	SEVERITY	EVIDENCE
ACENOCOUMAROL Concurrent use may result in an increased risk of bleeding.	2	3	3
AMPRENAVIR Concurrent use may result in increased nortriptyline serum concentrations and potential toxicity (anticholinergic effects, sedation, confusion, cardiac arrhythmias).	2	2	3
ANISINDIONE Concurrent use may result in an increased risk of bleeding.	2	3	3
BEPRIDIL Concurrent use may result in an increased risk of cardiotoxicity (QT prolongation, torsade de pointes, cardiac arrest).	1	1	3

INTERACTION	ONSET	SEVERITY	EVIDENCE
BETHANIDINE Concurrent use may result in decreased antihypertensive effectiveness.	1	3	3
CIMETIDINE Concurrent use may result in nortriptyline toxicity (dry mouth, blurred vision, urinary retention).	2	3	2
CISAPRIDE Concurrent use may result in cardiotoxicity (QT prolongation, torsade de pointes, cardiac arrest).	1	1	3
CLONIDINE Concurrent use may result in decreased antihypertensive effectiveness.	2	2	3
CLORGYLINE Concurrent use may result in neurotoxicity, seizures, or serotonin syndrome (hypertension, hyperthermia, myoclonus, mental status changes).	2	2	3
DICUMAROL Concurrent use may result in an increased risk of bleeding.	2	3	3
DROPERIDOL Concurrent use may result in an increased risk of cardiotoxicity (QT prolongation, torsade de pointes, cardiac arrest).	0	2	3
EPINEPHRINE Concurrent use may result in hypertension, cardiac arrhythmias, and tachycardia.	1	2	2
ETILEFRINE Concurrent use may result in hypertension, cardiac arrhythmias, and tachycardia.	1	2	2
FLUOXETINE Concurrent use may result in nortriptyline antidepressant toxicity (dry mouth, urinary retention, sedation) and an increased risk of cardiotoxicity (QT prolongation, torsade de pointes, cardiac arrest).	0	2	3
GREPAFLOXACIN Concurrent use may result in an increased risk of cardiotoxicity (QT prolongation, torsade de pointes, cardiac arrest).	2	1	3
GUANADREL Concurrent use may result in decreased antihypertensive effectiveness.	2	3	3
GUANETHIDINE Concurrent use may result in decreased antihypertensive effectiveness.	2	3	2

Onset: 0=Unspecified 1=Rapid 2=Delayed
Severity: 1=Contraindicated 2=Major 3=Moderate 4=Minor
Evidence: 1=Excellent 2=Good 3=Fair 4=Poor

INTERACTION	ONSET	SEVERITY	EVIDENCE
HALOFANTRINE Concurrent use may result in an increased risk of cardiotoxicity (QT prolongation, torsade de pointes, cardiac arrest).	2	2	3
ISOCARBOXAZID Concurrent use may result in neurotoxicity, seizures, or serotonin syndrome (hypertension, hyperthermia, myoclonus, mental status changes).	2	1	3
LEVOMETHADYL Concurrent use may result in an increased risk of cardiotoxicity (QT prolongation, torsade de pointes, cardiac arrest).	2	1	3
METHOXAMINE Concurrent use may result in hypertension, cardiac arrhythmias, and tachycardia.	1	2	2
MIDODRINE Concurrent use may result in hypertension, cardiac arrhythmias, and tachycardia.	1	2	2
MOCLOBEMIDE Concurrent use may result in neurotoxicity, seizures, or serotonin syndrome (hypertension, hyperthermia, myoclonus, mental status changes).	2	2	3
NOREPINEPHRINE Concurrent use may result in hypertension, cardiac arrhythmias, and tachycardia.	1	2	2
OXILOFRINE Concurrent use may result in hypertension, cardiac arrhythmias, and tachycardia.	1	2	2
PHENELZINE Concurrent use may result in neurotoxicity, seizures, or serotonin syndrome (hypertension, hyperthermia, myoclonus, mental status changes).	2	2	3
PHENINDIONE Concurrent use may result in an increased risk of bleeding.	2	3	3
PHENPROCOUMON Concurrent use may result in an increased risk of bleeding.	2	3	3
PHENYLEPHRINE Concurrent use may result in hypertension, cardiac arrhythmias, and tachycardia.	1	2	2
PIMOZIDE Concurrent use may result in an increased risk of cardiotoxicity (QT prolongation, torsade de pointes, cardiac arrest).	0	1	3
PROCARBAZINE Concurrent use may result in neurotoxicity, seizures.	2	2	3

INTERACTION	ONSET	SEVERITY	EVIDENCE
SELEGILINE Concurrent use may result in neurotoxicity, seizures, or serotonin syndrome (hypertension, hyperthermia, myoclonus, mental status changes).	2	2	3
SERTRALINE Concurrent use may result in elevated nortriptyline serum levels or possible serotonin syndrome (hypertension, hyperthermia, myoclonus, mental status changes).	2	2	3
SPARFLOXACIN Concurrent use may result in prolongation of the QTc interval and/or torsade de pointes.	2	1	3
TOBACCO Concurrent use may result in decreased nortriptyline concentrations.	2	3	3
TRAMADOL Concurrent use may result in an increased risk of seizures.	1	2	3
TRANYLCYPROMINE Concurrent use may result in neurotoxicity, seizures, or serotonin syndrome (hypertension, hyperthermia, myoclonus, mental status changes).	2	2	3
WARFARIN Concurrent use may result in an increased risk of bleeding.	2	3	3

Olanzapine

INTERACTION	ONSET	SEVERITY	EVIDENCE
CLOMIPRAMINE Concurrent use may result in an increased risk of seizures.	2	2	2
ETHANOL Concurrent use may result in excessive central nervous system depression.	1	3	3
FLUVOXAMINE Concurrent use may result in an increased risk of olanzapine adverse effects.	2	3	3
LEVOMETHADYL Concurrent use may result in an increased risk of cardiotoxicity (QT prolongation, torsade de pointes, cardiac arrest).	2	1	3
LITHIUM Concurrent use may result in weakness, dyskinesias, increased extrapyramidal symptoms, encephalopathy, and brain damage.	2	2	1

Onset:　　0=Unspecified 1=Rapid 2=Delayed
Severity:　1=Contraindicated 2=Major 3=Moderate 4=Minor
Evidence:　1=Excellent 2=Good 3=Fair 4=Poor

Oxazepam

INTERACTION	ONSET	SEVERITY	EVIDENCE
BIFONAZOLE Concurrent use may result in increased oxazepam serum concentrations and potential oxazepam toxicity (sedation, slurred speech, central nervous system depression).	2	1	3
BUTOCONAZOLE Concurrent use may result in increased oxazepam serum concentrations and potential oxazepam toxicity (sedation, slurred speech, central nervous system depression).	2	1	3
CABBAGE Concurrent use may result in reduced oxazepam effectiveness.	1	3	3
CLOTRIMAZOLE Concurrent use may result in increased oxazepam serum concentrations and potential oxazepam toxicity (sedation, slurred speech, central nervous system depression).	2	1	3
CROCONAZOLE Concurrent use may result in increased oxazepam serum concentrations and potential oxazepam toxicity (sedation, slurred speech, central nervous system depression).	2	1	3
ECONAZOLE Concurrent use may result in increased oxazepam serum concentrations and potential oxazepam toxicity (sedation, slurred speech, central nervous system depression).	2	1	3
FENTICONAZOLE Concurrent use may result in increased oxazepam serum concentrations and potential oxazepam toxicity (sedation, slurred speech, central nervous system depression).	2	1	3
FLUCONAZOLE Concurrent use may result in increased oxazepam serum concentrations and potential oxazepam toxicity (sedation, slurred speech, central nervous system depression).	2	1	3
FOSPHENYTOIN Concurrent use may result in loss of oxazepam efficacy.	2	4	3
ITRACONAZOLE Concurrent use may result in increased oxazepam serum concentrations and potential oxazepam toxicity (sedation, slurred speech, central nervous system depression).	2	1	3
KAVA Concurrent use may result in increased central nervous system depression.	2	3	3
KETOCONAZOLE Concurrent use may result in increased oxazepam serum concentrations and potential oxazepam toxicity (sedation, slurred speech, central nervous system depression).	2	1	3

INTERACTION	ONSET	SEVERITY	EVIDENCE
MICONAZOLE Concurrent use may result in increased oxazepam serum concentrations and potential oxazepam toxicity (sedation, slurred speech, central nervous system depression).	2	1	3
OMOCONAZOLE Concurrent use may result in increased oxazepam serum concentrations and potential oxazepam toxicity (sedation, slurred speech, central nervous system depression).	2	1	3
OXICONAZOLE Concurrent use may result in increased oxazepam serum concentrations and potential oxazepam toxicity (sedation, slurred speech, central nervous system depression).	2	1	3
PHENYTOIN Concurrent use may result in loss of oxazepam efficacy.	2	4	3
ST. JOHN'S WORT Concurrent use may result in reduced oxazepam effectiveness.	2	3	2
SULCONAZOLE Concurrent use may result in increased oxazepam serum concentrations and potential oxazepam toxicity (sedation, slurred speech, central nervous system depression).	2	1	3
TERCONAZOLE Concurrent use may result in increased oxazepam serum concentrations and potential oxazepam toxicity (sedation, slurred speech, central nervous system depression).	2	1	3
THEOPHYLLINE Concurrent use may result in decreased oxazepam effectiveness.	1	3	2
TIOCONAZOLE Concurrent use may result in increased oxazepam serum concentrations and potential oxazepam toxicity (sedation, slurred speech, central nervous system depression).	2	1	3
VORICONAZOLE Concurrent use may result in increased oxazepam serum concentrations and potential oxazepam toxicity (sedation, slurred speech, central nervous system depression).	2	1	3

Paroxetine

INTERACTION	ONSET	SEVERITY	EVIDENCE
ALMOTRIPTAN Concurrent use may result in weakness, hyperreflexia, and/or incoordination.	0	3	3
CIMETIDINE Concurrent use may result in increased paroxetine serum concentrations and possibly paroxetine toxicity (dizziness, somnolence, nausea, headache).	2	3	3

Onset: 0=Unspecified 1=Rapid 2=Delayed
Severity: 1=Contraindicated 2=Major 3=Moderate 4=Minor
Evidence: 1=Excellent 2=Good 3=Fair 4=Poor

INTERACTION	ONSET	SEVERITY	EVIDENCE
CLORGYLINE Concurrent use may result in central nervous system toxicity or serotonin syndrome (hypertension, hyperthermia, myoclonus, mental status changes).	1	1	2
DEXFENFLURAMINE Concurrent use may result in serotonin syndrome (hypertension, hyperthermia, myoclonus, mental status changes).	1	2	3
DEXTROMETHORPHAN Concurrent use may result in possible dextromethorphan toxicity (nausea, vomiting, blurred vision, hallucinations) or serotonin syndrome (hypertension, hyperthermia, myoclonus, mental status changes).	1	2	3
DROPERIDOL Concurrent use may result in an increased risk of cardiotoxicity (QT prolongation, torsade de pointes, cardiac arrest).	1	2	3
ENCAINIDE Concurrent use may result in an increased risk of encainide toxicity (cardiac arrhythmia).	1	3	3
ETHANOL Concurrent use may result in an increased risk of impairment of mental and motor skills.	1	4	3
FENFLURAMINE Concurrent use may result in serotonin syndrome (hypertension, hyperthermia, myoclonus, mental status changes).	1	2	3
FOSPHENYTOIN Concurrent use may result in reduced paroxetine efficacy.	2	3	3
FURAZOLIDONE Concurrent use may result in weakness, hyperreflexia, and incoordination.	2	1	3
HYDROXYTRYPTOPHAN Concurrent use may result in an increased risk of serotonin syndrome (hypertension, hyperthermia, myoclonus, mental status changes).	1	3	3
IPRONIAZID Concurrent use may result in central nervous system toxicity or serotonin syndrome (hypertension, hyperthermia, myoclonus, mental status changes).	1	1	2
ISOCARBOXAZID Concurrent use may result in central nervous system toxicity or serotonin syndrome (hypertension, hyperthermia, myoclonus, mental status changes).	1	1	2
MOCLOBEMIDE Concurrent use may result in central nervous system toxicity or serotonin syndrome (hypertension, hyperthermia, myoclonus, mental status changes).	1	1	2

INTERACTION	ONSET	SEVERITY	EVIDENCE
NIALAMIDE Concurrent use may result in central nervous system toxicity or serotonin syndrome (hypertension, hyperthermia, myoclonus, mental status changes).	1	1	2
PARGYLINE Concurrent use may result in central nervous system toxicity or serotonin syndrome (hypertension, hyperthermia, myoclonus, mental status changes).	1	1	2
PERPHENAZINE Concurrent use may result in increased plasma concentrations and side effects of perphenazine.	1	3	3
PHENELZINE Concurrent use may result in central nervous system toxicity or serotonin syndrome (hypertension, hyperthermia, myoclonus, mental status changes).	1	1	2
PHENOBARBITAL Concurrent use may result in reduced paroxetine effectiveness.	1	4	3
PHENYTOIN Concurrent use may result in reduced phenytoin and paroxetine efficacy.	2	3	3
PROCARBAZINE Concurrent use may result in central nervous system toxicity or serotonin syndrome (hypertension, hyperthermia, myoclonus, mental status changes).	1	1	2
PROCYCLIDINE Concurrent use may result in an increased risk of anticholinergic effects (dry mouth, sedation, mydriasis).	1	3	3
PROPAFENONE Concurrent use may result in an increased risk of propafenone toxicity (cardiac arrhythmia).	1	3	3
RISPERIDONE Concurrent use may result in an increased risk for serotonin syndrome (hypertension, hyperthermia, myoclonus, mental status changes).	2	2	2
SELEGILINE Concurrent use may result in central nervous system toxicity or serotonin syndrome (hypertension, hyperthermia, myoclonus, mental status changes).	1	1	2
SIBUTRAMINE Concurrent use may result in an increased risk of serotonin syndrome (hypertension, hypothermia, myoclonus, mental status changes).	1	2	3
THEOPHYLLINE Concurrent use may result in an increased risk of theophylline toxicity.	2	3	3

Onset: 0=Unspecified 1=Rapid 2=Delayed
Severity: 1=Contraindicated 2=Major 3=Moderate 4=Minor
Evidence: 1=Excellent 2=Good 3=Fair 4=Poor

INTERACTION	ONSET	SEVERITY	EVIDENCE
THIORIDAZINE Concurrent use may result in an increased risk of thioridazine toxicity, cardiotoxicity (QT prolongation, torsade de pointes, cardiac arrest).	1	1	3
TOLOXATONE Concurrent use may result in central nervous system toxicity or serotonin syndrome (hypertension, hyperthermia, myoclonus, mental status changes).	1	1	2
TRAMADOL Concurrent use may result in an increased risk of seizures and serotonin syndrome (hypertension, hyperthermia, myoclonus, mental status changes).	1	2	2
TRANYLCYPROMINE Concurrent use may result in central nervous system toxicity or serotonin syndrome (hypertension, hyperthermia, myoclonus, mental status changes).	1	1	2
TRYPTOPHAN Concurrent use may result in serotonin syndrome (hypertension, hyperthermia, myoclonus, mental status changes).	2	2	3

Pentobarbital

INTERACTION	ONSET	SEVERITY	EVIDENCE
ALPRENOLOL Concurrent use may result in decreased alprenolol effectiveness.	2	3	2
DICUMAROL Concurrent use may result in decreased anticoagulant effectiveness.	2	2	2
ETHANOL Concurrent use may result in excessive central nervous system depression.	1	3	1
METOPROLOL Concurrent use may result in decreased metoprolol effectiveness.	2	3	3
PREDNISOLONE Concurrent use may result in decreased therapeutic effect of prednisolone.	2	3	2
PREDNISONE Concurrent use may result in decreased therapeutic effect of prednisone.	2	3	2
THEOPHYLLINE Concurrent use may result in decreased theophylline effectiveness.	2	3	3
VALERIAN Concurrent use may result in increased central nervous system depression.	1	3	3

Perphenazine

INTERACTION	ONSET	SEVERITY	EVIDENCE
BELLADONNA Concurrent use may result in increased manic, agitated reactions, or enhanced anticholinergic effects resulting in cardiorespiratory failure, especially in cases of belladonna overdose.	1	3	2
BENZTROPINE Concurrent use may result in decreased perphenazine serum concentrations, decreased perphenazine effectiveness, enhanced anticholinergic effects (ileus, hyperpyrexia, sedation, dry mouth).	2	3	3
CABERGOLINE Concurrent use may result in the decreased therapeutic effect of both drugs.	1	3	3
CISAPRIDE Concurrent use may result in cardiotoxicity (QT prolongation, torsade de pointes, cardiac arrest).	1	1	3
DROPERIDOL Concurrent use may result in an increased risk of cardiotoxicity (QT prolongation, torsade de pointes, cardiac arrest).	1	1	3
ETHANOL Concurrent use may result in increased central nervous system depression and an increased risk of extrapyramidal reactions.	1	3	2
FOSPHENYTOIN Concurrent use may result in increased or decreased phenytoin levels and possibly reduced perphenazine levels.	2	4	3
GREPAFLOXACIN Concurrent use may result in an increased risk of cardiotoxicity (QT prolongation, torsade de pointes, cardiac arrest).	2	1	3
LEVODOPA Concurrent use may result in loss of levodopa efficacy.	1	3	2
LITHIUM Concurrent use may result in weakness, dyskinesias, increased extrapyramidal symptoms, encephalopathy, and brain damage.	2	2	1
MEPERIDINE Concurrent use may result in an increase in central nervous system and respiratory depression.	1	3	2
ORPHENADRINE Concurrent use may result in decreased perphenazine serum concentrations, decreased perphenazine effectiveness, enhanced anticholinergic effects (ileus, hyperpyrexia, sedation, dry mouth).	2	3	3

Onset: 0=Unspecified 1=Rapid 2=Delayed
Severity: 1=Contraindicated 2=Major 3=Moderate 4=Minor
Evidence: 1=Excellent 2=Good 3=Fair 4=Poor

INTERACTION	ONSET	SEVERITY	EVIDENCE
PAROXETINE Concurrent use may result in increased plasma concentrations and side effects of perphenazine.	1	3	3
PHENYTOIN Concurrent use may result in increased or decreased phenytoin levels and possibly reduced perphenazine levels.	2	4	3
PORFIMER Concurrent use may result in excessive intracellular damage in photosensitized tissues.	2	3	3
PROCYCLIDINE Concurrent use may result in decreased perphenazine serum concentrations, decreased perphenazine effectiveness, enhanced anticholinergic effects (ileus, hyperpyrexia, sedation, dry mouth).	2	3	3
TRAMADOL Concurrent use may result in an increased risk of seizures.	1	2	3
TRIHEXYPHENIDYL Concurrent use may result in decreased perphenazine serum concentrations, decreased perphenazine effectiveness, enhanced anticholinergic effects (ileus, hyperpyrexia, sedation, dry mouth).	2	3	3

Phenelzine

INTERACTION	ONSET	SEVERITY	EVIDENCE
ACARBOSE Concurrent use may result in excessive hypoglycemia, central nervous system depression, and seizures.	1	3	2
ACETOHEXAMIDE Concurrent use may result in excessive hypoglycemia, central nervous system depression, and seizures.	1	3	2
ALBUTEROL Concurrent use may result in an increased risk of tachycardia, agitation, or hypomania.	2	2	2
AMITRIPTYLINE Concurrent use may result in neurotoxicity, seizures, or serotonin syndrome (hypertension, hyperthermia, myoclonus, mental status changes).	2	1	3
AMOXAPINE Concurrent use may result in neurotoxicity, seizures, or serotonin syndrome (hypertension, hyperthermia, myoclonus, mental status changes).	2	2	3
AMPHETAMINE Concurrent use may result in hypertensive crisis (headache, hyperpyrexia, hypertension).	1	1	2
APRACLONIDINE Concurrent use may result in potentiation of phenelzine effects.	1	1	3

INTERACTION	ONSET	SEVERITY	EVIDENCE
BAMBUTEROL Concurrent use may result in an increased risk of tachycardia, agitation, or hypomania.	2	2	2
BENFLUOREX Concurrent use of may result in excessive hypoglycemia, central nervous system depression, and seizures.	1	3	2
BENZPHETAMINE Concurrent use may result in hypertensive crisis (headache, hyperpyrexia, hypertension).	1	1	2
BITOLTEROL Concurrent use may result in an increased risk of tachycardia, agitation, or hypomania.	2	2	2
BROXATEROL Concurrent use may result in an increased risk of tachycardia, agitation, or hypomania.	2	2	2
BUPROPION Concurrent use may result in bupropion toxicity (seizures, agitation, psychotic changes).	1	1	3
BUSPIRONE Concurrent use may result in hypertensive crisis.	1	1	3
CARBAMAZEPINE Concurrent use may result in hypertensive urgency, hyperpyrexia, and seizures.	1	1	3
CHLORPROPAMIDE Concurrent use may result in excessive hypoglycemia, central nervous system depression, and seizures.	1	3	2
CITALOPRAM Concurrent use may result in central nervous system toxicity or serotonin syndrome (hypertension, hyperthermia, myoclonus, mental status changes).	1	1	3
CLENBUTEROL Concurrent use may result in an increased risk of tachycardia, agitation, or hypomania.	2	2	2
CLOMIPRAMINE Concurrent use may result in neurotoxicity, seizures, or serotonin syndrome (hypertension, hyperthermia, myoclonus, mental status changes).	2	2	3
CLORGYLINE Concurrent use may result in hypertensive crisis (headache, palpitation, neck stiffness).	1	1	3
CLOVOXAMINE Concurrent use may result in central nervous system toxicity or serotonin syndrome (hypertension, hyperthermia, myoclonus, mental status changes).	1	1	3

Onset: 0=Unspecified 1=Rapid 2=Delayed
Severity: 1=Contraindicated 2=Major 3=Moderate 4=Minor
Evidence: 1=Excellent 2=Good 3=Fair 4=Poor

INTERACTION	ONSET	SEVERITY	EVIDENCE
COCAINE			
Concurrent use may result in hypertensive crisis (headache, hyperpyrexia, hypertension).	1	1	3
CYCLOBENZAPRINE			
Concurrent use may result in hypertensive crises (headache, hyperpyrexia, hypertension) or severe convulsive seizures.	1	1	3
CYPROHEPTADINE			
Concurrent use may result in prolonged and intensified anticholinergic effects.	2	1	3
DESIPRAMINE			
Concurrent use may result in neurotoxicity, seizures, or serotonin syndrome (hypertension, hyperthermia, myoclonus, mental status changes).	2	2	3
DEXFENFLURAMINE			
Concurrent use may result in central nervous system toxicity or serotonin syndrome (hypertension, hyperthermia, myoclonus, mental status changes).	1	1	3
DEXMETHYLPHENIDATE			
Concurrent use may result in hypertensive crisis (headache, palpitation, neck stiffness).	1	1	3
DEXTROAMPHETAMINE			
Concurrent use may result in a hypertensive crisis (headache, hyperpyrexia, hypertension).	1	1	3
DEXTROMETHORPHAN			
Concurrent use may result in an increased risk of serotonin syndrome (hypertension, hyperthermia, myoclonus, mental status changes).	1	1	3
DIETHYLPROPION			
Concurrent use may result in hypertensive crisis (headache, hyperpyrexia, hypertension).	1	1	2
DOPAMINE			
Concurrent use may result in hypertensive crisis (headache, hyperpyrexia, hypertension).	1	1	1
DOPAMINE FOODS			
Concurrent use may result in increased blood pressure.	1	1	1
DOTHIEPIN			
Concurrent use may result in neurotoxicity, seizures, or serotonin syndrome (hypertension, hyperthermia, myoclonus, mental status changes).	2	2	3
DOXEPIN			
Concurrent use may result in neurotoxicity, seizures, or serotonin syndrome (hypertension, hyperthermia, myoclonus, mental status changes).	2	2	3
DROPERIDOL			
Concurrent use may result in an increased risk of cardiotoxicity (QT prolongation, torsade de pointes, cardiac arrest).	1	2	3

INTERACTION	ONSET	SEVERITY	EVIDENCE
EPHEDRINE Concurrent use may result in hypertensive crisis (headache, hyperpyrexia, hypertension).	1	2	3
EPINEPHRINE Concurrent use may result in increased hypertensive effects.	1	1	3
FEMOXETINE Concurrent use may result in central nervous system toxicity or serotonin syndrome (hypertension, hyperthermia, myoclonus, mental status changes).	1	1	3
FENFLURAMINE Concurrent use may result in serotonin syndrome (hypertension, hyperthermia, myoclonus, mental status changes).	1	1	3
FENOTEROL Concurrent use may result in an increased risk of tachycardia, agitation, or hypomania.	2	2	2
FLUOXETINE Concurrent use may result in central nervous system toxicity or serotonin syndrome (hypertension, hyperthermia, myoclonus, mental status changes).	1	1	2
FLUVOXAMINE Concurrent use may result in central nervous system toxicity or serotonin syndrome (hypertension, hyperthermia, myoclonus, mental status changes).	1	1	2
FORMOTEROL Concurrent use may result in an increased risk of tachycardia, agitation, or hypomania.	2	2	2
FURAZOLIDONE Concurrent use may result in hypertensive crisis (headache, palpitation, neck stiffness).	1	1	3
GLICLAZIDE Concurrent use may result in excessive hypoglycemia, central nervous system depression, and seizures.	1	3	2
GLIMEPIRIDE Concurrent use may result in excessive hypoglycemia, central nervous system depression, and seizures.	1	3	2
GLIPIZIDE Concurrent use may result in excessive hypoglycemia, central nervous system depression, and seizures.	1	3	2
GLIQUIDONE Concurrent use may result in excessive hypoglycemia, central nervous system depression, and seizures.	1	3	2
GLYBURIDE Concurrent use may result in excessive hypoglycemia, central nervous system depression, and seizures.	1	3	2

Onset: 0=Unspecified 1=Rapid 2=Delayed
Severity: 1=Contraindicated 2=Major 3=Moderate 4=Minor
Evidence: 1=Excellent 2=Good 3=Fair 4=Poor

INTERACTION	ONSET	SEVERITY	EVIDENCE
GUANADREL Concurrent use may result in decreased antihypertensive response to guanadrel or hypertensive crisis when guanadrel is initiated in a patient already receiving phenelzine.	1	1	3
GUAR GUM Concurrent use may result in excessive hypoglycemia, central nervous system depression, and seizures.	1	3	2
HEXOPRENALINE Concurrent use may result in an increased risk of tachycardia, agitation, or hypomania.	2	2	2
IMIPRAMINE Concurrent use may result in neurotoxicity, seizures, or serotonin syndrome (hypertension, hyperthermia, myoclonus, mental status changes).	2	2	3
INSULIN Concurrent use may result in excessive hypoglycemia, central nervous system depression, and seizures.	1	3	2
IPRONIAZID Concurrent use may result in hypertensive crisis (headache, palpitation, neck stiffness).	1	1	3
ISOCARBOXAZID Concurrent use may result in hypertensive crisis (headache, palpitation, neck stiffness).	1	1	3
ISOETHARINE Concurrent use may result in an increased risk of tachycardia, agitation, or hypomania.	2	2	2
ISOMETHEPTENE Concurrent use may result in severe headache, hypertensive crisis, cardiac arrhythmias.	1	1	1
ISOPROTERENOL Concurrent use may result in increased hypertensive effects.	1	3	3
LAZABEMIDE Concurrent use may result in hypertensive crisis (headache, palpitation, neck stiffness).	1	1	3
LEVALBUTEROL Concurrent use may result in an increased risk of tachycardia, agitation, or hypomania.	2	2	2
LEVODOPA Concurrent use may result in hypertensive response.	1	1	3
LEVOMETHADYL Concurrent use may result in increased levels of levomethadyl or its active metabolites.	2	1	3

INTERACTION	ONSET	SEVERITY	EVIDENCE
LOFEPRAMINE Concurrent use may result in neurotoxicity, seizures, or serotonin syndrome (hypertension, hyperthermia, myoclonus, mental status changes).	2	2	3
MA HUANG Concurrent use may result in increased risk for excessive phenelzine activity including headache, hyperpyrexia, arrhythmias, and hypertensive crisis.	1	2	3
MAPROTILINE Concurrent use may result in neurotoxicity, seizures.	2	1	3
MAZINDOL Concurrent use may result in hypertensive crisis.	1	1	3
MEPERIDINE Concurrent use may result in cardiovascular instability, hyperpyrexia, coma, or death.	1	1	2
METARAMINOL Concurrent use may result in hypertensive crisis (headache, hyperpyrexia, hypertension).	1	2	3
METFORMIN Concurrent use may result in excessive hypoglycemia, central nervous system depression, and seizures.	1	3	2
METHAMPHETAMINE Concurrent use may result in hypertensive crisis.	1	1	3
METHOTRIMEPRAZINE Concurrent use may result in possibly prolonged effect of methotrimeprazine, with potentially increased side effects.	2	1	3
METHYLDOPA Concurrent use may result in hypertensive crisis (headache, palpitation, neck stiffness).	1	1	3
METHYLPHENIDATE Concurrent use may result in hypertensive crisis (headache, palpitation, neck stiffness).	1	1	3
MIGLITOL Concurrent use may result in excessive hypoglycemia, central nervous system depression, and seizures.	1	3	2
MIRTAZAPINE Concurrent use may result in neurotoxicity, seizures.	2	1	3
MOCLOBEMIDE Concurrent use may result in hypertensive crisis (headache, palpitation, neck stiffness).	1	1	3
MORPHINE Concurrent use may result in hypotension and exaggeration of central nervous system and respiratory depressant effects.	1	1	3

Onset: 0=Unspecified 1=Rapid 2=Delayed
Severity: 1=Contraindicated 2=Major 3=Moderate 4=Minor
Evidence: 1=Excellent 2=Good 3=Fair 4=Poor

INTERACTION	ONSET	SEVERITY	EVIDENCE
NEFAZODONE Concurrent use may result in hyperthermia, rigidity, myoclonus, seizures, fluctuations of vital signs, or mental status changes.	1	1	2
NIALAMIDE Concurrent use may result in hypertensive crisis (headache, palpitation, neck stiffness).	1	1	3
NOREPINEPHRINE Concurrent use may result in increased hypertensive effects.	1	1	3
NORTRIPTYLINE Concurrent use may result in neurotoxicity, seizures, or serotonin syndrome (hypertension, hyperthermia, myoclonus, mental status changes).	2	2	3
OPIPRAMOL Concurrent use may result in neurotoxicity, seizures, or serotonin syndrome (hypertension, hyperthermia, myoclonus, mental status changes).	2	1	3
OXYCODONE Concurrent use may result in anxiety, confusion and significant respiratory depressant effects or coma.	2	2	3
PARGYLINE Concurrent use may result in hypertensive crisis (headache, palpitation, neck stiffness).	1	1	3
PAROXETINE Concurrent use may result in central nervous system toxicity or serotonin syndrome (hypertension, hyperthermia, myoclonus, mental status changes).	1	1	2
PHENDIMETRAZINE Concurrent use may result in hypertensive crisis (headache, hyperpyrexia, hypertension).	1	1	2
PHENMETRAZINE Concurrent use may result in hypertensive crisis (headache, hyperpyrexia, hypertension).	1	1	2
PHENTERMINE Concurrent use may result in hypertensive crisis (headache, hyperpyrexia, hypertension).	1	1	1
PHENYLALANINE Concurrent use may result in hypertensive crisis (headache, palpitation, neck stiffness).	1	1	3
PHENYLEPHRINE Concurrent use may result in hypertensive crisis (headache, hyperpyrexia, hypertension).	1	1	2
PHENYLPROPANOLAMINE Concurrent use may result in hypertensive crisis (headache, hyperpyrexia, hypertension).	1	1	1

INTERACTION	ONSET	SEVERITY	EVIDENCE
PIRBUTEROL Concurrent use may result in an increased risk of tachycardia, agitation, or hypomania.	2	2	2
PROCARBAZINE Concurrent use may result in hypertensive crisis (headache, palpitation, neck stiffness).	1	1	3
PROCATEROL Concurrent use may result in an increased risk of tachycardia, agitation, or hypomania.	2	2	2
PROTRIPTYLINE Concurrent use may result in neurotoxicity, seizures, or serotonin syndrome (hypertension, hyperthermia, myoclonus, mental status changes).	2	2	3
PSEUDOEPHEDRINE Concurrent use may result in hypertensive crisis (headache, hyperpyrexia, hypertension).	1	1	3
REBOXETINE Concurrent use may result in hyperthermia, rigidity, myoclonus, seizures, fluctuations of vital signs, or mental status changes.	1	2	3
RESERPINE Concurrent use may result in elevated catecholamine levels.	1	1	3
RIMITEROL Concurrent use may result in an increased risk of tachycardia, agitation, or hypomania.	2	2	2
RITODRINE Concurrent use may result in an increased risk of tachycardia, agitation, or hypomania.	2	2	2
SALMETEROL Concurrent use may result in an increased risk of tachycardia, agitation, or hypomania.	2	2	2
SELEGILINE Concurrent use may result in hypertensive crisis (headache, palpitation, neck stiffness).	1	1	3
SERTRALINE Concurrent use may result in central nervous system toxicity or serotonin syndrome (hypertension, hyperthermia, myoclonus, mental status changes).	1	1	2
SIBUTRAMINE Concurrent use may result in central nervous system toxicity or serotonin syndrome (hypertension, hyperthermia, myoclonus, mental status changes).	1	1	3
SUMATRIPTAN Concurrent use may result in an increased risk of serotonin syndrome (hypertension, hyperthermia, myoclonus, mental status changes).	1	1	2

Onset: 0=Unspecified 1=Rapid 2=Delayed
Severity: 1=Contraindicated 2=Major 3=Moderate 4=Minor
Evidence: 1=Excellent 2=Good 3=Fair 4=Poor

INTERACTION	ONSET	SEVERITY	EVIDENCE
TERBUTALINE Concurrent use may result in an increased risk of tachycardia, agitation, or hypomania.	2	2	2
TOLAZAMIDE Concurrent use may result in excessive hypoglycemia, central nervous system depression, and seizures.	1	3	2
TOLBUTAMIDE Concurrent use may result in excessive hypoglycemia, central nervous system depression, and seizures.	1	3	2
TOLCAPONE Concurrent use may result in decreased catecholamine metabolism.	1	2	3
TOLOXATONE Concurrent use may result in hypertensive crisis (headache, palpitation, neck stiffness).	1	1	3
TRAMADOL Concurrent use may result in nausea, vomiting, cardiovascular collapse, respiratory depression, seizures.	1	2	3
TRANYLCYPROMINE Concurrent use may result in hypertensive crisis (headache, palpitation, neck stiffness).	1	1	3
TRIMIPRAMINE Concurrent use may result in neurotoxicity, seizures, or serotonin syndrome (hypertension, hyperthermia, myoclonus, mental status changes).	2	2	3
TROGLITAZONE Concurrent use may result in excessive hypoglycemia, central nervous system depression, and seizures.	1	3	2
TRYPTOPHAN Concurrent use may result in delirium and serotonin syndrome (hypertension, hyperthermia, myoclonus, mental status changes).	1	1	3
TULOBUTEROL Concurrent use may result in an increased risk of tachycardia, agitation, or hypomania.	2	2	2
TYRAMINE FOODS Concurrent use may result in increased blood pressure.	1	1	1
VENLAFAXINE Concurrent use may result in central nervous system toxicity or serotonin syndrome (hypertension, hyperthermia, myoclonus, mental status changes).	1	1	2

Phenobarbital

INTERACTION	ONSET	SEVERITY	EVIDENCE
ACENOCOUMAROL Concurrent use may result in decreased anticoagulant effectiveness.	2	2	2

INTERACTION	ONSET	SEVERITY	EVIDENCE
ALPRENOLOL Concurrent use may result in decreased alprenolol effectiveness.	2	3	3
ANISINDIONE Concurrent use may result in decreased anticoagulant effectiveness.	2	2	2
BETAMETHASONE Concurrent use may result in decreased betamethasone effectiveness.	2	3	3
CHLORPROMAZINE Concurrent use may result in decreased chlorpromazine effectiveness.	1	3	3
CLOZAPINE Concurrent use may result in decreased clozapine plasma levels associated with marked worsening of psychosis.	2	3	3
CORTISONE Concurrent use may result in decreased cortisone effectiveness.	2	3	3
CYCLOSPORINE Concurrent use may result in decreased cyclosporine effectiveness.	2	3	3
DEFLAZACORT Concurrent use may result in decreased corticosteroid effectiveness.	2	3	2
DEXAMETHASONE Concurrent use may result in decreased dexamethasone effectiveness.	2	3	2
DEXMETHYLPHENIDATE Concurrent use may result in an increase in phenobarbital plasma concentrations.	1	3	3
DICUMAROL Concurrent use may result in decreased anticoagulant effectiveness.	2	2	2
DIGITOXIN Concurrent use may result in decreased digitoxin levels.	2	3	3
DISOPYRAMIDE Concurrent use may result in decreased disopyramide effectiveness.	2	3	3
ETHANOL Concurrent use may result in excessive central nervous system depression.	1	3	1
ETHOSUXIMIDE Concurrent use may result in decreased ethosuximide serum concentrations.	2	3	3

Onset: 0=Unspecified 1=Rapid 2=Delayed
Severity: 1=Contraindicated 2=Major 3=Moderate 4=Minor
Evidence: 1=Excellent 2=Good 3=Fair 4=Poor

INTERACTION	ONSET	SEVERITY	EVIDENCE
FELODIPINE Concurrent use may result in decreased felodipine effectiveness.	2	3	3
FLUDROCORTISONE Concurrent use may result in decreased corticosteroid effectiveness.	2	3	2
FOSPHENYTOIN Concurrent use may result in increased or decreased phenytoin levels.	2	4	3
GRISEOFULVIN Concurrent use may result in decreased effectiveness of griseofulvin.	1	3	3
GUANFACINE Concurrent use may result in decreased guanfacine effectiveness.	2	3	3
HYDROCORTISONE Concurrent use may result in decreased corticosteroid effectiveness.	2	3	2
ITRACONAZOLE Concurrent use may result in loss of itraconazole efficacy.	2	3	3
LAMOTRIGINE Concurrent use may result in reduced lamotrigine efficacy, loss of seizure control.	2	3	2
METHOXYFLURANE Concurrent use may result in nephrotoxicity.	1	2	3
METHYLPREDNISOLONE Concurrent use may result in decreased methylprednisolone effectiveness.	2	3	2
METOPROLOL Concurrent use may result in decreased metoprolol effectiveness.	2	3	3
METRONIDAZOLE Concurrent use may result in decreased metronidazole effectiveness.	2	4	3
ORAL CONTRACEPTIVE Concurrent use may result in decreased contraceptive effectiveness.	2	2	2
PARAMETHASONE Concurrent use may result in decreased corticosteroid effectiveness.	2	3	2
PAROXETINE Concurrent use may result in reduced paroxetine effectiveness.	1	4	3
PHENINDIONE Concurrent use may result in decreased anticoagulant effectiveness.	2	2	2

INTERACTION	ONSET	SEVERITY	EVIDENCE
PHENPROCOUMON Concurrent use may result in decreased anticoagulant effectiveness.	2	2	2
PHENYTOIN Concurrent use may result in increased or decreased phenytoin levels.	2	4	3
PREDNISOLONE Concurrent use may result in decreased prednisolone effectiveness.	2	3	2
PREDNISONE Concurrent use may result in decreased therapeutic effect of prednisone.	2	3	2
PROPRANOLOL Concurrent use may result in decreased propranolol effectiveness.	2	3	3
QUINIDINE Concurrent use may result in decreased quinidine effectiveness.	2	3	2
TACROLIMUS Concurrent use may result in decreased tacrolimus efficacy.	2	3	3
TENIPOSIDE Concurrent use may result in increased teniposide clearance.	2	3	3
THEOPHYLLINE Concurrent use may result in decreased theophylline effectiveness.	2	3	2
TOPIRAMATE Concurrent use may result in a decrease in serum concentrations of topiramate.	2	3	3
TRIAMCINOLONE Concurrent use may result in decreased corticosteroid effectiveness.	2	3	2
VALERIAN Concurrent use may result in increased central nervous system depression.	1	3	3
VALPROIC ACID Concurrent use may result in phenobarbital toxicity or decreased valproic acid effectiveness.	2	3	1
VERAPAMIL Concurrent use may result in decreased verapamil effectiveness.	2	3	3
WARFARIN Concurrent use may result in decreased anticoagulant effectiveness.	2	3	1

Onset: 0=Unspecified 1=Rapid 2=Delayed
Severity: 1=Contraindicated 2=Major 3=Moderate 4=Minor
Evidence: 1=Excellent 2=Good 3=Fair 4=Poor

Prochlorperazine

INTERACTION	ONSET	SEVERITY	EVIDENCE
BELLADONNA Concurrent use may result in increased manic, agitated reactions, or enhanced anticholinergic effects resulting in cardiorespiratory failure, especially in cases of belladonna overdose.	1	3	2
BENZTROPINE Concurrent use may result in decreased prochlorperazine serum concentrations, decreased prochlorperazine effectiveness, and enhanced anticholinergic effects (ileus, hyperpyrexia, sedation, dry mouth).	2	3	3
CABERGOLINE Concurrent use may result in the decreased therapeutic effect of both drugs.	1	3	3
CISAPRIDE Concurrent use may result in cardiotoxicity (QT prolongation, torsade de pointes, cardiac arrest).	1	1	3
ETHANOL Concurrent use may result in increased central nervous system depression and an increased risk of extrapyramidal reactions.	1	3	2
FOSPHENYTOIN Concurrent use may result in increased or decreased phenytoin levels and possibly reduced prochlorperazine levels.	2	4	3
GREPAFLOXACIN Concurrent use may result in an increased risk of cardiotoxicity (QT prolongation, torsade de pointes, cardiac arrest).	2	1	3
GUANETHIDINE Concurrent use may result in decreased guanethidine effectiveness.	1	3	2
HALOFANTRINE Concurrent use may result in an increased risk of cardiotoxicity (QT prolongation, torsade de pointes, cardiac arrest).	0	2	3
LEVODOPA Concurrent use may result in loss of levodopa efficacy.	1	3	2
LITHIUM Concurrent use may result in weakness, dyskinesias, increased extrapyramidal symptoms, encephalopathy, and brain damage.	2	2	1
MEPERIDINE Concurrent use may result in an increase in central nervous system and respiratory depression.	1	3	2

INTERACTION	ONSET	SEVERITY	EVIDENCE
ORPHENADRINE Concurrent use may result in decreased prochlorperazine serum concentrations, decreased prochlorperazine effectiveness, and enhanced anticholinergic effects (ileus, hyperpyrexia, sedation, dry mouth).	2	3	3
PHENYTOIN Concurrent use may result in increased or decreased phenytoin levels and possibly reduced prochlorperazine levels.	2	4	3
PORFIMER Concurrent use may result in excessive intracellular damage in photosensitized tissues.	2	3	3
PROCYCLIDINE Concurrent use may result in decreased prochlorperazine serum concentrations, decreased prochlorperazine effectiveness, enhanced anticholinergic effects (ileus, hyperpyrexia, sedation, dry mouth).	2	3	3
TRIHEXYPHENIDYL Concurrent use may result in decreased prochlorperazine serum concentrations, decreased prochlorperazine effectiveness, and enhanced anticholinergic effects (ileus, hyperpyrexia, sedation, dry mouth).	2	3	3

Promethazine

INTERACTION	ONSET	SEVERITY	EVIDENCE
BELLADONNA Concurrent use may result in increased manic, agitated reactions, or enhanced anticholinergic effects resulting in cardiorespiratory failure, especially in cases of belladonna overdose.	1	3	2
BENZTROPINE Concurrent use may result in decreased promethazine serum concentrations, decreased promethazine effectiveness, and enhanced anticholinergic effects (ileus, hyperpyrexia, sedation, dry mouth).	2	3	3
CABERGOLINE Concurrent use may result in the decreased therapeutic effect of both drugs.	1	3	3
CISAPRIDE Concurrent use may result in cardiotoxicity (QT prolongation, torsade de pointes, cardiac arrest).	1	1	3
FOSPHENYTOIN Concurrent use may result in increased or decreased phenytoin levels and possibly reduced phenothiazine levels.	2	4	3

Onset: 0=Unspecified 1=Rapid 2=Delayed
Severity: 1=Contraindicated 2=Major 3=Moderate 4=Minor
Evidence: 1=Excellent 2=Good 3=Fair 4=Poor

INTERACTION	ONSET	SEVERITY	EVIDENCE
GREPAFLOXACIN Concurrent use may result in an increased risk of cardiotoxicity (QT prolongation, torsade de pointes, cardiac arrest).	2	1	3
LITHIUM Concurrent use may result in weakness, dyskinesias, increased extrapyramidal symptoms, encephalopathy, and brain damage.	2	2	1
MEPERIDINE Concurrent use may result in an increase in central nervous system and respiratory depression.	1	3	2
ORPHENADRINE Concurrent use may result in decreased promethazine serum concentrations, decreased promethazine effectiveness, and enhanced anticholinergic effects (ileus, hyperpyrexia, sedation, dry mouth).	2	3	3
PHENYTOIN Concurrent use may result in increased or decreased phenytoin levels and possibly reduced promethazine levels.	2	4	3
PORFIMER Concurrent use may result in excessive intracellular damage in photosensitized tissues.	2	3	3
PROCYCLIDINE Concurrent use may result in decreased promethazine serum concentrations, decreased promethazine effectiveness, and enhanced anticholinergic effects (ileus, hyperpyrexia, sedation, dry mouth).	2	3	3
TRAMADOL Concurrent use may result in an increased risk of seizures.	1	2	3
TRIHEXYPHENIDYL Concurrent use may result in decreased promethazine serum concentrations, decreased promethazine effectiveness, and enhanced anticholinergic effects (ileus, hyperpyrexia, sedation, dry mouth).	2	3	3

Protriptyline

INTERACTION	ONSET	SEVERITY	EVIDENCE
ACENOCOUMAROL Concurrent use may result in increased risk of bleeding.	2	3	3
AJMALINE Concurrent use may result in an increased risk of cardiotoxicity (QT prolongation, torsade de pointes, cardiac arrest).	0	2	3
AMISULPRIDE Concurrent use may result in an increased risk of cardiotoxicity (QT prolongation, torsade de pointes, cardiac arrest).	0	2	3

INTERACTION	ONSET	SEVERITY	EVIDENCE
AMITRIPTYLINE Concurrent use of more than one tricyclic antidepressant may result in an increased risk of cardiotoxicity (QT prolongation, torsade de pointes, cardiac arrest).	0	2	3
AMOXAPINE Concurrent use of more than one tricyclic antidepressant may result in an increased risk of cardiotoxicity (QT prolongation, torsade de pointes, cardiac arrest).	0	2	3
AMPRENAVIR Concurrent use may result in increased protriptyline serum concentrations and potential toxicity (anticholinergic effects, sedation, confusion, cardiac arrhythmias).	2	2	3
ANISINDIONE Concurrent use may result in increased risk of bleeding.	2	3	3
ASTEMIZOLE Concurrent use may result in an increased risk of cardiotoxicity (QT prolongation, torsade de pointes, cardiac arrest).	0	2	3
BEPRIDIL Concurrent use may result in an increased risk of cardiotoxicity (QT prolongation, torsade de pointes, cardiac arrest).	1	1	3
BETHANIDINE Concurrent use may result in decreased antihypertensive effectiveness.	1	3	2
CARBAMAZEPINE Concurrent use may result in decreased protriptyline plasma concentrations and increased carbamazepine plasma concentrations and possible toxicity (ataxia, nystagmus, apnea, seizures, coma).	2	3	3
CIMETIDINE Concurrent use may result in protriptyline toxicity (dry mouth, blurred vision, urinary retention).	2	3	3
CISAPRIDE Concurrent use may result in cardiotoxicity (QT prolongation, torsade de pointes, cardiac arrest).	1	1	3
CLONIDINE Concurrent use may result in decreased antihypertensive effectiveness.	2	2	3
CLORGYLINE Concurrent use may result in neurotoxicity, seizures, or serotonin syndrome (hypertension, hyperthermia, myoclonus, mental status changes).	2	2	3

Onset: 0=Unspecified 1=Rapid 2=Delayed
Severity: 1=Contraindicated 2=Major 3=Moderate 4=Minor
Evidence: 1=Excellent 2=Good 3=Fair 4=Poor

INTERACTION	ONSET	SEVERITY	EVIDENCE
DESIPRAMINE Concurrent use of more than one tricyclic antidepressant may result in an increased risk of cardiotoxicity (QT prolongation, torsade de pointes, cardiac arrest).	0	2	3
DIBENZEPIN Concurrent use of more than one tricyclic antidepressant may result in an increased risk of cardiotoxicity (QT prolongation, torsade de pointes, cardiac arrest).	0	2	3
DICUMAROL Concurrent use may result in increased risk of bleeding.	2	3	3
DISOPYRAMIDE Concurrent use may result in an increased risk of cardiotoxicity (QT prolongation, torsade de pointes, cardiac arrest).	0	2	3
DOXEPIN Concurrent use of more than one tricyclic antidepressant may result in an increased risk of cardiotoxicity (QT prolongation, torsade de pointes, cardiac arrest).	0	2	3
DROPERIDOL Concurrent use may result in an increased risk of cardiotoxicity (QT prolongation, torsade de pointes, cardiac arrest).	0	2	3
EPINEPHRINE Concurrent use may result in hypertension, cardiac arrhythmias, and tachycardia.	1	2	2
ETILEFRINE Concurrent use may result in hypertension, cardiac arrhythmias, and tachycardia.	1	2	2
FOSCARNET Concurrent use may result in an increased risk of cardiotoxicity (QT prolongation, torsade de pointes, cardiac arrest).	0	2	3
GREPAFLOXACIN Concurrent use may result in an increased risk of cardiotoxicity (QT prolongation, torsade de pointes, cardiac arrest).	2	1	3
GUANADREL Concurrent use may result in decreased antihypertensive effectiveness.	2	3	3
GUANETHIDINE Concurrent use may result in decreased antihypertensive effectiveness.	2	3	1
HALOFANTRINE Concurrent use may result in an increased risk of cardiotoxicity (QT prolongation, torsade de pointes, cardiac arrest).	2	2	3

INTERACTION	ONSET	SEVERITY	EVIDENCE
HALOPERIDOL Concurrent use may result in an increased risk of cardiotoxicity (QT prolongation, torsade de pointes, cardiac arrest).	0	2	3
HYDROQUINIDINE Concurrent use may result in an increased risk of cardiotoxicity (QT prolongation, torsade de pointes, cardiac arrest).	0	2	3
IMIPRAMINE Concurrent use of more than one tricyclic antidepressant may result in an increased risk of cardiotoxicity (QT prolongation, torsade de pointes, cardiac arrest).	0	2	3
IPRONIAZID Concurrent use may result in neurotoxicity, seizures, or serotonin syndrome (hypertension, hyperthermia, myoclonus, mental status changes).	2	2	3
ISOCARBOXAZID Concurrent use may result in neurotoxicity, seizures, or serotonin syndrome (hypertension, hyperthermia, myoclonus, mental status changes).	2	1	3
LEVOMETHADYL Concurrent use may result in an increased risk of cardiotoxicity (QT prolongation, torsade de pointes, cardiac arrest).	0	1	3
MESORIDAZINE Concurrent use may result in an increased risk of cardiotoxicity (QT prolongation, torsade de pointes, cardiac arrest).	0	1	3
METHOXAMINE Concurrent use may result in hypertension, cardiac arrhythmias, and tachycardia.	1	2	2
MIDODRINE Concurrent use may result in hypertension, cardiac arrhythmias, and tachycardia.	1	2	2
MOCLOBEMIDE Concurrent use may result in neurotoxicity, seizures, or serotonin syndrome (hypertension, hyperthermia, myoclonus, mental status changes).	2	2	3
NIALAMIDE Concurrent use may result in neurotoxicity, seizures, or serotonin syndrome (hypertension, hyperthermia, myoclonus, mental status changes).	2	2	3
NOREPINEPHRINE Concurrent use may result in hypertension, cardiac arrhythmias, and tachycardia.	1	2	2

Onset: 0=Unspecified 1=Rapid 2=Delayed
Severity: 1=Contraindicated 2=Major 3=Moderate 4=Minor
Evidence: 1=Excellent 2=Good 3=Fair 4=Poor

INTERACTION	ONSET	SEVERITY	EVIDENCE
NORTRIPTYLINE Concurrent use of more than one tricyclic antidepressant may result in an increased risk of cardiotoxicity (QT prolongation, torsade de pointes, cardiac arrest).	0	2	3
OXILOFRINE Concurrent use may result in hypertension, cardiac arrhythmias, and tachycardia.	1	2	2
PARGYLINE Concurrent use may result in neurotoxicity, seizures, or serotonin syndrome (hypertension, hyperthermia, myoclonus, mental status changes).	2	2	3
PAROXETINE Concurrent use may result in protriptyline toxicity (dry mouth, sedation, urinary retention).	2	3	3
PHENELZINE Concurrent use may result in neurotoxicity, seizures, or serotonin syndrome (hypertension, hyperthermia, myoclonus, mental status changes).	2	2	3
PHENINDIONE Concurrent use may result in increased risk of bleeding.	2	3	3
PHENPROCOUMON Concurrent use may result in increased risk of bleeding.	2	3	3
PHENYLEPHRINE Concurrent use may result in hypertension, cardiac arrhythmias, and tachycardia.	1	2	2
PIMOZIDE Concurrent use may result in an increased risk of cardiotoxicity (QT prolongation, torsade de pointes, cardiac arrest).	0	1	3
PIRMENOL Concurrent use may result in an increased risk of cardiotoxicity (QT prolongation, torsade de pointes, cardiac arrest).	0	2	3
PRAJMALINE Concurrent use may result in an increased risk of cardiotoxicity (QT prolongation, torsade de pointes, cardiac arrest).	0	2	3
PROCAINAMIDE Concurrent use may result in an increased risk of cardiotoxicity (QT prolongation, torsade de pointes, cardiac arrest).	0	2	3
PROCARBAZINE Concurrent use may result in neurotoxicity, seizures.	2	2	3
QUETIAPINE Concurrent use may result in an increased risk of cardiotoxicity (QT prolongation, torsade de pointes, cardiac arrest).	0	2	3

INTERACTION	ONSET	SEVERITY	EVIDENCE
QUINIDINE Concurrent use may result in protriptyline toxicity (dry mouth, sedation) and an increased risk of cardiotoxicity (QT prolongation, torsade de pointes, cardiac arrest).	2	3	3
QUINIDINE Concurrent use may result in an increased risk of cardiotoxicity (QT prolongation, torsade de pointes, cardiac arrest).	0	2	3
RISPERIDONE Concurrent use may result in an increased risk of cardiotoxicity (QT prolongation, torsade de pointes, cardiac arrest).	0	2	3
S-ADENOSYLMETHIONINE Concurrent use may result in an increased risk of serotonin syndrome (hypertension, hyperthermia, myoclonus, mental status changes).	2	3	3
SELEGILINE Concurrent use may result in neurotoxicity, seizures, or serotonin syndrome (hypertension, hyperthermia, myoclonus, mental status changes).	2	2	3
SERTINDOLE Concurrent use may result in an increased risk of cardiotoxicity (QT prolongation, torsade de pointes, cardiac arrest).	0	2	3
SERTRALINE Concurrent use may result in modest elevations in protriptyline serum levels or possible serotonin syndrome (hypertension, hyperthermia, myoclonus, mental status changes).	2	2	3
SULTOPRIDE Concurrent use may result in an increased risk of cardiotoxicity (QT prolongation, torsade de pointes, cardiac arrest).	0	2	3
THIORIDAZINE Concurrent use may result in an increased risk of cardiotoxicity (QT prolongation, torsade de pointes, cardiac arrest).	0	1	3
TOLOXATONE Concurrent use may result in neurotoxicity, seizures, or serotonin syndrome (hypertension, hyperthermia, myoclonus, mental status changes).	2	2	3
TRAMADOL Concurrent use may result in an increased risk of seizures.	1	2	3
TRANYLCYPROMINE Concurrent use may result in neurotoxicity, seizures, or serotonin syndrome (hypertension, hyperthermia, myoclonus, mental status changes).	2	2	3

Onset: 0=Unspecified 1=Rapid 2=Delayed
Severity: 1=Contraindicated 2=Major 3=Moderate 4=Minor
Evidence: 1=Excellent 2=Good 3=Fair 4=Poor

INTERACTION	ONSET	SEVERITY	EVIDENCE
TRIMIPRAMINE Concurrent use of more than one tricyclic antidepressant may result in an increased risk of cardiotoxicity (QT prolongation, torsade de pointes, cardiac arrest).	0	2	3
WARFARIN Concurrent use may result in an increased risk of bleeding.	2	3	3
ZIPRASIDONE Concurrent use may result in an increased risk of cardiotoxicity (QT prolongation, torsade de pointes, cardiac arrest).	0	1	3
ZOTEPINE Concurrent use may result in an increased risk of cardiotoxicity (QT prolongation, torsade de pointes, cardiac arrest).	0	2	3

Quazepam

INTERACTION	ONSET	SEVERITY	EVIDENCE
CIMETIDINE Concurrent use may result in quazepam toxicity (central nervous system depression).	1	4	3
KETOCONAZOLE Concurrent use may result in increased quazepam serum concentrations and potential quazepam toxicity (sedation, slurred speech, central nervous system depression).	2	1	3
THEOPHYLLINE Concurrent use may result in decreased quazepam effectiveness.	1	3	2

Quetiapine

INTERACTION	ONSET	SEVERITY	EVIDENCE
ETHANOL Concurrent use may result in potentiation of the cognitive and motor effects of alcohol.	1	3	3

Risperidone

INTERACTION	ONSET	SEVERITY	EVIDENCE
DROPERIDOL Concurrent use may result in an increased risk of cardiotoxicity (QT prolongation, torsade de pointes, cardiac arrest).	0	2	3
LEVOMETHADYL Concurrent use may result in an increased risk of cardiotoxicity (QT prolongation, torsade de pointes, cardiac arrest).	2	1	3
LITHIUM Concurrent use may result in weakness, dyskinesias, increased extrapyramidal symptoms, encephalopathy, and brain damage.	2	2	1

INTERACTION	ONSET	SEVERITY	EVIDENCE
PAROXETINE Concurrent use may result in an increased risk for serotonin syndrome (hypertension, hyperthermia, myoclonus, mental status changes).	2	2	2
TRAMADOL Concurrent use may result in an increased risk of seizures.	1	2	3

Secobarbital

INTERACTION	ONSET	SEVERITY	EVIDENCE
DICUMAROL Concurrent use may result in decreased anticoagulant effectiveness.	2	2	2
ETHANOL Concurrent use may result in excessive central nervous system depression.	1	3	1
FOSPHENYTOIN Concurrent use may result in increased or decreased phenytoin levels.	2	3	3
METHOXYFLURANE Concurrent use may result in nephrotoxicity.	1	3	3
ORAL CONTRACEPTIVE Concurrent use may result in decreased contraceptive effectiveness.	2	2	2
PHENYTOIN Concurrent use may result in increased or decreased phenytoin levels.	2	4	3
PREDNISOLONE Concurrent use may result in decreased therapeutic effect of prednisolone.	2	3	2
PREDNISONE Concurrent use may result in decreased therapeutic effect of prednisone.	2	3	2
THEOPHYLLINE Concurrent use may result in decreased theophylline effectiveness.	2	3	3
VALERIAN Concurrent use may result in increased central nervous system depression.	1	3	3
WARFARIN Concurrent use may result in decreased anticoagulant effectiveness.	2	3	1

Onset: 0=Unspecified 1=Rapid 2=Delayed
Severity: 1=Contraindicated 2=Major 3=Moderate 4=Minor
Evidence: 1=Excellent 2=Good 3=Fair 4=Poor

Sertraline

INTERACTION	ONSET	SEVERITY	EVIDENCE
ALMOTRIPTAN Concurrent use may result in weakness, hyperreflexia, and/or incoordination.	0	3	3
AMITRIPTYLINE Concurrent use may result in elevated amitriptyline serum levels or possible serotonin syndrome (hypertension, hyperthermia, myoclonus, mental status changes).	2	2	3
CARBAMAZEPINE Concurrent use may result in an increased risk of carbamazepine toxicity (ataxia, nystagmus, diplopia, headache, vomiting, apnea, seizures, coma) and decreased sertraline efficacy.	2	3	3
CIMETIDINE Concurrent use may result in elevated sertraline serum concentrations and increased risk of adverse side effects.	1	3	3
CLORGYLINE Concurrent use may result in central nervous system toxicity or serotonin syndrome (hypertension, hyperthermia, myoclonus, mental status changes).	1	1	2
CLOZAPINE Concurrent use may result in an increased risk of clozapine toxicity (sedation, seizures, hypotension).	2	3	3
DEXFENFLURAMINE Concurrent use may result in serotonin syndrome (hypertension, hyperthermia, myoclonus, mental status changes).	1	2	3
DROPERIDOL Concurrent use may result in an increased risk of cardiotoxicity (QT prolongation, torsade de pointes, cardiac arrest).	1	2	3
FENFLURAMINE Concurrent use may result in serotonin syndrome (hypertension, hyperthermia, myoclonus, mental status changes).	1	2	3
FURAZOLIDONE Concurrent use may result in weakness, hyperreflexia, and incoordination.	2	1	3
HYDROXYTRYPTOPHAN Concurrent use may result in an increased risk of serotonin syndrome (hypertension, hyperthermia, myoclonus, mental status changes).	1	3	3
IPRONIAZID Concurrent use may result in central nervous system toxicity or serotonin syndrome (hypertension, hyperthermia, myoclonus, mental status changes).	1	1	2

INTERACTION	ONSET	SEVERITY	EVIDENCE
ISOCARBOXAZID Concurrent use may result in central nervous system toxicity or serotonin syndrome (hypertension, hyperthermia, myoclonus, mental status changes).	1	1	2
LEVOMETHADYL Concurrent use may result in an increased risk of cardiotoxicity (QT prolongation, torsade de pointes, cardiac arrest).	2	1	3
MOCLOBEMIDE Concurrent use may result in central nervous system toxicity or serotonin syndrome (hypertension, hyperthermia, myoclonus, mental status changes).	1	1	2
NIALAMIDE Concurrent use may result in central nervous system toxicity or serotonin syndrome (hypertension, hyperthermia, myoclonus, mental status changes).	1	1	2
NORTRIPTYLINE Concurrent use may result in elevated nortriptyline serum levels or possible serotonin syndrome (hypertension, hyperthermia, myoclonus, mental status changes).	2	2	3
PARGYLINE Concurrent use may result in central nervous system toxicity or serotonin syndrome (hypertension, hyperthermia, myoclonus, mental status changes).	1	1	2
PHENELZINE Concurrent use may result in central nervous system toxicity or serotonin syndrome (hypertension, hyperthermia, myoclonus, mental status changes).	1	1	2
PROCARBAZINE Concurrent use may result in central nervous system toxicity or serotonin syndrome (hypertension, hyperthermia, myoclonus, mental status changes).	1	1	2
SELEGILINE Concurrent use may result in central nervous system toxicity or serotonin syndrome (hypertension, hyperthermia, myoclonus, mental status changes).	1	1	2
SIBUTRAMINE Concurrent use may result in an increased risk of serotonin syndrome (hypertension, hypothermia, myoclonus, mental status changes).	1	2	3
TERFENADINE Concurrent use may result in cardiotoxicity (QT prolongation, torsade de pointes, cardiac arrest).	1	2	3
TOLOXATONE Concurrent use may result in central nervous system toxicity or serotonin syndrome (hypertension, hyperthermia, myoclonus, mental status changes).	1	1	2

Onset: 0=Unspecified 1=Rapid 2=Delayed
Severity: 1=Contraindicated 2=Major 3=Moderate 4=Minor
Evidence: 1=Excellent 2=Good 3=Fair 4=Poor

INTERACTION	ONSET	SEVERITY	EVIDENCE
TRAMADOL Concurrent use may result in an increased risk of seizures and serotonin syndrome (hypertension, hyperthermia, myoclonus, mental status changes).	1	2	2
TRANYLCYPROMINE Concurrent use may result in central nervous system toxicity or serotonin syndrome (hypertension, hyperthermia, myoclonus, mental status changes).	1	1	2

Tacrine

INTERACTION	ONSET	SEVERITY	EVIDENCE
CIMETIDINE Concurrent use may result in tacrine toxicity (nausea, vomiting, loss of appetite).	1	4	2
FLUVOXAMINE Concurrent use may result in an increase in the plasma concentration of tacrine.	1	3	3
THEOPHYLLINE Concurrent use may result in theophylline toxicity (nausea, vomiting, palpitations, seizures).	2	3	3

Temazepam

INTERACTION	ONSET	SEVERITY	EVIDENCE
ETHANOL Concurrent use may result in impaired psychomotor functions.	1	3	2
THEOPHYLLINE Concurrent use may result in decreased temazepam effectiveness.	1	3	2

Thioridazine

INTERACTION	ONSET	SEVERITY	EVIDENCE
ACETYLCHOLINE Concurrent use may result in an increased risk of cardiotoxicity (QT prolongation, torsade de pointes, cardiac arrest).	2	1	3
AJMALINE Concurrent use may result in an increased risk of cardiotoxicity (QT prolongation, torsade de pointes, cardiac arrest).	0	1	3
AMIODARONE Concurrent use may result in an increased risk of cardiotoxicity (QT prolongation, torsade de pointes, cardiac arrest).	0	1	3
APRINDINE Concurrent use may result in an increased risk of cardiotoxicity (QT prolongation, torsade de pointes, cardiac arrest).	0	1	3

INTERACTION	ONSET	SEVERITY	EVIDENCE
ARSENIC TRIOXIDE Concurrent use may result in an increased risk of cardiotoxicity (QT prolongation, torsade de pointes, cardiac arrest).	0	1	3
ASTEMIZOLE Concurrent use may result in an increased risk of cardiotoxicity (QT prolongation, torsade de pointes, cardiac arrest).	0	1	3
BELLADONNA Concurrent use may result in increased manic, agitated reactions, or enhanced anticholinergic effects resulting in cardiorespiratory failure, especially in cases of belladonna overdose.	1	3	2
BENZTROPINE Concurrent use may result in decreased thioridazine serum concentrations, decreased thioridazine effectiveness, enhanced anticholinergic effects (ileus, hyperpyrexia, sedation, dry mouth).	2	3	3
CABERGOLINE Concurrent use may result in the decreased therapeutic effect of both drugs.	1	3	3
CISAPRIDE Concurrent use may result in cardiotoxicity (QT prolongation, torsade de pointes, cardiac arrest).	1	1	3
CLINDAMYCIN Concurrent use may result in an increased risk of cardiotoxicity (QT prolongation, torsade de pointes, cardiac arrest).	2	1	3
DIETHYLPROPION Concurrent use may result in an increased risk of cardiotoxicity (QT prolongation, torsade de pointes, cardiac arrest).	2	1	3
DROPERIDOL Concurrent use may result in an increased risk of cardiotoxicity (QT prolongation, torsade de pointes, cardiac arrest).	0	1	3
ETHANOL Concurrent use may result in increased central nervous system depression and an increased risk of extrapyramidal reactions.	1	3	2
FLUOXETINE Concurrent use may result in an increased risk of cardiotoxicity (QT prolongation, torsade de pointes, cardiac arrest).	1	1	3

Onset: 0=Unspecified 1=Rapid 2=Delayed
Severity: 1=Contraindicated 2=Major 3=Moderate 4=Minor
Evidence: 1=Excellent 2=Good 3=Fair 4=Poor

INTERACTION	ONSET	SEVERITY	EVIDENCE
FLUVOXAMINE Concurrent use may result in an increased risk of thioridazine toxicity, cardiotoxicity (QT prolongation, torsade de pointes, cardiac arrest).	1	1	3
FOSPHENYTOIN Concurrent use may result in increased or decreased phenytoin levels and possibly reduced thioridazine levels.	2	4	3
GREPAFLOXACIN Concurrent use may result in an increased risk of cardiotoxicity (QT prolongation, torsade de pointes, cardiac arrest).	2	1	3
HALOFANTRINE Concurrent use may result in an increased risk of cardiotoxicity (QT prolongation, torsade de pointes, cardiac arrest).	0	1	3
IOPAMIDOL Concurrent use may result in an increased risk of cardiotoxicity (QT prolongation, torsade de pointes, cardiac arrest).	2	1	3
KETANSERIN Concurrent use may result in an increased risk of cardiotoxicity (QT prolongation, torsade de pointes, cardiac arrest).	2	1	3
LEVODOPA Concurrent use may result in loss of levodopa efficacy.	1	3	2
LEVOMETHADYL Concurrent use may result in an increased risk of cardiotoxicity (QT prolongation, torsade de pointes, cardiac arrest).	0	1	3
LITHIUM Concurrent use may result in weakness, dyskinesias, increased extrapyramidal symptoms, encephalopathy, and brain damage.	2	2	1
LUBELUZOLE Concurrent use may result in an increased risk of cardiotoxicity (QT prolongation, torsade de pointes, cardiac arrest).	2	1	3
MEPERIDINE Concurrent use may result in an increase in central nervous system and respiratory depression.	1	3	2
ORPHENADRINE Concurrent use may result in decreased thioridazine serum concentrations, decreased thioridazine effectiveness, enhanced anticholinergic effects (ileus, hyperpyrexia, sedation, dry mouth).	2	3	3

INTERACTION	ONSET	SEVERITY	EVIDENCE
PAROXETINE Concurrent use may result in an increased risk of thioridazine toxicity, cardiotoxicity (QT prolongation, torsade de pointes, cardiac arrest).	1	1	3
PENTAMIDINE Concurrent use may result in an increased risk of cardiotoxicity (QT prolongation, torsade de pointes, cardiac arrest).	0	1	3
PHENYTOIN Concurrent use may result in increased or decreased phenytoin levels and possibly reduced thioridazine levels.	2	4	3
PORFIMER Concurrent use may result in excessive intracellular damage in photosensitized tissues.	2	3	3
PROBUCOL Concurrent use may result in an increased risk of cardiotoxicity (QT prolongation, torsade de pointes, cardiac arrest).	2	1	3
PROCATEROL Concurrent use may result in an increased risk of cardiotoxicity (QT prolongation, torsade de pointes, cardiac arrest).	2	1	3
PROCYCLIDINE Concurrent use may result in decreased thioridazine serum concentrations, decreased thioridazine effectiveness, enhanced anticholinergic effects (ileus, hyperpyrexia, sedation, dry mouth).	2	3	3
PROPRANOLOL Concurrent use may result in an increased risk of thioridazine toxicity, cardiotoxicity (QT prolongation, torsade de pointes, cardiac arrest).	2	1	3
PROTIRELIN Concurrent use may result in decreased TSH response.	2	3	3
ROXITHROMYCIN Concurrent use may result in an increased risk of cardiotoxicity (QT prolongation, torsade de pointes, cardiac arrest).	2	1	3
SEMATILIDE Concurrent use may result in an increased risk of cardiotoxicity (QT prolongation, torsade de pointes, cardiac arrest).	0	1	3
SPARFLOXACIN Concurrent use may result in prolongation of the QTc interval and/or torsade de pointes.	2	1	3

Onset: 0=Unspecified 1=Rapid 2=Delayed
Severity: 1=Contraindicated 2=Major 3=Moderate 4=Minor
Evidence: 1=Excellent 2=Good 3=Fair 4=Poor

INTERACTION	ONSET	SEVERITY	EVIDENCE
SPIRAMYCIN Concurrent use may result in an increased risk of cardiotoxicity (QT prolongation, torsade de pointes, cardiac arrest).	0	1	3
TERFENADINE Concurrent use may result in an increased risk of cardiotoxicity (QT prolongation, torsade de pointes, cardiac arrest).	2	1	3
TRAMADOL Concurrent use may result in an increased risk of seizures.	1	2	3
TRIHEXYPHENIDYL Concurrent use may result in decreased thioridazine serum concentrations, decreased thioridazine effectiveness, enhanced anticholinergic effects (ileus, hyperpyrexia, sedation, dry mouth).	2	3	3
ZIPRASIDONE Concurrent use may result in an increased risk of cardiotoxicity (QT prolongation, torsade de pointes, cardiac arrest).	0	1	3

Thiothixene

INTERACTION	ONSET	SEVERITY	EVIDENCE
CABERGOLINE Concurrent use may result in the decreased therapeutic effect of both drugs.	1	3	3
LITHIUM Concurrent use may result in weakness, dyskinesias, increased extrapyramidal symptoms, encephalopathy, and brain damage.	2	2	1
TRAMADOL Concurrent use may result in an increased risk of seizures.	1	2	3

Tranylcypromine

INTERACTION	ONSET	SEVERITY	EVIDENCE
ACARBOSE Concurrent use may result in excessive hypoglycemia, central nervous system depression, and seizures.	1	3	2
ACETOHEXAMIDE Concurrent use may result in excessive hypoglycemia, central nervous system depression, and seizures.	1	3	2
ALBUTEROL Concurrent use may result in an increased risk of tachycardia, agitation, or hypomania.	2	2	2
ALTRETAMINE Concurrent use may result in an increased risk of severe orthostatic hypotension.	2	2	3

INTERACTION	ONSET	SEVERITY	EVIDENCE
AMITRIPTYLINE Concurrent use may result in neurotoxicity, seizures, or serotonin syndrome (hypertension, hyperthermia, myoclonus, mental status changes).	2	1	3
AMOXAPINE Concurrent use may result in neurotoxicity, seizures, or serotonin syndrome (hypertension, hyperthermia, myoclonus, mental status changes).	2	2	3
AMPHETAMINE Concurrent use may result in hypertensive crisis (headache, hyperpyrexia, hypertension).	1	1	2
APRACLONIDINE Concurrent use may result in potentiation of tranylcypromine effects.	1	1	3
ATOMOXETINE Concurrent use may result in an increased risk of serotonin syndrome (hypertension, hyperthermia, myoclonus, mental status changes).	0	1	3
BAMBUTEROL Concurrent use may result in an increased risk of tachycardia, agitation, or hypomania.	2	2	2
BENFLUOREX Concurrent use may result in excessive hypoglycemia, central nervous system depression, and seizures.	1	3	2
BENZPHETAMINE Concurrent use may result in hypertensive crisis (headache, hyperpyrexia, hypertension).	1	1	2
BITOLTEROL Concurrent use may result in an increased risk of tachycardia, agitation, or hypomania.	2	2	2
BROXATEROL Concurrent use may result in an increased risk of tachycardia, agitation, or hypomania.	2	2	2
BUPROPION Concurrent use may result in bupropion toxicity (seizures, agitation, psychotic changes).	1	1	3
BUSPIRONE Concurrent use may result in hypertensive crisis.	1	1	3
CARBAMAZEPINE Concurrent use may result in hypertensive urgency, hyperpyrexia, and seizures.	1	1	3
CHLORPROPAMIDE Concurrent use may result in excessive hypoglycemia, central nervous system depression, and seizures.	1	3	2

Onset: 0=Unspecified 1=Rapid 2=Delayed
Severity: 1=Contraindicated 2=Major 3=Moderate 4=Minor
Evidence: 1=Excellent 2=Good 3=Fair 4=Poor

INTERACTION	ONSET	SEVERITY	EVIDENCE
CITALOPRAM Concurrent use may result in central nervous system toxicity or serotonin syndrome (hypertension, hyperthermia, myoclonus, mental status changes).	1	1	3
CLENBUTEROL Concurrent use may result in an increased risk of tachycardia, agitation, or hypomania.	2	2	2
CLOMIPRAMINE Concurrent use may result in neurotoxicity, seizures, or serotonin syndrome (hypertension, hyperthermia, myoclonus, mental status changes).	2	2	3
CLOVOXAMINE Concurrent use may result in central nervous system toxicity or serotonin syndrome (hypertension, hyperthermia, myoclonus, mental status changes).	1	1	3
CYCLOBENZAPRINE Concurrent use may result in hypertensive crises (headache, hyperpyrexia, hypertension) or severe convulsive seizures.	1	1	3
CYPROHEPTADINE Concurrent use may result in prolonged and intensified anticholinergic effects.	2	1	3
DESIPRAMINE Concurrent use may result in neurotoxicity, seizures, or serotonin syndrome (hypertension, hyperthermia, myoclonus, mental status changes).	2	2	3
DEXFENFLURAMINE Concurrent use may result in central nervous system toxicity or serotonin syndrome (hypertension, hyperthermia, myoclonus, mental status changes).	1	1	3
DEXMETHYLPHENIDATE Concurrent use may result in hypertensive crisis (headache, palpitation, neck stiffness).	1	1	3
DEXTROAMPHETAMINE Concurrent use may result in hypertensive crisis (headache, hyperpyrexia, hypertension).	1	1	3
DEXTROMETHORPHAN Concurrent use may result in an increased risk of serotonin syndrome (hypertension, hyperthermia, myoclonus, mental status changes).	1	1	3
DIETHYLPROPION Concurrent use may result in hypertensive crisis (headache, hyperpyrexia, hypertension).	1	1	2
DOPAMINE Concurrent use may result in hypertensive crisis (headache, hyperpyrexia, hypertension).	1	1	1

INTERACTION	ONSET	SEVERITY	EVIDENCE
DOTHIEPIN Concurrent use may result in neurotoxicity, seizures, or serotonin syndrome (hypertension, hyperthermia, myoclonus, mental status changes).	2	2	3
DOXEPIN Concurrent use may result in neurotoxicity, seizures, or serotonin syndrome (hypertension, hyperthermia, myoclonus, mental status changes).	2	2	3
DROPERIDOL Concurrent use may result in an increased risk of cardiotoxicity (QT prolongation, torsade de pointes, cardiac arrest).	1	2	3
ENTACAPONE Concurrent use may result in decreased catecholamine metabolism.	1	2	3
EPHEDRINE Concurrent use may result in hypertensive crisis (headache, hyperpyrexia, hypertension).	1	2	3
EPINEPHRINE Concurrent use may result in increased hypertensive effects.	1	3	3
ESCITALOPRAM Concurrent use may result in central nervous system toxicity or serotonin syndrome (hypertension, hyperthermia, myoclonus, mental status changes).	1	1	3
FEMOXETINE Concurrent use may result in central nervous system toxicity or serotonin syndrome (hypertension, hyperthermia, myoclonus, mental status changes).	1	1	3
FENFLURAMINE Concurrent use may result in serotonin syndrome (hypertension, hyperthermia, myoclonus, mental status changes).	1	1	3
FENOTEROL Concurrent use may result in an increased risk of tachycardia, agitation, or hypomania.	2	2	2
FLUOXETINE Concurrent use may result in central nervous system toxicity or serotonin syndrome (hypertension, hyperthermia, myoclonus, mental status changes).	1	1	2
FLUVOXAMINE Concurrent use may result in central nervous system toxicity or serotonin syndrome (hypertension, hyperthermia, myoclonus, mental status changes).	1	2	2

Onset: 0=Unspecified 1=Rapid 2=Delayed
Severity: 1=Contraindicated 2=Major 3=Moderate 4=Minor
Evidence: 1=Excellent 2=Good 3=Fair 4=Poor

INTERACTION	ONSET	SEVERITY	EVIDENCE
FORMOTEROL Concurrent use may result in an increased risk of tachycardia, agitation, or hypomania.	2	2	2
FURAZOLIDONE Concurrent use may result in an increased risk of a hypertensive crisis or convulsive seizures.	1	1	3
GLICLAZIDE Concurrent use may result in excessive hypoglycemia, central nervous system depression, and seizures.	1	3	2
GLIMEPIRIDE Concurrent use may result in excessive hypoglycemia, central nervous system depression, and seizures.	1	3	2
GLIPIZIDE Concurrent use may result in excessive hypoglycemia, central nervous system depression, and seizures.	1	3	2
GLIQUIDONE Concurrent use may result in excessive hypoglycemia, central nervous system depression, and seizures.	1	3	2
GLYBURIDE Concurrent use may result in excessive hypoglycemia, central nervous system depression, and seizures.	1	3	2
GUANADREL Concurrent use may result in decreased antihypertensive response to guanadrel or hypertensive crisis when guanadrel is initiated in a patient already receiving tranylcypromine therapy.	1	1	3
GUANETHIDINE Concurrent use may result in decreased antihypertensive response to guanethidine or hypertensive crisis when guanethidine is initiated in a patient already receiving tranylcypromine therapy.	1	1	3
GUAR GUM Concurrent use may result in excessive hypoglycemia, central nervous system depression, and seizures.	1	3	2
HEXOPRENALINE Concurrent use may result in an increased risk of tachycardia, agitation, or hypomania.	2	2	2
IMIPRAMINE Concurrent use may result in neurotoxicity, seizures, or serotonin syndrome (hypertension, hyperthermia, myoclonus, mental status changes).	2	2	3
INSULIN Concurrent use may result in excessive hypoglycemia, central nervous system depression, and seizures.	1	3	2

INTERACTION	ONSET	SEVERITY	EVIDENCE
INSULIN LISPRO, HUMAN Concurrent use may result in excessive hypoglycemia, central nervous system depression, and seizures.	1	3	2
ISOCARBOXAZID Concurrent use may result in an increased risk of a hypertensive crisis or convulsive seizures.	1	1	3
ISOETHARINE Concurrent use may result in an increased risk of tachycardia, agitation, or hypomania.	2	2	2
ISOMETHEPTENE Concurrent use may result in severe headache, hypertensive crisis, cardiac arrhythmias.	1	1	1
ISOPROTERENOL Concurrent use may result in increased hypertensive effects.	1	3	3
LEVALBUTEROL Concurrent use may result in an increased risk of tachycardia, agitation, or hypomania.	2	2	2
LEVODOPA Concurrent use may result in hypertensive crisis.	1	1	3
LEVOMETHADYL Concurrent use may result in increased levels of levomethadyl or its active metabolites.	2	1	3
LOFEPRAMINE Concurrent use may result in neurotoxicity, seizures, or serotonin syndrome (hypertension, hyperthermia, myoclonus, mental status changes).	2	2	3
MA HUANG Concurrent use may result in increased risk for excessive tranylcypromine activity including headache, hyperpyrexia, arrhythmias, and hypertensive crisis.	1	2	3
MAPROTILINE Concurrent use may result in neurotoxicity, seizures.	2	1	3
MAZINDOL Concurrent use may result in hypertensive crisis.	1	1	3
MEPERIDINE Concurrent use may result in cardiovascular instability, hyperpyrexia, coma.	1	1	2
METARAMINOL Concurrent use may result in hypertensive crisis (headache, hyperpyrexia, hypertension).	1	2	3
METFORMIN Concurrent use may result in excessive hypoglycemia, central nervous system depression, and seizures.	1	3	2

Onset: 0=Unspecified 1=Rapid 2=Delayed
Severity: 1=Contraindicated 2=Major 3=Moderate 4=Minor
Evidence: 1=Excellent 2=Good 3=Fair 4=Poor

INTERACTION	ONSET	SEVERITY	EVIDENCE
METHAMPHETAMINE Concurrent use may result in hypertensive crisis.	1	1	3
METHOTRIMEPRAZINE Concurrent use may result in possibly prolonged effect of the methotrimeprazine, with potentially increased side effects.	2	1	3
METHOXAMINE Concurrent use may result in hypertensive crisis (headache, hyperpyrexia, hypertension).	1	2	3
METHYLDOPA Concurrent use may result in hypertensive crisis (headache, palpitation, neck stiffness).	1	1	3
METHYLPHENIDATE Concurrent use may result in hypertensive crisis (headache, palpitation, neck stiffness).	1	1	3
MIGLITOL Concurrent use may result in excessive hypoglycemia, central nervous system depression, and seizures.	1	3	2
MIRTAZAPINE Concurrent use may result in neurotoxicity, seizures.	2	1	3
MORPHINE Concurrent use may result in hypotension and exaggeration of central nervous system and respiratory depressant effects.	1	1	3
NEFAZODONE Concurrent use may result in hyperthermia, rigidity, myoclonus, seizures, fluctuations of vital signs, or mental status changes.	1	2	2
NOREPINEPHRINE Concurrent use may result in increased hypertensive effects.	1	3	3
NORTRIPTYLINE Concurrent use may result in neurotoxicity, seizures, or serotonin syndrome (hypertension, hyperthermia, myoclonus, mental status changes).	2	2	3
OPIPRAMOL Concurrent use may result in neurotoxicity, seizures, or serotonin syndrome (hypertension, hyperthermia, myoclonus, mental status changes).	2	1	3
OXYCODONE Concurrent use may result in anxiety, confusion and significant respiratory depressant effects or coma.	2	2	3
PARGYLINE Concurrent use may result in an increased risk of a hypertensive crisis or convulsive seizures.	1	1	3
PAROXETINE Concurrent use may result in central nervous system toxicity or serotonin syndrome (hypertension, hyperthermia, myoclonus, mental status changes).	1	1	2

INTERACTION	ONSET	SEVERITY	EVIDENCE
PHENDIMETRAZINE Concurrent use may result in hypertensive crisis (headache, hyperpyrexia, hypertension).	1	1	2
PHENELZINE Concurrent use may result in hypertensive crisis (headache, palpitation, neck stiffness).	1	1	3
PHENMETRAZINE Concurrent use may result in hypertensive crisis (headache, hyperpyrexia, hypertension).	1	1	2
PHENTERMINE Concurrent use may result in hypertensive crisis (headache, hyperpyrexia, hypertension).	1	1	1
PHENYLEPHRINE Concurrent use may result in hypertensive crisis (headache, hyperpyrexia, hypertension).	1	1	3
PHENYLPROPANOLAMINE Concurrent use may result in hypertensive crisis (headache, hyperpyrexia, hypertension).	1	1	3
PIRBUTEROL Concurrent use may result in an increased risk of tachycardia, agitation, or hypomania.	2	2	2
PROCARBAZINE Concurrent use may result in an increased risk of hypertensive crisis or convulsive seizures.	1	1	3
PROCATEROL Concurrent use may result in an increased risk of tachycardia, agitation, or hypomania.	2	2	2
PROTRIPTYLINE Concurrent use may result in neurotoxicity, seizures, or serotonin syndrome (hypertension, hyperthermia, myoclonus, mental status changes).	2	2	3
PSEUDOEPHEDRINE Concurrent use may result in severe hypertension, hyperpyrexia, headache.	1	1	3
REBOXETINE Concurrent use may result in hyperthermia, rigidity, myoclonus, seizures, fluctuations of vital signs, or mental status changes.	1	2	3
RESERPINE Concurrent use may result in elevated catecholamine levels.	1	1	3
RIMITEROL Concurrent use may result in an increased risk of tachycardia, agitation, or hypomania.	2	2	2

Onset: 0=Unspecified 1=Rapid 2=Delayed
Severity: 1=Contraindicated 2=Major 3=Moderate 4=Minor
Evidence: 1=Excellent 2=Good 3=Fair 4=Poor

INTERACTION	ONSET	SEVERITY	EVIDENCE
RITODRINE Concurrent use may result in an increased risk of tachycardia, agitation, or hypomania.	2	2	2
RIZATRIPTAN Concurrent use may result in serotonin syndrome (hypertension, hyperthermia, myoclonus, mental status changes).	2	1	3
SALMETEROL Concurrent use may result in an increased risk of tachycardia, agitation, or hypomania.	2	2	2
SERTRALINE Concurrent use may result in central nervous system toxicity or serotonin syndrome (hypertension, hyperthermia, myoclonus, mental status changes).	1	1	2
SIBUTRAMINE Concurrent use may result in central nervous system toxicity or serotonin syndrome (hypertension, hyperthermia, myoclonus, mental status changes).	1	1	3
SUMATRIPTAN Concurrent use may result in an increased risk of serotonin syndrome (hypertension, hyperthermia, myoclonus, mental status changes).	1	1	3
SUMATRIPTAN Concurrent use may result in serotonin syndrome (hypertension, hyperthermia, myoclonus, mental status changes).	1	1	2
TERBUTALINE Concurrent use may result in an increased risk of tachycardia, agitation, or hypomania.	2	2	2
TOLAZAMIDE Concurrent use may result in excessive hypoglycemia, central nervous system depression, and seizures.	1	3	2
TOLBUTAMIDE Concurrent use may result in excessive hypoglycemia, central nervous system depression, and seizures.	1	3	2
TOLCAPONE Concurrent use may result in decreased catecholamine metabolism.	1	2	3
TRAMADOL Concurrent use may result in nausea, vomiting, cardiovascular collapse, respiratory depression, seizures.	1	2	3
TRIMIPRAMINE Concurrent use may result in neurotoxicity, seizures, or serotonin syndrome (hypertension, hyperthermia, myoclonus, mental status changes).	2	2	3
TROGLITAZONE Concurrent use may result in excessive hypoglycemia, central nervous system depression, and seizures.	1	3	2

INTERACTION	ONSET	SEVERITY	EVIDENCE
TRYPTOPHAN Concurrent use may result in an increased risk of hypertension, memory impairment, and disorientation.	1	1	3
TULOBUTEROL Concurrent use may result in an increased risk of tachycardia, agitation, or hypomania.	2	2	2
TYRAMINE FOODS Concurrent use may result in increased blood pressure.	1	1	1
VENLAFAXINE Concurrent use may result in central nervous system toxicity or serotonin syndrome (hypertension, hyperthermia, myoclonus, mental status changes).	1	1	2
ZOLMITRIPTAN Concurrent use may result in serotonin syndrome (hypertension, hyperthermia, myoclonus, mental status changes).	2	1	3

Trazodone

INTERACTION	ONSET	SEVERITY	EVIDENCE
DROPERIDOL Concurrent use may result in an increased risk of cardiotoxicity (QT prolongation, torsade de pointes, cardiac arrest).	1	2	3
FLUOXETINE Concurrent use may result in trazodone toxicity (sedation, dry mouth, urinary retention) or serotonin syndrome (hypertension, hyperthermia, myoclonus, mental status changes).	2	2	3
FOOD Concurrent use may result in increased time to peak levels.	1	4	2

Triazolam

INTERACTION	ONSET	SEVERITY	EVIDENCE
AMPRENAVIR Concurrent use may result in an increased risk of triazolam toxicity (excessive sedation, confusion).	1	1	3
AZITHROMYCIN Concurrent use may result in decreased clearance of triazolam and increased pharmacologic effect of triazolam.	0	4	3
CIMETIDINE Concurrent use may result in triazolam toxicity (excessive sedation, confusion).	1	4	3
CLARITHROMYCIN Concurrent use may result in increased triazolam toxicity (central nervous system depression, ataxia, lethargy).	2	3	3

Onset: 0=Unspecified 1=Rapid 2=Delayed
Severity: 1=Contraindicated 2=Major 3=Moderate 4=Minor
Evidence: 1=Excellent 2=Good 3=Fair 4=Poor

INTERACTION	ONSET	SEVERITY	EVIDENCE
DEHYDROEPIANDROSTERONE Concurrent use may result in increased central nervous system depression.	1	3	2
EFAVIRENZ Concurrent use may result in an increased risk of triazolam toxicity (excessive sedation, confusion).	2	1	3
ETHANOL Concurrent use may result in increased sedation.	1	3	1
FLUCONAZOLE Concurrent use may result in increased triazolam serum concentrations and potential triazolam toxicity (sedation, slurred speech, central nervous system depression).	2	1	3
FLUVOXAMINE Concurrent use may result in elevated serum triazolam concentrations.	2	3	3
GRAPEFRUIT JUICE Concurrent use may result in increased bioavailability of triazolam.	1	4	3
INDINAVIR Concurrent use may result in an increased risk of serious triazolam adverse effects (excessive or prolonged sedation).	1	1	3
ITRACONAZOLE Concurrent use may result in increased triazolam serum concentrations and potential triazolam toxicity (sedation, slurred speech, central nervous system depression).	2	1	3
JOSAMYCIN Concurrent use may result in increased triazolam toxicity (central nervous system depression, ataxia, lethargy).	2	3	3
KETOCONAZOLE Concurrent use may result in increased triazolam serum concentrations and potential triazolam toxicity (sedation, slurred speech, central nervous system depression).	2	1	3
MIBEFRADIL Concurrent use may result in an increased risk of triazolam toxicity (excessive sedation, confusion).	1	2	3
NEFAZODONE Concurrent use may result in psychomotor impairment and excessive sedation.	1	3	2
OMEPRAZOLE Concurrent use may result in triazolam toxicity (central nervous system depression, ataxia, lethargy).	2	3	3
RIFAMPIN Concurrent use may result in loss of triazolam efficacy.	1	3	3
RITONAVIR Concurrent use may result in an increased risk of extreme sedation and respiratory depression.	2	1	3

INTERACTION	ONSET	SEVERITY	EVIDENCE
ROXITHROMYCIN Concurrent use may result in increased triazolam toxicity (central nervous system depression, ataxia, lethargy).	2	3	3
SAQUINAVIR Concurrent use may result in an increased risk of triazolam toxicity (excessive sedation, respiratory depression).	1	1	3
THEOPHYLLINE Concurrent use may result in decreased triazolam effectiveness.	1	3	2
TROLEANDOMYCIN Concurrent use may result in increased triazolam toxicity (central nervous system depression, ataxia, lethargy).	2	3	3

Trifluoperazine

INTERACTION	ONSET	SEVERITY	EVIDENCE
BELLADONNA Concurrent use may result in increased manic, agitated reactions, or enhanced anticholinergic effects resulting in cardiorespiratory failure, especially in cases of belladonna overdose.	1	3	2
BENZTROPINE Concurrent use may result in decreased trifluoperazine serum concentrations, decreased trifluoperazine effectiveness, enhanced anticholinergic effects (ileus, hyperpyrexia, sedation, dry mouth).	2	3	3
CABERGOLINE Concurrent use may result in the decreased therapeutic effect of both drugs.	1	3	3
CISAPRIDE Concurrent use may result in cardiotoxicity (QT prolongation, torsade de pointes, cardiac arrest).	1	1	3
DROPERIDOL Concurrent use may result in an increased risk of cardiotoxicity (QT prolongation, torsade de pointes, cardiac arrest).	0	2	3
ETHANOL Concurrent use may result in increased central nervous system depression and an increased risk of extrapyramidal reactions.	1	3	2
FOSPHENYTOIN Concurrent use may result in increased or decreased phenytoin levels and possibly reduced trifluoperazine levels.	2	4	3
GREPAFLOXACIN Concurrent use may result in an increased risk of cardiotoxicity (QT prolongation, torsade de pointes, cardiac arrest).	2	1	3

Onset: 0=Unspecified 1=Rapid 2=Delayed
Severity: 1=Contraindicated 2=Major 3=Moderate 4=Minor
Evidence: 1=Excellent 2=Good 3=Fair 4=Poor

INTERACTION	ONSET	SEVERITY	EVIDENCE
HALOFANTRINE Concurrent use may result in an increased risk of cardiotoxicity (QT prolongation, torsade de pointes, cardiac arrest).	0	2	3
LEVODOPA Concurrent use may result in loss of levodopa efficacy.	1	3	2
LEVOMETHADYL Concurrent use may result in an increased risk of cardiotoxicity (QT prolongation, torsade de pointes, cardiac arrest).	2	2	3
LITHIUM Concurrent use may result in weakness, dyskinesias, increased extrapyramidal symptoms, encephalopathy, and brain damage.	2	2	1
MEPERIDINE Concurrent use may result in an increase in central nervous system and respiratory depression.	1	3	2
ORPHENADRINE Concurrent use may result in decreased trifluoperazine serum concentrations, decreased trifluoperazine effectiveness, enhanced anticholinergic effects (ileus, hyperpyrexia, sedation, dry mouth).	2	3	3
PHENYTOIN Concurrent use may result in increased or decreased phenytoin levels and possibly reduced trifluoperazine levels.	2	4	3
PORFIMER Concurrent use may result in excessive intracellular damage in photosensitized tissues.	2	3	3
PROCYCLIDINE Concurrent use may result in decreased trifluoperazine serum concentrations, decreased trifluoperazine effectiveness, enhanced anticholinergic effects (ileus, hyperpyrexia, sedation, dry mouth).	2	3	3
TRAMADOL Concurrent use may result in an increased risk of seizures.	1	2	3
TRIHEXYPHENIDYL Concurrent use may result in decreased trifluoperazine serum concentrations, decreased trifluoperazine effectiveness, enhanced anticholinergic effects (ileus, hyperpyrexia, sedation, dry mouth).	2	3	3

Trimipramine

INTERACTION	ONSET	SEVERITY	EVIDENCE
ACENOCOUMAROL Concurrent use may result in increased risk of bleeding.	2	3	3

INTERACTION	ONSET	SEVERITY	EVIDENCE
AMPRENAVIR Concurrent use may result in increased trimipramine serum concentrations and potential toxicity (anticholinergic effects, sedation, confusion, cardiac arrhythmias).	2	2	3
ANISINDIONE Concurrent use may result in an increased risk of bleeding.	2	3	3
BEPRIDIL Concurrent use may result in an increased risk of cardiotoxicity (QT prolongation, torsade de pointes, cardiac arrest).	1	1	3
BETHANIDINE Concurrent use may result in decreased antihypertensive effectiveness.	1	3	3
CISAPRIDE Concurrent use may result in cardiotoxicity (QT prolongation, torsade de pointes, cardiac arrest).	1	1	3
CLONIDINE Concurrent use may result in decreased antihypertensive effectiveness.	2	2	3
CLORGYLINE Concurrent use may result in neurotoxicity, seizures, or serotonin syndrome (hypertension, hyperthermia, myoclonus, mental status changes).	2	2	3
DICUMAROL Concurrent use may result in an increased risk of bleeding.	2	3	3
DROPERIDOL Concurrent use may result in an increased risk of cardiotoxicity (QT prolongation, torsade de pointes, cardiac arrest).	0	2	3
EPINEPHRINE Concurrent use may result in hypertension, cardiac arrhythmias, and tachycardia.	1	2	2
ETILEFRINE Concurrent use may result in hypertension, cardiac arrhythmias, and tachycardia.	1	2	2
FLUOXETINE Concurrent use may result in trimipramine antidepressant toxicity (dry mouth, urinary retention, sedation) and an increased risk of cardiotoxicity (QT prolongation, torsade de pointes, cardiac arrest).	0	2	3
GREPAFLOXACIN Concurrent use may result in an increased risk of cardiotoxicity (QT prolongation, torsade de pointes, cardiac arrest).	2	1	3

Onset: 0=Unspecified 1=Rapid 2=Delayed
Severity: 1=Contraindicated 2=Major 3=Moderate 4=Minor
Evidence: 1=Excellent 2=Good 3=Fair 4=Poor

INTERACTION	ONSET	SEVERITY	EVIDENCE
GUANADREL			
Concurrent use may result in decreased antihypertensive effectiveness.	2	3	3
HALOFANTRINE			
Concurrent use may result in an increased risk of cardiotoxicity (QT prolongation, torsade de pointes, cardiac arrest).	2	2	3
ISOCARBOXAZID			
Concurrent use may result in neurotoxicity, seizures, or serotonin syndrome (hypertension, hyperthermia, myoclonus, mental status changes).	2	1	3
LEVOMETHADYL			
Concurrent use may result in an increased risk of cardiotoxicity (QT prolongation, torsade de pointes, cardiac arrest).	2	1	3
METHOXAMINE			
Concurrent use may result in hypertension, cardiac arrhythmias, and tachycardia.	1	2	2
MIDODRINE			
Concurrent use may result in hypertension, cardiac arrhythmias, and tachycardia.	1	2	2
MOCLOBEMIDE			
Concurrent use may result in neurotoxicity, seizures, or serotonin syndrome (hypertension, hyperthermia, myoclonus, mental status changes).	2	2	3
NOREPINEPHRINE			
Concurrent use may result in hypertension, cardiac arrhythmias, and tachycardia.	1	2	2
OXILOFRINE			
Concurrent use may result in hypertension, cardiac arrhythmias, and tachycardia.	1	2	2
PHENELZINE			
Concurrent use may result in neurotoxicity, seizures, or serotonin syndrome (hypertension, hyperthermia, myoclonus, mental status changes).	2	2	3
PHENINDIONE			
Concurrent use may result in an increased risk of bleeding.	2	3	3
PHENPROCOUMON			
Concurrent use may result in an increased risk of bleeding.	2	3	3
PHENYLEPHRINE			
Concurrent use may result in hypertension, cardiac arrhythmias, and tachycardia.	1	2	2
PIMOZIDE			
Concurrent use may result in an increased risk of cardiotoxicity (QT prolongation, torsade de pointes, cardiac arrest).	0	1	3

INTERACTION	ONSET	SEVERITY	EVIDENCE
PROCARBAZINE Concurrent use may result in neurotoxicity, seizures.	2	2	3
SELEGILINE Concurrent use may result in neurotoxicity, seizures, or serotonin syndrome (hypertension, hyperthermia, myoclonus, mental status changes).	2	2	3
TRANYLCYPROMINE Concurrent use may result in neurotoxicity, seizures, or serotonin syndrome (hypertension, hyperthermia, myoclonus, mental status changes).	2	2	3
WARFARIN Concurrent use may result in an increased risk of bleeding.	2	3	3

Valproic acid

INTERACTION	ONSET	SEVERITY	EVIDENCE
CHOLESTYRAMINE Concurrent use may result in decreased serum valproic acid concentrations.	1	3	3
FELBAMATE Concurrent use may result in increased valproic acid concentrations.	2	3	3
FOSPHENYTOIN Concurrent use may result in altered valproate levels or altered phenytoin levels.	2	3	3
LAMOTRIGINE Concurrent use increased elimination half-life of lamotrigine leading to lamotrigine toxicity (fatigue, drowsiness, ataxia) and an increased risk of life-threatening rashes.	2	2	3
PHENOBARBITAL Concurrent use may result in phenobarbital toxicity or decreased valproic acid effectiveness.	2	3	1
PHENYTOIN Concurrent use may result in altered valproate levels or altered phenytoin levels.	2	3	3
PRIMIDONE Concurrent use may result in severe central nervous system depression.	1	2	3
TOPIRAMATE Concurrent use may result in decreased topiramate or valproic acid concentrations.	2	3	3
ZIDOVUDINE Concurrent use may result in increased zidovudine plasma concentrations and potential zidovudine toxicity (asthenia, fatigue, nausea, hematologic abnormalities).	2	3	3

Onset: 0=Unspecified 1=Rapid 2=Delayed
Severity: 1=Contraindicated 2=Major 3=Moderate 4=Minor
Evidence: 1=Excellent 2=Good 3=Fair 4=Poor

Venlafaxine

INTERACTION	ONSET	SEVERITY	EVIDENCE
ALMOTRIPTAN Concurrent use may result in weakness, hyperreflexia, and/or incoordination.	0	3	3
CIMETIDINE Concurrent use may result in an increased risk of venlafaxine toxicity (nausea, drowsiness, dizziness, ejaculatory disturbances).	2	4	3
CLORGYLINE Concurrent use may result in central nervous system toxicity or serotonin syndrome (hypertension, hyperthermia, myoclonus, mental status changes).	1	1	2
DEXFENFLURAMINE Concurrent use may result in serotonin syndrome (hypertension, hyperthermia, myoclonus, mental status changes).	1	2	3
ETHANOL Concurrent use may result in an increased risk of central nervous system effects.	1	4	3
FENFLURAMINE Concurrent use may result in serotonin syndrome (hypertension, hyperthermia, myoclonus, mental status changes).	1	2	3
FURAZOLIDONE Concurrent use may result in weakness, hyperreflexia, and incoordination.	2	1	3
IPRONIAZID Concurrent use may result in central nervous system toxicity or serotonin syndrome (hypertension, hyperthermia, myoclonus, mental status changes).	1	1	2
ISOCARBOXAZID Concurrent use may result in central nervous system toxicity or serotonin syndrome (hypertension, hyperthermia, myoclonus, mental status changes).	1	1	2
MOCLOBEMIDE Concurrent use may result in central nervous system toxicity or serotonin syndrome (hypertension, hyperthermia, myoclonus, mental status changes).	1	1	2
NIALAMIDE Concurrent use may result in central nervous system toxicity or serotonin syndrome (hypertension, hyperthermia, myoclonus, mental status changes).	1	1	2
PARGYLINE Concurrent use may result in central nervous system toxicity or serotonin syndrome (hypertension, hyperthermia, myoclonus, mental status changes).	1	1	2

INTERACTION	ONSET	SEVERITY	EVIDENCE
PHENELZINE Concurrent use may result in central nervous system toxicity or serotonin syndrome (hypertension, hyperthermia, myoclonus, mental status changes).	1	1	2
PROCARBAZINE Concurrent use may result in central nervous system toxicity or serotonin syndrome (hypertension, hyperthermia, myoclonus, mental status changes).	1	1	2
SELEGILINE Concurrent use may result in central nervous system toxicity or serotonin syndrome (hypertension, hyperthermia, myoclonus, mental status changes).	1	1	2
SIBUTRAMINE Concurrent use may result in an increased risk of serotonin syndrome (hypertension, hypothermia, myoclonus, mental status changes).	1	2	3
TOLOXATONE Concurrent use may result in central nervous system toxicity or serotonin syndrome (hypertension, hyperthermia, myoclonus, mental status changes).	1	1	2
TRAMADOL Concurrent use may result in an increased risk of seizures and serotonin syndrome (hypertension, hyperthermia, myoclonus, mental status changes).	1	2	2
TRANYLCYPROMINE Concurrent use may result in central nervous system toxicity or serotonin syndrome (hypertension, hyperthermia, myoclonus, mental status changes).	1	1	2

Zaleplon

INTERACTION	ONSET	SEVERITY	EVIDENCE
ETHANOL Concurrent use may result in impaired psychomotor functions.	1	3	3

Ziprasidone

INTERACTION	ONSET	SEVERITY	EVIDENCE
ACECAINIDE Concurrent use may result in an increased risk of cardiotoxicity (QT prolongation, torsade de pointes, cardiac arrest).	0	1	3
AJMALINE Concurrent use may result in an increased risk of cardiotoxicity (QT prolongation, torsade de pointes, cardiac arrest).	0	1	3

Onset: 0=Unspecified 1=Rapid 2=Delayed
Severity: 1=Contraindicated 2=Major 3=Moderate 4=Minor
Evidence: 1=Excellent 2=Good 3=Fair 4=Poor

INTERACTION	ONSET	SEVERITY	EVIDENCE
AMIODARONE			
Concurrent use may result in an increased risk of cardiotoxicity (QT prolongation, torsade de pointes, cardiac arrest).	0	1	3
ARSENIC TRIOXIDE			
Concurrent use may result in an increased risk of cardiotoxicity (QT prolongation, torsade de pointes, cardiac arrest).	0	1	3
AZIMILIDE			
Concurrent use may result in an increased risk of cardiotoxicity (QT prolongation, torsade de pointes, cardiac arrest).	0	1	3
BRETYLIUM			
Concurrent use may result in an increased risk of cardiotoxicity (QT prolongation, torsade de pointes, cardiac arrest).	0	1	3
CHLORPROMAZINE			
Concurrent use may result in an increased risk of cardiotoxicity (QT prolongation, torsade de pointes, cardiac arrest).	0	1	3
DISOPYRAMIDE			
Concurrent use may result in an increased risk of cardiotoxicity (QT prolongation, torsade de pointes, cardiac arrest).	0	1	3
DOFETILIDE			
Concurrent use may result in an increased risk of cardiotoxicity (QT prolongation, torsade de pointes, cardiac arrest).	0	1	3
DOLASETRON			
Concurrent use may result in an increased risk of cardiotoxicity (QT prolongation, torsade de pointes, cardiac arrest).	2	1	3
DROPERIDOL			
Concurrent use may result in an increased risk of cardiotoxicity (QT prolongation, torsade de pointes, cardiac arrest).	0	1	3
GATIFLOXACIN			
Concurrent use may result in an increased risk of cardiotoxicity (QT prolongation, torsade de pointes, cardiac arrest).	2	1	3
HALOFANTRINE			
Concurrent use may result in an increased risk of cardiotoxicity (QT prolongation, torsade de pointes, cardiac arrest).	0	1	3
IBUTILIDE			
Concurrent use may result in an increased risk of cardiotoxicity (QT prolongation, torsade de pointes, cardiac arrest).	0	1	3

INTERACTION	ONSET	SEVERITY	EVIDENCE
LEVOMETHADYL Concurrent use may result in an increased risk of cardiotoxicity (QT prolongation, torsade de pointes, cardiac arrest).	2	1	3
MEFLOQUINE Concurrent use may result in an increased risk of cardiotoxicity (QT prolongation, torsade de pointes, cardiac arrest).	2	1	3
MESORIDAZINE Concurrent use may result in an increased risk of cardiotoxicity (QT prolongation, torsade de pointes, cardiac arrest).	0	1	3
MOXIFLOXACIN Concurrent use may result in an increased risk of cardiotoxicity (QT prolongation, torsade de pointes, cardiac arrest).	2	1	3
PENTAMIDINE Concurrent use may result in an increased risk of cardiotoxicity (QT prolongation, torsade de pointes, cardiac arrest).	0	1	3
PIMOZIDE Concurrent use may result in an increased risk of cardiotoxicity (QT prolongation, torsade de pointes, cardiac arrest).	2	1	3
PIRMENOL Concurrent use may result in an increased risk of cardiotoxicity (QT prolongation, torsade de pointes, cardiac arrest).	0	1	3
PRAJMALINE Concurrent use may result in an increased risk of cardiotoxicity (QT prolongation, torsade de pointes, cardiac arrest).	0	1	3
PROBUCOL Concurrent use may result in an increased risk of cardiotoxicity (QT prolongation, torsade de pointes, cardiac arrest).	2	1	3
PROCAINAMIDE Concurrent use may result in an increased risk of cardiotoxicity (QT prolongation, torsade de pointes, cardiac arrest).	0	1	3
QUINIDINE Concurrent use may result in an increased risk of cardiotoxicity (QT prolongation, torsade de pointes, cardiac arrest).	0	1	3

Onset: 0=Unspecified 1=Rapid 2=Delayed
Severity: 1=Contraindicated 2=Major 3=Moderate 4=Minor
Evidence: 1=Excellent 2=Good 3=Fair 4=Poor

INTERACTION	ONSET	SEVERITY	EVIDENCE
SEMATILIDE Concurrent use may result in an increased risk of cardiotoxicity (QT prolongation, torsade de pointes, cardiac arrest).	0	1	3
SOTALOL Concurrent use may result in an increased risk of cardiotoxicity (QT prolongation, torsade de pointes, cardiac arrest).	0	1	3
SPARFLOXACIN Concurrent use may result in an increased risk of cardiotoxicity (QT prolongation, torsade de pointes, cardiac arrest).	2	1	3
TACROLIMUS Concurrent use may result in an increased risk of cardiotoxicity (QT prolongation, torsade de pointes, cardiac arrest).	2	1	3
TEDISAMIL Concurrent use may result in an increased risk of cardiotoxicity (QT prolongation, torsade de pointes, cardiac arrest).	0	1	3
THIORIDAZINE Concurrent use may result in an increased risk of cardiotoxicity (QT prolongation, torsade de pointes, cardiac arrest).	0	1	3

Zolpidem

INTERACTION	ONSET	SEVERITY	EVIDENCE
ETHANOL Concurrent use may result in increased sedation.	1	3	3
KETOCONAZOLE Concurrent use may result in increased plasma concentrations and pharmacodynamic effects of zolpidem.	1	3	3
RIFAMPIN Concurrent use may result in decreased plasma concentration and pharmacodynamic effect of zolpidem.	1	3	3

Section 3

Street Drug Profiles

As elaborated in the *Foreword*, many individuals who are prescribed psychotropic medications also have problems with substance abuse. To aid clinicians in this area, the *PDR® Drug Guide for Mental Health Professionals* has included this new section on street drugs. More than 100 substances of abuse are discussed, divided into three categories:

- *Part 1:* Commercial products, including alcohol, nitrites, and inhaled substances such as aerosol propellants and gases.
- *Part 2:* Commonly abused prescription drugs, including benzodiazepines and other central nervous system depressants, barbiturates, stimulants, narcotic analgesics, and anabolic steroids.
- *Part 3:* Illegal drugs, including cannabis, cocaine, heroin, and hallucinogens such as LSD.

Each profile is listed alphabetically by generic name and includes brand names (if available), common street names, a detailed description, common side effects of abuse, symptoms of overdose and withdrawal, and other pertinent facts. Please note that while every attempt has been made to provide the most current information, the data on street drugs are constantly changing in all of the related aspects discussed.

The profiles also include the Drug Enforcement Administration (DEA) classification, which is based on the Controlled Substances Act of 1970. **Class I** drugs are illegal, have a high potential for abuse, and have no accepted medical use in the United States. Drugs in the remaining classes are legal and have a currently accepted medical or research use, along with the following designations: **Class II** drugs have a high potential for abuse; **Class III** drugs have some potential for abuse; **Class IV** drugs have a relatively low potential for abuse; and **Class V** have the lowest potential for abuse.

This section does not include information on drug screening, due to numerous variations in laboratory testing methods and collection procedures. The window of opportunity to detect a drug is dependent on many factors, including the user's metabolic rate, dose size, how the drug was taken, and the cutoff concentration used by the laboratory to detect the drug. Generally, the drugs chosen for workplace screenings are detectable for several days after use. For specific information, contact the Substance Abuse and Mental Health Services Administration at 800-967-5752 or the website at www.workplace.samhsa.gov; and the DEA at 202-307-1000 or www.dea.gov.

Part 1.
Commercial Products

AEROSOLS AND GASES
COMMON STREET NAMES: Air blast, discorama, huff, laughing gas, moon gas, Oz, toncho, whippets
DEA CLASS: Not classified
PHARMACOLOGIC CLASS: Inhalants

Description: Except for medical anesthetics, aerosols and gases are not classified as drugs because they are not manufactured for pharmacologic use. Abused substances include household and commercial products such as butane lighters, propane tanks, and refrigerant gases; household aerosol propellants such as spray paints, hair or deodorant sprays, cooking oil, whipping cream, and fabric protectors; and medical anesthetic gases such as ether, chloroform, halothane, and nitrous oxide or "laughing gas." Most of these products produce short-term psychoactive effects similar to alcohol.

Method of use: Inhaled through the mouth or nose. In addition to inhaling directly from aerosol cans, users sniff the fumes from a plastic bag or through a cloth saturated with the substance (known as huffing). Users also inhale directly from balloons filled with nitrous oxide.

Duration of action: Onset is rapid but effects last only a short time. Inhaled nitrous oxide is rapidly eliminated by the lungs as unchanged gas.

Psychological effects: Aggressive behavior, apathy, delusions, distorted perception of reality, euphoria, hallucinations, impaired thinking and spatial judgment, loss of coordination, and loss of inhibition.

Physical effects: Depressed reflexes, dizziness, drowsiness, gait disturbance, head rush, headache, inattentiveness, limb spasm, loss of equilibrium and coordination, loss of sensation, nausea, rapid heartbeat followed by lethargy, slurred speech, vomiting, and wheezing. Long-term use may cause irreversible brain or nervous system damage, hearing loss, certain types of anemia, and bone marrow damage. Frequent use can cause tolerance and physical dependence. Serious burn injuries were reported because of the highly flammable nature of these products.

Overdose symptoms: Because these products are short-acting, users tend to inhale the fumes repeatedly for several hours, which increases the risk of overdosing. Symptoms may include impaired muscle tone, numbness and tingling in the extremities, respiratory depression, and heart and lung damage. Chronic exposure may induce heart failure and death within minutes of use, known as sudden sniffing death (SSD). High concentrations of inhalants can cause death from suffocation by displacing oxygen in the lungs. Nitrous oxide may cause sudden death by restricting oxygen to the brain. Death is usually related to asphyxia rather than a specific nitrous oxide level.

Withdrawal symptoms: Withdrawal symptoms may develop within several hours to a few days after the last use. Symptoms may include profuse sweating, rapid pulse, weight loss, disorientation, irritability, depression, sleeplessness, nausea, vomiting, physical agitation, anxiety, tremors, hallucinations, and seizures.

ALCOHOL

COMMON STREET NAMES: Booze, hooch
DEA CLASS: Not classified
PHARMACOLOGIC CLASS: CNS depressant

Description: Alcohol is a liquid made by yeast fermentation of carbohydrates such as grain or fruit. There are many varieties of alcohol, but ethanol (ethyl alcohol) is the type used to make alcoholic beverages and the one that is most commonly abused.

Method of use: Ingested

Duration of action: Onset and duration depend on various factors: the amount ingested, the type(s) of alcohol used, whether it was taken with or without food, and whether the individual is a chronic or occasional user.

Detection in blood screening: Alcohol use is best confirmed by breath or blood analysis. Blood alcohol content (BAC) helps determine the individual's intoxication level. BAC is influenced by the individual's weight, gender, height, tolerance, how quickly the alcohol was consumed, and whether it was taken with or without food. Most of the alcohol consumed is processed by the liver. A healthy liver metabolizes about 0.015 grams per deciliter per hour, which means that three-fourths of an ounce of pure alcohol is metabolized in 2 hours (this is equivalent to one 5-ounce glass of wine, one 12-ounce can of beer, or one 1.5-ounce shot of hard liquor). If the BAC is more than 100 milligrams per deciliter, the individual is considered intoxicated. Heavy drinkers have more active livers and may be able to metabolize up to three drinks an hour.

Psychological effects: Initial effects may include confusion, euphoria, and a false sense of well-being, which is replaced by anxiety, restlessness, mood changes, and depression as the BAC increases. Chronic use can cause psychological dependence.

Physical effects: Chronic alcohol abuse may cause anemia and other blood disorders, color-blindness, constipation, diarrhea, elevated blood pressure, inflammation of the pancreas, inflammation of the stomach lining, irregular heart rhythm, liver damage, low blood sugar, muscle weakness, and seizures. Chronic use can cause tolerance and physical dependence.

Overdose symptoms: The effects of alcohol intoxication vary among users. Some individuals may become intoxicated at a much lower BAC than others. The following data are based on clinical studies:

1. BAC of 0.02-0.03: Slight euphoria and loss of shyness.
2. BAC of 0.04-0.06: Sense of well-being, relaxation, lowered inhibitions, euphoria, and minor impairment of memory.
3. BAC of 0.07-0.09: Slight impairment of balance, speech, vision, reaction time, memory, and hearing. Loss of judgment and self-control are also noticeable at this stage.
4. BAC of 0.10-0.125: Significant impairment of balance, motor coordination, vision, speech, reaction time, and hearing. Euphoria is still apparent.
5. BAC of 0.13-0.15: Lack of physical control, blurred vision, and major loss of balance. Euphoria is reduced and replaced by anxiety and restlessness.
6. BAC of 0.16-0.20: Significant anxiety and restlessness, glossy eyes, and nausea. Pupils are slow to respond to stimuli.
7. BAC of 0.25: Significant anxiety and restlessness, nausea and vomiting, irregular "drunken" gait, loss of fine motor coordination, and mental confusion.
8. BAC of 0.30: Loss of consciousness.
9. BAC of 0.40 and up: Onset of stupor, coma, and possibly death due to respiratory depression.

Other symptoms of intoxication include constricted pupils, decreased heart rate, low blood pressure and respiration rate, diminished reflexes, and profuse sweating. Binge drinking is the most dangerous way to get severely intoxicated and is alarmingly prevalent among high school and college students. A binge is usually defined as having four or more drinks (for women) or five or more drinks (for men) in about 2 hours.

Withdrawal symptoms: Abruptly stopping use may cause strong alcohol cravings, nausea, excessive sweating, shakiness, depression, mood changes, headache, insomnia, unstable heart rate or blood pressure, tremors, anxiety or panic attacks, confusion and/or hallucinations (delirium tremens), and in extreme cases, seizures.

NITRITES (nonprescription products)

COMMON STREET NAMES: Ames, Amys, aroma of men, bolt, boppers, climax, hardware, pearls, poppers, quicksilver, rush, snappers, thrust, whiteout
DEA CLASS: Not classified
PHARMACOLOGIC CLASS: Inhalants

Description: Nitrites are volatile liquids that are readily absorbed from the lungs. Unlike other inhalants, they work primarily by dilating blood vessels and relaxing the muscles. Amyl nitrite and glyceryl trinitrate are used medically to treat acute chest pain (angina) and severe heart murmurs (see the prescription nitrites entry listed on page 426). Industrial nitrites that are reportedly abused are cyclohexyl nitrite, an ingredient found in room deodorizers, and butyl nitrite, which was used previously in the manufacturing of perfumes and antifreeze but is now considered illegal. Most of these products are used as sexual enhancers.

Method of use: Inhaled through the mouth or nose. In addition to inhaling directly from aerosol cans, users sniff the fumes from a plastic bag or through a cloth saturated with the substance (known as huffing).

Duration of action: Onset is rapid but effects last only a short time, usually 30 to 60 minutes.

Psychological effects: Loss of inhibition, distorted perception of reality, aggressive behavior, apathy, impaired judgment, euphoria, hallucinations, loss of coordination, and delusions.

Physical effects: Rapid heartbeat followed by lethargy, head rush, headaches, nausea, vomiting, slurred speech, loss of coordination, and wheezing. Frequent use can cause tolerance and physical dependence. Serious but reversible physical effects may include liver or kidney damage and blood oxygen depletion. Chronic use can cause serious damage to the heart and lungs and suppress the immune system, increasing the risk of infection. Prolonged use can also lead to poor muscle tone, muscle wasting, and numbness and tingling in the extremities.

Overdose symptoms: Because these products are short-acting, users tend to inhale the fumes repeatedly for several hours, which increases the risk of overdosing. Prolonged inhalation of nitrites may cause irregular and rapid heart rhythm, heart failure, and death within minutes of use.

Withdrawal symptoms: Abrupt discontinuation of use may cause sweating, rapid pulse, hand tremors, insomnia, nausea, vomiting, physical agitation, anxiety, hallucinations, and seizures.

Part 2.
Prescription Drugs

ACETAMINOPHEN WITH CODEINE PHOSPHATE
BRAND NAME: Tylenol with Codeine
COMMON STREET NAMES: Dreamer, God's drug, mister blue
DEA CLASS: Class III (tablets) and Class V (suspensions and elixirs)
PHARMACOLOGIC CLASS: Antipyretic analgesic, narcotic analgesic

Description: This medication is a fixed-dose combination of acetaminophen, an antipyretic (fever-reducing) analgesic; and codeine, a narcotic analgesic. It is prescribed for the relief of mild to moderately severe pain.

Method of use: Ingested

Duration of action: The analgesic effects usually last 4 to 6 hours after ingestion.

Psychological effects of abuse: Euphoria alternating with depression, confusion, nervousness, and hallucinations. The psychological dependence associated with narcotic addiction is complex. Long after physical dependence has ended, the addict may continue to think and talk about the drug and feel unable to manage daily activities without it.

Physical effects of abuse: Light-headedness, dizziness, nausea, vomiting, constipation, stomach discomfort, shortness of breath, and elevated blood pressure. Physical dependence can occur after prolonged use. Chronic use of acetaminophen is associated with liver damage. Abusing codeine may lead to breathing difficulties followed by respiratory arrest.

Overdose symptoms: Tolerance develops rapidly, and the progressively higher doses needed are often in the toxic range. Acute acetaminophen overdose can potentially result in fatal liver toxicity. Early symptoms include nausea, vomiting, sweating, and weakness. Clinical and laboratory evidence of liver toxicity may not be apparent until 48 to 72 hours after ingestion.

Overdose symptoms related to codeine include cold and clammy skin, severe drowsiness, constricted pupils, severe weakness, low blood pressure, respiratory depression, and coma.

Withdrawal symptoms: Although withdrawal is painful physically and emotionally, it is rarely life-threatening if adequate hydration and nutritional support are maintained. Withdrawal symptoms are similar to those of morphine but are considerably less intense. Abruptly stopping use can cause excessive tearing, yawning, and sweating in about 12 to 14 hours after the last dose. Additional symptoms may include diminished appetite, irritability, tremor, seizures, and loss of consciousness.

Adderall *see Dextroamphetamine, page 391*

Adipex-P *see Phentermine, page 440*

ALPRAZOLAM

BRAND NAME: Xanax
COMMON STREET NAMES: Candy, downers, sleeping pills, tranks, xanies
DEA CLASS: Class IV
PHARMACOLOGIC CLASS: Benzodiazepine, antianxiety

Description: Alprazolam is used to treat anxiety disorders with or without depression, acute stress reactions such as anxiety prior to surgery, and panic attacks with or without irrational fear. Abuse of benzodiazepines is particularly high among heroin and cocaine users.

Method of use: Ingested

Duration of action: 6 to 12 hours, but may persist longer in obese individuals.

Psychological effects of abuse: Amnesia, depression, difficulty concentrating, diminished sexual desire, impaired judgment, reduced inhibition, pressured speech, and suicidal ideation. Paradoxical reactions may include aggressive and agitated behavior. Prolonged use leads to psychological dependence and may cause behavior problems such as extreme aggression and hostility.

Physical effects of abuse: Change in appetite, constipation, difficulty urinating, dizziness, impaired muscle coordination, irregular gait, lightheadedness, low blood pressure, menstrual irregularities, and slurred speech. Long-term use may cause physical dependence.

Overdose symptoms: The most severe signs of overdose are respiratory depression and loss of consciousness. Other symptoms may include confusion, rapid and slurred speech, extreme sleepiness, diminished reflexes, and loss of muscle coordination. Death from overdose of a single benzodiazepine is extremely rare. However, there is an increased risk of toxicity when benzodiazepines are combined with alcohol and/or other CNS depressants. Fatalities have been reported in individuals who have overdosed with a combination of a single benzodiazepine and alcohol.

Withdrawal symptoms: Abrupt termination following long-term use may precipitate withdrawal symptoms and require hospitalization. Symptoms may include abdominal and muscle cramps, depression, insomnia, sweating, vomiting, tremors, and seizures.

Alurate *see Aprobarbital, page 381*

Ambien *see Zolpidem, page 454*

AMOBARBITAL SODIUM
BRAND NAME: Amytal sodium
COMMON STREET NAMES: Blue heavens, dolls, downers, goofballs, M&Ms, rainbows, red and blues, red devils, yellows
DEA CLASS: Class II
PHARMACOLOGIC CLASS: Barbiturate, hypnotic, sedative, anticonvulsant

Description: Barbiturates depress the sensory cortex, decrease motor activity, alter brain function, and produce drowsiness, sedation, and hypnosis. Amobarbital is used for the short-term treatment of insomnia. It is also used as a sedating agent for reducing anxiety prior to surgery.

Method of use: Injected IV or IM

Duration of action: 6 to 8 hours following a standard therapeutic dose.

Psychological effects of abuse: Barbiturates can cause psychological dependence, especially following prolonged use of high doses. Principal psychological effects include confusion, alternating euphoria and depression, and memory loss.

Physical effects of abuse: The most frequent physical effects are due to CNS depression, including dizziness, headache, excessive sleepiness, drowsiness, and irregular gait. Other physical symptoms may include headache, stomach pain, and skin rash. Paradoxical excitement and irritability may also occur. In chronic users, blood disorders such as megaloblastic anemia may develop. Physical dependence is a significant risk, since it can develop after short-term use.

Overdose symptoms: Overdosing with amobarbital may result in severe CNS depression. Initial symptoms include eye gazing, contracted pupils, slurred speech, irregular gait, and interrupted breathing. More serious overdose may result in respiratory and cardiovascular depression, severely low blood pressure and body temperature, coma, and shock that can lead to death. Reddish, bleeding blisters ("barb-burns") may occur on the hands, buttocks, and back of knees in about 6 percent of users; however, barbiturate overdose is not the sole cause of such blisters. All harmful effects are enhanced when barbiturates are taken with alcohol and/or other CNS depressants.

Withdrawal symptoms: Amobarbital is one of the most commonly abused barbiturates. Symptoms are similar to those of alcohol withdrawal and characterized by severe apprehension, weakness, elevated anxiety, irritability, dizziness, headache, sleeplessness, muscle twitching, nausea and vomiting, distortion of visual perception, and rapid pulse. Severely low blood pressure and convulsions may develop after a day or two, which eventually leads to hallucinations, delirium, and continuous seizures, followed by coma and death.

AMOBARBITAL AND SECOBARBITAL
BRAND NAME: Tuinal
COMMON STREET NAMES: Dolls, downers, goofballs, M&Ms, rainbows, red and blues, red birds, red devils, yellows
DEA CLASS: Class II
PHARMACOLOGIC CLASS: Barbiturate

Description: Barbiturates depress the sensory cortex, decrease motor activity, alter brain function, and produce drowsiness, sedation, and hypnosis. This drug combination is used as a sedative to relieve anxiety before surgery and as a supplemental agent for the short-term treatment of insomnia.

Method of use: Ingested

Duration of action: 6 to 8 hours following a standard therapeutic dose.

Psychological effects of abuse: Barbiturates may cause psychological dependence, especially following prolonged use of high doses. Psychological effects may include confusion, alternating euphoria and depression, and memory loss.

Physical effects of abuse: The most frequent physical effects are due to CNS depression, including dizziness, headache, excessive sleepiness, drowsiness, and irregular gait. Other symptoms may include headache, stomach pain, and skin rash. Paradoxical excitement and irritability may also occur. In chronic users, blood disorders such as megaloblastic anemia may develop. Physical dependence is a significant risk, since it can develop after short-term use.

Overdose symptoms: Overdosing with this drug may result in severe CNS depression. Initial symptoms include eye gazing, constricted pupils, slurred speech, irregular gait, and interrupted breathing. More serious overdose may result in respiratory and cardiovascular depression, severely low blood pressure and body temperature, coma, and shock that can lead to death. Reddish, bleeding blisters ("barb-burns") may occur on the hands, buttocks, and back of the knees in about 6 percent of users; however, barbiturate overdose is not the sole cause of such blisters. All harmful effects are enhanced when barbiturates are taken with alcohol and/or other CNS depressants.

Withdrawal symptoms: Amobarbital, one of the ingredients in Tuinal, is a commonly abused barbiturate. Symptoms are similar to those of alcohol withdrawal and characterized by severe apprehension, weakness, elevated anxiety, irritability, dizziness, headache, sleeplessness, muscle twitching, nausea and vomiting, distortion of visual perception, and rapid pulse. Severely low blood pressure and convulsions may develop after a day or two, which eventually leads to hallucinations, delirium, and continuous seizures, followed by coma and death.

Amytal see Amobarbital, page 379

Anadrol see Oxymetholone, page 431

Anavar see Oxandrolone, page 428

Android see Methyltestosterone, page 419

Anolor see Butalbital, page 384

APROBARBITAL

BRAND NAME: Alurate
COMMON STREET NAMES: Dolls, downers, goofballs, M&Ms, rainbows, red and blues, red devils, yellows
DEA CLASS: Class III
PHARMACOLOGIC CLASS: Barbiturate, hypnotic, sedative

Description: Aprobarbital is used for the short-term treatment of insomnia. It is also used as a sedating agent for reducing anxiety prior to surgery.

Method of use: Ingested

Duration of action: About 6 to 8 hours following a standard therapeutic dose.

Psychological effects of abuse: Barbiturates may cause psychological dependence, especially following prolonged use of high doses. Principal psychological effects may include confusion, alternating euphoria and depression, and memory loss.

Physical effects of abuse: The most frequent physical effects are due to CNS depression, including dizziness, headache, excessive sleepiness, drowsiness, and irregular gait. Other symptoms may include headache, stomach pain, and skin rash. Paradoxical excitement and irritability may also occur. In chronic users, blood disorders such as megaloblastic anemia may develop. Physical dependence is a significant risk, since it can develop after short-term use.

Overdose symptoms: Overdosing with aprobarbital can cause severe CNS depression. Initial symptoms may include eye gazing, contracted pupils, slurred speech, irregular gait, and interrupted breathing. More serious overdose may result in respiratory and cardiovascular depression, severely low blood pressure and body temperature, coma, and shock that can lead to death. Reddish, bleeding blisters ("barb-burns") may occur on the hands, buttocks, and back of knees in about 6 percent of users; however, barbiturate overdose is not the sole cause of such blisters. All harmful effects are enhanced when barbiturates are taken with alcohol and/or other CNS depressants.

Withdrawal symptoms: Aprobarbital is one of the most commonly abused barbiturates. Symptoms are similar to those of alcohol withdrawal and characterized by severe apprehension, weakness, elevated anxiety, irritability, dizziness, headache, sleeplessness, muscle twitching, nausea and vomiting, distortion of visual perception, and rapid pulse. Severely low blood pressure and convulsions may develop after a day or two, which eventually leads to hallucinations, delirium, and continuous seizures, followed by coma and death.

Aquachloral *see Chloral hydrate, page 386*

Astramorph PF *see Morphine, page 423*

Ativan *see Lorazepam, page 410*

Avinza *see Morphine, page 423*

BENZPHETAMINE HYDROCHLORIDE
BRAND NAME: Didrex
COMMON STREET NAMES: Chalk, crystal, crank, glass, meth, ice, speed
DEA CLASS: Class III
PHARMACOLOGIC CLASS: Amphetamine, CNS stimulant

Description: Benzphetamine is prescribed as a supplemental agent for weight loss. It is meant to be used along with caloric restriction, exercise, and behavior modification.

Method of use: Ingested and snorted

Duration of action: 8 to 24 hours

Psychological effects of abuse: Depression, hyperactivity, irritability, personality changes, and restlessness. Psychological dependence develops with chronic use.

Physical effects of abuse: Abdominal cramps, diarrhea, fatigue, insomnia, nausea, and vomiting. Long-term use may lead to physical dependence.

Overdose symptoms: Tolerance develops rapidly in chronic users, and progressively higher doses are needed to obtain the same effects as before. Overdose symptoms may include confusion, aggressiveness, hallucinations, panic state, severely elevated body temperature, tremors, rapid breathing, and muscle rigidity. Cardiovascular effects may include irregular heartbeat, severely low or high blood pressure, and circulatory collapse. The most severe symptom is psychosis that is clinically indistinguishable from schizophrenia. A fatal overdose is usually preceded by convulsions and coma.

Withdrawal symptoms: Benzphetamine is highly addictive, and physical dependence develops rapidly. Abrupt cessation of use may cause anxiety, extreme fatigue, paranoia, aggressive behavior, and strong drug cravings. Severe depression and suicidal ideation have also been reported.

Bontril *see Phendimetrazine, page 437*

BUTABARBITAL SODIUM
BRAND NAME: Butisol sodium
COMMON STREET NAMES: Barbs, downers, goofballs
DEA CLASS: Class III
PHARMACOLOGIC CLASS: Barbiturate, sedative, hypnotic

Description: Barbiturates depress the sensory cortex, decrease motor activity, alter brain function, and produce drowsiness, sedation, and hypnosis. Butabarbital is used primarily for daytime sedation.

Method of use: Ingested

Duration of action: Effects start within an hour and last for about 6 to 8 hours.

Psychological effects of abuse: Alternating euphoria and depression, confusion, and memory loss. Barbiturates may cause psychological dependence, especially following prolonged use of high doses.

Physical effects of abuse: Decreased blood pressure, unusual tiredness, nausea and vomiting, dizziness, drowsiness, heartburn, excessive sleepiness, shortness of breath, and dose-dependent respiratory depression. Prolonged use may cause tolerance and physical dependence.

Overdose symptoms: Unsteady gait, slurred speech, eye gazing, confusion, low blood pressure and body temperature, rapid heartbeat, and dose-dependent respiratory depression. All toxic effects are enhanced when butabarbital is taken with alcohol and/or other CNS depressant drugs.

Withdrawal symptoms: Symptoms are similar to those of alcohol withdrawal and characterized by severe apprehension, weakness, heightened anxiety, irritability, dizziness, headache, sleeplessness, muscle twitching, nausea and vomiting, distortion of visual perception, and rapid pulse. Severely low blood pressure and convulsions may develop after a day or two, which eventually leads to hallucinations, delirium, and continuous seizures, followed by coma and death.

BUTALBITAL COMBINATION PRODUCTS

GENERIC NAMES: Butalbital, aspirin, and caffeine (Fiorinal); butalbital, codeine phosphate, aspirin, and caffeine (Fiorinal with Codeine); and butalbital, acetaminophen, and caffeine (Anolor, Esgic, Fioricet, Repan, Zebutal)

COMMON STREET NAMES: Barbs, downers, goofballs

DEA CLASS: Class III (Fiorinal only)

PHARMACOLOGIC CLASS: Barbiturate, sedative, hypnotic

Description: These products are used primarily to relieve muscle and tension headache.

Method of use: Ingested

Duration of action: Effects start within an hour and last for about 12 hours.

Psychological effects of abuse: Confusion, hallucinations, depression, and feelings of intoxication. Barbiturates may cause psychological dependence, especially following prolonged use of high doses.

Physical effects of abuse: Decreased blood pressure, unusual tiredness, nausea and vomiting, dizziness, drowsiness, heartburn, excessive sleepiness, shortness of breath, and dose-dependent respiratory depression. Prolonged use may cause tolerance and physical dependence.

Overdose symptoms: Symptoms may include unsteady gait, slurred speech, eye gazing, confusion, low blood pressure and body temperature, rapid heart rate, and dose-dependent respiratory depression. All toxic effects are enhanced when these products are taken with alcohol and/or other CNS depressants. In cases of serious overdose, respiratory depression may lead to Cheyne-Stokes respiration (abnormal breathing patterns characterized by alternating periods of shallow and deep breathing) as well as respiratory arrest and coma, followed by death. In extreme cases, electrical activities in the brain may cease and electroencephalogram (EEG) readings may be "flat," although this does not necessarily indicate clinical death and may be fully reversible.

Withdrawal symptoms: Symptoms are similar to those of alcohol withdrawal and characterized by severe apprehension, strong drug cravings, weakness, heightened anxiety, irritability, dizziness, headache, sleeplessness, muscle twitching, nausea and vomiting, distortion of visual perception, and rapid pulse. Severely low blood pressure and convulsions may develop after a day or two, which eventually leads to hallucinations, delirium, and continuous seizures, followed by coma and death.

Butisol sodium *see Butabarbital, page 383*

BUTORPHANOL TARTRATE
BRAND NAME: Stadol
COMMON STREET NAMES: Not known
DEA CLASS: Class IV
PHARMACOLOGIC CLASS: Narcotic analgesic

Description: Butorphanol is a mixed narcotic agonist/antagonist and produces generalized CNS depression. It is used to help manage moderate to severe pain, as a sedative prior to surgery, and as a supplemental agent during anesthesia.

Method of use: Injected IV or IM and sniffed via nasal spray

Duration of action: Depends on dose and method of use. The effects persist for about 3 to 4 hours after injection, and about 4 to 5 hours after nasal application.

Psychological effects of abuse: Anxiety, apathy, confusion, depression, euphoria, general sense of well-being, hallucinations, inability to concentrate, nightmares, paradoxical excitement, and psychological dependence (after prolonged use). The psychological dependence associated with narcotic addiction is complex. Long after physical dependence has ended, the addict may continue to think and talk about the drug and feel unable to manage daily activities without it.

Physical effects of abuse: Blurred vision, constipation, dizziness, drowsiness, constricted pupils, excessive sleepiness, excessive sweating, flu-like symptoms, headache, light-headedness, low blood pressure, nausea, respiratory depression, respiratory tract infection, shortness of breath, slow pulse, tremors, unpleasant taste, vomiting, and weakness. Prolonged use may cause tolerance and physical dependence. Signs of tolerance include euphoria, sedation, shorter duration of action, and weaker painkilling effect.

Overdose symptoms: Chronic use can lead to tolerance, with the user needing progressively higher doses to obtain the same effects as before. Signs of overdose include constricted pupils, cold and clammy skin, confusion, severe drowsiness, slow or labored breathing, CNS and cardiac depression, and convulsions.

Withdrawal symptoms: Abruptly stopping the drug after long-term use may precipitate withdrawal symptoms. Intensity of symptoms is directly related to total daily dose, frequency and duration of use, and health of the user. Withdrawal from narcotics is rarely life-threatening. Without medical intervention, most of the physical symptoms of butorphanol withdrawal disappear within 7 to 10 days. Early symptoms may include watery eyes, runny nose, repeated yawning, and excessive sweating. Later-stage symptoms may include nervousness, muscle twitching, drug cravings, restlessness, irritability, loss of appetite, chills alternating with flushing, nausea, vomiting, bone and muscle pain in the back and extremities, tremors, elevated heart rate and blood pressure, and severe depression.

CHLORAL HYDRATE

BRAND NAMES: Aquachloral, Noctec, Somnote, Supprettes
COMMON STREET NAMES: Jellies, jellybeans, joy juice, knockout drops, Mickey, Mickey Finn, Peter, torpedo
DEA CLASS: Class IV
PHARMACOLOGIC CLASS: Sedative, hypnotic

Description: Chloral hydrate has properties similar to those of barbiturates. It is used for short-term sedation before diagnostic procedures, as a supplemental agent to manage pain following surgery, and for the short-term treatment of insomnia.

Method of use: Ingested or administered rectally

Duration of action: Chloral hydrate usually takes effect within 30 minutes and will induce sleep in about an hour following administration. The effects may last 4 to 8 hours.

Psychological effects of abuse: Confusion, disorientation, hallucinations, "hangover" effects, impaired judgment and concentration, nightmares, and paradoxical excitement.

Physical effects of abuse: Diarrhea, dizziness, headache, light-headedness, nausea, slow reflexes, stomach pain, unsteadiness, and vomiting. Chronic use can lead to addiction, severe withdrawal symptoms, and possibly liver damage.

Overdose symptoms: Tolerance develops rapidly after prolonged use, and the progressively higher doses needed are often in the toxic range. Signs of overdose may include severe drowsiness, nausea, vomiting, severe stomach pain, slurred speech, irregular gait, difficulty swallowing, severe weakness, dilated pupils, shortness of breath or other breathing problems, low blood pressure, irregular heart rate, low body temperature, respiratory depression, convulsions, and coma.

Withdrawal symptoms: Abruptly stopping use may precipitate withdrawal symptoms such as anorexia, nausea, vomiting, muscle weakness, low blood pressure, tremors, and seizures.

CLORAZEPATE DIPOTASSIUM

BRAND NAME: Tranxene
COMMON STREET NAMES: Candy, downers, sleeping pills, tranks
DEA CLASS: Class IV

PHARMACOLOGIC CLASS: Benzodiazepine, sedative, anticonvulsant

Description: Clorazepate is used to treat anxiety disorders, alcohol withdrawal, and as a supplemental agent in certain types of seizure disorders. Abuse of benzodiazepines is particularly high among heroin and cocaine users.

Method of use: Ingested

Duration of action: 8 to 24 hours

Psychological effects of abuse: Confusion, depression, impaired judgment and thinking abilities, mild euphoria, pressured speech, reduced inhibition, and suicidal ideation. Prolonged use may cause psychological dependence.

Physical effects of abuse: Change in appetite, constipation, difficulty urinating, dizziness, drowsiness, dry mouth, impaired muscle coordination, insomnia, irregular gait, light-headedness, low blood pressure, menstrual irregularities, nausea, slurred speech, tremor, and vomiting. Long-term use may cause physical dependence.

Overdose symptoms: The most severe signs of overdose are respiratory depression and coma. Other symptoms may include confusion, diminished reflexes, paradoxical euphoria, extreme sleepiness, and impaired coordination. Death from overdose of a single benzodiazepine is extremely rare. However, there is an increased risk of toxicity when benzodiazepines are combined with alcohol and/or other CNS depressants. Fatalities have been reported in individuals who have overdosed with a combination of a single benzodiazepine and alcohol.

Withdrawal symptoms: Abrupt termination following long-term use may precipitate withdrawal symptoms and require hospitalization. Symptoms may include abdominal and muscle cramps, depression, insomnia, sweating, vomiting, tremors, and seizures.

CHLORDIAZEPOXIDE
BRAND NAME: Librium
COMMON STREET NAMES: Candy, downers, sleeping pills, tranks
DEA CLASS: Class IV
PHARMACOLOGIC CLASS: Benzodiazepine, sedative, hypnotic

Description: Chlordiazepoxide is used to treat anxiety disorders with or without depression, alcohol withdrawal, and acute stress reactions such as anxiety prior to surgery. Abuse of benzodiazepines is particularly high among heroin and cocaine users.

Method of use: Ingested and injected IM or IV

Duration of action: 5 to 30 hours

Psycological effects of abuse: Confusion, depression, impaired judgment, mild euphoria, pressured speech, reduced inhibition, and suicidal ideation. Long-term use may cause psychological dependence.

Physical effects of abuse: Changes in appetite and body weight, dizziness, drowsiness, dry mouth, impaired muscle coordination, insomnia, irregular gait, light-headedness, low blood pressure, menstrual irregularities, nausea, slurred speech, and vomiting. Long-term use may cause physical dependence.

Overdose symptoms: The most severe signs of overdose are respiratory depression and coma. Other symptoms may include confusion, diminished reflexes, extreme sleepiness, unrealistic euphoria, and impaired muscle coordination. Death from overdose of a single benzodiazepine is extremely rare. However, there is an increased risk of toxicity when benzodiazepines are combined with alcohol and/or other CNS depressants. Fatalities have been reported in individuals who have overdosed with a combination of a single benzodiazepine and alcohol.

Withdrawal symptoms: Abrupt termination following long-term use may precipitate withdrawal symptoms and require hospitalization. Symptoms may include abdominal and muscle cramps, depression, insomnia, sweating, vomiting, tremors, and seizures.

CLONAZEPAM

BRAND NAME: Klonopin
COMMON STREET NAMES: Candy, downers, sleeping pills, tranks
DEA CLASS: Class IV
PHARMACOLOGIC CLASS: Benzodiazepine, anticonvulsant

Description: Clonazepam is used to treat panic disorder with or without irrational fears. It is also prescribed for certain types of seizures, either as monotherapy or an adjunct. Abuse of benzodiazepines is particularly high among heroin and cocaine users.

Method of use: Ingested

Duration of action: 18 to 50 hours

Psychological effects of abuse: Amnesia, confusion, depression, impaired judgment and thinking abilities, reduced inhibition, and suicidal ideation. Paradoxical effects include euphoria, hyperactivity, and extreme aggression. Prolonged use may cause psychological dependence.

Physical effects of abuse: Changes in sexual desire, constipation, decreased blood pressure, dizziness, drowsiness, fatigue, impaired physical capabilities, irregular gait, loss of muscle tone, sleepiness, slowed psychomotor performance, urinary retention, and visual disturbances. Prolonged use may cause physical dependence.

Overdose symptoms: The most severe signs of overdose are respiratory depression, loss of consciousness, and coma. Other symptoms may include confusion, diminished reflexes, slurred speech, impaired coordination, apnea, extreme sleepiness, loss of muscle tone, and severely low blood pressure. Death from overdose of a single benzodiazepine is extremely rare. However, there is an increased risk of toxicity when benzodiazepines are combined with alcohol and/or other CNS depressants. Fatalities have been reported in patients who have overdosed with a combination of a single benzodiazepine and alcohol.

Withdrawal symptoms: Abrupt termination following long-term use may precipitate withdrawal symptoms and require hospitalization. Symptoms may include abdominal and muscle cramps, depression, insomnia, sweating, vomiting, tremors, and seizures.

CODEINE PHOSPHATE and CODEINE SULFATE

BRAND NAMES: Capital and Codeine, Contin, Tylenol with Codeine
COMMON STREET NAMES: Hillbilly heroin, killers, percs, poor man's heroin, schoolboy
DEA CLASS: Class II (single agent), Class III (combined with Tylenol), and Class V (cough suppressant products)
PHARMACOLOGIC CLASS: Narcotic analgesic, cough suppressant

Description: Codeine is produced by the chemical manipulation of morphine. However, codeine produces less analgesia and sedation than morphine, and is less likely to cause respiratory depression. Codeine is indicated for mild to moderate pain. In lower doses, it is used as a cough suppressant. Codeine is also indicated for the symptomatic relief of acute diarrhea.

Method of use: Ingested and injected IM or SC

Duration of action: Depends on the dose and method of use. In general, codeine's analgesic effects last 4 to 6 hours following administration.

Psychological effects of abuse: Confusion, false sense of well-being, inability to concentrate, and psychological dependence (after prolonged use). The psychological dependence associated with narcotic addiction is complex. Long after physical dependence has ended, the addict may continue to think and talk about the drug and feel unable to manage daily activities without it.

Physical effects of abuse: Blurred vision, change in heart rhythm, constipation, constriction of pupils, drowsiness, dry mouth, flushing of the face, low blood pressure, headache, nausea, respiratory depression, urinary urgency or retention, and vomiting. *High doses:* Lethargy, seizures, and coma may occur. Prolonged use can cause physical dependence, but codeine produces less euphoria and sedation than morphine.

Overdose symptoms: Tolerance can develop rapidly, and progressively higher doses are needed to obtain the same effects as before. Signs of overdose may include constipation, stomach cramps, nausea, vomiting, drowsiness, dizziness, slurred speech, extreme sleepiness, low body temperature, low blood pressure, swelling, cold and clammy skin, nonreactive pupils, pulmonary edema, CNS and respiratory depression, convulsions, and coma. Death may result from respiratory failure 2 to 4 hours postingestion. Risk of overdose increases significantly when the drug is taken with alcohol.

Withdrawal symptoms: Although withdrawal is painful physically and emotionally, it's rarely life-threatening if adequate hydration and nutritional support are maintained. The symptoms are similar to those of morphine withdrawal but are considerably less intense. Abruptly stopping use can cause excessive tearing, yawning, and sweating about 12 to 14 hours after the last dose. Additional symptoms may include diminished appetite, gooseflesh, irritability, tremors, seizures, and loss of consciousness.

Concerta *see Methylphenidate, page 418*

Cylert *See Pemoline, page 434*

Dalmane *see Flurazepam, page 403*

Darvon *see Propoxyphene, page 441*

Delatestryl *see Testosterone, page 448*

Demerol *see Meperidine, page 411*

Desoxyn *see Methamphetamine, page 415*

Dexedrine *see Dextroamphetamine, page 391*

DEXMETHYLPHENIDATE HYDROCHLORIDE
BRAND NAME: Focalin
COMMON STREET NAME: Working man's cocaine
DEA CLASS: Class II
PHARMACOLOGIC CLASS: CNS stimulant, nonamphetamine

Description: This drug has pharmacologic actions similar to those of dextroamphetamine. It is used to treat attention deficit hyperactivity disorder (ADHD) and excessive daytime sleepiness (narcolepsy). Severe complications can occur when dexmethylphenidate tablets are crushed and diluted in water for injection. The tablets contain insoluble fillers that can block small blood vessels, causing serious damage to the lungs and eye retina. In addition, there have been reports of fatalities among drug users who combined dexmethylphenidate with pentazocine, a narcotic analgesic.

Method of use: Ingested; tablets are also crushed and snorted or diluted in water and injected.

Duration of action: 4 to 5 hours following a standard therapeutic dose.

Psychological effects of abuse: Depression, nervousness, and psychotic behavior.

Physical effects of abuse: Abdominal cramps, chronic insomnia, diarrhea, loss of appetite, nausea, rapid heart rate, tiredness, vomiting, and weight loss. Severe blockage in the blood vessels of the lungs and eye retina can occur when the drug is injected.

Overdose symptoms: Signs of overdose may include excessive sweating and hyperactivity, vomiting, agitation, tremors, severely elevated body temperature and blood pressure, rapid heart rate, and hallucinations.

Withdrawal symptoms: Withdrawal reactions are less common than with other CNS stimulants. Symptoms may include severe fatigue, depression, nausea, vomiting, stomach cramps, insomnia, and nightmares.

DEXTROAMPHETAMINE
BRAND NAMES: Adderall, Dexedrine
COMMON STREET NAMES: Bennies, black beauties, crosses, hearts, LA turn-around, speed, truck drivers, uppers
DEA CLASS: Class II
PHARMACOLOGIC CLASS: Amphetamine, CNS stimulant, anorexiant

Description: Dextroamphetamine has a marked CNS stimulant effect, particularly on the cerebral cortex. It is used to treat excessive daytime sleepiness (narcolepsy) and attention deficit hyperactivity disorder (ADHD).

Method of use: Ingested, snorted, smoked, and injected

Duration of action: About 4 hours for short-acting forms and 6 to 12 hours for long-acting forms.

Psychological effects of abuse: Aggression, confusion, depression, anxiety, delusions, agitation, paranoia, hallucinations, drug craving, and impulsive behavior. Tolerance and psychological dependence may develop after chronic use.

Physical effects of abuse: Blood-vessel inflammation in the brain, elevated blood pressure, fever, muscle pain, poor blood circulation, rapid heart rate, and weight loss.

Overdose symptoms: Overdose syndromes are characterized by circulatory collapse, seizures, irregular heart rate, significantly elevated body temperature, severe muscle weakness and pain, kidney and liver injuries, and coma. In some cases, severe psychosis was reported within 24 hours following IV administration.

Withdrawal symptoms: Abruptly stopping the drug after long-term use may cause extreme fatigue, overeating, depression, and stupor.

DIAZEPAM

BRAND NAME: Valium
COMMON STREET NAMES: Candy, downers, sleeping pills, tranks
DEA CLASS: Class IV
PHARMACOLOGIC CLASS: Benzodiazepine, sedative, antianxiety, anticonvulsant

Description: Diazepam is used to treat anxiety disorders with or without depression, acute stress reactions such as anxiety prior to surgery, panic attacks with or without irrational fear, alcohol withdrawal, and certain types of seizure disorders. Abuse of benzodiazepines is particularly high among heroin and cocaine users.

Method of use: Ingested and injected IM or IV

Duration of action: Effects can linger up to 4 days, but may persist longer in chronic users.

Psychological effects of abuse: Confusion, impaired judgment and thinking abilities, irritability, mild euphoria, pressured speech, reduced inhibition, and suicidal ideation. Long-term use may cause psychological dependence.

Physical effects of abuse: Changes in appetite and body weight, constipation, dizziness, impaired muscle coordination, low blood pressure, and vertigo. Long-term use may cause physical dependence.

Overdose symptoms: The most severe signs of overdose are respiratory depression and coma. Other symptoms may include confusion, diminished reflexes, unrealistic euphoria, extreme sleepiness, and impaired muscle coordination. Death from overdose of a single benzodiazepine is extremely rare. However, there is an increased risk of toxicity when benzodiazepines are combined with alcohol and/or other CNS depressants. Fatalities have been reported in individuals who have overdosed with a combination of a single benzodiazepine and alcohol.

Withdrawal symptoms: Abrupt termination following long-term use may precipitate withdrawal symptoms and require hospitalization. Symptoms may include abdominal and muscle cramps, depression, insomnia, sweating, vomiting, tremors, and seizures.

Didrex *see Benzphetamine, page 382*

DIETHYLPROPION HYDROCHLORIDE
BRAND NAMES: Dospan, Tenuate
COMMON STREET NAMES: Bam, bambita, beans, black beauties, Christmas trees, dolls, jellybeans, little bomb
DEA CLASS: Class IV
PHARMACOLOGIC CLASS: CNS stimulant and indirect-acting sympathomimetic, anorexiant

Description: Diethylpropion is related to amphetamines both chemically and pharmacologically. It is used as a supplemental agent to help promote weight loss in conjunction with caloric restriction, exercise, and behavior modification.

Method of use: Ingestion

Duration of action: 6 to 8 hours

Psychological effects of abuse: Mental depression, restlessness, talkativeness, uncontrollable excitement, personality changes, and psychosis.

Physical effects of abuse: Constipation, dry mouth, nausea, vomiting, stomach cramps, dizziness, light-headedness, sleeplessness, headache, elevated blood pressure, rapid heartbeat, blurred vision, dilated pupils, and intermittent or painful urination.

Overdose symptoms: Signs of overdose include confusion, restlessness, rapid breathing, stomach cramps, exaggerated reflexes, extremely high fever, irregular heartbeat, elevated blood pressure, hallucinations, panic state, convulsions, and coma.

Withdrawal symptoms: Physical dependence is not common. However, abruptly stopping use can occasionally cause insomnia, tiredness, depression, stomach cramps, convulsions, and nightmares.

Dilaudid *see Hydromorphone, page 407*

Dolophine *see Methadone, page 414*

Dopram *see Doxapram, page 394*

Doral *see Quazepam, page 443*

DOXAPRAM HYDROCHLORIDE
BRAND NAME: Dopram
COMMON STREET NAMES: Not known
DEA CLASS: Not classified
PHARMACOLOGIC CLASS: CNS and respiratory stimulant, nonamphetamine

Description: This drug is used to manage respiratory depression due to anesthesia. It is also used to manage abnormally high levels of carbon monoxide in the blood secondary to chronic obstructive pulmonary disease (COPD). Doxapram may raise blood pressure and stimulate the nervous system.

Method of use: Ingested and injected IV

Duration of action: About 6 to 8 hours

Psychological effects of abuse: Confusion, delirium, and hallucinations.

Physical effects of abuse: Shortness of breath, coughing, respiratory problems such as hyperventilation, convulsions, headache, dizziness, hiccup, hyperactivity, sweating, flushing, fever, nausea, vomiting, diarrhea, excessive sweating, flushing, difficulty urinating, and sudden high or low blood pressure.

Overdose symptoms: Signs of overdose include anorexia, high fever, excessive sweating, flushing, muscle rigidity, delirium, hallucinations, seizures, coma, and respiratory failure.

Withdrawal symptoms: To date, there are no reports of withdrawal effects following a standard therapeutic dose.

DRONABINOL and NABILONE
BRAND NAME: Marinol (dronabinol); also known as delta-9-tetrahydrocannabinol (THC)
COMMON STREET NAMES: Bud, endo, grass, herb, kind bud, Mary Jane, pot, shake, sinsemilla, weed
DEA CLASS: Class III
PHARMACOLOGIC CLASS: Antiemetic

Description: Dronabinol and nabilone are chemically related to THC, the active ingredient in marijuana. They are used to treat the nausea and vomiting associated with cancer chemotherapy and are prescribed only when other antiemetic drugs have failed to work. Dronabinol is also used to treat anorexia associated with weight loss in AIDS patients.

Method of use: Ingested

Duration of action: Onset of action occurs within 1 hour after ingestion and effects persist for 20 to 24 hours.

Psychological effects of abuse: Anxiety, confusion, depression, detachment from reality, hallucinations, memory loss, and mood changes.

Physical effects of abuse: Blurred vision, diarrhea, dizziness, drowsiness, dry eyes, dry mouth, feeling faint, headache, high blood pressure, increased appetite, irregular gait, rapid heartbeat, ringing in the ears, and vertigo. Chronic users may develop tolerance and physical dependence.

Overdose symptoms: Heavy users may develop tolerance rapidly and need progressively larger doses to obtain the same effects as before. Signs of overdose may include dizziness, drowsiness, slurred speech, irregular gait, decreased motor coordination and muscle strength, extreme tiredness or weakness, rapid heartbeat, high or low blood pressure, and rarely, psychosis.

Withdrawal symptoms: Abruptly stopping use may cause drug cravings, irritability, agitation, apprehension, insomnia, excessive sweating, aggressiveness, and extreme anxiety.

DTO *see Opium, page 427*

Duramorph PF *see Morphine, page 423*

Esgic *See Butalbital, page 384*

ESTAZOLAM
BRAND NAME: ProSom
COMMON STREET NAMES: Candy, downers, sleeping pills, tranks
DEA CLASS: Class IV
PHARMACOLOGIC CLASS: Benzodiazepine, sedative, hypnotic

Description: Estazolam is used for the short-term treatment of sleep disorders such as difficulty falling asleep or staying asleep. Abuse of benzodiazepines is particularly high among heroin and cocaine users.

Method of use: Ingested

Duration of action: Up to 30 hours

Psychological effects of abuse: Confusion, impaired judgment and thinking abilities, irritability, mild euphoria, pressured speech, reduced inhibition, and suicidal ideation. Long-term use may cause psychological dependence.

Physical effects of abuse: Changes in appetite and body weight, constipation, dizziness, impaired muscle coordination, and low blood pressure. Long-term use may cause physical dependence.

Overdose symptoms: The most severe signs of overdose are respiratory depression and coma. Other symptoms may include confusion, diminished reflexes, extreme sleepiness, unrealistic euphoria, and impaired muscle coordination. Death from overdose of a single benzodiazepine is extremely rare. However, there is an increased risk of toxicity when benzodiazepines are combined with alcohol and/or other CNS depressants. Fatalities have been reported in patients who have overdosed with a combination of a single benzodiazepine and alcohol.

Withdrawal symptoms: Abrupt termination following long-term use may precipitate withdrawal symptoms and require hospitalization. Symptoms may include abdominal and muscle cramps, depression, insomnia, sweating, vomiting, tremors, and seizures.

ETHCHLORVYNOL
BRAND NAME: Placidyl
COMMON STREET NAMES: Not known
DEA CLASS: Class IV
PHARMACOLOGIC CLASS: Sedative, hypnotic

Description: Ethchlorvynol is used for the short-term treatment of sleep disorders, but it is not superior to the benzodiazepines. For the most part, benzodiazepines have replaced the use of ethchlorvynol because of its high potential for causing addiction and toxic overdose.

Methodic of use: Ingested

Duration of action: Hypnotic effects last about 5 hours following ingestion of a single therapeutic dose. If given in high doses, the effects may persist for up to 35 hours.

Psychological effects of abuse: Confusion, feelings of intoxication, hallucinations, and depression. Prolonged use of high doses may cause psychological dependence.

Physical effects of abuse: Dizziness, irregular gait, facial numbness, low blood pressure, vomiting, nausea, visual changes, cough, shortness of breath, respiratory distress, and accumulation of fluid in the lungs (with IV injections only). Prolonged use may cause intense physical addiction and withdrawal symptoms.

Overdose symptoms: Tolerance develops rapidly, and the progressively higher doses needed are often in the toxic range. Symptoms include severely low blood pressure, accumulation of fluid in the lungs, and liver damage.

Withdrawal symptoms: Abrupt cessation of use may cause weakness, heightened anxiety, irritability, dizziness, headache, sleeplessness, nausea and vomiting, distortion of visual perception, rapid pulse, and convulsions.

ETHINAMATE
BRAND NAME: Valmid
COMMON STREET NAMES: Not known
DEA CLASS: Class IV
PHARMACOLOGIC CLASS: Sedative, hypnotic

Description: Ethinamate is marketed in other countries for the short-term treatment of insomnia. The drug was withdrawn from the U.S. market in 1990 after safer and more effective agents became available.

Method of use: Ingested

Duration of action: The hypnotic effects start within 20 minutes and last 3 to 5 hours.

Psychological effects of abuse: Behavioral changes, excessive irritability, and paradoxical excitement. Prolonged use may cause psychological dependence.

Physical effects of abuse: Dizziness, drowsiness, confusion, irregular gait, nausea, vomiting, and "hangover" effects. Prolonged use may cause tolerance and physical dependence.

Overdose symptoms: Tolerance develops rapidly, and the progressively higher doses needed are often in the toxic range. Toxicity reactions are similar to barbiturates. Major symptoms of overdose are CNS and respiratory depression, severely low blood pressure, and coma (after high doses). Additional symptoms include severe weakness, confusion, slurred speech, irregular gait, shortness of breath, breathing difficulties, and slowed heartbeat.

Withdrawal symptoms: Abrupt cessation of use may cause confusion, restlessness, nervousness, irritability, trembling, sleeplessness, agitation, dizziness, hyperactive reflexes, hallucinations, and seizures.

ETHYLESTRENOL
BRAND NAME: Orabolin
COMMON STREET NAMES: Arnolds, gym candy, juice, pumpers, roids, stackers, weight trainers
DEA CLASS: Class III
PHARMACOLOGIC CLASS: Anabolic-androgenic steroid

Description: Androgens are steroid hormones that develop and maintain male sex characteristics. They are used primarily to replace insufficient levels of testosterone due to poor functioning of the testes. When used in combination with exercise and a high-protein diet, androgens can promote increased muscle size and strength, improve stamina, and decrease recovery time between workouts. Androgens are also used to promote the development of puberty in males with clearly delayed onset. Additionally, androgens are sometimes prescribed for women with advancing, inoperable metastatic breast cancer who are 1 to 5 years postmenopausal.

Method of use: Ingested. Chronic users tend to rotate steroids using various methods known as cycling, stacking, and pyramiding. Sporadic discontinuation of use is believed to allow testosterone levels and sperm counts to return to normal. Taking steroids regularly with periodic "drug-free times" is called cycling. Stacking refers to the concomitant use of two or more steroids at high doses. Pyramiding is when the dose, frequency, or number of steroids taken is gradually increased, followed by progressive tapering of the drug(s).

Duration of action: Depends on the formulation, frequency, and method of use. In general, effects may last up to 6 days.

Psychological effects of abuse: Mood changes, depression, uncontrollable aggressive behavior, euphoria, anxiety, irritability, increased sex drive, and rarely, psychosis. Psychological dependence may also occur.

Physical effects of abuse: Angry or hostile feelings, elevated blood pressure and cholesterol, headache, insomnia, premature balding, psychotic reactions, severe acne, sexual dysfunction, and violent behavior. *In men:* Breast development, impotence, intermittent or painful urination, painful or persistent erections, reduced sperm production, and shrinking of the testicles. *In women:* Decreased body fat and breast size, deepening of the voice, enlarged clitoris, excessive growth of body hair, and menstrual changes. *In adolescents:* Premature termination of growth.

Prolonged use can lead to tolerance. While the long-term effects are not completely known, chronic steroid abuse has been associated with damage to the heart, liver, and brain.

Overdose symptoms: There have been no reports of serious overdose with this drug. Chronic use of high doses may cause excessive sexual stimulation, reduced sperm production, enlarged breasts in males, uncontrolled painful erection, jaundice, and deteriorating liver function. Excessive fluid retention may occur in users who have heart, liver, or kidney disease.

Withdrawal symptoms: Abrupt discontinuation may cause mood changes, tiredness, restlessness, loss of appetite, dissatisfaction with body image, sleeplessness, reduced sex drive, paranoia, and severe depression that can lead to suicide attempts.

FENFLURAMINE
BRAND NAME: Pondomin
COMMON STREET NAMES: Pep pills, speed, uppers
DEA CLASS: Class IV
PHARMACOLOGIC CLASS: CNS stimulant

Description: Fenfluramine was previously used as a supplemental agent to help promote weight loss. It was withdrawn from the market worldwide due to its serious adverse effect on heart valves, but can still be found among drug users. Fenfluramine is an indirect-acting sympathomimetic agent related to amphetamines, but at standard doses it usually depresses rather than stimulates the central nervous system.

Method of use: Ingested

Duration of action: Following a single dose, effects may last 4 to 6 hours.

Psychological effects of abuse: Confusion, agitation, depression, restlessness, combative behavior, and hallucinations. Acute paranoia and other psychotic behavior were also reported with the use of this product.

Physical effects of abuse: Constipation, dry mouth, nausea, vomiting, stomach cramps, dizziness, light-headedness, sleeplessness, headache, elevated blood pressure, rapid heartbeat, blurred vision, dilated pupils, and intermittent or painful urination. Valvular heart disease was reported with prolonged use, particularly when ingested with phentermine.

Overdose symptoms: Tolerance may develop after 12 weeks of chronic use, and progressively larger doses are needed to obtain the same effects as before. Toxicity can persist for up to 3 days following a single large dose. Overdose symptoms may include dilated and nonreactive pupils, double vision, rapid and irregular pulse, irregular heart rhythm, respiratory failure, seizures, and coma.

Withdrawal symptoms: Withdrawal symptoms following cessation of fenfluramine are rare, but agitation, irritability, hyperactivity, and interrupted sleep patterns have been reported.

FENTANYL and FENTANYL CITRATE
BRAND NAMES: Actiq, Duragesic, Sublimaze
COMMON STREET NAMES: China girl, China white, dance fever, friend, goodfellas, king ivory
DEA CLASS: Class II
PHARMACOLOGIC CLASS: Narcotic analgesic

Description: Fentanyl is used as a sedative prior to surgery, as a supplemental agent to induce general or local anesthesia, and to help manage moderate to severe pain. Transdermal fentanyl is used for chronic pain. Actiq, a raspberry-flavored lozenge, is indicated only for treating break-through cancer pain in opiate-tolerant individuals. Actiq is about 80 times more potent than morphine. Although the pharmacologic effects of fentanyl are the same as those of heroin, fentanyl is 50 to 100 times more potent. U.S. authorities have identified at least 12 analogues of fentanyl being produced clandestinely.

Method of use: The most common method is IV injection; other methods include transdermal (absorbed through the skin), transmucosal (buccal, or absorbed through the gums), smoked, and snorted.

Duration of action: Depends on dose and method of use. In general, the effects last for only 1 to 2 hours following administration. However, repeated administration of large doses may result in accumulation and a longer duration of action.

Psychological effects of abuse: Confusion, depression, and hallucinations. Psychological dependence can result after prolonged use, especially with high doses. The psychological dependence associated with narcotic addiction is complex. Long after physical dependence has ended, the addict may continue to think and talk about the drug and feel unable to manage daily activities without it.

Physical effects of abuse: Low blood pressure, drowsiness, dizziness, headache, restlessness, fatigue, muscle rigidity, seizures, paradoxical CNS stimulation, nausea, constipation, vomiting, diminished appetite, dry mouth, stomach cramps, decreased urination, and shortness of breath. Chronic use may cause physical dependence.

Overdose symptoms: The main symptoms are constricted pupils, CNS depression, and slow or labored breathing. Severe overdose may result in interrupted breathing, circulatory depression, severely low blood pressure, muscle rigidity, slow heart rate, seizures, delirium, and shock. Physical activity, such as strenuous exercise or dancing, may cause increased absorption of transdermal fentanyl. Toxicity has been reported with transdermal patches due to heat-induced changes in the delivery system. Risk of overdose increases significantly when the drug is taken with alcohol.

Withdrawal symptoms: Abruptly stopping the drug after chronic use may precipitate withdrawal. The intensity of symptoms is directly related to the total daily dose, frequency and duration of use, and the health of the user. Although withdrawal from narcotics is painful physically and emotionally, it is rarely life-threatening if adequate hydration and nutritional support are maintained. Early symptoms include watery eyes, runny nose, repeated yawning, and excessive sweating. Later-stage symptoms may include restlessness, irritability, loss of appetite, nausea, vomiting, diarrhea, shivering, drug cravings, tremors, and severe depression. Advanced withdrawal symptoms may include chills alternating with flushing, muscle and bone pain in the back and extremities, and elevated heart rate and blood pressure.

Finaject *see Trenbolone, page 450*

Fioricet *see Butalbital, page 384*

Fiorinal *see Butalbital, page 384*

FLUNITRAZEPAM
BRAND NAME: Rohypnol
COMMON STREET NAMES: Forget-me pill, Mexican valium, R2, Roche, roofies, roofinol, rope, rophies
DEA CLASS: Class IV
PHARMACOLOGIC CLASS: Benzodiazepine, sedative, hypnotic

Description: Flunitrazepam is neither approved nor manufactured in the U.S. It is used in other countries for the short-term treatment of insomnia, as a muscle relaxant prior to surgery, and as an aid in the induction of anesthesia. There is widespread abuse of flunitrazepam among drug users, especially those who use opioids or cocaine. Flunitrazepam has also gained a reputation as a "date rape" drug. Victims who are unknowingly given the drug become incapacitated and unable to resist sexual assault.

Method of use: Ingested, snorted, and injected IM or IV

Duration of action: 9 to 30 hours, depending on method of use and dose size.

Psychological effects of abuse: Amnesia, confusion, impaired mental capabilities, mania or hypomania, and suicidal ideation. Long-term use may cause psychological dependence.

Physical effects of abuse: Constipation, decreased blood pressure, dizziness, drowsiness, impaired physical capabilities, loss of muscle tone, sleepiness, slowed psychomotor performance, urinary retention, and visual disturbances. Long-term use may cause physical dependence. Neurological effects can persist for years, particularly in older people.

Overdose symptoms: Overdose with flunitrazepam is particularly dangerous since respiratory arrest can develop rapidly. Other symptoms may include confusion, diminished reflexes, disorientation, impaired coordination, extreme sleepiness, slurred speech, visual disturbances, loss of muscle tone, lowered blood pressure and pulse, and loss of consciousness. Death from overdose of a single benzodiazepine is extremely rare. However, there is an increased risk of toxicity when benzodiazepines are combined with alcohol and/or other CNS depressants. Fatalities have been reported in patients who have overdosed with a combination of a single benzodiazepine and alcohol.

Withdrawal symptoms: Abrupt termination following long-term use may precipitate withdrawal symptoms and require hospitalization. Symptoms may include abdominal and muscle cramps, agitation, delirium, depression, insomnia, rapid pulse, sweating, vomiting, hallucinations, tremors, and seizures.

FLUOXYMESTERONE
BRAND NAME: Halotestin
COMMON STREET NAMES: Arnolds, gym candy, juice, pumpers, roids, stackers, weight trainers
DEA CLASS: Class III
PHARMACOLOGIC CLASS: Anabolic-androgenic steroid

Description: Androgens are steroid hormones that develop and maintain male sex characteristics. They are used primarily to replace insufficient levels of testosterone due to poor functioning of the testes. When used in combination with exercise and a high-protein diet, androgens can promote increased muscle size and strength, improve stamina, and decrease recovery time between workouts. Androgens are also used to promote the development of puberty in males with clearly delayed onset. Additionally, androgens are sometimes prescribed for women with advancing, inoperable metastatic breast cancer who are 1 to 5 years postmenopausal. Fluoxymesterone has also been used in the management of anemias caused by certain cancers or chemotherapy.

Method of use: Ingested. Chronic users tend to rotate steroids using various methods known as cycling, stacking, and pyramiding. Sporadic discontinuation of use is believed to allow testosterone levels and sperm counts to return to normal. Taking steroids regularly with periodic "drug-free times" is called cycling. Stacking refers to the concomitant use of two or more steroids at high doses. Pyramiding is when the dose, frequency, or number of steroids taken is gradually increased, followed by progressive tapering of the drug(s).

Duration of action: Depends on the formulation, frequency, and method of use. In general, effects may last up to 6 days.

Psychological effects of abuse: Anxiety, changes in sex drive, and depression. Psychological dependence may also occur.

Physical effects of abuse: Angry or hostile feelings, elevated blood pressure and cholesterol, headache, insomnia, premature balding, psychotic reactions, severe acne, sexual dysfunction, and violent behavior. ***In men:*** Breast development, impotence, intermittent or painful urination, painful or persistent erections, reduced sperm production, and shrinking of the testicles. *In women:* Decreased body fat and breast size, deepening of the voice, enlarged clitoris, excessive growth of body hair, and menstrual changes. *In adolescents:* Premature termination of growth.

Prolonged use can lead to tolerance. While the long-term effects are not completely known, chronic steroid abuse has been associated with damage to the heart, liver, and brain.

Overdose symptoms: There have been no reports of serious overdose with this drug. Chronic use of high doses may cause excessive sexual stimulation, reduced sperm production, enlarged breasts in males, uncontrolled painful erection, jaundice, and deteriorating liver function. Excessive fluid retention may occur in users who have heart, liver, or kidney disease.

Withdrawal symptoms: Abrupt discontinuation may cause mood changes, tiredness, restlessness, loss of appetite, dissatisfaction with body image, sleeplessness, reduced sex drive, paranoia, and severe depression that can lead to suicide attempts.

FLURAZEPAM
BRAND NAME: Dalmane
COMMON STREET NAMES: Candy, downers, sleeping pills, tranks
DEA CLASS: Class IV
PHARMACOLOGIC CLASS: Benzodiazepine, sedative, hypnotic

Description: Flurazepam is used for the short-term treatment of sleep disorders such as insomnia. Abuse of benzodiazepines is particularly high among heroin and cocaine users.

Method of use: Ingested

Duration of action: 6 to 8 hours

Psychological effects of abuse: Confusion, impaired judgment and thinking abilities, irritability, mild euphoria, pressured speech, reduced inhibition, and suicidal ideation. Long-term use may cause psychological dependence.

Physical effects of abuse: Changes in appetite and body weight, constipation, dizziness, impaired muscle coordination, and low blood pressure. Long-term use may cause physical dependence.

Overdose symptoms: The most severe signs of overdose are respiratory depression and coma. Other symptoms may include confusion, diminished reflexes, unsteady gait, unrealistic euphoria, extreme sleepiness, and impaired muscle coordination. Death from overdose of a single benzodiazepine is extremely rare. However, there is an increased risk of toxicity when benzodiazepines are combined with alcohol and/or other CNS depressants. Fatalities have been reported in patients who have overdosed with a combination of a single benzodiazepine and alcohol.

Withdrawal symptoms: Abrupt termination following long-term use may precipitate withdrawal symptoms and require hospitalization. Symptoms may include abdominal and muscle cramps, depression, insomnia, sweating, vomiting, tremors, and seizures.

Focalin *see Dexmethylphenidate, page 390*

GHB (GAMMA HYDROXYBUTYRATE or SODIUM OXYBATE)
BRAND NAME: Xyrem
COMMON STREET NAMES: Bodily harm, cherry meth, fantasy, Georgia home boy, grievous bodily harm, liquid ecstasy, liquid E, liquid X, organic quaalude, salty water, scoop, sleep-500, somatomaz, vita-G
DEA CLASS: GHB is Class I; Xyrem is Class III for medical use.
PHARMACOLOGIC CLASS: CNS depressant

Description: GHB is produced naturally in small amounts by the body, but its function is unclear. The drug is used in Europe as a supplemental agent during anesthesia. It is also marketed as a drug that promotes muscle growth. In 2002, the FDA approved GHB to help reduce the number of cataplexy attacks (a condition marked by weak or paralyzed muscles) in patients with narcolepsy, but only under strict distribution control. When produced in clandestine laboratories, its effects are unpredictable. Drug abusers use GHB to reduce the stimulant effects of cocaine, methamphetamine, ephedrine, LSD, and mescaline, as well as to prevent the withdrawal symptoms of these agents. According to government reports, GHB has surpassed Rohypnol as the most common substance used in drug-facilitated sexual assaults. GBL (gamma butyrolactone), an analog of GHB, is also abused.

Method of use: Ingested

Duration of action: GHB is extremely short-acting and quickly leaves the user's system.

Psychological effects of abuse: Agitation, amnesia, confusion, delusion, depression, hallucinations, paranoia, and psychosis.

Physical effects of abuse: GHB is highly addictive, particularly with prolonged use. Early physical effects may include breathing problems, dizziness, excessive sweating, headache, loss of muscle tone, lowered blood pressure, nausea, reduced inhibition, sleepiness, sleepwalking, slowed heart rate and respiration, vertigo, and vomiting. Higher doses may cause complete loss of muscle coordination, decreased level of consciousness, slurred speech, seizures, coma, and death. Mixing GHB with alcohol greatly increases the CNS depressant effects, including respiratory arrest, unconsciousness, and coma.

Overdose symptoms: GHB is frequently combined with alcohol, which increases the risk of severe overdose. Symptoms depend on the amount ingested, whether any other CNS depressants were taken concurrently, and whether the drug was taken with or without food. Signs of overdose may include confusion, agitation, increased combativeness, excessive sweating, headache, impaired coordination, irregular gait, vomiting, blurred vision, memory loss, shortness of breath, respiratory depression, hallucinations, lowered body temperature, slow heart rate, seizures, and death.

Withdrawal symptoms: Abruptly stopping use may cause anxiety, agitation, insomnia, tremors, abnormally fast heart rate, and delirium within 1 to 6 hours after the last dose was taken, and the symptoms can last for months afterward.

GLUTETHIMIDE
COMMON STREET NAMES: Doors; when combined with codeine: doors & fours, loads, pancakes and syrup
DEA CLASS: Class II
PHARMACOLOGIC CLASS: Sedative, hypnotic

Description: Glutethimide has properties similar to those of barbiturates. It was used previously for the short-term treatment of insomnia, but safer and more effective products have now replaced it. Currently, there is little medical use of the drug in the U.S.

Method of use: Ingested

Duration of action: Sedation occurs 15 to 30 minutes following ingestion, with peak serum levels occurring 1 to 6 hours later.

Psychological effects of abuse: Confusion, false sense of well-being, and impaired perception. Psychological dependence may occur with prolonged use of high doses.

Physical effects of abuse: Anxiety, difficulty swallowing, excessive sleepiness, low blood pressure, loss of coordination, sexual dysfunction, and slowed heart rate and breathing. Excessive use leads to tolerance, physical dependence, and withdrawal symptoms similar to those of the barbiturates.

Overdose symptoms: Tolerance develops rapidly, and progressively higher doses are needed to obtain the same effects as before. Signs of overdose may include extreme tiredness, irregular gait, muscle rigidity, muscular hyperactivity, rapid heart rate, low blood pressure, respiratory failure, heart failure, seizures, and possibly coma.

Withdrawal symptoms: Severity of withdrawal symptoms are similar to those of barbiturates, including weakness, abdominal cramps, nausea, vomiting, disorientation, anxiety, restlessness, elevated body temperature, rapid heart rate, stupor, delirium, visual hallucinations, tremors, seizures, and possibly death.

Halcion *see Triazolam, page 451*

Halotestin *see Fluoxymesterone, page 402*

HYDROCODONE COMBINATION PRODUCTS

GENERIC NAMES: Hydrocodone with acetaminophen (Anexsia, Lorcet, Lortab, Maxidone, Norco, Vicodin, Zydone); hydrocodone with chlorpheniramine (Tussionex); hydrocodone with guaifenesin (Vicodin Tuss); hydrocodone with ibuprofen (Vicoprofen); and hydrocodone with chlorpheniramine and phenylephrine (Hycomine)

COMMON STREET NAMES: Hillbilly heroin, killers, percs, poor man's heroin, schoolboy

DEA CLASS: Class III for combination products; Class II for hydrocodone

PHARMACOLOGIC CLASS: Narcotic analgesic (hydrocodone as a single agent); combination products are classified as cough suppressant, decongestant, expectorant, or antihistamine.

Description: Hydrocodone is used to manage mild to moderate pain and as a cough suppressant.

Method of use: Ingested

Duration of action: Depends on the dose and drug(s) used. In general, when hydrocodone is combined with other analgesics, the painkilling effects may last for up to 8 hours following ingestion.

Psychological effects of abuse: Anxiety, confusion, false sense of well-being, inability to concentrate, mood changes, psychological dependence (after prolonged use). The psychological dependence associated with narcotic addiction is complex. Long after physical dependence has ended, the addict may continue to think and talk about the drug and feel unable to manage daily activities without it.

Physical effects of abuse: Constipation, dizziness, irregular breathing, light-headedness, nausea, respiratory depression, urinary retention, and vomiting. Physical tolerance develops rapidly and is marked by euphoria, sedation, shorter duration of action, and weaker painkilling effects.

Overdose symptoms: Chronic use leads to tolerance, and progressively higher doses are needed to obtain the same effects as before. Signs of overdose may include bluish skin, cold and clammy skin, excessive perspiration, limp muscles, low blood pressure, slow heartbeat, breathing problems, and extreme sleepiness that could progress to a state of nonresponsiveness or coma. Risk of overdose increases significantly when the drug is taken with alcohol.

Withdrawal symptoms: Although the symptoms are similar to those of morphine withdrawal, they are considerably less intense. Abruptly stopping use may cause excessive tearing, yawning, and sweating about 12 to 14 hours after the last dose. Additional symptoms may include diminished appetite, gooseflesh, irritability, confusion, irregular breathing, tremors, seizures and loss of consciousness.

HYDROMORPHONE
BRAND NAMES: Dilaudid, Dilaudid-HP
COMMON STREET NAMES: D, dillies, dust, juice, smack
DEA CLASS: Class II
PHARMACOLOGIC CLASS: Narcotic analgesic, cough suppressant

Description: Hydromorphone is used to help manage moderate to severe pain. In lower doses, it's used as a cough suppressant. Compared with morphine, hydromorphone is two to eight times more potent, has a shorter duration of action, and produces more sedation.

Method of use: Ingested, used rectally, and injected IM, IV, or SC. Narcotic addicts often dissolve the tablets and inject the solution as a substitute for heroin.

Duration of action: About 4 to 5 hours

Psychological effects of abuse: Confusion, depression, hallucination, moodiness, nervousness, psychological dependence (after prolonged use), restlessness, and paradoxical CNS stimulation. The psychological dependence associated with narcotic addiction is complex. Long after physical dependence has ended, the addict may continue to think and talk about the drug and feel unable to manage daily activities without it.

Physical effects of abuse: Constricted pupils, decreased urination, diminished appetite, dry mouth, dizziness, headache, irregular breathing, low blood pressure, light-headedness, nausea, paradoxical CNS stimulation, rash, respiratory depression, seizures, severe constipation, stomach cramps, tiredness, and vomiting. Physical dependence may develop after prolonged use.

Overdose symptoms: Although tolerance develops slowly, the risk of overdose eventually increases as progressively larger doses are needed to obtain the same effects as before. Symptoms of overdose may include severe drowsiness, clammy skin, confusion, constricted pupils, low blood pressure, interrupted breathing, slow pulse, tremors, respiratory depression, convulsions, and coma. Risk of overdose increases significantly when the drug is taken with alcohol.

Withdrawal symptoms: Withdrawal begins slowly, with peak effects occurring 5 days after the last dose; however, sleep disturbances can persist for 13 days afterward. Although withdrawal is painful physically and emotionally, it's rarely life-threatening if adequate hydration and nutritional support are maintained. Early symptoms may include irritability, insomnia, diminished appetite, severe yawning, severe sneezing, tearing, and cold-like symptoms. Later-stage symptoms include nausea, vomiting, diarrhea, abdominal cramps, paradoxical excitability, bone and muscle pain in the back and extremities, fever, chills, excessive sweating, depression, and elevated heart rate and blood pressure.

Infumorph *see Morphine, page 423*

Intensol *see Oxycodone, page 430*

Ionamin *see Phentermine, page 440*

Kadian *see Morphine, page 423*

KETAMINE
BRAND NAME: Ketalar
COMMON STREET NAMES: Cat Valiums, jet, K, K-hole, keets, Lady K, new ecstasy, Special K, super C, vitamin K
DEA CLASS: Class III
PHARMACOLOGIC CLASS: General anesthetic; also identified as a dissociative anesthetic

Description: Ketamine's chemical structure and pharmacologic action are similar to those of phencyclidine (PCP), but it is significantly less potent. The drug's delusional effects are similar to LSD and mescaline. Ketamine produces "dissociative anesthesia," characterized by pain relief and amnesia without causing loss of consciousness. Legally, it is used to induce and maintain general anesthesia, especially when a cardiovascular depression needs to be prevented. Due to its disassociative effects and the fact that it is tasteless and odorless, ketamine is reportedly used as a date-rape drug.

Method of use: Ingested, snorted, used rectally, smoked, and rarely, injected IM or IV

Duration of action: About 2 to 4 hours following the standard dose. Effects of chronic use may take anywhere from several months to 2 years to wear off completely.

Psychological effects of abuse: Visual hallucinations, out-of-body experience, confusion, anxiety, depression, delirium, long-term memory loss, amnesia, aggressive or violent behavior, and vivid dreams. Long-term use may cause tolerance and psychological dependence.

Physical effects of abuse: Ketamine's physical effects are similar to PCP, and it has the same visual effects as LSD. The drug causes impaired motor function, exaggerated sense of strength, elevated blood pressure, rapid heart rate, tremors, slurred speech, nausea, vomiting, loss of appetite, rapid eye movement, and respiratory depression. Rarely, seizures and respiratory arrest may occur.

Overdose symptoms: Disorientation, irrational behavior, hallucinations, rapid heart rate, elevated blood pressure, convulsions, muscle rigidity, respiratory depression, and coma. Death is rare following ketamine abuse or overdose, but 1 gram may cause death.

Withdrawal symptoms: None are reported, since no evidence of physical dependence can be detected when the drug is abruptly withdrawn.

Klonopin *see Clonazepam, page 388*

Levo-Dromoran *see Levorphanol, page 409*

LEVORPHANOL TARTRATE
BRAND NAME: Levo-Dromoran
COMMON STREET NAMES: Dreamer, M, Miss Emma, morph
DEA CLASS: Class II
PHARMACOLOGIC CLASS: Narcotic analgesic

Description: Levorphanol is a potent synthetic opioid that is classified as a morphine derivative. It is used to help manage moderate to severe pain, as a sedative prior to surgery, and as a supplemental agent to nitrous oxide/oxygen anesthesia.

Method of use: Ingested, snorted, and injected IV, IM, or SC

Duration of action: Depends on the dose. Effects generally last 4 to 8 hours but can persist significantly longer in chronic users.

Psychological effects of abuse: Confusion, depression, hallucinations, mood changes, psychological dependence (after prolonged use), and restlessness. The psychological dependence associated with narcotic addiction is complex. Long after physical dependence has ended, the addict may continue to think and talk about the drug and feel unable to manage daily activities without it.

Physical effects of abuse: Blurred vision, constipation, dizziness, excessive sleepiness, low blood pressure, nausea, respiratory depression, slow pulse, and vomiting.

Overdose symptoms: Signs of overdose may include anxiety, cold and clammy skin, confusion, weakness, severe drowsiness and dizziness, constricted pupils, low blood pressure, slow heart rate, CNS and cardiac depression, convulsions, respiratory depression, and unconsciousness.

Withdrawal symptoms: Abruptly stopping the drug after long-term use may precipitate withdrawal symptoms. The intensity and duration of symptoms are directly related to the total daily dose, frequency of use, and health of the user. Although withdrawal from narcotics is painful physically and emotionally, it is rarely life-threatening if adequate hydration and nutritional support are maintained. Early withdrawal symptoms may include watery eyes, runny nose, repeated yawning, and excessive sweating. Later-stage symptoms may include nervousness, muscle twitching, drug cravings, restlessness, irritability, loss of appetite, chills alternating with flushing, nausea, vomiting, bone and muscle pain in the back and extremities, tremors, elevated heart rate and blood pressure, and severe depression.

Librium *see Chlordiazepoxide, page 387*

LORAZEPAM
BRAND NAME: Ativan
COMMON STREET NAMES: Candy, downers, sleeping pills, tranks
DEA CLASS: Class IV
PHARMACOLOGIC CLASS: Benzodiazepine, sedative, antianxiety, antiemetic, anticonvulsant

Description: Lorazepam is used to treat anxiety disorders, including anxiety associated with depression. In addition, it is used intravenously to treat severe epileptic seizures, as a sedative to induce relaxation before anesthesia, and as a supplemental therapy to prevent vomiting. Abuse of benzodiazepines is particularly high among heroin and cocaine users.

Method of use: Ingested and injected IM or IV

Duration of action: 8 to 25 hours

Psychological effects of abuse: Confusion, impaired judgment and thinking abilities, irritability, mild euphoria, pressured speech, reduced inhibition, and suicidal ideation. Long-term use may cause psychological dependence.

Physical effects of abuse: Changes in appetite and body weight, constipation, dizziness, impaired muscle coordination, labored breathing, and low blood pressure. Long-term use may cause physical dependence.

Overdose symptoms: The most severe signs of overdose are respiratory depression and coma. Other symptoms may include confusion, diminished reflexes, unrealistic euphoria, extreme sleepiness, and impaired muscle coordination. Death from overdose of a single benzodiazepine is extremely rare. However, there is an increased risk of toxicity when benzodiazepines are combined with alcohol and/or other CNS depressants. Fatalities have been reported in patients who have overdosed with a combination of a single benzodiazepine and alcohol.

Withdrawal symptoms: Abrupt termination following long-term use may precipitate withdrawal symptoms and require hospitalization. Symptoms may include abdominal and muscle cramps, depression, insomnia, sweating, vomiting, tremors, and seizures.

Lorcet *see Hydrocodone, page 406*

Lortab *see Hydrocodone, page 406*

Luminal *see Phenobarbital, page 439*

Margesic *see Hydrocodone, page 406*

Marinol *see Dronabinol, page 394*

Maxidone *see Hydrocodone, page 406*

Mebaral *see Mephobarbital, page 412*

Mepergan *see Meperidine, page 411*

MEPERIDINE HYDROCHLORIDE
BRAND NAMES: Demerol, Meperitab, Mepergan
COMMON STREET NAMES: D, dillies, dust, juice, smack
DEA CLASS: Class II
PHARMACOLOGIC CLASS: Narcotic analgesic

Description: Meperidine is used as a sedative before surgery, as a supplemental agent to induce anesthesia, and to help manage moderate to severe pain. Although it has effects similar to morphine, meperidine has a shorter duration of action and weaker cough suppressing and antidiarrheal activities.

Method of use: Ingested and injected IM, IV, or SC

Duration of action: Depends on the dose and method of use. In general, effects persist 2 to 4 hours following administration.

Psychological effects of abuse: Confusion, depression, and hallucinations. The psychological dependence associated with narcotic addiction is complex. Long after physical dependence has ended, the addict may continue to think and talk about the drug and feel unable to manage daily activities without it. Psychological addiction is a major problem with meperidine, particularly when used in higher doses for prolonged periods.

Physical effects of abuse: Low blood pressure, drowsiness, dizziness, headache, light-headedness, feeling faint, restlessness, fatigue, seizures, nausea, constipation, vomiting, diminished appetite, dry mouth, abdominal cramps, stomach cramps, urine retention, and shortness of breath. Higher doses and long-term use is associated with paradoxical CNS excitement, tremors, and seizures due to the accumulation of the active metabolite normeperidine. Meperidine use has also been associated with symptoms that resemble Parkinson's disease, including jerky movements and tremors. Physical tolerance and addiction can develop, particularly when used in higher doses for prolonged periods.

Overdose symptoms: Chronic use leads to tolerance, and progressively larger doses are needed to obtain the same effects as before. Symptoms of overdose may include severe drowsiness, constricted pupils, clammy skin, confusion, slow pulse, slow or labored breathing, CNS depression, tremors, and seizures. Risk of overdose increases significantly when the drug is taken with alcohol.

Withdrawal symptoms: The intensity of symptoms is directly related to the total daily dose, frequency and duration of use, and the health of the user. Withdrawal symptoms may persist for up to 5 days after the last dose. Although withdrawal from narcotics is painful physically and emotionally, it is rarely life-threatening. Early symptoms appear within 3 hours after the last dose and may include watery eyes, runny nose, yawning, and sweating. Later-stage symptoms may include nervousness, muscle twitching, drug cravings, restlessness, irritability, loss of appetite, chills alternating with flushing, excessive sweating, nausea, vomiting, bone and muscle pain in the back and extremities, tremors, rapid heart rate, elevated blood pressure, and severe depression.

Meperitab *see Meperidine, page 411*

MEPHOBARBITAL
BRAND NAME: Mebaral
COMMON STREET NAME: Downers
DEA CLASS: Class IV
PHARMACOLOGIC CLASS: Barbiturate, sedative, anticonvulsant

Description: Barbiturates depress the sensory cortex, decrease motor activity, alter brain function, and produce drowsiness, sedation, and hypnosis. Mephobarbital is used primarily for daytime sedation and the management of seizure disorders.

Method of use: Ingested

Duration of action: Effects start within an hour and last for about 12 hours.

Psychological effects of abuse: Barbiturates may cause psychological dependence, especially following prolonged use of high doses. Effects may include confusion, alternating euphoria and depression, memory loss, impaired judgment, nervousness, nightmares, and hallucinations.

Physical effects of abuse: The most frequent physical effects are due to CNS depression, including dizziness, headache, excessive sleepiness, drowsiness, and irregular gait. Other symptoms may include headache, stomach pain, and skin rash. Paradoxical excitement and irritability may also occur. In chronic users, blood disorders such as megaloblastic anemia may develop. Short-term therapy has been associated with the development of Stevens-Johnson syndrome and toxic skin eruptions. Rarely, necrotic ulcer of the mouth may occur within 10 days of ingestion. Physical dependence is a significant risk, since it can develop after short-term use.

Overdose symptoms: Unsteady gait, slurred speech, confusion, low body temperature and blood pressure, and dose-dependent respiratory depression. Toxic effects are enhanced when the drug is taken with alcohol and/or other CNS depressants.

Withdrawal symptoms: Symptoms are similar to those of alcohol withdrawal and characterized by severe apprehension, weakness, heightened anxiety, irritability, dizziness, headache, sleeplessness, muscle twitching, nausea and vomiting, distortion of visual perception, and rapid pulse. Severely low blood pressure and convulsions may develop after a day or two, which eventually leads to hallucinations and delirium followed by coma and death.

MEPROBAMATE and CARISOPRODOL
BRAND NAMES: Miltown (meprobamate), Soma (carisoprodol)
COMMON STREET NAMES: Not known
DEA CLASS: Class IV (meprobamate only)
PHARMACOLOGIC CLASS: Antianxiety agent (meprobamate); muscle relaxant (carisoprodol)

Description: Meprobamate is used to treat anxiety, tension, and muscle spasms associated with tension. Carisoprodol is a muscle relaxant that the body metabolically converts to meprobamate, which probably accounts for some of the drug's pharmacologic properties as well as its tendency to be abused.

Method of use: Ingested

Duration of action: Onset and duration of action of meprobamate are similar to those of the intermediate-acting barbiturates. Its effects peak 2 hours following ingestion and persist for about 10 hours.

Psychological effects of abuse: Confusion, euphoria, and impaired mental abilities. Psychological dependence may develop after prolonged use.

Physical effects of abuse: Chills, diarrhea, drowsiness, elevated heart rate, feeling faint, headache, impaired physical abilities, loss of appetite, nausea, numbness in the extremities, slurred speech, stomach pain, vertigo, and vomiting. Tolerance and physical dependence may develop after excessive use.

Overdose symptoms: Overdose can cause death due to respiratory failure and/or severely low blood pressure. Other signs of overdose may include drowsiness, irregular gait, tiredness, weakness, nausea, vomiting, blurred vision, low blood pressure, shock, and coma.

Withdrawal symptoms: Abruptly stopping use may cause confusion, memory loss, excessive sweating, nervousness, elevated blood pressure, hallucinations, and psychosis.

Metadate *see Methylphenidate, page 418.*

METHADONE

BRAND NAMES: Dolophine, Methadone Intensol, Methadose
COMMON STREET NAMES: D, dillies, dolls, done, dust, frizzies, juice, smack
DEA CLASS: Class II
PHARMACOLOGIC CLASS: Narcotic nalgesic

Description: Although methadone's chemical structure is different from morphine and heroin, its pharmacologic effects are the same. It's used for detoxification and maintenance treatment of narcotic addiction and to help manage severe pain. High-dose methadone is useful for treating heroin addicts because it can block the drug's effects.

Method of use: Ingested and injected IM, IV, or SC

Duration of action: About 6 to 8 hours, although effects can last 24 to 48 hours in chronic users.

Psychological effects of abuse: Agitation, change in sexual desires, confusion, depression, disorientation, euphoria, and psychological depedence (after prolonged use). The psychological dependence associated with narcotic addiction is complex. Long after physical dependence has ended, the addict may continue to think and talk about the drug and feel unable to manage daily activities without it.

Physical effects of abuse: Blurred vision, CNS and respiratory depression, constricted pupils, constipation, diminished appetite, dizziness, drowsiness, faintness, headache, insomnia, light-headedness, loss of appetite, low blood pressure, nausea, seizures, slow heartbeat, slow or troubled breathing, stomach cramps, tremors, and vomiting. Chronic use results in tolerance and physical dependence.

Overdose symptoms: Chronic use leads to tolerance, and progressively higher doses are needed to obtain the same effects as before. Signs of overdose include low body temperature, constricted pupils, cold and clammy skin, confusion, severe drowsiness, slow or troubled breathing, CNS and respiratory depression, slow heartbeat, tremors, and seizures.

Withdrawal symptoms: Abruptly stopping the drug after chronic use may precipitate withdrawal symptoms. Although withdrawal from narcotics is painful physically and emotionally, it is rarely life-threatening if adequate hydration and nutritional support are maintained. Methadone withdrawal starts 24 hours after the last dose and can persist for several weeks. The intensity of symptoms is directly related to the total daily dose, frequency and duration of use, and the health of the user.

Early withdrawal symptoms may include watery eyes, runny nose, repeated yawning, and excessive sweating. Later-stage symptoms include restlessness, irritability, loss of appetite, nausea, vomiting, diarrhea, tremors, severe depression, shivering, and drug cravings. Advanced withdrawal symptoms may include elevated heart rate and blood pressure, chills alternating with flushing, and bone and muscle pain in the back and extremities.

Methadone Intensol *see Methadone, page 414*

Methadose *see Methadone, page 414*

METHAMPHETAMINE HYDROCHLORIDE
BRAND NAME: Desoxyn
COMMON STREET NAMES: Chalk, crank, crystal, fire, glass, go fast, ice, meth, speed
DEA CLASS: Class II
PHARMACOLOGIC CLASS: Amphetamine, CNS stimulant

Description: Amphetamine, methamphetamine, and dextroamphetamine are collectively referred to as amphetamines; they have similar chemical properties and pharmacologic actions. Methamphetamine is used as a supplemental agent for treating attention deficit hyperactivity disorder

(ADHD). It is also used as a short-term aid for weight loss when combined with caloric restriction, exercise, and behavior modification.

Method of use: Ingested, snorted, smoked (most common use), and injected IV

Duration of action: 8 to 24 hours

Psychological effects of abuse: Anxiety, heightened energy, increased alertness, irritability, restlessness, and talkativeness. Large doses can cause confusion, delusion, rage, violence, visual and auditory hallucinations, delirium, self-destructive behavior, aggressiveness, and panic. Chronic use leads to psychotic behavior, including paranoia, hallucinations, and psychotic rages that may result in violence. Psychological dependence develops rapidly in chronic users.

Physical effects of abuse: Amphetamines are known to increase energy and decrease appetite. Other physical symptoms may include diarrhea, dilated pupils, elevated body temperature, excessive sweating, headache, insomnia, muscle rigidity, rapid heartbeat, rapid breathing, stomach cramps, tremors, and vomiting. Chronic abuse may lead to permanent brain damage. There are characteristic sores on the bodies of chronic users from scratching at "bugs" (the delusional belief that bugs are crawling under the skin). Acute lead poisoning may also develop due to the method of production of methamphetamines that uses lead acetate as a reagent.

Overdose symptoms: Tolerance to the anorectic effect of methamphetamine usually develops within a few weeks. Individuals may need progressively larger doses to obtain the same effects as before. Symptoms of overdose may include nausea, vomiting, diarrhea, restlessness, severe high blood pressure, dangerously high body temperature, tremors, hyperactivity, rapid and irregular heartbeat, rapid breathing, muscle rigidity, severe psychosis, serotonin syndrome, seizures, and coma. High doses may cause stroke. Fatality rates increase significantly if high blood pressure and seizures occur.

Withdrawal symptoms: Methamphetamine is a powerfully addictive drug, and physical and psychological dependence develop rapidly. Abrupt cessation of use may cause anxiety, fatigue, paranoia, aggressive behavior, and strong drug cravings. Severe depression and suicidal ideation have also been reported. Psychotic behavior may persist for months or years after discontinuation of use.

METHENOLONE
BRAND NAME: Primobolan
COMMON STREET NAMES: Arnolds, gym candy, juice, pumpers, roids, stackers, weight trainers
DEA CLASS: Class III
PHARMACOLOGIC CLASS: Anabolic-androgenic steroid

Description: Androgens are steroid hormones that develop and maintain male sex characteristics. They are used primarily to replace insufficient levels of testosterone due to poor functioning of the testes. When used in combination with exercise and a high-protein diet, androgens can promote increased muscle size and strength, improve stamina, and decrease recovery time between workouts. Androgens are also used to promote the development of puberty in males with clearly delayed onset. Additionally, androgens are sometimes prescribed for women with advancing, inoperable metastatic breast cancer who are 1 to 5 years postmenopausal. Methenolone has also been effective in the management of aplastic anemia.

Method of use: Ingested and injected IM

Duration of action: Not entirely known but is believed to remain in the body for at least a week.

Psychological effects of abuse: Mood changes, depression, uncontrollable aggressive behavior, euphoria, anxiety, irritability, increased sex drive, and rarely, psychosis. Psychological dependence may also occur.

Physical effects of abuse: Angry or hostile feelings, elevated blood pressure and cholesterol, headache, insomnia, premature balding, psychotic reactions, severe acne, sexual dysfunction, and violent behavior. *In men:* Breast development, impotence, intermittent or painful urination, painful or persistent erections, reduced sperm production, and shrinking of the testicles. *In women:* Decreased body fat and breast size, deepening of the voice, enlarged clitoris, excessive growth of body hair, and menstrual changes. *In adolescents:* Premature termination of growth.

Prolonged use can lead to tolerance. While the long-term effects are not completely known, chronic steroid abuse has been associated with damage to the heart, liver, and brain.

Overdose symptoms: There have been no reports of serious overdose with androgenic steroids. Chronic use of high doses may cause excessive sexual stimulation, reduced sperm production, enlarged breasts in males, uncontrollable painful erection, jaundice, and deteriorating liver function. Excessive fluid retention may occur in users who have heart, liver, or kidney disease.

Withdrawal symptoms: Abrupt discontinuation may cause mood changes, tiredness, restlessness, loss of appetite, dissatisfaction with body image, sleeplessness, reduced sex drive, paranoia, and severe depression that can lead to suicide attempts.

Methitest *see Methyltestosterone, page 419*

Methylin *see Methylphenidate, page 418*

METHYLPHENIDATE HYDROCHLORIDE
BRAND NAMES: Concerta, Metadate, Methylin, Ritalin
COMMON STREET NAMES: R-ball, Rit, vitamin R, working man's cocaine
DEA CLASS: Class II
PHARMACOLOGIC CLASS: CNS stimulant, nonamphetamine

Description: Methylphenidate is used to treat attention deficit hyperactivity disorder (ADHD). In addition, it is the preferred drug for treating excessive daytime sleepiness (narcolepsy) due to its rapid action and fewer side effects than other CNS stimulants. Severe complications can occur when methylphenidate tablets are crushed and diluted in water for injection. The tablets contain soluble fibers that can block small blood vessels, causing serious damage to the lungs and eye retina.

Method of use: Ingested; tablets are also crushed and snorted or diluted in water and injected.

Duration of action: 4 to 5 hours following a standard therapeutic dose.

Psychological effects of abuse: Depression, nervousness, and psychotic behavior.

Physical effects of abuse: Anorexia, blurred vision, dizziness, elevated blood pressure, elevated or lowered pulse, headache, high body temperature, insomnia, irregular heart rhythm, nausea, stomach pain, Tourette's syndrome, toxic psychosis, vomiting, and weight loss. Severe blockage in the blood vessels of the lungs and eye retina can occur when the drug is injected.

Overdose symptoms: Signs of overdose include excessive sweating and hyperactivity, vomiting, agitation, tremors, severely elevated body temperature and blood pressure, rapid heart rate, and hallucinations.

Withdrawal symptoms: Withdrawal reactions are less common than with other CNS stimulants. Symptoms may include severe fatigue, depression, nausea, vomiting, stomach cramps, insomnia, and nightmares.

METHYLTESTOSTERONE

BRAND NAMES: Android, Methitest, Oreton, Testred, Virilon
COMMON STREET NAMES: Arnolds, gym candy, juice, pumpers, roids, stackers, weight trainers
DEA CLASS: Class III
PHARMACOLOGIC CLASS: Anabolic-androgenic steroid

Description: Androgens are steroid hormones that develop and maintain male sex characteristics. They are used primarily to replace insufficient levels of testosterone due to poor functioning of the testes. When used in combination with exercise and a high-protein diet, androgens can promote increased muscle size and strength, improve stamina, and decrease recovery time between workouts. Androgens are also used to promote the development of puberty in males with clearly delayed onset. Additionally, androgens are sometimes prescribed for women with advancing, inoperable metastatic breast cancer who are 1 to 5 years post-menopausal.

Method of use: Ingested and absorbed through the cheek and gum (buccal administration). Chronic users tend to rotate steroids using various methods known as cycling, stacking, and pyramiding. Sporadic discontinuation of use is believed to allow testosterone levels and sperm counts to return to normal. Taking steroids regularly with periodic "drug-free times" is called cycling. Stacking refers to the concomitant use of two or more steroids at high doses. Pyramiding is when the dose, frequency, or number of steroids taken is gradually increased, followed by progressive tapering of the drug(s).

Duration of action: Depends on the dose and method of use. Methyltestosterone remains active for up to 22 hours following use.

Psychological effects of abuse: Mood changes, depression, uncontrollable aggressive behavior, euphoria, anxiety, irritability, increased sex drive, and rarely, psychosis. Psychological dependence may occur.

Physical effects of abuse: Angry or hostile feelings, elevated blood pressure and cholesterol, headache, insomnia, premature balding, psychotic reactions, severe acne, sexual dysfunction, and violent behavior. *In men:* Breast development, impotence, intermittent or painful urination, painful or persistent erections, reduced sperm production, and shrinking of the testicles. *In women:* Decreased body fat and breast size, deepening of the voice, enlarged clitoris, excessive growth of body hair, and menstrual changes. *In adolescents:* Premature termination of growth.

Prolonged use can lead to tolerance. While the long-term effects are not completely known, chronic steroid abuse has been associated with damage to the heart, liver, and brain.

Overdose symptoms: There are no documented reports of overdose with androgens. Chronic use of high doses may cause excessive sexual stimulation, reduced sperm production, enlarged breasts in males, uncontrollable painful erection, jaundice, and deteriorating liver function. Excessive fluid retention may occur in users who have heart, liver, or kidney disease.

Withdrawal symptoms: Abrupt discontinuation may cause mood changes, tiredness, restlessness, loss of appetite, dissatisfaction with body image, sleeplessness, reduced sex drive, paranoia, and severe depression that can lead to suicide attempts.

METHYPRYLON
BRAND NAME: Noludar
COMMON STREET NAMES: Not known
DEA CLASS: Class III
PHARMACOLOGIC CLASS: Sedative, hypnotic (nonbarbiturate)

Description: Methyprylon is chemically related to glutethimide and causes CNS depression similar to barbiturates. The drug is marketed in other countries for the short-term treatment of insomnia. Methyprylon was withdrawn from the U.S. market after safer and more effective agents became available.

Method of use: Ingested, used rectally

Duration of action: Usually 5 to 8 hours following a standard therapeutic dose.

Psychological effects of abuse: Confusion, depression, paradoxical excitement, hallucinations, nightmares, and restlessness. Prolonged use may lead to psychological dependence.

Physical effects of abuse: Blurred or double vision, dizziness, drowsiness, fever, headache, insomnia, irregular gait, nausea, vomiting, diarrhea, constipation, stomach cramps, trembling, and weakness. Prolonged use may cause liver damage and/or soft bones or rickets. Respiratory depression, seizures, and coma have also been reported. Prolonged use may lead to tolerance and physical dependence.

Overdose symptoms: Complications with sedative overdose—such as pneumonia, fluid accumulation in the lungs, heart arrhythmias, and heart or kidney failure—may occur in rare cases. Life-threatening signs of overdose include severe confusion, dilated pupils, rapid heartbeat, excessive CNS and respiratory depression, severe drowsiness, loss of reflexes, coma, respiratory arrest, and death. Additional symptoms may include constricted pupils, slurred speech, irregular gait, weakness, and low body temperature.

Withdrawal symptoms: Abrupt cessation of use may cause severe confusion, nightmares, restlessness, paradoxical excitement, sleeplessness, excessive sweating, hallucinations, and seizures. Death has also been reported in individuals not receiving medical treatment during withdrawal.

MIDAZOLAM HYDROCHLORIDE
BRAND NAME: Versed
COMMON STREET NAMES: Candy, downers, sleeping pills, tranks
DEA CLASS: Class IV
PHARMACOLOGIC CLASS: Benzodiazepine, sedative, hypnotic

Description: Midazolam is used to produce drowsiness and relieve anxiety before surgery or diagnostic procedures. It is also used to induce loss of consciousness and amnesia in patients having surgery or those in critical-care settings. It is three to four times more potent than Valium. Abuse of benzodiazepines is particularly high among heroin and cocaine users.

Method of use: Ingested, snorted, and injected IM or IV

Duration of action: Up to 6 hours

Psychological effects of abuse: Amnesia, confusion, depression, impaired judgment and thinking abilities, reduced inhibition, and suicidal ideation. Paradoxical effects include euphoria, hyperactivity, and extreme aggression. Prolonged use may cause psychological dependence.

Physical effects of abuse: Constipation, decreased blood pressure, dizziness, drowsiness, impaired physical capabilities, irregular gait, loss of muscle tone, sleepiness, slowed psychomotor performance, urinary retention, and visual disturbances. Prolonged use may cause physical dependence.

Overdose symptoms: The most severe signs of overdose are respiratory depression, loss of consciousness, and coma. Other symptoms may include confusion, depression, diminished reflexes, slurred speech, impaired coordination, apnea, extreme sleepiness, loss of muscle tone, and severely low blood pressure. Death from overdose of a single benzodiazepine is extremely rare. However, there is an increased risk of toxicity when benzodiazepines are combined with alcohol and/or other CNS depressants. Fatalities have been reported in patients who have overdosed with a combination of a single benzodiazepine and alcohol.

Withdrawal symptoms: Abrupt termination following long-term use may precipitate withdrawal symptoms and require hospitalization. Symptoms may include abdominal and muscle cramps, depression, insomnia, sweating, vomiting, tremors, and seizures.

Miltown *see Meprobamate, page 413*

MODAFINIL
BRAND NAME: Provigil
COMMON STREET NAMES: Not known
DEA CLASS: Class IV
PHARMACOLOGIC CLASS: CNS stimulant, nonamphetamine

Description: Modafinil is used to improve wakefulness in those with excessive daytime sleepiness (narcolepsy). It is also used to treat obstructive sleep apnea/hypopnea syndrome and shift work sleep disorder. The drug is chemically and pharmacologically unrelated to other CNS stimulants such as methylphenidate or amphetamines.

Method of use: Ingested

Duration of action: About 10 to 12 hours

Psychological effects of abuse: Psychoactive and euphoric effects, as well as alterations of mood and perception, are the most common psychological effects of modafinil. Other effects may include anxiety, depression, confusion, paranoid delusions, auditory hallucinations, and amnesia. Eye problems such as floaters and dryness have also been reported.

Physical effects of abuse: High or low blood pressure, irregular heartbeats, headache, nervousness, dizziness, sleeplessness, irregular gait, nausea, diarrhea, vomiting, dry mouth, reduced appetite, ejaculatory difficulties, urinary difficulties, neck pain, tremor, abnormal involuntary movements, tingling sensation, abnormal vision, increased liver enzymes, shortness of breath, and nasal congestion.

Overdose symptoms: Overdose information is limited. The following have been reported with high doses: agitation, irritability, confusion, nervousness, tremor, sleeplessness, and heart palpitations.

Withdrawal symptoms: To date, physical dependence on this drug has not been reported. However, experience with modafinil is limited, and the potential for dependence still exists.

Mogadon *see Nitrazepam, page 425*

MORPHINE SULFATE

BRAND NAMES: Astramorph PF, Avinza, Duramorph PF, Infumorph, Kadian, MS Contin, MSIR, Oramorph SR, RMS, Roxanol
COMMON STREET NAMES: Dreamer, M, Miss Emma, morph
DEA CLASS: Class II
PHARMACOLOGIC CLASS: Narcotic analgesic

Description: Morphine is the principal constituent of opium. It is used as a sedative prior to surgery, as a supplemental agent to induce anesthesia, and to manage moderate to severe pain. Morphine can also be used to relieve pain associated with heart attack and to relieve anxiety in patients who have shortness of breath due to pulmonary edema or acute heart failure.

Method of use: Ingested, used rectally, and injected IM, IV, or SC

Duration of action: Depends on the dose and method of use. In general, the effects last 3 to 6 hours following administration. However, in chronic users the effects may last significantly longer.

Psychological effects of abuse: Confusion, disorientation, false sense of well-being, hallucinations, and thought disturbances. The psychological dependence associated with narcotic addiction is complex. Long after physical dependence has ended, the addict may continue to think and talk about the drug and feel unable to manage daily activities without it. Psychological dependence on morphine is known to develop slowly.

Physical effects of abuse: Blurred vision, CNS and respiratory depression, constipation, diminished appetite, dizziness, drowsiness, dry mouth, flushing, headache, low blood pressure and pulse, muscle rigidity, nausea, paradoxical CNS stimulation, restlessness, seizures, shortness of breath, stomach cramps, tiredness, urine retention, and vomiting. Physical dependence on morphine develops progressively.

Overdose symptoms: Although tolerance develops slowly, the risk of overdose eventually increases as progressively larger doses are needed to obtain the same effects as before. Signs of overdose may include severe drowsiness, constricted pupils, clammy skin, confusion, low blood pressure, interrupted breathing, slow pulse, tremors, respiratory depression, convulsions, and coma. Risk of overdose increases significantly when the drug is taken with alcohol.

Withdrawal symptoms: Although withdrawal from morphine is painful physically and emotionally, it's rarely life-threatening if adequate hydration and nutritional support are maintained. Symptoms begin slowly, with peak effects observed 5 days after cessation of use; however, sleep disturbances can persist up to 13 days following the last dose. Early withdrawal symptoms may include irritability, sleeplessness, diminished appetite, excessive yawning, severe sneezing, tearing, and head cold. Later-stage symptoms may include nausea, vomiting, severe diarrhea, paradoxical excitability, abdominal cramps, bone and muscle pain in the back and extremities, fever and chills, excessive sweating, and depression. Muscle spasms and kicking movements can also occur, which may explain the expression "kicking the habit."

MS Contin *see Morphine, page 423*

MSIR *see Morphine, page 423*

Mysoline *see Primidone, page 441*

NANDROLONE DECANOATE and NANDROLONE PHENPROPIONATE

COMMON STREET NAMES: Arnolds, gym candy, juice, pumpers, roids, stackers, weight trainers

DEA CLASS: Class III

PHARMACOLOGIC CLASS: Anabolic-androgenic steroid

Description: Androgens are steroid hormones that develop and maintain male sex characteristics. They are used primarily to replace insufficient levels of testosterone due to poor functioning of the testes. When used in combination with exercise and a high-protein diet, androgens can promote increased muscle size and strength, improve stamina, and decrease recovery time between workouts. Androgens are also used to promote the development of puberty in males with clearly delayed onset. Additionally, androgens are sometimes prescribed for women with advancing, inoperable metastatic breast cancer who are 1 to 5 years postmenopausal. Nandrolone has also been shown to positively influence calcium metabolism and increase bone mass in people with osteoporosis.

Method of use: Injected IM. Chronic users tend to rotate steroids using various methods known as cycling, stacking, and pyramiding. Sporadic discontinuation of use is believed to allow testosterone levels and sperm counts to return to normal. Taking steroids regularly with periodic "drug-free times" is called cycling. Stacking refers to the concomitant use of two or more steroids at high doses. Pyramiding is when the dose, frequency, or number of steroids taken is gradually increased, followed by progressive tapering of the drug(s).

Duration of action: Approximately 3 to 4 weeks.

Psychological effects of abuse: Mood changes, depression, and increased sex drive. Psychological dependence may also develop.

Physical effects of abuse: Angry or hostile feelings, elevated blood pressure and cholesterol, headache, insomnia, premature balding, psychotic reactions, severe acne, sexual dysfunction, and violent behavior. *In men:* Breast development, impotence, intermittent or painful urination, painful or persistent erections, reduced sperm production, and shrinking of the testicles. *In women:* Decreased body fat and breast size, deepening of the voice, enlarged clitoris, excessive growth of body hair, and menstrual changes. *In adolescents:* Premature termination of growth.

Prolonged use can lead to tolerance. While the long-term effects are not completely known, chronic steroid abuse has been associated with damage to the heart, liver, and brain.

Overdose symptoms: There have been no reports of serious overdose with this product. Chronic exposure to high doses may cause serious acne, excessive growth of body hair, hoarseness, changes in sex drive, poor sperm production, and menstrual problems in women.

Withdrawal symptoms: Abrupt discontinuation can cause mood changes, tiredness, restlessness, loss of appetite, dissatisfaction with body image, sleeplessness, reduced sex drive, paranoia, and severe depression that can lead to suicide attempts.

Nembutal *see Pentobarbital, page 436*

NITRAZEPAM
BRAND NAME: Mogadon
COMMON STREET NAMES: Candy, downers, sleeping pills, tranks
DEA CLASS: Class IV
PHARMACOLOGIC CLASS: Benzodiazepine, sedative, hypnotic

Description: Nitrazepam is neither approved nor manufactured in the U.S. It has similar pharmacologic properties as diazepam (Valium). Nitrazepam is used in other countries for the short-term treatment of insomnia. It has also been used in epilepsy, particularly in infants. Abuse of benzodiazepines is particularly high among heroin and cocaine users.

Method of use: Ingested and injected IM or IV

Duration of action: Up to 30 hours

Psychological effects of abuse: Amnesia, confusion, depression, euphoria, impaired judgment and thinking abilities, mild euphoria, pressured speech, reduced inhibition, and suicidal ideation. Long-term use may cause psychological dependence.

Physical effects of abuse: Constipation, decreased blood pressure, dizziness, drowsiness, impaired physical capabilities, loss of muscle tone, sleepiness, slowed psychomotor performance, urinary retention, and visual disturbances.

Overdose symptoms: The most severe signs of overdose are respiratory depression, loss of consciousness, and coma. Other symptoms may include sensitivity to light, diminished reflexes, slurred speech, impaired coordination, apnea, extreme sleepiness, loss of muscle tone, severely low blood pressure, and tremors. Death from overdose of a single benzodiazepine is extremely rare. However, there is an increased risk of toxicity when benzodiazepines are combined with alcohol and/or other CNS depressants. Fatalities have been reported in patients who have overdosed with a combination of a single benzodiazepine and alcohol.

Withdrawal symptoms: Abrupt termination following long-term use may precipitate withdrawal symptoms and require hospitalization. Symptoms may include abdominal and muscle cramps, depression, insomnia, severe drowsiness, sweating, vomiting, tremors, respiratory depression, seizures, and coma.

NITRITES (amyl nitrite and glyceryl trinitrate)
COMMON STREET NAME: Poppers
DEA CLASS: Not classified
PHARMACOLOGIC CLASS: Coronary vasodilator

Description: Nitrites are volatile liquids that are readily absorbed from the lungs. Amyl nitrite has an action similar to glyceryl trinitrate (also known as nitroglycerin). Nitrites relax and open the blood vessels to the heart and are used therapeutically to relieve acute chest pain (angina) and to help manage heart murmurs. In addition, nitrites are used as supplemental agents to counteract cyanide poisoning, although their effectiveness for this use is still in question. These drugs are often abused because users believe they expand creativity, stimulate music appreciation, promote a sense of abandon in dancing, and intensify sexual experiences.

Method of use: Inhalation

Duration of action: Therapeutic effects of short-acting products usually occur within 30 seconds and last for 3 to 5 minutes.

Psychological effects of abuse: Aggressive behavior, anxiety, restlessness, and rarely, psychosis.

Physical effects of abuse: Anemia and other blood disorders, blurred vision, coma, cough, dizziness, elevated pressure in the eye, face rash, flushing, loss of coordination, low blood pressure or pulse, nausea, paralysis of the face, throbbing headache, rapid heartbeat, shortness of breath, throat irritation, vomiting, weakness, and rarely, death. Cerebrovascular disease can occur due to severely low blood pressure. Tolerance may develop with prolonged use.

Overdose symptoms: Seizures have been reported following severe overdose. Fatalities from nitrite toxicity have occurred due to uncontrolled artery spasm (vasodilation) and/or methemoglobinemia, which causes dangerously low oxygenation of the tissues. Other signs of overdose include bluish skin color, fainting, shortness of breath, increased pressure in the eye, stomach irritation accompanied by nausea and vomiting, severe abdominal pain, muscular weakness, weakness that effects only one side of the body, psychosis, coma, and rarely, death.

Withdrawal symptoms: Sudden withdrawal may cause sharp or persistent contractions of the heart arteries (coronary vasospasm), possibly leading to reduced blood flow and heart damage.

Noctec *see Chloral hydrate, page 386*

Norco *see Hydrocodone, page 406*

Numorphan *see Oxymorphone, page 432*

OPIUM

BRAND NAMES: DTO (diluted tincture of opium), Opium Tincture (also known as deodorized tincture of opium), Papaveretum, Paregoric

COMMON STREET NAMES: Gee, God's medicine, gondola, great tobacco, gum, gumma

DEA CLASS: Class II for extracts, tinctures, and poppy; Class III for opium combination products such as Paregoric (opium with camphor).

PHARMACOLOGIC CLASS: Narcotic analgesic, antidiarrheal

Description: In the U.S., opium is used in the paregoric form to treat severe diarrhea. Rarely, it's used to relieve pain. Drug traffickers harvest opium from the poppy plant and refine the drug to make morphine or heroin.

Method of use: Ingested

Duration of action: Generally 4 to 5 hours

Psychological effects of abuse: Anxiety, confusion, depression, false sense of well-being, mood changes, psychological dependence (after prolonged use), and restlessness. The psychological dependence associated with narcotic addiction is complex. Long after physical dependence has ended, the addict may continue to think and talk about the drug and feel unable to manage daily activities without it.

Physical effects of abuse: Constipation, dizziness, headache, irregular breathing, light-headedness, loss of appetite, muscle weakness, low blood pressure, nausea, respiratory depression, sleeplessness, slowed heart rate, stomach cramps, urinary retention, and vomiting. Prolonged use may cause physical dependence.

Overdose symptoms: Chronic use leads to tolerance, and progressively higher doses are needed to obtain the same effects as before. Signs of overdose may include constipation, stomach cramps, nausea, vomiting, extreme sleepiness, nonreactive pupils, drowsiness, dizziness, slurred speech, cold and clammy skin, lowered body temperature and blood pressure, CNS and respiratory depression, convulsions, and coma. Death rarely occurs.

Withdrawal symptoms: Opiate withdrawal is considered to be fairly mild. The symptoms begin slowly, with peak effects observed after about 5 days, although sleep disturbances can persist for 13 days following abrupt cessation of use. Symptoms may include excessive yawning, nasal congestion, nausea, vomiting, diarrhea, excessive perspiration, muscle and joint pain, anxiety, fear, mildly elevated blood pressure, and rapid heartbeat. Other signs of withdrawal may include excessive tearing, restlessness, dilated pupils, involuntary twitching, abdominal pain, dehydration, and elevated blood sugar levels.

Orabolin *see Ethylestrenol, page 397*

Oramorph SR *see Morphine, page 423*

Oreton *see Methyltestosterone, page 419*

Oxandrin *see Oxandrolone, page 428*

OXANDROLONE

BRAND NAMES: Anavar, Oxandrin
COMMON STREET NAMES: Arnolds, gym candy, juice, pumpers, roids, stackers, weight trainers
DEA CLASS: Class III
PHARMACOLOGIC CLASS: Anabolic-androgenic steroids

Description: Androgens are steroid hormones that develop and maintain male sex characteristics. Oxandrolone is used as a supplemental treatment to promote weight gain following extensive weight loss due to surgery, chronic infections, or severe trauma. It is also used to treat patients who fail to gain or maintain normal weight for unknown medical reasons.

Method of use: Ingested. Chronic users tend to rotate steroids using various methods known as cycling, stacking, and pyramiding. Sporadic discontinuation of use is believed to allow testosterone levels and sperm counts to return to normal. Taking steroids regularly with periodic "drug-free times" is called cycling. Stacking refers to the concomitant use of two or more steroids at high doses. Pyramiding is when the dose, frequency, or number of steroids taken is gradually increased, followed by progressive tapering of the drug(s).

Duration of action: Depends on the formulation, frequency, and method of use. In general, effects last up to 6 days.

Psychological effects of abuse: Altered sex drive, depression, and mood changes. Psychological dependence may also develop.

Physical effects of abuse: Angry or hostile feelings, elevated blood pressure and cholesterol, headache, insomnia, premature balding, psychotic reactions, severe acne, sexual dysfunction, and violent behavior. *In men:* Breast development, impotence, intermittent or painful urination, painful or persistent erections, reduced sperm production, and shrinking of the testicles. *In women:* Decreased body fat and breast size, deepening of the voice, enlarged clitoris, excessive growth of body hair, and menstrual changes. *In adolescents:* Premature termination of growth.

Prolonged use can lead to tolerance. While the long-term effects are not completely known, chronic steroid abuse has been associated with damage to the heart, liver, and brain.

Overdose symptoms: There have been no reports of serious overdose with this drug, but excessive sodium and water retention may occur.

Withdrawal symptoms: Abrupt discontinuation may cause mood changes, tiredness, restlessness, loss of appetite, dissatisfaction with body image, sleeplessness, reduced sex drive, paranoia, and severe depression that can lead to suicide attempts.

OXAZEPAM

BRAND NAME: Serax
COMMON STREET NAMES: Candy, downers, sleeping pills, tranks
DEA CLASS: Class IV
PHARMACOLOGIC CLASS: Benzodiazepine, antianxiety, anticonvulsant

Description: Oxazepam is used to treat anxiety disorders and alcohol withdrawal. Abuse of benzodiazepines is particularly high among heroin and cocaine users.

Method of use: Ingested

Duration of action: 5 to 15 hours

Psychological effects of abuse: Amnesia, confusion, impaired judgment and thinking capabilities, mania or hypomania, pressured speech, reduced inhibition, and suicidal ideation. Long-term use may cause psychological dependence.

Physical effects of abuse: Constipation, dizziness, drowsiness, impaired physical capabilities, low blood pressure, muscle relaxation, sleepiness, slowed psychomotor performance, urinary retention, and visual disturbances. Long-term use may cause physical dependence.

Overdose symptoms: The most severe signs of overdose are respiratory depression and loss of consciousness. Other symptoms may include confusion, diminished reflexes, impaired coordination, slurred speech, extreme sleepiness, and loss of muscle tone. Death from overdose of a single benzodiazepine is extremely rare. However, there is an increased risk of toxicity when benzodiazepines are combined with alcohol and/or other CNS depressants. Fatalities have been reported in patients who have overdosed with a combination of a single benzodiazepine and alcohol.

Withdrawal symptoms: Abrupt termination following long-term use may precipitate withdrawal symptoms and require hospitalization. Symptoms may include abdominal and muscle cramps, depression, insomnia, sweating, vomiting, tremors, and seizures.

OXYCODONE HYDROCHLORIDE

BRAND NAMES: Intensol, OxyContin, OxyDose, OxyFast, OxyIR, Percocet, Percodan, Percolone, Roxicodone, Tylox

COMMON STREET NAMES: Hillbilly heroin, killers, OC's, Oxycotton, Oxy's, Percs, Poor man's heroin

DEA CLASS: Class II

PHARMACOLOGIC CLASS: Narcotic analgesic

Description: Oxycodone is a semisynthetic opioid derived from the opium alkaloid thebaine. It is used for the management of moderate to severe pain. Oxycodone has pharmacologic actions similar to codeine, heroin, and morphine. It elevates levels of the neurotransmitter dopamine, which is linked to pleasurable experiences. Opiate addicts use oxycodone to control withdrawal symptoms when heroin or morphine is unavailable. The brand OxyContin is especially prone to abuse because it contains higher doses of the medication in a timed-release tablet.

Method of use: Tablets are chewed or crushed into a powder that is snorted or diluted in water for injection. Chewing, crushing, or diluting long-acting tablets disables the timed-release action and allows high doses of the drug to enter the bloodstream quickly. Using oxycodone like this dramatically increases the risk of overdose.

Duration of action: Depends on the dose and method of use. In general, the effects last 4 to 6 hours following administration. The effects of timed-release tablets can persist for 12 hours or more.

Psychological effects of abuse: Abnormal dreams, anxiety, confusion, psychological dependence (after prolonged use), and thought disturbances. The psychological dependence associated with narcotic addiction is complex. Long after physical dependence has ended, the addict may continue to think and talk about the drug and feel unable to manage daily activities without it.

Physical effects of abuse: Abdominal cramps, constipation, decreased urination, diminished appetite, dizziness, dry mouth, euphoria, excessive sweating, gastrointestinal inflammation, headache, hiccups, light-head-edness, low blood pressure, nausea, respiratory depression, restlessness, sedation, sleepiness, and vomiting. Chronic use may cause tolerance and physical dependence.

Overdose symptoms: Fatalities have been reported, mostly when the timed-release tablets were crushed and snorted. Signs of overdose include dizziness, constricted pupils, weakness, cold and clammy skin, CNS depression, slowed or interrupted breathing, seizures, loss of conscious-ness, and coma. Risk of overdose increases significantly when the drug is taken with alcohol.

Withdrawal symptoms: Although withdrawal from oxycodone is painful physically and emotionally, it's rarely life-threatening if adequate hydra-tion and nutritional support are maintained. Although the symptoms are similar to those of morphine withdrawal, they are considerably less intense. Abruptly stopping use may cause excessive tearing, yawning, and sweating about 12 to 14 hours after the last dose. Additional symptoms may include diminished appetite, irritability, restless sleep (sometimes called the "yen"), confusion, irregular breathing, tremors, seizures, and loss of consciousness.

OxyContin *see Oxycodone, page 430*

OxyDose *see Oxycodone, page 430*

OxyFast *see Oxycodone, page 430*

OxyIR *see Oxycodone, page 430*

OXYMETHOLONE
BRAND NAME: Anadrol
COMMON STREET NAMES: Arnolds, gym candy, juice, pumpers, roids, stack-ers, weight trainers
DEA CLASS: Class III
PHARMACOLOGIC CLASS: Anabolic-androgenic steroid

Description: Oxymetholone is a synthetic derivative of testosterone. It is used for the treatment of anemias caused by weak red blood cell produc-tion or bone marrow failure.

Method of use: Ingested. Chronic users tend to rotate steroids using various methods known as cycling, stacking, and pyramiding. Sporadic discontinuation of use is believed to allow testosterone levels and sperm counts to return to normal. Taking steroids regularly with periodic "drug-free times" is called cycling. Stacking refers to the concomitant use of two or more steroids at high doses. Pyramiding is when the dose, frequency, or number of steroids taken is gradually increased, followed by progressive tapering of the drug(s).

Duration of action: Depends on the formulation, frequency, and method used. In general, effects may last up to 6 days following use.

Psychological effects of abuse: Mood changes, depression, and reduced sex drive. Psychological dependence may occur.

Physical effects of abuse: Angry or hostile feelings, elevated blood pressure and cholesterol, headache, insomnia, premature balding, psychotic reactions, severe acne, sexual dysfunction, and violent behavior. *In men:* Breast development, impotence, intermittent or painful urination, painful or persistent erections, reduced sperm production, and shrinking of the testicles. *In women:* Decreased body fat and breast size, deepening of the voice, enlarged clitoris, excessive growth of body hair, and menstrual changes. *In adolescents:* Premature termination of growth.

Prolonged use can lead to tolerance. While the long-term effects are not completely known, chronic steroid abuse has been associated with damage to the heart, liver, and brain.

Overdose symptoms: There have been no reports of severe overdose with this drug, and toxicity is unlikely following acute overdose. Chronic exposure to high doses may result in severe acne, excessive growth of body hair, hoarseness, change in sex drive, poor sperm production, and menstrual problems in women.

Withdrawal symptoms: Abrupt discontinuation may cause mood changes, tiredness, restlessness, loss of appetite, dissatisfaction with body image, sleeplessness, reduced sex drive, paranoia, and severe depression that can lead to suicide attempts.

OXYMORPHONE HYDROCHLORIDE

BRAND NAME: Numorphan
COMMON STREET NAMES: Dreamer, M, Miss Emma
DEA CLASS: Class II
PHARMACOLOGIC CLASS: Narcotic analgesic

Description: Oxymorphone is used to help manage moderate to severe pain, as a sedative prior to surgery, and as a supplemental agent during anesthesia. It's also used to relieve anxiety in patients who have difficulty breathing due to pulmonary edema caused by heart dysfunction.

Method of use: Rectal and injected IV, IM, or SC

Duration of action: Generally 3 to 6 hours (rectal and IV administration)

Psychological effects of abuse: Confusion, depression, hallucinations, and paradoxical CNS stimulation. The psychological dependence associated with narcotic addiction is complex. Long after physical dependence has ended, the addict may continue to think and talk about the drug and feel unable to manage daily activities without it.

Physical effects of abuse: Blurred vision, CNS and respiratory depression, constipation, diminished appetite, dizziness, drowsiness, dry mouth, flushing, headache, low blood pressure, lowered pulse, muscle rigidity, nausea, paradoxical CNS stimulation, restlessness, seizures, shortness of breath, stomach cramps, tiredness, urinary retention, and vomiting. Physical dependence develops progressively.

Overdose symptoms: Although tolerance develops slowly, the user eventually needs progressively larger doses to obtain the same effects as before. Symptoms of overdose may include severe drowsiness, clammy skin, confusion, constricted pupils, low blood pressure, interrupted breathing, slow pulse, tremors, respiratory depression, convulsions, and coma. Risk of overdose increases significantly when the drug is taken with alcohol.

Withdrawal symptoms: Although withdrawal from narcotics is painful physically and emotionally, it's rarely life-threatening if adequate hydration and nutritional support are maintained. Symptoms begin slowly, with peak effects observed 5 days after cessation of use; however, sleep disturbances can persist up to 13 days following the last dose. Early withdrawal symptoms may include irritability, sleeplessness, diminished appetite, excessive yawning, severe sneezing, tearing, and head cold. Later-stage symptoms may include nausea, vomiting, severe diarrhea, paradoxical excitability, abdominal cramps, bone and muscle pain in the back and extremities, fever and chills, excessive sweating, and depression. Elevated heart rate and blood pressure may also develop.

Papaveretum *see Opium, page 427*

PARALDEHYDE
BRAND NAME: Paral
COMMON STREET NAMES: Blue angels, blue devils, downers, goofers, nebbies, Peter, pink ladies, rainbows, softballs, yellow bullets
DEA CLASS: Class IV
PHARMACOLOGIC CLASS: Sedative, hypnotic

Description: Paraldehyde is marketed in other countries for the short-term treatment of insomnia. It is also used for treating symptoms of alcohol, barbiturate, and opiate withdrawal. High doses have sometimes been used to treat delirium and seizures. Paraldehyde was withdrawn from the U.S. market after safer and more effective agents became available.

Method of use: Ingested, used rectally, and injected IM or IV. Intravenous administration is extremely hazardous and could cause internal bleeding, accumulation of fluid in the lungs, heart damage, and circulatory collapse. Intramuscular injections are painful and could cause severe tissue damage, skin infection, and nerve damage at the injection site. Oral use can cause mouth and stomach irritation; rectal use can also cause irritation.

Duration of action: Depends on method of use. Hypnotic effects generally last 8 to 12 hours following a standard therapeutic dose.

Psychological effects of abuse: Nervousness, restlessness, irritability, and severe anxiety. Prolonged use may cause psychological dependence.

Physical effects of abuse: Coughing, low blood pressure, rapid heartbeat, fluid in the lungs, increased blood clotting, infection at the injection site, drowsiness, dizziness, "hangover" effects, stomach pain, nausea, and seizures. Paraldehyde decomposes during long-term storage, and deaths from corrosive poisoning have occurred after use of the decomposed drug. Prolonged use can lead to tolerance and physical dependence, especially in alcoholics.

Overdose symptoms: Death due to heart failure has been reported. Signs of overdose include weakness, depression, nausea, vomiting, rapid or labored breathing, slowed heartbeat, severely low blood pressure, and kidney or liver damage. Severe overdose could lead to respiratory depression and stupor followed by coma.

Withdrawal symptoms: Abrupt discontinuation can cause muscle and stomach cramps, excessive sweating, nausea, vomiting, tremors, hallucinations, and convulsions.

PEMOLINE
BRAND NAME: Cylert
COMMON STREET NAMES: Not known
DEA CLASS: Class IV
PHARMACOLOGIC CLASS: CNS stimulant, nonamphetamine

Description: Pemoline works much like dextroamphetamine and is used to treat attention deficit hyperactivity disorder (ADHD). However, pemoline is not recommended as first-line therapy due to its possible connection with liver failure.

Method of use: Ingested

Duration of action: For children, 7 hours; in other patients effects may last up to 13 hours.

Psychological effects of abuse: Depression, irritability, mild euphoria, and paranoid psychosis.

Physical effects of abuse: Dizziness, drowsiness, seizures, sleeplessness, headache, hallucinations, liver problems, loss of appetite, movement disorders, nausea, stuttering, stomach discomfort, severe muscle weakness, Tourette's syndrome, and weight loss. Prolonged use can lead to physical dependence.

Overdose symptoms: Prolonged use can lead to tolerance, and the progressively higher doses needed are often in the toxic range. Signs of overdose include agitation, confusion, restlessness, excessive sweating, severe muscle weakness, vomiting, rapid heartbeat, high blood pressure or body temperature, and hallucinations.

Withdrawal symptoms: Abrupt cessation of use may cause severe fatigue, sleepiness, headache, nausea, vomiting, abdominal pain, depression, paranoid psychosis, and seizures.

PENTAZOCINE HYDROCHLORIDE
BRAND NAME: Talwin
COMMON STREET NAMES: Poor man's heroin, Ts and Bs, Ts and Blues
DEA CLASS: Class IV
PHARMACOLOGIC CLASS: Narcotic analgesic, sedative

Description: Pentazocine is an opioid-type pain medication. It is used to treat moderate to severe pain, as a sedative prior to surgery, and as a supplemental agent during anesthesia. Combined preparations with aspirin may also be used in the treatment of moderate pain.

Method of use: Ingested and injected IM, IV, or SC

Duration of action: After ingestion: 4 to 5 hours; after injection: 2 to 3 hours.

Psychological effects of abuse: Confusion, disorientation, hallucinations, nightmares, and thought disturbances. The psychological dependence associated with narcotic addiction is complex. Long after physical dependence has ended, the addict may continue to think and talk about the drug and feel unable to manage daily activities without it.

Physical effects of abuse: Abdominal pain, blurred vision, chills, constipation, diminished appetite, dry mouth, feeling faint, flushing, headache, light-headedness, low blood pressure, nausea, sleeplessness, and vomiting. High doses can lead to rapid heart rate and respiratory depression. Chronic use may cause physical dependence.

Overdose symptoms: Although tolerance develops slowly, the user eventually needs progressively larger doses to obtain the same effects as before. Signs of overdose may include severe drowsiness, constricted pupils, severe high blood pressure, interrupted breathing, slow pulse, tremors, respiratory depression, convulsions, and coma. Risk of overdose increases significantly when the drug is taken with alcohol.

Withdrawal symptoms: Although pentazocine may cause physical dependence, withdrawal symptoms are much less severe than those of morphine. Early withdrawal symptoms may include irritability, sleeplessness, diminished appetite, excessive yawning, severe sneezing, tearing, and head cold. Later-stage symptoms may include nausea, vomiting, severe diarrhea, abdominal cramps, bone and muscle pain in the back and extremities, fever and chills, excessive sweating, depression, and elevated heart rate and blood pressure.

Pentothal *see Thiopental, page 449*

PENTOBARBITAL SODIUM
BRAND NAME: Nembutal
COMMON STREET NAMES: Downers, jackets, yellows
DEA CLASS: Class II
PHARMACOLOGIC CLASS: Barbiturate, sedative, anticonvulsant

Description: Barbiturates depress the sensory cortex, decrease motor activity, alter cerebral function, and produce drowsiness, sedation, and hypnosis. Pentobarbital is used as a sedative prior to surgery and to help induce anesthesia and alleviate anxiety. In addition, it is used for the emergency treatment of acute convulsive episodes such as status epilepticus.

Method of use: Used rectally and injected IM or IV

Duration of action: 3 to 4 hours following administration of a standard therapeutic dose.

Psychological effects of abuse: Barbiturates may cause psychological dependence, especially following prolonged use of high doses. Principal side effects include confusion, alternating euphoria and depression, and memory loss.

Physical effects of abuse: The most frequent physical side effects are due to CNS depression, including dizziness, headache, excessive sleepiness, drowsiness, and irregular gait. Other symptoms may include headache, stomach pain, and skin rash. Paradoxical excitement and irritability may also occur. In chronic users, blood disorders such as megaloblastic anemia may develop. Physical dependence is a significant risk, since it can develop after short-term use.

Overdose symptoms: Pentobarbital overdose may be complicated by the development of kidney necrosis, muscle necrosis, skin lesions, pneumonia, and low blood sugar. Seizures are not expected, except upon abrupt withdrawal from the drug.

Withdrawal symptoms: Pentobarbital is one of the most commonly abused barbiturates. Severe and life-threatening symptoms may occur within 48 hours of abrupt withdrawal, including continuous seizures, acute delirium syndromes with toxic psychosis, and coma, eventually resulting in death.

Percocet *see Oxycodone, page 430*

Percodan *see Oxycodone, page 430*

Percolone *see Oxycodone, page 430*

PHENDIMETRAZINE TARTRATE
BRAND NAMES: Bontril, Prelu-2
COMMON STREET NAMES: Not known
DEA CLASS: Class III
PHARMACOLOGIC CLASS: CNS stimulant, anorexiant

Description: Phendimetrazine is related to amphetamines both chemically and pharmacologically. It is a CNS stimulant and an indirect-acting sympathomimetic with actions similar to those of dextroamphetamine. Phendimetrazine is used as a short-term aid to help promote weight loss in conjunction with caloric restriction, exercise, and behavior modification.

Method of use: Ingested

Duration of action: 9 to 12 hours

Psychological effects of abuse: Agitation, paranoia, delusions, and hyperactivity. Rarely, psychotic episodes may occur following a single dose.

Physical effects of abuse: Elevated blood pressure, rapid heart rate, sleep disturbances, headache, dizziness, dry mouth, thirst, constipation, nausea, diarrhea, and increased urinary frequency. Effects of chronic abuse include hyperactivity, severe sleeplessness, severe irritability, personality changes, and psychosis. Pulmonary hypertension and valvular heart defects have been reported in patients receiving phendimetrazine in combination with other weight-loss-promoting drugs.

Overdose symptoms: Although overdose with phendimetrazine is rare, the following symptoms have been reported: agitation, hyperactivity, significantly elevated blood pressure and body temperature, and seizures.

Withdrawal symptoms: Although there are no reports of withdrawal reactions, the potential still exists for long-term users.

PHENMETRAZINE
BRAND NAME: Preludin
COMMON STREET NAMES: Black Cadillacs, beans, blue devils, bolt, cartwheels, fives, hearts, jellybeans, pep pills, snap
DEA CLASS: Class II
PHARMACOLOGIC CLASS: CNS stimulant, appetite suppressant

Description: Phenmetrazine is related to amphetamines both chemically and pharmacologically. It is a CNS stimulant and indirect-acting sympathomimetic with actions similar to those of dextroamphetamine. It is used as a short-term aid to help promote weight loss in conjunction with caloric restriction, exercise, and behavior modification. Phenmetrazine is not recommended as first-line therapy due to the potential for serious CNS side effects.

Method of use: Ingested, used rectally, and injected IV

Duration of action: Depends on the formulation. The effects of shorter-acting agents can last 4 to 6 hours, while the sustained-release version can last for 24 hours or more.

Psychological effects of abuse: Mild euphoria, nervousness, irritability, altered sexual desire, depression, mania, and rarely, psychotic behavior. Prolonged use may cause psychological dependence.

Physical effects of abuse: Rapid heartbeat, high blood pressure, heart palpitations, sleeplessness, headache, tremor, dizziness, dry mouth, excessive thirst, constipation, stomach discomfort, diarrhea, frequent urination, impotence, and blurred vision. Severe physical effects may include pulmonary hypertension, heart murmurs, and valvular heart disease. Prolonged use may cause physical dependence.

Overdose symptoms: Tolerance develops rapidly, and the progressively higher doses needed are often in the toxic range. Overdose symptoms include sleeplessness, hyperactivity, personality changes, psychosis, hallucinations, irregular heart rhythm, aggressive behavior, panic state, elevated body temperature, hyperactive reflexes, convulsions, and coma. Fatalities due to heart failure have been reported with high doses.

Withdrawal symptoms: Abrupt cessation of high doses may cause extreme fatigue, depression, and sleeping problems. Additional symptoms include hyperactivity, irritability, nausea, vomiting, nightmares, and tremors.

PHENOBARBITAL SODIUM
BRAND NAME: Luminal sodium
COMMON STREET NAMES: Barbs, downers, goofballs
DEA CLASS: Class IV
PHARMACOLOGIC CLASS: Barbiturate, sedative, hypnotic, anticonvulsant

Description: Barbiturates depress the sensory cortex, decrease motor activity, alter brain function, and produce drowsiness, sedation, and hypnosis. Phenobarbital is used to treat grand-mal and partial seizures. In addition, the injected form is effective for inducing sedation prior to surgery and facilitating the induction of anesthesia.

Method of use: Ingested and injected IM, IV, or SC

Duration of action: Effects begin in 20 to 60 minutes and can last for days, depending on the dose.

Psychological effects of abuse: Barbiturates may cause psychological dependence, especially following prolonged use of high doses. Psychological side effects may include confusion, alternating euphoria and depression, memory loss, impaired judgment, nervousness, nightmares, and hallucinations.

Physical effects of abuse: The most frequent physical effects are due to CNS depression, including dizziness, headache, excessive sleepiness, drowsiness, and irregular gait. Other symptoms may include headache, stomach pain, and skin rash. Paradoxical excitement and irritability may also occur. Short-term therapy with phenobarbital has been associated with the development of Stevens-Johnson syndrome and toxic skin eruptions. Physical dependence is a significant risk, since it can develop after short-term use.

Overdose symptoms: Phenobarbital overdose is associated with unusual reactions, including red, blistering skin lesions and neurological problems, that can appear 1 to 2 hours after ingestion. Other symptoms of overdose may include unsteady gait, slurred speech, confusion, low body temperature and blood pressure, and dose-dependent respiratory depression. Toxic effects may be enhanced when the drug is taken with alcohol and/or other CNS depressant drugs.

Withdrawal symptoms: Phenobarbital is abused less frequently because it is a long-acting barbiturate. Nevertheless, abrupt withdrawal may cause continuous seizures. Withdrawal symptoms can occur following discontinuation of chronic phenobarbital use, but are rare following an acute overdose. Symptoms are similar to those of alcohol withdrawal and may include generalized weakness, heightened anxiety, irritability, dizziness, headache, sleeplessness, muscle twitching, nausea and vomiting, and rapid pulse. Severely low blood pressure and convulsions may develop after a day or two, which eventually leads to hallucinations and delirium followed by coma and death.

PHENTERMINE HYDROCHLORIDE

BRAND NAMES: Adipex-P, Ionamin
COMMON STREET NAMES: Pep pills, speed, uppers
DEA CLASS: Class IV
PHARMACOLOGIC CLASS: CNS stimulant, anorexiant

Description: Phentermine is related to amphetamines both chemically and pharmacologically. It is used as a short-term aid to help promote weight loss in conjunction with caloric restriction, exercise, and behavior modification.

Method of use: Ingested

Duration of action: Up to 20 hours

Psychological effects of abuse: Confusion, agitation, reduced sexual desire, and restlessness. Acute paranoia and other psychotic behavior have also been reported. Psychological dependence can occur after chronic abuse.

Physical effects of abuse: Elevated blood pressure, rapid heart rate, constipation, diarrhea, nausea, dry mouth, sleeplessness, headache, and dizziness. Pulmonary hypertension and valvular heart defects have been reported, particularly when given concomitantly with fenfluramine or dexfenfluramine. Ischemic cerebrovascular disease, severe headache, and numbness have been associated with the use of phentermine.

Overdose symptoms: Overdose with phentermine is rare, but symptoms may include agitation, hyperactivity, significantly elevated blood pressure and body temperature, and seizures.

Withdrawal symptoms: Abrupt withdrawal may cause extreme fatigue and depression.

Pondomin *see Fenfluramine, page 399*

Prelu-2 *see Phendimetrazine, page 437*

PRIMIDONE
BRAND NAME: Mysoline
COMMON STREET NAMES: Barb, downers, goofers
DEA CLASS: Not classified
PHARMACOLOGIC CLASS: Barbiturate, anticonvulsant

Description: Primidone is used in the management of grand-mal, psychomotor, and focal seizures. One of its active metabolites is phenobarbital.

Method of use: Ingested

Duration of action: Effects are age- and dose-dependent, but usually persist for up to 5 days due to the drug's active metabolites.

Psychological effects of abuse: Barbiturates may cause psychological dependence, especially following prolonged use of high doses. Psychological side effects may include behavioral changes and excessive irritability.

Physical effects of abuse: Drowsiness, vertigo, tiredness, irregular gait, loss of appetite, nausea, vomiting, sexual dysfunction, double vision, and rapid eye movements.

Overdose symptoms: Unsteady gait, confusion, slurred speech, low blood pressure, lowered or elevated body temperature, dose-dependent respiratory depression, and coma. The drug's toxic effects are enhanced when taken with alcohol and/or other CNS depressants.

Withdrawal symptoms: Symptoms are similar to those of alcohol withdrawal and characterized by severe apprehension, weakness, heightened anxiety, irritability, dizziness, headache, sleeplessness, muscle twitching, nausea and vomiting, distortion of visual perception, and rapid pulse. Severely low blood pressure and convulsions may develop after a day or two, which eventually leads to hallucinations, delirium, and continuous seizures, followed by coma and death.

Primobolan *see Methenolone, page 417*

PROPOXYPHENE HYDROCHLORIDE and PROPOXYPHENE NAPSYLATE
BRAND NAME: Darvon
COMMON STREET NAMES: D, dillies, dust, juice, smack
DEA CLASS: Class IV
PHARMACOLOGIC CLASS: Narcotic analgesic

Description: Propoxyphene is an opioid analgesic that is structurally related to methadone. It is used to alleviate mild to moderate pain.

Method of use: Ingested

Duration of action: Generally, effects persist 6 to 12 hours following use, but can last 30 to 36 hours in chronic users.

Psychological effects of abuse: Confusion, depression, hallucinations, nervousness, and paradoxical excitement. The psychological dependence associated with narcotic addiction is complex. Long after physical dependence has ended, the addict may continue to think and talk about the drug and feel unable to manage daily activities without it.

Physical effects of abuse: Blurred vision, CNS and respiratory depression, constricted pupils, constipation, diminished appetite, dizziness, drowsiness, faintness, headache, insomnia, light-headedness, loss of appetite, low blood pressure, nausea, seizures, slow heartbeat, slow or troubled breathing, stomach cramps, tremors, and vomiting. Chronic use results in tolerance and physical dependence.

Overdose symptoms: Chronic use can lead to tolerance, and progressively higher doses are needed to obtain the same effects as before. Toxic accumulations of propoxyphene and its metabolites can occur quickly with repeated doses, and the effects are often complicated by the addition of alcohol or other drugs. A disturbing number of fatalities have occurred from accidental or intentional overdose with propoxyphene; death within an hour of overdosing is not uncommon. Psychotic reactions and possibly fatal CNS depression—including decreased or labored breathing, temporary stoppage of breathing, and decreased heart function—can develop rapidly. Other symptoms of propoxyphene overdose may include bluish skin, extreme sleepiness, pupil constriction later followed by dilation, irregular heartbeat, low blood pressure, stupor, seizures, and coma.

Withdrawal symptoms: Severe withdrawal syndromes have been reported, particularly in older individuals. Symptoms may include restlessness, muscle and bone pain, severe diarrhea, sleeplessness, involuntary leg movements, chills alternating with hot flashes, depression, nausea, vomiting, elevated heart rate and blood pressure, convulsions, and coma.

ProSom *see Estazolam, page 395*

Provigil *see Modafinil, page 422*

QUAZEPAM
BRAND NAME: Doral
COMMON STREET NAMES: Candy, downers, sleeping pills, tranks
DEA CLASS: Class IV
PHARMACOLOGIC CLASS: Benzodiazepine, sedative, hypnotic

Description: Quazepam is used for the short-term treatment of sleep disorders such as insomnia. Abuse of benzodiazepines is particularly high among heroin and cocaine users.

Method of use: Ingested

Duration of action: 25 to 41 hours

Psychological effects of abuse: Confusion, impaired judgment and thinking abilities, irritability, mild euphoria, pressured speech, reduced inhibition, and suicidal ideation. Long-term use may cause psychological dependence.

Physical effects of abuse: Changes in appetite and body weight, constipation, dizziness, impaired muscle coordination, and low blood pressure. Long-term use may cause physical dependence.

Overdose symptoms: The most severe signs of overdose are respiratory depression and coma. Other symptoms may include confusion, diminished reflexes, manic behavior, unrealistic euphoria, extreme sleepiness, and impaired muscle coordination. Death from overdose of a single benzodiazepine is extremely rare. However, there is an increased risk of toxicity when benzodiazepines are combined with alcohol and/or other CNS depressants. Fatalities have been reported in patients who have overdosed with a combination of a single benzodiazepine and alcohol.

Withdrawal symptoms: Abrupt termination may lead to withdrawal symptoms and require hospitalization. Symptoms may include abdominal and muscle cramps, depression, insomnia, sweating, vomiting, tremors, and seizures.

Repan *see Butalbital, page 384*

Restoril *see Temazepam, page 447*

Ritalin *see Methylphenidate, page 418*

RMS *see Morphine, page 423*

Rohypnol *see Flunitrazepam, page 401*

Roxanol *see Morphine, page 423*

Roxicodone *see Oxycodone, page 430*

SECOBARBITAL

BRAND NAME: Seconal
COMMON STREET NAMES: Downers, reds, red devils
DEA CLASS: Class II
PHARMACOLOGIC CLASS: Barbiturate (short-acting), sedative, hypnotic, anti-convulsant

Description: Barbiturates depress the sensory cortex, decrease motor activity, alter brain function, and produce drowsiness, sedation, and hypnosis. Secobarbital is used as an emergency aid in the management of acute convulsive episodes. In addition, it is used for the short-term treatment of insomnia and as a sedative before surgery to help induce anesthesia and alleviate anxiety.

Method of use: Ingested and injected IV or IM

Duration of action: 3 to 4 hours

Psychological effects of abuse: Barbiturates may cause psychological dependence, especially following prolonged use of high doses. Psychological effects may include confusion, alternating euphoria and depression, and memory loss.

Physical effects of abuse: The most frequent physical effects are due to CNS depression, including dizziness, headache, excessive sleepiness, drowsiness, and irregular gait. Other symptoms may include headache, stomach pain, and skin rash. Paradoxical excitement and irritability may also occur. In chronic users, blood disorders such as megaloblastic anemia may develop. Physical dependence is a significant risk, since it can develop after short-term use.

Overdose symptoms: Symptoms may include unsteady gait, slurred speech, confusion, low body temperature and blood pressure, and dose-dependent respiratory depression. Toxic effects are enhanced when secobarbital is taken with alcohol and/or other CNS depressant drugs.

Withdrawal symptoms: Addiction may result following chronic use. Withdrawal symptoms may include anorexia, nausea, vomiting, muscle weakness, tremors, and low blood pressure, followed by seizures within 16 to 24 hours after the last dose. Acute delirium with toxic psychosis may occur within 48 hours following termination of use.

Seconal *see Secobarbital, page 444*

Serax *see Oxazepam, page 429*

Soma *see Meprobamate and Carisoprodol, page 413*

Somnote *see Chloral hydrate, page 386*

Sonata *see Zaleplon, page 453*

Stadol *see Butorphanol, page 385*

Sufenta *see Sufentanil, page 445*

SUFENTANIL CITRATE
BRAND NAME: Sufenta
COMMON STREET NAMES: China white, China girl, dance fever, friend, good-fellas, king ivory
DEA CLASS: Class II
PHARMACOLOGIC CLASS: Narcotic analgesic/agonist, general anesthetic

Description: Sufentanil has three main uses: 1) as a primary agent for induction and maintenance of anesthesia administered with oxygen; 2) as a supplemental agent during maintenance of general anesthesia; and 3) as a combined agent used with low-dose bupivacaine during labor.

Method of use: Injected IV

Duration of action: Depends on dose size and the user's weight (duration is longer in obese individuals). Effects generally last 2 to 3 hours, but repeated use of large doses may result in accumulation and a longer duration of action.

Psychological effects of abuse: Confusion, depression, hallucinations, and restlessness. Prolonged use causes psychological dependence, particularly when high doses are used.

Physical effects of abuse: Blurred vision, CNS depression, constipation, decreased urination, diminished appetite, dizziness, drowsiness, dry mouth, excessive sleepiness, headache, high blood pressure (depending on dose), muscle rigidity, nausea, respiratory depression (depending on dose), slow heart rate or pulse, stomach cramps, and vomiting. Chronic use may cause physical dependence.

Overdose symptoms: The primary signs of overdose include CNS and respiratory depression and constricted pupils. Serious overdose may result in interrupted breathing, circulatory depression, severely low blood pressure, muscle rigidity, slow heart rate, delirium, seizures, and shock.

Withdrawal symptoms: Abruptly stopping the drug after long-term use may precipitate withdrawal symptoms. The intensity of symptoms is directly related to the total daily dose, frequency and duration of use, and the health of the user. Although painful physically and emotionally, withdrawal from narcotics is rarely life-threatening. Early symptoms may include watery eyes, runny nose, yawning, and sweating. Later-stage symptoms may include nervousness, muscle twitching, drug cravings, restlessness, irritability, loss of appetite, chills alternating with flushing, nausea, vomiting, bone and muscle pain in the back and extremities, tremors, elevated heart rate and blood pressure, and severe depression.

Supprettes *see Chloral hydrate, page 386*

STANOZOLOL
COMMON STREET NAMES: Arnolds, gym candy, juice, pumpers, roids, stackers, weight trainers
DEA CLASS: Class III
PHARMACOLOGIC CLASS: Anabolic-androgenic steroid

Description: Androgens are steroid hormones that develop and maintain male sex characteristics. They are used primarily to replace insufficient levels of testosterone due to poor functioning of the testes. When used in combination with exercise and a high-protein diet, androgens can promote increased muscle size and strength, improve stamina, and decrease recovery time between workouts. Androgens are also used to promote the development of puberty in males with clearly delayed onset. Additionally, androgens are sometimes prescribed for women with advancing, inoperable metastatic breast cancer who are 1 to 5 years postmenopausal. This product is also effective for treating excessive swelling and welts below the skin (angioedema).

Method of use: Ingested. Chronic users tend to rotate steroids using various methods known as cycling, stacking, and pyramiding. Sporadic discontinuation of use is believed to allow testosterone levels and sperm counts to return to normal. Taking steroids regularly with periodic "drug-free times" is called cycling. Stacking refers to the concomitant use of two or more steroids at high doses. Pyramiding is when the dose, frequency, or number of steroids taken is gradually increased, followed by progressive tapering of the drug(s).

Duration of action: Depends on the formulation, frequency, and method used. In general, effects can last up to 6 days following use.

Psychological effects of abuse: Mood changes, decreased or increased sexual drive, anxiety, and depression. Psychological dependence may occur.

Physical effects of abuse: Angry or hostile feelings, elevated blood pressure and cholesterol, headache, insomnia, premature balding, psychotic reactions, severe acne, sexual dysfunction, and violent behavior. *In men:* Breast development, impotence, intermittent or painful urination, painful or persistent erections, reduced sperm production, and shrinking of the testicles. *In women:* Decreased body fat and breast size, deepening of the voice, enlarged clitoris, excessive growth of body hair, and menstrual changes. *In adolescents:* Premature termination of growth.

Prolonged use can lead to tolerance. While the long-term effects are not completely known, chronic steroid abuse has been associated with damage to the heart, liver, and brain.

Overdose symptoms: There have been no reports of severe overdose with this product. Chronic abuse of high doses may result in acne, excessive body hair, changes in hormonal and lipid metabolism, nausea, vomiting, jaundice, behavioral changes, stroke, heart function deterioration, psychosis, and sudden death.

Withdrawal symptoms: Abrupt discontinuation may cause mood changes, tiredness, restlessness, loss of appetite, dissatisfaction with body image, sleeplessness, reduced sex drive, paranoia, and severe depression that can lead to suicide attempts.

Talwin *see Pentazocine, page 435*

TEMAZEPAM
BRAND NAME: Restoril
COMMON STREET NAMES: Candy, downers, sleeping pills, tranks
DEA CLASS: Class IV
PHARMACOLOGIC CLASS: Benzodiazepine, sedative, hypnotic

Description: Temazepam is used for the short-term treatment of sleep disorders such as insomnia. Abuse of benzodiazepines is particularly high among heroin and cocaine users.

Method of use: Ingested

Duration of action: 5 to 17 hours

Psychological effects of abuse: Confusion, impaired judgment and thinking abilities, irritability, mild euphoria, pressured speech, reduced inhibition, and suicidal ideation. Long-term use may cause psychological dependence.

Physical effects of abuse: Changes in appetite and body weight, constipation, dizziness, impaired muscle coordination, impaired physical capabilities, and low blood pressure. Long-term use may cause physical dependence.

Overdose symptoms: The most severe signs of overdose are respiratory depression and coma. Other symptoms may include confusion, diminished reflexes, manic behavior, unrealistic euphoria, extreme sleepiness, and impaired coordination. Death from overdose of a single benzodiazepine is extremely rare. However, there is an increased risk of toxicity when benzodiazepines are combined with alcohol and/or other CNS depressants. Fatalities have been reported in patients who have overdosed with a combination of a single benzodiazepine and alcohol.

Withdrawal symptoms: Abrupt termination following long-term use may precipitate withdrawal symptoms and require hospitalization. Symptoms may include abdominal and muscle cramps, agitation, delirium, depression, insomnia, rapid pulse, sweating, vomiting, hallucinations, tremors, and seizures.

Tenuate *see Diethylpropion, page 393*

TESTOSTERONE ENANTHATE
BRAND NAME: Delatestryl
COMMON STREET NAMES: Arnolds, gym candy, juice, pumpers, roids, stackers, weight trainers
DEA CLASS: Class III
PHARMACOLOGIC CLASS: Anabolic-androgenic steroid

Description: Androgens are steroid hormones that develop and maintain male sex characteristics. Testosterone enanthate is a derivative of the male hormone testosterone. Androgens are used primarily to replace insufficient levels of testosterone due to poor functioning of the testes. When used in combination with exercise and a high-protein diet, androgens can promote increased muscle size and strength, improve stamina, and decrease recovery time between workouts. Androgens are also used to promote the development of puberty in males with clearly delayed onset. Additionally, androgens are sometimes prescribed for women with advancing, inoperable metastatic breast cancer who are 1 to 5 years postmenopausal. This product has also been used in premenopausal women with breast cancer who have benefited from removal of one or both ovaries and are considered to have a hormone-responsive tumor.

Method of use: Injected IM. Chronic users tend to rotate steroids using various methods known as cycling, stacking, and pyramiding. Sporadic discontinuation of use is believed to allow testosterone levels and sperm counts to return to normal. Taking steroids regularly with periodic "drug-free times" is called cycling. Stacking refers to the concomitant use of two or more steroids at high doses. Pyramiding is when the dose, frequency, or number of steroids taken is gradually increased, followed by progressive tapering of the drug(s).

Duration of action: Up to 24 hours following IM administration.

Psychological effects of abuse: Mood changes, depression, and reduced sex drive. Psychological dependence may occur.

Physical effects of abuse: Angry or hostile feelings, elevated blood pressure and cholesterol, headache, insomnia, premature balding, psychotic reactions, severe acne, sexual dysfunction, and violent behavior. *In men:* Breast development, impotence, intermittent or painful urination, painful or persistent erections, reduced sperm production, and shrinking of the testicles. *In women:* Decreased body fat and breast size, deepening of the voice, enlarged clitoris, excessive growth of body hair, and menstrual changes. *In adolescents:* Premature termination of growth.

Prolonged use can lead to tolerance. While the long-term effects are not completely known, chronic steroid abuse has been associated with damage to the heart, liver, and brain.

Overdose symptoms: There have been no reports of severe overdose with this product. Chronic abuse of high doses may result in blurred vision, headache, sudden and severe inability to speak, seizures, slurred speech, temporary blindness, and sudden, severe weakness in the arm and/or leg on one side of the body.

Withdrawal symptoms: Abrupt discontinuation may cause mood changes, tiredness, restlessness, loss of appetite, dissatisfaction with body image, sleeplessness, reduced sex drive, paranoia, and severe depression that can lead to suicide attempts.

Testred *see Methyltestosterone, page 419*

THIOPENTAL SODIUM
BRAND NAME: Pentothal
COMMON STREET NAMES:
DEA CLASS: Class III
PHARMACOLOGIC CLASS: Barbiturate, anticonvulsant, general anesthetic, sedative

Description: Barbiturates depress the sensory cortex, decrease motor activity, alter brain function, and produce drowsiness, sedation, and hypnosis. Thiopental is used to control convulsions by inducing anesthesia. It is also used to treat grand-mal, psychomotor, and focal seizures. One of the drug's active metabolites is phenobarbital.

Method of use: Ingested

Duration of action: Effects are age- and dose-dependent but are usually brief.

Psychological effects of abuse: Barbiturates may cause psychological dependence, especially following prolonged use of high doses. Effects may include behavioral changes, excessive irritability, nightmares, hallucinations, nervousness, anxiety, and impaired judgment.

Physical effects of abuse: Low heart rate and blood pressure, feeling faint, drowsiness, tiredness, dizziness, headache, chills, coughing, irregular gait, loss of appetite, excessive sleeplessness, nausea, vomiting, sexual dysfunction, double vision, rapid eye movements, respiratory depression, and interrupted breathing.

Overdose symptoms: Unsteady gait, confusion, slurred speech, low blood pressure, high or low body temperature, sleepiness, dose-dependent respiratory depression, shock, and coma. The drug's toxic effects are enhanced when taken with alcohol and/or other CNS depressants.

Withdrawal symptoms: Symptoms are similar to those of alcohol withdrawal and characterized by severe apprehension, weakness, heightened anxiety, irritability, dizziness, headache, sleeplessness, muscle twitching, nausea and vomiting, distortion of visual perception, and rapid pulse. Severely low blood pressure and convulsions may develop after a day or two, which eventually lead to hallucinations, delirium, and continuous seizures, followed by coma and death.

Tranxene *see Clorazepate, page 386*

TRENBOLONE ACETATE
BRAND NAME: Finaject
COMMON STREET NAMES: Arnolds, gym candy, juice, pumpers, roids, stackers, weight trainers
DEA CLASS: Class III
PHARMACOLOGIC CLASS: Anabolic-androgenic steroid

Description: Androgens are steroid hormones that develop and maintain male sex characteristics. They are used primarily to replace insufficient levels of testosterone due to poor functioning of the testes. When used in combination with exercise and a high-protein diet, androgens can promote increased muscle size and strength, improve stamina, and decrease recovery time between workouts. Androgens are also used to promote the development of puberty in males with clearly delayed onset. Additionally, androgens are sometimes precribed for women with advancing, inoperable metastatic breast cancer who are 1 to 5 years postmenopausal.

Method of use: Ingested. Chronic users tend to rotate steroids using various methods known as cycling, stacking, and pyramiding. Sporadic discontinuation of use is believed to allow testosterone levels and sperm counts to return to normal. Taking steroids regularly with periodic "drug-free times" is called cycling. Stacking refers to the concomitant use of two or more steroids at high doses. Pyramiding is when the dose, frequency, or number of steroids taken is gradually increased, followed by progressive tapering of the drug(s).

Duration of action: Depends on the formulation, frequency, and method of use. In general, effects may last up to 6 days.

Psychological effects of abuse: Mood changes, depression, uncontrollable aggressive behavior, euphoria, anxiety, irritability, increased sex drive, and rarely, psychosis. Psychological dependence may also occur.

Physical effects of abuse: Angry or hostile feelings, elevated blood pressure and cholesterol, headache, insomnia, premature balding, psychotic reactions, severe acne, sexual dysfunction, and violent behavior. *In men:* Breast development, impotence, intermittent or painful urination, painful or persistent erections, reduced sperm production, and shrinking of the testicles. *In women:* Decreased body fat and breast size, deepening of the voice, enlarged clitoris, excessive growth of body hair, and menstrual changes. *In adolescents:* Premature termination of growth.

Prolonged use can lead to tolerance. While the long-term effects are not completely known, chronic steroid abuse has been associated with damage to the heart, liver, and brain.

Overdose symptoms: There have been no reports of serious overdose with this drug. Chronic use of high doses may cause excessive sexual stimulation, reduced sperm production, enlarged breasts in males, uncontrolled painful erection, jaundice, and deteriorating liver function. Excessive fluid retention may occur in users who have heart, liver, or kidney disease.

Withdrawal symptoms: Abrupt discontinuation may cause mood changes, tiredness, restlessness, loss of appetite, dissatisfaction with body image, sleeplessness, reduced sex drive, paranoia, and severe depression that can lead to suicide attempts.

TRIAZOLAM
BRAND NAME: Halcion
COMMON STREET NAMES: Candy, downers, sleeping pills, tranks
DEA CLASS: Class IV
PHARMACOLOGIC CLASS: Benzodiazepine, sedative, hypnotic

Description: Triazolam is used for the short-term treatment of sleep disorders such as insomnia. Abuse of benzodiazepines is particularly high among heroin and cocaine users.

Method of use: Ingested

Duration of action: 6 to 7 hours

Psychological effects of abuse: Confusion, impaired judgment and thinking abilities, irritability, mild euphoria, pressured speech, reduced inhibition, and suicidal ideation. Long-term use may cause psychological dependence.

Physical effects of abuse: Changes in appetite and body weight, constipation, dizziness, impaired muscle coordination, and low blood pressure. Long-term use may cause physical dependence.

Overdose symptoms: The most severe signs of overdose are respiratory depression and coma. Other symptoms may include confusion, diminished reflexes, manic behavior, unrealistic euphoria, extreme sleepiness, and impaired coordination. Death from overdose of a single benzodiazepine is extremely rare. However, there is an increased risk of toxicity when benzodiazepines are combined with alcohol and/or other CNS depressants. Fatalities have been reported in patients who have overdosed with a combination of a single benzodiazepine and alcohol.

Withdrawal symptoms: Abrupt termination following long-term use may precipitate withdrawal symptoms and require hospitalization. Symptoms may include abdominal and muscle cramps, depression, insomnia, sweating, vomiting, tremors, and seizures.

Tuinal *see Amobarbital and Secobarbital, page 380*

Tylox *see Oxycodone, page 430*

Valium *see Diazepam, page 392*

Versed *see Midazolam, page 421*

Vicodin *see Hydrocodone, page 406*

Virilon *see Methyltestosterone, page 419*

Xanax *see Alprazolam, page 378*

Xyrem *see GHB, page 404*

ZALEPLON
BRAND NAME: Sonata
COMMON STREET NAMES: Candy, downers, sleeping pills, tranks
DEA CLASS: Class IV
PHARMACOLOGIC CLASS: Hypnotic (not a benzodiazepine, but interacts with the same receptors in the brain)

Description: Zaleplon is used for the short-term treatment of insomnia. Abuse of benzodiazepine-type hypnotics is particularly high among heroin and cocaine users.

Method of use: Ingested

Duration of action: 6 to 8 hours

Psychological effects of abuse: Abnormal dreams, amnesia, changes in sexual desire, confusion, depersonalization, depression, hallucinations, impaired judgment and thinking abilities, reduced inhibition, and suicidal ideation. Paradoxical effects include euphoria, hyperactivity, and extreme aggression. Prolonged use may cause psychological dependence.

Physical effects of abuse: Abdominal pain, constipation, decreased blood pressure, dizziness, drowsiness, fatigue, impaired physical capabilities, irregular gait, light-headedness, loss of appetite, menstrual irregularities, migraine, nausea, sleepiness, slowed psychomotor performance, urinary retention, vertigo, and visual disturbances. Prolonged use may cause physical dependence.

Overdose symptoms: The most severe signs of overdose with benzodiazepine-type hypnotics are respiratory depression, loss of consciousness, and coma. Other symptoms may include sensitivity to light, confusion, diminished reflexes, slurred speech, impaired coordination, apnea, extreme sleepiness, loss of muscle tone, and severely low blood pressure. Death from overdose of a single benzodiazepine-type hypnotic is extremely rare. However, there is an increased risk of toxicity when benzodiazepine-type drugs are combined with alcohol and/or other CNS depressants. Fatalities have been reported in patients who have overdosed with a combination of a single benzodiazepine-type hypnotic and alcohol.

Withdrawal symptoms: Abrupt termination following long-term use may precipitate withdrawal symptoms and require hospitalization. Symptoms may include abdominal and muscle cramps, depression, insomnia, severe drowsiness, sweating, vomiting, tremors, respiratory depression, seizures, and coma.

Zebutal *see Butalbital, page 384*
see Butalbital, page 384

ZOLPIDEM

BRAND NAME: Ambien

COMMON STREET NAMES: Candy, downers, sleeping pills, tranks

DEA CLASS: Class IV

PHARMACOLOGIC CLASS: Hypnotic, sedative (not a benzodiazepine, but interacts with the same receptors in the brain)

Description: Zolpidem is used for the short-term treatment of insomnia. Abuse of benzodiazepine-type hypnotics is particularly high among heroin and cocaine users.

Method of use: Ingested

Duration of action: 6 to 8 hours

Psychological effects of abuse: Abnormal dreams, amnesia, confusion, depression, impaired judgment and thinking abilities, reduced inhibition, and suicidal ideation. Paradoxical effects include euphoria, hyperactivity, and extreme aggression. Prolonged use may cause psychological dependence.

Physical effects of abuse: Changes in sexual desire, constipation, decreased blood pressure, dizziness, drowsiness, fatigue, impaired physical capabilities, irregular gait, light-headedness, sleepiness, slowed psychomotor performance, urinary retention, and visual disturbances. Prolonged use may cause physical dependence.

Overdose symptoms: The most severe signs of overdose with benzodiazepine-type hypnotics are respiratory depression, loss of consciousness, and coma. Other symptoms may include confusion, diminished reflexes, slurred speech, impaired coordination, apnea, extreme sleepiness, loss of muscle tone, and severely low blood pressure. Death from overdose of a single benzodiazepine-type hypnotic is extremely rare. However, there is an increased risk of toxicity when benzodiazepine-type drugs are combined with alcohol and/or other CNS depressants. Fatalities have been reported in patients who have overdosed with a combination of a single benzodiazepine-type hypnotic and alcohol.

Withdrawal symptoms: Abrupt termination following long-term use may precipitate withdrawal symptoms and require hospitalization. Symptoms may include abdominal and muscle cramps, depression, insomnia, sweating, vomiting, tremors, and seizures.

Part 3.
Illegal Drugs

AMT (ALPHA-METHYLTRYPTAMINE)
COMMON STREET NAMES: Amthrax, Amtrak, spirals
DEA CLASS: Class I
PHARMACOLOGIC CLASS: Hallucinogen

Description: AMT is a chemical found in a variety of South American plants. The drug has a similar structure and pharmacologic characteristics as other tryptamine-based Class I hallucinogens.

Method of use: Ingested (often as a tea), smoked or used as snuff, and rarely, injected.

Duration of action: 1 to 6 hours, but in chronic users the effects can last 18 to 24 hours.

Psychological effects: AMT can produce similar psychological effects as other hallucinogens, including changes in perception, visual distortions, agitation, hyperactivity, confusion, euphoria, anxiety, mood alterations, slowed thinking, delirium, and unpredictable behavior. Long-term use may cause tolerance and psychological dependence.

Physical effects: AMT can produce similar physical effects as other hallucinogens, including CNS depression or stimulation, nausea, vomiting, diarrhea, elevated blood pressure and body temperature, abnormally fast heart rate, blurred vision, excessive salivation, irregular gait, loss of appetite, irregular breathing, numbness in the extremities, dizziness, drowsiness, decreased REM sleep, enhanced color awareness, and time distortion.

Overdose symptoms: AMT is not considered addictive; it does not produce compulsive drug-seeking behavior as do cocaine, amphetamines, heroin, and alcohol. However, it does produce tolerance, and chronic users must take progressively higher doses to achieve the same effects as before. This is particularly dangerous due to the unpredictability of the drug's effects. Symptoms of overdose may include irregular gait, rapid heart rate, tremors, and elevated blood pressure and body temperature.

Withdrawal symptoms: None are reported, since no evidence of physical dependence can be detected when the drug is abruptly withdrawn.

4-BROMO-2,5-DIMETHOXYPHENETHYLAMINE
COMMON STREET NAMES: 2C-B, B-DMPEA, bromo, MFT, Nexus, two's
DEA CLASS: Class I
PHARMACOLOGIC CLASS: CNS stimulant

Description: This drug is an illegally manufactured variation of mescaline and amphetamine and has the same pharmacologic actions as amphetamine. Because the drug is manufactured in clandestine laboratories, it's rarely pure, and the amount of active drug in an oral dose can vary considerably.

Method of use: Ingested and snorted

Duration of action: Up to 8 hours; effects begin 20 to 30 minutes after use and reach their peak within 1 to 2 hours.

Psychological effects: Aggressive and impulsive behavior, agitation, anxiety, confusion, delusions, depression, drug cravings, hallucinations, and paranoia. Psychological dependence can develop rapidly.

Physical effects: Dilated pupils, elevated heart rate, and increased blood pressure. Long-term effects may include psychiatric disturbances, impaired cognitive functions, and memory loss.

Overdose symptoms: In general, toxicity results in mild symptoms that may include agitation, dilated pupils, fatigue, poor concentration, excessive sweating, elevated blood pressure, and rapid heart rate. Occasionally, severe depression, anxiety, and delirium can occur. Severe overdose may cause dangerously high body temperature, blood-clotting problems, severe muscle weakness and pain, seizures, and acute kidney failure.

Withdrawal symptoms: Abruptly stopping the drug after long-term use may cause extreme fatigue, overeating, depression, and stupor.

COCAINE and CRACK COCAINE
COMMON STREET NAMES: Big C, blow, coke, crack, crank, flake, lady, nose candy, rocks, snow, snowbirds, white, zip
DEA CLASS: Class II
PHARMACOLOGIC CLASS: CNS stimulant

Description: Cocaine is prepared from an extract of the coca plant. It is one of the most potent CNS stimulants and is widely abused. Crack cocaine is processed with baking soda or ammonia to produce a form that can be smoked. Currently, controlled doses of cocaine can be administered by a doctor for legitimate medical use, primarily as a local anesthetic for certain eye, ear, and throat surgeries.

Method of use: Ingested, snorted, smoked (also called "freebasing"), and injected IV. Each method has significant health risks for the user.

Duration of action: Depends on the method of use. Snorting produces a slow onset that lasts 15 to 30 minutes. The effects of smoking or IV injection last 5 to 10 minutes and produce a more intense high.

Psychological effects: Cocaine use causes psychological dependence. *Moderate doses:* Agitation, argumentative behavior, irritability, nervousness, and talkativeness. *High doses:* Anxiety, delusions, extreme irritability, paranoia, and restlessness.

Physical effects: Cocaine is highly addictive due to its rapid onset of action. Compulsive use appears to develop more quickly in smokers than in users who snort. *Moderate doses:* Abdominal pain, constricted blood vessels, decreased appetite, dilated pupils, disturbances in heart rhythm, elevated blood pressure, headaches, increased body temperature, nausea, and rapid heart and respiratory rates. *High doses:* Abdominal pain, blurred vision, chest pain, coma, convulsions, dizziness, excessive sweating, headaches, heart attacks, muscle spasms, nausea, respiratory failure, shortness of breath, and stroke. *Warning:* Cocaine use can cause sudden death, even after the first time the drug is taken.

Overdose symptoms: An overdose can be fatal. Tolerance develops rapidly, and chronic users must take progressively higher doses to obtain the same effects as before. Cocaine-related deaths are usually caused by cardiac arrest or seizures followed by respiratory arrest. Other symptoms of overdose include high body temperature, hallucinations, and convulsions. Smoking or injecting cocaine is more dangerous than snorting it. Risk of harmful effects also increases when the drug is combined with alcohol.

Withdrawal symptoms: Abruptly stopping chronic use of high doses may produce relatively mild withdrawal symptoms, including depression, anxiety, sleep disturbances, and increased appetite. These usually occur within 24 to 48 hours following the last dose and can last 7 to 10 days. Long-term users may develop acute tolerance and can suffer from depression, headache, fatigue, and irritability after they stop using the drug. Crack cocaine users appear to develop a greater dependence on the drug and therefore have more severe withdrawal symptoms, including major psychiatric complications and severe depression.

DOM (4-METHYL-2,5-DIMETHOXYAMPHETAMINE) and DOB (4-BROMO-2,5-DIMETHOXYAMPHETAMINE)

COMMON STREET NAME: STP, an acronym for Serenity, Tranquility, and Peace

DEA CLASS: Class I

PHARMACOLOGIC CLASS: CNS stimulant

Description: These drugs are an illegally manufactured variation of mescaline and amphetamine. They are sold as drug-laced pieces of paper. Because these drugs are manufactured in clandestine laboratories, they are rarely pure, and the amount of active drug in an oral dose can vary considerably.

Method of use: Ingested, snorted, and rarely, injected IV

Duration of action: Depends on method of use. Effects can last 12 to 36 hours. Symptoms start about an hour after use and reach their peak after 4 to 10 hours.

Psychological effects: The main effects are perceptual distortions that can vary with dose, setting, and the user's mood. Tolerance and psychological dependence can develop rapidly following chronic use.

Physical effects: The most common effects are elevated heart rate, increased blood pressure, and dilated pupils. Because DOB and DOM are hallucinogens, their effects are unpredictable and could be substantially different each time they are used.

Overdose symptoms: In general, toxicity with these drugs results in mild symptoms that may include agitation, elevated blood pressure, rapid heart rate, dilated pupils, and excessive sweating. Fatigue and poor concentration are also common. Occasionally, severe depression, anxiety, and delirium can occur. Severe overdose may cause dangerously high body temperature, blood-clotting problems, muscle weakness, seizures, and acute kidney failure.

Withdrawal symptoms: These drugs are highly addictive, and physical and psychological dependence develops rapidly. Abrupt cessation of use may cause anxiety, paranoia, aggressive behavior, and strong drug cravings. Suicidal ideation has been reported. Psychotic behavior may persist for months or years after discontinuation of use.

HASHISH

COMMON STREET NAMES: Boom, chronic, gangster, hash, hash oil, hemp

DEA CLASS: Class I

PHARMACOLOGIC CLASS: Cannabinoid

Description: Hashish contains the psychoactive chemical delta-9-tetrahydrocannabinol (THC). It is made from the THC-rich resinous material of the cannabis plant, which is collected, dried, and then compressed into a variety of forms, such as balls, cakes, or cookie-like sheets. Pieces are then broken off, placed in pipes, and smoked. The Middle East, North Africa, Pakistan, and Afghanistan are the main sources of hashish.

Hashish (and hash oil) are stronger forms of marijuana. The drug's effects depend on the potency of the THC content. Hashish averages 2 to 8 percent THC, but it can contain as much as 20 percent. The drug has no legitimate medical use, but THC and a synthetic cannabinol (nabilone) are used to prevent vomiting in patients receiving cancer chemotherapy. In some studies, cannabis was found to have effects similar to analgesics, muscle relaxants, and appetite stimulants.

Hash oil is a tar-like solution distilled from hashish; it can contain anywhere from 15 to 70 percent THC. Cannabis growers usually try to maximize the plant's THC content.

Method of use: Hashish is usually smoked as a cigarette (called a joint or nail) or in a pipe (bong).

Duration of action: Hashish produces an effect almost immediately and reaches its peak in about 30 minutes. The effects usually wear off after 3 to 4 hours. Chronic users may not experience anything until 30 to 90 minutes after the first inhalation, but the effects can last for up to 8 hours.

Psychological effects: Distortion of time and space, loss of memory, impaired judgment, panic and anxiety attacks, and a false sense of well-being. Users taking cannabis in large doses have had psychotic episodes with paranoid or schizophrenic characteristics. Prolonged use of cannabis may lead to tolerance and psychological dependence.

Physical effects: Early physical effects may include nausea and vomiting. Later-stage effects may include memory loss, poor coordination, impaired learning skills, elevated heart rate and blood pressure, dry mouth, dry eyes, and blurred vision. Experts continue to debate whether physical dependence can occur.

Overdose symptoms: Heavy users rapidly develop tolerance and need progressively higher doses to obtain the same effects as before. Symptoms of overdose may include increased appetite, red and swollen eyes, dry mouth, poor motor coordination, and elevated heart rate and blood pressure.

Withdrawal symptoms: Withdrawal symptoms may include loss of appetite, anxiety, sleeplessness, irritability, restlessness, visual abnormalities, excessive sweating, headache, and stomach upset.

HEROIN

COMMON STREET NAMES: Brown sugar, dope, H, horse, junk, skag, skunk, smack, white horse
DEA CLASS: Class I
PHARMACOLOGIC CLASS: Narcotic analgesic

Description: Heroin is derived from the resin of the poppy plant. Pure heroin is a white powder with a bitter taste but is rarely sold on the street. Most heroin is distributed as powder that varies in color due to additives and manufacturing impurities. Another form of heroin, "black tar," has become increasingly available in the United States. The color and consistency of black tar heroin results from the crude processing methods used to manufacture the substance in Mexico. Heroin, which is illegal in the United States, is used in very limited treatment applications in other countries.

Method of use: Ingested, snorted, smoked, and injected IV (also called mainlining), IM, or SC (also called skin popping). Injection is the most efficient way to administer low-purity heroin, and until recently was the preferred method of use. The availability of higher-purity heroin now allows users to snort or smoke the narcotic.

Duration of action: The euphoric effects usually occur 7 to 8 seconds after injection. IM injection produces a relatively slow onset, typically 5 to 8 minutes. When heroin is sniffed or smoked, the peak effects usually occur within 10 to 15 minutes.

Psychological effects: Enhanced sexual pleasure, euphoria, psychological dependence, and significantly impaired mental function. The psychological dependence associated with narcotic addiction is complex. Long after physical dependence has ended, the addict may continue to think and talk about the drug and feel unable to manage daily activities without it.

Physical effects: Short-term physical effects include drowsiness, dry mouth, flushing, and a heavy feeling in the extremities. Long-term effects may include alternating wakefulness and drowsiness, slowed breathing, and reduced mental functioning. The development of infectious diseases—such as HIV/AIDS, infection of the heart lining, various abscesses, pneumonia, and hepatitis—is a major problem in heroin users. In addition, the impurities in the drug—especially talc—may clog blood vessels and damage the lungs, liver, kidneys, and brain.

Overdose symptoms: Tolerance and physical dependence may develop after only 2 to 3 days of continued heroin use. This greatly increases the risk of overdose as progressively higher doses are needed to obtain the same effects as before. Overdose may cause shallow breathing, convulsions, coma, and possibly death. In addition, heroin suppresses breathing and can cause the lungs to fill with fluid, which may also lead to death. Since heroin is manufactured in clandestine laboratories and drug impurities are unknown, abusers are at great risk of overdose or death.

Withdrawal symptoms: Withdrawal from heroin is extremely painful and dangerous. Symptoms are worse in people who have used large doses for prolonged periods. Abrupt withdrawal of heroin in a chronic user may be fatal. Symptoms may begin to appear within 6 hours after the last dose and continue to manifest within 24 hours. Withdrawal symptoms reach their peak at 48 to 72 hours following the last dose but may continue for weeks. Early symptoms include irritability, insomnia, diminished appetite, gooseflesh, hot and cold flashes, dilated pupils, runny nose, severe yawning, severe sneezing, excessive tearing, and cold-like symptoms. Later-stage symptoms include abdominal cramps, bone and muscle pain in the back and extremities, pronounced depression, nausea, vomiting, diarrhea, alternating fever and chills, excessive sweating, and elevated heart rate and blood pressure. Muscle spasms and kicking movements can also occur, which may explain the expression "kicking the habit."

KHAT

COMMON STREET NAMES: Khat has more than 40 street names, including Cadillac express, cat, chat, ephedrine, gat, go fast, kat, qat, slick, sniff, superspeed, tohai, tschat, wonderstar
DEA CLASS: Class I (cathine, one of the ingredients in khat, is Class IV)
PHARMACOLOGIC CLASS: CNS stimulant

Description: Khat is a naturally occurring stimulant derived from the *Catha edulis* shrub. This shrub is cultivated mainly in East Africa and the Arabian Peninsula, where the use of khat is an established cultural tradition for many social occasions. Khat is illegal in the U.S. but is used in some countries to aid weight loss.

The stimulating effects of khat are due to cathinone (a phenylpropylamine agent) and, to a much lesser extent, cathine (a norpseudoephedrine agent). Cathinone is about 10 times more potent than cathine and is only present in fresh leaves. As the leaves mature or dry, cathinone is converted to cathine. The effects of these alkaloids resemble those of amphetamines, particularly cathinone.

Methcathinone is an illegal synthetic drug that is sold as an alternative to methamphetamine. It has a chemical structure similar to cathinone but has stronger addictive properties and side effects.

Method of use: Usually ingested but can be snorted. The leaves are often chewed like tobacco and the juice swallowed; occasionally the chewed leaves are also swallowed. In addition, khat can be brewed as a tea or crushed and mixed with honey to make a paste.

Duration of action: Several hours

Psychological effects: Aggressive verbal outbursts, behavioral changes, euphoria, pressured speech, and psychotic reactions. Rarely, schizophrenic behavior or manic-like psychosis may occur. Psychological dependence develops rapidly.

Physical effects: Anorexia, constipation, dilated pupils, dry mouth, elevated blood pressure and body temperature, headache, increased heart rate with palpitations, insomnia, mouth inflammation or infection, severe nausea, swollen cornea, and tremors. Rarely, abnormal heart rhythm and severe chest pain may occur. Cathinone is very addictive, and physical dependence develops rapidly with chronic use.

Overdose symptoms: The main symptoms are hyperactivity, severely elevated blood pressure and body temperature, and seizures. Serious overdose symptoms from chewing khat are due to the phenylpropylamine content of the leaves.

Withdrawal symptoms: Cathinone is highly addictive, and physical and psychological dependence develop rapidly. Abruptly stopping the drug may precipitate withdrawal symptoms such as anxiety, paranoia, aggressive behavior, and strong drug cravings. Suicidal ideation has also been reported. Psychotic behavior may persist for months or years after discontinuation of use.

LSD (LYSERGIC ACID DIETHYLAMIDE)

COMMON STREET NAMES: Acid, blotter, boomers, cubes, dots, L, mellow yello, microdots, tabs, trips, window pane, yellow sunshines
DEA CLASS: Class I
PHARMACOLOGIC CLASS: Hallucinogen

Description: LSD is a potent hallucinogenic substance. It has no legitimate medical use. LSD, commonly referred to as acid, is usually sold as "dots" on blotter paper, but it can also be found as tablets, square gel caps, and rarely, in liquid form. Rogue chemists manufacturer the drug as a crystalline powder that can be reduced to a clear liquid for dosing purposes.

Method of use: Ingested

Duration of action: Up to 12 hours

Psychological effects: Psychological effects depend on the individual. The user may feel various emotions at once or swing rapidly from one mood to another. Depending on the dose, the drug may produce delusions, visual hallucinations, flashbacks, severe depression, and panic attacks. The user often refers to this experience as a "bad trip." Some LSD users experience severe, terrifying thoughts, and become fearful of losing control, going insane, or dying. Long-term use may cause tolerance and psychological dependence.

Physical effects: The effects of LSD are unpredictable, but the drug is not physically addictive. Physical reactions to LSD depend on the dose; the user's personality, mood, and expectations; and the surroundings in which the drug is used. Initial effects may include dilated pupils, elevated body temperature, increased heart rate and blood pressure, excessive sweating, loss of appetite, sleeplessness, dry mouth, and tremors.

Overdose symptoms: LSD is not considered addictive; it does not produce compulsive drug-seeking behavior as do cocaine, amphetamines, heroin, and alcohol. However, it does produce tolerance, and chronic users must take progressively higher doses to achieve the same effects as before. This is particularly dangerous due to the unpredictability of LSD. Symptoms of overdose may include excessive tearing, irregular gait, dilated pupils, rapid heart rate, tremors, and elevated blood pressure and body temperature. Overdose with LSD can be frightening and cause panic. Injuries and fatal accidents have been reported during states of LSD intoxication.

Withdrawal symptoms: None are reported, since no evidence of physical dependence can be detected when the drug is abruptly withdrawn.

MARIJUANA

COMMON STREET NAMES: Blunt, dope, ganja, grass, herb, joints, Mary Jane, pot, reefer, sinsemilla, skunk, weed
DEA CLASS: Class I
PHARMACOLOGIC CLASS: Cannabinoid

Description: Marijuana is a green, brown, or gray mixture of dried, shredded leaves, stems, seeds, and flowers of the hemp plant (*Cannabis sativa*). Cannabis is a term that refers to marijuana and other drugs made from the same plant. The active ingredient in marijuana is delta-9-tetrahydrocannabinol (THC), which is responsible for its psychoactive effects.

Method of use: Smoked as a cigarette (joint) or in a pipe (bong). Users also smoke blunts, the street name for cigars that have had their tobacco contents replaced with marijuana and other illicit drugs such as crack. Marijuana can also be mixed into foods or used to brew a tea.

Duration of action: Effects begin as soon as the drug enters the brain and can last from 1 to 3 hours.

Psychological effects: All cannabis products are mind-altering drugs. Users initially feel euphoric but then become extremely sleepy and depressed. Other effects include distorted perception, mood changes, anxiety or panic attacks, and difficulty with thinking and problem solving.

Physical effects: Short-term effects may include memory loss, poor coordination, impaired learning skills, elevated heart rate and blood pressure, dry mouth, dry eyes, and blurred vision. The potential for heart attack increases within the first hour of use due to the drug's effects on heart rate and blood pressure. Marijuana may also impair the immune system, which greatly increases the risk of bacterial infections. Tolerance and physical dependence may develop with long-term use.

In addition, smoking marijuana causes similar effects on the lungs as smoking tobacco, including daily cough and phlegm production, frequent chest illnesses, heightened risk of lung infections, and greater tendency toward obstructed airways. Marijuana contains 50 to 70 percent more carcinogenic hydrocarbons than tobacco, and cancer of the respiratory tract and lungs can result from marijuana smoking.

Overdose symptoms: Heavy users rapidly develop tolerance and need progressively higher doses to obtain the same effects as before. Serious health effects are more likely to be secondary to impaired judgment and behavioral problems rather than direct overdose effects. Early symptoms of overdose may include excessive sleepiness, mild euphoria, short-term memory loss, difficulty in accomplishing tasks, and lapses of attention. Serious overdose effects may include extreme tiredness, severe weakness and drowsiness, dizziness, slurred speech, irregular gait, decreased motor coordination and muscle strength, and rarely, psychosis.

Withdrawal symptoms: Abrupt discontinuation of use may cause drug cravings, irritability, agitation, apprehension, aggressiveness, tremulousness, sleeplessness, excessive sweating, and elevated anxiety. Additional symptoms may include increased aggression that reaches its peak effects about a week after the last smoked dose.

MDMA (3,4-METHYLENEDIOXYMETHAMPHETAMINE)

COMMON STREET NAMES: Adam, clarity, ecstasy, Eve, lover's speed, peace, STP, X, XTC

DEA CLASS: Class I

PHARMACOLOGIC CLASS: Amphetamine, CNS stimulant

Description: MDMA is an illegally manufactured variation of mescaline and amphetamine. It has both psychedelic and stimulant effects. It is a so-called "club drug" used at all-night dance parties known as "raves."

Because MDMA is manufactured in clandestine laboratories, it is rarely pure, and the amount of active drug in an oral dose can vary considerably.

Method of use: Ingested and snorted

Duration of action: Psychedelic effects last 4 to 6 hours.

Psychological effects: Anxiety, confusion, depression, paranoia, drug craving, and aggressive and impulsive behavior. Tolerance and psychological dependence may develop with chronic use.

Physical effects: High blood pressure, increased heart rate, elevated body temperature, jaw and teeth clenching, muscle tension, chills and/or sweating, nausea, blurred vision, faintness, dizziness, and drug craving. MDMA can increase heart rate significantly during strenuous physical activity, but the heart does not respond normally. Since MDMA use is associated with such strenuous activities as dancing for hours, the drug's effects on the heart could increase the risk of heart damage and cardiovascular collapse.

Overdose symptoms: Large doses may cause extremely high fever, severely high blood pressure, rapid heart rate, and kidney and heart failure. *Warning:* Drinking too much water after taking MDMA can be lethal. MDMA significantly increases the blood levels of vasopressin (an antidiuretic hormone). Vasopressin causes the body to retain more water, which dilutes the amount of sodium and other salts in the blood. This can swell the brain, causing damage to the brain and nerve tissue.

Withdrawal symptoms: MDMA is a powerfully addictive drug, and physical and psychological dependence develops rapidly. Abrupt cessation may precipitate withdrawal symptoms such as anxiety, paranoia, aggressive behavior, and strong drug cravings. Suicidal ideation has been reported. Psychotic behavior may persist for months or years after discontinuation of use.

MESCALINE (PEYOTE CACTUS)
COMMON STREET NAMES: Buttons, cactus, mesc
DEA CLASS: Class I
PHARMACOLOGIC CLASS: Hallucinogen

Description: Peyote is a small cactus whose principal active ingredient is mescaline (3, 4, 5-trimethoxyphenethylamine), a compound that is structurally similar to amphetamines. It can be either extracted from the plant or produced synthetically.

Method of use: Ingested (sometimes brewed as a tea) and smoked

Duration of action: 6 to 12 hours

Psychological effects: Common effects include visual and auditory hallucinations, abnormal sensory perception, amnesia, and anxiety. The following may also occur: suicidal thoughts, emotional instability, fear, anxiety, paranoia, and flashbacks.

Physical effects: Dizziness, drowsiness, headache, light-headedness, excessive salivation, tremors, weakness, increased muscle tone, blurred vision, dilated pupils, irregular gait, elevated blood pressure, stomach cramps, nausea, vomiting, abnormal reflexes, shivering, feelings of hot or cold, and respiratory depression. The drug can also cause numbness of the tongue and mouth. Tolerance has been documented but decreases rapidly within a few days following cessation of use. Although physiological drug addiction generally does not occur, cross-tolerance with other hallucinogens can develop.

Overdose symptoms: Overdose can cause death due to homicidal, psychotic, or suicidal behavior. Signs of mescaline overdose resemble those of LSD. A wide range of symptoms can be present, since users often take other drugs simultaneously with mescaline. Concomitant administration of alcohol with mescaline may produce prolonged seizures and coma.

Withdrawal symptoms: None are reported, since no evidence of physical dependence can be detected when the drug is abruptly withdrawn.

METHAQUALONE
COMMON STREET NAMES: Ludes, mandrex, Quaalude, quad, quay
DEA CLASS: Class I
PHARMACOLOGIC CLASS: Sedative, hypnotic

Description: Methaqualone has properties similar to those of barbiturates. It was used previously for the short-term treatment of insomnia but was withdrawn from the market in the U.S. and other countries due to a high risk of abuse.

Method of use: Ingested

Duration of action: Methaqualone absorbs rapidly following ingestion. The drug reaches peak serum levels within 2 hours, with the effects lasting 5 to 8 hours.

Psychological effects: Anxiety, confusion, false sense of well-being, and impaired perception. Psychological dependence may occur with prolonged use of high doses.

Physical effects: Excessive sleepiness, loss of coordination, low blood pressure, sexual dysfunction, and slowed heart rate and breathing.

Excessive use leads to tolerance, physical dependence, and withdrawal symptoms similar to those of barbiturates.

Overdose symptoms: Tolerance develops rapidly, and progressively higher doses are needed to obtain the same effects as before. Signs of overdose may include extreme tiredness, irregular gait, muscle rigidity, muscular hyperactivity, rapid heart rate, low blood pressure, respiratory failure, heart failure, seizures, and coma.

Withdrawal symptoms: Methaqualone withdrawal may lead to death if left untreated. Symptoms include weakness, abdominal cramps, nausea, vomiting, disorientation, anxiety, restlessness, rapid heart rate, visual hallucinations, stupor, delirium, tremors, and seizures.

5-MeO-DIPT (5-METHOXY-N, N-DIISOPROPYLTRYPTAMINE)
COMMON STREET NAMES: Foxy, foxy methoxy
DEA CLASS: Class I
PHARMACOLOGIC CLASS: Hallucinogen

Description: This drug has the same chemical properties and effects as other tryptamine-based Class I hallucinogens.

Method of use: Ingested, snorted, and smoked

Duration of action: 3 to 6 hours

Psychological effects: This drug can cause the same psychological effects as other hallucinogens, including changes in perception, visual distortions, agitation, hyperactivity, confusion, euphoria, anxiety, mood alterations, slowed thinking, delirium, and unpredictable behavior. Long-term use may cause tolerance and psychological dependence.

Physical effects: This drug can produce the same physical effects as other hallucinogens, including CNS depression or stimulation, nausea, vomiting, diarrhea, elevated blood pressure and body temperature, abnormally fast heart rate, blurred vision, excessive salivation, irregular gait, loss of appetite, irregular breathing, numbness in the extremities, dizziness, drowsiness, decreased REM sleep, enhanced color awareness, and time distortion.

Overdose symptoms: This drug is not considered addictive; it does not produce compulsive drug-seeking behavior as do cocaine, amphetamine, heroin, and alcohol. However, it does produce tolerance, and chronic users must take progressively higher doses to achieve the same effects as before. This is particularly dangerous due to the unpredictability of the drug's effects. Symptoms of overdose may include irregular gait, rapid heart rate, tremors, and elevated blood pressure and body temperature.

Withdrawal symptoms: None are reported, since no evidence of physical dependence can be detected when the drug is abruptly withdrawn.

PCP (PHENCYCLIDINE)
COMMON STREET NAMES: Angel dust, boat, hog, love boat, peace pill
DEA CLASS: Class I and II
PHARMACOLOGIC CLASS: Hallucinogen

Description: PCP is a dissociative anesthetic with sympathomimetic and hallucinogenic properties. It is a bitter-tasting, white crystalline powder that can dissolve in water and be mixed with dyes. PCP is manufactured illegally by rogue chemists in places known as "bucket labs." It is related chemically to ketamine and is a potent analgesic and anesthetic. The drug was originally developed as a tranquilizer for animals. PCP was formerly used in humans as an intravenous anesthetic, but severe adverse effects—especially postoperative psychosis—precluded its use. However, the drug still has some veterinary applications.

Method of use: Ingested, smoked, snorted, and injected IV. The most popular method is to apply the drug to a marijuana joint or menthol cigarette and smoke it, known as a "kool-dip."

Duration of action: If smoked, the effects start in 2 to 5 minutes and last about 15 to 30 minutes. In chronic users the effects can last 4 to 6 hours but may also linger for 1 to 2 days.

Psychological effects: PCP is a highly addictive drug that can cause psychological dependence. Frequent use can result in tolerance and drug craving. Effects may include mood and perception alteration, paranoia, panic attacks, anxiety, decreased awareness, compulsive drug-seeking behavior, and suicidal ideation. It can induce psychosis that is indistinguishable from schizophrenia. The following have also been reported: hallucinations, euphoria, agitation, hyperactivity, disorientation, and violent delusional behavior.

Physical effects: The physical effects of PCP are unpredictable, but the following have been reported: elevated pulse and heart rate, increased blood pressure and body temperature, muscle relaxation, dilated pupils, rapid eye movement, nausea, vomiting, blurred vision, dizziness, tremors, shallow breathing, loss of coordination, excessive salivation, excessive perspiration, convulsions, numbness and tingling in the extremities, and occasionally, excessively high fever. Constricted pupils and seizures are more common in children. Substantially increased blood pressure is the hallmark sign that usually resolves within 4 hours but can persist for more than 24 hours. Respiratory effects are uncommon without concurrent use of sedatives, narcotics, or alcohol.

Overdose symptoms: An overdose can cause death due to respiratory depression and coma. Other symptoms include unpredictable behavior, depression, convulsions, flashbacks, psychosis, delusions, and dangerously high fever.

Withdrawal symptoms: None are reported, since no evidence of physical dependence can be detected when the drug is abruptly withdrawn.

PMA (PARAMETHOXYAMPHETAMINE)
COMMON STREET NAMES: Death, Mitsubishi, double-stack
DEA CLASS: Class I
PHARMACOLOGIC CLASS: Amphetamine, hallucinogen, CNS stimulant

Description: PMA is a synthetic hallucinogen that is structurally related to MDMA but is significantly more lethal, even in smaller doses. It is produced legally in the U.S. for limited commercial applications and scientific research.

Method of use: Ingested, but the powder form may be injected or snorted.

Duration of action: Up to 8 hours; effects begin 30 to 60 minutes after use and reach their peak after approximately 90 minutes.

Psychological effects: Initial feelings include a rush of euphoria followed by a general sense of happiness and well-being. These effects are followed by a "coming down" phase 3 to 6 hours later, resulting in depression, anxiety, and general negativity that can persist for several days. Prolonged use may cause tolerance and psychological dependence.

Physical effects: Depends on the dose. A single small dose can cause labored breathing, erratic eye movement, elevated pulse rate and body temperature, high blood pressure, muscle spasms, nausea, and heightened visual stimulation. Larger doses may cause irregular heart rhythm, serious breathing difficulties, severely elevated body temperature, vomiting, kidney failure, and cardiac arrest.

Overdose symptoms: Illicit drug makers sometimes stamp MDMA logos on their PMA "products" in order to pass them off as MDMA. This could increase the risk of fatal overdose because users may unknownly mix PMA with MDMA. Signs of overdose can include vomiting, severely elevated body temperature, convulsions, coma, and death.

Withdrawal symptoms: None are reported, since no evidence of physical dependence can be detected when the drug is abruptly withdrawn.

PSILOCYBIN

COMMON STREET NAMES: Magic mushroom, musk, purple passion, shrooms
DEA CLASS: Class I
PHARMACOLOGIC CLASS: Hallucinogen

Description: Psilocybin, or psilocyn, is obtained from certain mush-rooms indigenous to tropical and subtropical regions of South America, Mexico, and the United States. These mushrooms are available fresh or dried. The effects produced by dried or brewed mushrooms are far less predictable and largely depend on the particular mushrooms used and the age and preservation of the extract. Psilocybin has properties similar to LSD but is less potent. It has no legitimate medical use.

Method of use: Ingested; the mushrooms are sometimes brewed as a tea or added to food to mask the bitter flavor.

Duration of action: 4 to 6 hours

Psychological effects: Vivid visual and auditory hallucinations, panic attacks, and emotional disturbances. Long-term use may cause tolerance and psychological dependence.

Physical effects: There are many species of mushrooms that contain varying amounts of psilocybin as well as uncertain amounts of other chemicals. It is nearly impossible to predict the physical effects of this compound. The most commonly reported effects include drowsiness, vomiting, muscle weakness, and panic attacks. The exact mechanism of action and extent of toxicity are unknown.

Overdose symptoms: Symptoms of overdose may occur 30 to 60 minutes (and sometimes as late as 3 hours) following ingestion. Signs include a pleasant yet apprehensive mood, impaired judgment, compulsive move-ments, vertigo, dilated pupils, irregular gait, tingling sensations, muscle weakness, loss of muscle tone, and drowsiness that almost progresses to sleep. Children may develop high temperatures with seizures.

Withdrawal symptoms: None are reported, since no evidence of physical dependence can be detected when the drug is abruptly withdrawn.

SALVIA DIVINORUM

COMMON STREET NAMES: Diviner's sage, herbal ecstasy, Mexican mint, ska Maria Pastora
DEA CLASS: Not classified
PHARMACOLOGIC CLASS: Hallucinogen

Description: *S. divinorum* is a perennial herb in the mint family. It's one of several vision-inducing plants used by the Mazatec Indians of Mexico.

The herb's active ingredient is Salvinorin A, a psychoactive chemical that can cause intense hallucinations.

Method of use: Ingested (usually as a tea), smoked, and chewed. The herb is most effective when it's vaporized and inhaled.

Duration of action: Hallucinogenic effects can last up to 1 hour.

Psychological effects: S. divinorum may cause similar psychological effects as ketamine, mescaline, and psilocybin, including changes in perception, hallucinations, and delirium. Long-term use may cause tolerance and psychological dependence.

Physical effects: S. divinorum may induce similar physical effects as ketamine, mescaline, and psilocybin, including CNS depression or stimulation, nausea, vomiting, diarrhea, elevated blood pressure, and abnormally fast heart rate.

Overdose symptoms: This drug is not considered addictive; it does not produce compulsive drug-seeking behavior as do cocaine, amphetamines, heroin, and alcohol. However, it does produce tolerance, and chronic users must take progressively higher doses to achieve the same effects as before. This is particularly dangerous due to the unpredictability of the drug's effects. Signs of overdose may include irregular gait, rapid heart rate, tremors, and elevated blood pressure and body temperature.

Withdrawal symptoms: None are reported, since no evidence of physical dependence can be detected when the drug is abruptly withdrawn.

Section 4

Common Prescription Drugs

Because patients with psychological disorders are often under simultaneous treatment for other medical problems, this section presents you with brief descriptions of the most commonly prescribed drugs and their customary uses. Based primarily on government-approved product labeling as submitted for publication in *Physicians' Desk Reference*®, the information is organized alphabetically by each medication's leading brand name and cross-referenced by the generic name. To see whether a drug is likely to interact with a patient's psychotropic regimen, check the appropriate listings in Section 2 of this book.

Abacavir *See Ziagen, page 641.*

Abacavir, Lamivudine, and Zidovudine *See Trizivir, page 627.*

Acarbose *See Precose, page 594.*

ACCOLATE
Zafirlukast

Accolate is prescribed to prevent asthma attacks. Unlike some of the inhaled medications used to relieve attacks in progress, it is not a steroid. Instead, it works by blocking the action of certain types of leukotrienes—natural compounds that cause swelling and constriction in the lungs. Taken in tablet form, it is used for long-term treatment.

Accuneb *See Proventil, page 599.*

ACCUPRIL
Quinapril

Accupril is used in the treatment of high blood pressure. It can be taken alone or in combination with a thiazide type of water pill such as HydroDIURIL. Accupril is in a family of drugs known as "ACE inhibitors." It works by preventing a chemical in the blood called angiotensin I from converting into a more potent form that increases salt and water retention in the body. Accupril also enhances blood flow throughout the blood vessels. Along with other drugs, Accupril is also prescribed in the treatment of congestive heart failure.

ACCURETIC
Quinapril with Hydrochlorothiazide

Accuretic combines two types of blood pressure medication. The first, quinapril hydrochloride, is an ACE (angiotensin-converting enzyme) inhibitor. It works by preventing a chemical in the blood called angiotensin I from converting into a more potent form (angiotensin II) that increases salt and water retention in the body and causes the blood vessels to constrict—two actions that tend to increase blood pressure.

To aid in clearing excess water from the body, Accuretic also contains hydrochlorothiazide, a diuretic that promotes production of urine. Diuretics often wash too much potassium out of the body along with the water. However, the ACE inhibitor part of Accuretic tends to keep potassium in the body, thereby canceling this unwanted effect.

Accuretic is not used for the initial treatment of high blood pressure. It is saved for later use, when a single blood pressure medication is not sufficient for the job. In addition, some doctors are using Accuretic along with other drugs to treat congestive heart failure.

ACCUTANE
Isotretinoin
Other brand name: Amnesteem

Accutane, a chemical cousin of vitamin A, is prescribed for the treatment of severe, disfiguring cystic acne that has not cleared up in response to milder medications such as antibiotics. It works on the oil glands within the skin, shrinking them and diminishing their output. The patient takes Accutane by mouth every day for several months, then stops. The antiacne effect can last even after the course of medication is finished.

Acebutolol *See Sectral, page 609.*

ACEON
Perindopril

Aceon is used in the treatment of high blood pressure. It can be taken alone or in combination with thiazide diuretics that help rid the body of excess water. Aceon belongs to a family of drugs called angiotensin converting enzyme (ACE) inhibitors. It works by preventing a chemical in the blood called angiotensin I from converting into a more potent form that increases salt and water retention in the body. Aceon also improves the flow of blood through the circulatory system.

Acetaminophen with Codeine *See Tylenol with Codeine, page 628.*

Acetaminophen with Oxycodone *See Percocet, page 588.*

Acetazolamide *See Diamox, page 519.*

Acetic acid *See Aci-Jel, page 477.*

Acetic acid and Hydrocortisone *See VoSoL HC, page 636.*

Achromycin V *See Tetracycline, page 619.*

ACI-JEL
Acetic acid

In some cases of vaginitis, the level of acidity in the vagina becomes too low. Applying Aci-Jel internally restores the acidity and keeps it within the normal range.

ACIPHEX
Rabeprazole

AcipHex blocks acid production in the stomach. It is prescribed for the short-term (4 to 8 weeks) treatment of sores and inflammation in the upper digestive canal (esophagus). This condition, known as gastro-esophageal reflux disease (GERD), is caused by the backflow of stomach acid into the esophagus over a prolonged period of time. Because GERD can be chronic, doctors sometimes continue to prescribe AcipHex to prevent a relapse after the initial course of treatment.

AcipHex can also be prescribed for the short-term (up to 4 weeks) treatment of duodenal ulcers (ulcers that form just outside the stomach at the top of the small intestine), and for Zollinger-Ellison syndrome, a disease which causes the stomach to produce too much acid. The drug is classified as a "proton pump inhibitor." It works by blocking a specific enzyme essential to the production of stomach acid. It begins reducing acid within an hour of administration.

AcipHex is sometimes combined with the antibiotics amoxicillin and clarithromycin to treat infections caused by *H. pylori*, a type of bacteria that lives in the digestive tract and is often associated with recurrent ulcers.

ACLOVATE
Alclometasone

Aclovate, a synthetic steroid medication of the cortisone family, is spread on the skin to relieve certain types of itchy rashes, including psoriasis.

Acrivastine with Pseudoephedrine *See Semprex-D, page 609.*

ACTIGALL
Ursodiol
Other brand name: Urso 250

Actigall is used to help dissolve certain kinds of gallstones. For people who suffer from gallstones but do not want to undergo surgery to remove them, Actigall treatment may be a good alternative. It is also recommended if age, infirmity, or a poor reaction to anesthesia makes someone a poor candidate for surgery.

Actigall is also used to prevent gallstones in people on rapid-weight-loss diets. And under the brand name Urso 250, its active ingredient is prescribed to treat liver disease caused by hardening and blockage of the bile ducts (primary biliary cirrhosis).

ACTIVELLA AND FEMHRT
Estrogen with Progestin
Other brand name: Prefest

These medications are designed for use in hormone replacement therapy. Both combine a form of estrogen with a substance that acts like progesterone. Both relieve the symptoms of menopause, and both are prescribed to prevent osteoporosis in postmenopausal women. (Activella is also used for vaginal atrophy.)

Estrogen, when taken by itself, poses an increased risk of uterine cancer. The progestin in these products largely counteracts this effect.

ACTONEL
Risedronate

Although our bones seem solid and stable, they actually undergo constant renewal. Specialized cells called *osteoclasts* draw used calcium out of the bones while other cells called *osteoblasts* replace it. Especially after menopause, this process can get out of balance. Calcium starts to leach out of the bones faster than it can be replaced, leading to the brittle-bone disease called osteoporosis.

Actonel combats this problem by reducing the activity of the osteoclasts and slowing the loss of calcium from the bones. It is prescribed for postmenopausal women, both to prevent osteoporosis and to strengthen the bones once the disease has begun. It is also used to prevent or treat osteoporosis resulting from therapy with steroid medications, and it is used in the treatment of Paget's disease, a condition in which patches of bone become softened and enlarged.

Both Actonel and a similar drug called Fosamax are members of the family of drugs called bisphosphonates.

ACTOS
Pioglitazone

Actos is used to control high blood sugar in type 2 diabetes. This form of the illness usually stems from the body's inability to make good use of insulin, the natural hormone that helps to transfer sugar out of the blood and into the cells, where it's converted to energy. Actos works by improving the body's response to its natural supply of insulin, rather than increasing its insulin output. Actos also reduces the production of unneeded sugar in the liver.

Actos (and the similar drug Avandia) can be used alone or in combination with insulin injections or other oral diabetes medications such as DiaBeta, Micronase, Glucotrol, or Glucophage.

ACULAR
Ketorolac, ocular

Acular relieves the itchy eyes brought on by seasonal allergies. Doctors also prescribe it to reduce inflammation after cataracts have been removed from the eyes. A preservative-free formulation (Acular PF) is used to reduce pain and light-sensitivity following operations to correct vision. Acular belongs to the class of medications called nonsteroidal anti-inflammatory drugs.

Acyclovir *See Zovirax, page 643.*

Adalat *See Procardia, page 597.*

Adapalene *See Differin, page 520.*

ADIPEX-P
Phentermine
Other brand name: Ionamin

Adipex-P, an appetite suppressant, is prescribed for short-term use (a few weeks) as part of an overall weight reduction program that also includes dieting, exercise, and counseling. The drug is for use only by excessively overweight individuals who have a condition—such as diabetes, high blood pressure, or high cholesterol—that could lead to serious medical problems.

ADVAIR DISKUS
Fluticasone and Salmeterol

Advair Diskus is an oral inhaler that contains two types of asthma medication. One is fluticasone propionate, a steroid that reduces inflammation in the lungs. The other, salmeterol, is a long-acting bronchodilator that opens up the airways. Together, the two ingredients provide better control of asthma than either does individually.

ADVICOR
Lovastatin and Extended-Release niacin

Advicor is a cholesterol-lowering drug. Excess cholesterol in the bloodstream can lead to hardening of the arteries and heart disease. Advicor lowers total cholesterol and LDL ("bad") cholesterol, while raising the amount of HDL ("good") cholesterol.

Advicor is a combination of two cholesterol-fighting ingredients: extended-release niacin and lovastatin (Mevacor). It is prescribed only when other drugs and a program of diet, exercise, and weight reduction have been unsuccessful in lowering cholesterol levels.

Advil *See Motrin, page 571.*

AEROBID
Flunisolide
Other brand names: AeroBid-M, Nasalide

AeroBid is prescribed for people who need long-term treatment to control and prevent the symptoms of asthma. It contains an anti-inflammatory steroid type of medication and may reduce or eliminate the need for other corticosteroids. A nasal-spray form of the drug (Nasalide) is available for relief of hay fever.

AGENERASE
Amprenavir

Agenerase is one of the many drugs now used to combat human immunodeficiency virus (HIV) infection. HIV undermines the immune system, reducing the body's ability to fight off other infections and eventually leading to the deadly condition known as acquired immune deficiency syndrome (AIDS).

Agenerase slows the progress of HIV by interfering with an important step in the virus's reproductive cycle. The drug is a member of the group of "protease inhibitors" famous for having successfully halted the advance of the virus in many HIV-positive individuals. Agenerase is prescribed only as part of a "drug cocktail" that attacks the virus on several fronts. It is not used alone.

AGGRENOX
Aspirin with Extended-release dipyridamole

Aggrenox is prescribed to stave off a stroke in people who have had a "mini-stroke" (transient ischemic attack) or a full-scale stroke due to a blood clot blocking an artery in the brain.

Both the ingredients in Aggrenox prevent the formation of clots by interfering with the tendency of blood platelets to clump together. However, the two ingredients together are more effective at preventing strokes than either ingredient taken alone. Aggrenox doesn't eliminate the possibility of a stroke; but it does reduce the odds by almost six percentage points during the first two years of treatment.

Aktob *See Tobrex, page 622.*

ALAMAST
Pemirolast

Alamast is taken to prevent the itchy eyes caused by allergies such as hay fever. It works by inhibiting the release of certain inflammatory agents, such as histamine and leukotrienes, that the body produces in response to an allergen.

Albuterol *See Proventil, page 599.*

Alclometasone *See Aclovate, page 477.*

ALDACTAZIDE
Spironolactone with Hydrochlorothiazide

Aldactazide is used in the treatment of high blood pressure and other conditions that require the elimination of excess fluid from the body. These conditions include congestive heart failure, cirrhosis of the liver, and kidney disease. Aldactazide combines two diuretic drugs that help the body produce and eliminate more urine. Spironolactone, one of the ingredients, helps to minimize the potassium loss that can be caused by the hydrochlorothiazide component.

ALDACTONE
Spironolactone

Aldactone flushes excess salt and water from the body and controls high blood pressure. It is used in the diagnosis and treatment of hyperaldosteronism, a condition in which the adrenal gland secretes too much aldosterone (a hormone that regulates the body's salt and potassium levels). It is also used in treating other conditions that require the elimination of excess fluid from the body. These conditions include congestive heart failure, high blood pressure, cirrhosis of the liver, kidney disease, and unusually low potassium levels in the blood. When used for high blood pressure, Aldactone can be taken alone or with other high blood pressure medications.

ALDOMET
Methyldopa

Aldomet is used to treat high blood pressure. It is effective when used alone or with other high blood pressure medications.

Alendronate *See Fosamax, page 538.*

Alesse *See Oral Contraceptives, page 582.*

Aleve *See Anaprox, page 485.*

Alfuzosin *See Uroxatral, page 630.*

ALLEGRA
Fexofenadine
Other brand name: Allegra-D

Allegra relieves the itchy, runny nose, sneezing, and itchy, red, watery eyes that come with hay fever. Its effect begins in 1 hour and lasts 12 hours, peaking around the second or third hour. Allegra is one of the new type of antihistamines that rarely cause drowsiness. It is also used to relieve the itching and welts of hives.

In addition, to the antihistamine in Allegra, Allegra-D also contains the nasal decongestant pseudoephedrine.

Allopurinol *See Zyloprim, page 644.*

Almotriptan *See Axert, page 492.*

Alora *See Estrogen Patches, page 531.*

ALPHAGAN P
Brimonidine

Alphagan P lowers high pressure in the eye, a problem typically caused by the condition known as open-angle glaucoma. Alphagan P works in two ways: it reduces production of the liquid that fills the eyeball, and it promotes drainage of this liquid.

Alprostadil *See Caverject, page 503.*

ALTACE
Ramipril

Altace is used in the treatment of high blood pressure. It is effective when used alone or in combination with other high blood pressure medications, especially thiazide-type water pills (diuretics). Altace works by preventing the conversion of a chemical in the blood called angiotensin I into a more potent substance that increases salt and water retention in the body. It also enhances blood flow in the circulatory system. It is a member of the group of drugs called ACE inhibitors.

Altace is also prescribed to reduce the chances of heart attack, stroke, and heart-related death in people 55 years or older who are in danger of such an event. Typical candidates include those who suffer from coronary artery disease, poor circulation, stroke, or diabetes and have at least one other risk factor, such as high blood pressure, high cholesterol levels, low HDL ("good") cholesterol, or cigarette smoking.

For those who do suffer a heart attack and develop heart failure, Altace can be prescribed to prevent the condition from getting worse.

ALTOCOR
Lovastatin, extended release

Altocor is an extended-release form of the cholesterol-lowering drug lovastatin. By releasing small amounts of the drug throughout the day, Altocor maintains a relatively steady level of lovastatin in the bloodstream.

In many people, high cholesterol levels contribute to the development of clogged arteries and heart disease. Altocor is prescribed to slow the clogging process in people who already have heart disease, and to fend off clogged arteries in people at risk of developing the disease.

Like other drugs in its class, Altocor reduces the level of "bad" LDL cholesterol and raises the level of "good" HDL cholesterol. For people at high risk of heart disease, current guidelines suggest drug therapy when the LDL level reaches 130. For people at lower risk, the cut-off is 160. For those at little or no risk, it is 190.

ALUPENT
Metaproterenol

Alupent is a bronchodilator prescribed for the prevention and relief of bronchial asthma and bronchial spasms (wheezing) associated with bronchitis and emphysema. Alupent Inhalation Solution is also used to treat acute asthmatic attacks in children 6 years of age and older.

Amantadine *See Symmetrel, page 614.*

AMARYL
Glimepiride

Amaryl is an oral medication used to treat type 2 (non-insulin-dependent) diabetes when diet and exercise alone fail to control abnormally high levels of blood sugar. Like other diabetes drugs classified as sulfonylureas, Amaryl lowers blood sugar by stimulating the pancreas to produce more insulin. Amaryl is often prescribed along with the insulin-boosting drug Glucophage. It may also be used in conjunction with insulin and other diabetes drugs.

Amcinonide *See Cyclocort, page 513.*

AMERGE
Naratriptan

Amerge is used for relief of classic migraine headaches. It's helpful whether or not the headache is preceded by an aura (visual disturbances, usually sensations of halos or flickering lights). The drug works only during an actual attack. It will not reduce the number of headaches that develop.

Amiloride with Hydrochlorothiazide *See Moduretic, page 569.*

Amlodipine *See Norvasc, page 580.*

Amlodipine with Benazepril *See Lotrel, page 558.*

Ammonium lactate *See Lac-Hydrin, page 550.*

Amnesteem *See Accutane, page 476.*

Amoxicillin *See Amoxil, page 485.*

Amoxicillin, Clarithromycin, and Lansoprazole *See Prevpac, page 596.*

Amoxicillin with Clavulanate *See Augmentin, page 489.*

AMOXIL
Amoxicillin

Amoxil, an antibiotic, is used to treat a wide variety of infections, including: gonorrhea, middle ear infections, skin infections, upper and lower respiratory tract infections, and infections of the genital and urinary tract. In combination with other drugs such as Prilosec, Prevacid, and/or Biaxin, it is also used to treat duodenal ulcers caused by *H. pylori* bacteria (sores in the wall of the small intestine near the exit from the stomach).

AMPICILLIN
Brand name: Principen

Ampicillin is a penicillin-like antibiotic prescribed for a wide variety of infections, including gonorrhea and other genital and urinary infections, respiratory infections, and gastrointestinal infections, as well as meningitis (inflamed membranes of the spinal cord or brain).

Amprenavir *See Agenerase, page 480.*

Anakinra *See Kineret, page 550.*

ANAPROX
Naproxen sodium
Other brand names: Aleve, Naprelan

Anaprox and Naprelan are nonsteroidal anti-inflammatory drugs used to relieve mild to moderate pain and menstrual cramps. They are also prescribed for relief of the inflammation, swelling, stiffness, and joint pain associated with rheumatoid arthritis and osteoarthritis (the most common form of arthritis), and for ankylosing spondylitis (spinal arthritis), tendinitis, bursitis, acute gout, and other conditions. Anaprox also may be prescribed for juvenile arthritis.

The over-the-counter form of naproxen sodium, Aleve, is used for temporary relief of minor aches and pains, and to reduce fever.

Anaspaz *See Levsin, page 553.*

Anastrozole *See Arimidex, page 487.*

Androderm *See Testosterone Patches, page 619.*

ANDROGEL
Testosterone gel

AndroGel is a hormone replacement product for men suffering from hypogonadism, a low level of the male hormone testosterone. This condition is marked by symptoms such as impotence and decreased interest in sex, lowered mood, fatigue, and decreases in bone density and lean body mass. Testosterone replacement therapy helps correct these problems. AndroGel, applied daily to the skin, provides an especially convenient way of taking the hormone, which was previously administered only by injection or skin patch.

ANDROID
Methyltestosterone
Other brand name: Testred

Android, a synthetic male sex hormone, is given to help develop and/or maintain male sex characteristics in boys and men who, for some reason, are not producing enough of the hormone on their own. A relatively short course of Android is sometimes used to try to trigger changes in boys whose puberty seems delayed. Android may also be given to women who have certain advanced, inoperable forms of breast cancer.

Anexsia *See Vicodin, page 634.*

Anolor 300 *See Fioricet, page 534.*

ANSAID
Flurbiprofen

Ansaid, a nonsteroidal anti-inflammatory drug, is used to relieve the inflammation, swelling, stiffness, and joint pain associated with rheumatoid arthritis and osteoarthritis (the most common form of arthritis).

ANTIVERT
Meclizine
Other brand name: Bonine

Antivert, an antihistamine, is prescribed for the management of nausea, vomiting, and dizziness associated with motion sickness.

Antivert may also be prescribed for the management of vertigo (a spinning sensation or a feeling that the ground is tilted) due to diseases affecting the vestibular system (the bony labyrinth of the ear, which contains the sensors that control balance).

ANZEMET
Dolasetron

Anzemet is used to prevent the nausea and vomiting that often accompany cancer chemotherapy and usually trouble patients who've received anesthesia during surgery. The drug works by blocking the action of one of the brain's chemical messengers, serotonin, on the nerves that trigger vomiting.

Apri *See Oral Contraceptives, page 582.*

ARAVA
Leflunomide

Arava is used in the treatment of rheumatoid arthritis. It reduces the pain, stiffness, inflammation, and swelling associated with this disease, and staves off the joint damage that ultimately results.

ARIMIDEX
Anastrozole

Arimidex is a first-line treatment of breast cancer in postmenopausal women. It slows the growth of advanced cancer within the breast and cancer that has spread to other parts of the body. Arimidex is also used to treat advanced breast cancer in postmenopausal women whose disease has spread to other parts of the body following treatment with tamoxifen (Nolvadex), another anticancer drug. Arimidex can also be prescribed along with other drugs to treat the early stages of breast cancer in postmenopausal women.

   Arimidex combats the kind of breast cancer that thrives on estrogen. One of the hormones produced by the adrenal gland is converted to a form of estrogen by an enzyme called aromatase. Arimidex suppresses this enzyme and thereby reduces the level of estrogen circulating in the body.

ARMOUR THYROID
Thyroid hormones

Armour Thyroid is prescribed when the thyroid gland is unable to produce enough hormone. It is also used to treat or prevent goiter (enlargement of the thyroid gland), and is given in a "suppression test" to diagnose an overactive thyroid.

ARTANE
Trihexyphenidyl

Artane is used, in conjunction with other drugs, for the relief of certain symptoms of Parkinson's disease, a brain disorder that causes muscle tremor, stiffness, and weakness. It is also used to control certain side effects induced by antipsychotic drugs such as Thorazine and Haldol. Artane works by correcting the chemical imbalance that causes Parkinson's disease.

ARTHROTEC
Diclofenac with Misoprostol

Arthrotec is designed to relieve the symptoms of arthritis in people who are also prone to ulcers. It contains diclofenac, a nonsteroidal anti-inflammatory drug (NSAID) for control of the inflammation, swelling, stiffness, and joint pain associated with rheumatoid arthritis and osteoarthritis. However, since NSAIDs can cause stomach ulcers in susceptible people, Arthrotec also contains misoprostol, a synthetic prostaglandin that serves to reduce the production of stomach acid, thereby protecting the stomach lining and thus preventing ulcers.

Asacol *See Rowasa, page 607.*

Aspirin with Extended-release dipyridamole *See Aggrenox, page 481.*

ASTELIN
Azelastine nasal spray

Astelin is an antihistamine nasal spray. It is prescribed for the relief of hay fever symptoms such as itchy, runny nose and sneezing, and can also be used to relieve cases of congested, runny nose and postnasal drip unrelated to allergies.

ATACAND
Candesartan

Atacand controls high blood pressure. It works by blocking the effect of a hormone called angiotensin II. Unopposed, this substance prompts the blood vessels to contract, an action that tends to raise blood pressure. Atacand relaxes and expands the blood vessels, allowing pressure to drop. The drug may be prescribed alone or with other blood pressure medications.

ATACAND HCT
Candesartan with Hydrochlorothiazide

Atacand HCT is a combination medication used in the treatment of high blood pressure. One component, candesartan, belongs to a class of blood pressure medications that work by preventing the hormone angiotensin II from constricting the blood vessels. This allows the blood to flow more freely and helps keep blood pressure down. The other component, hydrochlorothiazide, is a diuretic that increases the output of urine. This removes excess fluid from the body and helps lower blood pressure. Doctors usually prescribe Atacand HCT in place of its individual components. It can also be prescribed along with other blood pressure medications.

Atazanavir *See Reyataz, page 604.*

Atenolol *See Tenormin, page 618.*

Atenolol with Chlorthalidone *See Tenoretic, page 617.*

Atorvastatin *See Lipitor, page 555.*

ATROVENT
Ipratropium

Atrovent inhalation aerosol and solution are prescribed for long-term treatment of bronchial spasms (wheezing) associated with chronic obstructive pulmonary disease, including chronic bronchitis and emphysema. When inhaled, Atrovent opens the air passages, allowing more oxygen to reach the lungs.

Atrovent nasal spray relieves runny nose. The 0.03% spray is used for year-round runny nose due to allergies and other causes. The 0.06% spray is prescribed for hay fever and for runny nose due to colds. The spray does not relieve nasal congestion or sneezing.

A/T/S *See Erythromycin, Topical, page 530.*

AUGMENTIN
Amoxicillin with Clavulanate
Other brand name: Augmentin XR

Augmentin is used in the treatment of lower respiratory, middle ear, sinus, skin, and urinary tract infections that are caused by certain specific bacteria. These bacteria produce a chemical enzyme called beta lactamase that makes some infections particularly difficult to treat.

Augmentin ES-600, a stronger, oral-suspension form of the drug, is prescribed for certain stubborn ear infections that previous treatment has failed to clear up in children two and under, or those attending day care.

Augmentin XR is an extended-release form of the drug used to treat pneumonia and sinus infections.

Auranofin *See Ridaura, page 605.*

AVALIDE
Irbesartan with Hydrochlorothiazide

Avalide is a combination medication used to treat high blood pressure. One component, irbesartan, belongs to a class of blood pressure medications that prevents the hormone angiotensin II from constricting the blood vessels, thereby allowing blood to flow more freely and keeping blood pressure down. The other component, hydrochlorothiazide, is a diuretic that increases the output of urine, removing excess fluid from the body and thus lowering blood pressure.

Combinations such as Avalide are usually prescribed only when treatment with a single medication fails to lower blood pressure sufficiently. Avalide can be combined with yet other blood pressure medicines if pressure remains too high.

AVANDAMET
Rosiglitazone with Metformin

Avandamet is an oral medication used to control blood sugar levels in people with type 2 (non-insulin-dependent) diabetes. It contains two drugs commonly used to lower blood sugar, rosiglitazone (Avandia) and metformin (Glucophage). Avandamet replaces the need to take these two drugs separately. It is also used when treatment with Glucophage alone doesn't work. Avandamet is not, however, meant to take the place of weight loss or diet and exercise.

Blood sugar levels are ordinarily controlled by the body's natural supply of insulin, which helps sugar move out of the bloodstream and into the cells to be used for energy. People who have type 2 diabetes do not make enough insulin or do not respond normally to the insulin their bodies make, causing a buildup of unused sugar in the bloodstream. Avandamet helps remedy this problem in two ways: by decreasing the body's production of sugar and making the body more sensitive to its own insulin supply. Avandamet does not increase the body's production of insulin.

AVANDIA
Rosiglitazone

Avandia is used to hold down blood sugar levels in people with type 2 diabetes (also known as "non-insulin dependent" or "adult onset" diabetes).

Blood sugar levels are ordinarily controlled by the body's natural supply of insulin, which helps sugar move out of the bloodstream and into the cells. In type 2 diabetes, the buildup of sugar in the blood is often due not to a lack of insulin, but to the body's inability to make proper use of it. Avandia works first by decreasing sugar production, then by helping the body make more efficient use of whatever insulin is available. It does not increase the actual amount of insulin in circulation.

Avandia can be used alone or in conjunction with insulin, metformin (Glucophage), or a member of the sulfonylurea class of diabetes drugs (Diabinese, Micronase, Orinase). It takes effect slowly. Patients may not see a reduction in blood sugar levels for the first 2 weeks of therapy, and it may take 2 to 3 months for the medication to deliver maximum results.

AVAPRO
Irbesartan

Avapro is used to treat high blood pressure. A member of the family of drugs called angiotensin II receptor antagonists, it works by preventing the hormone angiotensin II from narrowing the blood vessels, an action that tends to raise blood pressure. Avapro may be prescribed alone or with other blood pressure medications.

In people with type 2 diabetes and high blood pressure, Avapro is also prescribed to stave off damage to the kidneys, often delaying the need for dialysis and a kidney transplant.

AVC
Sulfanilamide

AVC is used to treat yeast infections caused by *Candida albicans*, a type of fungus. AVC rapidly relieves vulvovaginitis—the itching, redness, and irritation of the external sex organs (vulva) and the thick, cottage cheese-like discharge that usually accompany yeast infections.

AVELOX
Moxifloxacin

Avelox, an antibiotic, is prescribed to treat sinus and lung infections. It kills bacteria that can cause sinusitis, pneumonia, and secondary infections in chronic bronchitis. It also fights skin infections caused by staph or strep.

Avelox is a member of the quinolone family of antibiotics. Like all antibiotics, Avelox works only against bacteria. It will not cure an infection caused by a virus.

Avita *See Retin-A and Renova, page 604.*

AVODART
Dutasteride

Avodart is used to treat prostate enlargement, a condition that is medically known as benign prostatic hyperplasia, or BPH.

The prostate is a chestnut-shaped gland that is part of the male reproductive system. It produces a liquid that forms part of the semen. This gland completely encloses the upper part of the urethra, the tube through which urine flows out of the bladder. Many men over age 50 suffer from a benign (noncancerous) enlargement of the prostate. The enlarged gland squeezes the urethra, obstructing the normal flow of urine. Resulting problems may include difficulty in starting urination, weak flow of urine, and the need to urinate urgently or more frequently. Sometimes surgical removal of the prostate is necessary.

By shrinking the enlarged prostate, Avodart may alleviate the various urinary symptoms, making surgery unnecessary. Periodic examinations by the doctor will be necessary to assess treatment response. It may take several months to notice symptom improvement.

AXERT
Almotriptan

Axert is a migraine treatment. It relieves the type of migraine that's accompanied by an aura (a set of symptoms that includes visual disturbances, speech difficulties, tingling, numbness, and weakness), as well as the kind that lacks an aura.

Axert is a member of a family of drugs called selective serotonin receptor agonists. These medications are thought to work by stopping abnormal dilation of blood vessels in the head, fighting inflammation, and reducing pain transmissions along certain nerve pathways near the brain.

Axert relieves migraines already in progress, but it won't prevent them from starting. It has not been tested for other types of headache, such as cluster headache, and should be used only for migraine attacks.

AXID
Nizatidine

Axid is prescribed for the treatment of duodenal ulcers and noncancerous stomach ulcers. Full-dose therapy for these problems lasts no longer than 8 weeks. However, doctors sometimes prescribe Axid at a reduced dosage after a duodenal ulcer has healed. The drug is also prescribed for the heartburn and the inflammation that result when acid stomach contents flow backward into the esophagus. Axid belongs to a class of drugs known as histamine H_2 blockers.

Azatadine with Pseudoephedrine *See Trinalin, page 627.*

Azelaic acid for acne *See Azelex, page 493.*

Azelaic acid for rosacea *See Finacea, page 534.*

Azelastine eye drops *See Optivar, page 582.*

Azelastine nasal spray *See Astelin, page 488.*

AZELEX
Azelaic acid for acne
Other brand name: Finevin

Azelex helps clear up mild to moderate acne. The skin eruptions and inflammation of acne typically begin during puberty, when oily secretions undergo an increase.

Azithromycin *See Zithromax, page 641.*

AZMACORT
Triamcinolone
Other brand names: Nasacort, Nasacort AQ

Azmacort and Nasacort are metered-dose inhalers containing the anti-inflammatory steroid medication, triamcinolone acetonide; Nasacort AQ is a metered-dose pump spray. Azmacort is used as long-term therapy to control bronchial asthma attacks. Nasacort and Nasacort AQ are prescribed to relieve the symptoms of hay fever and other nasal allergies. Nasacort is also used in the treatment of nasal polyps (projecting masses of tissue in the nose).

AZULFIDINE
Sulfasalazine

Azulfidine, an anti-inflammatory medicine, is prescribed for the treatment of mild to moderate ulcerative colitis (a long-term, progressive bowel disease) and as an added treatment in severe ulcerative colitis (chronic inflammation and ulceration of the lining of large bowel and rectum, the main symptom of which is bloody diarrhea).

Azulfidine EN-tabs are prescribed for people with ulcerative colitis who cannot take the regular Azulfidine tablet because of symptoms of stomach and intestinal irritation such as nausea and vomiting when taking the first few doses of the drug, or for those in whom a reduction in dosage does not lessen the stomach or intestinal side effects. The EN-tabs are also prescribed for adults and children with rheumatoid arthritis who fail to get relief from salicylates (such as aspirin) or other nonsteroidal anti-inflammatory drugs (such as ibuprofen).

Baclofen *See Lioresal, page 555.*

BACTRIM
Trimethoprim with Sulfamethoxazole
Other brand name: Septra

Bactrim, an antibacterial combination drug, is prescribed for the treatment of certain urinary tract infections, severe middle ear infections in children, long-lasting or frequently recurring bronchitis in adults that has increased in seriousness, inflammation of the intestine due to a severe bacterial infection, and travelers' diarrhea in adults. Bactrim is also prescribed for the treatment of *Pneumocystis carinii* pneumonia, and for prevention of this type of pneumonia in people with weakened immune systems.

BACTROBAN
Mupirocin

Bactroban is prescribed for the treatment of impetigo, a bacterial infection of the skin. An antibiotic ointment applied to the skin, it kills the staph and strep germs responsible for the problem.

Balsalazide *See Colazal, page 507.*

BECLOMETHASONE

Brand names: Beclovent, Beconase AQ Nasal Spray, Beconase Inhalation Aerosol, Qvar Inhalation Aerosol, Vancenase AQ Nasal Spray and Double Strength Nasal Spray, Vancenase Nasal Inhaler and PocketHaler Nasal Inhaler, Vanceril Inhalation Aerosol and Double Strength Inhalation Aerosol, Vanceril Inhaler

Beclomethasone is a type of steroid used for respiratory problems. Beclovent and Vanceril are prescribed for the prevention of recurring symptoms of bronchial asthma. Beconase and Vancenase are used to relieve the symptoms of hay fever and to prevent regrowth of nasal polyps following surgical removal.

Beclovent *See Beclomethasone, page 495.*

Beconase *See Beclomethasone, page 495.*

Bellatal *See Donnatal, page 523.*

Benazepril *See Lotensin, page 558.*

Benazepril with Hydrochlorothiazide *See Lotensin HCT, page 558.*

BENICAR

Olmesartan

Benicar controls high blood pressure. It works by blocking the effect of a hormone called angiotensin II. Unopposed, this substance prompts the blood vessels to contract, an action that tends to raise blood pressure. Benicar relaxes and expands the blood vessels, allowing pressure to drop. The drug may be prescribed alone or with other blood pressure medications.

BENTYL

Dicyclomine

Bentyl is prescribed for the treatment of functional bowel/irritable bowel syndrome (abdominal pain, accompanied by diarrhea and constipation associated with stress). It works by quelling the spasms associated with this condition.

BENZACLIN

Clindamycin and Benzoyl peroxide

BenzaClin is an acne treatment. Both its ingredients—the antibiotic clindamycin and the antibacterial agent benzoyl peroxide—attack the bacteria that help cause acne.

Benzac W *See Desquam-E, page 518.*

Benzagel *See Desquam-E, page 518.*

BENZAMYCIN
Erythromycin with Benzoyl peroxide

A combination of the antibiotic erythromycin and the antibacterial agent benzoyl peroxide, Benzamycin is effective in stopping the bacteria that cause acne and in reducing acne infection.

BenzaShave *See Desquam-E, page 518.*

Benzonatate *See Tessalon, page 619.*

Benzoyl peroxide *See Desquam-E, page 518.*

Bepridil *See Vascor, page 632.*

BETAGAN
Levobunolol

Betagan eyedrops are given to treat chronic open-angle glaucoma (increased pressure inside the eye). This medication is in a class called beta blockers. It works by lowering pressure within the eyeball.

Betamethasone *See Diprolene, page 522.*

Betaxolol *See Betoptic, page 496.*

Betimol *See Timoptic, page 621.*

BETOPTIC
Betaxolol

Betoptic Ophthalmic Solution and Betoptic S Ophthalmic Suspension contain a medication that lowers internal eye pressure. They are used to treat open-angle glaucoma (high pressure of the fluid in the eye).

BEXTRA
Valdecoxib

Bextra is a member of the relatively new class of painkillers called COX-2 inhibitors. It is prescribed for the relief of osteoarthritis, rheumatoid arthritis, and painful menstruation (dysmenorrhea).

COX-2 inhibitors are part of a larger group of medications called non-steroidal anti-inflammatory drugs (NSAIDs). All the drugs in this category (including such familiar remedies as aspirin, Motrin, and Naprosyn) relieve pain and inflammation by limiting the effect of a natural enzyme called COX-2. Unlike the older NSAIDs, however, the new COX-2 inhibitors do not interfere with COX-1, a related enzyme that exerts a protective effect on the lining of the stomach. As a result, Bextra and other COX-2 inhibitors are less likely to cause the bleeding and ulcers that sometimes accompany sustained use of the older NSAIDs.

BIAXIN

Clarithromycin
Other brand name: Biaxin XL

Biaxin, an antibiotic chemically related to erythromycin, is used to treat certain bacterial infections of the respiratory tract, including:

Strep throat
Pneumonia
Sinusitis (inflamed sinuses)
Tonsillitis (inflamed tonsils)
Acute middle ear infections
Acute flare-ups of chronic bronchitis (inflamed airways)

Biaxin is also prescribed to treat infections of the skin. Combined with Prilosec or Prevacid and amoxicillin, it is used to cure ulcers near the exit from the stomach (duodenal ulcers) caused by *H. pylori* bacteria. It can also be prescribed to combat *Mycobacterium avium* infections in people with AIDS.

Biaxin is available in tablet and suspension form, and in extended-release tablets (Biaxin XL). The extended-release form is used only for sinus inflammation and flare-ups of bronchitis.

Bicalutamide *See Casodex, page 502.*

Bimatoprost *See Lumigan, page 559.*

Bismuth subsalicylate, Metronidazole, and Tetracycline *See Helidac Therapy, page 542.*

Bisoprolol *See Zebeta, page 639.*

Bisoprolol with Hydrochlorothiazide *See Ziac, page 641.*

Bleph-10 *See Sodium Sulamyd, page 611.*

Bonine *See Antivert, page 486.*

BRETHINE
Terbutaline

Brethine is a bronchodilator (a medication that opens the bronchial tubes), prescribed for the prevention and relief of the bronchial spasms that constrict the airway in asthma patients. This medication is also used for the relief of bronchial spasm associated with bronchitis and emphysema.

Brevicon *See Oral Contraceptives, page 582.*

Brimonidine *See Alphagan P, page 482.*

Bromocriptine *See Parlodel, page 585.*

Brontex *See Tussi-Organidin NR, page 628.*

Budesonide *See Rhinocort Aqua, page 605.*

Budesonide inhalation powder *See Pulmicort Turbuhaler, page 601.*

Budesonide inhalation suspension *See Pulmicort Respules, page 600.*

Budesonide, oral *See Entocort EC, page 528.*

Bumetanide *See Bumex, page 498.*

BUMEX
Bumetanide

Bumex is used to lower the amount of excess salt and water in the body by increasing the output of urine. It is prescribed in the treatment of edema, or fluid retention, associated with congestive heart failure and liver or kidney disease. It is also occasionally prescribed, along with other drugs, to treat high blood pressure.

Bupropion for smoking *See Zyban, page 643.*

Butalbital, Acetaminophen, and Caffeine *See Fioricet, page 534.*

Butalbital, Aspirin, and Caffeine *See Fiorinal, page 535.*

Butalbital, Codeine, Aspirin, and Caffeine
See Fiorinal with Codeine, page 535.

Butoconazole *See Mycelex-3, page 572.*

CAFERGOT
Ergotamine with Caffeine

Cafergot is prescribed for the relief or prevention of vascular headaches—for example, migraine, migraine variants, or cluster headaches.

CALAN
Verapamil
Other brand names: Calan SR, Covera-HS, Isoptin, Isoptin SR, Verelan, Verelan PM

Verapamil-based medications can be prescribed for several heart and blood pressure problems. The fast-acting brands (Calan and Isoptin) are taken for angina (chest pain due to clogged cardiac arteries), as well as irregular heartbeat and high blood pressure. The longer-acting brands (Calan SR, Isoptin SR, Verelan, and Verelan PM) are typically used only for high blood pressure. Covera-HS is prescribed for both high blood pressure and angina.

Verapamil is a type of medication called a calcium channel blocker. It eases the heart's workload by slowing down the passage of nerve impulses through it, and hence the contractions of the heart muscle. This improves blood flow through the heart and throughout the body, reduces blood pressure, corrects irregular heartbeat, and helps prevent angina pain.

Some doctors also prescribe verapamil to prevent migraine headache and asthma and to treat manic depression and panic attacks, but the drug is not officially approved for these purposes.

Calcipotriene *See Dovonex, page 524.*

Calcitonin-salmon *See Miacalcin, page 565.*

Calcitriol *See Rocaltrol, page 606.*

Canasa *See Rowasa, page 607.*

Candesartan *See Atacand, page 488.*

Candesartan with Hydrochlorothiazide *See Atacand HCT, page 489.*

CAPOTEN
Captopril

Capoten is used in the treatment of high blood pressure and congestive heart failure. When prescribed for high blood pressure, it is effective used alone or combined with diuretics. If it is prescribed for congestive heart failure, it is used in combination with digitalis and diuretics. Capoten is in a family of drugs known as "ACE (angiotensin converting enzyme) inhibitors." It works by preventing a chemical in the blood called angiotensin I from converting into a more potent form that increases salt and water retention in the body. Capoten also enhances blood flow throughout the blood vessels.

In addition, Capoten is used to improve survival in certain people who have suffered heart attacks and to treat kidney disease in diabetics.

Some doctors also prescribe Capoten for angina pectoris (crushing chest pain), Raynaud's phenomenon (a disorder of the blood vessels that causes the fingers to turn white when exposed to cold), and rheumatoid arthritis.

CAPOZIDE
Captopril with Hydrochlorothiazide

Capozide is used in the treatment of high blood pressure. It combines an ACE inhibitor with a thiazide diuretic. Captopril, the ACE inhibitor, works by preventing a chemical in the blood called angiotensin I from converting into a more potent form that increases salt and water retention in the body. Captopril also enhances blood flow throughout the blood vessels. Hydrochlorothiazide, the diuretic, helps the body produce and eliminate more urine, which helps in lowering blood pressure.

Captopril *See Capoten, page 499.*

Captopril with Hydrochlorothiazide *See Capozide, page 500.*

Carac *See Efudex, page 526.*

CARAFATE
Sucralfate

Carafate Tablets and Suspension are used for the short-term treatment (up to 8 weeks) of an active duodenal ulcer (an open sore in the intestinal wall near the exit from the stomach). Carafate Tablets are also used for longer-term therapy at a reduced dosage after a duodenal ulcer has healed.

Carafate helps ulcers heal by forming a protective coating over them. Some doctors also prescribe Carafate for ulcers in the mouth and esophagus that develop during cancer therapy, for digestive tract irritation caused by drugs, for long-term treatment of stomach ulcers, and to relieve pain following tonsil removal.

Carbamazepine *See Tegretol, page 617.*

Carbatrol *See Tegretol, page 617.*

Carbidopa with Levodopa *See Sinemet CR, page 610.*

Carbinoxamine or Brompheniramine and Pseudoephedrine
See Rondec, page 607.

CARDENE
Nicardipine

Cardene, a type of medication called a calcium channel blocker, is prescribed for the treatment of chronic stable angina (chest pain that results when clogged arteries reduce the heart's oxygen supply, brought on by exertion) and for high blood pressure. When used to treat angina, Cardene is sometimes combined with beta-blocking medications such as Tenormin or Inderal. If it is used to treat high blood pressure, Cardene may be combined with other high blood pressure medications. Calcium channel blockers ease the workload of the heart by slowing down the passage of nerve impulses through the heart and its resulting muscle contractions. This improves blood flow through the heart and throughout the body. By expanding the blood vessels, calcium channel blockers also reduce blood pressure.

Cardene SR, a long-acting form of the drug, is prescribed only for high blood pressure.

Some doctors also prescribe Cardene to prevent migraine headache and to treat congestive heart failure. In combination with other drugs, such as Amicar, Cardene is also prescribed to manage neurological problems following certain kinds of stroke.

CARDIZEM
Diltiazem
Other brand names: Cardizem CD, Cardizem SR, Dilacor XR, Tiazac

Cardizem and Cardizem CD (a controlled release form of diltiazem) are used in the treatment of angina pectoris (chest pain that results when clogged arteries reduce the heart's oxygen supply) and chronic stable angina (a type brought on by exertion). Cardizem CD is also used to treat high blood pressure. Another controlled release form, Cardizem SR, is used only in the treatment of high blood pressure. Cardizem, a calcium channel blocker, dilates blood vessels and slows the heart to reduce blood pressure and the pain of angina.

Doctors sometimes prescribe Cardizem for loss of circulation in the fingers and toes (Raynaud's phenomenon), for involuntary movements (tardive dyskinesia), and to prevent heart attack.

Tiazac and Dilacor XR are used in the treatment of high blood pressure and chronic stable angina. They may be taken alone or combined with other blood pressure medications.

CARDURA
Doxazosin

Cardura is used in the treatment of benign prostatic hyperplasia, a condition in which the prostate gland grows larger, pressing on the urethra and threatening to block the flow of urine from the bladder. The drug relieves symptoms such as a weak stream, dribbling, incomplete emptying of the bladder, frequent urination, and burning during urination.

Cardura is also used in the treatment of high blood pressure. It is effective when used alone or in combination with other blood pressure medications, such as diuretics, beta-blocking medications, calcium channel blockers or ACE inhibitors.

Doctors also prescribe Cardura, along with other drugs such as digitalis and diuretics, for treatment of congestive heart failure.

Carisoprodol *See Soma, page 611.*

Carvedilol *See Coreg, page 510.*

CASODEX
Bicalutamide

Casodex is used in the treatment of advanced prostate cancer. It belongs to a class of drugs known as antiandrogens. These drugs block the effect of male hormones.

Casodex is prescribed along with a drug, such as Lupron, that mimics the effect of natural luteinizing hormone-releasing hormone (LHRH).

Cataflam *See Voltaren, page 636.*

CATAPRES
Clonidine

Catapres is prescribed for high blood pressure. It is effective when used alone or with other high blood pressure medications.

Doctors also prescribe Catapres for alcohol, nicotine, or benzodiazepine (tranquilizer) withdrawal; migraine headaches; smoking cessation programs; Tourette's syndrome (tics and uncontrollable utterances); narcotic/methadone detoxification; premenstrual tension; and diabetic diarrhea.

CAVERJECT
Alprostadil
Other brand names: Edex, Muse

Caverject is used to treat male impotence. Doctors also use the drug to help diagnose the exact nature of a patient's impotence.

Caverject and the similar brand Edex are both taken by injection. A third brand, Muse, is taken as a small suppository inserted in the penis.

CECLOR
Cefaclor

Ceclor, a cephalosporin antibiotic, is used in the treatment of ear, nose, throat, respiratory tract, urinary tract, and skin infections caused by specific bacteria, including staph, strep, and *E. coli*. Uses include treatment of sore or strep throat, pneumonia, and tonsillitis. Ceclor CD, an extended release form of the drug, is also used for flare-ups of chronic bronchitis.

CEDAX
Ceftibuten

Cedax cures mild-to-moderate bacterial infections of the throat, ear, and respiratory tract. Among these infections are strep throat, tonsillitis, and acute otitis media (middle ear infection) in children and adults. Cedax is also prescribed for acute flare-ups of chronic bronchitis in adults. Cedax is a cephalosporin antibiotic.

Cefaclor *See Ceclor, page 503.*

Cefadroxil *See Duricef, page 524.*

Cefdinir *See Omnicef, page 582.*

Cefditoren *See Spectracef, page 611.*

Cefixime *See Suprax, page 613.*

Cefprozil *See Cefzil, page 504.*

Ceftibuten *See Cedax, page 503.*

CEFTIN
Cefuroxime

Ceftin, a cephalosporin antibiotic, is prescribed for mild to moderately severe bacterial infections of the throat, lungs, ears, skin, sinuses, and urinary tract, and for gonorrhea. Ceftin tablets are also prescribed in the early stages of Lyme disease.

Ceftriaxone *See Rocephin, page 607.*

Cefuroxime *See Ceftin, page 503.*

CEFZIL
Cefprozil

Cefzil, a cephalosporin antibiotic, is prescribed for mild to moderately severe bacterial infections of the throat, ear, sinuses, respiratory tract, and skin. Among these infections are strep throat, tonsillitis, bronchitis, and pneumonia.

CELEBREX
Celecoxib

Celebrex is prescribed for acute pain, menstrual cramps, and the pain and inflammation of osteoarthritis and rheumatoid arthritis. It is the first of a new class of nonsteroidal anti-inflammatory drugs (NSAIDs) called "COX-2 inhibitors." Like older NSAIDs such as Motrin and Naprosyn, Celebrex is believed to fight pain and inflammation by inhibiting the effect of a natural enzyme called COX-2. Unlike the older medications, however, it does not interfere with a similar substance, called COX-1, which exerts a protective effect on the lining of the stomach. Celebrex is therefore less likely to cause the bleeding and ulcers that sometimes accompany sustained use of the older NSAIDs.

Celebrex has also been found to reduce the number of colorectal polyps (growths in the wall of the lower intestine and rectum) in people who suffer from the condition called familial adenomatous polyposis (FAP), an inherited tendency to develop large numbers of colorectal polyps that eventually become cancerous.

Celecoxib *See Celebrex, page 504.*

Cenestin *See Premarin, page 595.*

Cephalexin *See Keflex, page 549.*

Cephradine *See Velosef, page 633.*

Cetacort *See Hydrocortisone Skin Preparations, page 543.*

Cetirizine *See Zyrtec, page 644.*

Cetirizine with Pseudoephedrine *See Zyrtec-D, page 645.*

Chlordiazepoxide with Clidinium *See Librax, page 555.*

Chlorhexidine *See Peridex, page 589.*

Chlorothiazide *See Diuril, page 523.*

Chlorpheniramine with Pseudoephedrine *See Deconamine, page 516.*

Chlorpropamide *See Diabinese, page 519.*

Chlorthalidone *See Thalitone, page 620.*

Chlorzoxazone *See Parafon Forte DSC, page 585.*

Cholestyramine *See Questran, page 601.*

Choline magnesium trisalicylate *See Trilisate, page 626.*

CIALIS
Tadalafil

Cialis is an oral drug for male impotence, also known as erectile dysfunction (ED). It works by dilating blood vessels in the penis, allowing the inflow of blood needed for an erection.

Ciclopirox *See Loprox, page 557.*

Ciclopirox nail lacquer *See Penlac, page 587.*

Cilostazol *See Pletal, page 592.*

CILOXAN
Ciprofloxacin, ocular

Ciloxan is an antibiotic used in the treatment of eye infections. The ointment form of the drug is prescribed for eye inflammations. The solution can also be used to treat ulcers or sores on the cornea (the transparent covering over the pupil). Ciprofloxacin, the active ingredient, is a member of the quinolone family of antibiotics.

Cimetidine *See Tagamet, page 615.*

CIPRO
Ciprofloxacin

Cipro is used to treat infections of the lower respiratory tract, the abdomen, the skin, the bones and joints, and the urinary tract, including cystitis (bladder inflammation) in women. It is also prescribed for severe sinus or bronchial infections, infectious diarrhea, typhoid fever, inhalational anthrax, infections of the prostate gland, and some sexually transmitted diseases such as gonorrhea. Additionally, some doctors prescribe Cipro for certain serious ear infections, tuberculosis, and some of the infections common in people with AIDS.

Because Cipro is effective only for certain types of bacterial infections, before beginning treatment the doctor may perform tests to identify the specific organisms causing the infection.

Cipro is available as a tablet and an oral suspension and as a suspension to be used externally in the ear.

Ciprofloxacin *See Cipro, page 505.*

Ciprofloxacin, ocular *See Ciloxan, page 505.*

CLARINEX
Desloratadine

Clarinex is an antihistamine used to relieve the symptoms of hay fever (seasonal and perennial allergic rhinitis). Like many of the newer members of the antihistamine family, Clarinex causes less drowsiness than do older products such as Benadryl.

Clarithromycin *See Biaxin, page 497.*

CLEOCIN T
Clindamycin

Cleocin T is an antibiotic used to treat acne.

CLEOCIN VAGINAL
Clindamycin

Cleocin Vaginal products (cream and ovules) are used to treat bacterial vaginosis, an infection of the vagina. The infection, which is probably sexually transmitted, often produces a gray or yellow discharge with a fishy smell that increases if the external genitals are washed with alkaline soap.

Before prescribing Cleocin, doctors typically test the vaginal discharge in the laboratory and examine it under the microscope to make certain that the patient does not have a yeast infection or another sexually transmitted disease (STD) such as chlamydia, gonorrhea, or herpes simplex.

Climara *See Estrogen Patches, page 531.*

Clinac BPO *See Desquam-E, page 518.*

Clindamycin *See Cleocin T, page 506.*
See Cleocin Vaginal, page 506.

Clindamycin and Benzoyl peroxide *See BenzaClin, page 495.*

CLINORIL
Sulindac

Clinoril, a nonsteroidal anti-inflammatory drug, is used to relieve the inflammation, swelling, stiffness, and joint pain associated with rheumatoid arthritis, osteoarthritis (the most common form of arthritis), and ankylosing spondylitis (stiffness and progressive arthritis of the spine). It is also used to treat bursitis, tendinitis, acute gouty arthritis, and other types of pain.

The safety and effectiveness of this medication in the treatment of people with severe, incapacitating rheumatoid arthritis have not been established.

Clobetasol *See Temovate, page 617.*

Clomid *See Clomiphene Citrate, page 507.*

CLOMIPHENE CITRATE
Brand names: Clomid, Serophene

Clomiphene is prescribed for the treatment of ovulatory failure in women who wish to become pregnant and whose husbands are fertile and potent.

Clonidine *See Catapres, page 502.*

Clopidogrel *See Plavix, page 591.*

Clotrimazole *See Gyne-Lotrimin, page 542.*

Clotrimazole with Betamethasone *See Lotrisone, page 559.*

Co-Gesic *See Vicodin, page 634.*

COLAZAL
Balsalazide

Colazal is used in the treatment of mild to moderate ulcerative colitis (chronic inflammation and ulceration of the lower intestine). It is an anti-inflammatory medicine specially formulated to release the active ingredient, mesalamine, directly to the lining of the colon. Its ability to provide relief without the severe side effects found with similar drugs is believed to be due to this localized drug delivery mechanism.

Colesevelam *See WelChol, page 636.*

COLESTID
Colestipol

Colestid, in conjunction with diet, is used to help lower high levels of cholesterol in the blood. This reduces the chances of developing clogged arteries and heart disease. The drug is available in plain and orange-flavored granules and in tablet form.

Colestipol *See Colestid, page 508.*

Colistin, Neomycin, Hydrocortisone, and Thonzonium
See Cortisporin-TC Otic, page 510.

COLYTE
Polyethylene glycol with Electrolytes
Other brand name: GoLYTELY

Colyte is used to clean the bowel before an examination of the upper part of the rectum (colonoscopy) or a barium enema X-ray.

COMBIPATCH
Estradiol and Norethindrone acetate

A remedy for the symptoms of menopause, CombiPatch combines the hormones estrogen (estradiol) and progestin (norethindrone acetate) in a slow-release patch that's applied to the skin. The product eases such symptoms of menopause as feelings of warmth in the face, neck, and chest, and the sudden intense episodes of heat and sweating known as "hot flashes." It is also prescribed to relieve external vaginal irritation and internal vaginal dryness.

CombiPatch can also be used as an estrogen supplement by women unable to produce sufficient amounts of estrogen on their own. Problems prompting the need for supplementation include ovarian failure, hypogonadism (impaired hormone production), and surgical removal of the ovaries.

COMBIVENT
Ipratropium with Albuterol

Combivent is prescribed for people with chronic obstructive pulmonary disease (COPD) if they are already taking one airway-opening medication and need another. The product's two active ingredients act in distinctly different ways. Ipratropium quells airway-closing spasms in the bronchial walls. Albuterol relaxes the muscles in the walls, permitting them to expand. When used together, the two ingredients provide more relief than either can do alone.

Combivent is supplied in an aerosol canister for use only with the special Combivent mouthpiece.

COMBIVIR
Lamivudine and Zidovudine

Combivir is used to fight the human immunodeficiency virus (HIV) that causes AIDS. It is a combination product containing the two AIDS drugs, lamivudine (Epivir) and zidovudine (Retrovir). It is intended for use with additional AIDS drugs.

HIV does its damage by slowly destroying the immune system, eventually leaving the body defenseless against infections. The drugs in Combivir interfere with the virus's ability to reproduce, thus staving off the decline of the immune system and preserving better health.

COMTAN
Entacapone

Comtan is used for Parkinson's disease. It is prescribed when doses of the combination drug levodopa/carbidopa (Sinemet) begin to wear off too soon. By extending the effect of each dose of Sinemet, it frees the patient from the stiffness and tremors of Parkinson's for a longer period of time.

Comtan works by inhibiting the effect of an enzyme that breaks down the levodopa in Sinemet. It has no effect on Parkinson's disease when used by itself.

CONDYLOX
Podofilox

Condylox solution and gel are used to treat external genital warts. The gel formulation is also used to treat warts around the anus.

Conjugated estrogens *See Premarin, page 595.*

COREG
Carvedilol

Coreg lowers blood pressure and increases the output of the heart. It is prescribed for people with congestive heart failure to increase survival and reduce the need for hospitalization. Coreg may be prescribed if you have survived a heart attack and now suffer from left ventricular dysfunction, a condition where the left side of the heart no longer pumps properly. It is also used to control high blood pressure. When prescribed for heart failure, it can be used alone or with other drugs such as digitalis. For hypertension , it is often prescribed along with a diuretic. Coreg is a member of the beta blocker family of drugs.

CORGARD
Nadolol

Corgard is used in the treatment of angina pectoris (chest pain, usually caused by lack of oxygen to the heart due to clogged arteries) and to reduce high blood pressure.

When prescribed for high blood pressure, it is effective when used alone or in combination with other high blood pressure medications. Corgard is a type of drug known as a beta blocker. It decreases the force and rate of heart contractions, reducing the heart's demand for oxygen and lowering blood pressure.

Cormax *See Temovate, page 617.*

CORTISPORIN OPHTHALMIC SUSPENSION
Polymyxin B, Neomycin, and Hydrocortisone

Cortisporin Ophthalmic Suspension is a combination of the steroid drug, hydrocortisone, and two antibiotics. It is prescribed to relieve inflammatory conditions such as irritation, swelling, redness, and general eye discomfort, and to treat superficial bacterial infections of the eye.

CORTISPORIN-TC OTIC
Colistin, Neomycin, Hydrocortisone, and Thonzonium

Cortisporin-TC is a liquid suspension used to treat external ear infections. They may also be prescribed after ear surgery such as a mastoidectomy.

The ingredients colistin sulfate and neomycin sulfate are antibiotics used to treat the bacterial infection itself, while hydrocortisone acetate is a steroid that helps reduce the inflammation, swelling, itching, and other skin reactions associated with an ear infection; thonzonium bromide facilitates the drug's effects.

CORZIDE
Nadolol with Bendroflumethiazide

Corzide is a combination drug used in the treatment of high blood pressure. It combines a beta blocker and a thiazide diuretic. Nadolol, the beta blocker, decreases the force and rate of heart contractions, thereby reducing blood pressure. Bendroflumethiazide, the diuretic, helps the body produce and eliminate more urine, which removes excess fluid and thus helps to lower blood pressure.

COSOPT
Dorzolamide with Timolol

Cosopt lowers high pressure in the eye, a problem typically caused by the condition known as open-angle glaucoma. Cosopt works by reducing production of the liquid that fills the eyeball.

COUMADIN
Warfarin

Coumadin is an anticoagulant (blood thinner). It is prescribed to:

Prevent and/or treat a blood clot that has formed within a blood vessel or in the lungs.

Prevent and/or treat blood clots associated with certain heart conditions or replacement of a heart valve.

Aid in the prevention of blood clots that may form in blood vessels anywhere in the body after a heart attack.

Reduce the risk of death, another heart attack, or stroke after a heart attack.

Covera-HS *See Calan, page 499.*

COZAAR
Losartan

Cozaar is used in the treatment of high blood pressure. It is effective when used alone or with other high blood pressure medications, such as diuretics that help the body get rid of water.

Cozaar is also used to slow the progress of kidney disease caused by type 2 diabetes (the type of diabetes that doesn't require insulin shots).

This angiotensin II receptor antagonist works, in part, by preventing the hormone angiotensin II from constricting the blood vessels, which tends to raise blood pressure.

Creon *See Pancrease, page 585.*

CRESTOR
Rosuvastatin

Crestor is used to lower cholesterol levels when diet and exercise alone have failed to work. The drug can help lower the total cholesterol count as well as harmful levels of low-density lipoprotein (LDL) cholesterol. It can also lower triglycerides, a type of fat that is carried through the bloodstream and can end up being stored as body fat. Sometimes Crestor may be combined with another type of cholesterol-lowering drug such as Colestid, Questran, or WelChol.

In addition, Crestor can help increase the amount of "good" cholesterol known as high-density lipoprotein (HDL).

It's especially important to keep LDL cholesterol under control, since high levels are associated with heart disease. Federal guidelines recommend considering drug therapy when LDL levels reach 130 in people at high risk for heart disease. For people with a lower risk, the cutoff is 160. For those with little or no risk, it is 190.

CRIXIVAN
Indinavir

Crixivan is used in the treatment of human immunodeficiency virus (HIV) infection. HIV causes the immune system to break down so that it can no longer fight off other infections. This leads to the fatal disease known as acquired immune deficiency syndrome (AIDS).

HIV thrives by taking over the immune system's vital CD4 cells (white blood cells) and using their inner workings to make additional copies of itself. Crixivan belongs to a class of HIV drugs called protease inhibitors, which work by interfering with an important step in the virus's reproductive cycle. Although Crixivan cannot eliminate HIV already present in the body, it can reduce the amount of virus available to infect other cells.

Crixivan can be taken alone or in combination with other HIV drugs such as Retrovir. Because Crixivan and Retrovir attack the virus in different ways, the combination is likely to be more effective than either drug alone.

CROLOM
Cromolyn, ocular

Crolom is an eyedrop that relieves the itching, tearing, discharge, and redness caused by seasonal and chronic allergies. The drug works by preventing certain cells in the body from releasing histamine and other substances that can cause an allergic reaction. It may be prescribed alone or with a steroid medication.

Cromolyn, inhaled *See Intal, page 547.*

Cromolyn, ocular *See Crolom, page 513.*

CUTIVATE
Fluticasone topical

Cutivate cream and ointment are prescribed for relief of inflamed, itchy rashes and other inflammatory skin conditions.

Cyclessa *See Oral Contraceptives, page 582.*

Cyclobenzaprine *See Flexeril, page 535.*

CYCLOCORT
Amcinonide

Cyclocort is prescribed for the relief of the inflammatory and itchy symptoms of skin disorders that are responsive to corticosteroid treatment.

Cyclophosphamide *See Cytoxan, page 514.*

Cyclosporine *See Sandimmune, page 608.*

Cyproheptadine *See Periactin, page 589.*

CYTOTEC
Misoprostol

Cytotec, a synthetic prostaglandin (hormone-like substance), reduces the production of stomach acid and protects the stomach lining. People who take nonsteroidal anti-inflammatory drugs (NSAIDs) may be given Cytotec tablets to help prevent stomach ulcers.

Aspirin and other NSAIDs such as Motrin, Naprosyn, Feldene, and others, which are widely used to control the pain and inflammation of arthritis, are generally hard on the stomach. If an NSAID is needed for a prolonged period of time and the patient is elderly or has ever had a stomach ulcer, the doctor may prescribe Cytotec for as long as the patient takes the NSAID.

CYTOXAN

Cyclophosphamide

Cytoxan, an anticancer drug, works by interfering with the growth of malignant cells. It may be used alone but is often given with other anticancer medications. Cytoxan is used in the treatment of the following types of cancer:

Breast cancer
Leukemias (cancers affecting the white blood cells)
Malignant lymphomas (Hodgkin's disease or cancer of the lymph nodes)
Multiple myeloma (a malignant condition or cancer of the plasma cells)
Advanced mycosis fungoides (cancer of the skin and lymph nodes)
Neuroblastoma (a malignant tumor of the adrenal gland or sympathetic
  nervous system)
Ovarian cancer (adenocarcinoma)
Retinoblastoma (a malignant tumor of the retina)

In addition, Cytoxan may sometimes be given to children who have "minimal change" nephrotic syndrome (kidney damage resulting in loss of protein in the urine) and who have not responded well to treatment with steroid medications.

DANTRIUM

Dantrolene

Dantrium is given to relieve muscle spasm caused by conditions such as cerebral palsy, multiple sclerosis, spinal cord injury, or stroke. Dantrium does not cure these conditions, but it may enhance the effect of other treatments, such as physical therapy.

In addition, Dantrium is used to prevent or manage malignant hyperthermia, a life-threatening rapid rise in body temperature that sometimes develops as a reaction to anesthesia. Some doctors also prescribe Dantrium for heat stroke and muscle pain caused by exercise.

Dantrolene *See Dantrium, page 514.*

DARVOCET-N

Propoxyphene napsylate, Acetaminophen
Other brand names: Darvon-N (propoxyphene napsylate), Darvon (propoxyphene hydrochloride), Darvon Compound-65 (propoxyphene hydrochloride, aspirin, and caffeine)

Darvocet-N and its companion products all contain propoxyphene, a mild narcotic painkiller, and all are prescribed for the relief of mild to moderate pain. In addition, Darvocet-N and Darvon Compound-65 contain extra ingredients capable of reducing fever.

Darvon *See Darvocet-N, page 515.*

Darvon Compound-65 *See Darvocet-N, page 515.*

Darvon-N *See Darvocet-N, page 515.*

DAYPRO

Oxaprozin

Daypro is a nonsteroidal anti-inflammatory drug used to relieve the inflammation, swelling, stiffness, and joint pain associated with rheumatoid arthritis and osteoarthritis (the most common kind of arthritis).

DDAVP

Desmopressin
Other brand name: Stimate

DDAVP nasal spray, nose drops, and tablets are given to prevent or control the frequent urination and loss of water associated with diabetes insipidus (a rare condition characterized by very large quantities of diluted urine and excessive thirst). They are also used to treat frequent passage of urine and increased thirst in people with certain brain injuries, and those who have undergone surgery in the pituitary region of the brain. DDAVP nasal spray and nose drops are also prescribed to help stop some types of bedwetting.

Stimate nasal spray is used to stop bleeding in certain types of hemophilia (failure of the blood to clot).

DECADRON TABLETS

Dexamethasone

Decadron, a corticosteroid drug, is used to reduce inflammation and relieve symptoms in a variety of disorders, including rheumatoid arthritis and severe cases of asthma. It may be given to people to treat primary or secondary adrenal cortex insufficiency (lack of sufficient adrenal hormone). It is also given to help treat the following disorders:

Severe allergic conditions such as drug-induced allergies
Blood disorders such as various anemias
Certain cancers (along with other drugs)
Skin diseases such as severe psoriasis
Collagen (connective tissue) diseases such as systemic lupus
 erythematosus
Digestive tract disease such as ulcerative colitis
High serum levels of calcium associated with cancer
Fluid retention due to nephrotic syndrome (a condition in which
 damage to the kidneys causes the body to lose protein in the urine)
Eye diseases such as allergic conjunctivitis
Lung diseases such as tuberculosis (along with other drugs)

DECONAMINE

Chlorpheniramine with Pseudoephedrine

Deconamine is an antihistamine and decongestant used for the temporary relief of persistent runny nose, sneezing, and nasal congestion caused by upper respiratory infections (the common cold), sinus inflammation, or hay fever. It is also used to help clear nasal passages and shrink swollen membranes and to drain the sinuses and relieve sinus pressure.

DELTASONE

Prednisone

Deltasone, a steroid drug, is used to reduce inflammation and alleviate symptoms in a variety of disorders, including rheumatoid arthritis and severe cases of asthma. It may be given to treat primary or secondary adrenal cortex insufficiency (lack of sufficient adrenal hormone in the body). It is used in treating all of the following:

Abnormal adrenal gland development
Allergic conditions (severe)
Blood disorders
Certain cancers (along with other drugs)
Diseases of the connective tissue including systemic lupus erythematosus
Eye diseases of various kinds
Flare-ups of multiple sclerosis
Fluid retention due to "nephrotic syndrome" (a condition in which damage to the kidneys causes protein to be lost in the urine)
Lung diseases, including tuberculosis

Meningitis (inflamed membranes around the brain)
Prevention of organ rejection
Rheumatoid arthritis and related disorders
Severe flare-ups of ulcerative colitis or enteritis (inflammation of the
  intestines)
Skin diseases
Thyroid gland inflammation
Trichinosis (with complications)

DEMADEX
Torsemide

Demadex is a diuretic drug. It flushes excess water from the body by
promoting the production of urine.

Demadex is prescribed to reduce the water retention and swelling that
often accompany congestive heart failure, chronic kidney failure, and cirrhosis of the liver. It is also prescribed for high blood pressure, either
alone or with other medications.

DEMEROL
Meperidine

Demerol, a narcotic analgesic, is prescribed for the relief of moderate to
severe pain. Like other painkillers in this category, it can lead to mental
and physical dependence if taken too long.

Demulen *See Oral Contraceptives, page 582.*

DENAVIR
Penciclovir

Denavir cream is used to treat recurrent cold sores on the lips and face. It
works by interfering with the growth of the herpesvirus responsible for
the sores.

DEPAKENE
Valproic acid

Depakene, an epilepsy medicine, is used to treat certain types of seizures
and convulsions. It may be prescribed alone or with other anticonvulsant
medications.

DEPO-PROVERA
Medroxyprogesterone acetate

Depo-Provera Contraceptive Injection is given in the buttock or upper arm to prevent pregnancy. It is more than 99 percent effective; the chances of becoming pregnant during the first year of use are less than 1 in 100. The injection is given every 3 months (13 weeks) by a doctor. Depo-Provera works by preventing the release of hormones called gonadotropins from the pituitary gland in the brain. Without these hormones, the monthly release of an egg from the ovary cannot occur. If no egg is released, pregnancy is impossible. Depo-Provera also causes changes in the lining of the uterus that make pregnancy less likely even if an egg is released.

In higher doses, Depo-Provera is also used in the treatment of certain cancers including cancer of the endometrium (lining of the uterus) and kidney cancer.

Desloratadine *See Clarinex, page 506.*

Desmopressin *See DDAVP, page 515.*

Desogen *See Oral Contraceptives, page 582.*

Desonide *See Tridesilon, page 626.*

DesOwen *See Tridesilon, page 626.*

Desoximetasone *See Topicort, page 624.*

DESQUAM-E
Benzoyl peroxide
Other brand names: Benzac W, Benzagel, BenzaShave, Clinac BPO, Triaz

Desquam-E gel is used to treat acne. It can be used alone or with other treatments, including antibiotics and products that contain retinoic acid, sulfur, or salicylic acid.

DETROL
Tolterodine
Other brand name: Detrol LA

Detrol combats symptoms of overactive bladder, including frequent urination, urgency (increased need to urinate), and urge incontinence (inability to control urination). The drug works by blocking the nerve impulses that prompt the bladder to contract.

Dexamethasone *See Decadron Tablets, page 515.*

Dexamethasone with Neomycin *See Neodecadron Ophthalmic Ointment and Solution, page 574.*

Dexchlorpheniramine *See Polaramine, page 592.*

DiaBeta *See Micronase, page 567.*

DIABINESE
Chlorpropamide

Diabinese is an oral antidiabetic medication used to treat type 2 (non-insulin-dependent) diabetes. Diabetes (a buildup of sugar in the blood) occurs when the body fails to produce enough insulin or is unable to use it properly. Insulin expedites the transfer of sugar into the cells, where it's converted to energy.

There are two forms of diabetes: type 1 (insulin-dependent) and type 2 (non-insulin-dependent). Type 1 usually requires insulin injection for life, while type 2 diabetes can usually be treated by dietary changes and oral antidiabetic medications such as Diabinese. Diabinese is thought to control diabetes by stimulating the pancreas to secrete more insulin. Occasionally, type 2 diabetics must take insulin injections on a temporary basis, especially during stressful periods or times of illness.

DIAMOX
Acetazolamide

Diamox controls fluid secretion. It is used in the treatment of glaucoma (excessive pressure in the eyes), epilepsy (for both brief and unlocalized seizures), and fluid retention due to congestive heart failure or drugs. It is also used to prevent or relieve the symptoms of acute mountain sickness in climbers attempting a rapid climb and those who feel sick even though they are making a gradual climb.

Diclofenac *See Voltaren, page 636.*

Diclofenac with Misoprostol *See Arthrotec, page 488.*

Dicyclomine *See Bentyl, page 495.*

Didanosine *See Videx, page 634.*

DIDRONEL
Etidronate

Didronel tablets are prescribed for the treatment of Paget's bone disease, which causes pain, bone fractures, and problems in the circulatory and nervous systems. Didronel can decrease pain, increase the ability to move, and slow the progression of the disease.

Didronel is also prescribed following hip replacement and spinal cord injury to prevent abnormal bone formation and inflammation.

Diethylpropion *See Tenuate, page 618.*

DIFFERIN
Adapalene

Differin is prescribed for the treatment of acne. Its exact mode of action is unknown, but it appears to modulate the cellular differentiation, hardening, and inflammatory processes that contribute to acne.

Diflorasone *See Psorcon, page 600.*

DIFLUCAN
Fluconazole

Diflucan is used to treat fungal infections called candidiasis (also known as thrush or yeast infections). These include vaginal infections, throat infections, and fungal infections elsewhere in the body, such as infections of the urinary tract, peritonitis (inflammation of the lining of the abdomen), and pneumonia. Diflucan is also prescribed to guard against candidiasis in some people receiving bone marrow transplants, and is used to treat meningitis (brain or spinal cord inflammation) caused by another type of fungus.

In addition, Diflucan is now being prescribed for fungal infections in kidney and liver transplant patients, and fungal infections in patients with AIDS.

Diflunisal *See Dolobid, page 523.*

Digitek *See Lanoxin, page 551.*

Digoxin *See Lanoxin, page 551.*

Dihydrocodeine, Aspirin, and Caffeine *See Synalgos-DC, page 614.*

Dihydroergotamine *See Migranal, page 567.*

Dilacor XR *See Cardizem, page 501.*

DILANTIN
Phenytoin

Dilantin is an antiepileptic drug, prescribed to control grand mal seizures (a type of seizure in which the individual experiences a sudden loss of consciousness immediately followed by generalized convulsions) and temporal lobe seizures (a type of seizure caused by disease in the cortex of the temporal [side] lobe of the brain affecting smell, taste, sight, hearing, memory, and movement).

   Dilantin may also be used to prevent and treat seizures occurring during and after neurosurgery (surgery of the brain and spinal cord).

DILAUDID
Hydromorphone

Dilaudid, a narcotic analgesic, is prescribed for the relief of moderate to severe pain such as that due to:

Biliary colic (pain caused by an obstruction in the gallbladder or bile duct)
Burns
Cancer
Heart attack
Injury (soft tissue and bone)
Renal colic (sharp lower back and groin pain usually caused by the passage of a stone through the ureter)
Surgery

Diltiazem *See Cardizem, page 501.*

DIOVAN
Valsartan
Other brand name: Diovan HCT

Diovan is one of a new class of blood pressure medications called angiotensin II receptor antagonists. Diovan works by preventing the hormone angiotensin II from narrowing the blood vessels, which tends to raise blood pressure. Diovan may be prescribed alone or with other blood pressure medications, such as diuretics that help the body get rid of excess water. Diovan HCT is just such a combination. It contains Diovan plus the common diuretic hydrochlorothiazide.

DIPENTUM
Olsalazine

Dipentum is an anti-inflammatory drug used to maintain long-term freedom from symptoms of ulcerative colitis (chronic inflammation and ulceration of the large intestine and rectum). It is prescribed for people who cannot take sulfasalazine (Azulfidine).

Diphenoxylate with Atropine *See Lomotil, page 556.*

Dipivefrin *See Propine, page 598.*

DIPROLENE
Betamethasone
Other brand name: Diprosone

Diprolene, a synthetic cortisone-like steroid available in cream, gel, lotion, or ointment form, is used to treat certain itchy rashes and other inflammatory skin conditions. Its sister product Diprosone is available only as a cream.

Diprosone *See Diprolene, page 522.*

Dipyridamole *See Persantine, page 589.*

Dirithromycin *See Dynabac, page 525.*

DISALCID
Salsalate

Disalcid, a nonsteroidal anti-inflammatory drug, is used to relieve the symptoms of rheumatoid arthritis, osteoarthritis (the most common form of arthritis), and other rheumatic disorders (conditions that involve pain and inflammation in joints and the tissues around them).

Disopyramide *See Norpace, page 579.*

DITROPAN
Oxybutynin
Other brand name: Ditropan XL

Ditropan relaxes the bladder muscle and reduces spasms. It is used to treat the urgency, frequency, leakage, incontinence, and painful or difficult urination caused by neurogenic bladder (altered bladder function due to a nervous system abnormality).

DIURIL
Chlorothiazide

Diuril is used in the treatment of high blood pressure and other conditions that require the elimination of excess fluid from the body. These conditions include congestive heart failure, cirrhosis of the liver, corticosteroid and estrogen therapy, and kidney disease. When used for high blood pressure, Diuril can be used alone or with other high blood pressure medications. Diuril contains a form of thiazide, a diuretic that prompts the body to eliminate more fluid, which helps lower blood pressure.

Dolasetron *See Anzemet, page 487.*

DOLOBID
Diflunisal

Dolobid, a nonsteroidal anti-inflammatory drug, is used to treat mild to moderate pain and to relieve the inflammation, swelling, stiffness, and joint pain associated with rheumatoid arthritis and osteoarthritis (the most common form of arthritis).

DONNATAL
Phenobarbital, Hyoscyamine, Atropine, and Scopolamine
Other brand name: Bellatal

Donnatal is a mild antispasmodic medication; it has been used with other drugs for relief of cramps and pain associated with various stomach, intestinal, and bowel disorders, including irritable bowel syndrome, acute colitis, and duodenal ulcer.

One of its ingredients, phenobarbital, is a mild sedative.

Dornase alfa *See Pulmozyme, page 601.*

DORYX
Doxycycline
Other brand names: Vibramycin, Vibra-Tabs

Doxycycline is a broad-spectrum tetracycline antibiotic used against a wide variety of bacterial infections, including Rocky Mountain spotted fever and other fevers caused by ticks, fleas, and lice; urinary tract infections; trachoma (chronic infections of the eye); and some gonococcal infections in adults. It is an approved treatment for inhalational anthrax. It is also used with other medications to treat severe acne and amoebic dysentery (diarrhea caused by severe parasitic infection of the intestines).

Doxycycline may also be taken for the prevention of malaria on foreign trips of less than 4 months' duration.

Occasionally doctors prescribe doxycycline to treat early Lyme disease and to prevent "traveler's diarrhea." These are not yet officially approved uses for this drug.

Dorzolamide *See Trusopt, page 628.*

Dorzolamide with Timolol *See Cosopt, page 511.*

DOVONEX
Calcipotriene

Dovonex is prescribed to help clear up the scaly skin condition known as psoriasis. A synthetic form of vitamin D, it is available in cream and ointment form, and in a liquid for the scalp.

Doxazosin *See Cardura, page 502.*

Doxycycline *See Doryx, page 523.*

DURAGESIC
Fentanyl

Duragesic patches deliver a continuous dose of the potent narcotic painkiller fentanyl for a period of three days. The patches are prescribed for chronic pain when short-acting narcotics and other types of painkillers fail to provide relief.

DURICEF
Cefadroxil

Duricef, a cephalosporin antibiotic, is used in the treatment of nose, throat, urinary tract, and skin infections that are caused by specific bacteria, including staph, strep, and *E. coli.*

Dutasteride *See Avodart, page 492.*

DYAZIDE

Hydrochlorothiazide with Triamterene
Other brand names: Maxzide, Maxzide-25 MG

Dyazide is a combination of diuretic drugs used in the treatment of high blood pressure and other conditions that require the elimination of excess fluid from the body. When used for high blood pressure, Dyazide can be taken alone or with other high blood pressure medications. Diuretics help the body produce and eliminate more urine, which helps lower blood pressure. Triamterene, one of the ingredients of Dyazide, helps to minimize the potassium loss that can be caused by the other component, hydrochlorothiazide. Maxzide and Maxzide-25 MG contain the same combination of ingredients.

DYNABAC

Dirithromycin

Dynabac cures certain mild-to-moderate skin infections and respiratory infections such as strep throat, tonsillitis, pneumonia, and flare-ups of chronic bronchitis. Dynabac is part of the same family of drugs as the commonly prescribed antibiotic erythromycin.

Dynacin *See Minocin, page 568.*

DYNACIRC

Isradipine
Other brand name: DynaCirc CR

DynaCirc, a type of medication called a calcium channel blocker, is prescribed for the treatment of high blood pressure. It is effective when used alone or with a thiazide-type diuretic to flush excess water from the body. Calcium channel blockers ease the workload of the heart by slowing down the passage of nerve impulses through the heart muscle, thereby slowing the beat. This improves blood flow through the heart and throughout the body and reduces blood pressure. A controlled-release version of this drug (DynaCirc CR) maintains lower blood pressure for 24 hours.

Echothiophate *See Phospholine Iodide, page 590.*

EC-Naprosyn *See Naprosyn, page 573.*

Econazole *See Spectazole Cream, page 611.*

Edex *See Caverject, page 503.*

E.E.S. *See Erythromycin, Oral, page 529.*

Efalizumab *See Raptiva, page 602.*

Efavirenz *See Sustiva, page 613.*

EFUDEX

Fluorouracil
Other brand name: Carac

Efudex and Carac are prescribed for the treatment of actinic or solar ker-atoses (small red horny growths or flesh-colored wartlike growths caused by overexposure to ultraviolet radiation or the sun). Such growths may develop into skin cancer. When conventional methods are impractical—as when the affected sites are hard to get at—the 5 percent strength of Efudex is useful in the treatment of superficial basal cell carcinomas, or slow-growing malignant tumors of the face usually found at the edge of the nostrils, eyelids, or lips. Efudex is available in cream and solution forms. Carac comes in cream form only.

ELDEPRYL

Selegiline

Eldepryl is prescribed along with Sinemet (levodopa/carbidopa) for peo-ple with Parkinson's disease. It is used when Sinemet no longer seems to be working well. Eldepryl has no effect when taken by itself; it works only in combination with levodopa or Sinemet.

Parkinson's disease, which causes muscle rigidity and difficulty with walking and talking, involves the progressive degeneration of a particular type of nerve cell. Early on, levodopa or Sinemet alone may alleviate the symptoms of the disease. In time, however, these medications begin to lose their effect; their action seems to switch on and off at random, and the individual may begin to experience side effects such as involuntary movements and "freezing" in mid-motion.

Eldepryl may be prescribed at this stage of the disease to help restore the effectiveness of Sinemet. When a patient begins to take Eldepryl, the dosage of Sinemet may need to be reduced.

ELESTAT

Epinastine

Elestat is an antihistamine prescribed to relieve the itchy eyes caused by an allergic trigger such as pollen or animal dander. It starts to work with-in 3 to 5 minutes of placing the drops in the eye, and its effects usually last for 8 hours.

Eletriptan *See Relpax, page 603.*

ELIDEL
Pimecrolimus

Elidel is a non-steroidal cream that relieves mild to moderate symptoms of eczema, a skin condition marked by itchy red patches that often crust, scale, and ooze. Elidel is approved for use in adults and children over 2 years old; it can be used for short-term treatment or on-and-off treatment over longer periods of time. Elidel is considered an effective alternative for people who cannot tolerate or do not respond to conventional eczema therapies.

ELOCON
Mometasone furoate

Elocon is a cortisone-like steroid available in cream, ointment, and lotion form. It is used to treat certain itchy rashes and other inflammatory skin conditions.

E-Mycin *See Erythromycin, Oral, page 529.*

Enalapril *See Vasotec, page 633.*

Enalapril with Felodipine *See Lexxel, page 554.*

Enalapril with Hydrochlorothiazide *See Vaseretic, page 632.*

ENBREL
Etanercept

Enbrel is used to relieve the symptoms and slow the progress of moderate to severe rheumatoid arthritis. It's also prescribed to relieve the symptoms of psoriatic arthritis. It can be added to methotrexate (Rheumatrex) therapy when methotrexate fails to provide adequate relief. Prescribed alone, it is also used for juvenile rheumatoid arthritis when other drugs have failed.

Enbrel is the first in a class of drugs designed to block the action of tumor necrosis factor (TNF), a naturally occurring protein responsible for much of the joint inflammation that plagues the victims of rheumatoid arthritis. In clinical trials, Enbrel provided the majority of patients with significant relief.

Enbrel is also used to reduce the symptoms of active ankylosing spondylitis, an inflammatory condition that results in stiffness and immobility and can sometimes cause joints and bones to fuse together.

Endocet *See Percocet, page 588.*

ENDURON
Methyclothiazide

Enduron is used in the treatment of high blood pressure and other conditions that require the elimination of excess fluid from the body. These conditions include congestive heart failure, cirrhosis of the liver, side effects of steroid and estrogen therapy, and kidney disease. When used for high blood pressure, Enduron can be used alone or with other high blood pressure medications. Enduron contains a form of thiazide, a diuretic that prompts the body to produce and eliminate more urine, which helps lower blood pressure.

Entacapone *See Comtan, page 509.*

ENTOCORT EC
Budesonide, oral

Entocort EC is used to treat Crohn's disease, a chronic intestinal inflammation that causes sustained diarrhea and abdominal pain. The drug contains the anti-inflammatory steroid budesonide in a special formulation that concentrates in the intestines, thereby reducing its impact on the rest of the body.

Epinastine *See Elestat, page 526.*

Epitol *See Tegretol, page 617.*

EPIVIR
Lamivudine

Epivir is one of the drugs used to fight infection with the human immunodeficiency virus (HIV), the deadly cause of AIDS. Doctors turn to Epivir as the infection gets worse. The drug is taken along with Retrovir, another HIV medication.

HIV does its damage by slowly destroying the immune system, eventually leaving the body defenseless against infections. Like other drugs for HIV, Epivir interferes with the virus's ability to reproduce. This staves off the collapse of the immune system.

Eplerenone *See Inspra, page 546.*

Eprosartan *See Teveten, page 619.*

Eprosartan with Hydrochlorothiazide *See Teveten HCT, page 620.*

ERGOLOID MESYLATES

This drug helps relieve symptoms of declining mental capacity seen in some people over age 60. The symptoms include reduced understanding and motivation, and a decline in self-care and interpersonal skills.

Ergotamine with Caffeine *See Cafergot, page 499.*

Eryc *See Erythromycin, Oral, page 529.*

Erycette *See Erythromycin, Topical, page 530.*

Ery-Tab *See Erythromycin, Oral, page 529.*

Erythrocin *See Erythromycin, Oral, page 529.*

ERYTHROMYCIN, ORAL
Brand names: E.E.S., E-Mycin, Eryc, Ery-Tab, Erythrocin, PCE

Erythromycin is an antibiotic used to treat many kinds of infections, including:

Acute pelvic inflammatory disease
Gonorrhea
Intestinal parasitic infections
Legionnaires' disease
Listeriosis
Pinkeye
Rectal infections
Reproductive tract infections
Skin infections
Syphilis
Upper and lower respiratory tract infections
Urinary tract infections
Whooping cough

Erythromycin is also prescribed to prevent rheumatic fever in people who are allergic to penicillin and sulfa drugs. It is prescribed before colo-rectal surgery to prevent infection.

ERYTHROMYCIN, TOPICAL
Brand names: A/T/S, Erycette, T-Stat

Topical erythromycin (applied directly to the skin) is used for the treatment of acne.

Erythromycin with Benzoyl peroxide *See Benzamycin, page 496.*

Erythromycin ethylsuccinate with Sulfisoxazole *See Pediazole, page 587.*

Eryzole *See Pediazole, page 587.*

Esclim *See Estrogen Patches, page 531.*

Esgic *See Fioricet, page 534.*

Esidrix *See HydroDIURIL, page 543.*

Esomeprazole *See Nexium, page 574.*

Esterified estrogens and Methyltestosterone *See Estratest, page 530.*

Estraderm *See Estrogen Patches, page 531.*

Estradiol *See Estrogen Patches, page 531.*

Estradiol and Norethindrone acetate *See CombiPatch, page 508.*

Estradiol topical lotion *See Estrasorb, page 530.*

Estradiol vaginal ring *See Estring, page 531.*

Estradiol vaginal tablets *See Vagifem, page 631.*

ESTRASORB
Estradiol topical lotion

Estrasorb is a topical lotion that contains the hormone estrogen. It's used to reduce the symptoms of moderate to severe hot flashes associated with menopause. The most common symptoms during a hot flash include sudden sweating, intense feelings of body heat, and sudden feelings of warmth spreading to the face, neck, and chest.

ESTRATEST
Esterified estrogens and Methyltestosterone

Estratest tablets quell the flushing, sweating, "hot flashes," and vaginal irritation that trouble three-quarters of all women when they reach menopause. Estratest works by replacing some of the estrogen that is lost when the reproductive system shuts down. Although it relieves the physical symptoms of menopause, it won't help emotional symptoms such as depression if the physical symptoms are absent. It combines supplemental estrogen with a synthetic form of the male hormone testosterone, and is prescribed when estrogen alone fails to relieve menopausal symptoms.

ESTRING
Estradiol vaginal ring

Estring is an estrogen replacement system for relief of the vaginal problems that often occur after menopause, including vaginal dryness, burning, and itching, and difficult or painful intercourse. Estring is also prescribed for postmenopausal urinary problems such as difficulty urinating or urinary urgency.

ESTROGEN PATCHES
Estradiol
Brand names: Alora, Climara, Esclim, Estraderm, Vivelle, Vivelle-Dot

All of these products are used to reduce symptoms of menopause, including feelings of warmth in the face, neck, and chest; the sudden intense episodes of heat and sweating known as "hot flashes"; dry, itchy external genitals; and vaginal irritation. They are also prescribed for other conditions that cause low levels of estrogen, and some doctors prescribe them for teenagers who fail to mature at the usual rate.

Along with diet, calcium supplements, and exercise, Alora, Estraderm, Climara, Vivelle, and Vivelle-Dot are prescribed to prevent osteoporosis, a condition in which the bones become brittle and easily broken.

Estrogen with Progestin *See Activella and femhrt, page 478.*

Estropipate *See Ogen, page 581.*

Estrostep *See Oral contraceptives, page 582.*

Etanercept *See Enbrel, page 527.*

Ethinyl estradiol and Norelgestromin *See Ortho Evra, page 583.*

Etidronate *See Didronel, page 520.*

Etodolac *See Lodine, page 556.*

Etonogestrel and Ethinyl estradiol *See NuvaRing, page 581.*

EULEXIN
Flutamide

Eulexin is used along with drugs such as Lupron to treat prostate cancer. Eulexin belongs to a class of drugs known as antiandrogens. It blocks the effect of the male hormone testosterone. Giving Eulexin with Lupron, which reduces the body's testosterone levels, is one way of treating prostate cancer. For some forms of prostate cancer, radiation therapy is administered along with the drugs.

EVISTA
Raloxifene

Evista is prescribed to treat and prevent osteoporosis, the brittle-bone disease that strikes some women after menopause. A variety of factors promote osteoporosis. The more factors that apply to an individual, the greater her chances of developing the disease. These factors include:

Caucasian or Asian descent
Slender build
Early menopause
Smoking
Drinking
A diet low in calcium
An inactive lifestyle
Osteoporosis in the family

Ezetimibe *See Zetia, page 640.*

FACTIVE
Gemifloxacin

Factive is an antibiotic that is used to treat infections of the respiratory tract, such as bronchitis and pneumonia.

Famciclovir *See Famvir, page 532.*

Famotidine *See Pepcid, page 587.*

FAMVIR
Famciclovir

Famvir tablets are used to treat herpes zoster, commonly referred to as "shingles," in adults. Shingles is a painful rash with raised, red pimples on the trunk of the body, usually the back. Because it is caused by the same virus that causes chickenpox, only people who have had chicken-pox can get shingles. When prescribed for shingles, Famvir works best in people age 50 or over.

Famvir is also prescribed to treat attacks of genital herpes and to prevent future flare-ups. For people with HIV infections, it is used as a treatment for both genital and oral herpes.

FARESTON
Toremifene

Fareston is used to treat advanced breast cancer in women who have passed menopause. Some forms of breast cancer are stimulated by estrogen. Fareston slows the progression of such cancers by blocking the sites where estrogen normally acts on the tumor.

Felbamate *See Felbatol, page 533.*

FELBATOL
Felbamate

Felbatol, a relatively new epilepsy medication, is used alone or with other drugs to treat partial seizures with or without generalization (seizures in which consciousness may be retained or lost). It is also used with other medications to treat seizures associated with Lennox-Gastaut syndrome (a childhood condition characterized by brief loss of awareness and muscle tone).

Felbatol is prescribed only when other medications have failed to control severe cases of epilepsy.

FELDENE
Piroxicam

Feldene, a nonsteroidal anti-inflammatory drug, is used to relieve the inflammation, swelling, stiffness, and joint pain associated with rheumatoid arthritis and osteoarthritis (the most common form of arthritis). It is prescribed both for sudden flare-ups and for long-term treatment.

Felodipine *See Plendil, page 592.*

femhrt *See Activella and femhrt, page 478.*

Fenofibrate *See Tricor, page 625.*

Fenoprofen *See Nalfon, page 572.*

Fentanyl *See Duragesic, page 524.*

FERTINEX
Urofollitropin

Fertinex contains the female hormone called follicle-stimulating hormone (FSH). It is used to promote development of eggs in the ovaries of women who have difficulty producing eggs on their own. Fertinex therapy is usually followed by an injection of another hormone, human chorionic gonadotropin (Profasi), which triggers release of the egg. Fertinex is also given to produce many eggs in women going through in vitro fertilization.

Before prescribing Fertinex, the doctor will do a careful workup to make certain that the patient's infertility is not the result of a problem outside the ovaries, and that there's no other reason, such as pregnancy, to avoid the use of Fertinex.

Fexofenadine *See Allegra, page 482.*

FINACEA
Azelaic acid for rosacea

Finacea is an ointment used to treat mild to moderate rosacea (a skin condition marked by red eruptions, usually on the cheeks and nose). In advanced cases—and usually only in men—the nose becomes red and bulbous. Doctors aren't sure what causes rosacea, but the condition may be aggravated by stress, infection, vitamin deficiencies, and hormonal problems.

Finasteride for baldness *See Propecia, page 598.*

Finasteride for prostate problems *See Proscar, page 599.*

Finevin *See Azelex, page 493.*

FIORICET
Butalbital, Acetaminophen, and Caffeine
Other brand names: Anolor 300, Esgic, Esgic-Plus

Fioricet, a strong, non-narcotic pain reliever and relaxant, is prescribed for the relief of tension headache symptoms caused by muscle contractions in the head, neck, and shoulder area. It combines a sedative barbiturate (butalbital), a non-aspirin pain reliever (acetaminophen), and caffeine.

FIORINAL
Butalbital, Aspirin, and Caffeine

Fiorinal, a strong, non-narcotic pain reliever and muscle relaxant, is prescribed for the relief of tension headache symptoms caused by stress or muscle contraction in the head, neck, and shoulder area. It combines a non-narcotic, sedative barbiturate (butalbital) with a pain reliever (aspirin) and a stimulant (caffeine).

FIORINAL WITH CODEINE
Butalbital, Codeine, Aspirin, and Caffeine

Fiorinal with Codeine, a strong narcotic pain reliever and muscle relaxant, is prescribed for the relief of tension headache caused by stress and muscle contraction in the head, neck, and shoulder area. It combines a sedative-barbiturate (butalbital), a narcotic pain reliever and cough suppressant (codeine), a non-narcotic pain and fever reliever (aspirin), and a stimulant (caffeine).

FLAGYL
Metronidazole

Flagyl is an antibacterial drug prescribed for certain vaginal and urinary tract infections in men and women; amebic dysentery and liver abscess; and infections of the abdomen, skin, bones and joints, brain, lungs, and heart caused by certain bacteria.

Flavoxate *See Urispas, page 630.*

Flecainide *See Tambocor, page 615.*

FLEXERIL
Cyclobenzaprine

Flexeril is a muscle relaxant prescribed to relieve muscle spasms resulting from injuries such as sprains, strains, or pulls. Combined with rest and physical therapy, Flexeril provides relief of muscular stiffness and pain.

FLOMAX
Tamsulosin

Flomax is used to treat the symptoms of an enlarged prostate—a condition technically known as benign prostatic hyperplasia or BPH. The walnut-sized prostate gland surrounds the urethra (the duct that drains the bladder). If the gland becomes enlarged, it can squeeze the urethra, interfering with the flow of urine. This can cause difficulty in starting urination, a weak flow of urine, and the need to urinate urgently or more frequently. Flomax doesn't shrink the prostate. Instead, it relaxes the muscle around it, freeing the flow of urine and decreasing urinary symptoms.

Flonase *See Fluticasone, page 536.*

Flovent *See Fluticasone, page 536.*

FLOXIN
Ofloxacin

Floxin is an antibiotic. Floxin tablets have been used effectively to treat lower respiratory tract infections, including chronic bronchitis and pneumonia, sexually transmitted diseases (except syphilis), pelvic inflammatory disease, and infections of the urinary tract, prostate gland, and skin. Floxin Otic solution is used to treat ear infections.

Fluconazole *See Diflucan, page 520.*

Flunisolide *See AeroBid, page 480.*

Fluocinonide *See Lidex, page 555.*

Fluorometholone *See FML, page 537.*

Fluorouracil *See Efudex, page 526.*

Fluoxymesterone *See Halotestin, page 542.*

Flurbiprofen *See Ansaid, page 486.*

Flutamide *See Eulexin, page 532.*

FLUTICASONE
Brand names: Flonase, Flovent, Flovent Diskus, Flovent Rotadisk

Flonase nasal spray is a remedy for the stuffy, runny, itchy nose that plagues many allergy-sufferers. It can be used either for seasonal attacks of hay fever or for year-round allergic conditions. Flonase is a steroid medication. It works by relieving inflammation within the nasal passages.

The Flovent, Flovent Rotadisk, and Flovent Diskus oral inhalers are used to prevent flare-ups of asthma. (They will not, however, relieve an acute attack.) They sometimes serve as a replacement for the steroid tablets that many people take to control asthma.

Fluticasone and Salmeterol *See Advair Diskus, page 479.*

Fluticasone, topical *See Cutivate, page 513.*

Fluvastatin *See Lescol, page 552.*

FML
Fluorometholone

FML is a steroid (cortisone-like) eye ointment that is used to treat inflammation of the eyelid and the eye itself.

FOLLISTIM
Follitropin beta for injection

Follistim contains "follicle stimulating hormone" (FSH). This is the natural hormone that prompts a new egg to ripen inside a follicle (egg sac) within the ovaries each month. Follistim injections are given to stimulate production of eggs for use in Assisted Reproductive Technology (ART), a procedure in which the egg is removed from the body and fertilized in the laboratory. Follistim is also used to promote ovulation and pregnancy in infertile patients if the problem is not due to primary ovarian failure (lack of viable eggs).

A second hormone—human chorionic gonadotropin (HCG)—is needed to bring an egg to full maturity. Follistim treatments therefore end with an injection of HCG.

Follitropin beta for injection *See Follistim, page 537.*

FORADIL
Formoterol

Foradil is an asthma medication. It relaxes the muscles in the walls of the airways, allowing them to expand. Taken on a twice-daily basis, it helps to control asthma in people who need regular treatment with short-acting inhalers, including people with nighttime asthma. Regular twice-daily use can also relieve tightening of the airways in people with Chronic Obstructive Pulmonary Disease, including chronic bronchitis and emphysema.

Taken on an as-needed basis, Foradil can also be used to prevent exercise-induced tightening of the airways (also called "exercise-induced asthma") in adults and children 12 years of age and older.

Formoterol *See Foradil, page 537.*

FORTOVASE
Saquinavir

Fortovase is used in the treatment of advanced human immunodeficiency virus (HIV) infection. HIV causes the immune system to break down so that it can no longer fight off other infections. This leads to the fatal disease known as acquired immune deficiency syndrome (AIDS).

Fortovase belongs to a class of HIV drugs called protease inhibitors, which work by interfering with an important step in the virus's reproductive cycle. Fortovase is used in combination with other HIV drugs called nucleoside analogues (Retrovir or Hivid, for example). The combination produces an increase in the immune system's vital CD4 cells (white blood cells) and reduces the amount of virus in the bloodstream.

FOSAMAX
Alendronate

Fosamax is prescribed for the prevention and treatment of osteoporosis, the brittle bone disease, in postmenopausal women. It is also used to increase bone mass in men with osteoporosis, and is prescribed for both men and women who have developed a form of osteoporosis sometimes caused by steroid medications such as prednisone. This drug can also be used to relieve Paget's disease of bone, a painful condition that weakens and deforms the bones.

Fosamprenavir *See Lexiva, page 554.*

Fosfomycin *See Monurol, page 571.*

Fosinopril *See Monopril, page 570.*

Fosinopril with Hydrochlorothiazide *See Monopril-HCT, page 570.*

FROVA
Frovatriptan

Frova is used to relieve attacks of migraine headache. It's helpful whether or not the headache is preceded by an aura (visual disturbances such as seeing halos or flickering lights).

Experts think that migraines are caused by the expansion of blood vessels serving the brain, and that this expansion is triggered by a decline in the level of serotonin, one of the brain's chief chemical messengers. Frova works by restoring serotonin levels to normal. It belongs to a class of drugs called "serotonin agonists."

Frovatriptan *See Frova, page 538.*

Fulvicin P/G *See Gris-PEG, page 541.*

Furosemide *See Lasix, page 551.*

Gabapentin *See Neurontin, page 574.*

GANTRISIN
Sulfisoxazole

Gantrisin is a children's medication prescribed for the treatment of severe, repeated, or long-lasting urinary tract infections. These include pyelonephritis (bacterial kidney inflammation), pyelitis (inflammation of the part of the kidney that drains urine into the ureter), and cystitis (inflammation of the bladder).

This drug is also used to treat bacterial meningitis, and is prescribed as a preventive measure for children who have been exposed to meningitis.

Some middle ear infections are treated with Gantrisin in combination with penicillin or erythromycin.

Toxoplasmosis (parasitic disease transmitted by infected cats, their feces or litter boxes, and by undercooked meat) can be treated with Gantrisin in combination with pyrimethamine (Daraprim).

Malaria that does not respond to the drug chloroquine (Aralen) can be treated with Gantrisin in combination with other drug treatment.

Gantrisin is also used in the treatment of bacterial infections such as trachoma and inclusion conjunctivitis (eye infections), nocardiosis (bacterial disease affecting the lungs, skin, and brain), and chancroid (venereal disease causing enlargement and ulceration of lymph nodes in the groin).

GARAMYCIN OPHTHALMIC
Gentamicin

Garamycin Ophthalmic, an antibiotic, is applied to the eye for treatment of infections such as conjunctivitis (pinkeye) and other eye infections.

Gatifloxacin *See Tequin, page 618.*

Gatifloxacin eye drops *See Zymar, page 644.*

Gemfibrozil *See Lopid, page 556.*

Gemifloxacin *See Factive, page 532.*

Gentamicin *See Garamycin Ophthalmic, page 539.*

Glimepiride *See Amaryl, page 484.*

Glipizide *See Glucotrol, page 540.*

Glipizide with Metformin *See Metaglip, page 563.*

GLUCOPHAGE
Metformin

Glucophage is an oral antidiabetic medication used to treat type 2 (non-insulin-dependent) diabetes. Diabetes develops when the body proves unable to burn sugar and the unused sugar builds up in the bloodstream. Glucophage lowers the amount of sugar in the blood by decreasing sugar production and absorption and helping the body respond better to its own insulin, which promotes the burning of sugar. It does not, however, increase the body's production of insulin.

Glucophage is sometimes prescribed along with insulin or certain other oral antidiabetic drugs such as Micronase or Glucotrol. It is also used alone.

Standard Glucophage tablets are taken two or three times daily. An extended-release form (Glucophage XR) is available for once-daily dosing.

Glucophage is an aid to, not a substitute for, good diet and exercise. Failure to follow a sound diet and exercise plan can lead to serious complications such as dangerously high or low blood sugar levels. Glucophage is not an oral form of insulin and cannot be used in place of insulin.

GLUCOTROL
Glipizide

Glucotrol is an oral antidiabetic medication used to treat type 2 (non-insulin-dependent) diabetes. In diabetics either the body does not make enough insulin or the insulin that is produced no longer works properly.

There are actually two forms of diabetes: type 1 (insulin-dependent) and type 2 (non-insulin-dependent). Type 1 usually requires insulin injections for life, while type 2 diabetes can usually be treated by dietary changes and/or oral antidiabetic medications such as Glucotrol. Glucotrol is thought to control diabetes by stimulating the pancreas to secrete more insulin. If you suffer from type 1 diabetes, you will need to use insulin and will not be able to use Glucotrol. Occasionally, type 2 diabetics must take insulin injections on a temporary basis, especially during stressful periods or times of illness.

GLUCOVANCE
Glyburide with Metformin

Glucovance is used in the treatment of type 2 (noninsulin dependent) diabetes. Diabetes develops when the body's ability to burn sugar declines and the unused sugar builds up in the bloodstream. Ordinarily, sugar is moved out of the blood and into the body's cells by the hormone insulin. A buildup occurs when the body either fails to make enough insulin or doesn't respond to it properly.

Glucovance is a combination of 2 drugs—glyburide (DiaBeta, Micronase) and metformin (Glucophage)—that attack high blood sugar levels in several ways. The glyburide component stimulates the pancreas to produce more insulin and helps the body use it properly. The metformin component also encourages proper insulin utilization, and in addition works to decrease sugar production and absorption.

Glucovance is prescribed when diet and exercise prove insufficient to keep sugar levels under control. Glucovance can also be combined with other diabetes drugs such as Avandia.

Glyburide *See Micronase, page 567.*

Glyburide with Metformin *See Glucovance, page 541.*

Glynase *See Micronase, page 567.*

GoLYTELY *See Colyte, page 508.*

Goserelin *See Zoladex, page 642.*

Granisetron *See Kytril, page 550.*

Griseofulvin *See Gris-PEG, page 541.*

GRIS-PEG
Griseofulvin
Other brand name: Fulvicin P/G

Gris-PEG is prescribed for the treatment of the following ringworm infections:

Athlete's foot
Barber's itch (inflammation of the facial hair follicles)
Ringworm of the body
Ringworm of the groin and thigh
Ringworm of the nails
Ringworm of the scalp

Because Gris-PEG is effective for only certain types of fungal infections, before treatment the doctor may perform tests to identify the source of infection.

Guaifenesin with Codeine *See Tussi-Organidin NR, page 628.*

GYNE-LOTRIMIN
Clotrimazole
Other brand names: Lotrimin, Mycelex, Mycelex-7

Clotrimazole, the active ingredient in these medications, is used to treat fungal infections. In preparations for the skin, it is effective against ringworm, athlete's foot, and jock itch. In vaginal creams and tablets, it is used against vaginal yeast infections. In lozenge form, it is prescribed to treat oral yeast infections and to prevent them in people with weak immune systems.

Habitrol *See Nicotine Patches, page 575.*

Halobetasol *See Ultravate, page 629.*

HALOTESTIN
Fluoxymesterone

Halotestin is a male hormone used to ease the symptoms of advanced, recurrent breast cancer in women who are between 1 and 5 years past menopause or who have a type of breast tumor that is promoted by female hormones. Halotestin is also prescribed for men who have too little of the male hormone testosterone.

HELIDAC THERAPY
Bismuth subsalicylate, Metronidazole, and Tetracycline

Helidac is a drug combination that cures the infection responsible for most stomach ulcers. Although ulcers used to be blamed on stress and spicy food, doctors now know that a germ called *Helicobacter pylori* is the actual culprit in a majority of cases.

HIVID
Zalcitabine
Hivid is one of the drugs used against the human immunodeficiency virus (HIV)—the deadly cause of AIDS. HIV does its damage by slowly undermining the immune system, finally leaving the body without any

defense against infection. Hivid staves off collapse of the immune system by interfering with the virus's ability to reproduce.

Hivid is often combined with a protease inhibitor (Crixivan, Invirase, and Norvir) as part of the "cocktail" of drugs that has proven so effective in halting or even reversing the progress of HIV. Hivid can also be combined with the HIV drug Retrovir, provided the patient has not already been taking Retrovir for more than 3 months. For people with advanced cases of HIV, Hivid is sometimes prescribed by itself when other drugs don't work or can't be tolerated.

Humalog *See Insulin, page 546.*

Human chorionic gonadotropin *See Profasi, page 597.*

Humegon *See Pergonal, page 588.*

Humulin *See Insulin, page 546.*

Hydrocet *See Vicodin, page 634.*

Hydrochlorothiazide *See HydroDIURIL, page 543.*

Hydrochlorothiazide with Triamterene *See Dyazide, page 525.*

Hydrocodone with Acetaminophen *See Vicodin, page 634.*

Hydrocodone with Chlorpheniramine polistirex *See Tussionex, page 628.*

Hydrocodone with Ibuprofen *See Vicoprofen, page 634.*

HYDROCORTISONE SKIN PREPARATIONS
Brand names: Cetacort, Hytone, Nutracort

Hydrocortisone creams and lotions contain a steroid medication that relieves a variety of itchy rashes and inflammatory skin conditions.

HYDRODIURIL
Hydrochlorothiazide
Other brand name: Esidrix

HydroDIURIL is used in the treatment of high blood pressure and other conditions that require the elimination of excess fluid (water) from the body. These conditions include congestive heart failure, cirrhosis of the liver, corticosteroid and estrogen therapy, and kidney disorders. When used for high blood pressure, HydroDIURIL can be used alone or with other high blood pressure medications. HydroDIURIL contains a form of thiazide, a diuretic that prompts the body to produce and eliminate more urine, which helps lower blood pressure.

Hydromorphone *See Dilaudid, page 521.*

Hydroxychloroquine *See Plaquenil, page 591.*

Hyoscyamine *See Levsin, page 553.*

Hytone *See Hydrocortisone Skin Preparations, page 543.*

HYTRIN
Terazosin

Hytrin is prescribed to reduce high blood pressure. It may be used alone or in combination with other blood pressure lowering drugs, such as HydroDIURIL (a diuretic) or Inderal, a beta blocker.

Hytrin is also prescribed to relieve the symptoms of benign prostatic hyperplasia or BPH. BPH is an enlargement of the prostate gland that surrounds the urinary canal. It leads to the following symptoms:

a weak or interrupted stream when urinating
a feeling that the bladder cannot be completely emptied
a delay when starting to urinate
a need to urinate often, especially at night
a feeling that urgency when urination is needed

Hytrin relaxes the tightness of a certain type of muscle in the prostate and at the opening of the bladder. This can reduce the severity of the symptoms.

HYZAAR
Losartan with Hydrochlorothiazide

Hyzaar is a combination medication used in the treatment of high blood pressure. One component, losartan, belongs to a new class of blood pressure medications that work by preventing the hormone angiotensin II from constricting the blood vessels, thus allowing blood to flow more freely and keeping the blood pressure down. The other component, hydrochlorothiazide, is a diuretic that increases the output of urine, removing excess fluid from the body and thus lowering blood pressure.

Ibuprofen *See Motrin, page 571.*

Iletin *See Insulin, page 546.*

IMDUR

Isosorbide mononitrate
Other brand names: Ismo, Monoket

Imdur is prescribed to prevent angina pectoris (crushing chest pain that results when partially clogged arteries restrict the flow of needed oxygen-rich blood to the heart muscle). This medication does not relieve angina attacks already underway.

IMITREX

Sumatriptan

Imitrex is prescribed for the treatment of a migraine attack with or without the presence of an aura (visual disturbances, usually sensations of halos or flickering lights, which precede an attack). The injectable form is also used to relieve cluster headache attacks. (Cluster headaches come on in waves, then disappear for long periods of time. They are limited to one side of the head, and occur mainly in men.)

   Imitrex cuts headaches short. It will not reduce the number of attacks.

IMODIUM

Loperamide

Imodium controls symptoms of diarrhea, including Traveler's Diarrhea. It works by slowing the activity of the intestines and affecting the movement of water and chemicals through the bowel. It can be purchased over the counter in liquid and capsule form under the brand name Imodium A-D.

Indapamide *See Lozol, page 559.*

INDERAL

Propranolol
Other brand name: Inderal LA

Inderal, a type of medication known as a beta blocker, is used in the treatment of high blood pressure, angina pectoris (chest pain, usually caused by lack of oxygen to the heart due to clogged arteries), changes in heart rhythm, prevention of migraine headache, hereditary tremors, hypertrophic subaortic stenosis (a condition related to exertional angina), and tumors of the adrenal gland. It is also used to reduce the risk of death from recurring heart attack.

   When used for the treatment of high blood pressure, it is effective alone or combined with other high blood pressure medications, particularly thiazide-type diuretics. Beta blockers decrease the force and rate of heart contractions, reducing the heart's demand for oxygen and lowering blood pressure.

INDERIDE

Propranolol with Hydrochlorothiazide
Other brand name: Inderide LA

Inderide is used in the treatment of high blood pressure. It combines a beta blocker (propranolol) with a thiazide diuretic (hydrochlorothiazide). Beta blockers decrease the force and rate of heart contractions, thus lowering blood pressure. Diuretics help the body produce and eliminate more urine, which also helps lower blood pressure.

Indinavir *See Crixivan, page 512.*

INDOCIN

Indomethacin

Indocin, a nonsteroidal anti-inflammatory drug, is used to relieve the inflammation, swelling, stiffness and joint pain associated with moderate or severe rheumatoid arthritis and osteoarthritis (the most common form of arthritis), and ankylosing spondylitis (arthritis of the spine). It is also used to treat bursitis, tendinitis (acute painful shoulder), acute gouty arthritis, and other kinds of pain.

Indomethacin *See Indocin, page 546.*

INSPRA

Eplerenone

Inspra is prescribed to improve survival in patients who have congestive heart failure following a heart attack. It is also used to treat high blood pressure. Inspra may be used alone or with other antihypertensive agents. Inspra lowers blood pressure by blocking the actions of the hormone aldosterone.

INSULIN

Brand names: Humalog, Humulin, Iletin, Novolin

Insulin is prescribed for diabetes mellitus when diet modifications and oral medications fail to correct the condition. Insulin is a hormone produced by the pancreas, a large gland that lies near the stomach. This hormone is necessary for the body's correct use of food, especially sugar.

Insulin apparently works by helping sugar penetrate the cell wall, where it is then utilized by the cell. In people with diabetes, the body either does not make enough insulin, or the insulin that is produced cannot be used properly.

There are actually two forms of diabetes: type 1 (insulin-dependent) and type 2 (non-insulin-dependent). Type 1 usually requires insulin injections for life, while type 2 diabetes can usually be treated by dietary changes and/or oral antidiabetic medications such as Diabinese, Glucotrol, and Glucophage. Occasionally, type 2 diabetics must take insulin injections on a temporary basis, especially during stressful periods or times of illness.

The various available types of insulin differ in several ways: in the source (animal, human, or genetically engineered), in the time requirements for the insulin to take effect, and in the length of time the insulin remains working.

Regular insulin manufactured from beef and pork pancreas, begins working within 30 to 60 minutes, and lasts for 6 to 8 hours. Variations of insulin have been developed to satisfy the needs of individual patients. For example, zinc suspension insulin is an intermediate-acting insulin that starts working within 1 to 1-1/2 hours and lasts approximately 24 hours. Insulin combined with zinc and protamine is a longer-acting insulin that takes effect within 4 to 6 hours and lasts up to 36 hours. The time and course of action may vary considerably in different individuals or at different times in the same individual. The genetically engineered insulin lispro injection works faster and for a shorter length of time than human regular insulin and should be used along with a longer-acting insulin. It is available only by prescription.

Animal-based insulin is a very safe product. However, some components may cause an allergic reaction. Therefore, genetically engineered human insulin has been developed to lessen the chance of an allergic reaction. It is structurally identical to the insulin produced by the human pancreas. However, some human insulin may be produced in a semi-synthetic process that begins with animal-based ingredients, and may cause an allergic reaction.

INTAL

Cromolyn, inhaled
Other brand name: Nasalcrom

Intal contains the antiasthmatic/antiallergic medication cromolyn sodium.

Different forms of the drug are used to manage bronchial asthma, to prevent asthma attacks, and to prevent and treat seasonal and chronic allergies.

The drug works by preventing certain cells in the body from releasing substances that can cause allergic reactions or prompt too much bronchial activity. It also helps prevent bronchial constriction caused by exercise, aspirin, cold air, and certain environmental pollutants such as sulfur dioxide.

Ionamin *See Adipex-P, page 479.*

Ipratropium *See Atrovent, page 489.*

Ipratropium with Albuterol *See Combivent, page 509.*

Irbesartan *See Avapro, page 491.*

Irbesartan with Hydrochlorothiazide *See Avalide, page 490.*

Ismo *See Imdur, page 545.*

Isometheptene, Dichloralphenazone, and Acetaminophen
See Midrin, page 567.

Isoptin *See Calan, page 499.*

Isopto Carpine *See Pilocar, page 590.*

ISORDIL
Isosorbide dinitrate
Other brand name: Sorbitrate

Isordil is prescribed to relieve or prevent angina pectoris (suffocating chest pain). Angina pectoris occurs when the arteries and veins become constricted and sufficient oxygen does not reach the heart. Isordil dilates the blood vessels by relaxing the muscles in their walls. Oxygen flow improves as the vessels relax, and chest pain subsides.

In swallowed capsules or tablets, Isordil helps to increase the amount of exercise patients can do before chest pain begins.

In chewable or sublingual (held under the tongue) tablets, Isordil can help relieve chest pain that has already started or prevent pain expected from a strenuous activity such as walking up a hill or climbing stairs.

Isosorbide dinitrate *See Isordil, page 548.*

Isosorbide mononitrate *See Imdur, page 545.*

Isotretinoin *See Accutane, page 476.*

Isradipine *See DynaCirc, page 525.*

Itraconazole *See Sporanox, page 612.*

Kadian *See MS Contin, page 571.*

KALETRA
Lopinavir and Ritonavir

Kaletra combats the human immunodeficiency virus (HIV). HIV is the deadly virus that undermines the infection-fighting capacity of the body's immune system, eventually leading to AIDS.

Kaletra is a combination of two drugs, lopinavir and ritonavir (Norvir), both of which fall into the drug category known as protease inhibitors. When taken along with other HIV drugs, Kaletra lowers the amount of the virus circulating in the bloodstream. However, it does not completely eradicate the virus, and the patient may continue to develop the rare infections that attack when the immune system weakens. It's also important to remember that Kaletra does not eliminate the danger of transmitting the virus to others.

Kaon-CL *See Micro-K, page 566.*

K-Dur *See Micro-K, page 566.*

KEFLEX
Cephalexin
Other brand name: Keftab

Keflex and Keftab are cephalosporin antibiotics. They are prescribed for bacterial infections of the respiratory tract, the middle ear, the bones, the skin, and the reproductive and urinary systems. Because the drugs are effective for only certain types of bacterial infections, before beginning treatment the doctor may perform tests to identify the organisms causing the infection.

Keflex is available in capsules and an oral suspension form for use in children. Keftab, available only in tablet form, is prescribed exclusively for adults.

Keftab *See Keflex, page 549.*

KEPPRA
Levetiracetam

Keppra helps reduce the frequency of partial epileptic seizures, a form of epilepsy in which neural disturbances are limited to a specific region of the brain and the victim remains conscious throughout the attack. The drug is used along with other epilepsy medications, never by itself.

Ketoconazole *See Nizoral, page 578.*

Ketoprofen *See Oruvail, page 584.*

Ketorolac *See Toradol, page 624.*

Ketorolac, ocular *See Acular, page 479.*

Ketotifen *See Zaditor, page 638.*

KINERET
Anakinra

Kineret is used to relieve the symptoms of rheumatoid arthritis. It is usually prescribed after other antirheumatic drugs have failed to make an improvement. Kineret can be prescribed alone or in combination with other drugs for rheumatoid arthritis.

Kineret works by blocking the effects of interleukin-1, an inflammatory compound released by the immune system. While fighting inflammation, Kineret may also affect the immune system's ability to fight infection.

Klor-Con *See Micro-K, page 566.*

K-Tab *See Micro-K, page 566.*

KYTRIL
Granisetron

Kytril is prescribed to prevent the nausea and vomiting associated with radiation therapy and chemotherapy for cancer. It is available in tablet and liquid forms.

Labetalol *See Normodyne, page 579.*

LAC-HYDRIN
Ammonium lactate

Lac-Hydrin is used in the treatment of dry, scaly skin, including the genetic condition called ichthyosis vulgaris. Available in cream and lotion form, the drug moisturizes the skin and breaks up the scales.

LACTULOSE

Lactulose treats constipation. In people who are chronically constipated, Lactulose increases the number and frequency of bowel movements.

LAMISIL
Terbinafine

Lamisil fights fungal infections. In tablet form, it's used for fungus of the toenail or fingernail. The cream and the solution are used for other fungal infections such as athlete's foot, jock itch, and ringworm. The solution is also used to treat tinea versicolor, a fungal infection that produces brown, tan, or white spots on the trunk of the body.

Lamivudine *See Epivir, page 528.*

Lamivudine and Zidovudine *See Combivir, page 509.*

LANOXIN
Digoxin
Other brand name: Digitek

Lanoxin is used in the treatment of congestive heart failure, certain types of irregular heartbeat, and other heart problems. It improves the strength and efficiency of the heart, which leads to better circulation of blood and reduction of the uncomfortable swelling that is common in people with congestive heart failure. Lanoxin is usually prescribed along with a water pill (to help relieve swelling) and a drug called an ACE inhibitor (to further improve circulation). It belongs to a class of drugs known as digitalis glycosides.

Lansoprazole *See Prevacid, page 595.*

LASIX
Furosemide

Lasix is a diuretic (water pill) used in the treatment of high blood pressure and other conditions that require the elimination of excess fluid from the body. These conditions include congestive heart failure, cirrhosis of the liver, and kidney disease. When used to treat high blood pressure, Lasix is effective alone or in combination with other high blood pressure medications. Diuretics help the body produce and eliminate more urine, which helps lower blood pressure. Lasix is classified as a "loop diuretic" because of its point of action in the kidneys.

   Lasix is also used with other drugs in people with fluid accumulation in the lungs.

Latanoprost *See Xalatan, page 637.*

Leflunomide *See Arava, page 487.*

LESCOL
Fluvastatin

Lescol reduces "bad" LDL cholesterol—and increases "good" HDL cholesterol—in the blood, and can lower the risk of developing clogged arteries and heart disease. It is also prescribed to slow the accumulation of
plaque in the arteries of people who already have coronary heart disease,
and can also be prescribed when a patient is released from the hospital
after a heart attack.

Also, if you have coronary heart disease you may be prescribed Lescol
to reduce the risk of undergoing coronary revascularization procedures
(angioplasty, bypass surgery, or stent insertion).

Doctors prescribe Lescol only when patients have been unable to
reduce their blood cholesterol level sufficiently with a low-fat, low-
cholesterol diet alone. For people at high risk of heart disease, current
guidelines call for considering drug therapy when LDL levels reach 130.
For people at lower risk, the cut-off is 160. For those at little or no risk,
it's 190.

Leuprolide *See Lupron Depot, page 559.*

Levalbuterol *See Xopenex, page 637.*

LEVAQUIN
Levofloxacin

Levaquin cures a variety of bacterial infections, including several types
of sinus infection and pneumonia. It is also prescribed for flare-ups of
chronic bronchitis, acute kidney infections, certain urinary or chronic
prostate and skin infections. Levaquin is a member of the quinolone
family of antibiotics.

Levbid *See Levsin, page 553.*

Levetiracetam *See Keppra, page 549.*

LEVITRA
Vardenafil

Levitra is an oral drug for male impotence, also known as erectile dysfunction (ED). It works by dilating blood vessels in the penis, allowing
the inflow of blood needed for an erection.

Levlen *See Oral Contraceptives, page 582.*

Levlite *See Oral Contraceptives, page 582.*

Levobunolol *See Betagan, page 496.*

LEVODOPA

Levodopa (L-dopa) relieves the symptoms of parkinsonism (a nerve disorder characterized by tremors, drooling, stooped posture, a shuffling walk, and muscle weakness). Levodopa is also used in elderly people whose parkinsonism is related to hardening of the arteries in the brain.

Some doctors also prescribe levodopa for male sexual dysfunction, shingles, restless leg syndrome, and periodic leg movements.

Levofloxacin *See Levaquin, page 552.*

Levonorgestrel and Ethinyl Estradiol *See Preven, page 596.*

Levonorgestrel implants *See Norplant, page 580.*

Levora *See Oral Contraceptives, page 582.*

Levothroid *See Synthroid, page 614.*

Levothyroxine *See Synthroid, page 614.*

Levoxyl *See Synthroid, page 614.*

LEVSIN

Hyoscyamine
Other brand names: Anaspaz, Levbid, Levsinex, NuLev

Levsin is an antispasmodic medication given to help treat various stomach, intestinal, and urinary tract disorders that involve cramps, colic, or other painful muscle contractions. Because Levsin has a drying effect, it may also be used to dry a runny nose or to dry excess secretions before anesthesia is administered.

Together with morphine or other narcotics, Levsin is prescribed for the pain of gallstones or kidney stones. For inflammation of the pancreas, Levsin may be used to help control excess secretions and reduce pain. Levsin may also be taken in Parkinson's disease to help reduce muscle rigidity and tremors and to help control drooling and excess sweating. The drug is sometimes prescribed during treatment for peptic ulcer.

Doctors also give Levsin as part of the preparation for certain diagnostic x-rays (for example, of the stomach, intestines, or kidneys).

Levsin comes in several forms, including regular tablets, tablets to be dissolved under the tongue, tablets that dissolve on the tongue (NuLev), sustained-release capsules (Levsinex Timecaps), and sustained-release tablets (Levbid), as well as liquid, drops, and an injectable solution.

Levsinex *See Levsin, page 553.*

LEXIVA
Fosamprenavir

Lexiva is prescribed for adults with human immunodeficiency virus (HIV) infection. HIV undermines the immune system, reducing the body's ability to fight off other infections and eventually leading to the deadly condition known as acquired immune deficiency syndrome (AIDS).

Lexiva slows the progression of HIV by interfering with an important step in the virus's reproductive cycle. The drug is a member of the group of "protease inhibitors." Lexiva is prescribed only as part of a "drug cocktail" that attacks the virus on several fronts. It is not to be used alone.

Lexiva is not a cure for HIV infection or AIDS. It does not completely eliminate HIV from the body, nor does it totally restore the immune system. There is still a danger of developing serious opportunistic infections (that is, infections that develop when the immune system falters). It is important, therefore, for the patient to continue to see a doctor for regular blood counts and tests. Notify the healthcare provider immediately of any change in the patient's general health.

LEXXEL
Enalapril with Felodipine

Lexxel is used to treat high blood pressure. It combines two blood pressure drugs: an ACE inhibitor and a calcium channel blocker. The ACE inhibitor (enalapril) lowers blood pressure by preventing a chemical in the blood called angiotensin I from converting to a more potent form that narrows the blood vessels and increases salt and water retention. The calcium channel blocker (felodipine) also works to keep the blood vessels open, and eases the heart's workload by reducing the force and rate of the heartbeat.

Lexxel can be prescribed alone or in combination with other blood pressure medicines, especially water pills (diuretics) such as HydroDIURIL or Esidrix.

LIBRAX
Chlordiazepoxide with Clidinium

Librax is used, in combination with other therapy, for the treatment of peptic ulcer, irritable bowel syndrome (spastic colon), and acute enterocolitis (inflammation of the colon and small intestine). Librax is a combination of a benzodiazepine (chlordiazepoxide) and an antispasmodic medication (clidinium).

LIDEX
Fluocinonide

Lidex is a steroid medication that relieves the itching and inflammation of a wide variety of skin problems, including redness and swelling.

Linezolid *See Zyvox, page 645.*

LIORESAL
Baclofen

Lioresal is a muscle relaxant that helps relieve the symptoms and pain of muscle spasms caused by multiple sclerosis (MS), particularly in muscles that control joints. It also relieves pain due to rhythmic expansion and contraction of muscles (clonus) and pain due to muscular stiffness. Lioresal may also be of some help to people with spinal cord injuries and diseases.

LIPITOR
Atorvastatin

Lipitor is a cholesterol-lowering drug. Doctors may prescribe it along with a special diet if blood cholesterol or triglyceride levels are high enough to pose a risk of heart disease, and the patient has been unable to lower the readings by diet alone.

The drug works by helping to clear harmful low density lipoprotein (LDL) cholesterol out of the blood and by limiting the body's ability to form new LDL cholesterol.

For people at high risk of heart disease, the doctor may suggest a cholesterol-lowering medication if LDL readings are 130 or more. For those at low risk, a medication is considered at readings of 190 or more.

Lisinopril *See Zestril, page 640.*

Lisinopril with Hydrochlorothiazide *See Zestoretic, page 640.*

LODINE
Etodolac

Lodine, a nonsteroidal anti-inflammatory drug, is available in regular and extended-release forms (Lodine XL). Both forms are used to relieve the inflammation, swelling, stiffness, and joint pain of osteoarthritis (the most common form of arthritis) and rheumatoid arthritis. Regular Lodine is also used to relieve pain in other situations.

Loestrin *See Oral Contraceptives, page 582.*

Lofibra *See Tricor, page 625.*

Lomefloxacin *See Maxaquin, page 561.*

LOMOTIL
Diphenoxylate with Atropine

Lomotil is used, along with other drugs, in the treatment of diarrhea. It should not be used for antibiotic-induced diarrhea (pseudomembranous colitis) or diarrhea caused by enterotoxin-producing bacteria.

Lo/Ovral *See Oral Contraceptives, page 582.*

Loperamide *See Imodium, page 545.*

LOPID
Gemfibrozil

Lopid is prescribed, along with a special diet, for treatment of people with very high levels of serum triglycerides (a fatty substance in the blood) who are at risk of developing pancreatitis (inflammation of the pancreas) and who do not respond adequately to a strict diet.

This drug can also be used to reduce the risk of coronary heart disease in people who have failed to respond to weight loss, diet, exercise, and other triglyceride- or cholesterol-lowering drugs.

Lopinavir and Ritonavir *See Kaletra, page 549.*

LOPRESSOR
Metoprolol
Other brand name: Toprol-XL

Lopressor, a type of medication known as a beta blocker, is used in the treatment of high blood pressure, angina pectoris (chest pain, usually caused by lack of oxygen to the heart due to clogged arteries), and heart attack. When prescribed for high blood pressure, it is effective when used alone or in combination with other high blood pressure medications. Beta blockers decrease the force and rate of heart contractions, thereby reducing the demand for oxygen and lowering blood pressure.

Occasionally doctors prescribe Lopressor for the treatment of aggressive behavior, prevention of migraine headache, and relief of temporary anxiety.

An extended-release form of this drug, called Toprol-XL, is prescribed for high blood pressure, angina, and heart failure.

LOPROX
Ciclopirox

Loprox cream, lotion, and topical solution are prescribed for the treatment of the following fungal skin infections:

Athlete's foot
Fungal infection of the groin (jock itch)
Fungal infection of non-hairy parts of the skin
Candidiasis (yeastlike fungal infection of the skin)
Tinea versicolor—infection of the skin that is characterized by brown or
    tan patches on the trunk.

Loprox gel is used for athlete's foot, fungal infections of the non-hairy parts of the skin, and certain scalp inflammations (seborrheic dermatitis of the scalp).

LORABID
Loracarbef

Lorabid is a carbacephem antibiotic. It is used to treat mild-to-moderate bacterial infections of the lungs, ears, throat, sinuses, skin, urinary tract, and kidneys.

Loracarbef *See Lorabid, page 557.*

Lorcet *See Vicodin, page 634.*

Lortab *See Vicodin, page 634.*

Losartan *See Cozaar, page 511.*

Losartan with Hydrochlorothiazide *See Hyzaar, page 544.*

LOTENSIN
Benazepril

Lotensin is used in the treatment of high blood pressure. It is effective when used alone or in combination with thiazide diuretics. Lotensin is in a family of drugs called ACE (angiotensin-converting enzyme) inhibitors. It works by preventing a chemical in the blood called angiotensin I from converting into a more potent form that increases salt and water retention in the body. Lotensin also enhances blood flow throughout the circulatory system.

LOTENSIN HCT
Benazepril with Hydrochlorothiazide

Lotensin HCT combines two types of blood pressure medication. The first, benazepril hydrochloride, is an ACE (angiotensin-converting enzyme) inhibitor. It works by preventing a chemical in the blood called angiotensin I from converting into a more potent form (angiotensin II) that increases salt and water retention in the body and causes the blood vessels to constrict—two actions that tend to increase blood pressure.

To aid in clearing excess water from the body, Lotensin HCT also contains hydrochlorothiazide, a diuretic that promotes production of urine. Diuretics often wash too much potassium out of the body along with the water. However, the ACE inhibitor part of Lotensin HCT tends to keep potassium in the body, thereby canceling this unwanted effect.

Lotensin HCT is not used for the initial treatment of high blood pressure. It is saved for later use, when a single blood pressure medication is not sufficient for the job. In addition, some doctors are using Lotensin HCT along with other drugs to treat congestive heart failure.

LOTREL
Amlodipine with Benazepril

Lotrel is used in the treatment of high blood pressure. It is a combination medicine that is used when treatment with a single drug has not been successful or has caused side effects.

One component, amlodipine, is a calcium channel blocker. It eases the workload of the heart by slowing down the passage of nerve impulses and hence the contractions of the heart muscle. This improves blood flow through the heart and throughout the body and reduces blood pressure. The other component, benazepril, is an angiotensin-converting enzyme (ACE) inhibitor. It works by preventing the transformation of a hormone called angiotensin I into a more potent substance that increases salt and water retention in the body.

Lotrimin *See Gyne-Lotrimin, page 542.*

LOTRISONE
Clotrimazole with Betamethasone

Lotrisone cream and lotion contain a combination of a steroid (betamethasone) and an antifungal drug (clotrimazole). Lotrisone is used to treat skin infections caused by fungus, such as athlete's foot, jock itch, and ringworm of the body.

Betamethasone treats symptoms (such as itching, redness, swelling, and inflammation) that result from fungus infections, while clotrimazole treats the cause of the infection by inhibiting the growth of certain yeast and fungus organisms. If the infection is not inflamed, the doctor may prescribe a different medication.

Lovastatin *See Mevacor, page 565.*

Lovastatin, extended release *See Altocor, page 483.*

Lovastatin and Extended-release niacin *See Advicor, page 480.*

Low-Ogestrel *See Oral Contraceptives, page 582.*

LOZOL
Indapamide

Lozol is used in the treatment of high blood pressure, either alone or in combination with other high blood pressure medications. Lozol is also used to relieve salt and fluid retention. During pregnancy, doctors may prescribe Lozol to relieve fluid retention caused by a specific condition or when fluid retention causes extreme discomfort that is not relieved by rest.

LUMIGAN
Bimatoprost

Lumigan is an eye drop that combats high pressure inside the eyeball. It is prescribed for a condition called open-angle glaucoma (a gradual increase of pressure in the eye). It is typically used after other remedies have caused problems or fail to work. It lowers pressure by promoting drainage of the fluid (aqueous humor) that fills the eye.

LUPRON DEPOT
Leuprolide

Lupron is a synthetic version of the naturally occurring gonadotropin releasing hormone (GnRH). Lupron suppresses shedding of the endometrium (lining of the uterus) during menstruation and is used to treat endometriosis, a condition in which cells from the endometrium grow outside of the uterus. Endometriosis causes painful growths to form around the outside of the uterus, fallopian tubes, and ovaries.

Two forms of Lupron—Lupron Depot 3.75 and Lupron Depot 11.25—are prescribed to relieve the pain of endometriosis and shrink the growths. (The hormonal medication norethindrone acetate is often added to the regimen.) Three other forms of Lupron—Lupron Depot 7.5, Lupron Depot 22.5, and Lupron Depot 30—are prescribed to relieve the symptoms of advanced prostate cancer.

The first two forms of Lupron are also used before surgery, along with iron, to treat anemia caused by fibroids (tumors) in the uterus when iron alone is not effective. Some doctors also prescribe Lupron for infertility and for early puberty.

LURIDE
Sodium fluoride

Luride is prescribed to strengthen children's teeth against decay during the period when the teeth are still developing.

Studies have shown that children who live where the drinking water contains a certain level of fluoride have fewer cavities than others. Fluoride helps prevent cavities in three ways: by increasing the teeth's resistance to dissolving on contact with acid, by strengthening teeth, and by slowing down the growth of mouth bacteria.

Luride may be given to children who live where the water fluoride level is 0.6 parts per million or less.

Macrobid *See Macrodantin, page 560.*

MACRODANTIN
Nitrofurantoin
Other brand name: Macrobid

Nitrofurantoin, an antibacterial drug, is prescribed for the treatment of urinary tract infections caused by certain strains of bacteria.

MAVIK
Trandolapril

Mavik controls high blood pressure. It is effective when used alone or combined with other high blood pressure medications such as diuretics that help rid the body of excess water. Mavik is also used to treat heart failure or dysfunction following a heart attack.

Mavik is in a family of drugs known as ACE (angiotensin converting enzyme) inhibitors. It works by preventing a chemical in the blood called angiotensin I from converting into a more potent form that increases salt and water retention in the body. ACE inhibitors also expand the blood vessels, further reducing blood pressure.

MAXALT
Rizatriptan
Other brand name: Maxalt-MLT

Maxalt is prescribed for the treatment of a migraine attack with or without the presence of an aura (visual disturbances, usually sensations of halos or flickering lights, which precede an attack). It cuts headaches short, but won't prevent attacks.

MAXAQUIN
Lomefloxacin

Maxaquin is a quinolone antibiotic used to treat lower respiratory infections, including chronic bronchitis, and urinary tract infections, including cystitis (inflammation of the inner lining of the bladder). Maxaquin is also given before bladder surgery and prostate biopsy to prevent the infections that sometimes follow these operations.

Maxidone *See Vicodin, page 634.*

Maxzide *See Dyazide, page 525.*

Meclizine *See Antivert, page 486.*

MECLOFENAMATE

Meclofenamate, a nonsteroidal anti-inflammatory drug, is used for the relief of mild to moderate pain. It is also used in the treatment of menstrual pain and heavy menstrual blood loss (when the cause is unknown) and to relieve the inflammation, swelling, stiffness, and joint pain associated with rheumatoid arthritis and osteoarthritis (the most common form of arthritis).

MEDROL
Methylprednisolone

Medrol, a corticosteroid drug, is used to reduce inflammation and improve symptoms in a variety of disorders, including rheumatoid arthritis, acute gouty arthritis, and severe cases of asthma. Medrol may be prescribed to treat primary or secondary adrenal cortex insufficiency (inability of the adrenal gland to produce sufficient hormone). It is also given to help treat the following disorders:

Severe allergic conditions (including drug-induced allergic states)
Blood disorders (leukemia and various anemias)
Certain cancers (along with other drugs)
Skin diseases (including severe psoriasis)
Connective tissue diseases such as systemic lupus erythematosus
Digestive tract diseases such as ulcerative colitis
High serum levels of calcium associated with cancer
Fluid retention due to nephrotic syndrome (a condition in which
  damage to the kidney causes loss of protein in urine)
Various eye diseases
Lung diseases such as tuberculosis
Worsening of multiple sclerosis

Medroxyprogesterone for contraception *See Depo-Provera, page 518.*

Medroxyprogesterone for menstrual problems *See Provera, page 600.*

Mefenamic acid *See Ponstel, page 593.*

MEGACE
Megestrol acetate

Megace is a synthetic drug that has the same effect as the female hormone progesterone. In tablet form it is used to treat cancer of the breast and uterus. Megace is usually prescribed when a tumor cannot be removed by surgery or has recurred after surgery, or when other drugs or radiation therapy are ineffective. Megace Oral Suspension is used to treat lack or loss of appetite, malnutrition and wasting away, and unexplained, significant weight loss in people with AIDS.

Megestrol acetate *See Megace, page 562.*

Meloxicam *See Mobic, page 569.*

Menotropins *See Pergonal, page 588.*

Meperidine *See Demerol, page 517.*

MERIDIA
Sibutramine

Meridia helps the seriously overweight shed pounds and keep them off. It is especially recommended for those who in addition to being overweight have other health problems such as high blood pressure, diabetes, or high cholesterol. It is used in conjunction with a low-calorie diet.

Meridia works by boosting levels of certain chemical messengers in the nervous system, including serotonin, dopamine, and norepinephrine.

Mesalamine *See Rowasa, page 607.*

METAGLIP
Glipizide with Metformin

Metaglip is an oral medication used to control blood sugar levels in people with type 2 (non-insulin-dependent) diabetes. It contains two drugs commonly used to lower blood sugar, glipizide (Glucotrol) and metformin (Glucophage). Metaglip replaces the need to take these two drugs separately. It is prescribed when diet and exercise alone do not control blood sugar levels, or when treatment with another antidiabetic medication does not work.

Blood sugar levels are ordinarily controlled by the body's natural supply of insulin, which helps sugar move out of the bloodstream and into the cells to be used for energy. People who have type 2 diabetes do not make enough insulin or do not respond normally to the insulin their bodies make, causing a buildup of unused sugar in the bloodstream. Metaglip helps remedy this problem in two ways: by causing the body to release more insulin and by helping the body use insulin more effectively.

Metaproterenol *See Alupent, page 484.*

Metaxalone *See Skelaxin, page 610.*

Metformin *See Glucophage, page 540.*

Methazolamide *See Neptazane, page 574.*

Methenamine *See Urised, page 630.*

METHERGINE
Methylergonovine

Methergine, a blood-vessel constrictor, is given to prevent or control excessive bleeding following childbirth. It works by causing the uterine muscles to contract, thereby reducing the mother's blood loss.

Methergine comes in tablet and injectable forms.

Methocarbamol *See Robaxin, page 606.*

METHOTREXATE
Brand names: Rheumatrex, Trexall

Methotrexate is an anticancer drug used in the treatment of lymphoma (cancer of the lymph nodes) and certain forms of leukemia. It is also given to treat some forms of cancers of the uterus, breast, lung, head, neck, and ovary. Methotrexate is also given to treat rheumatoid arthritis when other treatments have proved ineffective, and is sometimes used to treat very severe and disabling psoriasis (a skin disease characterized by thickened patches of red, inflamed skin often covered by silver scales).

Methyclothiazide *See Enduron, page 528.*

Methyldopa *See Aldomet, page 482.*

Methylergonovine *See Methergine, page 564.*

Methylprednisolone *See Medrol, page 561.*

Methyltestosterone *See Android, page 486.*

Methysergide *See Sansert, page 608.*

Metoclopramide *See Reglan, page 602.*

Metolazone *See Zaroxolyn, page 639.*

Metoprolol *See Lopressor, page 556.*

MetroCream *See MetroGel, page 564.*

METROGEL
Metronidazole
Other brand names: MetroCream, MetroLotion

MetroGel is a preparation of the drug metronidazole used for the treatment of a skin condition called rosacea (red eruptions, usually on the face). The cream and lotion forms of metronidazole are used for the same problem. All are for external (topical) use only.

METROGEL-VAGINAL
Metronidazole

Metrogel-Vaginal is used to treat bacterial vaginosis, a bacteria-caused inflammation of the vagina accompanied by pain and a vaginal discharge.

MetroLotion *See MetroGel, page 564.*

Metronidazole *See Flagyl, page 535.*

Metronidazole cream, gel, and lotion *See MetroGel, page 564.*

Metronidazole vaginal gel *See Metrogel-Vaginal, page 565.*

MEVACOR
Lovastatin

Mevacor is used, along with diet, to lower cholesterol levels in people with primary hypercholesterolemia (too much cholesterol in the bloodstream). High cholesterol levels foster the buildup of artery-clogging plaque, which can be especially dangerous when it collects in the vessels serving the muscles of the heart. Mevacor is prescribed to prevent this problem—called coronary heart disease—or to slow its advance if the arteries are already clogging up.

Mexiletine *See Mexitil, page 565.*

MEXITIL
Mexiletine

Mexitil is used to treat severe irregular heartbeat (arrhythmia). Irregular heart rhythms are generally divided into two main types: heartbeats that are faster than normal (tachycardia) and heartbeats that are slower than normal (bradycardia). Arrhythmias are often caused by drugs or disease but can occur in otherwise healthy people with no history of heart disease or other illness.

MIACALCIN
Calcitonin-salmon

Miacalcin is a synthetic form of calcitonin, a naturally occurring hormone produced by the thyroid gland. Miacalcin reduces the rate of calcium loss from bones. Since less calcium passes from the bones to the blood, Miacalcin also helps control blood calcium levels.

Miacalcin Nasal Spray is used to treat postmenopausal osteoporosis (bone loss occurring after menopause) in women who cannot or will not take estrogen.

MICARDIS

Telmisartan

Micardis controls high blood pressure. It works by blocking the effects of a hormone called angiotensin II. Unopposed, this substance tends to constrict the blood vessels while promoting retention of salt and water—actions that tend to raise blood pressure. Micardis prevents these effects and thus keeps blood pressure lower. It can be prescribed alone or with other high blood pressure medications, such as diuretics that help rid the body of excess water.

MICARDIS HCT

Telmisartan with Hydrochlorothiazide

Micardis HCT is a combination medication used in the treatment of high blood pressure. One component, telmisartan, belongs to a class of blood pressure medications that work by preventing the hormone angiotensin II from constricting the blood vessels. This allows the blood to flow more freely and helps keep blood pressure down. The other component of Micardis HCT, hydrochlorothiazide, is a diuretic that increases the output of urine. This removes excess fluid from the body and helps lower blood pressure. Doctors usually prescribe Micardis HCT in place of its individual components. It can also be prescribed along with other blood pressure medications.

Miconazole *See Monistat, page 570.*

MICRO-K

Potassium chloride
Other brand names: Kaon-CL, K-Dur, Klor-Con, K-Tab, Slow-K

Micro-K is used to treat or prevent low potassium levels in people who may face potassium loss caused by digitalis (Lanoxin), non-potassium-sparing diuretics (such as Diuril and Dyazide), and certain diseases.

Potassium plays an essential role in the proper functioning of a wide range of systems in the body, including the kidneys, muscles, and nerves. As a result, a potassium deficiency may have a wide range of effects, including dry mouth, thirst, reduced urination, weakness, fatigue, drowsiness, low blood pressure, restlessness, muscle cramps, abnormal heart rate, nausea, and vomiting.

Micro-K and its sister products are slow-release potassium formulations.

MICRONASE
Glyburide
Other brand names: DiaBeta, Glynase

Micronase is an oral antidiabetic medication used to treat type 2 diabetes, the kind that occurs when the body either does not make enough insulin or fails to use insulin properly. Insulin transfers sugar from the blood-stream to the body's cells, where it is then used for energy.

There are two forms of diabetes: type 1 and type 2. Type 1 diabetes results from a complete shutdown of normal insulin production and usually requires insulin injections for life, while type 2 diabetes can usually be treated by dietary changes, exercise, and/or oral antidiabetic medications such as Micronase. This medication controls diabetes by stimulating the pancreas to produce more insulin and by helping insulin to work better. Type 2 diabetics may need insulin injections, sometimes only temporarily during stressful periods such as illness, or on a long-term basis if an oral antidiabetic medication fails to control blood sugar.

Micronase can be used alone or along with a drug called metformin (Glucophage) if diet plus either drug alone fails to control sugar levels.

Micronor *See Oral Contraceptives, page 582.*

MIDRIN
Isometheptene, Dichloralphenazone, and Acetaminophen

Midrin is prescribed for the treatment of tension headaches. It is also used to treat vascular headaches such as migraine.

MIGRANAL
Dihydroergotamine

Migranal Nasal Spray is used for relief of migraine headache attacks, whether or not preceded by an aura (visual disturbances, usually including sensations of halos or flickering lights).

This nasally administered remedy contains the same active ingredient as D.H.E. 45, an injectable form of the drug. It constricts the blood vessels, and may defeat migraine through this action.

MINIPRESS
Prazosin

Minipress is used to treat high blood pressure. It is effective used alone or with other high blood pressure medications such as diuretics or beta-blocking medications (drugs that ease heart contractions) such as Tenormin.

Minipress is also prescribed for the treatment of benign prostatic hyperplasia (BPH), an abnormal enlargement of the prostate gland.

MINOCIN
Minocycline
Other brand name: Dynacin

Minocin is a form of the antibiotic tetracycline. It is given to help treat many different kinds of infection, including:

Acne
Amebic dysentery
Anthrax (when penicillin cannot be given)
Cholera
Gonorrhea (when penicillin cannot be given)
Plague
Respiratory infections such as pneumonia
Rocky Mountain spotted fever
Syphilis (when penicillin cannot be given)
Urinary tract infections, rectal infections, and infections of the cervix caused by certain microbes

Minocycline *See Minocin, page 568.*

MIRALAX
Polyethylene glycol

MiraLax is a remedy for constipation. It works by retaining water in the stool, softening it and increasing the frequency of bowel movements. It may take up to 2 to 4 days to work.

Mircette *See Oral Contraceptives, page 582.*

MIRAPEX
Pramipexole

Although it is not a cure, Mirapex eases the symptoms of Parkinson's disease—a progressive disorder marked by muscle rigidity, weakness, shaking, tremor, and eventually difficulty with walking and talking. Parkinson's disease results from a shortage of the chemical messenger dopamine in certain areas of the brain. Mirapex is believed to work by boosting the action of whatever dopamine is available. The drug can be used with other Parkinson's medications such as Eldepryl and Sinemet.

Misoprostol *See Cytotec, page 513.*

MOBIC
Meloxicam

Mobic is a nonsteroidal anti-inflammatory drug (NSAID) in prescription form. It is used to relieve the pain and stiffness of osteoarthritis.

Modicon *See Oral Contraceptives, page 582.*

MODURETIC
Amiloride with Hydrochlorothiazide

Moduretic is a diuretic combination used in the treatment of high blood pressure and congestive heart failure, conditions which require the elimination of excess fluid (water) from the body. When used for high blood pressure, Moduretic can be used alone or with other high blood pressure medications. Diuretics help the body produce and eliminate more urine, which helps lower blood pressure. Amiloride, one of the ingredients, helps minimize the potassium loss that can be caused by the other component, hydrochlorothiazide.

Moexipril *See Univasc, page 630.*

Moexipril with Hydrochlorothiazide *See Uniretic, page 629.*

Mometasone furoate *See Elocon, page 527.*

Mometasone furoate monohydrate *See Nasonex, page 573.*

MONISTAT
Miconazole

Monistat is available in several formulations, including Monistat 3 vaginal suppositories, Monistat 7 vaginal cream and suppositories, and Monistat-Derm skin cream. Monistat's active ingredient, Miconazole, fights fungal infections.

Monistat 3 and Monistat 7 are used for vaginal yeast infections. Monistat-Derm is used for skin infections such as athlete's foot, ringworm, jock itch, yeast infection on the skin (cutaneous candidiasis), and tinea versicolor (a common skin condition that produces patches of white, tan, or brown finely flaking skin over the neck and trunk).

Monoket *See Imdur, page 545.*

MONOPRIL
Fosinopril

Monopril is a high blood pressure medication known as an ACE inhibitor. It is effective when used alone or in combination with other medications for the treatment of high blood pressure. Monopril is also prescribed for heart failure.

Monopril works by preventing the conversion of a chemical in the blood called angiotensin I into a more potent substance that increases salt and water retention in the body and causes blood vessels to constrict—two actions that tend to increase blood pressure. Monopril also enhances blood flow in the circulatory system.

MONOPRIL-HCT
Fosinopril with Hydrochlorothiazide

Monopril-HCT is used to treat high blood pressure. It usually is prescribed after other blood pressure medications have failed to do the job. Monopril-HCT combines two types of blood pressure medicine. The first, fosinopril sodium, is an ACE (angiotensin-converting enzyme) inhibitor. It works by preventing a chemical in the blood called angiotensin I from converting into a more potent form (angiotensin II) that increases salt and water retention in the body and causes blood vessels to constrict—two actions that tend to increase blood pressure. To aid in clearing water from the body, Monopril-HCT also contains hydrochlorothiazide, a diuretic that promotes the production of urine.

Montelukast *See Singulair, page 610.*

MONUROL
Fosfomycin

Monurol is an antibiotic used to treat bladder infections (cystitis) in women. Produced in dry granule form, Monurol is taken as a single dose mixed with water.

Morphine *See MS Contin, page 571.*

MOTRIN
Ibuprofen
Other brand name: Advil

Motrin is a nonsteroidal anti-inflammatory drug available in both prescription and nonprescription forms. Prescription Motrin is used in adults for relief of the symptoms of rheumatoid arthritis and osteoarthritis, treatment of menstrual pain, and relief of mild to moderate pain. In children aged 6 months and older it can be given to reduce fever and relieve mild to moderate pain. It is also used to relieve the symptoms of juvenile arthritis.

Motrin IB tablets, caplets, and gelcaps; Children's Motrin Suspension; and Advil tablets and caplets are available without a prescription. Check the packages for uses, dosage, and other information on these products.

Moxifloxacin *See Avelox, page 491.*

MS CONTIN
Morphine
Other brand name: Kadian

MS Contin, a controlled-release tablet containing morphine, is used to relieve moderate to severe pain. While regular morphine is usually given every 4 hours, MS Contin is typically taken every 12 hours—only twice a day. The Kadian brand may be taken once or twice a day. The drugs are intended for people who need a morphine painkiller for more than just a few days.

Mupirocin *See Bactroban, page 494.*

Muse *See Caverject, page 503.*

Mycelex *See Gyne-Lotrimin, page 542.*

MYCELEX-3
Butoconazole

Mycelex-3 Vaginal Cream is an antifungal medication that cures yeast-like infections of the vulva and vagina.

MYCOLOG-II
Nystatin with Triamcinolone
Other brand names: Myco-Triacet II, Mytrex

Mycolog-II Cream and Ointment are prescribed for the treatment of candidiasis (a yeast-like fungal infection) of the skin. The combination of an antifungal (nystatin) and a steroid (triamcinolone acetonide) provides greater benefit than nystatin alone during the first few days of treatment. Nystatin kills the fungus or prevents its growth; triamcinolone helps relieve the redness, swelling, itching, and other discomfort that can accompany a skin infection.

Myco-Triacet II *See Mycolog-II, page 572.*

Mykrox *See Zaroxolyn, page 639.*

MYSOLINE
Primidone

Mysoline is used to treat epileptic and other seizures. It can be used alone or with other anticonvulsant drugs. It is chemically similar to barbiturates.

Mytrex *See Mycolog-II, page 572.*

Nabumetone *See Relafen, page 603.*

Nadolol *See Corgard, page 510.*

Nadolol with Bendroflumethiazide *See Corzide, page 511.*

Nafarelin *See Synarel, page 614.*

NALFON
Fenoprofen

Nalfon, a nonsteroidal anti-inflammatory drug, is used to relieve the inflammation, swelling, stiffness, and joint pain associated with rheumatoid arthritis and osteoarthritis (the most common form of arthritis). It is also used to relieve mild to moderate pain.

Naltrexone *See ReVia, page 604.*

Naphazoline with Pheniramine *See Naphcon-A, page 573.*

NAPHCON-A
Naphazoline with Pheniramine
Other brand name: Opcon-A

Naphcon-A, an eyedrop containing both a decongestant and an antihistamine, is used to relieve itchy, red eyes caused by ragweed, pollen, and animal hair.

Naprelan *See Anaprox, page 485.*

NAPROSYN
Naproxen
Other brand name: EC-Naprosyn

Naprosyn, a nonsteroidal anti-inflammatory drug, is used to relieve the inflammation, swelling, stiffness, and joint pain associated with rheumatoid arthritis, osteoarthritis (the most common form of arthritis), juvenile arthritis, ankylosing spondylitis (spinal arthritis), tendinitis, bursitis, and acute gout; it is also used to relieve menstrual cramps and other types of mild to moderate pain.

Naproxen *See Naprosyn, page 573.*

Naproxen sodium *See Anaprox, page 485.*

Naratriptan *See Amerge, page 484.*

Nasacort *See Azmacort, page 493.*

Nasalcrom *See Intal, page 547.*

Nasalide *See AeroBid, page 480.*

NASONEX
Mometasone furoate monohydrate

Nasonex nasal spray prevents and relieves the runny, stuffy nose that accompanies hay fever and year-round allergies. It contains a steroid medication that fights inflammation.

Nateglinide *See Starlix, page 612.*

Necon *See Oral Contraceptives, page 582.*

Nedocromil *See Tilade, page 621.*

Nelfinavir *See Viracept, page 635.*

NEODECADRON OPHTHALMIC OINTMENT AND SOLUTION
Dexamethasone with Neomycin

Neodecadron is a steroid and antibiotic combination that is used to treat inflammatory eye conditions in which there is also a bacterial infection or the possibility of a bacterial infection. Dexamethasone (the steroid) decreases inflammation. Neomycin, the antibiotic, kills some of the more common bacteria.

Neoral *See Sandimmune, page 608.*

NEPTAZANE
Methazolamide

Neptazane, anhydrase is used to treat the eye condition called chronic open-angle glaucoma. This type of glaucoma is caused by a gradual blockage of the outflow of fluid in the front compartment of the eye over a period of years, causing a slow rise in pressure. It rarely occurs before the age of 40. Neptazane is also used for the type called acute angle-closure glaucoma when pressure within the eye must be lowered before surgery.

NEURONTIN
Gabapentin

Neurontin has two uses. First, it may be prescribed with other medications to treat partial seizures (the type in which symptoms are limited). It can be used whether or not the seizures eventually become general and result in loss of consciousness.

Second, it can be used to relieve the burning nerve pain that sometimes persists for months or even years after an attack of shingles (herpes zoster).

Nevirapine *See Viramune, page 635.*

NEXIUM
Esomeprazole

Nexium relieves heartburn and other symptoms caused by the backflow of stomach acid into the canal to the stomach (the esophagus)—a condition known as gastroesophageal reflux disease. It is also prescribed to heal the damage (erosive esophagitis) that reflux disease can cause.

Prescribed in combination with the antibiotics Biaxin and Amoxil, Nexium is also used to treat the infection that causes most duodenal ulcers (ulcers occurring just beyond the exit from the stomach).

Like its sister drug Prilosec, Nexium works by reducing the production of stomach acid.

Niacin *See Niaspan, page 575.*

NIASPAN
Niacin

Although the niacin in Niaspan is one of the B-complex vitamins, this drug isn't taken to prevent deficiencies. In large doses, niacin also lowers cholesterol, and Niaspan extended-release tablets are designed specifically for this purpose.

Excessive levels of cholesterol in the blood can lead to clogged arteries and increased risk of heart attack. Niaspan is prescribed, along with a low-fat, low cholesterol diet, to reduce blood cholesterol levels, combat clogged arteries, and lower the chance of repeated heart attacks. It is used only when diet alone fails to do the job, and is often taken along with another type of cholesterol-lowering drug known as a bile acid sequestrant (Colestid, Questran, WelChol). It can also be combined with any of the cholesterol-lowering "statin" drugs (Lescol, Lipitor, Mevacor, Pravachol, Zocor).

Niaspan is also used to reduce very high levels of the blood fats known as triglycerides, a condition that can cause painful inflammation of the pancreas.

Nicardipine *See Cardene, page 501.*

NicoDerm CQ *See Nicotine Patches, page 575.*

Nicotine Inhalation System *See Nicotrol Inhaler, page 576.*

Nicotine nasal spray *See Nicotrol NS, page 576.*

NICOTINE PATCHES
Brand names: Habitrol, NicoDerm CQ, Nicotrol

Nicotine patches, which are available under several brand names, are designed to help people quit smoking by reducing the craving for tobacco. Each adhesive patch contains a specific amount of nicotine embedded in a pad or gel.

Nicotine, the habit-forming ingredient in tobacco, is a stimulant and a mood lifter. When people give up smoking, lack of nicotine makes them crave cigarettes and may also cause anger, anxiety, concentration problems, irritability, frustration, or restlessness.

When a nicotine patch is worn, a specific amount of nicotine steadily travels out of the patch, through the skin, and into the bloodstream, keeping a constant low level of nicotine in the body. Although the resulting level of nicotine is less than smoking would deliver, it may be enough to prevent craving for cigarettes or development of other withdrawal symptoms.

Habitrol patches are round and come in three strengths: 21, 14, or 7 milligrams of nicotine per patch. Habitrol patches are worn 24 hours a day.

NicoDerm CQ patches are rectangular and come in three strengths: 21, 14, or 7 milligrams of nicotine per patch. NicoDerm CQ patches are worn 24 hours a day.

Nicotrol patches are rectangular and deliver 15 milligrams of nicotine per patch. Nicotrol patches are applied in the morning, worn all day, and removed at bedtime. They are not worn during sleep. Nicotrol is available over-the-counter.

Nicotrol *See Nicotine Patches, page 575.*

NICOTROL INHALER
Nicotine inhalation system

A quit-smoking aid, the Nicotrol Inhaler provides a substitute source of nicotine when people first give up cigarettes. A sudden decline in nicotine levels can cause such withdrawal symptoms as nervousness, restlessness, irritability, anxiety, depression, dizziness, drowsiness, concentration problems, sleep disturbances, increased appetite, weight gain, headache, constipation, fatigue, muscle aches, and a craving for tobacco. Nicotrol Inhaler prevents these symptoms and, through a familiar hand-to-mouth ritual, acts as a replacement for cigarettes. (Most of the nicotine in the product is, however, deposited in the mouth instead of the lungs.)

NICOTROL NS
Nicotine nasal spray

Nicotrol NS is used to relieve withdrawal symptoms in people who are attempting to give up smoking. A sudden decline in nicotine levels can cause such withdrawal symptoms as nervousness, restlessness, irritability, anxiety, depression, dizziness, drowsiness, concentration problems, sleep disturbances, increased appetite, weight gain, headache, constipation, fatigue, muscle aches, and a craving for tobacco. Used as part of a comprehensive smoking cessation program, Nicotrol Inhaler prevents these symptoms.

Nifedipine *See Procardia, page 597.*

NILANDRON
Nilutamide

Nilandron is used for advanced prostate cancer—cancer that has begun to spread beyond the prostate gland. An "antiandrogen" drug, it blocks the effects of the male hormone testosterone, which is known to encourage prostate cancer. The drug is part of a treatment program that begins with removal of the testes, a major—but not the only—source of testosterone.

Nilutamide *See Nilandron, page 577.*

Nimodipine *See Nimotop, page 577.*

NIMOTOP
Nimodipine

Nimotop is used to prevent and treat problems caused by a burst blood vessel in the head (subarachnoid hemorrhage).

It is also occasionally prescribed for certain types of migraine headaches, stroke, and age-related memory problems such as Alzheimer's disease.

Nimotop belongs to a class of drugs known as calcium channel blockers which are frequently prescribed for high blood pressure and the crushing chest pain of angina.

Nisoldipine *See Sular, page 613.*

Nitro-Bid *See Nitroglycerin, page 577.*

Nitro-Dur *See Nitroglycerin, page 577.*

Nitrofurantoin *See Macrodantin, page 560.*

NITROGLYCERIN
Brand names: Nitro-Bid, Nitro-Dur, Nitrolingual Spray, Nitrostat Tablets, Transderm-Nitro

Nitroglycerin is prescribed to prevent and treat angina pectoris (suffocating chest pain). This condition occurs when the coronary arteries become constricted and are not able to carry sufficient oxygen to the heart muscle.

Nitroglycerin is thought to improve oxygen flow by relaxing muscles in the walls of arteries and veins, thus allowing them to dilate.

Nitroglycerin is used in different forms. As a patch or ointment, nitroglycerin may be applied to the skin. The patch and the ointment are for *prevention* of chest pain.

Swallowing nitroglycerin in capsule or tablet form also helps to *prevent* chest pain from occurring.

In the form of sublingual (held under the tongue) or buccal (held in the cheek) tablets, or in oral spray (sprayed on or under the tongue), nitroglycerin helps relieve chest pain that has *already begun*. The spray can also prevent anginal pain. The type of nitroglycerin prescribed depends on the patient's condition.

Nitrolingual Spray *See Nitroglycerin, page 577.*

Nitrostat Tablets *See Nitroglycerin, page 577.*

Nizatidine *See Axid, page 493.*

NIZORAL
Ketoconazole

Nizoral, a broad-spectrum antifungal drug available in tablet form, may be given to treat several fungal infections within the body, including oral thrush and candidiasis.

It may also be given to treat severe, hard-to-treat fungal skin infections that have not cleared up after treatment with creams, ointments, or the oral drug griseofulvin (Fulvicin, Grisactin).

NOLVADEX
Tamoxifen citrate

Nolvadex, an anticancer drug, is given to treat breast cancer. It also has proved effective when cancer has spread to other parts of the body. Nolvadex is most effective in stopping the kind of breast cancer that thrives on estrogen.

Nolvadex is also prescribed to reduce the risk of invasive breast cancer following surgery and radiation therapy for ductal carcinoma in situ (a localized cancer that can be totally removed surgically). The drug can also be used to reduce the odds of breast cancer in women at high risk of developing the disease. It does not completely eliminate the risk, but in a five-year study of over 1,500 high-risk women, it slashed the number of cases by 44 percent.

Norco *See Vicodin, page 634.*

Nordette *See Oral Contraceptives, page 582.*

Norfloxacin *See Noroxin, page 579.*

NORGESIC
Orphenadrine, Aspirin, and Caffeine
Other brand name: Norgesic Forte

Norgesic is prescribed, along with rest, physical therapy, and other measures, for the relief of mild to moderate pain caused by severe muscle disorders.

Norinyl *See Oral Contraceptives, page 582.*

NORMODYNE
Labetalol
Other brand name: Trandate

Normodyne is used in the treatment of high blood pressure. It is effective when used alone or in combination with other high blood pressure medications, especially thiazide diuretics such as HydroDIURIL and "loop" diuretics such as Lasix.

NOROXIN
Norfloxacin

Noroxin is an antibacterial medication used to treat infections of the urinary tract, including cystitis (inflammation of the inner lining of the bladder caused by a bacterial infection), prostatitis (inflammation of the prostate gland), and certain sexually transmitted diseases, such as gonorrhea.

NORPACE
Disopyramide
Other brand name: Norpace CR

Norpace is used to treat severe irregular heartbeat. It relaxes an overactive heart and improves the efficiency of the heart's pumping action.

NORPLANT
Levonorgestrel implants

Norplant is a birth control method consisting of 6 thin, flexible plastic capsules implanted just beneath the skin in a woman's upper, inner arm. The implants are inserted by a physician. Each set prevents pregnancy for 5 years, but can be removed by the doctor at any time. The Norplant capsules contain progestin, a synthetic version of the naturally occurring female hormone progesterone, which they release slowly and continuously into the bloodstream. This constant release of progestin prevents the ovaries from releasing eggs for fertilization. Norplant also works by thickening the mucus in the vagina near the opening of the uterus. The thick mucus makes it difficult for sperm to enter the uterus during sexual intercourse.

Norplant is more than 99 percent effective in preventing pregnancy. Overall, fewer than one woman in 100 becomes pregnant during the first year of Norplant use.

Nor-QD *See Oral Contraceptives, page 582.*

NORVASC
Amlodipine

Norvasc is prescribed for angina, a condition characterized by episodes of crushing chest pain that usually results from a lack of oxygen in the heart muscle due to clogged arteries. Norvasc is also prescribed for high blood pressure. It is a type of medication called a calcium channel blocker. These drugs dilate blood vessels and slow the heart to reduce blood pressure and the pain of angina.

NORVIR
Ritonavir

Norvir is prescribed to slow the progress of HIV (human immunodeficiency virus) infection. HIV causes the immune system to break down so that it can no longer respond effectively to infection, leading to the fatal disease known as acquired immune deficiency syndrome (AIDS). Without treatment, HIV takes over certain human cells, especially white blood cells, and uses the inner workings of the infected cell to make additional copies of itself. Norvir belongs to a class of HIV drugs called protease inhibitors, which work by interfering with an important step in this reproduction process. Although Norvir cannot get rid of HIV already present in the body, it can reduce the amount of virus available to infect other cells.

Norvir is used in combination with other HIV drugs called nucleoside analogues (Retrovir, Hivid, and others). These two types of drugs act against HIV in different ways, thus improving the odds of success.

Novolin *See Insulin, page 546.*

NuLev *See Levsin, page 553.*

Nutracort *See Hydrocortisone Skin Preparations, page 543.*

NUVARING
Etonogestrel and Ethinyl estradiol

NuvaRing is a contraceptive device. Like oral contraceptives ("The Pill"), it prevents pregnancy by providing a steady level of the female hormones estrogen and progestin. This eliminates the hormonal surge that ordinarily triggers the release of an egg. Hormonal contraceptives such as NuvaRing are extremely reliable when used exactly as directed.

Nystatin with Triamcinolone *See Mycolog-II, page 572.*

OCUFLOX
Ofloxacin, ocular

Ocuflox is an antibiotic used in the treatment of eye infections. It is prescribed for eye inflammations and for ulcers or sores on the cornea (the transparent covering over the pupil). Ofloxacin, the active ingredient, is a member of the quinolone family of antibiotics.

Ofloxacin *See Floxin, page 536.*

Ofloxacin, ocular *See Ocuflox, page 581.*

OGEN
Estropipate
Other brand name: Ortho-Est

Ogen and Ortho-Est are estrogen replacement drugs. The tablets are used to reduce symptoms of menopause, including feelings of warmth in face, neck, and chest, and the sudden intense episodes of heat and sweating known as "hot flashes." They also may be prescribed for teenagers who fail to mature at the usual rate.

In addition, either the tablets or Ogen vaginal cream can be used for other conditions caused by lack of estrogen, such as dry, itchy external genitals and vaginal irritation.

Along with diet, calcium supplements, and exercise, Ogen and Ortho-Est tablets are also prescribed to prevent osteoporosis, a condition in which the bones become brittle and easily broken.

Some doctors also prescribe these drugs to treat breast cancer and cancer of the prostate.

Ogestrel *See Oral Contraceptives, page 582.*

Olmesartan *See Benicar, page 495.*

Olopatadine *See Patanol, page 586.*

Olsalazine *See Dipentum, page 522.*

Omeprazole *See Prilosec, page 596.*

OMNICEF
Cefdinir

Omnicef is a member of the family of antibiotics known as cephalosporins. It is used to treat mild to moderate infections, including:

Acute flare-ups of chronic bronchitis
Middle ear infections (otitis media)
Throat and tonsil infections (pharyngitis/tonsillitis)
Pneumonia
Sinus infections
Skin infections

Ondansetron *See Zofran, page 642.*

Opcon-A *See Naphcon-A, page 573.*

OPTIVAR
Azelastine eye drops

Optivar is taken to relieve and prevent the itchy eyes brought on by seasonal allergies. The drug usually starts to work within 3 minutes of placing the drops in the eye, and its effects usually last for about 8 hours.

ORAL CONTRACEPTIVES
Brand names: Alesse, Apri, Brevicon, Cyclessa, Demulen, Desogen, Estrostep, Levlen, Levlite, Levora, Loestrin, Lo/Ovral, Low-Ogestrel, Micronor, Mircette, Modicon, Necon, Nordette, Norinyl, Nor-QD,

Ogestrel, Ortho-Cept, Ortho-Cyclen, Ortho-Novum, Ortho Tri-Cyclen, Ovcon, Ovral, Tri-Levlen, Tri-Norinyl, Triphasil, Trivora, Yasmin, Zovia

Oral contraceptives (also known as "The Pill") are highly effective means of preventing pregnancy. Oral contraceptives consist of synthetic forms of two hormones produced naturally in the body: either progestin alone or estrogen and progestin. Estrogen and progestin regulate a woman's menstrual cycle, and the fluctuating levels of these hormones play an essential role in fertility.

To reduce side effects, oral contraceptives are available in a wide range of estrogen and progestin concentrations. Progestin-only products (such as Micronor) are usually prescribed for women who should avoid estrogens; however, they may not be as effective as estrogen/progestin contraceptives.

One variety of the Pill—the Ortho Tri-Cyclen 28-day Dialpak—is also used in the treatment of moderate acne in women aged 15 and older. It is taken just as it would be for contraception.

ORAP
Pimozide

Orap is prescribed for people with severe cases of the neurological disorder known as Tourette's syndrome if they have not been helped sufficiently by Haldol (haloperidol), the first-choice medication. Orap helps suppress the physical and verbal symptoms—twitches, jerks, and bizarre outbursts—that are associated with Tourette's syndrome.

Orlistat *See Xenical, page 637.*

Orphenadrine, Aspirin, and Caffeine *See Norgesic, page 579.*

Ortho-Cept *See Oral Contraceptives, page 582.*

Ortho-Cyclen *See Oral Contraceptives, page 582.*

Ortho-Est *See Ogen, page 581.*

ORTHO EVRA
Ethinyl estradiol and Norelgestromin

Ortho Evra is a contraceptive skin patch. It contains estrogen and progestin, the same hormones found in many birth control pills. Fertility depends on regular fluctuations in the levels of these hormones. Contraceptives such as Ortho Evra reduce fertility by eliminating the fluctuations. Once applied to the skin, the Ortho Evra patch releases a steady supply of estrogen and progestin through the skin and into the bloodstream.

Ortho-Novum *See Oral Contraceptives, page 582.*

Ortho Tri-Cyclen *See Oral Contraceptives, page 582.*

Orudis KT *See Oruvail, page 584.*

ORUVAIL
Ketoprofen
Other brand names: Orudis KT

Oruvail is an extended-release, nonsteroidal anti-inflammatory drug used to relieve the inflammation, swelling, stiffness, and joint pain associated with rheumatoid arthritis and osteoarthritis (the most common form of arthritis). This form of the drug is for long-term treatment, not for severe attacks that come on suddenly. It is also used to relieve mild to moderate pain, as well as menstrual pain.

Actron and Orudis KT are over-the-counter forms of the drug. They are used to relieve minor aches and pains associated with the common cold, headache, toothache, muscle aches, backache, minor arthritis, and menstrual cramps. They are also used to reduce fever.

Oseltamivir *See Tamiflu, page 615.*

Ovcon *See Oral Contraceptives, page 582.*

Ovral *See Oral Contraceptives, page 582.*

Oxaprozin *See Daypro, page 515.*

Oxcarbazepine *See Trileptal, page 626.*

Oxiconazole *See Oxistat, page 584.*

OXISTAT
Oxiconazole

Oxistat is used to treat fungal skin diseases, including athlete's foot (tinea pedis), jock itch (tinea cruris), ringworm (tinea corporis), and tinea versicolor, which appears as patches on the skin. It is available as a cream or lotion.

Oxybutynin *See Ditropan, page 522.*

Oxycodone *See OxyContin, page 585.*

Oxycodone with Aspirin *See Percodan, page 588.*

OXYCONTIN
Oxycodone

OxyContin is a controlled-release form of the narcotic painkiller oxycodone. It is prescribed for moderate to severe pain when continuous, around-the-clock relief is needed for an extended period of time.

Paclitaxel *See Taxol, page 616.*

PANCREASE
Pancrelipase
Other brand names: Creon, Pancrease MT, Viokase, Ultrase

Pancrease is used to treat pancreatic enzyme deficiency. It is often prescribed for people with cystic fibrosis, chronic inflammation of the pancreas, or blockages of the pancreas or common bile duct caused by cancer. It is also taken by people who have had their pancreas removed or who have had gastrointestinal bypass surgery. Pancrease helps with the digestion of proteins, starches, and fats.

Pancrelipase *See Pancrease, page 585.*

Pantoprazole *See Protonix, page 599.*

PARAFON FORTE DSC
Chlorzoxazone

Parafon Forte DSC is prescribed, along with rest and physical therapy, for the relief of discomfort associated with severe, painful muscle spasms.

PARLODEL
Bromocriptine

Parlodel inhibits the secretion of the hormone prolactin from the pituitary gland. It also mimics the action of dopamine, a shortage of which leads to Parkinson's disease. It is used to treat a variety of medical conditions, including:

Infertility in some women

Menstrual problems such as the abnormal stoppage or absence of flow, with or without excessive production of milk

Growth hormone overproduction leading to acromegaly, a condition characterized by an abnormally large skull, jaw, hands, and feet

Parkinson's disease

Pituitary gland tumors

Some doctors also prescribe Parlodel to treat cocaine addiction, the eye condition known as glaucoma, erection problems in certain men, restless leg syndrome, and a dangerous reaction to major tranquilizers called neuroleptic malignant syndrome.

PATANOL

Olopatadine

Patanol is an antihistamine that relieves the red, itchy eyes often caused by allergies.

PCE *See Erythromycin, Oral, page 529.*

PEDIAPRED

Prednisolone sodium phosphate

Pediapred, a steroid drug, is used to reduce inflammation and improve symptoms in a variety of disorders, including rheumatoid arthritis, acute gouty arthritis, and severe cases of asthma. It may be given to people to treat primary or secondary adrenal cortex insufficiency (lack of or insufficient adrenal cortical hormone in the body). It is also given to help treat the following disorders:

Blood disorders such as leukemia and various anemias

Certain cancers (along with other drugs)

Connective tissue diseases such as systemic lupus erythematosus

Digestive tract diseases such as ulcerative colitis

Eye diseases of various kinds

Fluid retention due to nephrotic syndrome (a condition in which damage to the kidneys causes a loss of protein in the urine)

High blood levels of calcium associated with cancer

Lung diseases such as tuberculosis

Severe allergic conditions such as drug-induced allergic reactions

Severe skin eruptions

Studies have shown that high doses of Pediapred are effective in controlling severe symptoms of multiple sclerosis, although they do not affect the ultimate outcome or natural history of the disease.

PEDIAZOLE
Erythromycin ethylsuccinate with Sulfisoxazole
Other brand name: Eryzole

Pediazole is a combination of two antibacterial agents, the macrolide antibiotic erythromycin and the sulfa drug sulfisoxazole. It is prescribed for the treatment of severe middle ear infections in children.

Pemirolast *See Alamast, page 481.*

Penciclovir *See Denavir, page 517.*

Penicillin VK *See Penicillin V Potassium, page 587.*

PENICILLIN V POTASSIUM
Brand names: Penicillin VK, Veetids

Penicillin V potassium is used to treat infections, including dental infection, infections in the heart, middle ear infections, rheumatic fever, scarlet fever, skin infections, and upper and lower respiratory tract infections.

Penicillin V works against only certain types of bacteria—it is ineffective against fungi, viruses, and parasites.

PENLAC
Ciclopirox nail lacquer

Penlac is a nail lacquer used in the treatment of nail infections caused by the fungus *Trichophyton rubrum* (ringworm of the nails). It is prescribed only if the pale semicircle at the base of the nail is free of infection. It is part of a comprehensive treatment plan that includes professional removal of the unattached infected nails as frequently as monthly

Pentasa *See Rowasa, page 607.*

Pentoxifylline *See Trental, page 625.*

PEPCID
Famotidine
Other brand name: Pepcid AC

Pepcid is prescribed for the short-term treatment of active duodenal ulcer (in the upper intestine) for 4 to 8 weeks and for active, benign gastric ulcer (in the stomach) for 6 to 8 weeks. It is prescribed for maintenance therapy, at reduced dosage, after a duodenal ulcer has healed. It is also used for short-term treatment of GERD, a condition in which the acid contents of the stomach flow back into the food canal (esophagus), and for the resulting inflammation of the esophagus. And it is prescribed for certain diseases that cause the stomach to produce excessive quantities of acid, such as Zollinger-Ellison syndrome. Pepcid belongs to a class of drugs known as histamine H_2 blockers.

An over-the-counter formulation, Pepcid AC, is used to relieve and prevent heartburn, acid indigestion, and sour stomach. Pepcid RPD is a preparation that dissolves rapidly in the mouth.

PERCOCET

Acetaminophen with Oxycodone
Other brand names: Endocet, Roxicet, Tylox

Percocet, a narcotic analgesic, is used to treat moderate to moderately severe pain. It contains two drugs—acetaminophen and oxycodone. Acetaminophen is used to reduce both pain and fever. Oxycodone, a narcotic analgesic, is used for its calming effect and for pain.

PERCODAN

Oxycodone with Aspirin

Percodan combines two pain-killing drugs: the narcotic analgesic oxycodone, and the common pain reliever aspirin. It is prescribed for moderate to moderately severe pain.

Pergolide *See Permax, page 589.*

PERGONAL

Menotropins
Other brand name: Humegon

Pergonal is a synthetic version of two female hormones, luteinizing hormone (LH) and follicle-stimulating hormone (FSH). It is used to stimulate the follicles in the ovaries to cause ovulation, or release of an egg, in women who are having difficulty getting pregnant. It is usually followed by 1 injection of human chorionic gonadotropin (Profasi). In addition, Pergonal is given to produce many eggs in women undergoing *in vitro* fertilization.

Pergonal is also used to stimulate the production of sperm in men with some forms of male infertility.

PERIACTIN
Cyproheptadine

Periactin is an antihistamine given to help relieve cold- and allergy-related symptoms such as hay fever, nasal inflammation, stuffy nose, red and inflamed eyes, hives, and swelling. Periactin may also be given after epinephrine to help treat anaphylaxis, a life-threatening allergic reaction.

Some doctors prescribe Periactin to treat cluster headache and to stimulate appetite in underweight people.

PERIDEX
Chlorhexidine

Peridex is an oral rinse used to treat gingivitis, a condition in which the gums become red and swollen. Peridex is also used to control gum bleeding caused by gingivitis. It is not effective for the more serious form of gum disease known as periodontitis

Perindopril *See Aceon, page 476.*

PERMAX
Pergolide

Permax is given, along with another drug, to help relieve the symptoms of Parkinson's disease.

In Parkinson's disease, the brain cells receive too little of a natural chemical messenger called dopamine. This results in tremor, rigid muscles, difficulty with walking and talking, and other distressing symptoms.

People with Parkinson's disease are given medication to increase the amount of dopamine reaching their brain; the medication may be levodopa, or, more commonly, a levodopa-carbidopa combination, such as Sinemet.

The role of Permax is to increase the effectiveness of Sinemet so that people need less of it.

PERSANTINE
Dipyridamole

Persantine helps reduce the formation of blood clots in people who have had heart valve surgery. It is used in combination with blood thinners such as Coumadin.

Some doctors also prescribe Persantine in combination with other drugs, such as aspirin, to reduce the damage from a heart attack and prevent a recurrence, to treat angina, and to prevent complications during heart bypass surgery.

Phenaphen with Codeine *See Tylenol with Codeine, page 628.*

Phenazopyridine *See Pyridium, page 601.*

PHENERGAN WITH CODEINE
Promethazine with Codeine

Phenergan with Codeine is used to relieve coughs and other symptoms of allergies and the common cold. Promethazine, an antihistamine, helps reduce itching and swelling and dries up secretions from the nose, eyes, and throat. It also has sedative effects and helps control nausea and vomiting. Codeine, a narcotic analgesic, helps relieve pain and stops coughing.

Phenobarbital, Hyoscyamine, Atropine, and Scopolamine
See Donnatal, page 523.

Phentermine *See Adipex-P, page 479.*

Phenytoin *See Dilantin, page 521.*

PHOSPHOLINE IODIDE
Echothiophate

Phospholine Iodide is used to treat chronic open-angle glaucoma, a partial loss of vision or blindness resulting from a gradual increase in pressure of fluid in the eye. Because the vision loss occurs slowly, people often do not experience any symptoms and do not realize that their vision has declined. By the time the loss is noticed, it may be irreversible. Phospholine Iodide helps by reducing fluid pressure in the eye.

Phospholine Iodide is also used to treat secondary glaucoma (such as glaucoma following surgery to remove cataracts), for subacute or chronic angle-closure glaucoma after iridectomy (surgical removal of a portion of the iris) or when someone cannot have surgery or refuses it. The drug is also prescribed for children with accommodative esotropia ("cross-eye").

PILOCAR
Pilocarpine
Other brand names: Isopto Carpine, Pilopine HS Gel

Pilocar causes constriction of the pupils (miosis) and reduces pressure within the eye. It is used to treat the increased pressure of open-angle glaucoma and to lower eye pressure before surgery for the more severe condition called acute angle-closure glaucoma. It can be used alone or in combination with other medications. Glaucoma, one of the leading causes of blindness in the United States, is characterized by increased pressure in the eye that can damage the optic nerve and cause loss of vision. It results from insufficient drainage of the eyeball through a field called the "angle."

Pilocarpine *See Pilocar, page 590.*

Pilopine HS Gel *See Pilocar, page 590.*

Pimecrolimus *See Elidel, page 527.*

Pimozide *See Orap, page 583.*

PINDOLOL

Pindolol, a type of medication known as a beta blocker, is used in the treatment of high blood pressure. It is effective alone or combined with other high blood pressure medications, particularly with a thiazide-type diuretic (a "water pill" that increases urine output to remove excess fluid from the body). Beta blockers decrease the force and rate of heart contractions.

Pioglitazone *See Actos, page 478.*

Piroxicam *See Feldene, page 533.*

PLAQUENIL
Hydroxychloroquine

Plaquenil is prescribed for the prevention and treatment of certain forms of malaria. Plaquenil is also used to treat the symptoms of rheumatoid arthritis such as swelling, inflammation, stiffness, and joint pain. It is also prescribed for lupus erythematosus, a chronic inflammation of the connective tissue.

PLAVIX
Clopidogrel

Plavix keeps blood platelets slippery and discourages formation of clots, thereby improving blood flow to the heart, brain, and body. The drug is prescribed to reduce the risk of heart attack, stroke, and serious circulation problems in people with hardening of the arteries or unstable angina (dangerous chest pain), and in people who've already suffered a heart attack or stroke.

PLENDIL
Felodipine

Plendil is prescribed for the treatment of high blood pressure. It is effective alone or in combination with other high blood pressure medications. A type of medication called a calcium channel blocker, Plendil eases the workload of the heart by slowing down the passage of nerve impulses through the heart, thereby reducing the rate its beats. This improves blood flow through the heart and throughout the body, reduces blood pressure, and helps prevent angina pain (chest pain, often accompanied by a feeling of choking, usually caused by lack of oxygen in the heart due to clogged arteries).

PLETAL
Cilostazol

Pletal helps relieve the painful leg cramps caused by "intermittent claudication," a condition that results when arteries clogged with fatty plaque are unable to deliver an adequate blood supply to the muscles of the legs. Pletal helps the blood get through by dilating the blood vessels and preventing blood cells from clumping together.

Podofilox *See Condylox, page 509.*

POLARAMINE
Dexchlorpheniramine

Polaramine is an antihistamine that relieves allergy symptoms, including: nasal stuffiness and inflammation and eye irritation caused by hay fever and other allergies; itching, swelling, and redness from hives and other rashes; allergic reactions to blood transfusions; and, with other medications, anaphylactic shock (severe allergic reaction).

Antihistamines work by decreasing the effects of histamine, a chemical the body releases in response to certain irritants. Histamine narrows air passages in the lungs and contributes to inflammation. Antihistamines reduce itching and swelling and dry up secretions from the nose, eyes, and throat.

Polyethylene glycol *See MiraLax, page 568.*

Polyethylene glycol with Electrolytes *See Colyte, page 508.*

Polymyxin B, Neomycin, and Hydrocortisone *See Cortisporin Ophthalmic Suspension, page 510.*

PONSTEL
Mefenamic acid

Ponstel, a nonsteroidal anti-inflammatory drug, is used for the relief of moderate pain (when treatment will not last for more than 7 days) and for the treatment of menstrual pain.

Potassium chloride *See Micro-K, page 566.*

Pramipexole *See Mirapex, page 569.*

PRANDIN
Repaglinide

Prandin is used to reduce blood sugar levels in people with type 2 diabetes (the kind that does not require insulin shots). It works by promoting the production of insulin, the hormone responsible for transporting sugar out of the bloodstream and into the cells, where it supplies energy. Prandin is prescribed when diet and exercise alone fail to correct the problem. A combination of Prandin and a second diabetes drug called Glucophage can be prescribed if either drug alone proves insufficient.

PRAVACHOL
Pravastatin

Pravachol is a cholesterol-lowering drug. A doctor will prescribe it along with a cholesterol-lowering diet when blood cholesterol levels are dangerously high and the patient has not been able to lower it by diet alone.

High cholesterol can lead to heart problems. By lowering cholesterol, Pravachol improves a patient's chances of avoiding a heart attack, heart surgery, and death from heart disease. In people who already have hardening of the arteries, it slows progression of the disease and cuts the risk of acute attacks.

The drug works by helping to clear harmful low-density lipoprotein (LDL) cholesterol out of the blood and by limiting the body's ability to form new LDL cholesterol. For people at high risk of heart disease, current guidelines call for considering drug therapy when LDL levels reach 130. For people at lower risk, the cut-off is 160. For those at little or no risk, it's 190.

Pravachol can also be prescribed for children ages 8 and older when diet alone fails to lower their cholesterol levels.

Pravastatin *See Pravachol, page 593.*

Pravastatin with Aspirin *See Pravigard PAC, page 594.*

PRAVIGARD PAC
Pravastatin with Aspirin

Each Pravigard PAC contains a single dose of two medications—one tablet of aspirin and one tablet of the cholesterol-lowering drug Pravachol (pravastatin sodium). Both Pravachol and aspirin are prescribed for people with heart disease to help reduce the risk of heart attack and stroke, as well as reduce the risk of dying from heart disease. They're also used to improve the chances of avoiding heart surgery and procedures such as angioplasty.

In addition, Pravachol is used to lower cholesterol levels and slow the buildup of fatty deposits in the arteries. It's important to remember, however, that Pravigard PAC is not a substitute for diet, exercise, and weight loss. To get the full benefit of the medication, it is necessary to stick to the diet and exercise program prescribed by the doctor.

Prazosin *See Minipress, page 568.*

PRECOSE
Acarbose

Precose is an oral medication used to treat type 2 (noninsulin-dependent) diabetes when high blood sugar levels cannot be controlled by diet alone. Precose works by slowing the body's digestion of carbohydrates so that blood sugar levels won't surge upward after a meal. Precose may be taken alone or in combination with certain other diabetes medications such as Diabinese, Micronase, Glucophage, and Insulin.

PRED FORTE
Prednisolone acetate

Pred Forte contains a steroid medication that eases redness, irritation, and swelling due to inflammation of the eye.

Prednisolone acetate *See Pred Forte, page 594.*

Prednisolone sodium phosphate *See Pediapred, page 586.*

Prednisone *See Deltasone, page 516.*

Prefest *See Activella and femhrt, page 478.*

PREMARIN
Conjugated estrogens
Other brand names: Cenestin, Premphase, Prempro,

Premarin is an estrogen replacement drug. The tablets are used to reduce moderate to servere symptoms of menopause, including feelings of warmth in the face, neck, and chest, and the sudden intense episodes of heat and sweating known as "hot flashes." Cenestin tablets, containing a synthetic form of conjugated estrogens, may also be prescribed for these symptoms.

In addition to the symptoms of menopause, Premarin tablets are prescribed for teenagers who fail to mature at the usual rate, and to relieve the symptoms of certain types of cancer, including some forms of breast and prostate cancer.

In addition, either the tablets or Premarin vaginal cream can be used for other conditions caused by lack of estrogen, such as dry, itchy external genitals and vaginal irritation.

Along with diet, calcium supplements, and exercise, Premarin tablets are also prescribed to prevent postmenopausal osteoporosis, a condition in which the bones become brittle and easily broken. Before taking Premarin solely for this purpose, you should carefully consider using alternative, nonestrogen therapies.

The addition of progesterone to estrogen-replacement therapy has been shown to reduce the risk of uterine cancer. Prempro combines estrogen and progesterone in a single tablet taken once daily. Premphase is a 28-day supply of tablets. The first 14 contain only estrogen. The second 14 supply both estrogen and progesterone. Both Prempro and Premphase are prescribed to reduce the symptoms of menopause, including vaginal problems, and to prevent osteoporosis.

Premphase *See Premarin, page 595.*

Prempro *See Premarin, page 595.*

PREVACID
Lansoprazole

Prevacid blocks the production of stomach acid. It is prescribed for the short-term treatment (up to 4 weeks) of duodenal ulcers, (ulcers in the intestinal wall near the exit from the stomach). It is also used for up to 8 weeks in the treatment of stomach ulcers, gastroesophageal reflux disease (backflow of acid into the canal to the stomach), and a condition called erosive esophagitis (severe inflammation of the canal). Once a duodenal ulcer or case of esophagitis has cleared up, the doctor may continue prescribing Prevacid to prevent a relapse. Prevacid is also prescribed to reduce the risk of stomach ulcers in people who develop this problem while taking nonsteroidal anti-inflammatory drugs such as Advil, Motrin, and Naprosyn. The drug is also used for long-term treatment of certain diseases marked by excessive acid production, such as Zollinger-Ellison syndrome.

Prevacid is also prescribed as part of a combination treatment to eliminate the *H. pylori* infection that causes most cases of duodenal ulcer.

PREVEN
Levonorgestrel and Ethinyl Estradiol

The Preven Emergency Contraception Kit provides "morning after" birth control following a contraceptive failure (for instance, a broken condom) or unprotected intercourse.

The hormone pills in the Preven kit can prevent a pregnancy, but will not end one that's already begun. They work primarily by inhibiting ovulation (release of an egg) and possibly by blocking fertilization and implantation of the egg in the lining of the uterus.

PREVPAC
Amoxicillin, Clarithromycin, and Lansoprazole

Prevpac is a prepackaged combination of drugs designed to cure duodenal ulcers (ulcers in the intestinal wall near the exit from the stomach) caused by *H. pylori* bacteria, the most common source of ulcers. With two antibiotics and an acid-blocking agent, Prevpac will eradicate the *H. pylori* infection and improve the odds of remaining ulcer-free. This type of therapy is usually reserved for people with an active ulcer and those who've had one for at least a year.

PRILOSEC
Omeprazole

Prilosec is prescribed for the short-term treatment (4 to 8 weeks) of stomach ulcer, duodenal ulcer (near the exit from the stomach), and erosive esophagitis (inflammation of the esophagus), and for the treatment of heartburn and other symptoms of gastroesophageal reflux disease (backflow of acid stomach contents into the canal leading to the stomach). It is also used to maintain healing of erosive esophagitis and for the long-term treatment of conditions in which too much stomach acid is secreted, including Zollinger-Ellison syndrome, multiple endocrine adenomas (benign tumors), and systemic mastocytosis (cancerous cells).

Combined with the antibiotic clarithromycin (Biaxin) (and sometimes with the antibiotic amoxicillin as well), Prilosec is also used to cure patients whose ulcers are caused by infection with the germ *H. pylori*, the most common source of duodenal ulcers.

Primidone *See Mysoline, page 572.*

Principen *See Ampicillin, page 485.*

Prinivil *See Zestril, page 640.*

Prinzide *See Zestoretic, page 640.*

Procainamide *See Procanbid, page 597.*

PROCANBID
Procainamide
Other brand names: Pronestyl, Pronestyl-SR

Procanbid is used to treat severe irregular heartbeats (arrhythmias). Arrhythmias are generally divided into two main types: heartbeats that are faster than normal (tachycardia), and heartbeats that are slower than normal (bradycardia). Irregular heartbeats are often caused by drugs or disease but can occur in otherwise healthy people with no history of heart disease or other illness.

PROCARDIA
Nifedipine
Other brand names: Procardia XL, Adalat, Adalat CC

Procardia and Procardia XL are used to treat angina (chest pain caused by lack of oxygen to the heart due to clogged arteries or spasm of the arteries). Procardia XL is also used to treat high blood pressure. Procardia and Procardia XL are calcium channel blockers. They ease the workload of the heart by relaxing the muscles in the walls of the arteries, allowing them to dilate. This improves blood flow through the heart and throughout the body, reduces blood pressure, and helps prevent angina. Procardia XL is taken once a day and provides a steady rate of medication over a 24-hour period.

PROFASI
Human chorionic gonadotropin

Profasi is an infertility treatment that brings on ovulation, or release of an egg from the ovary, in women who do not ovulate on their own. It is used after therapy with another drug, Pergonal or Humegon (menotropins).

Profasi is also given to boys to treat undescended or underdeveloped testicles. It is used in men to stimulate the production of testosterone.

Some doctors also use human chorionic gonadotropin in men with erection problems or lack of sexual desire, and in the therapy of male "menopause."

Progesterone *See Prometrium, page 598.*

Promethazine with Codeine *See Phenergan with Codeine, page 590.*

PROMETRIUM
Progesterone

Prometrium is prescribed for postmenopausal women who are taking estrogen (hormone replacement therapy); it prevents a buildup of the lining of the uterus and abnormal bleeding. Prometrium also may be prescribed to restore menstruation if a woman's menstrual periods have stopped.

Pronestyl *See Procanbid, page 597.*

Propafenone *See Rythmol, page 608.*

PROPECIA
Finasteride for baldness

Propecia is a remedy for baldness in men with mild to moderate hair loss on the top of the head and the front of the mid-scalp area. It increases hair growth, improves hair regrowth, and slows down hair loss. It works only on scalp hair and does not affect hair on other parts of the body.

Improvement can be seen as early as 3 months after starting therapy with Propecia, but for many men it takes longer. The improvement lasts only as long as therapy continues; when it stops, new hair growth ceases and hair loss resumes.

Propecia is a low-dose form of Proscar, a drug prescribed for prostate enlargement.

PROPINE
Dipivefrin

Propine is used to treat chronic open-angle glaucoma, the most common form of the disease. In glaucoma, the fluid inside the eyeball is under abnormally high pressure, a condition which can cause vision problems or even blindness.

Propine belongs to a class of medication called "prodrugs," drugs that generally are not active by themselves, but are converted in the body to an active form. This makes for better absorption, stability, and comfort and reduces side effects.

Propoxyphene *See Darvocet-N, page 515.*

Propranolol *See Inderal, page 545.*

Propranolol with Hydrochlorothiazide *See Inderide, page 546.*

PROSCAR
Finasteride for prostate problems

Proscar is prescribed to help shrink an enlarged prostate.

The prostate, a chestnut-shaped gland present in males, produces a liquid that forms part of the semen. This gland completely surrounds the upper part of the urethra, the tube through which urine flows out of the bladder. Many men over age 50 suffer from a benign (noncancerous) enlargement of the prostate. The enlarged gland squeezes the urethra, obstructing the normal flow of urine. Resulting problems may include difficulty in starting urination, weak flow of urine, and the need to urinate urgently or frequently. Sometimes surgical removal of the prostate is necessary.

By shrinking the enlarged prostate, Proscar may alleviate the various associated urinary problems, making surgery unnecessary.

Some doctors are also prescribing Proscar for baldness and as a preventive measure against prostate cancer.

PROTONIX
Pantoprazole

Protonix blocks the production of stomach acid. It is prescribed to heal a condition called erosive esophagitis (a severe inflammation of the passage to the stomach) brought on by a persistent backflow of stomach acid (gastroesophageal reflux disease). Later, it may be prescribed to maintain healing and prevent a relapse.

Protonix is a member of the "proton pump inhibitor" class of acid blockers, which includes AcipHex, Nexium, Prilosec, and Prevacid.

PROVENTIL
Albuterol
Other brand names: AccuNeb, Proventil HFA, Ventolin HFA, Volmax Extended-Release Tablets, VoSpire Extended-Release Tablets

Drugs containing albuterol are prescribed for the prevention and relief of bronchial spasms that narrow the airway. This especially applies to the treatment of asthma. Some brands of this medication are also used for the prevention of bronchial spasm due to exercise.

PROVERA
Medroxyprogesterone acetate

Provera is derived from the female hormone progesterone. It is prescribed for problems such as failure to menstruate or abnormal menstruation. Provera is also prescribed to prevent abnormal growth of the uterine lining in women taking estrogen replacement therapy.

Other forms of medroxyprogesterone, such as Depo-Provera, are used as a contraceptive injection and are prescribed in the treatment of endometrial cancer.

Some doctors also prescribe Provera to treat endometriosis, menopausal symptoms, premenstrual tension, sexual aggressive behavior in men, and sleep apnea (temporary failure to breath while sleeping).

PSORCON
Diflorasone

Psorcon is prescribed for the relief of the inflammation and itching of skin disorders that respond to the application of steroids (hormones produced by the body that have potent anti-inflammatory effects).

Psorcon is available in ointment and cream forms, and in emollient ointment and cream.

PULMICORT RESPULES
Budesonide inhalation suspension

Budesonide, the active ingredient in Pulmicort Respules, is an anti-inflammatory steroid medication. Inhaled on a regular basis, Pulmicort helps prevent asthma attacks.

Pulmicort Respules are prescribed for children 12 months to 8 years of age. They are given by nebulizer (a device that produces a fine spray). Adults and children over 6 can use another form of budesonide, Pulmicort Turbuhaler, that's taken with an inhaler. Both types of Pulmicort are preventive medicines. They will not relieve an acute or life-threatening episode of asthma.

PULMICORT TURBUHALER
Budesonide inhalation powder

Budesonide, the active ingredient in Pulmicort Turbuhaler, is an anti-inflammatory steroid medication. Inhaled on a regular basis, Pulmicort helps prevent asthma attacks. It is sometimes prescribed in addition to oral steroids, and may reduce or eliminate the need for them.

Pulmicort Turbuhaler is used to treat asthma in adults and children over age 6. Children 12 months to 8 years of age can be treated with another form of budesonide, Pulmicort Respules, which is given by nebulizer. Both types of Pulmicort are preventive medicines. They will not relieve an acute or life-threatening episode of asthma.

PULMOZYME
Dornase alfa

Pulmozyme inhalation solution reduces the number of respiratory infections that require injectable antibiotics in people with cystic fibrosis. It is also used to make breathing easier by thinning the mucus in the lungs.

PYRIDIUM
Phenazopyridine

Pyridium is a urinary tract analgesic that helps relieve the pain, burning, urgency, frequency, and irritation caused by infection, trauma, catheters, or various surgical procedures in the lower urinary tract. Pyridium is indicated for short-term use and can only relieve symptoms; it is not a treatment for the underlying cause of the symptoms.

QUESTRAN
Cholestyramine
Other brand name: Questran Light

Questran is used to lower cholesterol levels in the blood of people with primary hypercholesterolemia (too much LDL cholesterol). Hypercholesterolemia is a genetic condition characterized by a lack of the LDL receptors that remove cholesterol from the bloodstream.

This drug can be used to lower cholesterol levels in people who also have hypertriglyceridemia, a condition in which an excess of fat is stored in the body.

This drug may also be prescribed to relieve itching associated with gallbladder obstruction.

It is available in two forms: Questran and Questran Light.

Quibron-T/SR *See Theo-Dur, page 620.*

Quinapril *See Accupril, page 475.*

Quinapril with Hydrochlorothiazide *See Accuretic, page 475.*

QUINIDEX EXTENTABS
Quinidine sulfate

Quinidex Extentabs are used to correct certain types of irregular heart rhythms and to slow an abnormally fast heartbeat.

Quinidine sulfate *See Quinidex Extentabs, page 602.*

Qvar Inhalation Aerosol *See Beclomethasone, page 495.*

Rabeprazole *See AcipHex, page 477.*

Raloxifene *See Evista, page 532.*

Ramipril *See Altace, page 483.*

Ranitidine *See Zantac, page 638.*

RAPTIVA
Efalizumab

Psoriasis is a skin disease that is caused, in part, by an overactive immune system. Raptiva belongs to a class of drugs called immunosuppressives, which decrease the activity of the immune system. It is prescribed for patients with severe plaque psoriasis who can no longer control their disease with medications applied to the skin.

REBETOL
Ribavirin

In combination with the interferon drugs Intron A or PEG-Intron, Rebetol is prescribed to treat chronic hepatitis C. Rebetol is always used with one of the other drugs. By itself, it is ineffective against hepatitis C.

REGLAN
Metoclopramide

Reglan increases the contractions of the stomach and small intestine, helping the passage of food. It is given to treat the symptoms of diabetic gastroparesis, a condition in which the stomach does not contract. These symptoms include vomiting, nausea, heartburn, feeling of indigestion, persistent fullness after meals, and appetite loss. Reglan is also used, for short periods, to treat heartburn in people with gastroesophageal reflux disease (backflow of stomach contents into the esophagus). In addition, it is given to prevent nausea and vomiting caused by cancer chemotherapy and surgery.

RELAFEN
Nabumetone

Relafen, a nonsteroidal anti-inflammatory drug, is used to relieve the inflammation, swelling, stiffness, and joint pain associated with rheumatoid arthritis and osteoarthritis (the most common form of arthritis).

RELENZA
Zanamivir

Relenza is an antiviral drug that hastens recovery from the flu. Victims who begin taking Relenza within the first 2 days of their illness typically start to feel improvement a day earlier than they would otherwise. The drug is believed to work by interfering with the spread of virus particles inside the respiratory tract.

RELPAX
Eletriptan

Relpax is used to treat migraine headaches with or without the presence of auras (visual disturbances that precede an attack, such as halos or flickering lights). It shortens the duration of the headache but will not prevent attacks.

Renova *See Retin-A and Renova, page 604.*

Repaglinide *See Prandin, page 593.*

REQUIP
Ropinirole

Requip helps relieve the signs and symptoms of Parkinson's disease. Caused by a deficit of dopamine (one of the brain's chief chemical messengers), this disorder is marked by progressive muscle stiffness, tremor, and fatigue. Requip works by stimulating dopamine receptors in the brain, thus promoting better, easier movement.

Requip can be taken with or without levodopa (usually prescribed as Sinemet), another drug used to treat the symptoms of Parkinson's disease.

RETIN-A AND RENOVA
Tretinoin
Other brand name: Avita

Retin-A, Avita, and Renova contain the skin medication tretinoin. Retin-A and Avita are used in the treatment of acne. Renova is prescribed to reduce fine wrinkles, discoloration, and roughness on facial skin (as part of a comprehensive program of skin care and sun avoidance).

Retin-A is available in liquid, cream, or gel form, and in a stronger gel called Retin-A Micro. Avita comes only as a gel. Renova is available in cream form only.

RETROVIR
Zidovudine

Retrovir is prescribed for adults infected with human immunodeficiency virus (HIV). HIV causes the immune system to break down so that it can no longer respond effectively to infection, leading to the fatal disease known as acquired immune deficiency syndrome (AIDS). Retrovir slows down the progress of HIV. Combining Retrovir with other drugs such as Epivir and Crixivan can further slow the progression.

Retrovir is also prescribed for HIV-infected children over 3 months of age who have symptoms of HIV or who have no symptoms but, through testing, have shown evidence of impaired immunity.

Retrovir taken during pregnancy often prevents transmission of HIV from mother to child.

Signs and symptoms of HIV disease are significant weight loss, fever, diarrhea, infections, and problems with the nervous system.

REVIA
Naltrexone

ReVia is prescribed to treat alcohol dependence and narcotic addiction. ReVia is not a cure. Patients must be ready to make a change and be willing to undertake a comprehensive treatment program that includes professional counseling, support groups, and close medical supervision.

REYATAZ
Atazanavir

Reyataz is used with other medications to treat human immunodeficiency virus (HIV) infection. HIV causes the immune system to break down so that it can no longer fight off other infections. This leads to acquired immune deficiency syndrome (AIDS).

HIV thrives by taking over the immune system's vital CD4 cells (white blood cells) and using their inner workings to make additional copies of itself. Reyataz belongs to a class of HIV drugs called protease inhibitors, which work by interfering with an important step in the virus's reproductive cycle.

Reyataz is approved for used only in combination with other anti-HIV medications.

Rheumatrex *See Methotrexate, page 564.*

RHINOCORT AQUA
Budesonide

Rhinocort Aqua is an anti-inflammatory steroid nasal spray. It is prescribed to relieve the symptoms of hay fever and similar allergic nasal inflammations.

Ribavirin *See Rebetol, page 602.*

RIDAURA
Auranofin

Ridaura, a gold preparation, is given to help treat rheumatoid arthritis. Ridaura is taken by mouth, unlike other gold compounds, which are given by injection. It is recommended only for people who have not been helped sufficiently by nonsteroidal anti-inflammatory drugs (Anaprox, Dolobid, Indocin, Motrin, and others). Ridaura should be part of a comprehensive arthritis treatment program that includes non-drug forms of therapy.

The patients most likely to benefit from Ridaura are those with active joint inflammation, especially in the early stages.

RIFADIN
Rifampin
Other brand name: Rimactane

Rifadin is used to treat all forms of tuberculosis. Rifadin is used in combination with two other antituberculosis drugs at the start of therapy: isoniazid and pyrazinamide. Later, streptomycin or ethambutol may be added. Rifadin is also used to eliminate a meningitis-causing bacteria in people who are carriers of the disease but have no symptoms of the illness. Rifadin is not effective as a treatment for active meningitis.

Occasionally doctors prescribe rifampin to treat leprosy or Legionnaires' disease.

Rifampin *See Rifadin, page 605.*

Rifampin, Isoniazid, and Pyrazinamide *See Rifater, page 606.*

RIFATER
Rifampin, Isoniazid, and Pyrazinamide

Rifater is a combination antibiotic used to treat the initial phase of tuberculosis. After a 2-month period, the doctor may prescribe another combination of antituberculosis drugs (Rifamate), which can be continued for longer periods.

Rimactane *See Rifadin, page 605.*

Risedronate *See Actonel, page 478.*

Ritonavir *See Norvir, page 580.*

Rizatriptan *See Maxalt, page 561.*

ROBAXIN
Methocarbamol

Robaxin is prescribed, along with rest, physical therapy, and other measures, for the relief of pain due to severe muscular injuries, sprains, and strains.

ROCALTROL
Calcitriol

Rocaltrol is a synthetic form of vitamin D used to treat people on dialysis who have hypocalcemia (abnormally low blood calcium levels) and resulting bone damage. Rocaltrol is also prescribed to treat low blood calcium levels in people who have hypoparathyroidism (decreased functioning of the parathyroid glands). When functioning correctly, these glands help control the level of calcium in the blood.

Rocaltrol is also prescribed for *hyper*parathyroidism (*increased* functioning of the parathyroid glands) and resulting bone disorders in people with kidney disease who are not yet on dialysis.

ROCEPHIN
Ceftriaxone

Rocephin is a member of the cephalosporin family of antibiotics. It is used to treat infections of the skin, blood, bones, joints, ears, respiratory tract, abdomen, and urinary tract. It is also prescribed for gonorrhea, pelvic inflammatory disease, and meningitis (brain infection), and to protect against infection after surgery.

Rofecoxib *See Vioxx, page 634.*

RONDEC
Carbinoxamine or Brompheniramine and Pseudoephedrine

Rondec is an antihistamine/decongestant that relieves nasal inflammation and runny nose and the symptoms of hay fever and other allergies. Carbinoxamine and brompheniramine, the antihistamines, fight the effects of histamine, a chemical released by the body in response to certain irritants. Histamine narrows air passages in the lungs and contributes to inflammation. Antihistamines reduce itching and swelling and dry up secretions from the nose, eyes, and throat. Pseudoephedrine, the decongestant, reduces nasal congestion and makes breathing easier.

Ropinirole *See Requip, page 603.*

Rosiglitazone *See Avandia, page 491.*

Rosiglitazone with Metformin *See Avandamet, page 490.*

Rosuvastatin *See Crestor, page 512.*

ROWASA
Mesalamine
Other brand names: Asacol, Canasa, Pentasa

Rowasa Suspension Enema, Pentasa, and Asacol are used to treat mild to moderate ulcerative colitis (inflammation of the large intestine and rectum). Rowasa Suspension Enema is also prescribed for inflammation of the lower colon, and inflammation of the rectum.

Rowasa Suppositories and Canasa Suppositories are used to treat inflammation of the rectum.

Roxicet *See Percocet, page 588.*

Rynatan *See Trinalin, page 627.*

RYTHMOL
Propafenone

Rythmol is used to help correct certain life-threatening heartbeat irregularities (ventricular arrhythmias) by reducing the excitability of the heart muscle.

Salmeterol *See Serevent, page 609.*

Salsalate *See Disalcid, page 522.*

SANDIMMUNE
Cyclosporine
Other brand name: Neoral

Sandimmune suppresses the body's immune system. It is given after transplant surgery to help prevent rejection of organs (kidney, heart, or liver). It is also used to avoid long-term rejection in people previously treated with other immunosuppressant drugs, such as Imuran.

Neoral is a newer formulation of Sandimmune's active ingredient, cyclosporine. In addition to prevention of organ rejection, it is prescribed for certain severe cases of rheumatoid arthritis and psoriasis.

Some doctors also prescribe Sandimmune to treat alopecia areata (localized areas of hair loss), aplastic anemia (shortage of red and white blood cells and platelets), Crohn's disease (chronic inflammation of the digestive tract), and nephropathy (kidney disease). Sandimmune is sometimes used in the treatment of severe skin disorders, including psoriasis and dermatomyositis (inflammation of the skin and muscles causing weakness and rash). The drug is also used in procedures involving bone marrow, the pancreas, and the lungs.

Sandimmune is always given with prednisone or a similar steroid. It is available in capsules and liquid, or as an injection.

SANSERT
Methysergide

Sansert tablets are prescribed to prevent or reduce the intensity and frequency of severe "vascular" headaches (the kind caused by constriction and dilation of arteries within the head). Doctors usually prescribe Sansert only if a patient has one or more severe headaches per week, or the headaches are extremely severe and uncontrollable.

Sansert is preventive medication. Sansert is not a painkiller and cannot diminish a headache that has already developed. It should not be used for acute migraine attacks.

Saquinavir *See Fortovase, page 538.*

SECTRAL
Acebutolol

Sectral, a type of medication known as a beta blocker, is used in the treatment of high blood pressure and abnormal heart rhythms. When used to treat high blood pressure, it is effective used alone or in combination with other high blood pressure medications, particularly with a thiazide-type diuretic. Beta blockers decrease the force and rate of heart contractions, thus reducing pressure within the circulatory system.

Selegiline *See Eldepryl, page 526.*

SEMPREX-D
Acrivastine with Pseudoephedrine

Semprex-D is an antihistamine and decongestant drug that relieves sneezing, running nose, itching, watery eyes, and stuffy nose caused by seasonal allergies such as hay fever.

Septra *See Bactrim, page 494.*

SEREVENT
Salmeterol
Other brand name: Serevent Diskus

Serevent relaxes the muscles in the walls of the bronchial tubes, allowing the passageways to expand and carry more air. Taken regularly (twice a day), the drug is used in the treatment of asthma and chronic obstructive pulmonary disease (COPD), including emphysema and chronic bronchitis. A relatively long-acting medication, it is recommended only for the type of asthma patient who needs shorter-acting bronchodilators such as Alupent and Ventolin on a frequent, regular basis.

Serevent is available in an aerosol inhaler and as Serevent Diskus inhalation powder. Both forms of Serevent can be used with or without inhaled or oral steroid therapy.

Serophene *See Clomiphene Citrate, page 507.*

Sibutramine *See Meridia, page 563.*

Sildenafil *See Viagra, page 633.*

SILVADENE CREAM 1%
Silver sulfadiazine

Silvadene Cream 1% is applied directly to the skin. The cream is used along with other medications to prevent and treat wound infections in people with second- and third-degree burns. It is effective against a variety of bacteria as well as yeast.

Silver sulfadiazine *See Silvadene Cream 1%, page 610.*

Simvastatin *See Zocor, page 642.*

SINEMET CR
Carbidopa with Levodopa

Sinemet CR is a controlled-release tablet that may be given to help relieve the muscle stiffness, tremor, and weakness caused by Parkinson's disease. It may also be given to relieve Parkinson-like symptoms caused by encephalitis (brain fever), carbon monoxide poisoning, or manganese poisoning.

Sinemet CR contains two drugs, carbidopa and levodopa. The drug that actually produces the anti-Parkinson's effect is levodopa. Carbidopa prevents vitamin B-6 from destroying levodopa, thus allowing levodopa to work more efficiently.

Parkinson's drugs such as Sinemet CR relieve the symptoms of the disease, but are not a permanent cure.

SINGULAIR
Montelukast

Singulair is used for long-term prevention of asthma. It reduces the swelling and inflammation that tend to close up the airways, and relaxes the walls of the bronchial tubes, expanding the airways and permitting more air to pass through.

Singulair is also used to relieve the stuffy, runny nose and sneezing caused by seasonal allergies.

SKELAXIN
Metaxalone

Along with rest and physical therapy, Skelaxin is prescribed for the relief of painful musculoskeletal conditions. Researchers aren't sure how the drug works, but suspect that its effectiveness stems from its sedative properties.

Slo-bid *See Theo-Dur, page 620*

Slow-K *See Micro-K, page 566.*

Sodium fluoride *See Luride, page 560.*

SODIUM SULAMYD
Sulfacetamide
Other brand name: Bleph-10

Sodium Sulamyd is used in the treatment of eye inflammations, corneal ulcer, and other eye infections. It may be used along with an oral sulfa drug to treat a serious eye infection called trachoma.

SOMA
Carisoprodol

Soma is used, along with rest, physical therapy, and other measures, for the relief of acute, painful muscle strains and spasms.

Sorbitrate *See Isordil, page 548.*

SPECTAZOLE CREAM
Econazole

Spectazole cream is prescribed for fungal skin diseases commonly called ringworm (tinea). It is used to treat athlete's foot (tinea pedis), "jock itch" (tinea cruris), a fungus infection of the entire body (tinea corporis), and a skin infection that causes yellow- or brown-colored skin eruptions (tinea versicolor). It is also prescribed for yeast infections of the skin caused by candida fungus (cutaneous candidiasis).

SPECTRACEF
Cefditoren

Spectracef cures mild-to-moderate bacterial infections of the skin, throat, and respiratory tract. Among these infections are pneumonia, strep throat, and tonsillitis. Spectracef is also prescribed for acute flare-ups of chronic bronchitis. Spectracef is a cephalosporin antibiotic.

Spironolactone *See Aldactone, page 481.*

Spironolactone with Hydrochlorothiazide *See Aldactazide, page 481.*

SPORANOX
Itraconazole

Sporanox capsules are used to treat three types of serious fungal infections: blastomycosis, histoplasmosis, and aspergillosis. Blastomycosis can affect the lungs, bones, and skin. Histoplasmosis can affect the lungs, heart, and blood. Aspergillosis can affect the lungs, kidneys, and other organs. The drug is also prescribed for onychomycosis, which infects the toenails and fingernails. Additionally, Sporanox is used against fungal infections in people with weak immune systems, such as AIDS patients.

Sporanox oral solution is used to treat candidiasis (fungal infection) of the mouth, throat, and gullet (esophagus), and for other fungal infections in people with weakened immunity and fever.

STARLIX
Nateglinide

Starlix combats high blood sugar levels in people with type 2 diabetes (the kind that does not require insulin shots). Insulin speeds the transfer of sugar from the bloodstream to the body's cells, where it's burned to produce energy. In diabetes, the body either fails to make enough insulin, or proves unable to properly use what's available. Starlix attacks the problem from the production angle, stimulating the pancreas to secrete more insulin.

Starlix can be used alone or combined with another diabetes drug, called Glucophage, that tackles the other part of the problem, working to improve the body's response to whatever insulin it makes. Starlix is prescribed only when diet and exercise—or Glucophage alone—have failed to control blood sugar levels.

Stavudine *See Zerit, page 639.*

Stimate *See DDAVP, page 515.*

STRIANT
Testosterone buccal system, oral

Striant is a hormone replacement product for men who have hypogonadism, a low level of the male hormone testosterone. The condition is marked by symptoms such as impotence and decreased interest in sex, lowered mood, fatigue, and decreases in bone density and lean body mass. Testosterone replacement therapy helps correct these problems.

The term "buccal" refers to the cheek. When the Striant buccal system is applied to the gum, medication is absorbed through the cheek.

Sucralfate *See Carafate, page 500.*

SULAR
Nisoldipine

Sular controls high blood pressure. A long-acting tablet, Sular may be used alone or in combination with other blood pressure medications.

Sular is a type of medication called a calcium channel blocker. It inhibits the flow of calcium through the smooth muscles of the heart, delaying the passage of nerve impulses, slowing down the heart, and expanding the blood vessels. This eases the heart's workload and reduces blood pressure.

Sulfacetamide *See Sodium Sulamyd, page 611.*

Sulfanilamide *See AVC, page 491.*

Sulfasalazine *See Azulfidine, page 494.*

Sulfisoxazole *See Gantrisin, page 539.*

Sulindac *See Clinoril, page 507.*

Sumatriptan *See Imitrex, page 545.*

Sumycin *See Tetracycline, page 619.*

SUPRAX
Cefixime

Suprax, a cephalosporin antibiotic, is prescribed for bacterial infections of the chest, ears, urinary tract, and throat, and for uncomplicated gonorrhea.

SUSTIVA
Efavirenz

Sustiva is one of the growing number of drugs used to fight HIV infection. HIV, the human immunodeficiency virus, weakens the immune system until it can no longer fight off infections, leading to the fatal disease known as AIDS (acquired immune deficiency syndrome).

Like other drugs for HIV, Sustiva works by impairing the virus's ability to multiply. However, when taken alone it may prompt the virus to become resistant. Sustiva is therefore always taken with at least one other HIV medication, such as Retrovir or Crixivan. Even when used properly, it may remain effective for only a limited time.

SYMMETREL
Amantadine

Symmetrel is used to treat or prevent flu caused by the Influenza A virus; to treat Parkinson's disease; and to relieve tremors, jerks, or writhing caused by treatment with other drugs.

Hospital workers—and others in close contact with someone who has or is likely to get flu caused by the Influenza A virus—should have a flu shot each year. If a flu shot is impossible or contraindicated, preventive treatment with Symmetrel may be advisable. A flu shot can still be taken after starting treatment with Symmetrel. Once the body has manufactured enough antibodies to the Influenza A virus, Symmetrel will no longer be needed.

SYNALGOS-DC
Dihydrocodeine, Aspirin, and Caffeine

Synalgos-DC is a narcotic analgesic prescribed for the relief of moderate to moderately severe pain.

SYNAREL
Nafarelin

Synarel is used to relieve the symptoms of endometriosis, including menstrual cramps or low back pain during menstruation, painful intercourse, painful bowel movements, and abnormal and heavy menstrual bleeding. Endometriosis is a condition in which fragments of the tissue that lines the uterus are found in the other parts of the pelvic cavity.

Synarel is also used to treat unusually early puberty in children of both sexes. Some doctors prescribe Synarel as a contraceptive for both men and women.

SYNTHROID
Levothyroxine
Other brand names: Levothroid, Levoxyl, Unithroid

Synthroid, a synthetic thyroid hormone may be given in any of the following cases:

If the thyroid gland is not making enough hormone;
If the thyroid is enlarged (a goiter) or there is a risk for developing a goiter;
If the patient has certain cancers of the thyroid;

If thyroid production is low due to surgery, radiation, certain drugs, or disease of the pituitary gland or the hypothalamus in the brain.

Tadalafil *See Cialis, page 505.*

TAGAMET
Cimetidine
Other brand name: Tagamet HB

Tagamet is prescribed for the treatment of certain kinds of stomach and intestinal ulcers and related conditions. These include: active duodenal (upper intestinal) ulcers; active benign stomach ulcers; erosive gastro-esophageal reflux disease (backflow of acid stomach contents); prevention of upper abdominal bleeding in those who are critically ill; and excess-acid conditions such as Zollinger-Ellison syndrome (a form of peptic ulcer with too much acid). It is also used to prevent a relapse after the healing of active ulcers. Tagamet is a histamine blocker.

Some doctors also use Tagamet to treat acne and to prevent stress-induced ulcers. It may also be used to treat chronic hives, herpesvirus infections (including shingles), abnormal hair growth in women, and overactivity of the parathyroid gland.

An over-the-counter version of the drug, Tagamet HB, is used to relieve heartburn, acid indigestion, and sour stomach.

TAMBOCOR
Flecainide

Tambocor is prescribed to treat certain heart rhythm disturbances, including paroxysmal atrial fibrillation (a sudden attack or worsening of irregular heartbeat in which the upper chamber of the heart beats irregularly and very rapidly) and paroxysmal supraventricular tachycardia (a sudden attack or worsening of an abnormally fast but regular heart rate that occurs in intermittent episodes).

TAMIFLU
Oseltamivir

Tamiflu speeds recovery from the flu. When started during the first 2 days of the illness, it hastens improvement by at least a day. It also can prevent the flu if treatment is started within 2 days after exposure to a flu victim. Tamiflu is one of a new class of antiviral drugs called neuraminidase inhibitors.

As the flu virus takes hold in the body, it forms new copies of itself and spreads from cell to cell. Neuraminidase inhibitors fight the virus by preventing the release of new copies from infected cells. The other drug in this class, Relenza, is taken by inhalation. Tamiflu is taken in liquid or capsule form.

Tamoxifen *See Nolvadex, page 578.*

Tamsulosin *See Flomax, page 535.*

TARKA
Trandolapril with Verapamil

Tarka is used to treat high blood pressure. It combines two blood pressure drugs: an ACE inhibitor and a calcium channel blocker. The ACE inhibitor (trandolapril) lowers blood pressure by preventing a chemical in the blood called angiotensin I from converting to a more potent form that narrows the blood vessels and increases salt and water retention. The calcium channel blocker (verapamil hydrochloride) also works to keep the blood vessels open, and eases the heart's workload by reducing the force and rate of the heartbeat.

TASMAR
Tolcapone

Tasmar helps to relieve the muscle stiffness, tremor, and weakness caused by Parkinson's disease. When taken with Sinemet (levodopa/carbidopa), it sustains the blood levels of dopamine needed for normal muscle function. Because Tasmar has been known to cause liver failure, it is prescribed only when other Parkinson's drugs fail to control the symptoms.

Like all Parkinson's medications, Tasmar can provide long-term relief of symptoms, but won't cure the underlying disease. If symptoms do not improve after 3 weeks of Tasmar therapy, the doctor will discontinue the drug.

TAXOL
Paclitaxel

Taxol is used to treat cancer of the ovary and breast cancer that does not respond to other drugs. An extract of the bark of the Pacific yew tree, it works by interfering with the growth of cancer cells.

Some doctors also prescribe Taxol to treat certain kinds of lung cancer.

Tazarotene *See Tazorac, page 617.*

TAZORAC
Tazarotene

Tazorac gel comes in two strengths, 0.05% and 0.1%. Both strengths are used to treat the type of psoriasis that causes large plaques on the skin. The 0.1% strength is also used to treat mild to moderate facial acne. The drug is chemically related to vitamin A.

Tegaserod *See Zelnorm, page 639.*

TEGRETOL
Carbamazepine
Other brand names: Carbatrol, Epitol, Tegretol-XR

Tegretol is used in the treatment of seizure disorders, including certain types of epilepsy. It is also prescribed for trigeminal neuralgia (severe pain in the jaws) and pain in the tongue and throat.

Without official approval, Tegretol is also used to treat alcohol withdrawal, cocaine addiction, and emotional disorders such as depression and abnormally aggressive behavior. The drug is also used to treat migraine headache and "restless legs."

Telmisartan *See Micardis, page 566.*

Telmisartan with Hydrochlorothiazide *See Micardis HCT, page 566.*

TEMOVATE
Clobetasol
Other brand name: Cormax

Temovate and Cormax relieve the itching and inflammation of moderate to severe skin conditions. The scalp application is used for short-term treatment of scalp conditions; the cream, ointment, emollient cream, and gel are used for short-term treatment of skin conditions on the body. The products contain a steroid medication for external use only.

Tenofovir disoproxil *See Viread, page 636*

TENORETIC
Atenolol with Chlorthalidone

Tenoretic is used in the treatment of high blood pressure. It combines a beta-blocker drug and a diuretic. Tenoretic can be used alone or in combination with other high blood pressure medications. Atenolol, the beta blocker, decreases the force and rate of heart contractions. Chlorthalidone, the diuretic, helps the body produce and eliminate more urine, which clears excess fluid from the body and tends to lower blood pressure.

TENORMIN
Atenolol

Tenormin, a type of medication known as a beta-blocker, is used in the treatment of high blood pressure, angina pectoris (chest pain, usually caused by lack of oxygen in the heart muscle due to clogged arteries), and heart attack. When used for high blood pressure it is effective alone or combined with other high blood pressure medications, particularly with a thiazide-type water pill (diuretic). Beta-blockers decrease the force and rate of heart contractions.

Without official approval, Tenormin is also used for treatment of alcohol withdrawal, prevention of migraine headache, and bouts of anxiety.

TENUATE
Diethylpropion

Tenuate, an appetite suppressant, is prescribed for short-term use (a few weeks) as part of an overall diet plan for weight reduction. It is available in two forms: immediate-release tablets (Tenuate) and controlled-release tablets (Tenuate Dospan). Tenuate should be used with a behavior modification program.

TEQUIN
Gatifloxacin

Tequin is a member of the "quinolone" family of antibiotics. It is used to treat acute sinus infections, skin infections, pneumonia, complications of chronic bronchitis, kidney and urinary tract infections, and gonorrhea.

TERAZOL
Terconazole

Terazol is an antifungal medication. It is prescribed to treat candidiasis (a yeast-like fungal infection) of the vulva and vagina.

Terazosin *See Hytrin, page 544.*

Terbinafine *See Lamisil, page 551.*

Terbutaline *See Brethine, page 498.*

Terconazole *See Terazol, page 618.*

TESSALON
Benzonatate

Tessalon is taken for relief of a cough. It works by deadening certain receptors in the respiratory tract, thereby dampening the cough reflex.

Testim *See AndroGel, page 486.*

Testoderm *See Testosterone Patches, page 619.*

Testosterone buccal system, oral *See Striant, page 612.*

Testosterone gel *See AndroGel, page 486.*

TESTOSTERONE PATCHES
Brand names: Androderm, Testoderm

These patches are prescribed for men with low levels of the male hormone, testosterone. Lack of testosterone can lead to declining interest in sex, as well as impotence, fatigue, depression, and loss of masculine characteristics.

Testred *See Android, page 486.*

TETRACYCLINE
Brand names: Achromycin V, Sumycin

Tetracycline, a "broad-spectrum" antibiotic, is used to treat bacterial infections such as Rocky Mountain spotted fever, typhus fever, and tick fevers; upper respiratory infections; pneumonia; gonorrhea; amoebic infections; and urinary tract infections. It is also used to help treat severe acne and to treat trachoma (a chronic eye infection) and conjunctivitis (pinkeye). Tetracycline is often a viable alternative for people who are allergic to penicillin.

TEVETEN
Eprosartan

Teveten is used to treat high blood pressure. It is a member of the family of drugs called angiotensin II receptor blockers. The hormone angiotensin II makes the blood vessels constrict, causing blood pressure to rise. Teveten works by blocking the receptors that respond to this hormone. The drug may be prescribed alone or in combination with other medications that help lower blood pressure, such as water pills (diuretics) or calcium channel blockers.

TEVETEN HCT
Eprosartan with Hydrochlorothiazide

Teveten HCT is a combination medication used in the treatment of high blood pressure. One component, eprosartan, belongs to a class of blood pressure medications that work by preventing the hormone angiotensin II from constricting the blood vessels, thus allowing blood to flow more freely and keeping blood pressure down. The other component, hydrochlorothiazide, is a diuretic that increases the output of urine, removing excess fluid from the body and thus lowering blood pressure.

THALITONE
Chlorthalidone

Thalitone is a diuretic (water pill) used to treat high blood pressure and fluid retention associated with congestive heart failure, cirrhosis of the liver (a disease of the liver caused by damage to its cells), corticosteroid and estrogen therapy, and kidney disease. When used for high blood pressure, Thalitone may be used alone or in combination with other high blood pressure medications. Diuretics rid the body of excess fluid by stiulating the production of urine. This tends to lower blood pressure.

Theo-24 *See Theo-Dur, page 620.*

Theochron *See Theo-Dur, page 620.*

THEO-DUR
Theophylline
Other brand names: Quibron-T/SR, Slo-bid, T-Phyl, Theo-24, Theochron, Uni-Dur, Uniphyl

Theo-Dur, an oral bronchodilator medication, is given to treat symptoms of asthma, chronic bronchitis, and emphysema. The active ingredient of Theo-Dur, theophylline, is a chemical cousin of caffeine. It opens the airways by relaxing the smooth muscle that circles the tubes and blood vessels in the lungs.

Theophylline *See Theo-Dur, page 620.*

Thyroid Hormones *See Armour Thyroid, page 487.*

Tiazac *See Cardizem, page 501.*

TICLID
Ticlopidine

Ticlid makes the blood less likely to clot. It is prescribed to reduce the risk of stroke in people who have already suffered a stroke or had warning signs of stroke, and who either cannot take aspirin or fail to benefit from aspirin therapy.

Ticlid is also given, along with aspirin, to reduce the chances of a clot forming after a stent (a metal mesh tube) has been inserted in a coronary artery (a procedure used to keep the artery open and relieve the chest pain of angina).

Ticlopidine *See Ticlid, page 621.*

TIGAN
Trimethobenzamide

Tigan is prescribed to control nausea and vomiting.

TILADE
Nedocromil

Tilade is an anti-inflammatory medication prescribed for use on a regular basis to control symptoms of mild to moderate asthma.

Timolol *See Timoptic, page 621.*

TIMOPTIC
Timolol
Other brand names: Betimol, Timoptic-XE

Timoptic is an eyedrop that effectively reduces internal pressure in the eye. Timoptic is used in the treatment of open-angle glaucoma (potentially damaging chronic high pressure in the eye).

Tioconazole *See Vagistat-1, page 631.*

Tizanidine *See Zanaflex, page 638.*

TOBRADEX

Tobramycin and Dexamethasone

Tobradex combines a steroid drug, dexamethasone, and an antibiotic, tobramycin. It is prescribed to control inflammation and infection in the eye.

Tobramycin *See Tobrex, page 622.*

Tobramycin and Dexamethasone *See Tobradex, page 622.*

TOBREX

Tobramycin
Other brand name: Aktob

Tobrex is an antibiotic applied to the eye to treat bacterial infections.

Tocainide *See Tonocard, page 623.*

Tolazamide *See Tolinase, page 623.*

TOLBUTAMIDE

Tolbutamide is an oral antidiabetic medication used to treat type 2 (non-insulin-dependent) diabetes. Diabetes occurs when the body does not make enough insulin, or when the insulin that is produced no longer works properly. Insulin works by helping sugar get inside the body's cells, where it is then used for energy.

There are two forms of diabetes: type 1 (insulin-dependent) and type 2 (non-insulin-dependent). Type 1 diabetes usually requires taking insulin injections for life, while type 2 diabetes can usually be treated by dietary changes, exercise, and/or oral antidiabetic medications such as tolbutamide. This drug controls diabetes by stimulating the pancreas to secrete more insulin and by helping insulin work better.

Occasionally, type 2 diabetics must take insulin injections temporarily during stressful periods or times of illness. When diet, exercise, and an oral antidiabetic medication fail to reduce symptoms and/or blood sugar levels, a person with type 2 diabetes may require long-term insulin injections.

Tolcapone *See Tasmar, page 616.*

TOLECTIN
Tolmetin

Tolectin is a nonsteroidal anti-inflammatory drug used to relieve the inflammation, swelling, stiffness, and joint pain associated with rheumatoid arthritis and osteoarthritis (the most common form of arthritis). It is used for both acute episodes and long-term treatment. It is also used to treat juvenile rheumatoid arthritis.

TOLINASE
Tolazamide

Tolinase is an oral antidiabetic drug available in tablet form. It lowers the high blood sugar levels found in diabetics by stimulating the pancreas to release insulin, the hormone that helps transport sugar into the cells, where it is burned to produce energy. Tolinase may be given as a supplement to diet therapy to help control type 2 (non-insulin-dependent) diabetes.

There are two types of diabetes: type 1 (insulin-dependent) and type 2 (non-insulin-dependent). Type 1 diabetes usually requires insulin injection for life; type 2 can usually be controlled by dietary changes, exercise, and oral diabetes medications. Occasionally—during stressful periods or times of illness, or if oral medications fail to work—a type 2 diabetic may need insulin injections.

Tolmetin See Tolectin, page 623.

Tolterodine See Detrol, page 518.

TONOCARD
Tocainide

Tonocard is used to treat severe irregular heartbeat (arrhythmias). Arrhythmias are generally divided into two main types: heartbeats that are faster than normal (tachycardia), or heartbeats that are slower than normal (bradycardia). Irregular heartbeats are often caused by drugs or disease but can occur in otherwise healthy people with no history of heart disease or other illness. Tonocard works differently from other antiarrhythmic drugs, such as quinidine (Quinidex), procainamide (Procan SR), and disopyramide (Norpace). It is similar to lidocaine (Xylocaine) and is effective in treating severe ventricular arrhythmias (irregular heartbeats that occur in the main chambers of the heart).

TOPAMAX
Topiramate

Topamax is an antiepileptic drug, prescribed to control both the mild attacks known as partial seizures and the severe tonic-clonic convulsions known as grand mal seizures. It is typically added to the treatment regimen when other drugs fail to fully control a patient's attacks.

TOPICORT
Desoximetasone

Topicort is a synthetic steroid medication in cream, gel, or ointment form that relieves the inflammation and itching caused by a variety of skin conditions.

Topiramate *See Topamax, page 624.*

Toprol-XL *See Lopressor, page 556.*

TORADOL
Ketorolac

Toradol, a nonsteroidal anti-inflammatory drug, is used to relieve moderately severe, acute pain. It is prescribed for a limited amount of time (no more than 5 days for adults and as a single dose for children), not for long-term therapy.

Toremifene *See Fareston, page 533.*

Torsemide *See Demadex, page 517.*

T-Phyl *See Theo-Dur, page 620.*

Tramadol *See Ultram, page 629.*

Tramadol and Acetaminophen *See Ultracet, page 629.*

Trandate *See Normodyne, page 579.*

Trandolapril *See Mavik, page 560.*

Trandolapril with Verapamil *See Tarka, page 616.*

Transderm-Nitro *See Nitroglycerin, page 577.*

TRAVATAN
Travoprost

Travatan is an eyedrop that reduces excessive pressure in the eye (often a result of the condition called open-angle glaucoma). Travatan works by promoting drainage of the fluid that fills the eye. It is usually prescribed when other remedies cannot be used or the other drugs have not been effective.

Travoprost *See Travatan, page 625.*

TRENTAL
Pentoxifylline

Trental is a medication that reduces the viscosity or "stickiness" of the blood, allowing it to flow more freely. It helps relieve the painful leg cramps caused by "intermittent claudication," a condition that results when hardening of the arteries reduces the leg muscles' blood supply.

Some doctors also prescribe Trental for dementia, strokes, circulatory and nerve problems caused by diabetes, and Raynaud's syndrome (a disorder of the blood vessels in which exposure to cold causes the fingers and toes to turn white). The drug is also used to treat impotence and to increase sperm motility in infertile men.

Tretinoin *See Retin-A and Renova, page 604.*

Trexall *See Methotrexate, page 564.*

Triamcinolone *See Azmacort, page 493.*

Triaz *See Desquam-E, page 518.*

TRICOR
Fenofibrate
Other brand name: Lofibra

Tricor is used, along with a special diet, to treat people with very high levels of triglycerides (a fatty substance in the blood). Tricor also improves cholesterol levels by lowering total cholesterol—including "bad" LDL cholesterol—and raising "good" HDL cholesterol. It works by promoting the dissolution and elimination of fat particles in the blood.

Tricor is usually added to a treatment regimen only when other measures have failed to produce adequate results. Often, diet and exercise are enough to bring blood fats under control. Likewise, it's sometimes sufficient to simply treat an underlying problem such as diabetes, underactive thyroid, kidney disease, liver dysfunction, or alcoholism. And in some cases, just discontinuing a medication is enough to do the job. For instance, certain water pills and "beta-blocker" heart medications are capable of causing a massive increase in triglyceride levels. Estrogen replacement therapy is another potential culprit.

Whatever the other treatment measures may be, it's important to remember that Tricor is intended to supplement them, rather than replace them outright. To get the full benefit of the medication, patients need to stick to the diet, exercise program, and other treatments the doctor prescribes. All these efforts to keep cholesterol and triglyceride levels normal are important because together they may lower the risk of heart disease.

For people at high risk of heart disease, current guidelines call for considering drug therapy when LDL levels reach 130. For people at lower risk, the cut-off is 160. For those at little or no risk, it's 190.

TRIDESILON
Desonide
Other brand name: DesOwen

Tridesilon is a steroid preparation that relieves the itching and inflammation of a variety of skin problems. It is applied directly to the skin.

Trihexyphenidyl *See Artane, page 488.*

TRILEPTAL
Oxcarbazepine

Trileptal helps reduce the frequency of partial epileptic seizures, a form of epilepsy in which neural disturbances are limited to a specific region of the brain and the victim remains conscious throughout the attack. Trileptal may be prescribed by itself to treat the problem in adults. It can also be used in combination with other seizure medications in adults and in children as young as four years old.

Tri-Levlen *See Oral Contraceptives, page 582.*

TRILISATE
Choline magnesium trisalicylate

Trilisate, a nonsteroidal, anti-inflammatory medication, is prescribed for the relief of the signs and symptoms of rheumatoid arthritis (chronic joint inflammation disease), osteoarthritis (degenerative joint disease), and other forms of arthritis. This drug is used in the long-term management of these diseases and especially for flare-ups of severe rheumatoid arthritis.

Trilisate may also be prescribed for the treatment of acute painful shoulder, for mild to moderate pain in general, and for fever.

In children, this medication is prescribed for severe conditions—such as juvenile rheumatoid arthritis—that require relief of pain and inflammation.

Trimethobenzamide *See Tigan, page 621.*

Trimethoprim with Sulfamethoxazole *See Bactrim, page 494.*

TRINALIN
Azatadine with Pseudoephedrine
Other brand name: Rynatan

Trinalin and Rynatan are long-acting antihistamine/decongestants that relieve nasal stuffiness and middle ear congestion caused by hay fever and ongoing nasal inflammation. They can be used alone or with antibiotics and analgesics such as aspirin or acetaminophen. Azatadine, the antihistamine in these products, reduces itching and swelling and dries up secretions from the nose, eyes, and throat. Pseudoephedrine, the decongestant, reduces nasal congestion and makes breathing easier.

Tri-Norinyl *See Oral Contraceptives, page 582.*

Triphasil *See Oral Contraceptives, page 582.*

Trivora *See Oral Contraceptives, page 582.*

TRIZIVIR
Abacavir, Lamivudine, and Zidovudine

Trizivir combines three drugs used to fight HIV, the deadly virus that undermines the immune system, leaving the body ever more vulnerable to infection, and eventually leading to AIDS. The components of Trizivir are all members of the category of HIV drugs known as nucleoside analogs:

Abacavir (also called Ziagen)
Lamivudine (also called Epivir or 3TC)
Zidovudine (also called Retrovir, AZT, or ZDV)

Trizivir may be prescribed alone or in combination with other HIV drugs. It reduces the amount of HIV in the bloodstream, but does not completely cure the disease. Patients may still develop the rare infections and other complications that accompany HIV. Remember, too, that Trizivir does not reduce the risk of transmitting the virus to others.

TRUSOPT
Dorzolamide

Trusopt eye drops are prescribed for the treatment of the excessive pressure in the eyeball known as open-angle glaucoma.

T-Stat *See Erythromycin, Topical, page 530.*

TUSSIONEX
Hydrocodone with Chlorpheniramine polistirex

Tussionex Extended-Release Suspension is a cough-suppressant/antihistamine combination used to relieve coughs and the upper respiratory symptoms of colds and allergies. Hydrocodone, a mild narcotic similar to codeine, is believed to work directly on the cough center. Chlorpheniramine, an antihistamine, reduces itching and swelling and dries up secretions from the eyes, nose, and throat.

TUSSI-ORGANIDIN NR
Guaifenesin with Codeine
Other brand name: Brontex

Tussi-Organidin NR is used to relieve coughs and chest congestion in adults and children. It contains guaifenesin, which helps thin and loosen mucus in the lungs, making it easier to cough up. It also contains a cough suppressant, the narcotic codeine.

TYLENOL WITH CODEINE
Acetaminophen with Codeine
Other brand name: Phenaphen with Codeine

Tylenol with Codeine, a narcotic analgesic, is used to treat mild to moderately severe pain. It contains two drugs—acetaminophen and codeine. Acetaminophen, an antipyretic (fever-reducing) analgesic, is used to reduce pain and fever. Codeine, a narcotic analgesic, relieves moderate to severe pain.

People who are allergic to aspirin can take Tylenol with Codeine.

Tylox *See Percocet, page 588.*

ULTRACET
Tramadol and Acetaminophen

Ultracet is used to treat moderate to severe pain for a period of five days or less. It contains two pain-relieving agents. Tramadol, known technically as an opioid analgesic, is a narcotic pain reliever. Acetaminophen is the active ingredient in the over-the-counter pain remedy Tylenol.

ULTRAVATE
Halobetasol

Ultravate is a high-potency steroid medication that relieves the itching and inflammation caused by a wide variety of skin disorders. It is available in cream and ointment formulations.

ULTRAM
Tramadol

Ultram, known technically as an opioid analgesic, is a narcotic painkiller. It is prescribed to relieve moderate to moderately severe pain.

Ultrase *See Pancrease, page 585.*

Uni-Dur *See Theo-Dur, page 620.*

Uniphyl *See Theo-Dur, page 620.*

UNIRETIC
Moexipril with Hydrochlorothiazide

Uniretic combines two types of blood pressure medication. The first, moexipril hydrochloride, is an ACE (angiotensin-converting enzyme) inhibitor. It works by preventing a chemical in the blood called angiotensin I from converting into a more potent form (angiotensin II) that increases salt and water retention in the body and causes the blood vessels to constrict—two actions that tend to increase blood pressure.

To aid in clearing excess water from the body, Uniretic also contains hydrochlorothiazide, a diuretic that promotes production of urine. Diuretics often wash too much potassium out of the body along with the water. However, the ACE inhibitor part of Uniretic tends to keep potassium in the body, thereby canceling this unwanted effect.

Uniretic is not used for the initial treatment of high blood pressure. It is saved for later use, when a single blood pressure medication is not sufficient for the job.

Unithroid *See Synthroid, page 614.*

UNIVASC
Moexipril

Univasc is used in the treatment of high blood pressure. It is effective when used alone or with thiazide diuretics that help rid the body of excess water. Univasc belongs to a family of drugs called angiotensin-converting enzyme (ACE) inhibitors. It works by preventing the transformation of a hormone in the blood called angiotensin I into a more potent substance that increases salt and water retention in the body and causes the blood vessels to constrict—two actions that tend to increase blood pressure.

URISED
Methenamine

Urised relieves lower urinary tract discomfort caused by inflammation or diagnostic procedures. It is used to treat urinary tract infections including cystitis (inflammation of the bladder and ureters), urethritis (inflammation of the urethra), and trigonitis (inflammation of the mucous membrane of the bladder). Methenamine, the major component of this drug, acts as a mild antiseptic by changing into formaldehyde in the urinary tract when it comes in contact with acidic urine.

URISPAS
Flavoxate

Urispas prevents spasms in the urinary tract and relieves the painful or difficult urination, urinary urgency, excessive nighttime urination, pubic area pain, frequency of urination, and inability to hold urine caused by urinary tract infections. Urispas is taken in combination with antibiotics to treat the infection.

Urofollitropin *See Fertinex, page 534.*

UROXATRAL
Alfuzosin

Uroxatral is used to treat the symptoms of an enlarged prostate--a condition technically known as benign prostatic hyperplasia or BPH. The walnut-sized prostate gland surrounds the urethra (the duct that drains the bladder). If the gland becomes enlarged, it can squeeze the urethra, interfering with the flow of urine. This can cause difficulty in starting urination, a weak flow of urine, and the need to urinate urgently or more frequently. Uroxatral doesn't shrink the prostate. Instead, it relaxes the muscle around it, freeing the flow of urine and decreasing urinary symptoms.

Ursodiol *See Actigall, page 477.*

Urso 250 *See Actigall, page 477.*

VAGIFEM
Estradiol vaginal tablets

As estrogen levels decline during menopause, vaginal tissues tend to shrink and lose their elasticity--sometimes producing a condition known as atrophic vaginitis. Inserted in the vagina on a regular basis, Vagifem tablets provide a local source of estrogen replacement without passing through the rest of the system. This helps relieve such symptoms of atrophic vaginitis as vaginal dryness, soreness, and itching.

VAGISTAT-1
Tioconazole

Vagistat-1 ointment is used to treat repeated bouts of vaginal yeast infection (candidiasis of the vagina). Symptoms include irritation and discharge. Women experiencing these symptoms for the first time should see their doctor to make certain the problem is yeast. If they've had them before, they can use this over-the-counter medication without another trip to the doctor.

Valacyclovir *See Valtrex, page 632.*

VALCYTE
Valganciclovir

Valcyte tablets are used in the treatment of an eye disease called cytomegalovirus (CMV) retinitis, one of the many infections that take hold when the immune system is undermined by AIDS.

Valcyte is also used to prevent CMV disease in people who've had a kidney, heart, or kidney-pancreas transplant. Valcyte is not approved for use in liver transplant patients.

Valcyte is very similar to the CMV medication Cytovene (ganciclovir).

Valdecoxib *See Bextra, page 496.*

Valganciclovir *See Valcyte, page 631.*

Valproic acid *See Depakene, page 517.*

Valsartan *See Diovan, page 521.*

VALTREX
Valacyclovir

Valtrex is used to treat certain herpes infections, including herpes zoster (the painful rash known as shingles), genital herpes, and herpes cold sores on the face and lips.

Vancenase *See Beclomethasone, page 495.*

Vanceril *See Beclomethasone, page 495.*

Vardenafil *See Levitra, page 552.*

VASCOR
Bepridil

Vascor, a type of medication called a calcium channel blocker, is prescribed for the treatment of chronic stable angina (severe chest pain, often accompanied by a feeling of choking, brought on by exertion). Vascor is effective used alone or in combination with beta-blocking drugs and/or nitrates. Calcium channel blockers slow down the passage of nerve impulses through the heart and blood vessels. This slows the heartbeat and dilates the blood vessels to reduce blood pressure—actions that ease the workload on the heart and help prevent angina pain.

VASERETIC
Enalapril with Hydrochlorothiazide

Vaseretic is used in the treatment of high blood pressure. It combines an ACE inhibitor with a thiazide diuretic. Enalapril, the ACE inhibitor, works by preventing a chemical in the blood called angiotensin I from converting into a more potent form that increases salt and water retention in the body and constricts the blood vessels—actions that tend to increase blood pressure. Hydrochlorothiazide, a diuretic, rids the body of excess fluid by promoting the production of urine, which also helps in lowering blood pressure.

VASOTEC
Enalapril

Vasotec is a high blood pressure medication known as an ACE inhibitor. It works by preventing a chemical in the blood called angiotensin I from converting into a more potent form that increases salt and water retention in the body and constricts the blood vessels—actions that tend to increase blood pressure. It is effective when used alone or in combination with other medications, especially thiazide-type diuretics. It is also used in the treatment of congestive heart failure, usually in combination with diuretics and digitalis, and is prescribed as a preventive measure in certain conditions that could lead to heart failure.

Veetids *See Penicillin V Potassium, page 587.*

VELOSEF
Cephradine

Velosef, a broad-spectrum cephalosporin antibiotic available in capsule or liquid form, is similar to penicillin. Velosef is given to treat certain infections of the upper or lower respiratory tract, including pharyngitis (strep throat) and pneumonia, as well as middle ear, skin, or urinary tract infections.

Ventolin HFA *See Proventil, page 599.*

Verapamil *See Calan, page 499.*

Verelan *See Calan, page 499.*

VIAGRA
Sildenafil

Viagra is an oral drug for male impotence, also known as erectile dysfunction (ED). It works by dilating blood vessels in the penis, allowing the inflow of blood needed for an erection.

Vibramycin *See Doryx, page 523.*

Vibra-Tabs *See Doryx, page 523.*

VICODIN
Hydrocodone with Acetaminophen
Other brand names: Anexsia, Co-Gesic, Hydrocet, Lorcet, Lortab,
Maxidone, Norco, Zydone

Vicodin combines a narcotic analgesic (painkiller) and cough reliever with a non-narcotic analgesic for the relief of moderate to moderately severe pain.

VICOPROFEN
Hydrocodone with Ibuprofen

Vicoprofen is a chemical cousin of the well-known painkiller Vicodin. Both products contain the prescription pain medication hydrocodone. However, while Vicodin also includes acetaminophen (the active ingredient in Tylenol), Vicoprofen replaces it with ibuprofen (the active ingredient in Advil).

Vicoprofen relieves acute pain. It is generally prescribed for less than 10 days, and cannot be used in the long-term treatment of osteoarthritis or rheumatoid arthritis.

VIDEX
Didanosine

Videx is one of the drugs used to fight the human immunodeficiency virus (HIV)—the deadly cause of AIDS. Over a period of years, HIV slowly destroys the immune system, leaving the body defenseless against infection. Videx disrupts reproduction of HIV, thereby staving off the immune system's collapse.

Signs and symptoms of advanced HIV infection include diarrhea, fever, headache, infections, problems with the nervous system, rash, sore throat, and significant weight loss.

Viokase *See Pancrease, page 585.*

VIOXX
Rofecoxib

Vioxx is a new kind of painkiller used in the treatment of osteoarthritis, rheumatoid arthritis, painful menstruation (dysmenorrhea), and other types of acute pain. It is a member of the family of nonsteroidal anti-inflammatory drugs (NSAIDs) called "COX-2 inhibitors." Other drugs in this family include Celebrex and Bextra.

Like older NSAIDs such as aspirin, Motrin, and Naprosyn, these newer drugs are believed to fight pain and inflammation by inhibiting the effect of a natural enzyme called COX-2. Unlike the older medications, however, the newer drugs do not interfere with a similar substance, called COX-1, which exerts a protective effect on the lining of the stomach. The COX-2 inhibitors are therefore less likely to cause the bleeding and ulcers that sometimes accompany sustained use of the older NSAIDs.

Although COX-2 inhibitors offer many of the same benefits as aspirin, they do not share its blood-thinning effects. People taking low-dose aspirin to reduce the risk of a heart attack will need to continue taking it in addition to Vioxx.

VIRACEPT
Nelfinavir

Viracept is one of the drugs prescribed to fight HIV, the human immuno-deficiency virus that causes AIDS (acquired immune deficiency syndrome). Once inside the body, HIV spreads through certain key cells in the immune system, weakening the body's ability to fight off other infections. Viracept works by interfering with an important step in the virus's reproductive cycle. This slows the spread of the virus and prolongs the strength of the immune system.

Viracept belongs to the new class of drugs that has successfully reversed the course of HIV infection in many people. Called protease inhibitors, these drugs work better when used in combination with other HIV medications called nucleoside analogues (Retrovir, Hivid, and others) that act against the virus in other ways.

VIRAMUNE
Nevirapine

Viramune is prescribed for advanced cases of HIV. HIV—the human immunodeficiency virus that causes AIDS—undermines the immune system over a period of years, eventually leaving the body defenseless against infection. Viramune is generally prescribed only after the immune system has declined and infections have begun to appear. It is always taken with at least one other HIV medication such as Retrovir or Videx. If taken alone, it can cause the virus to become resistant. Even if used properly, it may be effective for only a limited time.

Like other drugs for HIV, Viramune works by impairing the virus's ability to multiply.

VIREAD
Tenofovir disoproxil

Viread is one of the drugs prescribed to fight HIV, the human immuno-deficiency virus that causes AIDS (acquired immune deficiency syndrome). HIV attacks the immune system, slowly destroying the body's ability to fight off infection. Viread staves off the attack by interfering with HIV reverse transcriptase, an enzyme the virus needs to reproduce.

Viread lowers the amount of HIV in the blood and may help increase the number of T cells, important agents of the immune system that kill microscopic foreign invaders. It is used in combination with other anti-HIV drugs when these drugs are not effective by themselves.

Vivelle *See Estrogen Patches, page 531.*

Volmax *See Proventil, page 599.*

VOLTAREN
Diclofenac
Other brand name: Cataflam (Diclofenac potassium)

Voltaren and Cataflam are nonsteroidal anti-inflammatory drugs used to relieve the inflammation, swelling, stiffness, and joint pain associated with rheumatoid arthritis, osteoarthritis (the most common form of arthritis), and ankylosing spondylitis (arthritis and stiffness of the spine). Voltaren-XR, the extended-release form of Voltaren, is used only for long-term treatment. Cataflam is also prescribed for immediate relief of pain and menstrual discomfort.

VOSOL HC
Acetic acid and Hydrocortisone

VoSoL HC is prescribed for infection and inflammation of the external ear canal.

VoSpire *See Proventil, page 599.*

Warfarin *See Coumadin, page 511.*

WELCHOL
Colesevelam

WelChol is used to lower blood cholesterol levels when diet and exercise prove insufficient. It works by binding with cholesterol-based bile acids to take them out of circulation. This prompts the liver to produce a replacement supply of bile acids, drawing the extra cholesterol it needs out of the bloodstream.

WelChol is sometimes prescribed along with one of the popular "statin" drugs that fight cholesterol in a different way. Among these drugs are Lescol, Lipitor, Mevacor, Pravachol, and Zocor.

XALATAN
Latanoprost

Xalatan is used to relieve high pressure within the eye (a hallmark of the condition known as open-angle glaucoma). It can be prescribed alone or with other glaucoma medications.

XENICAL
Orlistat

Xenical blocks absorption of dietary fat into the bloodstream, thereby reducing the number of calories obtained from a meal. At the usual dosage level, it cuts fat absorption by almost one-third. Combined with a low-calorie diet, it is used to promote weight loss and discourage the return of unwanted pounds.

The drug is prescribed for the frankly obese and for merely overweight people who have other health problems such as high blood pressure, diabetes, or high cholesterol levels. Weight status is determined by the body mass index (BMI), a comparison of height to weight.

XOPENEX
Levalbuterol

Xopenex is a "bronchodilator." It works by relaxing the muscles in the walls of the lungs' many tiny airways (bronchioles), allowing them to expand so patients can get more air. It is prescribed for asthma.

Yasmin *See Oral Contraceptives, page 582.*

YOCON
Yohimbine
Other brand name: Yohimex

Yocon is used in the treatment of male impotence. The drug is thought to work by stimulating the release of norepinephrine, one of the body's natural chemical regulators. This results in increased blood flow to the penis.

Yohimbine *See Yocon, page 637.*

Yohimex *See Yocon, page 637.*

ZADITOR
Ketotifen

Zaditor combats the release of chemicals that trigger allergic reactions. Available in eyedrop form, it works within minutes to relieve the itchy eyes brought on by allergies.

Zafirlukast *See Accolate, page 475.*

Zalcitabine *See Hivid, page 542.*

ZANAFLEX
Tizanidine

Zanaflex relaxes the tense, rigid muscles caused by spasticity. It is prescribed for people with multiple sclerosis, spinal cord injuries, and other disorders that produce protracted muscle spasms. The effect of the drug peaks 1 to 2 hours after each dose and is gone within 3 to 6 hours, so it's best to schedule doses for shortly before the daily activities when relief of spasticity is most important.

Zanamivir *See Relenza, page 603.*

ZANTAC
Ranitidine

Zantac is prescribed for the short-term treatment (4 to 8 weeks) of active duodenal ulcer (near the exit from the stomach) and active benign gastric ulcer (in the stomach itself), and as maintenance therapy for gastric or duodenal ulcer, at a reduced dosage, after the ulcer has healed. It is also used for the treatment of conditions in which the stomach produces too much acid, such as Zollinger-Ellison syndrome and systemic mastocytosis, for gastroesophageal reflux disease (backflow of acid stomach contents into the entry to the stomach) and for healing—and maintaining healing of—erosive esophagitis (severe inflammation of the esophagus).

Some doctors prescribe Zantac to prevent damage to the stomach and duodenum from long-term use of nonsteroidal anti-inflammatory drugs such as Indocin and Motrin, and to treat bleeding of the stomach and intestine. Zantac is also sometimes prescribed for stress-induced ulcers.

ZAROXOLYN
Metolazone
Other brand name: Mykrox

Zaroxolyn is a diuretic used in the treatment of high blood pressure and other conditions that require the elimination of excess fluid from the body. These conditions include congestive heart failure and kidney disease. When used for high blood pressure, Zaroxolyn can be used alone or with other high blood pressure medications. Diuretics prompt the body to produce and eliminate more urine, which helps lower blood pressure.

ZEBETA
Bisoprolol

Zebeta, a type of medication known as a beta-blocker, is used to treat high blood pressure. Beta-blockers lower blood pressure by decreasing the force and rate of heart contractions, which reduces the heart's demand for oxygen. Zebeta can be used alone or in combination with other high blood pressure medications

ZELNORM
Tegaserod

Zelnorm provides relief for many women suffering from the type of irritable bowel syndrome marked by constipation. It works by mimicking the effect that serotonin has on the intestines.

Serotonin is one of the nervous system's chief chemical messengers. When it activates certain receptors in the walls of the intestines, it stimulates digestive activity and reduces intestinal sensitivity. Women using Zelnorm report less abdominal pain, bloating, and discomfort, and an increase in the frequency of bowel movements.

ZERIT
Stavudine

Zerit is one of the drugs used to fight the human immunodeficiency virus (HIV)—the deadly cause of AIDS. It is usually prescribed for people who have already been taking the HIV drug Retrovir for an extended period. HIV attacks the immune system, slowly destroying the body's ability to fight off infection. Zerit helps stave off the attack by disrupting the virus's ability to reproduce.

Signs and symptoms of HIV infection include diarrhea, fever, headache, infections, problems with the nervous system, rash, sore throat, and significant weight loss.

ZESTORETIC

Lisinopril with Hydrochlorothiazide
Other brand name: Prinzide

Zestoretic is used in the treatment of high blood pressure. It combines an ACE inhibitor drug with a diuretic. Lisinopril, the ACE inhibitor, works by limiting production of a substance that promotes salt and water retention in the body. Hydrochlorothiazide, a diuretic, prompts the body to produce and eliminate more urine, which helps in lowering blood pressure. Combination products such as Zestoretic are usually not prescribed until therapy is already under way.

ZESTRIL

Lisinopril
Other brand name: Prinivil

Lisinopril is used in the treatment of high blood pressure. It is effective when used alone or when combined with other high blood pressure medications. It may also be used with other medications in the treatment of heart failure, and may be given within 24 hours of a heart attack to improve chances of survival.

Lisinopril is a type of drug called an ACE inhibitor. It works by reducing production of a substance that increases salt and water retention in the body.

ZETIA

Ezetimibe

Zetia is a new kind of cholesterol-lowering drug. The older cholesterol-lowering drugs called "statins" reduce cholesterol by interfering with its production in the body. Zetia acts by diminishing the absorption of dietary cholesterol through the intestines.

Zetia may be taken alone or with a statin drug. Because the two drugs fight cholesterol in different ways, the Zetia/statin combination has a greater impact than either drug alone.

Cholesterol—especially "bad" LDL cholesterol—promotes clogged arteries, increasing the risk of heart attack and stroke. "Good" HDL cholesterol helps to prevent clogged arteries. Zetia lowers the bad cholesterol and raises the good. It also lowers total cholesterol readings and reduces levels of triglycerides (fats in the blood).

Cholesterol-lowering drugs are typically prescribed for people who either have heart disease or are in danger of developing it. For people at high risk of heart disease, current guidelines call for considering drug therapy when LDL levels reach 130. For people at lower risk, the cut-off is 160. For those at little or no risk, it is 190.

ZIAC
Bisoprolol with Hydrochlorothiazide

Ziac is used to treat high blood pressure. It combines a beta-blocker (bisoprolol, which is the ingredient in the drug Zebeta) with a thiazide diuretic (hydrochlorothiazide). Beta-blockers decrease the force and rate of heart contractions, thus lowering blood pressure. Diuretics help the body produce and eliminate more urine, which also helps lower blood pressure.

ZIAGEN
Abacavir

Ziagen helps to halt the inroads of the human immunodeficiency virus (HIV). Without treatment, HIV gradually undermines the body's immune system, encouraging other infections to take hold until the body succumbs to full-blown acquired immune deficiency syndrome (AIDS).

Like other anti-HIV drugs, Ziagen holds back the advance of the virus by disrupting its reproductive cycle. This medication is used only as part of a "drug cocktail" that attacks the virus on several fronts. It is not prescribed alone.

Zidovudine *See Retrovir, page 604.*

Zileuton *See Zyflo, page 644.*

ZITHROMAX
Azithromycin

Zithromax is an antibiotic related to erythromycin. For adults, it is prescribed to treat certain mild to moderate skin infections; upper and lower respiratory tract infections, including pharyngitis (strep throat), tonsillitis, worsening of chronic obstructive pulmonary disease, and pneumonia; sexually transmitted infections of the cervix or urinary tract; and genital ulcer disease in men. In children, Zithromax is used to treat middle ear infection, pneumonia, tonsillitis, and strep throat.

ZOCOR
Simvastatin

Zocor is a cholesterol-lowering drug. Doctors prescribe Zocor in addition to a cholesterol-lowering diet when blood cholesterol levels are too high and a patient has been unable to lower it by diet alone. For people at high risk of heart disease, current guidelines call for considering drug therapy when LDL levels reach 130. For people at lower risk, the cut-off is 160. For those at little or no risk, it's 190.

In people with high cholesterol and heart disease, Zocor reduces the risk of heart attack, stroke, and "mini-stroke" (transient ischemic attack) and can stave off the need for bypass surgery or angioplasty to clear clogged arteries. Zocor can also reduce these risks in people with diabetes, peripheral vascular disease, and a history of stroke.

ZOFRAN
Ondansetron
Other brand name: Zofran ODT

Zofran is used for the prevention of nausea and vomiting caused by radiation therapy and chemotherapy for cancer. In some cases, it is also used to prevent these problems following surgery.

ZOLADEX
Goserelin

Zoladex relieves the symptoms of advanced prostate cancer in men and advanced breast cancer in premenopausal women. In combination with other forms of therapy, it is also prescribed during treatment of early prostate cancer.

In addition, it can be used in the treatment of endometriosis, a condition in which tissue from the lining of the uterus invades the abdomen. If a woman is scheduled for surgical removal of the lining, the drug may be used to thin the lining prior to the operation.

Zoladex works by reducing levels of testosterone in men and estrogen in women. These hormones can encourage the growth of certain cancers.

Zolmitriptan *See Zomig, page 642.*

ZOMIG
Zolmitriptan

Zomig relieves migraine headaches. It's effective whether or not the headache is preceded by an aura (visual disturbances such as halos and flickering lights). For most people Zomig provides relief within 2 hours, but it will not abort an attack or reduce the number of headaches experienced.

Migraines are thought to be caused by expansion and inflammation of blood vessels in the head. Zomig ends a migraine attack by constricting these blood vessels and reducing inflammation.

ZONEGRAN
Zonisamide

Zonegran helps reduce the frequency of partial epileptic seizures, a form of epilepsy in which neural disturbances are limited to a specific region of the brain and the victim remains conscious throughout the attack. The drug is used in combination with other antiseizure medications, not by itself.

Zonisamide *See Zonegran, page 643.*

Zovia *See Oral Contraceptives, page 582.*

ZOVIRAX
Acyclovir

Zovirax liquid, capsules, and tablets are used in the treatment of certain infections with herpesviruses. These include genital herpes, shingles, and chickenpox. This drug may not be appropriate for everyone, and its use should be thoroughly discussed with the doctor. Zovirax ointment is used to treat initial episodes of genital herpes and certain herpes simplex infections of the skin and mucous membranes. Zovirax cream is used for herpes cold sores on the lips and face only.

Some doctors use Zovirax, along with other drugs, in the treatment of AIDS, and for unusual herpes infections such as those following kidney and bone marrow transplants.

ZYBAN
Bupropion

Zyban is a nicotine-free quit-smoking aid. Instead of nicotine, it contains the same active ingredient as the antidepressant medication Wellbutrin. It works by boosting the levels of several chemical messengers in the brain. With more of these chemicals at work, patients experience a reduction in nicotine withdrawal symptoms and a weakening of the urge to smoke. More than a third of the people who take Zyban while participating in a support program are able to quit smoking for at least 1 month. Zyban can also prove helpful when people with conditions such as chronic bronchitis and emphysema decide it's time to quit.

Zydone *See Vicodin, page 634.*

ZYFLO
Zileuton

Zyflo tablets prevent and relieve the symptoms of chronic asthma. The drug works by relaxing the muscles in the walls of the airways, allowing them to open wider, and by reducing inflammation, swelling, and mucus secretion in the lungs.

ZYLOPRIM
Allopurinol

Zyloprim is used in the treatment of many symptoms of gout, including acute attacks, tophi (collection of uric acid crystals in the tissues, especially around joints), joint destruction, and uric acid stones. Gout is a form of arthritis characterized by increased blood levels of uric acid. Zyloprim works by reducing uric acid production in the body, thus preventing crystals from forming.

Zyloprim is also used to manage increased uric acid levels in the blood of people with certain cancers, such as leukemia. It is also prescribed to manage some types of kidney stones.

ZYMAR
Gatifloxacin eye drops

Zymar is an antibiotic used in the treatment of eye infections such as conjunctivitis (pinkeye) and other bacterial infections. Gatifloxacin, the active ingredient, is a member of the quinolone family of antibiotics.

ZYRTEC
Cetirizine

Zyrtec is an antihistamine. It is prescribed to treat the sneezing; itchy, runny nose; and itchy, red, watery eyes caused by seasonal allergies such as hay fever. Zyrtec also relieves the symptoms of year-round allergies due to dust, mold, and animal dander. This medication is also used in the treatment of chronic itchy skin and hives.

ZYRTEC-D
Cetirizine with Pseudoephedrine

Zyrtec-D contains the same antihistamine found in regular Zyrtec, plus the decongestant pseudoephedrine. The drug is prescribed to relieve the symptoms of hay fever and similar allergies, whether seasonal or year-round.

ZYVOX
Linezolid

Zyvox is a member of a new class of antibiotics called oxazolidinones. It is used to treat certain types of pneumonia, some forms of skin infection, and infections involving certain strains of a germ called *Enterococcus faecium*.

Section 5

Mental and Emotional Side Effects

Psychological symptoms are sometimes the result of medications prescribed for an entirely unrelated purpose. These unwanted side effects can confound diagnosis and complicate therapy, leading to additional and perhaps unnecessary medication. Part 1 of this section lists alphabetically some 175 mental and emotional symptoms and the drugs that can cause them. (For example, you will see here a list of all the drugs that can trigger or exacerbate depression.) Part 2 lists alphabetically the potential psychological side effects of each drug (for example, all the symptoms that can be caused by the antibiotic Cipro).

The information in this section is extracted from the Side Effects Index of *Physicians' Desk Reference®*, a compilation of all adverse events reported in official product labeling as published in *PDR*. The reported incidence of a particular side effect for some drugs is shown in parentheses following the entry. Side effects known to occur in 3% of patients or more are marked with a ▲ symbol. Entries are limited to reactions that may be expected to occur at recommended dosage levels in the general patient population. Effects of overdose are not included.

Part 1.
Side Effects by Symptom

Aggression

Accutane Capsules
Advair Diskus 100/50
Advair Diskus 250/50
Advair Diskus 500/50
Ambien Tablets (Rare)
Amerge Tablets (Rare)
Amnesteem Capsules
Aricept Tablets (Frequent)
Celexa Oral Solution (Infrequent)
Celexa Tablets (Infrequent)
Celontin Capsules
Copegus Tablets (Less than 1%)
▲ Crinone 4% Gel (Less than 5%)
▲ Crinone 8% Gel (Less than 5%)
Depacon Injection
Depakene Capsules
Depakene Syrup
Depakote ER Tablets
Depakote Sprinkle Capsules
Depakote Tablets
Evoxac Capsules
▲ Exelon Capsules (3%)
▲ Exelon Oral Solution (3%)
Felbatol Oral Suspension (Frequent)
Felbatol Tablets (Frequent)
Flexeril Tablets
Flovent 44 mcg Inhalation Aerosol
Flovent 110 mcg Inhalation Aerosol
Flovent 220 mcg Inhalation Aerosol
Flovent Rotadisk 50 mcg
Flovent Rotadisk 100 mcg
Flovent Rotadisk 250 mcg
Floxin Tablets
▲ Foscavir Injection (Between 1% and 5%)
Genotropin Lyophilized Powder
Halcion Tablets
Imitrex Injection
Imitrex Tablets (Rare)
▲ Intron A for Injection (Less than 5%)
Klonopin Tablets (Infrequent)
Klonopin Wafers (Infrequent)
Levaquin in 5% Dextrose Injection (0.1% to 1%)
Levaquin Injection (0.1% to 1%)
Levaquin Tablets (0.1% to 1%)
Lexapro Oral Solution (Infrequent)
Lexapro Tablets (Infrequent)
Neurontin Capsules
Neurontin Oral Solution
Neurontin Tablets
PEG-Intron Powder for Injection (Less than or equal to 1%)
Priftin Tablets (Less than 1%)
Prilosec Delayed-Release Capsules (Less than 1%)
Prilosec OTC Tablets (Less than 1%)
Prochieve 4% Gel
Prochieve 8% Gel
Pulmicort Respules (Less than 1%)
Pulmicort Turbuhaler Inhalation Powder (Rare)
Reminyl Oral Solution
Reminyl Tablets
Requip Tablets (Infrequent)
▲ Risperdal M-Tab Tablets (1% to 3%)
▲ Risperdal Oral Solution (1% to 3%)
▲ Risperdal Tablets (1% to 3%)
Singulair Chewable Tablets
Singulair Oral Granules
Singulair Tablets
Soriatane Capsules
Strattera Capsules (0.5%)
Symmetrel Syrup
Symmetrel Tablets
▲ Topamax Sprinkle Capsules (2% to 9%)
▲ Topamax Tablets
Trileptal Oral Suspension
Trileptal Tablets
Xanax Tablets (Rare)
Xanax XR Tablets (Rare to infrequent)
Zarontin Capsules
Zarontin Syrup
Zoloft Oral Concentrate (Infrequent to 2%)
Zoloft Tablets (Infrequent to 2%)

Agitation

Abilify Tablets (2% or greater)
Aciphex Tablets (Rare)
Actiq (Less than 1%)
Advair Diskus 100/50
Advair Diskus 250/50
Advair Diskus 500/50
Aggrenox Capsules (Less than 1%)
Allegra-D Extended-Release Tablets (1.9%)
Aloprim for Injection (Less than 1%)

Ambien Tablets (Infrequent)
AmBisome for Injection (Less common)
Amerge Tablets (Rare)
Amoxil Capsules (Rare)
Amoxil Chewable Tablets (Rare)
Amoxil for Oral Suspension (Rare)
Amoxil Pediatric Drops for Oral Suspension (Rare)
Amoxil Tablets (Rare)
▲ Amphotec (1% to 5%)
▲ Anafranil (3%)
Anzemet Injection (Infrequent)
Anzemet Tablets (Infrequent)
Aricept Tablets
Ativan Injection
Augmentin Chewable Tablets (Rare)
Augmentin ES-600 Powder for Oral Suspension (Rare)
Augmentin Powder for Oral Suspension (Rare)
Augmentin Tablets (Rare)
Augmentin XR Tablets (Rare)
Avelox I.V. (Less than 0.1%)
Avelox Tablets (Less than 0.1%)
▲ Avinza Capsules (Less than 5%)
Bicillin L-A Injection
Brevibloc Concentrate (About 2%)
Brevibloc Double Strength Injection (About 2%)
Brevibloc Double Strength Premixed Injection (About 2%)
Brevibloc Injection (About 2%)
Brevibloc Premixed Injection (About 2%)
Buprenex Injectable (Rare)
Busulfex Injection (2%)
Caduet Tablets (Less than or equal to 0.1%)
Carbatrol Capsules
Cardura Tablets (0.5% to 1%)
Catapres Tablets (About 3 in 100 patients)
Catapres-TTS (0.5% or less)
Cedax Oral Suspension (0.1% to 1%)
▲ Celexa Oral Solution (3%)
▲ Celexa Tablets (3%)
▲ CellCept Capsules (3% to less than 20%)
▲ CellCept Intravenous (3% to less than 20%)
▲ CellCept Oral Suspension (3% to less than 20%)
▲ CellCept Tablets (3% to less than 20%)

▲ Cerebyx Injection (3.3% to 9.5%)
Chlorpromazine
Cipro I.V.
Cipro I.V. Pharmacy Bulk Package
Cipro Oral Suspension
Cipro Tablets
Cipro XR Tablets
Clorpres Tablets (About 3%)
▲ Clozapine Tablets (4%)
▲ Clozaril Tablets (4%)
▲ Cognex Capsules (7%)
Comtan Tablets
Comvax
▲ Copaxone for Injection (4%)
Crixivan Capsules (Less than 2%)
Cuprimine Capsules
Demerol Syrup
Demerol Tablets
Depacon Injection (1% or more)
Depakene Capsules (1% or more)
Depakene Syrup (1% or more)
Depakote ER Tablets (Greater than 1%)
Depakote Sprinkle Capsules
▲ Depakote Tablets (1% to 5%)
Dexedrine Spansule Capsules
Dexedrine Tablets
Dilaudid Ampules
Dilaudid Injection
Dilaudid Multiple Dose Vials
Dilaudid Non-Sterile Powder
Dilaudid Oral Liquid (Less frequent)
Dilaudid Rectal Suppositories
Dilaudid Tablets
Dilaudid Tablets - 8 mg (Less frequent)
Dilaudid-HP Injection (Less frequent)
Dilaudid-HP Lyophilized Powder 250 mg (Less frequent)
Diprivan Injectable Emulsion (Less than 1%)
Doral
Duragesic Transdermal System (1% or greater)
Ecotrin Enteric Coated Aspirin Low, Regular and Maximum Strength Tablets
▲ Effexor Tablets (2% to 4.5%)
▲ Effexor XR Capsules (4%)
Eldepryl Capsules
Elspar for Injection
Engerix-B Vaccine (Less than 1%)
▲ Entocort EC Capsules (Less than 5%)
Evoxac Capsules (Less than 1%)
Exelon Capsules (2% or more)

Exelon Oral Solution (2% or more)
Felbatol Oral Suspension (Frequent)
Felbatol Tablets (Frequent)
Ferrlecit Injection (Greater than 1%)
Flexeril Tablets (Less than 1%)
▲ Flolan for Injection (11%)
Flovent 44 mcg Inhalation Aerosol
Flovent 110 mcg Inhalation Aerosol
Flovent 220 mcg Inhalation Aerosol
Flovent Rotadisk 50 mcg
Flovent Rotadisk 100 mcg
Flovent Rotadisk 250 mcg
Floxin Tablets
Fludara for Injection
Flumadine Syrup (0.3% to 1%)
Flumadine Tablets (0.3% to 1%)
Fortovase Capsules (Less than 2%)
▲ Foscavir Injection (Between 1% and 5%)
Frova Tablets (Infrequent)
Gabitril Tablets (1%)
Geodon Capsules (Frequent)
Guanfacine
Halcion Tablets
Haldol Decanoate 50 Injection
Haldol Decanoate 100 Injection
Hivid Tablets (Less than 1%)
Imitrex Injection (Infrequent)
Imitrex Nasal Spray (Infrequent)
Imitrex Tablets (Up to 2%)
▲ Indapamide Tablets (Greater than or equal to 5%)
▲ Infergen (4% to 6%)
▲ Intron A for Injection (Less than 5%)
▲ Invanz for Injection (3.3% to 5.1%)
Invirase Capsules (Less than 2%)
Kadian Capsules (Less than 3%)
Kaletra Capsules (Less than 2%)
Kaletra Oral Solution (Less than 2%)
Keflex Pulvules
Klonopin Tablets
Klonopin Wafers
Kytril Injection (Less than 2%)
Lamictal Chewable Dispersible Tablets (Infrequent)
Lamictal Tablets (Infrequent)
Lariam Tablets (Occasional)
Leukeran Tablets (Rare)
Levaquin in 5% Dextrose Injection (0.1% to 1%)
Levaquin Injection (0.1% to 1%)
Levaquin Tablets (0.1% to 1%)
Lexapro Oral Solution (Infrequent)
Lexapro Tablets (Infrequent)

Lexxel Tablets
Loxitane Capsules
▲ Lupron Depot 7.5 mg (Less than 5%)
Lupron Depot—3 Month 11.25 mg
Maxalt Tablets (Infrequent)
Maxalt-MLT Orally Disintegrating Tablets (Infrequent)
Mebaral Tablets (Less than 1 in 100 patients)
Mellaril
Meridia Capsules (Greater than or equal to 1%)
Merrem I.V. (Greater than 0.1% to 1%)
Miacalcin Nasal Spray (Less than 1%)
Mirapex Tablets (Less than 1%; 1.1%)
MS Contin Tablets (Less frequent)
MSIR Oral Capsules (Less frequent)
MSIR Oral Solution Concentrate (Less frequent)
MSIR Oral Tablets (Less frequent)
Namenda Tablets (Greater than or equal to 2%)
Narcan Injection
Nardil Tablets (Uncommon)
Naropin Injection (Less than 1%)
Navane Capsules
Navane Concentrate
Navane Intramuscular
Nefazodone
Nembutal Sodium Solution (Less than 1%)
Neurontin Capsules (Infrequent)
Neurontin Oral Solution (Infrequent)
Neurontin Tablets (Infrequent)
Norflex Extended-Release Tablets
Norflex Injection
Norpramin Tablets
Norvasc Tablets (Less than or equal to 0.1%)
Norvir Oral Solution (Less than 2%)
Norvir Soft Gelatin Capsules (Less than 2%)
Nubain Injection
Orthoclone OKT3 Sterile Solution
OxyContin Tablets (Less than 1%)
Pamelor
Parnate Tablets
Paxil CR Controlled-Release Tablets (2%)
▲ Paxil Oral Suspension (1.1% to 5%)
▲ Paxil Tablets (1.1% to 5%)
PEG-Intron Powder for Injection (2%)
Pepcid for Oral Suspension (Infrequent)

Pepcid Injection (Infrequent)
Pepcid Injection Premixed (Infrequent)
Pepcid Tablets (Infrequent)
Permax Tablets (Infrequent)
Phenergan Suppositories
Phenergan Tablets
Phenobarbital (Less than 1%)
Prevacid Delayed-Release Capsules
  (Less than 1%)
Prevacid for Delayed-Release Oral
  Suspension (Less than 1%)
Prevacid NapraPAC 375 (Less than
  1%)
Prevacid NapraPAC 500 (Less than
  1%)
Prevacid SoluTab Delayed-Release
  Tablets (Less than 1%)
PREVPAC (Less than 1%)
Prochlorperazine
▲ Prograf Capsules and Injection (3% to
  15%)
Proleukin for Injection
ProSom Tablets (Infrequent)
Provigil Tablets (1%)
Prozac Pulvules and Liquid (At least
  2%)
▲ Rebetol Capsules (5% to 8%)
▲ Rebetol Oral Solution (5% to 8%)
Recombivax HB
Relafen Tablets (1%)
Relpax Tablets (Infrequent)
Remeron SolTab Tablets (Frequent)
Reminyl Oral Solution (Greater than
  or equal to 2%)
Reminyl Tablets (Greater than or
  equal to 2%)
ReoPro Vials (0.7%)
Requip Tablets (Infrequent)
Rescriptor Tablets
Reyataz Capsules (Less than 3%)
▲ Ribavirin Capsules (5%)
Rilutek Tablets (Frequent)
Risperdal Consta Injection (Frequent)
▲ Risperdal M-Tab Tablets (22% to 26%)
▲ Risperdal Oral Solution (22% to 26%)
▲ Risperdal Tablets (8% to 26%)
▲ Rituxan for Infusion (1% to 5%)
▲ Rituxan I.V. (1% to 5%)
Roferon-A Injection
▲ Romazicon Injection (3% to 9%)
Salagen Tablets (Rare)
Sarafem Pulvules (Frequent)
Seconal (Less than 1%)
Sedapap Tablets 50 mg/650 mg
  (Infrequent)

Serentil Ampuls
Serentil Concentrate
Serentil Tablets
▲ Seroquel Tablets (4%)
▲ Simulect for Injection (3% to 10%)
Singulair Chewable Tablets
Singulair Oral Granules
Singulair Tablets
Soma Tablets
Sonata Capsules (Infrequent)
St. Joseph 81 mg Aspirin
Stadol Injection (Less than 1%)
Stadol NS (Less than 1%)
Stalevo Tablets (1%)
Suprane Liquid for Inhalation (Less
  than 1%)
Surmontil Capsules
Sustiva Capsules (Less than 2%)
▲ Symmetrel Syrup (1% to 5%)
▲ Symmetrel Tablets (1% to 5%)
Tagamet Injection
Tagamet Liquid
Tagamet Tablets
Targretin Capsules
Tasmar Tablets (1%)
Tegretol Chewable Tablets
Tegretol Suspension
Tegretol Tablets
Tegretol-XR Tablets
Tequin Injection (Less than 0.1%)
Tequin Tablets (Less than 0.1%)
Thalomid Capsules
Thioridazine Hydrochloride Tablets
Thiothixene Capsules
▲ Topamax Sprinkle Capsules (3%)
▲ Topamax Tablets (3%)
Trasylol Injection (1% to 2%)
Trental Tablets
Trifluoperazine
Trileptal Oral Suspension (1% to 2%)
Trileptal Tablets (1% to 2%)
▲ Trisenox Injection (5%)
Trovan I.V. (Less than 1%)
Trovan Tablets (Less than 1%)
Twinrix Vaccine (Less than 1%)
▲ Ultram Tablets (1% to 14%)
▲ Valcyte Tablets (Less than 5%)
Valtrex Caplets
▲ Vesanoid Capsules (9%)
VFEND I.V. (Less than 1%)
VFEND Oral Suspension (Less than
  1%)
VFEND Tablets (Less than 1%)
Vicoprofen Tablets (Less than 1%)

Vistide Injection
Vivactil Tablets
▲ Wellbutrin SR Sustained-Release Tablets (3% to 9%)
▲ Wellbutrin Tablets (31.9%)
▲ Wellbutrin XL Extended-Release Tablets (3% to 9%)
Xanax Tablets (Rare; 2.9%)
Xanax XR Tablets (Rare to frequent)
Xyrem Oral Solution (Frequent)
Zanaflex Tablets (Infrequent)
Zantac 150 EFFERdose Granules (Rare)
Zantac 150 EFFERdose Tablets (Rare)
Zantac 150 Tablets (Rare)
Zantac 300 Tablets (Rare)
Zantac Injection
Zantac Injection Premixed
Zantac Syrup (Rare)
Zithromax Capsules, 250 mg (1% or less)
Zithromax for Oral Suspension, 300 mg, 600 mg, 900 mg, 1200 mg (1% or less)
Zithromax Tablets, 250 mg, 500 mg (1% or less)
▲ Zofran Injection (2% to 6%)
▲ Zofran Injection Premixed (2% to 6%)
▲ Zofran ODT Orally Disintegrating Tablets (6%)
▲ Zofran Oral Solution (6%)
▲ Zofran Tablets (6%)
▲ Zoloft Oral Concentrate (1% to 6%)
▲ Zoloft Tablets (1% to 6%)
▲ Zometa for Intravenous Infusion (12.8%)
Zomig Nasal Spray (Infrequent to less than 2%)
Zomig Tablets (Infrequent)
Zomig-ZMT Tablets (Infrequent)
▲ Zonegran Capsules (9%)
▲ Zosyn (2.1% to 7.1%)
▲ Zosyn in Galaxy Containers (2.1% to 7.1%)
Zovirax Capsules
Zovirax for Injection (Approximately 1%)
Zovirax Suspension
Zovirax Tablets
Zyban Sustained-Release Tablets (Frequent)
▲ Zyprexa Tablets (23%)
▲ Zyprexa ZYDIS Orally Disintegrating Tablets (23%)
Zyrtec Syrup (Less than 2%)

Zyrtec Tablets (Less than 2%)
Zyrtec-D 12 Hour Extended Relief Tablets (Less than 2%)

Agoraphobia
Fluvoxamine maleate (Infrequent)

Alcohol abuse
BuSpar Tablets (Rare)
Effexor Tablets (Rare)
Effexor XR Capsules (Rare)
Paxil Oral Suspension (Infrequent)
Paxil Tablets (Infrequent)
Zyprexa Tablets (Infrequent)
Zyprexa ZYDIS Orally Disintegrating Tablets (Infrequent)

Anger
BuSpar Tablets (2%)
Meridia Capsules
Xanax XR Tablets (Infrequent)

Antisocial reaction
Prozac Pulvules and Liquid (Rare)
Zyprexa Tablets (Infrequent)
Zyprexa ZYDIS Orally Disintegrating Tablets (Infrequent)

Anxiety
▲ Abilify Tablets (25%)
Aceon Tablets 2 mg, 4 mg, 8 mg (0.3% to 1%)
Aciphex Tablets
Actonel Tablets (0.6% to 4.3%)
Adalat CC Tablets (Less than 1%)
Advicor Tablets
▲ Aerobid Inhaler System (1% to 3%)
▲ Aerobid-M Inhaler System (1% to 3%)
Allegra-D Extended-Release Tablets (1.4%)
▲ Alora Transdermal System (Up to 9%)
Aloxi Injection (1%)
Altace Capsules (Less than 1%)
Altocor Extended-Release Tablets
Ambien Tablets (1%)
▲ AmBisome for Injection (7.4% to 13.7%)
Amerge Tablets (Infrequent)
Amoxil Capsules (Rare)
Amoxil Chewable Tablets (Rare)
Amoxil for Oral Suspension (Rare)
Amoxil Pediatric Drops for Oral Suspension (Rare)
Amoxil Tablets (Rare)
▲ Anafranil (9%)

Androderm Transdermal System (Less than 1%)
AndroGel (Fewer than 1%)
▲ Angiomax for Injection (6%)
Anzemet Injection (Infrequently)
Anzemet Tablets (Infrequently)
▲ Arava Tablets (1% to 3%)
▲ Aredia for Injection (14.3%)
▲ Arimidex Tablets (2% to 5%)
▲ Aromasin Tablets (10%)
Arthrotec Tablets (Rare)
Asacol Delayed-Release Tablets (2% or greater)
Astelin Nasal Spray (Infrequent)
Astramorph/PF Injection, (Preservative-Free)
Atacand HCT 16-12.5 Tablets (0.5% or greater)
Atacand HCT 32-12.5 Tablets (0.5% or greater)
Atacand Tablets (0.5% or greater)
Augmentin Chewable Tablets (Rare)
Augmentin ES-600 Powder for Oral Suspension (Rare)
Augmentin Powder for Oral Suspension (Rare)
Augmentin Tablets (Rare)
Augmentin XR Tablets (Rare)
Avalide Tablets (1% or greater)
Avapro Tablets (Less than 1%)
Avelox I.V. (0.05% to 1%)
Avelox Tablets (0.05% to 1%)
▲ Avinza Capsules (Less than 5%)
Axert Tablets (Infrequent)
▲ Betaseron for SC Injection (10%)
Bextra Tablets (0.1% to 1.9%)
Biaxin Filmtab Tablets
Biaxin Granules
Biaxin XL Filmtab Tablets
Bicillin C-R 900/300 Injection
Bicillin C-R Injection
Bicillin L-A Injection
Brevibloc Concentrate (Less than 1%)
Brevibloc Double Strength Injection (Less than 1%)
Brevibloc Double Strength Premixed Injection (Less than 1%)
Brevibloc Injection (Less than 1%)
Brevibloc Premixed Injection (Less than 1%)
Brevital Sodium for Injection
▲ Busulfex Injection (72% to 75%)
Caduet Tablets (Greater than 0.1% to less than or equal to 1%)

Cardura Tablets (1.1%)
Carnitor Injection (1% to 2%)
▲ Casodex Tablets (2% to 5%)
Cataflam Tablets (Occasional)
Catapres Tablets
Catapres-TTS (0.5% or less)
Celebrex Capsules (0.1% to 1.9%)
▲ Celexa Oral Solution (4%)
▲ Celexa Tablets (4%)
▲ CellCept Capsules (3% to 28.4%)
▲ CellCept Intravenous (3% to 28.4%)
▲ CellCept Oral Suspension (3% to 28.4%)
▲ CellCept Tablets (3% to 28.4%)
▲ Cenestin Tablets, 0.45 mg, 0.625 mg, 0.9 mg, 1.25 mg (5.7%)
Cipro I.V. (1% or less)
Cipro I.V. Pharmacy Bulk Package (Less than 1%)
Cipro Oral Suspension
Cipro Tablets
Cipro XR Tablets
Clomid Tablets
Clorpres Tablets
Clozapine Tablets (1%)
Clozaril Tablets (1%)
▲ Cognex (3%)
Colazal Capsules
Comtan Tablets (2%)
▲ Copaxone for Injection (23%)
▲ Copegus Tablets (33%)
Cosopt Sterile Ophthalmic Solution
Cozaar Tablets (Less than 1%)
Crestor Tablets (Greater than or equal to 1%)
Crixivan Capsules (Less than 2%)
Cubicin for Injection (1% to 2%)
Cuprimine Capsules
Cytotec Tablets (Infrequent)
Cytovene Capsules (At least 3 subjects)
Cytovene-IV (At least 3 subjects)
▲ Daptacel (23.6% to 39.6%)
▲ DaunoXome Injection (Less than or equal to 5%)
Delatestryl Injection
Demser Capsules
▲ Depacon Injection (1% to 5%)
▲ Depakene Capsules (1% to 5%)
▲ Depakene Syrup (1% to 5%)
▲ Depakote ER Tablets (1% to 5%)
▲ Depakote Sprinkle Capsules (1% to 5%)
▲ Depakote Tablets (1% to 5%)
Detrol LA Capsules (1%)

Digitek Tablets
Dilaudid Ampules
Dilaudid Injection
Dilaudid Multiple Dose Vials
Dilaudid Non-Sterile Powder
Dilaudid Rectal Suppositories
Dilaudid Tablets
Diovan HCT Tablets (Greater than 0.2%)
Diovan Tablets
Diprivan Injectable Emulsion (Less than 1%)
Doral
▲ Dostinex Tablets (1% to less than 10%)
▲ Doxil Injection (Less than 1% to 5%)
▲ Duragesic Transdermal System (3% to 10%)
▲ Effexor Tablets (2% to 11.2%)
Effexor XR Capsules (1%)
Elavil
Eldepryl Capsules (1 of 49 patients)
▲ Eloxatin for Injection (2% to 5%)
Emcyt Capsules (1%)
Emend Capsules (Greater than 0.5%)
EpiPen Auto-Injector
EpiPen Jr. Auto-Injector
▲ Epogen for Injection (2% to 7%)
Ergamisol Tablets (1%)
▲ Esclim Transdermal System (Up to 8.3%)
Estratest H.S. Tablets
Estratest Tablets
▲ Estring Vaginal Ring (1% to 3%)
Evoxac Capsules (1.3%)
▲ Exelon Capsules (5%)
▲ Exelon Oral Solution (5%)
▲ Fabrazyme for Intravenous Infusion (8%)
▲ Faslodex Injection (5%)
Felbatol Oral Suspension (5.2% to 5.3%)
▲ Felbatol Tablets (5.2% to 5.3%)
Feldene Capsules (Occasional)
Femara Tablets (Less frequent)
Flexeril Tablets (Less than 1%)
▲ Flolan for Injection (7% to 21%)
Floxin Tablets (Less than 1%)
▲ Fluvoxamine maleate (1% to 5%)
Fortovase Capsules (2.2%)
▲ Foscavir Injection (5% or greater)
Frova Tablets (Frequent)
▲ Fuzeon Injection (5.7%)
Gabitril Tablets (1% or more)
Gamimune N, 10% Solvent/Detergent Treated

Gammar-P I.V.
Gastrocrom Oral Concentrate (Less common)
Gengraf Capsules (1% to less than 3%)
Geodon Capsules
Geodon for Injection (Up to 2%)
Gleevec Tablets (Infrequent)
Glucotrol XL Extended Release Tablets (Less than 3%)
Gonal-F for Injection
Guanfacine (Less frequent)
Haldol Decanoate 50 Injection
Haldol Decanoate 100 Injection
Hivid Tablets (Less than 1%)
Hycodan Syrup
Hycodan Tablets
Hycomine Compound Tablets
Hycotuss Expectorant Syrup
Hytrin Capsules (At least 1%)
Hyzaar 50-12.5 Tablets
Hyzaar 100-25 Tablets
Imitrex Injection (1.1%)
Imitrex Nasal Spray (Infrequent)
Imitrex Tablets
▲ Indapamide Tablets (Greater than or equal to 5%)
Indocin Capsules (Less than 1%)
Indocin Oral Suspension (Less than 1%)
Indocin Suppositories (Less than 1%)
▲ Infanrix Vaccine (3.3% to 9.2%)
▲ Infergen (10% to 19%)
▲ Intron A for Injection (Up to 5%)
Invanz for Injection (0.8% to 1.1%)
Invirase Capsules (Greater than or equal to 2%)
▲ Kadian Capsules (Less than 3% to 6%)
Kaletra Capsules (Less than 2%)
Kaletra Oral Solution (Less than 2%)
Keppra Oral Solution (2%)
Keppra Tablets (2%)
Ketek Tablets (Less than 0.2%)
Klonopin Tablets (Infrequent)
Klonopin Wafers (Infrequent)
Kytril Injection (Less than 2%)
Kytril Tablets (2%)
▲ Lamictal Chewable Dispersible Tablets (3.8%)
▲ Lamictal Tablets (3.8%)
Lanoxicaps Capsules
Lanoxin Elixir Pediatric
Lanoxin Injection

Lanoxin Injection Pediatric
Lanoxin Tablets
Lariam Tablets (Occasional)
Lescol Capsules
Lescol XL Tablets
▲ Leukine (11%)
Levaquin in 5% Dextrose Injection (0.1% to 1%)
Levaquin Injection (0.1% to 1%)
Levaquin Tablets (0.1% to 1%)
Levothroid Tablets
Levoxyl Tablets
Lexapro Oral Solution (At least 2%)
Lexapro Tablets (At least 2%)
Lexxel Tablets
Lofibra Capsules
Lortab 2.5/500 Tablets
Lortab 5/500 Tablets
Lortab 7.5/500 Tablets
Lortab 10/500 Tablets
Lortab Elixir
Lotensin Tablets (Less than 1%)
Lotrel Capsules
Lotronex Tablets (Infrequent)
▲ Ludiomil (3%)
▲ Lupron Depot 3.75 mg (3%)
▲ Lupron Depot—3 Month 11.25 mg (3%)
▲ Lupron Depot—3 Month 22.5 mg (Less than 5%)
▲ Lupron Injection (Less than 5%)
M.V.I. Pediatric for Injection (Rare)
Malarone Pediatric Tablets (Less than 1%)
Malarone Tablets (Less than 1%)
Marinol Capsules (Greater than 1%)
Mavik Tablets (0.3% to 1%)
Maxair Autohaler
Maxalt Tablets (Infrequent)
Maxalt-MLT Orally Disintegrating Tablets (Infrequent)
Maxidone Tablets
Maxzide Tablets
Maxzide-25 mg Tablets
Mebaral Tablets (Less than 1 in 100 patients)
▲ Mepron Suspension (7%)
▲ Meridia Capsules (4.5%)
Merrem I.V. (Greater than 0.1% to 1%)
Mevacor Tablets (0.5% to 1%)
Miacalcin Nasal Spray (Less than 1%)
Micardis HCT Tablets
Micardis Tablets (More than 0.3%)

Mirapex Tablets (1% or more)
Mobic Tablets (Less than 2%)
Namenda Tablets (Greater than or equal to 2%)
Naprelan Tablets (Less than 1%)
Nardil Tablets (Less frequent)
▲ Naropin Injection (1% to 5%)
▲ Natrecor for Injection (3%)
Nefazodone
Nembutal Sodium Solution (Less than 1%)
Neoral Oral Solution (1% to less than 3%)
Neoral Soft Gelatin Capsules (1% to less than 3%)
Nesacaine Injection
Nesacaine-MPF Injection
Neurontin Capsules (Frequent)
Neurontin Oral Solution (Frequent)
Neurontin Tablets (Frequent)
▲ Nipent for Injection (3% to 10%)
Norco 5/325 Tablets
Norco 7.5/325 Tablets
Norco 10/325 Tablets
Noroxin Tablets (Less frequent)
Norpramin Tablets
Norvasc Tablets (More than 0.1% to 1%)
Norvir Oral Solution (Less than 2%)
Norvir Soft Gelatin Capsules (Less than 2%)
▲ OxyContin Tablets (Between 1% and 5%)
Pamelor
Parnate Tablets
▲ Paxil CR Controlled-Release Tablets (2% to 5%)
▲ Paxil Oral Suspension (1% to 5.9%)
▲ Paxil Tablets (1% to 5.9%)
Pediazole Suspension
▲ Pegasys (19%)
▲ PEG-Intron Powder for Injection (28%)
Pepcid for Oral Suspension (Infrequent)
Pepcid Injection (Infrequent)
Pepcid Injection Premixed (Infrequent)
Pepcid Tablets (Infrequent)
▲ Permax Tablets (6.4%)
Phenobarbital (Less than 1%)
▲ Photofrin for Injection (7%)
Plavix Tablets (1% to 2.5%)
Plendil Extended-Release Tablets (0.5% to 1.5%)

Pletal Tablets (Less than 2%)
Polocaine Injection
Polocaine-MPF Injection
Pravachol Tablets
Prefest Tablets
▲ Premphase Tablets (2% to 5%)
▲ Prempro Tablets (2% to 5%)
Prevacid Delayed-Release Capsules (Less than 1%)
Prevacid for Delayed-Release Oral Suspension (Less than 1%)
Prevacid NapraPAC 375 (Less than 1%)
Prevacid NapraPAC 500 (Less than 1%)
Prevacid SoluTab Delayed-Release Tablets (Less than 1%)
PREVPAC (Less than 1%)
Prilosec Delayed-Release Capsules (Less than 1%)
Prilosec OTC Tablets (Less than 1%)
ProAmatine Tablets (Less frequent)
Procardia XL Extended Release Tablets (1% or less)
▲ Procrit for Injection (2% to 11%)
▲ Prograf Capsules and Injection (3% to 15%)
▲ Proleukin for Injection (12%)
▲ Prometrium Capsules 100 mg, 200 mg (Less than 5%)
ProSom Tablets (Frequent)
Protonix I.V. (Greater than or equal to 1%)
Protonix Tablets (Greater than or equal to 1%)
▲ Provigil Tablets (5%)
▲ Prozac Pulvules and Liquid (4% to 17%)
Pulmicort Respules (Less than 1%)
Pulmicort Turbuhaler Inhalation Powder (Rare)
▲ Rapamune Oral Solution and Tablets (3% to 20%)
▲ Rebetol Capsules (47%)
▲ Rebetol Oral Solution (47%)
Relafen Tablets (Less than 1%)
Relpax Tablets (Infrequent)
Remeron SolTab Tablets (Frequent)
Reminyl Oral Solution (Greater than or equal to 2%)
Reminyl Tablets (Greater than or equal to 2%)
ReoPro Vials (1.7%)
Requip Tablets (1% or more)
▲ Rescriptor Tablets (2.4% to 6.7%)

Retrovir Capsules
Retrovir IV Infusion
Retrovir Syrup
Retrovir Tablets
Reyataz Capsules (Less than 3%)
▲ Ribavirin Capsules (47%)
Rifater Tablets
Risperdal Consta Injection (Frequent)
▲ Risperdal M-Tab Tablets (12% to 20%)
▲ Risperdal Oral Solution (12% to 20%)
▲ Risperdal Tablets (4% to 20%)
▲ Roferon-A Injection (5% to 6%)
▲ Romazicon Injection (3% to 9%)
Rythmol Tablets (1.5% to 2%)
Salagen Tablets (Less than 1%)
Sandimmune I.V. Ampuls for Infusion (Rare)
Sandimmune Oral Solution (Rare)
Sandimmune Soft Gelatin Capsules (Rare)
Sandostatin Injection (Less than 1%)
▲ Sandostatin LAR Depot (5% to 15%)
▲ Sarafem Pulvules (3% to 13%)
Seconal (Less than 1%)
▲ Serevent Diskus (1% to 3%)
▲ Seroquel Tablets (4%)
▲ Serostim for Injection (1% to 5%)
▲ Simulect for Injection (3% to 10%)
Sonata Capsules (Frequent)
Soriatane Capsules (Less than 1%)
▲ Sporanox Capsules (3%)
Stadol Injection (Greater than or equal to 1%)
Stadol NS (Greater than or equal to 1%)
Stalevo Tablets (2%)
Striant Mucoadhesive
▲ Suboxone Tablets (12%)
▲ Subutex Tablets (12%)
Sular Tablets (Less than or equal to 1%)
Surmontil Capsules
Sustiva Capsules (Less than 2%)
▲ Symmetrel Syrup (1% to 5%)
▲ Symmetrel Tablets (1% to 5%)
Synercid I.V. (Less than 1%)
Synvisc
Tagamet Injection
Tagamet Liquid
Tagamet Tablets
▲ Tambocor Tablets (1% to 3%)
Tarka Tablets (0.3% or more)
Tasmar Tablets (1% or more)
▲ Temodar Capsules (7%)

Tequin Injection (Less than 0.1%)
Tequin Tablets (Less than 0.1%)
Testred Capsules, 10 mg
Teveten HCT Tablets (Less than 1%)
Teveten Tablets (Less than 1%)
Thalomid Capsules
Tikosyn Capsules (Greater than 2%)
Timoptic in Ocudose (Less frequent)
Timoptic Sterile Ophthalmic Solution (Less frequent)
Timoptic-XE Sterile Ophthalmic Gel Forming Solution
▲ Topamax Sprinkle Capsules (More than 1% to 10%)
▲ Topamax Tablets (More than 1% to 10%)
Trasylol Injection (1% to 2%)
▲ Travatan Ophthalmic Solution (1% to 5%)
Trental Tablets (Less than 1%)
Triavil Tablets
Tricor Tablets (Less than 1%)
▲ Trileptal Oral Suspension (5% to 7%)
▲ Trileptal Tablets (5% to 7%)
▲ Trisenox Injection (30%)
Trovan I.V. (Less than 1%)
Trovan Tablets (Less than 1%)
Tussionex Pennkinetic Extended-Release Suspension
Ultracet Tablets (At least 1%)
▲ Ultram Tablets (1% to 14%)
Uniretic Tablets (Less than 1%)
Vantin Tablets and Oral Suspension (Less than 1%)
▲ Velcade for Injection (14%)
▲ Vesanoid Capsules (17%)
VFEND I.V. (Less than 1%)
VFEND Oral Suspension (Less than 1%)
VFEND Tablets (Less than 1%)
Viadur Implant (Less than 2%)
Viagra Tablets
Vicodin ES Tablets
Vicodin HP Tablets
Vicodin Tablets
▲ Vicoprofen Tablets (3% to 9%)
Vioxx Oral Suspension (Greater than 0.1% to 1.9%)
Vioxx Tablets (Greater than 0.1% to 1.9%)
Viracept Oral Powder (Less than 2%)
Viracept Tablets (Less than 2%)
Vistide Injection
Vivactil Tablets
Vivelle-Dot Transdermal System

Voltaren Tablets (Occasional)
Voltaren-XR Tablets (Occasional)
▲ Wellbutrin SR Sustained-Release Tablets (5% to 6%)
▲ Wellbutrin Tablets (3.1%)
▲ Wellbutrin XL Extended-Release Tablets (5% to 6%)
▲ Xanax Tablets (16.6%)
▲ Xanax XR Tablets (1.1% to 7.8%)
▲ Xenical Capsules (2.8% to 4.4%)
Xopenex Inhalation Solution (2.7%)
▲ Xyrem Oral Solution (3% to 6%)
Zanaflex Tablets (Frequent)
Zebeta Tablets
▲ Zenapax for Injection (2% to 5%)
▲ Zevalin Injection (4%)
Ziac Tablets
Zocor Tablets
▲ Zofran Injection (2% to 6%)
▲ Zofran Injection Premixed (2% to 6%)
▲ Zofran ODT Orally Disintegrating Tablets (6%)
▲ Zofran Oral Solution (6%)
▲ Zofran Tablets (6%)
▲ Zoladex (1% to 5%)
Zoladex 3-month
▲ Zoloft Oral Concentrate (4%)
▲ Zoloft Tablets 4%
▲ Zometa for Intravenous Infusion (9% to 14%)
Zomig Nasal Spray (Infrequent)
Zomig Tablets (Infrequent)
Zomig-ZMT Tablets (Infrequent)
▲ Zonegran Capsules (3%)
▲ Zosyn (1.2% to 3.2%)
▲ Zosyn in Galaxy Containers (1.2% to 3.2%)
▲ Zyban Sustained-Release Tablets (8%)
Zydone Tablets
▲ Zyprexa Tablets (9%)
▲ Zyprexa ZYDIS Orally Disintegrating Tablets (9%)
Zyrtec Syrup (Less than 2%)
Zyrtec Tablets (Less than 2%)
Zyrtec-D 12 Hour Extended Relief Tablets (Less than 2%)

Anxiety, paradoxical
Halcion Tablets
Valium Tablets
Vivactil Tablets

Apathy
Abilify Tablets (1% or less)
Ambien Tablets (Rare)
Bicillin C-R 900/300 Injection
Bicillin C-R Injection

BuSpar Tablets (Infrequent)
Caduet Tablets (Less than or equal to 0.1%)
Campath Ampules
Celexa Oral Solution (Infrequent)
Celexa Tablets (Infrequent)
Cognex Capsules (Infrequent)
Digitek Tablets
Effexor Tablets (Infrequent)
Effexor XR Capsules (Infrequent)
Eldepryl Capsules
Evoxac Capsules
Exelon Capsules (Infrequent)
Exelon Oral Solution (Infrequent)
Felbatol Oral Suspension
Felbatol Tablets
Fluvoxamine maleate (Frequent)
Gabitril Tablets (Infrequent)
Imitrex Injection
Imitrex Nasal Spray (Rare)
Imitrex Tablets (Rare)
▲ Intron A for Injection (Less than 5%)
Kadian Capsules (Less than 3%)
Klonopin Tablets (Infrequent)
Klonopin Wafers (Infrequent)
Lamictal Chewable Dispersible Tablets (Infrequent)
Lamictal Tablets (Infrequent)
Lanoxicaps Capsules
Lanoxin Elixir Pediatric
Lanoxin Injection
Lanoxin Injection Pediatric
Lanoxin Tablets
Lexapro Oral Solution (Infrequent)
Lexapro Tablets (Infrequent)
Mirapex Tablets (1% or more)
Namenda Tablets (Infrequent)
Nefazodone
Neurontin Capsules (Infrequent)
Neurontin Oral Solution (Infrequent)
Neurontin Tablets (Infrequent)
Nexium Delayed-Release Capsules (Less than 1%)
Norvasc Tablets (Less than or equal to 0.1%)
Permax Tablets (Infrequent)
Prevacid Delayed-Release Capsules (Less than 1%)
Prevacid for Delayed-Release Oral Suspension (Less than 1%)
Prevacid NapraPAC 375 (Less than 1%)
Prevacid NapraPAC 500 (Less than 1%)

Prevacid SoluTab Delayed-Release Tablets (Less than 1%)
PREVPAC (Less than 1%)
Prilosec Delayed-Release Capsules (Less than 1%)
Prilosec OTC Tablets (Less than 1%)
ProSom Tablets (Infrequent)
Prozac Pulvules and Liquid (Infrequent)
Relpax Tablets (Infrequent)
Remeron SolTab Tablets (Frequent)
Reminyl Oral Solution (Infrequent)
Reminyl Tablets (Infrequent)
Requip Tablets (Infrequent)
Rilutek Tablets (Infrequent)
Risperdal Consta Injection (Frequent)
Risperdal M-Tab Tablets (Infrequent)
Risperdal Oral Solution (Infrequent)
Risperdal Tablets (Infrequent)
Rocaltrol Capsules
Rocaltrol Oral Solution
Roferon-A Injection (Infrequent)
Sarafem Pulvules (Infrequent)
Septra DS Tablets
Septra Grape Suspension
Septra Suspension
Septra Tablets
Seroquel Tablets (Infrequent)
Sonata Capsules (Frequent)
Sustiva Capsules (Less than 2%)
Tambocor Tablets (Less than 1%)
Tasmar Tablets (Infrequent)
▲ Topamax Sprinkle Capsules (1% to 3%)
▲ Topamax Tablets (1% to 3%)
Trileptal Oral Suspension
Trileptal Tablets
Xanax XR Tablets (Infrequent)
Xyrem Oral Solution (Infrequent)
Zoloft Oral Concentrate (Infrequent)
Zoloft Tablets (Infrequent)
Zomig Nasal Spray (Rare)
Zomig Tablets (Rare)
Zomig-ZMT Tablets (Rare)
Zyprexa Tablets
Zyprexa ZYDIS Orally Disintegrating Tablets

Auditory disturbances
Aralen Tablets
Navelbine Injection
▲ Wellbutrin Tablets (5.3%)

Awareness, altered
Diprivan Injectable Emulsion (Less than 1%)
Halcion Tablets

Awareness, heightened
Demser Capsules
Imitrex Tablets (Rare)
▲ Marinol Capsules (8% to 24%)

Behavior, hypochondriacal
Ativan Injection (Occasional)
Celontin Capsules

Behavior, inappropriate
Diprivan Injectable Emulsion (Less
  than 1%)
Halcion Tablets
Phenergan Suppositories
Phenergan Tablets
ProSom Tablets
Ritalin Hydrochloride Tablets
Ritalin LA Capsules
Ritalin-SR Tablets
Serentil Ampuls
Serentil Concentrate
Serentil Tablets
Symmetrel Syrup
Symmetrel Tablets
Tessalon Capsules (Isolated instances)
Tessalon Perles (Isolated instances)
Xanax Tablets (Rare)
Zovirax for Injection

Behavior, schizophrenic
Zonegran Capsules (2%)

Behavior, violent
Accutane Capsules
Amnesteem Capsules
Guanfacine
Invanz for Injection (Greater than 0.1%)
Prozac Pulvules and Liquid
Sarafem Pulvules
Zovirax Capsules
Zovirax Suspension
Zovirax Tablets

Behavioral changes
Ambien Tablets
Amoxil Capsules (Rare)
Amoxil Chewable Tablets (Rare)
Amoxil for Oral Suspension (Rare)
Amoxil Pediatric Drops for Oral
  Suspension (Rare)
Amoxil Tablets (Rare)
Augmentin Chewable Tablets (Rare)
Augmentin ES-600 Powder for Oral
  Suspension (Rare)
Augmentin Powder for Oral
  Suspension (Rare)

Augmentin Tablets (Rare)
Augmentin XR Tablets (Rare)
Biaxin Filmtab Tablets
Biaxin Granules
Biaxin XL Filmtab Tablets
Catapres Tablets
Catapres-TTS (0.5% or less)
Clorpres Tablets
Cosopt Sterile Ophthalmic Solution
Cytotec Tablets (Infrequent)
Eldepryl Capsules
Fortovase Capsules (Less than 2%)
Gastrocrom Oral Concentrate (Less
  common)
▲ Klonopin Tablets (5% to 25%)
▲ Klonopin Wafers (5% to 25%)
Mellaril
Nadolol Tablets (6 of 1000 patients)
Neurontin Capsules
Neurontin Oral Solution
Neurontin Tablets
▲ Orap Tablets (27.7%)
PREVPAC
Priftin Tablets
Rifadin Capsules
Rifadin IV
Rifater Tablets
▲ Roferon-A Injection (3%)
Thioridazine Hydrochloride Tablets
Timoptic in Ocudose (Less frequent)
Timoptic Sterile Ophthalmic Solution
  (Less frequent)
Timoptic-XE Sterile Ophthalmic Gel
  Forming Solution
Uniphyl 400 mg and 600 mg Tablets
Valtrex Caplets
Zyprexa Tablets
Zyprexa ZYDIS Orally Disintegrating
  Tablets

Behavioral deterioration
Depacon Injection
Depakene Capsules
Depakene Syrup
Depakote ER Tablets
Depakote Sprinkle Capsules
Depakote Tablets

Bulimia
Paxil CR Controlled-Release Tablets
Paxil Oral Suspension (Rare)
Paxil Tablets (Rare)

Catatonia
Blocadren Tablets

Celexa Oral Solution (Rare)
Celexa Tablets (Rare)
Chlorpromazine (Rare)
Corzide 40/5 Tablets
Corzide 80/5 Tablets
Cosopt Sterile Ophthalmic Solution
Depacon Injection (1% or more)
Depakene Capsules (1% or more)
Depakene Syrup (1% or more)
Depakote ER Tablets (Greater than 1%)
Depakote Sprinkle Capsules
▲ Depakote Tablets (1% to 5%)
Effexor Tablets
Effexor XR Capsules
Haldol Decanoate 50 Injection
Haldol Decanoate 100 Injection
Inderal LA Long-Acting Capsules
Nadolol Tablets
Phenergan Suppositories
Phenergan Tablets
Prochlorperazine
Relpax Tablets (Rare)
Risperdal M-Tab Tablets (Infrequent)
Risperdal Oral Solution (Infrequent)
Risperdal Tablets (Infrequent)
Seroquel Tablets (Infrequent)
Tenormin I.V. Injection
Tenormin Tablets
Timolide Tablets
Timoptic in Ocudose
Timoptic Sterile Ophthalmic Solution
Timoptic-XE Sterile Ophthalmic Gel Forming Solution
Toprol-XL Tablets
Triavil Tablets
Trifluoperazine
Trilafon
Zebeta Tablets
Ziac Tablets

Central nervous system depression

Anaprox DS Tablets (Less than 1%)
Anaprox Tablets (Less than 1%)
Ativan Injection
Cerebyx Injection (Infrequent)
Depacon Injection
Depakene Capsules
Depakene Syrup
Depakote ER Tablets
Depakote Tablets
EC-Naprosyn Delayed-Release Tablets (Less than 1%)

EMLA Anesthetic Disc (Unlikely with disc)
EMLA Cream (Unlikely with cream)
Fluvoxamine maleate (Infrequent)
▲ Klonopin Tablets (Most frequent)
▲ Klonopin Wafers (Most frequent)
Lamictal Chewable Dispersible Tablets (Infrequent)
Lamictal Tablets (Infrequent)
Mebaral Tablets (Less than 1 in 100 patients)
Naprosyn Suspension (Less than 1%)
Naprosyn Tablets (Less than 1%)
Nembutal Sodium Solution (Less than 1%)
Neurontin Capsules
Neurontin Oral Solution
Neurontin Tablets
Prozac Pulvules and Liquid (Infrequent)
Rilutek Tablets (Rare)
Sarafem Pulvules (Infrequent)
Seconal (Less than 1%)
▲ Vesanoid Capsules (3%)
▲ Xanax Tablets (13.8% to 13.9%)
Xanax XR Tablets

Central nervous system depression, neonatal

Halcion Tablets
Streptomycin Sulfate Injection

Central nervous system reactions

Attenuvax
Azulfidine EN-tabs Tablets
BuSpar Tablets
▲ Cipro I.V. Pharmacy Bulk Package (Among most frequent)
Clozapine Tablets
Clozaril Tablets
Digitek Tablets
Hexalen Capsules
▲ Intron A for Injection (Less than 5%)
Lanoxicaps Capsules (Rare)
Lanoxin Elixir Pediatric
Lanoxin Injection
Lanoxin Injection Pediatric
Lanoxin Tablets
Lariam Tablets
▲ Leukine (11%)
▲ Nipent for Injection (1% to 11%)
Noroxin Tablets
Orap Tablets
Orthoclone OKT3 Sterile Solution

▲ Paraplatin for Injection (5%)
Prochlorperazine
▲ Roferon-A Injection (Less than 5%)
Serentil Ampuls
Serentil Concentrate
Serentil Tablets
Silvadene Cream (1%)
Stalevo Tablets
Trifluoperazine

Central nervous system stimulation

Adipex-P Capsules
Adipex-P Tablets
Avelox I.V.
Avelox Tablets
Axert Tablets (Infrequent)
Balamine DM Oral Drops
Balamine DM Syrup
Cipro I.V.
Cipro Oral Suspension
Cipro Tablets
Cipro XR Tablets
Combivent Inhalation Aerosol
Effexor Tablets (Infrequent)
Effexor XR Capsules (Infrequent)
EMLA Anesthetic Disc (Unlikely with disc)
EMLA Cream (Unlikely with cream)
Floxin Tablets
Fluvoxamine maleate (2%)
Kytril Injection (Less than 2%)
Lamictal Chewable Dispersible Tablets (Rare)
Lamictal Tablets (Rare)
Lidoderm Patch
Lindane Lotion 1%
Lindane Shampoo 1%
Meridia Capsules (1.5%)
Mirapex Tablets (Less than 1%)
Nefazodone
Noroxin Tablets
Paxil Oral Suspension (Frequent)
Paxil Tablets (Frequent)
Prozac Pulvules and Liquid (Infrequent)
Sarafem Pulvules (Infrequent)
Tequin Injection
Tequin Tablets
Trovan I.V.
Trovan Tablets
▲ Ultram Tablets (7% to 14%)
Ventolin HFA Inhalation Aerosol
VoSpire Extended-Release Tablets

Wellbutrin SR Sustained-Release Tablets (1% to 2%)
Wellbutrin XL Extended-Release Tablets (1% to 2%)
Zyban Sustained-Release Tablets (Infrequent)
Zyprexa Tablets (Infrequent)
Zyprexa ZYDIS Orally Disintegrating Tablets (Infrequent)
Zyrtec-D 12 Hour Extended Relief Tablets

Central nervous system stimulation, paradoxical

Halcion Tablets
Numorphan Injection
Numorphan Suppositories

Cognitive dysfunction

Ambien Tablets (Infrequent)
Amerge Tablets (Infrequent)
Anaprox DS Tablets (Less than 1%)
Anaprox Tablets (Less than 1%)
EC-Naprosyn Delayed-Release Tablets (Rare)
Floxin Tablets (Less than 1%)
▲ Naprelan Tablets (3% to 9%)
Naprosyn Suspension (Less than 1%)
Naprosyn Tablets (Less than 1%)
Orthoclone OKT3 Sterile Solution
Prevacid NapraPAC 375 (Less than 1%)
Prevacid NapraPAC 500 (Less than 1%)
Rescriptor Tablets
Risperdal M-Tab Tablets
Risperdal Oral Solution
Risperdal Tablets
Trexall Tablets
Ultracet Tablets
Ultram Tablets (Less than 1%)
▲ Xanax Tablets (28.8%)

Coma

Aciphex Tablets
Aggrenox Capsules (Less than 1%)
Aloprim for Injection (Less than 1%)
AmBisome for Injection (Less common)
Arthrotec Tablets (Rare)
Ativan Injection (Less than 1%)
▲ Avinza Capsules (Less than 5%)
Bicillin C-R 900/300 Injection
Bicillin C-R Injection
Bicillin L-A Injection

Buprenex Injectable (Infrequent)
Busulfex Injection (One patient)
Campath Ampules
Cataflam Tablets (Rarely)
Cerebyx Injection (Infrequent)
Cognex Capsules (Rare)
Copaxone for Injection (Infrequent)
Copegus Tablets (Less than 1%)
Dalmane Capsules
DDAVP Injection 4 mcg/mL (Rare)
DDAVP Nasal Spray (Rare)
Depacon Injection (Rare)
Depakene Capsules (Rare)
Depakene Syrup (Rare)
Depakote ER Tablets (Rare)
Depakote Sprinkle Capsules (Rare)
Depakote Tablets (Rare)
Desmopressin Acetate Injection (Rare)
Ecotrin Enteric Coated Aspirin Low,
  Regular and Maximum Strength
  Tablets
Elavil
Elspar for Injection
Ergamisol Tablets
Eskalith Capsules
Eskalith CR Controlled-Release
  Tablets
Evoxac Capsules (Less than 1%)
Felbatol Oral Suspension
Felbatol Tablets
Feldene Capsules (Rare)
Fludara for Injection
Fluvoxamine maleate (Rare)
Fortaz for Injection
Fortaz Injection
Foscavir Injection (Less than 1%)
Gabitril Tablets (Infrequent)
Indocin Capsules (Less than 1%)
Indocin I.V. (Less than 1%)
Indocin Oral Suspension (Less than
  1%)
Indocin Suppositories (Less than 1%)
▲ Intron A for Injection (Less than 5%)
Klonopin Tablets
Klonopin Wafers
Levaquin in 5% Dextrose Injection
  (0.1% to 1%)
Levaquin Injection (0.1% to 1%)
Levaquin Tablets (0.1% to 1%)
Matulane Capsules
Motrin Suspension, Oral Drops,
  Chewable Tablets, and Caplets (Rare;
  less than 1%)
Nardil Tablets (Less frequent)

Naropin Injection (Less than 1%)
Oncaspar
Orthoclone OKT3 Sterile Solution
Permax Tablets (Infrequent)
Pfizerpen for Injection
PhosLo Gelcaps
PhosLo Tablets
Ponstel Capsules (Rare)
Prochlorperazine
Prograf Capsules and Injection
Proleukin for Injection (1%)
Prozac Pulvules and Liquid (Rare)
ReoPro Vials (0.4%)
Requip Tablets (Infrequent)
Rilutek Tablets (Infrequent)
Risperdal M-Tab Tablets (Rare)
Risperdal Oral Solution (Rare)
Risperdal Tablets (Rare)
Roferon-A Injection (Rare to
  infrequent)
Rythmol Tablets (Less than 1%)
Sarafem Pulvules (Rare)
St. Joseph 81 mg Aspirin
Streptomycin Sulfate Injection
  (Occasional)
Stromectol Tablets
Symbyax Capsules (Infrequent)
Symmetrel Syrup
Symmetrel Tablets
Tigan Capsules
Tigan Injectable
Tigan Suppositories
Triavil Tablets
▲ Trisenox Injection (5%)
Ultram Tablets
Valtrex Caplets
▲ Vesanoid Capsules (3%)
VFEND I.V. (Less than 1%)
VFEND Oral Suspension (Less than
  1%)
VFEND Tablets (Less than 1%)
Voltaren Tablets (Rare)
Voltaren-XR Tablets (Rare)
Wellbutrin SR Sustained-Release
  Tablets
Wellbutrin Tablets
Wellbutrin XL Extended-Release
  Tablets
Xyrem Oral Solution (Infrequent)
Zoloft Oral Concentrate (Rare)
Zoloft Tablets (Rare)
Zovirax Capsules
Zovirax for Injection (Approximately
  1%)

Zovirax Suspension
Zovirax Tablets
Zyban Sustained-Release Tablets
Zyprexa Tablets (Infrequent)
Zyprexa ZYDIS Orally Disintegrating
Tablets (Infrequent)

Combativeness

Diprivan Injectable Emulsion (Less
than 1%)
Orthoclone OKT3 Sterile Solution
Zosyn (1% or less)
Zosyn in Galaxy Containers (1.0% or
less)

Confusion

Abilify Tablets (1% or greater)
Aciphex Tablets (Rare)
Actimmune (Rare)
▲ Actiq (1% to 6%)
Adalat CC Tablets (Less than 1%)
Aggrenox Capsules (1.1%)
▲ Agrylin Capsules (1% to 5%)
Aldoclor Tablets
Aldoril Tablets
Alferon N Injection (One patient to
3%)
Ambien Tablets (Frequent)
▲ AmBisome for Injection (8.6% to
12.9%)
Amerge Tablets (Rare)
Amicar Injection
Amicar Syrup, 25%
Amicar Tablets
Amoxil Capsules (Rare)
Amoxil Chewable Tablets (Rare)
Amoxil for Oral Suspension (Rare)
Amoxil Pediatric Drops for Oral
Suspension (Rare)
Amoxil Tablets (Rare)
▲ Amphotec (5% or more)
▲ Anafranil (3%)
Ancobon Capsules
Androderm Transdermal System (Less
than 1%)
Angiomax for Injection (Rare)
Anzemet Injection (Infrequent)
Anzemet Tablets (Infrequent)
Aricept Tablets
▲ Arimidex Tablets (2% to 5%)
▲ Arixtra Injection (1.2% to 3.1%)
▲ Aromasin Tablets (2% to 5%)
Arthrotec Tablets (Rare)
Asacol Delayed-Release Tablets
Astelin Nasal Spray

Ativan Injection (1.3%)
Augmentin Chewable Tablets (Rare)
Augmentin ES-600 Powder for Oral
Suspension (Rare)
Augmentin Powder for Oral
Suspension (Rare)
Augmentin Tablets (Rare)
Augmentin XR Tablets (Rare)
Avalide Tablets
Avelox I.V. (0.05% to 1%)
Avelox Tablets (0.05% to 1%)
▲ Avinza Capsules (Less than 5%)
Benztropine
Betaseron for SC Injection
Bextra Tablets (0.1% to 1.9%)
Biaxin Filmtab Tablets
Biaxin Granules
Biaxin XL Filmtab Tablets
Bicillin C-R 900/300 Injection
Bicillin C-R Injection
Bicillin L-A Injection
Brevibloc Concentrate (About 2%)
Brevibloc Double Strength Injection
(About 2%)
Brevibloc Double Strength Premixed
Injection (About 2%)
Brevibloc Injection (About 2%)
Brevibloc Premixed Injection (About
2%)
BuSpar Tablets (2%)
▲ Busulfex Injection (11%)
Campath Ampules
▲ Camptosar Injection (Up to 7%)
Captopril Tablets
Carbatrol Capsules
Cardene I.V. (Rare)
Cardura Tablets (Less than 0.5%)
▲ Casodex Tablets (2% to 5%)
Cataflam Tablets (Occasional)
Ceclor Pulvules (Rare)
Ceclor Suspension (Rare)
Cefzil for Oral Suspension (Less than
1%)
Cefzil Tablets (Less than 1%)
Celexa Oral Solution (Frequent)
Celexa Tablets (Frequent)
▲ CellCept Capsules (3% to less than
20%)
▲ CellCept Intravenous (3% to less than
20%)
▲ CellCept Oral Suspension (3% to less
than 20%)
▲ CellCept Tablets (3% to less than
20%)
Celontin Capsules

Cerebyx Injection (Infrequent)
Cipro I.V. (1% or less)
Cipro I.V. Pharmacy Bulk Package (Less than 1%)
Cipro Oral Suspension
Cipro Tablets
Cipro XR Tablets
▲ Clozapine Tablets (3%)
▲ Clozaril Tablets (3%)
▲ Cognex Capsules (7%)
Copaxone for Injection (2%)
Cosopt Sterile Ophthalmic Solution
Covera-HS Tablets (Less than 2%)
Cozaar Tablets (Less than 1%)
Cubicin for Injection (1% to 2%)
Cytotec Tablets
Cytovene Capsules (At least 3 subjects)
Cytovene-IV (At least 3 subjects)
Dalmane Capsules (Rare)
Dantrium Capsules (Less frequent)
Daranide Tablets
▲ DaunoXome Injection (Less than or equal to 5%)
Demser Capsules
▲ Depacon Injection (1% to 5%)
▲ Depakene Capsules (1% to 5%)
▲ Depakene Syrup (1% to 5%)
▲ Depakote ER Tablets (1% to 5%)
▲ Depakote Sprinkle Capsules (1% to 5%)
▲ Depakote Tablets (1% to 5%)
▲ DepoCyt Injection (4% to 14%)
▲ Desyrel (4.9%)
Diamox Sequels Sustained-Release Capsules
Didronel Tablets
Digitek Tablets
▲ Dilantin Infatabs (Among most common)
▲ Dilantin Kapseals (Among most common)
▲ Dilantin-125 Oral Suspension (Among most common)
Diovan HCT Tablets
Diprivan Injectable Emulsion (Less than 1%)
▲ Ditropan XL Extended Release Tablets (2% to 5%)
Diuril Oral Suspension
Diuril Sodium Intravenous
Diuril Tablets
Dolobid Tablets (Less than 1 in 100)
Doral
Dostinex Tablets

Doxil Injection (Less than 1%)
▲ Duragesic Transdermal System (10% or more)
Dyazide Capsules
Ecotrin Enteric Coated Aspirin Low, Regular and Maximum Strength Tablets
Edecrin Sodium Intravenous
Edecrin Tablets
Effexor Tablets (2%)
Effexor XR Capsules (Frequent)
Elavil
▲ Eldepryl Capsules (3 of 49 patients)
Elspar for Injection
Emend Capsules (Greater than 0.5%)
EMLA Anesthetic Disc (Unlikely with disc)
EMLA Cream (Unlikely with cream)
▲ Entocort EC Capsules (Less than 5%)
Ergamisol Tablets (Less frequent)
Ery-Tab Tablets (Isolated reports)
Erythrocin Stearate Filmtab Tablets (Isolated reports)
Erythromycin Base Filmtab Tablets (Isolated reports)
Erythromycin Delayed-Release Capsules (Isolated reports)
Eskalith Capsules
Eskalith CR Controlled-Release Tablets
Evoxac Capsules (Less than 1%)
▲ Exelon Capsules (8%)
▲ Exelon Oral Solution (8%)
Famvir Tablets (Infrequent)
Felbatol Oral Suspension
Felbatol Tablets
Feldene Capsules (Occasional)
▲ Flolan for Injection (6%)
Floxin Tablets (Less than 1%)
Fludara for Injection
Flumadine Syrup (Less than 0.3%)
Flumadine Tablets (Less than 0.3%)
Fluvoxamine maleate
Fortovase Capsules (Less than 2%)
▲ Foscavir Injection (5% or greater)
Frova Tablets (Infrequent)
▲ Gabitril Tablets (5%)
Ganite Injection
Gengraf Capsules (1% to less than 3%)
Geodon Capsules (Frequent)
Glucotrol XL Extended Release Tablets (Less than 1%)
Grifulvin V Tablets Microsize and Oral Suspension Microsize (Occasional)

Gris-PEG Tablets (Occasional)
Guanfacine (3% or less)
Guanidine Hydrochloride Tablets
Halcion Tablets (0.5% to 0.9%)
Haldol Decanoate 50 Injection
Haldol Decanoate 100 Injection
Herceptin I.V. (At least one of the 958
  patients)
Hivid Tablets (Less than 1%)
▲ Humira Injection (Less than 5%)
HydroDIURIL Tablets
Hyzaar 50-12.5 Tablets
Hyzaar 100-25 Tablets
Imitrex Injection (Infrequent)
Imitrex Nasal Spray (Infrequent)
Imitrex Tablets (Infrequent)
Indocin Capsules (Less than 1%)
Indocin Oral Suspension (Less than
  1%)
Indocin Suppositories (Less than 1%)
▲ Infergen (4%)
▲ Intron A for Injection (Up to 12%)
▲ Invanz for Injection (3.3% to 5.1%)
Invirase Capsules (Less than 2%)
Isoptin SR Tablets (1% or less)
Kadian Capsules (Less than 3%)
Kaletra Capsules (Less than 2%)
Kaletra Oral Solution (Less than 2%)
Keflex Pulvules
Keppra Oral Solution (1% or more)
Keppra Tablets (1% or more)
Klonopin Tablets (1%)
Klonopin Wafers (1%)
K-Phos Neutral Tablets
K-Phos Original (Sodium Free)
  Tablets (Less frequent)
Lamictal Chewable Dispersible
  Tablets (1.8%)
Lamictal Tablets (1.8%)
Lanoxicaps Capsules
Lanoxin Elixir Pediatric
Lanoxin Injection
Lanoxin Injection Pediatric
Lanoxin Tablets
Lariam Tablets (Occasional)
Leukeran Tablets (Rare)
Levaquin in 5% Dextrose Injection
  (0.1% to 1%)
Levaquin Injection (0.1% to 1%)
Levaquin Tablets (0.1% to 1%)
Lexapro Oral Solution (Infrequent)
Lexapro Tablets (Infrequent)
Lexxel Tablets
Librium Capsules

Lidoderm Patch
Limbitrol (Less common)
Lopid Tablets
Lotronex Tablets (Rare)
Lovenox Injection (2.2%)
Loxitane Capsules
Lupron Depot 3.75 mg
▲ Lupron Depot—4 Month 30 mg (Less
  than 5%)
Macrobid Capsules (Rare)
Macrodantin Capsules (Rare)
Marinol Capsules (Greater than 1%)
Matulane Capsules
Maxair Autohaler
Maxalt Tablets (Infrequent)
Maxalt-MLT Orally Disintegrating
  Tablets (Infrequent)
Mebaral Tablets (Less than 1 in 100
  patients)
Meridia Capsules
Merrem I.V. (Greater than 0.1% to 1%)
Mexitil Capsules (1.9% to 2.6%)
Midamor Tablets (Less than or equal
  to 1%)
Mintezol Chewable Tablets
Mintezol Suspension
▲ Mirapex Tablets (4% to 10%)
Mobic Tablets (Less than 2%)
Moduretic Tablets (Less than or equal
  to 1%)
Motrin Suspension, Oral Drops,
  Chewable Tablets, and Caplets (Less
  than 1%)
Mycobutin Capsules (More than one
  patient)
▲ Namenda Tablets (6%)
Naprelan Tablets (Less than 1%)
Naropin Injection (Less than 1%)
Natrecor for Injection (At least 1%)
▲ Nefazodone (7% to 8%)
Nembutal Sodium Solution (Less than
  1%)
Neoral Oral Solution (1% to less than
  3%)
Neoral Soft Gelatin Capsules (1% to
  less than 3%)
Neumega for Injection
Neurontin Capsules
Neurontin Oral Solution
Neurontin Tablets
Nexium Delayed-Release Capsules
  (Less than 1%)
Norflex Extended-Release Tablets
  (Infrequent)

Norflex Injection (Infrequent)
Noroxin Tablets
Norpramin Tablets
Norvir Oral Solution (Less than 2%)
Norvir Soft Gelatin Capsules (Less than 2%)
Nubain Injection (1% or less)
NuLev Orally Disintegrating Tablets
Numorphan Injection
Numorphan Suppositories
Oncaspar (Less than 1%)
▲ Ontak Vials (8%)
Orthoclone OKT3 Sterile Solution
▲ OxyContin Tablets (Between 1% and 5%)
Pamelor
Parnate Tablets
Paxil CR Controlled-Release Tablets (1%)
Paxil Oral Suspension (1%)
Paxil Tablets (1%)
Pepcid for Oral Suspension (Infrequent)
Pepcid Injection (Infrequent)
Pepcid Injection Premixed (Infrequent)
Pepcid Tablets (Infrequent)
Periactin Tablets
▲ Permax Tablets (11.1%)
Phenergan Suppositories
Phenobarbital (Less than 1%)
▲ Phenytek Capsules (Among most common)
PhosLo Gelcaps
PhosLo Tablets
▲ Photofrin for Injection (8%)
Plavix Tablets
Ponstel Capsules (Occasional)
Prevacid Delayed-Release Capsules (Less than 1%)
Prevacid for Delayed-Release Oral Suspension (Less than 1%)
Prevacid NapraPAC 375 (Less than 1%)
Prevacid NapraPAC 500 (Less than 1%)
Prevacid SoluTab Delayed-Release Tablets (Less than 1%)
▲ PREVPAC (Less than 1% to 3%)
Prilosec Delayed-Release Capsules (Less than 1%)
Prilosec OTC Tablets (Less than 1%)
Primaxin I.M.
Primaxin I.V. (Less than 0.2%)

Prinivil Tablets (0.3% to 1%)
Prinzide Tablets
ProAmatine Tablets (Less frequent)
▲ Prograf Capsules and Injection (3% to 15%)
▲ Proleukin for Injection (34%)
▲ Prometrium Capsules (100 mg, 200 mg) (Less than 5%)
ProSom Tablets (2%)
Protonix I.V. (Less than 1%)
Protonix Tablets (Less than 1%)
Provigil Tablets (1%)
Prozac Pulvules and Liquid (Frequent)
▲ Rapamune Oral Solution and Tablets (3% to 20%)
Relafen Tablets (Less than 1%)
Relpax Tablets (Infrequent)
Remeron SolTab Tablets (2%)
Remicade for IV Injection (Greater than or equal to 0.2%)
Reminyl Oral Solution (Greater than or equal to 2%)
Reminyl Tablets (Greater than or equal to 2%)
ReoPro Vials (0.6%)
▲ Requip Tablets (5%)
Rescriptor Tablets
Retrovir Capsules
Retrovir IV Infusion
Retrovir Syrup
Retrovir Tablets
Reyataz Capsules (Less than 3%)
Rifadin Capsules
Rifadin IV
Rifamate Capsules
Rifater Tablets
Rilutek Tablets (Infrequent)
Risperdal Consta Injection (Infrequent)
Risperdal M-Tab Tablets (Infrequent)
Risperdal Oral Solution (Infrequent)
Risperdal Tablets (Infrequent)
▲ Roferon-A Injection (Less than 4% to 8%)
Romazicon Injection (Less than 1%)
Rythmol Tablets (Less than 1%)
Salagen Tablets (Less than 1%)
Sandimmune I.V. Ampuls for Infusion (2% or less)
Sandimmune Oral Solution (2% or less)
Sandimmune Soft Gelatin Capsules (2% or less)
▲ Sandostatin LAR Depot (5% to 15%)
Sarafem Pulvules (Frequent)

Seconal (Less than 1%)
Sedapap Tablets 50 mg/650 mg (Infrequent)
Serentil Ampuls
Serentil Concentrate
Serentil Tablets
Seroquel Tablets (Infrequent)
Sinequan Capsules (Infrequent)
Sinequan Oral Concentrate (Infrequent)
Soma Tablets
Sonata Capsules (1% or less)
St. Joseph 81 mg Aspirin
Stadol Injection (Greater than or equal to 1%)
Stadol NS (Greater than or equal to 1%)
Stalevo Tablets
Stromectol Tablets
Sular Tablets (Less than or equal to 1%)
Surmontil Capsules
Sustiva Capsules (Less than 2%)
Symbyax Capsules (Infrequent)
▲ Symmetrel Syrup (0.1% to 5%)
▲ Symmetrel Tablets (0.1% to 5%)
Synercid I.V. (Less than 1%)
Tagamet Injection (Occasional)
Tagamet Liquid (Occasional)
Tagamet Tablets (Occasional)
Tambocor Tablets (Less than 1%)
Tamiflu Capsules
Tamiflu Oral Suspension
Targretin Capsules
Tarka Tablets
▲ Tasmar Tablets (10% to 11%)
Taxotere Injection Concentrate
Tegretol Chewable Tablets
Tegretol Suspension
Tegretol Tablets
Tegretol-XR Tablets
▲ Temodar Capsules (5%)
Tequin Injection (Less than 0.1%)
Tequin Tablets (Less than 0.1%)
Tessalon Capsules
Tessalon Perles
Thalomid Capsules
Timolide Tablets (Less than 1%)
Timoptic in Ocudose (Less frequent)
Timoptic Sterile Ophthalmic Solution (Less frequent)
Timoptic-XE Sterile Ophthalmic Gel Forming Solution
Tofranil

Tofranil-PM
▲ Topamax Sprinkle Capsules (4% to 14%)
▲ Topamax Tablets (4% to 14%)
Toprol-XL Tablets
Transderm Scop Transdermal Therapeutic System (Infrequent)
Tranxene T-TAB Tablets (Less common)
Tranxene-SD Half Strength Tablets (Less common)
Tranxene-SD Tablets (Less common)
▲ Trasylol Injection (4%)
Trental Tablets (Less than 1%)
Trexall Tablets
Triavil Tablets
Tricor Tablets (Less than 1%)
Trileptal Oral Suspension (1% to 2%)
Trileptal Tablets (1% to 2%)
Trilisate Liquid (Rare)
Trilisate Tablets (Rare)
▲ Trisenox Injection (5%)
Trovan I.V. (Less than 1%)
Trovan Tablets (Less than 1%)
Ultracet Tablets (At least 1%)
▲ Ultram Tablets (1% to 5%)
Uroqid-Acid No. 2 Tablets
▲ Valcyte Tablets (Less than 5%)
Valium Tablets (Infrequent)
Valtrex Caplets
Vantin Tablets and Oral Suspension (Less than 1%)
Vaseretic Tablets
Vasotec I.V. Injection (0.5% to 1%)
Verelan PM Capsules (2% or less)
▲ Vesanoid Capsules (14%)
VFEND I.V. (Less than 1%)
VFEND Oral Suspension (Less than 1%)
VFEND Tablets (Less than 1%)
Vicoprofen Tablets (Less than 3%)
Vioxx Oral Suspension
Vioxx Tablets
Vistide Injection
Vivactil Tablets
Voltaren Tablets (Occasional)
Voltaren-XR Tablets (Occasional)
Wellbutrin SR Sustained-Release Tablets
▲ Wellbutrin Tablets (8.4%)
Wellbutrin XL Extended-Release Tablets
▲ Xanax Tablets (9.9% to 10.4%)
Xanax XR Tablets (1.5%)

▲ Xeloda Tablets (Less than 5%)
Xylocaine 2% Jelly
▲ Xyrem Oral Solution (3% to 13%)
Zantac 150 EFFERdose Granules
(Rare)
Zantac 150 EFFERdose Tablets (Rare)
Zantac 150 Tablets (Rare)
Zantac 300 Tablets (Rare)
Zantac Injection (Rare)
Zantac Injection Premixed (Rare)
Zantac Syrup (Rare)
Zestoretic Tablets
Zestril Tablets (0.3% to 1.0%)
Zoloft Oral Concentrate (Infrequent)
Zoloft Tablets (Infrequent)
▲ Zometa for Intravenous Infusion
(12.8%)
Zomig Nasal Spray (Infrequent)
▲ Zonegran Capsules (6%)
Zosyn (1% or less)
Zosyn in Galaxy Containers (1% or
less)
Zovirax Capsules
Zovirax for Injection (Approximately
1%)
Zovirax Suspension
Zovirax Tablets
Zyban Sustained-Release Tablets
(Infrequent)
Zyprexa IntraMuscular (Infrequent)
Zyprexa Tablets
Zyprexa ZYDIS Orally Disintegrating
Tablets
Zyrtec Syrup (Less than 2%)
Zyrtec Tablets (Less than 2%)
Zyrtec-D 12 Hour Extended Relief
Tablets (Less than 2%)

Confusion, nocturnal
Mellaril
Thioridazine Hydrochloride Tablets
(Extremely rare)
Trilafon

Consciousness, disorders of
Amerge Tablets (Rare)
Comtan Tablets
Hexalen Capsules
▲ Intron A for Injection (Less than 5%)
Neoral Oral Solution
Neoral Soft Gelatin Capsules
Permax Tablets
Sandimmune I.V. Ampuls for Infusion
Sandimmune Oral Solution
Sandimmune Soft Gelatin Capsules

Symmetrel Syrup (Uncommon)
Symmetrel Tablets (Uncommon)
Tasmar Tablets (Four cases)
Valtrex Caplets
Zovirax Capsules
Zovirax Suspension
Zovirax Tablets

Delirium
Abilify Tablets (Rare)
Aciphex Tablets
Amicar Injection
Amicar Syrup, 25%
Amicar Tablets
Ativan Injection (1.3%)
▲ Avinza Capsules (Less than 5%)
Brevital Sodium for Injection
Busulfex Injection (2%)
Catapres Tablets
Catapres-TTS (0.5% or less)
Celexa Oral Solution
Celexa Tablets
▲ CellCept Capsules (3% to less than
20%)
▲ CellCept Intravenous (3% to less than
20%)
▲ CellCept Oral Suspension (3% to less
than 20%)
▲ CellCept Tablets (3% to less than
20%)
Cerebyx Injection
Cipro I.V.
Cipro I.V. Pharmacy Bulk Package
Cipro Oral Suspension
Cipro Tablets
Cipro XR Tablets
Clorpres Tablets
Clozapine Tablets
Clozaril Tablets
Cognex Capsules (Infrequent)
Digitek Tablets
Diprivan Injectable Emulsion (Less
than 1%)
Effexor Tablets
Effexor XR Capsules
Evoxac Capsules
Exelon Capsules (Infrequent)
Exelon Oral Solution (Infrequent)
Famvir Tablets (Infrequent)
Fluvoxamine maleate (Infrequent)
Geodon Capsules (Frequent)
Lamictal Chewable Dispersible
Tablets (Rare)
Lamictal Tablets (Rare)
Lanoxicaps Capsules

Lanoxin Elixir Pediatric
Lanoxin Injection
Lanoxin Injection Pediatric
Lanoxin Tablets
Levaquin in 5% Dextrose Injection
  (0.1% to 1%)
Levaquin Injection (0.1% to 1%)
Levaquin Tablets (0.1% to 1%)
Lexapro Oral Solution
Lexapro Tablets
Merrem I.V. (Greater than 0.1% to
  1%)
Namenda Tablets (Infrequent)
Nardil Tablets (Less frequent)
Orthoclone OKT3 Sterile Solution
  (Less than 1%)
Paxil CR Controlled-Release Tablets
Paxil Oral Suspension (Rare)
Paxil Tablets (Rare)
Phenergan Suppositories
Phenergan Tablets
Phenobarbital
PhosLo Gelcaps
PhosLo Tablets
Prograf Capsules and Injection
Remeron SolTab Tablets (Infrequent)
Reminyl Oral Solution (Infrequent)
Reminyl Tablets (Infrequent)
Requip Tablets (Infrequent)
Rilutek Tablets (Infrequent)
Risperdal Consta Injection
  (Infrequent)
Risperdal M-Tab Tablets (Rare)
Risperdal Oral Solution (Rare)
Risperdal Tablets (Rare)
Romazicon Injection (Less than 1%)
Seroquel Tablets (Rare)
Symmetrel Syrup
Symmetrel Tablets
Tasmar Tablets (Rare)
Topamax Sprinkle Capsules
  (Infrequent)
Topamax Tablets (Infrequent)
Trileptal Oral Suspension
Trileptal Tablets
VFEND I.V. (Less than 1%)
VFEND Oral Suspension (Less than
  1%)
VFEND Tablets (Less than 1%)
Vistide Injection
Wellbutrin SR Sustained-Release
  Tablets
Wellbutrin Tablets
Wellbutrin XL Extended-Release
  Tablets

Zovirax Capsules
Zovirax for Injection
Zovirax Suspension
Zovirax Tablets
Zyban Sustained-Release Tablets
Zyprexa Tablets (Infrequent)
Zyprexa ZYDIS Orally Disintegrating
  Tablets (Infrequent)

Delusions

Ambien Tablets (Rare)
Aricept Tablets (Frequent)
Celexa Oral Solution (Rare)
Celexa Tablets (Rare)
Clozapine Tablets (Less than 1%)
Clozaril Tablets (Less than 1%)
Effexor Tablets (Rare)
Effexor XR Capsules (Rare)
Elavil
Eldepryl Capsules
Evoxac Capsules
Exelon Capsules (2% or more)
Exelon Oral Solution (2% or more)
Felbatol Oral Suspension
Felbatol Tablets
Flexeril Tablets (Rare)
Fluvoxamine maleate (Infrequent)
Gabitril Tablets (Infrequent)
Halcion Tablets
Lamictal Chewable Dispersible
  Tablets (Rare)
Lamictal Tablets (Rare)
Limbitrol
▲ Lupron Depot 3.75 mg (Among most
  frequent)
▲ Lupron Depot—3 Month 11.25 mg
  (Less than 5%)
▲ Lupron Depot—3 Month 22.5 mg
  (Less than 5%)
Mirapex Tablets (1%)
Namenda Tablets (Infrequent)
Norpramin Tablets
Nubain Injection (1% or less)
Pamelor
Paxil CR Controlled-Release Tablets
Paxil Oral Suspension (Rare)
Paxil Tablets (Rare)
Permax Tablets (Infrequent)
Prozac Pulvules and Liquid (Rare)
Remeron SolTab Tablets (Infrequent)
Requip Tablets (Infrequent)
Rilutek Tablets (Infrequent)
Risperdal Consta Injection (Frequent)
Salagen Tablets (Rare)
Sarafem Pulvules (Rare)

Seroquel Tablets (Infrequent)
Sonata Capsules (Rare)
Stadol Injection
Stadol NS
Stalevo Tablets
Surmontil Capsules
Sustiva Capsules
Symmetrel Syrup
Symmetrel Tablets
Tasmar Tablets (Infrequent)
Topamax Sprinkle Capsules (Infrequent)
Topamax Tablets (Infrequent)
Triavil Tablets
Trileptal Oral Suspension
Trileptal Tablets
Vivactil Tablets
Wellbutrin SR Sustained-Release Tablets
Wellbutrin Tablets (1.2%)
Wellbutrin XL Extended-Release Tablets
Zoloft Oral Concentrate (Infrequent)
Zoloft Tablets (Infrequent)
Zyban Sustained-Release Tablets

Dementia

Ambien Tablets (Rare)
Depacon Injection (Several reports)
Depakene Capsules (Several reports)
Depakene Syrup (Several reports)
Depakote ER Tablets (Several reports)
Depakote Sprinkle Capsules (Several reports)
Depakote Tablets (Several reports)
Effexor Tablets (Rare)
Effexor XR Capsules (Rare)
Evoxac Capsules
Exelon Capsules (Infrequent)
Exelon Oral Solution (Infrequent)
▲ Foscavir Injection (Between 1% and 5%)
Hivid Tablets (Less than 1%)
▲ Lupron Depot—4 Month 30 mg (Less than 5%)
Premarin Tablets
Premphase Tablets
Prempro Tablets
Relpax Tablets (Rare)
Remeron SolTab Tablets (Rare)
Requip Tablets (Infrequent)
Rilutek Tablets (Rare)
Risperdal Consta Injection (Infrequent)
Stalevo Tablets

▲ Vesanoid Capsules (3%)
VFEND I.V. (Less than 1%)
VFEND Oral Suspension (Less than 1%)
VFEND Tablets (Less than 1%)
Vistide Injection
Zanaflex Tablets (Rare)

Depersonalization

Abilify Tablets (1% or less)
Ambien Tablets (Rare)
Anzemet Injection (Infrequent)
Anzemet Tablets (Infrequent)
Astelin Nasal Spray (Infrequent)
Avelox I.V. (Less than 0.1%)
Avelox Tablets (Less than 0.1%)
Betaseron for SC Injection
Biaxin Filmtab Tablets
Biaxin Granules
Biaxin XL Filmtab Tablets
Buprenex Injectable (Infrequent)
BuSpar Tablets (Infrequent)
Caduet Tablets (Greater than 0.1% to less than or equal to 1%)
Cardura Tablets (Less than 0.5%)
Celexa Oral Solution (Infrequent)
Celexa Tablets (Infrequent)
Cerebyx Injection (Infrequent)
Cipro I.V. (1% or less)
Cipro I.V. Pharmacy Bulk Package (Less than 1%)
Cipro Oral Suspension (Less than 1%)
Cipro Tablets (Less than 1%)
Cipro XR Tablets (Less than 1%)
Copaxone for Injection (Infrequent)
Duragesic Transdermal System (Less than 1%)
Effexor Tablets (1%)
Effexor XR Capsules (Frequent)
Evoxac Capsules (Less than 1%)
Exelon Capsules (Infrequent)
Exelon Oral Solution (Infrequent)
Fluvoxamine maleate (Infrequent)
Frova Tablets (Infrequent)
Gabitril Tablets (Frequent)
Halcion Tablets
Hivid Tablets (Less than 1%)
Indocin Capsules (Less than 1%)
Indocin Oral Suspension (Less than 1%)
Indocin Suppositories (Less than 1%)
Klonopin Tablets (Infrequent)
Klonopin Wafers (Infrequent)
Kogenate FS

Lamictal Chewable Dispersible Tablets (Infrequent)
Lamictal Tablets (Infrequent)
Lexapro Oral Solution (Infrequent)
Lexapro Tablets (Infrequent)
Marinol Capsules (Greater than 1%)
Maxalt Tablets (Rare)
Maxalt-MLT Orally Disintegrating Tablets (Rare)
Namenda Tablets (Infrequent)
Nefazodone (Infrequent)
Neurontin Capsules (Infrequent)
Neurontin Oral Solution (Infrequent)
Neurontin Tablets (Infrequent)
Norvasc Tablets (More than 0.1% to 1%)
Nubain Injection (1% or less)
OxyContin Tablets (Less than 1%)
Paxil CR Controlled-Release Tablets (Infrequent)
Paxil Oral Suspension (Infrequent)
Paxil Tablets (Infrequent)
Prevacid Delayed-Release Capsules (Less than 1%)
Prevacid for Delayed-Release Oral Suspension (Less than 1%)
Prevacid NapraPAC 375 (Less than 1%)
Prevacid NapraPAC 500 (Less than 1%)
Prevacid SoluTab Delayed-Release Tablets (Less than 1%)
PREVPAC
Prozac Pulvules and Liquid (Infrequent)
Relpax Tablets (Infrequent)
Remeron SolTab Tablets (Infrequent)
Requip Tablets (Infrequent)
Rilutek Tablets (Infrequent)
Risperdal Consta Injection (Infrequent)
▲ Romazicon Injection (1% to 3%)
Sarafem Pulvules (Infrequent)
Seroquel Tablets (Infrequent)
Sonata Capsules (Less than 1% to 2%)
Symbyax Capsules (Infrequent)
Tambocor Tablets (Less than 1%)
Tequin Injection (Less than 0.1%)
Tequin Tablets (Less than 0.1%)
Topamax Sprinkle Capsules (1% to 2%)
Topamax Tablets (1% to 2%)
Trovan I.V. (Less than 1%)

Trovan Tablets (Less than 1%)
Ultracet Tablets (Less than 1%)
VFEND I.V. (Less than 1%)
VFEND Oral Suspension (Less than 1%)
VFEND Tablets (Less than 1%
Wellbutrin SR Sustained-Release Tablets (Infrequent)
Wellbutrin Tablets (Infrequent)
Wellbutrin XL Extended-Release Tablets (Infrequent)
Xanax Tablets
▲ Xanax XR Tablets (5.7%)
Xyrem Oral Solution (Infrequent)
Zanaflex Tablets (Infrequent)
Zoloft Oral Concentrate (Infrequent)
Zoloft Tablets (Infrequent)
Zomig Nasal Spray (Infrequent)
Zyban Sustained-Release Tablets (Infrequent)
Zyprexa Tablets (Infrequent)
Zyprexa ZYDIS Orally Disintegrating Tablets (Infrequent)
Zyrtec Syrup (Less than 2%)
Zyrtec Tablets (Less than 2%)
Zyrtec-D 12 Hour Extended Relief Tablets (Less than 2%)

Depression
Abilify Tablets (1% or greater)
Accupril Tablets (0.5% to 1%)
Accuretic Tablets (Greater than 0.5%)
Accutane Capsules
Aceon Tablets 2 mg, 4 mg, 8 mg (2.0%)
Aciphex Tablets
▲ Actimmune (3%)
Activella Tablets
▲ Actonel Tablets (2.3% to 6.8%)
Adalat CC Tablets (Less than 1%)
Adderall XR Capsules (0.7%)
Advair Diskus 100/50
Advair Diskus 250/50
Advair Diskus 500/50
▲ Aerobid Inhaler System (1% to 3%)
▲ Aerobid-M Inhaler System (1% to 3%)
▲ Agenerase Capsules (9% to 16%)
▲ Agenerase Oral Solution (4% to 16%)
▲ Agrylin Capsules (1% to 5%)
Aldoclor Tablets
Aldoril Tablets
Alesse-28 Tablets
Alferon N Injection (One patient to 3%)
▲ Alimta for Injection (14%)

▲ Alora Transdermal System (1% to 6%)
Altace Capsules (Less than 1%)
Altocor Extended-Release Tablets
Ambien Tablets (2%)
AmBisome for Injection (Less common
Amerge Tablets (Infrequent)
Amnesteem Capsules
▲ Amphotec (1% to 5%)
▲ Anafranil (5%)
▲ Androderm Transdermal System (3%)
AndroGel (Up to 1%)
▲ Arava Tablets (1% to 3%)
▲ Aricept Tablets (3%)
▲ Arimidex Tablets (2% to 11%)
▲ Aromasin Tablets (13%)
Arthrotec Tablets (Rare)
Asacol Delayed-Release Tablets
Astelin Nasal Spray (Infrequent)
Atacand HCT 16-12.5 Tablets (0.5% or greater)
Atacand HCT 32-12.5 Tablets (0.5% or greater)
Atacand Tablets (0.5% or greater)
Ativan Injection (1.3%)
Avalide Tablets
Avapro Tablets (Less than 1%)
Avelox I.V.
Avelox Tablets
▲ Avonex (18% to 20%)
Axert Tablets (Rare)
Aygestin Tablets
Azmacort Inhalation Aerosol
Azulfidine EN-tabs Tablets (Rare)
Beconase AQ Nasal Spray
Benztropine
▲ Betaseron for SC Injection (34%)
Betimol Ophthalmic Solution
Betoptic S Ophthalmic Suspension (Rare)
Bextra Tablets (0.1% to 1.9%)
Blocadren Tablets
Bravelle for Intramuscular or Subcutaneous Injection (2.7%)
Brevibloc Concentrate (Less than 1%)
Brevibloc Double Strength Injection (Less than 1%)
Brevibloc Double Strength Premixed Injection (Less than 1%)
Brevibloc Injection (Less than 1%)
Brevibloc Premixed Injection (Less than 1%)
Brevicon 28-Day Tablets

BuSpar Tablets (2%)
▲ Busulfex Injection (23%)
Caduet Tablets (Greater than 0.1% to less than 2%)
▲ Campath Ampules (1% to 7%)
Captopril Tablets
Carbatrol Capsules
Cardizem LA Extended Release Tablets (Less than 2%)
Cardura Tablets (1%)
▲ Carnitor Injection (5% to 6%)
▲ Casodex Tablets (4%)
Cataflam Tablets (Occasional)
Catapres Tablets (About 1 in 100 patients)
Catapres-TTS (0.5% or less)
Celebrex Capsules (0.1% to 1.9%)
Celexa Oral Solution (Frequent)
Celexa Tablets (Frequent)
▲ CellCept Capsules (3% to less than 20%)
▲ CellCept Intravenous (3% to less than 20%)
▲ CellCept Oral Suspension (3% to less than 20%)
▲ CellCept Tablets (3% to less than 20%)
Celontin Capsules
Cenestin Tablets, 0.3mg
▲ Cenestin Tablets, 0.45 mg, 0.625 mg, 0.9 mg, 1.25 mg (3.8% to 28%)
Cerebyx Injection (Infrequent)
Cipro I.V. (1% or less)
Cipro I.V. Pharmacy Bulk Package (Less than 1%)
Cipro Oral Suspension (Less than 1%)
Cipro Tablets (Less than 1%)
Cipro XR Tablets (Less than 1%)
▲ Climara Transdermal System (1% to 8%)
Clinoril Tablets (Less than 1%)
Clomid Tablets (Fewer than 1%)
Clorpres Tablets (About 1%)
Clozapine Tablets (1%)
Clozaril Tablets (1%)
▲ Cognex Capsules (4%)
Colazal Capsules
▲ CombiPatch Transdermal System (8% to 9%)
Concerta Extended-Release Tablets
Copaxone for Injection (At least 2%)
▲ Copegus Tablets (20%)
▲ Coreg Tablets (Greater than 1% to 3%)
Corzide 40/5 Tablets

Corzide 80/5 Tablets
Cosopt Sterile Ophthalmic Solution (Less than 1%)
Cozaar Tablets (Less than 1%)
Crestor Tablets (Greater than or equal to 2%)
▲ Crinone 4% Gel (19%)
▲ Crinone 8% Gel (11% to 15%)
Crixivan Capsules (Less than 2%)
Cylert Chewable Tablets
Cylert Tablets
Cytovene Capsules (At least 3 subjects)
Cytovene-IV (At least 3 subjects)
Dalmane Capsules (Rare)
Dantrium Capsules (Less frequent)
Daranide Tablets
▲ DaunoXome Injection (3% to 7%)
DDAVP Nasal Spray
Decadron Phosphate Injection
Decadron Tablets
Delatestryl Injection
Delestrogen Injection
Demser Capsules
▲ Depacon Injection (4% to 5%)
▲ Depakene Capsules (5%)
▲ Depakene Syrup (5%)
▲ Depakote ER Tablets (4% to 5%)
▲ Depakote Sprinkle Capsules (4% to 5%)
▲ Depakote Tablets (1% to 5%)
Desmopressin Acetate Rhinal Tube
Diamox Sequels Sustained-Release Capsules
Didronel Tablets
Digitek Tablets
Dilaudid Oral Liquid (Less frequent)
Dilaudid Tablets - 8 mg (Less frequent)
Dilaudid-HP Injection (Less frequent)
Dilaudid-HP Lyophilized Powder 250 mg (Less frequent)
Diovan HCT Tablets (Greater than 0.2%)
Dipentum Capsules (1.5%)
Diprivan Injectable Emulsion (Less than 1%)
Dolobid Tablets (Less than 1 in 100)
Doral
▲ Dostinex Tablets (3%)
▲ Doxil Injection (Less than 1% to 5%)
▲ Duragesic Transdermal System (3% to 10%)
DynaCirc Capsules (0.5% to 1%)
DynaCirc CR Tablets (0.5% to 1%)

8-MOP Capsules
Effexor Tablets (1%)
▲ Effexor XR Capsules (3%)
Eldepryl Capsules
Eligard 30 mg (1.1%)
Eligard 7.5 mg (Less than 2%)
Elmiron Capsules
▲ Eloxatin for Injection (2% to 5%)
Elspar for Injection
Emend Capsules (Greater than 0.5%)
▲ Emtriva Capsules (6% to 9%)
Enbrel for Injection (Infrequent)
Ergamisol Tablets (1% to 2%)
Esclim Transdermal System
Estrace Tablets
Estrace Vaginal Cream
Estrasorb Topical Emulsion
Estratest H.S. Tablets
Estratest Tablets
Estring Vaginal Ring (At least 1 report)
Estrostep 21 Tablets
Estrostep Fe Tablets
▲ Evista Tablets (6.4%)
▲ Evoxac Capsules (1% to 3%)
▲ Exelon Capsules (6%)
▲ Exelon Oral Solution (6%)
▲ Fabrazyme for Intravenous Infusion 3%)
Fareston Tablets
▲ Faslodex Injection (5.7%)
▲ Felbatol Oral Suspension (5.3%)
▲ Felbatol Tablets (5.3%)
Feldene Capsules (Occasional)
Femara Tablets (Less frequent
▲ femhrt Tablets (5.8%)
Femring Vaginal Ring
Flexeril Tablets (Less than 1%)
▲ Flolan for Injection (13% to 37%)
Florinef Acetate Tablets
Flovent 44 mcg Inhalation Aerosol
Flovent 110 mcg Inhalation Aerosol
Flovent 220 mcg Inhalation Aerosol
Flovent Rotadisk 50 mcg
Flovent Rotadisk 100 mcg
Flovent Rotadisk 250 mcg
Floxin Tablets (Less than 1%)
Fludara for Injection (Up to 1%)
Flumadine Syrup (0.3% to 1%)
Flumadine Tablets (0.3% to 1%)
Fluvoxamine maleate (2%)
Focalin Tablets
▲ Forteo Injection (4.1%)
Fortovase Capsules (2.7%)
▲ Foscavir Injection (5% or greater)

Frova Tablets (Infrequent)
▲ Fuzeon Injection (8.6%)
▲ Gabitril Tablets (3%)
Gastrocrom Oral Concentrate (Less common)
Gengraf Capsules (Rare)
Gleevec Tablets (Infrequent)
Glucotrol XL Extended Release Tablets (Less than 3%)
Guanfacine (3% or less)
Halcion Tablets (0.5% to 0.9%)
Haldol Decanoate 50 Injection
Haldol Decanoate 100 Injection
▲ Herceptin I.V. (6%)
Hivid Tablets (0.4%)
Hydrocortone Phosphate Injection, Sterile
Hydrocortone Tablets
Hytrin Capsules (0.3%)
Hyzaar 50-12.5 Tablets
Hyzaar 100-25 Tablets
Imitrex Injection (Rare)
Imitrex Nasal Spray (Infrequent)
Imitrex Tablets (Infrequent)
▲ Indapamide Tablets (Less than 5%)
Inderal LA Long-Acting Capsules
Indocin Capsules (Greater than 1%)
Indocin Oral Suspension (Greater than 1%)
Indocin Suppositories (Greater than 1%)
▲ Infergen (18% to 26%)
▲ Intron A for Injection (2% to 40%)
Invanz for Injection (Greater than 0.1%)
Invirase Capsules (Greater than or equal to 2%)
Kadian Capsules (Less than 3%)
Kaletra Capsules (Less than 2%)
Kaletra Oral Solution (Less than 2%)
▲ Keppra Oral Solution (4%)
▲ Keppra Tablets (4%)
▲ Klonopin Tablets (4% to 7%)
▲ Klonopin Wafers (4% to 7%)
▲ Lamictal Chewable Dispersible Tablets (4.2%)
▲ Lamictal Tablets (4.2%)
Lanoxicaps Capsules
Lanoxin Elixir Pediatric
Lanoxin Injection
Lanoxin Injection Pediatric
Lanoxin Tablets
Lariam Tablets (Occasional)
Lescol Capsules
Lescol XL Tablets

Levaquin in 5% Dextrose Injection (0.1% to 1%)
Levaquin Injection (0.1% to 1%)
Levaquin Tablets (0.1% to 1%)
Levlen 21 Tablets
Levlen 28 Tablets
Levlite 28 Tablets
Levora Tablets
Lexapro Oral Solution (Infrequent)
Lexapro Tablets (Infrequent)
▲ Lexiva Tablets (Less than 1% to 11%)
Lexxel Tablets
Lidoderm Patch
Lipitor Tablets (Less than 2%)
Lo/Ovral-28 Tablets
Loestrin 21 Tablets
Loestrin Fe Tablets
Lofibra Capsules
Lopid Tablets
Lotronex Tablets (2%)
Low-Ogestrel-28 Tablets
Lunelle Monthly Injection
▲ Lupron Depot 3.75 mg (16%)
▲ Lupron Depot—3 Month 11.25 mg (16%)
▲ Lupron Depot—3 Month 22.5 mg (Less than 5%)
▲ Lupron Depot—4 Month 30 mg (Less than 5%)
▲ Lupron Injection (Less than 5%)
Macrobid Capsules (Rare)
Macrodantin Capsules (Rare)
Malarone Pediatric Tablets (Less than 1%)
Malarone Tablets (Less than 1%)
Marinol Capsules (Less than 1%)
Matulane Capsules
Maxair Autohaler
Maxalt Tablets (Infrequent)
Maxalt-MLT Orally Disintegrating Tablets (Infrequent)
Maxzide Tablets
Maxzide-25 mg Tablets
Menest Tablets
▲ Meridia Capsules (4.3%)
Merrem I.V. (Greater than 0.1% to 1%)
Metadate CD Capsules
Metadate ER Tablets
MetroGel-Vaginal Gel (Less than 1%)
Mevacor Tablets (0.5% to 1%)
Mexitil Capsules (2.4%)
▲ Miacalcin Nasal Spray (1% to 3%)
Micardis HCT Tablets
Micardis Tablets (More than 0.3%)
Microgestin 1/20 Tablets

Microgestin 1.5/30 Tablets
Microgestin Fe 1/20 Tablets
Microgestin Fe 1.5/30 Tablets
Midamor Tablets (Less than or equal to 1%)
▲ Minipress Capsules (1% to 4%)
Minizide Capsules (Rare)
Mintezol Chewable Tablets
Mintezol Suspension
Mirapex Tablets (1% or more)
▲ Mirena Intrauterine System (5% or more)
Mithracin for Intravenous Use
Moban Oral Concentrate (Less frequent)
Moban Tablets (Less frequent)
Mobic Tablets (Less than 2%)
Moduretic Tablets (Less than or equal to 1%)
Motrin Suspension, Oral Drops, Chewable Tablets, and Caplets (Less than 1%)
MS Contin Tablets (Less frequent)
MSIR Oral Capsules (Less frequent)
MSIR Oral Solution Concentrate (Less frequent)
MSIR Oral Tablets (Less frequent)
▲ Mylotarg for Injection (8% to 13%)
Nadolol Tablets
Namenda Tablets (Greater than or equal to 2%)
Naprelan Tablets (Less than 1%)
Naropin Injection
Necon 0.5/35 Tablets
Necon 1/35 Tablets
Necon 1/50 Tablets
Necon 10/11 Tablets
Nefazodone
Neoral Oral Solution (Rare)
Neoral Soft Gelatin Capsules (Rare)
Nesacaine Injection
Nesacaine-MPF Injection
Neurontin Capsules (1.8%)
Neurontin Oral Solution (1.8%)
Neurontin Tablets (1.8%)
▲ Nilandron Tablets (8.6%)
Nimotop Capsules (Up to 1.4%)
▲ Nipent for Injection (3% to 10%)
Nizoral Tablets (Rare)
Nolvadex Tablets (Infrequent)
Nordette-28 Tablets
Norinyl 1 + 35 28-Day Tablets
Norinyl 1 + 50 28-Day Tablets
Noroxin Tablets (Less frequent)

Norvasc Tablets (More than 0.1% to 1%)
Norvir Oral Solution (Less than 2%)
Norvir Soft Gelatin Capsules (Less than 2%)
Novarel for Injection
Nubain Injection (1% or less)
Numorphan Injection
Numorphan Suppositories
Ogestrel 0.5/50-28 Tablets
▲ Orap Tablets (2 of 20 patients)
Orapred Oral Solution
Ortho Evra Transdermal System
Ortho Tri-Cyclen Lo Tablets
Ortho Tri-Cyclen Tablets
Ortho-Cept Tablets
Ortho-Cyclen Tablets
Ortho-Est Tablets
Ovcon 35 Tablets
Ovcon 50 Tablets
Ovrette Tablets
Oxandrin Tablets
Oxsoralen-Ultra Capsules
OxyContin Tablets (Less than 1%)
Paxil CR Controlled-Release Tablets (Frequent to 2%)
Paxil Oral Suspension (Frequent)
Paxil Tablets (Frequent)
Pediazole Suspension
▲ Pegasys (18%)
▲ PEG-Intron Powder for Injection (29%)
Pentasa Capsules (Less than 1%)
Pepcid for Oral Suspension (Infrequent)
Pepcid Injection (Infrequent)
Pepcid Injection Premixed (Infrequent)
Pepcid Tablets (Infrequent)
▲ Permax Tablets (3.2%)
▲ Plavix Tablets (3.6%)
Plendil Extended-Release Tablets (0.5% to 1.5%)
Polocaine Injection
Polocaine-MPF Injection
Ponstel Capsules (Occasional)
Pravachol Tablets
▲ Prefest Tablets (5%)
Pregnyl for Injection
Premarin Intravenous
▲ Premarin Tablets (5% to 8%)
Premarin Vaginal Cream
▲ Premphase Tablets (6% to 11%)
▲ Prempro Tablets (6% to 11%)

Prevacid Delayed-Release Capsules (Less than 1%)
Prevacid for Delayed-Release Oral Suspension (Less than 1%)
Prevacid NapraPAC 375 (Less than 1%)
Prevacid NapraPAC 500 (Less than 1%)
Prevacid SoluTab Delayed-Release Tablets (Less than 1%)
PREVPAC (Less than 1%)
Prilosec Delayed-Release Capsules (Less than 1%)
Prilosec OTC Tablets (Less than 1%)
Prinivil Tablets (Greater than 1%)
Prinzide Tablets (0.3% to 1%)
Procanbid Extended-Release Tablets (Occasional)
Procardia Capsules (Less than 0.5%)
Procardia XL Extended Release Tablets (1% or less)
▲ Prochieve 4% Gel (8% to 11%)
▲ Prochieve 8% Gel (8% to 11%)
▲ Prograf Capsules and Injection (3% to 15%)
Proleukin for Injection (Less than 1%)
▲ Prometrium Capsules (100 mg, 200 mg) (Less than 5% to 19%)
ProSom Tablets (2%)
Protonix I.V. (Less than 1%)
Protonix Tablets (Less than 1%)
Protopic Ointment (Greater than or equal to 1%)
▲ Provigil Tablets (2%)
Prozac Pulvules and Liquid
Pulmicort Respules (Less than 1%)
Pulmicort Turbuhaler Inhalation Powder (Rare)
▲ Rapamune Oral Solution and Tablets (3% to 20%)
▲ Rebetol Capsules (13% to 36%)
▲ Rebetol Oral Solution (13% to 36%)
▲ Rebetron Combination Therapy (23% to 36%)
▲ Rebif Injection (25%)
Relafen Tablets (Less than 1%)
Relpax Tablets (Infrequent)
Remeron SolTab Tablets (Frequent)
▲ Remicade for IV Injection (8%)
▲ Reminyl Oral Solution (7%)
▲ Reminyl Tablets (7%)
Requip Tablets (1% or more)
Retrovir Capsules
Retrovir IV Infusion
Retrovir Syrup

Retrovir Tablets
▲ Reyataz Capsules (3% to 8%)
▲ Ribavirin Capsules (23% to 36%)
▲ Rilutek Tablets (4.2% to 6.1%)
Risperdal Consta Injection (Frequent)
Risperdal M-Tab Tablets (Infrequent)
Risperdal Oral Solution (Infrequent)
Risperdal Tablets (Infrequent)
Ritalin Hydrochloride Tablets
Ritalin LA Capsules
Ritalin-SR Tablets
▲ Rituxan for Infusion (Among most frequent)
▲ Rituxan I.V. (Among most frequent)
▲ Roferon-A Injection (16% to 28%)
▲ Romazicon Injection (1% to 3%)
Rythmol Tablets (Less than 1%)
Salagen Tablets (Less than 1%)
Sandimmune I.V. Ampuls for Infusion (Rare)
Sandimmune Oral Solution (Rare)
Sandimmune Soft Gelatin Capsules (Rare)
▲ Sandostatin Injection (1% to 4%)
▲ Sandostatin LAR Depot (5% to 15%)
Seasonale Tablets
Sedapap Tablets 50 mg/650 mg (Infrequent)
Septra DS Tablets
Septra Grape Suspension
Septra Suspension
Septra Tablets
▲ Serostim for Injection (1% to 5%)
▲ Simulect for Injection (3% to 10%)
Solu-Medrol Sterile Powder
Sonata Capsules (Frequent)
▲ Soriatane Capsules (1% to 10%)
▲ Spiriva HandiHaler (1% to 3%)
Sporanox Capsules (Infrequent)
Sporanox Oral Solution (1.1% to 2%)
Stadol Injection (Less than 1%)
Stadol NS (Less than 1%)
Stalevo Tablets
▲ Strattera Capsules (2% to 6%)
Striant Mucoadhesive
▲ Suboxone Tablets (11%)
▲ Subutex Tablets (11%)
Sular Tablets (Less than or equal to 1%)
▲ Sustiva Capsules (2% to 3%)
▲ Symmetrel Syrup (1% to 5%)
▲ Symmetrel Tablets (1% to 5%)
▲ Synarel Nasal Solution for Endometriosis (3% of patients)
Tagamet Injection

Tagamet Liquid
Tagamet Tablets
▲ Tambocor Tablets (1% to 3%)
Targretin Capsules
Tasmar Tablets (Frequent)
Tegretol Chewable Tablets
Tegretol Suspension
Tegretol Tablets
▲ Temodar Capsules (6%)
▲ Tenormin I.V. Injection (0.6% to 12%)
▲ Tenormin Tablets (0.6% to 12%)
Tequin Injection (Less than 0.1%)
Tequin Tablets (Less than 0.1%)
Testim 1% Gel
Testred Capsules, 10 mg
Teveten HCT Tablets (Less than 1%)
Teveten Tablets (1%)
Thalomid Capsules
Tiazac Capsules (Less than 2%)
Tigan Capsules
Tigan Injectable
Tigan Suppositories
Timolide Tablets
Timoptic in Ocudose (Less frequent)
Timoptic Sterile Ophthalmic Solution
 (Less frequent)
Timoptic-XE Sterile Ophthalmic Gel
 Forming Solution
▲ Topamax Sprinkle Capsules (5% to
 13%)
▲ Topamax Tablets (5% to 13%)
▲ Toprol-XL Tablets (About 5 of 100
 patients)
Toradol IM Injection, IV Injection
 (1% or less)
Toradol Tablets (1% or less)
Tranxene T-TAB Tablets
Tranxene-SD Half Strength Tablets
Tranxene-SD Tablets
▲ Travatan Ophthalmic Solution (1% to
 5%)
Trecator-SC Tablets
Trental Tablets (Less than 1%)
Tricor Tablets
Tri-Levlen 21 Tablets
Tri-Levlen 28 Tablets
Tri-Norinyl-28 Tablets
Triphasil-28 Tablets
▲ Trisenox Injection (20%)
Trivora-28 Tablets
▲ Trizivir Tablets (9%)
Trovan I.V. (Less than 1%)
Trovan Tablets (Less than 1%)
Ultracet Tablets (Less than 1%)
Ultram Tablets (Less than 1%)

Uniretic Tablets (Less than 1%)
▲ Valcyte Tablets (Less than 5%)
Valium Tablets (Infrequent)
▲ Valtrex Caplets (Less than 1% to 7%)
Vaseretic Tablets
Vasotec I.V. Injection (0.5% to 1%)
▲ Vesanoid Capsules (14%)
VFEND I.V. (Less than 1%)
VFEND Oral Suspension (Less than
 1%)
VFEND Tablets (Less than 1%)
▲ Viadur Implant (5.3%)
Viagra Tablets (Less than 2%)
Vicoprofen Tablets (Less than 1%)
Vioxx Oral Suspension (Greater than
 0.1% to 1.9%)
Vioxx Tablets (Greater than 0.1% to
 1.9%)
Viracept Oral Powder (Less than 2%)
Viracept Tablets (Less than 2%)
Vistide Injection
Vivelle Transdermal System
▲ Vivelle-Dot Transdermal System (3%
 to 10.6%)
Voltaren Tablets (Occasional)
Voltaren-XR Tablets (Occasional)
Wellbutrin Tablets (Frequent)
▲ Xanax Tablets (13.8% to 13.9%)
▲ Xanax XR Tablets (1.3% to 12.1%)
▲ Xeloda Tablets (Less than 5%)
▲ Xenical Capsules (3.4%)
▲ Xyrem Oral Solution (6%)
Yasmin 28 Tablets (Greater than 1%)
Zanaflex Tablets (Frequent)
Zantac 150 EFFERdose Granules
 (Rare)
Zantac 150 EFFERdose Tablets (Rare)
Zantac 150 Tablets (Rare)
Zantac 300 Tablets (Rare)
Zantac Injection (Rare)
Zantac Injection Premixed (Rare)
Zantac Syrup (Rare)
Zarontin Capsules (Rare)
Zarontin Syrup (Rare)
Zaroxolyn Tablets
Zebeta Tablets (Up to 0.2%)
Zelnorm Tablets
▲ Zenapax for Injection (2% to 5%)
Zestoretic Tablets (0.3% to 1%)
Zestril Tablets (Greater than 1%)
Ziac Tablets
Zocor Tablets
▲ Zoladex (1% to 54%)
Zoladex 3-month
Zoloft Oral Concentrate (Infrequent)

Zoloft Tablets (Infrequent)
▲ Zometa for Intravenous Infusion (12%)
Zomig Nasal Spray (Infrequent)
Zomig Tablets (Infrequent)
Zomig-ZMT Tablets (Infrequent)
▲ Zonegran Capsules (6%)
Zosyn (1% or less)
Zosyn in Galaxy Containers (1% or less)
Zovia 1/35E Tablets
Zovia 1/50E Tablets
Zyban Sustained-Release Tablets (Frequent)
Zyprexa Tablets
Zyprexa ZYDIS Orally Disintegrating Tablets
Zyrtec Syrup (Less than 2%)
Zyrtec Tablets (Less than 2%)
Zyrtec-D 12 Hour Extended Relief Tablets (Less than 2%)

Depression aggravation of
Bextra Tablets (0.1% to 1.9%)
Celexa Oral Solution (Frequent)
Celexa Tablets (Frequent)
Coreg Tablets (Greater than 0.1% to 1%)
Evoxac Capsules (Less than 1%)
Frova Tablets (Rare)
Halcion Tablets
▲ Intron A for Injection (Less than 5%)
Lexapro Oral Solution (Infrequent)
Lexapro Tablets (Infrequent)
Lupron Depot 3.75 mg
Lupron Depot—3 Month 11.25 mg (Possible)
Meridia Capsules
Nexium Delayed-Release Capsules (Less than 1%)
Sustiva Capsules (Less than 2%)
Tegretol-XR Tablets
Zoloft Oral Concentrate (Infrequent)
Zoloft Tablets (Infrequent)

Depression, psychotic
Celexa Oral Solution (Infrequent)
Celexa Tablets (Infrequent)
Copaxone for Injection (Infrequent)
Effexor Tablets (Rare)
Effexor XR Capsules (Infrequent)
Paxil CR Controlled-Release Tablets
Paxil Oral Suspension (Rare)
Paxil Tablets (Rare)
Relpax Tablets (Rare)
Remeron SolTab Tablets (Rare)

Rilutek Tablets (Rare)
Risperdal Consta Injection (Infrequent)

Depressive reactions
▲ Combivir Tablets (9%)
▲ Epivir Oral Solution (9%)
▲ Epivir Tablets (9%)
▲ Rescriptor Tablets (4.9% to 12.6%)
Soma Tablets
Xanax Tablets

Disordered sense of smell
Ambien Tablets (Rare)
Astelin Nasal Spray
Avelox I.V. (Less than 0.1%)
Avelox Tablets (Less than 0.1%)
Axert Tablets (Rare)
Caduet Tablets (Less than 2%)
Cardura Tablets (Less than 0.5%)
Cerebyx Injection (Infrequent)
Colazal Capsules
Doxil Injection (Less than 1%)
Effexor Tablets (Infrequent)
Effexor XR Capsules (Infrequent)
Evoxac Capsules (Less than 1%)
Flumadine Syrup (Less than 0.3%)
Flumadine Tablets (Less than 0.3%)
Fluvoxamine maleate (Infrequent)
Gabitril Tablets (Infrequent)
Hivid Tablets (Less than 1%)
▲ Intron A for Injection (Less than 5%)
Lamictal Chewable Dispersible Tablets (Rare)
Lamictal Tablets (Rare)
Levaquin in 5% Dextrose Injection (0.1% to 1%)
Levaquin Injection (0.1% to 1%)
Levaquin Tablets (0.1% to 1%)
Lipitor Tablets (Less than 2%)
Miacalcin Nasal Spray (Less than 1%)
Nexium Delayed-Release Capsules (Less than 1%)
Norvasc Tablets (Less than or equal to 0.1%)
Norvir Oral Solution (Less than 2%)
Norvir Soft Gelatin Capsules (Less than 2%)
Paxil CR Controlled-Release Tablets
Paxil Oral Suspension (Rare)
Paxil Tablets (Rare)
Prevacid Delayed-Release Capsules (Less than 1%)
Prevacid for Delayed-Release Oral Suspension (Less than 1%)

Prevacid NapraPAC 375 (Less than 1%)
Prevacid NapraPAC 500 (Less than 1%)
Prevacid SoluTab Delayed-Release Tablets (Less than 1%)
PREVPAC (Less than 1%)
Prozac Pulvules and Liquid (Rare)
Relpax Tablets (Rare)
Remeron SolTab Tablets (Rare)
Remeron Tablets (Rare)
Rescriptor Tablets
Sarafem Pulvules (Rare)
Sonata Capsules (Less than 1% to 2%)
Sustiva Capsules (Less than 2%)
Tasmar Tablets (Infrequent)
Tequin Injection (Less than 0.1%)
Tequin Tablets (Less than 0.1%)
Topamax Sprinkle Capsules (Infrequent)
Topamax Tablets (Infrequent)
Zomig Nasal Spray (Infrequent)
Zomig Tablets (Infrequent)
Zomig-ZMT Tablets (Infrequent)
Zonegran Capsules (Infrequent)
Zyrtec Syrup (Less than 2%)
Zyrtec Tablets (Less than 2%)
Zyrtec-D 12 Hour Extended Relief Tablets (Less than 2%)

Disorientation
Aciphex Tablets
Actimmune (Rare)
Alferon N Injection (1%)
Arthrotec Tablets (Rare)
Asacol Delayed-Release Tablets
Biaxin Filmtab Tablets
Biaxin Granules
Biaxin XL Filmtab Tablets
Botox Purified Neurotoxin Complex
Cosopt Sterile Ophthalmic Solution
Dalmane Capsules
Daranide Tablets
Demerol Syrup
Demerol Tablets
Demser Capsules
Dilaudid Ampules
Dilaudid Injection
Dilaudid Multiple Dose Vials
Dilaudid Non-Sterile Powder
Dilaudid Oral Liquid (Less frequent)
Dilaudid Rectal Suppositories
Dilaudid Tablets

Dilaudid Tablets - 8 mg (Less frequent)
Dilaudid-HP Injection (Less frequent)
Dilaudid-HP Lyophilized Powder 250 mg (Less frequent)
Dolobid Tablets (Less than 1 in 100)
Elavil
Eldepryl Capsules
Emend Capsules (Isolated cases)
Famvir Tablets (Infrequent)
Flexeril Tablets (Less than 1%)
Floxin Tablets
Halcion Tablets
INFeD Injection
▲ Invanz for Injection (3.3% to 5.1%)
Lexapro Oral Solution (Infrequent)
Lexapro Tablets (Infrequent)
Maxalt Tablets (Infrequent)
Maxalt-MLT Orally Disintegrating Tablets (Infrequent)
MS Contin Tablets (Less frequent)
MSIR Oral Capsules (Less frequent)
MSIR Oral Solution Concentrate (Less frequent)
MSIR Oral Tablets (Less frequent)
Norpramin Tablets
Oncaspar
Orthoclone OKT3 Sterile Solution
Pamelor
Parnate Tablets
Pediazole Suspension
Phenergan Suppositories
PREVPAC
Rescriptor Tablets
Sinequan Capsules (Infrequent)
Sinequan Oral Concentrate (Infrequent)
Soma Tablets
Stalevo Tablets
Surmontil Capsules
Tagamet Injection
Tagamet Liquid
Tagamet Tablets
Tigan Capsules
Tigan Injectable
Tigan Suppositories
Timoptic in Ocudose (Less frequent)
Timoptic Sterile Ophthalmic Solution (Less frequent)
Timoptic-XE Sterile Ophthalmic Gel Forming Solution
Transderm Scop Transdermal Therapeutic System (Infrequent)
Triavil Tablets

Vivactil Tablets
Xanax XR Tablets (1.5%)

Disorientation, place
Blocadren Tablets
Corzide 40/5 Tablets
Corzide 80/5 Tablets
Cosopt Sterile Ophthalmic Solution
Inderal LA Long-Acting Capsules
Nadolol Tablets
Tenormin I.V. Injection
Tenormin Tablets
Timolide Tablets
Timoptic in Ocudose
Timoptic Sterile Ophthalmic Solution
Timoptic-XE Sterile Ophthalmic Gel
  Forming Solution
Toprol-XL Tablets
Zebeta Tablets
Ziac Tablets

Disorientation, time
Blocadren Tablets
Corzide 40/5 Tablets
Corzide 80/5 Tablets
Cosopt Sterile Ophthalmic Solution
Inderal LA Long-Acting Capsules
Nadolol Tablets
Tenormin I.V. Injection
Tenormin Tablets
Timolide Tablets
Timoptic in Ocudose
Timoptic Sterile Ophthalmic Solution
Timoptic-XE Sterile Ophthalmic Gel
  Forming Solution
Toprol-XL Tablets
Zebeta Tablets
Ziac Tablets

Double vision
Abelcet Injection
Abilify Tablets (Rare)
Aciphex Tablets
Adalat CC Tablets (Less than 1%)
▲ Agrylin Capsules (1% to 5%)
Ambien Tablets (Frequent)
Arthrotec Tablets (Rare)
Ativan Injection (Occasional)
Axert Tablets (Rare)
Azopt Ophthalmic Suspension (Less
  than 1%)
Balamine DM Oral Drops
Balamine DM Syrup
Betimol Ophthalmic Solution
Blocadren Tablets

Botox Purified Neurotoxin Complex
  (Rare)
Brevicon 28-Day Tablets (Rare)
Buprenex Injectable (Less than 1%)
Caduet Tablets (Greater than 0.1% to
  less than or equal to 1%)
Carbatrol Capsules
Celexa Oral Solution (Rare)
Celexa Tablets (Rare)
▲ Cerebyx Injection (3.3%)
Cipro I.V. (1% or less)
Cipro I.V. Pharmacy Bulk Package
  (Less than 1%)
Cipro Oral Suspension (Less than 1%)
Cipro Tablets (Less than 1%)
Cipro XR Tablets (Less than 1%)
Clomid Tablets (1.5%)
Cognex Capsules (Infrequent)
Copaxone for Injection (At least 2%)
Cosopt Sterile Ophthalmic Solution
Dantrium Capsules (Less frequent)
▲ Depacon Injection (16%)
▲ Depakene Capsules (16%)
▲ Depakene Syrup (16%)
▲ Depakote ER Tablets (16%)
▲ Depakote Sprinkle Capsules (16%)
▲ Depakote Tablets (1% to 16%)
Dilaudid Ampules
Dilaudid Injection
Dilaudid Multiple Dose Vials
Dilaudid Non-Sterile Powder
Dilaudid Oral Liquid (Less frequent)
Dilaudid Rectal Suppositories
Dilaudid Tablets
Dilaudid Tablets - 8 mg (Less frequent
Dilaudid-HP Injection (Less frequent)
Dilaudid-HP Lyophilized Powder
  250 mg (Less frequent)
Diprivan Injectable Emulsion (Less
  than 1%)
Effexor Tablets (Infrequent)
Effexor XR Capsules (Infrequent)
Eldepryl Capsules
EMLA Anesthetic Disc (Unlikely with
  disc)
EMLA Cream (Unlikely with cream)
Evoxac Capsules (Less than 1%)
Exelon Capsules (Infrequent)
Exelon Oral Solution (Infrequent)
Fareston Tablets
▲ Felbatol Oral Suspension (3.4% to
  6.1%)
▲ Felbatol Tablets (3.4% to 6.1%)
  femhrt Tablets

Flexeril Tablets (Less than 1%)
Floxin Tablets
Fluvoxamine maleate (Infrequent)
Gabitril Tablets (1% or more)
Geodon Capsules (Frequent)
Indocin Capsules (Less than 1%)
Indocin Oral Suspension (Less than 1%)
Indocin Suppositories (Less than 1%)
▲ Intron A for Injection (Less than 5%)
Kadian Capsules (Less than 3%)
Keppra Oral Solution (2%)
Keppra Tablets (2%)
Ketek Tablets (Greater than or equal to 0.2% to less than 2%)
Klonopin Tablets (Infrequent)
Klonopin Wafers (Infrequent)
▲ Lamictal Chewable Dispersible Tablets (5% to 49%)
▲ Lamictal Tablets (5% to 49%)
Levaquin in 5% Dextrose Injection (0.1% to 1%)
Levaquin Injection (0.1% to 1%)
Levaquin Tablets (0.1% to 1%)
Levlen 21 Tablets (Rare)
Levlen 28 Tablets (Rare)
Levlite 28 Tablets (Rare)
Lidoderm Patch
M.V.I. Pediatric for Injection (Rare)
Matulane Capsules
Mirapex Tablets (1% or more)
Motrin Suspension, Oral Drops, Chewable Tablets, and Caplets (Less than 1%)
MS Contin Tablets (Less frequent)
MSIR Oral Capsules (Less frequent)
MSIR Oral Solution Concentrate (Less frequent)
MSIR Oral Tablets (Less frequent)
Namenda Tablets (Infrequent)
Naprelan Tablets (Less than 1%)
Nefazodone (Infrequent)
▲ Neurontin Capsules (1.2% to 5.9%)
▲ Neurontin Oral Solution (1.2 to 5.9%)
▲ Neurontin Tablets (1.2% to 5.9%)
Norinyl 1 + 35 28-Day Tablets
Norinyl 1 + 50 28-Day Tablets
Noroxin Tablets
Norvasc Tablets (More than 0.1% to 1%)
Norvir Oral Solution (Less than 2%)
Norvir Soft Gelatin Capsules (Less than 2%)
Numorphan Injection

Numorphan Suppositories
Ortho Tri-Cyclen Lo Tablets
Ortho Tri-Cyclen Tablets (Rare)
Orthoclone OKT3 Sterile Solution
Ortho-Cyclen Tablets (Rare)
Ovcon 35 Tablets
Ovcon 50 Tablets
Paxil CR Controlled-Release Tablets (Rare)
Paxil Oral Suspension (Rare)
Paxil Tablets (Rare)
Peganone Tablets
Periactin Tablets
Permax Tablets (2.1%)
Phenergan Suppositories
Phenergan Tablets
Photofrin for Injection
Pletal Tablets (Less than 2%)
Premphase Tablets
Prempro Tablets
Prevacid Delayed-Release Capsules (Less than 1%)
Prevacid for Delayed-Release Oral Suspension (Less than 1%)
Prevacid NapraPAC 375 (Less than 1%)
Prevacid NapraPAC 500 (Less than 1%)
Prevacid SoluTab Delayed-Release Tablets (Less than 1%)
PREVPAC (Less than 1%)
Prilosec Delayed-Release Capsules (Less than 1%)
Prilosec OTC Tablets (Less than 1%)
Prinivil Tablets (0.3% to 1%)
Prinzide Tablets
ProSom Tablets (Rare)
Protonix I.V. (Less than 1%)
Protonix Tablets (Less than 1%)
Prozac Pulvules and Liquid (Rare)
Relpax Tablets (Rare)
Remeron SolTab Tablets (Rare)
ReoPro Vials (0.1%)
Requip Tablets (2%)
Rescriptor Tablets
Rilutek Tablets (Rare)
Risperdal M-Tab Tablets (Rare)
Risperdal Oral Solution (Rare)
Risperdal Tablets (Rare)
▲ Romazicon Injection (1% to 3%)
Sarafem Pulvules (Rare)
Soma Tablets
Sonata Capsules (Infrequent)
▲ Soriatane Capsules (1% to 5%)

Stalevo Tablets
Sustiva Capsules (Less than 2%)
Symbyax Capsules (Infrequent)
▲ Tambocor Tablets (1% to 3%)
Tasmar Tablets (Infrequent)
Tegretol Chewable Tablets
Tegretol Suspension
Tegretol Tablets
Tegretol-XR Tablets
▲ Temodar Capsules (5%)
Thalomid Capsules
Timolide Tablets
Timoptic in Ocudose (Less frequent)
Timoptic Sterile Ophthalmic Solution
(Less frequent)
Timoptic-XE Sterile Ophthalmic Gel
Forming Solution
▲ Topamax Sprinkle Capsules (1% to
10%)
▲ Topamax Tablets (1% to 10%)
Tranxene T-TAB Tablets
Tranxene-SD Half Strength Tablets
Tranxene-SD Tablets
Trecator-SC Tablets (Rare)
▲ Trileptal Oral Suspension (5% to 40%)
▲ Trileptal Tablets (5% to 40%)
Tri-Levlen 21 Tablets (Rare)
Tri-Levlen 28 Tablets (Rare)
Tri-Norinyl-28 Tablets
Valium Tablets (Infrequent)
VFEND I.V. (Less than 1%)
VFEND Oral Suspension (Less than
1%)
VFEND Tablets (Less than 1%)
Viagra Tablets
Vistide Injection
Wellbutrin SR Sustained-Release
Tablets
Wellbutrin Tablets (Rare)
Wellbutrin XL Extended-Release
Tablets
Xalatan Sterile Ophthalmic Solution
(Less than 1%)
Xanax Tablets
Xylocaine 2% Jelly
Zestoretic Tablets
Zestril Tablets (0.3% to 1.0%)
Zoloft Oral Concentrate (Rare)
Zoloft Tablets (Rare)
Zomig Tablets (Rare)
Zomig-ZMT Tablets (Rare)
▲ Zonegran Capsules (6%)
Zyban Sustained-Release Tablets
Zyprexa Tablets (Infrequent)

Zyprexa ZYDIS Orally Disintegrating
Tablets (Infrequent)

Dreaming

Amerge Tablets (Rare)
Dilaudid Oral Liquid (Less frequent)
Dilaudid Tablets - 8 mg (Less
frequent)
Limbitrol (Less common)
▲ Malarone Pediatric Tablets (2% to 7%)
▲ Malarone Tablets (2% to 7%)
MS Contin Tablets (Less frequent)
MSIR Oral Capsules (Less frequent)
MSIR Oral Solution Concentrate
(Less frequent)
MSIR Oral Tablets (Less frequent)
▲ Tenormin I.V. Injection (Up to 3%)
▲ Tenormin Tablets (Up to 3%)

Dreaming abnormalities

Aciphex Tablets
Actiq (Less than 1%)
Ambien Tablets (1%)
▲ Anafranil (3%)
Anaprox DS Tablets (Less than 1%)
Anaprox Tablets (Less than 1%)
Anzemet Injection (Infrequent)
Anzemet Tablets (Infrequent)
▲ Aricept Tablets (3%)
Arthrotec Tablets (Rare)
Avelox I.V. (Less than 0.1%)
Avelox Tablets (Less than 0.1%)
▲ Avinza Capsules (Less than 5%)
Axert Tablets (Rare)
Blocadren Tablets (Less than 1%)
Buprenex Injectable (Less than 1%)
BuSpar Tablets (Frequent)
Caduet Tablets (Greater than 0.1% to
less than 2%)
Cardizem LA Extended Release
Tablets (Less than 2%)
Cataflam Tablets (Occasional)
Catapres Tablets
Catapres-TTS (0.5% or less)
Cipro XR Tablets (Less than 1%)
Clorpres Tablets
Cognex Capsules (Infrequent)
Copaxone for Injection (Frequent)
Cozaar Tablets (Less than 1%)
Crixivan Capsules (Less than 2%)
Cytovene Capsules (At least 3
subjects)
Cytovene-IV (At least 3 subjects)
▲ Depacon Injection (1% to 5%)
▲ Depakene Capsules (1% to 5%)

▲ Depakene Syrup (1% to 5%)
▲ Depakote ER Tablets (1% to 5%)
▲ Depakote Sprinkle Capsules (1% to 5%)
▲ Depakote Tablets (1% to 5%)
Dilaudid-HP Injection (Less frequent)
Dilaudid-HP Lyophilized Powder 250 mg (Less frequent)
Diprivan Injectable Emulsion (Less than 1%)
Duragesic Transdermal System (1% or greater)
EC-Naprosyn Delayed-Release Tablets (Less than 1%)
▲ Effexor Tablets (4%)
▲ Effexor XR Capsules (3% to 7%)
Elavil
▲ Eldepryl Capsules (2 of 49 patients)
▲ Emtriva Capsules (2% to 11%)
Evoxac Capsules (Less than 1%)
Exelon Capsules (Infrequent)
Exelon Oral Solution (Infrequent)
Feldene Capsules (Occasional)
Flexeril Tablets (Less than 1%)
Floxin Tablets (Less than 1%)
Fluvoxamine maleate
Fortovase Capsules (Less than 2%)
Frova Tablets (Rare)
Gabitril Tablets (Infrequent)
Ganite Injection
Halcion Tablets (Rare)
Hyzaar 50-12.5 Tablets
Hyzaar 100-25 Tablets
Inderal LA Long-Acting Capsules
▲ Intron A for Injection (Less than 5%)
Invirase Capsules (Less than 2%)
Kadian Capsules (Less than 3%)
Kaletra Capsules (Less than 2%)
Kaletra Oral Solution (Less than 2%)
Klonopin Tablets (Infrequent)
Klonopin Wafers (Infrequent)
Lamictal Chewable Dispersible Tablets (Infrequent)
Lamictal Tablets (Infrequent)
▲ Lariam Tablets (Among most frequent)
Levaquin in 5% Dextrose Injection (0.1% to 1%)
Levaquin Injection (0.1% to 1%)
Levaquin Tablets (0.1% to 1%)
▲ Lexapro Oral Solution (3%)
▲ Lexapro Tablets (3%)
Lipitor Tablets (Less than 2%)
Lotensin HCT Tablets (0.3% or more)
Lotronex Tablets (Rare)

Maxalt Tablets (Infrequent)
Maxalt-MLT Orally Disintegrating Tablets (Infrequent)
Mellaril
Meridia Capsules
▲ Mirapex Tablets (Greater than or equal to 1% to 11%)
Motrin Suspension, Oral Drops, Chewable Tablets, and Caplets (Less than 1%)
▲ Naprelan Tablets (3% to 9%)
Naprosyn Suspension (Less than 1%)
Naprosyn Tablets (Less than 1%)
▲ Nefazodone (3%)
Neurontin Capsules (Infrequent)
Neurontin Oral Solution (Infrequent)
Neurontin Tablets (Infrequent)
Nipent for Injection (Less than 3%)
Norvasc Tablets (More than 0.1% to 1%)
Norvir Oral Solution (Less than 2%)
Norvir Soft Gelatin Capsules (Less than 2%)
Nubain Injection (1% or less)
Orap Tablets (2.7%)
▲ OxyContin Tablets (Between 1% and 5%)
Paxil CR Controlled-Release Tablets (1%)
▲ Paxil Oral Suspension (3% to 4%)
▲ Paxil Tablets (3% to 4%)
Permax Tablets (2.7%)
Ponstel Capsules (Occasional)
Prevacid Delayed-Release Capsules (Less than 1%)
Prevacid for Delayed-Release Oral Suspension (Less than 1%)
Prevacid NapraPAC 375 (Less than 1%)
Prevacid NapraPAC 500 (Less than 1%)
Prevacid SoluTab Delayed-Release Tablets (Less than 1%)
PREVPAC (Less than 1%)
Prilosec Delayed-Release Capsules (Less than 1%)
Prilosec OTC Tablets (Less than 1%)
▲ Prograf Capsules and Injection (3% to 15%)
ProSom Tablets (2%)
Protonix I.V. (Less than 1%)
Protonix Tablets (Less than 1%)
▲ Prozac Pulvules and Liquid (1% to 5%)
Relpax Tablets (Infrequent)

▲ Remeron SolTab Tablets (4%)
▲ Requip Tablets (11%)
Rescriptor Tablets
Reyataz Capsules (Less than 3%)
Rilutek Tablets (Rare)
Risperdal Consta Injection (Up to 2%)
Risperdal M-Tab Tablets (Frequent)
Risperdal Oral Solution (Frequent)
Risperdal Tablets (Frequent)
Rythmol Tablets (Less than 1%)
Salagen Tablets (Less than 1%)
▲ Sarafem Pulvules (3%)
Serentil Ampuls
Serentil Concentrate
Serentil Tablets
Seroquel Tablets (Infrequent)
Singulair Chewable Tablets (Very rare)
Singulair Oral Granules (Very rare)
Singulair Tablets (Very rare)
Spectracef Tablets (0.1% to 1%)
Sporanox Capsules (2%)
Stadol Injection (Less than 1%)
Stadol NS (Less than 1%)
Stalevo Tablets
▲ Strattera Capsules (4%)
Sular Tablets (Less than or equal to 1%)
▲ Sustiva Capsules (1% to 4%)
▲ Symmetrel Syrup (1% to 5%)
▲ Symmetrel Tablets (1% to 5%)
Tambocor Tablets (Less than 1%)
▲ Tasmar Tablets (16% to 21%)
▲ Tequin Injection (0.1% to 3%)
▲ Tequin Tablets (0.1% to 3%)
Thioridazine Hydrochloride Tablets
Tiazac Capsules (Less than 2%)
Topamax Sprinkle Capsules (Infrequent)
Topamax Tablets (Infrequent)
Toradol IM Injection, IV Injection (1% or less)
Toradol Tablets (1% or less)
Triavil Tablets
Trilafon
Trovan I.V. (Less than 1%)
Trovan Tablets (Less than 1%)
Vantin Tablets and Oral Suspension (Less than 1%)
Vaseretic Tablets
Vasotec I.V. Injection (0.5% to 1%)
VFEND I.V. (Less than 1%)
VFEND Oral Suspension (Less than 1%)
VFEND Tablets (Less than 1%)

Viagra Tablets (Less than 2%)
Vicoprofen Tablets (Less than 1%)
Vistide Injection
Voltaren Tablets (Occasional)
Voltaren-XR Tablets (Occasional)
Wellbutrin SR Sustained-Release Tablets (At least 1%)
Wellbutrin Tablets
Wellbutrin XL Extended-Release Tablets (At least 1%)
Xanax Tablets (1.8%)
Xanax XR Tablets (Infrequent)
▲ Xyrem Oral Solution (3% to 9%)
Zanaflex Tablets (Infrequent)
Zebeta Tablets
Ziac Tablets
Zoloft Oral Concentrate (Infrequent)
Zoloft Tablets (Infrequent)
Zomig Nasal Spray (Rare)
Zonegran Capsules (Infrequent)
▲ Zyban Sustained-Release Tablets (5%)
Zyprexa Tablets
Zyprexa ZYDIS Orally Disintegrating Tablets

Elation
▲ Marinol Capsules (8% to 24%)

Emotional disturbances
Accutane Capsules
Avalide Tablets
Avapro Tablets (Less than 1%)
Depacon Injection
Depakene Capsules
Depakene Syrup
Depakote ER Tablets
Depakote Sprinkle Capsules
Depakote Tablets
Efudex Cream (Infrequent)
Efudex Topical Solutions (Infrequent)
Imitrex Nasal Spray (Rare)
Lariam Tablets (Less than 1%)
Orapred Oral Solution
Paxil Oral Suspension (Infrequent)
Paxil Tablets (Infrequent)
Plaquenil Tablets

Emotional lability
Accutane Capsules
Actiq (Less than 1%)
Activella Tablets (0% to 6%)
▲ Adderall XR Capsules (1% to 9%)
Adenoscan (Less than 1%)
Ambien Tablets (Infrequent)
Amnesteem Capsules

▲ AndroGel (Up to 3%)
Aricept Tablets (Infrequent)
Asacol Delayed-Release Tablets
Avelox I.V. (Less than 0.1%)
Avelox Tablets (Less than 0.1%)
Betaseron for SC Injection
Blocadren Tablets
Bravelle for Intramuscular or Subcutaneous Injection (2% to 2.7%)
BuSpar Tablets (Rare)
Caduet Tablets (Less than 2%)
Cardura Tablets (Less than 0.5%)
Celexa Oral Solution (Infrequent)
Celexa Tablets (Infrequent)
▲ CellCept Capsules (3% to less than 20%)
▲ CellCept Intravenous (3% to less than 20%)
▲ CellCept Oral Suspension (3% to less than 20%)
▲ CellCept Tablets (3% to less than 20%)
Cerebyx Injection (Infrequent)
Copaxone for Injection (At least 2%)
Coreg Tablets (Greater than 0.1% to 1%)
Corzide 40/5 Tablets
Corzide 80/5 Tablets
Cosopt Sterile Ophthalmic Solution
▲ Crinone 4% Gel (23%)
▲ Crinone 8% Gel (22%)
DaunoXome Injection (Less than or equal to 5%)
▲ Depacon Injection (6%)
▲ Depakene Capsules (6%)
▲ Depakene Syrup (6%)
▲ Depakote ER Tablets (6%)
▲ Depakote Sprinkle Capsules (6%)
▲ Depakote Tablets (1% to 6%)
Diprivan Injectable Emulsion (Less than 1%)
▲ Doxil Injection (1% to 5%)
Effexor Tablets (Frequent)
Effexor XR Capsules (Infrequent)
Elmiron Capsules
Emcyt Capsules (2%)
▲ Esclim Transdermal System (2.1% to 8.3%)
Evoxac Capsules (Less than 1%)
Exelon Capsules (Infrequent)
Exelon Oral Solution (Infrequent)
▲ Felbatol Oral Suspension (6.5%)
▲ Felbatol Tablets (6.5%)
Floxin Tablets
Fluvoxamine maleate (Infrequent)

Frova Tablets (Infrequent)
▲ Gabitril Tablets (3%)
Gengraf Capsules (1% to less than 3%)
▲ Gonal-F for Injection (5.1%)
Guanidine Hydrochloride Tablets
Hivid Tablets (Less than 1%)
Inderal LA Long-Acting Capsules
▲ Infergen (6% to 12%)
▲ Intron A for Injection (Less than 5%)
Kaletra Capsules (Less than 2%)
Kaletra Oral Solution (Less than 2%)
Keppra Oral Solution (2%)
Keppra Tablets (2%)
Klonopin Tablets (1%)
Klonopin Wafers (1%)
▲ Lamictal Chewable Dispersible Tablets (4%)
▲ Lamictal Tablets (4%)
Levaquin in 5% Dextrose Injection (0.1% to 1%)
Levaquin Injection (0.1% to 1%)
Levaquin Tablets (0.1% to 1%)
Levothroid Tablets
Levoxyl Tablets
Lexapro Oral Solution (Infrequent)
Lexapro Tablets (Infrequent)
Lipitor Tablets (Less than 2%)
Lunelle Monthly Injection
▲ Lupron Depot 3.75 mg (16%)
▲ Lupron Depot—3 Month 11.25 mg (16%)
Lupron Depot-PED 7.5 mg, 11.25 mg and 15 mg (Less than 2%)
Lupron Injection Pediatric (Less than 2%)
Meridia Capsules (1.3%)
Motrin Suspension, Oral Drops, Chewable Tablets, and Caplets (Less than 1%)
Nadolol Tablets
Namenda Tablets (Infrequent)
Naprelan Tablets (Less than 1%)
Naropin Injection (Less than 1%)
Nefazodone
Neoral Oral Solution (1% to less than 3%)
Neoral Soft Gelatin Capsules (1% to less than 3%)
▲ Neurontin Capsules (4.2% to 6%)
▲ Neurontin Oral Solution (4.2% to 6%)
▲ Neurontin Tablets (4.2% to 6%)
Nipent for Injection (Less than 3%)
Norvir Oral Solution (Less than 2%)
Norvir Soft Gelatin Capsules (Less than 2%)

Oncaspar (Less than 1%)
Ovidrel for Injection (Less than 2%)
OxyContin Tablets (Less than 1%)
Paxil CR Controlled-Release Tablets (Infrequent)
Paxil Oral Suspension (Frequent)
Paxil Tablets (Frequent)
Pediapred Oral Solution
▲ PEG-Intron Powder for Injection (28%)
Permax Tablets (Infrequent)
Prevacid Delayed-Release Capsules (Less than 1%)
Prevacid for Delayed-Release Oral Suspension (Less than 1%)
Prevacid NapraPAC 375 (Less than 1%)
Prevacid NapraPAC 500 (Less than 1%)
Prevacid SoluTab Delayed-Release Tablets (Less than 1%)
PREVPAC (Less than 1%)
Prochieve 4% Gel
Prochieve 8% Gel
▲ Prograf Capsules and Injection (3% to 15%)
▲ Prometrium Capsules (100 mg, 200 mg) (6%)
ProSom Tablets (Infrequent)
Protonix I.V. (Less than 1%)
Protonix Tablets (Less than 1%)
Provigil Tablets (1%)
Prozac Pulvules and Liquid (Frequent)
▲ Pulmicort Respules (1% to 3%)
▲ Rapamune Oral Solution and Tablets (3% to 20%)
▲ Rebetol Capsules (7% to 47%)
▲ Rebetol Oral Solution (7% to 47%)
▲ Rebetron Combination Therapy (7% to 12%)
Relpax Tablets (Infrequent)
Remeron SolTab Tablets (Infrequent)
Requip Tablets (Infrequent)
Rescriptor Tablets
Retrovir Capsules
Retrovir IV Infusion
Retrovir Syrup
Retrovir Tablets
Reyataz Capsules (Less than 3%)
▲ Ribavirin Capsules (7% to 47%)
Rilutek Tablets (Infrequent)
Risperdal Consta Injection (Infrequent)
Risperdal M-Tab Tablets (Rare)
Risperdal Oral Solution (Rare)
Risperdal Tablets (Rare)

Roferon-A Injection (Less than 3%)
▲ Romazicon Injection (1% to 3%)
Salagen Tablets (Less than 1%)
Sarafem Pulvules (Frequent)
Seroquel Tablets (Rare)
Sonata Capsules (Frequent)
Striant Mucoadhesive
Sustiva Capsules (Less than 2%)
Symbyax Capsules (Infrequent)
▲ Synarel Nasal Solution for Central Precocious Puberty (6%)
▲ Synarel Nasal Solution for Endometriosis (15% of patients)
Tasmar Tablets (Frequent)
Tenormin I.V. Injection
Tenormin Tablets
Thalomid Capsules
Timolide Tablets
Timoptic in Ocudose
Timoptic Sterile Ophthalmic Solution
Timoptic-XE Sterile Ophthalmic Gel Forming Solution
▲ Topamax Sprinkle Capsules (3%)
▲ Topamax Tablets (3%)
Toprol-XL Tablets
▲ Trileptal Oral Suspension (2% to 3%)
▲ Trileptal Tablets (2% to 3%)
Trovan I.V. (Less than 1%)
Trovan Tablets (Less than 1%)
Ultracet Tablets (Less than 1%)
▲ Ultram Tablets (7% to 14%)
Uniretic Tablets (Less than 1%)
Viracept Oral Powder (Less than 2%)
Viracept Tablets (Less than 2%)
Wellbutrin SR Sustained-Release Tablets (Infrequent)
Wellbutrin XL Extended-Release Tablets (Infrequent)
Yasmin 28 Tablets
Zanaflex Tablets (Infrequent)
Zebeta Tablets
Zelnorm Tablets
Ziac Tablets
▲ Zoladex (60%)
Zoladex 3-month
Zoloft Oral Concentrate (Infrequent)
Zoloft Tablets (Infrequent)
Zomig Tablets (Infrequent)
Zomig-ZMT Tablets (Infrequent)
Zyban Sustained-Release Tablets (Infrequent)
Zyprexa IntraMuscular (Infrequent)
Zyprexa Tablets
Zyprexa ZYDIS Orally Disintegrating Tablets

Zyrtec Syrup (Less than 2%)
Zyrtec Tablets (Less than 2%)
Zyrtec-D 12 Hour Extended Relief
Tablets (Less than 2%)

Euphoria

Abilify Tablets (Rare)
Actiq (Less than 1%)
Adderall Tablets
Adderall XR Capsules
Adipex-P Capsules
Adipex-P Tablets
Alacol DM Syrup
Ambien Tablets (Frequent)
Astramorph/PF Injection,
(Preservative-Free)
▲ Avinza Capsules (Less than 5%)
Axert Tablets (Rare)
Bicillin C-R 900/300 Injection
Bicillin C-R Injection
Bicillin L-A Injection
BuSpar Tablets (Infrequent)
Celexa Oral Solution (Infrequent)
Celexa Tablets (Infrequent)
Copaxone for Injection (At least 2%)
Dalmane Capsules (Rare)
Darvocet-N 50 Tablets
Darvocet-N 100 Tablets
Darvon Capsules
Darvon Compound-65 Capsules
Darvon-N Tablets
Decadron Phosphate Injection
Decadron Tablets
Demerol Syrup
Demerol Tablets
Depacon Injection (0.9%)
Desoxyn Tablets
Dexedrine Spansule Capsules
Dexedrine Tablets
DextroStat Tablets
Dilaudid Ampules
Dilaudid Injection
Dilaudid Multiple Dose Vials
Dilaudid Non-Sterile Powder
Dilaudid Oral Liquid
Dilaudid Rectal Suppositories
Dilaudid Tablets
Dilaudid Tablets - 8 mg
Dilaudid-HP Injection (Less frequent)
Dilaudid-HP Lyophilized Powder
250 mg (Less frequent)
Diprivan Injectable Emulsion (Less
than 1%)
Doral

▲ Duragesic Transdermal System (3% to
10%)
Effexor Tablets (Infrequent)
Effexor XR Capsules (Infrequent)
Eldepryl Capsules
EMLA Anesthetic Disc (Unlikely with
disc)
EMLA Cream (Unlikely with cream)
Ergamisol Tablets
Felbatol Oral Suspension (Infrequent)
Felbatol Tablets (Infrequent)
Floxin Tablets (Less than 1%)
Flumadine Syrup (Less than 0.3%)
Flumadine Tablets (Less than 0.3%)
Fluvoxamine maleate (Infrequent)
Fortovase Capsules (Less than 2%)
Frova Tablets (Infrequent)
Gabitril Tablets (Frequent)
Halcion Tablets (0.5% to 0.9%)
Haldol Decanoate 50 Injection
Haldol Decanoate 100 Injection
Hivid Tablets (Less than 1%)
Hydrocortone Phosphate Injection,
Sterile
Hydrocortone Tablets
Imitrex Injection (Infrequent)
Imitrex Nasal Spray (Infrequent)
Imitrex Tablets (Infrequent)
Invirase Capsules (Less than 2%)
Ionamin Capsules
Kadian Capsules (Less than 3%)
Lamictal Chewable Dispersible
Tablets (Infrequent)
Lamictal Tablets (Infrequent)
Lidoderm Patch
Limbitrol
▲ Marinol Capsules (3% to 10%)
Maxalt Tablets (Frequent)
Maxalt-MLT Orally Disintegrating
Tablets (Frequent)
Miltown Tablets
Moban Oral Concentrate (Less
frequent)
Moban Tablets (Less frequent)
▲ MS Contin Tablets (Among most
frequent)
▲ MSIR Oral Capsules (Among most
frequent)
▲ MSIR Oral Solution Concentrate
(Among most frequent)
▲ MSIR Oral Tablets (Among most
frequent)
Nardil Tablets (Less common)
Nefazodone (Infrequent)

Neurontin Capsules (Infrequent)
Neurontin Oral Solution (Infrequent)
Neurontin Tablets (Infrequent)
Norvir Oral Solution (Less than 2%)
Norvir Soft Gelatin Capsules (Less than 2%)
Nubain Injection (1% or less)
Numorphan Injection
Numorphan Suppositories
Oraped Oral Solution
▲ OxyContin Tablets (Between 1% and 5%)
OxyFast Oral Concentrate Solution
OxyIR Capsules
Paxil CR Controlled-Release Tablets
Paxil Oral Suspension (Rare)
Paxil Tablets (Rare)
Percocet Tablets
Percodan Tablets
Periactin Tablets
Permax Tablets (Infrequent)
Phenergan Suppositories
Phenergan Tablets
ProSom Tablets (Infrequent)
Prozac Pulvules and Liquid (Infrequent)
Relpax Tablets (Infrequent)
Remeron SolTab Tablets (Infrequent)
Requip Tablets (Infrequent)
Rescriptor Tablets
Rilutek Tablets (Rare)
Risperdal Consta Injection (Infrequent)
Risperdal M-Tab Tablets (Infrequent)
Risperdal Oral Solution (Infrequent)
Risperdal Tablets (Infrequent)
▲ Romazicon Injection (1% to 3%)
Sarafem Pulvules (Infrequent)
Sedapap Tablets 50 mg/650 mg (Infrequent)
Seroquel Tablets (Rare)
Solu-Medrol Sterile Powder
Soma Tablets
Sonata Capsules (Frequent)
Stadol Injection (Greater than or equal to 1%)
Stadol NS (Greater than or equal to 1%)
Stalevo Tablets
Sustiva Capsules (Less than 2%)
Symbyax Capsules (Infrequent)
Symmetrel Syrup (0.1% to 1%)
Symmetrel Tablets (0.1% to 1%)
Tambocor Tablets (Less than 1%)
Tasmar Tablets (1%)
Tequin Injection (Less than 0.1%)

Tequin Tablets (Less than 0.1%)
Thalomid Capsules
Topamax Sprinkle Capsules (Frequent)
Topamax Tablets (Frequent)
Toradol IM Injection, IV Injection (1% or less)
Toradol Tablets (1% or less)
Trileptal Oral Suspension
Trileptal Tablets
Trovan I.V. (Less than 1%)
Trovan Tablets (Less than 1%)
Tussionex Pennkinetic Extended-Release Suspension
Tylenol with Codeine Elixir
Tylenol with Codeine Tablets
Ultracet Tablets (At least 1%)
▲ Ultram Tablets (1% to 14%)
VFEND I.V. (Less than 1%)
VFEND Oral Suspension (Less than 1%)
VFEND Tablets (Less than 1%)
Vicoprofen Tablets (Less than 1%)
Wellbutrin SR Sustained-Release Tablets
Wellbutrin Tablets (1.2%)
Wellbutrin XL Extended-Release Tablets
Xanax XR Tablets (Infrequent)
Xylocaine 2% Jelly
Xyrem Oral Solution (Infrequent)
Zanaflex Tablets (Infrequent)
Zarontin Capsules
Zarontin Syrup
Zoloft Oral Concentrate (Infrequent)
Zoloft Tablets (Infrequent)
Zomig Nasal Spray (Rare)
Zomig Tablets (Rare)
Zomig-ZMT Tablets (Rare)
Zonegran Capsules (Infrequent)
Zyban Sustained-Release Tablets
Zyprexa Tablets (2%)
Zyprexa ZYDIS Orally Disintegrating Tablets (2%)
Zyrtec Syrup (Less than 2%)
Zyrtec Tablets (Less than 2%)
Zyrtec-D 12 Hour Extended Relief Tablets (Less than 2%)

Excitability
Anadrol-50 Tablets
Astramorph/PF Injection (Preservative-Free)
Balamine DM Oral Drops (Rare)

Balamine DM Syrup (Rare)
Benztropine
BuSpar Tablets (2%)
Crixivan Capsules (Less than 2%)
Elavil
Extendryl Chewable Tablets
Extendryl SR. & JR. Capsules
Extendryl Syrup
Flexeril Tablets (Less than 1%)
Klonopin Tablets (Infrequent)
Klonopin Wafers (Infrequent)
Lexapro Oral Solution (Infrequent)
Lexapro Tablets (Infrequent)
Narcan Injection
Naropin Injection
Nesacaine Injection
Nesacaine-MPF Injection
NuLev Orally Disintegrating Tablets
Orap Tablets
Oxandrin Tablets
Periactin Tablets
Phenergan Suppositories
Phenergan Tablets
Phenobarbital
Polocaine Injection
Polocaine-MPF Injection
Sedapap Tablets 50 mg/650 mg
  (Infrequent)
Serentil Ampuls
Serentil Concentrate
Serentil Tablets
Serevent Inhalation Aerosol
Triavil Tablets
Tylenol, Children's, Plus Cold,
Tylenol, Children's, Plus Cold
  & Cough,
Tylenol, Maximum Strength, Allergy
  Sinus Day Time Caplets, Gelcaps,
  and Geltabs
Tylenol, Maximum Strength, Flu
  NightTime Gelcaps
Tylenol, Maximum Strength, Severe
  Cold & Flu NightTime Liquid
Tylenol, Multi-Symptom, Cold
  Night Time Complete Formula
  Caplets
Vicks 44m, Pediatric, Cough & Cold
  Relief
Vicks NyQuil, Children's, Cold/Cough
  Relief,
Vicks NyQuil LiquiCaps
Vicks NyQuil Liquid
Zyrtec-D 12 Hour Extended Relief
  Tablets

Excitement, paradoxical
Diamox Sequels Sustained-Release
  Capsules
Halcion Tablets
Miltown Tablets
ProSom Tablets
Serax
Triavil Tablets
Valium Tablets

Fear
Bicillin L-A Injection
BuSpar Tablets (Infrequent)
Dilaudid Ampules
Dilaudid Injection
Dilaudid Multiple Dose Vials
Dilaudid Non-Sterile Powder
Dilaudid Rectal Suppositories
Dilaudid Tablets
Hycodan Syrup
Hycodan Tablets
Hycomine Compound Tablets
Hycotuss Expectorant Syrup
Lortab 2.5/500 Tablets
Lortab 5/500 Tablets
Lortab 7.5/500 Tablets
Lortab 10/500 Tablets
Lortab Elixir
Maxidone Tablets
Norco 5/325 Tablets
Norco 7.5/325 Tablets
Norco 10/325 Tablets
Tussionex Pennkinetic Extended-
  Release Suspension
Vicodin ES Tablets
Vicodin HP Tablets
Vicodin Tablets
Xanax Tablets (1.4%)
Zydone Tablets
Zyrtec-D 12 Hour Extended Relief
  Tablets

Feeling, drugged
▲ Ambien Tablets (3%)
Neurontin Capsules (Infrequent)
Neurontin Oral Solution (Infrequent)
Neurontin Tablets (Infrequent)
Paxil Oral Suspension (2%)
Paxil Tablets (2%)

Feeling, high
Neurontin Capsules (Rare)
Neurontin Oral Solution (Rare)
Neurontin Tablets (Rare)

Feeling, intoxicated
Ambien Tablets (Rare)
Effexor XR Capsules (Rare)
Imitrex Injection (Rare)
▲ Sedapap Tablets 50 mg/650 mg
  (Among the most frequent)
Trileptal Oral Suspension
Trileptal Tablets
Xanax XR Tablets (Infrequent)

Feeling, strange
Ambien Tablets (Rare)
Amerge Tablets (Infrequent)
Imitrex Injection (2.2%)
Imitrex Nasal Spray (Infrequent)
Imitrex Tablets
Lexapro Oral Solution (Infrequent)
Lexapro Tablets (Infrequent)
MS Contin Tablets (Less frequent)
Neurontin Capsules (Rare)
Neurontin Oral Solution (Rare)
Neurontin Tablets (Rare)
Trileptal Oral Suspension (1% to 2%)
Trileptal Tablets (1% to 2%)

Floating feeling
Dilaudid Oral Liquid (Less frequent)
Dilaudid Tablets - 8 mg (Less
  frequent)
Dilaudid-HP Injection (Less frequent)
Dilaudid-HP Lyophilized Powder
  250 mg (Less frequent)
Mintezol Chewable Tablets
Mintezol Suspension
MS Contin Tablets (Less frequent)
MSIR Oral Capsules (Less frequent)
MSIR Oral Solution Concentrate
  (Less frequent)
MSIR Oral Tablets (Less frequent)
Nubain Injection (1% or less)

Frigidity, unspecified
Wellbutrin Tablets (Infrequent)

Hallucinations
Seconal (Less than 1%)
Actimmune (Rare)
Actiq (1% to 2%)
Allegra-D Extended-Release Tablets
Ambien Tablets (Infrequent)
AmBisome for Injection (Less
  common)
Amerge Tablets (Rare)
Amicar Injection
Amicar Syrup, 25%
Amicar Tablets

▲ Amphotec (1% to 5%)
Ancobon Capsules
Aricept Tablets
Arthrotec Tablets (Rare)
Ativan Injection (1%)
Avelox I.V. (Less than 1%)
Avelox Tablets (Less than 1%)
▲ Avinza Capsules (Less than 5%)
Azulfidine EN-tabs Tablets (Rare)
Balamine DM Oral Drops
Balamine DM Syrup
Benztropine
Biaxin Filmtab Tablets
Biaxin Granules
Biaxin XL Filmtab Tablets
Blocadren Tablets (Less than 1%)
Buprenex Injectable (Infrequent)
BuSpar Tablets (Infrequent)
▲ Busulfex Injection (5%)
Campath Ampules
Cardizem LA Extended Release
  Tablets (Less than 2%)
Cataflam Tablets (Rarely)
Catapres Tablets
Ceclor Pulvules (Rare)
Ceclor Suspension (Rare)
Celexa Oral Solution (Infrequent)
Celexa Tablets (Infrequent)
▲ CellCept Capsules (3% to less than
  20%)
▲ CellCept Intravenous (3% to less than
  20%)
▲ CellCept Oral Suspension (3% to less
  than 20%)
▲ CellCept Tablets (3% to less than
  20%)
Celontin Capsules (Rare)
Cipro I.V. (1% or less)
Cipro I.V. Pharmacy Bulk Package
  (Less than 1%)
Cipro Oral Suspension (Less than 1%)
Cipro Tablets (Less than 1%)
Cipro XR Tablets
Clozapine Tablets (Less than 1%)
Clozaril Tablets (Less than 1%)
Cognex Capsules (2%)
Comtan Tablets
Copaxone for Injection (Infrequent)
Corzide 40/5 Tablets
Corzide 80/5 Tablets
Cosopt Sterile Ophthalmic Solution
Cylert Chewable Tablets
Cylert Tablets
Cytovene Capsules

Cytovene-IV
Dalmane Capsules (Rare)
Darvocet-N 50 Tablets
Darvocet-N 100 Tablets
Darvon Capsules
Darvon Compound-65 Capsules
Darvon-N Tablets
DaunoXome Injection (Less than or
equal to 5%)
Demerol Syrup
Demerol Tablets
Demser Capsules
Depacon Injection
Depakene Capsules
Depakene Syrup
Depakote ER Tablets (Greater than
1%)
Depakote Sprinkle Capsules
▲ Depakote Tablets (1% to 5%)
Detrol Tablets
Didronel Tablets
Digitek Tablets
Dilaudid Ampules
Dilaudid Injection
Dilaudid Multiple Dose Vials
Dilaudid Non-Sterile Powder
Dilaudid Oral Liquid (Less frequent)
Dilaudid Rectal Suppositories
Dilaudid Tablets
Dilaudid Tablets - 8 mg (Less
frequent)
Dilaudid-HP Injection (Less frequent)
Dilaudid-HP Lyophilized Powder
250 mg (Less frequent)
Diprivan Injectable Emulsion (Less
than 1%)
Dolobid Tablets (Less than 1 in 100)
Doral
Dostinex Tablets
▲ Duragesic Transdermal System (3% to
10%)
Effexor Tablets (Infrequent)
Effexor XR Capsules (Infrequent)
Elavil
▲ Eldepryl Capsules (3 of 49 patients
Elspar for Injection
Ergamisol Tablets (Less frequent)
Ery-Tab Tablets (Isolated reports)
Erythrocin Stearate Filmtab Tablets
(Isolated reports)
Erythromycin Base Filmtab Tablets
(Isolated reports)
Erythromycin Delayed-Release
Capsules, (Isolated reports)

Eskalith Capsules
Eskalith CR Controlled-Release
Tablets
Evoxac Capsules (Less than 1%)
▲ Exelon Capsules (4%)
▲ Exelon Oral Solution (4%)
Famvir Tablets (Infrequent)
Felbatol Oral Suspension (Infrequent)
Felbatol Tablets (Infrequent)
Feldene Capsules (Rare)
Flexeril Tablets (Less than 1%)
Floxin Tablets (Less than 1%)
Flumadine Syrup (Less than 0.3%)
Flumadine Tablets (Less than 0.3%)
Fluvoxamine maleate (Infrequent)
Focalin Tablets
Fortovase Capsules (Less than 2%)
▲ Foscavir Injection Between (1% and
5%)
Gabitril Tablets (Frequent)
Ganite Injection
Gastrocrom Oral Concentrate (Less
common)
Guanidine Hydrochloride Tablets
Halcion Tablets
Haldol Decanoate 50 Injection
Haldol Decanoate 100 Injection
Hivid Tablets (Less than 1%)
Imitrex Injection
Imitrex Tablets (Rare)
Inderal LA Long-Acting Capsules
Invanz for Injection (Very rare)
Invirase Capsules (Less than 2%)
Kadian Capsules (Less than 3%)
Keflex Pulvules
Klonopin Tablets
Klonopin Wafers
Lamictal Chewable Dispersible
Tablets (Infrequent)
Lamictal Tablets (Infrequent)
Lanoxicaps Capsules
Lanoxin Elixir Pediatric
Lanoxin Injection
Lanoxin Injection Pediatric
Lanoxin Tablets
Lariam Tablets (Occasional)
Leukeran Tablets (Rare)
Levaquin in 5% Dextrose Injection
(0.1% to 1%)
Levaquin Injection (0.1% to 1%)
Levaquin Tablets (0.1% to 1%)
Limbitrol
Marinol Capsules (Greater than 1%)
Matulane Capsules

Mebaral Tablets (Less than 1 in 100 patients

Merrem I.V. (Greater than 0.1% to 1%)

Mexitil Capsules (About 3 in 1,000)

Minipress Capsules (Less than 1%)

Minizide Capsules (Rare)

▲ Mirapex Tablets (9% to 17%)

Motrin Suspension, Oral Drops, Chewable Tablets, and Caplets (Less than 1%)

MS Contin Tablets (Less frequent)

MSIR Oral Capsules (Less frequent)

MSIR Oral Solution Concentrate (Less frequent)

MSIR Oral Tablets (Less frequent)

Nadolol Tablets

Narcan Injection

Naropin Injection (Less than 1%)

Nefazodone (Infrequent)

Nembutal Sodium Solution (Less than 1%)

Neurontin Capsules (Infrequent)

Neurontin Oral Solution (Infrequent)

Neurontin Tablets (Infrequent)

Nipent for Injection (Less than 3%)

Norflex Extended-Release Tablets

Norflex Injection

Noroxin Tablets

Norpramin Tablets

Norvir Oral Solution (Less than 2%)

Norvir Soft Gelatin Capsules (Less than 2%)

Nubain Injection (1% or less)

Numorphan Injection

Numorphan Suppositories

OxyContin Tablets (Less than 1%)

Pamelor

Paxil CR Controlled-Release Tablets (Infrequent)

Paxil Oral Suspension (Infrequent)

Paxil Tablets (Infrequent)

Pediazole Suspension

Pepcid for Oral Suspension (Infrequent)

Pepcid Injection (Infrequent)

Pepcid Injection Premixed (Infrequent)

Pepcid Tablets (Infrequent)

Periactin Tablets

▲ Permax Tablets (13.8%)

Phenergan Suppositories

Phenergan Tablets

Phenobarbital (Less than 1%)

Plavix Tablets

Ponstel Capsules (Rare)

Prevacid Delayed-Release Capsules (Less than 1%)

Prevacid for Delayed-Release Oral Suspension (Less than 1%)

Prevacid NapraPAC 375 (Less than 1%)

Prevacid NapraPAC 500 (Less than 1%)

Prevacid SoluTab Delayed-Release Tablets (Less than 1%)

PREVPAC (Less than 1%)

Prilosec Delayed-Release Capsules (Less than 1%)

Prilosec OTC Tablets (Less than 1%)

Primaxin I.M.

Primaxin I.V.

Procanbid Extended-Release Tablets (Occasional)

▲ Prograf Capsules and Injection (3% to 15%)

ProSom Tablets (Rare)

Protonix I.V. (Less than 1%)

Protonix Tablets (Less than 1%)

Provigil Tablets (At least 1%)

Prozac Pulvules and Liquid (Infrequent)

Relpax Tablets (Rare)

Remeron SolTab Tablets (Infrequent)

Reminyl Oral Solution (Greater than or equal to 2%)

Reminyl Tablets (Greater than or equal to 2%)

▲ Requip Tablets (5% to 10%)

Rescriptor Tablets

Reyataz Capsules (Less than 3%)

Rilutek Tablets (Infrequent)

▲ Risperdal Consta Injection (6% to 7%)

Roferon-A Injection (Infrequent)

▲ Sandostatin LAR Depot (1% to 4%)

Sarafem Pulvules (Infrequent)

Septra DS Tablets

Septra Grape Suspension

Septra Suspension

Septra Tablets

Seroquel Tablets (Infrequent)

Sinequan Capsules (Infrequent)

Sinequan Oral Concentrate (Infrequent)

Singulair Chewable Tablets

Singulair Oral Granules

Singulair Tablets

Sonata Capsules (Less than 1%)

Stadol Injection (Less than 1%)
Stadol NS (Less than 1%)
▲ Stalevo Tablets (4%)
Surmontil Capsules
Sustiva Capsules (Less than 2%)
▲ Symmetrel Syrup (1% to 5%)
▲ Symmetrel Tablets (1% to 5%)
Tagamet Injection
Tagamet Liquid
Tagamet Tablets
▲ Tasmar Tablets (8% to 10%)
Tenormin I.V. Injection
Tenormin Tablets
Tequin Injection (Less than 0.1%)
Tequin Tablets (Less than 0.1%)
Tiazac Capsules (Less than 2%)
Timolide Tablets
Timoptic in Ocudose (Less frequent)
Timoptic Sterile Ophthalmic Solution
(Less frequent)
Timoptic-XE Sterile Ophthalmic Gel
Forming Solution
Tofranil
Tofranil-PM
Topamax Sprinkle Capsules
(Frequent)
Topamax Tablets (Frequent)
Toradol IM Injection, IV Injection
(1% or less)
Toradol Tablets (1% or less)
Transderm Scop Transdermal
Therapeutic System (Infrequent)
Triavil Tablets
Trilisate Liquid (Rare)
Trilisate Tablets (Rare)
Trovan I.V. (Less than 1%)
Trovan Tablets (Less than 1%)
Ultracet Tablets (Less than 1%)
▲ Ultram Tablets (Less than 1% to 14%)
▲ Valcyte Tablets (Less than 5%)
Valium Tablets
Vantin Tablets and Oral Suspension
(Less than 1%)
▲ Vesanoid Capsules (6%)
▲ VFEND I.V. (2.5% to 5.1%)
▲ VFEND Oral Suspension (2.5% to
5.1%)
▲ VFEND Tablets (2.5% to 5.1%)
Vioxx Oral Suspension (Less than
0.1%)
Vioxx Tablets (Less than 0.1%)
Vistide Injection
Vivactil Tablets
Voltaren Tablets (Rare)
Voltaren-XR Tablets (Rare)

Wellbutrin SR Sustained-Release
Tablets
Wellbutrin Tablets (Frequent)
Wellbutrin XL Extended-Release
Tablets
Xanax Tablets (Rare)
Xanax XR Tablets (Rare to
(infrequent)
Xyrem Oral Solution
Zantac 150 EFFERdose Granules
(Rare)
Zantac 150 EFFERdose Tablets (Rare)
Zantac 150 Tablets (Rare)
Zantac 300 Tablets (Rare)
Zantac Injection
Zantac Injection Premixed
Zantac Syrup (Rare)
Zebeta Tablets
Ziac Tablets
Zoloft Oral Concentrate (Infrequent)
Zoloft Tablets (Infrequent)
Zomig Tablets (Rare)
Zomig-ZMT Tablets (Rare)
Zosyn (1% or less)
Zosyn in Galaxy Containers (1.0% or
less)
Zovirax Capsules
Zovirax for Injection (Approximately
1%)
Zovirax Suspension
Zovirax Tablets
Zyban Sustained-Release Tablets
Zyprexa Tablets
Zyprexa ZYDIS Orally Disintegrating
Tablets
Zyrtec-D 12 Hour Extended Relief
Tablets

Hallucinations, auditory

Bicillin C-R 900/300 Injection
Bicillin C-R Injection
Bicillin L-A Injection
Catapres Tablets (Rare)
Catapres-TTS (0.5% or less)
Clorpres Tablets
Lexapro Oral Solution (Infrequent)
Lexapro Tablets (Infrequent)
Orthoclone OKT3 Sterile Solution
Valtrex Caplets

Hallucinations, visual

Benztropine
Bicillin C-R 900/300 Injection
Bicillin C-R Injection
Bicillin L-A Injection

Carbatrol Capsules
Catapres Tablets (Rare)
Catapres-TTS (0.5% or less)
Clorpres Tablets
Orthoclone OKT3 Sterile Solution
Salagen Tablets (Rare)
Tegretol Chewable Tablets
Tegretol Suspension
Tegretol Tablets
Tegretol-XR Tablets
Tessalon Capsules
Tessalon Perles
Valtrex Caplets

Hangover

Aciphex Tablets (Rare)
Effexor Tablets (Infrequent)
Effexor XR Capsules (Infrequent)
Maxalt Tablets (Infrequent)
Maxalt-MLT Orally Disintegrating
  Tablets (Infrequent)
Nefazodone (Infrequent)
Neurontin Capsules (Rare)
Neurontin Oral Solution (Rare)
Neurontin Tablets (Rare)
Nipent for Injection (Less than 3%)
Phenobarbital
▲ ProSom Tablets (3%)
Restoril
Sonata Capsules (Infrequent)
Thalomid Capsules
Xanax XR Tablets (Infrequent)
Xyrem Oral Solution (Infrequent)
Zyprexa Tablets (Infrequent)
Zyprexa ZYDIS Orally Disintegrating
  Tablets (Infrequent)

Hostility

Abilify Tablets (1% or greater)
Amerge Tablets (Rare)
Aricept Tablets (Infrequent)
BuSpar Tablets (2%)
Cerebyx Injection (Infrequent)
Cognex Capsules (2%)
Copaxone for Injection (Infrequent)
Depacon Injection
Depakene Capsules
Depakene Syrup
Depakote ER Tablets
Depakote Sprinkle Capsules
Depakote Tablets
Duragesic Transdermal System (Less
  than 1%)
Effexor Tablets (Infrequent)
Effexor XR Capsules (Infrequent)

Floxin Tablets
Fluvoxamine maleate (Infrequent)
Gabitril Tablets (2%)
Geodon Capsules (Frequent)
Keppra Oral Solution (2%)
Keppra Tablets (2%)
Klonopin Tablets
Klonopin Wafers
Lamictal Chewable Dispersible
  Tablets (Frequent)
Lamictal Tablets (Frequent)
Nefazodone (Infrequent)
▲ Neurontin Capsules (5.2% to 7.6%)
▲ Neurontin Oral Solution (5.2% to
  7.6%)
▲ Neurontin Tablets (5.2% to 7.6%)
Nipent for Injection (Less than 3%)
Nubain Injection (1% or less)
Paxil CR Controlled-Release Tablets
  (Rare)
Paxil Oral Suspension (Infrequent)
Paxil Tablets (Infrequent)
Permax Tablets (Infrequent)
Prevacid Delayed-Release Capsules
  (Less than 1%)
Prevacid for Delayed-Release Oral
  Suspension (Less than 1%)
Prevacid NapraPAC 375 (Less than
  1%)
Prevacid NapraPAC 500 (Less than
  1%)
Prevacid SoluTab Delayed-Release
  Tablets (Less than 1%)
PREVPAC (Less than 1%)
ProSom Tablets (Infrequent)
Prozac Pulvules and Liquid
  (Infrequent)
Remeron SolTab Tablets (Infrequent)
Reyataz Capsules (Less than 3%)
Rilutek Tablets (Frequent)
Sarafem Pulvules (Infrequent)
Sonata Capsules (Rare)
Stadol Injection (Less than 1%)
Stadol NS (Less than 1%)
Symbyax Capsules (Infrequent)
Tasmar Tablets (Infrequent)
Tequin Injection (Less than 0.1%)
Tequin Tablets (Less than 0.1%)
Thalomid Capsules
Wellbutrin SR Sustained-Release
  Tablets (Infrequent)
▲ Wellbutrin Tablets (5.6%)
Wellbutrin XL Extended-Release
  Tablets (Infrequent)

Xanax Tablets (Rare)
Xanax XR Tablets (Rare)
Zyban Sustained-Release Tablets
  (Infrequent)
▲ Zyprexa Tablets (15%)
▲ Zyprexa ZYDIS Orally Disintegrating
  Tablets (15%)

Hyperactivity
Abilify Tablets (1% or less)
▲ Aerobid Inhaler System (1% to 3%)
▲ Aerobid-M Inhaler System (1% to
  3%)
Amerge Tablets (Rare)
Amoxil Capsules (Rare)
Amoxil Chewable Tablets (Rare)
Amoxil for Oral Suspension (Rare)
Amoxil Pediatric Drops for Oral
  Suspension (Rare)
Amoxil Tablets (Rare)
Augmentin Chewable Tablets (Rare)
Augmentin ES-600 Powder for Oral
  Suspension (Rare)
Augmentin Powder for Oral
  Suspension (Rare)
Augmentin Tablets (Rare)
Augmentin XR Tablets (Rare)
Ceclor Pulvules (Rare)
Ceclor Suspension (Rare)
Ceftin for Oral Suspension (0.1% to
  1%)
Cefzil for Oral Suspension (Less than
  1%)
Cefzil Tablets (Less than 1%)
Dalmane Capsules (Rare)
Depacon Injection
Depakene Capsules
Depakene Syrup
Depakote ER Tablets
Depakote Sprinkle Capsules
Depakote Tablets
Klonopin Tablets (Infrequent)
Klonopin Wafers (Infrequent)
Levothroid Tablets
Levoxyl Tablets
Mellaril
Moban Oral Concentrate (Less
  frequent)
Moban Tablets (Less frequent)
Neurontin Capsules
Neurontin Oral Solution
Neurontin Tablets
PREVPAC
Roferon-A Injection (Infrequent)
Spectracef Tablets

Tasmar Tablets (1%)
Thioridazine Hydrochloride Tablets
  (Extremely rare)
Trilafon
Zarontin Capsules
Zarontin Syrup

Hyperexcitability
Phenergan Suppositories
Phenergan Tablets

Hyperirritability
Mintezol Chewable Tablets
Mintezol Suspension

Hypnotic effects
Trilafon

Hypoactivity
▲ Aerobid Inhaler System (1% to 3%)
▲ Aerobid-M Inhaler System (1% to 3%)
▲ Flumist Vaccine (10.6 to 14%)

Hysteria
Ambien Tablets (Rare)
Cognex Capsules (Rare)
Diprivan Injectable Emulsion (Less
  than 1%)
Fluvoxamine maleate (Infrequent)
Imitrex Injection (Rare)
Imitrex Tablets (Rare)
Klonopin Tablets
Klonopin Wafers
Neurontin Capsules (Rare)
Neurontin Oral Solution (Rare)
Neurontin Tablets (Rare)
Paxil Oral Suspension (Rare)
Paxil Tablets (Rare)
Periactin Tablets
Phenergan Suppositories
Phenergan Tablets
Relpax Tablets (Rare)
Trileptal Oral Suspension
Trileptal Tablets

Illusion, unspecified
Ambien Tablets (Infrequent)
Evoxac Capsules
Klonopin Tablets (Infrequent)
Klonopin Wafers (Infrequent)
Zoloft Oral Concentrate (Rare)
Zoloft Tablets (Rare)

Impairment of sensation
AmBisome for Injection (Less
  common
▲ Astelin Nasal Spray (7.9%)

Cognex Capsules (Rare)
Copaxone for Injection (At least 2%)
Crixivan Capsules (Less than 2%)
Cytovene Capsules
Cytovene-IV
Evoxac Capsules (Less than 1%)
Floxin Otic Solution (Single report)
Fortovase Capsules (Less than 2%)
Frova Tablets (Frequent)
Halcion (Rare)
Hivid Tablets
Imitrex Injection (Rare)
Imitrex Nasal Spray (Rare)
Imitrex Tablets (Rare)
Invirase Capsules (Less than 2%)
Lexxel Tablets
Maxalt Tablets (Rare)
Maxalt-MLT Orally Disintegrating
   Tablets (Rare)
Neurontin Capsules (Infrequent)
Neurontin Oral Solution (Infrequent)
Neurontin Tablets (Infrequent)
Prinivil Tablets (0.3% to 1%)
Prinzide Tablets
▲ Taxotere Injection Concentrate (7 of
   134 patients)
Thalomid Capsules
Vaseretic Tablets
Vasotec I.V. Injection (0.5% to 1%)
▲ Velcade for Injection (23%)
Zestril Tablets (0.3% to 1.0%)

Impairment of sensation, one side of face
Prilosec Delayed-Release Capsules
   (Less than 1%)
Prilosec OTC Tablets (Less than 1%)

Inebriated feeling
Klonopin Tablets (Infrequent)
Klonopin Wafers (Infrequent)

Insomnia
▲ Abilify Tablets (24%)
Accupril Tablets (0.5% to 1%)
Accuretic Tablets (1.2%)
Accutane Capsules
Aciphex Tablets
Actigall Capsules (1.9%)
Actiq (1% to 2%)
▲ Activella Tablets (0% to 6%)
▲ Actonel Tablets (4.7%)
Adalat CC Tablets (Less than 1%)
Adderall Tablets
▲ Adderall XR Capsules (1.5% to 17%)

Adipex-P Capsules
Adipex-P Tablets
Advicor Tablets
▲ Aerobid Inhaler System (1% to 3%)
▲ Aerobid-M Inhaler System (1% to
   3%)
▲ Agrylin Capsules (1% to 5%)
Alacol DM Syrup
Alferon N Injection (2%)
Allegra Capsules (Less than 1%)
Allegra Tablets (Less than 1%)
▲ Allegra-D Extended-Release Tablets
   (12.6%)
▲ Alora Transdermal System (1% to
   8%)
Aloxi Injection (Less than 1%)
Alphagan P Ophthalmic Solution
   (Less than 1%)
Altace Capsules (Less than 1%)
Altocor Extended-Release Tablets
Ambien Tablets (Frequent)
Amnesteem Capsules
Amoxil Capsules (Rare)
Amoxil Chewable Tablets (Rare)
Amoxil for Oral Suspension (Rare)
Amoxil Pediatric Drops for Oral
   Suspension (Rare)
Amoxil Tablets (Rare)
▲ Amphotec (5% or more)
Anadrol-50 Tablets
▲ Anafranil (25%)
Anaprox DS Tablets (Less than 1%)
Anaprox Tablets (Less than 1%)
▲ Angiomax for Injection (7%)
▲ Arava Tablets (1% to 3%)
▲ Aredia for Injection (22.2%)
▲ Aricept Tablets (9%)
▲ Arimidex Tablets (2% to 6%)
▲ Arixtra Injection (0.9% to 5.0%)
▲ Aromasin Tablets (11%)
Arthrotec Tablets (Rare)
Asacol Delayed-Release Tablets (2%)
Atacand HCT 16-12.5 Tablets (0.5%
   or greater)
Atacand HCT 32-12.5 Tablets (0.5%
   or greater)
Atrovent Inhalation Aerosol (Less
   than 1%)
Atrovent Inhalation Solution (0.9%)
Augmentin Chewable Tablets (Rare)
Augmentin ES-600 Powder for Oral
   Suspension (Rare)
Augmentin Powder for Oral
   Suspension (Rare)
Augmentin Tablets (Rare)

Augmentin XR Tablets (Rare)
Avelox I.V. (0.1% to less than 3%)
Avelox Tablets (0.1% to less than 3%)
▲ Avinza Capsules (5% to 10%)
Axert Tablets (Infrequent)
Aygestin Tablets
Azulfidine EN-tabs Tablets (Rare)
Balamine DM Oral Drops
Balamine DM Syrup
Benicar Tablets (Greater than 0.5%)
▲ Betaseron for SC Injection (24%)
Betoptic S Ophthalmic Suspension
(Rare)
Bextra Tablets (0.1% to 1.9%)
Biaxin Filmtab Tablets
Biaxin Granules
Biaxin XL Filmtab Tablets
Blocadren Tablets (Less than 1%)
▲ BuSpar Tablets (3%)
▲ Busulfex Injection (84%)
Caduet Tablets (Greater than 0.1%)
▲ Campath Ampules (10%)
▲ Camptosar Injection (Up to 19.4%)
Captopril Tablets (About 0.5 to 2%)
Carafate Suspension (Less than 0.5%)
Carafate Tablets (Less than 0.5%)
Cardizem LA Extended Release
Tablets (Less than 2%)
Cardura Tablets (1% to 1.2%)
▲ Carnitor Injection (1% to 3%)
▲ Casodex Tablets (5%)
Cataflam Tablets (Occasional)
Catapres Tablets (About 5 in 1,000
patients)
Catapres-TTS (2 of 101 patients)
Ceclor Pulvules (Rare)
Ceclor Suspension (Rare)
Cedax Oral Suspension (0.1% to 1%)
Cefzil for Oral Suspension (Less than
1%)
Cefzil Tablets (Less than 1%)
Celebrex Capsules (2.3%)
▲ Celexa Oral Solution (15%)
▲ Celexa Tablets (15%)
▲ CellCept Capsules (40.8%)
▲ CellCept Intravenous (40.8%)
▲ CellCept Oral Suspension (40.8%)
▲ CellCept Tablets (40.8%)
Celontin Capsules
▲ Cenestin Tablets, 0.45 mg, 0.625 mg,
0.9 mg, 1.25 mg (42%)
Cerebyx Injection (Infrequent)
Chlorpromazine
Cialis Tablets (Less than 2%)
Cipro I.V. (1% or less)

Cipro I.V. Pharmacy Bulk Package
(Less than 1%)
Cipro Oral Suspension (Less than 1%)
Cipro Tablets (Less than 1%)
Cipro XR Tablets (Less than 1%)
Clinoril Tablets (Less than 1%)
Clomid Tablets (Fewer than 1%)
Clorpres Tablets (About 5 in 1,000)
Clozapine Tablets (2%)
▲ Clozaril Tablets (2% to 20%)
▲ Cognex Capsules (6%)
Colazal Capsules (2%)
Colestid Tablets (Infrequent)
▲ CombiPatch Transdermal System (6%
to 8%)
Combivent Inhalation Aerosol (Less
than 2%)
Combivir Tablets (11%)
▲ Concerta Extended-Release Tablets
(4%)
▲ Condylox Topical Solution (Less than
5%)
Copaxone for Injection (At least 2%)
▲ Copegus Tablets (30%)
Coreg Tablets (2%)
Cosopt Sterile Ophthalmic Solution
Covera-HS Tablets (Less than 2%)
Cozaar Tablets (1% or greater)
Crestor Tablets (Greater than or equal
to 2%)
▲ Crinone 4% Gel (Less than 5%)
▲ Crinone 8% Gel (Less than 5%)
▲ Crixivan Capsules (3.1%)
▲ Cubicin for Injection (4.5%)
▲ Cylert Chewable Tablets (Most
frequent)
▲ Cylert Tablets (Most frequent)
Cytovene Capsules (At least 3
subjects)
Cytovene-IV (At least 3 subjects)
Dantrium Capsules (Less frequent)
Dapsone Tablets
▲ DaunoXome Injection (Up to 6%)
Decadron Phosphate Injection
Decadron Tablets
Demadex Tablets and Injection (1.2%)
Demser Capsules
▲ Depacon Injection (9% to 15%)
▲ Depakene Capsules (15%)
▲ Depakene Syrup (15%)
▲ Depakote ER Tablets (1% to 15%)
▲ Depakote Sprinkle Capsules (9% to
15%)
▲ Depakote Tablets (1% to 15%)
Desoxyn Tablets

▲ Desyrel (9.9%)
Dexedrine Spansule Capsules
Dexedrine Tablets
DextroStat Tablets
Dilantin Infatabs
Dilantin Kapseals
Dilantin-125 Oral Suspension
Dilaudid Ampules
Dilaudid Injection
Dilaudid Multiple Dose Vials
Dilaudid Non-Sterile Powder
Dilaudid Oral Liquid (Less frequent)
Dilaudid Rectal Suppositories
Dilaudid Tablets
Dilaudid Tablets - 8 mg (Less frequent)
Dilaudid-HP Injection (Less frequent)
Dilaudid-HP Lyophilized Powder 250 mg (Less frequent)
Diovan HCT Tablets (Greater than 0.2%)
Diovan Tablets
Dipentum Capsules (Rare)
Diprivan Injectable Emulsion (Less than 1%)
▲ Ditropan XL Extended Release Tablets (2% to 5%)
Dolobid Tablets (Greater than 1 in 100)
▲ Dostinex Tablets (1% to less than 10%)
▲ Doxil Injection (Less than 1% to 5%)
▲ Duragesic Transdermal System (3% to 10%)
DynaCirc Capsules (0.5% to 1%)
DynaCirc CR Tablets (0.5% to 1%)
8-MOP Capsules
EC-Naprosyn Delayed-Release Tablets (Less than 1%)
▲ Effexor Tablets (3% to 22.5%)
▲ Effexor XR Capsules (3% to 23%)
Efudex Cream
Efudex Topical Solutions
Elavil
Eldepryl Capsules (1 of 49 patients)
Eligard 30 mg (1.1%)
Eligard 7.5 mg (Less than 2%)
Elmiron Capsules
▲ Eloxatin for Injection (9% to 11%)
▲ Emcyt Capsules (3%)
Emend Capsules (2.9%)
▲ Emtriva Capsules (7% to 16%)
Engerix-B Vaccine (Less than 1%)
▲ Entocort EC Capsules (Less than 5%)
▲ Epivir Oral Solution (11%)
▲ Epivir Tablets (11%)

▲ Epogen for Injection (13% to 16%)
Ergamisol Tablets (1%)
▲ Estring Vaginal Ring (4%)
▲ Evista Tablets (5.5%)
Evoxac Capsules (2.4%)
Excedrin Extra-Strength Caplets
Excedrin Extra-Strength Geltabs
Excedrin Extra-Strength Tablets
▲ Exelon Capsules (9%)
▲ Exelon Oral Solution (9%)
Factive Tablets (0.1% to 1%)
Famvir Tablets (1.5% to 2.5%)
▲ Faslodex Injection (6.9%)
▲ Felbatol Oral Suspension (8.6% to 17.5%)
▲ Felbatol Tablets (8.6% to 17.5%)
Feldene Capsules (Occasional)
▲ Femara Tablets (7%)
femhrt Tablets
Ferrlecit Injection (Greater than 1%)
Flexeril Tablets (Less than 1%)
▲ Flolan for Injection (4% to 9%)
Flomax Capsules (1.4% to 2.4%)
Florinef Acetate Tablets
▲ Flovent 44 mcg Inhalation Aerosol (3% to 13%)
▲ Flovent 110 mcg Inhalation Aerosol (3% to 13%)
▲ Flovent 220 mcg Inhalation Aerosol (3% to 13%)
Flovent Rotadisk 50 mcg
Flovent Rotadisk 100 mcg
Flovent Rotadisk 250 mcg
Floxin Otic Solution (Single report)
▲ Floxin Tablets (3% to 7%)
Flumadine Syrup (2.1% to 3.4%)
Flumadine Tablets (2.1% to 3.4%)
▲ Fluvoxamine maleate (4% to 21%)
▲ Focalin Tablets (Among most common)
▲ Forteo Injection (4.3%)
▲ Fortovase Capsules (5.6%)
▲ Foscavir Injection (Between 1% and 5%)
Frova Tablets (Frequent)
Fuzeon Injection (11.3%)
▲ Gabitril Tablets (6%)
Gastrocrom Oral Concentrate (Less common)
Gemzar for Injection (Infrequent)
Gengraf Capsules (1% to less than 3%)
▲ Geodon for Injection (Up to 3%)
▲ Gleevec Tablets (Up to 13%)
Glucotrol XL Extended Release Tablets (Less than 3%)

Grifulvin V Tablets Microsize and Oral Suspension Microsize (Occasional)
Gris-PEG Tablets (Occasional)
Guanfacine (Less than 3% to 4%)
Halcion Tablets (Rare)
Haldol Decanoate 50 Injection
Haldol Decanoate 100 Injection
Havrix Vaccine (Less than 1%)
▲ Herceptin I.V. (14%)
Hivid Tablets (Less than 1%)
Hydrocortone Phosphate Injection, Sterile
Hydrocortone Tablets
Hytrin Capsules (At least 1%)
Hyzaar 50-12.5 Tablets
Hyzaar 100-25 Tablets
▲ Indapamide Tablets (Less than 5%)
Inderal LA Long-Acting Capsules
Indocin Capsules (Less than 1%)
Indocin Oral Suspension (Less than 1%)
Indocin Suppositories (Less than 1%)
▲ Infergen (24% to 39%)
▲ Intron A for Injection (Up to 12%)
▲ Invanz for Injection (3% to 3.2%)
Invirase Capsules (Greater than or equal to 2%)
Ionamin Capsules
Isoptin SR Tablets (1% or less)
Kadian Capsules (Less than 3%)
Kaletra Capsules (1.1% to 2.4%)
Kaletra Oral Solution (1.1% to 2.4%)
Keppra Oral Solution (1% or more)
Keppra Tablets (1% or more)
Ketek Tablets (Greater than or equal to 0.2% to less than 2%)
Klonopin Tablets (Infrequent)
Klonopin Wafers (Infrequent)
Kytril Injection (Less than 2%)
▲ Kytril Tablets (3% to 5%)
▲ Lamictal Chewable Dispersible Tablets (5.6%)
▲ Lamictal Tablets (5.6%)
▲ Lariam Tablets (Among most frequent)
Lescol Capsules (2.7%)
Lescol XL Tablets (1.8%)
▲ Leukine (11%)
▲ Leustatin Injection (7%)
▲ Levaquin in 5% Dextrose Injection (0.4% to 4.3%)
▲ Levaquin Injection (0.4% to 4.3%)
▲ Levaquin Tablets (0.4% to 4.3%)
Levitra Tablets (Less than 2%)
Levlen 21 Tablets
Levlen 28 Tablets
Levlite 28 Tablets
Levothroid Tablets
Levoxyl Tablets
▲ Lexapro Oral Solution (5% to 14%)
▲ Lexapro Tablets (5% to 14%)
Lexxel Tablets
Lipitor Tablets (Greater than or equal to 2%)
Lofibra Capsules
Lotensin HCT Tablets (0.3% to 1%)
Lotensin Tablets (Less than 1%)
Lotrel Capsules
Loxitane Capsules
▲ Lupron Depot 3.75 mg (16%)
▲ Lupron Depot 7.5 mg (Less than 5%)
▲ Lupron Depot—3 Month 11.25 mg (16%)
▲ Lupron Depot—3 Month 22.5 mg (8.5%)
▲ Lupron Depot—4 Month 30 mg (Less than 5%)
▲ Lupron Injection (5% or more)
▲ Malarone Pediatric Tablets (2% to 3%)
▲ Malarone Tablets (2% to 3%)
Matulane Capsules
Mavik Tablets (0.3% to 1%)
Maxair Autohaler
Maxalt Tablets (Infrequent)
Maxalt-MLT Orally Disintegrating Tablets (Infrequent)
Maxzide Tablets
Maxzide-25 mg Tablets
Mebaral Tablets (Less than 1 in 100 patients)
▲ Mepron Suspension (10% to 19%)
▲ Meridia Capsules (10.7%)
Merrem I.V. (Greater than 0.1% to 1%)
▲ Metadate CD Capsules (5%)
▲ Metadate ER Tablets (Among most common)
Mevacor Tablets (0.5% to 1%)
Miacalcin Nasal Spray (Less than 1%)
Micardis HCT Tablets
Micardis Tablets (More than 0.3%)
Midamor Tablets (Less than or equal to 1%)
Minipress Capsules
▲ Mirapex Tablets (17% to 27%)
Mobic Tablets (0.4% to 3.6%)
Moduretic Tablets (Less than or equal to 1%)
Monurol Sachet (Less than 1%)

Motrin Cold & Sinus Caplets
Motrin Suspension, Oral Drops, Chewable Tablets, and Caplets (Less than 1%)
MS Contin Tablets (Less frequent)
MSIR Oral Capsules (Less frequent)
MSIR Oral Solution Concentrate (Less frequent)
MSIR Oral Tablets (Less frequent)
Mycobutin Capsules (1%)
▲ Mylotarg for Injection (14% to 22%)
Namenda Tablets (Greater than or equal to 2%)
Naprelan Tablets (Less than 3%)
Naprosyn Suspension (Less than 1%)
Naprosyn Tablets (Less than 1%)
Nardil Tablets (Common)
Naropin Injection (Less than 1%)
Natrecor for Injection (2%)
Navane Capsules
Navane Concentrate
Navane Intramuscular
▲ Nefazodone (11%)
Nembutal Sodium Solution (Less than 1%)
Neoral Oral Solution (1% to less than 3%)
Neoral Soft Gelatin Capsules (1% to less than 3%)
▲ Neulasta Injection (15% to 72%)
▲ Neumega for Injection (33%)
Neurontin Capsules
Neurontin Oral Solution
Neurontin Tablets
Nexium Delayed-Release Capsules (Less than 1%)
Niaspan Extended-Release Tablets
▲ Nilandron Tablets (16.3%)
▲ Nipent for Injection (3% to 10%)
Noroxin Tablets (Less frequent)
Norpramin Tablets
Norvasc Tablets (More than 0.1% to 1%)
Norvir Oral Solution (1.3% to 2.6%)
Norvir Soft Gelatin Capsules (1.3% to 2.6%)
NuLev Orally Disintegrating Tablets
Omnicef Capsules (0.2%)
Omnicef for Oral Suspension (0.2%)
▲ Ontak Vials (9%)
▲ Orap Tablets (2 of 20 patients)
Orapred Oral Solution
Ortho Tri-Cyclen Lo Tablets
Ortho Tri-Cyclen Tablets

Ortho-Cyclen Tablets
Ovidrel for Injection (Less than 2%)
Oxandrin Tablets
Oxsoralen-Ultra Capsules
▲ OxyContin Tablets (Between 1% and 5%)
▲ Pacerone Tablets (1% to 3%)
Pamelor
Parnate Tablets
▲ Paxil CR Controlled-Release Tablets (7% to 20%)
▲ Paxil Oral Suspension (1.3% to 24%)
▲ Paxil Tablets (1.3% to 24%)
Pediazole Suspension
Peganone Tablets
▲ Pegasys (19%)
▲ PEG-Intron Powder for Injection (23%)
Pentasa Capsules (Less than 1%)
Pepcid for Oral Suspension (Infrequent)
Pepcid Injection (Infrequent)
Pepcid Injection Premixed (Infrequent)
Pepcid Tablets (Infrequent)
Periactin Tablets
▲ Permax Tablets (7.9%)
Phenergan Suppositories
Phenergan Tablets
Phenobarbital (Less than 1%)
Phenytek Capsules
▲ Photofrin for Injection (14%)
Plavix Tablets (1% to 2.5%)
Plendil Extended-Release Tablets (0.5% to 1.5%)
Pletal Tablets (Less than 2%)
Ponstel Capsules (Occasional)
Pravachol Tablets
Prefest Tablets
▲ Premarin Tablets (6% to 7%)
▲ Premphase Tablets (6% to 7%)
▲ Prempro Tablets (6% to 7%)
Prevacid NapraPAC 375 (Less than 1%)
Prevacid NapraPAC 500 (Less than 1%)
PREVPAC
Prilosec Delayed-Release Capsules (Less than 1%)
Prilosec OTC Tablets (Less than 1%)
Prinivil Tablets (0.3% to 1%)
Prinzide Tablets
ProAmatine Tablets (Rare)
Procardia XL Extended Release Tablets (Less than 3%)

Prochieve 4% Gel
Prochieve 8% Gel
Prochlorperazine (Sometimes)
▲ Procrit for Injection (13% to 21%)
▲ Prograf Capsules and Injection (32% to 64%)
Proleukin for Injection
▲ Prometrium Capsules (100 mg, 200 mg) (Less than 5%)
Protonix I.V. (Greater than or equal to 1%)
Protonix Tablets (Less than or equal to 1%)
▲ Protopic Ointment (Up to 4%)
▲ Provigil Tablets (5%)
▲ Prozac Pulvules and Liquid (10% to 33%)
▲ Pulmicort Turbuhaler Inhalation Powder (1% to 3%)
▲ Rapamune Oral Solution and Tablets (13% to 22%)
▲ Rebetol Capsules (14% to 41%)
▲ Rebetol Oral Solution (14% to 41%)
▲ Rebetron Combination Therapy (26% to 39%)
Recombivax HB (Less than to greater than 1%)
ReFacto Vials
▲ Relafen Tablets (1% to 3%)
Relpax Tablets (Infrequent)
▲ Remicade for IV Injection (6%)
▲ Reminyl Oral Solution (5%)
▲ Reminyl Tablets (5%)
ReoPro Vials (0.3%)
Requip Tablets (1% or more)
▲ Rescriptor Tablets (1.2% to 5%)
▲ Retrovir Capsules (2.4% to 5%)
▲ Retrovir IV Infusion (3% to 5%)
▲ Retrovir Syrup (2.4% to 5%)
▲ Retrovir Tablets (2.4% to 5%)
▲ Reyataz Capsules (Less than 1% to 5%)
▲ Ribavirin Capsules (26% to 41%)
Rifater Tablets
Rilutek Tablets (2.1% to 2.9%)
▲ Risperdal Consta Injection (13% to 16%)
▲ Risperdal M-Tab Tablets (23% to 26%)
▲ Risperdal Oral Solution (23% to 26%)
▲ Risperdal Tablets (23% to 26%)
▲ Ritalin Hydrochloride Tablets (One of the two most common)
▲ Ritalin LA Capsules (3.1%)
▲ Ritalin-SR Tablets (One of the two most common)

▲ Rituxan for Infusion (1% to 5%)
▲ Rituxan I.V. (1% to 5%)
▲ Roferon-A Injection (14%)
▲ Romazicon Injection (3% to 9%)
Rowasa Rectal Suspension Enema (0.12%)
Rythmol Tablets (1.5%)
Salagen Tablets (Less than 1%)
▲ Sandostatin LAR Depot (5% to 15%)
▲ Sarafem Pulvules (9% to 24%)
Seconal (Less than 1%)
▲ Semprex-D Capsules (4%)
Septra DS Tablets
Septra Grape Suspension
Septra Suspension
Septra Tablets
▲ Serevent Inhalation Aerosol (1% to 3%)
▲ Serostim for Injection (3.9% to 5.9%)
▲ Simulect for Injection (Greater than or equal to 10%)
Singulair Chewable Tablets
Singulair Oral Granules
Singulair Tablets
Solu-Medrol Sterile Powder
Soma Tablets
Sonata Capsules (Infrequent)
▲ Soriatane Capsules (1% to 10%)
Spectracef Tablets (0.1% to 1%)
Sporanox Capsules (Infrequent)
Sporanox Oral Solution (Less than 2%)
▲ Stadol Injection (Greater than or equal to 1% to 11%)
▲ Stadol NS (Greater than or equal to 1% to 11%)
Stalevo Tablets
▲ Strattera Capsules (5% to 16%)
▲ Suboxone Tablets (14% to 25%)
▲ Subutex Tablets (21.4% to 25%)
Sular Tablets (Less than or equal to 1%)
Surmontil Capsules
▲ Sustiva Capsules (1% to 7%)
▲ Symmetrel Syrup (5% to 10%)
▲ Symmetrel Tablets (5% to 10%)
▲ Synarel Nasal Solution for Endometriosis (8% of patients)
Synercid I.V. (Less than 1%)
Tambocor Tablets (1% to 3%)
Tamiflu Capsules (1.1% to 1.2%)
Tamiflu Oral Suspension (1.1% to 1.2%)
▲ Targretin Capsules (4.8% to 11.3%)
Tarka Tablets (Less frequent)

▲ Temodar Capsules (10%)
▲ Tequin Injection (0.1% to 3%)
▲ Tequin Tablets (0.1% to 3%)
Testim 1% Gel (1% or less)
Teveten HCT Tablets (Less than 1%)
Teveten Tablets (Less than 1%)
Thalomid Capsules
Thiothixene Capsules
Tiazac Capsules (Less than 2%)
▲ Tikosyn Capsules (4%)
Timolide Tablets (Less than 1%)
Timoptic in Ocudose (Less frequent)
Timoptic Sterile Ophthalmic Solution
Timoptic-XE Sterile Ophthalmic Gel
Forming Solution
▲ Topamax Sprinkle Capsules (Frequent to 8%)
▲ Topamax Tablets (Frequent to 8%)
Toprol-XL Tablets
Toradol IM Injection, IV Injection (1% or less)
Toradol Tablets (1% or less)
Tranxene T-TAB Tablets
Tranxene-SD Half Strength Tablets
Tranxene-SD Tablets
▲ Trasylol Injection (3%)
Trental Tablets
Triavil Tablets
Tricor Tablets (1%)
Trifluoperazine
Trilafon
▲ Trileptal Oral Suspension (2% to 4%)
▲ Trileptal Tablets (2% to 4%)
Tri-Levlen 21 Tablets
Tri-Levlen 28 Tablets
▲ Trisenox Injection (43%)
▲ Trizivir Tablets (7% to 13%)
Trovan I.V. (Less than 1%)
Trovan Tablets (Less than 1%)
Twinrix Vaccine (Less than 1%)
Tylenol, Children's, Plus Cold
Tylenol, Maximum Strength, Severe Cold & Flu NightTime Liquid
Tylenol, Maximum Strength, Sinus Day Non-Drowsy Geltabs, Gelcaps, and Caplets
Tylenol, Maximum Strength, Sinus Night Time Caplets
Tylenol, Multi-Symptom, Cold Day Non-Drowsy Caplets and Gelcaps
Tylenol, Multi-Symptom, Cold Night Time Complete Formula Caplets
Tylenol Sinus Severe Congestion Caplets
Ultracet Tablets (2%)

Uniphyl 400 mg and 600 mg Tablets
Uniretic Tablets (Less than 1%)
▲ Vagifem Tablets (3% to 5%)
▲ Valcyte Tablets (16%)
Valium Tablets
Vantin Tablets and Oral Suspension (Less than 1%)
Vaseretic Tablets (0.5% to 2%)
Vasotec I.V. Injection (0.5% to 1%)
▲ Velcade for Injection (27%)
Ventolin HFA Inhalation Aerosol
Verelan PM Capsules (2% or less)
▲ Vesanoid Capsules (14%)
VFEND I.V. (Less than 1%)
VFEND Oral Suspension (Less than 1%)
VFEND Tablets (Less than 1%)
Viagra Tablets (Less than 2%)
Vicks 44D Cough & Head Congestion Relief
Vicks 44m, Pediatric, Cough & Cold Relief
Vicks DayQuil Multi-Symptom Cold/Flu Relief Liquid & LiquiCaps
Vicks NyQuil, Children's, Cold/Cough Relief
▲ Vicoprofen Tablets (3% to 9%)
Vioxx Oral Suspension (Greater than (0.1% to 1.9%)
Vioxx Tablets (Greater than 0.1% to 1.9%)
Viracept Oral Powder (Less than 2%)
Viracept Tablets (Less than 2%)
Vistide Injection
Vivactil Tablets
▲ Vivelle-Dot Transdermal System (1.5% to 6.4%)
Voltaren Tablets (Occasional)
Voltaren-XR Tablets (Occasional)
VoSpire Extended-Release Tablets (2.4%)
▲ Wellbutrin SR Sustained-Release Tablets (5% to 16%)
▲ Wellbutrin Tablets (18.6%)
▲ Wellbutrin XL Extended-Release Tablets (5% to 16%)
▲ Xanax Tablets (8.9% to 29.4%)
▲ Xanax XR Tablets (24.2%)
▲ Xeloda Tablets (Less than 5%)
Xopenex Inhalation Solution
▲ Xyrem Oral Solution (5%)
Zantac 150 EFFERdose Granules (Rare)
Zantac 150 EFFERdose Tablets (Rare)
Zantac 150 Tablets (Rare)

Zantac 300 Tablets (Rare)
Zantac Injection
Zantac Injection Premixed
Zantac Syrup (Rare)
Zaroxolyn Tablets
Zebeta Tablets (1.5% to 2.5%)
▲ Zenapax for Injection (Greater than 5%)
▲ Zerit Capsules (29%)
▲ Zerit for Oral Solution (29%)
Zestoretic Tablets
Zestril Tablets (0.3% to 1.0%)
▲ Zevalin Injection (5%)
Ziac Tablets (1.1% to 1.2%)
▲ Ziagen Oral Solution (7% to 13%)
▲ Ziagen Tablets (7% to 13%)
Zithromax Capsules, 250 mg (1% or less)
Zithromax for IV Infusion (1% or less)
Zithromax for Oral Suspension, 300 mg, 600 mg, 900 mg, 1200 mg (1% or less)
Zithromax Tablets, 250 mg, 500 mg (1% or less)
Zocor Tablets
▲ Zoladex (5% to 11%)
Zoladex (3-month)
▲ Zoloft Oral Concentrate (12% to 28%)
▲ Zoloft Tablets (12% to 28%)
▲ Zometa for Intravenous Infusion (14% to 15.1%)
Zomig Nasal Spray (Infrequent to less than 2%)
Zomig Tablets (Infrequent)
Zomig-ZMT Tablets (Infrequent)
▲ Zonegran Capsules (6%)
▲ Zosyn (4.5% to 6.6%)
▲ Zosyn in Galaxy Containers (4.5% to 6.6%)
▲ Zyban Sustained-Release Tablets (31% to 40%)
▲ Zyprexa Tablets (20%)

▲ Zyprexa ZYDIS Orally Disintegrating Tablets (20%)
▲ Zyrtec Syrup (Less than 2% to 9%)
▲ Zyrtec Tablets (Less than 2% to 9%)
▲ Zyrtec-D 12 Hour Extended Relief Tablets (4%)
Zyvox for Oral Suspension (2.5%)
Zyvox Injection (2.5%)
Zyvox Tablets (2.5%)

Intoxication, chronic
Miltown Tablets

Irritability
▲ Aerobid Inhaler System (3% to 9%)
▲ Aerobid-M Inhaler System (3% to 9%)
Alacol DM Syrup
Aricept Tablets (Frequent)
Arthrotec Tablets (Rare)
Attenuvax
Catapres-TTS (0.5% or less)
Cedax Oral Suspension (0.1% to 1%)
Ceftin for Oral Suspension (0.1% to 1%)
Celontin Capsules
Cenestin Tablets, 0.3 mg
Cenestin Tablets, 0.45 mg, 0.625 mg, 0.9 mg, 1.25 mg
Cipro I.V. (1% or less)
Cipro I.V. Pharmacy Bulk Package (Less than 1%)
Cipro Oral Suspension (Less than 1%)
Cipro Tablets (Less than 1%)
Cipro XR Tablets
Clomid Tablets
Clozapine Tablets (Less than 1%)
Clozaril Tablets (Less than 1%)
▲ Comvax (32.2% to 57.0%)
▲ Copegus Tablets (33%)
Cylert Chewable Tablets
Cylert Tablets
Cytovene Capsules
Cytovene-IV
Dalmane Capsules
▲ Daptacel (36.9% to 41.4%)
Dipentum Capsules (Rare)
Efudex Cream
Efudex Topical Solutions
Elavil
Eldepryl Capsules
Elspar for Injection
Engerix-B Vaccine (Less than 1%)
Excedrin Extra-Strength Caplets
Excedrin Extra-Strength Geltabs
Excedrin Extra-Strength Tablets
Extendryl Chewable Tablets
Extendryl SR. & JR. Capsules
Extendryl Syrup
Femring Vaginal Ring
▲ Flumist Vaccine (9.9% to 19.5%)
Fortovase Capsules (Less than 2%)
▲ Gabitril Tablets (10%)
▲ Gamimune N, 10% Solvent/Detergent Treated (Among most common)
Gastrocrom Oral Concentrate (2 of 87 patients)

Guanidine Hydrochloride Tablets
Halcion Tablets
HibTITER (133 of 1,118 vaccinations)
▲ Indapamide Tablets (Greater than or equal to 5%)
▲ Infanrix Vaccine (28.8% to 61.5%)
▲ Intron A for Injection (Up to 16%)
Invirase Capsules (Less than 2%)
▲ Lamictal Chewable Dispersible Tablets (3%)
▲ Lamictal Tablets (3%)
Levothroid Tablets
Levoxyl Tablets
Lexapro Oral Solution (Frequent)
Lexapro Tablets (Frequent)
Lexxel Tablets
Maxalt Tablets (Infrequent)
Maxalt-MLT Orally Disintegrating Tablets (Infrequent)
Meruvax II
M-M-R II
Mumpsvax
Narcan Injection
Novarel for Injection
Paxil CR Controlled-Release Tablets
▲ Pediarix Vaccine (1.7% to 63.8%)
Pedvax HIB, liquid
▲ Pegasys (19%)
▲ PEG-Intron Powder for Injection (28%)
Periactin Tablets
Plaquenil Tablets
Plendil Extended-Release Tablets (0.5% to 1.5%)
Prefest Tablets
Pregnyl for Injection
Premarin Tablets
Premphase Tablets
Prempro Tablets
▲ Prevnar for Injection (68.9% to 72.8%)
Prinivil Tablets (0.3% to 1%)
Prinzide Tablets
Proleukin for Injection
▲ Prometrium Capsules (100 mg, 200 mg)
Pulmicort Respules (Less than 1%)
Pulmicort Turbuhaler Inhalation Powder (Rare)
▲ Rebetol Capsules (10% to 47%)
▲ Rebetol Oral Solution (10% to 47%)
▲ Rebetron Combination Therapy (23% to 32%)
Recombivax HB (Greater than 1%)

Retrovir Capsules (1.6%)
Retrovir IV Infusion (2%)
Retrovir Syrup (1.6%)
Retrovir Tablets (1.6%)
▲ Ribavirin Capsules (23% to 47%)
▲ Roferon-A Injection (Less than 5% to 15%)
Singulair Chewable Tablets (Very rare)
Singulair Oral Granules (Very rare)
Singulair Tablets (Very rare)
▲ Skelaxin Tablets (Most frequent)
Soma Tablets
▲ Strattera Capsules (0.5% to 8%)
▲ Symmetrel Syrup (1% to 5%)
▲ Symmetrel Tablets (1% to 5%)
Tasmar Tablets (1%)
Tranxene T-TAB Tablets
Tranxene-SD Half Strength Tablets
Tranxene-SD Tablets
Triavil Tablets
Twinrix Vaccine (Less than 1%)
Uniphyl 400 mg and 600 mg Tablets
Varivax (Greater than or equal to 1%)
VoSpire Extended-Release Tablets (Less frequent)
▲ Wellbutrin SR Sustained-Release Tablets (2% to 3%)
▲ Wellbutrin XL Extended-Release Tablets (2% to 3%)
▲ Xanax Tablets (33.1%)
Xanax XR Tablets (Rare) to frequent
▲ Xeloda Tablets (Less than 5%)
Zarontin Capsules
Zarontin Syrup
Zestoretic Tablets
Zestril Tablets (0.3% to 1.0%)
Zomig Nasal Spray (Rare)
Zomig Tablets (Rare)
Zomig-ZMT Tablets (Rare)
▲ Zonegran Capsules (9%)
Zyban Sustained-Release Tablets (Frequent)
Zyrtec Syrup
Zyrtec Tablets

Jitteriness

Chlorpromazine
Cubicin for Injection (Less than 1%)
Guanidine Hydrochloride Tablets
Lexapro Oral Solution (Infrequent)
Lexapro Tablets (Infrequent)
Nardil Tablets (Less common)
Procardia Capsules (2% or less)
Prochlorperazine
Trifluoperazine

Language problems, unspecified

▲ Topamax Sprinkle Capsules (2% to 10%)
▲ Topamax Tablets (2% to 10%)

Laughing, easy

▲ Marinol Capsules (8% to 24%)

Libido decreased

Abilify Tablets (1% or less)
Aciphex Tablets
Actiq (Less than 1%)
Adalat CC Tablets (Less than 1.0%)
Aldoclor Tablets
Aldoril Tablets
Ambien Tablets (Rare)
Amerge Tablets (Rare)
Anadrol-50 Tablets
Androderm Transdermal System (Less than 1%)
▲ AndroGel (Up to 3%)
Aricept Tablets (Infrequent)
Asacol Delayed-Release Tablets
▲ Avinza Capsules (Less than 5%)
Avodart Soft Gelatin Capsules (0.3% to 3%)
Blocadren Tablets (0.6%)
BuSpar Tablets (Infrequent)
Caduet Tablets (Less than 2%)
Calcijex Injection
Cardura Tablets (0.8%)
▲ Casodex Tablets (2% to 5%)
Celexa Oral Solution (2%)
Celexa Tablets (2%)
Clozapine Tablets (Less than 1%)
Clozaril Tablets (Less than 1%)
Copaxone for Injection (Infrequent)
Coreg Tablets (Greater than 0.1% to 1%)
Corzide 40/5 Tablets (1 to 5 of 1000 patients)
Corzide 80/5 Tablets (1 to 5 of 1000 patients)
Cosopt Sterile Ophthalmic Solution
Cozaar Tablets (Less than 1%)
▲ Crinone 8% Gel (10%)
Cytotec Tablets (Infrequent)
Delatestryl Injection
Diovan HCT Tablets (Greater than 0.2%)
Doral
DynaCirc Capsules (0.5% to 1%)
DynaCirc CR Tablets (0.5% to 1%)
▲ Effexor Tablets (2% to 5.7%)

▲ Effexor XR Capsules (3% to 9%)
▲ Eligard 30 mg (3.3%)
Eligard 7.5 mg (Less than 2%)
Estring Vaginal Ring (At least 1 report)
Exelon Capsules (Infrequent)
Exelon Oral Solution (Infrequent)
Flomax Capsules (1.0% to 2.0%)
Fluvoxamine maleate (2%)
Gabitril Tablets (Infrequent)
Gengraf Capsules (1% to less than 3%)
Glucotrol XL Extended Release Tablets (Less than 1%)
Guanfacine (3% or less)
Hectorol Capsules
Hectorol Injection
Hytrin Capsules (0.6%)
Hyzaar 50-12.5 Tablets
Hyzaar 100-25 Tablets
▲ Indapamide Tablets (Less than 5%)
▲ Infergen (5%)
▲ Intron A for Injection (Up to 5%)
Inversine Tablets
Kadian Capsules (Less than 3%)
Kaletra Capsules (Less than 2%)
Kaletra Oral Solution (Less than 2%)
Klonopin Tablets (1%)
Klonopin Wafers (1%)
Lamictal Chewable Dispersible Tablets (Rare)
Lamictal Tablets (Rare)
▲ Lexapro Oral Solution (3% to 7%)
▲ Lexapro Tablets (3% to 7%)
Lexxel Tablets
Librium Capsules
Lipitor Tablets (Less than 2%)
Lofibra Capsules
Lopid Tablets
Lotensin HCT Tablets (0.3% to 1%)
Lotrel Capsules
▲ Lupron Depot 3.75 mg (Less than 5%)
▲ Lupron Depot 7.5 mg (5.4%)
▲ Lupron Depot—3 Month 11.25 mg (1.8% to 11%)
▲ Lupron Depot—3 Month 22.5 mg (Less than 5%)
▲ Lupron Depot—4 Month 30 mg (Less than 5%)
▲ Lupron Injection (Less than 5%)
Mavik Tablets (0.3% to 1%)
Meridia Capsules
Mexitil Capsules (Less than 1% or about 4 in 1,000)

Midamor Tablets (Less than or equal to 1%)
Mirapex Tablets (1%)
▲ Mirena Intrauterine System (5% or more)
Moduretic Tablets
MS Contin Tablets (Less frequent)
MSIR Oral Capsules (Less frequent)
MSIR Oral Solution Concentrate (Less frequent)
MSIR Oral Tablets (Less frequent)
Nadolol Tablets (1 to 5 of 1000 patients)
Nefazodone (1%)
Neoral Oral Solution (1% to less than 3%)
Neoral Soft Gelatin Capsules (1% to less than 3%)
Neurontin Capsules (Infrequent)
Neurontin Oral Solution (Infrequent)
Neurontin Tablets (Infrequent)
▲ Nilandron Tablets (11%)
Norpramin Tablets
Norvir Oral Solution (Less than 2%)
Norvir Soft Gelatin Capsules (Less than 2%)
Ovrette Tablets
OxyContin Tablets
▲ Pacerone Tablets (1% to 3%)
Pamelor
▲ Paxil CR Controlled-Release Tablets (7% to 12%)
▲ Paxil Oral Suspension (3% to 9%)
▲ Paxil Tablets (3% to 9%)
Pepcid for Oral Suspension (Infrequent)
Pepcid Injection (Infrequent)
Pepcid Injection Premixed (Infrequent)
Pepcid Tablets (Infrequent)
Permax Tablets (Infrequent)
Plendil Extended-Release Tablets (0.5% to 1.5%)
Prevacid Delayed-Release Capsules (Less than 1%)
Prevacid for Delayed-Release Oral Suspension (Less than 1%)
Prevacid NapraPAC 375 (Less than 1%)
Prevacid NapraPAC 500 (Less than 1%)
Prevacid SoluTab Delayed-Release Tablets (Less than 1%)
PREVPAC (Less than 1%)

Prinivil Tablets (0.4%)
Prinzide Tablets (0.3% to 1%)
Procardia XL Extended Release Tablets (1% or less)
▲ Prochieve 4% Gel (10%)
▲ Prochieve 8% Gel (10%)
Propecia Tablets (1.8%)
▲ Proscar Tablets (3.3%)
ProSom Tablets (Rare)
Protonix I.V. (Less than 1%)
Protonix Tablets (Less than 1%)
Provigil Tablets (At least 1%)
▲ Prozac Pulvules and Liquid (1% to 11%)
Requip Tablets (Infrequent)
Rescriptor Tablets
Reyataz Capsules (Less than 3%)
Rilutek Tablets (Infrequent)
Risperdal Consta Injection (Infrequent)
Rocaltrol Capsules
Rocaltrol Oral Solution
Sandostatin Injection (Less than 1%)
Sandostatin LAR Depot (Rare)
▲ Sarafem Pulvules (3% to 9%)
Seroquel Tablets (Rare)
Sonata Capsules (Infrequent)
Soriatane Capsules (Less than 1%)
Sporanox Capsules (0.2% to 1.2%)
▲ Strattera Capsules (5% or greater)
Sular Tablets (Less than or equal to 1%)
Surmontil Capsules
▲ Symbyax Capsules (2% to 4%)
Symmetrel Syrup (0.1% to 1%)
Symmetrel Tablets (0.1% to 1%)
▲ Synarel Nasal Solution for Endometriosis (22% of patients)
Tambocor Tablets (Less than 1%)
Tarka Tablets
Tasmar Tablets (Infrequent)
Testred Capsules, 10 mg
Thalomid Capsules
Timolide Tablets (Less than 1%)
Timoptic in Ocudose
Timoptic Sterile Ophthalmic Solution
Timoptic-XE Sterile Ophthalmic Gel Forming Solution
Topamax Sprinkle Capsules (Less than 1% to 2%)
Topamax Tablets (Less than 1% to 2%)
Toprol-XL Tablets
Tricor Tablets (2%)

Trileptal Oral Suspension
Trileptal Tablets
Trovan I.V. (Less than 1%)
Trovan Tablets (Less than 1%)
Uniretic Tablets (Less than 1%)
Vaseretic Tablets (0.5% to 2%)
VFEND I.V. (Less than 1%)
VFEND Oral Suspension (Less than 1%)
VFEND Tablets (Less than 1%)
Vicoprofen Tablets (Less than 1%)
Wellbutrin SR Sustained-Release Tablets (Infrequent)
▲ Wellbutrin Tablets (3.1%)
Wellbutrin XL Extended-Release Tablets (Infrequent)
▲ Xanax Tablets (14.4%)
▲ Xanax XR Tablets (6%)
Xyrem Oral Solution (Infrequent)
Zantac Injection
Zantac Injection Premixed
Zebeta Tablets
Zestoretic Tablets (0.3% to 1%)
Zestril Tablets (0.4%)
▲ Zoladex (61%)
▲ Zoloft Oral Concentrate (1% to 11%)
▲ Zoloft Tablets (1% to 11%)
Zonegran Capsules (Infrequent)
Zyban Sustained-Release Tablets (Infrequent)
Zyprexa Tablets (Infrequent)
Zyprexa ZYDIS Orally Disintegrating Tablets (Infrequent)
Zyrtec Syrup (Less than 2%)
Zyrtec Tablets (Less than 2%)
Zyrtec-D 12 Hour Extended Relief Tablets (Less than 2%)

Libido increased

Abilify Tablets (1% or less)
Anadrol-50 Tablets
Androderm Transdermal System
AndroGel (One patient)
Aricept Tablets (Frequent)
BuSpar Tablets (Infrequent)
Celexa Oral Solution (Infrequent)
Celexa Tablets (Infrequent)
Clozapine Tablets (Less than 1%)
Clozaril Tablets (Less than 1%)
Cognex Capsules (Infrequent)
Delatestryl Injection
▲ Dostinex Tablets (Less than 10%)
Effexor Tablets (Infrequent)
Effexor XR Capsules (Infrequent)
Exelon Capsules (Infrequent)

Exelon Oral Solution (Infrequent)
Fluvoxamine maleate (Infrequent)
Gabitril Tablets (Infrequent)
Gengraf Capsules (1% to less than 3%)
Haldol Decanoate 50 Injection
Haldol Decanoate 100 Injection
Klonopin Tablets (Infrequent)
Klonopin Wafers (Infrequent)
Lamictal Chewable Dispersible Tablets (Rare)
Lamictal Tablets (Rare)
Librium Capsules
Lotensin Tablets (Less than 1%)
Lupron Injection
Meridia Capsules
Moban Oral Concentrate
Moban Tablets
Namenda Tablets (Infrequent)
Nefazodone (Infrequent)
Neoral Oral Solution (1% to less than 3%)
Neoral Soft Gelatin Capsules (1% to less than 3%)
Neurontin Capsules (Rare)
Neurontin Oral Solution (Rare)
Neurontin Tablets (Rare)
Norpramin Tablets
Pamelor
Paxil CR Controlled-Release Tablets (Infrequent)
Paxil Oral Suspension (Rare)
Paxil Tablets (Rare)
Permax Tablets (Infrequent)
Prevacid Delayed-Release Capsules (Less than 1%)
Prevacid for Delayed-Release Oral Suspension (Less than 1%)
Prevacid NapraPAC 375 (Less than 1%)
Prevacid NapraPAC 500 (Less than 1%)
Prevacid SoluTab Delayed-Release Tablets (Less than 1%)
PREVPAC (Less than 1%)
Prozac Pulvules and Liquid (Infrequent)
Remeron SolTab Tablets (Infrequent)
Reminyl Oral Solution (Infrequent)
Reminyl Tablets (Infrequent)
Requip Tablets (Infrequent)
Rilutek Tablets (Infrequent)
Risperdal M-Tab Tablets (Infrequent)
Risperdal Oral Solution (Infrequent)

Risperdal Tablets (Infrequent)
Sarafem Pulvules (Infrequent)
Seroquel Tablets (Infrequent)
Stalevo Tablets
Surmontil Capsules
Symbyax Capsules (Rare)
Synarel Nasal Solution for
  Endometriosis (1% of patients)
Tasmar Tablets (Infrequent)
Testred Capsules, 10 mg
Topamax Sprinkle Capsules (Rare)
Topamax Tablets (Rare)
Trileptal Oral Suspension
Trileptal Tablets
Vistide Injection
Wellbutrin SR Sustained-Release
  Tablets
Wellbutrin Tablets (Frequent)
Wellbutrin XL Extended-Release
  Tablets
▲ Xanax Tablets (7.7%)
Xanax XR Tablets (Frequent)
Zarontin Capsules (Rare)
Zarontin Syrup (Rare)
▲ Zoladex (12%)
Zoloft Oral Concentrate (Rare)
Zoloft Tablets (Rare)
Zyban Sustained-Release Tablets
Zyprexa Tablets
Zyprexa ZYDIS Orally Disintegrating
  Tablets

Libido, changes
Activella Tablets
Adderall Tablets
Adderall XR Capsules
Adipex-P Capsules
Adipex-P Tablets
Alesse-28 Tablets
Alora Transdermal System
▲ Anafranil (21%)
Avalide Tablets
Avapro Tablets (Less than 1%)
Brevicon 28-Day Tablets
Cenestin Tablets, 0.3 mg
Cenestin Tablets, 0.45 mg, 0.625 mg,
  0.9 mg, 1.25 mg
Climara Transdermal System
Delestrogen Injection
Desoxyn Tablets
Dexedrine Spansule Capsules
Dexedrine Tablets
DextroStat Tablets
Doral

Elavil
Esclim Transdermal System
Estrace Tablets
Estrace Vaginal Cream
Estrasorb Topical Emulsion
Estratest H.S. Tablets
Estratest Tablets
Estrostep 21 Tablets
Estrostep Fe Tablets
femhrt Tablets
Femring Vaginal Ring
Flexeril Tablets (Rare)
▲ Fortovase Capsules (3.3%)
Halcion Tablets
Invirase Capsules (Greater than or
  equal to 2%)
Ionamin Capsules
Levlen 21 Tablets
Levlen 28 Tablets
Levlite 28 Tablets
Levora Tablets
Limbitrol
Lo/Ovral-28 Tablets
Loestrin 21 Tablets
Loestrin Fe Tablets
Low-Ogestrel-28 Tablets
Lunelle Monthly Injection
▲ Lupron Depot 3.75 mg (16%)
▲ Lupron Depot—3 Month 11.25 mg
  (16%)
Mellaril
Menest Tablets
Microgestin 1/20 Tablets
Microgestin 1.5/30 Tablets
Microgestin Fe 1/20 Tablets
Microgestin Fe 1.5/30 Tablets
Necon 0.5/35 Tablets
Necon 1/35 Tablets
Necon 1/50 Tablets
Necon 10/11 Tablets
Neurontin Capsules (Infrequent)
Neurontin Oral Solution (Infrequent)
Neurontin Tablets (Infrequent)
Nipent for Injection (Less than 3%)
Nordette-28 Tablets
Norinyl 1 + 35 28-Day Tablets
Norinyl 1 + 50 28-Day Tablets
Ogestrel 0.5/50-28 Tablets
Ortho Evra Transdermal System
Ortho Tri-Cyclen Lo Tablets
Ortho Tri-Cyclen Tablets
Ortho-Cept Tablets
Ortho-Cyclen Tablets
Ortho-Est Tablets

Ovcon 35 Tablets
Ovcon 50 Tablets
Ovral-28 Tablets
Oxandrin Tablets
Prefest Tablets
Premarin Intravenous
Premarin Tablets
Premarin Vaginal Cream
Premphase Tablets
Prempro Tablets
▲ Roferon-A Injection (Less than 4%)
Seasonale Tablets
Serentil Ampuls
Serentil Concentrate
Serentil Tablets
Sinequan Capsules
Sinequan Oral Concentrate
Thioridazine Hydrochloride Tablets
Triavil Tablets
Trilafon
Tri-Levlen 21 Tablets
Tri-Levlen 28 Tablets
Tri-Norinyl-28 Tablets
Triphasil-28 Tablets
Trivora-28 Tablets
Valium Tablets (Infrequent)
Vivactil Tablets
Vivelle Transdermal System
Vivelle-Dot Transdermal System
▲ Xanax Tablets (7.1%)
Yasmin 28 Tablets
Zovia 1/35E Tablets
Zovia 1/50E Tablets

Libido, loss of

Advicor Tablets
Altocor Extended-Release Tablets
Catapres Tablets (About 3 in 100 patients)
Catapres-TTS (0.5% or less)
Clorpres Tablets (About 3%)
Klonopin Tablets (Infrequent)
Klonopin Wafers (Infrequent)
Lescol Capsules
Lescol XL Tablets
Mevacor Tablets (0.5% to 1%)
Nolvadex Tablets
Orap Tablets
Pravachol Tablets
Roferon-A Injection (Infrequent)
Trexall Tablets
Zantac 150 EFFERdose Granules (Occasional)
Zantac 150 EFFERdose Tablets (Occasional)

Zantac 150 Tablets (Occasional)
Zantac 300 Tablets (Occasional)
Zantac Syrup (Occasional)
Ziac Tablets (0.4%)
Zocor Tablets

Listlessness

Aricept Tablets (Infrequent)
Indocin Capsules (Greater than 1%)
Indocin Oral Suspension (Greater than 1%)
Indocin Suppositories (Greater than 1%)
Synvisc

Manic behavior

Abilify Tablets (Greater than 1%)
Ambien Tablets (Rare)
Bextra Tablets (Rare)
Celexa Oral Solution
Celexa Tablets
Cipro I.V. (1% or less)
Cipro I.V. Pharmacy Bulk Package (Less than 1%)
Cipro Oral Suspension (Less than 1%)
Cipro Tablets (Less than 1%)
Cipro XR Tablets
Copaxone for Injection (Infrequent)
Effexor Tablets (0.5%)
Effexor XR Capsules (0.5%)
Elavil (Rare)
Evoxac Capsules (Less than 1%)
Felbatol Oral Suspension
Felbatol Tablets
Floxin Tablets
Fluvoxamine maleate (Approximately 1%)
Guanfacine
Halcion Tablets
Herceptin I.V. (At least one of the 958 patients)
Hivid Tablets (Less than 1%)
▲ Intron A for Injection (Less than 5%)
Lamictal Chewable Dispersible Tablets (Rare)
Lamictal Tablets (Rare)
Levaquin in 5% Dextrose Injection (0.1% to 1%)
Levaquin Injection (0.1% to 1%)
Levaquin Tablets (0.1% to 1%)
Nardil Tablets (Less frequent)
Nefazodone (0.3% to 1.6%)
Neurontin Capsules (Rare)
Neurontin Oral Solution (Rare)
Neurontin Tablets (Rare)
Orthoclone OKT3 Sterile Solution (Less than 1%)

Parnate Tablets
Paxil CR Controlled-Release Tablets
  (Approximately 1%)
Paxil Oral Suspension (Infrequent)
Paxil Tablets (Infrequent)
Permax Tablets (Infrequent)
Provigil Tablets
Relpax Tablets (Rare)
Remeron SolTab Tablets
  (Approximately 0.2%)
Requip Tablets (Infrequent)
Rescriptor Tablets
Retrovir IV Infusion
Rilutek Tablets (Infrequent)
Risperdal Consta Injection
  (Infrequent)
Risperdal M-Tab Tablets
Risperdal Oral Solution
▲ Risperdal Tablets (8%)
Roferon-A Injection
Rythmol Tablets (Less than 1%)
Seroquel Tablets (Infrequent)
Sustiva Capsules
Symmetrel Syrup
Symmetrel Tablets
Tasmar Tablets (Infrequent)
Topamax Sprinkle Capsules (Rare)
Topamax Tablets (Rare)
Triavil Tablets (Rare)
Trileptal Oral Suspension
Trileptal Tablets
Valtrex Caplets
Wellbutrin SR Sustained-Release
  Tablets
Wellbutrin Tablets (Frequent)
Wellbutrin XL Extended-Release
  Tablets
Xanax Tablets
Xanax XR Tablets (Infrequent)
Zomig Nasal Spray (Rare)
Zyban Sustained-Release Tablets

Manic behavior, mild

Celexa Oral Solution
Celexa Tablets
Effexor Tablets (0.5%)
Effexor XR Capsules (0.3%)
Elavil Injection (Rare)
Elavil Tablets (Rare)
Fluvoxamine maleate (Approximately
  1%)
Lamictal Chewable Dispersible
  Tablets (Rare)
Lamictal Tablets (Rare)

Limbitrol
▲ Nardil Tablets (Most common)
Nefazodone (0.3% to 1.6%)
Norpramin Tablets
Pamelor
Paxil CR Controlled-Release Tablets
  (Approximately 1%)
Paxil Oral Suspension (Approximately
  1%)
Paxil Tablets (Approximately 1%)
Prozac Pulvules and Liquid (0.1% to
  1.8%)
Remeron SolTab Tablets
  (Approximately 0.2%)
Remeron Tablets (Approximately 0.2%)
Sarafem Pulvules
Surmontil Capsules
Triavil Tablets (Rare)
Vivactil Tablets
Wellbutrin SR Sustained-Release
  Tablets (Rare)
Wellbutrin Tablets (Frequent)
Wellbutrin XL Extended-Release
  Tablets (Rare)
Xanax Tablets
Xanax XR Tablets (Infrequent)
Zoloft Oral Concentrate
  (Approximately 0.4%)
Zoloft Tablets (Approximately 0.4%)
Zyban Sustained-Release Tablets
  (Rare)

Melancholia

Celexa Oral Solution (Rare)
Celexa Tablets (Rare)

Memory impairment

Abilify Tablets (1% or less)
▲ Anafranil (9%)
Benztropine
BuSpar Tablets (Rare)
Copaxone for Injection (Infrequent)
▲ Copegus Tablets (6%)
Cozaar Tablets (Less than 1%)
Eldepryl Capsules
Eskalith Capsules
Eskalith CR Controlled-Release
  Tablets
Gleevec Tablets (Infrequent)
Halcion Tablets (0.5% to 0.9%)
Hyzaar 50-12.5 Tablets
Hyzaar 100-25 Tablets
Imitrex Nasal Spray (Rare)
Imitrex Tablets (Rare)
▲ Klonopin Tablets (4%)

▲ Klonopin Wafers (4%)
Lamictal Chewable Dispersible
  Tablets (2.4%)
Lamictal Tablets (2.4%)
▲ Lupron Depot 3.75 mg (Among most
  frequent)
▲ Lupron Depot—3 Month 11.25 mg
  (Less than 5%)
▲ Lupron Injection (Less than 5%)
Maxalt Tablets (Infrequent)
Maxalt-MLT Orally Disintegrating
  Tablets (Infrequent)
▲ Nefazodone (4%)
▲ Pegasys (5%)
Prinivil Tablets (0.3% to 1%)
Prinzide Tablets
Rifamate Capsules (Uncommon)
Rifater Tablets (Uncommon)
▲ Roferon-A Injection (Less than 4%)
Serax
Stalevo Tablets
Timolide Tablets
▲ Topamax Sprinkle Capsules (2% to
  14%)
▲ Topamax Tablets (2% to 14%)
Transderm Scop Transdermal
  Therapeutic System (Infrequent)
▲ Vesanoid Capsules (3%)
▲ Wellbutrin SR Sustained-Release
  Tablets (Up to 3%)
Wellbutrin Tablets (Infrequent)
▲ Wellbutrin XL Extended-Release
  Tablets (Up to 3%)
▲ Xanax Tablets (33.1%)
▲ Xanax XR Tablets (15.4%)
Zestoretic Tablets
Ziac Tablets
▲ Zonegran Capsules (6%)
Zyban Sustained-Release Tablets
  (Infrequent)

Memory loss, short-term

Altocor Extended-Release Tablets
Blocadren Tablets
Clozapine Tablets (Less than 1%)
Clozaril Tablets (Less than 1%)
Corzide 40/5 Tablets
Corzide 80/5 Tablets
Cosopt Sterile Ophthalmic Solution
▲ Crinone 4% Gel (Less than 5%)
▲ Crinone 8% Gel (Less than 5%)
Cytovene Capsules
Cytovene-IV
Ergamisol Tablets (10 out of 463
  patients)

Hivid Tablets (Less than 1%)
Inderal LA Long-Acting Capsules
Lescol Capsules
Lescol XL Tablets
Meridia Capsules
Mevacor Tablets (0.5% to 1%)
Mexitil Capsules (Less than 1% to
  about 9 in 1,000)
Nadolol Tablets
Parnate Tablets
Pravachol Tablets
Rythmol Tablets (Less than 1%)
Tenormin I.V. Injection
Tenormin Tablets
Timoptic in Ocudose
Timoptic Sterile Ophthalmic Solution
Timoptic-XE Sterile Ophthalmic Gel
  Forming Solution
Toprol-XL Tablets
Zocor Tablets

Mental acuity, loss of
Crixivan Capsules (Less than 2%)
Retrovir Capsules
Retrovir IV Infusion
Retrovir Syrup
Retrovir Tablets
Stalevo Tablets
Tasmar Tablets (1%)

Mental clouding
Dilaudid Ampules
Dilaudid Non-Sterile Powder
Dilaudid Rectal Suppositories
Dilaudid Tablets
Halcion Tablets
Hycodan Syrup
Hycodan Tablets
Hycomine Compound Tablets
Hycotuss Expectorant Syrup
Lortab 2.5/500 Tablets
Lortab 5/500 Tablets
Lortab 7.5/500 Tablets
Lortab 10/500 Tablets
Lortab Elixir
Maxidone Tablets
Norco 5/325 Tablets
Norco 7.5/325 Tablets
Norco 10/325 Tablets
Numorphan Injection
Numorphan Suppositories
Prochlorperazine
Tussionex Pennkinetic Extended-
  Release Suspension
Vicodin ES Tablets

Vicodin HP Tablets
Vicodin Tablets
Vioxx Oral Suspension (Greater than 0.1% to 1.9%)
Vioxx Tablets (Greater than 0.1% to 1.9%)
Zydone Tablets

Mental performance, impairment

Aldoclor Tablets
Aldoril Tablets
Alferon N Injection (1%)
Ambien Tablets (Infrequent)
Amerge Tablets (Infrequent)
Anaprox DS Tablets (Less than 1%)
Anaprox Tablets (Less than 1%)
Arthrotec Tablets (Rare)
Ativan Injection
BuSpar Tablets (2%)
Cardura Tablets (Less than 0.5%)
Celexa Oral Solution (Frequent)
Celexa Tablets (Frequent)
Clozapine Tablets
Clozaril Tablets
Copaxone for Injection (Infrequent)
Cosopt Sterile Ophthalmic Solution
Demerol Syrup
Demerol Tablets
Dilaudid Ampules
Dilaudid Injection
Dilaudid Multiple Dose Vials
Dilaudid Non-Sterile Powder
Dilaudid Rectal Suppositories
Dilaudid Tablets
Dostinex Tablets (1%)
EC-Naprosyn Delayed-Release Tablets (Less than 1%)
Elavil
Ergamisol Tablets (Less frequent)
Eskalith Capsules
Eskalith CR Controlled-Release Tablets
Exelon Capsules (Infrequent)
Exelon Oral Solution (Infrequent)
Felbatol Oral Suspension
Felbatol Tablets
Fludara for Injection (Up to 1%)
Flumadine Syrup (0.3% to 2.1%)
Flumadine Tablets (0.3% to 2.1%)
Fortovase Capsules (Less than 2%)
Frova Tablets (Infrequent)
▲ Gabitril Tablets (6%)
Gengraf Capsules (1% to less than 3%)

Grifulvin V Tablets Microsize and Oral Suspension Microsize
Hivid Tablets (Less than 1%)
Hycodan Syrup
Hycodan Tablets
Hycomine Compound Tablets
Hycotuss Expectorant Syrup
Imitrex Injection (Rare)
Imitrex Nasal Spray (Rare)
Imitrex Tablets (Infrequent)
▲ Intron A for Injection (Up to 14%)
Inversine Tablets
Invirase Capsules (Less than 2%)
Kadian Capsules (Less than 3%)
Klonopin Tablets (1% to 2%)
Klonopin Wafers (1% to 2%)
Lamictal Chewable Dispersible Tablets (1.7%)
Lamictal Tablets (1.7%)
Levaquin in 5% Dextrose Injection (0.1% to 1%)
Levaquin Injection (0.1% to 1%)
Levaquin Tablets (0.1% to 1%)
Lexapro Oral Solution (Frequent)
Lexapro Tablets (Frequent)
Limbitrol
Lortab 2.5/500 Tablets
Lortab 5/500 Tablets
Lortab 7.5/500 Tablets
Lortab 10/500 Tablets
Lortab Elixir
Loxitane Capsules
Maxalt Tablets (Frequent)
Maxalt-MLT Orally Disintegrating Tablets (Infrequent)
Maxidone Tablets
Meridia Capsules
Miltown Tablets
MS Contin Tablets
▲ Naprelan Tablets (3% to 9%)
Naprosyn Suspension (Less than 1%)
Naprosyn Tablets (Less than 1%)
▲ Nefazodone (3%)
Neoral Oral Solution (1% to less than 3%)
Neoral Soft Gelatin Capsules (1% to less than 3%)
Norco 5/325 Tablets
Norco 7.5/325 Tablets
Norco 10/325 Tablets
Norpramin Tablets
Orap Tablets
Paxil Oral Suspension (Frequent)
Paxil Tablets (Frequent)

Percocet Tablets
Percodan Tablets
Phenergan Suppositories
Phenergan Tablets
Prochlorperazine
▲ Prometrium Capsules (100 mg, 200 mg) (Less than 5%)
ProSom Tablets
Rebetron Combination Therapy
Remeron SolTab Tablets
Requip Tablets (Infrequent)
Rifadin Capsules
Rifadin IV
Rifamate Capsules
Rifater Tablets
Risperdal M-Tab Tablets (Infrequent)
Risperdal Oral Solution (Infrequent)
Risperdal Tablets (Infrequent)
▲ Roferon-A Injection (4%)
Seroquel Tablets
Surmontil Capsules
▲ Sustiva Capsules (1% to 9%)
Tarka Tablets (Less frequent)
Timolide Tablets
Timoptic in Ocudose
Timoptic Sterile Ophthalmic Solution
Timoptic-XE Sterile Ophthalmic Gel Forming Solution
▲ Topamax Sprinkle Capsules (5% to 14%)
▲ Topamax Tablets (5% to 14%)
Toradol IM Injection, IV Injection (1% or less)
Toradol Tablets (1% or less)
Trovan I.V. (Less than 1%)
Trovan Tablets (Less than 1%)
Tussionex Pennkinetic Extended-Release Suspension
Tylenol with Codeine Elixir
Tylenol with Codeine Tablets
Ultracet Tablets
Ultram Tablets (Less than 1%)
Vicodin ES Tablets
Vicodin HP Tablets
Vicodin Tablets
Vistaril Intramuscular Solution (Seldom)
Vivactil Tablets
Xanax Tablets
▲ Xanax XR Tablets (7.2%)
Zarontin Capsules
Zarontin Syrup
Zebeta Tablets
Zelnorm Tablets

Zestril Tablets (0.3% to 1.0%)
Ziac Tablets
Zoloft Oral Concentrate (1.3% to 2%)
Zoloft Tablets (1.3% to 2%)
▲ Zonegran Capsules (6%)
▲ Zyban Sustained-Release Tablets (9%)
Zydone Tablets
Zyrtec Syrup (Less than 2%)
Zyrtec Tablets (Less than 2%)
Zyrtec-D 12 Hour Extended Relief Tablets (Less than 2%)

Mental slowness

BuSpar Tablets (Infrequent)
Celontin Capsules
▲ Topamax Sprinkle Capsules (8% to 15.4%)
▲ Topamax Tablets (8% to 15.4%)
▲ Zonegran Capsules (4%)

Mental status, altered

Clozapine Tablets
Clozaril Tablets
Cubicin for Injection (Less than 1%)
Cuprimine Capsules
▲ Digitek Tablets (5%)
Elavil
Eldepryl Capsules
Haldol Decanoate 50 Injection
Haldol Decanoate 100 Injection
▲ Idamycin PFS Injection (41%)
▲ Invanz for Injection (3.3% to 5.1%)
Lanoxicaps Capsules
Lanoxin Elixir Pediatric
Lanoxin Injection
Lanoxin Injection Pediatric
Lanoxin Tablets
Moban Oral Concentrate
Moban Tablets
Navane Capsules
Navane Concentrate
Navane Intramuscular
Neumega for Injection
Oncaspar
Orap Tablets
Orthoclone OKT3 Sterile Solution (Less than 1%)
▲ Prograf Capsules and Injection Approximately (55%)
▲ Proleukin for Injection (73%)
Risperdal M-Tab Tablets
Risperdal Oral Solution
Risperdal Tablets
▲ Roferon-A Injection (10% to 17%)
Serentil Ampuls

Serentil Concentrate
Serentil Tablets
Seroquel Tablets
Stalevo Tablets
Stromectol Tablets
Triavil Tablets
Trifluoperazine

Mood changes

Adalat CC Tablets (Rare)
▲ Aerobid Inhaler System (1% to 3%)
▲ Aerobid-M Inhaler System (1% to 3%)
▲ Agenerase Oral Solution (4% to 9%)
Alesse-28 Tablets
▲ Alimta for Injection (14%)
Aloxi Injection (Less than 1%)
▲ Arimidex Tablets (17%)
Aygestin Tablets
Cenestin Tablets, 0.3 mg
Cenestin Tablets, 0.45 mg, 0.625 mg, 0.9 mg, 1.25 mg
Clomid Tablets
▲ Copegus Tablets (5%)
Decadron Phosphate Injection
Decadron Tablets
Dilaudid Ampules
Dilaudid Injection
Dilaudid Multiple Dose Vials
Dilaudid Non-Sterile Powder
Dilaudid Oral Liquid (Less frequent)
Dilaudid Rectal Suppositories
Dilaudid Tablets
Dilaudid Tablets - 8 mg (Less frequent)
Dilaudid-HP Injection (Less frequent)
Dilaudid-HP Lyophilized Powder 250 mg (Less frequent)
Dipentum Capsules (Rare)
Eldepryl Capsules
Enbrel for Injection
Feldene Capsules (Rare)
Femring Vaginal Ring
Florinef Acetate Tablets
Guanidine Hydrochloride Tablets
Hexalen Capsules
Hivid Tablets (Less than 1%)
Hycodan Syrup
Hycodan Tablets
Hycomine Compound Tablets
Hycotuss Expectorant Syrup
Hydrocortone Phosphate Injection, Sterile
Hydrocortone Tablets
Lariam Tablets (Occasional)

Levlen 21 Tablets
Levlen 28 Tablets
Levlite 28 Tablets
▲ Lexiva Tablets (Less than 1% to 11%)
Lo/Ovral-28 Tablets
Lortab 2.5/500 Tablets
Lortab 5/500 Tablets
Lortab 7.5/500 Tablets
Lortab 10/500 Tablets
Lortab Elixir
Lupron Depot 3.75 mg
▲ Lupron Injection (Less than 5%)
Marinol Capsules
Maxidone Tablets
Meridia Capsules
MS Contin Tablets (Less frequent)
MSIR Oral Capsules (Less frequent)
MSIR Oral Solution Concentrate (Less frequent)
MSIR Oral Tablets (Less frequent)
Norco 5/325 Tablets
Norco 7.5/325 Tablets
Norco 10/325 Tablets
Oncaspar
Orapred Oral Solution
Ortho Tri-Cyclen Lo Tablets
Ortho Tri-Cyclen Tablets
Orthoclone OKT3 Sterile Solution
Ortho-Cyclen Tablets
Ovral-28 Tablets
Ovrette Tablets
▲ Pegasys (3%)
Prefest Tablets
Premarin Tablets
Premphase Tablets
Prempro Tablets
▲ Procardia Capsules (7%)
▲ Procardia XL Extended Release Tablets (7%)
Seasonale Tablets
Solu-Medrol Sterile Powder
▲ Strattera Capsules (2% to 5%)
Testim 1% Gel (1% or less)
▲ Topamax Sprinkle Capsules (4% to 9%)
▲ Topamax Tablets (4% to 9%)
Trexall Tablets
Tri-Levlen 21 Tablets
Tri-Levlen 28 Tablets
Triphasil-28 Tablets
Tussionex Pennkinetic Extended-Release Suspension
Vicodin ES Tablets
Vicodin HP Tablets
Vicodin Tablets

Vicoprofen Tablets (Less than 1%)
Wellbutrin Tablets (Infrequent)
Xanax XR Tablets (Infrequent)
▲ Xeloda Tablets (5%)
Zydone Tablets

Nervousness

Abilify Tablets (1% or greater)
Accupril Tablets (0.5% to 1%)
Accuretic Tablets (0.5% to 1%)
Accutane Capsules
Aceon Tablets 2 mg, 4 mg, 8 mg
 (1.1%)
Aciphex Tablets
Actiq (1% to 2%)
Activella Tablets
Adalat CC Tablets (Rare)
▲ Adderall XR Capsules (6%)
Adenoscan (2%)
▲ Aerobid Inhaler System (3% to 9%)
▲ Aerobid-M Inhaler System (3% to
 9%)
▲ Agrylin Capsules (1% to 5%)
Alacol DM Syrup
Alesse-28 Tablets
Alferon N Injection (1%)
Allegra Capsules (Less than 1%)
Allegra Tablets (Less than 1%)
Allegra-D Extended-Release Tablets
 (1.4%)
Altace Capsules (Less than 1%)
▲ Alupent Inhalation Aerosol (14.1%)
Ambien Tablets (1%)
AmBisome for Injection (Less
 common)
Amnesteem Capsules
▲ Amphotec (1% to 5%)
▲ Anafranil (18%)
▲ AndroGel (Up to 3%)
▲ Angiomax for Injection (5%)
Aricept Tablets (Frequent)
▲ Arimidex Tablets (2% to 5%)
Arthrotec Tablets (Rare)
Asacol Delayed-Release Tablets (2%
 or greater)
Astelin Nasal Spray (Infrequent)
▲ Atrovent Inhalation Aerosol (3.1%)
▲ Atrovent Inhalation Solution (0.5%)
Avalide Tablets (1% or greater)
Avapro Tablets (1% or greater)
Avelox I.V. (0.1% to less than 3%)
Avelox Tablets (0.1% to less than 3%)
▲ Avinza Capsules (Less than 5%)
Axert Tablets (Rare)
Balamine DM Oral Drops
Balamine DM Syrup

Benztropine
▲ Betaseron for SC Injection (7%)
Bextra Tablets (0.1% to 1.9%)
Bicillin C-R 900/300 Injection
Bicillin C-R Injection
Bicillin L-A Injection
Blocadren Tablets (Less than 1%)
Brevicon 28-Day Tablets
▲ BuSpar Tablets (5%)
Caduet Tablets (Greater than 0.1% to
 less than or equal to 1%)
Campath Ampules
Captopril Tablets
Cardizem LA Extended Release
 Tablets (Less than 2%)
Cardura Tablets (2%)
▲ Casodex Tablets (2% to 5%)
Cataflam Tablets (Occasional)
▲ Catapres Tablets (About 3 in 100
 patients)
Catapres-TTS (1 of 101 patients)
Ceclor Pulvules (Rare)
Ceclor Suspension (Rare)
Cefzil for Oral Suspension (Less than
 1%)
Cefzil Tablets (Less than 1%)
Celebrex Capsules (0.1% to 1.9%)
▲ CellCept Capsules (3% to less than
 20%)
▲ CellCept Intravenous (3% to less than
 20%)
▲ CellCept Oral Suspension (3% to less
 than 20%)
▲ CellCept Tablets (3% to less than
 20%)
Celontin Capsules
Cenestin Tablets, 0.3 mg
▲ Cenestin Tablets, 0.45 mg, 0.625 mg,
 0.9 mg, 1.25 mg (3.8% to 28%)
Cerebyx Injection (Frequent)
Cipro I.V.
Cipro I.V. Pharmacy Bulk Package
Cipro Oral Suspension
Cipro Tablets
Cipro XR Tablets
Clinoril Tablets (Greater than 1%)
▲ Clorpres Tablets (About 3%)
Cognex Capsules (Frequent)
Colazal Capsules
▲ CombiPatch Transdermal System (5%
 to 6%)
Combivent Inhalation Aerosol (Less
 than 2%)
▲ Concerta Extended-Release Tablets
 (Among most common)

Copaxone for Injection (2%)
▲ Copegus Tablets (33%)
Coreg Tablets (Greater than 0.1% to 1%)
Cosopt Sterile Ophthalmic Solution
▲ Cozaar Tablets (Less than 1% to 4%)
▲ Crinone 8% Gel (16%)
Crixivan Capsules (Less than 2%)
Dalmane Capsules
Dantrium Capsules (Less frequent)
Daranide Tablets
Demadex Tablets and Injection (1.1%)
▲ Depacon Injection (0.9% to 11%)
▲ Depakene Capsules (11%)
▲ Depakene Syrup (11%)
▲ Depakote ER Tablets (1% to 11%)
▲ Depakote Sprinkle Capsules (7% to 11%)
▲ Depakote Tablets (1% to 11%)
▲ Desyrel (14.8%)
Detrol Tablets (1.1%)
Dilantin Infatabs
Dilantin Kapseals
Dilantin-125 Oral Suspension
Dilaudid Oral Liquid (Less frequent)
Dilaudid Tablets - 8 mg (Less frequent)
Dilaudid-HP Injection
Dilaudid-HP Lyophilized Powder 250 mg
▲ Ditropan XL Extended Release Tablets (2% to 5%)
Dolobid Tablets (Less than 1 in 100)
Doral
▲ Dostinex Tablets (1% to less than 10%)
Doxil Injection (Less than 1%)
▲ Duragesic Transdermal System (3% to 10%)
DynaCirc Capsules (0.5% to 1%)
DynaCirc CR Tablets (0.5% to 1%)
8-MOP Capsules
▲ Effexor Tablets (2% to 21.3%)
▲ Effexor XR Capsules (5% to 11%)
Eldepryl Capsules
▲ Eloxatin for Injection (2% to 5%)
EMLA Anesthetic Disc (Unlikely with disc)
EMLA Cream (Unlikely with cream)
▲ Entocort EC Capsules (Less than 5%)
EpiPen Jr. Auto-Injector
Ergamisol Tablets (1% to 2%)
Estrasorb Topical Emulsion
Estring Vaginal Ring (At least 1 report)
Estrostep 21 Tablets

Estrostep Fe Tablets
Excedrin Extra-Strength Caplets
Excedrin Extra-Strength Geltabs
Excedrin Extra-Strength Tablets
Exelon Capsules (2% or more)
Exelon Oral Solution (2% or more)
Factive Tablets (Less than or equal to 0.1%)
▲ Felbatol Oral Suspension (7.0% to 16.1%)
▲ Felbatol Tablets (7.0% to 16.1%)
Feldene Capsules (Occasional)
▲ femhrt Tablets (5.4%)
Femring Vaginal Ring
Ferrlecit Injection (Two or more patients)
▲ Flexeril Tablets (1% to 3%)
▲ Flolan for Injection (7% to 21%)
▲ Flovent Rotadisk 50 mcg (1% to 3%)
▲ Flovent Rotadisk 100 mcg (1% to 3%)
▲ Flovent Rotadisk 250 mcg (1% to 3%)
▲ Floxin Tablets (1% to 3%)
Flumadine Syrup (1.3% to 2.1%)
Flumadine Tablets (1.3% to 2.1%)
▲ Fluvoxamine maleate (2% to 12%)
▲ Focalin Tablets (Among most common)
▲ Foscavir Injection (Between 1% and 5%)
Frova Tablets (Infrequent)
▲ Gabitril Tablets (10%)
Gastrocrom Oral Concentrate (Less common)
Gengraf Capsules (1% to less than 3%)
▲ Glucotrol XL Extended Release Tablets (3.6%)
Guanfacine (Less frequent)
▲ Halcion Tablets (5.2%)
Hivid Tablets (Less than 1%)
Hytrin Capsules (2.3%)
Hyzaar 50-12.5 Tablets
Hyzaar 100-25 Tablets
▲ Indapamide Tablets (Less than 5%)
Indocin Capsules (Less than 1%)
Indocin Oral Suspension (Less than 1%)
Indocin Suppositories (Less than 1%)
▲ Infergen (16% to 31%)
▲ Intron A for Injection (Up to 3%)
Invanz for Injection (Greater than 0.1%)
Kaletra Capsules (Less than 2%)
Kaletra Oral Solution (Less than 2%)
▲ Keppra Oral Solution (4%)
▲ Keppra Tablets (4%)

▲ Klonopin Tablets (1% to 3%)
▲ Klonopin Wafers (1% to 3%)
Lamictal Chewable Dispersible Tablets (2%)
Lamictal Tablets (2%)
Levaquin in 5% Dextrose Injection (0.1% to 1%)
Levaquin Injection (0.1% to 1%)
Levaquin Tablets (0.1% to 1%)
Levlen 21 Tablets
Levlen 28 Tablets
Levlite 28 Tablets
Levora Tablets
Levothroid Tablets
Levoxyl Tablets
Lexapro Oral Solution (Infrequent)
Lexapro Tablets (Infrequent)
Lexxel Tablets
Lidoderm Patch
Lo/Ovral-28 Tablets
Loestrin 21 Tablets
Loestrin Fe Tablets
Lofibra Capsules
Lotensin HCT Tablets (0.3% to 1%)
Lotensin Tablets (Less than 1%)
Lotrel Capsules
Low-Ogestrel-28 Tablets
▲ Ludiomil (6%)
Lunelle Monthly Injection
▲ Lupron Depot 3.75 mg (4%)
▲ Lupron Depot—3 Month 11.25 mg (4%)
▲ Lupron Depot—3 Month 22.5 mg (Less than 5%)
Lupron Depot-PED 7.5 mg, 11.25 mg and 15 mg (Less than 2%)
▲ Lupron Injection (Less than 5%)
Lupron Injection Pediatric (Less than 2%)
Marinol Capsules (Greater than 1%)
Matulane Capsules
▲ Maxair Autohaler (4.5% to 6.9%)
Maxalt Tablets (Infrequent)
Maxalt-MLT Orally Disintegrating Tablets (Infrequent)
Mebaral Tablets (Less than 1 in 100 patients)
▲ Meridia Capsules (5.2%)
Merrem I.V. (Greater than 0.1% to 1%)
▲ Metadate CD Capsules (Among most common)
▲ Metadate ER Tablets (Among most common)
▲ Mexitil Capsules (5% to 11.3%)
Micardis HCT Tablets

Microgestin 1/20 Tablets
Microgestin 1.5/30 Tablets
Microgestin Fe 1/20 Tablets
Microgestin Fe 1.5/30 Tablets
Midamor Tablets (Less than or equal to 1%)
▲ Minipress Capsules (1% to 4%)
Minizide Capsules
Mirapex Tablets (1% or more)
▲ Mirena Intrauterine System (5% or more)
Mobic Tablets (Less than 2%)
Moduretic Tablets (Less than or equal to 1%)
Monurol Sachet (Less than 1%)
Motrin Cold & Sinus Caplets
Motrin Suspension, Oral Drops, Chewable Tablets, and Caplets (1% to less than 3%)
MS Contin Tablets (Less frequent)
MSIR Oral Capsules (Less frequent)
MSIR Oral Solution Concentrate (Less frequent)
MSIR Oral Tablets (Less frequent)
Namenda Tablets (Infrequent)
Naprelan Tablets (Less than 1%)
Narcan Injection
Naropin Injection (Less than 1%)
Necon 0.5/35 Tablets
Necon 1/35 Tablets
Necon 1/50 Tablets
Necon 10/11 Tablets
Nembutal Sodium Solution (Less than 1%)
Neoral Oral Solution (1% to less than 3%)
Neoral Soft Gelatin Capsules (1% to less than 3%)
▲ Neumega for Injection (Greater than or equal to 10%)
Neurontin Capsules (2.4%)
Neurontin Oral Solution (2.4%)
Neurontin Tablets (2.4%)
Nexium Delayed-Release Capsules (Less than 1%)
Nilandron Tablets (2%)
▲ Nipent for Injection (3% to 10%)
Nordette-28 Tablets
Norinyl 1 + 35 28-Day Tablets
Norinyl 1 + 50 28-Day Tablets
Norvasc Tablets (More than 0.1% to 1%)
Norvir Oral Solution (Less than 2%)
Norvir Soft Gelatin Capsules (Less than 2%)

Nubain Injection (1% or less)
NuLev Orally Disintegrating Tablets
Numorphan Injection
Numorphan Suppositories
Ogestrel 0.5/50-28 Tablets
▲ Ontak Vials (11%)
▲ Orap Tablets (8.3%)
Ortho Evra Transdermal System
Ortho Tri-Cyclen Lo Tablets
Ortho Tri-Cyclen Tablets
Ortho-Cept Tablets
Ortho-Cyclen Tablets
Ovcon 35 Tablets
Ovcon 50 Tablets
Ovral-28 Tablets
Ovrette Tablets
Oxsoralen-Ultra Capsules
▲ OxyContin Tablets (Between 1% and 5%)
▲ Paxil CR Controlled-Release Tablets (2% to 3%)
▲ Paxil Oral Suspension (4% to 9%)
▲ Paxil Tablets (4% to 9%)
▲ Pegasys (19%)
▲ PEG-Intron Powder for Injection (4%)
Periactin Tablets
Permax Tablets (Frequent)
Phenergan Suppositories
Phenergan Tablets
Phenobarbital (Less than 1%)
Phenytek Capsules
Plaquenil Tablets
Plendil Extended-Release Tablets (0.5% to 1.5%)
Ponstel Capsules (Occasional)
Prefest Tablets
▲ Premarin Tablets (2% to 5%)
▲ Premphase Tablets (2% to 3%)
▲ Prempro Tablets (2% to 3%)
Prevacid Delayed-Release Capsules (Less than 1%)
Prevacid for Delayed-Release Oral Suspension (Less than 1%)
Prevacid NapraPAC 375 (Less than 1%)
Prevacid NapraPAC 500 (Less than 1%)
Prevacid SoluTab Delayed-Release Tablets (Less than 1%)
PREVPAC (Less than 1%)
Prilosec Delayed-Release Capsules (Less than 1%)
Prilosec OTC Tablets (Less than 1%)
Prinivil Tablets (0.3% to 1%)
Prinzide Tablets
ProAmatine Tablets (Less frequent)

▲ Procardia Capsules (2% or less to 7%)
▲ Procardia XL Extended Release Tablets (Less than 3% to 7%)
▲ Prochieve 4% Gel (16%)
▲ Prochieve 8% Gel (16%)
Prochlorperazine
▲ Prograf Capsules and Injection (3%)
Prometrium Capsules (100 mg, 200 mg)
▲ ProSom Tablets (8%)
Protonix I.V. (Less than 1%)
Protonix Tablets (Less than 1%)
▲ Provigil Tablets (7%)
▲ Prozac Pulvules and Liquid (8% to 16%)
▲ Rebetol Capsules (3% to 6%)
▲ Rebetol Oral Solution (3% to 6%)
▲ Rebetron Combination Therapy (4% to 5%)
▲ Relafen Tablets (1% to 3%)
Relpax Tablets (Infrequent)
Requip Tablets (1% or more)
Rescriptor Tablets
▲ Restoril (4.6%)
Retrovir Capsules (1.6%)
Retrovir IV Infusion (2%)
Retrovir Syrup (1.6%)
Retrovir Tablets (1.6%)
Reyataz Capsules (Less than 3%)
▲ Ribavirin Capsules (4% to 6%)
Risperdal Consta Injection (Frequent)
Risperdal M-Tab Tablets (Frequent)
Risperdal Oral Solution (Frequent)
Risperdal Tablets (Frequent)
▲ Ritalin Hydrochloride Tablets (One of the two most common)
▲ Ritalin LA Capsules (Among most common)
▲ Ritalin-SR Tablets (One of the two most common)
▲ Rituxan for Infusion (1% to 5%)
▲ Rituxan I.V. (1% to 5%)
Roferon-A Injection (Less than 3% to less than 5%)
▲ Romazicon Injection (3% to 9%)
Salagen Tablets (Less than 1%)
▲ Sandostatin LAR Depot (1% to 4%)
▲ Sarafem Pulvules (3% to 14%)
Seasonale Tablets
Seconal (Less than 1%)
▲ Semprex-D Capsules (3%)
Septra DS Tablets
Septra Grape Suspension
Septra Suspension
Septra Tablets

▲ Serevent Inhalation Aerosol (1% to 3%)
▲ Skelaxin Tablets (Most frequent)
Sonata Capsules (Frequent)
Spectracef Tablets (0.1% to 1%)
Stadol Injection (Greater than or equal to 1%)
Stadol NS (Greater than or equal to 1%)
Stalevo Tablets
▲ Suboxone Tablets (6%)
▲ Subutex Tablets (6%)
Sular Tablets (Less than or equal to 1%)
Sustiva Capsules (1% to 2%)
▲ Symmetrel Syrup (1% to 5%)
▲ Symmetrel Tablets (1% to 5%)
Synagis Intramuscular (More than 1%)
Tasmar Tablets (Infrequent)
Tequin Injection (Less than 0.1%)
Tequin Tablets (Less than 0.1%)
Teveten HCT Tablets (Less than 1%)
Teveten Tablets (Less than 1%)
▲ Thalomid Capsules (2.8% to 9.4%)
Tiazac Capsules (Less than 2%)
Timolide Tablets (Less than 1%)
Timoptic in Ocudose (Less frequent)
Timoptic Sterile Ophthalmic Solution (Less frequent)
Timoptic-XE Sterile Ophthalmic Gel Forming Solution
▲ Topamax Sprinkle Capsules (9% to 19%)
▲ Topamax Tablets (9% to 19%)
Toradol IM Injection, IV Injection (1% or less)
Toradol Tablets (1% or less)
Tranxene T-TAB Tablets (Less common)
Tranxene-SD Half Strength Tablets (Less common)
Tranxene-SD Tablets (Less common)
Trental Tablets
Tricor Tablets
▲ Trileptal Oral Suspension (2% to 4%)
▲ Trileptal Tablets (2% to 4%)
Tri-Levlen 21 Tablets
Tri-Levlen 28 Tablets
Tri-Norinyl-28 Tablets
Triphasil-28 Tablets
Trivora-28 Tablets
Tylenol, Children's, Plus Cold
Tylenol, Maximum Strength, Severe Cold & Flu NightTime Liquid
Tylenol, Maximum Strength, Sinus Day Non-Drowsy Geltabs, Gelcaps, and Caplets
Tylenol, Maximum Strength, Sinus Night Time Caplets
Tylenol, Multi-Symptom, Cold Day Non-Drowsy Caplets and Gelcaps
Tylenol, Multi-Symptom, Cold Night Time Complete Formula Caplets
Tylenol Sinus Severe Congestion Caplets
Ultracet Tablets (At least 1%)
▲ Ultram Tablets (1% to 14%)
Uniretic Tablets (Less than 1%)
Vantin Tablets and Oral Suspension (Less than 1%)
Varivax (Greater than or equal to 1%)
Vaseretic Tablets (0.5% to 2%)
Vasotec I.V. Injection (0.5% to 1%)
Vicks 44D Cough & Head Congestion Relief
Vicks 44m, Pediatric, Cough & Cold Relief
Vicks DayQuil Multi-Symptom Cold/Flu Relief Liquid & LiquiCaps
Vicks NyQuil, Children's, Cold/Cough Relief
▲ Vicoprofen Tablets (3% to 9%)
Vistide Injection
Voltaren Tablets (Occasional)
Voltaren-XR Tablets (Occasional)
▲ VoSpire Extended-Release Tablets (8.5%)
▲ Wellbutrin SR Sustained-Release Tablets (3% to 5%)
▲ Wellbutrin XL Extended-Release Tablets (3% to 5%)
▲ Xanax Tablets (4.1%)
▲ Xanax XR Tablets (22%)
▲ Xopenex Inhalation Solution (2.8% to 9.6%)
Xylocaine 2% Jelly
▲ Xyrem Oral Solution (7%)
Yasmin 28 Tablets (Greater than 1%)
▲ Zanaflex Tablets (3%)
Zaroxolyn Tablets (Less than 2%)
Zestoretic Tablets
Zestril Tablets (0.3% to 1.0%)
Zithromax Capsules, 250 mg (1% or less)
Zithromax for IV Infusion (1% or less)
Zithromax for Oral Suspension, 300 mg, 600 mg, 900 mg, 1200 mg (1% or less)
Zithromax Tablets, 250 mg, 500 mg (1% or less)

▲ Zoladex (3% to 5%)
  Zoladex 3-month
▲ Zoloft Oral Concentrate (6%)
▲ Zoloft Tablets (6%)
  Zomig Nasal Spray (Infrequent)
  Zonegran Capsules (2%)
  Zovia 1/35E Tablets
  Zovia 1/50E Tablets
▲ Zyban Sustained-Release Tablets (4%)
▲ Zyprexa Tablets (16%)
▲ Zyprexa ZYDIS Orally Disintegrating
  Tablets (16%)
  Zyrtec Syrup (Less than 2%)
  Zyrtec Tablets (Less than 2%)
  Zyrtec-D 12 Hour Extended Relief
  Tablets (Less than 2%)

Neuropsychiatric disorders, life-threatening, aggravation of
Roferon-A Injection

Neuropsychometrics performance, decrease
Blocadren Tablets
Corzide 40/5 Tablets
Corzide 80/5 Tablets
Cosopt Sterile Ophthalmic Solution
Inderal LA Long-Acting Capsules
Nadolol Tablets
Tenormin I.V. Injection
Tenormin Tablets
Timoptic in Ocudose
Timoptic Sterile Ophthalmic Solution
Timoptic-XE Sterile Ophthalmic Gel
  Forming Solution
Toprol-XL Tablets

Neurosis, unspecified
Ambien Tablets (Rare)
Cerebyx Injection (Infrequent)
Cognex Capsules (Infrequent)
Evoxac Capsules
Exelon Capsules (Infrequent)
Exelon Oral Solution (Infrequent)
Gabitril Tablets (Infrequent)
▲ Intron A for Injection (Less than 5%)
  Lamictal Chewable Dispersible
  Tablets (Rare)
  Lamictal Tablets (Rare)
  Namenda Tablets (Infrequent)
  Neurontin Capsules (Rare)
  Neurontin Oral Solution (Rare)
  Neurontin Tablets (Rare)
  Nipent for Injection (Less than 3%)

Paxil Oral Suspension (Infrequent)
Paxil Tablets (Infrequent)
Permax Tablets (Infrequent)
Prevacid Delayed-Release Capsules
  (Less than 1%)
Prevacid for Delayed-Release Oral
  Suspension (Less than 1%)
Prevacid NapraPAC 375 (Less than
  1%)
Prevacid NapraPAC 500 (Less than
  1%)
Prevacid SoluTab Delayed-Release
  Tablets (Less than 1%)
PREVPAC (Less than 1%)
Prozac Pulvules and Liquid
  (Infrequent)
Relpax Tablets (Rare)
Remeron SolTab Tablets (Infrequent)
Requip Tablets (Infrequent)
Sarafem Pulvules (Infrequent)
Sustiva Capsules
Symbyax Capsules (Infrequent)
Topamax Sprinkle Capsules
  (Infrequent)
Topamax Tablets (Infrequent)
Uniretic Tablets (Less than 1%)

Nightmares
Aldoclor Tablets
Aldoril Tablets
Axert Tablets (Rare)
Biaxin Filmtab Tablets
Biaxin Granules
Biaxin XL Filmtab Tablets
Blocadren Tablets
Catapres Tablets
Catapres-TTS (0.5% or less)
Cipro I.V. (1% or less)
Cipro I.V. Pharmacy Bulk Package
  (Less than 1%)
Cipro Oral Suspension (Less than 1%)
Cipro Tablets (Less than 1%)
Cipro XR Tablets
Clorpres Tablets
▲ Clozapine Tablets (4%)
▲ Clozaril Tablets (4%)
  Cosopt Sterile Ophthalmic Solution
  Doral
▲ Effexor XR Capsules (4% to 7%)
  Elavil
  Eldepryl Capsules
  Floxin Tablets
  Halcion Tablets (Rare)
  Klonopin Tablets (Infrequent)

Klonopin Wafers (Infrequent)
Levaquin in 5% Dextrose Injection
Levaquin Injection
Levaquin Tablets
Marinol Capsules (Less than 1%)
Matulane Capsules
Mebaral Tablets (Less than 1 in 100 patients)
Meridia Capsules
Nardil Tablets (Infrequent)
Naropin Injection (Less than 1%)
Nembutal Sodium Solution (Less than 1%)
Norpramin Tablets
Pamelor
Phenergan Suppositories
Phenergan Tablets
Phenobarbital (Less than 1%)
Plaquenil Tablets
PREVPAC
Relafen Tablets (Less than 1%)
Risperdal M-Tab Tablets (Rare)
Risperdal Oral Solution (Rare)
Risperdal Tablets (Rare)
Seconal (Less than 1%)
Stalevo Tablets
Surmontil Capsules
Tequin Injection
Tequin Tablets
Timolide Tablets
Timoptic in Ocudose
Timoptic Sterile Ophthalmic Solution
Timoptic-XE Sterile Ophthalmic Gel Forming Solution
Toprol-XL Tablets
Triavil Tablets
Trovan I.V.
Trovan Tablets
Vantin Tablets and Oral Suspension (Less than 1%)
Vivactil Tablets
Xanax XR Tablets (Frequent)

Obsessive compulsive symptoms

Zyprexa Tablets (Infrequent)
Zyprexa ZYDIS Orally Disintegrating Tablets (Infrequent)

Orgasmic dysfunction, female

▲ Effexor XR Capsules (2% to 8%)
Sarafem Pulvules

Overstimulation

Adderall Tablets

Adderall XR Capsules
Adipex-P Capsules
Adipex-P Tablets
Desoxyn Tablets
Dexedrine Spansule Capsules
Dexedrine Tablets
DextroStat Tablets
Eldepryl Capsules
Halcion Tablets
Ionamin Capsules
Miltown Tablets
Parnate Tablets

Panic attack

Abilify Tablets (1% or less)
Ambien Tablets (Rare)
Amerge Tablets (Rare)
Celexa Oral Solution (Infrequent)
Celexa Tablets (Infrequent)
Cozaar Tablets (Less than 1%)
Effexor Tablets
Effexor XR Capsules
Hyzaar 50-12.5 Tablets
Hyzaar 100-25 Tablets
Imitrex Injection
Imitrex Nasal Spray
Imitrex Tablets
Lamictal Chewable Dispersible Tablets (Infrequent)
Lamictal Tablets (Infrequent)
Lariam Tablets (Occasional)
Lexapro Oral Solution (Infrequent)
Lexapro Tablets (Infrequent)
Pamelor
Tasmar Tablets (1%)
Trileptal Oral Suspension
Trileptal Tablets

Paranoia

Adalat CC Tablets (Rare)
Allegra-D Extended-Release Tablets (Less than 1%)
Aricept Tablets (Infrequent)
Arthrotec Tablets (Rare)
Celexa Oral Solution (Infrequent)
Celexa Tablets (Infrequent)
Cipro I.V. (1% or less)
Cipro I.V. Pharmacy Bulk Package (Less than 1%)
Cipro Oral Suspension
Cipro Tablets
Cipro XR Tablets
Clozapine Tablets (Less than 1%)
Clozaril Tablets (Less than 1%)
Cognex Capsules (Infrequent)

Copaxone for Injection (Infrequent)
Doral
Duragesic Transdermal System (1% or greater)
Effexor Tablets (Infrequent)
Effexor XR Capsules (Infrequent)
Evoxac Capsules
Exelon Capsules (2% or more)
Exelon Oral Solution (2% or more)
Felbatol Oral Suspension
Felbatol Tablets
Flexeril Tablets
Floxin Tablets
Fluvoxamine maleate (Infrequent)
Gabitril Tablets (Frequent)
Hivid Tablets (Less than 1%)
Lamictal Chewable Dispersible Tablets (Infrequent)
Lamictal Tablets (Infrequent)
Lariam Tablets (Occasional)
Levaquin in 5% Dextrose Injection (0.1% to 1%)
Levaquin Injection (0.1% to 1%)
Levaquin Tablets (0.1% to 1%)
▲ Marinol Capsules (3% to 10%)
Mirapex Tablets (Less than 1%)
Nefazodone (Infrequent)
Neurontin Capsules (Infrequent)
Neurontin Oral Solution (Infrequent)
Neurontin Tablets (Infrequent)
Orthoclone OKT3 Sterile Solution (Less than 1%)
Paxil CR Controlled-Release Tablets (Rare)
Paxil Oral Suspension (Infrequent)
Paxil Tablets (Infrequent)
Permax Tablets (Frequent)
Procardia Capsules (Less than 0.5%)
Prozac Pulvules and Liquid (Infrequent)
Remeron SolTab Tablets (Infrequent)
Reminyl Oral Solution (Infrequent)
Reminyl Tablets (Infrequent)
Requip Tablets (Infrequent)
Rescriptor Tablets
Rilutek Tablets (Infrequent)
▲ Romazicon Injection (1% to 3%)
Sandostatin Injection (Less than 1%)
Sandostatin LAR Depot (Rare)
Sarafem Pulvules (Infrequent)
Seroquel Tablets (Infrequent)
Stalevo Tablets
Sustiva Capsules
Symmetrel Syrup

Symmetrel Tablets
Tasmar Tablets (Infrequent)
Tequin Injection (Less than 0.1%)
Tequin Tablets (Less than 0.1%)
Topamax Sprinkle Capsules (Infrequent)
Topamax Tablets (Infrequent)
Trilafon
Trileptal Oral Suspension
Trileptal Tablets
Trovan I.V. (Less than 1%)
Trovan Tablets (Less than 1%)
Ultracet Tablets (Less than 1%)
Wellbutrin SR Sustained-Release Tablets
Wellbutrin Tablets (Infrequent)
Wellbutrin XL Extended-Release Tablets
Zoloft Oral Concentrate (Infrequent)
Zoloft Tablets (Infrequent)
Zyban Sustained-Release Tablets
Zyprexa Tablets
Zyprexa ZYDIS Orally Disintegrating Tablets

Personality changes

Ambien Tablets (Rare)
Cardizem LA Extended Release Tablets (Less than 2%)
Cerebyx Injection (Infrequent)
Decadron Tablets
▲ Depacon Injection (1% to 5%)
▲ Depakene Capsules (1% to 5%)
▲ Depakene Syrup (1% to 5%)
▲ Depakote ER Tablets (1% to 5%)
▲ Depakote Sprinkle Capsules (1% to 5%)
▲ Depakote Tablets (1% to 5%)
Eldepryl Capsules
Enbrel for Injection
Evoxac Capsules
Exelon Capsules (Infrequent)
Exelon Oral Solution (Infrequent)
Florinef Acetate Tablets
Frova Tablets (Rare)
Gabitril Tablets (Frequent)
Geodon for Injection (Up to 2%)
Hydrocortone Phosphate Injection, Sterile
Hydrocortone Tablets
Imitrex Tablets (Rare)
▲ Intron A for Injection (Less than 5%)
Lamictal Chewable Dispersible Tablets (Infrequent)
Lamictal Tablets (Infrequent)

▲ Lupron Depot 3.75 mg (Among most frequent)
▲ Lupron Depot—3 Month 11.25 mg (Less than 5%)
Lupron Depot-PED 7.5 mg, 11.25 mg and 15 mg (Less than 2%)
Lupron Injection Pediatric (Less than 2%)
Namenda Tablets (Infrequent)
Neurontin Capsules (Rare)
Neurontin Oral Solution (2.8%)
Neurontin Tablets (Rare)
Norvir Oral Solution (Less than 2%)
Norvir Soft Gelatin Capsules (Less than 2%)
Permax Tablets (2.1%)
▲ Prometrium Capsules (100 mg, 200 mg) (Less than 5%)
Prozac Pulvules and Liquid (At least 2%)
Requip Tablets (Infrequent)
Rilutek Tablets (Infrequent)
Sarafem Pulvules (Infrequent)
Solu-Medrol Sterile Powder
Tiazac Capsules (Less than 2%)
Topamax Sprinkle Capsules (Frequent)
Topamax Tablets (Frequent)
Trileptal Oral Suspension
Trileptal Tablets
Vistide Injection
▲ Zyprexa Tablets (8%)
▲ Zyprexa ZYDIS Orally Disintegrating Tablets (8%)

Phobia, unspecified
Cipro XR Tablets
Imitrex Injection

Phobic disorder
Cipro I.V. (1% or less)
Cipro I.V. Pharmacy Bulk Package (Less than 1%)
Cipro Oral Suspension (Less than 1%)
Cipro Tablets (Less than 1%)
Floxin Tablets
Fluvoxamine maleate (Infrequent)
Imitrex Tablets (Rare)
Zyprexa Tablets (Infrequent)
Zyprexa ZYDIS Orally Disintegrating Tablets (Infrequent)

Phonophobia
Imitrex Tablets (Frequent)

Photophobia
Abilify Tablets (Rare)
Accutane Capsules
▲ Alocril Ophthalmic Solution (1% to 10%)
▲ Alphagan P Ophthalmic Solution (1% to 4%)
Amerge Tablets (Frequent)
Amnesteem Capsules
▲ Betimol Ophthalmic Solution (More than 5%)
Betoptic S Ophthalmic Suspension (Small number of patients)
Botox Purified Neurotoxin Complex
Calcijex Injection
Cardura Tablets (Less than 0.5%)
Celexa Oral Solution (Infrequent)
Celexa Tablets (Infrequent)
Celontin Capsules
Cerebyx Injection (Infrequent)
Ciloxan Ophthalmic Ointment (Less than 1%)
Ciloxan Ophthalmic Solution (Less than 1%)
Clomid Tablets (1.5%)
Copaxone for Injection (Infrequent)
Cosopt Sterile Ophthalmic Solution (Less than 1%)
CytoGam Intravenous (Infrequent)
Depakote ER Tablets (Greater than 1%)
Effexor Tablets (Infrequent)
Effexor XR Capsules (Infrequent)
Ergamisol Tablets
Floxin Tablets (Less than 1%)
Fluvoxamine maleate
Gabitril Tablets (Infrequent)
Gamimune N, 10% Solvent/Detergent Treated (Infrequent)
Geodon Capsules (Infrequent)
Havrix Vaccine (Less than 1%)
Hectorol Capsules
Hectorol Injection
Hivid Tablets (Less than 1%)
Imitrex Injection (Infrequent)
Imitrex Tablets (Frequent)
▲ Intron A for Injection (Less than 5%)
Lacrisert Sterile Ophthalmic Insert
Lamictal Chewable Dispersible Tablets (Infrequent)
Lamictal Tablets (Infrequent)
Levitra Tablets (Less than 2%)
Lotronex Tablets (Rare)
▲ Lumigan Ophthalmic Solution (1% to 3%)

Matulane Capsules
Maxalt Tablets (Rare)
Maxalt-MLT Orally Disintegrating
Tablets (Rare)
Nefazodone (Infrequent)
Neurontin Capsules (Infrequent)
Neurontin Oral Solution (Infrequent)
Neurontin Tablets (Infrequent)
Nilandron Tablets (2%)
Nipent for Injection (Less than 3%)
Nizoral Tablets (Less than 1%)
Norvir Oral Solution (Less than 2%)
Norvir Soft Gelatin Capsules (Less
than 2%)
Ocuflox Ophthalmic Solution
▲ Orthoclone OKT3 Sterile Solution
(10%)
▲ Pacerone Tablets (4% to 9%)
Paxil CR Controlled-Release Tablets
(Infrequent)
Paxil Oral Suspension (Rare)
Paxil Tablets (Rare)
Permax Tablets (Infrequent)
Photofrin for Injection
Plaquenil Tablets (Fairly common)
Prevacid Delayed-Release Capsules
(Less than 1%)
Prevacid for Delayed-Release Oral
Suspension (Less than 1%)
Prevacid NapraPAC 375 (Less than
1%)
Prevacid NapraPAC 500 (Less than
1%)
Prevacid SoluTab Delayed-Release
Tablets (Less than 1%)
PREVPAC (Less than 1%)
Prinivil Tablets (0.3% to 1%)
Prinzide Tablets
ProSom Tablets (Infrequent)
Prozac Pulvules and Liquid
(Infrequent)
▲ Quixin Ophthalmic Solution (1% to
3%)
Relpax Tablets (Infrequent)
Requip Tablets (Infrequent)
Rescriptor Tablets
Retrovir Capsules
Retrovir IV Infusion
Retrovir Syrup
Retrovir Tablets
Rilutek Tablets (Rare)
Risperdal M-Tab Tablets (Rare)
Risperdal Oral Solution (Rare)
Risperdal Tablets (Rare)

Rocaltrol Capsules
Rocaltrol Oral Solution
Sarafem Pulvules (Infrequent)
Serentil Ampuls
Serentil Concentrate
Serentil Tablets
Sonata Capsules (Infrequent)
▲ Soriatane Capsules (1% to 10%)
Tambocor Tablets (Less than 1%)
Tequin Injection (Less than 0.1%)
Tequin Tablets (Less than 0.1%)
Topamax Sprinkle Capsules
(Infrequent)
Topamax Tablets (Infrequent)
▲ Travatan Ophthalmic Solution (1% to
4%)
Triavil Tablets
Trilafon
Trileptal Oral Suspension
Trileptal Tablets
Trovan I.V. (Less than 1%)
Trovan Tablets (Less than 1%)
▲ Trusopt Sterile Ophthalmic Solution
(Approximately 1% to 5%)
Twinrix Vaccine (Less than 1%)
▲ VFEND I.V. (2.4% to 30%)
▲ VFEND Oral Suspension 2.4% to
30%)
▲ VFEND Tablets (2.4% to 30%)
Viagra Tablets (Less than 2%)
▲ Xalatan Sterile Ophthalmic Solution
(1% to 4%)
Xanax XR Tablets (Infrequent)
▲ Zaditor Ophthalmic Solution 0.025%
(Less than 5%)
Zestoretic Tablets
Zestril Tablets (0.3% to 1.0%)
Zoloft Oral Concentrate (Rare)
Zoloft Tablets (Rare)
Zomig Nasal Spray (Rare)
Zonegran Capsules (Rare)
Zosyn (1% or less)
Zosyn in Galaxy Containers (1% or
less)

Psychiatric disturbances
Accutane Capsules
Advicor Tablets
Aldoclor Tablets
Aldoril Tablets
Altocor Extended-Release Tablets
Aralen Tablets
Arthrotec Tablets (Rare)
Avonex
Benztropine

Clinoril Tablets (Less than 1 in 100)
Cosopt Sterile Ophthalmic Solution
Cuprimine Capsules
Decadron Phosphate Injection
Decadron Tablets
Didronel Tablets
Florinef Acetate Tablets
Fortovase Capsules (Less than 2%)
▲ Gengraf Capsules (5%)
Hydrocortone Phosphate Injection,
  Sterile
Hydrocortone Tablets
Indocin Capsules (Less than 1%)
Indocin Oral Suspension (Less than
  1%)
Indocin Suppositories (Less than 1%)
Infergen
Invirase Capsules (Less than 2%)
Lariam Tablets (Occasional)
Lescol Capsules
Lescol XL Tablets
▲ Leukine (15%)
Mebaral Tablets (Less than 1 in 100
  patients)
Mellaril
Mintezol Chewable Tablets
Mintezol Suspension
Nembutal Sodium Solution (Less than
  1%)
Neoral Oral Solution
Neoral Soft Gelatin Capsules
Nizoral Tablets (Rare)
Noroxin Tablets
Pepcid for Oral Suspension
  (Infrequent)
Pepcid Injection (Infrequent)
Pepcid Injection Premixed
  (Infrequent)
Pepcid Tablets (Infrequent)
Phenobarbital (Less than 1%)
Prilosec Delayed-Release Capsules
  (Less than 1%)
Prilosec OTC Tablets (Less than 1%)
Primaxin I.M.
Primaxin I.V. (Less than 0.2%)
Pulmicort Respules (Less than 1%)
Pulmicort Turbuhaler Inhalation
  Powder (Rare)
Sandimmune I.V. Ampuls for Infusion
Sandimmune Oral Solution
Sandimmune Soft Gelatin Capsules
Seconal (Less than 1%)
Solu-Medrol Sterile Powder
Thioridazine Hydrochloride Tablets
  (Extremely rare)

Timoptic in Ocudose (Less frequent)
Timoptic Sterile Ophthalmic Solution
  (Less frequent)
Timoptic-XE Sterile Ophthalmic Gel
  Forming Solution
Trecator-SC Tablets
Zarontin Capsules
Zarontin Syrup

Psychoses

Abilify Tablets (2% or greater)
Accutane Capsules
Adderall Tablets (Rare)
Adderall XR Capsules
Adipex-P Capsules
Adipex-P Tablets
Aldoclor Tablets
Aldoril Tablets
▲ Amphotec (1% to 5%)
Ancobon Capsules
Antabuse Tablets
Aralen Tablets (Rare)
▲ Aredia for Injection (Up to 4%)
Avelox I.V.
Avelox Tablets
Avonex
Bextra Tablets (Rare)
Biaxin Filmtab Tablets
Biaxin Granules
Biaxin XL Filmtab Tablets
Bicillin L-A Injection
Buprenex Injectable (Less than 1%)
BuSpar Tablets (Rare)
Cedax Capsules
Cedax Oral Suspension
Celexa Oral Solution (Infrequent)
Celexa Tablets (Infrequent)
▲ CellCept Capsules (3% to less than
  20%)
▲ CellCept Intravenous (3% to less than
  20%)
▲ CellCept Oral Suspension (3% to less
  than 20%)
▲ CellCept Tablets (3% to less than
  20%)
Celontin Capsules (Rare)
Cerebyx Injection (Infrequent)
Clinoril Tablets (Less than 1 in 100)
Clomid Tablets
Cognex Capsules (Rare)
Copegus Tablets (Less than 1%)
Covera-HS Tablets (Less than 2%)
Dapsone Tablets
Decadron Phosphate Injection
Decadron Tablets

Depacon Injection
Depakene Capsules
Depakene Syrup
Depakote ER Tablets (Greater than 1%)
Depakote Sprinkle Capsules
Depakote Tablets
Desoxyn Tablets (Rare)
Dexedrine Spansule Capsules (Rare at recommended doses)
Dexedrine Tablets (Rare at recommended doses)
DextroStat Tablets (Rare)
Effexor Tablets (Rare)
Effexor XR Capsules (Infrequent)
Exelon Capsules (Infrequent)
Exelon Oral Solution (Infrequent)
Felbatol Oral Suspension
Felbatol Tablets
Floxin Tablets
Fluvoxamine maleate (Infrequent to frequent)
Fortovase Capsules (Less than 2%)
Gabitril Tablets (Infrequent)
Gastrocrom Oral Concentrate (Less common)
Geodon for Injection (Up to 1%)
Guanidine Hydrochloride Tablets
Hivid Tablets (Less than 1%)
Hydrocortone Phosphate Injection, Sterile
Hydrocortone Tablets
Indocin Capsules (Less than 1%)
Indocin Oral Suspension (Less than 1%)
Indocin Suppositories (Less than 1%)
Invirase Capsules (Less than 2%)
Ionamin Capsules (Rare)
Isoptin SR Tablets (1% or less)
Klonopin Tablets
Klonopin Wafers
Lamictal Chewable Dispersible Tablets (Infrequent)
Lamictal Tablets (Infrequent)
Lanoxicaps Capsules
Lanoxin Elixir Pediatric
Lanoxin Injection
Lanoxin Injection Pediatric
Lariam Tablets (Occasional)
Macrobid Capsules (Rare)
Macrodantin Capsules (Rare)
Mexitil Capsules (Less than 1% or about 2 in 1,000)
Mirapex Tablets (Less than or greater than or equal to 1%)

Namenda Tablets (Infrequent)
Nardil Tablets (Infrequent)
Neurontin Capsules (Infrequent)
Neurontin Oral Solution (Infrequent)
Neurontin Tablets (Infrequent)
Noroxin Tablets
Orapred Oral Solution
Orthoclone OKT3 Sterile Solution
Paxil CR Controlled-Release Tablets
Paxil Oral Suspension (Rare)
Paxil Tablets (Rare)
Pediapred Oral Solution
Pediazole Suspension
PEG-Intron Powder for Injection (Less than or equal to 1%)
Permax Tablets (2.1%; frequent)
Plaquenil Tablets
PREVPAC
Procanbid Extended-Release Tablets (Occasional)
▲ Prograf Capsules and Injection (3% to 15%)
Provigil Tablets
Prozac Pulvules and Liquid (Infrequent)
Pulmicort Respules (Less than 1%)
Pulmicort Turbuhaler Inhalation Powder (Rare)
Reyataz Capsules (Less than 3%)
Rifadin Capsules (Rare)
Rifadin IV (Rare)
Rilutek Tablets (Rare)
Ritalin Hydrochloride Tablets
Ritalin LA Capsules
Ritalin-SR Tablets
Rocaltrol Capsules (Rare)
Rocaltrol Oral Solution (Rare)
Roferon-A Injection
Rythmol Tablets (Less than 1%)
Sarafem Pulvules (Infrequent)
Solu-Medrol Sterile Powder
Stalevo Tablets
Sustiva Capsules (Less than 2%)
Symmetrel Syrup (0.1% to 1%)
Symmetrel Tablets (0.1% to 1%)
Tagamet Injection
Tagamet Liquid
Tagamet Tablets
Tarka Tablets
Tasmar Tablets (Infrequent)
Tenormin I.V. Injection
Tenormin Tablets
Tequin Injection (Less than 0.1%)
Tequin Tablets (Less than 0.1%)

Thalomid Capsules
Topamax Sprinkle Capsules
(Frequent)
Topamax Tablets (Frequent)
Toradol IM Injection, IV Injection
Toradol Tablets
Trilafon
▲ Valcyte Tablets (Less than 5%)
Valtrex Caplets
Verelan PM Capsules (2% or less)
VFEND I.V. (Less than 1%)
VFEND Oral Suspension (Less than 1%)
VFEND Tablets (Less than 1%)
Wellbutrin SR Sustained-Release
Tablets
Wellbutrin Tablets (Infrequent)
Wellbutrin XL Extended-Release
Tablets
Zarontin Capsules
Zarontin Syrup
Zoloft Oral Concentrate
Zoloft Tablets
Zomig Nasal Spray (Rare)
Zovirax Capsules
Zovirax for Injection
Zovirax Suspension
Zovirax Tablets
Zyban Sustained-Release Tablets

Psychoses, aggravation
Clozapine Tablets
Clozaril Tablets
Decadron Phosphate Injection
Decadron Tablets
Hydrocortone Phosphate Injection,
Sterile
Hydrocortone Tablets
Mellaril
Norpramin Tablets
Pamelor
Pediapred Oral Solution
Serentil Ampuls
Serentil Concentrate
Serentil Tablets
Seroquel Tablets (Infrequent)
Solu-Medrol Sterile Powder
Surmontil Capsules
Thioridazine Hydrochloride Tablets
Vivactil Tablets

Psychoses, toxic
Astramorph/PF Injection
(Preservative-Free)
Cipro I.V. (1% or less)

Cipro I.V. Pharmacy Bulk Package
(Less than 1%)
Cipro Oral Suspension
Cipro Tablets
Cipro XR Tablets
Concerta Extended-Release Tablets
Floxin Tablets
Focalin Tablets (Rare)
Levaquin in 5% Dextrose Injection
Levaquin Injection
Levaquin Tablets
Metadate CD Capsules
Metadate ER Tablets
Rifamate Capsules (Uncommon)
Rifater Tablet (Uncommon)
Ritalin Hydrochloride Tablets
Ritalin LA Capsules
Ritalin-SR Tablets

Psychosis, activation
Amnesteem Capsules
Carbatrol Capsules
Prochlorperazine
Risperdal Consta Injection (Frequent)
Tegretol Chewable Tablets
Tegretol Suspension
Tegretol Tablets
Tegretol-XR Tablets
Triavil Tablets
Trifluoperazine (trifluoperazine tablets)
Wellbutrin SR Sustained-Release
Tablets
Wellbutrin XL Extended-Release
Tablets
Zyban Sustained-Release Tablets

Psychosis, paranoid
Zarontin Capsules (Rare)
Zarontin Syrup (Rare)

Psychotic symptoms, paradoxical exacerbation
Haldol Decanoate 50 Injection
Haldol Decanoate 100 Injection
Navane Capsules (Infrequent)
Navane Concentrate (Infrequent)
Navane Intramuscular (Infrequent)
Thiothixene Capsules

Rage
Valium Tablets
Xanax Tablets (Rare)
Xanax XR Tablets (Rare)

Schizophrenia, precipitation
Nardil Tablets (Less frequent)

Zyprexa Tablets
Zyprexa ZYDIS Orally
  Disintegrating Tablets

Sedation

▲ Alacol DM Syrup (Among most
  frequent)
Aldoclor Tablets
Aldoril Tablets
Amerge Tablets (Rare)
Ancobon Capsules
Ativan Injection
Balamine DM Oral Drops
Balamine DM Syrup
▲ Buprenex Injectable (Most frequent)
▲ Catapres Tablets (About 10 in 100
  patients)
Catapres-TTS (3 of 101 patients)
▲ Clorpres Tablets (About 10%)
▲ Clozapine Tablets (More than 5% to
  39%)
▲ Clozaril Tablets (More than 5% to
  39%)
Corzide 40/5 Tablets (6 of 1000
  patients)
Corzide 80/5 Tablets (6 of 1000
  patients)
Dalmane Capsules
▲ Darvocet-N 50 Tablets (Among most
  frequent)
▲ Darvocet-N 100 Tablets (Among most
  frequent)
▲ Darvon Capsules (Among most
  frequent)
▲ Darvon Compound-65 Capsules
  (Among most frequent)
▲ Darvon-N Tablets (Among most
  frequent)
▲ Demerol Syrup (Among most
  frequent)
▲ Demerol Tablets (Among most
  frequent)
▲ Demser Capsules (Almost all
  patients)
Depacon Injection
Depakene Capsules
Depakene Syrup
Depakote ER Tablets
Depakote Tablets
Dilaudid Ampules
Dilaudid Injection
Dilaudid Multiple Dose Vials
Dilaudid Non-Sterile Powder
Dilaudid Oral Liquid
Dilaudid Rectal Suppositories
Dilaudid Tablets

Dilaudid Tablets - 8 mg
▲ Dilaudid-HP Injection (Among most
  frequent)
▲ Dilaudid-HP Lyophilized Powder 250
  mg (Among most frequent)
▲ Guanfacine (5% to 39%)
Halcion Tablets
Hycodan Syrup
Hycodan Tablets
Hycomine Compound Tablets
Hycotuss Expectorant Syrup
Imitrex Injection (2.7%)
Imitrex Nasal Spray (Infrequent)
Imitrex Tablets
Inversine Tablets
Kadian Capsules (Less than 3%)
▲ Lortab 2.5/500 Tablets (Among most
  frequent)
▲ Lortab 5/500 Tablets (Among most
  frequent)
▲ Lortab 7.5/500 Tablets (Among most
  frequent)
▲ Lortab 10/500 Tablets (Among most
  frequent)
▲ Lortab Elixir (Among most frequent)
Lotronex Tablets (Rare)
▲ Maxidone Tablets (Among most
  frequent)
▲ MS Contin Tablets (Among most
  frequent)
▲ MSIR Oral Capsules (Among most
  frequent)
▲ MSIR Oral Solution Concentrate
  (Among most frequent)
▲ MSIR Oral Tablets (Among most
  frequent)
Nadolol Tablets (6 of 1000 patients)
Navane Capsules
Navane Concentrate
Navane Intramuscular
▲ Norco 5/325 Tablets (Among most
  frequent)
▲ Norco 7.5/325 Tablets (Among most
  frequent)
▲ Norco 10/325 Tablets (Among most
  frequent)
▲ Nubain Injection (36%)
▲ Orap Tablets (14 of 20 patients)
▲ OxyFast Oral Concentrate Solution
  (Among most frequent)
▲ OxyIR Capsules (Among most
  frequent)
▲ Percocet Tablets (Among most
  frequent)
▲ Percodan Tablets (Among most
  frequent)

Periactin Tablets
Phenergan Suppositories
Roferon-A Injection (Infrequent)
▲ Sedapap Tablets 50 mg/650 mg
(Among the most frequent)
▲ Semprex-D Capsules (6% more
common than with placebo)
Sonata Capsules
▲ Strattera Capsules (2% to 4%)
▲ Synalgos-DC Capsules (Among most
frequent)
Tessalon Capsules
Tessalon Perles
Thiothixene Capsules
Triavil Tablets
Tussionex Pennkinetic Extended-
Release Suspension
▲ Tylenol with Codeine Elixir (Among
most frequent)
▲ Tylenol with Codeine Tablets (Among
most frequent)
Valcyte Tablets
▲ Vicodin ES Tablets (Among most
frequent)
▲ Vicodin HP Tablets (Among most
frequent)
▲ Vicodin Tablets (Among most
frequent)
▲ Wellbutrin Tablets (19.8%)
Xanax Tablets
▲ Xanax XR Tablets (45.2%)
▲ Xeloda Tablets (Less than 5%)
▲ Zanaflex Tablets (48%)
▲ Zofran Injection (8%)
▲ Zofran Injection Premixed (8%)
▲ Zofran ODT Orally Disintegrating
Tablets (20%)
▲ Zofran Oral Solution (20%)
▲ Zofran Tablets (20%)
▲ Zydone Tablets (Among most
frequent)

Sensorium, clouded
Blocadren Tablets
Corzide 40/5 Tablets
Corzide 80/5 Tablets
Cosopt Sterile Ophthalmic Solution
Inderal LA Long-Acting Capsules
Mexitil Capsules (1.9% to 2.6%)
Nadolol Tablets
Tenormin I.V. Injection
Tenormin Tablets
Timolide Tablets
Timoptic in Ocudose
Timoptic Sterile Ophthalmic Solution

Timoptic-XE Sterile Ophthalmic Gel
Forming Solution
Toprol-XL Tablets
Xanax Tablets
Zebeta Tablets
Ziac Tablets

Sensory deficit, persistent
Nesacaine Injection
Nesacaine-MPF Injection

Sensory disturbances
Depo-Medrol Single-Dose Vial
▲ Foscavir Injection (Between 1% and
5%)
▲ Leukine (6%)
▲ Paraplatin for Injection (4% to 6%)
Paxil Oral Suspension
Paxil Tablets
▲ Prograf Capsules and Injection
(Approximately 55%)
▲ Proleukin for Injection (10%)
Rocaltrol Capsules
Rocaltrol Oral Solution
▲ Wellbutrin Tablets (4%)
Xanax Tablets

Serotonin syndrome
BuSpar Tablets
Celexa Oral Solution
Celexa Tablets
Effexor Tablets
Effexor XR Capsules
Elavil Very rare
Fluvoxamine maleate
Imitrex Injection
Imitrex Tablets
Lexapro Oral Solution
Lexapro Tablets
Meridia Capsules
Paxil CR Controlled-Release Tablets
Paxil Oral Suspension
Paxil Tablets
Prozac Pulvules and Liquid
Ultram Tablets
Zoloft Oral Concentrate
Zoloft Tablets

Sexual activity, decrease
▲ Catapres Tablets (About 3 in 100
patients)
Catapres-TTS (0.5% or less)
Clorpres Tablets (About 3%)
Risperdal M-Tab Tablets (Frequent)
Risperdal Oral Solution (Frequent)
Risperdal Tablets (Frequent)

Sexual dysfunction

Aceon Tablets (2 mg, 4 mg, 8 mg)
(0.3% to 1.4%)
Avalide Tablets
Avapro Tablets (Less than 1%)
Caduet Tablets (Greater that 0.1% to
2%)
Cardizem LA Extended Release
Tablets (Less than 2%)
Cardura Tablets (2%)
Catapres-TTS (2 of 101 patients)
Celexa Oral Solution
Celexa Tablets
Copaxone for Injection (Infrequent)
Effexor Tablets (2%)
Effexor XR Capsules
Eldepryl Capsules
Eskalith Capsules
Eskalith CR Controlled-Release
Tablets
Evoxac Capsules (Less than 1%)
Fluvoxamine maleate
Geodon Capsules (Infrequent)
Gleevec Tablets (Infrequent)
Hivid Tablets (Less than 1%)
Lexapro Oral Solution
Lexapro Tablets
Lotronex Tablets (Rare)
Maxzide Tablets
Maxzide-25 mg Tablets
Nardil Tablets (Common)
Naropin Injection
Nesacaine Injection
Nesacaine-MPF Injection
Neurontin Capsules (Infrequent)
Neurontin Oral Solution (Infrequent)
Neurontin Tablets (Infrequent)
Norvasc Tablets (Less than 1% to 2%)
▲ Paxil Oral Suspension (3.7% to 10%)
▲ Paxil Tablets (3.7% to 10%)
Polocaine Injection
Polocaine-MPF Injection
Procardia Capsules (2% or less)
Risperdal M-Tab Tablets (Frequent)
Risperdal Oral Solution (Frequent)
Risperdal Tablets (Frequent)
Roferon-A Injection (Infrequent)
Sarafem Pulvules
▲ Strattera Capsules (3% or greater)
Tiazac Capsules (Less than 2%)
Viracept Oral Powder (Less than 2%)
Viracept Tablets (Less than 2%)
Wellbutrin Tablets (Frequent)
▲ Xanax Tablets (7.4%)

Xanax XR Tablets (2.4%)
Ziac Tablets
▲ Zoladex (21%)
▲ Zoladex 3-month (One of the two
most common)
Zoloft Oral Concentrate (Frequent)
Zoloft Tablets (Frequent)

Sleep disturbances

Aceon Tablets 2 mg, 4 mg, 8 mg
(2.5%)
Adalat CC Tablets (Rare)
▲ Advair Diskus 100/50 (1% to 3%)
▲ Advair Diskus 250/50 (1% to 3%)
▲ Advair Diskus 500/50 (1% to 3%)
Allegra-D Extended-Release Tablets
(Less than 1%)
Ambien Tablets (Infrequent)
Amerge Tablets (Infrequent)
Anzemet Injection (Infrequent)
Anzemet Tablets (Infrequent)
▲ Arava Tablets (1% to 3%)
Astelin Nasal Spray (Infrequent)
Avalide Tablets
Avapro Tablets (Less than 1%)
Avelox I.V. (Less than 0.1%)
Avelox Tablets (Less than 0.1%)
Celexa Oral Solution (At least 2%)
Celexa Tablets (At least 2%)
▲ Clozapine Tablets (4%)
▲ Clozaril Tablets (4%)
▲ Combivir Tablets (11%)
Copaxone for Injection (At least 2%)
Coreg Tablets (Greater than 0.1% to
1%)
Corzide 40/5 Tablets
Corzide 80/5 Tablets
Cozaar Tablets (Less than 1%)
▲ Crinone 4% Gel (18%)
▲ Crinone 8% Gel (18%)
Crixivan Capsules (Less than 2%)
Depakote ER Tablets (Greater than 1%)
Doral
Effexor Tablets (Infrequent)
Elavil
Eldepryl Capsules
▲ Entocort EC Capsules (Less than 5%)
▲ Epivir Oral Solution (11%)
▲ Epivir Tablets (11%)
▲ Floxin Tablets (1% to 3%)
▲ Fludara for Injection (1% to 3%)
Fluvoxamine maleate (Infrequent)
Halcion Tablets
▲ Hectorol Capsules (3.3%)
▲ Hectorol Injection (3.3%)

HibTITER
Hyzaar 50-12.5 Tablets
Hyzaar 100-25 Tablets
Imitrex Injection (Rare)
Imitrex Nasal Spray (Infrequent)
Imitrex Tablets (Rare to Infrequent)
Klonopin Tablets (Infrequent)
Klonopin Wafers (Infrequent)
Lamictal Chewable Dispersible
    Tablets (1.4%)
Lamictal Tablets (1.4%)
▲ Lariam Tablets (Among most
    frequent)
Levaquin in 5% Dextrose Injection
    (0.1% to 1%)
Levaquin Injection (0.1% to 1%)
Levaquin Tablets (0.1% to 1%)
▲ Lotronex Tablets (3%)
▲ Lupron Depot 3.75 mg (16%)
▲ Lupron Depot 7.5 mg (Less than 5%)
▲ Lupron Depot—3 Month 11.25 mg
    (16%)
▲ Lupron Depot—3 Month 22.5 mg
    (8.5%)
▲ Lupron Depot—4 Month 30 mg (Less
    than 5%)
▲ Lupron Injection (5% or more)
▲ Mexitil Capsules (7.1% to 7.5%)
Mirapex Tablets (Less than or equal to
    1%)
Nadolol Tablets
Namenda Tablets (Infrequent)
Nardil Tablets (Common)
Nexium Delayed-Release Capsules
    (Less than 1%)
Noroxin Tablets (Less frequent)
Numorphan Injection
Numorphan Suppositories
▲ Pacerone Tablets (1% to 3%)
▲ Pediarix Vaccine (0.4% to 46.7%)
Prevacid Delayed-Release Capsules
    (Less than 1%)
Prevacid for Delayed-Release Oral
    Suspension (Less than 1%)
Prevacid NapraPAC 375 (Less than
    1%)
Prevacid NapraPAC 500 (Less than
    1%)
Prevacid SoluTab Delayed-Release
    Tablets (Less than 1%)
▲ Prevnar for Injection (18.1% to
    33.3%)
PREVPAC (Less than 1%)
Procardia Capsules (2% or less)
Prochieve 4% Gel

Prochieve 8% Gel
ProSom Tablets (Infrequent)
Protonix I.V. (Less than 1%)
Protonix Tablets (Less than 1%)
Provigil Tablets (At least 1%)
Prozac Pulvules and Liquid (Frequent)
Recombivax HB (Less than 1%)
Relpax Tablets (Rare)
Rescriptor Tablets
Reyataz Capsules (Less than 3%)
Risperdal M-Tab Tablets (Frequent)
Risperdal Oral Solution (Frequent)
Risperdal Tablets (Frequent)
▲ Roferon-A Injection (5% to 11%)
Sarafem Pulvules (Frequent)
▲ Serevent Diskus (1% to 3%)
Sonata Capsules (Rare)
▲ Strattera Capsules (4%)
Symbyax Capsules (1% to 2%)
▲ Tasmar Tablets (24% to 25%)
Triavil Tablets
Tricor Tablets (Less than 1%)
▲ Trizivir Tablets (7% to 11%)
▲ Ultram Tablets (1% to 5%)
Valium Tablets
Varivax (Greater than or equal to
    1%)
Viracept Oral Powder (Less than 2%)
Viracept Tablets (Less than 2%)
▲ Wellbutrin Tablets (4%)
Xanax Tablets (Rare)
Xanax XR Tablets (Rare)
▲ Xenical Capsules (3.9%)
▲ Xyrem Oral Solution (6% to 14%)
Zarontin Capsules
Zarontin Syrup
Zebeta Tablets
Zelnorm Tablets
Ziac Tablets
▲ Ziagen Oral Solution (7%)
▲ Ziagen Tablets (7%)
Zyrtec Syrup (Less than 2%)
Zyrtec Tablets (Less than 2%)
Zyrtec-D 12 Hour Extended Relief
    Tablets (Less than 2%)

Sleep talking

Sonata Capsules (Rare)
Xanax XR Tablets (Infrequent)

Sleep walking

Halcion
Neurontin Capsules
Neurontin Oral Solution
Neurontin Tablets

Sonata Capsules (Rare)
▲ Xyrem Oral Solution (7%)

Sleep-inducing effects
▲ Advair Diskus 100/50 (1% to 3%)
▲ Advair Diskus 250/50 (1% to 3%)
▲ Advair Diskus 500/50 (1% to 3%)
Lotronex Tablets (Infrequent)

Sleeping, excessive
Aloxi Injection (Less than 1%)
Fluvoxamine maleate (Infrequent)
Maxalt Tablets (Rare)
Maxalt-MLT Orally Disintegrating
Tablets (Rare)
Nardil Tablets (Common)
Permax Tablets
Prinivil Tablets (0.3% to 1%)
Prinzide Tablets
Xanax XR Tablets (1.3%)
Zestoretic Tablets
Zestril Tablets (0.3% to 1%)

Sluggishness
Lexapro Oral Solution (Infrequent)
Lexapro Tablets (Infrequent)
Sedapap Tablets 50 mg/650 mg
(Infrequent)
Xanax XR Tablets (Infrequent)

Smell disturbances
Amerge Tablets (Infrequent)
Beconase AQ Nasal Spray (Rare)
Biaxin Filmtab Tablets
Biaxin Granules
Biaxin XL Filmtab Tablets
BuSpar Tablets (Infrequent)
Eligard 7.5 mg (Less than 2%)
Ergamisol Tablets (1%)
Flonase Nasal Spray
Floxin Tablets
Hivid Tablets (Less than 1%)
Imitrex Injection (Rare)
Imitrex Nasal Spray (Infrequent)
Imitrex Tablets (Infrequent)
Lotronex Tablets (Rare)
Maxair Autohaler (0.6%)
Maxalt Tablets (Rare)
Maxalt-MLT Orally Disintegrating
Tablets (Rare)
Nasonex Nasal Spray (Very rare)
▲ Pacerone Tablets (1% to 3%)
PREVPAC
▲ Roferon-A Injection (3%)
Rythmol Tablets (Less than 1%)
Testim 1% Gel (1% or less)

Timentin ADD-Vantage
Timentin Galaxy Container
Timentin IV Infusion
Timentin Pharmacy Bulk Package
Xanax Tablets

Sociopathy
BuSpar Tablets (Infrequent)
DextroStat Tablets
Neurontin Capsules (Rare)
Neurontin Oral Solution (Rare)
Neurontin Tablets (Rare)
Paxil Oral Suspension (Rare)
Paxil Tablets (Rare)
Sarafem Pulvules (Rare)
Zyprexa Tablets (Infrequent)
Zyprexa ZYDIS Orally Disintegrating
Tablets (Infrequent)

Speech difficulties
Clozapine Tablets (Less than 1%)
Clozaril Tablets (Less than 1%)
▲ Demser Capsules (10%)
Geodon for Injection (Up to 2%)
Marinol Capsules (Less than 1%)
Mexitil Capsules (2.6%)
Nubain Injection (1% or less)
Zyprexa Tablets (2%)
Zyprexa ZYDIS Orally Disintegrating
Tablets (2%)

Speech disturbances
Accuretic Tablets
Actiq (Less than 1%)
Ambien Tablets (Infrequent)
▲ Amphotec (1% to 5%)
Anafranil (3%)
Avelox I.V. (Less than 0.1%)
Avelox Tablets (Less than 0.1%)
Brevibloc Concentrate (Less than 1%)
Brevibloc Double Strength Injection
(Less than 1%)
Brevibloc Double Strength Premixed
Injection (Less than 1%)
Brevibloc Injection (Less than 1%)
Brevibloc Premixed Injection (Less
than 1%)
Carbatrol Capsules
Cerebyx Injection (Frequent)
Copaxone for Injection (2%)
Dantrium Capsules (Less frequent)
▲ Depakote ER Tablets (1% to 5%)
▲ Depakote Tablets (1% to 5%)
Doral
Duragesic Transdermal System (1% or
greater)

Effexor Tablets (Infrequent)
Effexor XR Capsules (Infrequent)
Eldepryl Capsules
Ergamisol Tablets
Estrace Tablets
Estrace Vaginal Cream
Evoxac Capsules (Less than 1%)
Fortovase Capsules (Less than 2%)
Frova Tablets (Infrequent)
▲ Gabitril Tablets (4%)
Hivid Tablets (Less than 1%)
Imitrex Injection
▲ Intron A for Injection (Less than 5%)
Invirase Capsules (Less than 2%)
Lamictal Chewable Dispersible
   Tablets (2.5%)
Lamictal Tablets (2.5%)
Levaquin in 5% Dextrose Injection
   (0.1% to 1%)
Levaquin Injection (0.1% to 1%)
Levaquin Tablets (0.1% to 1%)
Levlen 21 Tablets
Levlen 28 Tablets
Levlite 28 Tablets
Meridia Capsules
Mirapex Tablets (1% or more)
Neurontin Capsules (Infrequent)
Neurontin Oral Solution (Infrequent)
Neurontin Tablets (Infrequent)
NuLev Orally Disintegrating Tablets
▲ Orap Tablets (2 of 20 patients)
Ortho Tri-Cyclen Lo Tablets
Ortho Tri-Cyclen Tablets
Ortho-Cyclen Tablets
Ortho-Est Tablets
OxyContin Tablets (Less than 1%)
Permax Tablets (1.1%)
Prevacid Delayed-Release Capsules
   (Less than 1%)
Prevacid for Delayed-Release Oral
   Suspension (Less than 1%)
Prevacid NapraPAC 375
Prevacid NapraPAC 500
Prevacid SoluTab Delayed-Release
   Tablets (Less than 1%)
PREVPAC
▲ Proleukin for Injection (7%)
▲ Prometrium Capsules (100 mg,
   200 mg) (Less than 5%)
Protonix I.V.
Relpax Tablets (Infrequent)
Romazicon Injection (Less than 1%)
Rythmol Tablets (Less than 1%)
Salagen Tablets (Less than 1%)

Symbyax Capsules (Up to 2%)
Tambocor Tablets (Less than 1%)
Tasmar Tablets (Frequent)
Tegretol Chewable Tablets
Tegretol Suspension
Tegretol Tablets
Tegretol-XR Tablets
▲ Topamax Sprinkle Capsules (4% to 13%)
▲ Topamax Tablets (4% to 13%)
▲ Trileptal Oral Suspension (1% to 3%)
▲ Trileptal Tablets (1% to 3%)
Tri-Levlen 21 Tablets
Tri-Levlen 28 Tablets
Trovan I.V. (Less than 1%)
Trovan Tablets (Less than 1%)
Ultram Tablets (Infrequent)
▲ Vesanoid Capsules (3%)
Vistide Injection
▲ Zanaflex Tablets (3%)
Zomig Nasal Spray (Infrequent)
▲ Zonegran Capsules (5%)
Zyprexa Tablets (2%)
Zyprexa ZYDIS Orally Disintegrating
   Tablets (2%)

Speech, incoherent
Clozapine Tablets (Less than 1%)
Clozaril Tablets (Less than 1%)

Speech, slurring
BuSpar Tablets (Rare)
Clozapine Tablets (1%)
Clozaril Tablets (1%)
Coly-Mycin M Parenteral
Corzide 40/5 Tablets (1 to 5 of 1000
   patients)
Corzide 80/5 Tablets (1 to 5 of 1000
   patients)
Dalmane Capsules (Rare)
▲ Dilantin Infatabs (Among most
   common)
▲ Dilantin Kapseals (Among most
   common)
▲ Dilantin-125 Oral Suspension (Among
   most common)
Doral
Eskalith Capsules
Eskalith CR Controlled-Release
   Tablets
Fluvoxamine maleate (Rare)
Halcion Tablets
Kadian Capsules (Less than 3%)
Klonopin Tablets
Klonopin Wafers
Loxitane Capsules

Matulane Capsules
Miltown Tablets
Nadolol Tablets (1 to 5 of 1000 patients)
▲ Phenytek Capsules (Among most common)
Serentil Ampuls
Serentil Concentrate
Serentil Tablets
Sonata Capsules (Rare)
Symmetrel Syrup (0.1% to 1%)
Symmetrel Tablets (0.1% to 1%)
Tranxene T-TAB Tablets
Tranxene-SD Half Strength Tablets
Tranxene-SD Tablets
Trilafon
Valium Tablets (Infrequent)
Vicoprofen Tablets (Less than 1%)
Xanax Tablets

Stimulation

Dalmane Capsules (Rare)
Sonata Capsules (Rare)
Stalevo Tablets
Valium Tablets
Xanax Tablets (Rare)
Xanax XR Tablets (Rare)

Stupor

Abilify Tablets (1% or less)
Ambien Tablets (Infrequent)
▲ Amphotec (1% to 5%)
Ativan Injection (1.2%)
BuSpar Tablets (Rare)
Celexa Oral Solution (Rare)
Celexa Tablets (Rare)
▲ Cerebyx Injection (7.7%)
Copaxone for Injection (Frequent)
Duragesic Transdermal System (Less than 1%)
Effexor Tablets (Infrequent)
Effexor XR Capsules (Infrequent)
Eskalith Capsules
Eskalith CR Controlled-Release Tablets
Felbatol Oral Suspension (2.6%)
Felbatol Tablets (2.6%)
Fluvoxamine maleate (Infrequent)
▲ Foscavir Injection (Between 1% and 5%)
Gabitril Tablets (Frequent)
Hivid Tablets (Less than 1%)
▲ Invanz for Injection (3.3% to 5.1%)
Lamictal Chewable Dispersible Tablets (Infrequent)

Lamictal Tablets (Infrequent)
Levaquin in 5% Dextrose Injection (0.1% to 1%)
Levaquin Injection (0.1% to 1%)
Levaquin Tablets (0.1% to 1%)
Moduretic Tablets (Less than or equal to 1%)
Namenda Tablets (Infrequent)
Naropin Injection (Less than 1%)
Neurontin Capsules (Infrequent)
Neurontin Oral Solution (Infrequent)
Neurontin Tablets (Infrequent)
Orthoclone OKT3 Sterile Solution
OxyContin Tablets (Less than 1%)
Paxil CR Controlled-Release Tablets
Paxil Oral Suspension (Rare)
Paxil Tablets (Rare)
Permax Tablets (Rare)
PhosLo Gelcaps
PhosLo Tablets
ProSom Tablets (Infrequent)
Prozac Pulvules and Liquid (Rare)
Relpax Tablets (Infrequent)
Remeron SolTab Tablets (Rare)
Requip Tablets (Infrequent)
Rilutek Tablets (Infrequent)
Risperdal M-Tab Tablets (Infrequent)
Risperdal Oral Solution (Infrequent)
Risperdal Tablets (Infrequent)
Romazicon Injection (Less than 1%)
Sarafem Pulvules (Rare)
Seroquel Tablets (Infrequent)
Sonata Capsules (Rare)
Streptomycin Sulfate Injection
Stromectol Tablets
Symmetrel Syrup
Symmetrel Tablets
Tambocor Tablets (Less than 1%)
Topamax Sprinkle Capsules (1% to 2%)
Topamax Tablets (1% to 2%)
Toradol IM Injection, IV Injection (1% or less)
Toradol Tablets (1% or less)
Trileptal Oral Suspension
Trileptal Tablets
Ultracet Tablets (Less than 1%)
Xanax XR Tablets (Infrequent)
Xyrem Oral Solution (Frequent)
Zanaflex Tablets (Infrequent)
Zyprexa Tablets (Infrequent)
Zyprexa ZYDIS Orally Disintegrating Tablets (Infrequent)

Stuttering

Seroquel Tablets (Rare)
Zyprexa Tablets (Infrequent)
Zyprexa ZYDIS Orally Disintegrating
  Tablets (Infrequent)

Suicidal ideation

Abilify Tablets (1% or greater)
Accutane Capsules
Ambien Tablets
Amnesteem Capsules
Avelox I.V.
Avelox Tablets
▲ Avonex (4%)
Betaseron for SC Injection
BuSpar Tablets (Infrequent)
Celontin Capsules (Rare)
Cipro XR Tablets (Rare)
Cognex Capsules (Rare)
Copegus Tablets (Less than 1%)
Depakote Tablets
Effexor Tablets (Rare)
Effexor XR Capsules (Rare)
Exelon Capsules (Infrequent)
Exelon Oral Solution (Infrequent)
Floxin Tablets (Rare)
Halcion Tablets
Infergen
Intron A for Injection (Rare)
Klonopin Tablets (Infrequent)
Klonopin Wafers (Infrequent)
Lamictal Chewable Dispersible
  Tablets (Rare)
Lamictal Tablets (Rare)
Lariam Tablets (Rare)
Levaquin in 5% Dextrose Injection
  (Rare)
Levaquin Injection (Rare)
Levaquin Tablets (Rare)
Lexapro Oral Solution (Infrequent)
Lexapro Tablets (Infrequent)
Lupron Depot 3.75 mg (Very rare)
Lupron Depot—3 Month 11.25 mg
  (Very rare)
Miltown Tablets
Nefazodone (Infrequent)
Neurontin Capsules (Infrequent)
Neurontin Oral Solution (Infrequent)
Neurontin Tablets (Infrequent)
Nizoral Tablets (Rare)
Pegasys
PEG-Intron Powder for Injection
  (Less than or equal to 1%)
Prozac Pulvules and Liquid
Rebetron Combination Therapy (Less
  than 1%)

Rebif Injection
Remeron SolTab Tablets
Roferon-A Injection
Sarafem Pulvules
Soriatane Capsules
Stalevo Tablets
Symmetrel Syrup (Less than 0.1%)
Symmetrel Tablets (Less than 0.1%)
Trilafon
Ultram Tablets (Infrequent)
VFEND I.V. (Less than 1%)
VFEND Oral Suspension (Less than
  1%)
VFEND Tablets (Less than 1%)
Viracept Oral Powder (Less than 2%)
Viracept Tablets (Less than 2%)
Wellbutrin SR Sustained-Release
  Tablets (Infrequent)
Wellbutrin Tablets (Rare)
Wellbutrin XL Extended-Release
  Tablets (Infrequent)
Xanax Tablets
Xanax XR Tablets (Infrequent)
Zarontin Capsules (Rare)
Zarontin Syrup (Rare)
Zoloft Oral Concentrate (Rare)
Zoloft Tablets (Rare)
Zyban Sustained-Release Tablets
  (Infrequent)

Suicide, attempt of

Abilify Tablets (1% or less)
Accutane Capsules
Ambien Tablets (Rare)
Amnesteem Capsules
Celexa Oral Solution (Frequent)
Celexa Tablets (Frequent)
Copaxone for Injection (Infrequent)
Effexor Tablets (Infrequent)
Effexor XR Capsules (Infrequent)
Exelon Capsules (Infrequent)
Exelon Oral Solution (Infrequent)
Felbatol Oral Suspension (Infrequent)
Felbatol Tablets (Infrequent)
Floxin Tablets (Rare)
Fluvoxamine maleate (Infrequent)
Fortovase Capsules (Rare)
Gabitril Tablets (Infrequent)
Hivid Tablets (Less than 1%)
Imitrex Tablets (Rare)
Infergen
Intron A for Injection (Rare;
  less than 5%)
Invirase Capsules (Rare)

Klonopin Tablets (Infrequent)
Klonopin Wafers (Infrequent)
Lamictal Chewable Dispersible
  Tablets (Rare)
Lamictal Tablets (Rare)
Lariam Tablets (Rare)
Levaquin in 5% Dextrose Injection
  (Rare)
Levaquin Injection (Rare)
Levaquin Tablets (Rare)
Lexapro Oral Solution (Infrequent)
Lexapro Tablets (Infrequent)
Lupron Depot 3.75 mg (Very rare)
Lupron Depot—3 Month 11.25 mg
  (Very rare)
Mirapex Tablets (Less than 1%)
Namenda Tablets (Infrequent)
Nefazodone (Infrequent)
Neurontin Capsules (Rare)
Neurontin Oral Solution (Rare)
Neurontin Tablets (Rare)
Paxil Oral Suspension
Paxil Tablets
PEG-Intron Powder for Injection
  (Less than or equal to 1%)
Proleukin for Injection
Prozac Pulvules and Liquid
  (Infrequent)
Rebetron Combination Therapy (Less
  than 1%)
Rebif Injection
Remicade for IV Injection (Greater
  than or equal to 0.2%)
Requip Tablets (Rare)
Reyataz Capsules (Less than 3%)
Rilutek Tablets (Infrequent)
▲ Risperdal Consta Injection (1% to
  4%)
Risperdal M-Tab Tablets (1.2%)
Risperdal Oral Solution (1.2%)
Risperdal Tablets (1.2%)
Roferon-A Injection
Sandostatin LAR Depot (Rare)
Sarafem Pulvules (Infrequent)
Seroquel Tablets (Infrequent)
Sustiva Capsules
Symbyax Capsules (Infrequent)
Symmetrel Syrup (Less than 0.1%)
Symmetrel Tablets (Less than 0.1%)
Thalomid Capsules
Topamax Sprinkle Capsules
  (Frequent)
Topamax Tablets (Frequent)
Vivactil Tablets

Xanax Tablets
Zanaflex Tablets (Rare)
Zelnorm Tablets
Zoloft Oral Concentrate
Zoloft Tablets
Zyprexa Tablets (Frequent)
Zyprexa ZYDIS Orally Disintegrating
  Tablets (Frequent)

Talkativeness
Carbatrol Capsules
Dalmane Capsules
Tegretol Chewable Tablets
Tegretol Suspension
Tegretol Tablets
Tegretol-XR Tablets
Xanax Tablets (2.2%)
Xanax XR Tablets (Infrequent)

Tenseness
Allegra-D Extended-Release Tablets
Clomid Tablets (Fewer than 1%)
▲ Indapamide Tablets (Greater than or
  equal to 5%)
Loxitane Capsules
Prostin E2 Suppositories
Zelnorm Tablets
Zyrtec-D 12 Hour Extended Relief
  Tablets

Thinking abnormality
Actiq (1% to 2%)
Ambien Tablets (Rare)
AmBisome for Injection (Less
  common)
▲ Amphotec (5% or more)
Androderm Transdermal System (Less
  than 1%)
Astelin Nasal Spray (Infrequent)
Ativan Injection (Less than 1%)
Avelox I.V. (Less than 0.1%)
Avelox Tablets (Less than 0.1%)
▲ Avinza Capsules (Less than 5%)
Brevibloc Concentrate (Less than 1%)
Brevibloc Double Strength Injection
  (Less than 1%)
Brevibloc Double Strength Premixed
  Injection (Less than 1%)
Brevibloc Injection (Less than 1%)
Brevibloc Premixed Injection (Less
  than 1%)
Campath Ampules
Cardura Tablets (Less than 0.5%)
▲ CellCept Capsules (3% to less than
  20%)

▲ CellCept Intravenous (3% to less than 20%)

▲ CellCept Oral Suspension (3% to less than 20%)

▲ CellCept Tablets (3% to less than 20%)

Cerebyx Injection (Frequent)

▲ Cognex Capsules (3%)

Coreg Tablets (Greater than 0.1% to 1%)

Cytovene Capsules (At least 3 subjects)

Cytovene-IV (At least 3 subjects)

▲ DaunoXome Injection (Less than or equal to 5%)

DDAVP Tablets

▲ Depacon Injection (6%)

▲ Depakene Capsules (6%)

▲ Depakene Syrup (6%)

▲ Depakote ER Tablets (6%)

▲ Depakote Sprinkle Capsules (6%)

▲ Depakote Tablets (1% to 6%)

Diprivan Injectable Emulsion (Less than 1%)

Doral

Doxil Injection (Less than 1%)

Duragesic Transdermal System (1% or greater)

Effexor Tablets (2%)

Effexor XR Capsules (Frequent)

Evoxac Capsules (Less than 1%)

▲ Felbatol Oral Suspension (6.5%)

▲ Felbatol Tablets (6.5%)

Flexeril Tablets (Less than 1%)

Fluvoxamine maleate

Frova Tablets (Infrequent)

▲ Gabitril Tablets (6%)

Halcion Tablets

Hivid Tablets (Less than 1%)

▲ Infergen (8% to 10%)

▲ Intron A for Injection (Less than 5%)

Kadian Capsules (Less than 3%)

Kaletra Capsules (Less than 2%)

Kaletra Oral Solution (Less than 2%)

Keppra Oral Solution (1% or more)

Keppra Tablets (1% or more)

▲ Lamictal Chewable Dispersible Tablets (3%)

▲ Lamictal Tablets (3%)

▲ Lupron Depot—4 Month 30 mg (Less than 5%)

▲ Marinol Capsules (3% to 10%)

Mebaral Tablets (Less than 1 in 100 patients)

Meridia Capsules (Greater than or equal to 1%)

▲ Mirapex Tablets (2% to 3%)

Namenda Tablets (Infrequent)

Nefazodone (Infrequent)

Nembutal Sodium Solution (Less than 1%)

Neurontin Capsules (1.7% to 2.7%)

Neurontin Oral Solution (1.7% to 2.7%)

Neurontin Tablets (1.7% to 2.7%)

Nipent for Injection (Less than 3%)

Norvir Oral Solution (Up to 0.7%)

Norvir Soft Gelatin Capsules (Up to 0.7%)

▲ OxyContin Tablets (Between 1% and 5%)

Paxil CR Controlled-Release Tablets

Paxil Oral Suspension (Infrequent)

Paxil Tablets (Infrequent)

Permax Tablets (Frequent)

Phenobarbital (Less than 1%)

Prevacid Delayed-Release Capsules (Less than 1%)

Prevacid for Delayed-Release Oral Suspension (Less than 1%)

Prevacid NapraPAC 375 (Less than 1%)

Prevacid NapraPAC 500 (Less than 1%)

Prevacid SoluTab Delayed-Release Tablets (Less than 1%)

PREVPAC (Less than 1%)

ProAmatine Tablets (Less frequent)

▲ Prograf Capsules and Injection (3% to 15%)

ProSom Tablets (2%)

Protonix I.V. (Less than 1%)

Protonix Tablets (Less than 1%)

Provigil Tablets (At least 1%)

Prozac Pulvules and Liquid (2%)

Relpax Tablets (Infrequent)

▲ Remeron SolTab Tablets (3%)

ReoPro Vials (2.1%)

Rilutek Tablets (Infrequent)

▲ Risperdal Consta Injection (Up to 3%)

Salagen Tablets (Less than 1%)

▲ Sarafem Pulvules (3% to 6%)

Seconal (Less than 1%)

Seroquel Tablets (Infrequent)

Sonata Capsules (Frequent)

Sular Tablets (Less than or equal to 1%)

▲ Symbyax Capsules (Greater than or equal to 5% to 6%)

Symmetrel Syrup (0.1% to 1%)
Symmetrel Tablets (0.1% to 1%)
Tasmar Tablets (Infrequent)
Tequin Injection (Less than 0.1%)
Tequin Tablets (Less than 0.1%)
Thalomid Capsules
Toradol IM Injection, IV Injection
  (1% or less)
Toradol Tablets (1% or less)
Trileptal Oral Suspension (2%)
Trileptal Tablets (2%)
Trovan I.V. (Less than 1%)
Trovan Tablets (Less than 1%)
Ultracet Tablets (Less than 1%)
Vicoprofen Tablets (Less than 3%)

Wellbutrin Tablets (Infrequent)
Xyrem Oral Solution
Zanaflex Tablets (Infrequent)
Zoladex (1% or greater)
Zoladex 3-month
Zomig Nasal Spray (Infrequent)
Zyban Sustained-Release Tablets (1%)
Zyprexa Tablets
Zyprexa ZYDIS Orally Disintegrating
  Tablets
Zyrtec Syrup (Less than 2%)
Zyrtec Tablets (Less than 2%)
Zyrtec-D 12 Hour Extended Relief
  Tablets (Less than 2%)

Part 2.
Side Effects by Brand

Abelcet Injection
Double vision

Abilify Tablets
Agitation (2% or greater)
▲ Anxiety (25%)
Apathy (1% or less)
Confusion (1% or greater)
Delirium (Rare)
Depersonalization (1% or less)
Depression (1% or greater)
Double vision (Rare)
Euphoria (Rare)
Hostility (1% or greater)
Hyperactivity (1% or less)
▲ Insomnia (24%)
Libido decreased (1% or less)
Libido increased (1% or less)
Manic behavior (Greater than 1%)
Memory impairment (1% or less)
Nervousness (1% or greater)
Panic attack (1% or less)
Photophobia (Rare)
Psychoses (2% or greater)
Stupor (1% or less)
Suicidal ideation (1% or greater)
Suicide, attempt of (1% or less)

Accupril Tablets
Depression (0.5% to 1%)
Insomnia (0.5% to 1%)
Nervousness (0.5% to 1%)

Accuretic Tablets
Depression (Greater than 0.5%)
Insomnia (1.2%)
Nervousness (0.5% to 1%)
Speech disturbances

Accutane Capsules
Aggression
Behavior, violent
Depression
Emotional disturbances
Emotional lability
Insomnia
Nervousness
Photophobia
Psychiatric disturbances
Psychoses

Suicidal ideation
Suicide, attempt of

Aceon Tablets
Anxiety (0.3% to 1%)
Depression (2%)
Nervousness (1.1%)
Sexual dysfunction (0.3% to 1.4%)
Sleep disturbances (2.5%)

Aciphex Tablets
Agitation (Rare)
Anxiety
Coma
Confusion (Rare)
Delirium
Depression
Disorientation
Double vision
Dreaming abnormalities
Hangover (Rare)
Insomnia
Libido decreased
Nervousness

Actigall Capsules
Insomnia (1.9%)

Actimmune
Confusion (Rare)
▲ Depression (3%)
Disorientation (Rare)
Hallucinations (Rare)

Actiq
Agitation (Less than 1%)
▲ Confusion (1% to 6%)
Dreaming abnormalities (Less than 1%)
Emotional lability (Less than 1%)
Euphoria (Less than 1%)
Hallucinations (1% to 2%)
Insomnia (1% to 2%)
Libido decreased (Less than 1%)
Nervousness (1% to 2%)
Speech disturbances (Less than 1%)
Thinking abnormality (1% to 2%)

Activella Tablets
Depression
Emotional lability (0% to 6%)
▲ Insomnia (0% to 6%)

Libido, changes
Nervousness

Actonel Tablets
Anxiety (0.6% to 4.3%)
▲ Depression (2.3% to 6.8%)
▲ Insomnia (4.7%)

Adalat CC Tablets
Anxiety (Less than 1%)
Confusion (Less than 1%)
Depression (Less than 1%)
Double vision (Less than 1%)
Insomnia (Less than 1%)
Libido decreased (Less than 1%)
Mood changes (Rare)
Nervousness (Rare)
Paranoia (Rare)
Sleep disturbances (Rare)

Adderall Tablets
Euphoria
Insomnia
Libido, changes
Overstimulation
Psychoses (Rare)

Adderall XR Capsules
Depression (0.7%)
▲ Emotional lability (1% to 9%)
Euphoria
▲ Insomnia (1.5% to 17%)
Libido, changes
▲ Nervousness (6%)
Overstimulation
Psychoses

Adenoscan
Emotional lability (Less than 1%)
Nervousness (2%)

Adipex-P
Central nervous system stimulation
Euphoria
Insomnia
Libido, changes
Overstimulation
Psychoses

Advair Diskus
Aggression
Agitation
Depression
▲ Sleep disturbances (1% to 3%)
▲ Sleep-inducing effects (1% to 3%)

Advicor Tablets
Anxiety
Insomnia
Libido, loss of
Psychiatric disturbances

Aerobid
▲ Anxiety (1% to 3%)
▲ Depression (1% to 3%)
▲ Hyperactivity (1% to 3%)
▲ Hypoactivity (1% to 3%)
▲ Insomnia (1% to 3%)
▲ Irritability (3% to 9%)
▲ Mood changes (1% to 3%)
▲ Nervousness (3% to 9%)

Agenerase Capsules
▲ Depression (9% to 16%)

Agenerase Oral Solution
▲ Depression (4% to 16%)
▲ Mood changes (4% to 9%)

Aggrenox Capsules
Agitation (Less than 1%)
Coma (Less than 1%)
Confusion (1.1%)

Agrylin Capsules
▲ Confusion (1% to 5%)
▲ Depression (1% to 5%)
▲ Double vision (1% to 5%)
▲ Insomnia (1% to 5%)
▲ Nervousness (1% to 5%)

Alacol DM Syrup
Euphoria
Insomnia
Irritability
Nervousness
▲ Sedation (Among most frequent)

Aldoclor Tablets
Confusion
Depression
Libido decreased
Mental performance, impairment
Nightmares
Psychiatric disturbances
Psychoses
Sedation

Aldoril Tablets
Confusion
Depression
Libido decreased
Mental performance, impairment
Nightmares

Psychiatric disturbances
Psychoses
Sedation

Alesse-28 Tablets
Depression
Libido, changes
Mood changes
Nervousness

Alferon N Injection
Confusion (One patient to 3%)
Depression (One patient to 3%)
Disorientation (1%)
Insomnia (2%)
Mental performance, impairment (1%)
Nervousness (1%)

Alimta for Injection
▲ Depression (14%)
▲ Mood changes (14%)

Allegra
Insomnia (Less than 1%)
Nervousness (Less than 1%)

Allegra-D
Agitation (1.9%)
Anxiety (1.4%)
Hallucinations
▲ Insomnia (12.6%)
Nervousness (1.4%)
Paranoia (Less than 1%)
Sleep disturbances (Less than 1%)
Tenseness

Alocril Ophthalmic Solution
▲ Photophobia (1% to 10%)

Aloprim for Injection
Agitation (Less than 1%)
Coma (Less than 1%)

Alora Transdermal System
▲ Anxiety (Up to 9%)
▲ Depression (1% to 6%)
▲ Insomnia (1% to 8%)
Libido, changes

Aloxi Injection
Anxiety (1%)
Insomnia (Less than 1%)
Mood changes (Less than 1%)
Sleeping, excessive (Less than 1%)

Alphagan P Ophthalmic Solution
Insomnia (Less than 1%)
▲ Photophobia (1% to 4%)

Altace Capsules
Anxiety (Less than 1%)
Depression (Less than 1%)
Insomnia (Less than 1%)
Nervousness (Less than 1%)

Altocor Extended-Release Tablets
Anxiety
Depression
Insomnia
Libido, loss of
Memory loss, short-term
Psychiatric disturbances

Alupent Inhalation Aerosol
▲ Nervousness (14.1%)

Ambien Tablets
Aggression (Rare)
Agitation (Infrequent)
Anxiety (1%)
Apathy (Rare)
Behavioral changes
Cognitive dysfunction (Infrequent)
Confusion (Frequent)
Delusions (Rare)
Dementia (Rare)
Depersonalization (Rare)
Depression (2%)
Disordered sense of smell (Rare)
Double vision (Frequent)
Dreaming abnormalities (1%)
Emotional lability (Infrequent)
Euphoria (Frequent)
▲ Feeling, drugged (3%)
Feeling, intoxicated (Rare)
Feeling, strange (Rare)
Hallucinations (Infrequent)
Hysteria (Rare)
Illusion, unspecified (Infrequent)
Insomnia (Frequent)
Libido decreased (Rare)
Manic behavior (Rare)
Mental performance, impairment (Infrequent)
Nervousness (1%)
Neurosis, unspecified (Rare)
Panic attack (Rare)
Personality changes (Rare)
Sleep disturbances (Infrequent)
Speech disturbances (Infrequent)
Stupor (Infrequent)
Suicidal ideation
Suicide, attempt of (Rare)
Thinking abnormalities (Rare)

AmBisome for Injection
Agitation (Less common)
▲ Anxiety (7.4% to 13.7%)
Coma (Less common)
▲ Confusion (8.6% to 12.9%)
Depression (Less common)
Hallucinations (Less common)
Impairment of sensation (Less common)
Nervousness (Less common)
Thinking abnormality (Less common)

Amerge Tablets
Aggression (Rare)
Agitation (Rare)
Anxiety (Infrequent)
Cognitive dysfunction (Infrequent)
Confusion (Rare)
Consciousness, disorders of (Rare)
Depression (Infrequent)
Dreaming (Rare)
Feeling, strange (Infrequent)
Hallucinations (Rare)
Hostility (Rare)
Hyperactivity (Rare)
Libido decreased (Rare)
Mental performance, impairment
  (Infrequent)
Panic attack (Rare)
Photophobia (Frequent)
Sedation (Rare)
Sleep disturbances (Infrequent)
Smell disturbances (Infrequent)

Amicar
Confusion
Delirium
Hallucinations

Amnesteem Capsules
Aggression
Behavior, violent
Depression
Emotional lability
Insomnia
Nervousness
Photophobia
Psychosis, activation
Suicidal ideation
Suicide, attempt of

Amoxil
Agitation (Rare)
Anxiety (Rare)
Behavioral changes (Rare)
Confusion (Rare)
Hyperactivity (Rare)
Insomnia (Rare)

Amphotec
▲ Agitation (1% to 5%)
▲ Confusion (5% or more)
▲ Depression (1% to 5%)
▲ Hallucinations (1% to 5%)
▲ Insomnia (5% or more)
▲ Nervousness (1% to 5%)
▲ Psychoses (1% to 5%)
▲ Speech disturbances (1% to 5%)
▲ Stupor (1% to 5%)
▲ Thinking abnormality (5% or more)

Anadrol-50 Tablets
Excitability
Insomnia
Libido decreased
Libido increased

Anafranil
▲ Agitation (3%)
▲ Anxiety (9%)
▲ Confusion (3%)
▲ Depression (5%)
▲ Dreaming abnormalities (3%)
▲ Insomnia (25%)
▲ Libido, changes (21%)
▲ Memory impairment (9%)
▲ Nervousness (18%)
▲ Speech disturbances (3%)

Anaprox
Central nervous system depression
  (Less than 1%)
Cognitive dysfunction (Less than 1%)
Dreaming abnormalities (Less than 1%)
Insomnia (Less than 1%)
Mental performance, impairment
  (Less than 1%)

Ancobon Capsules
Confusion
Hallucinations
Psychoses
Sedation

Androderm Transdermal System
Anxiety (Less than 1%)
Confusion (Less than 1%)
▲ Depression (3%)
Libido decreased (Less than 1%)
Libido increased
Thinking abnormality (Less than 1%)

AndroGel
Anxiety (Fewer than 1%)
Depression (Up to 1%)

▲ Emotional lability (Up to 3%)
▲ Libido decreased (Up to 3%)
  Libido increased (One patient)
▲ Nervousness (Up to 3%)

Angiomax for Injection
▲ Anxiety (6%)
  Confusion (Rare)
▲ Insomnia (7%)
▲ Nervousness (5%)

Antabuse Tablets
  Psychoses

Anzemet
  Agitation (Infrequent)
  Anxiety (Infrequent)
  Confusion (Infrequent)
  Depersonalization (Infrequent)
  Dreaming abnormalities
    (Infrequent)
  Sleep disturbances (Infrequent)

Aralen Tablets
  Auditory disturbances
  Psychiatric disturbances
  Psychoses (Rare)

Arava Tablets
▲ Anxiety (1% to 3%)
▲ Depression (1% to 3%)
▲ Insomnia (1% to 3%)
▲ Sleep disturbances (1% to 3%)

Aredia for Injection
▲ Anxiety (14.3%)
▲ Insomnia (22.2%)
▲ Psychoses (Up to 4%)

Aricept Tablets
  Aggression (Frequent)
  Agitation
  Confusion
  Delusions (Frequent)
▲ Depression (3%)
▲ Dreaming abnormalities (3%)
  Emotional lability (Infrequent)
  Hallucinations
  Hostility (Infrequent)
▲ Insomnia (9%)
  Irritability (Frequent)
  Libido decreased (Infrequent)
  Libido increased (Frequent)
  Listlessness (Infrequent)
  Nervousness (Frequent)
  Paranoia (Infrequent)

Arimidex Tablets
▲ Anxiety (2% to 5%)
▲ Confusion (2% to 5%)
▲ Depression (2% to 11%)
▲ Insomnia (2% to 6%)
▲ Mood changes (17%)
▲ Nervousness (2% to 5%)

Arixtra Injection
▲ Confusion (1.2% to 3.1%)
▲ Insomnia (0.9% to 5.0%)

Aromasin Tablets
▲ Anxiety (10%)
▲ Confusion (2% to 5%)
▲ Depression (13%)
▲ Insomnia (11%)

Arthrotec Tablets
  Anxiety (Rare)
  Coma (Rare)
  Confusion (Rare)
  Depression (Rare)
  Disorientation (Rare)
  Double vision (Rare)
  Dreaming abnormalities (Rare)
  Hallucinations (Rare)
  Insomnia (Rare)
  Irritability (Rare)
  Mental performance, impairment
    (Rare)
  Nervousness (Rare)
  Paranoia (Rare)
  Psychiatric disturbances (Rare)

Asacol Delayed-Release Tablets
  Anxiety (2% or greater)
  Confusion
  Depression
  Disorientation
  Emotional lability
  Insomnia (2%)
  Libido decreased
  Nervousness (2% or greater)

Astelin Nasal Spray
  Anxiety (Infrequent)
  Confusion
  Depersonalization (Infrequent)
  Depression (Infrequent)
  Disordered sense of smell
▲ Impairment of sensation (7.9%)
  Nervousness (Infrequent)
  Sleep disturbances (Infrequent)
  Thinking abnormality (Infrequent)

Astramorph/PF Injection
Anxiety
Euphoria
Excitability
Psychoses, toxic

Atacand HCT Tablets
Anxiety (0.5% or greater)
Depression (0.5% or greater)
Insomnia (0.5% or greater)

Atacand Tablets
Anxiety (0.5% or greater)
Depression (0.5% or greater)

Ativan Injection
Agitation (Infrequent)
Behavior, inappropriate
(Occasional)
Central nervous system depression
Coma (Less than 1%)
Confusion (1.3%)
Delirium (1.3%)
Depression (1.3%)
Double vision (Occasional)
Hallucinations (1%)
Mental performance, impairment
Sedation
Stupor (1.2%)
Thinking abnormality (Less than 1%)

Atrovent Inhalation Aerosol
Insomnia (Less than 1%)
▲ Nervousness (3.1%)

Atrovent Inhalation Solution
Insomnia (0.9%)
Nervousness (0.5%)

Attenuvax
Central nervous system reactions
Irritability

Augmentin
Agitation (Rare)
Anxiety (Rare)
Behavioral changes (Rare)
Confusion (Rare)
Hyperactivity (Rare)
Insomnia (Rare)

Avalide Tablets
Anxiety (1% or greater)
Confusion
Depression
Emotional disturbances
Libido, changes

Nervousness (1% or greater)
Sexual dysfunction
Sleep disturbances

Avapro Tablets
Anxiety (Less than 1%)
Depression (Less than 1%)
Emotional disturbances (Less than 1%)
Libido, changes (Less than 1%)
Nervousness (1% or greater)
Sexual dysfunction (Less than 1%)
Sleep disturbances (Less than 1%)

Avelox
Agitation (Less than 0.1%)
Anxiety (0.05% to 1%)
Central nervous system stimulation
Confusion (0.05% to 1%)
Depersonalization (Less than 0.1%)
Depression
Disordered sense of smell (Less than 0.1%)
Dreaming abnormalities (Less than 0.1%)
Emotional lability (Less than 0.1%)
Hallucinations (Less than 1%)
Insomnia (0.1% to less than 3%)
Nervousness (0.1% to less than 3%)
Psychoses
Sleep disturbances (Less than 0.1%)
Speech disturbances (Less than 0.1%)
Suicidal ideation
Thinking abnormality (Less than 0.1%)

Avinza Capsules
▲ Agitation (Less than 5%)
▲ Anxiety (Less than 5%)
▲ Coma (Less than 5%)
▲ Confusion (Less than 5%)
▲ Delirium (Less than 5%)
▲ Dreaming abnormalities (Less than 5%)
▲ Euphoria (Less than 5%)
▲ Hallucinations (Less than 5%)
▲ Insomnia (5% to 10%)
▲ Libido decreased (Less than 5%)
▲ Nervousness (Less than 5%)
▲ Thinking abnormality (Less than 5%)

Avodart Soft Gelatin Capsules
Libido decreased (0.3% to 3%)

Avonex
▲ Depression (18% to 20%)
Psychiatric disturbances

Psychoses
▲ Suicidal ideation (4%)

Axert Tablets
Anxiety (Infrequent)
Central nervous system stimulation
(Infrequent)
Depression (Rare)
Disordered sense of smell (Rare)
Double vision (Rare)
Dreaming abnormalities (Rare)
Euphoria (Rare)
Insomnia (Infrequent)
Nervousness (Rare)
Nightmares (Rare)

Aygestin Tablets
Depression
Insomnia
Mood changes

Azmacort Inhalation Aerosol
Depression

Azopt Ophthalmic Suspension
Double vision (Less than 1%)

Azulfidine EN-tabs Tablets
Central nervous system reactions
Depression (Rare)
Hallucinations (Rare)
Insomnia (Rare)

Balamine
Central nervous system stimulation
Double vision
Excitability (Rare)
Hallucinations
Insomnia
Nervousness
Sedation

Beconase AQ Nasal Spray
Depression
Smell disturbances (Rare)

Benicar Tablets
Insomnia (Greater than 0.5%)

Benztropine
Confusion
Depression
Excitability
Hallucinations
Hallucinations, visual
Memory impairment
Nervousness
Psychiatric disturbances

Betaseron for SC Injection
▲ Anxiety (10%)
Confusion
Depersonalization
▲ Depression (34%)
Emotional lability
▲ Insomnia (24%)
▲ Nervousness (7%)
Suicidal ideation

Betimol Ophthalmic Solution
Depression
Double vision
▲ Photophobia (More than 5%)

Betoptic S Ophthalmic Suspension
Depression (Rare)
Insomnia (Rare)
Photophobia (Small number of
patients)

Bextra Tablets
Anxiety (0.1% to 1.9%)
Confusion (0.1% to 1.9%)
Depression (0.1% to 1.9%)
Depression, aggravation of (0.1% to
1.9%)
Insomnia (0.1% to 1.9%)
Manic behavior (Rare)
Nervousness (0.1% to 1.9%)
Psychoses (Rare)

Biaxin
Anxiety
Behavioral changes
Confusion
Depersonalization
Disorientation
Hallucinations
Insomnia
Nightmares
Psychoses
Smell disturbances

Bicillin C-R Injection
Anxiety
Apathy
Coma
Confusion
Euphoria
Hallucinations, auditory
Hallucinations, visual
Nervousness

Bicillin L-A Injection
Agitation
Anxiety
Coma
Confusion
Euphoria
Fear
Hallucinations, auditory
Hallucinations, visual
Nervousness
Psychoses

Blocadren Tablets
Catatonia
Depression
Disorientation, place
Disorientation, time
Double vision
Dreaming abnormalities (Less than 1%)
Emotional lability
Hallucinations (Less than 1%)
Insomnia (Less than 1%)
Libido decreased (0.6%)
Memory loss, short-term
Nervousness (Less than 1%)
Neuropsychometrics performance, decrease
Nightmares
Sensorium, clouded

Botox
Disorientation
Double vision (Rare)
Photophobia

Bravelle for Injection
Depression (2.7%)
Emotional lability (2% to 2.7%)

Brevibloc Injection
Agitation (About 2%)
Anxiety (Less than 1%)
Confusion (About 2%)
Depression (Less than 1%)
Speech disturbances (Less than 1%)
Thinking abnormality (Less than 1%)

Brevicon 28-Day Tablets
Depression
Double vision (Rare)
Libido, changes
Nervousness

Brevital Sodium for Injection
Anxiety
Delirium

Buprenex Injectable
Agitation (Rare)
Coma (Infrequent)
Depersonalization (Infrequent)
Double vision (Less than 1%)
Dreaming abnormalities (Less than 1%)
Hallucinations (Infrequent)
Psychoses (Less than 1%)
▲ Sedation (Most frequent)

BuSpar Tablets
Alcohol abuse (Rare)
Anger (2%)
Apathy (Infrequent)
Central nervous system reactions
Confusion (2%)
Depersonalization (Infrequent)
Depression (2%)
Dreaming abnormalities (Frequent)
Emotional lability (Rare)
Euphoria (Infrequent)
Excitability (2%)
Fear (Infrequent)
Hallucinations (Infrequent)
Hostility (2%)
▲ Insomnia (3%)
Libido decreased (Infrequent)
Libido increased (Infrequent)
Memory impairment (Rare)
Mental performance, impairment (2%)
Mental slowness (Infrequent)
▲ Nervousness (5%)
Psychoses (Rare)
Serotonin syndrome
Smell disturbances (Infrequent)
Sociopathy (Infrequent)
Speech, slurring (Rare)
Stupor (Rare)
Suicidal ideation (Infrequent)

Busulfex Injection
Agitation (2%)
▲ Anxiety (72% to 75%)
Coma (One patient)
▲ Confusion (11%)
Delirium (2%)
▲ Depression (23%)
▲ Hallucinations (5%)
▲ Insomnia (84%)

Caduet Tablets
Agitation (Less than or equal to 0.1%)

Anxiety (Greater than 0.1% to less than or equal to 1%)
Apathy (Less than or equal to 0.1%)
Depersonalization (Greater than 0.1% to less than or equal to 1%)
Depression (Greater than 0.1% to less than 2%)
Disordered sense of smell (Less than 2%)
Double vision (Greater than 0.1% to less than or equal to 1%)
Dreaming abnormalities (Greater than 0.1% to less than 2%)
Emotional lability (Less than 2%)
Insomnia (Greater than 0.1%)
Libido decreased (Less than 2%)
Nervousness (Greater than 0.1% to less than or equal to 1%)
Sexual dysfunction (Greater that 0.1% to 2%)

Calcijex Injection
Libido decreased
Photophobia

Campath Ampules
Apathy
Coma
Confusion
▲ Depression (1% to 7%)
Hallucinations
▲ Insomnia (10%)
Nervousness
Thinking abnormality

Camptosar Injection
▲ Confusion (Up to 7%)
▲ Insomnia (Up to 19.4%)

Captopril Tablets
Confusion
Depression
Insomnia (About 0.5 to 2%)
Nervousness

Carafate
Insomnia (Less than 0.5%)

Carbatrol Capsules
Agitation
Confusion
Depression
Double vision
Hallucinations, visual
Psychosis, activation

Speech disturbances
Talkativeness

Cardene I.V.
Confusion (Rare)

Cardizem LA Tablets
Depression (Less than 2%)
Dreaming abnormalities (Less than 2%)
Hallucinations (Less than 2%)
Insomnia (Less than 2%)
Nervousness (Less than 2%)
Personality changes (Less than 2%)
Sexual dysfunction (Less than 2%)

Cardura Tablets
Agitation (0.5% to 1%)
Anxiety (1.1%)
Confusion (Less than 0.5%)
Depersonalization (Less than 0.5%)
Depression (1%)
Disordered sense of smell (Less than 0.5%)
Emotional lability (Less than 0.5%)
Insomnia (1% to 1.2%)
Libido decreased (0.8%)
Mental performance, impairment (Less than 0.5%)
Nervousness (2%)
Photophobia (Less than 0.5%)
Sexual dysfunction (2%)
Thinking abnormality (Less than 0.5%)

Carnitor Injection
Anxiety (1% to 2%)
▲ Depression (5% to 6%)
▲ Insomnia (1% to 3%)

Casodex Tablets
▲ Anxiety (2% to 5%)
▲ Confusion (2% to 5%)
▲ Depression (4%)
▲ Insomnia (5%)
▲ Libido decreased (2% to 5%)
▲ Nervousness (2% to 5%)

Cataflam Tablets
Anxiety (Occasional)
Coma (Rare)
Confusion (Occasional)
Depression (Occasional)
Dreaming abnormalities (Occasional)
Hallucinations (Rare)

Insomnia (Occasional)
Nervousness (Occasional)

Catapres Tablets

Agitation (About 3 in 100 patients)
Anxiety
Behavioral changes
Delirium
Depression (About 1 in 100 patients)
Dreaming abnormalities
Hallucinations
Hallucinations, auditory (Rare)
Hallucinations, visual (Rare)
Insomnia (About 5 in 1,000 patients)
Libido, loss of (About 3 in 100 patients)
▲ Nervousness (About 3 in 100 patients)
Nightmares
▲ Sedation (About 10 in 100 patients)
▲ Sexual activity, decrease (About 3 in 100 patients)

Catapres-TTS

Agitation (0.5% or less)
Anxiety (0.5% or less)
Behavioral changes (0.5% or less)
Delirium (0.5% or less)
Depression (0.5% or less)
Dreaming abnormalities (0.5% or less)
Hallucinations, auditory (0.5% or less)
Hallucinations, visual (0.5% or less)
Insomnia (2 of 101 patients)
Irritability (0.5% or less)
Libido, loss of (0.5% or less)
Nervousness (1 of 101 patients)
Nightmares (0.5% or less)
Sedation (3 of 101 patients)
Sexual activity, decrease (0.5% or less)
Sexual dysfunction (2 of 101 patients)

Ceclor

Confusion (Rare)
Hallucinations (Rare)
Hyperactivity (Rare)
Insomnia (Rare)
Nervousness (Rare)

Cedax Capsules

Psychoses

Cedax Oral Suspension

Agitation (0.1% to 1%)
Insomnia (0.1% to 1%)

Irritability (0.1% to 1%)
Psychoses

Ceftin for Oral Suspension

Hyperactivity (0.1% to 1%)
Irritability (0.1% to 1%)

Cefzil

Confusion (Less than 1%)
Hyperactivity (Less than 1%)
Insomnia (Less than 1%)
Nervousness (Less than 1%)

Celebrex Capsules

Anxiety (0.1% to 1.9%)
Depression (0.1% to 1.9%)
Insomnia (2.3%)
Nervousness (0.1% to 1.9%)

Celexa

Aggression (Infrequent)
▲ Agitation (3%)
▲ Anxiety (4%)
Apathy (Infrequent)
Catatonia (Rare)
Confusion (Frequent)
Delirium
Delusions (Rare)
Depersonalization (Infrequent)
Depression (Frequent)
Depression, aggravation of (Frequent)
Depression, psychotic (Infrequent)
Double vision (Rare)
Emotional lability (Infrequent)
Euphoria (Infrequent)
Hallucinations (Infrequent)
▲ Insomnia (15%)
Libido decreased (2%)
Libido increased (Infrequent)
Manic behavior
Manic behavior, mild
Melancholia (Rare)
Mental performance, impairment (Frequent)
Panic attack (Infrequent)
Paranoia (Infrequent)
Photophobia (Infrequent)
Psychoses (Infrequent)
Serotonin syndrome
Sexual dysfunction
Sleep disturbances (At least 2%)
Stupor (Rare)
Suicide, attempt of (Frequent)

CellCept

▲ Agitation (3% to less than 20%)

▲ Anxiety (3% to 28.4%)
▲ Confusion (3% to less than 20%)
▲ Delirium (3% to less than 20%)
▲ Depression (3% to less than 20%)
▲ Emotional lability (3% to less than 20%)
▲ Hallucinations (3% to less than 20%)
▲ Insomnia (40.8%)
▲ Nervousness (3% to less than 20%)
▲ Psychoses (3% to less than 20%)
▲ Thinking abnormality (3% to less than 20%)

Celontin Capsules
Aggression
Behavior, hypochondriacal
Confusion
Depression
Hallucinations (Rare)
Insomnia
Irritability
Mental slowness
Nervousness
Photophobia
Psychoses (Rare)
Suicidal ideation (Rare)

Cenestin Tablets
▲ Anxiety (5.7%)
▲ Depression (3.8% to 28%)
▲ Insomnia (42%)
Irritability
Libido, changes
Mood changes
▲ Nervousness (3.8% to 28%)

Cenestin Tablets, 0.3 mg
Depression
Irritability
Libido, changes
Mood changes
Nervousness

Cerebyx Injection
▲ Agitation (3.3% to 9.5%)
Central nervous system depression (Infrequent)
Coma (Infrequent)
Confusion (Infrequent)
Delirium
Depersonalization (Infrequent)
Depression (Infrequent)
Disordered sense of smell (Infrequent)
▲ Double vision (3.3%)
Emotional lability (Infrequent)
Hostility (Infrequent)

Insomnia (Infrequent)
Nervousness (Frequent)
Neurosis, unspecified (Infrequent)
Personality changes (Infrequent)
Photophobia (Infrequent)
Psychoses (Infrequent)
Speech disturbances (Frequent)
▲ Stupor (7.7%)
Thinking abnormality (Frequent)

Chlorpromazine
Agitation
Catatonia (Rare)
Insomnia
Jitteriness

Cialis Tablets
Insomnia (Less than 2%)

Ciloxan Ophthalmic Ointment
Photophobia (Less than 1%)

Ciloxan Ophthalmic Solution
Photophobia (Less than 1%)

Cipro I.V.
Agitation
Anxiety (1% or less)
Central nervous system stimulation
Confusion (1% or less)
Delirium
Depersonalization (1% or less)
Depression (1% or less)
Double vision (1% or less)
Hallucinations (1% or less)
Insomnia (1% or less)
Irritability (1% or less)
Manic behavior (1% or less)
Nervousness
Nightmares (1% or less)
Paranoia (1% or less)
Phobic disorder (1% or less)
Psychoses, toxic (1% or less)

Cipro I.V. Pharmacy Bulk Package
Agitation
Anxiety (Less than 1%)
▲ Central nervous system reactions (Among most frequent)
Confusion (Less than 1%)
Delirium
Depersonalization (Less than 1%)
Depression (Less than 1%)
Double vision (Less than 1%)
Hallucinations (Less than 1%)

Insomnia (Less than 1%)
Irritability (Less than 1%)
Manic behavior (Less than 1%)
Nervousness
Nightmares (Less than 1%)
Paranoia (Less than 1%)
Phobic disorder (Less than 1%)
Psychoses, toxic (Less than 1%)

Cipro Tablets & Oral Suspension

Agitation
Anxiety
Central nervous system stimulation
Confusion
Delirium
Depersonalization (Less than 1%)
Depression (Less than 1%)
Double vision (Less than 1%)
Hallucinations (Less than 1%)
Insomnia (Less than 1%)
Irritability (Less than 1%)
Manic behavior (Less than 1%)
Nervousness
Nightmares (Less than 1%)
Paranoia
Phobic disorder (Less than 1%)
Psychoses, toxic

Cipro XR Tablets

Agitation
Anxiety
Central nervous system stimulation
Confusion
Delirium
Depersonalization (Less than 1%)
Depression (Less than 1%)
Double vision (Less than 1%)
Dreaming abnormalities (Less than 1%)
Hallucinations
Insomnia (Less than 1%)
Irritability
Manic behavior
Nervousness
Nightmares
Paranoia
Phobia, unspecified
Psychoses, toxic
Suicidal ideation (Rare)

Climara Transdermal System

▲ Depression (1% to 8%)
Libido, changes

Clinoril Tablets

Depression (Less than 1%)
Insomnia (Less than 1%)
Nervousness (Greater than 1%)
Psychiatric disturbances (Less than 1 in 100)
Psychoses (Less than 1 in 100)

Clomid Tablets

Anxiety
Depression (Fewer than 1%)
Double vision (1.5%)
Insomnia (Fewer than 1%)
Irritability
Mood changes
Photophobia (1.5%)
Psychoses
Tenseness (Fewer than 1%)

Clorpres Tablets

Agitation (About 3%)
Anxiety
Behavioral changes
Delirium
Depression (About 1%)
Dreaming abnormalities
Hallucinations, auditory
Hallucinations, visual
Insomnia (About 5 in 1,000)
Libido, loss of (About 3%)
▲ Nervousness (About 3%)
Nightmares
▲ Sedation (About 10%)
Sexual activity, decrease (About 3%)

Clozapine Tablets

▲ Agitation (4%)
Anxiety (1%)
Central nervous system reactions
▲ Confusion (3%)
Delirium
Delusions (Less than 1%)
Depression (1%)
Hallucinations (Less than 1%)
Insomnia (2%)
Irritability (Less than 1%)
Libido decreased (Less than 1%)
Libido increased (Less than 1%)
Memory loss, short-term (Less than 1%)
Mental performance, impairment
Mental status, altered
▲ Nightmares (4%)
Paranoia (Less than 1%)
Psychoses, aggravation

▲ Sedation (More than 5% to 39%)
▲ Sleep disturbances (4%)
  Speech difficulties (Less than 1%)
  Speech, incoherent (Less than 1%)
  Speech, slurring (1%)

Clozaril Tablets
▲ Agitation (4%)
  Anxiety (1%)
  Central nervous system reactions
▲ Confusion (3%)
  Delirium
  Delusions (Less than 1%)
  Depression (1%)
  Hallucinations (Less than 1%)
▲ Insomnia (2% to 20%)
  Irritability (Less than 1%)
  Libido decreased (Less than 1%)
  Libido increased (Less than 1%)
  Memory loss, short-term (Less than 1%)
  Mental performance, impairment
  Mental status, altered
▲ Nightmares (4%)
  Paranoia (Less than 1%)
  Psychoses, aggravation
▲ Sedation (More than 5% to 39%)
▲ Sleep disturbances (4%)
  Speech difficulties (Less than 1%)
  Speech, incoherent (Less than 1%)
  Speech, slurring (1%)

Cognex Capsules
▲ Agitation (7%)
▲ Anxiety (3%)
  Apathy (Infrequent)
  Coma (Rare)
▲ Confusion (7%)
  Delirium (Infrequent)
▲ Depression (4%)
  Double vision (Infrequent)
  Dreaming abnormalities (Infrequent)
  Hallucinations (2%)
  Hostility (2%)
  Hysteria (Rare)
  Impairment of sensation (Rare)
▲ Insomnia (6%)
  Libido increased (Infrequent)
  Nervousness (Frequent)
  Neurosis, unspecified (Infrequent)
  Paranoia (Infrequent)
  Psychoses (Rare)
  Suicidal ideation (Rare)
▲ Thinking abnormality (3%)

Colazal Capsules
  Anxiety
  Depression
  Disordered sense of smell
  Insomnia (2%)
  Nervousness

Colestid Tablets
  Insomnia (Infrequent)

Coly-Mycin M Parenteral
  Speech, slurring

CombiPatch Transdermal System
▲ Depression (8% to 9%)
▲ Insomnia (6% to 8%)
▲ Nervousness (5% to 6%)

Combivent Inhalation Aerosol
  Central nervous system stimulation
  Insomnia (Less than 2%)
  Nervousness (Less than 2%)

Combivir Tablets
▲ Depressive reactions (9%)
▲ Insomnia (11%)
▲ Sleep disturbances (11%)

Comtan Tablets
  Agitation (1%)
  Anxiety (2%)
  Consciousness, disorders of
  Hallucinations

Comvax
  Agitation
▲ Irritability (32.2% to 57.0%)

Concerta Tablets
  Depression
▲ Insomnia (4%)
▲ Nervousness (Among most common)
  Psychoses, toxic

Condylox Topical Solution
▲ Insomnia (Less than 5%)

Copaxone for Injection
▲ Agitation (4%)
▲ Anxiety (23%)
  Coma (Infrequent)
  Confusion (2%)
  Depersonalization (Infrequent)
  Depression (At least 2%)
  Depression, psychotic (Infrequent)
  Double vision (At least 2%)
  Dreaming abnormalities (Frequent)

Emotional lability (At least 2%)
Euphoria (At least 2%)
Hallucinations (Infrequent)
Hostility (Infrequent)
Impairment of sensation (At least 2%)
Insomnia (At least 2%)
Libido decreased (Infrequent)
Manic behavior (Infrequent)
Memory impairment (Infrequent)
Mental performance, impairment (Infrequent)
Nervousness (2%)
Paranoia (Infrequent)
Photophobia (Infrequent)
Sexual dysfunction (Infrequent)
Sleep disturbances (At least 2%)
Speech disturbances (2%)
Stupor (Frequent)
Suicide, attempt of (Infrequent)

Copegus Tablets
Aggression (Less than 1%)
▲ Anxiety (33%)
Coma (Less than 1%)
▲ Depression (20%)
▲ Insomnia (30%)
▲ Irritability (33%)
▲ Memory impairment (6%)
▲ Mood changes (5%)
▲ Nervousness (33%)
Psychoses (Less than 1%)
Suicidal ideation (Less than 1%)

Coreg Tablets
▲ Depression (Greater than 1% to 3%)
Depression, aggravation of (Greater than 0.1% to 1%)
Emotional lability (Greater than 0.1% to 1%)
Insomnia (2%)
Libido decreased (Greater than 0.1% to 1%)
Nervousness (Greater than 0.1% to 1%)
Sleep disturbances (Greater than 0.1% to 1%)
Thinking abnormality (Greater than 0.1% to 1%)

Corzide Tablets
Catatonia
Depression
Disorientation, place
Disorientation, time
Emotional lability
Hallucinations
Libido decreased (1 to 5 of 1000 patients)

Memory loss, short-term
Neuropsychometrics performance, decrease
Sedation (6 of 1000 patients)
Sensorium, clouded
Sleep disturbances
Speech, slurring (1 to 5 of 1000 patients)

Cosopt Ophthalmic Solution
Anxiety
Behavioral changes
Catatonia
Confusion
Depression (Less than 1%)
Disorientation
Disorientation, place
Disorientation, time
Double vision
Emotional lability
Hallucinations
Insomnia
Libido decreased
Memory loss, short-term
Mental performance, impairment
Nervousness
Neuropsychometrics performance, decrease
Nightmares
Photophobia (Less than 1%)
Psychiatric disturbances
Sensorium, clouded

Covera-HS Tablets
Confusion (Less than 2%)
Insomnia (Less than 2%)
Psychoses (Less than 2%)

Cozaar Tablets
Anxiety (Less than 1%)
Confusion (Less than 1%)
Depression (Less than 1%)
Dreaming abnormalities (Less than 1%)
Insomnia (1% or greater)
Libido decreased (Less than 1%)
Memory impairment (Less than 1%)
▲ Nervousness (Less than 1% to 4%)
Panic attack (Less than 1%)
Sleep disturbances (Less than 1%)

Crestor Tablets
Anxiety (Greater than or equal to 1%)
Depression (Greater than or equal to 2%)
Insomnia (Greater than or equal to 2%)

Crinone 4% Gel
▲ Aggression (Less than 5%)
▲ Depression (19%)
▲ Emotional lability (23%)
▲ Insomnia (Less than 5%)
▲ Memory loss, short-term (Less than 5%)
▲ Sleep disturbances (18%)

Crinone 8% Gel
▲ Aggression (Less than 5%)
▲ Depression (11% to 15%)
▲ Emotional lability (22%)
▲ Insomnia (Less than 5%)
▲ Libido decreased (10%)
▲ Memory loss, short-term (Less than 5%)
▲ Nervousness (16%)
▲ Sleep disturbances (18%)

Crixivan Capsules
Agitation (Less than 2%)
Anxiety (Less than 2%)
Depression (Less than 2%)
Dreaming abnormalities (Less than 2%)
Excitability (Less than 2%)
Impairment of sensation (Less than 2%)
▲ Insomnia (3.1%)
Mental acuity, loss of (Less than 2%)
Nervousness (Less than 2%)
Sleep disturbances (Less than 2%)

Cubicin for Injection
Anxiety (1% to 2%)
Confusion (1% to 2%)
▲ Insomnia (4.5%)
Jitteriness (Less than 1%)
Mental status, altered (Less than 1%)

Cuprimine Capsules
Agitation
Anxiety
Mental status, altered
Psychiatric disturbances

Cylert
Depression
Hallucinations
▲ Insomnia (Most frequent)
Irritability

CytoGam Intravenous
Photophobia (Infrequent)

Cytotec Tablets
Anxiety (Infrequent)

Behavioral changes (Infrequent)
Confusion
Libido decreased (Infrequent)

Cytovene
Anxiety (At least 3 subjects)
Confusion (At least 3 subjects)
Depression (At least 3 subjects)
Dreaming abnormalities (At least 3 subjects)
Hallucinations
Impairment of sensation
Insomnia (At least 3 subjects)
Irritability
Memory loss, short-term
Thinking abnormality (At least 3 subjects)

Dalmane Capsules
Coma
Confusion (Rare)
Depression (Rare)
Disorientation
Euphoria (Rare)
Hallucinations (Rare)
Hyperactivity (Rare)
Irritability
Nervousness
Sedation
Speech, slurring (Rare)
Stimulation (Rare)
Talkativeness

Dantrium Capsules
Confusion (Less frequent)
Depression (Less frequent)
Double vision (Less frequent)
Insomnia (Less frequent)
Nervousness (Less frequent)
Speech disturbances (Less frequent)

Dapsone Tablets
Insomnia
Psychoses

Daptacel
▲ Anxiety (23.6% to 39.6%)
▲ Irritability (36.9% to 41.4%)

Daranide Tablets
Confusion
Depression
Disorientation
Nervousness

Darvocet-N
Euphoria

Hallucinations
▲ Sedation (Among most frequent)

Darvon Capsules
Euphoria
Hallucinations
▲ Sedation (Among most frequent)

Darvon Compound-65 Capsules
Euphoria
Hallucinations
▲ Sedation (Among most frequent)

Darvon-N Tablets
Euphoria
Hallucinations
▲ Sedation (Among most frequent)

DaunoXome Injection
▲ Anxiety (Less than or equal to 5%)
▲ Confusion (Less than or equal to 5%)
▲ Depression (3% to 7%)
Emotional lability (Less than or equal to 5%)
Hallucinations (Less than or equal to 5%)
▲ Insomnia (Up to 6%)
▲ Thinking abnormality (Less than or equal to 5%)

DDAVP Injection 4 mcg/mL
Coma (Rare)

DDAVP Nasal Spray
Coma (Rare)
Depression

DDAVP Tablets
Thinking abnormality

Decadron
Depression
Euphoria
Insomnia
Mood changes
Personality changes (Decadron Tablets)
Psychiatric disturbances
Psychoses
Psychoses, aggravation

Delatestryl Injection
Anxiety
Depression
Libido decreased
Libido increased

Delestrogen Injection
Depression
Libido, changes

Demadex Tablets and Injection
Insomnia (1.2%)
Nervousness (1.1%)

Demerol
Agitation
Disorientation
Euphoria
Hallucinations
Mental performance, impairment
▲ Sedation (Among most frequent)

Demser Capsules
Anxiety
Awareness, heightened
Confusion
Depression
Disorientation
Hallucinations
Insomnia
▲ Sedation (Almost all patients)
▲ Speech difficulties (10%)

Depacon Injection
Aggression
Agitation (1% or more)
▲ Anxiety (1% to 5%)
Behavioral deterioration
Catatonia (1% or more)
Central nervous system depression
Coma (Rare)
▲ Confusion (1% to 5%)
Dementia (Several reports)
▲ Depression (4% to 5%)
▲ Double vision (16%)
▲ Dreaming abnormalities (1% to 5%)
Emotional disturbances
▲ Emotional lability (6%)
Euphoria (0.9%)
Hallucinations
Hostility
Hyperactivity
▲ Insomnia (9% to 15%)
▲ Nervousness (0.9% to 11%)
▲ Personality changes (1% to 5%)
Psychoses
Sedation
▲ Thinking abnormality (6%)

Depakene
Aggression
Agitation (1% or more)

▲ Anxiety (1% to 5%)
Behavioral deterioration
Catatonia (1% or more)
Central nervous system depression
Coma (Rare)
▲ Confusion (1% to 5%)
Dementia (Several reports)
▲ Depression (5%)
▲ Double vision (16%)
▲ Dreaming abnormalities (1% to 5%)
Emotional disturbances
▲ Emotional lability (6%)
Hallucinations
Hostility
Hyperactivity
▲ Insomnia (15%)
▲ Nervousness (11%)
▲ Personality changes (1% to 5%)
Psychoses
Sedation
▲ Thinking abnormality (6%)

Depakote ER Tablets
Aggression
Agitation (Greater than 1%)
▲ Anxiety (1% to 5%)
Behavioral deterioration
Catatonia (Greater than 1%)
Central nervous system depression
Coma (Rare)
▲ Confusion (1% to 5%)
Dementia (Several reports)
▲ Depression (4% to 5%)
▲ Double vision (16%)
▲ Dreaming abnormalities (1% to 5%)
Emotional disturbances
▲ Emotional lability (6%)
Hallucinations (Greater than 1%)
Hostility
Hyperactivity
▲ Insomnia (1% to 15%)
▲ Nervousness (1% to 11%)
▲ Personality changes (1% to 5%)
Photophobia (Greater than 1%)
Psychoses (Greater than 1%)
Sedation
Sleep disturbances (Greater than 1%)
▲ Speech disturbances (1% to 5%)
▲ Thinking abnormality (6%)

Depakote Sprinkle Capsules
Aggression
Agitation
▲ Anxiety (1% to 5%)
Behavioral deterioration
Catatonia

Coma (Rare)
▲ Confusion (1% to 5%)
Dementia (Several reports)
▲ Depression (4% to 5%)
▲ Double vision (16%)
▲ Dreaming abnormalities (1% to 5%)
Emotional disturbances
▲ Emotional lability (6%)
Hallucinations
Hostility
Hyperactivity
▲ Insomnia (9% to 15%)
▲ Nervousness (7% to 11%)
▲ Personality changes (1% to 5%)
Psychoses
▲ Thinking abnormality (6%)

Depakote Tablets
Aggression
▲ Agitation (1% to 5%)
▲ Anxiety (1% to 5%)
Behavioral deterioration
▲ Catatonia (1% to 5%)
Central nervous system depression
Coma (Rare)
▲ Confusion (1% to 5%)
Dementia (Several reports)
▲ Depression (1% to 5%)
▲ Double vision (1% to 16%)
▲ Dreaming abnormalities (1% to 5%)
Emotional disturbances
▲ Emotional lability (1% to 6%)
▲ Hallucinations (1% to 5%)
Hostility
Hyperactivity
▲ Insomnia (1% to 15%)
▲ Nervousness (1% to 11%)
▲ Personality changes (1% to 5%)
Psychoses
Sedation
▲ Speech disturbances (1% to 5%)
Suicidal ideation
▲ Thinking abnormality (1% to 6%)

DepoCyt Injection
▲ Confusion (4% to 14%)

Depo-Medrol Single-Dose Vial
Sensory disturbances

Desmopressin Acetate Injection
Coma (Rare)

Desmopressin Acetate Rhinal Tube
Depression

Desoxyn Tablets
Euphoria
Insomnia
Libido, changes
Overstimulation
Psychoses (Rare)

Desyrel
▲ Confusion (4.9%)
▲ Insomnia (9.9%)
▲ Nervousness (14.8%)

Detrol LA Capsules
Anxiety (1%)

Detrol Tablets
Hallucinations
Nervousness (1.1%)

Dexedrine
Agitation
Euphoria
Insomnia
Libido, changes
Overstimulation
Psychoses (Rare at recommended
doses)

DextroStat Tablets
Euphoria
Insomnia
Libido, changes
Overstimulation
Psychoses (Rare)
Sociopathy

Diamox Capsules
Confusion
Depression
Excitement, paradoxical

Didronel Tablets
Confusion
Depression
Hallucinations
Psychiatric disturbances

Digitek Tablets
Anxiety
Apathy
Central nervous system reactions
Confusion
Delirium
Depression
Hallucinations
▲ Mental status, altered (5%)

Dilantin
▲ Confusion (Among most common)
Insomnia
Nervousness
▲ Speech, slurring (Among most
common)

Dilaudid Injection
Agitation
Anxiety
Disorientation
Double vision
Euphoria
Fear
Hallucinations
Insomnia
Mental clouding (Dilaudid Ampules/
Dilaudid Non-Sterile Powder)
Mental performance, impairment
Mood changes
Sedation

Dilaudid Rectal Suppositories & Tablets
Agitation
Anxiety
Disorientation
Double vision
Euphoria
Fear
Hallucinations
Insomnia
Mental clouding
Mental performance, impairment
Mood changes
Sedation

Dilaudid Tablets - 8 mg & Oral Liquid
Agitation (Less frequent)
Depression (Less frequent)
Disorientation (Less frequent)
Double vision (Less frequent)
Dreaming (Less frequent)
Euphoria
Floating feeling (Less frequent)
Hallucinations (Less frequent)
Insomnia (Less frequent)
Mood changes (Less frequent)
Nervousness (Less frequent)
Sedation

Dilaudid-HP
Agitation (Less frequent)
Depression (Less frequent)

Disorientation (Less frequent)
Double vision (Less frequent)
Dreaming abnormalities (Less frequent)
Euphoria (Less frequent)
Floating feeling (Less frequent)
Hallucinations (Less frequent)
Insomnia (Less frequent)
Mood changes (Less frequent)
Nervousness
▲ Sedation (Among most frequent)

Diovan HCT Tablets
Anxiety (Greater than 0.2%)
Confusion
Depression (Greater than 0.2%)
Insomnia (Greater than 0.2%)
Libido decreased (Greater than 0.2%)

Diovan Tablets
Anxiety
Insomnia

Dipentum Capsules
Depression (1.5%)
Insomnia (Rare)
Irritability (Rare)
Mood changes (Rare)

Diprivan Injectable Emulsion
Agitation (Less than 1%)
Anxiety (Less than 1%)
Awareness, altered (Less than 1%)
Behavior, inappropriate (Less than 1%)
Combativeness (Less than 1%)
Confusion (Less than 1%)
Delirium (Less than 1%)
Depression (Less than 1%)
Double vision (Less than 1%)
Dreaming abnormalities (Less than 1%)
Emotional lability (Less than 1%)
Euphoria (Less than 1%)
Hallucinations (Less than 1%)
Hysteria (Less than 1%)
Insomnia (Less than 1%)
Thinking abnormality (Less than 1%)

Ditropan XL Tablets
▲ Confusion (2% to 5%)
▲ Insomnia (2% to 5%)
▲ Nervousness (2% to 5%)

Diuril
Confusion

Dolobid Tablets
Confusion (Less than 1 in 100)

Depression (Less than 1 in 100)
Disorientation (Less than 1 in 100)
Hallucinations (Less than 1 in 100)
Insomnia (Greater than 1 in 100)
Nervousness (Less than 1 in 100)

Doral
Agitation
Anxiety
Confusion
Depression
Euphoria
Hallucinations
Libido changes
Libido decreased
Nervousness
Nightmares
Paranoia
Sleep disturbances
Speech disturbances
Speech, slurring
Thinking abnormality

Dostinex Tablets
▲ Anxiety (1% to less than 10%)
Confusion
▲ Depression (3%)
Hallucinations
▲ Insomnia (1% to less than 10%)
▲ Libido increased (Less than 10%)
Mental performance, impairment (1%)
▲ Nervousness (1% to less than 10%)

Doxil Injection
▲ Anxiety (Less than (1% to 5%)
Confusion (Less than 1%)
▲ Depression (Less than 1% to 5%)
Disordered sense of smell (Less than 1%)
▲ Emotional lability (1% to 5%)
▲ Insomnia (Less than 1% to 5%)
Nervousness (Less than 1%)
Thinking abnormality (Less than 1%)

Duragesic Transdermal System
Agitation (1% or greater)
▲ Anxiety (3% to 10%)
▲ Confusion (10% or more)
Depersonalization (Less than 1%)
▲ Depression (3% to 10%)
Dreaming abnormalities (1% or greater)
▲ Euphoria (3% to 10%)
▲ Hallucinations (3% to 10%)
Hostility (Less than 1%)

▲ Insomnia (3% to 10%)
▲ Nervousness (3% to 10%)
Paranoia (1% or greater)
Speech disturbances (1% or greater)
Stupor (Less than 1%)
Thinking abnormality (1% or greater)

Dyazide Capsules
Confusion

DynaCirc
Depression (0.5% to 1%)
Insomnia (0.5% to 1%)
Libido decreased (0.5% to 1%)
Nervousness (0.5% to 1%)

8-MOP Capsules
Depression
Insomnia
Nervousness

EC-Naprosyn Tablets
Central nervous system depression
(Less than 1%)
Cognitive dysfunction (Rare)
Dreaming abnormalities (Less than 1%)
Insomnia (Less than 1%)
Mental performance, impairment
(Less than 1%)

Ecotrin Enteric Coated Aspirin Tablets
Agitation
Coma
Confusion

Edecrin
Confusion

Effexor Tablets
▲ Agitation (2% to 4.5%)
Alcohol abuse (Rare)
▲ Anxiety (2% to 11.2%)
Apathy (Infrequent)
Catatonia
Central nervous system stimulation
(Infrequent)
Confusion (2%)
Delirium
Delusions (Rare)
Dementia (Rare)
Depersonalization (1%)
Depression (1%)
Depression, psychotic (Rare)
Disordered sense of smell (Infrequent)
Double vision (Infrequent)

▲ Dreaming abnormalities (4%)
Emotional lability (Frequent)
Euphoria (Infrequent)
Hallucinations (Infrequent)
Hangover (Infrequent)
Hostility (Infrequent)
▲ Insomnia (3% to 22.5%)
▲ Libido decreased (2% to 5.7%)
Libido increased (Infrequent)
Manic behavior (0.5%)
Manic behavior, mild (0.5%)
▲ Nervousness (2% to 21.3%)
Panic attack
Paranoia (Infrequent)
Photophobia (Infrequent)
Psychoses (Rare)
Serotonin syndrome
Sexual dysfunction (2%)
Sleep disturbances (Infrequent)
Speech disturbances (Infrequent)
Stupor (Infrequent)
Suicidal ideation (Rare)
Suicide, attempt of (Infrequent)
Thinking abnormality (2%)

Effexor XR Capsules
▲ Agitation (4%)
Alcohol abuse (Rare)
Anxiety (1%)
Apathy (Infrequent)
Catatonia
Central nervous system stimulation
(Infrequent)
Confusion (Frequent)
Delirium
Delusions (Rare)
Dementia (Rare)
Depersonalization (Frequent)
▲ Depression (3%)
Depression, psychotic (Infrequent)
Disordered sense of smell (Infrequent)
Double vision (Infrequent)
▲ Dreaming abnormalities (3% to 7%)
Emotional lability (Infrequent)
Euphoria (Infrequent)
Feeling, intoxicated (Rare)
Hallucinations (Infrequent)
Hangover (Infrequent)
Hostility (Infrequent)
▲ Insomnia (3% to 23%)
▲ Libido decreased (3% to 9%)
Libido increased (Infrequent)
Manic behavior (0.5%)
Manic behavior, mild (0.3%)
▲ Nervousness (5% to 11%)

▲ Nightmares (4% to 7%)
▲ Orgasmic dysfunction, female (2% to 8%)
Panic attack
Paranoia (Infrequent)
Photophobia (Infrequent)
Psychoses (Infrequent)
Serotonin syndrome
Sexual dysfunction
Speech disturbances (Infrequent)
Stupor (Infrequent)
Suicidal ideation (Rare)
Suicide, attempt of (Infrequent)
Thinking abnormality (Frequent)

Efudex
Emotional disturbances (Infrequent)
Insomnia
Irritability

Elavil
Anxiety
Coma
Confusion
Delusions
Disorientation
Dreaming abnormalities
Excitability
Hallucinations
Insomnia
Irritability
Libido, changes
Manic behavior (Rare)
Manic behavior, mild (Rare)
Mental performance, impairment
Mental status, altered
Nightmares
Serotonin syndrome (Very rare)
Sleep disturbances

Eldepryl Capsules
Agitation
Anxiety (1 of 49 patients)
Apathy
Behavioral changes
▲ Confusion (3 of 49 patients)
Delusions
Depression
Disorientation
Double vision
▲ Dreaming abnormalities (2 of 49 patients)
Euphoria
▲ Hallucinations (3 of 49 patients)
Insomnia (1 of 49 patients)

Irritability
Memory impairment
Mental status, altered
Mood changes
Nervousness
Nightmares
Overstimulation
Personality changes
Sexual dysfunction
Sleep disturbances
Speech disturbances

Eligard 7.5 mg
Depression (Less than 2%)
Insomnia (Less than 2%)
Libido decreased (Less than 2%)
Smell disturbances (Less than 2%)

Eligard 30 mg
Depression (1.1%)
Insomnia (1.1%)
▲ Libido decreased (3.3%)

Elmiron Capsules
Depression
Emotional lability
Insomnia

Eloxatin for Injection
▲ Anxiety (2% to 5%)
▲ Depression (2% to 5%)
▲ Insomnia (9% to 11%)
▲ Nervousness (2% to 5%)

Elspar for Injection
Agitation
Coma
Confusion
Depression
Hallucinations
Irritability

Emcyt Capsules
Anxiety (1%)
Emotional lability (2%)
▲ Insomnia (3%)

Emend Capsules
Anxiety (Greater than 0.5%)
Confusion (Greater than 0.5%)
Depression (Greater than 0.5%)
Disorientation (Isolated cases)
Insomnia (2.9%)

EMLA
Central nervous system depression (Unlikely)

Central nervous system stimulation
(Unlikely)
Confusion (Unlikely)
Double vision (Unlikely)
Euphoria (Unlikely)
Nervousness (Unlikely)

Emtriva Capsules

▲ Depression (6% to 9%)
▲ Dreaming abnormalities (2% to 11%)
▲ Insomnia (7% to 16%)

Enbrel for Injection

Depression (Infrequent)
Mood changes
Personality changes

Engerix-B Vaccine

Agitation (Less than 1%)
Insomnia (Less than 1%)
Irritability (Less than 1%)

Entocort EC Capsules

▲ Agitation (Less than 5%)
▲ Confusion (Less than 5%)
▲ Insomnia (Less than 5%)
▲ Nervousness (Less than 5%)
▲ Sleep disturbances (Less than 5%)

EpiPen Auto-Injector

Anxiety

EpiPen Jr. Auto-Injector

Anxiety
Nervousness

Epivir Oral Solution

▲ Depressive reactions (9%)
▲ Insomnia (11%)
▲ Sleep disturbances (11%)

Epivir Tablets

▲ Depressive reactions (9%)
▲ Insomnia (11%)
▲ Sleep disturbances (11%)

Epogen for Injection

▲ Anxiety (2% to 7%)
▲ Insomnia (13% to 16%)

Ergamisol Tablets

Anxiety (1%)
Coma
Confusion (Less frequent)
Depression (1% to 2%)
Euphoria
Hallucinations (Less frequent)
Insomnia (1%)
Memory loss, short-term (10 out of

463 patients)
Mental performance, impairment
(Less frequent)
Nervousness (1% to 2%)
Photophobia
Smell disturbances (1%)
Speech disturbances

Ery-Tab Tablets

Confusion (Isolated reports)
Hallucinations (Isolated reports)

Erythrocin Stearate Tablets

Confusion (Isolated reports)
Hallucinations (Isolated reports)

Erythromycin

Confusion (Isolated reports))
Hallucinations (Isolated reports)

Esclim Transdermal System

▲ Anxiety (Up to 8.3%)
Depression
▲ Emotional lability (2.1% to 8.3%)
Libido, changes

Eskalith

Coma
Confusion
Hallucinations
Memory impairment
Mental performance, impairment
Sexual dysfunction
Speech, slurring
Stupor

Estrace

Depression
Libido, changes
Speech disturbances

Estrasorb Topical Emulsion

Depression
Libido, changes
Nervousness

Estratest

Anxiety
Depression
Libido, changes

Estring Vaginal Ring

▲ Anxiety (1% to 3%)
Depression (At least 1 report)
▲ Insomnia (4%)
Libido decreased (At least 1 report)
Nervousness (At least 1 report)

Estrostep 21/Estrostep Fe Tablets
Depression
Libido, changes
Nervousness

Evista Tablets
▲ Depression (6.4%)
▲ Insomnia (5.5%)

Evoxac Capsules
Aggression
Agitation (Less than 1%)
Anxiety (1.3%)
Apathy
Coma (Less than 1%)
Confusion (Less than 1%)
Delirium
Delusions
Dementia
Depersonalization (Less than 1%)
▲ Depression (1% to 3%)
Depression, aggravation of (Less than 1%)
Disordered sense of smell (Less than 1%)
Double vision (Less than 1%)
Dreaming abnormalities (Less than 1%)
Emotional lability (Less than 1%)
Hallucinations (Less than 1%)
Illusion, unspecified
Impairment of sensation (Less than 1%)
Insomnia (2.4%)
Manic behavior (Less than 1%)
Neurosis, unspecified
Paranoia
Personality changes
Sexual dysfunction (Less than 1%)
Speech disturbances (Less than 1%)
Thinking abnormality (Less than 1%)

Excedrin Extra-Strength
Insomnia
Irritability
Nervousness

Exelon
▲ Aggression (3%)
Agitation (2% or more)
▲ Anxiety (5%)
Apathy (Infrequent)
▲ Confusion (8%)
Delirium (Infrequent)
Delusions (2% or more)
Dementia (Infrequent)

Depersonalization (Infrequent)
▲ Depression (6%)
Double vision (Infrequent)
Dreaming abnormalities (Infrequent)
Emotional lability (Infrequent)
▲ Hallucinations (4%)
▲ Insomnia (9%)
Libido decreased (Infrequent)
Libido increased (Infrequent)
Mental performance, impairment (Infrequent)
Nervousness (2% or more)
Neurosis, unspecified (Infrequent)
Paranoia (2% or more)
Personality changes (Infrequent)
Psychoses (Infrequent)
Suicidal ideation (Infrequent)
Suicide, attempt of (Infrequent)

Extendryl
Excitability
Irritability

Fabrazyme for Intravenous Infusion
▲ Anxiety (8%)
▲ Depression (3%)

Factive Tablets
Insomnia (0.1% to 1%)
Nervousness (Less than or equal to 0.1%)

Famvir Tablets
Confusion (Infrequent)
Delirium (Infrequent)
Disorientation (Infrequent)
Hallucinations (Infrequent)
Insomnia (1.5% to 2.5%)

Fareston Tablets
Depression
Double vision

Faslodex Injection
▲ Anxiety (5%)
▲ Depression (5.7%)
▲ Insomnia (6.9%)

Felbatol
Aggression (Frequent)
Agitation (Frequent)
▲ Anxiety (5.2% to 5.3%)
Apathy
Coma
Confusion
Delusions

▲ Depression (5.3%)
▲ Double vision (3.4% to 6.1%)
▲ Emotional lability (6.5%)
  Euphoria (Infrequent)
  Hallucinations (Infrequent)
▲ Insomnia (8.6% to 17.5%)
  Manic behavior
  Mental performance, impairment
▲ Nervousness (7.0% to 16.1%)
  Paranoia
  Psychoses
  Stupor (2.6%)
  Suicide, attempt of (Infrequent)
▲ Thinking abnormality (6.5%)

Feldene Capsules
  Anxiety (Occasional)
  Coma (Rare)
  Confusion (Occasional)
  Depression (Occasional)
  Dreaming abnormalities (Occasional)
  Hallucinations (Rare)
  Insomnia (Occasional)
  Mood changes (Rare)
  Nervousness (Occasional)

Femara Tablets
  Anxiety (Less frequent)
  Depression (Less frequent)
▲ Insomnia (7%)

femhrt Tablets
▲ Depression (5.8%)
  Double vision
  Insomnia
  Libido, changes
▲ Nervousness (5.4%)

Femring Vaginal Ring
  Depression
  Irritability
  Libido, changes
  Mood changes
  Nervousness

Ferrlecit Injection
  Agitation (Greater than 1%)
  Insomnia (Greater than 1%)
  Nervousness (Two or more patients)

Flexeril Tablets
  Aggression
  Agitation (Less than 1%)
  Anxiety (Less than 1%)
  Delusions (Rare)
  Depression (Less than 1%)
  Disorientation (Less than 1%)

  Double vision (Less than 1%)
  Dreaming abnormalities (Less than 1%)
  Excitability (Less than 1%)
  Hallucinations (Less than 1%)
  Insomnia (Less than 1%)
  Libido, changes (Rare)
▲ Nervousness (1% to 3%)
  Paranoia
  Thinking abnormality (Less than 1%)

Flolan for Injection
▲ Agitation (11%)
▲ Anxiety (7% to 21%)
▲ Confusion (6%)
▲ Depression (13% to 37%)
▲ Insomnia (4% to 9%)
▲ Nervousness (7% to 21%)

Flomax Capsules
  Insomnia (1.4% to 2.4%)
  Libido decreased (1% to 2%)

Flonase Nasal Spray
  Smell disturbances

Florinef Acetate Tablets
  Depression
  Insomnia
  Mood changes
  Personality changes
  Psychiatric disturbances

Flovent Inhalation Aerosol
  Aggression
  Agitation
  Depression
▲ Insomnia (3% to 13%)

Flovent Rotadisk
  Aggression
  Agitation
  Depression
  Insomnia
▲ Nervousness (1% to 3%)

Floxin Otic Solution
  Impairment of sensation (Single report)
  Insomnia (Single report)

Floxin Tablets
  Aggression
  Agitation
  Anxiety (Less than 1%)
  Central nervous system stimulation
  Cognitive dysfunction (Less than 1%)
  Confusion (Less than 1%)
  Depression (Less than 1%)

Disorientation
Double vision
Dreaming abnormalities (Less than 1%)
Emotional lability
Euphoria (Less than 1%)
Hallucinations (Less than 1%)
Hostility
▲ Insomnia (3% to 7%)
Manic behavior
▲ Nervousness (1% to 3%)
Nightmares
Paranoia
Phobic disorder
Photophobia (Less than 1%)
Psychoses
Psychoses, toxic
▲ Sleep disturbances (1% to 3%)
Smell disturbances
Suicidal ideation (Rare)
Suicide, attempt of (Rare)

Fludara for Injection
Agitation
Coma
Confusion
Depression (Up to 1%)
Mental performance, impairment (Up to 1%)
▲ Sleep disturbances (1% to 3%)

Flumadine
Agitation (0.3% to 1%)
Confusion (Less than 0.3%)
Depression (0.3% to 1%)
Disordered sense of smell (Less than 0.3%)
Euphoria (Less than 0.3%)
Hallucinations (Less than 0.3%)
Insomnia (2.1% to 3.4%)
Mental performance, impairment (0.3% to 2.1%)
Nervousness (1.3% to 2.1%)

Flumist Vaccine
▲ Hypoactivity (10.6% to 14%)
▲ Irritability (9.9% to 19.5%)

Fluvoxamine maleate
Agitation (2%)
Agoraphobia (Infrequent)
▲ Anxiety (1% to 5%)
Apathy (Frequent)
Central nervous system depression (Infrequent)
Central nervous system stimulation (2%)

Coma (Rare)
Confusion
Delirium (Infrequent)
Delusions (Infrequent)
Depersonalization (Infrequent)
Depression (2%)
Disordered sense of smell (Infrequent)
Double vision (Infrequent)
Dreaming abnormalities
Emotional lability (Infrequent)
Euphoria (Infrequent)
Hallucinations (Infrequent)
Hostility (Infrequent)
Hysteria (Infrequent)
▲ Insomnia (4% to 21%)
Libido decreased (2%)
Libido increased (Infrequent)
Manic behavior (Approximately 1%)
Manic behavior, mild (Approximately 1%)
▲ Nervousness (2% to 12%)
Paranoia (Infrequent)
Phobic disorder (Infrequent)
Photophobia
Psychoses (Infrequent to frequent)
Serotonin syndrome
Sexual dysfunction
Sleep disturbances (Infrequent)
Sleeping, excessive (Infrequent)
Speech, slurring (Rare)
Stupor (Infrequent)
Suicide, attempt of (Infrequent)
Thinking abnormality

Focalin Tablets
Depression
Hallucinations
▲ Insomnia (Among most common)
▲ Nervousness (Among most common)
Psychoses, toxic (Rare)

Fortaz Injection
Coma

Forteo Injection
▲ Depression (4.1%)
▲ Insomnia (4.3%)

Fortovase Capsules
Agitation (Less than 2%)
Anxiety (2.2%)
Behavioral changes (Less than 2%)
Confusion (Less than 2%)
Depression (2.7%)

Dreaming abnormalities (Less than 2%)
Euphoria (Less than 2%)
Hallucinations (Less than 2%)
Impairment of sensation (Less than 2%)
▲ Insomnia (5.6%)
Irritability (Less than 2%)
▲ Libido, changes (3.3%)
Mental performance, impairment (Less than 2%)
Psychiatric disturbances (Less than 2%)
Psychoses (Less than 2%)
Speech disturbances (Less than 2%)
Suicide, attempt of (Rare)

Foscavir Injection
▲ Aggression (Between 1% and 5%)
▲ Agitation (Between 1% and 5%)
▲ Anxiety (5% or greater)
Coma (Less than 1%)
▲ Confusion (5% or greater)
▲ Dementia (Between 1% and 5%)
▲ Depression (5% or greater)
▲ Hallucinations (Between 1% and 5%)
▲ Insomnia (Between 1% and 5%)
▲ Nervousness (Between 1% and 5%)
▲ Sensory disturbances (Between 1% and 5%)
▲ Stupor (Between 1% and 5%)

Frova Tablets
Agitation (Infrequent)
Anxiety (Frequent)
Confusion (Infrequent)
Depersonalization (Infrequent)
Depression (Infrequent)
Depression, aggravation of (Rare)
Dreaming abnormalities (Rare)
Emotional lability (Infrequent)
Euphoria (Infrequent)
Impairment of sensation (Frequent)
Insomnia (Frequent)
Mental performance, impairment (Infrequent)
Nervousness (Infrequent)
Personality changes (Rare)
Speech disturbances (Infrequent)
Thinking abnormality (Infrequent)

Fuzeon Injection
▲ Anxiety (5.7%)
▲ Depression (8.6%)
Insomnia (11.3%)

Gabitril Tablets
Agitation (1%)
Anxiety (1% or more)
Apathy (Infrequent)
Coma (Infrequent)
▲ Confusion (5%)
Delusions (Infrequent)
Depersonalization (Frequent)
▲ Depression (3%)
Disordered sense of smell (Infrequent)
Double vision (1% or more)
Dreaming abnormalities (Infrequent)
▲ Emotional lability (3%)
Euphoria (Frequent)
Hallucinations (Frequent)
Hostility (2%)
▲ Insomnia (6%)
▲ Irritability (10%)
Libido decreased (Infrequent)
Libido increased (Infrequent)
▲ Mental performance, impairment (6%)
▲ Nervousness (10%)
Neurosis, unspecified (Infrequent)
Paranoia (Frequent)
Personality changes (Frequent)
Photophobia (Infrequent)
Psychoses (Infrequent)
▲ Speech disturbances (4%)
Stupor (Frequent)
Suicide, attempt of (Infrequent)
▲ Thinking abnormality (6%)

Gamimune N, 10%
Anxiety
▲ Irritability (Among most common)
Photophobia (Infrequent)

Gammar-P I.V.
Anxiety

Ganite Injection
Confusion
Dreaming abnormalities
Hallucinations

Gastrocrom Oral Concentrate
Anxiety (Less common)
Behavioral changes (Less common)
Depression (Less common)
Hallucinations (Less common)
Insomnia (Less common)
Irritability (2 of 87 patients)
Nervousness (Less common)
Psychoses (Less common)

Gemzar for Injection
Insomnia (Infrequent)

Gengraf Capsules
Anxiety (1% to less than 3%)
Confusion (1% to less than 3%)
Depression (Rare)
Emotional lability (1% to less than 3%)
Insomnia (1% to less than 3%)
Libido decreased (1% to less than 3%)
Libido increased (1% to less than 3%)
Mental performance, impairment (1% to less than 3%)
Nervousness (1% to less than 3%)
▲ Psychiatric disturbances (5%)

Genotropin Lyophilized Powder
Aggression

Geodon Capsules
Agitation (Frequent)
Anxiety
Confusion (Frequent)
Delirium (Frequent)
Double vision (Frequent)
Hostility (Frequent)
Photophobia (Infrequent)
Sexual dysfunction (Infrequent)

Geodon for Injection
Anxiety (Up to 2%)
▲ Insomnia (Up to 3%)
Personality changes (Up to 2%)
Psychoses (Up to 1%)
Speech difficulties (Up to 2%)

Gleevec Tablets
Anxiety (Infrequent)
Depression (Infrequent)
▲ Insomnia (Up to 13%)
Memory impairment (Infrequent)
Sexual dysfunction (Infrequent)

Glucotrol XL Tablets
Anxiety (Less than 3%)
Confusion (Less than 1%)
Depression (Less than 3%)
Insomnia (Less than 3%)
Libido decreased (Less than 1%)
▲ Nervousness (3.6%)

Gonal-F for Injection
Anxiety
▲ Emotional lability (5.1%)

Grifulvin V Tablets and Oral Suspension
Confusion (Occasional)
Insomnia (Occasional)
Mental performance, impairment

Gris-PEG Tablets
Confusion (Occasional)
Insomnia (Occasional)

Guanfacine
Agitation (Less frequent)
Anxiety (Less frequent)
Behavior, violent
Confusion (3% or less)
Depression (3% or less)
Insomnia (Less than 3% to 4%)
Libido decreased (3% or less)
Manic behavior
Nervousness (Less frequent)
▲ Sedation (5% to 39%)

Guanidine HCl Tablets
Confusion
Emotional lability
Hallucinations
Irritability
Jitteriness
Mood changes
Psychoses

Halcion Tablets
Aggression
Agitation
Anxiety, paradoxical
Awareness, altered
Behavior, inappropriate
Central nervous system depression, neonatal
Central nervous system stimulation, paradoxical
Confusion (0.5% to 0.9%)
Delusions
Depersonalization
Depression (0.5% to 0.9%)
Depression, aggravation of
Disorientation
Dreaming abnormalities (Rare)
Euphoria (0.5% to 0.9%)
Excitement, paradoxical
Hallucinations
Impairment of sensation (Rare)
Insomnia (Rare)
Irritability
Libido, changes

Manic behavior
Memory impairment (0.5% to 0.9%)
Mental clouding
▲ Nervousness (5.2%)
Nightmares (Rare)
Overstimulation
Sedation
Sleep disturbances
Sleep walking
Speech, slurring
Suicidal ideation
Thinking abnormality

Haldol Decanoate Injection
Agitation
Anxiety
Catatonia
Confusion
Depression
Euphoria
Hallucinations
Insomnia
Libido increased
Mental status, altered
Psychotic symptoms, paradoxical
  exacerbation

Havrix Vaccine
Insomnia (Less than 1%)
Photophobia (Less than 1%)

Hectorol
Libido decreased
Photophobia
▲ Sleep disturbances (3.3%)

Herceptin I.V.
Confusion (At least one of the 958
  patients)
▲ Depression (6%)
▲ Insomnia (14%)
Manic behavior (At least one of the
  958 patients)

Hexalen Capsules
Central nervous system reactions
Consciousness, disorders of
Mood changes

HibTITER
Irritability (133 of 1,118 vaccinations)
Sleep disturbances

Hivid Tablets
Agitation (Less than 1%)
Anxiety (Less than 1%)
Confusion (Less than 1%)

Dementia (Less than 1%)
Depersonalization (Less than 1%)
Depression (0.4%)
Disordered sense of smell (Less than
  1%)
Emotional lability (Less than 1%)
Euphoria (Less than 1%)
Hallucinations (Less than 1%)
Impairment of sensation
Insomnia (Less than 1%)
Manic behavior (Less than 1%)
Memory loss, short-term (Less than
  1%)
Mental performance, impairment
  (Less than 1%)
Mood changes (Less than 1%)
Nervousness (Less than 1%)
Paranoia (Less than 1%)
Photophobia (Less than 1%)
Psychoses (Less than 1%)
Sexual dysfunction (Less than 1%)
Smell disturbances (Less than 1%)
Speech disturbances (Less than 1%)
Stupor (Less than 1%)
Suicide, attempt of (Less than 1%)
Thinking abnormality (Less than 1%)

Humira Injection
▲ Confusion (Less than 5%)

Hycodan
Anxiety
Fear
Mental clouding
Mental performance, impairment
Mood changes
Sedation

Hycomine Compound Tablets
Anxiety
Fear
Mental clouding
Mental performance, impairment
Mood changes
Sedation

Hycotuss Expectorant Syrup
Anxiety
Fear
Mental clouding
Mental performance, impairment
Mood changes
Sedation

Hydrocortone
Depression

Euphoria
Insomnia
Mood changes
Personality changes
Psychiatric disturbances
Psychoses
Psychoses, aggravation

HydroDIURIL Tablets
Confusion

Hytrin Capsules
Anxiety (At least 1%)
Depression (0.3%)
Insomnia (At least 1%)
Libido decreased (0.6%)
Nervousness (2.3%)

Hyzaar Tablets
Anxiety
Confusion
Depression
Dreaming abnormalities
Insomnia
Libido decreased
Memory impairment
Nervousness
Panic attack
Sleep disturbances

Idamycin PFS Injection
▲ Mental status, altered (41%)

Imitrex Injection
Aggression
Agitation (Infrequent)
Anxiety (1.1%)
Apathy
Confusion (Infrequent)
Depression (Rare)
Euphoria (Infrequent)
Feeling, intoxicated (Rare)
Feeling, strange (2.2%)
Hallucinations
Hysteria (Rare)
Impairment of sensation (Rare)
Mental performance, impairment
  (Rare)
Panic attack
Phobia, unspecified
Photophobia (Infrequent)
Sedation (2.7%)
Serotonin syndrome
Sleep disturbances (Rare)
Smell disturbances (Rare)
Speech disturbances

Imitrex Nasal Spray
Agitation (Infrequent)
Anxiety (Infrequent)
Apathy (Rare)
Confusion (Infrequent)
Depression (Infrequent)
Emotional disturbances (Rare)
Euphoria (Infrequent)
Feeling, strange (Infrequent)
Impairment of sensation (Rare)
Memory impairment (Rare)
Mental performance, impairment
  (Rare)
Panic attack
Sedation (Infrequent)
Sleep disturbances (Infrequent)
Smell disturbances (Infrequent)

Imitrex Tablets
Aggression (Rare)
Agitation (Up to 2%)
Anxiety
Apathy (Rare)
Awareness, heightened (Rare)
Confusion (Infrequent)
Depression (Infrequent)
Euphoria (Infrequent)
Feeling, strange
Hallucinations (Rare)
Hysteria (Rare)
Impairment of sensation
  (Rare)
Memory impairment (Rare)
Mental performance, impairment
  (Infrequent)
Panic attack
Personality changes (Rare)
Phobic disorder (Rare)
Phonophobia (Frequent)
Photophobia (Frequent)
Sedation
Serotonin syndrome
Sleep disturbances (Rare to
  Infrequent)
Smell disturbances (Infrequent)
Suicide, attempt of (Rare)

Indapamide Tablets
▲ Agitation (Greater than or equal to
  5%)
▲ Anxiety (Greater than or equal to 5%)
▲ Depression (Less than 5%)
▲ Insomnia (Less than 5%)
▲ Irritability (Greater than or equal to
  5%)

▲ Libido decreased (Less than 5%)
▲ Nervousness (Less than 5%)
▲ Tenseness (Greater than or equal to 5%)

Inderal LA Capsules
Catatonia
Depression
Disorientation, place
Disorientation, time
Dreaming abnormalities
Emotional lability
Hallucinations
Insomnia
Memory loss, short-term
Neuropsychometrics performance, decrease
Sensorium, clouded

Indocin Capsules, Oral Suspension & Suppositories
Anxiety (Less than 1%)
Coma (Less than 1%)
Confusion (Less than 1%)
Depersonalization (Less than 1%)
Depression (Greater than 1%)
Double vision (Less than 1%)
Insomnia (Less than 1%)
Listlessness (Greater than 1%)
Nervousness (Less than 1%)
Psychiatric disturbances (Less than 1%)
Psychoses (Less than 1%)

Indocin I.V.
Coma (Less than 1%)

Infanrix Vaccine
▲ Anxiety (3.3% to 9.2%)
▲ Irritability (28.8% to 61.5%)

INFeD Injection
Disorientation

Infergen
▲ Agitation (4% to 6%)
▲ Anxiety (10% to 19%)
▲ Confusion (4%)
▲ Depression (18% to 26%)
▲ Emotional lability (6% to 12%)
▲ Insomnia (24% to 39%)
▲ Libido decreased (5%)
▲ Nervousness (16% to 31%)
Psychiatric disturbances
Suicidal ideation
Suicide, attempt of
▲ Thinking abnormality (8% to 10%)

Intron A for Injection
▲ Aggression (Less than 5%)
▲ Agitation (Less than 5%)
▲ Anxiety (Up to 5%)
▲ Apathy (Less than 5%)
▲ Central nervous system reactions (Less than 5%)
▲ Coma (Less than 5%)
▲ Confusion (Up to 12%)
▲ Consciousness, disorders of (Less than 5%)
▲ Depression (2% to 40%)
▲ Depression, aggravation of (Less than 5%)
▲ Disordered sense of smell (Less than 5%)
▲ Double vision (Less than 5%)
▲ Dreaming abnormalities (Less than 5%)
▲ Emotional lability (Less than 5%)
▲ Insomnia (Up to 12%)
▲ Irritability (Up to 16%)
▲ Libido decreased (Up to 5%)
▲ Manic behavior (Less than 5%)
▲ Mental performance, impairment (Up to 14%)
▲ Nervousness (Up to 3%)
▲ Neurosis, unspecified (Less than 5%)
▲ Personality changes (Less than 5%)
▲ Photophobia (Less than 5%)
▲ Speech disturbances (Less than 5%)
Suicidal ideation (Rare)
Suicide, attempt of (Rare; less than 5%)
▲ Thinking abnormality (Less than 5%)

Invanz for Injection
▲ Agitation (3.3% to 5.1%)
Anxiety (0.8% to 1.1%)
Behavior, violent (Greater than 0.1%)
▲ Confusion (3.3% to 5.1%)
Depression (Greater than 0.1%)
▲ Disorientation (3.3% to 5.1%)
Hallucinations (Very rare)
▲ Insomnia (3% to 3.2%)
▲ Mental status, altered (3.3% to 5.1%)
Nervousness (Greater than 0.1%)
▲ Stupor (3.3% to 5.1%)

Inversine Tablets
Libido decreased
Mental performance, impairment
Sedation

Invirase Capsules
Agitation (Less than 2%)
Anxiety (Greater than or equal to 2%)

Confusion (Less than 2%)
Depression (Greater than or equal to 2%)
Dreaming abnormalities (Less than 2%)
Euphoria (Less than 2%)
Hallucinations (Less than 2%)
Impairment of sensation (Less than 2%)
Insomnia (Greater than or equal to 2%)
Irritability (Less than 2%)
Libido, changes (Greater than or equal to 2%)
Mental performance, impairment (Less than 2%)
Psychiatric disturbances (Less than 2%)
Psychoses (Less than 2%)
Speech disturbances (Less than 2%)
Suicide, attempt of (Rare)

Ionamin Capsules
Euphoria
Insomnia
Libido, changes
Overstimulation
Psychoses (Rare)

Isoptin SR Tablets
Confusion (1% or less)
Insomnia (1% or less)
Psychoses (1% or less)

Kadian Capsules
Agitation (Less than 3%)
▲ Anxiety (Less than 3% to 6%)
Apathy (Less than 3%)
Confusion (Less than 3%)
Depression (Less than 3%)
Double vision (Less than 3%)
Dreaming abnormalities (Less than 3%)
Euphoria (Less than 3%)
Hallucinations (Less than 3%)
Insomnia (Less than 3%)
Libido decreased (Less than 3%)
Mental performance, impairment (Less than 3%)
Sedation (Less than 3%)
Speech, slurring (Less than 3%)
Thinking abnormality (Less than 3%)

Kaletra
Agitation (Less than 2%)
Anxiety (Less than 2%)

Confusion (Less than 2%)
Depression (Less than 2%)
Dreaming abnormalities (Less than 2%)
Emotional lability (Less than 2%)
Insomnia (1.1% to 2.4%)
Libido decreased (Less than 2%)
Nervousness (Less than 2%)
Thinking abnormality (Less than 2%)

Keflex Pulvules
Agitation
Confusion
Hallucinations

Keppra
Anxiety (2%)
Confusion (1% or more)
▲ Depression (4%)
Double vision (2%)
Emotional lability (2%)
Hostility (2%)
Insomnia (1% or more)
▲ Nervousness (4%)
Thinking abnormality (1% or more)

Ketek Tablets
Anxiety (Less than 0.2%)
Double vision (Greater than or equal 0.2% to less than 2%)
Insomnia (Greater than or equal 0.2% to less than 2%)

Klonopin
Aggression (Infrequent)
Agitation
Anxiety (Infrequent)
Apathy (Infrequent)
▲ Behavioral changes (5% to 25%)
▲ Central nervous system depression (Most frequent)
Coma
Confusion (1%)
Depersonalization (Infrequent)
▲ Depression (4% to 7%)
Double vision (Infrequent)
Dreaming abnormalities (Infrequent)
Emotional lability (1%)
Excitability (Infrequent)
Hallucinations
Hostility
Hyperactivity (Infrequent)
Hysteria
Illusion, unspecified (Infrequent)
Inebriated feeling (Infrequent)
Insomnia (Infrequent)

Libido decreased (1%)
Libido increased (Infrequent)
Libido, loss of (Infrequent)
▲ Memory impairment (4%)
Mental performance, impairment (1% to 2%)
▲ Nervousness (1% to 3%)
Nightmares (Infrequent)
Psychoses
Sleep disturbances (Infrequent)
Speech, slurring
Suicidal ideation (Infrequent)
Suicide, attempt of (Infrequent)

Kogenate FS
Depersonalization

K-Phos Tablets
Confusion

Kytril Injection
Agitation (Less than 2%)
Anxiety (Less than 2%)
Central nervous system stimulation (Less than 2%)
Insomnia (Less than 2%)

Kytril Tablets
Anxiety (2%)
▲ Insomnia (3% to 5%)

Lacrisert Sterile Ophthalmic Insert
Photophobia

Lamictal
Agitation (Infrequent)
▲ Anxiety (3.8%)
Apathy (Infrequent)
Central nervous system depression (Infrequent)
Central nervous system stimulation (Rare)
Confusion (1.8%)
Delirium (Rare)
Delusions (Rare)
Depersonalization (Infrequent)
▲ Depression (4.2%)
Disordered sense of smell (Rare)
▲ Double vision (5% to 49%)
Dreaming abnormalities (Infrequent)
▲ Emotional lability (4%)
Euphoria (Infrequent)
Hallucinations (Infrequent)
Hostility (Frequent)
▲ Insomnia (5.6%)
▲ Irritability (3%)

Libido decreased (Rare)
Libido increased (Rare)
Manic behavior (Rare)
Manic behavior, mild (Rare)
Memory impairment (2.4%)
Mental performance, impairment (1.7%)
Nervousness (2%)
Neurosis, unspecified (Rare)
Panic attack (Infrequent)
Paranoia (Infrequent)
Personality changes (Infrequent)
Photophobia (Infrequent)
Psychoses (Infrequent)
Sleep disturbances (1.4%)
Speech disturbances (2.5%)
Stupor (Infrequent)
Suicidal ideation (Rare)
Suicide, attempt of (Rare)
▲ Thinking abnormality (3%)

Lanoxicaps Capsules
Anxiety
Apathy
Central nervous system reactions (Rare)
Confusion
Delirium
Depression
Hallucinations
Mental status, altered
Psychoses

Lanoxin
Anxiety
Apathy
Central nervous system reactions
Confusion
Delirium
Depression
Hallucinations
Mental status, altered
Psychoses (Lanoxin Injection/Lanoxin Pediatric Injection/Lanoxin Pediatric Elixir)

Lariam Tablets
Agitation (Occasional)
Anxiety (Occasional)
Central nervous system reactions
Confusion (Occasional)
Depression (Occasional)
▲ Dreaming abnormalities (Among most frequent)
Emotional disturbances (Less than 1%)

Hallucinations (Occasional)
▲ Insomnia (Among most frequent)
Mood changes (Occasional)
Panic attack (Occasional)
Paranoia (Occasional)
Psychiatric disturbances (Occasional)
Psychoses (Occasional)
▲ Sleep disturbances (Among most frequent)
Suicidal ideation (Rare)
Suicide, attempt of (Rare)

Lescol Capsules
Anxiety
Depression
Insomnia (2.7%)
Libido, loss of
Memory loss, short-term
Psychiatric disturbances

Lescol XL Tablets
Anxiety
Depression
Insomnia (1.8%)
Libido, loss of
Memory loss, short-term
Psychiatric disturbances

Leukeran Tablets
Agitation (Rare)
Confusion (Rare)
Hallucinations (Rare)

Leukine
▲ Anxiety (11%)
▲ Central nervous system reactions (11%)
▲ Insomnia (11%)
▲ Psychiatric disturbances (15%)
▲ Sensory disturbances (6%)

Leustatin Injection
▲ Insomnia (7%)

Levaquin
Aggression (0.1% to 1%)
Agitation (0.1% to 1%)
Anxiety (0.1% to 1%)
Coma (0.1% to 1%)
Confusion (0.1% to 1%)
Delirium (0.1% to 1%)
Depression (0.1% to 1%)
Disordered sense of smell (0.1% to 1%)
Double vision (0.1% to 1%)
Dreaming abnormalities (0.1% to 1%)
Emotional lability (0.1% to 1%)
Hallucinations (0.1% to 1%)

▲ Insomnia (0.4% to 4.3%)
Manic behavior (0.1% to 1%)
Mental performance, impairment (0.1% to 1%)
Nervousness (0.1% to 1%)
Nightmares
Paranoia (0.1% to 1%)
Psychoses, toxic
Sleep disturbances (0.1% to 1%)
Speech disturbances (0.1% to 1%)
Stupor (0.1% to 1%)
Suicidal ideation (Rare)
Suicide, attempt of (Rare)

Levitra Tablets
Insomnia (Less than 2%)
Photophobia (Less than 2%)

Levlen 21/Levlen 28 Tablets
Depression
Double vision (Rare)
Insomnia
Libido, changes
Mood changes
Nervousness
Speech disturbances

Levlite 28 Tablets
Depression
Double vision (Rare)
Insomnia
Libido, changes
Mood changes
Nervousness
Speech disturbances

Levora Tablets
Depression
Libido, changes
Nervousness

Levothroid Tablets
Anxiety
Emotional lability
Hyperactivity
Insomnia
Irritability
Nervousness

Levoxyl Tablets
Anxiety
Emotional lability
Hyperactivity
Insomnia
Irritability
Nervousness

Lexapro

Aggression (Infrequent)
Agitation (Infrequent)
Anxiety (At least 2%)
Apathy (Infrequent)
Confusion (Infrequent)
Delirium
Depersonalization (Infrequent)
Depression (Infrequent)
Depression, aggravation of
  (Infrequent)
Disorientation (Infrequent)
▲ Dreaming abnormalities (3%)
Emotional lability (Infrequent)
Excitability (Infrequent)
Feeling, strange (Infrequent)
Hallucinations, auditory (Infrequent)
▲ Insomnia (5% to 14%)
Irritability (Frequent)
Jitteriness (Infrequent)
▲ Libido decreased (3% to 7%)
Mental performance, impairment
  (Frequent)
Nervousness (Infrequent)
Panic attack (Infrequent)
Serotonin syndrome
Sexual dysfunction
Sluggishness (Infrequent)
Suicidal ideation (Infrequent)
Suicide, attempt of (Infrequent)

Lexiva Tablets

▲ Depression (Less than 1% to 11%)
▲ Mood changes (Less than 1% to 11%)

Lexxel Tablets

Agitation
Anxiety
Confusion
Depression
Impairment of sensation
Insomnia
Irritability
Libido decreased
Nervousness

Librium Capsules

Confusion
Libido decreased
Libido increased

Lidoderm Patch

Central nervous system stimulation
Confusion
Depression
Double vision

Euphoria
Nervousness

Limbitrol

Confusion (Less common)
Delusions
Dreaming (Less common)
Euphoria
Hallucinations
Libido, changes
Manic behavior, mild
Mental performance, impairment

Lindane Lotion & Shampoo

Central nervous system stimulation

Lipitor Tablets

Depression (Less than 2%)
Disordered sense of smell (Less than
  2%)
Dreaming abnormalities (Less than
  2%)
Emotional lability (Less than 2%)
Insomnia (Greater than or equal to 2%)
Libido decreased (Less than 2%)

Lo/Ovral-28 Tablets

Depression
Libido, changes
Mood changes
Nervousness

Loestrin 21/Loestrin Fe Tablets

Depression
Libido, changes
Nervousness

Lofibra Capsules

Anxiety
Depression
Insomnia
Libido decreased
Nervousness

Lopid Tablets

Confusion
Depression
Libido decreased

Lortab

Anxiety
Fear
Mental clouding
Mental performance, impairment
Mood changes
▲ Sedation (Among most frequent)

Lotensin HCT Tablets
Dreaming abnormalities (0.3% or more)
Insomnia (0.3% to 1%)
Libido decreased (0.3% to 1%)
Nervousness (0.3% to 1%)

Lotensin Tablets
Anxiety (Less than 1%)
Insomnia (Less than 1%)
Libido increased (Less than 1%)
Nervousness (Less than 1%)

Lotrel Capsules
Anxiety
Insomnia
Libido decreased
Nervousness

Lotronex Tablets
Anxiety (Infrequent)
Confusion (Rare)
Depression (2%)
Dreaming abnormalities (Rare)
Photophobia (Rare)
Sedation (Rare)
Sexual dysfunction (Rare)
▲ Sleep disturbances (3%)
Sleep-inducing effects (Infrequent)
Smell disturbances (Rare)

Lovenox Injection
Confusion (2.2%)

Low-Ogestrel-28 Tablets
Depression
Libido, changes
Nervousness

Loxitane Capsules
Agitation
Confusion
Insomnia
Mental performance, impairment
Speech, slurring
Tenseness

Ludiomil
▲ Anxiety (3%)
▲ Nervousness (6%)

Lumigan Ophthalmic Solution
▲ Photophobia (1% to 3%)

Lunelle Monthly Injection
Depression
Emotional lability

Libido, changes
Nervousness

Lupron Depot 3.75 mg
▲ Anxiety (3%)
Confusion
▲ Delusions (Among most frequent)
▲ Depression (16%)
Depression, aggravation of
▲ Emotional lability (16%)
▲ Insomnia (16%)
▲ Libido decreased (Less than 5%)
▲ Libido, changes (16%)
▲ Memory impairment (Among most frequent)
Mood changes
▲ Nervousness (4%)
▲ Personality changes (Among most frequent)
▲ Sleep disturbances (16%)
Suicidal ideation (Very rare)
Suicide, attempt of (Very rare)

Lupron Depot 7.5 mg
▲ Agitation (Less than 5%)
▲ Insomnia (Less than 5%)
▲ Libido decreased (5.4%)
▲ Sleep disturbances (Less than 5%)

Lupron Depot–3 Month 11.25 mg
Agitation
▲ Anxiety (3%)
▲ Delusions (Less than 5%)
▲ Depression (16%)
Depression, aggravation of (Possible)
▲ Emotional lability (16%)
▲ Insomnia (16%)
▲ Libido decreased (1.8% to 11%)
▲ Libido, changes (16%)
▲ Memory impairment (Less than 5%)
▲ Nervousness (4%)
▲ Personality changes (Less than 5%)
▲ Sleep disturbances (16%)
Suicidal ideation (Very rare)
Suicide, attempt of (Very rare)

Lupron Depot–3 Month 22.5 mg
▲ Anxiety (Less than 5%)
▲ Delusions (Less than 5%)
▲ Depression (Less than 5%)
▲ Insomnia (8.5%)
▲ Libido decreased (Less than 5%)
▲ Nervousness (Less than 5%)
▲ Sleep disturbances (8.5%)

Lupron Depot–4 Month 30 mg
▲ Confusion (Less than 5%)

▲ Dementia (Less than 5%)
▲ Depression (Less than 5%)
▲ Insomnia (Less than 5%)
▲ Libido decreased (Less than 5%)
▲ Sleep disturbances (Less than 5%)
▲ Thinking abnormality (Less than 5%)

Lupron Depot-PED
Emotional lability (Less than 2%)
Nervousness (Less than 2%)
Personality changes (Less than 2%)

Lupron Injection
▲ Anxiety (Less than 5%)
▲ Depression (Less than 5%)
▲ Insomnia (5% or more)
▲ Libido decreased (Less than 5%)
Libido increased
▲ Memory impairment (Less than 5%)
▲ Mood changes (Less than 5%)
▲ Nervousness (Less than 5%)
▲ Sleep disturbances (5% or more)

Lupron Injection Pediatric
Emotional lability (Less than 2%)
Nervousness (Less than 2%)
Personality changes (Less than 2%)

M.V.I. Pediatric for Injection
Anxiety (Rare)
Double vision (Rare)

Macrobid Capsules
Confusion (Rare)
Depression (Rare)
Psychoses (Rare)

Macrodantin Capsules
Confusion (Rare)
Depression (Rare)
Psychoses (Rare)

Malarone
Anxiety (Less than 1%)
Depression (Less than 1%)
▲ Dreaming (2% to 7%)
▲ Insomnia (2% to 3%)

Marinol Capsules
Anxiety (Greater than 1%)
▲ Awareness, heightened (8% to 24%)
Confusion (Greater than 1%)
Depersonalization (Greater than 1%)
Depression (Less than 1%)
▲ Elation (8% to 24%)
▲ Euphoria (3% to 10%)
Hallucinations (Greater than 1%)

▲ Laughing, easy (8% to 24%)
Mood changes
Nervousness (Greater than 1%)
Nightmares (Less than 1%)
▲ Paranoia (3% to 10%)
Speech difficulties (Less than 1%)
▲ Thinking abnormality (3% to 10%)

Matulane Capsules
Coma
Confusion
Depression
Double vision
Hallucinations
Insomnia
Nervousness
Nightmares
Photophobia
Speech, slurring

Mavik Tablets
Anxiety (0.3% to 1%)
Insomnia (0.3% to 1%)
Libido decreased (0.3% to 1%)

Maxair Autohaler
Anxiety
Confusion
Depression
Insomnia
▲ Nervousness (4.5% to 6.9%)
Smell disturbances (0.6%)

Maxalt
Agitation (Infrequent)
Anxiety (Infrequent)
Confusion (Infrequent)
Depersonalization (Rare)
Depression (Infrequent)
Disorientation (Infrequent)
Dreaming abnormalities (Infrequent)
Euphoria (Frequent)
Hangover (Infrequent)
Impairment of sensation (Rare)
Insomnia (Infrequent)
Irritability (Infrequent)
Memory impairment (Infrequent)
Mental performance, impairment (Frequent—Maxalt Tablets; Infrequent—Maxalt-MLT Tablets)
Nervousness (Infrequent)
Photophobia (Rare)
Sleeping, excessive (Rare)
Smell disturbances (Rare)

Maxidone Tablets
Anxiety
Fear
Mental clouding
Mental performance, impairment
Mood changes
▲ Sedation (Among most frequent)

Maxzide
Anxiety
Depression
Insomnia
Sexual dysfunction

Mebaral Tablets
Agitation (Less than 1 in 100 patients)
Anxiety (Less than 1 in 100 patients)
Central nervous system depression
  (Less than 1 in 100 patients)
Confusion (Less than 1 in
  100 patients)
Hallucinations (Less than 1 in 100
  patients)
Insomnia (Less than 1 in 100 patients)
Nervousness (Less than 1 in 100
  patients)
Nightmares (Less than 1 in 100
  patients)
Psychiatric disturbances (Less than 1
  in 100 patients)
Thinking abnormality (Less than 1 in
  100 patients)

Mellaril
Agitation
Behavioral changes
Confusion, nocturnal
Dreaming abnormalities
Hyperactivity
Libido, changes
Psychiatric disturbances
Psychoses, aggravation

Menest Tablets
Depression
Libido, changes

Mepron Suspension
▲ Anxiety (7%)
▲ Insomnia (10% to 19%)

Meridia Capsules
Agitation (Greater than or equal to
  1%)
Anger
▲ Anxiety (4.5%)

Central nervous system stimulation
  (1.5%)
Confusion
▲ Depression (4.3%)
Depression, aggravation of
Dreaming abnormalities
Emotional lability (1.3%)
▲ Insomnia (10.7%)
Libido decreased
Libido increased
Memory loss, short-term
Mental performance, impairment
Mood changes
▲ Nervousness (5.2%)
Nightmares
Serotonin syndrome
Speech disturbances
Thinking abnormality (Greater than or
  equal to 1%)

Merrem I.V.
Agitation (Greater than 0.1% to 1%)
Anxiety (Greater than 0.1% to 1%)
Confusion (Greater than 0.1% to 1%)
Delirium (Greater than 0.1% to 1%)
Depression (Greater than 0.1% to 1%)
Hallucinations (Greater than 0.1% to
  1%)
Insomnia (Greater than 0.1% to 1%)
Nervousness (Greater than 0.1% to
  1%)

Meruvax II
Irritability

Metadate CD Capsules
Depression
▲ Insomnia (5%)
▲ Nervousness (Among most common)
Psychoses, toxic

Metadate ER Tablets
Depression
▲ Insomnia (Among most common)
▲ Nervousness (Among most
  common)
Psychoses, toxic

MetroGel-Vaginal Gel
Depression (Less than 1%)

Mevacor Tablets
Anxiety (0.5% to 1%)
Depression (0.5% to 1%)
Insomnia (0.5% to 1%)
Libido, loss of (0.5% to 1%)
Memory loss, short-term (0.5% to 1%)

Mexitil Capsules

Confusion (1.9% to 2.6%)
Depression (2.4%)
Hallucinations (About 3 in 1,000)
Libido decreased (Less than 1% or
  about 4 in 1,000)
Memory loss, short-term (Less than
  1% to about 9 in 1,000)
▲ Nervousness (5% to 11.3%)
Psychoses (Less than 1% or about
  2 in 1,000)
Sensorium, clouded (1.9% to 2.6%)
▲ Sleep disturbances (7.1% to 7.5%)
Speech difficulties (2.6%)

Miacalcin Nasal Spray

Agitation (Less than 1%)
Anxiety (Less than 1%)
▲ Depression (1% to 3%)
Disordered sense of smell (Less than
  1%)
Insomnia (Less than 1%)

Micardis HCT Tablets

Anxiety
Depression
Insomnia
Nervousness

Micardis Tablets

Anxiety (More than 0.3%)
Depression (More than 0.3%)
Insomnia (More than 0.3%)

Microgestin/Microgestin Fe

Depression
Libido, changes
Nervousness

Midamor Tablets

Confusion (Less than or equal to 1%)
Depression (Less than or equal to 1%)
Insomnia (Less than or equal to 1%)
Libido decreased (Less than or equal
  to 1%)
Nervousness (Less than or equal to 1%)

Miltown Tablets

Euphoria
Excitement, paradoxical
Intoxication, chronic
Mental performance, impairment
Overstimulation
Speech, slurring
Suicidal ideation

Minipress Capsules

▲ Depression (1% to 4%)
Hallucinations (Less than 1%)
Insomnia
▲ Nervousness (1% to 4%)

Minizide Capsules

Depression (Rare)
Hallucinations (Rare)
Nervousness

Mintezol

Confusion
Depression
Floating feeling
Hyperirritability
Psychiatric disturbances

Mirapex Tablets

Agitation (Less than 1%; 1.1%)
Anxiety (1% or more)
Apathy (1% or more)
Central nervous system stimulation
  (Less than 1%)
▲ Confusion (4% to 10%)
Delusions (1%)
Depression (1% or more)
Double vision (1% or more)
▲ Dreaming abnormalities (Greater than
  or equal to 1% to 11%)
▲ Hallucinations (9% to 17%)
▲ Insomnia (17% to 27%)
Libido decreased (1%)
Nervousness (1% or more)
Paranoia (Less than 1%)
Psychoses (Less than 1%; 1% or more)
Sleep disturbances (Less than or equal
  to 1%)
Speech disturbances (1% or more)
Suicide, attempt of (Less than 1%)
▲ Thinking abnormality (2% to 3%)

Mirena Intrauterine System

▲ Depression (5% or more)
▲ Libido decreased (5% or more)
▲ Nervousness (5% or more)

Mithracin for Intravenous Use

Depression

M-M-R II

Irritability

Moban

Depression (Less frequent)
Euphoria (Less frequent)
Hyperactivity (Less frequent)

Libido increased
Mental status, altered

Mobic Tablets
Anxiety (Less than 2%)
Confusion (Less than 2%)
Depression (Less than 2%)
Insomnia (0.4% to 3.6%)
Nervousness (Less than 2%)

Moduretic Tablets
Confusion (Less than or equal to 1%)
Depression (Less than or equal to 1%)
Insomnia (Less than or equal to 1%)
Libido decreased
Nervousness (Less than or equal to 1%)
Stupor (Less than or equal to 1%)

Monurol Sachet
Insomnia (Less than 1%)
Nervousness (Less than 1%)

Motrin
Coma (Rare; less than 1%)
Confusion (Less than 1%)
Depression (Less than 1%)
Double vision (Less than 1%)
Dreaming abnormalities (Less than 1%)
Emotional lability (Less than 1%)
Hallucinations (Less than 1%)
Insomnia (Less than 1%)
Nervousness (1% to less than 3%)

Motrin Cold & Sinus Caplets
Insomnia
Nervousness

MS Contin Tablets
Agitation (Less frequent)
Depression (Less frequent)
Disorientation (Less frequent)
Double vision (Less frequent)
Dreaming (Less frequent)
▲ Euphoria (Among most frequent)
Feeling, strange (Less frequent)
Floating feeling (Less frequent)
Hallucinations (Less frequent)
Insomnia (Less frequent)
Libido decreased (Less frequent)
Mental performance, impairment
Mood changes (Less frequent)
Nervousness (Less frequent)
▲ Sedation (Among most frequent)

MSIR
Agitation (Less frequent)

Depression (Less frequent)
Disorientation (Less frequent)
Double vision (Less frequent)
Dreaming (Less frequent)
▲ Euphoria (Among most frequent)
Floating feeling (Less frequent)
Hallucinations (Less frequent)
Insomnia (Less frequent)
Libido decreased (Less frequent)
Mood changes (Less frequent)
Nervousness (Less frequent)
▲ Sedation (Among most frequent)

Mumpsvax
Irritability

Mycobutin Capsules
Confusion (More than one patient)
Insomnia (1%)

Mylotarg for Injection
▲ Depression (8% to 13%)
▲ Insomnia (14% to 22%)

Nadolol Tablets
Behavioral changes (6 of 1000 patients)
Catatonia
Depression
Disorientation, place
Disorientation, time
Emotional lability
Hallucinations
Libido decreased (1 to 5 of 1000 patients)
Memory loss, short-term
Neuropsychometrics performance, decrease
Sedation (6 of 1000 patients)
Sensorium, clouded
Sleep disturbances
Speech, slurring (1 to 5 of 1000 patients)

Namenda Tablets
Agitation (Greater than or equal to 2%)
Anxiety (Greater than or equal to 2%)
Apathy (Infrequent)
▲ Confusion (6%)
Delirium (Infrequent)
Delusions (Infrequent)
Depersonalization (Infrequent)
Depression (Greater than or equal to 2%)
Double vision (Infrequent)
Emotional lability (Infrequent)

Insomnia (Greater than or equal to 2%)
Libido increased (Infrequent)
Nervousness (Infrequent)
Neurosis, unspecified (Infrequent)
Personality changes (Infrequent)
Psychoses (Infrequent)
Sleep disturbances (Infrequent)
Stupor (Infrequent)
Suicide, attempt of (Infrequent)
Thinking abnormality (Infrequent)

Naprelan Tablets
Anxiety (Less than 1%)
▲ Cognitive dysfunction (3% to 9%)
Confusion (Less than 1%)
Depression (Less than 1%)
Double vision (Less than 1%)
▲ Dreaming abnormalities (3% to 9%)
Emotional lability (Less than 1%)
Insomnia (Less than 3%)
▲ Mental performance, impairment (3% to 9%)
Nervousness (Less than 1%)

Naprosyn
Central nervous system depression (Less than 1%)
Cognitive dysfunction (Less than 1%)
Dreaming abnormalities (Less than 1%)
Insomnia (Less than 1%)
Mental performance, impairment (Less than 1%)

Narcan Injection
Agitation
Excitability
Hallucinations
Irritability
Nervousness

Nardil Tablets
Agitation (Uncommon)
Anxiety (Less frequent)
Coma (Less frequent)
Delirium (Less frequent)
Euphoria (Less common)
Insomnia (Common)
Jitteriness (Less common)
Manic behavior (Less frequent)
▲ Manic behavior, mild (Most common)
Nightmares (Infrequent)
Psychoses (Infrequent)
Schizophrenia, precipitation (Less frequent)
Sexual dysfunction (Common)

Sleep disturbances (Common)
Sleeping, excessive (Common)

Naropin Injection
Agitation (Less than 1%)
▲ Anxiety (1% to 5%)
Coma (Less than 1%)
Confusion (Less than 1%)
Depression
Emotional lability (Less than 1%)
Excitability
Hallucinations (Less than 1%)
Insomnia (Less than 1%)
Nervousness (Less than 1%)
Nightmares (Less than 1%)
Sexual dysfunction
Stupor (Less than 1%)

Nasonex Nasal Spray
Smell disturbances (Very rare)

Natrecor for Injection
▲ Anxiety (3%)
Confusion (At least 1%)
Insomnia (2%)

Navane
Agitation
Insomnia
Mental status, altered
Psychotic symptoms, paradoxical exacerbation (Infrequent)
Sedation

Navelbine Injection
Auditory disturbances

Necon Tablets
Depression
Libido, changes
Nervousness

Nefazodone
Agitation
Anxiety
Apathy (Infrequent)
Central nervous system stimulation
▲ Confusion (7% to 8%)
Depersonalization (Infrequent)
Depression
Double vision (Infrequent)
▲ Dreaming abnormalities (3%)
Emotional lability
Euphoria (Infrequent)
Hallucinations (Infrequent)
Hangover (Infrequent)
Hostility (Infrequent)

▲ Insomnia (11%)
 Libido decreased (1%)
 Libido increased (Infrequent)
 Manic behavior (0.3% to 1.6%)
 Manic behavior, mild (0.3% to 1.6%)
▲ Memory impairment (4%)
▲ Mental performance, impairment (3%)
 Paranoia (Infrequent)
 Photophobia (Infrequent)
 Suicidal ideation (Infrequent)
 Suicide, attempt of (Infrequent)
 Thinking abnormality (Infrequent)

Nembutal Sodium Solution
 Agitation (Less than 1%)
 Anxiety (Less than 1%)
 Central nervous system depression
  (Less than 1%)
 Confusion (Less than 1%)
 Hallucinations (Less than 1%)
 Insomnia (Less than 1%)
 Nervousness (Less than 1%)
 Nightmares (Less than 1%)
 Psychiatric disturbances (Less than 1%)
 Thinking abnormality (Less than 1%)

Neoral
 Anxiety (1% to less than 3%)
 Confusion (1% to less than 3%)
 Consciousness, disorders of
 Depression (Rare)
 Emotional lability (1% to less than 3%)
 Insomnia (1% to less than 3%)
 Libido decreased (1% to less than 3%)
 Libido increased (1% to less than 3%)
 Mental performance, impairment (1%
  to less than 3%)
 Nervousness (1% to less than 3%)
 Psychiatric disturbances

Nesacaine/Nesacaine-MPF
 Anxiety
 Depression
 Excitability
 Sensory deficit, persistent
 Sexual dysfunction

Neulasta Injection
▲ Insomnia (15% to 72%)

Neumega for Injection
 Confusion
▲ Insomnia (33%)
 Mental status, altered
▲ Nervousness (Greater than or equal to
 10%)

Neurontin
 Aggression
 Agitation (Infrequent)
 Anxiety (Frequent)
 Apathy (Infrequent)
 Behavioral changes
 Central nervous system depression
 Confusion
 Depersonalization (Infrequent)
 Depression (1.8%)
▲ Double vision (1.2% to 5.9%)
 Dreaming abnormalities (Infrequent)
▲ Emotional lability (4.2% to 6%)
 Euphoria (Infrequent)
 Feeling, drugged (Infrequent)
 Feeling, high (Rare)
 Feeling, strange (Rare)
 Hallucinations (Infrequent)
 Hangover (Rare)
▲ Hostility (5.2% to 7.6%)
 Hyperactivity
 Hysteria (Rare)
 Impairment of sensation (Infrequent)
 Insomnia
 Libido decreased (Infrequent)
 Libido increased (Rare)
 Libido, changes (Infrequent)
 Manic behavior (Rare)
 Nervousness (2.4%)
 Neurosis, unspecified (Rare)
 Paranoia (Infrequent)
 Personality changes (Rare)
 Photophobia (Infrequent)
 Psychoses (Infrequent)
 Sexual dysfunction (Infrequent)
 Sleep walking
 Sociopathy (Rare)
 Speech disturbances (Infrequent)
 Stupor (Infrequent)
 Suicidal ideation (Infrequent)
 Suicide, attempt of (Rare)
 Thinking abnormality (1.7% to 2.7%)

Nexium Capsules
 Apathy (Less than 1%)
 Confusion (Less than 1%)
 Depression, aggravation of (Less than
  1%)
 Disordered sense of smell (Less than
  1%)
 Insomnia (Less than 1%)
 Nervousness (Less than 1%)
 Sleep disturbances (Less than 1%)

Niaspan Tablets
Insomnia

Nilandron Tablets
▲ Depression (8.6%)
▲ Insomnia (16.3%)
▲ Libido decreased (11%)
Nervousness (2%)
Photophobia (2%)

Nimotop Capsules
Depression (Up to 1.4%)

Nipent for Injection
▲ Anxiety (3% to 10%)
▲ Central nervous system reactions (1% to 11%)
▲ Depression (3% to 10%)
Dreaming abnormalities (Less than 3%)
Emotional lability (Less than 3%)
Hallucinations (Less than 3%)
Hangover (Less than 3%)
Hostility (Less than 3%)
▲ Insomnia (3% to 10%)
Libido, changes (Less than 3%)
▲ Nervousness (3% to 10%)
Neurosis, unspecified (Less than 3%)
Photophobia (Less than 3%)
Thinking abnormality (Less than 3%)

Nizoral Tablets
Depression (Rare)
Photophobia (Less than 1%)
Psychiatric disturbances (Rare)
Suicidal ideation (Rare)

Nolvadex Tablets
Depression (Infrequent)
Libido, loss of

Norco Tablets
Anxiety
Fear
Mental clouding
Mental performance, impairment
Mood changes
▲ Sedation (Among most frequent)

Nordette-28 Tablets
Depression
Libido, changes
Nervousness

Norflex
Agitation
Confusion (Infrequent)
Hallucinations

Norinyl 28-Day Tablets
Depression
Double vision
Libido, changes
Nervousness

Noroxin Tablets
Anxiety (Less frequent)
Central nervous system reactions
Central nervous system stimulation
Confusion
Depression (Less frequent)
Double vision
Hallucinations
Insomnia (Less frequent)
Psychiatric disturbances
Psychoses
Sleep disturbances (Less frequent)

Norpramin Tablets
Agitation
Anxiety
Confusion
Delusions
Disorientation
Hallucinations
Insomnia
Libido decreased
Libido increased
Manic behavior, mild
Mental performance, impairment
Nightmares
Psychoses, aggravation

Norvasc Tablets
Agitation (Less than or equal to 0.1%)
Anxiety (More than 0.1% to 1%)
Apathy (Less than or equal to 0.1%)
Depersonalization (More than 0.1% to 1%)
Depression (More than 0.1% to 1%)
Disordered sense of smell (Less than or equal to 0.1%)
Double vision (More than 0.1% to 1%)
Dreaming abnormalities (More than 0.1% to 1%)
Insomnia (More than 0.1% to 1%)
Nervousness (More than 0.1% to 1%)
Sexual dysfunction (Less than 1% to 2%)

Norvir
Agitation (Less than 2%)
Anxiety (Less than 2%)
Confusion (Less than 2%)

Depression (Less than 2%)
Disordered sense of smell (Less than 2%)
Double vision (Less than 2%)
Dreaming abnormalities (Less than 2%)
Emotional lability (Less than 2%)
Euphoria (Less than 2%)
Hallucinations (Less than 2%)
Insomnia (1.3% to 2.6%)
Libido decreased (Less than 2%)
Nervousness (Less than 2%)
Personality changes (Less than 2%)
Photophobia (Less than 2%)
Thinking abnormality (Up to 0.7%)

Novarel for Injection
Depression
Irritability

Nubain Injection
Agitation
Confusion (1% or less)
Delusions (1% or less)
Depersonalization (1% or less)
Depression (1% or less)
Dreaming abnormalities (1% or less)
Euphoria (1% or less)
Floating feeling (1% or less)
Hallucinations (1% or less)
Hostility (1% or less)
Nervousness (1% or less)
▲ Sedation (36%)
Speech difficulties (1% or less)

NuLev Tablets
Confusion
Excitability
Insomnia
Nervousness
Speech disturbances

Numorphan
Central nervous system stimulation, paradoxical
Confusion
Depression
Double vision
Euphoria
Hallucinations
Mental clouding
Nervousness
Sleep disturbances

Ocuflox Ophthalmic Solution
Photophobia

Ogestrel Tablets
Depression
Libido, changes
Nervousness

Omnicef
Insomnia (0.2%)

Oncaspar
Coma
Confusion (Less than 1%)
Disorientation
Emotional lability (Less than 1%)
Mental status, altered
Mood changes

Ontak Vials
▲ Confusion (8%)
▲ Insomnia (9%)
▲ Nervousness (11%)

Orap Tablets
▲ Behavioral changes (27.7%)
Central nervous system reactions
▲ Depression (2 of 20 patients)
Dreaming abnormalities (2.7%)
Excitability
▲ Insomnia (2 of 20 patients)
Libido, loss of
Mental performance, impairment
Mental status, altered
▲ Nervousness (8.3%)
▲ Sedation (14 of 20 patients)
▲ Speech disturbances (2 of 20 patients)

Orapred Oral Solution
Depression
Emotional disturbances
Euphoria
Insomnia
Mood changes
Psychoses

Ortho Evra Transdermal System
Depression
Libido, changes
Nervousness

Ortho Tri-Cyclen Lo Tablets
Depression
Double vision
Insomnia
Libido, changes
Mood changes
Nervousness
Speech disturbances

Ortho Tri-Cyclen Tablets
Depression
Double vision (Rare)
Insomnia
Libido, changes
Mood changes
Nervousness
Speech disturbances

Ortho-Cept Tablets
Depression
Libido, changes
Nervousness

Orthoclone OKT3 Sterile Solution
Agitation
Central nervous system reactions
Cognitive dysfunction
Coma
Combativeness
Confusion
Delirium (Less than 1%)
Disorientation
Double vision
Hallucinations, auditory
Hallucinations, visual
Manic behavior (Less than 1%)
Mental status, altered (Less than 1%)
Mood changes
Paranoia (Less than 1%)
▲ Photophobia (10%)
Psychoses
Stupor

Ortho-Cyclen Tablets
Depression
Double vision (Rare)
Insomnia
Libido, changes
Mood changes
Nervousness
Speech disturbances

Ortho-Est Tablets
Depression
Libido, changes
Speech disturbances

Ovcon Tablets
Depression
Double vision
Libido, changes
Nervousness

Ovidrel for Injection
Emotional lability (Less than 2%)
Insomnia (Less than 2%)

Ovral-28 Tablets
Libido, changes
Mood changes
Nervousness

Ovrette Tablets
Depression
Libido decreased
Mood changes
Nervousness

Oxandrin Tablets
Depression
Excitability
Insomnia
Libido, changes

Oxsoralen-Ultra Capsules
Depression
Insomnia
Nervousness

OxyContin Tablets
Agitation (Less than 1%)
▲ Anxiety (Between 1% and 5%)
▲ Confusion (Between 1% and 5%)
Depersonalization (Less than 1%)
Depression (Less than 1%)
▲ Dreaming abnormalities (Between 1% and 5%)
Emotional lability (Less than 1%)
▲ Euphoria (Between 1% and 5%)
Hallucinations (Less than 1%)
▲ Insomnia (Between 1% and 5%)
Libido decreased
▲ Nervousness (Between 1% and 5%)
Speech disturbances (Less than 1%)
Stupor (Less than 1%)
▲ Thinking abnormality (Between 1% and 5%)

OxyFast Oral Concentrate Solution
Euphoria
▲ Sedation (Among most frequent)

OxyIR Capsules
Euphoria
▲ Sedation (Among most frequent)

Pacerone Tablets
▲ Insomnia (1% to 3%)
▲ Libido decreased (1% to 3%)

▲ Photophobia (4% to 9%)
▲ Sleep disturbances (1% to 3%)
▲ Smell disturbances (1% to 3%)

Pamelor
Agitation
Anxiety
Confusion
Delusions
Disorientation
Hallucinations
Insomnia
Libido decreased
Libido increased
Manic behavior, mild
Nightmares
Panic attack
Psychoses, aggravation

Paraplatin for Injection
▲ Central nervous system reactions
  (5%)
▲ Sensory disturbances (4% to 6%)

Parnate Tablets
Agitation
Anxiety
Confusion
Disorientation
Insomnia
Manic behavior
Memory loss, short-term
Overstimulation

Paxil CR Tablets
Agitation (2%)
▲ Anxiety (2% to 5%)
Bulimia
Confusion (1%)
Delirium
Delusions
Depersonalization (Infrequent)
Depression (Frequent to 2%)
Depression, psychotic
Disordered sense of smell
Double vision (Rare)
Dreaming abnormalities (1%)
Emotional lability (Infrequent)
Euphoria
Hallucinations (Infrequent)
Hostility (Rare)
▲ Insomnia (7% to 20%)
Irritability
▲ Libido decreased (7% to 12%)
Libido increased (Infrequent)
Manic behavior (Approximately 1%)

Manic behavior, mild (Approximately
  1%)
▲ Nervousness (2% to 3%)
Paranoia (Rare)
Photophobia (Infrequent)
Psychoses
Serotonin syndrome
Stupor
Thinking abnormality

Paxil Oral Suspension & Tablets
▲ Agitation (1.1% to 5%)
Alcohol abuse (Infrequent)
▲ Anxiety (1% to 5.9%)
Bulimia (Rare)
Central nervous system stimulation
  (Frequent)
Confusion (1%)
Delirium (Rare)
Delusions (Rare)
Depersonalization (Infrequent)
Depression (Frequent)
Depression, psychotic (Rare)
Disordered sense of smell (Rare)
Double vision (Rare)
▲ Dreaming abnormalities (3% to 4%)
Emotional disturbances (Infrequent)
Emotional lability (Frequent)
Euphoria (Rare)
Feeling, drugged (2%)
Hallucinations (Infrequent)
Hostility (Infrequent)
Hysteria (Rare)
▲ Insomnia (1.3% to 24%)
▲ Libido decreased (3% to 9%)
Libido increased (Rare)
Manic behavior (Infrequent)
Manic behavior, mild (Approximately
  1%)
Mental performance, impairment
  (Frequent)
▲ Nervousness (4% to 9%)
Neurosis, unspecified (Infrequent)
Paranoia (Infrequent)
Photophobia (Rare)
Psychoses (Rare)
Sensory disturbances
Serotonin syndrome
▲ Sexual dysfunction (3.7% to 10%)
Sociopathy (Rare)
Stupor (Rare)
Suicide, attempt of
Thinking abnormality (Infrequent)

Pediapred Oral Solution
Emotional lability
Psychoses
Psychoses, aggravation

Pediarix Vaccine
▲ Irritability (1.7% to 63.8%)
▲ Sleep disturbances (0.4% to 46.7%)

Pediazole Suspension
Anxiety
Depression
Disorientation
Hallucinations
Insomnia
Psychoses

PedvaxHIB, Liquid
Irritability

Peganone Tablets
Double vision
Insomnia

Pegasys
▲ Anxiety (19%)
▲ Depression (18%)
▲ Insomnia (19%)
▲ Irritability (19%)
▲ Memory impairment (5%)
▲ Mood changes (3%)
▲ Nervousness (19%)
Suicidal ideation

PEG-Intron Powder for Injection
Aggression (Less than or equal to 1%)
Agitation (2%)
▲ Anxiety (28%)
▲ Depression (29%)
▲ Emotional lability (28%)
▲ Insomnia (23%)
▲ Irritability (28%)
▲ Nervousness (4%)
Psychoses (Less than or equal to 1%)
Suicidal ideation (Less than or equal to 1%)
Suicide, attempt of (Less than or equal to 1%)

Pentasa Capsules
Depression (Less than 1%)
Insomnia (Less than 1%)

Pepcid
Agitation (Infrequent)
Anxiety (Infrequent)
Confusion (Infrequent)

Depression (Infrequent)
Hallucinations (Infrequent)
Insomnia (Infrequent)
Libido decreased (Infrequent)
Psychiatric disturbances (Infrequent)

Percocet Tablets
Euphoria
Mental performance, impairment
▲ Sedation (Among most frequent)

Percodan Tablets
Euphoria
Mental performance, impairment
▲ Sedation (Among most frequent)

Periactin Tablets
Confusion
Double vision
Euphoria
Excitability
Hallucinations
Hysteria
Insomnia
Irritability
Nervousness
Sedation

Permax Tablets
Agitation (Infrequent)
▲ Anxiety (6.4%)
Apathy (Infrequent)
Coma (Infrequent)
▲ Confusion (11.1%)
Consciousness, disorders of
Delusions (Infrequent)
▲ Depression (3.2%)
Double vision (2.1%)
Dreaming abnormalities (2.7%)
Emotional lability (Infrequent)
Euphoria (Infrequent)
▲ Hallucinations (13.8%)
Hostility (Infrequent)
▲ Insomnia (7.9%)
Libido decreased (Infrequent)
Libido increased (Infrequent)
Manic behavior (Infrequent)
Nervousness (Frequent)
Neurosis, unspecified (Infrequent)
Paranoia (Frequent)
Personality changes (2.1%)
Photophobia (Infrequent)
Psychoses (2.1%; frequent)
Sleeping, excessive
Speech disturbances (1.1%)
Stupor (Rare)
Thinking abnormality (Frequent)

Pfizerpen for Injection
Coma

Phenergan
Agitation
Behavior, inappropriate
Catatonia
Confusion (Phenergan Suppositories)
Delirium
Disorientation (Phenergan
  Suppositories)
Double vision
Euphoria
Excitability
Hallucinations
Hyperexcitability
Hysteria
Insomnia
Mental performance, impairment
Nervousness
Nightmares
Sedation (Phenergan Suppositories)

Phenobarbital
Agitation (Less than 1%)
Anxiety (Less than 1%)
Confusion (Less than 1%)
Delirium
Excitability
Hallucinations (Less than 1%)
Hangover
Insomnia (Less than 1%)
Nervousness (Less than 1%)
Nightmares (Less than 1%)
Psychiatic disturbances (Less than 1%)
Thinking abnormality (Less than 1%)

Phenytek Capsules
▲ Confusion (Among most common)
Insomnia
Nervousness
▲ Speech, slurring (Among most
  common)

PhosLo
Coma
Confusion
Delirium
Stupor

Photofrin for Injection
▲ Anxiety (7%)
▲ Confusion (8%)
Double vision
▲ Insomnia (14%)
Photophobia

Plaquenil Tablets
Emotional disturbances
Irritability
Nervousness
Nightmares
Photophobia (Fairly common)
Psychoses

Plavix Tablets
Anxiety (1% to 2.5%)
Confusion
▲ Depression (3.6%)
Hallucinations
Insomnia (1% to 2.5%)

Plendil Tablets
Anxiety (0.5% to 1.5%)
Depression (0.5% to 1.5%)
Insomnia (0.5% to 1.5%)
Irritability (0.5% to 1.5%)
Libido decreased (0.5% to 1.5%)
Nervousness (0.5% to 1.5%)

Pletal Tablets
Anxiety (Less than 2%)
Double vision (Less than 2%)
Insomnia (Less than 2%)

Polocaine/Polocaine-MPF
Anxiety
Depression
Excitability
Sexual dysfunction

Ponstel Capsules
Coma (Rare)
Confusion (Occasional)
Depression (Occasional)
Dreaming abnormalities
  (Occasional)
Hallucinations (Rare)
Insomnia (Occasional)
Nervousness (Occasional)

Pravachol Tablets
Anxiety
Depression
Insomnia
Libido, loss of
Memory loss, short-term

Prefest Tablets
Anxiety
▲ Depression (5%)
Insomnia
Irritability
Libido, changes

Mood changes
Nervousness

Pregnyl for Injection
Depression
Irritability

Premarin Intravenous
Depression
Libido, changes

Premarin Tablets
Dementia
▲ Depression (5% to 8%)
▲ Insomnia (6% to 7%)
Irritability
Libido, changes
Mood changes
▲ Nervousness (2% to 5%)

Premarin Vaginal Cream
Depression
Libido, changes

Premphase Tablets
▲ Anxiety (2% to 5%)
Dementia
▲ Depression (6% to 11%)
Double vision
▲ Insomnia (6% to 7%)
Irritability
Libido, changes
Mood changes
▲ Nervousness (2% to 3%)

Prempro Tablets
▲ Anxiety (2% to 5%)
Dementia
▲ Depression (6% to 11%)
Double vision
▲ Insomnia (6% to 7%)
Irritability
Libido, changes
Mood changes
▲ Nervousness (2% to 3%)

Prevacid
Agitation (Less than 1%)
Anxiety (Less than 1%)
Apathy (Less than 1%)
Cognitive dysfunction (Less than 1%)
Confusion (Less than 1%)
Depersonalization (Less than 1%)
Depression (Less than 1%)
Disordered sense of smell (Less than 1%)
Double vision (Less than 1%)

Dreaming abnormalities (Less than 1%)
Emotional lability (Less than 1%)
Hallucinations (Less than 1%)
Hostility (Less than 1%)
Insomnia (Less than 1%—Prevacid NapraPAC)
Libido decreased (Less than 1%)
Libido increased (Less than 1%)
Nervousness (Less than 1%)
Neurosis, unspecified (Less than 1%)
Photophobia (Less than 1%)
Sleep disturbances (Less than 1%)
Speech disturbances
Thinking abnormality (Less than 1%)

Prevnar for Injection
▲ Irritability (68.9% to 72.8%)
▲ Sleep disturbances (18.1% to 33.3%)

PREVPAC
Agitation (Less than 1%)
Anxiety (Less than 1%)
Apathy (Less than 1%)
Behavioral changes
▲ Confusion (Less than 1% to 3%)
Depersonalization
Depression (Less than 1%)
Disordered sense of smell (Less than 1%)
Disorientation
Double vision (Less than 1%)
Dreaming abnormalities (Less than 1%)
Emotional lability (Less than 1%)
Hallucinations (Less than 1%)
Hostility (Less than 1%)
Hyperactivity
Insomnia
Libido decreased (Less than 1%)
Libido increased (Less than 1%)
Nervousness (Less than 1%)
Neurosis, unspecified (Less than 1%)
Nightmares
Photophobia (Less than 1%)
Psychoses
Sleep disturbances (Less than 1%)
Smell disturbances
Speech disturbances
Thinking abnormality (Less than 1%)

Priftin Tablets
Aggression (Less than 1%)
Behavioral changes

Prilosec/Prilosec OTC
Aggression (Less than 1%)
Anxiety (Less than 1%)

Apathy (Less than 1%)
Confusion (Less than 1%)
Depression (Less than 1%)
Double vision (Less than 1%)
Dreaming abnormalities (Less than 1%)
Hallucinations (Less than 1%)
Impairment of sensation, one side of face (Less than 1%)
Insomnia (Less than 1%)
Nervousness (Less than 1%)
Psychiatric disturbances (Less than 1%)

Primaxin
Confusion
Hallucinations
Psychiatric disturbances

Prinivil Tablets
Confusion (0.3% to 1%)
Depression (Greater than 1%)
Double vision (0.3% to 1%)
Impairment of sensation (0.3% to 1%)
Insomnia (0.3% to 1%)
Irritability (0.3% to 1%)
Libido decreased (0.4%)
Memory impairment (0.3% to 1%)
Nervousness (0.3% to 1%)
Photophobia (0.3% to 1%)
Sleeping, excessive (0.3% to 1%)

Prinzide Tablets
Confusion
Depression (0.3% to 1%)
Double vision
Impairment of sensation
Insomnia
Irritability
Libido decreased (0.3% to 1%)
Memory impairment
Nervousness
Photophobia
Sleeping, excessive

ProAmatine Tablets
Anxiety (Less frequent)
Confusion (Less frequent)
Insomnia (Rare)
Nervousness (Less frequent)
Thinking abnormality (Less frequent)

Procanbid Tablets
Depression (Occasional)
Hallucinations (Occasional)
Psychoses (Occasional)

Procardia Capsules
Depression (Less than 0.5%)
Jitteriness (2% or less)
▲ Mood changes (7%)
▲ Nervousness (2% or less to 7%)
Paranoia (Less than 0.5%)
Sexual dysfunction (2% or less)
Sleep disturbances (2% or less)

Procardia XL Tablets
Anxiety (1% or less)
Depression (1% or less)
Insomnia (Less than 3%)
Libido decreased (1% or less)
▲ Mood changes (7%)
▲ Nervousness (Less than 3% to 7%)

Prochieve Gel
Aggression
▲ Depression (8% to 11%)
Emotional lability
Insomnia
▲ Libido decreased (10%)
▲ Nervousness (16%)
Sleep disturbances

Prochlorperazine
Agitation
Catatonia
Central nervous system reactions
Coma
Insomnia (Sometimes)
Jitteriness
Mental clouding
Mental performance, impairment
Nervousness
Psychosis, activation

Procrit for Injection
▲ Anxiety (2% to 11%)
▲ Insomnia (13% to 21%)

Prograf
▲ Agitation (3% to 15%)
▲ Anxiety (3% to 15%)
Coma
▲ Confusion (3% to 15%)
Delirium
▲ Depression (3% to 15%)
▲ Dreaming abnormalities (3% to 15%)
▲ Emotional lability (3% to 15%)
▲ Hallucinations (3% to 15%)
▲ Insomnia (32% to 64%)
▲ Mental status, altered (Approximately 55%)
▲ Nervousness (3%)
▲ Psychoses (3% to 15%)

▲ Sensory disturbances (Approximately 55%)
▲ Thinking abnormality (3% to 15%)

Proleukin for Injection
Agitation
▲ Anxiety (12%)
Coma (1%)
▲ Confusion (34%)
Depression (Less than 1%)
Insomnia
Irritability
▲ Mental status, altered (73%)
▲ Sensory disturbances (10%)
▲ Speech disturbances (7%)
Suicide, attempt of

Prometrium Capsules
▲ Anxiety (Less than 5%)
▲ Confusion (Less than 5%)
▲ Depression (Less than 5% to 19%)
▲ Emotional lability (6%)
▲ Insomnia (Less than 5%)
▲ Irritability (5% to 8%)
▲ Mental performance, impairment (Less than 5%)
Nervousness
▲ Personality changes (Less than 5%)
▲ Speech disturbances (Less than 5%)

Propecia Tablets
Libido decreased (1.8%)

Proscar Tablets
▲ Libido decreased (3.3%)

ProSom Tablets
Agitation (Infrequent)
Anxiety (Frequent)
Apathy (Infrequent)
Behavior, inappropriate
Confusion (2%)
Depression (2%)
Double vision (Rare)
Dreaming abnormalities (2%)
Emotional lability (Infrequent)
Euphoria (Infrequent)
Excitement, paradoxical
Hallucinations (Rare)
▲ Hangover (3%)
Hostility (Infrequent)
Libido decreased (Rare)
Mental performance, impairment
▲ Nervousness (8%)
Photophobia (Infrequent)
Sleep disturbances (Infrequent)

Stupor (Infrequent)
Thinking abnormality (2%)

Prostin E2 Suppositories
Tenseness

Protonix
Anxiety (Greater than or equal to 1%)
Confusion (Less than 1%)
Depression (Less than 1%)
Double vision (Less than 1%)
Dreaming abnormalities (Less than 1%)
Emotional lability (Less than 1%)
Hallucinations (Less than 1%)
Insomnia (Greater than or equal to 1%)
Libido decreased (Less than 1%)
Nervousness (Less than 1%)
Sleep disturbances (Less than 1%)
Speech disturbances
Thinking abnormality (Less than 1%)

Protopic Ointment
Depression (Greater than or equal to 1%)
▲ Insomnia (Up to 4%)

Provigil Tablets
Agitation (1%)
▲ Anxiety (5%)
Confusion (1%)
▲ Depression (2%)
Emotional lability (1%)
Hallucinations (At least 1%)
▲ Insomnia (5%)
Libido decreased (At least 1%)
Manic behavior
▲ Nervousness (7%)
Psychoses
Sleep disturbances (At least 1%)
Thinking abnormality (At least 1%)

Prozac
Agitation (At least 2%)
Antisocial reaction (Rare)
▲ Anxiety (4% to 17%)
Apathy (Infrequent)
Behavior, violent
Central nervous system depression (Infrequent)
Central nervous system stimulation (Infrequent)
Coma (Rare)
Confusion (Frequent)
Delusions (Rare)
Depersonalization (Infrequent)

Depression
Disordered sense of smell (Rare)
Double vision (Rare)
▲ Dreaming abnormalities (1% to 5%)
Emotional lability (Frequent)
Euphoria (Infrequent)
Hallucinations (Infrequent)
Hostility (Infrequent)
▲ Insomnia (10% to 33%)
▲ Libido decreased (1% to 11%)
Libido increased (Infrequent)
Manic behavior, mild (0.1% to 1.8%)
▲ Nervousness (8% to 16%)
Neurosis, unspecified (Infrequent)
Paranoia (Infrequent)
Personality changes (At least 2%)
Photophobia (Infrequent)
Psychoses (Infrequent)
Serotonin syndrome
Sleep disturbances (Frequent)
Stupor (Rare)
Suicidal ideation
Suicide, attempt of (Infrequent)
Thinking abnormality (2%)

Pulmicort Respules
Aggression (Less than 1%)
Anxiety (Less than 1%)
Depression (Less than 1%)
▲ Emotional lability (1% to 3%)
Irritability (Less than 1%)
Psychiatric disturbances (Less than 1%)
Psychoses (Less than 1%)

Pulmicort Turbuhaler Powder
Aggression (Rare)
Anxiety (Rare)
Depression (Rare)
▲ Insomnia (1% to 3%)
Irritability (Rare)
Psychiatric disturbances (Rare)
Psychoses (Rare)

Quixin Ophthalmic Solution
▲ Photophobia (1% to 3%)

Rapamune
▲ Anxiety (3% to 20%)
▲ Confusion (3% to 20%)
▲ Depression (3% to 20%)
▲ Emotional lability (3% to 20%)
▲ Insomnia (13% to 22%)

Rebetol
▲ Agitation (5% to 8%)
▲ Anxiety (47%)
▲ Depression (13% to 36%)

▲ Emotional lability (7% to 47%)
▲ Insomnia (14% to 41%)
▲ Irritability (10% to 47%)
▲ Nervousness (3% to 6%)

Rebetron Combination Therapy
▲ Depression (23% to 36%)
▲ Emotional lability (7% to 12%)
▲ Insomnia (26% to 39%)
▲ Irritability (23% to 32%)
Mental performance, impairment
▲ Nervousness (4% to 5%)
Suicidal ideation (Less than 1%)
Suicide, attempt of (Less than 1%)

Rebif Injection
▲ Depression (25%)
Suicidal ideation
Suicide, attempt of

Recombivax HB
Agitation
Insomnia (Less to greater than 1%)
Irritability (Greater than 1%)
Sleep disturbances (Less than 1%)

ReFacto Vials
Insomnia

Relafen Tablets
Agitation (1%)
Anxiety (Less than 1%)
Confusion (Less than 1%)
Depression (Less than 1%)
▲ Insomnia (1% to 3%)
▲ Nervousness (1% to 3%)
Nightmares (Less than 1%)

Relpax Tablets
Agitation (Infrequent)
Anxiety (Infrequent)
Apathy (Infrequent)
Catatonia (Rare)
Confusion (Infrequent)
Dementia (Rare)
Depersonalization (Infrequent)
Depression (Infrequent)
Depression, psychotic (Rare)
Disordered sense of smell (Rare)
Double vision (Rare)
Dreaming abnormalities (Infrequent)
Emotional lability (Infrequent)
Euphoria (Infrequent)
Hallucinations (Rare)
Hysteria (Rare)
Insomnia (Infrequent)

Manic behavior (Rare)
Nervousness (Infrequent)
Neurosis, unspecified (Rare)
Photophobia (Infrequent)
Sleep disturbances (Rare)
Speech disturbances (Infrequent)
Stupor (Infrequent)
Thinking abnormality (Infrequent)

Remeron

Agitation (Frequent)
Anxiety (Frequent)
Apathy (Frequent)
Confusion (2%)
Delirium (Infrequent)
Delusions (Infrequent)
Dementia (Rare)
Depersonalization (Infrequent)
Depression (Frequent)
Depression, psychotic (Rare)
Disordered sense of smell (Rare)
Double vision (Rare)
▲ Dreaming abnormalities (4%)
Emotional lability (Infrequent)
Euphoria (Infrequent)
Hallucinations (Infrequent)
Hostility (Infrequent)
Libido increased (Infrequent)
Manic behavior (Approximately 0.2%)
Manic behavior, mild (Approximately 0.2%)
Mental performance, impairment
Neurosis, unspecified (Infrequent)
Paranoia (Infrequent)
Stupor (Rare)
Suicidal ideation
▲ Thinking abnormality (3%)

Remicade for IV Injection

Confusion (Greater than or equal to 0.2%)
▲ Depression (8%)
▲ Insomnia (6%)
Suicide, attempt of (Greater than or equal to 0.2%)

Reminyl

Aggression
Agitation (Greater than or equal to 2%)
Anxiety (Greater than or equal to 2%)
Apathy (Infrequent)
Confusion (Greater than or equal to 2%)

Delirium (Infrequent)
▲ Depression (7%)
Hallucinations (Greater than or equal to 2%)
▲ Insomnia (5%)
Libido increased (Infrequent)
Paranoia (Infrequent)

ReoPro Vials

Agitation (0.7%)
Anxiety (1.7%)
Coma (0.4%)
Confusion (0.6%)
Double vision (0.1%)
Insomnia (0.3%)
Thinking abnormality (2.1%)

Requip Tablets

Aggression (Infrequent)
Agitation (Infrequent)
Anxiety (1% or more)
Apathy (Infrequent)
Coma (Infrequent)
▲ Confusion (5%)
Delirium (Infrequent)
Delusions (Infrequent)
Dementia (Infrequent)
Depersonalization (Infrequent)
Depression (1% or more)
Double vision (2%)
▲ Dreaming abnormalities (11%)
Emotional lability (Infrequent)
Euphoria (Infrequent)
▲ Hallucinations (5% to 10%)
Insomnia (1% or more)
Libido decreased (Infrequent)
Libido increased (Infrequent)
Manic behavior (Infrequent)
Mental performance, impairment (Infrequent)
Nervousness (1% or more)
Neurosis, unspecified (Infrequent)
Paranoia (Infrequent)
Personality changes (Infrequent)
Photophobia (Infrequent)
Stupor (Infrequent)
Suicide, attempt of (Rare)

Rescriptor Tablets

Agitation
▲ Anxiety (2.4% to 6.7%)
Cognitive dysfunction
Confusion

▲ Depressive reactions (4.9% to 12.6%)
Disordered sense of smell
Disorientation
Double vision
Dreaming abnormalities
Emotional lability
Euphoria
Hallucinations
▲ Insomnia (1.2% to 5%)
Libido decreased
Manic behavior
Nervousness
Paranoia
Photophobia
Sleep disturbances

Restoril
Hangover
▲ Nervousness (4.6%)

Retrovir Capsules, Tablets & Syrup
Anxiety
Confusion
Depression
Emotional lability
▲ Insomnia (2.4% to 5%)
Irritability (1.6%)
Mental acuity, loss of
Nervousness (1.6%)
Photophobia

Retrovir IV Infusion
Anxiety
Confusion
Depression
Emotional lability
▲ Insomnia (3% to 5%)
Irritability (2%)
Manic behavior
Mental acuity, loss of
Nervousness (2%)
Photophobia

Reyataz Capsules
Agitation (Less than 3%)
Anxiety (Less than 3%)
Confusion (Less than 3%)
▲ Depression (3% to 8%)
Dreaming abnormalities (Less than 3%)
Emotional lability (Less than 3%)
Hallucinations (Less than 3%)
Hostility (Less than 3%)
▲ Insomnia (Less than (1% to 5%)

Libido decreased (Less than 3%)
Nervousness (Less than 3%)
Psychoses (Less than 3%)
Sleep disturbances (Less than 3%)
Suicide, attempt of (Less than 3%)

Ribavirin Capsules
▲ Agitation (5%)
▲ Anxiety (47%)
▲ Depression (23% to 36%)
▲ Emotional lability (7% to 47%)
▲ Insomnia (26% to 41%)
▲ Irritability (23% to 47%)
▲ Nervousness (4% to 6%)

Rifadin
Behavioral changes
Confusion
Mental performance, impairment
Psychoses (Rare)

Rifamate Capsules
Confusion
Memory impairment (Uncommon)
Mental performance, impairment
Psychoses, toxic (Uncommon)

Rifater Tablets
Anxiety
Behavioral changes
Confusion
Insomnia
Memory impairment (Uncommon)
Mental performance, impairment
Psychoses, toxic (Uncommon)

Rilutek Tablets
Agitation (Frequent)
Apathy (Infrequent)
Central nervous system depression (Rare)
Coma (Infrequent)
Confusion (Infrequent)
Delirium (Infrequent)
Delusions (Infrequent)
Dementia (Rare)
Depersonalization (Infrequent)
▲ Depression (4.2% to 6.1%)
Depression, psychotic (Rare)
Double vision (Rare)
Dreaming abnormalities (Rare)
Emotional lability (Infrequent)
Euphoria (Rare)
Hallucinations (Infrequent)
Hostility (Frequent)

Insomnia (2.1% to 2.9%)
Libido decreased (Infrequent)
Libido increased (Infrequent)
Manic behavior (Infrequent)
Paranoia (Infrequent)
Personality changes (Infrequent)
Photophobia (Rare)
Psychoses (Rare)
Stupor (Infrequent)
Suicide, attempt of (Infrequent)
Thinking abnormality (Infrequent)

Risperdal Consta Injection

Agitation (Frequent)
Anxiety (Frequent)
Apathy (Frequent)
Confusion (Infrequent)
Delirium (Infrequent)
Delusions (Frequent)
Dementia (Infrequent)
Depersonalization (Infrequent)
Depression (Frequent)
Depression, psychotic (Infrequent)
Dreaming abnormalities (Up to 2%)
Emotional lability (Infrequent)
Euphoria (Infrequent)
▲ Hallucinations (6% to 7%)
▲ Insomnia (13% to 16%)
Libido decreased (Infrequent)
Manic behavior (Infrequent)
Nervousness (Frequent)
Psychosis, activation (Frequent)
▲ Suicide, attempt of (1% to 4%)
▲ Thinking abnormality (Up to 3%)

Risperdal M-Tab Tablets & Oral Solution

▲ Aggression (1% to 3%)
▲ Agitation (22% to 26%)
▲ Anxiety (12% to 20%)
Apathy (Infrequent)
Catatonia (Infrequent)
Cognitive dysfunction
Coma (Rare)
Confusion (Infrequent)
Delirium (Rare)
Depression (Infrequent)
Double vision (Rare)
Dreaming abnormalities (Frequent)
Emotional lability (Rare)
Euphoria (Infrequent)
▲ Insomnia (23% to 26%)
Libido increased (Infrequent)
Manic behavior

Mental performance, impairment (Infrequent)
Mental status, altered
Nervousness (Frequent)
Nightmares (Rare)
Photophobia (Rare)
Sexual activity, decrease (Frequent)
Sexual dysfunction (Frequent)
Sleep disturbances (Frequent)
Stupor (Infrequent)
Suicide, attempt of (1.2%)

Risperdal Tablets

▲ Aggression (1% to 3%)
▲ Agitation (8% to 26%)
▲ Anxiety (4% to 20%)
Apathy (Infrequent)
Catatonia (Infrequent)
Cognitive dysfunction
Coma (Rare)
Confusion (Infrequent)
Delirium (Rare)
Depression (Infrequent)
Double vision (Rare)
Dreaming abnormalities (Frequent)
Emotional lability (Rare)
Euphoria (Infrequent)
▲ Insomnia (23% to 26%)
Libido increased (Infrequent)
▲ Manic behavior (8%)
Mental performance, impairment (Infrequent)
Mental status, altered
Nervousness (Frequent)
Nightmares (Rare)
Photophobia (Rare)
Sexual activity, decrease (Frequent)
Sexual dysfunction (Frequent)
Sleep disturbances (Frequent)
Stupor (Infrequent)
Suicide, attempt of (1.2%)

Ritalin LA Capsules

Behavior, inappropriate
Depression
▲ Insomnia (3.1%)
▲ Nervousness (Among most common)
Psychoses
Psychoses, toxic

Ritalin/Ritalin-SR

Behavior, inappropriate
Depression
▲ Insomnia (One of the two most common)

▲ Nervousness (One of the two most
  common)
  Psychoses
  Psychoses, toxic

Rituxan
▲ Agitation (1% to 5%)
▲ Depression (Among most frequent)
▲ Insomnia (1% to 5%)
▲ Nervousness (1% to 5%)

Rocaltrol
  Apathy
  Libido decreased
  Photophobia
  Psychoses (Rare)
  Sensory disturbances

Roferon-A Injection
  Agitation
▲ Anxiety (5% to 6%)
  Apathy (Infrequent)
▲ Behavioral changes (3%)
▲ Central nervous system reactions
  (Less than 5%)
  Coma (Rare to Infrequent)
▲ Confusion (Less than 4% to 8%)
▲ Depression (16% to 28%)
  Emotional lability (Less than 3%)
  Hallucinations (Infrequent)
  Hyperactivity (Infrequent)
▲ Insomnia (14%)
▲ Irritability (Less than 5% to 15%)
▲ Libido, changes (Less than 4%)
  Libido, loss of (Infrequent)
  Manic behavior
▲ Memory impairment (Less than 4%)
▲ Mental performance, impairment (4%)
▲ Mental status, altered (10% to 17%)
  Nervousness (Less than 3% to less
  than 5%)
  Neuropsychiatric disorders, life-
  threatening, aggravation of
  Psychoses
  Sedation (Infrequent)
  Sexual dysfunction (Infrequent)
▲ Sleep disturbances (5% to 11%)
▲ Smell disturbances (3%)
  Suicidal ideation
  Suicide, attempt of

Romazicon Injection
▲ Agitation (3% to 9%)
▲ Anxiety (3% to 9%)
  Confusion (Less than 1%)
  Delirium (Less than 1%)
▲ Depersonalization (1% to 3%)

▲ Depression (1% to 3%)
▲ Double vision (1% to 3%)
▲ Emotional lability (1% to 3%)
▲ Euphoria (1% to 3%)
▲ Insomnia (3% to 9%)
▲ Nervousness (3% to 9%)
▲ Paranoia (1% to 3%)
  Speech disturbances (Less than 1%)
  Stupor (Less than 1%)

Rowasa Rectal Suspension Enema
  Insomnia (0.12%)

Rythmol Tablets
  Anxiety (1.5% to 2%)
  Coma (Less than 1%)
  Confusion (Less than 1%)
  Depression (Less than 1%)
  Dreaming abnormalities (Less than
  1%)
  Insomnia (1.5%)
  Manic behavior (Less than 1%)
  Memory loss, short-term (Less than
  1%)
  Psychoses (Less than 1%)
  Smell disturbances (Less than 1%)
  Speech disturbances (Less than 1%)

Salagen Tablets
  Agitation (Rare)
  Anxiety (Less than 1%)
  Confusion (Less than 1%)
  Delusions (Rare)
  Depression (Less than 1%)
  Dreaming abnormalities (Less than
  1%)
  Emotional lability (Less than 1%)
  Hallucinations, visual (Rare)
  Insomnia (Less than 1%)
  Nervousness (Less than 1%)
  Speech disturbances (Less than 1%)
  Thinking abnormality (Less than 1%)

Sandimmune
  Anxiety (Rare)
  Confusion (2% or less)
  Consciousness, disorders of
  Depression (Rare)
  Psychiatric disturbances

Sandostatin Injection
  Anxiety (Less than 1%)
▲ Depression (1% to 4%)
  Libido decreased (Less than 1%)
  Paranoia (Less than 1%)

Sandostatin LAR Depot

▲ Anxiety (5% to 15%)
▲ Confusion (5% to 15%)
▲ Depression (5% to 15%)
▲ Hallucinations (1% to 4%)
▲ Insomnia (5% to 15%)
Libido decreased (Rare)
▲ Nervousness (1% to 4%)
Paranoia (Rare)
Suicide, attempt of (Rare)

Sarafem Pulvules

Agitation (Frequent)
▲ Anxiety (3% to 13%)
Apathy (Infrequent)
Behavior, violent
Central nervous system depression
(Infrequent)
Central nervous system stimulation
(Infrequent)
Coma (Rare)
Confusion (Frequent)
Delusions (Rare)
Depersonalization (Infrequent)
Disordered sense of smell (Rare)
Double vision (Rare)
▲ Dreaming abnormalities (3%)
Emotional lability (Frequent)
Euphoria (Infrequent)
Hallucinations (Infrequent)
Hostility (Infrequent)
▲ Insomnia (9% to 24%)
▲ Libido decreased (3% to 9%)
Libido increased (Infrequent)
Manic behavior, mild
▲ Nervousness (3% to 14%)
Neurosis, unspecified (Infrequent)
Orgasmic dysfunction, female
Paranoia (Infrequent)
Personality changes (Infrequent)
Photophobia (Infrequent)
Psychoses (Infrequent)
Sexual dysfunction
Sleep disturbances (Frequent)
Sociopathy (Rare)
Stupor (Rare)
Suicidal ideation
Suicide, attempt of (Infrequent)
▲ Thinking abnormality (3% to 6%)

Seasonale Tablets

Depression
Libido, changes
Mood changes
Nervousness

Seconal

Agitation (Less than 1%)
Anxiety (Less than 1%)
Central nervous system depression
(Less than 1%)
Confusion (Less than 1%)
Hallucinations (Less than 1%)
Insomnia (Less than 1%)
Nervousness (Less than 1%)
Nightmares (Less than 1%)
Psychiatric disturbances (Less than 1%)
Thinking abnormality (Less than 1%)

Sedapap Tablets

Agitation (Infrequent)
Confusion (Infrequent)
Depression (Infrequent)
Euphoria (Infrequent)
Excitability (Infrequent)
▲ Feeling, intoxicated (Among the most
frequent)
▲ Sedation (Among the most frequent)
Sluggishness (Infrequent)

Semprex-D Capsules

▲ Insomnia (4%)
▲ Nervousness (3%)
▲ Sedation (6% more common than with
placebo)

Septra

Apathy
Depression
Hallucinations
Insomnia
Nervousness

Serax

Excitement, paradoxical
Memory impairment

Serentil

Agitation
Behavior, inappropriate
Central nervous system reactions
Confusion
Dreaming abnormalities
Excitability
Libido, changes
Mental status, altered
Photophobia
Psychoses, aggravation
Speech, slurring

Serevent Diskus

▲ Anxiety (1% to 3%)
▲ Sleep disturbances (1% to 3%)

Serevent Inhalation Aerosol

Excitability
▲ Insomnia (1% to 3%)
▲ Nervousness (1% to 3%)

Seroquel Tablets

▲ Agitation (4%)
▲ Anxiety (4%)
Apathy (Infrequent)
Catatonia (Infrequent)
Confusion (Infrequent)
Delirium (Rare)
Delusions (Infrequent)
Depersonalization (Infrequent)
Dreaming abnormalities (Infrequent)
Emotional lability (Rare)
Euphoria (Rare)
Hallucinations (Infrequent)
Libido decreased (Rare)
Libido increased (Infrequent)
Manic behavior (Infrequent)
Mental performance, impairment
Mental status, altered
Paranoia (Infrequent)
Psychoses, aggravation (Infrequent)
Stupor (Infrequent)
Stuttering (Rare)
Suicide, attempt of (Infrequent)
Thinking abnormality (Infrequent)

Serostim for Injection

▲ Anxiety (1% to 5%)
▲ Depression (1% to 5%)
▲ Insomnia (3.9% to 5.9%)

Silvadene Cream 1%

Central nervous system reactions

Simulect for Injection

▲ Agitation (3% to 10%)
▲ Anxiety (3% to 10%)
▲ Depression (3% to 10%)
▲ Insomnia (Greater than or equal to 10%)

Sinequan

Confusion (Infrequent)
Disorientation (Infrequent)
Hallucinations (Infrequent)
Libido, changes

Singulair

Aggression
Agitation
Dreaming abnormalities (Very rare)
Hallucinations
Insomnia
Irritability (Very rare)

Skelaxin Tablets

▲ Irritability (Most frequent)
▲ Nervousness (Most frequent)

Solu-Medrol Sterile Powder

Depression
Euphoria
Insomnia
Mood changes
Personality changes
Psychiatric disturbances
Psychoses
Psychoses, aggravation

Soma Tablets

Agitation
Confusion
Depressive reactions
Disorientation
Double vision
Euphoria
Insomnia
Irritability

Sonata Capsules

Agitation (Infrequent)
Anxiety (Frequent)
Apathy (Frequent)
Confusion (1% or less)
Delusions (Rare)
Depersonalization (Less than 1% to 2%)
Depression (Frequent)
Disordered sense of smell (Less than 1% to 2%)
Double vision (Infrequent)
Emotional lability (Frequent)
Euphoria (Frequent)
Hallucinations (Less than 1%)
Hangover (Infrequent)
Hostility (Rare)
Insomnia (Infrequent)
Libido decreased (Infrequent)
Nervousness (Frequent)
Photophobia (Infrequent)
Sedation
Sleep disturbances (Rare)
Sleep talking (Rare)
Sleep walking (Rare)
Speech, slurring (Rare)
Stimulation (Rare)
Stupor (Rare)
Thinking abnormality (Frequent)

Soriatane Capsules

Aggression

Anxiety (Less than 1%)
▲ Depression (1% to 10%)
▲ Double vision (1% to 5%)
▲ Insomnia (1% to 10%)
Libido decreased (Less than 1%)
▲ Photophobia (1% to 10%)
Suicidal ideation

Spectracef Tablets
Dreaming abnormalities (0.1% to 1%)
Hyperactivity
Insomnia (0.1% to 1%)
Nervousness (0.1% to 1%)

Spiriva HandiHaler
▲ Depression (1% to 3%)

Sporanox Capsules
▲ Anxiety (3%)
Depression (Infrequent)
Dreaming abnormalities (2%)
Insomnia (Infrequent)
Libido decreased (0.2% to 1.2%)

Sporanox Oral Solution
Depression (1.1% to 2%)
Insomnia (Less than 2%)

St. Joseph 81 mg Aspirin
Agitation
Coma
Confusion

Stadol
Agitation (Less than 1%)
Anxiety (Greater than or equal to 1%)
Confusion (Greater than or equal to 1%)
Delusions
Depression (Less than 1%)
Dreaming abnormalities (Less than 1%)
Euphoria (Greater than or equal to 1%)
Floating feeling (Greater than or equal to 1%)
Hallucinations (Less than 1%)
Hostility (Less than 1%)
▲ Insomnia (Greater than or equal to 1% to 11%)
Nervousness (Greater than or equal to 1%)

Stalevo Tablets
Agitation (1%)
Anxiety (2%)
Central nervous system reactions
Confusion
Delusions
Dementia

Depression
Disorientation
Double vision
Dreaming abnormalities
Euphoria
▲ Hallucinations (4%)
Insomnia
Libido increased
Memory impairment
Mental acuity, loss of
Mental status, altered
Nervousness
Nightmares
Paranoia
Psychoses
Stimulation
Suicidal ideation

Strattera Capsules
Aggression (0.5%)
▲ Depression (2% to 6%)
▲ Dreaming abnormalities (4%)
▲ Insomnia (5% to 16%)
▲ Irritability (0.5% to 8%)
▲ Libido decreased (5% or greater)
▲ Mood changes (2% to 5%)
▲ Sedation (2% to 4%)
▲ Sexual dysfunction (3% or greater)
▲ Sleep disturbances (4%)

Streptomycin Sulfate Injection
Central nervous system depression, neonatal
Coma (Occasional)
Stupor

Striant Mucoadhesive
Anxiety
Depression
Emotional lability

Stromectol Tablets
Coma
Confusion
Mental status, altered
Stupor

Suboxone Tablets
▲ Anxiety (12%)
▲ Depression (11%)
▲ Insomnia (14% to 25%)
▲ Nervousness (6%)

Subutex Tablets
▲ Anxiety (12%)
▲ Depression (11%)

▲ Insomnia (21.4% to 25%)
▲ Nervousness (6%)

Sular Tablets

Anxiety (Less than or equal to 1%)
Confusion (Less than or equal to 1%)
Depression (Less than or equal to 1%)
Dreaming abnormalities (Less than or equal to 1%)
Insomnia (Less than or equal to 1%)
Libido decreased (Less than or equal to 1%)
Nervousness (Less than or equal to 1%)
Thinking abnormality (Less than or equal to 1%)

Suprane Liquid for Inhalation

Agitation (Less than 1%)

Surmontil Capsules

Agitation
Anxiety
Confusion
Delusions
Disorientation
Hallucinations
Insomnia
Libido decreased
Libido increased
Manic behavior, mild
Mental performance, impairment
Nightmares
Psychoses, aggravation

Sustiva Capsules

Agitation (Less than 2%)
Anxiety (Less than 2%)
Apathy (Less than 2%)
Confusion (Less than 2%)
Delusions
▲ Depression (2% to 3%)
Depression, aggravation of (Less than 2%)
Disordered sense of smell (Less than 2%)
Double vision (Less than 2%)
▲ Dreaming abnormalities (1% to 4%)
Emotional lability (Less than 2%)
Euphoria (Less than 2%)
Hallucinations (Less than 2%)
▲ Insomnia (1% to 7%)
Manic behavior
▲ Mental performance, impairment (1% to 9%)
Nervousness (1% to 2%)

Neurosis, unspecified
Paranoia
Psychoses (Less than 2%)
Suicide, attempt of

Symbyax Capsules

Coma (Infrequent)
Confusion (Infrequent)
Depersonalization (Infrequent)
Double vision (Infrequent)
Emotional lability (Infrequent)
Euphoria (Infrequent)
Hostility (Infrequent)
▲ Libido decreased (2% to 4%)
Libido increased (Rare)
Neurosis, unspecified (Infrequent)
Sleep disturbances (1% to 2%)
Speech disturbances (Up to 2%)
Suicide, attempt of (Infrequent)
▲ Thinking abnormality (Greater than or equal to 5% to 6%)

Symmetrel

Aggression
▲ Agitation (1% to 5%)
▲ Anxiety (1% to 5%)
Behavior, inappropriate
Coma
▲ Confusion (0.1% to 5%)
Consciousness, disorders of (Uncommon)
Delirium
Delusions
▲ Depression (1% to 5%)
▲ Dreaming abnormalities (1% to 5%)
Euphoria (0.1% to 1%)
▲ Hallucinations (1% to 5%)
▲ Insomnia (5% to 10%)
▲ Irritability (1% to 5%)
Libido decreased (0.1% to 1%)
Manic behavior
▲ Nervousness (1% to 5%)
Paranoia
Psychoses (0.1% to 1%)
Speech, slurring (0.1% to 1%)
Stupor
Suicidal ideation (Less than 0.1%)
Suicide, attempt of (Less than 0.1%)
Thinking abnormality (0.1% to 1%)

Synagis Intramuscular

Nervousness (More than 1%)

Synalgos-DC Capsules

▲ Sedation (Among most frequent)

Synarel Nasal Solution for Central Precocious Puberty
▲ Emotional lability (6%)

Synarel Nasal Solution for Endometriosis
▲ Depression (3% of patients)
▲ Emotional lability (15% of patients)
▲ Insomnia (8% of patients)
▲ Libido decreased (22% of patients)
Libido increased (1% of patients)

Synercid I.V.
Anxiety (Less than 1%)
Confusion (Less than 1%)
Insomnia (Less than 1%)

Synvisc
Anxiety
Listlessness

Tagamet
Agitation
Anxiety
Confusion (Occasional)
Depression
Disorientation
Hallucinations
Psychoses

Tambocor Tablets
▲ Anxiety (1% to 3%)
Apathy (Less than 1%)
Confusion (Less than 1%)
Depersonalization (Less than 1%)
▲ Depression (1% to 3%)
▲ Double vision (1% to 3%)
Dreaming abnormalities (Less than 1%)
Euphoria (Less than 1%)
Insomnia (1% to 3%)
Libido decreased (Less than 1%)
Photophobia (Less than 1%)
Speech disturbances (Less than 1%)
Stupor (Less than 1%)

Tamiflu
Confusion
Insomnia (1.1% to 1.2%)

Targretin Capsules
Agitation
Confusion
Depression
▲ Insomnia (4.8% to 11.3%)

Tarka Tablets
Anxiety (0.3% or more)

Confusion
Insomnia (Less frequent)
Libido decreased
Mental performance, impairment (Less frequent)
Psychoses

Tasmar Tablets
Agitation (1%)
Anxiety (1% or more)
Apathy (Infrequent)
▲ Confusion (10% to 11%)
Consciousness, disorders of (Four cases)
Delirium (Rare)
Delusions (Infrequent)
Depression (Frequent)
Disordered sense of smell (Infrequent)
Double vision (Infrequent)
▲ Dreaming abnormalities (16% to 21%)
Emotional lability (Frequent)
Euphoria (1%)
▲ Hallucinations (8% to 10%)
Hostility (Infrequent)
Hyperactivity (1%)
Irritability (1%)
Libido decreased (Infrequent)
Libido increased (Infrequent)
Manic behavior (Infrequent)
Mental acuity, loss of (1%)
Nervousness (Infrequent)
Panic attack (1%)
Paranoia (Infrequent)
Psychoses (Infrequent)
▲ Sleep disturbances (24% to 25%)
Speech disturbances (Frequent)
Thinking abnormality (Infrequent)

Taxotere Injection Concentrate
Confusion
▲ Impairment of sensation (7 of 134 patients)

Tegretol
Agitation
Confusion
Depression
Depression, aggravation of (Tegretol-XR Tablets)
Double vision
Hallucinations, visual
Psychosis, activation

Speech disturbances
Talkativeness

Temodar Capsules
▲ Anxiety (7%)
▲ Confusion (5%)
▲ Depression (6%)
▲ Double vision (5%)
▲ Insomnia (10%)

Tenormin
Catatonia
▲ Depression (0.6% to 12%)
Disorientation, place
Disorientation, time
▲ Dreaming (Up to 3%)
Emotional lability
Hallucinations
Memory loss, short-term
Neuropsychometrics performance,
  decrease
Psychoses
Sensorium, clouded

Tequin
Agitation (Less than 0.1%)
Anxiety (Less than 0.1%)
Central nervous system stimulation
Confusion (Less than 0.1%)
Depersonalization (Less than 0.1%)
Depression (Less than 0.1%)
Disordered sense of smell (Less than
  0.1%)
▲ Dreaming abnormalities (0.1% to 3%)
Euphoria (Less than 0.1%)
Hallucinations (Less than 0.1%)
Hostility (Less than 0.1%)
▲ Insomnia (0.1% to 3%)
Nervousness (Less than 0.1%)
Nightmares
Paranoia (Less than 0.1%)
Photophobia (Less than 0.1%)
Psychoses (Less than 0.1%)
Thinking abnormality (Less than
  0.1%)

Tessalon
Behavior, inappropriate (Isolated
  instances)
Confusion
Hallucinations, visual
Sedation

Testim 1% Gel
Depression
Insomnia (1% or less)

Mood changes (1% or less)
Smell disturbances (1% or less)

Testred Capsules
Anxiety
Depression
Libido decreased
Libido increased

Teveten HCT Tablets
Anxiety (Less than 1%)
Depression (Less than 1%)
Insomnia (Less than 1%)
Nervousness (Less than 1%)

Teveten Tablets
Anxiety (Less than 1%)
Depression (1%)
Insomnia (Less than 1%)
Nervousness (Less than 1%)

Thalomid Capsules
Agitation
Anxiety
Confusion
Depression
Double vision
Emotional lability
Euphoria
Hangover
Hostility
Impairment of sensation
Insomnia
Libido decreased
▲ Nervousness (2.8% to 9.4%)
Psychoses
Suicide, attempt of
Thinking abnormality

Thioridazine HCl Tablets
Agitation
Behavioral changes
Confusion, nocturnal (Extremely rare)
Dreaming abnormalities
Hyperactivity (Extremely rare)
Libido, changes
Psychiatric disturbances (Extremely
  rare)
Psychoses, aggravation

Thiothixene Capsules
Agitation
Insomnia
Psychotic symptoms, paradoxical
  exacerbation
Sedation

Tiazac Capsules
Depression (Less than 2%)
Dreaming abnormalities (Less than 2%)
Hallucinations (Less than 2%)
Insomnia (Less than 2%)
Nervousness (Less than 2%)
Personality changes (Less than 2%)
Sexual dysfunction (Less than 2%)

Tigan
Coma
Depression
Disorientation

Tikosyn Capsules
Anxiety (Greater than 2%)
▲ Insomnia (4%)

Timentin
Smell disturbances

Timolide Tablets
Catatonia
Confusion (Less than 1%)
Depression
Disorientation, place
Disorientation, time
Double vision
Emotional lability
Hallucinations
Insomnia (Less than 1%)
Libido decreased (Less than 1%)
Memory impairment
Mental performance, impairment
Nervousness (Less than 1%)
Nightmares
Sensorium, clouded

Timoptic
Anxiety (Less frequent)
Behavioral changes (Less frequent)
Catatonia
Confusion (Less frequent)
Depression (Less frequent)
Disorientation (Less frequent)
Disorientation, place
Disorientation, time
Double vision (Less frequent)
Emotional lability
Hallucinations (Less frequent)
Insomnia (Timoptic Sterile
  Ophthalmic Solution) (Less
  frequent—Timoptic in Ocudose)
Libido decreased
Memory loss, short-term

Mental performance, impairment
Nervousness (Less frequent)
Neuropsychometrics performance,
  decrease
Nightmares
Psychiatric disturbances (Less
  frequent)
Sensorium, clouded

Timoptic-XE Sterile Ophthalmic Gel Forming Solution
Anxiety
Behavioral changes
Catatonia
Confusion
Depression
Disorientation
Disorientation, place
Disorientation, time
Double vision
Emotional lability
Hallucinations
Insomnia
Libido decreased
Memory loss, short-term
Mental performance, impairment
Nervousness
Neuropsychometrics performance,
  decrease
Nightmares
Psychiatric disturbances
Sensorium, clouded

Tofranil
Confusion
Hallucinations

Topamax
▲ Aggression (2% to 9%)
▲ Agitation (3%)
▲ Anxiety (More than 1% to 10%)
▲ Apathy (1% to 3%)
▲ Confusion (4% to 14%)
Delirium (Infrequent)
Delusions (Infrequent)
Depersonalization (1% to 2%)
▲ Depression (5% to 13%)
Disordered sense of smell (Infrequent)
▲ Double vision (1% to 10%)
Dreaming abnormalities (Infrequent)
▲ Emotional lability (3%)
Euphoria (Frequent)
Hallucinations (Frequent)
▲ Insomnia (Frequent to 8%)

▲ Language problems, unspecified (2% to 10%)
Libido decreased (Less than 1% to 2%)
Libido increased (Rare)
Manic behavior (Rare)
▲ Memory impairment (2% to 14%)
▲ Mental performance, impairment (5% to 14%)
▲ Mental slowness (8% to 15.4%)
▲ Mood changes (4% to 9%)
▲ Nervousness (9% to 19%)
Neurosis, unspecified (Infrequent)
Paranoia (Infrequent)
Personality changes (Frequent)
Photophobia (Infrequent)
Psychoses (Frequent)
▲ Speech disturbances (4% to 13%)
Stupor (1% to 2%)
Suicide, attempt of (Frequent)

Toprol-XL Tablets
Catatonia
Confusion
▲ Depression (About 5 of 100 patients)
Disorientation, place
Disorientation, time
Emotional lability
Insomnia
Libido decreased
Memory loss, short-term
Neuropsychometrics performance, decrease
Nightmares
Sensorium, clouded

Toradol
Depression (1% or less)
Dreaming abnormalities (1% or less)
Euphoria (1% or less)
Hallucinations (1% or less)
Insomnia (1% or less)
Mental performance, impairment (1% or less)
Nervousness (1% or less)
Psychoses
Stupor (1% or less)
Thinking abnormality (1% or less)

Transderm Scōp Transdermal System
Confusion (Infrequent)
Disorientation (Infrequent)
Hallucinations (Infrequent)
Memory impairment (Infrequent)

Tranxene
Confusion (Less common)
Depression
Double vision
Insomnia
Irritability
Nervousness (Less common)
Speech, slurring

Trasylol Injection
Agitation (1% to 2%)
Anxiety (1% to 2%)
▲ Confusion (4%)
▲ Insomnia (3%)

Travatan Ophthalmic Solution
▲ Anxiety (1% to 5%)
▲ Depression (1% to 5%)
▲ Photophobia (1% to 4%)

Trecator-SC Tablets
Depression
Double vision (Rare)
Psychiatric disturbances

Trental Tablets
Agitation
Anxiety (Less than 1%)
Confusion (Less than 1%)
Depression (Less than 1%)
Insomnia
Nervousness

Trexall Tablets
Cognitive dysfunction
Confusion
Libido, loss of
Mood changes

Triavil Tablets
Anxiety
Catatonia
Coma
Confusion
Delusions
Disorientation
Dreaming abnormalities
Excitability
Excitement, paradoxical
Hallucinations
Insomnia
Irritability
Libido, changes
Manic behavior (Rare)
Manic behavior, mild (Rare)

Mental status, altered
Nightmares
Photophobia
Psychosis, activation
Sedation
Sleep disturbances

Tricor Tablets
Anxiety (Less than 1%)
Confusion (Less than 1%)
Depression
Insomnia (1%)
Libido decreased (2%)
Nervousness
Sleep disturbances (Less than 1%)

Trifluoperazine
Agitation
Catatonia
Central nervous system reactions
Insomnia
Jitteriness
Mental status, altered
Psychosis, activation (trifluoperazine tablets)

Trilafon
Catatonia
Confusion, nocturnal
Dreaming abnormalities
Hyperactivity
Hypnotic effects
Insomnia
Libido, changes
Paranoia
Photophobia
Psychoses
Speech, slurring
Suicidal ideation

Trileptal
Aggression
Agitation (1% to 2%)
▲ Anxiety (5% to 7%)
Apathy
Confusion (1% to 2%)
Delirium
Delusions
▲ Double vision (5% to 40%)
▲ Emotional lability (2% to 3%)
Euphoria
Feeling, intoxicated
Feeling, strange (1% to 2%)
Hysteria
▲ Insomnia (2% to 4%)
Libido decreased

Libido increased
Manic behavior
▲ Nervousness (2% to 4%)
Panic attack
Paranoia
Personality changes
Photophobia
▲ Speech disturbances (1% to 3%)
Stupor
Thinking abnormality (2%)

Tri-Levlen-21/Tri-Levlen-28
Depression
Double vision (Rare)
Insomnia
Libido, changes
Mood changes
Nervousness
Speech disturbances

Trilisate
Confusion (Rare)
Hallucinations (Rare)

Tri-Norinyl-28 Tablets
Depression
Double vision
Libido, changes
Nervousness

Triphasil-28 Tablets
Depression
Libido, changes
Mood changes
Nervousness

Trisenox Injection
▲ Agitation (5%)
▲ Anxiety (30%)
▲ Coma (5%)
▲ Confusion (5%)
▲ Depression (20%)
▲ Insomnia (43%)

Trivora-28 Tablets
Depression
Libido, changes
Nervousness

Trizivir Tablets
▲ Depression (9%)
▲ Insomnia (7% to 13%)
▲ Sleep disturbances (7% to 11%)

Trovan
Agitation (Less than 1%)
Anxiety (Less than 1%)
Central nervous system stimulation

Confusion (Less than 1%)
Depersonalization (Less than 1%)
Depression (Less than 1%)
Dreaming abnormalities (Less than 1%)
Emotional lability (Less than 1%)
Euphoria (Less than 1%)
Hallucinations (Less than 1%)
Insomnia (Less than 1%)
Libido decreased (Less than 1%)
Mental performance, impairment (Less than 1%)
Nightmares
Paranoia (Less than 1%)
Photophobia (Less than 1%)
Speech disturbances (Less than 1%)
Thinking abnormality (Less than 1%)

Trusopt Sterile Ophthalmic Solution
▲ Photophobia (Approximately 1% to 5%)

Tussionex Pennkinetic Suspension
Anxiety
Euphoria
Fear
Mental clouding
Mental performance, impairment
Mood changes
Sedation

Twinrix Vaccine
Agitation (Less than 1%)
Insomnia (Less than 1%)
Irritability (Less than 1%)
Photophobia (Less than 1%)

Tylenol, Children's, Plus Cold
Excitability
Insomnia
Nervousness

Tylenol, Children's, Plus Cold & Cough
Excitability

Tylenol, Maximum Strength, Allergy Sinus Day Time
Excitability

Tylenol, Maximum Strength, Flu NightTime
Excitability

Tylenol, Maximum Strength, Severe Cold & Flu NightTime Liquid
Excitability
Insomnia
Nervousness

Tylenol, Maximum Strength, Sinus Day Non-Drowsy/Sinus NightTime
Insomnia
Nervousness

Tylenol, Multi-Symptom, Cold Day Non-Drowsy
Insomnia
Nervousness

Tylenol, Multi-Symptom, Cold NightTime Complete Formula
Excitability
Insomnia
Nervousness

Tylenol Sinus Severe Congestion Caplets
Insomnia
Nervousness

Tylenol with Codeine
Euphoria
Mental performance, impairment
▲ Sedation (Among most frequent)

Ultracet
Anxiety (At least 1%)
Cognitive dysfunction
Confusion (At least 1%)
Depersonalization (Less than 1%)
Depression (Less than 1%)
Emotional lability (Less than 1%)
Euphoria (At least 1%)
Hallucinations (Less than 1%)
Insomnia (2%)
Mental performance, impairment
Nervousness (At least 1%)
Paranoia (Less than 1%)
Stupor (Less than 1%)
Thinking abnormality (Less than 1%)

Ultram Tablets
▲ Agitation (1% to 14%)
▲ Anxiety (1% to 14%)
▲ Central nervous system stimulation (7% to 14%)
Cognitive dysfunction (Less than 1%)

Coma
▲ Confusion (1% to 5%)
Depression (Less than 1%)
▲ Emotional lability (7% to 14%)
▲ Euphoria (1% to 14%)
▲ Hallucinations (Less than 1% to 14%)
Mental performance, impairment (Less than 1%)
▲ Nervousness (1% to 14%)
Serotonin syndrome
▲ Sleep disturbances (1% to 5%)
Speech disturbances (Infrequent)
Suicidal ideation (Infrequent)

Uniphyl Tablets
Behavioral changes
Insomnia
Irritability

Uniretic Tablets
Anxiety (Less than 1%)
Depression (Less than 1%)
Emotional lability (Less than 1%)
Insomnia (Less than 1%)
Libido decreased (Less than 1%)
Nervousness (Less than 1%)
Neurosis, unspecified (Less than 1%)

Uroqid-Acid No. 2 Tablets
Confusion

Vagifem Tablets
▲ Insomnia (3% to 5%)

Valcyte Tablets
▲ Agitation (Less than 5%)
▲ Confusion (Less than 5%)
▲ Depression (Less than 5%)
▲ Hallucinations (Less than 5%)
▲ Insomnia (16%)
▲ Psychoses (Less than 5%)
Sedation

Valium Tablets
Anxiety, paradoxical
Confusion (Infrequent)
Depression (Infrequent)
Double vision (Infrequent)
Excitement, paradoxical
Hallucinations
Insomnia
Libido, changes (Infrequent)
Rage
Sleep disturbances
Speech, slurring (Infrequent)
Stimulation

Valtrex Caplets
Agitation
Behavioral changes
Coma
Confusion
Consciousness, disorders of
▲ Depression (Less than 1% to 7%)
Hallucinations, auditory
Hallucinations, visual
Manic behavior
Psychoses

Vantin Tablets and Oral Suspension
Anxiety (Less than 1%)
Confusion (Less than 1%)
Dreaming abnormalities (Less than 1%)
Hallucinations (Less than 1%)
Insomnia (Less than 1%)
Nervousness (Less than 1%)
Nightmares (Less than 1%)

Varivax
Irritability (Greater than or equal to 1%)
Nervousness (Greater than or equal to 1%)
Sleep disturbances (Greater than or equal to 1%)

Vaseretic Tablets
Confusion
Depression
Dreaming abnormalities
Impairment of sensation
Insomnia (0.5% to 2%)
Libido decreased (0.5% to 2%)
Nervousness (0.5% to 2%)

Vasotec I.V. Injection
Confusion (0.5% to 1%)
Depression (0.5% to 1%)
Dreaming abnormalities (0.5% to 1%)
Impairment of sensation (0.5% to 1%)
Insomnia (0.5% to 1%)
Nervousness (0.5% to 1%)

Velcade for Injection
▲ Anxiety (14%)
▲ Impairment of sensation (23%)
▲ Insomnia (27%)

Ventolin HFA Inhalation Aerosol
Central nervous system stimulation
Insomnia

Verelan PM Capsules
Confusion (2% or less)
Insomnia (2% or less)
Psychoses (2% or less)

Vesanoid Capsules
▲ Agitation (9%)
▲ Anxiety (17%)
▲ Central nervous system depression (3%)
▲ Coma (3%)
▲ Confusion (14%)
▲ Dementia (3%)
▲ Depression (14%)
▲ Hallucinations (6%)
▲ Insomnia (14%)
▲ Memory impairment (3%)
▲ Speech disturbances (3%)

VFEND
Agitation (Less than 1%)
Anxiety (Less than 1%)
Coma (Less than 1%)
Confusion (Less than 1%)
Delirium (Less than 1%)
Dementia (Less than 1%)
Depersonalization (Less than 1%)
Depression (Less than 1%)
Double vision (Less than 1%)
Dreaming abnormalities (Less than 1%)
Euphoria (Less than 1%)
▲ Hallucinations (2.5% to 5.1%)
Insomnia (Less than 1%)
Libido decreased (Less than 1%)
▲ Photophobia (2.4% to 30%)
Psychoses (Less than 1%)
Suicidal ideation (Less than 1%)

Viadur Implant
Anxiety (Less than 2%)
▲ Depression (5.3%)

Viagra Tablets
Anxiety
Depression (Less than 2%)
Double vision
Dreaming abnormalities (Less than 2%)
Insomnia (Less than 2%)
Photophobia (Less than 2%)

Vicks 44D Cough & Head Congestion Relief
Insomnia
Nervousness

Vicks 44m, Pediatric, Cough & Cold Relief
Excitability
Insomnia
Nervousness

Vicks DayQuil Multi-Symptom Cold/Flu Relief
Insomnia
Nervousness

Vicks NyQuil
Excitability

Vicks NyQuil, Children's, Cold/Cough Relief
Excitability
Insomnia
Nervousness

Vicodin
Anxiety
Fear
Mental clouding
Mental performance, impairment
Mood changes
▲ Sedation (Among most frequent)

Vicoprofen Tablets
Agitation (Less than 1%)
▲ Anxiety (3% to 9%)
Confusion (Less than 3%)
Depression (Less than 1%)
Dreaming abnormalities (Less than 1%)
Euphoria (Less than 1%)
▲ Insomnia (3% to 9%)
Libido decreased (Less than 1%)
Mood changes (Less than 1%)
▲ Nervousness (3% to 9%)
Speech, slurring (Less than 1%)
Thinking abnormality (Less than 3%)

Vioxx
Anxiety (Greater than 0.1% to 1.9%)
Confusion
Depression (Greater than 0.1% to 1.9%)
Hallucinations (Less than 0.1%)
Insomnia (Greater than 0.1% to 1.9%)
Mental clouding (Greater than 0.1% to 1.9%)

Viracept
Anxiety (Less than 2%)
Depression (Less than 2%)
Emotional lability (Less than 2%)
Insomnia (Less than 2%)
Sexual dysfunction (Less than 2%)
Sleep disturbances (Less than 2%)
Suicidal ideation (Less than 2%)

Vistaril Intramuscular Solution
Mental performance,
  impairment (Seldom)

Vistide Injection
Agitation
Anxiety
Confusion
Delirium
Dementia
Depression
Double vision
Dreaming abnormalities
Hallucinations
Insomnia
Libido increased
Nervousness
Personality changes
Speech disturbances

Vivactil Tablets
Agitation
Anxiety
Anxiety, paradoxical
Confusion
Delusions
Disorientation
Hallucinations
Insomnia
Libido, changes
Manic behavior, mild
Mental performance, impairment
Nightmares
Psychoses, aggravation
Suicide, attempt of

Vivelle Transdermal System
Depression
Libido, changes

Vivelle-Dot Transdermal System
Anxiety
▲ Depression (3% to 10.6%)
▲ Insomnia (1.5% to 6.4%)
Libido, changes

Voltaren
Anxiety (Occasional)
Coma (Rare)
Confusion (Occasional)
Depression (Occasional)
Dreaming abnormalities (Occasional)
Hallucinations (Rare)
Insomnia (Occasional)
Nervousness (Occasional)

VoSpire Tablets
Central nervous system stimulation
Insomnia (2.4%)
Irritability (Less frequent)
▲ Nervousness (8.5%)

Wellbutrin SR/Wellbutrin XL
▲ Agitation (3% to 9%)
▲ Anxiety (5% to 6%)
Central nervous system stimulation
  (1% to 2%)
Coma
Confusion
Delirium
Delusions
Depersonalization (Infrequent)
Double vision
Dreaming abnormalities (At least 1%)
Emotional lability (Infrequent)
Euphoria
Hallucinations
Hostility (Infrequent)
▲ Insomnia (5% to 16%)
▲ Irritability (2% to 3%)
Libido decreased (Infrequent)
Libido increased
Manic behavior
Manic behavior, mild (Rare)
▲ Memory impairment (Up to 3%)
▲ Nervousness (3% to 5%)
Paranoia
Psychoses
Psychosis, activation
Suicidal ideation (Infrequent)

Wellbutrin Tablets
▲ Agitation (31.9%)
▲ Anxiety (3.1%)
▲ Auditory disturbances (5.3%)
Coma
▲ Confusion (8.4%)
Delirium
Delusions (1.2%)
Depersonalization (Infrequent)
Depression (Frequent)
Double vision (Rare)

Dreaming abnormalities
Euphoria (1.2%)
Frigidity, unspecified (Infrequent)
Hallucinations (Frequent)
▲ Hostility (5.6%)
▲ Insomnia (18.6%)
▲ Libido decreased (3.1%)
Libido increased (Frequent)
Manic behavior (Frequent)
Manic behavior, mild (Frequent)
Memory impairment (Infrequent)
Mood changes (Infrequent)
Paranoia (Infrequent)
Psychoses (Infrequent)
▲ Sedation (19.8%)
▲ Sensory disturbances (4%)
Sexual dysfunction (Frequent)
▲ Sleep disturbances (4%)
Suicidal ideation (Rare)
Thinking abnormality (Infrequent)

Xalatan Ophthalmic Solution
Double vision (Less than 1%)
▲ Photophobia (1% to 4%)

Xanax Tablets
Aggression (Rare)
Agitation (Rare; 2.9%)
▲ Anxiety (16.6%)
Behavior, inappropriate (Rare)
▲ Central nervous system depression
(13.8% to 13.9%)
▲ Cognitive dysfunction (28.8%)
▲ Confusion (9.9% to 10.4%)
Depersonalization
▲ Depression (13.8% to 13.9%)
Depressive reactions
Double vision
Dreaming abnormalities (1.8%)
Fear (1.4%)
Hallucinations (Rare)
Hostility (Rare)
▲ Insomnia (8.9% to 29.4%)
▲ Irritability (33.1%)
▲ Libido decreased (14.4%)
▲ Libido increased (7.7%)
▲ Libido, changes (7.1%)
Manic behavior
Manic behavior, mild
▲ Memory impairment (33.1%)
Mental performance, impairment
▲ Nervousness (4.1%)
Rage (Rare)
Sedation
Sensorium, clouded
Sensory disturbances

▲ Sexual dysfunction (7.4%)
Sleep disturbances (Rare)
Smell disturbances
Speech, slurring
Stimulation (Rare)
Suicidal ideation
Suicide, attempt of
Talkativeness (2.2%)

Xanax XR Tablets
Aggression (Rare to Infrequent)
Agitation (Rare to frequent)
Anger (Infrequent)
▲ Anxiety (1.1% to 7.8%)
Apathy (Infrequent)
Central nervous system depression
Confusion (1.5%)
▲ Depersonalization (5.7%)
▲ Depression (1.3% to 12.1%)
Disorientation (1.5%)
Dreaming abnormalities (Infrequent)
Euphoria (Infrequent)
Feeling, intoxicated (Infrequent)
Hallucinations (Rare to Infrequent)
Hangover (Infrequent)
Hostility (Rare)
▲ Insomnia (24.2%)
Irritability (Rare to frequent)
▲ Libido decreased (6%)
Libido increased (Frequent)
Manic behavior (Infrequent)
Manic behavior, mild (Infrequent)
▲ Memory impairment (15.4%)
▲ Mental performance, impairment
(7.2%)
Mood changes (Infrequent)
▲ Nervousness (22%)
Nightmares (Frequent)
Photophobia (Infrequent)
Rage (Rare)
▲ Sedation (45.2%)
Sexual dysfunction (2.4%)
Sleep disturbances (Rare)
Sleep talking (Infrequent)
Sleeping, excessive (1.3%)
Sluggishness (Infrequent)
Stimulation (Rare)
Stupor (Infrequent)
Suicidal ideation (Infrequent)
Talkativeness (Infrequent)

Xeloda Tablets
▲ Confusion (Less than 5%)
▲ Depression (Less than 5%)
▲ Insomnia (Less than 5%)

▲ Irritability (Less than 5%)
▲ Mood changes (5%)
▲ Sedation (Less than 5%)

Xenical Capsules
▲ Anxiety (2.8% to 4.4%)
▲ Depression (3.4%)
▲ Sleep disturbances (3.9%)

Xopenex Inhalation Solution
Anxiety (2.7%)
Insomnia
▲ Nervousness (2.8% to 9.6%)

Xylocaine 2% Jelly
Confusion
Double vision
Euphoria
Nervousness

Xyrem Oral Solution
Agitation (Frequent)
▲ Anxiety (3% to 6%)
Apathy (Infrequent)
Coma (Infrequent)
▲ Confusion (3% to 13%)
Depersonalization (Infrequent)
▲ Depression (6%)
▲ Dreaming abnormalities (3% to 9%)
Euphoria (Infrequent)
Hallucinations
Hangover (Infrequent)
▲ Insomnia (5%)
Libido decreased (Infrequent)
▲ Nervousness (7%)
▲ Sleep disturbances (6% to 14%)
▲ Sleep walking (7%)
Stupor (Frequent)
Thinking abnormality

Yasmin 28 Tablets
Depression (Greater than 1%)
Emotional lability
Libido, changes
Nervousness (Greater than 1%)

Zaditor Ophthalmic Solution
▲ Photophobia (Less than 5%)

Zanaflex Tablets
Agitation (Infrequent)
Anxiety (Frequent)
Dementia (Rare)
Depersonalization (Infrequent)
Depression (Frequent)
Dreaming abnormalities (Infrequent)
Emotional lability (Infrequent)

Euphoria (Infrequent)
▲ Nervousness (3%)
▲ Sedation (48%)
▲ Speech disturbances (3%)
Stupor (Infrequent)
Suicide, attempt of (Rare)
Thinking abnormality (Infrequent)

Zantac Injection
Agitation
Confusion (Rare)
Depression (Rare)
Hallucinations
Insomnia
Libido decreased

Zantac Tablets, Granules & Syrup
Agitation (Rare)
Confusion (Rare)
Depression (Rare)
Hallucinations (Rare)
Insomnia (Rare)
Libido, loss of (Occasional)

Zarontin
Aggression
Depression (Rare)
Euphoria
Hyperactivity
Irritability
Libido increased (Rare)
Mental performance, impairment
Psychiatric disturbances
Psychoses
Psychosis, paranoid (Rare)
Sleep disturbances
Suicidal ideation (Rare)

Zaroxolyn Tablets
Depression
Insomnia
Nervousness (Less than 2%)

Zebeta Tablets
Anxiety
Catatonia
Depression (Up to 0.2%)
Disorientation, place
Disorientation, time
Dreaming abnormalities
Emotional lability
Hallucinations
Insomnia (1.5% to 2.5%)
Libido decreased
Mental performance, impairment

Sensorium, clouded
Sleep disturbances

Zelnorm Tablets
Depression
Emotional lability
Mental performance, impairment
Sleep disturbances
Suicide, attempt of
Tenseness

Zenapax for Injection
▲ Anxiety (2% to 5%)
▲ Depression (2% to 5%)
▲ Insomnia (Greater than 5%)

Zerit
▲ Insomnia (29%)

Zestoretic Tablets
Confusion
Depression (0.3% to 1%)
Double vision
Insomnia
Irritability
Libido decreased (0.3% to 1%)
Memory impairment
Nervousness
Photophobia
Sleeping, excessive

Zestril Tablets
Confusion (0.3% to 1%)
Depression (Greater than 1%)
Double vision (0.3% to 1%)
Impairment of sensation (0.3% to 1%)
Insomnia (0.3% to 1%)
Irritability (0.3% to 1%)
Libido decreased (0.4%)
Mental performance, impairment
  (0.3% to 1%)
Nervousness (0.3% to 1%)
Photophobia (0.3% to 1%)
Sleeping, excessive (0.3% to 1%)

Zevalin Injection
▲ Anxiety (4%)
▲ Insomnia (5%)

Ziac Tablets
Anxiety
Catatonia
Depression
Disorientation, place
Disorientation, time
Dreaming abnormalities
Emotional lability

Hallucinations
Insomnia (1.1% to 1.2%)
Libido, loss of (0.4%)
Memory impairment
Mental performance, impairment
Sensorium, clouded
Sexual dysfunction
Sleep disturbances

Ziagen
▲ Insomnia (7% to 13%)
▲ Sleep disturbances (7%)

Zithromax
Agitation (1% or less—Zithromax
  Capsules, Tablets & Oral
  Suspension)
Insomnia (1% or less)
Nervousness (1% or less)

Zocor Tablets
Anxiety
Depression
Insomnia
Libido, loss of
Memory loss, short-term

Zofran Injection
▲ Agitation (2% to 6%)
▲ Anxiety (2% to 6%)
▲ Sedation (8%)

Zofran Tablets & Oral Solution
▲ Agitation (6%)
▲ Anxiety (6%)
▲ Sedation (20%)

Zoladex
▲ Anxiety (1% to 5%)
▲ Depression (1% to 54%)
▲ Emotional lability (60%)
▲ Insomnia (5% to 11%)
▲ Libido decreased (61%)
▲ Libido increased (12%)
▲ Nervousness (3% to 5%)
▲ Sexual dysfunction (21%)
  Thinking abnormality (1% or greater)

Zoladex 3-month
Anxiety
Depression
Emotional lability
Insomnia
Nervousness
▲ Sexual dysfunction (One of the two
  most common)
  Thinking abnormality

Zoloft

Aggression (Infrequent to 2%)
▲ Agitation (1% to 6%)
▲ Anxiety (4%)
Apathy (Infrequent)
Coma (Rare)
Confusion (Infrequent)
Delusions (Infrequent)
Depersonalization (Infrequent)
Depression (Infrequent)
Depression, aggravation of (Infrequent)
Double vision (Rare)
Dreaming abnormalities (Infrequent)
Emotional lability (Infrequent)
Euphoria (Infrequent)
Hallucinations (Infrequent)
Illusion, unspecified (Rare)
▲ Insomnia (12% to 28%)
▲ Libido decreased (1% to 11%)
Libido increased (Rare)
Manic behavior, mild (Approximately 0.4%)
Mental performance, impairment (1.3% to 2%)
▲ Nervousness (6%)
Paranoia (Infrequent)
Photophobia (Rare)
Psychoses
Serotonin syndrome
Sexual dysfunction (Frequent)
Suicidal ideation (Rare)
Suicide, attempt of

Zometa for Intravenous Infusion

▲ Agitation (12.8%)
▲ Anxiety (9% to 14%)
▲ Confusion (12.8%)
▲ Depression (12%)
▲ Insomnia (14% to 15.1%)

Zomig Nasal Spray

Agitation (Infrequent to less than 2%)
Anxiety (Infrequent)
Apathy (Rare)
Confusion (Infrequent)
Depersonalization (Infrequent)
Depression (Infrequent)
Disordered sense of smell (Infrequent)
Dreaming abnormalities (Rare)
Euphoria (Rare)
Insomnia (Infrequent to less than 2%)
Irritability (Rare)
Manic behavior (Rare)

Nervousness (Infrequent)
Photophobia (Rare)
Psychoses (Rare)
Speech disturbances (Infrequent)
Thinking abnormality (Infrequent)

Zomig/Zomig-ZMT Tablets

Agitation (Infrequent)
Anxiety (Infrequent)
Apathy (Rare)
Depression (Infrequent)
Disordered sense of smell (Infrequent)
Double vision (Rare)
Emotional lability (Infrequent)
Euphoria (Rare)
Hallucinations (Rare)
Insomnia (Infrequent)
Irritability (Rare)

Zonegran Capsules

▲ Agitation (9%)
▲ Anxiety (3%)
Behavior, schizophrenic (2%)
▲ Confusion (6%)
▲ Depression (6%)
Disordered sense of smell (Infrequent)
▲ Double vision (6%)
Dreaming abnormalities (Infrequent)
Euphoria (Infrequent)
▲ Insomnia (6%)
▲ Irritability (9%)
Libido decreased (Infrequent)
▲ Memory impairment (6%)
▲ Mental performance, impairment (6%)
▲ Mental slowness (4%)
Nervousness (2%)
Photophobia (Rare)
▲ Speech disturbances (5%)

Zosyn

▲ Agitation (2.1% to 7.1%)
▲ Anxiety (1.2% to 3.2%)
Combativeness (1% or less)
Confusion (1% or less)
Depression (1% or less)
Hallucinations (1% or less)
▲ Insomnia (4.5% to 6.6%)
Photophobia (1% or less)

Zovia Tablets

Depression
Libido, changes
Nervousness

Zovirax Capsules, Tablets & Suspension

Agitation

Behavior, violent
Coma
Confusion
Consciousness, disorders of
Delirium
Hallucinations
Psychoses

Zovirax for Injection

Agitation (Approximately 1%)
Behavior, inappropriate
Coma (Approximately 1%)
Confusion (Approximately 1%)
Delirium
Hallucinations (Approximately 1%)
Psychoses

Zyban Tablets

Agitation (Frequent)
▲ Anxiety (8%)
Central nervous system stimulation
(Infrequent)
Coma
Confusion (Infrequent)
Delirium
Delusions
Depersonalization (Infrequent)
Depression (Frequent)
Double vision
▲ Dreaming abnormalities (5%)
Emotional lability (Infrequent)
Euphoria
Hallucinations
Hostility (Infrequent)
▲ Insomnia (31% to 40%)
Irritability (Frequent)
Libido decreased (Infrequent)
Libido (increased)
Manic (behavior)
Manic behavior, mild (Rare)
Memory impairment (Infrequent)
▲ Mental performance, impairment (9%)
▲ Nervousness (4%)
Paranoia
Psychoses
Psychosis, activation
Suicidal ideation (Infrequent)
Thinking abnormality (1%)

Zydone Tablets

Anxiety
Fear
Mental clouding
Mental performance, impairment
Mood changes
▲ Sedation (Among most frequent)

Zyprexa/Zyprexa ZYDIS

▲ Agitation (23%)
Alcohol abuse (Infrequent)
Antisocial reaction (Infrequent)
▲ Anxiety (9%)
Apathy
Behavioral changes
Central nervous system stimulation
(Infrequent)
Coma (Infrequent)
Confusion
Delirium (Infrequent)
Depersonalization (Infrequent)
Depression
Double vision (Infrequent)
Dreaming abnormalities
Emotional lability
Euphoria (2%)
Hallucinations
Hangover (Infrequent)
▲ Hostility (15%)
▲ Insomnia (20%)
Libido decreased (Infrequent)
Libido increased
▲ Nervousness (16%)
Obsessive compulsive symptoms
(Infrequent)
Paranoia
▲ Personality changes (8%)
Phobic disorder (Infrequent)
Schizophrenia, precipitation
Sociopathy (Infrequent)
Speech difficulties (2%)
Speech disturbances (2%)
Stupor (Infrequent)
Stuttering (Infrequent)
Suicide, attempt of (Frequent)
Thinking abnormality

Zyrtec

Agitation (Less than 2%)
Anxiety (Less than 2%)
Confusion (Less than 2%)
Depersonalization (Less than 2%)
Depression (Less than 2%)
Disordered sense of smell (Less than
(2%)
Emotional lability (Less than 2%)
Euphoria (Less than 2%)
▲ Insomnia (Less than 2% to 9%)
Irritability
Libido decreased (Less than 2%)
Mental performance, impairment
(Less than 2%)
Nervousness (Less than 2%)

Sleep disturbances (Less than 2%)
Thinking abnormality (Less than 2%)

Zyrtec-D

Agitation (Less than 2%)
Anxiety (Less than 2%)
Central nervous system stimulation
Confusion (Less than 2%)
Depersonalization (Less than 2%)
Depression (Less than 2%)
Disordered sense of smell (Less than (2%)
Emotional lability (Less than 2%)
Euphoria (Less than 2%)

Excitability
Fear
Hallucinations
▲ Insomnia (4%)
Libido decreased (Less than (2%)
Mental performance, impairment (Less than 2%)
Nervousness (Less than 2%)
Sleep disturbances (Less than 2%)
Tenseness
Thinking abnormality (Less than 2%)

Zyvox

Insomnia (2.5%)

Psychotropic Herbs and Supplements

Some 35 herbs and nutritional supplements are currently being used to relieve a variety of mental and emotional problems, ranging from memory loss to nervousness and depression. The profiles in this section describe the verified effects of these products, as well as other claims made by their proponents. Also included is a brief discussion of their proposed mechanism of action and the contraindications, precautions, and potential interactions associated with their use. Information on use in pregnancy, typical dosage, and the effects of overdosage can be found as well. The profiles are organized alphabetically by the substance's most commonly used name.

The information in these profiles is drawn from in-depth monographs in two alternative medicine handbooks published by *Physicians' Desk Reference®—PDR® for Herbal Medicines* and *PDR® for Nutritional Supplements*.

5-HTP

Why people take it

5-HTP (5-hydroxytryptophan) is valued primarily for its effect on depression. In one carefully designed study, it was found to work slightly better than the serotonin-boosting drug Luvox. Other trials, however, have been less encouraging.

5-HTP is also an effective weight-loss aid. In one carefully controlled clinical trial—and again in a follow-up study—it trimmed 5 percent off the subjects' body weight in a matter of weeks.

Although more research is needed, 5-HTP also seems to act as a mild painkiller. Clinical studies have shown it to be helpful for treating insomnia, fibromyalgia, and chronic tension headache.

What it is; how it works

As the name suggests, 5-HTP is a chemical cousin of the amino acid tryptophan. In fact, the body needs tryptophan to make 5-HTP, which is then converted to serotonin in the brain. Scientists believe it is this conversion that accounts for the antidepressant effects of 5-HTP.

5-HTP is commercially derived from the seeds of an African plant. Small amounts are also found in food, including bananas, tomatoes, plums, avocados, eggplant, walnuts, and pineapples.

Avoid if...

5-HTP should be strictly avoided by anyone with carcinoid tumors (small growths usually found in the intestinal tract). It is not recommended for people with heart disease, chest pain, or high blood pressure, as well as those who have suffered heart attacks. It should not be taken by patients who show signs of an allergic reaction to any component of the supplement. It should also be avoided during treatment with, or within 2 weeks of stopping, a drug classified as an MAO inhibitor, such as the antidepressants Nardil and Parnate.

Special cautions

A severe, life-threatening condition known as eosinophilia-myalgia syndrome (EMS) has been reported in a few people taking 5-HTP. Marked by muscle pain and excessive white blood cell counts, the syndrome has been linked to contaminants in the 5-HTP preparation, rather than 5-HTP itself. Switching preparations in one group of patients resolved the problem.

Supplemental 5-HTP has been know to cause side effects such as nausea, diarrhea, loss of appetite, vomiting, difficulty breathing, and irregular heartbeat. In high doses it can also cause neurological problems such as dilated pupils, abnormally sensitive reflexes, loss of muscle coordination, and blurred vision.

Possible drug interactions

Remember that 5-HTP should never be used while taking a prescription MAO inhibitor such as Nardil or Parnate, or within 2 weeks of stopping an MAO inhibitor. At least in theory, a dangerous interaction is possible.

It's also best to avoid combining 5-HTP with serotonin-boosting drugs such as Luvox and the antidepressant medications Paxil, Prozac, Serzone, and Zoloft. The excessive levels of serotonin that may result can trigger sweating, tremors, flushing, confusion, and agitation. Likewise, 5-HTP should not be combined with tricyclic antidepressants such as Elavil and Tofranil or with the antidepressant herb St. John's wort.

Similarly, patients should not use 5-HTP while taking migraine drugs such as Amerge, Imitrex, and Zomig, since the combination could increase the risk of adverse reactions. In addition, combining 5-HTP with the migraine remedy Sansert reduces its effectiveness; and 5-HTP can also decrease the effectiveness of the antihistamine Periactin.

Patients should also be aware that certain drugs, such as the blood pressure drugs Aldomet and Dibenzyline, inhibit 5-HTP's effect, while Carbidopa enhances its delivery to the brain.

Special information about pregnancy and breastfeeding

Pregnant women and nursing mothers should not take 5-HTP.

Available preparations and dosage

Because of its potential side effects, experts advise against taking 5-HTP by itself. In Europe, doctors prescribe 5-HTP along with carbidopa, which suppresses the conversion of 5-HTP to serotonin outside the brain, reducing serotonin-induced side effects in the body. High daily doses of 100 milligrams to 2 grams of 5-HTP are needed to gain the desired effects; and only when taken with carbidopa are such doses considered reasonably safe. The lower doses of 5-HTP found in dietary supplements are not likely to have any effect.

Overdosage

No overdoses have been reported. However, the first symptoms of overdose would likely be those of excessive serotonin levels, such as sweating, tremors, flushing, confusion, agitation, and rapid heartbeat. Untreated, the patient's condition could progress to coma, seizures, and death. If an overdose is suspected, seek medical help immediately.

Acetylcysteine

Why people take it

Acetylcysteine—also known as N-acetylcysteine or NAC—is available as a supplement and as a prescription drug. Doctors use it to treat acetaminophen overdose. They also prescribe it to thin the excess mucus that occurs with certain lung disorders, such as acute and chronic bronchitis.

As a nutritional supplement, acetylcysteine shows potential as a treatment for age-related memory loss, and may be helpful for a broad range of disorders. The evidence so far shows that it is an effective treatment for chronic obstructive pulmonary disease. Preliminary studies suggest supplemental acetylcysteine may be helpful for treating, and possibly preventing, heart disease. It also shows promise in treating diabetes, certain cancers, and immune system disorders, although more studies are needed.

Because of its liver-protecting abilities, some researchers suggest that acetylcysteine could help treat infectious liver diseases such as hepatitis C, although this remains to be seen.

What it is; how it works

Acetylcysteine is derived from the amino acid L-cysteine. It is preferred over L-cysteine because it is more stable and possibly better absorbed. As a drug, acetylcysteine is well known for its ability to increase liver stores of the antioxidant glutathione, which is why it's routinely given to treat liver damage due to acetaminophen poisoning. This versatile drug is also available as an inhalant called Mucomyst, which binds to mucus proteins, making the gluey substance more watery.

When given as a supplement, acetylcysteine may protect certain cells from damage and even death by increasing levels of L-cysteine and glutathione. Researchers believe this is why it may be helpful for diabetes, heart disease, and cancer, among other things. One study, however, suggested that acetylcysteine might have actually caused DNA damage in certain cells, leading the researchers to believe that the supplement may promote some cancers while inhibiting others.

Avoid if...

There are no known reasons to avoid acetylcysteine at recommended dosages.

Special cautions

Acetylcysteine may be harmful if given early in the treatment of critically ill patients and should therefore be used cautiously, if at all. Caution is also advised for patients with a history of peptic ulcers, since the supplement's mucus-thinning properties could disrupt the stomach's protective mucosal lining. In addition, acetylcysteine metabolism is reduced in patients with chronic liver disease as well as in preterm newborns.

Potential side effects of acetylcysteine include nausea, vomiting, diarrhea, headaches, and rashes. It could also interfere with certain tests for diabetes.

There is a small possibility that acetylcysteine could cause kidney stones. Patients who tend to form kidney stones, especially those caused by excess cystine, should not take this supplement.

Possible drug interactions
Acetylcysteine can cause headaches in those taking nitrates for the treatment of chest pain. It could also decrease blood levels of certain anti-seizure drugs such as Tegretol and Carbatrol.

Special information about pregnancy and breastfeeding
Pregnant women should use acetylcysteine only if prescribed by a doctor, and nursing mothers should avoid the supplement entirely.

Available preparations and dosage
When taking a prescription form of acetylcysteine such as Mucomyst, patients should follow their doctor's instructions.

As a dietary supplement, the usual dose is 600 milligrams, taken anywhere from once daily to 3 times a day. It is available in capsule and tablet form. Common brands include NAC Fuel by TwinLab and N-A-C Sustain by Jarrow Formulas. Various generic brands are also available. Patients should follow the manufacturer's labeling whenever possible.

An important note: Patients should be sure to drink at least 6 to 8 glasses of water a day to prevent the formation of kidney stones.

Overdosage
No information on overdosage with oral supplements is available. When given intravenously for acetaminophen poisoning, high doses can produce symptoms similar to those of a severe allergic reaction, including swelling of the face and throat and heart and blood pressure irregularities.

Acetyl-L-Carnitine

Why people take it
Acetyl-L-carnitine may help slow the progression of Alzheimer's disease in some patients, especially younger ones. In one of its larger clinical trials, researchers found that acetyl-L-carnitine provided the most benefit for patients less than 62 years old. Other, smaller studies showed benefits for patients with mild to moderate symptoms. None of the studies, however, found that the supplement could reverse Alzheimer's disease.

Acetyl-L-carnitine also shows some promise in treating stroke, diabetes-related nerve disorders, and Down's syndrome. Although more research is needed, preliminary evidence suggests it may also help slow the aging process, improve depression in the elderly, treat the mental decline associated with alcoholism, and improve sperm motility.

What it is; how it works

Acetyl-L-carnitine is a close chemical relative of the amino acid compound L-carnitine. The body makes acetyl-L-carnitine in the brain, liver, and kidneys. It also occurs naturally in meat and dairy products.

Acetyl-L-carnitine helps the body's cells produce energy. It also promotes production of acetylcholine, a chemical messenger that plays a role in memory and learning. In lab studies, acetyl-L-carnitine also appears to protect cells from the damage that often occurs during aging.

Researchers aren't sure how acetyl-L-carnitine helps improve memory and nerve disorders. Some speculate it may boost brain levels of acetylcholine, which is deficient in patients with age-related dementias like Alzheimer's. Others suggest it may slow the death of nerve cells in the brain and other parts of the body.

Avoid if...

There are no known reasons to avoid acetyl-L-carnitine at recommended dosages.

Special cautions

People with seizure disorders should take acetyl-L-carnitine only under a doctor's supervision. Although the incidence is rare, a few patients have experienced an increase in the number or severity of their seizures while taking this supplement.

Caregivers of patients with Alzheimer's should be aware that acetyl-L-carnitine has caused increased agitation in some patients.

Acetyl-L-carnitine may also cause stomach upsets, including nausea, vomiting, diarrhea, and cramping.

Possible drug interactions

Certain drugs may cause a decrease in the body's acetyl-L-carnitine levels. These include the anti-HIV drugs Videx, Hivid, and Zerit, and anti-seizure drugs such as Depakote. Antibiotics that contain pivalic acid, such as Spectracef, may also decrease acetyl-L-carnitine levels, although this shouldn't pose a problem if treatment is only for a short period.

Special information about pregnancy and breastfeeding

Because the safety of acetyl-L-carnitine supplements during pregnancy hasn't been tested, women who are pregnant or breastfeeding should not take this substance.

Available preparations and dosage

Typical dosages range from 500 milligrams to 2 grams daily, given in several smaller doses. Some studies, including those for Alzheimer's, used 3 grams a day. There is no consensus on how long treatment must continue before results are observed. Patients should follow the manufacturer's labeling whenever available.

Acetyl-L-carnitine is available in tablets and capsules from various companies, including TwinLab, Now Foods, and Jarrow Formulas. It is also a common ingredient in "brain boosting" supplements.

Overdosage
There are no reports of overdosage.

Alpha-GPC

Why people take it
Alpha-GPC (L-alpha-glycerylphosphorylcholine) is promoted as a "cognitive enhancer" that helps treat age-related memory disorders, including Alzheimer's disease and the aftereffects of stroke. It is also popular among athletes and bodybuilders because of its reputed ability to boost levels of human growth hormone. Although some preliminary research does support these claims, more convincing evidence is needed before this supplement can be considered effective.

What it is; how it works
Alpha-GPC is made from a naturally occurring soybean fat known as lecithin. It is closely related to phosphatidylcholine and serves a similar purpose, acting as a source of the essential nutrient choline. (Alpha-GPC is 40 percent choline.) In theory, the body could use this to make acetylcholine, a chemical messenger that plays a role in memory and learning and also encourages the body to secrete human growth hormone.

Whether alpha-GPC does indeed get converted into acetylcholine, and how much of it actually reaches the brain, is unknown. Animal studies suggest that the conversion does occur, but researchers aren't certain whether this would have any therapeutic effect on the body. Further clinical studies, as well as safety data, are needed to confirm any potential benefits of using this supplement.

Avoid if...
Unless patients have an allergic reaction, there are no known reasons to avoid alpha-GPC supplements.

Special cautions
There are no reported precautions for alpha-GPC, although it should probably not be given to children due to the lack of safety data.

Possible drug interactions
There are no known drug interactions.

Special information about pregnancy and breastfeeding
Due to the lack of safety data, pregnant and breastfeeding women should not take alpha-GPC.

Available preparations and dosage

Typical daily dosages range from 500 milligrams to 1 gram. No information is available on how long treatment should last. Patients should follow the manufacturer's labeling whenever available.

Overdosage

No information on overdosage is available.

Arginine Pyroglutamate

Why people take it

Preliminary research suggests that arginine pyroglutamate may help improve verbal memory in the elderly. One study also found that it may be useful for treating the memory problems associated with chronic alcohol abuse. Definitive evidence for both claims, however, is still lacking.

This supplement is also used by some bodybuilders because the arginine it contains tends to promote the production of human growth hormone. Enthusiasts believe this hormone builds muscle mass and promotes endurance. Many experts, however, warn against adult use of human growth hormone—or substances that promote its release.

What it is; how it works

Arginine pyroglutamate is a water-soluble molecule made from the naturally occurring acids L-arginine and pyroglutamate. The supplement is absorbed by the small intestine, where its two acids are split and sent to various metabolic pathways in the body. Some of the pyroglutamate appears to enter the brain, although more studies are needed to confirm this.

Scientists aren't sure how arginine pyroglutamate may help memory problems, but it appears to be structurally related to the experimental drug piracetam. Piracetam has been studied in Europe as a possible "cognitive enhancer," although clinical trials give mixed results on its effectiveness. Piracetam seems to enhance membrane fluidity in the brain and also appears to interact with glutamate receptors in the brain. Some researchers speculate that arginine pyroglutamate may work in a similar fashion.

In addition to stimulating the production of human growth hormone, the arginine in this compound serves as raw material for nitric oxide, one of the factors that promotes the dilation of blood vessels.

Avoid if...

Unless patients have an allergic reaction, there are no known reasons to completely avoid arginine pyroglutamate. However, due to its impact on the production of human growth hormone, it is not recommended for children, pregnant women, or nursing mothers.

Special cautions

Arginine pyroglutamate may cause minor stomach upsets. Because the arginine it contains affects insulin secretion, people with diabetes should take this compound with care. Arginine may also aggravate schizophrenia. Patients with this problem would be wise to avoid the substance.

Possible drug interactions

Because arginine tends to dilate blood vessels, it's best to avoid combining this supplement with Viagra, heart medicines such as nitroglycerin, and some blood pressure medicines. Patients should also check with their doctor before combining arginine pyroglutamate with any psychotropic medication.

Special information about pregnancy and breastfeeding

Due to its impact on human growth hormone, pregnant and breastfeeding women should not take arginine pyroglutamate.

Available preparations and dosage

Typical dosages range from 500 milligrams to 1,000 milligrams a day. A 500-milligram dose delivers about 150 milligrams of L-arginine and 350 milligrams of pyroglutamate. Patients should follow the manufacturer's labeling whenever available.

Overdosage

No information on overdosage is available.

Bugleweed

Latin name: Lycopus virginicus
Other names: Gypsywort, Sweet Bugle, Water Bugle, Virginia Water Horehound

Why people take it

Bugleweed is used in cases of mildly overactive thyroid, a condition which often leads to nervousness and insomnia. Bugleweed also relieves tension and pain in the breast.

What it is; how it works

Bugleweed does its work by inhibiting the action of thyroid hormones and the reproductive hormones associated with the menstrual cycle. It also reduces levels of prolactin, the hormone that triggers breast milk production.

The herb is a creeping perennial that grows to about 2 feet in height and has a mint-like smell. It was discovered on the banks of streams in

Virginia, but now grows throughout North America. A closely related plant called Gypsywort is found in Europe. Bugleweed's medicinal value lies in its fresh or dried above-ground parts collected during the flowering season.

Avoid if...
Bugleweed should not be used by people with thyroid insufficiency, those taking a thyroid medication, or anyone who will be undergoing a diagnostic test that employs radioactive isotopes.

Special cautions
Warn patients against stopping use of this herb abruptly. This could lead to excessive thyroid activity and symptoms such as breast pain.

Possible drug interactions
Do not use bugleweed if you are taking any thyroid medications.

Special information about pregnancy and breastfeeding
No harmful effects are known.

Available preparations and dosage
Bugleweed is available as a crushed dry herb, as a freshly pressed juice, and in liquid extract form. The dried herb may be used to make tea.

The best dosage of bugleweed varies according to the patient's age and weight. The daily dosage for an adult usually lies between 1 and 2 grams of bugleweed for tea. Liquid extracts should supply approximately 20 milligrams of the active ingredient.

Overdosage
Extremely high doses of bugleweed can cause enlargement of the thyroid gland. Suddenly stopping use of the herb can make the problem worse.

CDP-Choline

Why people take it
Touted as a stronger type of choline (see separate entry), CDP-choline is said to offer many of the same benefits. Like choline, it may sharpen the memory and boost learning, two traits that might help stall aging in the brain. Also like choline, it promises to alleviate some movement disorders. It has been tested in people who have trouble carrying out voluntary movements such as walking—people with Parkinson's disease, for example. And it has also been studied as a treatment for involuntary movements such as the continual chewing or writhing motions (called *tardive dyskinesia*) occasionally triggered by long-term use of antipsy-

chotic drugs. In addition, some evidence hints that it may be useful for treating stroke, brain injury, and vision problems.

Unfortunately, results to date have been less than spectacular. A number of studies have detected small improvements when people with Alzheimer's disease, head injury, or tardive dyskinesia were treated with large doses of the substance. Minor benefits have also been observed in studies of people with multi-infarct dementia or stroke. Likewise, some people with Parkinson's disease have enjoyed small improvements in their symptoms when CDP-choline was added to their regular drug regimen. On balance, though, experts agree that bigger and better studies are needed before CDP-choline can win a passing grade.

(Note, however, that although CDP-choline may still be considered experimental in the U.S., it's sold widely under a variety of brand names in Europe and Japan for treatment of all the disorders discussed above.)

What it is; how it works

Routinely present throughout the body, CDP-choline is a necessary ingredient in the production of compounds known as phospholipids, especially the phospholipid known as phosphatidylcholine. (See separate entry for more on the use of this compound as a dietary supplement.) In turn, phosphatidylcholine and other phospholipids are used to manufacture cell membranes, the barriers protecting the intricate machinery that allows cells to function properly.

Some research suggests that CDP-choline, like other forms of choline, boosts production of acetylcholine, a chemical messenger (neurotransmitter) that's deficient in the brains of people with Alzheimer's disease. Other studies indicate that the drug promotes formation and repair of cell membranes, thereby limiting nerve damage and aiding in recovery from stroke and head injury. To some degree, CDP-choline may also increase the circulation in the brain. At this point, however, all of these possible effects need further verification.

Avoid if...

Because of its potential impact on neurotransmitters, patients who suffer from bipolar disorder or Parkinson's disease should check with their doctor before using CDP-choline. The product should not be used by patients who are allergic to choline. It is also unwise to give it to children due to the lack of safety data.

Special cautions

People in research studies have taken as much as 1,000 milligrams of CDP-choline per day with few ill effects. The most common complaints have been gastrointestinal reactions (nausea, vomiting, diarrhea, stomach pain), dizziness, rash, headache, and fatigue. A small number of people have suffered low blood pressure and changes in heart rate after taking CDP-choline.

Possible drug interactions

CDP-choline could theoretically interfere with the action of drugs that work by blocking the effect of acetylcholine (for example, the antinausea medication scopolamine). Patients who are taking such drugs should check with their doctor before using CDP-choline.

Special information about pregnancy and breastfeeding

Because the safety of CDP-choline supplements during pregnancy hasn't been evaluated, it's best for pregnant and breastfeeding women to avoid them.

Available preparations and dosage

Typically, CDP-choline is sold in capsule form in strengths of 200 to 250 milligrams. Daily dosages of 500 to 2,000 milligrams are typical. Patients should follow the manufacturer's labeling whenever available.

Overdosage

No information on overdosage is available.

Choline

Why people take it

Choline is a vitamin-like compound that has recently gained acceptance as an essential nutrient. It is so important, in fact, that the National Academy of Sciences has increased the recommended intake for pregnant and nursing women in order to ensure normal brain development in the baby. Although the body can produce a certain amount of choline on its own, we also need to get an adequate supply from food. Studies have found that a dietary deficiency can lead to liver and kidney disorders, high blood pressure, and heart disease.

Choline is one of the building blocks of acetylcholine, a key chemical messenger in the nervous system. This fact has led researchers to study it for a wide variety of neurologic disorders, including the tremors and rigidity of Parkinson's disease, the memory loss of Alzheimer's disease, and the involuntary movements of tardive dyskinesia and Huntington's disease.

Choline shows promise as a way to control mood swings and reduce memory loss. Increases in acetylcholine in the brain seem to improve mood, alertness, and mental energy, while low levels are linked to depression and lack of concentration. Many people who use choline notice an improvement in overall disposition. Athletes who take choline-based supplements report greater energy and less fatigue. And researchers have also found that choline boosts the mood of at least some Alzheimer's patients. (Choline will not, however, cure Alzheimer's, though it might play a role in staving it off.)

Choline is also reported to help prevent or treat liver disorders such as cirrhosis, fatty liver, hepatitis, and damage due to drugs or toxic substances. In addition, it may confer some benefit to those with eczema, kidney and gallbladder disorders, and manic depression. It also appears to have some positive impact on cholesterol levels, although not to the extent of two related compounds, phosphatidylcholine and lecithin.

What it is; how it works

Closely related to the B-complex family of vitamins, choline is found in all living cells, where it supports the integrity of cell membranes. In addition to its role in the production of acetylcholine, it aids in the transport of fats into the body's cells. An adequate supply of choline is essential for proper liver function. It is also needed to hold down levels of the amino acid homocysteine—which plays a role in heart disease.

Avoid if...

People suffering from ulcers should avoid choline supplements, since they can increase stomach acid. And because of its potential impact on neurotransmitters, patients who have manic depression or Parkinson's disease should check with their doctor before using choline.

Special cautions

Choline is generally safe and nontoxic even at high levels, although megadoses are usually reserved for treating manic depression and other serious psychiatric disorders. High doses (more than 3.5 grams a day) can be counterproductive, actually causing depression in some people, and can lead to a fishy body odor and other side effects such as dizziness, low blood pressure, excessive sweating, nausea, diarrhea, and abdominal cramps. Excess consumption can also overstimulate muscles, leading to tightening in the shoulders and neck and, ultimately, a tension headache.

Certain patients should be particularly cautious of high doses, including those with liver or kidney disease, depression, Parkinson's disease, and trimethylaminuria (a rare genetic disorder that interferes with choline metabolism).

Possible drug interactions

Choline could theoretically interfere with the action of drugs that work by blocking the effect of acetylcholine (for example, the antinausea medication scopolamine). It's best to check with the doctor before combining choline with such drugs.

On the other hand, the anticancer drug methotrexate could interfere with choline metabolism and possibly block its beneficial effects. Animal studies show that choline supplementation may help offset this problem.

Special information about pregnancy and breastfeeding

For healthy women who eat a balanced diet, choline supplements are usually unnecessary during pregnancy and breastfeeding.

Available preparations and dosage

The new RDI for choline ranges from 425 to 550 milligrams per day for adults. Few people suffer an outright deficiency, since Americans' average dietary intake ranges from 500 to 1,000 milligrams daily. However, since many of the foods richest in choline, such as egg yolks and liver, are also high in cholesterol, intake may be falling among people who watch their cholesterol levels.

Choline is available as tablets, capsules, softgels, powder, and liquids. The different forms of Choline (bitartrate, chloride, and dihydrogencitate) vary in potency from 36 to 75 percent choline. The optimal daily supplemental dose of choline is often pegged at 250 to 350 milligrams, although some studies have used as much as 1,200 milligrams. To lower homocysteine levels, choline requires the vitamins B_6, B_{12}, and folic acid. Aside from eggs and liver, good dietary sources of choline are wheat germ, lentils, peanuts, soybeans, iceberg lettuce, cabbage, and cauliflower. Supplements such as lecithin and phosphatidylcholine supply significant amounts of basic choline. It's also found in brewer's yeast, and is often included in B-complex and multinutrient vitamins or sold in combination with vitamin B_6 or inositol. It should be taken with meals.

Overdosage

A dose of 200 grams or more (100 times the typical dose) could prove dangerous. Sustained megadoses of 3,500 milligrams daily or more tend to cause muscle stiffness and digestive upsets.

DHA

Why people take it

DHA (docosahexaenoic acid) is an essential fatty acid that has piqued interest in the medical community due to its abundant presence in fish oil (see separate entry). Researchers suspect that DHA supplements could prove useful for treating certain brain and mood disorders. DHA deficiencies have been noted in people with attention deficit disorder, dyslexia, depression, age-related mental decline, and Alzheimer's disease. DHA levels are also inadequate in those suffering from postpartum depression or the cognitive decline associated with alcoholism. In addition, DHA has gained a reputation as a "brain booster." Japanese students, for example, take DHA supplements to improve their performance on exams.

Researchers are also studying DHA as a potential treatment for vision disorders such as age-related macular degeneration, and for certain serious congenital disorders such as cystic fibrosis. Like the fish oil in which it's found, DHA is also used to reduce triglyceride levels and protect against heart disease

What it is; how it works

One of the two omega-3 fatty acids found in fish oil, DHA is essential for proper brain and eye development in infants. DHA is abundant in breast milk, and many studies have linked breast-feeding to better vision and higher IQ in children, particularly those born prematurely. Scientists in the U.S. are still debating whether adding DHA to commercial infant formulas confers similar benefits, but the World Health Organization already recommends it. In fact, DHA-enriched formulas are widely available in Japan and countries throughout Europe, and were finally approved for use in the U.S. in 2001.

The science backing DHA supplementation for children and adults is far more questionable. While most nutritionists agree that it's important to get enough omega-3 fats from the diet, the value of supplements is unknown. In theory, DHA could be helpful for various psychiatric disorders because it's one of the main fatty acids in brain and eye tissue, and it appears to be necessary for proper brain-cell signaling. However, most of the research is preliminary, and many of the findings contradict each other. Although some studies, for example, have revealed low DHA levels in people with attention deficit disorders and Alzheimer's disease, clinical trials of DHA supplements failed to improve these conditions.

Avoid if...

Because of possible blood-thinning effects, DHA supplements should not be used by patients who have a bleeding disorder such as hemophilia or a tendency to hemorrhage.

Special cautions

There have been no reports of serious reactions, even in those taking up to 6 grams of DHA a day for 3 months. Potential minor side effects include a fishy odor or taste, belching, upset stomach, nausea, and diarrhea. Infants and children should not take DHA supplements unless monitored by a physician.

Because DHA supplements may slightly increase the risk of hemorrhage, patients should stop taking them before any type of surgery. It is also advisable to check the Special Cautions in the entry on Fish Oil. In theory, the same warnings could apply to DHA supplements.

Possible drug interactions

There have been no reported interactions to date. But patients who are taking a blood-thinning drug such as aspirin or Coumadin should still check with their doctor before taking DHA supplements, which could further thin the blood. Increased bleeding could also occur if DHA is taken with supplemental garlic or the herb ginkgo. Possible signs of an interaction could include increased bruising and nosebleeds.

Special information about pregnancy and breastfeeding
Pregnant and breastfeeding women should check with their doctor before using DHA supplements.

Available preparations and dosage
DHA supplements are made from fish or algae and are available in capsule form; a common brand is Neuromins. Typical dosages for pregnant and nursing women are 100 to 200 milligrams a day. The dosages needed to lower triglyceride levels are higher, ranging from 1 to 4 grams a day. DHA is also found in certain infant formulas and in specially raised eggs.

Patients should choose preparations that contain vitamin E to prevent oxidation of the easily damaged oil; they should also take a little extra vitamin E to prevent oxidation within the body. To prevent stomach upset, DHA supplements should be taken with meals.

Overdosage
No information on overdosage is available.

DHEA

Why people take it
Whether or not DHEA (dehydroepiandrosterone) should be taken at all as an unregulated over-the-counter supplement is a controversial issue. There is evidence that this steroid can improve feelings of well-being and increase sexual satisfaction—but only in people whose adrenal glands are functioning poorly. There are also preliminary results indicating that it may have a beneficial effect on some people with major depression.

Much of the controversy arises because DHEA is being promoted as a cure for many other ailments and has taken on the reputation of an anti-aging remedy—kind of a modern-day fountain of youth. Advocates claim that it can encourage weight loss; boost sex drive and the immune system; enhance mood, memory, and energy; and reverse the aging process. Some proponents even suggest using it as an adjunct to conventional cancer therapy. And a number of anti-aging clinics recommend taking it as early as your 40's or 50's to fight off old age and remain biologically young. Athletes take it in large doses to enhance their performance. However, much of the research behind these claims was done on laboratory animals, and experts caution that the results of such studies cannot be translated to humans. The long-term effects of DHEA supplementation are not known and since it is a powerful hormone, it should be used with great caution and only under a doctor's supervision.

What it is; how it works

DHEA is a steroid hormone produced primarily by the adrenal glands. It is the most abundant hormone in the body, with the highest concentrations found in the brain. The only known function of DHEA is as a precursor hormone, meaning that it is a source material which the body converts into other hormones, such as estrogen and testosterone. It peaks in production by the age of 25 and gradually declines until, by age 70, levels may be more than 80 percent below their earlier highs.

Low DHEA levels have been associated with certain diseases, such as Alzheimer's, cancer, diabetes, multiple sclerosis, lupus, and other immune function disorders. For this reason, researchers have been tempted to speculate that supplementation with a synthetic form of DHEA could reverse these diseases, much like hormone replacement therapy reduces some of the symptoms of menopause by returning the hormone balance to a premenopausal state. However, it has not yet been proven that either the diseases or the aging process itself are a result of lowered levels of DHEA, and it is not yet clear whether using DHEA is helpful or, in the long run, harmful.

Despite all this, there are physicians who recommend use of this hormone to treat a variety of ailments or combat the effects of aging. Anyone who decides to try DHEA should seek out a qualified physician willing to plan and monitor their treatment.

Avoid if...

DHEA should not be used by patients who have a hormone-related cancer—or a family history of one—including breast, cervical, uterine, ovarian, and prostate cancers. The hormone should also not be given to children.

Special cautions

DHEA has been known to cause acne, facial hair growth, and deepening of the voice in some women, and there are reports of breast enlargement in men taking high doses, probably because it triggers hormone production. The hormone may also lower levels of "good" HDL cholesterol and raise levels of cancer-promoting hormones. There have been a few reports of DHEA-related hepatitis and insulin resistance.

Possible drug interactions

Natural DHEA levels may be boosted by certain drugs, including Xanax, Cardizem, testosterone, and the sports supplement androstenedione. Adding even more DHEA through supplementation increases the risk of side effects.

Certain other drugs tend to lower natural DHEA levels. Drugs in this category include Danocrine (used to treat endometriosis), corticosteroids, insulin, and morphine.

Special information about pregnancy and breastfeeding
Because of its hormonal effects, DHEA should not be used during pregnancy or while breastfeeding.

Available preparations and dosage
DHEA is available in capsule, tablet, cream, and spray form in strengths ranging from 5 milligrams to 200 milligrams. The typical daily dose is 25 to 50 milligrams.

Dosage should be set by a physician following a blood test or saliva test can tell if a true deficiency exists and how much, if any, supplemental DHEA is needed. Individuals taking DHEA will also periodically need to visit their doctor to have their blood levels monitored and the dosage adjusted accordingly.

Overdosage
No information on overdosage is available.

DL-Phenylalanine

Why people take it
An "essential" amino acid that the body can't manufacture on its own, phenylalanine is one of the raw materials for three of the nervous system's most important chemical messengers: dopamine, epinephrine, and norepinephrine. The body can also convert it to phenylethylamine, a mood-boosting substance that's said to have pain-relieving effects as well.

In light of these properties, phenylalanine has been proposed as a treatment for depression, Parkinson's disease, and chronic-pain conditions such as arthritis. Trials for arthritis have yielded conflicting results, but preliminary trials for depression have proved encouraging. Phenylalanine has also been promoted as an appetite suppressant and sexual stimulant, but its effectiveness for these purposes remains unproven.

What it is; how it works
There are two types of phenylalanine: L-phenylalanine and D-phenylalanine. The "L" variety occurs primarily in animal protein and supports production of dopamine, epinephrine, norepinephrine, and the mood elevator phenylethylamine. The "D" form of the substance is typically found in plant protein and blocks an enzyme that degrades enkephalins, a group of natural substances that the body produces to deaden pain.

Because of this action, D-phenylalanine (but not L-phenylalanine) has been proposed as a treatment for chronic pain. L-phenylalanine, on the other hand, is usually taken to relieve depression. The "L" form of the substance has also been suggested as a treatment for vitiligo, a disease characterized by abnormal white blotches of skin due to loss of pigmentation.

D-phenylalanine alone is not available as a nutritional supplement, but both forms are created during the commercial manufacturing process and are typically sold as DL-phenylalanine or DLPA. Products containing only the "L" form are also available. Phenylalanine is also an ingredient of the popular artificial sweetener aspartame.

Avoid if...

Children born without the ability to process phenylalanine can build up dangerous levels of this amino acid, leading to mental retardation, seizures, extreme hyperactivity, and psychosis. Youngsters with this condition—called phenylketonuria—must follow a special diet designed to supply no more phenylalanine than necessary, and must be monitored regularly for excess phenylalanine in the blood.

Special cautions

L-phenylalanine has also been reported to exacerbate involuntary movements (tardive dyskinesia) in schizophrenic patients. Anyone with this disorder should therefore use DL-phenylalanine with extreme caution. Caution is also warranted for people with high blood pressure or an anxiety disorder; phenylalanine tends to aggravate these conditions.

DL-phenylalanine occasionally causes mild nausea, heartburn, or headache. Because it can have significant effects on mood, it's best to use this type of phenylalanine only under a doctor's supervision.

Possible drug interactions

Phenylalanine supplements should never be combined with drugs known as MAO inhibitors, including the antidepressants Nardil and Parnate; a surge in blood pressure could result. It is also best to avoid combining phenylalanine with antipsychotic drugs, since it increases the likelihood of tardive dyskinesia.

On the other hand, taking phenylalanine with the drug Eldepryl may boost the antidepressant activity of both agents.

Special information about pregnancy and breastfeeding

Phenylalanine supplements are not recommended during pregnancy and breastfeeding.

Available preparations and dosage

DL-phenylalanine is available in capsule, tablet, and powder form. Typical dosages range from 375 milligrams to 2.25 grams daily.

Overdosage
There are no reports of overdosage.

Fish Oil

Why people take it
Fish oil is one of those nutritional megastars that holds promise for a wide variety of chronic conditions. The latest buzz focuses on its potential to alleviate symptoms of several serious psychiatric illnesses, including bipolar disorder, schizophrenia, and severe depression. Preliminary research hints that it may also be helpful for warding off Alzheimer's disease and treating attention deficit disorder. Keep in mind, however, that most of this research is still in its infancy, and more definitive answers are needed before fish oil supplements can be recommended.

While the effects of fish oil on the brain are still being investigated, more is known about its benefits for the heart. Rich in omega-3 fatty acids, fish oil seems to help protect against cardiovascular disease. Studies have found that it lowers blood pressure, keeps arteries clear following angioplasty, and reduces the risk of sudden cardiac death, death from heart attack, and stroke. If all that weren't enough, there's some evidence that fish oil could be useful for treating arthritis (particularly rheumatoid arthritis), Crohn's disease, kidney disease, and ulcerative colitis.

What it is; how it works
The two omega-3 fatty acids contained in fish oil are eicosapentaenoic acid (EPA) and docosahexaenoic acid (DHA). These acids are especially prevalent in oily cold-water fish such as cod, tuna, mackerel, herring, and salmon. Because the omega-3s come from algae that are then eaten by krill that in turn are eaten by larger fish, farm-raised fish that have been fed grain alone may contain little or none of these beneficial acids.

Researchers speculate that because Western diets have changed drastically in the last century, Americans may be deficient in omega-3 fatty acids. The brain and nervous system rely on fatty acids like EPA and DHA to regulate cell membrane function. These acids may even play a role in the proper regulation of serotonin, a chemical messenger that has gained fame for its role in depression and other mental illnesses. Indeed, depression rates have soared in recent decades, and global studies show that depression is less likely to occur in countries that consume the most fish. But while the evidence so far is tantalizing, fish oil's effectiveness against psychiatric disorders has yet to be tested in major clinical trials.

In the prevention of heart disease, omega-3s are thought to work by lowering total cholesterol and triglyceride levels, raising "good" HDL cholesterol, and thinning the blood. They lower the level of fibrinogen, the blood clotting factor, and keep blood platelets from becoming too sticky, all of which helps to prevent the buildup of artery-clogging plaque. Fish oil also tends to dilate the blood vessels, which can help to lower blood pressure in those with hypertension.

Some researchers have found that the omega-3s have anti-inflammatory properties that appear to make them helpful in the treatment of arthritis, Crohn's disease, endometriosis, lupus, and ulcerative colitis. In addition, laboratory experiments suggest that these fatty acids may have an anti-cancer effect. They are also being studied for a variety of other disorders, including eczema, psoriasis, and Raynaud's phenomenon.

Avoid if...
Because of their blood-thinning effects, fish oil supplements should be used only with great caution by patients who have a bleeding disorder such as hemophilia or a tendency to hemorrhage.

Special cautions
Although fish oil tends to have beneficial effects on "good" HDL cholesterol and total cholesterol levels, high doses sometimes cause an increase in "bad" LDL cholesterol levels. A few studies have also suggested that fish oil supplements may cause an increase in the blood sugar levels of people with diabetes. Diabetics should discuss use of these supplements with their doctor and closely monitor their blood sugar for any change.

Because fish oil supplements may slightly increase the risk of hemorrhage, patients should stop taking them before any type of surgery. Patients who have had a stroke should check with their doctor before using fish oil. It could be dangerous if the stroke involved bleeding into the brain. Give fish oil supplements to children only under a doctor's supervision.

Potential side effects of fish oil capsules include a fishy odor or taste, belching, upset stomach, nausea, diarrhea, increased bleeding (including nosebleeds), and easy bruising.

To obtain the greatest heart benefits from the fatty acids found in fish and fish oils, patients should follow a low-fat diet.

Possible drug interactions
Patients who are taking a blood-thinning drug such as aspirin or Coumadin should check with their doctor before taking fish oil supplements, which could further thin the blood. Increased bleeding could also occur if fish oil is taken with supplemental garlic or the herb ginkgo. Signs to watch for include easy bruising, nosebleeds, spitting or vomiting up blood, and blood in the stool or urine. Note, however, that these reactions are rare and may be alleviated by reducing the dose of fish oil.

Special information about pregnancy and breastfeeding

Pregnant women and nursing mothers should use fish oil capsules only under a doctor's supervision.

Some types of fish can contain high amounts of mercury, which can hurt a developing baby's brain. The Food and Drug Administration advises pregnant and breastfeeding women, and those who might become pregnant, to avoid shark, swordfish, king mackerel, and tilefish.

Available preparations and dosage

Fish oil is available in liquid, softgel, or capsule form. Most fish oil supplements range in potency from 200 to 400 milligrams of omega-3 acids. Patients should check the labels carefully, since the number of milligrams in each capsule often refers to the total weight rather than its omega-3 content. Patients should choose preparations that contain vitamin E to prevent oxidation of the easily damaged oil; they should also take a little extra vitamin E to prevent oxidation within the body.

Supplements that contain 18 percent EPA and 12 percent DHA are generally considered standard. They should be taken in divided doses, with meals, to prevent stomach upset. Patients should pay attention to expiration dates and refrigerate the package after opening. Some preparations may contain pesticides.

There is no recommended dietary allowance (RDA) for omega-3 fatty acids. When taken to prevent arterial clogging after angioplasty, doses of 4 to 5 grams per day are typical. For arthritis and high blood pressure, doses of 3 grams daily are usually recommended. A dosage of 1 gram a day has been found to have a protective effect on heart attack victims. However, the American Heart Association suggests that it may be better for patients to boost their intake by eating fish 2 or 3 times a week, rather than taking large amounts of supplements. A 7-ounce serving of salmon or bluefish provides 2.4 grams of omega-3 acids. The same serving of herring contains 3.2 grams.

Overdosage

There are no reports of serious adverse effects, even with dosages as high as 15 grams a day taken for prolonged periods of time. However, it's important for patients to make sure they are using fish oil supplements rather than fish liver oils. The latter contain large amounts of vitamins A and D, which can build up in the body until they reach toxic levels. Symptoms of vitamin A toxicity include hair loss, headache, menstrual problems, stiffness, joint pain, weakness, and dry skin. Excessive intake of vitamin D can lead to irreversible kidney and cardiovascular damage.

Gamma-Tocopherol

Why people take it

Gamma-tocopherol is a member of the vitamin E family. Although *alpha*-tocopherol is the best known form of this vitamin, there is preliminary evidence that gamma-tocopherol may be more protective against cardiovascular disease and some cancers. As a form of vitamin E, gamma-tocopherol is also thought to slow the progress of Alzheimer's disease.

What it is; how it works

Gamma-tocopherol is the most common of the tocopherols. It is found in many seeds and nuts, including soybeans, corn, and walnuts, and is the principal tocopherol in the American diet.

Like other forms of vitamin E, gamma-tocopherol is an antioxidant, scavenging the free radicals that cause cellular damage. Researchers believe that it helps to prevent fat buildup in the arteries, protects cells in the artery walls, reduces the risk of blood clots, inhibits the development of certain cancers, and stimulates the immune system.

Avoid if...

Gamma-tocopherol must be avoided by anyone with a hypersensitivity to it. There are no medical conditions that completely preclude its use.

Special cautions

Those on the blood-thinning medication warfarin should be cautious in using high doses of gamma-tocopherol (doses greater than 100 milligrams daily). Also those with vitamin K deficiencies, such as people with liver failure, should be cautious about using high doses. Gamma-tocopherol must also be used cautiously by those with bleeding ulcers and similar bleeding problems, those with a history of hemorrhagic stroke, and those with hemophilia.

To reduce the risk of bleeding problems, people preparing for surgery should stop high-dose gamma-tocopherol supplementation 1 month before the procedure.

There is one study in which high blood levels of gamma-tocopherol was associated with an increased incidence of knee osteoarthritis, especially in African-Americans.

Possible drug interactions

High doses of gamma-tocopherol may boost the effects of blood-thinning drugs, such as aspirin. Some herbs, including garlic and ginkgo, also possess blood-thinning activity and high doses of gamma-tocopherol may enhance their action as well. The following drugs may reduce the impact of gamma-tocopherol:

Cholestyramine (Questran)

Colestipol (Colestid)
Isoniazid (Rifampin)
Mineral oil
Neomycin (Neosporin)
Orlistat (Xenical)
Sucralfate (Carafate)
Alpha-tocopherol
Iron

Vitamin C and selenium may increase the effectiveness of gamma-tocopherol.

Special information about pregnancy and breastfeeding

Since the effects of gamma-tocopherol during pregnancy have not been studied, the safest course is to forego supplementation.

Available preparations and dosage

Typical doses are about 200 milligrams daily.

Overdosage

There are no reports of gamma-tocopherol overdose.

Ginkgo

Latin name: Ginkgo biloba

Why people take it

Ginkgo is generally accepted as a remedy for minor deficits in brain function, such as those that occur with advancing age. It is used to improve concentration and combat short-term memory loss due to clogged arteries in the brain, and to treat dizziness, ringing in the ears, headache, and emotional hypersensitivity accompanied by anxiety. For people with intermittent circulation problems in the legs, it permits longer pain-free walks.

What it is; how it works

Although the ginkgo tree has been around for 200 million years, it's only during the last couple of decades that its true value has been recognized. Active compounds in ginkgo extract improve circulation, discourage clot formation, reinforce the walls of the capillaries, and protect nerve cells from harm when deprived of oxygen. These ingredients also appear to have an antioxidant effect, sparing brain tissue from the damage caused by free radicals. Because the active ingredients are limited to minute quantities in natural ginkgo leaves, only concentrated ginkgo extract is really effective.

The ginkgo tree grows over 100 feet high and can live for hundreds of years. The tree flowers for the first time when it is between 20 and 30 years old. Native to China, Japan, and Korea, it now grows worldwide, and is intensively cultivated in major plantations such as one in Sumter, South Carolina.

Avoid if...
Anyone who has been warned about the possibility of bleeding in the brain should avoid ginkgo. There have been reports of intracranial hemorrhage associated with this herb. It should also be avoided if it causes an allergic reaction.

Special cautions
Taken orally in customary doses, ginkgo is unlikely to have side effects. Spasms, cramps, and mild digestive problems are the most common reactions. On rare occasions, allergic skin problems may occur.

Possible drug interactions
Combining ginkgo with clot-busting drugs, blood-thinners, or aspirin may increase the risk of intracranial bleeding.

Special information about pregnancy and breastfeeding
There is no information available.

Available preparations and dosage
Ginkgo extract is produced in liquid, tablet, and capsule form, in strengths ranging from 30 to 500 milligrams. Tea made from ginkgo leaves, as in traditional Chinese medicine, is too weak to be effective.

A total daily intake of 120 milligrams is usually recommended, typically in three 40-milligram doses spaced throughout the day. Doses of up to 240 milligrams a day are taken by people with severe memory loss.

Strengths of commercial preparations may vary. Follow the manufacturer's labeling whenever available.

Overdosage
A massive overdose can reduce muscle tone, leading to severe weakness. If an overdose is suspected, seek medical attention immediately.

Glycine

Why people take it
In at least one carefully designed clinical trial, high-dose glycine has provided additional relief to schizophrenic patients taking antipsychotic drugs. Glycine has also been used successfully to help alleviate the symptoms of spasticity, primarily in patients with multiple sclerosis; and it has cured seizures caused by an inborn lack of the related amino acid L-serine.

Glycine is one of the many nutritional supplements adopted by body-builders to boost physical performance. Its popularity stems from its role in the formation of creatine, a key ingredient in the chemical reaction that powers muscles. Unfortunately, while there's some evidence that creatine may indeed be helpful during short bursts of physical activity, glycine alone does not seem to have the same effect. In fact, the American Dietetic Association notes that glycine and other supposedly ergogenic (energy-producing) substances may owe their standing more to psychological than to any physical effects.

Studies in laboratory animals suggest that glycine may combat certain types of cancer, including liver tumors and melanoma. Taken with other amino acids, it may also reduce the symptoms of benign prostatic hyperplasia (BPH), although the study suggesting this possibility has never been replicated.

What it is; how it works

Glycine is one of the "nonessential" amino acids that the body can produce for itself whenever they fall short in the diet. It's also available from high-protein foods such as meat, fish, beans, and dairy products.

Glycine combines with two other amino acids—arginine and methionine—to build energy-producing creatine. It also promotes the storage of blood sugar (glucose) in the form of glycogen. Together with the amino acids cysteine and glutamic acid, it produces the protective antioxidant glutathione. And on top of all these duties, it also serves as one of the nervous system's chemical regulators, inhibiting neurological responses in the spinal cord.

Glycine's beneficial effect on schizophrenia is believed to result from its ability to boost nerve impulses transmitted through N-methyl-D-aspartic acid (NMDA) receptors in the brain.

Avoid if...

Extra glycine and other amino acids increase the burden on the liver and kidneys, and should be avoided by anyone who has problems in these areas unless their doctor recommends otherwise.

Special cautions

Even when taken in megadoses, glycine rarely has unwanted side effects. Mild stomach problems are the most likely possibility.

Possible drug interactions

Theoretically glycine may add to the beneficial effects of antispastic drugs such as baclofen, diazepam (Valium), dantrolene (Dantrium), and tizanidine (Zanaflex). No other interactions are known.

Special information about pregnancy and breastfeeding

It's not known whether high levels of glycine are safe during pregnancy. As with any supplement not absolutely necessary for health, it's best to avoid glycine while pregnant or breastfeeding.

Available preparations and dosage

Glycine is available in tablet, capsule, and powder form in doses ranging from 100 to 600 milligrams. Those who use it as a performance-booster take up to 1 gram daily in divided doses. Doses for spasticity are 1 gram per day. Doses used for the management of schizophrenia have ranged from 40 to 90 grams daily.

Overdosage

There are no reports of glycine overdose.

Hops

Latin name: Humulus lupulus

Why people take it

This herb is an accepted remedy for edginess and insomnia. Effectiveness for its other uses—including stimulation of the appetite, increasing the flow of digestive juices, and treating ulcers, skin abrasions, and bladder inflammation—has never been scientifically verified.

What it is; how it works

Hops have long been associated with beer and ale, but the beverage originally called ale in English was made from fermented malt only, and contained no hops. The use of hops probably began in Holland in the early 14th century, and the resulting drink became known as "bier" or "beer." At first, there was much resistance to the use of hops, which was regarded as a "wicked weed that would spoil the taste… and endanger the people."

The plant's medicinal value lies in a set of light yellow scales adjoining the fruit. Compounds in these scales have a sedative effect. Hop tea induces calm, and pillows stuffed with hops assist sleep.

Avoid if...

No known medical conditions preclude the use of hops.

Special cautions

The fresh plant can occasionally cause a reaction. However, when taken at customary dosage levels, hops pose no problems.

Possible drug interactions

There are no known interactions.

Special information about pregnancy and breastfeeding
No harmful effects are known.

Available preparations and dosage
Hops are available in crushed and powdered form, and in commercial preparations for oral administration. A hop tea can be prepared by pouring boiling water over the ground herb and steeping for 10 to 15 minutes.

The usual single dose of Hops is 0.5 grams (about 1 heaping teaspoonful). The strength of commercial preparations may vary, so follow the manufacturer's directions whenever available.

Store hops protected from light and moisture.

Overdosage
No information on overdosage is available.

Huperzine A

Why people take it
Huperzine A shows considerable promise as a treatment for Alzheimer's disease and age-related memory impairment. Numerous studies suggest that it may be as effective as Cognex and Aricept, two of the prescription drugs currently available for Alzheimer's.

What it is; how it works
Alzheimer's disease is marked by declining activity in certain nerve cells that respond to acetylcholine, one of the key chemical messengers in the brain. Huperzine A, like Cognex and Aricept, inhibits the breakdown of acetylcholine, thereby boosting the amount available to these cells.

Huperzine A is a plant alkaloid derived from the Chinese club moss plant, *Huperzia serrata*. In Chinese folk medicine, this herb has long been used as treatment for fever and inflammation, though there's no scientific evidence that it's effective for these problems.

Avoid if...
Huperzine A has a number of potential cardiac and neurological side effects. It should be avoided by those with seizure disorders, heartbeat irregularities, or asthma. People with irritable bowel disease, inflammatory bowel disease, and malabsorption syndromes should also refrain from using this medication.

Special cautions
Huperzine A has potent pharmacological effects and its long-term safety has not been verified. It should be used only under medical supervision and should never be given to children.

Side effects reported with huperzine A include nausea and diarrhea, sweating, blurred vision, twitching, and dizziness. Other possible effects include vomiting, cramping, asthma attacks, slow or irregular heartbeat, seizures, urinary incontinence, increased urination, and excessive salivation.

Possible drug interactions

Combining huperzine A with other medications that boost acetylcholine levels increases the likelihood of side effects. Drugs in this category include Aricept, Cognex, neostigmine, physostigmine, and pyridostigmine. Side effects are also more likely when huperzine A is taken with drugs that mimic the effects of acetylcholine, such as the bladder stimulant Urecholine.

Special information about pregnancy and breastfeeding

Safety of this medication during pregnancy has not been confirmed. It should be avoided by pregnant women and nursing mothers.

Available preparations and dosage

Huperzine A is available in natural and synthetic forms. The natural substance is three times as potent as its synthetic counterpart. Doses of natural huperzine A used in clinical trials have ranged from 60 to 200 micrograms daily.

Overdosage

There are no reports of huperzine A overdose.

Kava Kava

Latin name: Piper methysticum

Why people take it

In the past, kava kava has been taken for a host of ailments on which it has no appreciable effect, including asthma, arthritis, indigestion, cystitis, syphilis, and gonorrhea. For anxiety and insomnia, however, it is now considered a proven remedy.

What it is; how it works

One of the "new" herbs that have recently gained considerable media attention, kava kava has actually been around for centuries in the South Seas, where it's used as a ceremonial beverage. The plant's fleshy underground stem is mildly intoxicating when chewed. Prepared as a nonalcoholic drink, it is said to foster a sense of contentment and well-being, while sharpening the mind, memory, and senses.

Research shows that the active ingredients in kava kava (kava pyrones) do in fact have a calming, sedative effect. They also appear to relax the muscles, relieve spasms, and prevent convulsions. At least two scientific studies have confirmed the herb's ability to significantly reduce symptoms of anxiety. In a third study, researchers rated it as effective as prescription tranquilizers.

Avoid if...

Kava kava should not be used by women who are pregnant or nursing. It should also be avoided by anyone with a depressive disorder; it can deepen a depressed mood.

Special cautions

Patients may notice a slightly tired feeling in the mornings when first taking kava kava.

In rare cases, kava kava can cause an allergic reaction, a slight yellowing of the skin, gastrointestinal complaints, impaired or abnormal movement, loss of balance, pupil dilation, and difficulty focusing. Because of the possibility of visual disturbances, it's important to drive with caution while using this herb.

High doses of the herb have been known to trigger hepatitis, cirrhosis, and liver failure. Heavy long-term use can also cause an unusual scaly rash, and may lead to unwanted weight loss. This herb should not be taken for more than 3 months without a doctor's approval.

Possible drug interactions

Kava kava should not be combined with other substances that act on the brain, such as alcohol, barbiturates, or other mood-altering drugs. It may increase their effect. Be especially wary of taking it with the tranquilizer Xanax; the combination has caused coma.

Kava kava has an antagonistic effect on dopamine. Patients taking a levodopa-based medication for Parkinson's disease should avoid this herb.

Special information about pregnancy and breastfeeding

Remember, kava kava should be avoided during pregnancy and nursing.

Available preparations and dosage

Commercial extracts are the predominant form of kava kava. The crushed root can also be used. Daily doses delivering between 50 and 240 milligrams of the active ingredients are the customary recommendation. Commercial capsules containing between 150 and 300 milligrams of root extract may be taken twice a day. Because the potency of commercial preparations may vary, follow the manufacturer's directions whenever available. The dosage should be administered with food or liquid.

Overdosage

An overdose is usually signaled by a lack of coordination, followed by tiredness and a tendency to sleep. If an overdose is suspected, seek medical attention immediately.

Lavender

Latin name: Lavandula angustifolia

Why people take it

In Europe, lavender is considered an effective remedy for nervousness, insomnia, nervous stomach, and loss of appetite. It is also used in mineral baths to treat circulatory disorders.

Other uses remain unproven. They include migraine, cramps, asthma, and arthritis. Lavender is used in aromatherapy for sleep induction, and is added to bathwater to help treat poorly healing wounds.

What it is; how it works

Because of its wonderful fragrance, from Roman times onward lavender has always been a popular bath additive. In fact, its name derives from the Latin "lavare" meaning "to wash." Over the centuries, it has been used in a variety of forms, including oil, distilled water, and alcohol solution (tincture). One species, spike lavender, is even an effective insect repellent.

Lavender's medicinal value lies in the essential oil, customarily extracted from the flowers. Taken internally, lavender has been found to stimulate the production and flow of bile. It also has a mildly sedating effect, and gets rid of gas. Used externally, it improves circulation and brings color to the skin.

Avoid if...

No known medical conditions preclude the use of lavender.

Special cautions

Taken at customary dosage levels, lavender presents no problems, although a few people do develop a sensitivity to the oil.

Possible drug interactions

No interactions have been reported.

Special information about pregnancy and breastfeeding

No harmful effects are known.

Available preparations and dosage

Extracts, bath additives, and crushed lavender flowers are all available.

To prepare a bath additive, boil 100 grams (about one-half cup) of lavender in 2 quarts of water, then add to the tub.

The usual daily dose of lavender for internal use is:
Crushed flowers: 3 to 5 grams
Essential oil: 1 to 4 drops

Overdosage
No information on overdosage is available.

Lemon Balm

Latin name: Melissa officinalis
Other names: Balm Mint, Bee Balm, Blue Balm, Cure-all, Garden Balm, Honey Plant, Sweet Balm, Sweet Mary

Why people take it
Lemon balm is officially recognized only for its ability to calm the nerves and promote sleep. In the past it has been taken for a wide variety of problems, including bloating and gas, mood disorders, bronchial inflammation, high blood pressure, palpitations, vomiting, toothache, earache, and headache. However, its effectiveness for these purposes has never been validated by clinical trials.

Applied externally, it has also been used for arthritis, nerve pains, and stiff neck—but again without clinical validation.

What it is; how it works
Lemon balm's medicinal properties have been held in high regard for nearly two millennia. The Roman scholar Pliny believed lemon balm could prevent infection in open wounds (an action that has been clinically proven for balsamic oils in general). The noted 16th century physician Paracelsus believed lemon balm could heal even patients close to death.

Modern research on lemon balm has revealed a mild sedative effect, antibacterial and antiviral properties, and an ability to quell spasms and relieve cramps and gas. Only the plant's leaves are medicinal.

A perennial herb, lemon balm grows up to 3 feet in height. It is native to the east Mediterranean region and west Asia, but is cultivated throughout central Europe. Before flowering, it has a lemon-like taste and smell; and the fresh leaves, in addition to their medicinal applications, are commonly used in cooking.

Avoid if...
No known medical conditions preclude the use of lemon balm.

Special cautions
When taken at customary dosage levels, lemon balm poses no hazards.

Possible drug interactions
There are no known interactions.

Special information about pregnancy and breastfeeding
No harmful effects are known.

Available preparations and dosage
Lemon balm can be found in the form of dried herb, herb powder, and liquid or dry extracts, as well as various liquid and solid commercial preparations.

To make a tea, pour a cup of hot water over 1.5 to 4.5 grams (about one-quarter to 1 teaspoonful) of crushed lemon balm, steep for 10 minutes, and strain.

The usual daily dose of lemon balm is 8 to 10 grams (about 2 teaspoonfuls) Because the strength of commercial preparations may vary, follow the manufacturer's instructions whenever available.

Lemon balm can be stored in a well-sealed, non-plastic container protected from light and moisture for up to 1 year.

Overdosage
No information on overdosage is available.

L-Phenylalanine

Why people take it
An "essential" amino acid that the body can't manufacture on its own, phenylalanine is one of the raw materials for three of the nervous system's most important chemical messengers: dopamine, epinephrine, and norepinephrine. The body can also convert it to phenylethylamine, a mood-boosting substance that's said to have pain-relieving effects as well.

L-phenylalanine, the form of the substance found naturally in the diet, has shown promise as a treatment for unipolar depression. It has also proven useful in the treatment of vitiligo, a disease characterized by abnormal white blotches of skin due to loss of pigmentation. Phenylalanine has also been promoted as an appetite suppressant and sexual stimulant, but its effectiveness for these purposes remains unproven.

What it is; how it works
Researchers believe that L-phenylalanine's impact on depression stems from its role in the production of dopamine and norepinephrine, two of the chemical messengers that regulate mood. It's value in the treatment of vitiligo is thought to rest on an ability to stimulate the production of pigment-producing melanin in the affected areas of skin.

Outright deficiencies of L-phenylalanine are rare, but have been known to strike people who don't eat enough protein. (Signs of deficiency include bloodshot eyes, cataracts, and behavioral changes.) Good sources of L-phenylalanine include protein foods such as poultry, meats, fish, dairy products, soybeans, nuts, and seeds. Phenylalanine is also an ingredient of the popular artificial sweetener aspartame.

Another form of phenylalanine—D-phenylalanine—has been proposed as a treatment for chronic pain. This substance is available only in combination with L-phenylalanine, in products known as DL-phenylalanine (see separate entry).

Avoid if...

Children born without the ability to process phenylalanine can build up dangerous levels of this amino acid, leading to mental retardation, seizures, extreme hyperactivity, and psychosis. Youngsters with this condition—called phenylketonuria—must follow a special diet designed to supply no more phenylalanine than necessary, and must be monitored regularly for excess phenylalanine in the blood.

Special cautions

L-phenylalanine has also been reported to exacerbate involuntary movements (tardive dyskinesia) in schizophrenic patients. Anyone with this disorder should therefore use L-phenylalanine supplements with extreme caution. Caution is also warranted for people with high blood pressure or an anxiety disorder; phenylalanine tends to aggravate these conditions.

It's best for patients with vitiligo to use L-phenylalanine under a doctor's supervision.

Possible drug interactions

L-phenylalanine supplements should never be combined with drugs known as MAO inhibitors, including the antidepressants Nardil and Parnate; a surge in blood pressure could result. It is also best to avoid combining L-phenylalanine with antipsychotic drugs, since it increases the likelihood of tardive dyskinesia.

On the other hand, taking L-phenylalanine with the drug Eldepryl may boost the antidepressant activity of both agents.

Special information about pregnancy and breastfeeding

Phenylalanine supplements are not recommended during pregnancy and breastfeeding.

Available preparations and dosage

The estimated adult daily requirement for L-phenylalanine and the related amino acid tyrosine combined is approximately 7 milligrams per pound of body weight. Infants require almost 9 times that amount; children need 10 milligrams per pound. Most people fulfill these requirements through diet alone, but commercial L-phenylalanine supplements are available in capsule and tablet form. Typical dosages range from 500 milligrams to 1.5 grams daily. The supplements should not be taken with other amino acids or protein foods. L-phenylalanine is most effective if taken on an empty stomach prior to meals. Vitamin B_6 is said to enhance its effectiveness.

Overdosage
No overdoses have been reported

Melatonin

Why people take it
In numerous clinical studies, the hormone we call melatonin has demonstrated its value as a treatment for insomnia. For example, in one study, 14 of 18 patients taking melatonin were able to give up the sedatives they had been relying on to sleep. There is also a possibility that melatonin may relieve jet lag, though the evidence for this is mixed.

Other claims made for this hormone range from wildly exaggerated to totally baseless. Despite some hints that it may be useful for cancer and immune disorders, clinical research has yet to verify its value. Assertions that melatonin can improve the symptoms of Alzheimer's disease, lower cholesterol levels, reduce high blood pressure, prevent heart attacks, improve sexual performance, and delay the onset of aging are entirely without foundation.

What it is; how it works
Melatonin is a product of the pineal gland, where it is synthesized from the amino acid tryptophan. Under normal conditions, melatonin levels foreshadow the sleep cycle, usually increasing rapidly from the late evening until midnight, then decreasing as morning approaches. In this way, melatonin helps regulate circadian rhythm, the body's 24-hour "dark-light clock" that governs the timing of hormone production, sleep, body temperature, and more.

Not surprisingly, people with high levels of melatonin usually sleep longer and more soundly than those with a deficiency. For example, the elderly, who produce less melatonin than the young and middle-aged, are typically more susceptible to insomnia. Similarly, events that throw melatonin levels out of synch—such as a jet trip between time zones—seem to interfere with production of the hormone and thus disrupt sleep. Consumption of alcohol, tobacco, and narcotics has a similar effect.

Avoid if...
Because melatonin sometimes causes depression, those who suffer from depression should avoid it. It has been known to trigger seizures, and should not be used by anyone with epilepsy or other seizure disorders. Couples who are trying to conceive a baby should avoid this hormone. It is also not for use in children or teenagers.

Special cautions

As with other medications that cause sleepiness, melatonin should be taken only at bedtime. Patients should not drive or operate hazardous machinery after taking a dose.

Side effects are more likely with higher doses. They include stomach discomfort, morning grogginess, daytime hangover, depression, headache, lethargy, disorientation, amnesia, inhibition of fertility, increased seizures, reduced male sexual drive, low body temperature, retinal damage, and breast enlargement.

Possible drug interactions

A number of drugs can reduce melatonin levels. Among them are aspirin, other nonsteroidal anti-inflammatory drugs, and beta blockers such as Inderal, Lopressor, and Tenormin. On the other hand, Luvox can increase the effect of melatonin supplements.

Use of melatonin with benzodiazepines, sedating antihistamines, sedating antidepressants and other sedating drugs may cause additive sedation and increase the likelihood of side effects. Melatonin should never be combined with Prozac.

There is a report of melatonin enhancing the activity of the tuberculosis drug isoniazid. It may also increase the anticancer effect of interleukin-2.

Special information about pregnancy and breastfeeding

Experts advise against the use of melatonin by pregnant women and nursing mothers.

Available preparations and dosage

Melatonin is available in capsules, tablets, lozenges, and liquid. Those who use melatonin for sleep disturbance or jet lag should take no more than 0.3 to 3 milligrams at bedtime for short periods of time (no longer than 2 weeks). It's best to check with a doctor before taking higher doses or dosing for longer periods of time.

Overdosage

There are no reports of melatonin overdose.

Myo-Inositol

Why people take it

In a number of clinical trials, *myo*-inositol has proven to be an effective treatment for some patients with depression, panic disorder, and obsessive-compulsive disorder. It does not, however, have any beneficial effects on Alzheimer's disease, schizophrenia, or autism. And when tested for attention deficit disorder, it made the problem worse.

What it is; how it works

Myo-inositol is a small, but significant, component of cell membranes. The body manufactures it from glucose, and it's also obtained from dietary intake of foods such as dried beans, chickpeas, lentils, citrus fruit, nuts, oats, rice, and whole-grain products.

Researchers have noted a shortage of *myo*-inositol in the cerebrospinal fluid of many patients with depression. They believe its effects on depression and anxiety may stem from its ability to activate serotonin receptors in the brain. As one of the brain's chief chemical messengers, serotonin appears to play a key role in the modulation of moods—a fact that accounts for the success of such serotonin-boosting drugs as Luvox, Paxil, and Prozac. While *myo*-inositol has similar therapeutic effects, hopes that it might enhance the effect of these drugs have failed to be realized.

Avoid if...

There are no known reasons to avoid *myo*-inositol at recommended dosage levels.

Special cautions

Due to the theoretical possibility that this substance could exacerbate the manic symptoms of bipolar disorder, patients suffering from this problem should use *myo*-inositol supplements with caution and only under a doctor's supervision.

Possible drug interactions

Although it has not been observed in clinical trials, there is a theoretical possibility that high doses of *myo*-inositol may improve the action of serotonin-boosting drugs such as Celexa, Luvox, Paxil, Prozac, and Zoloft, and migraine medications such as Amerge, Axert, Imitrex, Maxalt, and Zomig. It might also add to the effects of St. John's wort.

Special information about pregnancy and breastfeeding

Because the safety of *myo*-inositol during pregnancy has not been confirmed, it should be avoided by pregnant women and nursing mothers. In very high doses, it can trigger uterine contractions.

Available preparations and dosage

The dosage that produced positive effects in clinical studies was 12 grams a day, divided into several smaller doses. Improvement, if any, can be expected in about 1 month.

Overdosage

There are no reports of *myo*-inositol overdose.

NADH

Why people take it

A chemical cousin of vitamin B_3, NADH (nicontinamide adenine dinucleotide) is naturally present in each of the body's cells, where it's needed to trigger conversion of nutrients into the cellular "fuel" adenosine triphosphate (ATP). Proponents of NADH have tested it for several serious diseases, including Parkinson's, Alzheimer's, depression, and chronic fatigue syndrome. Although results have been mixed, it seems to be helpful for many patients with Parkinson's disease. Trials for Alzheimer's disease and chronic fatigue syndrome have also been encouraging. Additionally, in one recent study NADH was found to significantly lower blood pressure and cholesterol levels.

What it is; how it works

Because of its role in the synthesis of ATP, NADH is a key factor in the body's production of energy. There's also some evidence that high levels of NADH in the brain may enhance production of such chemical messengers as dopamine, norepinephrine, and serotonin. The body produces NADH continuously, using vitamin B_3 as raw material. It's also readily available from such dietary sources as fish, poultry, beef, and products made with yeast. Deficiencies of NADH in the U.S. are almost unknown, except in rare cases of alcoholism.

Research on the use of NADH for treatment of chronic fatigue syndrome has produced encouraging—though not spectacular—results. The study included 26 patients with chronic fatigue, and found that 31 percent of those taking 10 milligrams of NADH daily had fewer symptoms. The researchers theorize that a shortage of ATP may contribute to the symptoms of chronic fatigue, and that NADH works by helping to replenish depleted cellular stores of the compound.

Because Parkinson's disease is caused by a shortage of dopamine at certain locations in the brain, researchers have speculated that NADH's dopamine-boosting effect might relieve the tremors and rigidity the disease produces. Preliminary studies seem to indicate that for many Parkinson's patients this may be true. In one uncontrolled trial of NADH in 885 people with Parkinson's disease, nearly 80 percent showed improvement.

Since NADH supports production of other chemical messengers in the brain, scientists are also eyeing it for use against Alzheimer's disease and depression. In one small trial, 17 patients suffering from Alzheimer's showed improvement after taking NADH for 8 to 12 weeks. Likewise, a 10-month trial of NADH in 205 depressed patients ended in improvement for 93 percent. But since these studies were small, uncontrolled, and conducted by advocates of NADH, experts say more rigorous testing is needed before any firm conclusions can be drawn.

Avoid if...
Given the lack of conclusive research, it would be unwise to use NADH as a replacement for more promising treatments. Although there are no known reasons to avoid the supplement, it's best used as part of an overall treatment plan. It is not recommended for children.

Special cautions
Little is known about the effects of long-term, high-dose use of NADH, but excessive use of the related compound nicotinic acid can lead to liver damage, so caution is in order.

NADH appears to have few significant side effects, but there have been isolated reports of such gastrointestinal side effects as nausea and loss of appetite.

Possible drug interactions
No drug interactions are known.

Special information about pregnancy and breastfeeding
Because of lack of long-term safety studies, NADH should be avoided by pregnant women and nursing mothers.

Available preparations and dosage
NADH is available in 2.5- and 5-milligram tablets. A typical dosage recommendation is 5 milligrams once or twice daily, with water, on an empty stomach. An injectable form is used by physicians to treat complications of alcoholism.

Overdosage
No information is available on overdosage.

Passion Flower

Latin name: Passiflora incarnata
Other names: Granadilla, Maypop, Passion Vine

Why people take it
Although proven effective only for edginess and insomnia, passion flower has also been used as a remedy for depression and nervous stomach. Applied externally, it has been used for hemorrhoids.

What it is; how it works
This perennial vine, which reaches 30 feet in length, grows naturally from the southeastern U.S. to Brazil and Argentina, and is cultivated in Europe as a garden plant. The blossoms are considered symbolic of Christ's Passion (their central corona, for instance, represents the Crown of Thorns), accounting for their name.

The above-ground parts of the plant hold its medicinal value. In animal tests, researchers found that the plant lowers blood pressure and slows the passage of food through the digestive tract.

Avoid if...
No known medical conditions preclude the use of passion flower.

Special cautions
At customary dosage levels, Passion Flower poses no risks.

Possible drug interactions
No interactions have been reported.

Special information about pregnancy and breastfeeding
No harmful effects are known.

Available preparations and dosage
Passion flower is available as an herb for tea. It is also an ingredient in certain sedative bath additives.

To make tea, pour 150 milliliters (about two-thirds of a cup) of hot water over 1 teaspoonful of passion flower, steep for 10 minutes, then strain.

To prepare an external rinse, particularly for hemorrhoids, put 20 grams (about 3 tablespoonfuls) of Passion Flower into 200 grams (about 1 cup) of simmering water, allow to cool, then strain.

The typical oral dosage is 2 to 3 cups of tea during the day and one-half hour before bedtime.

Overdosage
No information on overdosage is available.

Phosphatidylcholine

Why people take it
Two potential benefits have attracted interest in phosphatidylcholine: its impact on cholesterol levels and its effect on memory loss. In both roles, the substance gets mixed reviews.

Hopes that phosphatidylcholine might combat memory loss have been based on its ability to increase levels of acetylcholine in the brain. This important chemical messenger appears to play a role in maintaining memory, and has been found to be in short supply in Alzheimer's patients. Unfortunately an analysis of 11 carefully controlled clinical experiments with lecithin, a food supplement rich in phosphatidyl-choline, was unable to detect any significant benefit. The supplement may have very modest effects on patients with impaired thinking or dementia, but it doesn't seem to yield any major improvement.

Similarly, some experts once believed that phosphatidylcholine might relieve the symptoms of tardive dyskinesia, a severe neurological disorder that's brought on by long-term use of certain antipsychotic drugs. But when schizophrenic patients suffering from the signs and symptoms of the disorder—involuntary movements of the muscles of the face, mouth, and cheeks—were put on lecithin or related compounds, they experienced only slight improvement.

Phosphatidylcholine's performance against high cholesterol has been equally unexciting. Although it has produced moderate reductions in some studies, it has had no significant effect in a number of others.

It has been suggested that phosphatidylcholine might eventually have some therapeutic role in some cancers. Phosphatidylcholine is essential for normal liver function, and there is ample evidence that liver cancer is promoted in various animals by choline-deficient diets. In addition, phosphatidylcholine has demonstrated protective effects against a number of other liver disorders, including alcoholic fibrosis and viral hepatitis.

What it is; how it works

Phosphatidylcholine is a combination of choline, fatty acids, glycerol, and phosphorus. Its choline component serves as a raw material in the production of acetylcholine and has recently been classified as an essential nutrient by the National Academy of Sciences. (See entry on Choline.) As a source of extra choline, phosphatidylcholine is a better delivery form and is better tolerated than choline itself.

Phosphatidylcholine is one of several phosphorus-based compounds contained in lecithin, a naturally occurring substance derived from beef liver, eggs, soybeans, and peanuts. Lecithin products are generally composed of from 5 to 30 percent phosphatidylcholine. Choline constitutes about 13 percent of the total.

Avoid if...

Phosphatidylcholine is generally considered safe for everyone.

Special cautions

No major side effects need be expected. A few people suffer mild side effects such as nausea, diarrhea, and increased salivation.

Possible drug interactions

It's best to avoid choline-containing supplements if one is taking a prescription drug such as scopolamine (an antinausea medication) that works by blocking the effects of acetylcholine.

Special information about pregnancy and breastfeeding

For healthy women who eat a balanced diet, choline supplements are usually unnecessary during pregnancy and breastfeeding.

Available preparations and dosage

There are several ways to obtain supplemental phosphatidylcholine. Typical commercial lecithin supplements contain 20 to 30 percent phosphatidylcholine. Softgel capsules containing 55 to 90 percent phosphatidylcholine are available. There's also a liquid containing 3 grams of phosphatidylcholine per 5 milliliters. Typical dosages range from 3 to 9 grams of phosphatidylcholine daily, taken in several smaller doses.

Overdosage

The upper tolerable limit of choline is 3.5 grams a day. (It takes approximately 27 grams of phosphatidylcholine to supply this amount.) Dosages above this level may bring on dizziness, nausea, diarrhea, cramps, and a fishy body odor.

Phosphatidylserine

Why people take it

Phosphatidylserine (PS) is found in high concentrations in the brain. It may help to preserve, or even improve, some aspects of mental functioning in the elderly. In the largest study to date, 200 milligrams of phosphatidylserine daily made a small but significant improvement in patients with Alzheimer's disease. Other smaller studies also found phosphatidylserine to be mildly helpful. Keep in mind, however, that these studies lasted just a few months, and while phosphatidylserine may reduce symptoms in the short term, at best it probably slows the rate of deterioration rather than halting the progression altogether. Preliminary evidence also suggests that phosphatidylserine can boost the immune system, and it may blunt the effects of the stress hormone cortisol during exercise.

What it is; how it works

Phosphatidylserine belongs to a special category of fat-soluble substances called phospholipids, which are essential components of cell membranes. Brain tissues are especially rich in phosphatidylserine, but aging causes a decline in the phosphatidylserine content of cells throughout the body. Research has shown that in addition to improving neural function, phosphatidylserine may enhance energy metabolism in all cells. It also seems to boost levels of the brain chemical acetylcholine, which has been linked to improved memory function.

Some controversy exists about the source of phosphatidylserine supplements. Most research has been conducted with phosphatidylserine derived from cow brain tissue. Due to concerns about mad-cow disease, soy-based phosphatidylserine supplements have generally replaced cow-based ones. The two types are not structurally identical, however, and some researchers think these differences could be important.

Phosphatidylserine is found in only trace amounts in a typical diet. Very small amounts are present in egg yolks and soybeans.

Avoid if...

Aside from an allergy to them, there are no known reasons to avoid phosphatidylserine supplements.

Special cautions

Due to the lack of safety studies, phosphatidylserine supplements should not be given to children. Those who have a rare genetic condition known as antiphospholipid-antibody syndrome should talk to their doctor before taking phosphatidylserine.

Occasional side effects, such as nausea and indigestion, have been reported.

Possible drug interactions

There are no reported drug interactions with phosphatidylserine.

Special information about pregnancy and breastfeeding

Due to the lack of safety data, pregnant and breastfeeding women should not use phosphatidylserine.

Available preparations and dosage

Most phosphatidylserine supplements are made from soy. Due to concerns about mad-cow disease, it's best to avoid those made from cow, or "bovine," sources. PS capsules are available in strengths of 50, 100, and 500 milligrams. Typical doses are 100 milligrams three times a day.

Overdosage

There are no reports of overdosage.

Rauwolfia

Latin name: Rauwolfia serpentina

Why people take it

Rauwolfia is officially recognized in Europe as a treatment for nervousness, insomnia, and high blood pressure. In folk medicine, it has also been used for vomiting, gas, liver problems, and wounds. However, its effectiveness for such conditions remains unverified.

Indian medicine uses it as an antidote for poisonous snake bites, and as a remedy for fever, abdominal cramps, slow and painful urination, and wounds.

What it is; how it works

Reserpine, an extract of rauwolfia, combats high blood pressure, and is found in such prescription blood pressure medications as Diupres and Hydropres. Reserpine also combats irregular heartbeat and has a sedative effect.

Rauwolfia, a small shrub sporting white to pink flowers, is native to India, Indochina, Borneo, Sri Lanka, and Sumatra. Its medicinal properties lie in the dried root. The fresh root has a very bitter and unpleasant taste.

Avoid if...

Rauwolfia can trigger severe depression. No one suffering from depression should take this herb. The drug also tends to stimulate the lining of the digestive tract, so it should be avoided if an ulcer or ulcerative colitis exists. Rauwolfia should also be avoided during pregnancy and nursing.

Special cautions

Side effects can include nasal congestion, depression, fatigue, impotence, and slowed reaction time. Patients should use caution when handling machinery or driving.

Possible drug interactions

Rauwolfia must never be combined with drugs classified as monoamine oxidase inhibitors, such as the antidepressants Nardil and Parnate.

Rauwolfia enhances the sedative effect of alcohol and barbiturates; the combination should be avoided. Rauwolfia also increases the effects of antipsychotic drugs.

Taken with digitalis-based drugs such as Lanoxin, or quinidine products such as Quinaglute and Quinidex, rauwolfia can slow the heart and cause irregular beats.

The drug is also likely to interact with levodopa (Sinemet), causing twitching and other involuntary movements. Combining it with many common flu remedies and appetite suppressants can lead to a sharp rise in blood pressure.

Special information about pregnancy and breastfeeding

Rauwolfia may cause birth defects when taken during pregnancy; and it appears in breast milk. Women should avoid this drug while pregnant or breastfeeding.

Available preparations and dosage

Rauwolfia is available in ground form and as a powder for internal use.

The usual daily dose of rauwolfia is 600 milligrams. (Recommended dosage of the active ingredient reserpine is far smaller; 0.25 milligram is the daily maximum.)

Overdosage

Symptoms of overdosage include mental depression, heavy sedation, and a severe drop in blood pressure. If an overdose is suspected, seek medical attention immediately.

SAMe

Why people take it

In a series of small but promising clinical trials, this over-the-counter remedy for depression has proved itself the equal of traditional prescription drugs. Though some authorities dismiss it as a mild mood-lifter, others regard it as an important new medication, since it has not only performed as well as potent "tricyclic" antidepressants, but also starts working faster (within one or two weeks, versus three to four weeks or longer for standard drugs). Outside the U.S., it has been sold for years as a prescription antidepressant, mainly under the name AdoMet.

SAMe (S-adenosylmethionine) has been studied as an aid to the effectiveness of other antidepressants, with promising results. It also has been found to provide at least some relief from postpartum depression and depression associated with Parkinson's disease and epilepsy. In addition, it has been tested for a number of other neurological disorders, including schizophrenia, Alzheimer's disease, and dementia. Although these tests are far from conclusive, they've produced encouraging results.

SAMe is also used to treat osteoarthritis, the type of arthritis caused by wear and tear on the protective cartilage in the joints. Preliminary studies appear to confirm its ability to relieve stiffness, pain, and swelling. However, there's no evidence to support manufacturers' claims that it can renew damaged cartilage. SAMe also shows promise as a treatment for the painful muscle condition called fibromyalgia. And studies show that supplementation with SAMe can improve liver function, making it a candidate for treatment of cirrhosis, impaired bile flow, and liver damage from drugs or alcohol.

Claims that SAMe is useful in the treatment of heart disease and cancer are currently unsubstantiated, though preliminary clinical studies are underway. Assertions that SAMe fights the effects of aging also remain unproven.

What it is; how it works

The body manufactures a natural supply of SAMe from the essential amino acid methionine. In turn, SAMe plays an important role in the production of a wide variety of hormones, amino acids, antioxidants, and chemical messengers in the brain. Researchers have noted low levels of SAMe in people with depression, and have found that SAMe rises as depression improves. SAMe also helps maintain the strength and flexibility of cell walls, and participates in the production of DNA and RNA.

SAMe supplements are especially helpful in cases of liver disease, which depletes the body's natural supply. Extra vitamin B_6, B_{12}, and folic acid are usually recommended with SAMe supplementation. In fact, some products already have them added.

Avoid if...

People who have bipolar disorder should use SAMe only under a doctor's supervision; SAMe can cause episodes of mania. Those taking antidepressants should not discontinue their medication or start taking SAMe without consulting a physician. SAMe is not recommended for children.

Special cautions

Patients taking a prescription antidepressant may need to reduce their dosage gradually when attempting to replace their medication with SAMe or adding SAMe to their regimen.

Patients with high homocysteine levels (a condition associated with increased risk of heart disease) should consider adding the homocysteine-lowering supplement TMG to the regimen. Homocysteine is a byproduct of SAMe.

Unlike some prescription antidepressants, SAMe is said to have no serious side effects. However, some people suffer mild digestive upsets, anxiety, insomnia, mania, and hyperactive muscles.

There is no reason to believe that SAMe could cause cancer. But because people who already have cancer might react differently to this substance, they should check with their doctor before taking SAMe.

Possible drug interactions

SAMe may reduce the effectiveness of some medications, including the Parkinson's disease medication L-dopa.

Special information about pregnancy and breastfeeding

The safety of SAMe supplements during pregnancy has not been determined; it should be used only under a doctor's supervision. SAMe supplementation is not recommended for nursing mothers.

Available preparations and dosage

Synthetic SAMe is available in tablets and capsules, usually in strengths of 100 or 200 milligrams. For depression, some authorities recommend dosages of 400 to 1,600 milligrams daily. For arthritis, recommendations vary from 200 to 1,200 milligrams daily. For liver disease, daily dosages of 1,600 milligrams are common. The daily total is divided into smaller doses. They should be taken 1 hour before or 2 hours after meals.

Some forms of SAMe tend to degrade quickly at any temperature above freezing. Look for a temperature-stable form in a coated tablet. Store away from moisture.

Overdosage

No information on overdosage is available.

St. John's Wort

Latin name: Hypericum perforatum

Why people take it

In many—but not all—clinical trials, St. John's wort has proven to be an effective treatment for mild to moderate depressive disorders. It also has a mildly tranquilizing and sedative effect. Oily preparations of the herb are useful in the treatment of wounds, burns, blunt injuries, and inflammation of the skin.

Although its effectiveness for other ailments has not been proven, St. John's wort has also been used to treat sleep disturbances, gallbladder disorders, gastritis, bronchitis, asthma, diarrhea, bed-wetting, rheumatism, muscle pain, and gout.

What it is; how it works

St. John's wort is believed to combat depression by boosting the levels of certain chemical messengers in the brain. Like the prescription antidepressant Prozac, it seems to increase the amount of serotonin available to the nervous system. It also tends to promote higher levels of the chemical messengers norepinephrine and dopamine. In clinical trials, daily doses of 800 to 900 milligrams of St. John's wort have proven to be as effective as 20 milligrams of Prozac or 75 milligrams of the antidepressant Tofranil.

Applied to the skin, oily preparations of the herb have an antibacterial and anti-inflammatory action, though they seem to have no effect on viruses.

St. John's wort is a golden yellow perennial flower that secretes a red liquid when pinched. Cut at the start of the flowering season and processed in bunches, it must be dried quickly to preserve its oil and secretions.

This plant has been used medicinally for over 2,000 years. Ancient Greeks believed that its odor repelled evil spirits. Early Christians named the plant in honor of St. John the Baptist because they believed it released its blood-red oil on the 29th of August, the day the saint was beheaded.

Avoid if...

There are no known reasons to avoid St. John's wort at recommended dosage levels.

Special cautions

With heavy use, St. John's wort increases sensitivity to sunlight. To avoid a sunburn, patients should minimize exposure to the sun while using this medication. This herb can also cause bloating and constipation.

Possible drug interactions

Patients should avoid St. John's wort while taking a prescription MAO inhibitor such as Nardil or Parnate. At least in theory, a dangerous interaction is possible.

It's also best to avoid combining St. John's wort with serotonin-boosting drugs such as Celexa, Luvox, Paxil, Prozac, Serzone, and Zoloft. The excessive levels of serotonin that may result can trigger sweating, tremors, flushing, confusion, and agitation.

Patients taking medications for HIV, the virus that causes AIDS, should not use St. John's wort. The herb is known to interfere with at least one HIV drug—Crixivan—and may reduce the effect of others, including Agenerase, Fortovase, Invirase, Norvir, and Viracept. St. John's wort should also be avoided by people taking Neoral, a drug used to keep transplant patients from rejecting their new organs. It can inhibit the drug's life-saving effect.

Patients who use a hormonal form of contraception should remember that oral contraceptive failure has occasionally been reported in women taking St. John's wort.

Special information about pregnancy and breastfeeding

No harmful effects are known.

Available preparations and dosage

For depression, the typical dosage of standardized extract is 300 milligrams taken 3 times a day. The extract is available in tablet, capsule, and liquid form. Common brands are made by Celestial Seasonings, Centrum Herbals, Nature's Way, and Schiff. Strengths of commercial preparations may vary. Patients should follow the manufacturer's labeling whenever available.

A treatment regimen of 4 to 6 weeks is typically recommended for depression. Patients should check with their doctor if they feel no improvement. They may need a different therapy.

Overdosage

No information on overdosage is available.

Tocotrienols

Why people take it

Tocotrienols are a form of vitamin E. In general, people take them for the same reasons they take other forms of the vitamin (see separate entry), including the prevention of Alzheimer's disease, heart disease, and cancer, particularly breast cancer.

Most scientific study has focused on the alpha-tocopherol form of vitamin E because it appears to be the most active in humans. However, proponents of tocotrienols claim that they are the "missing link" in the vitamin E story; and preliminary research does indeed suggest that they may yield impressive benefits. For example, some studies suggest that tocotrienols can lower blood cholesterol levels more effectively than alpha-tocopherol can. Others hint that tocotrienols can greatly inhibit tumor formation, especially in human breast cells. Animal studies also suggest tocotrienols may be useful for healing alcohol-induced stomach lesions.

While the evidence is promising, many questions remain. There are four different types of tocotrienols, and scientists still aren't sure which ones are best, or how much should be taken. Studies also need to be done to find out the effects of taking tocotrienols and tocopherols together. (Some researchers claim that taking the two at the same time negates some of the benefits of tocotrienols.) Whatever the case, experts agree that alpha-tocopherol is still an important form of vitamin E and should not be avoided in favor of tocotrienols.

What it is; how it works

Like other forms of vitamin E, tocotrienols seem to be potent antioxidants that protect the fats in cell membranes from oxidation, or spoilage. Oxidation is thought to be a significant factor in many diseases, as well as the aging process. The antioxidant abilities of tocotrienols may explain why they are helpful for protecting the cardiovascular and nervous systems. How this form of vitamin E works to prevent cancer is still unknown.

The richest sources of tocotrienols are palm, rice bran, and coconut oils. Other plant-based oils, such as corn and canola, contain very little. Like all forms of vitamin E, tocotrienols are fat soluble.

Avoid if...

Aside from an allergy to them, there are no known reasons to avoid tocotrienol supplements.

Special cautions

Because tocotrienols could interfere with blood clot formation, patients who have bleeding problems—including those with hemophilia, peptic ulcers, vitamin K deficiency, a tendency to hemorrhage, or a history of stroke—should take care not to overdose. Likewise, patients should avoid tocotrienols about 1 month before and for 2 weeks after any surgery.

Because tocotrienol supplements are relatively new, there is little information on side effects. In general, the same precautions should be followed as those for vitamin E (see separate entry).

Possible drug interactions

Patients who are taking a blood-thinning drug such as aspirin or Coumadin should check with their doctor before taking tocotrienols, which could further thin the blood. In general, patients on blood thinners should not take more than 100 milligrams of tocotrienols per day. Likewise, tocotrienols should be used cautiously by patients taking antiplatelet drugs such as Aggrenox, Plavix, and Ticlid. In theory, increased bleeding could also occur if tocotrienols are taken with supplemental garlic or the herb ginkgo.

Patients taking cholesterol-lowering drugs such as Lescol, Pravachol, and Zocor should be aware that tocotrienols may further lower their cholesterol.

Certain drugs may decrease the absorption of tocotrienols or interfere with their use in the body. These include the cholesterol-lowering drugs Colestid and Questran, the antibiotics isoniazid and neomycin, the weight-loss drug Xenical, and the ulcer medication Carafate. Other products that may decrease absorption include mineral oil, the fat substitute olestra, and cholesterol-lowering supplements, especially the plant-based phytosterols and phytostanols.

Because of possible oxidation, tocotrienols should not be taken at the same time as iron supplements.

Special information about pregnancy and breastfeeding

Due to the lack of safety data, pregnant and breastfeeding women should use tocotrienol supplements only with their doctor's approval.

Available preparations and dosage

Most supplements contain a mixture of tocotrienols in liquid softgel form. Some manufacturers also offer "mixed" vitamin E supplements that contain the tocopherol forms as well.

Unlike the alpha-tocopherol form of vitamin E, there are no governmental recommendations for tocotrienols. Dosages used in clinical studies range from 200 to 300 milligrams per day, although some researchers believe that daily doses of 30 to 50 milligrams are sufficient for general disease prevention.

Tocotrienol supplements may be listed as "esterified," which means the formulation was chemically altered to make them more stable. Unesterified tocotrienols should not be taken with supplemental iron, since the combination could actually encourage oxidation. All tocotrienol supplements should be stored at cool temperatures in a dark, tightly closed bottle. They should be taken with fat to enhance absorption.

Overdosage
Little information is available on overdosage; so far, no serious side effects have been reported.

Valerian

Latin name: Valeriana officinalis
Other names: All-heal, Amantilla, Capon's Tail, Heliotrope, Setwall, Vandal Root

Why people take it
Valerian is an accepted remedy for insomnia, and appears to calm nervousness as well. Although its other uses have not been formally verified, valerian is also taken for mental strain, lack of concentration, excitability, hysteria, stress, headache, epilepsy, premenstrual syndrome, symptoms of pregnancy, problems of menopause, nerve pain, fainting, stomach cramps, colic, and uterine spasms.

What it is; how it works
The Ancient Greek physician Galen referred to valerian as "Phu," an expression of disgust at the plant's smell. In medieval times, it was given the name "All-heal," reflecting its many purported healing properties. It was also used as a spice and an ingredient in perfume.

The medicinal parts are the carefully dried underground stem and the dried root. Rigorous clinical trials have verified that extracts of the root do indeed have a sleep-inducing effect. Researchers believe that this action stems from the herb's tendency to boost levels of GABA (gamma-aminobutyric acid), one of the chemical messengers in the brain. Valerian also seems to relax muscles and discourage spasms.

This plant, which produces bright pink to white flowers, grows 20 to 40 inches in height. It is native to Europe and the temperate regions of Asia, and is cultivated in Europe, Japan, and the U.S.

Avoid if...
Unless a doctor approves, anyone with a large skin injury, an acute skin disorder, a severe infection, heart problems, or severe muscle tension should avoid using valerian extract or oil as a bath additive.

Special cautions
In rare instances, valerian can cause digestive problems or an allergic reaction. Long-term use can lead to headache, restlessness, sleeplessness, pupil dilation, and heart problems.

Because of valerian's sedative effect, it's best to avoid operating machinery or driving for several hours after taking the herb.

Possible drug interactions

Valerian should not be combined with other sedatives, including barbiturates such as Seconal and benzodiazepine medications such as Ativan, Halcion, Librium, Valium, and Xanax. Although there is no evidence of an interaction with alcohol, it's considered best to avoid this combination as well.

Special information about pregnancy and breastfeeding

Use of valerian during pregnancy or breastfeeding is not recommended.

Available preparations and dosage

To prepare valerian tea, combine 3 to 5 grams (about 1 teaspoonful) of crushed Valerian with 150 milliliters of hot water (about two-thirds cup), steep for 10 to 15 minutes, then strain.

To make a bath additive, combine 100 grams (about one-half cup) of crushed valerian with 2 quarts of hot water for each full bath.

A variety of commercial preparations are available in capsule and tablet form. For relief of insomnia, typical doses of valerian extract range from 400 to 900 milligrams 30 minutes before bedtime. Because the potency of commercial tablets and capsules may vary, follow the manufacturer's directions whenever available.

For other forms of the herb, the following daily dosages are commonly recommended:

Powder: 15 grams (about 3 teaspoonfuls)
Tea: 2 to 3 cups daily, including 1 before bedtime
Alcohol solution: 1 to 3 milliliters (about one-half to one teaspoonful) 1
　　　　　or more times per day
Alcohol solution (1:5): 15 to 20 drops in water several times daily
Pressed juice: 1 tablespoonful 3 times daily for adults; 1 teaspoonful 3
　　　　　times daily for children

Valerian should be stored away from light. Alcohol solutions (tinctures) and extracts must be kept in tightly closed glass containers.

Overdosage

No information on overdosage is available.

Vinpocetine

Why people take it

A so-called "smart drug," vinpocetine is said to improve memory and mental function by increasing the blood supply to the brain. Advocates claim it can help healthy people, as well as those with some degree of brain impairment. It has not, however, proved capable of halting or even slowing the progress of Alzheimer's disease. Vinpocetine has also been described as a possible antioxidant, protecting cells from the damaging free radicals that can oxidize (burn) tissues throughout the body, including the brain.

Some preliminary research suggests that vinpocetine may have some protective effects in both sight and hearing. One study of patients with mild burn trauma in the eyes showed that vinpocetine enhanced healing, most likely as a result of increased blood flow to the damaged tissue. Vinpocetine has also been associated with improvements seen in retinas damaged by hepatitis B virus. Damage from acoustic trauma has been similarly been reduced by vinpocetine treatment.

Vinpocetine is sold as a drug in Germany, Japan, Mexico, and Portugal for the treatment of cerebrovascular disorders—ailments that interrupt blood circulation in the brain, starving it of oxygen. In Portugal, it's also used to treat general circulatory problems, as well as certain disorders of the eyes and ears. The drug is approved in Australia for the treatment of mental function disorders in the elderly and for other disorders of the brain. Though it has never been approved in the United States, it can be purchased here as a dietary supplement.

What it is; how it works

Like other members of the vinca alkaloid family of drugs, such as the cancer drugs vincristine, vinblastine, and vinorelbine, vinpocetine comes from the periwinkle plant. Limited research data show that vinpocetine does in fact relax the blood vessels of the brain, improve cerebral blood flow, and inhibit blood clotting to some extent. One study implies that the drug improves memory in healthy people. Studies in animals also indicate a protective effect when the brain is deprived of oxygen.

On the other hand, a number of trials have produced less encouraging results. To date, studies in people with Alzheimer's disease or stroke have been very disappointing. Trials in people with brain dysfunction due to other causes have produced mixed results, providing no clear answers for researchers. There is currently not enough evidence to determine whether vinpocetine does or does not reduce fatalities and dependence in ischemic stroke. It's evident that additional, wide-scale studies are needed before any firm conclusions can be drawn about vinpocetine's real value and most appropriate uses.

Avoid if...

Vinpocetine should not be taken if one has ever had an allergic reaction to one of the vinca-based anticancer drugs, or to vinpocetine itself.

Special cautions

It is a good idea for patients to get periodic checkups while taking vinpocetine whatever the status of their health. Blood pressure should be checked on a regular basis. A routine blood test is recommended from time to time to ensure that the liver is breaking down the drug properly. Don't forget that outside the U.S. vinpocetine is used like a potent prescription drug. A bit of extra caution is merited.

Side effects are relatively mild. People enrolled in research studies have taken up to 60 milligrams of vinpocetine per day without suffering serious adverse reactions. Some people found that their blood pressure dropped slightly, an effect that can cause dizziness. Facial flushing has also occurred among people taking vinpocetine. Other complaints reported include temporary sleep disturbances and restlessness (usually after 10 weeks of therapy), pressure headache, dry mouth, and stomach disturbances. Minor decreases in blood sugar have been noted, too, but it has not been determined whether this effect was actually caused by vinpocetine.

Possible drug interactions
Small changes in clotting time have been reported in people who combine the blood thinner warfarin with vinpocetine. While the combination does not seem to pose a great danger, more frequent monitoring of clotting time is a good idea.

Special information about pregnancy and breastfeeding
During pregnancy and breastfeeding it's best to avoid any medication that's not absolutely necessary for short-term health. Patients should forego vinpocetine throughout this period.

Available preparations and dosage
Vinpocetine is typically sold as 5-milligram tablets. Depending on the product purchased, the label may recommend anywhere from 5 to 30 milligrams daily. Do not exceed the recommended amount.

Overdosage
There are no reports of vinpocetine overdosage.

Vitamin E

Why people take it
Vitamin E has grabbed the headlines in recent years for its potential to treat—and possibly prevent—a host of devastating illnesses, including Alzheimer's disease, heart disease, peripheral nerve damage, and cancer. Researchers are particularly impressed by a study in the *New England Journal of Medicine* that showed supplemental vitamin E helped slow the progression of mild to moderate Alzheimer's disease. The results were so convincing that the American Psychiatric Association now includes the vitamin in its treatment guidelines for Alzheimer's.

The study's authors caution that one trial cannot tell the whole story, and they still don't know how vitamin E protects the brain, or whether it could stave off dementia in the first place. Also, the dose used in the study was high—2,000 International Units a day—and treatment at such high doses needs to be supervised by a doctor since, theoretically, it could cause bleeding and other problems. Even so, many researchers believe that the possible rewards of taking vitamin E seem to outweigh the risks, especially since we have so few effective treatments for Alzheimer's.

Much fanfare also surrounds the use of vitamin E for fighting heart disease and cancer. Unfortunately, for every reputable study that has found a link between vitamin E and lower rates of both diseases, another one comes along that casts doubt on the evidence. While nutritional surveys strongly suggest that vitamin E can help prevent heart disease and various cancers (including prostate, breast, and colon cancer), clinical trials of the supplement have been disappointing. It could be that some studies were too short or used a dosage that was too low. For now, the best course seems to be to get plenty of vitamin E from food and perhaps take modest amounts of supplements.

Vitamin E also gets attention for its role in strengthening the immune system and protecting the body from environmental toxins, including air pollution, tobacco smoke, and the sun's ultraviolet rays. For the same reasons, vitamin E supplements may be somewhat beneficial for treating asthma, diabetes, cataracts, and rheumatoid arthritis. It could also help relieve muscle cramps and some of the symptoms associated with premenstrual syndrome, although more research is needed. Claims that vitamin E can reverse skin aging, improve athletic abilities, and enhance fertility and sexual performance have never been substantiated.

What it is; how it works

Even though vitamin E is well known as an essential nutrient, scientists aren't sure how the body uses it. Part of the confusion stems from the vitamin's many forms. Vitamin E is actually a catchall term for a family of eight naturally occurring molecules. They are divided into two main groups, the tocopherols and the tocotrienols. The best known, and the one generally found in supplements, is alpha-tocopherol. The government bases its daily-allowance recommendation on alpha-tocopherol because, so far, it seems to be the most biologically usable form in humans. This does not, however, mean that the other forms of vitamin E are insignificant. In fact, some argue that certain tocotrienols (see separate entry) are more potent antioxidants, although the evidence is still being debated.

Scientists do know that vitamin E is a powerful antioxidant that protects the fats found in cell membranes throughout the body from oxidation, or spoilage. Oxidation is thought to play a role in numerous degenerative diseases as well as the aging process. For example, it is widely believed that the oxidation of "bad" LDL cholesterol leads to the formation of artery-clogging plaque. And oxidative stress has also been linked to many nervous system disorders because brain and nerve cells are rich in fats that are vulnerable to oxidation.

Although vitamin E's role as an antioxidant gets credit for most of its protective effects, it is not the vitamin's only beneficial property. This versatile nutrient also seems to act as a blood thinner and a cell-membrane stabilizer; and it plays an important role in the maintenance of a healthy immune system. A number of studies have shown that it can inhibit the development of certain cancers.

The richest sources of vitamin E, especially the tocopherol form, are vegetable and nut oils, including corn, sunflower, canola, soybean, and olive oils. Palm, rice bran, and coconut oils are high in the tocotrienols. Most nuts are high in vitamin E, as are fatty meats, unrefined cereal and grains, and wheat germ. Various fruits and vegetables—spinach, lettuce, onions, blackberries, apples, and pears—also contain this vitamin.

Vitamin E is fat soluble, which means that the body can store vitamin E for future use. Although high doses of fat-soluble vitamins could lead to toxic buildups in the body, vitamin E has proven safe even in much larger than standard doses.

Vitamin E deficiency is rare in humans but can occur in very premature infants. Individuals who may be deficient include those with cystic fibrosis, Crohn's disease, and certain rare genetic disorders. Vitamin E deficiency is also a concern for those who have had part of their gastrointestinal tract removed. People on a strict low-fat diet may be somewhat deficient since fatty nuts and oils are the best sources of vitamin E.

Avoid if...

Aside from an allergy to them, there are no known reasons to avoid vitamin E supplements.

Special cautions

Because vitamin E can prevent the formation of blood clots, patients who have bleeding problems—including those with hemophilia, peptic ulcers, vitamin K deficiency, a tendency to hemorrhage, or a history of stroke—should take care not to overdose. Likewise, patients should avoid vitamin E supplements about one month before and for 2 weeks after any surgery.

In general, the risk of side effects is low. Even at doses of 1,500 International Units (IU) per day, vitamin E appears to have no harmful effects. However, at doses of 2,400 IU or more bleeding problems may begin to appear. Too much vitamin E may also reduce the body's supply of vitamin A, alter the immune system, and impair sexual function.

Rare reactions to vitamin E supplements include fatigue, breast soreness, emotional disturbances, inflammation of the veins, stomach upset, altered blood fat levels, and thyroid problems.

Possible drug interactions

Patients who are taking a blood-thinning drug such as aspirin or Coumadin should check with their doctor before taking vitamin E supplements, which could further thin the blood. In general, patients taking these drugs should not exceed total daily doses of 100 milligrams of natural vitamin E or 200 milligrams of the synthetic version. Vitamin E should also be used cautiously with antiplatelet drugs such as Aggrenox, Plavix, and Ticlid. In theory, increased bleeding could also occur if vitamin E is taken with supplemental garlic or the herb ginkgo.

Certain drugs may decrease vitamin E absorption or interfere with its use in the body. These include anticonvulsants such as phenobarbital, Dilantin, and Tegretol; the cholesterol-lowering drugs Colestid and Questran; the antibiotics isoniazid and neomycin; and ulcer drugs such as Carafate. In some studies, the weight-loss drug Xenical reduced vitamin E absorption by up to 60 percent. Other products that may counter the effects of vitamin E include fiber supplements, mineral oil, the fat substitute Olestra, and cholesterol-lowering supplements, especially the plant-based phytosterols and phytostanols.

On the plus side, vitamin E may help alleviate the side effects of Cordarone, which is used to prevent abnormal heart rhythms. It may also inhibit Retrovir's harmful effects on bone marrow, and could be useful for treating the kidney damage caused by drugs used to prevent organ rejection, including the immunosuppressants Neoral and Sandimmune. Be aware, however, that in some studies vitamin E actually interfered with immunosuppressant drugs.

Because of possible oxidation, vitamin E should not be taken at the same time as iron supplements. Patients taking supplemental oils—including flaxseed, perilla, borage, blackcurrant, evening primrose, and fish oils—should take a little extra vitamin E to prevent oxidation.

The mineral selenium may boost the effectiveness of vitamin E. In addition, taking other antioxidants—such as vitamin C, glutathione, alpha-lipoic acid, and Coenzyme Q10—may help the body hold onto vitamin E.

Special information about pregnancy and breastfeeding

Pregnant women should not take more than the Recommended Dietary Allowance (RDA) of 15 milligrams (or 22 IU) of vitamin E a day. For breastfeeding women, the RDA is 19 milligrams (or 28 IU). For both cases, the RDA is measured using natural alpha-tocopherol.

Available preparations and dosage

There are several forms of vitamin E available commercially. Most consist of alpha-tocopherol in tablets, capsules, or liquid softgel form. Some manufacturers are now offering "mixed" formulations that include additional forms such as gamma-tocopherol and the tocotrienols.

Typical daily dosages for natural alpha-tocopherol range from 100 to 400 milligrams, with a recommended upper limit of 1,000 milligrams per day. The dosages for synthetic alpha-tocopherol are double that amount, since this form is not as easily stored by the body. Patients can spot the synthetic version by checking the letters listed *before* "alpha-tocopherol." The natural form lists "d," as in d-alpha-tocopherol, while the synthetic version lists "dl," as in dl-alpha-tocopherol. The RDA set by the government is much lower than the doses used in studies: 15 milligrams of natural alpha-tocopherol a day for adults.

Vitamin E is measured in milligrams or International Units (IU), with 1 milligram of alpha-tocopherol equal to approximately 1.5 IU. Therefore, to convert from milligrams to IU, multiply by 1.5. For example, the RDA for vitamin E is 15 milligrams or about 22 IU.

Vitamin E is often listed as "esterified," which means it was chemically altered to make it more stable. Unesterified vitamin E should not be taken with supplemental iron, since the combination could actually encourage oxidation. All vitamin E supplements should be stored at cool temperatures in a dark, tightly closed bottle.

Overdosage

There are no reports of overdosage with vitamin E in any form. However, extremely high doses (2,400 IU or more per day) could theoretically cause bleeding problems due to the vitamin's clot-preventing ability.

Zinc

Why people take it

Because zinc is vital for overall body function, a deficiency could lead to a host of problems. Low levels have been linked to poor brain function, delayed wound healing, a weak immune system, infertility, alcoholism, and anorexia. People who could benefit from zinc supplements include those who do not consume enough calories, vegetarians, some older infants and children with impaired growth, and people who suffer from alcoholism or digestive diseases that cause malabsorption and diarrhea. Vegetarians may need as much as 50 percent more zinc than meat eaters, since zinc is poorly absorbed from plant foods.

If taken during pregnancy, zinc may prevent certain birth defects and ensure proper fetal growth. Preliminary research suggests that zinc may be helpful for people with immune system problems such as rheumatoid arthritis and HIV. It may also slow vision loss due to macular degeneration.

Some evidence suggests that zinc may zap the common cold. In clinical trials, patients using zinc every 2 hours at the first sign of a cough or sniffle reduced their suffering by nearly 3 days. The trick is to use zinc in the form of throat lozenges or nasal spray, since these methods are thought to work by directly interfering with cold viruses in the nose and throat. Zinc capsules or tablets can also be taken to improve overall immunity, but this probably only works in people who have a zinc deficiency to begin with.

Some enthusiasts believe zinc could be beneficial for treating a wide range of other illnesses. The list includes Alzheimer's disease, attention deficit disorder, benign prostatic hyperplasia, bladder infection, cataracts, diabetes, Down's syndrome, and even baldness. While there is no doubt that a true zinc deficiency can lead to numerous problems, no credible evidence shows that zinc supplementation can benefit these conditions.

What it is; how it works
Zinc is an essential mineral that is found in almost every cell in the body. It stimulates the activity of some 100 enzymes, and plays an important role in regulating gene expression. It is needed to support normal growth and development during pregnancy, childhood, and adolescence. An adequate supply is needed for normal sperm production. Zinc is also important for maintaining a healthy immune system, healing cuts and wounds, and maintaining a normal sense of taste and smell.

How zinc works is somewhat of a mystery. Scientists do know that the mineral is needed to activate T-lymphocytes, a type of white blood cell that fights infection. Advocates suggest that it may also interfere with the replication of cold viruses. Some research suggests that zinc acts as an antioxidant and a cell-membrane stabilizer, which could explain why it's helpful for brain function.

Zinc is widely distributed in foods. Oysters are a particularly rich source, although red meat and poultry provide the majority of zinc in the American diet. Other sources include beans, nuts, certain seafood, whole grains, fortified breakfast cereals, and dairy products. Zinc absorption is greater from a diet high in animal protein than a diet rich in plant proteins, including soy. This is because plant-based compounds called phytates can decrease zinc absorption.

Even borderline zinc deficiency can have profound negative effects. General signs of zinc deficiency include growth retardation, hair loss, diarrhea, delayed sexual maturation and impotence, eye and skin lesions, and loss of appetite. There is also some evidence that weight loss, delayed healing of wounds, taste abnormalities, and mental lethargy can occur. Remember, however, that some of these symptoms can also result from a variety of medical conditions other than zinc deficiency.

Avoid if...
Aside from an allergy to the ingredients in a supplement, there are no known reasons to avoid zinc.

Special cautions
Zinc causes few problems in doses up to 30 milligrams a day. Higher doses may cause stomach problems, including pain, nausea, and vomiting. Other reactions include headache, drowsiness, and a metallic taste.

Possible drug interactions
Advise patients that zinc supplements could decrease the absorption of certain antibiotics, including penicillin, tetracycline, and quinolones such as Cipro and Floxin. The mineral could also decrease absorption of bone-building drugs such as Actonel, Fosamax, and Didronel. Likewise, these same drugs could inhibit the absorption of zinc.

Certain minerals can decrease zinc absorption, including phosphorus, calcium, and iron. Products that contain phosphates, such as the drug K-Phos and certain potassium supplements, also may decrease zinc levels. On the other hand, too much zinc can cause a copper deficiency.

Special information about pregnancy and breastfeeding
Pregnant women should not exceed the Recommended Dietary Allowance (RDA) of 11 milligrams of zinc a day. Nursing mothers can take up to 12 milligrams.

Available preparations and dosage
Zinc supplements are available in several forms as tablets, capsules, lozenges, and nasal sprays; the most common preparations use zinc gluconate and zinc picolinate. A typical dose is 15 milligrams per day, although daily RDA requirements are somewhat lower, at 8 milligrams for women and 11 milligrams for men. For colds, the usual dosage is 13 to 23 milligrams of zinc gluconate every 2 hours for a week or two (but no longer).

For best absorption, zinc should not be taken with food or beverages that contain caffeine, tea, oxalic acid (such as spinach, sweet potatoes, rhubarb, and beans), and phytic acid (unleavened bread, seeds, nuts, grains, and soy). Taking zinc supplements with foods rich in amino acids, especially meat, may enhance absorption.

Overdosage
The recommended upper limit for zinc intake by adults is 40 milligrams a day. Sustained megadoses can lead to nausea and vomiting. Intakes of more than 150 milligrams per day can cause copper deficiency, reduce "good" HDL cholesterol levels, and depress the immune system.

Prescription Drugs with Potential for Abuse

Over 500 legal prescription drug products—many of them psychotherapeutic—pose at least some danger of physical or psychological dependence leading to abuse. Such drugs are subject to the Controlled Substances Act of 1970, which assigns each drug to one of four categories of risk. Listed on the following pages are the products—both branded and generic—that fall under the Act. The meaning of their assignments is as follows:

CII = High Potential for Abuse: Use may lead to severe physical or psychological dependence. Prescriptions must be written or confirmed in writing. No renewals are permitted.

CIII = Some Potential for Abuse: Use may lead to low-to-moderate physical dependence or high psychological dependence. Prescriptions may be oral or written. Up to five renewals are permitted within six months.

CIV = Low Potential for Abuse: Use may lead to limited physical or psychological dependence. Prescriptions may be oral or written. Up to five renewals are permitted within six months.

CV = Subject to State and Local Regulation: Abuse potential is low; in some areas a prescription may not be required.

Category CII

Actiq
Adderall
Adderall XR
Alfenta
Alfentanil HCl
Alfentanil HCl Novation
Amphetamine Salt Combo
Amytal Sodium
APAP/Oxycodone
Aspirin/Oxycodone
Avinza
B & O Supprettes 15A
B & O Supprettes 16A
Belladonna/Opium
Bupivacaine/Fentanyl Citrate/Sodium
  Chloride
Bupivacaine/Hydromorphone/Sodium
  Chloride
Cocaine HCl
Codeine Phosphate
Codeine Sulfate
Concerta
Demerol Hydrochloride
Desoxyn
Dexedrine
Dexedrine Spansules
Dextroamphetamine Sulfate
Dextrose/Morphine Sulfate
Dextrostat
Dilaudid
Dilaudid-5
Dilaudid-HP
Diphenoxylate Hydrochloride
Dolophine HCl
Duragesic
Duramorph
Endocet
Endodan
Fentanyl Citrate
Fentanyl Citrate/Sodium Chloride
Focalin
Hydrocodone Bitartrate
Hydromorphone HCl
Hydromorphone HCl/Sodium
  Chloride
Kadian
Levo-Dromoran
Levorphanol Tartrate
Mepergan
Meperidine HCl
Meperidine HCl/Promethazine HCl
Meperidine HCl/Sodium Chloride
Meperitab

Meprozine
Metadate CD
Metadate ER
Methadone HCl
Methadone HCl Concentrate
Methadone HCl Intensol
Methadose
Methamphetamine HCl
Methylin
Methylin ER
Methylphenidate HCl
Morphine Sulfate
Morphine Sulfate/Sodium Chloride
MS Contin
MSIR
Nembutal Sodium
Numorphan HCl
Opium
Oramorph SR
Oxy IR
Oxycodone HCl
OxyContin
Oxydose
OxyFast
Pentobarbital Sodium
Percocet
Percodan
Ritalin
Ritalin LA
Ritalin-SR
RMS
Roxanol
Roxanol-T
Roxicet
Roxicodone
Roxicodone Intensol
Seconal Sodium
Sublimaze
Sufenta
Sufentanil Citrate
Sufentanil Citrate Novaplus
Tuinal
Tylox
Ultiva

Category CIII

4-Dihydrotestosterone
Acetaminophen/Butalbital/Caffeine/
  Codeine
Acetaminophen/Codeine
A-G Tussin
Anadrol-50
Anaplex HD
Androderm

Androgel
Android
Anexsia
APAP w/Codeine
APAP-Hydrocodone
APAP/Hydrocodone Bitartrate
APAP/Hydrocodone Bitartrate HS
Ascomp w/Codeine
Aspirin/Butalbital/Caffeine
Aspirin/Butalbital/Caffeine/Codeine
Aspirin/Carisoprodol/Codeine
Aspirin/Codeine
Atuss EX
Atuss G
Atuss HC
Atuss MR
Atuss MS
Atuss NX
Bancap HC
Bontril PDM
Bontril Slow-Release
Bromphenex HD
Bromplex HD
Brontex
Brovex HC
B-Tuss
Buprenex
Buprenorphine HCl
Butalbital
Butalbital Compound
Butalbital Compound w/Codeine
Butisol Sodium
Carbinoxamine/Hydrocodone/PSE
Ceta Plus
Codafed Expectorant
Codal-DH
Codeine Phosphate/Guaifenesin
Codeine/Guaifenesin
Codiclear DH
Codimal DH
Codituss DH
Co-Gesic
Coldcough
Coldcough EXP
Coldcough HC
Coldcough XP
Coldtuss
Co-Tussin
Cotuss-V
Coughtuss
CPM/Hydrocodone/Phenylephrine
Crantex HC
Cytuss HC
Damason-P

Deca-Durabolin
De-Chlor G
De-Chlor HC
De-Chlor HD
De-Chlor MR
De-Chlor NX
Decotuss-HD
Delatestryl
Depo-Testosterone
Detuss
Didrex
Dihydro-CP
Dihydro-GP
Dihydrotestosterone
Dolorex Forte
Donatussin DC
Drituss HD
Drocon-CS
Duradal HD
Duradal HD Plus
Dynatuss HC
Dynatuss HCG
Echotuss-HC
ED-TLC
ED-Tuss HC
Endacof HC
Endagen-HD
Endal HD
Endal HD Plus
Enditussin-HD
Endotuss-HD
Enplus-HD
Entex HC
Entuss Expectorant
Exo-Tuss
Fioricet w/Codeine
Fiorinal
Fiorinal w/Codeine
First-Testosterone
First-Testosterone MC
Fluoxymesterone
Flutuss HC
Fortabs
Genecof-HC
Genecof-XP
Giltuss HC
G-Tuss
Guaifenesin/Hydrocodone Bitartrate
Guaifenesin/Hydrocodone Bitartrate
  Phenylephrine HCl
Guaifenesin/Hydrocodone/
  Pseudoephedrine
Guapetex HC
Guiadex DH

H-C Tussive
H-C Tussive-D
Histex HC
Histinex HC
Histinex PV
Histuss HC
Histussin-D
Histussin-HC
Homatropine/Hydrocodone
Hybolin Decanoate
Hycodan
Hycomal DH
Hycomine Compound
Hycotuss Expectorant
Hydone
Hydro GP
Hydro PC
Hydro PC II
Hydro PC II Plus
Hydro Pro
Hydrocet
Hydrocodone Bitartrate/Ibuprofen
Hydrocodone Compound
Hydrocodone/Potassium
  Guaiacolsulfonate
Hydrocof-HC
Hydro-DP
Hydromet
Hydron CP
Hydron EX
Hydron KGS
Hydron PSC
Hydro-Tussin DHC
Hydro-Tussin EXP
Hydro-Tussin HC
Hydro-Tussin HD
Hydro-Tussin XP
HY-KXP
Hyphed
Jaycof Expectorant
Jaycof-HC
Jaycof-XP
Ketalar
Ketamine HCl
Kwelcof
Laniroif
Levall 5.0
Lorcet 10/650
Lorcet Plus
Lorcet-HD
Lortab
Lortab 2.5/500
Lortab 5/500
Lortab 7.5/500

Lortab 10/500
Lortab Asa
Lortuss HC
Marcof Expectorant
Margesic-H
Marinol
Maxidone
Maxi-Tuss HC
Maxi-Tuss HCX
M-Clear
Melfiat
M-End
Methitest
Methyltestosterone
Methyltestosterone Micronized
Mintuss EX
Mintuss G
Mintuss HC
Mintuss HD
Mintuss MR
Mintuss MS
Mintuss NX
Nalex DH
Nalex Expectorant
Nandrolone Decanoate
Norco
Notuss
Notuss PD
Nucodine
Nucodine Expectorant
Nucofed
Nucofed Expectorant
Obezine
Oxandrin
Pancof
Pancof EXP
Panlor DC
Panlor SS
Paregoric
Pediatex HC
Pentothal
Phanatuss-HC Diabetic Choice
Phendal-HD
Phendiet
Phendiet-105
Phendimetrazine Tartrate
Phenylephrine HD
Phrenilin w/Caffeine/Codeine
Pneumotussin
Pneumotussin 2.5
Poly-Tussin
Poly-Tussin HD
Poly-Tussin XP
Prelu-2

Pro-Clear
Pro-Cof
Pro-Cof D
Prolex DH
Pro-Red
Protex
Protex-D
Protuss
P-V-Tussin
Pyregesic-C
Qrp Tussin
Quintex HC
Q-V Tussin
Relacon-HC
Rhinacon DH
Rindal HD
Soma Compound w/Codeine
S-T Forte 2
Stagesic
Stanozolol
Statuss Green
Striant
Suboxone
Subutex
Su-Tuss HD
Synalgos-DC
Teslac
Testim
Testosterone
Testosterone Cypionate
Testosterone Enanthate
Testosterone Propionate
Testosterone Propionate Micronized
Testred
Testro AQ
T-Gesic
Triant-HC
Trimal DH
Tri-Vent HC
Tussadur-HD
Tussafed-HC
Tussafed-HCG
Tuss-AX
Tuss-DS
Tussend
Tussend Expectorant
Tuss-ES
Tuss-HC
Tussigon
Tussionex Pennkinetic
Tusso-DF
Tuss-PD
Tuss-S
Tylenol w/Codeine #3

Tylenol w/Codeine #4
Uni Cof
Uni Cof EXP
Uni Tuss HC
Valertest No. 1
Vanacet
Vanacon
Vanex-HD
Vicoclear
Vicodin
Vicodin ES
Vicodin HP
Vicoprofen
Vi-Q-Tuss
Virilon
Vitussin Expectorant
Vortex
Well-Tuss HD
Winstrol
Xyrem
Z-Cof HC
Ztuss
Ztuss Expectorant
Zydone

Category CIV

Acetaminophen/Pentazocine HCl
Acetaminophen/Propoxyphene HCl
Adipex-P
Alprazolam
Alprazolam Intensol
Ambien
Ambien PAK
Amidrine
Amitriptyline/Chlordiazepoxide
APAP/Dichloral/Isomethepene
APAP/Pentazocine HCl
APAP/Propoxyphene
APAP/Propoxyphene HCl
APAP/Propoxyphene Napsylate
Aquachloral Supprettes
Aspirin/Caffeine/Propoxyphene HCl
Ativan
Atti-Plex P Tablet #1
Barbital Sodium
Brevital Sodium
Butorphanol Tartrate
Butorphanol Tartrate Novation
Chloral Hydrate
Chlordiazepoxide HCl
Clonazepam
Clorazepate Dipotassium
Cylert
Dalmane

Darvocet A500
Darvocet-N 100
Darvocet-N 50
Darvon
Darvon Compound-65
Darvon-N
Diastat
Diastat Pediatric
Diazepam
Diazepam Intensol
Diethylpropion HCl
Doral
Duradrin
Epidrin
Equagesic
Estazolam
Fastin
Flurazepam HCl
Gen-Xene
Halcion
Ionamin
Iso-Acetazone
Klonopin
Klonopin Wafers
Librium
Limbitrol
Limbitrol DS
Lorazepam
Lorazepam Intensol
Luminal Sodium
MB-Tab
Mebaral
Meprobamate
Meridia
Micrainin
Midazolam
Midazolam HCl
Midazolam HCl Novation
Midrin
Migquin
Migratine
Migrazone
Migrin-A
Miltown
Motofen
Naloxone/Pentazocine
Oxazepam
Paraldehyde
PC-Cap
Pemoline
Phenobarbital
Phenobarbital Sodium
Phentercot
Phentermine HCl

Phentride
PP-Cap
Pro-Fast HS
Pro-Fast SA
Pro-Fast SR
Pronap-100
Propoxacet
Propoxacet-N
Propoxacet-N 100
Propoxyphene Compound
Propoxyphene HCl
Prosom
Provigil
Restoril
Sodium Phenobarbital
Somnote
Sonata
Stadol
Stadol NS
Talacen
Talwin Lactate
Talwin NX
Temazepam
Tenuate
Tenuate Dospan
Trancot
Tranxene-SD
Tranxene T-Tab
Triazolam
Valium
Va-Zone
Xanax
Xanax XR

Category CV

Acetaminophen/Codeine
Atropine Sulfate/Diphenoxylate HCl
Baltussin
Biotussin AC
Biotussin DAC
Brontex
Bron-Tuss
Capital w/Codeine
Cheracol w/Codeine
Cheratussin AC
Cheratussin DAC
Codafed Pediatric Expectorant
Codeine/Guaifenesin
Codeine/Guaifenesin/Pseudoephedrine
   Expectorant
Codeine/Phenylephrine HCl/
   Promethazine HCl
Codeine/Promethazine
Codeine/Pseudoephedrine/Triprolidine

Codimal PH
ColdCough PD
Diabetic Tussin C Expectorant
Dihistine DH
Dihistine Expectorant
Gani-Tuss NR
Giltuss Ped-C
Guaitussin AC
Guaitussin DAC
Guai-CO
Guaifen AC
Guaifen-C
Guaifensin AC
Guaifenesin AC Expectorant
Guaitussin AC
Guaitussin DAC
Guiatuscon A.C.
Guiatuss AC
Guiatuss DAC
Halotussin AC
Halotussin DAC
Iofen-C NF
Iophen C-NR
Kolephrin #1
Lomocot
Lomotil
Lonox
Mytussin AC Cough
Mytussin DAC
Novadyne Expectorant
Nucodine Pediatric
Nucofed Pediatric Expectorant
Orgadin-Tuss
Pancof PD
Pediacof
Phenhist Expectorant
Phenylhistine DH Expectorant
Phenylhistine Expectorant
Promethazine VC w/Codeine
Promethazine w/Codeine
Pseudo-Chlor/Codeine
Rid-A-Pain w/Codeine
Robafen AC
Romilar AC
Ryna-C
Sudatuss-2
Sudatuss-SF
Suttar-2
Suttar-SF
Tussi-Organidin NR
Tussi-Organidin-S NR
Tussirex
Tylenol w/Codeine
Vi-Atro

Indices

Psychotropic Drugs Indexed by Brand and Generic Name

Listed here are all psychotropic drugs profiled in the first section of the book. Cross-referenced generic names are shown in italics.

Psychotropic Drugs Indexed by Indication

Use this index to determine which drugs are available for a specific psychological problem. Both brand and generic names are listed; cross-referenced generic names are shown in italics. Only medications profiled in the first section of the book are included.

Psychotropic Drugs Indexed by Category

This index allows you to identify all the psychotropic alternatives in a particular pharmacological category. Remember, though, that even closely related drugs may differ in their therapeutic action and adverse effects. Both brand and generic names are listed; cross-referenced generic names are shown in italics. Only medications profiled in the first section of the book are included.

Psychotropic Herbs and Supplements Indexed by Indication

This index identifies the nutritional supplements and herbs generally deemed most promising for specific mental and emotional problems. These products are profiled in Section 6. Although many of them are also used for a variety of nonpsychological ailments, only their psychotropic effects are reflected here.

Age-related memory loss
Acetylcysteine, 818
Alpha-GPC, 822
Arginine Pyroglutamate, 823
CDP-Choline, 825
Choline, 827
DHA, 829
DHEA, 831
Ginkgo, 839
Huperzine A, 843
Phosphatidylcholine, 855
Phosphatidylserine, 857
Vinpocetine, 867

Alzheimer's disease
Acetyl-L-Carnitine, 820
CDP-Choline, 825
DHA, 829
Fish Oil, 835
Gamma-Tocopherol, 838
Huperzine A, 843
NADH, 853
Phosphatidylcholine, 855
Phosphatidylserine, 857
Tocotrienols, 864
Vitamin E, 869

Anxiety
Kava Kava, 844
St. John's Wort, 862

Attention deficit disorder
DHA, 829
Fish Oil, 835

Bipolar disorder
Fish Oil, 835

Brain function deficit
Ginkgo, 839
Zinc, 873

Depression
5-HTP, 817
Choline, 827
DHA, 829
DL-Phenylalanine, 833

Fish Oil, 835
L-Phenylalanine, 848
Myo-Inositol, 851
NADH, 853
SAMe, 860
St. John's Wort, 862

Insomnia
Bugleweed, 824
Hops, 842
Kava Kava, 844
Lavender, 846
Lemon Balm, 847
Melatonin, 850
Passion Flower, 854
Rauwolfia, 858
Valerian, 866

Movement disorders
CDP-Choline, 825
Choline, 827
Glycine, 840
NADH, 853
Phosphatidylcholine, 855

Nervousness
Bugleweed, 824
Hops, 842
Lavender, 846
Lemon Balm, 847
Passion Flower, 854
Rauwolfia, 858
Valerian, 866

Obsessive-compulsive disorder
Myo-Inositol, 851

Panic disorder
Myo-Inositol, 851

Schizophrenia
Fish Oil, 835
Glycine, 840

Stroke recovery
Alpha-GPC, 822
CDP-Choline, 825

Mental Health Internet Resources

General Resources

Community Psychology Net
www.cmmtypsych.net

FreeMedicalJournals.com: Full-Text Articles
www.freemedicaljournals.com

NetPsychology
www.netpsych.com

Psych Web
www.psychwww.com

PsychREF: Resources in Psychology on the Internet
www.psychref.com

Government Resources

National Institute of Mental Health (NIMH)
www.nimh.nih.gov

National Library of Medicine
www.nlm.nih.gov

National Mental Health Information Center
www.mentalhealth.org

Organizations

American Psychological Association (APA)
www.apa.org

American Psychology Society (APS)
www.psychologicalscience.org

National Association of Social Workers (NASW)
www.naswdc.org

National Association of State Mental Health Program Directors
www.nasmhpd.org

Patient Resources

Administration for Children and Families (ACF)
www.acf.dhhs.gov

National Empowerment Center (NEC)
www.power2u.org

National Mental Health Consumers' Self-Help Clearinghouse
www.mhselfhelp.org

New York Online Access to Health (NOAH): Support Groups
www.noah-health.org/english/support.html

Psychotherapy and Treatment

Association for Advancement of Behavior Therapy (AABT)
www.aabt.org

American Institute for Cognitive Therapy
www.cognitivetherapynyc.com

National Association of Cognitive-Behavioral Therapists
www.nacbt.org

National Coalition of Creative Arts Therapies Associations (NCATA)
www.nccata.org

Society for the Exploration of Psychotherapy Integration (SEPI)
www.cyberpsych.org/sepi

Substance Abuse

American Council for Drug Education
www.acde.org

American Society of Addiction Medicine (ASAM)
www.asam.org

Drug Enforcement Administration
www.dea.gov

National Institute on Alcohol Abuse and Alcoholism (NIAAA)
www.niaaa.nih.gov

National Institute on Drug Abuse (NIDA)
www.nida.nih.gov

Substance Abuse and Mental Health Services Administration (SAMHSA)
www.samhsa.gov

Suicide and Runaways

American Foundation for Suicide Prevention
www.afsp.org

Training Institute for Suicide Assessment
www.suicideassessment.com

National Runaway Switchboard
www.nrscrisisline.org

Visual Identification Guide

VISUAL IDENTIFICATION GUIDE

Use this section to quickly verify the identity of a capsule, tablet, or other solid oral medication. More than 200 leading tablets and capsules are shown in actual size and color, organized alphabetically by brand name. Each is labeled with its generic name, as well as its strength and the name of its supplier.

ABILIFY

RX   (Aripiprazole)
BRISTOL-MYERS
SQUIBB

5 mg   10 mg   15 mg

20 mg   30 mg

ABILIFY

RX   (Aripiprazole)
OTSUKA AMERICA

5 mg   10 mg   15 mg

20 mg   30 mg

ADDERALL

C-II (Amphetamine salt combo)
SHIRE

5 mg   7.5 mg   10 mg

12.5 mg   15 mg

20 mg   30 mg

ADDERALL XR

C-II (Amphetamine salt combo)
SHIRE

5 mg

10 mg

15 mg

20 mg

25 mg

25 mg

Extended-Release Capsules

AMBIEN

C-IV   (Zolpidem Tartrate)
SANOFI-SYNTHELABO

5401* 5 mg

5421* 10 mg

ANTABUSE

RX   (Disulfiram)
ODYSSEY

250 mg

ARICEPT

RX   (Donepezil HCl)
EISAI/PFIZER

5 mg   10 mg

CELEXA

RX (Citalopram Hydrobromide)
FOREST

10 mg

20 mg

40 mg

CLOZARIL

RX   (Clozapine)
NOVARTIS

25 mg   100 mg

Other side: engraved with a facilitated
score and the dosage strength.

* Manufacturer's Identification Code

CONCERTA

C-II (Methylphenidate HCl)
MCNEIL CONSUMER

alza 18	alza27
18 mg	27 mg

alza 36	alza 54
36 mg	54 mg

Extended-Release Tablets

CYLERT

C-IV (Pemoline Tablets)
ABBOTT

TH* 18.75 mg**   **TI*** 37.5 mg**

TJ* 75 mg**

CYLERT

C-IV (Pemoline)
ABBOTT

TK* 37.5 mg**

Chewable Tablets

DEPAKOTE

RX (Divalproex Sodium)
ABBOTT

NT* 125 mg   **NR*** 250 mg

NS* 500 mg

Delayed-Release Tablets

DEXEDRINE

C-II (Dextroamphetamine Sulfate)
GLAXOSMITHKLINE

15-mg Spansule®
Also available as 5-mg Spansule®
and 10-mg Spansule® capsules.

5 mg

DEXTROSTAT

C-II (Dextroamphetamine Sulfate)
SHIRE

5 mg

10 mg

▲ EFFEXOR

RX (Venlafaxine HCl)
WYETH

701** 25 mg

781** 37.5 mg

703** 50 mg

704** 75 mg

705** 100 mg

EFFEXOR XR

RX (Venlafaxine HCl)
WYETH

837* 37.5 mg

833* 75 mg

836* 150 mg

Extended-Release Capsules

ESKALITH

RX (Lithium Carbonate)
GLAXOSMITHKLINE

300 mg

ESKALITH CR

RX (Lithium Carbonate)
GLAXOSMITHKLINE

450 mg

Controlled-Release Tablets

†EXELON

RX (Rivastigmine Tartrate)
NOVARTIS

1.5 mg

3 mg

4.5 mg

6 mg

---

† Additional dosage forms and sizes available.
▲ The appearance of these tablets and capsules
   is a trademark of Wyeth Pharmaceuticals.

     * Manufacturer's Identification Code
     ** Product identification number on reverse side.

FOCALIN

C-II   (Dexmethylphenidate HCl)
NOVARTIS

2.5 mg

5 mg

10 mg

†GEODON

RX   (Ziprasidone HCl)
PFIZER

20 mg

40 mg

60 mg

80 mg

KLONOPIN

C-IV   (Clonazepam)
ROCHE

0.5 mg

1 mg

2 mg

KLONOPIN WAFERS

C-IV   (Clonazepam)
ROCHE

0.125 mg

0.25 mg

0.5 mg

1 mg

2 mg

Orally Disintegrating Tablets

LAMICTAL CHEWABLE DISPERSIBLE TABLETS

RX   (Lamotrigine)
GLAXOSMITHKLINE

2 mg

5 mg

25 mg

LAMICTAL

RX   (Lamotrigine)
GLAXOSMITHKLINE

25 mg

100 mg

150 mg

200 mg

†LEXAPRO

RX   (Escitalopram Oxalate)
FOREST

10 mg

20 mg

MOBAN

RX   (Molindone HCl)
ENDO

5 mg

10 mg

25 mg

50 mg

100 mg

NARDIL

RX   (Phenelzine Sulfate)
PARKE-DAVIS
A WARNER-LAMBERT DIVISION
A PFIZER COMPANY

15 mg

†NAVANE

RX   (Thiothixene)
PFIZER

571* 1 mg

572* 2 mg

573* 5 mg

574* 10 mg

577* 20 mg

---

† Additional dosage forms and sizes available.   * Manufacturer's Identification Code

NORPRAMIN

RX   (Desipramine HCl)
AVENTIS

10 mg   25 mg   50 mg

75 mg   100 mg   150 mg

PARNATE

RX   (Tranylcypromine Sulfate)
GLAXOSMITHKLINE

10 mg

†PAXIL

RX   (Paroxetine HCl)
GLAXOSMITHKLINE

10 mg

20 mg

30 mg

40 mg

PAXIL CR

RX   (Paroxetine HCl)
GLAXOSMITHKLINE

12.5 mg

25 mg

37.5 mg

Controlled-Release Tablets

PROVIGIL

C-IV   (Modafinil)
CEPHALON

100 mg

200 mg

PROZAC

RX   (Fluoxetine HCl)
ELI LILLY

10 mg

20 mg

PROZAC WEEKLY

RX   (Fluoxetine HCl)
ELI LILLY

90 mg

†REMINYL

RX   (Galantamine HBr)
JANSSEN

4 mg   8 mg   12 mg

†RISPERDAL

RX   (Risperidone)
JANSSEN

0.25 mg   0.5 mg

1 mg   2 mg

3 mg   4 mg

RISPERDAL M-TAB

RX   (Risperidone)
JANSSEN

0.5 mg   1 mg

2 mg
Orally Disintegrating Tablets

† Additional dosage forms and sizes available.

RITALIN

C-II (Methylphenidate HCl)
NOVARTIS

7* 5 mg   **3*** 10 mg

34* 20 mg

RITALIN LA

C-II (Methylphenidate HCl)
NOVARTIS

NVR R20
20 mg

NVR R30
30 mg

NVR R40
40 mg

Extended-Release Capsules

RITALIN-SR

C-II (Methylphenidate HCl)
NOVARTIS

CIBA 16
16* 20 mg

Sustained-Release Tablets

SEROQUEL

RX (Quetiapine Fumarate)
ASTRAZENECA

25 mg   100 mg   200 mg

300 mg

†SINEQUAN

RX (Doxepin HCl)
PFIZER

534* 10 mg

535* 25 mg

536* 50 mg

539* 75 mg

538* 100 mg

537* 150 mg

STRATTERA

RX (Atomoxetine HCl)
ELI LILLY

Lilly 3227   10 mg
10 mg

Lilly 3228   18 mg
18 mg

Lilly 3229   25 mg
25 mg

Lilly 3228   40 mg
40 mg

Lilly 3231   60 mg
60 mg

SURMONTIL

RX (Trimipramine Maleate)
ODYSSEY

OP 718
25 mg

OP 719
50 mg

OP 720
100 mg

†VALIUM

C-IV (Diazepam)
ROCHE

2 mg   5 mg

10 mg

VIVACTIL

RX (Protriptyline HCl)
ODYSSEY

OP 701
5 mg

OP 702
10 mg

WELLBUTRIN SR

RX (Bupropion HCl)
GLAXOSMITHKLINE

WELLBUTRIN SR 100
100 mg

WELLBUTRIN SR 150
150 mg

WELLBUTRIN SR 200
200 mg

Sustained-Release Tablets

† Additional dosage forms and sizes available.   * Manufacturer's Identification Code

WELLBUTRIN

RX   (Bupropion HCl)
GLAXOSMITHKLINE

75 mg

100 mg

WELLBUTRIN XL

RX   (Bupropion HCl)
GLAXOSMITHKLINE

WELLBUTRIN XL 150
WELLBUTRIN XL 300

150 mg   300 mg

Extended-Release Tablets

XANAX

C-IV   (Alprazolam)
PHARMACIA & UPJOHN

XANAX 0.25
29* 0.25 mg

55* 0.5 mg

XANAX
90* 1 mg

XANAX
GN
94* 2 mg

†ZOLOFT

RX   (Sertraline HCl)
PFIZER

ZOLOFT   25 MG
496* 25 mg

ZOLOFT   50 MG
490* 50 mg

ZOLOFT   100 MG
491* 100 mg

†ZYPREXA

RX   (Olanzapine)
ELI LILLY

LILLY 4112   LILLY 4115
2.5 mg   5 mg

LILLY 4116   LILLY 4117
7.5 mg   10 mg

LILLY   LILLY 4420
15 mg   20 mg

ZYPREXA ZYDIS

RX   (Olanzapine orally
disintegrating tablets)
ELI LILLY

5   10
5 mg   10 mg

Zydis® is a registered trademark of
R.P. Scherer Corp.

---

† Additional dosage forms and sizes available.   * Manufacturer's Identification Code